DISCARDED

Foreign Relations of the
United States, 1969–1976

Volume XXIII

Arab-Israeli Dispute, 1969–1972

Editor   Steven G. Galpern

General Editor   Adam M. Howard

United States Government Publishing Office
Washington
2015

DEPARTMENT OF STATE

Office of the Historian

Bureau of Public Affairs

For sale by the Superintendent of Documents, U.S. Government Publishing Office
Internet: bookstore.gpo.gov   Phone: toll free (866) 512-1800;   DC area (202) 512-1800
Fax: (202) 512-2104 Mail: Stop IDCC, Washington, DC 20402-0001

ISBN 978-0-16-092847-5

Preface

The *Foreign Relations of the United States* series presents the official documentary historical record of major foreign policy decisions and significant diplomatic activity of the United States Government. The Historian of the Department of State is charged with the responsibility for the preparation of the *Foreign Relations* series. The staff of the Office of the Historian, Bureau of Public Affairs, under the direction of the General Editor of the *Foreign Relations* series, plans, researches, compiles, and edits the volumes in the series. Secretary of State Frank B. Kellogg first promulgated official regulations codifying specific standards for the selection and editing of documents for the series on March 26, 1925. These regulations, with minor modifications, guided the series through 1991.

Public Law 102–138, the Foreign Relations Authorization Act, established a new statutory charter for the preparation of the series which was signed by President George H.W. Bush on October 28, 1991. Section 198 of P.L. 102–138 added a new Title IV to the Department of State's Basic Authorities Act of 1956 (22 USC 4351, et seq.).

The statute requires that the *Foreign Relations* series be a thorough, accurate, and reliable record of major United States foreign policy decisions and significant United States diplomatic activity. The volumes of the series should include all records needed to provide comprehensive documentation of major foreign policy decisions and actions of the United States Government. The statute also confirms the editing principles established by Secretary Kellogg: the *Foreign Relations* series is guided by the principles of historical objectivity and accuracy; records should not be altered or deletions made without indicating in the published text that a deletion has been made; the published record should omit no facts that were of major importance in reaching a decision, and nothing should be omitted for the purposes of concealing a defect in policy. The statute also requires that the *Foreign Relations* series be published not more than 30 years after the events recorded. The editors are convinced that this volume meets all regulatory, statutory, and scholarly standards of selection and editing.

Structure and Scope of the Foreign Relations *Series*

This volume is part of a subseries of volumes of the *Foreign Relations* series that documents the most important issues in the foreign policy of the administrations of Richard M. Nixon and Gerald R. Ford. This volume documents U.S. policy toward the Arab-Israeli dispute between January 1969 and December 1972. During his first term in office, President Richard Nixon was confronted with the challenges posed by the outcomes of the June 1967 Arab-Israeli War, most notably Israel's acquisition of territory from its Arab neighbors in the Sinai Peninsula, the Gaza Strip, the Golan Heights, and the West Bank; lingering hostilities between Israeli and Arab forces; the rise of the Palestine Liberation Organization under Yasser Arafat; and growing Soviet influence in the Arab states. Although this volume primarily traces the administration's efforts to broker an Egyptian-Israeli peace settlement while seeking to preserve a precarious regional balance of power between the belligerents, it also covers other aspects of U.S. bilateral relations with Israel, Egypt, Syria, Lebanon, and Jordan, including nuclear matters and arms sales. It should be noted that, because of the hour-by-hour nature of the decision-making among U.S. officials during the September 1970 Jordan Crisis, this event is covered separately in *Foreign Relations, 1969–1976*, volume XXIV, Middle East Region and Arabian Peninsula, 1969–1972; Jordan, September 1970. Moreover, to see how the Nixon administration's handling of the Arab-Israeli dispute fit in with its broader Middle East policy, this volume should be read in conjunction with the other Middle East compilations in the subseries. For documentation on the administration's broad view of the region, including regional defense, and its political relations with Saudi Arabia and the countries of the Arabian Peninsula, see *ibid*. The nexus of oil matters and the Arab-Israeli dispute, including the Arab oil embargo of 1973, is covered in *Foreign Relations*, volume XXXVI, Energy Crisis, 1969–1974. U.S. relations with Iran, with which the Nixon administration developed close ties, are covered in *Foreign Relations, 1969–1976*, volume E–4, Documents on Iran and Iraq, 1969–1972. Substantial documentation on U.S.-Soviet discussions of a Middle East settlement can also be found in *Foreign Relations, 1969–1976*, volumes XII–XV, Soviet Union, January 1969–October 1970; October 1970–October 1971; October 1971–May 1972; and June 1972–August 1974.

Focus of Research and Principles of Selection for Foreign Relations, Volume XXIII

The *Foreign Relations* series has documented U.S. policy toward the Arab-Israeli dispute since the establishment of the State of Israel in 1948. Until the Suez crisis in 1956, when Israel participated with Britain and France in the tripartite invasion of Egypt, the series dealt with the dispute in its "Near and Middle East" volumes as one among many regional issues that concerned U.S. policymaking. Since then, the series has dedicated entire volumes to the subject, focusing on U.S. efforts to manage crises, reduce the level of violence in the region, and provide support to its allies, namely Israel, Jordan, and Lebanon. This volume, which covers a majority of the period between the Arab-Israeli wars of

June 1967 and October 1973, documents the first Nixon administration's attempts to grapple with the intractable issues that frustrated previous Presidents and their staffs. In this case, however, Nixon and his advisors had to contend with the most important consequence of Israel's overwhelming victory in the 1967 war: its acquisition of neighboring Arab territory (including the Sinai Peninsula and the Gaza Strip from Egypt, the Golan Heights from Syria, and the West Bank from Jordan). Although Nixon's predecessor, Lyndon B. Johnson, certainly had to consider this issue during the last year and a half of his administration, land questions framed the policymaking environment from the moment Nixon took office and did so throughout his presidency. In common with all recent *Foreign Relations* volumes, the focus of the volume is devoted primarily to the policy formulation process whereby the Nixon administration addressed these challenges.

The administration's efforts to persuade Israel and the front-line Arab states to begin negotiations for a settlement—along the lines of the land-for-peace framework established by U.N. Security Council Resolution 242—occurred in a variety of arenas and were conducted by multiple parts of the bureaucracy. However, over the course of this volume, a number of salient themes are highlighted. The first is the bureaucratic balance of power within the Nixon administration's foreign policymaking apparatus. Somewhat uncharacteristically for foreign policymaking in the Nixon years, responsibility for Middle East policymaking initially resided largely with the Department of State. Indeed, the administration's first attempt to settle the simmering war of attrition between Egypt and Israel was named for its chief advocate, Secretary of State William P. Rogers. Over time, however, the influence of the White House and specifically that of the President's Assistant for National Security Affairs Henry A. Kissinger over U.S. policy toward the Arab-Israeli dispute continued to grow, reflecting the administration's concerns over the balance of power in the region following the collapse of the Rogers Plan. This influence exacerbated further the already tense relations between Kissinger and Rogers. By the end of Nixon's first term, Kissinger had circumvented the Department of State by opening a separate backchannel to Egypt in the hopes of breaking the diplomatic stalemate.

The second theme highlighted by this volume is the extent to which the Nixon administration viewed the Arab-Israeli dispute through the lens of the Cold War. For Nixon and Kissinger, in particular, no settlement was possible without taking into consideration the Soviet Union, whose influence—and indeed, presence—in Egypt had spiked dramatically following Israel's June 1967 victory. Beginning in 1969, the U.S. worked directly with the Soviet Union to bring Israel and Egypt to the negotiating table.

The first chapter of this volume predominantly concerns the Nixon administration's decision, early in 1969, to offer specific proposals for a settlement between Egypt and Israel. In January and February, National Security Study Memoranda (NSSM), the papers generated in response to them, and the National Security Council (NSC) meetings that considered the issues raised by the papers reveal the thinking that paved the way for the series of talks that occurred in April and May between Assistant Secretary of State for Near East and South Asian Affairs Joseph Sisco and Soviet Ambassador to the United States Anatoliy Dobrynin. In these discussions, Sisco unveiled, in piecemeal fashion, a U.S. proposal for the framework of an Israeli-Egyptian accord to be negotiated under the auspices of the Special Representative of the United Nations Middle East Mission, Gunnar Jarring, and co-sponsored by the United States and the Soviet Union. The plan, delivered to the Soviet Union on October 28 and publicly announced in Washington by Secretary of State Rogers on December 9, presented the specific outlines of a settlement. As his memoranda to the President make clear, Kissinger doubted the usefulness of such an approach, and, indeed, the chapter concludes with the Soviet Union rejecting the "Rogers Plan" because it considered the document "one-sided" and "pro-Israel." The Israeli Government also rejected the plan—as it did a proposal for a settlement between Israel and Jordan—because it believed that U.S. officials had gone too far in appeasing the Arab states. Nixon and Kissinger viewed the dispute between Egypt and Israel, in part, as a cold war proxy battle in which the Soviet Union and the United States could use their influence over their respective clients to achieve a settlement. However, the first chapter reveals there were limits to the extent that the President and his National Security Adviser were willing to push Israel to negotiate—a theme that persists through the volume.

While the U.S.-Soviet talks that culminated in the Rogers Plan and its eventual rejection provides the narrative thread that ties the first chapter together, there are also other, smaller, sub-narratives. One underlying storyline is the Nixon administration's efforts, beginning with NSSM 40 in April 1969, to assess Israel's nuclear program, in part by trying to persuade the country to sign the Nuclear Non-Proliferation Treaty (NPT). By February 1970, after making no headway in this effort beyond pressuring Israeli Ambassador Yitzhak Rabin into making the vague assurance that Israel would not be the first country to "introduce" nuclear weapons in the Middle East, Nixon and his advisors dropped the issue altogether. The administration's response to arms requests—particularly by Israel and to a lesser extent Jordan—is also a recurring theme, not only in this chapter but also in the rest of the volume. Another narrative thread is that of U.S. participation in attempts to reach a settlement between Israel and its neighbors in the U.N. context—that is, in the Four Power discussions with Britain, France, and the Soviet Union, in which U.S. Ambassador Charles Yost took part. The chapter also refers to Jarring's work on behalf of the United Nations, and it documents the Nixon administration's contingency planning in response to Palestinian fedayeen-instigated crises in Lebanon.

Chapter 2 focuses on the aftermath of the Rogers Plan's demise and the evolution of the process that led to the Egyptian-Israeli cease-fire in August 1970. The February Washington Special Actions Group (WSAG) meetings that considered Soviet moves to strengthen Egyptian military defenses sets the tone of the chapter, which finds the Nixon administration confronting balance-of-power issues in the region, particularly as it weighed giving additional financial and military assistance to Israel. Nixon's decision in March to defer Israeli aircraft requests greatly disappointed Israeli officials, who responded with an intelligence briefing on the participation of Soviet pilots in operational flights in Egypt—a new level of Soviet involvement in that country's air defenses. Consequently, in April, Nixon sought a re-examination of U.S. policy options in the Middle East, including possible political initiatives and a reassessment of Israeli assistance requests, in light of the recent Soviet activity in Egypt. At a June NSC meeting, Director of Central Intelligence Richard Helms confirmed that the Soviet Union was constructing surface-to-air missile sites and manning them with Soviet personnel. This prompted Nixon to approve steps recommended by Rogers in a June 9 memorandum to get Egypt and Israel to "stop shooting" and "start talking," resulting in a cease-fire accord on August 7—also referred to as "the standstill agreement." The transcript of an acrimonious telephone conversation between Kissinger and Rogers on the cusp of the agreement's announcement is one of the chapter's most provocative documents, laying bare the notoriously tense relationship between the President's chief foreign policy advisers.

As with the first chapter, other issues arise in chapter 2 that are not related to its larger narrative. The June WSAG meetings concerning a fedayeen uprising in Jordan foreshadowed the crisis that the Nixon administration would confront the following September. Along with Israeli arms requests, the administration also had to consider military requests from Jordan and Lebanon. And, finally, the United States continued to participate in the Four Power talks at the United Nations, where, after the failure of U.S. settlement proposals in December 1969, a state of paralysis—usually with the United States and the United Kingdom on one side and France and the Soviet Union on the other—prevented the forum from producing anything substantive.

Much of chapter 3 details U.S. efforts to monitor the cease-fire zone along the Suez Canal and then to grapple with the violations that were discovered, particularly the relocation of surface-to-air missile batteries within the zone. The violations prompted diplomatic approaches to both Egypt and the Soviet Union as well as a request by Nixon for two study memoranda: the first to outline how the United States could support Israel against Soviet and Egyptian missile defenses west of the Suez Canal; and a second to review U.S. options in the Middle East before the resumption of any significant activity to produce a diplomatic settlement. The President asked that the latter study take into account violations of the standstill agreement as well as the major Palestinian fedayeen uprising that occurred in Jordan that September and the Soviet response to it. In the three months following the uprising—and primarily in response to it—the administration considered policy options regarding the Palestinians. It also made contact with Fatah, the Palestinian Liberation Organization's leading faction, through the CIA, and discussed providing further military assistance to both Israel and Jordan. The second part of chapter 3 uses Presidential recordings to document U.S. attempts to broker an interim settlement between Egypt and Israel, as proposed by Sadat in a speech to Egypt's National Assembly in February. The administration's efforts were hampered by what U.S. officials described as Israel's inadequate response to Ambassador Jarring's attempts to restart talks between Egypt and Israel. While Rogers advocated pressuring Israel to be more conciliatory, Kissinger believed that Israel would reject such an approach and virtually end any chance of a negotiated agreement over the next year.

The fourth and final chapter documents the Department of State's mission to launch "proximity talks" between Egypt and Israel, while, unbeknownst to the Department, Kissinger carried on a secret back channel conversation with Hafez Ismail in Egypt. Concurrently, the President and Kissinger continued their dialogue with the Soviets, presenting to Chairman Leonid I. Brezhnev a new proposal for a Middle East settlement during the Moscow summit in May 1972. For its part, the Department of State pressed ahead with efforts to bring the Egyptians and Israelis to the negotiating table, a plan the NSC and White House viewed as unimaginative, even counterproductive. Other issues covered in the chapter include the administration's policy toward aircraft sales to Israel, Israeli clashes with fedayeen based in Lebanon, the killing of Israeli athletes at the Munich Olympics by members of the Palestinian group Black September, and Jordanian involvement in achieving a post-peace settlement arrangement in the West Bank.

Editorial Methodology

The documents are presented chronologically according to Washington time. Memoranda of conversation are placed according to the time and date of the conversation, rather than the date the memorandum was drafted.

Editorial treatment of the documents published in the Foreign Relations series follows Office style guidelines, supplemented by guidance from the General Editor and the chief technical editor. The source text is reproduced as exactly as possible, including marginalia or other notations, which are described in the footnotes. Texts are transcribed and printed according to accepted conventions for the publication of historical documents in the limitations of modern typography. A heading has been supplied by the editors for each document included in the volume. Spelling, capitalization, and punctuation are retained as found in the original text, except that obvious typographical errors are silently corrected. Other mistakes and omissions in the documents are corrected by bracketed insertions: a correction is set in italic type; an addition in roman type. Words or phrases underlined in the source text are printed in italics. Abbreviations and contractions are preserved as found in the original text, and a list of abbreviations is included in the front matter of each volume. In telegrams, the telegram number (including special designators such as Secto) is printed at the start of the text of the telegram.

Bracketed insertions are also used to indicate omitted text that deals with an unrelated subject (in roman type) or that remains classified after declassification review (in italic type). The amount and, where possible, the nature of the material not declassified has been noted by indicating the number of lines or pages of text that were omitted. Entire documents withheld for declassification purposes have been accounted for and are listed by headings, source notes, and number of pages not declassified in their chronological place. All brackets that appear in the source text are so identified by footnotes. All ellipses are in the original documents

The first footnote to each document indicates the source of the document, original classification, distribution, and drafting information. This note also provides the background of important documents and policies and indicates whether the President or his major policy advisers read the document.

Editorial notes and additional annotation summarize pertinent material not printed in the volume, indicate the location of additional documentary sources, provide references to important related documents printed in other volumes, describe key events, and provide summaries of and citations to public statements that supplement and elucidate the printed documents. Information derived from memoirs and other first-hand accounts has been used when appropriate to supplement or explicate the official record. The numbers in the index refer to document numbers rather than to page numbers.

Advisory Committee on Historical Diplomatic Documentation

The Advisory Committee on Historical Diplomatic Documentation, established under the Foreign Relations statute, reviews records, advises, and makes recommendations concerning the Foreign Relations series. The Advisory Committee monitors the overall compilation and editorial process of the series and advises on all aspects of the preparation and declassification of the series. The Advisory Committee does not necessarily review the contents of individual volumes in the series, but it makes recommendations on issues that come to its attention and review volumes, as it deems necessary to fulfill its advisory and statutory obligations.

Presidential Recordings and Materials Preservation Act Review

Under the terms of the Presidential Recordings and Materials Preservation Act (PRMPA) of 1974 (44 USC 2111 note), the National Archives and Records Administration (NARA) has custody of the Nixon Presidential historical materials. The requirements of the PRMPA and implementing regulations govern access to the Nixon Presidential historical materials. The PRMPA and implementing public access regulations require NARA to review for additional restrictions in order to ensure the protection of the privacy rights of former Nixon White House officials, since these officials were not given the opportunity to separate their personal materials from public papers. Thus, the PRMPA and implementing public access regulations require NARA formally to notify the Nixon estate and former Nixon White House staff members that the agency is scheduling for public release Nixon White House historical materials. The Nixon estate and former White House staff members have 30 days to contest the release of Nixon historical materials in which they were a participant or are mentioned. Further, the PRMPA and implementing regulations require NARA to segregate and return to the creator of files private and personal materials. All Foreign Relations volumes that include materials from NARA's Nixon Presidential Materials Staff are processed and released in accordance with the PRMPA.

Nixon White House Tapes

Access to the Nixon White House tape recordings is governed by the terms of the PRMPA and an access agreement with the Office of Presidential Libraries of the National Archives and Records Administration and the Nixon Estate. In February 1971, President Nixon initiated a voice activated taping system in the Oval Office of the White House and, subsequently, in the President's office in the Executive Office Building, Camp David, the Cabinet Room, and White House and Camp David telephones. The audiotapes include conversations of President Nixon with his Assistant for National Security Affairs, Henry Kissinger, other White House aides, Secretary of State Rogers, other Cabinet officers, members of Congress, and key foreign officials. The clarity of the voices on the tape recordings is often very poor, but the editor has made every effort to verify the accuracy of the transcripts produced here. Readers are advised that the tape recording is the official document; the transcript represents an interpretation of that document. Through the use of digital audio and other advances in technology, the Office of the Historian has been able to enhance the tape recordings and over time produce more accurate transcripts. The result is that some transcripts printed here may differ from transcripts of the same conversations printed in previous *Foreign Relations* volumes. The most accurate transcripts possible, however, cannot substitute for listening to the recordings. Readers are urged to consult the recordings themselves for a full appreciation of those aspects of the conversations that cannot be captured in a transcript, such as the speakers' inflections and emphases that may convey nuances of meaning, as well as the larger context of the discussion.

Declassification Review

The Office of Information Programs and Services, Bureau of Administration, conducted the declassification review for the Department of State of the documents published in this volume. The review was conducted in accordance with the standards set forth in Executive Order 12958 on Classified National Security Information, as amended, Executive Order 13526 on Classified National Security Information, and applicable laws.

The principle guiding declassification review is to release all information, subject only to the current requirements of national security as embodied in law and regulation. Declassification decisions entailed concurrence of the appropriate geographic and functional bureaus in the Department of State, other concerned agencies of the U.S. Government, and the appropriate foreign governments regarding specific documents of those governments. The declassification review of this volume, which began in 2006 and was completed in 2013, resulted in the decision to withhold 0 documents in full, excise a paragraph or more in 5 documents, and make minor excisions of less than a paragraph in 25 documents.

The Office of the Historian is confident, on the basis of the research conducted in preparing this volume and as a result of the declassification review process described above, that the documentation and editorial notes presented here provide an accurate and comprehensive—given limitations of space—account of the Nixon administration's policy toward the Arab-Israeli dispute from 1969 to 1972.

Acknowledgments

The editor wishes to acknowledge the assistance of officials at the Nixon Presidential Materials Project, located at the time of research at the National Archives and Records Administration (Archives II), at College Park, Maryland. The editor also wishes to acknowledge the

Richard Nixon Estate for allowing access to the Nixon presidential recordings and the Richard Nixon Library & Birthplace for facilitating that access. Special thanks are due to Scott Koch, formerly of the Historical Staff of the Central Intelligence Agency, who was extremely helpful in arranging full access to the files of the Central Intelligence Agency. John Haynes of the Library of Congress was responsible for expediting access to the Kissinger Papers, including the transcripts of Henry Kissinger's telephone conversations. The editor was able to use the Kissinger Papers, including the transcripts of telephone conversations, with the kind permission of Henry Kissinger. The editor would like also to thank Sandra Meagher at the Department of Defense.

Steven G. Galpern collected documentation for this volume and selected and edited it, under the supervision of Edward C. Keefer, the former General Editor of the *Foreign Relations* series. Susan C. Weetman, Carl Ashley, and Dean Weatherhead coordinated the declassification review. Keri E. Lewis, Kristen Ahlberg, Margaret Ball, Aaron Marrs, and Mandy Chalou did the copy and technical editing. Do Mi Stauber, Inc. prepared the index.

Stephen P. Randolph, Ph.D.
The Historian
Bureau of Public Affairs
August 2015

Contents

Preface	III
Sources	XV
Abbreviations and Terms	XXV
Persons	XXIX
Arab-Israeli Dispute, 1969–1972	
The Rogers Plan	1
The Cease-Fire Agreement	271
The Interim Settlement Proposal	554
Proximity Talks and the Backchannel: Separate Department of State and White House Negotiating Tracks	915
Index	1095

Sources

Sources for the Foreign Relations *Series*

The *Foreign Relations* statute requires that the published record in the *Foreign Relations* series include all records needed to provide comprehensive documentation of major U.S. foreign policy decisions and significant U.S. diplomatic activity. It further requires that government agencies, departments, and other entities of the U.S. Government engaged in foreign policy formulation, execution, or support cooperate with the Department of State historians by providing full and complete access pertinent to foreign policy decisions and actions and by providing copies of selected records. Most of the sources consulted in preparation of this volume have been declassified and are available for review at the National Archives and Records Administration. A few collections, mostly relating to intelligence matters or Henry Kissinger's Papers at the Manuscript Division of the Library of Congress, remain closed to the public. They were available to the editors of this volume and the documents chosen for publication have been declassified.

The editors of the *Foreign Relations* series have complete access to all the retired records and papers of the Department of State: the central files of the Department; the special decentralized files ("lot files") of the Department at the bureau, office, and division levels; the files of the Department's Executive Secretariat, which contain the records of international conferences and high-level official visits, correspondence with foreign leaders by the President and Secretary of State, and memoranda of conversations between the President and Secretary of State and foreign officials; and the files of overseas diplomatic posts. All the Department's indexed central files through December 1976 have been permanently transferred to the National Archives and Records Administration at College Park, Maryland (Archives II). Many of the Department's decentralized office (or lot) files covering the 1969–1976 period, which the National Archives deems worthy of permanent retention, have been transferred or are in the process of being transferred from the Department's custody to Archives II.

The editors of the *Foreign Relations* series also have full access to the papers of President Nixon and other White House foreign policy records. Presidential papers maintained and preserved at the Presidential libraries and previously at the Nixon Presidential Materials Project at Archives II include some of the most significant foreign affairs-related documentation from the Department of State and other Federal agencies including the National Security Council, the Central Intelligence Agency, the Department of Defense, and the Joint Chiefs of Staff. Dr. Henry Kissinger has approved access to his papers at the Library of Congress.

Research for this volume was completed through special access to restricted documents at the Nixon Presidential Materials Project, the Library of Congress, and other agencies. While all the material printed in this volume has been declassified, some of it is extracted from still-classified documents. The Nixon Presidential Materials Staff is processing and declassifying many of the documents used in this volume, but they might not be available in their entirety at the time of publication.

Sources for Foreign Relations, 1969–1976, Volume XXIII

In compiling this volume, the editor made extensive use of the Presidential papers and other White House records at the Nixon Presidential Materials Project. At the time of research, this collection was housed at the National Archives and Records Administration (NARA) in College Park, Maryland, but has subsequently been transferred to the Nixon Presidential Library and Museum in Yorba Linda, California. Since the most important documents on the Arab-Israeli dispute flowed to the President through his primary foreign policy advisor and bureaucratic gatekeeper, Henry Kissinger, this collection contains the richest and broadest spectrum of material. Within the Nixon papers, the National Security Council (NSC) Files are the best source for documents that, as a group, reveal how the administration conceived and executed policy.

The NSC Country Files for the Middle East were invaluable in the preparation of this volume. They were the working files of the NSC staff members responsible for analyzing information for Kissinger on individual Middle East countries, regional Middle East matters, and issues related to the Arab-Israeli dispute. The files not only contain the material that NSC staff members sent to Kissinger, but also the memoranda based on this material that he in turn sent to the President. They also include memoranda from cabinet officials to the President—which Kissinger summarized and analyzed for him—policy papers, and some of the most important Department of State telegrams. Of the countries involved in the Arab-Israeli dispute, Israel was by far the closest U.S. ally, and, as a result, its files are the most voluminous (7 Hollinger boxes). On the Arab side of the equation, the relevant country files include those for the United Arab Republic—renamed "Arab Republic of Egypt" in 1971 (5 Hollinger boxes)—Jordan (5 Hollinger boxes), Lebanon (2 Hollinger boxes), and Syria (1 Hollinger box). The small number of boxes for Lebanon corresponds to Nixon administration's diminished attention to the country, except during moments of crisis, while the absence of material on Syria reflects the lack of U.S. representation there from 1967–1974.

Given the inclination of President Nixon and his advisers to view the Arab-Israeli dispute within the context of Cold War, they worked directly with the Soviet Union to bring Israel and Egypt to the negotiating table, particularly in 1969, through talks between Assistant Secretary of State Joseph Sisco and Soviet Ambassador Anatoliy Dobrynin. The telegrams reporting those meetings, as well as other Soviet-related material on the Middle East, are located in both the Soviet Country Files (16 Hollinger boxes) and the general Middle East Country Files dedicated exclusively to Arab-Israeli negotiations (11 Hollinger boxes). The latter group contains some of the best Department of State telegrams and White House memoranda concerning the repeated efforts to launch discussions between Israel and the Arab states, as well as the administration's attempts to reduce the level of violence in the region. The more general Middle East Country Files, which focus on broader regional issues (4 Hollinger boxes), were useful, although much less so than the negotiations files.

For the minutes of meetings on the Middle East held by the NSC and its subgroups, the policy papers that informed those meetings, the "Study Memoranda" from Kissinger that initiated the production of the papers, and the "Decision Memoranda" that represented the culmination of the NSC policy-making process, the editor made extensive use of the National Security Council Institutional (H-Files). It is impossible to understand how the Nixon administration conceived and executed policy regarding the Arab-Israeli dispute without reviewing this material (315 Hollinger boxes, denoted by the letter "H" that precedes the box number, only a small portion of which are related to the Middle East). Until recently, the documents were under the custody of the NSC but have now been transferred to the National Archives. The documents are divided into minutes files and meeting files, with the former containing the minutes from the meetings of the Senior and Special Review Groups (SRG), the Washington Special Actions Group (WSAG), and the National Security Council. Chaired by Kissinger, the Special Review Group on the Middle East was an interdepartmental body of sub-Cabinet-level officials—including Richard Helms, the Director of Central Intelligence, and Harold Saunders, the member of the NSC staff most responsible for the Middle East—that helped formulate Middle East policy by producing and discussing papers on pressing issues. The WSAG, also chaired by Kissinger, consisted of representatives at the undersecretary level from the Departments of State and Defense, the Central Intelligence Agency (CIA), the Joint Chiefs of Staff (JCS), and members of the NSC staff, and handled contingency-planning for crises in the Middle East. Many of the papers, the analytical summaries of the papers, and the talking points for the meetings of both the SRG and the WSAG are contained in the meetings files. Finally, National Security Study Memoranda (NSSM) and National Security Decision Memoranda (NSDM) concerning the Arab-Israeli dispute can be located by finding their subject headings in the research guide, as can the Middle East-related SRG and WSAG meeting files.

Harold Saunders was virtually Kissinger's shadow for Middle East issues on the NSC staff, and, because he was a prodigious record-keeper, his files are both extensive and useful. In fact, many of his memoranda to Kissinger were forwarded to the President with only the name in the "From" column changed. The Saunders collection is divided into Middle East Negotiations files (19 Hollinger boxes) and Chronological Files—the latter being somewhat of a misnomer because the second half contains subject files subdivided by country and other topics, including the Middle East, Israel, and the individual Arab States. For administration policy toward the Arab-Israeli dispute, however, the "Middle East Negotiations" material is the much better of the two. It is separated into four major categories: 1) "June Initiative," which refers to the U.S. peace efforts in the summer of 1970; 2) "Four Power Talks," which refers to the U.N.-based discussions between the Permanent Representatives of the United States, the Soviet Union, Britain, and France; 3) "Jarring Talks," which refers to efforts by U.N. Special Representative Gunnar Jarring to jump-start negotiations; and 4) "U.S.-U.S.S.R. Talks." While many of the telegrams, memoranda, and papers in the Saunders Files can be found elsewhere in the NSC Files, this group remains enormously helpful to the researcher. First, by examining the "Middle East Negotiations" documents in the order in which they are organized, one can better see how administration policy evolved over time. Second, these files do, in fact, contain material not found elsewhere, especially the most relevant Department of State telegrams. Going first to the Saunders Files—or the Country Files for that matter—to find these telegrams, rather than to the Department of State Central Files at NARA (to be discussed later), might seem counterintuitive. But given the sheer volume of material in the Central Files, use of the Saunders files saves the researcher both time and energy.

The next place to look for Arab-Israeli-related material within the NSC collection is the Kissinger Office Files. They were maintained by Kissinger's immediate staff and contain the essential record of Kissinger's 1972 backchannel correspondence with Egypt's intelligence chief through which he tried to organize secret, high-level talks between the United States and Egypt. Important documents are also in the NSC Files, Agency Files, CIA, particularly Helms's memoranda to Kissinger. Finally, the NSC Files, Presidential Correspondence Files, include letters between Nixon and the leaders of Israel, Egypt, Jordan, Lebanon, and the Soviet Union, oftentimes with the President's handwritten signature.

There are three groups of records, two of which are unique to the Nixon administration, that not only add color and life to the telegrams, memoranda, and minutes of meetings but also serve as an essential backdrop to them by helping to explain some of the motivations and behavior of key figures, such as Nixon, Kissinger, and Secretary of State William Rogers. Transcripts of the Kissinger telephone conversations, which were produced by a secretary listening in on the phone at Kissinger's office at the White House or transcribed from tape recordings from his home telephone are in the Nixon Presidential Materials. They reveal Kissinger's unvarnished—and mostly negative—opinions of Department of State maneuverings regarding policy toward the Arab-Israeli dispute. Within the White House Special Files—outside of the NSC collection—are the papers of the President's Chief of Staff H R. Haldeman, who, at the end of each day, wrote, and then later dictated, a daily diary. The diary—available in CD form as *The Haldeman Diaries, the Multi-Media Edition* and published in an abridged book form by G. Putnam and Sons—contains blunt observations of the tensions between Kissinger and Rogers, showing how the nature of their relationship troubled Nixon because of the way in which it interfered with the execution of policy. Nixon's own views on the Kissinger-Rogers dynamic, as well as those regarding the Arab-Israeli dispute, are on full display in the White House Presidential Recordings, which begin in February 1971. Those that are transcribed or cited in this and other *Foreign Relations* volumes comprise only a small portion of what is available in the Nixon Presidential Materials, and, thus, represent what the editors and the Nixon Tape team at the Office of the Historian believe are the key recordings.

After the Nixon Presidential Materials, the compilation of this volume benefitted most from the records of the Department of State. The large and well-trammeled Record Group 59, Department of State Central Files at NARA, contain the most complete record of communications to and from posts in the Middle East. While documents related to the Arab-Israeli dispute are almost entirely in POL 27–14 ARAB–ISR and POL 27–14 ARAB–ISR/UN, others can be found in other POL and DEF files for Israel and the front-line Arab states. The Department of State Lot File for the Office of Israel and Arab-Israel Affairs, Bureau of Near Eastern and South Asian Affairs, contains copious background information but little material on policy-making—with the exception of two boxes of Middle East-related NSSMs, the contents of which are largely unavailable to the public. The Rogers Lot File is filled with speeches, personal correspondence, records of trips and state visits, statements before congressional committees, and documents concerning the Secretary's interactions with the media, while the Sisco Lot File is helpful for material on the 1969 two-power talks and NSC Interdepartmental Group memoranda. Most documents of value in the Department of State Lot Files are duplicated in the Nixon collection, and, ultimately, the researcher will get a better sense of the Department's role in policy-making (or lack thereof) from Rogers all the way down to embassy officials, through the NSC Files of the Nixon Presidential Materials.

The records of the Department of Defense, the CIA, and Henry Kissinger—at the Library of Congress—were useful to greater and lesser degrees for this volume, but it should be noted they are closed to the public. The Department of Defense files at the Washington National Records Center reveal how the views of Secretary of Defense Melvin Laird ran contrary to the White House's on U.S. military support for Israel, but his perspective can also be gleaned from Defense documents in the NSC Files. Nonetheless, the details of weapons discussions—and the deals that emerged from them—between Defense officials and their counterparts from other countries can sometimes be found only in the Department's own files. The CIA records, which are in Agency custody, contain intelligence estimates and memoranda on various Middle East topics that helped inform decision-making at the White House, and most of those documents are in National Intelligence Council (NIC) Files. Helms's memoranda to Kissinger and the President are in the Director of Central Intelligence (DCI) files and the Executive Registry, but, again, the most important memoranda and finished intelligence are in the NSC Files of the Nixon records. Finally, there are the Papers of Henry Kissinger at the Manuscript Division of the Library of Congress, a collection available, by permission of Kissinger himself, to the staff at the Office of the Historian for use in the *Foreign Relations* series. Many of the documents here are duplicates of those in the Nixon Presidential Materials, especially those in Kissinger's Chronological and Geopolitical Files. But for minutes of meetings missing from the Nixon NSC Files, the Kissinger Top Secret (TS) Files were critical for filling in these gaps.

The following list identifies the particular files and collections used in the preparation of this volume.

Unpublished Sources

Department of State, Record Group 59, Files of the Department of State

National Archives and Records Administration, College Park, Maryland

    Central Files. Central files are the general subject files for Department of State materials. The 1969-1972 period includes two sets of materials (1967–1969 and 1970–1973) organized by a subject-numeric system. This system consists of seven broad categories: Administration, Consular, Culture and Information, Economic, Political and Defense, Science, and Social. In particular, the Political (POL) and Defense (DEF) related files are important to this *Foreign Relations* volume. Within each of these divisions are subject subcategories. For example, Political and Defense contains four subtopics: POL (Politics), DEF (Defense), CSM (Communism) and INT (Intelligence). Numerical subdivisions further define the subtopics. The following represent the most important central files utilized for this volume:

        DEF 12 ISR
        DEF 12–5 ISR
        DEF 12–5 JORDAN
        DEF 12–5 LEB
        ORG 7 S AID [US] JORDAN
        POL 7 UAR
        POL 15–1 JORDAN
        POL 23–8 LEB
        POL 27–12 ARAB-ISR
        POL 27–14 ARAB-ISR
        POL IS–US/NIXON
        POL LEB–US

    Lot Files

        Bureau of Near Eastern and South Asian Affairs
        Office Files of William Rogers
        Office Files of Joseph J. Sisco

Lyndon B. Johnson Presidential Library

Austin, Texas

    National Security File
        Middle East

Nixon Presidential Materials, National Archives and Records Administration

College Park, Maryland

(Note: These files have been transferred to the Nixon Presidential Library and Museum in Yorba Linda, California)

    Kissinger Telephone Conversation Transcripts
    NSC Files:
        Agency Files
        Country Files
        Kissinger Office Files

NSC Institutional Files (H-Files)
President's Trip Files
Presidential Correspondence
Presidential Daily Briefings
Presidential/Kissinger Memcons
Saunders Files
Subject Files
VIP Visits
White House Special Files
White House Central Files:
The President's Daily Diary
White House Tapes

Henry A. Kissinger Papers

Library of Congress, Manuscripts Division, Washington, DC
Geopolitical File

Department of Defense

Washington National Records Center
Office of the Secretary of Defense (OSD) Files
International Security Affairs (ISA) Files

National Security Council

Washington, DC
Subject Files

Central Intelligence Agency

Langley, VA
Office of the Director of Central Intelligence Files
Office of Executive Registry Files

Published Sources

Beattie, Kirk. *Egypt During the Sadat Years*. New York: Palgrave, 2000.
Dobrynin, Anatoliy. *In Confidence: Moscow's Ambassador to America's Six Cold War Presidents*. New York: Times Books, 1995.
Geyer, David C., and Douglas Selvage, eds. *Soviet-American Relations: The Détente Years, 1969–1972*. Washington: Government Printing Office, 2007.
Haldeman, H.R. *The Haldeman Diaries: Inside the Nixon White House*. New York: Putnam, 1994.
———. *The Haldeman Diaries: Inside the Nixon White House, Multimedia Edition*
Kissinger, Henry A. *White House Years*. Boston: Little, Brown and Company, 1979.
Meir, Golda. *My Life*. London: Weidenfeld and Nicolson, 1075.
Rabin, Yitzhak. *The Rabin Memoirs*. Berkeley: University of California Press, 1996.
Sadat, Anwar. *In Search of Identity: An Autobiography*. New York: Harper and Row, 1978.
The New York Times
United Nations. *Yearbook of the United Nations*, 1969–1972.
United States. Department of State. *Bulletin*, 1969–1972.

———. National Archives and Records Administration. *The Public Papers of the Presidents of the United States: Lyndon Johnson, 1968-69*. Washington: Government Printing Office, 1970.
———. National Archives and Records Administration. *The Public Papers of the Presidents of the United States: Richard Nixon, 1969, 1970, 1971, 1972*. Washington: Government Printing Office, 1971–1974.
The Washington Post

Abbreviations and Terms

AF, Bureau of African Affairs, Department of State
AF/N, Office of Algeria, Libya, Morocco, Spanish Sahara, Tunisia, Sudan, Mauritania Affairs, Bureau of African Affairs, Department of State
AMB, Ambassador
ASU, Arab Socialist Union, Egypt's only political party
ASW, Anti-Submarine Warfare

BG, Brigadier General

CBU, Cluster Bomb
CENTO, Central Treaty Organization
CIA, Central Intelligence Agency
CINCMEAFSA, Commander in Chief Middle East/South Asia and Africa South of the Sahara
CJCS, Chairman of the Joint Chiefs of Staff
COMINT, Communications Intelligence

DAO, Defense Attaché's Office
DCI, Director of Central Intelligence
DCM, Deputy Chief of Mission
Dept, Department of State
DeptOff, Department of State officer
DIA, Defense Intelligence Agency
DOD, Department of Defense

ECM, Electronic Countermeasures
EDT, Eastern Daylight Time
ELINT, Electronic Intelligence
EmbOff, Embassy Officer
EST, Eastern Standard Time
EUR, Bureau of European Affairs, Department of State
EUR/SOV, Office of Soviet Union Affairs, Bureau of European Affairs, Department of State
Exdis, Exclusive Distribution

FBI, Federal Bureau of Investigation
FBIS, Foreign Broadcast Information Service
FMS, Foreign Military Sales
FonMin, Foreign Minister
FonOff, Foreign Office/Foreign Official
FY, fiscal year
FYI, for your information

GA, General Assembly
Gen., General
GMT, Greenwich Mean Time
GNP, Gross National Product

XXV

XXVI Abbreviations and Terms

GOI, Government of Israel
GOJ, Government of Jordan
GOL, Government of Lebanon
GUAR, Government of the United Arab Republic

HAK, Henry A. Kissinger
HHS, Harold H. Saunders

IAEA, International Atomic Energy Agency
IAF, Israeli Air Force
IAI, Office of Israel and Arab-Israeli Affairs, Bureau of Near Eastern and South Asian Affairs, Department of State
ICRC, International Committee of the Red Cross
IDAF, Israel Defense Air Forces
IDF, Israel Defense Forces
ILO, International Labor Organization
INR, Bureau of Intelligence and Research, Department of State
INR/DRR, Directorate for Regional Research, Bureau of Intelligence and Research, Department of State
INR/RNA/NE, Office of Research and Analysis for Near East and South Asia, Near East Division, Bureau of Intelligence and Research, Department of State
INR/RSE, Office of Research and Analysis for USSR and Eastern Europe, Bureau of Intelligence and Research, Department of State
IO, Bureau of International Organization Affairs, Department of State
IO/UNP, Office of United Nations Political Affairs, Bureau of International Organization Affairs, Department of State

JAF, Jordanian Air Force
JD, Jordanian Dollar

MAP, Military Assistance Program
ME, Middle East
Memcon, Memorandum of Conversation
MIG, A.I. Mikoyan i M.I. Gurevich (Soviet fighter aircraft named for aircraft designers Mikoyan and Gurevich)

NATO, North Atlantic Treaty Organization
NEA, Bureau of Near Eastern and South Asian Affairs, Department of State
NEA/ARN, Office of Lebanon, Jordan, Syrian Arab Republic, and Iraq Affairs, Bureau of Near Eastern and South Asian Affairs, Department of State
NEA/ARP, Office of Saudi Arabia, Kuwait, Yemen, and Aden Affairs, Bureau of Near Eastern and South Asian Affairs, Department of State
NEA/EGY, Office of Egyptian Affairs, Bureau of Near Eastern and South Asian Affairs, Department of State
NEA/IAI, Office of Israel and Arab-Israeli Affairs, Bureau of Near Eastern and South Asian Affairs, Department of State
NEA/RA, Office of Regional Affairs, Bureau of Near Eastern and South Asian Affairs, Department of State
NEA/UAR, Office of United Arab Republic Affairs, Bureau of Near Eastern and South Asian Affairs, Department of State
NPT, Nuclear Non-Proliferation Treaty
NSC, National Security Council
Nodis, No Distribution (other than to persons indicated)
Noforn, No Foreign Dissemination

NSDM, National Security Decision Memorandum
NSSM, National Security Study Memorandum

OAU, Organization of African Unity
OMB, Office of Management and Budget
OSD, Office of the Secretary of Defense
OSD/ISA, Office of the Secretary of Defense for International Security Affairs.

PA, Bureau of Public Affairs, Department of State
PFLP, Popular Front for the Liberation of Palestine
PLO, Palestine Liberation Organization
PM, Prime Minister
PM/MAS, Office of Military Assistance and Sales, Bureau of Poltico-Military Affairs, Department of State

Reftel, reference telegram
RES, Resolution
RG, Record Group
RN, Richard Nixon

S, Office of the Secretary of State
SA–2, Surface-to-Air Missile
SA–3, Surface-to-Air Missile
S/S, Executive Secretariat of the Department of State
SALT, Strategic Arms Limitation Treaty
SAM, Surface-to-Air Missile
SC, Security Council
Secto, series indicator for telegrams from the Secretary of State while away from Washington
Septel, separate telegram
SFRC, Senate Foreign Relations Committee
SRG, Senior Review Group
SSM, Surface-to-Surface Missile
SYG, United Nations Secretary General

Tosec, series indicator for telegrams to the Secretary of State while away from Washington

UAR, United Arab Republic
UK, United Kingdom
UN, United Nations
UNDP, United Nations Development Program
UNGA, United Nations General Assembly
UNRWA, United Nations Relief and Works Agency for Palestine Refugees in the Near East
UNSC, United Nations Security Council
USAF, United States Air Force
USDAO, United States Defense Attaché Office
USG, United States Government
USINT, United States Interests Section
USNATO, United States Mission to the North Atlantic Treaty Organization
USSR, Union of Soviet Socialist Republics
USUN, United States Mission at the United Nations

WHO, World Health Organization
WSAG, Washington Special Actions Group

Persons

Agnew, Spiro T., Vice President of the United States from January 20, 1969, until October 10, 1973
Allon, Yigal, Deputy Prime Minister of Israel; Acting Prime Minister from February until March 1969
Arafat, Yassir, Leader of Fatah and Chairman of the Executive Committee of the Palestine Liberation Organization
Argov, Shlomo, Minister of Israeli Embassy until August 1971
Asad (Assad), Hafez al-, President of Syria
Atherton, Alfred L., Jr., Country Director, Office of Israel and Arab-Israel Affairs, Bureau of Near East and South Asian Affairs, Department of State until March 1970; thereafter, Deputy Assistant Secretary of State for Near Eastern and South Asian Affairs

Bar-On, Lieutenant Colonel Aryeh, Aide to Israeli Defense Minister Dayan
Barbour, Walworth, U.S. Ambassador to Israel
Beam, Jacob D., U.S. Ambassador to the Soviet Union from March 1969
Begin, Menachem, leader, Herut Party
Behr, Colonel Robert M., USAF, senior staff member, National Security Council Operations Staff for Scientific Affairs from 1969 until 1971
Bérard, Armand, French Permanent Representative to the United Nations until February 1970
Bergus, Donald C., Principal Officer of the U.S. Interests Section in Cairo until February 1972
Bitan, Moshe, Assistant Director General, Israeli Ministry of Foreign Affairs
Brezhnev, Leonid Ilyich, General Secretary of the Communist Party of the Soviet Union
Brown, L. Dean, U.S. Ambassador to Jordan from September 1970
Buffum, William B., U.S. Deputy Permanent Representative to the United Nations until September 1970; U.S. Ambassador to Lebanon from September 1970
Bunche, Ralph, Under Secretary General of the United Nations until June 1971
Bush, George H.W., U.S. Permanent Representative to the United Nations from February 1971

Caradon, Lord (Hugh Mackintosh Foot), British Permanent Representative to the United Nations until 1970
Celler, Emanuel, Member, U.S. House of Representatives (D-New York) until 1973; Dean of the U.S. House of Representatives
Cline, Ray S., Director, Bureau of Intelligence and Research, Department of State

Davies, Rodger P., Deputy Assistant Secretary of State for Near Eastern and South Asian Affairs
Davis, Jeanne W., National Security Council Staff Secretary
Dayan, Moshe, Defense Minister of Israel
De Gaulle, Charles, President of France until April 1969
De Palma, Samuel, Assistant Secretary of State for International Organizations Affairs from February 1969 until June 1973
Dinitz, Simcha, Special Assistant to Golda Meir
Dobrynin, Anatoliy F., Soviet Ambassador to the United States
Dulles, John Foster, Secretary of State from January 1953 until April 1959

XXX Persons

Eban, Abba, Foreign Minister of Israel
Ehrlichman, John, Assistant to the President for Domestic Affairs
Eisenhower, Dwight D., President of the United States from 1953 until 1961
Eliot, Theodore L., Jr., Executive Secretary of the Department of State from August 1969
Elizur, Michael, Director of North American Affairs and Acting Assistant Director General, Israeli Minister of Foreign Affairs as of 1970

Fahmy, Ismail, Egyptian Under Secretary of Foreign Affairs
Faisal ibn Abd al-Aziz al Saud, King of Saudi Arabia
Fawzi, Mahmoud, Foreign Affairs Assistant to Gamal Abdel Nasser; Prime Minister of Egypt until January 1972
Fawzi, General Mohamed, Egyptian Minister of Defense from 1968 until 1971
Fulbright, J. William, Senator (D-Arkansas); Chairman, Senate Committee on Foreign Relations

Garment, Leonard, Adviser to President Nixon on Jewish Affairs
Gazit, Mordechai, Director General of the Israeli Prime Minister's Office under Golda Meir
Ghaleb, Mohammed Murad, Egyptian Ambassador to Moscow until January 1972; Foreign Minister of Egypt from February 1972
Ghorbal, Ashraf, Chief, Egyptian Interests Section, Foreign Ministry of the United Arab Republic
Greene, Joseph N., Jr., Principal Officer, U.S. Interests Section in Cairo from February 1972 until July 1973
Gromyko, Andrei A., Soviet Foreign Minister
Gur, Major General Mordechai, Military Attaché, Israeli Embassy in Washington

Haig, General Alexander M., Jr., Senior Military Adviser to the Assistant to the President for National Security Affairs from January 1969 until June 1970; Deputy Assistant to the President for National Security Affairs
Haldeman, H.R., Assistant to the President; White House Chief of Staff from January 1969 until April 1973
Hassan bin Talal, el-, Crown Prince of Jordan and younger brother of King Hussein
Hassan Muhammed ibn Yusuf, Mawlay al-, King of Morocco from 1961
Heikal, Mohamed Hasanayn, Editor and weekly columnist at Cairo daily newspaper, *Al Ahram*; adviser to Gamal Abdel Nasser and Anwar al-Sadat
Helms, Richard M., Director of Central Intelligence, Central Intelligence Agency from June 1966 until February 1973
Helou, Charles, President of Lebanon until September 1970
Herzog, General Chaim, Special Assistant to Golda Meir
Hoskinson, Samuel M., member, National Security Council Staff from 1970 until 1972
Hussein bin Talal, King of Jordan from 1953

Irwin, John N. II, Under Secretary of State from September 1970 until July 1972; thereafter, Deputy Secretary of State
Ismail, Hafez, Egyptian Chief of Intelligence

Jackson, Henry M. "Scoop", Senator (D-Washington)
Jarring, Gunnar V., Swedish Ambassador to the Soviet Union; detailed to the United Nations to serve as Special Representative, United Nations Middle East Mission
Johnson, Lyndon B., President of the United States from 1963 until 1969
Johnson, U. Alexis, Under Secretary of State for Political Affairs from February 1969

Karamessines, Thomas, Deputy Director for Plans, Central Intelligence Agency, until 1973
Kennedy, David M., Secretary of the Treasury from January 22, 1969, until February 11, 1971
Kennedy, Colonel Richard T., member, National Security Council Staff
Kissinger, Henry A., Assistant to the President for National Security Affairs from 1969
Knowles, Lieutenant General Richard T., USA, Assistant to the Chairman of the Joint Chiefs of Staff
Kosygin, Aleksei N., Chairman of the Council of Ministers of the Soviet Union

Laird, Melvin R., Secretary of Defense from 1969
Lincoln, General George A., Director, Office of Emergency Preparedness, from 1969 until 1973

Malik, Yakov A., Soviet Representative to the United Nations
McCloskey, Robert J., Deputy Assistant Secretary of State for Press Relations and Ambassador at Large from 1969
Meir, Golda, Prime Minister of Israel from March 1969
Mitchell, John N., Attorney General of the United States
Moorer, Admiral Thomas H., USN, Chief of Naval Operations until July 1970; thereafter Chairman of the Joint Chiefs of Staff

Narasimhan, C.V., Deputy Secretary General of the United Nations; Acting Administrator of the United Nations Development Program as of 1971; Under Secretary General for Inter-Agency Affairs and Coordination from 1972 until 1978; Chef de Cabinet to the Secretary General as of 1972
Nasser, Gamal Abdel, President of Egypt until September 1970
Newlin, Michael H., Political Affairs Counselor, U.S. Mission to the United Nations, from 1968 until 1972; Deputy Chief of Mission of the Embassy in Kinshasa from 1972 until 1975; U.S Consul General in Jerusalem from 1975 until 1980
Nixon, Richard M., President of the United States from January 20 1969 until August 9, 1974
Noyes, James H., Deputy Assistant Secretary of Defense for Near Eastern, African, and Southern Asian Affairs from 1970
Nutter, G. Warren, Assistant Secretary of Defense for International Security Affairs from March 1969 until January 1972

Packard, David, Deputy Secretary of Defense from January 1969 until December 1971
Pompidou, Georges, President of France from June 1969
Pranger, Robert J., Deputy Assistant Secretary of Defense for the Near East and South Asia, 1970; Deputy Assistant Secretary of Defense for Policy Plans and NSC Affairs, 1971

Qadhafi (Qaddafi, Kaddafi), Muammar al-, Chairman of the Libyan Revolutionary Command Council and Commander in Chief of the Libyan Armed Forces

Rabin, Lieutenant General Yitzhak, Israeli Ambassador to the United States
Riad, Mahmoud, Foreign Minister of Egypt until 1972
Riad, Mohammed, Counselor Egyptian Foreign Ministry
Richardson, Elliot L., Under Secretary of State until June 23, 1970; thereafter, Secretary of Health, Education, and Welfare
Rifai, Abdel Munim, Prime Minister of Jordan from March until August 1969; Foreign Minister from August 1969 until June 1970; Prime Minister from June until September 1970; thereafter Foreign Minister

XXXII   Persons

Rifai, Zaid, Secretary General of the Royal Court of Jordan; King Hussein's private secretary
Rogers, William P., Secretary of State from January 1969 until September 1973
Rostow, Eugene V., Under Secretary of State for Political Affairs until February 1969
Rush, Kenneth W., Deputy Secretary of Defense from February 1972 until January 1973
Rusk, Dean, Secretary of State until January 1969

Sadat, Anwar al-, President of Egypt from October 1970
Saint George, Rear Admiral William R., member, National Security Council Staff, as of 1970
Saunders, Harold H., member, National Security Council Staff from 1969 until 1971
Seelye, Talcott W., Country Director, Lebanon, Jordan, Syrian Arab Republic, and Iraq, Bureau of Near Eastern and South Asian Affairs, Department of State
Selden, Armistead I., Jr., Principal Deputy Assistant Secretary of Defense for International Security Affairs from 1970 until 1972
Shakespeare, Frank, Director, United States Information Agency, from 1969
Sharaf, Abdul Hamid, Jordanian Ambassador to the United States
Sisco, Joseph J., Assistant Secretary of State for Near East and South Asian Affairs from February 1969
Sonnenfeldt, Helmut, member, National Security Council Staff
Stackhouse, Heywood, Country Director, Office of Israel and Arab Israel Affairs, Department of State
Sterner, Michael, Country Director, Office of United Arab Republic Affairs, Department of State
Symmes, Harrison M., U.S. Ambassador to Jordan until May 1970

Tcherniakov, Yuri N., Chargé d'Affaires, Soviet Embassy, Washington
Tekoah, Yosef, Israeli Representative to the United Nations
Thant, U, Secretary General of the United Nations until December 1971
Thornton, Thomas, member, National Security Council Staff

Vinogradov, Vladimir M., Deputy Foreign Minister of the Soviet Union until 1970; thereafter Soviet Ambassador to Egypt

Waldheim, Kurt, Secretary General of the United Nations from December 1971
Warnke, Paul, Assistant Secretary of Defense for International Security Affairs
Wheeler, General Earle G., Chairman of the Joint Chiefs of Staff until July 1970
Wiley, Marshall W., Counselor, U.S. Interests Section, Cairo

Yariv, Major General Aharon, Chief of the Intelligence Corps, Israeli Defense Forces
Yost, Charles W., U.S. Permanent Representative to the United Nations from January 1969 until February 1971

Zayyat, Mohamed Hassan el-, Egyptian Representative to the United Nations until February 1972; thereafter Foreign Minister
Zeigler, Ronald, White House Press Secretary
Zurhellen, Joseph O., Deputy Chief of Mission, U.S. Embassy in Tel Aviv, until 1973

Arab-Israeli Dispute, 1969–1972

The Rogers Plan

1. Telegram From the Department of State to the Embassy in Israel[1]

Washington, January 2, 1969, 0259Z.

11. *Summary.* Under Secretary Rostow January 1 handed Israeli Chargé Argov copy of USSR peace Quote plan Unquote given Secretary by Soviet Chargé December 30 (septel).[2] Rostow noted that this latest Soviet approach, while reiterating many standard Soviet positions, also contained significant innovations responsive to U.S. insistence on need for agreement among parties to conflict. This could be important development, and we believed it imperative to proceed from hypothesis that Soviets wanted movement now toward Middle East settlement. Rostow outlined for Argov our preliminary analysis of Soviet memorandum and tentative views on how we should reply, emphasizing these not yet cleared within USG. This connection, Rostow assured Argov there would be no change in fundamentals of our policy. We would stress to Soviets need for parties themselves to agree on settlement and would cast reply in terms of what US and USSR

---

[1] Source: Johnson Library, National Security File, Middle East, Country File, Box 142, Israel, Cables and Memos, Vol. XI, 12/68–1/69. Secret; Exdis. Drafted by Atherton and approved by Rostow. Repeated to London, Paris, Moscow, Amman, Cairo, and USUN.

[2] A memorandum of conversation of Rusk's December 30 meeting with Soviet Chargé Uri Tcherniakov is in the National Archives, RG 59, Central Files 1967–69, POL 27–12 ARAB–ISR. For an unofficial translation of the Soviet "peace 'plan'," see *Foreign Relations, 1964–1968*, volume XX, Arab-Israeli Dispute, 1967–1968, Document 374. The same day, Tcherniakov also gave Robert Ellsworth, an assistant to President-elect Nixon, two notes outlining a Soviet plan for a political settlement in the Middle East. The notes given to Ellsworth were almost identical to those Tcherniakov handed to Secretary of State Dean Rusk. The memorandum of conversation between Ellsworth and Tcherniakov and the Soviet notes given Ellsworth are in the National Archives, Nixon Presidential Materials, NSC Files, Kissinger Office Files, Box 1, HAK Administrative and Staff Files—Transition, Robert Ellsworth.

might jointly do to help Jarring. Rostow agreed to Argov's request that US not repeat not reply to USSR until we had received GOI reaction to latest Soviet memorandum, which Argov thought should be available by end of week. *End summary.*

1. Under Secretary Rostow called in Israeli Chargé Argov January 1 to inform GOI of latest Soviet approach on Middle East made by Soviet Chargé Tcherniakov to Secretary December 30. Rostow told Argov Tcherniakov had left two papers: (A) A general statement of Soviet policy which contained nothing new, and (B) new Quote plan Unquote for Middle East settlement. Rostow gave Argov copy of latter document, noting that Tcherniakov had said Soviets did not repeat not plan publish it and that we desired it be held in confidence. Argov assured us there would be great care in handling information.

2. Tcherniakov had also made the comment, which seemed particularly significant since this Soviet approach followed Gromyko's Cairo visit, that USSR had reason to hope the UAR would accept new Soviet Quote plan Unquote if Israel did. In this connection, Rostow noted that we had report from Cairo that UARG had Quote lost Unquote paragraph of its reply to Secretary's seven points about Egyptian will to peace which we expected to receive shortly.[3]

3. Rostow said Tcherniakov had reported that similar approaches were being made to British and French. French Chargé Leprette had told Rostow yesterday that Soviet approach had been made to French Ambassador in Moscow by Semyanov, who had also made following points orally:

(A) If France considered conditions favorable for a four-power effort in Middle East, this would find favorable echo within Soviet Government. (Rostow noted in this connection that Soviets had been consistently cool to idea of four-power approach.)

(B) Soviets did not repeat not envisage imposition of solution on parties in which latter had not participated.

(C) Reopening of Suez Canal no longer linked to settlement of refugee problem.

(D) While avoiding direct reply to question of whether prior Israeli withdrawal was precondition for negotiations, Semyanov said USSR

---

[3] On November 2, 1968, Secretary Rusk presented to Egyptian Foreign Minister Riad an eight-point peace proposal. Seven points were written: 1) Israeli withdrawal from territory of UAR; 2) a formal termination of the state of war; 3) Suez Canal open to all flagships; 4) Palestinian refugees would have a choice of resettlement in 15 countries, including Israel; 5) international presence at Sharm el-Sheikh; 6) a general understanding about level of arms in area; 7) both UAR and Israel would be signatory to document. The eighth point was provided orally: Egypt would not have to accept the proposal until an agreement was worked out for the other Arab states. See *Foreign Relations, 1964–1968,* volume XX, Arab-Israeli Dispute, 1967–1968, Document 301.

was seeking Quote preliminary agreement of the parties on all of the elements of a final settlement Unquote.

4. Turning to latest Soviet Quote plan Unquote, Rostow said we were preparing careful analysis and had some preliminary views which we wanted to share with GOI. While many points in Soviet memorandum were repetitions of old positions and there were number of internal contradictions, we saw following significant changes:

(A) Soviets were now speaking of need for Quote agreed Unquote plan by means of contacts through Jarring at beginning of settlement process. Rostow said we interpreted this language as Soviet response to our emphasis on concept of agreement among parties. Semyanov's language seems to characterize Soviet conception of Quote plan Unquote as given in paper.

(B) This agreed plan, to be arrived at before any action is taken on the ground, is to cover entire Quote package Unquote of issues dealt with in November 1967 Security Council Resolution.[4]

(C) New Soviet memorandum contains clear implication that border rectifications are envisaged. This implication is contained in language that Quote provisions shall also be agreed upon which concern secure and recognized boundaries (with corresponding maps attached) Unquote. At same time, Rostow noted, Soviets have left themselves an out by including language from their September 4 note about withdrawal to pre-June 5 lines.[5]

(D) Soviets are no longer insisting that settlement process must begin with Israeli declaration of readiness to start partial withdrawal by a given date. Instead, Israel and Arab states are to issue declarations simultaneously of Quote readiness to achieve peaceful settlement Unquote.

(E) Soviets now describe purpose of agreement between parties as Quote establishment of just and lasting peace Unquote and not repeat not merely as Quote political settlement Unquote.

(F) Soviet memorandum appeared to suggest that settlement process could begin without Syrian participation. In this connection, French Chargé had reported that Soviet Ambassador in Cairo, in conversation with French Ambassador, had said that if agreement reached between UAR and Israel then Syria would be obliged to come along.

---

[4] UN Security Council Resolution 242, adopted unanimously on November 22, 1967, was passed in the wake of the Arab-Israeli war of 1967. The resolution established a "land-for-peace" framework to resolve the Arab-Israeli dispute. For the text of the resolution, see ibid., volume XIX, Arab-Israeli Crisis and War, 1967, Document 542.

[5] Dobrynin delivered the note in a meeting with Rusk and Deputy Under Secretary Bohlen. For a record of the meeting and a translation of the note, see ibid., volume XX, Arab-Israeli Dispute, 1967–1968, Document 245. "Pre-June 5 lines" refers to the borders between Israel and its neighbors that existed before the Arab-Israeli war of 1967.

5. Rostow said that the timing of this Soviet approach was of particular interest, coming as it did after Gromyko's Cairo visit and after Israeli attack on Beirut airport to which Soviets, however, have made no reference.[6] Question arose of why Soviets wanted to move now toward settlement without awaiting new U.S. administration. Rostow said we believed we must operate from hypothesis that Soviets wanted early movement toward settlement, perhaps because of concern about risks of military blow-up in area, and of situation they could not control. Soviets might also hope for concessions from present administration but, if so, they would be disappointed. While flexible and responsive, USG did not repeat not intend to abandon fundamental principles and did not repeat not wish to negotiate details of settlement with Soviets for parties.

6. Rostow said that our preliminary and as yet uncleared ideas about how to reply to latest Soviet approach were as follows: We would state that we were always prepared to discuss with others how we might help Jarring Mission. We do not want to take over negotiations from parties and would seek to cast our reply in terms of advice that USG and USSR could give to Jarring. We might, for example, revert to Jarring's March 10 formula,[7] seeking to persuade Soviets to join us in advising Jarring to call a meeting of the parties with revised Quote plan Unquote as agenda. While Soviets have never replied to Rostow's questions to Dobrynin on this point, they have never rejected the idea.[8] Our purpose was to encourage movement on Jarring's part, Rostow said, and we continued to believe that Israel should take initiatives with Jarring in order to preempt initiatives by others. Noting that Soviets appeared to be negotiating for Nasser, Rostow said we would prefer to make clear in our reply that we are not speaking for Israel, although we would handle that point in the light of our consultation with GOI. In response to question from Argov, Rostow said we were proceeding from hypothesis that what Soviets told us was binding on Cairo.

---

[6] Israeli commandos attacked the Beirut International Airport on December 28, 1968, in reprisal for an attack by Palestinian guerrillas on an Israeli commercial aircraft in the airport at Athens. See ibid., Document 367. Gromyko visited Cairo in late December 1968.

[7] Swedish Ambassador Gunnar V. Jarring was the UN Secretary General's Special Representative to the United Nation's Middle East Mission, a position established by Security Council Resolution 242. Jarring's formula stipulated that the Governments of the United Arab Republic and Israel accept that Resolution 242 provided the basis for settling their differences and that they would send representatives to negotiations on peace on that basis.

[8] Presumably a reference to a luncheon meeting between Rostow and Dobrynin on November 8, 1968, at which they discussed prospects for the Jarring Mission. (Telegram 269827 to Tel Aviv, November 9, 1968; National Archives, RG 59, Central Files 1967–69, POL 27 ARAB–ISR)

7. Rostow concluded by saying that we believed latest Soviet approach could represent important development, and we were desirous of consulting with GOI in this matter.

8. Noting that Israeli Cabinet and Ambassador Rabin were now reviewing entire situation with respect to Middle East settlement, Argov said that while he realized we wished to reply soonest to Soviets, he asked that USG delay replying until we had received Israeli reaction to latest Soviet approach. Rostow agreed if delay was no more than a few days. While reserving further comment, Argov observed that on quick perusal memorandum appeared to contain many old and unacceptable positions: e.g., with respect to nature of final peace settlement. If further study revealed that there had been movement on Soviet side, this demonstrated again that basic rule of world politics was that when U.S. was firm, Soviets always yielded in the end.

Rusk

2. Telegram From the Department of State to Certain Diplomatic Posts[1]

Washington, January 16, 1969, 0204Z.

7299. 1. Following is text our reply to recent Soviet approaches on Middle East which Secretary gave Soviet Chargé, Wednesday, January 15. Final version had been modified in minor respects to take account of some but not all comments received from Israelis and British (French comments not received at time final text prepared.)

2. Amman should give copies confidentially to GOJ. In doing so should note that it must be regarded as reply to specific Soviet communications and not as broad and comprehensive statement of US policy. (FYI The necessity to rebut and get straight Soviet arguments and assertions inevitably gives the reply a flavor which the Arabs may interpret as being unbalanced against them. We should endeavor make context clear without being defensive about text.) Amman should also emphasize US desire that US–USSR consultations and exchanges regarding ME be carried on in context of support for Jarring Mission and SC No-

---

[1] Source: Johnson Library, National Security File, Country File, Middle East, Box 147, Jordan, Cables, Vol. V, 3/68–1/69. Secret; Priority; Exdis. Drafted by Arthur R. Day (Deputy Director, Office of U.N. Political Affairs), cleared by Atherton, and approved by Sisco. Sent to Amman, Cairo, Tel Aviv, USUN, London, Paris, and Moscow.

vember 22 Res. All our efforts continue be directed to assisting Jarring in carrying out his mandate and are designed to improve his chances for success.

3. We are providing copies to Israelis, British and French here.

4. Embassy Moscow should make copy available to Jarring.

5. *Begin text:* We have studied the communications of the Soviet Government presented to Secretary Rusk on December 30.[2] These communications have been brought to the attention of President Johnson who requests that this response of the US Government be transmitted to Chairman Kosygin.

The United States Government has also studied the oral communication on the ME presented to Under Secretary Rostow by Minister Tcherniakov on December 19, 1968.[3]

The US Government welcomes the desire of the Soviet Government to cooperate with it in assisting Amb Jarring in his efforts to promote agreement on a peaceful and accepted settlement of the conflict in the ME. The United States values the continuing exchange of views with the Sov Govt concerning the ME, in particular since a continued impasse contains dangers of violence that could threaten the state interests of the United States.

The US Govt has noted certain constructive elements in the latest communications from the Govt of the Soviet Union, particularly the recognition reflected in those communications of the principle that a settlement should be based upon agreement among the parties to establish a just and lasting peace in the ME, in accordance with the provisions and principles of the SC Res of Nov 22, 1967.

The US Govt notes that certain other aspects of the Sov Govt's communications reiterate positions and opinions which do not accord with US views on responsibility for the hostilities in June, 1967, and for the impasse in the Jarring Mission, and on the proper interpretation of the SC Res. The US considers it important that there be no misunderstanding with the Soviet Union on this vital subject, and therefore offers the following comments:

1. The US regards it as a matter of the highest priority that the Soviet Union, and US and other countries use their full influence to arrest the dangerous increase in Arab terrorism in the area. Terrorism leads inevitably to reprisal. The cycle of terrorism and reprisal, in the judge-

---

[2] See footnote 2, Document 1.

[3] The note from the Soviet Union, handed to Rusk by Tcherniakov on December 19, 1968, was a formal response to "recent statements made by American officials in conversations with Soviet representatives in Washington and New York regarding the problems of a Middle East settlement." For the text of the note, see *Foreign Relations, 1964–1968,* volume XX, Arab-Israeli Dispute, 1967–1968, Document 354.

ment of the US, may imperil the very possibility of reaching a peaceful settlement pursuant to the SC Res of Nov 22, 1967. Terrorist activities supported or tolerated by some governments, and the reprisals they provoke, constitute a most serious violation of the cease-fire resolutions of the Security Council.

2. The Sov communications raise again the question of Israeli acceptance of the Nov 22 Res and its readiness to implement it. In the view of the US, Israel has accepted and agreed to implement the Res by means of agreement.

It seems evident that the Arabs interpret these terms differently from the Israelis. In the view of the US, the parties should now pursue the process of clarifying their positions on key substantive issues rather than debating this point further. The US takes the plan given to us by Min Tcherniakov on Dec 30 as an indication of Sov agreement with this position.

3. The US Govt is glad to note that the Sov Govt considers that the points made to FonMin Riad by Sect Rusk contain constructive considerations. It would like to emphasize, however, that all the points made by the Secretary, including specifically that related to Israeli withdrawal, were based on the assumption that withdrawal would be part of a settlement agreed between the parties which brought a just and lasting peace to the area. The US does not share the view, expressed in the Sov communication, that the UAR responded positively to Sect Rusk's remarks.[4] It had expected that the UAR would be prepared to move further in clarifying its position than it has so far been willing to do. The US continues to hope that the Secretary's statements will ultimately have this result.

4. Both the Sov communications of Dec 19 and Dec 30 misconstrue the views of the US on the significance of the Israeli reference to the armistice agreements in FonMin Eban's statement to Amb Jarring of Nov 4.[5] The armistice agreements clearly specified that the armistice demarcation lines were not definitive political boundaries but could be changed by agreement in the transition from armistice to a condition of true peace. As the US emphasized in its communication of Sept 29, 1968,[6] the heart of US policy since June 5, 1967 has been that this transition must take place. This continues to be US policy. At the same time, it has been and remains US policy, as Pres Johnson said on Sept 10,

---

[4] See footnote 3, Document 1.

[5] For a description of Jarring's discussion with Eban, see *Foreign Relations, 1964–1968*, volume XX, Arab-Israeli Dispute, 1967–1968, Document 307.

[6] Ibid., Document 266.

1968,[7] that the secure and recognized boundaries required by the SC Res of Nov 22, 1967, cannot and should not reflect the weight of conquest. These principles are reflected in the SC Res which calls for the establishment of a just and lasting peace but does not specify that the secure and recognized boundaries to which Israeli forces would withdraw should be identical with the lines held prior to June 5, 1967, or on any other date. In the view of the US, the essential purpose of the Res is to accomplish this transition to a condition of peace, and agreement between the parties on its elements, and not return to the status quo ante. The US is convinced that continuation of the fragile armistice of the last twenty years would be a burden to world peace. The US cannot speak for Israel, but believes it important to make its own views on this matter clear once more to the Sov Govt.

5. In its communication of Dec 30, the Sov Govt states that inner qte the fundamental problem End inner qte of a ME settlement is a withdrawal of Israeli forces from inner quote the End inner qte Arab territories they occupy pursuant to the cease-fire reses to the armistice demarcation lines of June 5, 1967. The US does not regard this as a correct interpretation of the Res of Nov 22, 1967: That Res does not use the language employed in the Soviet note. The Res, in the view of the US, requires Israeli withdrawal Begin inner qte from territories occupied in the recent conflict End inner qte to secure and recognized boundaries, to be established by an agreement of the parties pursuant to para 3 of the Res. We believe this is the intendment of para 2 of the Sov plan given the US on Dec 30.

6. That plan seems in form to be an agreement to make an agreement—a provisional agreement among the parties dealing with the issues specified in the SC Res of Nov 22, 1967. This provisional agreement expressly calls for further consultations between the parties, to be organized by Amb Jarring, through which the definitive provisions of the final agreement required by para 3 of the Res would be reached.

The US finds the idea of a preliminary agreement or understanding between the parties a useful one, which could make it possible for Amb Jarring to hold productive meetings with the parties, and assist them to reach agreement on a definitive plan for fulfilling all the provisions of the SC Res, and on an agreed time schedule for carrying out such a plan. The US is of the view that the agreement contemplated by the plan should comprise all aspects of the settlement between Israel and each of its neighbors, as a Begin inner qte package End inner qte, before any steps for implementing the settlement be carried out.

---

[7] In a speech that Johnson gave on the occasion of the 125th Anniversary Meeting of B'nai B'rith. The list of guests included Deputy Prime Minister of Israel Yigal Allon. (*Public Papers: Johnson, 1968–69*, Book II, pp. 944–950)

7. The US has found certain problems of textual interpretation in analyzing the Soviet draft plan. For example, para 2 speaks of agreed provisions with regard to secure and recognized boundaries (with corresponding maps attached), while para 4 contemplates withdrawal to the armistice demarcation lines of June 5. Paragraph 2, again, recognizes the possible utility of demilitarized zones, as mentioned in the Res. But para 4 calls for the introduction of Arab troops into territories from which Israel withdraws. Para 4 mentions restoring the situation on the frontier between Israel and the UAR which existed in May, 1967. But that situation, in the view of the US, was the proximate cause of the war. And the preamble of the Soviet plan calls for a condition of peace, not of armistice. Para 4 also makes no mention of freedom of navigation for Israeli vessels in the Suez Canal. Para 5 suggests that Israeli troop withdrawal should be completed before the obligations undertaken by the Arab governments become binding on the latter. This procedure appears inconsistent with para 2 which recognizes the principle of a Begin inner qte package End inner qte settlement, and with the secondary introductory para which recognizes the need for agreement on a plan for fulfillment of other provisions of the SC Res at the same time as there is agreement on a timetable and procedure for Israeli withdrawal.

8. The US is prepared to discuss the form in which the two governments could embody their views on how to achieve a Begin inner qte package End inner qte agreement among the parties, to be negotiated in detail not by the Soviet Union and the United States, but by the parties, meeting with Amb Jarring.

9. The United States and the Soviet Union are agreed that while both governments should do everything in their power to assist Amb Jarring and the parties to reach agreement, peace cannot be imposed by them, but should be established by the agreement of the parties. The United States has no objection to an agreed timetable for Israeli withdrawal, if such a timetable is made part of the agreement of the parties. It considers that a timetable for fulfilling the agreement of the parties should be one of the problems taken up by Ambassador Jarring with them.

The United States should, however, comment at this point on two problems of security raised in the Soviet communications.

10. The Soviet statement of December 19 in paragraph 2, refers to the United States comment of November 8 regarding Israeli territorial claims respecting the UAR and adds the remark that Israel has raised Qte the question about the necessity of stationing her forces at Sharm-al-Sheikh. Unqte In the view of the United States, the process of reaching agreement and achieving a peaceful and accepted settlement, as provided in the November 22, 1967, resolution, must involve negoti-

ation of the means for carrying out all the elements of a settlement as set forth in that resolution, including the guarantee of maritime rights dealt with in paragraph 2 (a) of the resolution. It must be clearly appreciated that the June, 1967, conflict was touched off by the issue of rights of passage through the Straits of Tiran. Only the most secure arrangements for the guarantee of these rights will make possible the realization of our hopes for peace. The choice among possible means of implementing paragraph 2(a) of the Security Council Resolution is for the parties, working with Ambassador Jarring.

11. With respect to demilitarization of the Sinai, the eventual decision on this point also will depend on the parties themselves. The United States finds it difficult to believe, however, that the partial demilitarization suggested by the Soviet Government would provide the conditions of security necessary for the establishment of peace. The 1967 war began as a direct result of events in Sinai, and activities in this area had led to the outbreak of hostilities ten years earlier. It is difficult to see, in the face of this history, how a lasting peace can be based on only partial demilitarization of this sensitive area.

12. The United States continues to believe that an understanding with respect to armament levels and arms limitation is a vital aspect of the quest for peace in the Middle East. It continues to regret Soviet policy in this regard, and urges that the problem be viewed as an indispensable element of the peaceful settlement of the Middle Eastern crisis. *End text.*

Rusk

3. National Security Study Memorandum 2[1]

Washington, January 21, 1969.

TO

The Secretary of State
The Secretary of Defense
The Director of Central Intelligence
The Chairman, Joint Chiefs of Staff

SUBJECT

Middle East Policy

The President has directed the preparation of two papers on Arab-Israel problems for consideration by the NSC. One paper should consider alternative US policy approaches aimed at securing a Middle East settlement, including (1) direct Arab-Israeli negotiations (2) U.S.-Soviet negotiations and (3) Four Power negotiations.[2] The paper should also consider the possibility that no early settlement will be reached, and US interests and policies in such a situation. The second paper should consider alternative views of basic US interests in the area and should include consideration of the issues listed in the attachment.[3]

---

[1] Source: National Archives, Nixon Presidential Materials, NSC Files, NSC Institutional Files (H-Files), Box H–126, National Security Study Memoranda. Secret.

[2] The February 1 paper, "The Arab-Israeli Dispute: Principal US Options," considered six policy scenarios: 1) "Let forces in the area play themselves out, leaving it mainly to the parties to work out a settlement if they can"; 2) "More active US diplomatic support for a renewed effort by Jarring"; 3) "US–USSR negotiations to help Jarring promote a settlement"; 4) "Four-Power approach"; 5) "A unilateral US effort to bring about a settlement"; and 6) "Settlement imposed by the major powers." (Ibid., Box H–020, National Security Council Meetings, NSC Meeting Briefing by Joint Staff: SIOP (Middle East Papers) 2/4/69)

[3] The January 24 paper, "Basic US Interests in the Middle East," examined the interests and assumptions that underlay U.S. policy formulation in the Middle East on the basis of six questions: "(1) How important are our interests in that area? (2) How grave is the Soviet threat to these interests? (3) To what extent does the expansion of Soviet influence in the Middle East threaten NATO? (4) What posture should the United States ideally adopt vis-à-vis the conflicting states and groupings of states in the area? (5) What is the present US position in the area? (6) How important is an early Arab-Israel settlement to the preservation of our interests?" (Ibid., Box H–126, National Security Study Memoranda, NSSM 2) According to an undated summary prepared by Saunders, the January 24 paper was "highlighted by two differing viewpoints": 1) "A broad Arab-Israeli settlement is very important and there is enough possibility of achieving it to make its continued pursuit worthwhile"; and 2) "A broad settlement, although desirable, is not possible in the near future." (Ibid., Box H–020, National Security Council Meetings, NSC Meeting Briefing by Joint Staff: SIOP (Middle East Papers) 2/4/69) Saunders sent the undated summary under cover of a January 28 memorandum to Kissinger. (Ibid., Box H–034, Senior Review Group Meetings, Review Group Middle East 1/28/69)

The President has directed that the NSC Interdepartmental Group for the Near East perform this study.

The first paper should be forwarded to the NSC Review Group by January 25, 1969. The second paper should be forwarded to the NSC Review Group by February 24, 1969.

Attachment

1. What is the role of the Middle East today in U.S. global strategy? What are the real U.S. interests there and how important are they?

2. What is the nature of the Soviet threat to the Middle East? How likely is Soviet dominance or predominance? What forces will tend to limit Soviet influence?

3. What is the precise nature of the Soviet threat to NATO via the Middle East?

4. What is the present state of the U.S. position in the Middle East? Is it eroding drastically? Or is there a level of common interests shared with some nations in the area which will prevent it from deteriorating beyond a certain point? Is an early Arab-Israel settlement essential to preserving the U.S. position?

5. In the light of answers to these questions, what is the most appropriate U.S. posture toward the Middle East? What level and kinds of involvement are appropriate in view of our interests and U.S. and Soviet capabilities?

4. Minutes of a National Security Council Meeting[1]

Washington, February 1, 1969.

PARTICIPANTS

The President
The Vice President
The Secretary of State, William P. Rogers
The Secretary of Defense, Melvin R. Laird
The Secretary of the Treasury, David M. Kennedy
The Chairman, Joint Chiefs of Staff, General Earle G. Wheeler
The Director of Central Intelligence, Richard M. Helms
Under Secretary of State, Elliot L. Richardson
State Department Counselor, Richard F. Pederson
US Ambassador to the UN, Charles Yost
Assistant Secretary of State, Joseph J. Sisco
Former Assistant Secretary of State, Parker T. Hart
Deputy Assistant Secretary of State, Rodger P. Davies
Director, Office of Emergency Preparedness, General George A. Lincoln
Colonel Alexander Haig
Harold H. Saunders
Dr. Henry A. Kissinger

NSC Meeting on Middle East

Briefings

Helms: *History* of Arab-Jewish relations and the course of Arab nationalism (disunity).

Fedayeen movement (Fatah, PLO, PFLP): adamantly opposed to any solution other than the destruction of Israel. Their influence makes it questionable whether any Arab government could reach settlement with Israel. Current significance is that terrorism brings on Israeli reprisals, which raise likelihood of broader conflict.

Military balance: Israelis will almost certainly retain military superiority for next year or so. Superiority qualitative—depends partly on pre-emptive strategy. Jericho missiles—10 or so could be deployed 1970–1. Arabs' 1967 losses just about made up—assume USSR believes equipment sent is about all Arabs can now absorb.

Soviet interests: USSR has leapfrogged Northern Tier. Soviet naval expansion—steadier, more effective than Khrushchev's rather opportunistic move to put missiles in Cuba.

---

[1] Source: National Archives, Nixon Presidential Materials, NSC Files, NSC Institutional Files (H-Files), Box H-109, NSC Meeting Minutes, NSC Minutes, Originals 1969. Top Secret. Drafted on May 1 by Saunders. All brackets are in the original except those indicating text that remains classified. According to the President's Daily Diary, the meeting was held in the Cabinet Room from 9:37 a.m. to 12:42 p.m. (Ibid., White House Central Files)

Question:

President: You talk about USSR's "measured, effective plan." Does this emanate from military strategy or something that just happens? Do they have a meeting like ours here today, decide on policy and then execute it? Or do they just muddle along?

Policy result of high-level decision—considered policy—or just happen?

Helms: Highest level decision. Considered policy.

Briefing (continued)

Helms: *Soviet peace plan.* Acknowledge that peace is a package plan. Arabs want imposed peace. These Arab objections main reason for Israeli rejection of plan.

Arab attitudes toward U.S.: Growing hostility—see us as backing Israel—Arab "gift for twisted analysis"—Arabs see even those things we do for them as somehow directed against them.

US image good in Israel. But Israel has its own brand of reservation about our inability to see the Arabs through Israeli eyes; tendency to rely only on themselves.

JCS briefing:

1. Significance of Soviet fleet.

—Sharp increase in 1967 and 1968 [President assured himself that trend was always low before 1963 and that present trend is new.]
—Primary concern: missile and torpedo threat.
—60 technicians at Mers-el-Kebir in Algeria.
—A "challenge" to US operations. Could affect future US decisions to commit forces in the area.

2. Strategic implications for US of renewed conflict.

—Arab-Israeli balance.

[President: Looking at chart showing 2 bombers in Israeli air force asked how Israel was able to take out Arab airfields with just 2 bombers. General Wheeler answered: "fighter-bombers." President nodded quickly.]

Vice President: How do present air inventories compare with those of June, 1967?

Wheeler: Qualitative differences here and there but generally comparable.

Lincoln: How do Soviet advisors operate in Units?

Wheeler: Strictly advisory. Arabs xenophobic and not likely to submit to Soviet command.

Briefing (continued)

JCS: Imbalance in supersonic aircraft could be dangerous to Israel by June 1969.

Strategic implications

—US intervention capability. US contingency plan designed to drive a wedge between opposing forces.

Questions

President: I understand your contingency plan is based on intelligence estimate that local conflict main possibility.

I agree that US–USSR conflict remote, but what if one of Arab countries where Soviet fleet present is attacked?

Wheeler: Contingency plan if US–USSR—

President: What if a more limited Soviet involvement?

Kissinger: What if Israeli raid on Aswan dam or Israeli city shelled by Soviet fleet?

President: Could you give some thought to that?

Wheeler: Possibilities we are examining:

—US attack on Soviet bases in Siberia.
—Sink one Soviet ship in Mediterranean.
—Seize Soviet intelligence trawler.

President: Could you consider what we could do indirectly through the Israelis?

Seems to me Soviet naval presence is primarily political. Therefore, we must be prepared for a less-than-military contingency.

Wheeler: Primarily political. But Soviet presence in ports puts a Soviet umbrella over those ports. In a tenuous sense, fleet therefore does have military use.

Briefing continued

Described plan for introduction of US ground forces—initial force, follow-on and on-call forces. Plan could be fulfilled but would degrade strategic reserve.

Final arrival of on-call forces 39 days; 18 days for follow-on; 2–17 days initial. Airlift.

Questions

President: Are we capable of repeating Lebanon-type operation?[2]

---

[2] Reference is to Operation Blue Bat of July 1958, when President Eisenhower sent 14,000 Marines to Beirut in response to a request by Lebanon's President Camille Chamoun. Chamoun asked for the U.S. forces in response to the "Bastille Day" coup in Baghdad, which toppled the pro-Western government in Iraq.

Wheeler: I believe so. Would modify this plan.

President: Any military exercises politically useful?

Wheeler: Continuous US bilateral and NATO exercise. NATO has just put together surveillance unit to keep track of subs.

President: Are Sovs, Israelis, Arabs aware of these things?

Wheeler: Yes. This is one purpose of exercises.

Laird: Sixth Fleet not as "ready" as it should be in manning levels. Have to look at this as situation heats up.

President: How is Malta being used?

Wheeler: NATO has returned small air surveillance unit to Malta. Tenuous relationship of Malta to NATO via Secretary General, mainly to keep Soviets out.

President: Is Sixth Fleet NATO-related?

Wheeler: US controlled in peace; in war under NATO.

President: In a Lebanon-type situation, who controls Sixth Fleet?

Wheeler: "You do sir."

President: Isn't there significant British and French presence?

Wheeler: Significant French and Italian presence. French navy in Mediterranean. Navy most cooperative since French withdrawal till de Gaulle blew whistle.

President: Could Italians and French block or compete with Soviet past presence?

Wheeler: Mers-el-Kebir main instance. Little opportunity for us to exercise influence.

French still have residual influence which, depending on de Gaulle, could be helpful. But unlikely France could swing Algerians away from Soviet backing.

President: What has happened to French political influence?

Lincoln: What if USSR says its fleet will screen UAR coast?

Wheeler: Have to go ashore in Israel.

President: Could we phase deployment?

Wheeler: Yes—move into Europe, for instance.

Vice President: Could we involve NATO instead of us?

Wheeler: We couldn't involve NATO. Only last few months that NATO concerned about Soviet presence.

President: NATO pathological on point of involvement. For instance, may even be problem if Berlin, one of their own cities, threatened.

Vice President: Is that true about political moves?

Wheeler: Not as true.

Kissinger: To what extent could Soviet fleet be used as a hostage in Berlin crisis?

Wheeler: Yes.

President: I'm just thinking about symbolic acts.

Lincoln: If Israeli port attacked, might be unclear who did it.

Wheeler: We have pretty fair surveillance activity. We could identify—though not necessarily prove. This political problem.

Briefing continued

JCS: Main military problem (Soviets would have same problems):

1.—Deployment routes and staging areas. Need Azores or equivalent.

—Transportation resources: would require "major revision of our worldwide program."

2. Would USSR intervene? Paratroops. Two routes—Western over Yugoslavia.

Questions

President: If Sovs flew troops into Cairo or Damascus, what could we do?

Wheeler: Fly into Crete, Italy, Athens. Turkey not possible. Incirlik not usable in 1967. Malta airfield not good enough. Greeks cooperative in 1967.

Briefing continued

JCS: [2½ *lines not declassified*]

By sealift using maritime fleet, could move 6–10 divisions from Baltic (transit 13 days), 3–10 divisions from northern division (15 days), Black Sea 6–10 divisions (3 days). They have exercised in small way in Black Sea.

Impact of local conflict on US commitments. Cause problems in NATO somewhat like Czechoslovakia.

Question

Lincoln: Are Soviets stockpiling?

Wheeler: Not in UAR but in Algeria there is equipment the Algerians can't possibly use.

President: In State briefing, could you include country-by-country relations with us.

Briefing continued

Hart: In *Turkey*, attitude not pro-Arab but rather pro-Israeli but Turkey focuses on Cyprus and that requires Arab votes. Tend favor moderate Arab states. Want good relationship with Iraq, because of

Kurds. Trying to bind Iraq quietly to Turkey (gas line). Relations with US basically good, though strains.

President: *Is* this one area for patting on back—a little preventive medicine? In terms of planning of visits, Turks and others, let's have meeting soon.

Hart: Yes, sir. We have strategic and intelligence installation. Conditions of use—Turkish permission.

Morocco—Algerian tension. Never broke with us, generally friendly relations. Get as much as it can from us. Some influence on other Arab states.

Libya—Considerable US influence. Fears Nasser. US–UK bulwark against radicals.

President: Get in best team we can in terms of ambassadorial appointments. "Get heavy weights in there."

Algeria—If we renewed relations with.

President: What influence does Tito[3] have? Could he be helpful?

Hart: Mainly in UAR.

Sisco: Shift in his view since Czechoslovakia.

President: I would be open to meeting with Tito if you recommend it.

Briefing continued

Hart: In principle, it would help with radical states—even Iraq—marginally.

Sudan—broke relations but represented there. Would be one of first to resume.

Lebanon—delicate democracy. Genesis based on fear of Muslim majority around it.

Syria—unstable. Will be last to resume relations with us.

Iraq—basic instability. Will not be quick to resume relations unless regime changes.

Arab-Israeli—The main interests involved—Arab fear of Israeli expansion and Israel wants formalized peace. Johnston and Johnson missions.[4]

---

[3] Josip Broz Tito, President of Yugoslavia from 1945 to 1980.

[4] The Johnston Mission, led by President Eisenhower's Special Representative Eric Johnston, was organized in October 1953 to secure an agreement among Lebanon, Syria, Jordan, and Israel to develop the Jordan River basin. The mission ended in October 1955, when the Arab League rejected the project because it would benefit Israel along with its Arab neighbors. The Johnson Mission, led by Joseph Johnson, President Kennedy's Special Representative to the Palestine Conciliation Commission, was established in July 1962 to help resolve the Palestinian refugee problem. Johnson formally resigned from the mission on January 31, 1963.

In 1948, no Arab *state* lost any territory; it was Palestinians who lost their homes.

Fedayeen riding groundswell of popularity.

In a way, Jordan and UAR have—by accepting UN resolution—accepted existence of Israel.

Jordan most committed to peace settlement but Hussein caught between radicals and need to get land back.

If we resume relations with Arabs, that will strengthen moderates.

Questions

President: If we have a Lebanon-type situation in Jordan, what capability would we have—if, for instance, we faced a fedayeen takeover in Jordan?

Wheeler: "Could probably—of course would have problems." Problem: Israelis not basically interested in survival of Hussein.

Hart: "I'm not sure they've made up their minds finally on this." If Jordan became a radical state, easier for Israel to move.

President: "That kind of thinking is a death wish. They must not be given any encouragement."

The political problem in the US—"we just can't tote that." Extremely difficult for us to move in to save Israel.

Laird: What's the possibility of Israel-Jordan settlement?

Hart Hard without UAR. Have to be simultaneous movement.

Rogers: We don't think Hussein could survive separate settlement.

Laird: Hope Israel doesn't misinterpret mood in U.S.

Rogers: On basis my talk with Rabin, "I don't think they misinterpret."

President: Dayan says we should have good relations with Arabs.

Lincoln: We should make clear to Israel and its friends importance of Hussein.

President: Harder to explain to Israel's friends in US.

Rabin-Dayan have fatalistic attitude—it will blow and they'll take care of it.

Wheeler: Rabin explained deep Israeli feelings against Hussein—in 6-day war Jordanians inflicted much heavier casualties.

Briefing continued

Hart: Israel suspicious of UAR intentions.

Politics in Israel will reduce Israeli flexibility between now and November.

Siege atmosphere in Israel. Don't trade territory for political agreements.

Status quo of today works against peace and even Israel's long-term security.

Settlement will require pressure on Israel—for arrangements that will include well-policed demilitarization.

President: Guaranteed by whom?

Hart: UN sanctified.

Lincoln: Who pay for UN forces?

Hart: Senator Javits[5] interest in refugee settlement.

Briefing continued

Hart: Have to be clear where Israeli and US coincide: We don't want Israel destroyed but don't have stake in boundaries. Want lasting settlement. Above all, want to avoid war with USSR.

In deciding how much pressure we apply on Israel, have to decide how UAR can be brought along.

Important to develop maximum public understanding in US.

Sisco: Elements in our policy as it evolved after June War:

—Commitment to territorial integrity.

—Nasser's May 1967 blockade, he was overturning post-Suez US arrangements.

—We wanted to try this time to achieve lasting peace.

—These combined in 5 principles of June 19, 1967.[6] "Parties to conflict, parties to peace." These incorporated in November 22 resolution.

The equation: withdrawal in return for end of belligerency.

While resolution adopted unanimously, there was not unanimous interpretations. We really passed these differences on to Jarring. Reflected in semantic argument "accepting and implementing" the resolution.

Rogers: Rabin says Arabs are trying to "force us into settlement short of peace."

Sisco: July 1968, we got Israel to soften stand on (1) direct negotiations as a precondition to exchanging substance, (2) peace treaty.[7] Parties have been exchanging views through Jarring. But Israel wants binding commitment on peace.

President: Israel insists on bilateral agreements. What is Israeli view toward outside participation?

---

[5] Jacob K. Javits (R–NY).

[6] In a speech on June 19, 1967, President Johnson set forth five principles for peace in the Middle East. For the text of his speech, see *Public Papers: Johnson, 1967*, Book I, pp. 630–634. See also *Foreign Relations, 1964–1968*, volume XIX, Arab-Israeli Crisis and War, 1967, Document 308.

[7] See ibid., volume XX, Arab-Israeli Dispute, 1967–1968, Document 213.

Sisco: Israel wants to be left alone to deal with Hussein—and the UAR.

Israel-Jordan exchanges. Allon Plan as non-starter with Hussein.[8]

Israel nervous about big-power intervention. Last Soviet note—"a five-legged horse that could move in any direction."

We don't honestly know what USSR intends.

Shall we await Soviet reply or develop a plan of our own to discuss.

Whatever we put in, we have to be sure we can produce Israel.

Israel's Cabinet divided—explains inability to decide on territorial objectives. Arabs made it easy for Israelis to avoid decision. Election will make flexibility difficult.

President: Javits or somebody mentioned USSR made propaganda hay. What's the answer?

Sisco: Soviets have had a propaganda ride. We didn't refute publicly because we wanted to work out our response without appearing to throw cold water.

Lincoln: Could Israel and Jordan consider Allon Plan with UN force?

Sisco: May be feasible.

President: Israel says it wants peace via bilateral agreements. Yet in intelligence we hear extremists so strong that Arab governments can't control them. Do sophisticated Israelis discount outside guarantees?

Rogers: Fedayeen raids not significant now. Could be handled if contractual peace.

Israelis afraid we'll be stampeded by tension. Say Russians are heating up atmosphere to panic us. Russians won't use nuclear weapons. Arabs won't start war. Sovs won't intervene; they don't have air cover over this fleet. Rabin says: Don't make decisions because you think you're on the brink of war. We're not going to take more territory. Permanent peace will be anti-Soviet.

President: When you come down to it, a peace that he (Rabin) negotiates with any of these wobbly governments, isn't a peace either with revolutionary movements there.

"I can see the symbolism there; they want recognition." But unless they have some outside recognition.

---

[8] Conceived by Israeli Foreign Minister Yigal Allon in the wake of the Arab-Israeli war of 1967, the plan proposed that Israel would relinquish political control of the West Bank to Jordan in exchange for military control of a strip of land along the eastern side of the Jordan River to secure the border between them.

Rogers: Israelis know they need guarantees.

Sisco: Four-power proposal has to be handled delicately. As proposed, it gives preference to Soviet plan and downplays Jarring.[9] We see Jarring and UN as central. Sovs and French disagree. UK wavers but waiting to see what we'll do.

Response will be one of your Administration's first moves. Jarring wants step by parties or anything four powers can. We're boxed in. Propose: informal, individual consultations but they will quickly become more formal. Might nudge Israelis, who are thinking of putting forward ideas through secret channel toward Jordan.

President: What's timing?

Rogers: I have a draft reply for you to consider quickly.[10]

Kissinger: Review Group has not seen proposal. Maybe 2-power approach better. This just one sub-choice in one of three options.

President: I want to tie this into announcement of NPT.[11] Get points with de Gaulle.

UN thinks this a good move?

Yost: Yes, Arabs prefer.

Rogers: Pressure on both sides.

President: Could Jarring make a significant contribution?

Yost: Not going get to first base by himself.

Yost: Hard keep Jarring and four-powers going same time—but possible.

President: Four-powers with Jarring?

Yost: Jarring wants to stay independent.

President: Don't like idea of saying "me too." Propose variant method of implementation.

---

[9] The French proposal reads: "The French Government considers that the Middle East crisis, far from easing as desired, has become aggravated to such an extent that it is necessary that the Security Council be enabled to face up to the responsibilities devolving upon it under the charter. To that end, the French Government proposes that the representatives of France, the United States, the U.S.S.R., and the United Kingdom on the Security Council meet at the end of January to seek, in conjunction with the Secretary General of the United Nations, a means whereby their governments could contribute to the establishment of a just and lasting peace in the Middle East, specifically by defining the terms of implementations of Council Resolution No. 242 of November 22, 1967." The rest of the note concerned the points on which "exchanges of views could bear." (Telegram 8744 to Paris, January 17; National Archives, Nixon Presidential Materials, NSC Files, NSC Institutional Files (H-Files), Box H–020, National Security Council Meetings, NSC Meeting Middle East 2/1/69)

[10] Sent as telegram 19022, Document 7.

[11] On February 5, Nixon sent the Nuclear Nonproliferation Treaty, which had been signed and opened for signature on July 1, 1968, to the Senate requesting its advice and consent to the treaty's ratification.

Kissinger: Choice may be between 2-power and 4-power not 4-power and nothing. May be Soviet talks be more fruitful.

President: Does 4-power rule out 2-power?

Rogers: No. Make it clear 4-power in framework of Jarring.

Yost: Maintain two-power element in four-power.

President: The real powers are the US and USSR.

Rogers: How do we say that?

President: Different—what we say and what we do.

Sisco: USSR has made clear US–USSR dialogue the prime one despite its acceptance of French proposal. Could have four sets of talks going on at same time. Four-powers could do some marginal work

President: "Trying to be devil's advocate," another element that appeals: reassure our NATO allies. You feel we should go on all four lines?

Sisco: Yes.

Laird: Must move soon. High expectancy of a US move because press aware that NSC discussing the issue.

President: We'll make a move.

Lincoln: What about Israelis?

President: Leave that to Secretary of State! (Laughter)

Yost: Israelis underestimate Fedayeen movement.

Kissinger: Have to distinguish between Israeli statements and what their situation is.

Israelis say they won't settle for less than a real peace, but they must know that isn't possible. They must really be saying that they find it hard to see how legal arrangement could increase their security. They must know that most wars start between countries who recognize each other and are at peace. The only peace arrangements that work are settlements that (1) increase will of the parties to peace, or (2) decrease ability to make war.

We haven't systematically discussed options. Must know what we want if we're going to try to get.

President: Our ability to deliver Israelis gets down to what we will do.

Richardson: Not only what we'll do but what we can do in de-escalating.

President: What will we do vis-à-vis the Russians? That's the heart.

Yost: Italians go along with Four-Power if in UN framework.

Lincoln: Have we gone into guarantees?

Rogers: That's down the road.

President: Have to get to that.

Kissinger: Why can't we go till Wednesday to review systematically?

President: Move Council up to Tuesday at 10:00 a.m.[12]

What we have in mind:

—Respond affirmatively.

Kissinger: Distribute draft reply to French note before Tuesday and meeting.

---

[12] Tuesday, February 4.

5. Minutes of a National Security Council Meeting[1]

Washington, February 4, 1969, 10 a.m.

PARTICIPANTS

The President
The Vice President
The Secretary of State, William P. Rogers
The Secretary of Defense, Melvin R. Laird
(For Joint Chiefs of Staff) General McConnell
Under Secretary of State, Elliot L. Richardson
Director, Office of Emergency Preparedness, General George A. Lincoln
US Ambassador to the UN, Charles Yost
Dr. Henry A. Kissinger
Colonel Alexander Haig
Harold H. Saunders
The Director of Central Intelligence, Richard M. Helms (for part of the meeting)

President: Mentioned effective Kissinger paper on options;[2] asked Kissinger to distribute to members of Council.

Kissinger: Presentation based on talking points.

President: Is it accurate to say that 1967 war came without the expectation or intention of any of parties?

Kissinger: Yes.

---

[1] Source: National Archives, Nixon Presidential Materials, NSC Files, NSC Institutional Files (H-Files), Box H–109, NSC Meeting Minutes, NSC Minutes Originals 1969. Top Secret. Drafted on May 1 by Saunders. All brackets are in the original. According to the President's Daily Diary, the meeting was held in the Cabinet Room from 10:07 a.m. to 11:45 a.m. (Ibid., White House Central Files)

[2] See footnote 2, Document 3.

Yost: Agree.

Rogers: Rusk told him he concerned about repeat because rumors similar to 1967 circulating again.

President: I ask because it relevant to contigency planning—shows necessity for planning to consider unexpected. The more we can let our minds—when we have the luxury of time—run to the unexpected.

Laird: Problem: We're spending time on procedure rather than on where we want to come out.

Our main purpose is to avoid war with USSR. Time coming when Israel will announce it has 10 missiles on the line just when we delivering F–4s. If we look at where we want to come out, we ought to begin putting some pressure on Israeli government. We have to be in position of pressing Israel but at same time promise to work with USSR to limit arms.

President: At end of meeting, talk about how to get plan for what we're after before negotiators sit down. Laird's point well taken. We must know what we want rather than saying we want whatever we can negotiate.

Yost: Agree. We may even want to put part of it on the table.

President: We tend in government too often to think too much about how we look in public.

Rogers: Procedures become substance.

President: One substantive decision we make is that we are going to take the initiative, which we haven't done before. That's a major decision. But we want to negotiate on our terms—not other peoples' terms.

An imposed settlement in the Mid-East—not in terms of the formality but in terms of the skill of our negotiation—is what has to be done.

Laird: We have to think what's going to happen with Israel. Our overriding purpose to avoid war with USSR. Israeli nuclear capability would increase risk.

Rogers: What makes you think Israel will announce?

Lincoln: Even if they don't, we have a responsibility if we know. And USSR will know.

President: Henry, proceed. Talk about how we meld 2-power and 4-power, "as frankly I feel we must do."

Kissinger: Intimate relationship among all these things. On overall settlement, I'll concentrate on 4-power and 2-power approaches. Other two options have little support—let Jarring go by himself or US mediation.

Spelled out pros and cons in February 3 memo, "The Middle East—Some Policy Considerations."[3]

Whichever way we go, we can still regulate the intensity via diplomatic and public handling.

Kissinger then turned to amerliorative steps in the absence of a settlement. Foremost is the Israeli nuclear problem, which could draw USSR even more into the Mid-East with some form guarantee for the Arabs.

Review Group has not addressed itself fully to these basic issues. Mainly concentrated on negotiating options.

President: We've gone down the road on procedures because events have moved us on.

French note[4]—have to respond. But poses a problem with Israel's friends.

How we set up this forum can be a major decision on substance.

We accept 4-power approach in principle but have bilateral discussions first.

Most important to move talks along with Russians.

On my trip,[5] four-power talks not high on agenda. But opportunity to use them to draw de Gaulle toward us.

Need talking paper: What they might bring up and what we want.[6]

Handle letter in low-key way. Don't announce, just acknowledge.

Rogers: State has never felt that four-power should supersede two-power.

Yost: Soviet ambassador said we must work closely.

President: "Don't be in any hurry to have anything done on the four-power front."

"At UN go to the two-power forum. Start talking with Soviets."

Rogers: When Dobrynin comes back (around February 7) may have instructions.

President: Harmful if we give impression that four-power forum where things will be settled. Main value as umbrella. Lip service to dealing with British and French.

---

[3] Kissinger's February 3 memorandum explored the "arguments for and against seeking a general settlement" immediately and considered "ways of trying for a general settlement," including the pros and cons of the Four- and Two-Power approaches. (National Archives, Nixon Presidential Materials, NSC Files, Box 651, Country Files, Middle East, Middle East through December 1969)

[4] See footnote 9, Document 4.

[5] Nixon traveled to Europe February 23-March 2.

[6] "The Points We Want to Leave in Europe," February 19. (National Archives, Nixon Presidential Materials, NSC Files, Box 442, President's Trip Files, President Nixon's Trip to Europe, February–March 1969 (2 of 2))

Laird raised Israeli nuclear question.

What are we going to guarantee Israel?

We have to face up to that question.

We have to tell Israelis what we're prepared to do.

Richardson: Rabin says:

1. Israel disinterested in international guarantees.

2. If US and USSR provide guarantees, this juxtaposes US and USSR in Mid-East in a dangerous way.

President: I'd make that point if I were Rabin. But I'd bet if Mid-East fighting breaks out again, there's a 50 percent chance we'll be dragged in.

It's "not necessarily" true the USSR will stay out, even if they should.

If Israel in danger and calls on us to do something.

Greater danger each time Mid-East fighting comes around. Greater in 1967 than in 1956. Rabin doesn't take account of this. ["Rabin reminds me of Radford."][7]

By the time we take this trip, be prepared to talk.

President: I have arranged that each week Presidents Eisenhower and Johnson to be briefed.

Briefing on Mid-East contingency plans.

Purpose of plans: to deter and then to force hostile forces to withdraw.

Soviets have capability to project force overseas as they did not five years ago.

[Comment: President again, as February 1, seems to be groping to understand Soviet intentions, degree of concertedness in decision making.]

Kissinger: Question raised whether we could repeat our approach to Cuban missile crisis.

President: This gets down to "mission Gerard Smith[8] has." [ACDA]

President: In looking at military contingency plan stages, could State prepare a comparable "diplomatic symphony" going at the same time.

---

[7] Admiral Arthur W. Radford, Chairman of the Joint Chiefs of Staff, 1953–1957.

[8] Gerard C. Smith, Director of the Arms Control and Disarmament Agency from 1969 until 1973 and Chief of the U.S. Delegation to the Strategic Arms Limitation Talks.

6. National Security Study Memorandum 17[1]

Washington, February 6, 1969.

TO
- The Secretary of State
- The Secretary of Defense
- The Director of Central Intelligence

SUBJECT
- Further Studies on Middle East Policy

Following the NSC meeting of February 4 on the Middle East,[2] the President directed that the NSC Interdepartmental Group for Near East, as a next step in developing a precise strategy, prepare the following papers for early discussion in the NSC Review Group and the NSC:

1. A description of an Arab-Israeli settlement which the US could support and which, if achieved, would reduce the likelihood of further Arab-Israeli hostilities. The following should also be included:

—Alternative terms of settlement where appropriate.

—Discussion of the respective contribution of the major alternatives described to reducing likelihood of future hostilities.

—A judgment on the likely acceptability of terms to the parties.

2. A discussion of alternative forms of US and international guarantees of a settlement and of Israeli security.

3. A plan of action which would relate the two-power and four-power negotiating tracks to each other and to our most significant bilateral relationships, including an estimate of chances of success and an analysis of where we would be if this course of action failed.

4. A possible plan of action detailing ameliorative steps to be taken if we judge that a general settlement is not possible now, including an estimate of chances of success and an analysis of where we would be if this course failed.[3]

---

[1] Source: National Archives, Nixon Presidential Materials, NSC Files, NSC Institutional Files (H-Files), Box H–135, National Security Study Memoranda. Secret; Exdis. A copy was sent to the Chairman, Joint Chiefs of Staff and the Director, Office of Emergency Preparedness.

[2] See Document 5.

[3] The Review Group met on February 18 to discuss the NSCIG/NEA paper, "Further Studies on Middle East Policy." The paper is in the National Archives, Nixon Presidential Materials, NSC Files, NSC Institutional Files (H-Files), Box H–135, National Security Study Memoranda, NSSM 17. No minutes of the NSC Review Group meeting have been found. A revised text of the paper is Document 8.

These papers should be forwarded to the NSC Review Group by February 13. The paper on basic US interests in the Middle East, requested in NSSM 2,[4] should be forwarded at the same time if possible.

Henry A. Kissinger

---

[4] See footnote 3, Document 3.

---

7. **Telegram From the Department of State to Certain Diplomatic Posts**[1]

Washington, February 6, 1969, 0214Z.

19022. Following for your information is full text of US reply to French proposal for meeting of UN reps of Four Powers on Middle East;[2] given to French Amb by Secy Feb 5:

Qte The United States Government has carefully considered the proposal of the French Government of January 16, 1969, for a meeting of the United Nations representatives of France, the USSR, the United Kingdom and the United States on the Middle East.

The United States has a deep and abiding interest in the establishment of an agreed peace in the Middle East which is in the interest of all peoples in the area. We have supported fully the mission of Ambassador Jarring to promote the agreement called for in the SC Resolution of November 22, 1967.

The United States is prepared in principle to consider favorably a meeting of United Nations representatives of the four governments within the framework of the Security Council to discuss ways and means to assist Ambassador Jarring to promote agreement between the parties in accordance with the Security Council Resolution of November 22, 1967. To this end, the United States suggests that there be prompt preliminary discussions, in the first instance on a bilateral basis, in order to develop the measure of understanding that would

---

[1] Source: National Archives, Nixon Presidential Materials, NSC Files, Box 1187, Saunders Files, Middle East Negotiations Files, Middle East Settlement—Jarring Cables, 1969. Confidential; Priority; Exdis. Drafted by Betty J. Jones (IO/UNP); cleared in NEA/IAI, NEA/UAR, and EUR; and approved by Sisco. Sent to Amman, Beirut, Jidda, London, Moscow, Paris, Rome, Tel Aviv, Cairo, and USUN.

[2] See footnote 9, Document 4.

make an early meeting of the representatives of the Four Powers a fruitful and constructive complement to Ambassador Jarring's mission. Unqte.[3]

Rogers

---

[3] Yost met French Ambassador to the United Nations Armand Bérard on February 12 to discuss establishing a Four-Power framework. (Telegram 414 from USUN, February 13; National Archives, Nixon Presidential Materials, NSC Files, Box 648, Country Files, Middle East, Middle East Negotiations)

---

8. **Paper Prepared by the Interdepartmental Group for Near East and South Asia**[1]

NSCIG/NEA 69–2A (Revised)   Washington, February 20, 1969.

Further Studies on Middle East Policy

In two previous NSC meetings[2] several principal options were considered:

A. Leaving the matter of a settlement of the Arab-Israeli dispute exclusively to the parties and to Jarring; this option was rejected.

B. Adopting a more active policy to achieve a general settlement using some combination of the following: (1) intensive US diplomatic efforts with the parties and Jarring; (2) possible US–USSR discussions to develop some new principles of a settlement which Jarring would be asked to try out on the parties; and (3) four-power discussions at the UN Permanent Representatives level.

C. Anticipating that a general settlement involving Israel, Jordan, and the UAR is not likely now and concentrating our efforts for the mo-

---

[1] Source: National Archives, Nixon Presidential Materials, NSC Files, NSC Institutional Files (H-Files), Box H–135, National Security Study Memoranda, NSSM 17. Secret; Exdis. In a February 20 memorandum sent separately to Kissinger, Sisco explained that this paper incorporated revisions that had been agreed upon at the Review Group meeting on February 18. (Ibid.) No minutes of the Review Group meeting have been found.

[2] See Documents 4 and 5.

ment on certain high-priority objectives short of a general settlement; a separate paper exploring this option is to be submitted later.[3]

In order to prepare further for the exploratory four-power discussions in New York, the President's talks in Europe and the eventual choice of policy, this paper presents:

—the elements of an overall settlement the US could support;

—alternative means of guaranteeing such a settlement;

—two possible approaches for injecting our views of a settlement into dialogue between the parties;

—the relation between Two Power and Four Power talks;

—the special question of dealing with Israel;

—objectives in the President's European talks.

Elements of Overall Settlement

We have been considering possible basic elements of an overall settlement intended to establish a permanent peace based on a binding agreement. The details of any feasible settlement will have to be worked out in the course of discussions. Whatever the eventual details, we see certain *major principles* as governing a settlement:

—The parties must somehow participate in the negotiation of terms. We do not believe face-to-face negotiations are essential at the outset, although we doubt the Israelis will agree to a settlement unless the Arabs sit down with them at some point (presumably under Jarring's auspices).

—The objective of negotiations is a binding agreement. We do not believe a peace treaty per se is required; the essential purpose could be met by signature of a common document by both sides, which could then be endorsed by the Security Council. But we doubt that any form of settlement is feasible, or desirable, unless it contains an element of contract which the Arabs have hitherto firmly resisted

—There must be withdrawal of forces to secure and recognized boundaries. We believe if a settlement is to be achieved this will mean that Israel will be required to withdraw its troops to the international boundary with Egypt, and there must be a special arrangement for Gaza; in the case of Jordan, it means Israeli evacuation of the West Bank except for (a) the minor border rectifications that the two parties may agree upon, and (b) Jerusalem which is a special problem.

---

[3] Not found.

—Certain critical areas will have to be demilitarized. We doubt that Israel will agree to substantial withdrawal from the occupied territories under arrangements which would permit their military occupation by the other side.

—Jordan will have to have a role—and more than just a religious role—in Jerusalem. But a settlement is unlikely unless the city remains united. Israel will probably resist giving up any authority in the city, but we do not believe the Arabs could accept any settlement which excluded the Jordanians entirely from Arab Jerusalem.

—No overall settlement is conceivable without some arrangement on the refugees. A refugee settlement is essential both for symbolic and humanitarian reasons and to provide an alternative to the fedayeen approach to recapture lost territory. Any refugee settlement must include a choice of "repatriation" as well as compensation, although we doubt that many of the refugees would opt to return to Israel. Israel will probably resist but might ultimately accede to token repatriation although it would require a veto over the number of refugees it accepts. In any event, solution of the refugee problem will take a long time; the parties will have to agree to a mechanism which can work on this key issue for an extended period.

—Free navigation (in Suez as well as the Gulf of Aqaba) must include ships of all flags. Israel will not accept less.

—Agreement on all elements of a settlement will be required before implementation of any part of the settlement can begin.

International Guarantees

The feasibility of a settlement plan will depend in large part on the guarantees of the settlement and of Israel's security, and the degree to which Israel considers them sufficient. Consideration of possible alternative forms of guarantees proceeds from the premise that a settlement plan will have to involve the participation of non-Middle Eastern countries in its implementation and that guarantees of an international character will be required. International assurances could be reflected in Security Council endorsement of an agreed settlement, making the settlement terms binding upon all members as Security Council decisions. Additionally, the Four Powers could declare their support of a Council resolution endorsing the settlement terms and committing the Four Powers to consult, in the event of a breach or violation of the settlement terms, on appropriate Four Power action either within or outside the Security Council.

Collective international assurances alone, however, will not be convincing to Israel. The only type of assurance it would have faith in would be a unilateral guarantee from the United States. But it would not be in our interest to offer a firm, formal guarantee of Israel's security. We should avoid any open-ended and uncontrollable commitment because it would subordinate the United States to Israeli concepts of defense and security, and because it would polarize the area between us and the USSR.

Short of a formal security guarantee, it is possible that some type of US assurance could be worked out that would go at least part-way in meeting Israel's problem, and still be acceptable in terms of our own national interests and Congressional concerns. We might, for example, make a unilateral public statement in conjunction with a Security Council endorsement or a Four Power collective declaration on a settlement plan not going beyond the sense or specific terms of the collective assurance but noting that we would not necessarily consider ourselves precluded from taking action consistent with the intent of that assurance merely because of the failure of all the other parties to act thereunder. Alternatively, a "sense of the Congress" resolution could underline our national obligation under a collective international assurance.

Apart from a specific guarantee, and in the absence of any arms limitation agreement with the USSR, we could give Israel a firm commitment to provide it the military equipment we believe needed to maintain a reasonable balance in the area. Such a commitment could be helpful in getting Israel to accept elements of an overall settlement.

Two Possible Approaches

Jarring is awaiting some further guidance from the major powers, and they are presently considering ways to assist him, including a Four Power procedural suggestion to him that he renew his discussions with the parties and direct further inquiries to them regarding substantive positions in order to elicit as comprehensive a response as possible. Such a move will only help Jarring keep afloat for a relatively brief time, and he can be expected to renew his discussions with the parties at a reasonably early date. However, if as is likely there will be no significant narrowing of the gap at an early date between the Arabs and the Israelis, pressures will build up for more direct involvement in the substantive settlement by the major powers.

Meanwhile the growing strength and importance of the Palestinian fedayeen make their attitude toward a settlement increasingly relevant. How long, in other words, will the assumption remain valid that Arab governments can speak for the Palestinians who are not a party to the negotiations but whose interests are deeply involved? It is uncertain, for example, how long King Hussein can maintain the necessary flexibility to enter into a settlement in the face of fedayeen opposition. The role of the fedayeen underscores both the urgency and the difficulty of achieving a settlement.

We have weighed two general approaches:

A. *Development and Submission by the United States of an Overall Arab-Israeli Settlement Plan.*

Although the elements of a settlement sketched out above might be the basis for a reasonable compromise, it is not recommended that the United States put forward any blueprint at this time. The gap between the two parties is still too great, and it would be premature for us alone or in concert with others to inject any far-reaching substantive plan into the negotiations. The parties would declare various parts of it unacceptable, and Israel would resist the entire concept of a plan drawn up by third parties. The concessions required of Israel would be substantial and seeking to achieve its concurrence, or at least acquiescence, at this stage is likely to result in an early crisis between us. We would be expected to produce Israel on such a plan, and this is unlikely at this point. Its feasibility in the long run will depend on whether we and the USSR are prepared to influence the UAR and Israel to this end and whether the principal parties can be moved in this direction. Our consideration of possible elements of a settlement plan is useful largely for internal purposes and to give us a clearer picture as to what might be feasible near the end of the road. It is intended as a yardstick to measure substantive proposals which the USSR and France can be expected to make in the weeks ahead and as a guide for the substantive views we may wish to express on various elements of a Security Council resolution.

B. *Step-by-Step Approach.*

Another approach would be a step-by-step injection of specific substantive views by the US on key parts of the settlement as discussions proceed between the parties under Jarring's auspices, possibly between ourselves and the USSR, and perhaps within the Four Power framework.

At the heart of the present impasse are two fundamental questions: (a) whether the UAR is prepared to conclude a binding agreement for a permanent peace in the Middle East; and (b) whether Israel is prepared to withdraw from Arab territories occupied in the 1967 war. It would therefore appear logical to attack first the two issues of withdrawal and permanent peace based on agreement between the parties.

There are several possible steps which might be considered, after the President's trip to Europe, and when we will have a clearer view of the attitude of the other three major powers as elucidated in the exploratory discussions being pursued by Ambassador Yost in New York. The following diplomatic steps would be designed to help move the parties closer and to facilitate Jarring's efforts. They involve a complicated but not infeasible complex of negotiations. It would be appropriate for decisions to be taken on one or more of the following courses of action shortly after the President's return from Europe.

First, on the occasion of the Eban visit[4] to explore with him and to encourage Israel to take two important steps with respect to the UAR part of the settlement:

(a) To submit to Jarring a new document on implementation of the November 1967 Security Council Resolution and on the UAR aspect of the settlement. This document should indicate an Israeli willingness to consider withdrawal of its forces from the present cease-fire lines to the former international boundaries between the mandated territory of Palestine and Egypt *conditioned* on achievement of a satisfactory agreement on all other elements of the Security Council Resolution, including a binding agreement to a permanent peace signed by the UAR. Such a document would not reduce Israel's leverage since it does not contemplate any Israeli withdrawal in the absence of a commitment by the UAR to a binding peace.

Such an Israeli statement is not likely to meet Nasser's demands for total withdrawal, but it would help keep Jarring in play, would improve the Israeli position abroad, would put us in a position to support it as a step forward, and buy more time for Israel to pursue its private contacts to achieve peace with Jordan. It could eventually lead to a process narrowing the gap between the UAR and Israel. A US discussion with Israel at this critical juncture is also important because a strain in our relations has developed in recent weeks. The strain results from our recent support in the Security Council of the strong condemnation of Israel[5] and our dissociation from Israel on the territorial aspect of the UAR settlement. In this latter connection, Secretary Rusk on November 2 informed UAR Foreign Minister Riad that, within the context of a binding peace agreement, we favor withdrawal of Israeli forces from the UAR to the international boundary line.[6] Israel believes this undermined its negotiating position.

(b) To renew and intensify its secret contacts with the Jordanians, keeping Jarring and the United States informed of their progress. In order to facilitate such talks, we should encourage Israel to announce an easing of its policy regarding displaced persons by allowing as many of the 350,000 who desire to return to their West Bank camps and villages. We should also encourage Israel to offer Jordan, in return for a binding commitment to peace signed by the GOJ and as part of a satis-

---

[4] Eban visited the United States in March. See Documents 13 and 14.

[5] UN Security Council Resolution 262, adopted unanimously on December 31, 1968, condemned Israel for its attack on the Beirut International Airport. (*Yearbook of the United Nations, 1968.* pp. 236–237)

[6] See footnote 3, Document 1.

factory agreement on all elements of Resolution 242, specific territorial terms which could be accepted by King Hussein—i.e., no unilateral concessions of territory, reciprocity with respect to territorial changes involved in adjusting the West Bank boundary, no Israeli garrisons or settlements on the West Bank and a reasonable compromise on Jerusalem which would give Jordan a meaningful rather than a purely symbolic role in the Arab sector of the city. While such terms could in the first instance be conveyed through the direct Israeli-Jordanian channel, Israel should be urged to use the Jarring channel more substantively than in the past if and when Jordan indicates a desire to do so. Hussein would welcome reaffirmation by the new Administration of the views expressed by the Johnson Administration regarding a Jordanian settlement. It would be psychologically advantageous to do this at an early date, even before any visit of Hussein to this country.

Second, we will wish to decide after the President's European trip whether to renew the US–USSR dialogue. If the decision is affirmative, we could submit to the Soviets an American document containing concrete proposals for settlement of the Israeli-UAR part of the overall settlement. Because we would be expected by the Soviets to produce Israeli concurrence, there should be a prior review of such a document with Israel. These proposals might also be presented to the UK and France for their review in order to keep them in the picture. They would also be discussed by us at an appropriate stage with the UAR and Jordan. Jarring and the UN should be kept in the center of the public stage as much as possible. If sufficient common ground between the US–USSR is achieved, the proposals would be presented to Jarring to try out on the parties.

Relation Between Two Power and Four Power Talks

If we should decide to give primacy to the bilateral discussions between ourselves and the Soviet Union, it raises the question of the relation of such discussions to possible Four Power meetings. The posture we adopted in our response to the French note provides a reasonable guide. While concentrating our principal efforts on the US–USSR dialogue, it will prove necessary and desirable to keep the French and the British abreast of these discussions. In the first place, the Soviets can be expected to reveal much of the contents of any discussions between us to the French whose position is likely to be closer to the Soviets than to ours. Secondly, the French themselves will be persistent in injecting themselves in the substance. This should prove manageable if we maintain the posture that any formal Four Power meetings, particularly on substance, must be preceded by individual consultations whose purpose would be to develop common ground. It is likely to be necessary therefore for the United States to take a very firm stand with the French and resist frequent and premature Four Power meetings on the substance before individual consultations have developed areas of common understanding.

The US–USSR dialogue would reflect the political realities of the situation in terms of power in the area and potential to influence the parties. The Soviets will try to apply pressure on us to induce Israel to be more forthcoming on withdrawal; we in turn will want to put the pressure on the USSR to move the UAR closer to a firm commitment to a permanent peace based on agreement between the parties.

While the probability of success is not very great, the deteriorating situation in the area requires such effort. The knowledge that such efforts are being made is of psychological importance in the area, regardless of the bleak prospects for success. The next several months are particularly important for increased diplomatic efforts. As a minimum, further explorations and testing of the Soviets will help determine more precisely whether they and the UAR are genuinely interested in arriving at some form of accommodation. At present, it appears that any accommodation which they would be prepared to accept would fall short of the binding peace settlement which Israel desires, and short even of the major principles we believe must govern a settlement. We may have to make a judgment at some point as to whether an accommodation which would be something more than the old Armistice arrangements and something less than the full-scale peace which Israel wants would represent a significant improvement over an indefinite prolongation of the stalemate. This would be a complex judgment to make, and we would have to take into account the fact that the Middle East is a dynamic situation which will not stand still. Our present assessment is that without progress towards a settlement, or at least evidence of major efforts being made towards this end, the situation will continue to deteriorate with the increased risk of a general renewal of hostilities. On the other hand, an inadequate settlement might not only fail to preserve peace but would render Israel more vulnerable, through loss of the military advantage of the occupied territories, if hostilities should recur.

How Much Leverage Do We Have with the Israelis?

Whatever the reasonableness—in our eyes—of an overall settlement such as we have in mind, we must face the fundamental truth that we will have very serious difficulty in "selling" it to Israel. We may count it as certain that any plan we could support as reasonable for *both* Israel and the Arabs will be viewed by Israel as jeopardizing its security.

As we discuss a settlement with others, then, there will be increasing strains in US-Israeli relations. Theoretically, we have a number of important levers with Israel: (a) its realization that in an ultimate sense Israel's national survival depends on the fundamental US concern for its security; (b) Israel's dependence on the United States for critical items of military hardware; and (c) the importance to Israel's economy of an unrestricted flow of private capital donations and loans from the United States. It is relevant to ask what effective, as opposed to theoretical, leverage do we have? Israel realizes that the United States alone or in concert with the other major powers would not use force to impose a settlement on it. Moreover, in addition to the domestic political factors involved, there is the more fundamental dilemma that United States pressure on Israel to make concessions on the key issue of territory will be viewed by Israel as a weakening of its capacity to safeguard its own security against a hostile Arab world. It would not be in our interests to contribute to a significant weakening of Israel's defensive capabilities, either through the relinquishment of territory or by withholding US arms, in circumstances where the UAR has been unwilling to make a credible commitment on peace. We and the Israelis are likely to differ on whether certain territorial concessions would jeopardize Israeli security.

An additional factor limiting our effective leverage is the relative fragility of the Israeli Government coalition. The Government might well find itself unable to take a given course of action without bringing about its own collapse. In fact, we may find that no reasonable solution can be accepted by Israel before its November elections determine its leadership. This analysis is not intended to indicate that our leverage on Israel is not substantial; but rather that it is more limited than would appear on the surface.

Explorations of the President During European Trip

President Nixon will have an opportunity during his European trip to discuss the Middle East fully with the NATO countries and in particular the UK, France, and Italy, all of whom have a special interest. In general, since we are not presently in a position to produce Israel on the specific key elements of a settlement, the President's discussions should be primarily exploratory.

With the United Kingdom, whose policy is ambivalent, the President will have an opportunity to impress on Wilson the importance we attach to its position and the need to maintain a common front. The United Kingdom is more anxious to open the Suez Canal than we are. Secondly, since resuming relations with the UAR, it has been carefully nurturing and seeking to improve its relations in the Arab world. Third, the United Kingdom will be very tempted to accept a limited accommodation even though it falls far short of the binding peace which Israel insists upon. Maintaining a common position with the United Kingdom will be difficult. If the President indicates our intention to maintain a special close relationship with the United Kingdom in our consultations on Middle East matters, this should help somewhat to keep the United Kingdom with us on substance.[7]

De Gaulle will be more difficult. The persistent thread that has run through France's policy on the Middle East since May 1967 has been its near obsession with seeking a great power solution to the region's problems and with proving to the world that France is one of the great powers concerned. De Gaulle has consistently feared that the US and the USSR, rather than the Big Four, will develop the principal elements of a settlement and encourage the parties through Jarring to make peace. We face therefore a very delicate tactical situation in the future as we consider both the two power and four power approach. It appears that the most feasible procedure may be to give primacy to the US–USSR dialogue, while at the same time continuing side talks with the UK and France. Willingness to commit ourselves to the Four Power structure as the principal center for discussion is not likely to have a decisive influence on the substantive position of the French.

The French favor an imposed settlement, but do not seem to accept the responsibilities and the implications of such an approach. Recent pronouncements by De Gaulle in support of the Arabs, in addition to the arms embargo, have destroyed in Israel's eyes any position of impartiality which the French may have enjoyed in earlier days. The French position on substance indicates a little more flexibility on the question of borders than in the past. Foreign Minister Debre said on January 31 that evacuation of the occupied territories, although the first step necessary towards settlement, should be to safe and recognized frontiers. This seems to imply rectification, delineation, and guarantees of the frontiers before Israel withdraws to them.

The President's discussions with De Gaulle will afford an opportunity to probe the views of the French Government on the specific elements of a settlement.[8] Our impression to date has been that De Gaulle is probably more interested in the way a settlement is arrived at than in the substance. He sees the area being polarized, and himself as the "depolarizer." He does, however, have an interest in seeing to it that the comparatively moderate regimes in Jordan and Lebanon and even the UAR's are not swept away in the increasingly revolutionary atmosphere of the Arab lands.

---

[7] President Nixon visited the United Kingdom February 24–26. He met with British Prime Minister Harold Wilson at the Prime Minister's country residence Chequers on February 24. See *Foreign Relations*, 1969–1976, volume XLI, Western Europe; NATO, 1969–1972, Document 310.

[8] Nixon discussed the Middle East with de Gaulle in the French President's office in the Elysée Palace in Paris on February 28. (Memorandum of conversation; National Archives, Nixon Presidential Materials, NSC Files, Box 1023, Presidential/HAK MemCons, MemCons—The President and General DeGaulle)

9. Memorandum From President Nixon to Secretary of State Rogers and the President's Assistant for National Security Affairs (Kissinger)[1]

Washington, February 22, 1969.

I have noted in reading the papers prepared by the State Department and by the Security Council Review Board on the Mideast,[2] references from time to time to "domestic political considerations."

The purpose of this memorandum is two fold:

(1) Under no circumstances will domestic political considerations have any bearing on the decisions I make with regard to the Mideast.

(2) The only consideration which will affect my decision on this policy will be the security interests of the United States.

In the future, I want no reference to domestic political considerations to be included in any papers and I do not want the subject of domestic political considerations to be brought up in discussions of this subject.

Will you please circulate this memorandum among all those who are working on this problem.

RN

---

[1] Source: National Archives, RG 59, Central Files 1967–69, POL IS–US/NIXON. Confidential; Exdis. A notation written in an unknown hand in the upper right-hand corner indicates that Rogers saw the memorandum.

[2] See, for example, Document 8.

10. Memorandum From Secretary of Defense Laird to Secretary of State Rogers, the President's Assistant for National Security Affairs (Kissinger), and Director of Central Intelligence Helms[1]

Washington, February 27, 1969.

SUBJECT

Stopping the Introduction of Nuclear Weapons Into the Middle East

From all of the available intelligence and from the intensive conversations here in Defense with Ambassador Rabin in the fall of 1968, [2 lines not declassified].[2] I do not believe this coincides with the interests of the United States, and, in fact, constitutes the single most dangerous phenomenon in an area dangerous enough without nuclear weapons.

The problem is how to stop this development. If the Israelis complete the development of a nuclear weapon within the next three to six months—which is quite possible—we will be powerless to do more than invoke sanctions, i.e., cease delivery of F–4s after the "introduction" of nuclear weapons into the area. Such a negative course would not take us very far. The Israelis would be unable and unwilling to reverse their course. Moreover, their requirement for conventional strength would be greater, not less, and the likelihood of our actually invoking the sanctions would not be great in such circumstances. Furthermore, at any time prior to such events, or certainly not long thereafter, we may well be faced with public knowledge of the essential facts. So far these facts have remained in the category of vague, unsubstantiated, and not fully accepted rumors; but we are depending primarily on luck. Once the public is made aware of the situation the Administration's delicate task will become even more difficult.

---

[1] Source: Washington National Records Center, OSD Files: FRC 330–75–0103, Box 12, Israel. Top Secret. All brackets are in the original except those indicating text that remains classified.

[2] Rabin was in Washington in November 1968 to negotiate the purchase of Phantom aircraft. As a condition to the purchase, Israel agreed that it would not be the first nation to introduce nuclear weapons into the Middle East. See *Foreign Relations, 1964–1968,* volume XX, Arab-Israeli Dispute, 1967–1968, Documents 332 and 333.

I believe we should meet very soon to consider how to proceed on this, followed by an early meeting with the President.[3] Because of the sensitivity and complexity of this issue, I suggest this not be dealt with through the regular NSC machinery.

Melvin R. Laird

---

[3] According to a follow-up memorandum from Laird to Rogers, Kissinger, and Helms, March 17, the four had not yet met, nor had they met with Nixon. Laird wrote, "Since February 27 I have seen additional evidence of activity that would enhance Israel's capability in [*less than 1 line not declassified*]. I refer to the granting, last June and October, of export licenses for two CDC 6400 computers and one IBM 360/65 computer for Israel. As Dave Packard indicated in his March 14, 1969, memorandum to the Secretary of State and the Secretary of Commerce, we believe the CDC 6400, in particular, could be a critical tool in [*less than 1 line not declassified*]." Laird repeated his request for a meeting on the issue, but it is unclear if the meeting occurred. (National Archives, Nixon Presidential Materials, NSC Files, Box 1236, Saunders Files, Middle East Negotiations Files)

---

11. Memorandum From the President's Assistant for National Security Affairs (Kissinger) to President Nixon[1]

Washington, March 8, 1969.

SUBJECT

    Next Steps on the Middle East

Attached is Secretary Rogers's recommendation on how we might relate our talks with Eban to those with the Russians both separately and together with the British and French.[2] I talked at length with Joe Sisco during its drafting and feel it comes out just about where we want to be.[3]

The essence of the plan is, *first*, to give Eban a detailed description, some of it in writing, of our views on the principles that should govern

---

[1] Source: National Archives, Nixon Presidential Materials, NSC Files, Box 651, Country Files, Middle East, Middle East through December 1969. Secret; Exdis. Sent for action.

[2] Rogers's March 7 memorandum to the President is attached but not printed.

[3] In a telephone conversation with Rogers at 12:30 p.m. on March 7, Kissinger said that he had met with Sisco to discuss the Department's recommendation and thought what State had is "really first rate." Kissinger added that he "really thinks this is the way to proceed. Secondly, bilateral talks should be here rather than New York." (National Archives, Nixon Presidential Materials, Henry Kissinger Telephone Conversation Transcripts, Box 1, Chronological File)

a settlement. (These are the principles formulated for your European talks modified to reflect the nuances in the diplomatic debates of the last twenty months. They are attached to the Secretary's memo.) While we will not give Eban a veto, we need to preserve the atmosphere of consultation. We would *then* begin point-by-point discussion with Dobrynin of our positions on the main items in the UN resolution. Meanwhile, we shall try to clarify further the French position, and Joe Sisco will be having talks with his British counterpart on the nuts and bolts of possible guarantees, forms of agreement and so on. After hearing Eban's reaction to our general principles, we would surface them in the four-power forum the week of March 17.

This seems to me the right way to proceed, provided everyone understands that our broad initial objectives are to use these talks (a) to bring the others as close as possible to our position and (b) to press on them—especially the USSR—co-responsibility for achieving success or sharing the blame for failure.

One final point should be called to your attention. If we achieve enough common ground in all these talks to warrant going on, it is implicit in the Secretary's recommendation that we would present any formal proposals through Jarring. The reason for insisting on this approach is to fend off possible French and Russian proposals that the big powers present proposals directly. That would pin responsibility on us alone to deliver Israel, while keeping Jarring in the middle would tend to pin the main responsibility on the parties themselves.

Recommendation: That you approve this general approach as a basis for the talking points to be written for the talks you and Secretary Rogers will have with Eban next week (March 12–13) and for following through with the Russians, French and British.[4]

---

[4] The President initialed his approval. Below his initials appears in an unknown hand: "3/10/69. 1. Notified Hal Saunders. 2. (ditto mark signifying repeat of "Notified") SS that Pres. approved memo as way for proceeding."

---

12. Editorial Note

During the first two weeks of March 1969, UN Special Representative Gunnar Jarring left texts of questions with the Foreign Ministers of the United Arab Republic, Jordan, Israel, and Lebanon, designed to restart negotiations between them. Jarring introduced the questions with this statement: "Security Council Resolution 242 (1967) sets out provisions and principles in accordance with which a peaceful and accepted settlement of the Middle East question should be achieved. Some of these provisions would impose obligations on both sides, some on one side, and some on the other; it has generally been accepted that they should be regarded as a whole. The following questions designed to elicit the attitude of the parties towards the provisions of the Security Council Resolution are based on this assumption and are to be understood in the context that each provision is regarded as part of a 'package deal.'" (Telegram 903 from Tel Aviv, March 11; National Archives, Nixon Presidential Materials, NSC Files, Box 648, Country Files, Middle East, Middle East Negotiations) The questions for Israel and Jordan were sent in telegrams 903 from Tel Aviv, March 11, and 1361 from Amman, March 20, respectively. (Ibid.) The questions for the United Arab Republic are in telegram 558 from Cairo, March 8 (ibid., Box 634, Country Files, Middle East, UAR, Vol. I), and those for Lebanon in telegram 2425 from Beirut, March 21. (Ibid., Box 1187, Saunders Files, Middle East Negotiations Files, Middle East Settlement—Jarring Cables)

At a March 20 meeting in Amman, Jordanian Foreign Minister Abdel Munim Rifai informed Ambassador Harrison Symmes that "a coordinated UAR/GOJ response had been developed in a series of lengthy meetings that he had in Cairo" with UAR Foreign Minister Mahmoud Riad. While the responses would be "essentially positive and affirmative," Rifai said, the Governments of Jordan and the United Arab Republic considered it vital that the responses also be "accurate and cautious" to avoid giving away "negotiating advantages." (Telegram 1360 from Amman, March 20; ibid., Box 648, Country Files, Middle East, Middle East Negotiations) Jarring received Jordan's answers to his questions on March 23. (Telegram 47456 to USUN, March 27; ibid., RG 59, Central Files 1967–69, POL 27 ARAB–ISR) Eban delivered Israel's replies to Jarring at an April 2 meeting in Jerusalem. In the letter accompanying the text of the responses, Eban wrote: "I now enclose specific replies in an affirmative spirit to the questions as formulated. It is my understanding that on the basis of the answers received from the three governments you propose to pursue further mutual clarifications in an effort to promote agreement on all the matters at issue in accordance with your mandate. We are ready to join in this process at any appropriate place." (Ibid., Nixon Presidential Materials, NSC Files, Box 1187, Saunders Files, Middle East Negotiations Files, Middle East Settlement—Jarring Cables)

13. Telegram From the Department of State to the Embassy in Israel[1]

Washington, March 13, 1969, 1732Z.

38852. 1. Following is uncleared account of Secretary's response to Eban's March 12 presentation reported septel,[2] and of Eban comments thereon. It is subject to change on review, FYI, Noforn.

2. After expressing condolences on Eshkol death and congratulations to Mrs. Meir,[3] Secretary said new administration fully aware of special US–Israeli relations which it has no intention of changing.

3. Secretary continued that he agreed with much of what Eban had said and could assure Eban there was no lessening of US support for Israel's objective of contractual settlement which is lasting and fully protects Israel's security.

4. US stands firmly on concept of agreement between parties. Our purpose in Two Power and Four Power talks is to support Jarring efforts with parties, not substitute for them.

5. Secretary said we do not think parties have made sufficient effort, however, to get into substance of a settlement. We do not wish to argue question of blame but want to move things along. We are not asking Israel to make proposals which undermine its negotiating position but feel we have obligation to help parties move toward permanent peace.

6. We hope Israel will be forthcoming in its replies to Jarring.[4] We also hope Arabs will say what they mean by peace. This is fundamental and we agree with Eban's analysis of the concept of peace.

7. In urging Israel to be forthcoming, we mean we hope Israel will be willing to specify boundaries to which it will withdraw. We will not

---

[1] Source: National Archives, Nixon Presidential Materials, NSC Files, Box 604, Country Files, Middle East, Israel, Vol. I. Secret; Priority; Exdis. Drafted by Atherton, cleared in IO, and approved by Sisco. Repeated priority to Amman and to London, Paris, Moscow, Cairo, USUN, Jidda, and Beirut.

[2] Telegram 38981 to Tel Aviv, March 13; ibid., Box 613, Country Files, Middle East, Jordan, Vol. I.

[3] Israeli Prime Minister Levi Eshkol suffered a fatal heart attack on February 26. The Labor Party selected Meir as the "consensus candidate" to succeed Eshkol rather than endure a fierce tug-of-war between Defense Minister Moshe Dayan and Deputy Prime Minister Yigal Allon for control of the party. "I honestly didn't want the responsibility, the awful stress of being Prime Minister," Meir wrote in her autobiography. But "I had no choice. . . . It was enough that we had a war with the Arabs on our hands; we could wait for that to end before we embarked on a war of the Jews." (Meir, *My Life*, pp. 350–352)

[4] See Document 12.

suggest to anyone, however, that Israel withdraw without receiving an Arab assurance on peace.

8. As concerns Israel's position, we see territorial question as guts of issue. We are convinced that agreement binding Arabs to peace, bulwarked by arrangements for demilitarization and by international guarantees, can more adequately insure Israel's security than can continuation of present unstable no-war, no-peace situation. On this point, Secretary said, we and Israel may have differences. We sometimes have impression Israel may think present situation is better than peace.

9. Secretary continued that now is time to make determined effort. We view Security Council Resolution and Jarring Mission as proper focus for search for peace settlement. We plan to move next week in bilateral and Four Power contexts since we believe Jarring has reached impasse and that major powers can now play helpful role.[5] We are making no conclusive judgments about Soviet and French intentions and realize we must be skeptical, particularly re Soviets, although latter may have their own reasons for wanting to move. We hope Israel will give French their detailed views on French proposals.[6]

10. Secretary then handed Eban copy of USG description of principles which we feel should govern peace settlement and which we plan to submit to other three powers next week.[7] (Text will be made available to posts after further discussion with Eban.) We would appreciate Israel's comments on these principles and could perhaps discuss them further next day.

11. Elaborating on statement of principles, Secretary said we do not favor imposed settlement and believe precise boundaries are for

---

[5] Sisco had his first substantive talk with Dobrynin on March 18 (see Document 15), and he spoke with French Ambassador Charles Lucet and British Chargé d'Affaires Edward Tompkins separately on March 20. (Telegram 43763 to Paris, March 21; National Archives, Nixon Presidential Materials, NSC Files, Box 614, Country Files, Middle East, Jordan, Vol. III, and telegram 43764 to London, March 21; ibid., Box 726, Country Files, Europe, United Kingdom, Vol. I)

[6] On March 14, Ambassador Sargent Shriver informed the Department that, since Nixon's visit to Paris, "serious" discussions about the Middle East had occurred at the highest levels of the French Government. The previous day, Luc de la Barre de Nanteuil, Chief of Levant Affairs at the French Foreign Ministry, had told Shriver that France's ideas on the Middle East would be put into final form before the next Four-Power meeting on March 24. (Telegram 3685 from Paris; ibid., Box 644, Country Files, Middle East, General, Vol. I)

[7] See Document 17.

parties to work out. As we have said before, however, we do not consider either Qte Allon Plan End qte or Israeli retention of territory at Sharm al-Sheikh consistent with our principles.

12. Secretary continued that we would find it useful to hear how Israel envisages relations with its neighbors following peace settlement. In our view, type of relations existing between neighboring states that have long lived in peace is unattainable in Middle East at this stage in history. We think juridical peace, buttressed by international guarantees, can be attained and could evolve into fully normal relations Israel seeks. It also possible that quite different relations might emerge between Israel and Jordan on one hand and between Israel and UAR on other.

13. Eban responded that, with respect to Secretary's suggestions about giving Arabs GOI concept of boundaries, question is at what stage this should be done. If Israel did so before Arabs reached decision to make peace, latter would simply reject Israeli proposals. Jarring himself has said that Israel should not give Arabs a map. Secretary commented that agreed boundaries must clearly be related to Israel's security.

14. In response to Eban's query re status of document handed him by Secretary, latter said it was still in-house document on which we want Israel's comments. Eban replied that, while he had no difficulty with our use of word Qte minimal End qte in discussing boundary changes among ourselves, to give this formulation to others as basis for discussions would erode US position further. On quick reading of our principles, Eban said several points caught his eye which would undermine Israel's position. Secretary agreed we could discuss principles paper further next day.[8]

15. Commenting on Secretary's statement re continuation of status quo, Eban said Israel by no means considers present situation perfect; it is better, however, than to withdraw from cease fire lines without peace. Israel agrees it should not simply stand pat. US should not be too impatient, however. Status quo can continue for some months without danger of hostilities.

---

[8] The paper that Rogers handed to Eban is not identified, but presumably it was a version of the paper prepared for the Four-Power talks, Document 17. According to the Israeli record of the March 13 meeting, Eban's response to the paper was negative: "The idea that the U.S. should submit a document of this kind to the other three powers or to anyone else is profoundly shocking. I request formally and solemnly that this not be done and I ask that this request be made known to the President." (Israel State Archive, Ministry of Foreign Affairs, 4780/2)

16. Secretary referred to indications that Israel believes face-to-face negotiations are necessary to make progress. We agree that direct negotiations desirable but believe agreement could also be produced by negotiations through Jarring which parties could then commit themselves to. Eban replied that Israel agreed some months ago to move from insistence on direct negotiations to a phased approach. Decision re when to move from indirect to direct negotiations could be made empirically but he could not see how peace could be achieved without meetings between parties. Eban added that GOI had even been prepared to give Jarring draft of what contractual agreement might look like and might still do so later, but for present would stay with Jarring's question and answer exercise.

17. Turning to French proposals, Eban said they were even further than Soviets from concept of agreement. Sisco noted that we had given French our preliminary comments and that French were refining their proposals and had given us some elaboration previous day. Sisco said we were aware of French-Israeli discussions in Paris and knew that GOI was weighing question of giving French substantive reactions. Eban replied that Israel had pointed out certain fatal flaws in French proposal which invalidated the rest.

18. Sisco made point that French will develop their position with or without Israeli views. We believe Israel can influence French position by making its substantive views known, regardless of what it thinks about procedure French are proposing.

19. In response to Ambassador Rabin's query why USG paying such attention to French, Secretary said we had made clear to French that settlement must be a package and we would not agree on phased approach. Was anything to be gained, however, by treating France as enemy? Rabin said Qte France is Israel's enemy End qte. Eban added that French are outside of European consensus re Middle East. Dutch Government, for example, does not like our giving France the role of representing Europe. In Israel's view US will get more cooperation from British. In response to Secretary's questions whether he had talked to British, Eban said he had seen Prime Minister Wilson briefly in transiting London and would have longer talk with him on return trip. Secretary noted that British seemed to wish to stay close to USG.

20. Eban asked if our position was that Four Power talks would take place only if and when bilateral talks became convergent. Secretary said this was not quite our position. We have said nothing is excluded but we want to have advance idea of what will happen before moving to Four Power forum. We have also made clear we will con-

tinue to consult with Israel and others. Four Powers have agreed their talks will be low-key and private. Eban expressed skepticism, saying anything we give Soviets will appear in Cairo press.

Rogers

14. Memorandum of Conversation[1]

Washington, March 14, 1969.

PARTICIPANTS

The President
Joseph J. Sisco
Henry A. Kissinger
Emil Mosbacher
Harold H. Saunders

Abba Eban
Yitzhak Rabin
Shlomo Argov

The President received Israeli Foreign Minister Eban in his office for fifty-five minutes on Friday, March 14, 1969.

After an exchange of pleasantries and a picture-taking session, the President explained his policy toward the four-power discussions on the Middle East. He frankly admitted that he had been "dragging his feet." He referred to his press conference statement[2] that the US did not wish to enter a negotiating situation where the cards would be stacked against us and added that his main purpose in the current exploratory bilateral talks is to see how far we can go in drawing the other three Governments closer to our position. The Soviets have been refueling one group of protagonists in the Middle East, and the French have been seeking a role as "spoilers." In a situation of this kind, he felt it was better to draw them into the process of trying to reach some sort of accommodation than to "leave them in left field." That said, the President assured Mr. Eban that we continue to support Ambassador Jarring but we felt we could usefully engage the other three governments in discussion of what guarantees might be possible for a settlement.

---

[1] Source: National Archives, Nixon Presidential Materials, NSC Files, Box 604, Country Files, Middle East, Israel, Vol. I. Secret; Nodis. Drafted by Saunders on March 17. According to the President's Daily Diary, the meeting was held from 3:06 to 3:50 p.m. (Ibid., White House Central Files)

[2] Made on March 4. The text of his statement is printed in *Public Papers: Nixon, 1969*, pp. 179–194.

The President concluded this part of his explanation by asking Eban disarmingly, "Don't you think we ought to try?" He said he realized that some of Eban's colleagues would argue that we should stand aloof. The President said he would not question that approach if we were dealing with stable governments and rational people. But we are not dealing with such people, and we feel we have a clear obligation to do what we reasonably can to make the situation less dangerous. We are particularly concerned, of course, with avoiding a clash with the Soviet Union.

The President assured Mr. Eban that we have Israel's interests at heart and that is why we have wanted to consult with Israel's representative this week before moving further in the four-power forum. But, he said, "We need your help. Don't make our role impossible."

Mr. Eban said that he had deeply appreciated the opportunity for a frank exchange of views. He said he felt that, after his three days of talks in Washington, our positions were close enough for us to work harmoniously together. He said that he had been asked at the Press Club whether he had noticed any distinct erosion in the American position and he had answered that he saw none. When he had been asked whether US and Israeli views were identical, he had replied that the views of two free Governments are never likely to be identical but that there can be enough harmony in the positions of each for close cooperation.

The President acknowledged that there are differences of view and that these differences are natural. "Just don't hit us too hard," he said.

The President went on to emphasize that, although he had been accused of many things, he had rarely been charged with being naive about Soviet intentions. "I know what they are up to." Having no illusions about the possibility of reaching full agreement with the USSR, he still felt it desirable to talk with the Soviets, keeping our guard up all the while, to see what common ground we and they might reach.

Mr. Eban then said he wanted to state his views on three subjects: the issue of war and peace, the four-power discussions, and Jordan.

On the issue of striving toward peace, he said that negotiations must continue; otherwise, a "war psychosis" would seize the people of the area. However, he did not see the present situation as capable of leading to a world conflagration because, first, the Arabs are in no position to wage a war and they know it, and, second, the Soviets do not want war. In a brief exchange on this point, the President pointed out that, while the Soviets may want continuation of enough tension for them to exploit, they had found out in 1967 that they are not capable of controlling their Arab friends and must therefore not draw too fine a line between the exploitable and the dangerous. Mr. Eban went on to say that the current situation is difficult for Israelis—with the persistent border-shelling and the occasional terrorist grenades—but it does not seriously threaten Israel. However unpleasant it may be, the present situation is better than "the great historic mistake" of retreating from present advantageous positions for less than a peace which would assure the existence of Israel.

On the four-power talks, Mr. Eban began by saying that only one of the four is really important for Israel—the U.S. Differences do exist between our positions, but he felt after his talks here this week that we have moved closer and they are close enough to make cooperation possible. The President interjected that it was important for us to engage in this process to give ourselves "some running room with the moderate Arabs." Mr. Eban nodded his understanding and went on to comment individually on the positions of the USSR and France.

The Soviets, he believed, "want us out without peace." Israel has a "robust skepticism" about the Soviet position. The Soviets' purpose is to cement their position in the Arab world and to undercut the US position as completely as possible.

The French position is "more tragic." A great deal of emotion is involved because the relationship has moved from a "romantic love affair" to a love-hate situation. President de Gaulle, he said, seemed incapable of anything but black or white feelings. Mr. Eban traced much of the current Israeli feeling toward President de Gaulle from his failure in May of 1967 to "understand our peril." Mr. Eban described how he had tried to convince de Gaulle on May 24, 1967, of the threat which Israel faced.[3] He said the Israeli man in the street feels that, if de Gaulle could not understand Israel's plight in that situation at a time when men in the street from Montevideo to Tokyo knew that Israel's very existence was threatened, Israelis could not trust guarantees which depended on the French because they would have no assurance that a French government would be any more likely in the future to understand Israel's peril than the French Government did in May 1967.

The President said he believed that the French position could be moved. He conceded that it would not be moved if the Middle East were the only issue we were discussing, but there are other issues which are perhaps even more important to France. The President did not say it in so many words, but the clear implication was that he felt that the French desire to participate with us in talks with the USSR would influence France to give on the Middle East. At any rate, the President said, "Let us give it a whack."

---

[3] Recalling his meeting with de Gaulle in Paris at his office in the Elysée Palace, Eban wrote that he did not believe that the French President took seriously the threat to Israel posed by the withdrawal of UNEF from the Sinai Peninsula and the Egyptian blockade of the Straits of Tiran. (*Abba Eban: An Autobiography*, pp. 341–344)

Mr. Eban returned to the question of guarantees for a peace settlement. "If two of the four guarantors are against us, why should we put our trust in guarantees?" Then he went on to argue against "globalizing" the Middle Eastern conflict. He felt that big-power guarantees would get the US "involved too early" in any crisis. He used the analogy of Berlin to point out how the whole world becomes involved by the smallest border incident which involves the US and the USSR. The President nodded seriously that this was "an important point."

After an off-the-record discussion of Mr. Eban's views of the possibilities of peace with Jordan, the President said that King Hussein would be coming to the United States on a visit in early April[4] and asked Mr. Eban what he felt we should say to the King. Mr. Eban said that what we tell him will be very important to the prospects of a settlement between Israel and Jordan because Hussein feels a need for international support. Mr. Eban suggested that we urge Hussein to enter serious negotiations with the Israelis and to tell him of our feeling—"if you believe it"—that we thought it possible for Jordan to win serious concessions from Israel if it negotiated seriously.

In a brief aside to this part of the conversation, the President asked Mr. Eban his views of the situation in Cairo and whether or not we should resume relations. Mr. Eban said he thought Nasser's internal situation was shaky—perhaps even more so than Hussein's. When the President stated his position as not setting conditions on the resumption of relations with Egypt, Mr. Eban said he felt this was exactly right. When the President asked whether we should do more, Mr. Eban said he felt that it would look too much as if we were running after Nasser. When the President asked directly whether Mr. Eban felt it was in Israel's interest for us to resume relations, Mr. Eban a couple of times avoided a direct answer.

The meeting closed with another exchange of pleasantries and with reiteration of a theme that the President struck throughout the meeting—that we intend to proceed in close cooperation with Israel.

Harold H. Saunders[5]

---

[4] King Hussein visited the United States during the second week of April and met with President Nixon on April 8. See Document 19.

[5] Saunders initialed "H.H.S." above his typed signature.

15. Telegram From the Department of State to the Embassy in the Soviet Union[1]

Washington, March 18, 1969, 0141Z.

42154. *Begin summary:* Assistant Secretary Sisco met with Ambassador Dobrynin today to resume US-Soviet Middle East talks.[2] The Soviets have brought a Middle East expert here from Moscow and clearly intend to pursue this dialogue in a serious manner. Mr. Sisco suggested that as immediate steps the Soviets parallel our efforts (a) to encourage scrupulous observance by the parties of the ceasefire and (b) to urge the parties to be responsive to Jarring's latest questions. He also stressed our belief that a UAR commitment to work for an agreed and lasting peace is necessary to get a meaningful negotiating process started. Dobrynin said the USSR concurred in our view that the terms of a settlement must be agreed to by the parties, must constitute a package and should be worked out through Jarring. He argued, however, that clarification of the Israeli position on boundaries would help elicit a clear expression of the Arab position on peace. He also made the point that, while there is no question of QUOTE imposing UNQUOTE a settlement, agreed positions by the US and USSR could constitute pressure on the parties.

Sisco told Dobrynin we hoped to present some ideas on the substance of a settlement shortly in New York. Once that decision was taken, we would make these ideas available to Dobrynin and hoped to get into further specifics in our next meeting with him.[3] Dobrynin and Sisco agreed that their meetings should continue at fairly frequent intervals on a quiet and informal but businesslike basis. If the press learns of these talks, we will confirm they are taking place but decline to discuss their substance. *End summary*

1. Asst. Secretary Sisco, NEA, (accompanied by Atherton) met with Soviet Ambassador Dobrynin at Soviet Embassy March 18 to resume US-Soviet dialogue on Middle East. Also present on Soviet side were

---

[1] Source: National Archives, Nixon Presidential Materials, NSC Files, Box 653, Country Files, Middle East, Sisco Middle East Talks. Secret; Nodis. Drafted by Atherton, cleared in EUR, and approved by Sisco. Repeated to Amman, Cairo, Tel Aviv, London, Paris, and USUN.

[2] This was the first of nine meetings between Sisco and Dobrynin, the last of which occurred on April 22. Brief summaries of most of the conversations are in an April 18 memorandum from Saunders to Kissinger, which is printed in *Foreign Relations,* 1969–1976, volume XII, Soviet Union, January 1969–October 1970, Document 38.

[3] At the next meeting on March 24, Sisco gave Dobrynin the U.S. working paper that Yost presented in the Four-Power forum the same day (see Document 17). (Telegram 46143 to Moscow, March 25; National Archives, Nixon Presidential Materials, NSC Files, Box 653, Country Files, Middle East, Sisco Middle East Talks)

V.V. Mikhailov, Counselor of Embassy, and A. Semiochkin, Chief of Near East Dept. who had arrived from Moscow previous evening.

2. In brief opening statement Dobrynin noted he had already had opportunity to convey Soviet concern re Middle East situation to President[4] and expressed hope that current talks would be constructive and productive. Dobrynin noted that Soviet December 30 plan provided both that Israel's existence as independent state should be guaranteed and that Arab territories occupied by Israel should be liberated.[5] Soviets wished to take US views into account to extent possible and had no objection to detailed discussion of all issues although Soviet interest focused primarily on Israeli withdrawal. Soviet plan did not contain answers to all questions and details should be worked out with parties concerned. He hoped, however, that US and USSR could agree on number of specifics. Dobrynin emphasized that Soviet plan calls for strong and lasting peace, not merely return to armistice situation, and envisages utilization of Jarring Mission. He would welcome US comments on Soviet plan and hoped to hear US ideas as well.

3. Sisco replied that we welcome opportunity to resume discussions, noting that he and Dobrynin had previously agreed these talks were of utmost importance and should be held quietly and in businesslike atmosphere. Sisco suggested and Dobrynin agreed that, if press learned of talks, both sides would confirm they had taken place but would make no comment on substance.

4. Sisco continued that we viewed these discussions with Soviets and consultations in New York among four powers as effort help Jarring narrow gap between parties within framework of SC Resolution. We hoped to get down to specifics, and did not preclude possibility that we might together produce informal QTE pieces of paper UNQTE on ad referendum basis if we reach point where common ideas emerge.

5. Sisco then suggested two immediate steps for Soviet consideration: (a) that, in view recent cease-fire violations in area, we counsel parties to scrupulously respect cease fire resolutions in effort develop better climate for negotiations; and (b) that Soviets encourage parties, as we have already done with Israeli and Arab friends, to respond positively to Jarring's latest questions.[6] This connection Sisco said we were concerned about press reports that UAR Foreign Minister Riad had recently expressed doubts about possibility of political settlement and had indicated that military solution needed.

---

[4] Dobrynin met with Nixon on February 17. See *Foreign Relations*, 1969–1976, volume XII, Soviet Union, January 1969–October 1970, Document 14.

[5] See Document 1.

[6] See Document 12.

6. Sisco continued that he wanted to stress following: goal of our efforts is just and lasting peace and we welcome Soviet views that peace must replace armistice agreements. In our view objective is a commitment to peace from all parties and agreement between parties on the components of peace. We emphasize need for agreement in belief that any lasting settlement must record parties obligations to each other in contractual form—i.e., as obligations to each other. Stated another way, we believe settlement must be reciprocally binding. We also believe settlement must be QUOTE package UNQUOTE in which there is agreement on all elements before any can be implemented. We understand this is also Soviet view.

7. Re Sisco's suggestions for immediate steps, Dobrynin said Soviets doing their best to help Jarring Mission and believe parties must work through Jarring. Re need to defuse situation in area, Dobrynin said he generally agreed but had no authority to make specific undertaking on this question which beyond scope of present talks. Fedayeen were fact of life, opposed to many things which were happening in occupied territories and inspired by desire to liberate those territories; and activities would continue until settlement reached.

8. Dobrynin agreed that settlement must be QUOTE binding UNQUOTE. Precise form (e.g., through Security Council or a four powers) was up to parties and we could discuss this aspect at a later stage. Soviets prepared discuss informally several ways in which settlement could be recorded.

9. Dobrynin said Soviets agreed on QUOTE package UNQUOTE concept; Soviet plan called for parties to deposit their declarations on same day troop withdrawal begins. In principle, therefore, he saw no difference between us on this point.

10. Turning to four-power discussions, Sisco said we expect Ambassador Yost will resume discussions on bilateral basis this week, we have some concrete ideas to submit in New York and, once we have decided to do so, these ideas will be passed to Dobrynin here probably later this week. Meanwhile we will examine points Dobrynin has made and hope to be able raise number of specifics at next meeting, perhaps sometime this week.

11. Dobrynin then asked why Israeli Foreign Minister Eban was opposed to four-power talks. Sisco replied by saying he wanted to give Dobrynin some sense of what Eban had said.[7] In brief, Eban had stressed four points: (a) Israel will withdraw only in context of peace, (b) peace must be in form of binding contractual agreement, (c) settlement must be a package and (d) secure and recognized borders must be

---

[7] See Documents 13 and 14.

different from Armistice Lines. Atherton added that, in clarifications to us, Eban had cited three factors which must govern determination of borders: (a) they must be agreed between parties which as practical matter ruled out present cease fire lines; (b) they must be based on Israel's security needs and not on historical or emotional consideration; and (c) they must preserve Jewish character of state which rules out incorporation into Israel of Arab population.

12. Sisco said he wanted to give Dobrynin some idea of what we mean by peace. We do not expect Arabs and Israelis suddenly to love each other. To us peace does mean, however, liquidation of Arab-Israeli conflict; transition from armistice situation to formal state of peace as provided for in Armistice Agreements; and end of belligerent claims, blockades and boycotts. In addition we do not accept views that Arab governments have no responsibility for fedayeen. There could not be peace if governments accept a settlement but fedayeen reject it.

13. Dobrynin replied that it necessary to distinguish between two situations; (a) in absence of settlement, he did not see how Arabs could be asked to give up efforts to liberate occupied territories. (b) Once settlement agreed and territorial dispute settled, there would be no basis for fedayeen to continue.

14. Re Dobrynin's question about Israeli attitude toward four-power talks, Sisco said GOI has reservations since it believes parties themselves must make the peace. For our part we see discussions with Soviets and in four-power context as assisting Jarring not as mechanism for dictating or imposing settlement.

15. Dobrynin agreed, asking whether Israelis really think four-power talks represent effort to impose settlement. Such talks might constitute pressure, but question of imposing settlement does not arise. Soviet plan speaks of agreed settlement, which means settlement agreed to by Israel and Arabs. Sisco said US-Soviet recommendations would certainly carry weight. Despite Israeli objections, we had told Israelis we intend to continue consultations with other powers which we see as being in overall US interest. For US and USSR, Sisco added, such interests go beyond Middle East. Dobrynin agreed and said Middle East appeared most promising area for US-Soviet agreement.

16. Sisco observed that we could proceed in two ways: (a) we could seek common ground while disregarding the parties and accomplish nothing; or (b) we could seek to bring the parties along. We assume both sides will attempt to follow latter course. Dobrynin commented that he assumed that we would both want to brief QTE our friends UNQTE on our talks but hoped certain delicate questions which might arise would be held by the two of us.

17. Dobrynin asked whether we had a clear idea of Israel's position on recognized borders, noting that Jarring had told Soviets in Moscow

they were not clear to him. Sisco said that, if UAR would make clear commitment to seek agreement on just and lasting peace, we had impression this would unlock the door and make it possible to get at all specific issues covered by Security Council Resolution, including withdrawal. Israeli willingness to be specific on borders is linked to Arab willingness make binding commitment to peace.

18. Dobrynin asked if this was not a two-sided process. Sisco agreed it was and suggested that, if UAR has difficulty indicating its position on peace through Jarring, it might help if UAR gave such indication to USSR. Dobrynin thought this would be difficult at present though not ultimately. Problem was that Israel would only speak of QUOTE secure and recognized borders UNQUOTE. Dobrynin noted that former Secretary Rusk and Under Secretary Rostow had said Israel seeks only demilitarization but no territory from UAR and Syria and wants only some corrections in border with Jordan. Without committing USG, Soviets have explained these views in discussing their plan with Arabs, but Israeli statements on territorial question continue to raise questions. It would unlock door for Arabs if Israel would clarify its position on territories. In such a case, Soviets could make recommendations to Arabs about stating their position on peace. Sisco agreed these were the two fundamental questions; Israel is convinced that Arabs do not want peace, and Arabs are convinced that Israel does not wish to return territories. These positions reflect suspicions rooted in history of problem but it should be possible with ingenuity to find way out of this vicious circle.

19. Dobrynin asked if Israelis had told USG what boundaries they wanted, noting that he was not asking what they had told us but only whether they had told us. Sisco said Israelis have not indicated to us precisely what they have in mind; they have shown us no maps. We believe Israel will not give precise indication until convinced that Arabs are ready to work out agreement on peace. Meanwhile their position is that boundaries should be final and different from Armistice Lines. Dobrynin asked if we could indicate whether Israeli position on boundaries is reasonable or unreasonable. Sisco said we have impression that, if it were possible to get Arab commitment to peace, GOI territorial decisions would be reasonable; this is only an impression Sisco repeated. We doubt that GOI has so far reached specific territorial decisions, given reluctance of all governments to avoid QUOTE iffy UNQUOTE decisions. Dobrynin said situation was also QUOTE iffy UNQUOTE on Arab side since Arabs were being asked to make decision on peace without knowing Israel's territorial demands. Problem would appear easier for Israel since it must have idea of what it will want when Arabs say they want peace.

20. Sisco replied that two situations were not equal. Israel would need to take concrete act of withdrawal in return for Arab commitment

on paper. Latter was also concrete act but not in same category. Feeling is deep in Israel that Arab agreement on peace represents act of recognition of Israel's right to exist in peace and security, which both we and Soviets accept. It can be argued that Arab signature on piece of paper is less important than substance, but for psychological and other reasons Israel attaches importance to formality of recognition.

21. Dobrynin commented that central point of Soviet proposal is that it is responsive to wishes of both sides. Withdrawal would not begin until parties had deposited documents recording agreement on all issues. In response to Sisco's comment that this raised prior question of what would be in those documents, Dobrynin said this would first have to be clarified among the parties.

Rogers

16. National Security Study Memorandum 33[1]

Washington, March 21, 1969.

TO

The Secretary of State
The Secretary of Defense
The Director of Central Intelligence

SUBJECT

Contingency Planning for the Middle East

The President has directed the preparation of studies for various contingencies in the Middle East. As directed in the guidelines for contingency planning these papers should include a careful orchestration of political and military actions. These studies should be performed by the Near East Interdepartmental Group and should be submitted to the Review Group by the dates indicated below:

—*Resumption of Arab-Israeli Hostilities.* This should examine possible U.S. actions in the event of renewed conflict in the Middle East provoked by either the Arabs or Israel. It should assume that the USSR

---

[1] Source: National Archives, Nixon Presidential Materials, NSC Files, NSC Institutional Files (H-Files), Box H–141, National Security Study Memoranda. Secret. A copy was sent to the Chairman of the Joint Chiefs of Staff and the Director of the United States Information Agency.

and the US do not become involved to the extent of engaging in actual hostilities in support of either side. (May 23, 1969)

—*Jordan.* This should explore the most likely crises as a result of internal or external pressures. (April 4, 1969)

—*Possible US-Soviet Confrontation.* This should cover contingencies relating to accidental or deliberate direct Soviet involvement in the Mideast which could lead toward US–USSR confrontation. (April 25, 1969)

Henry A. Kissinger

17. Telegram From the Department of State to the Mission to the United Nations[1]

Washington, March 22, 1969, 0430Z.

44729. Subject: Four-Power Consultations on ME.

1. Following is text of U.S. working paper to be given to other three major powers (guidance septel):[2]

Begin text: Views to be conveyed to Ambassador Jarring and to the principal parties on ways and means to achieve agreement in accordance with Security Council Resolution 242 of November 22, 1967.

The following views are conveyed to Ambassador Jarring and to the principal parties concerned with a view to helping promote agreement called for in Security Council Resolution of November 22, 1967:

1. That the parties accept SC Resolution 242 and state their willingness to implement it in all of its provisions in accordance with paragraph 3 of the resolution.

---

[1] Source: National Archives, Nixon Presidential Materials, NSC Files, Box 648, Country Files, Middle East, Middle East Negotiations. Secret; Priority; Exdis. Drafted by Arthur R. Day (IO/UNP), cleared by Sisco and De Palma, and approved by De Palma. Repeated Priority to Amman and to Jidda. Beirut, London, Kuwait, Moscow, Paris. Tel Aviv, and Cairo.

[2] In telegram 44730, March 22, the Department instructed the Ambassadors in Jordan, Lebanon, and Saudi Arabia, and the U.S. Minister in Egypt, to deliver copies of the U.S. working paper to their host governments on March 24, at which time Yost would be presenting the paper in the Four-Power meeting in New York scheduled for that day. The telegram also provided oral comments for the U.S. representatives to deliver as they distributed the working paper. (Ibid.)

2. There should be agreement between the parties on all elements of a settlement before implementation of any part of the package begins.

3. That the parties agree to exchange substantive views indirectly under the auspices of Ambassador Jarring, without prejudice to engaging in a more direct process at an appropriate stage. We believe that it will not be possible to reach a settlement without more direct Arab-Israeli contact at some point.

4. The objective should be a just and lasting peace based on agreement between the parties. The form of settlement must be contractually and reciprocally binding and may involve international participation as part of an overall guarantee of its terms.

5. A just and lasting peace will require withdrawal of Israeli forces to secure and recognized boundaries in the context of peace arrived at by agreement between the parties. The boundaries to be established under a just and lasting peace are intimately related to important security considerations for both sides: rectifications from pre-existing lines should be confined to those required for mutual security and should not reflect the weight of conquest. The question of Israeli withdrawal is intimately linked with a contractual commitment to peace from the Arabs and specific provisions for guarantees. Special arrangements should be considered for Gaza.

6. Certain critical areas should be demilitarized.

7. Jordan should have a defined role—civil, economic and religious—in Jerusalem which would remain a unified city. Arrangements would be made to assure the interest of all religions.

8. An overall settlement must provide for solution of the refugee problem. A refugee settlement should provide for the exercise of free choice by the refugees between resettlement with compensation and repatriation under conditions and controls acceptable to the two sides. The parties should agree to a mechanism which can work on this problem for an extended period.

9. Free navigation for the ships of all nations, including Israel, in the Suez Canal as well as the Gulf of Aqaba must be assured. Special arrangements will be required for Sharm al-Shaykh.

Rogers

18. Telegram From the Department of State to Certain Diplomatic Posts[1]

Washington, April 3, 1969, 2353Z.

51229. Sisco and Dobrynin had working lunch April 3 on Middle East in which following principal points emerged:

1. Dobrynin said he wished to state explicitly and categorically that Soviet Union wants peace in Middle East not simply an armistice. In response to Sisco's query, he did not elaborate on content of peace nor did he give any indication of USSR willingness to press UAR to make a binding commitment on peace. After expressing hope that we could make some progress, Sisco said there are some who believe that the USSR is not interested in real peace in Middle East. In support of this thesis is view that Soviet influence has not been on wane in the area and that all-out Soviet support for Arab cause is serving present Soviet interest. Sisco asked why should Soviets therefore want peace in the area when it may believe that it has things going for it? Dobrynin said this was a fair question. and he would answer it in this way: (a) Soviet Union does not like unstable situations. In Middle East, if another war were to occur, it could cause difficulties between us and we would once again have to be on the hot-line to see what the two of us could do. Situation in Middle East is beginning to look like it did in months before June [1967] war. Soviets think situation is too risky. (b) Soviets want to make progress because bilateral discussions between US and USSR on Middle East are first serious talks between Soviet Government and new Administration. We therefore believe it is important for progress to be made in the interest of overall US–USSR relations. Sisco took opportunity underscore point he has made at previous meetings with Dobrynin; namely, that unless Soviets can bring UAR around to make commitment [to] peace with Israel on basis of a binding agreement, it will be most difficult, if not impossible for US to influence Israelis to withdraw its forces to secure and recognized borders.

---

[1] Source: National Archives, Nixon Presidential Materials, NSC Files, Box 653, Country Files, Middle East, Sisco Middle East Talks, April–June (1969). Secret; Priority; Nodis. Drafted and approved by Sisco. Sent to Moscow, London, Paris, Amman, Tel Aviv, USUN, and Cairo. All brackets are in the original except "[1967]", "[to]". and "[sic]", added for clarity.

2. Dobrynin, who was aware of Secretary's appointment with Fawzi this morning,[2] asked if anything emerged from this talk. Sisco said two principal topics touched upon: (a) UAR desire to have Four Powers move ahead; and (b) indication that current UAR reaction to US working paper not as negative as public statement by Nasser on March 27.[3] Sisco said Fawzi found some good elements in paper as well as others which he did not like.

3. Sisco said he had impression that position of both sides had hardened somewhat, citing GOI Foreign Minister's emphasis on direct negotiations and peace treaty and Nasser's emphasis on Khartoum formula, i.e., no negotiations, no peace, no recognition.[4] Sisco said our impression of Israeli position is that they flexible on question of form provided undertakings are reciprocal and binding between parties. On negotiations, we continue to believe that indirect method can be pursued further but, we do not see a settlement being achieved unless Arabs at some point agree to direct discussion. Sisco stressed direct discussion procedure was an important element of Israeli thinking and reflected Arab recognition of GOI right to live in peace and security. Dobrynin agreed that position of both sides had probably hardened. He feels that there is some flexibility in form of settlement on Arab side, though he continues to shy away from any indication that Arabs would be willing to assume direct binding obligations to Israel. He continues to talk in terms of declarations deposited with the Security Council and obligations in relation to the Council and not between the parties.

4. Most interesting statement came from Dobrynin on the question of guarantees. He said plainly USSR has no interest in guarantees. If

---

[2] Telegram 51470 to Cairo, April 4, reported Rogers's April 3 meeting with Fawzi at which the two discussed "general questions relating to Arab-Israel settlement." The Secretary "pointed out necessity of UAR convincing rest of world it prepared recognize and live in peace with Israel by saying so explicitly." Fawzi was "unwilling say so even privately but said that UAR readiness recognize Israel's borders and renounce belligerency was sufficient proof of peaceful intentions." He added that if the United States "had some formula to propose on question recognizing Israel which would be short of formal, diplomatic recognition, UAR would be prepared to consider it." While the "withdrawal question was lost in shuffle," Rogers affirmed that the U.S. position on refugees "was consistent with UN resolutions on the subject, which "satisfied" Fawzi. (Ibid., RG 59, Central Files 1967–69, POL 7 UAR)

[3] In his March 27 speech, Nasser criticized the U.S. working paper and said that the Arabs would never agree to an "imposed settlement" by the Four Powers. (*New York Times*, March 28, 1969, p. 7)

[4] In a resolution adopted by the Arab League heads of state at a meeting in Khartoum August 29 to September 1, 1967, the heads of state "agreed to unified efforts at international and diplomatic levels to eliminate the consequences of aggression and to assure the withdrawal of the aggressor forces of Israel from Arab lands, but within the limits to which Arab states are committed: No peace with Israel, no negotiation with Israel, no recognition of Israel and maintenance of the rights of Palestinian people in their nation." (Ibid., September 2, 1967, p. 1)

Eban does not want Soviet Union to join in any guarantees, this is perfectly all right with them. He said positive reference to guarantees which Soviets have made have largely been in deference to US views. Soviets would be prepared to join in a Security Council endorsement, but if Soviet involvement in political guarantees gives Israelis any difficulty Soviets would not insist on being included. As far as they are concerned, important guarantees are practical arrangements on ground. In this connection, he expressed interest in possible UN role in Sharm-al-Sheik, Gaza, and in small demilitarized zone on both sides of international boundary between Egypt and Israel. He continued express very strong opposition to concept of demilitarization of entire Sinai.

5. Dobrynin was at great pains to explain that if the practical procedure for withdrawal which Soviets have suggested in December 30th Plan[5] is not acceptable, they are prepared to entertain alternative suggestions we might have.

6. Looking ahead, Dobrynin asked how US and USSR could be most useful. Sisco said speaking personally, once we have explored in detail specific points in Security Council resolution, we will want to take a look at Soviet position in totality to determine whether and how much movement has been made and where there are elements of agreement and disagreement. As we explored this, Dobrynin said, based on instructions from Moscow, he would be prepared to try to work out some new QTE practical plan UNQTE based on our combined thoughts. He asked Sisco what he meant when he said he speaking personally. Sisco said this is his own line of thinking and that whether we would want to try to put together a US/USSR QTE piece of paper UNQTE will depend on whether there are sufficient areas of agreement between us to make this a worthwhile exercise. Sisco expressed hope that this would be the case; but when he said he was speaking personally he was indicating that no such decision on a next step had been taken by the U.S. Government. This judgment would be made after we had compared our respective positions on all points. Dobrynin said his instructions go beyond merely exploring, but include objective of working out something with us. Sisco said that, too, is our objective. At same time Sisco stressed that one of things we will keep in foreground of our thinking on whether QTE combined thoughts UNQTE should be developed will be whether such ideas take sufficiently into account views of principal parties in area. If there was a reasonable chance that a common piece of paper would be a vehicle for helping to bring parties along, this might be worthwhile endeavor. We attach great importance to US–USSR talks on ME. Basically, this would mean USSR capacity to bring Egyptians along, and we to influence Israelis. We are not

---

[5] See Document 1.

interested in a propaganda exercise which would find us taking a position in disassociation from parties in the area; that would not be helpful in promoting a solution.

8 [sic]. Dobrynin asked if there had been any new development re US resumption of relations with UAR, making clear Soviets have no objections. Sisco said matter stands where it has been; our attitude is positive and we ready to discuss when UAR is ready.

Rogers

---

19. Memorandum of Conversation[1]

Washington, April 8, 1969, 10:30 a.m.

PARTICIPANTS

President Nixon
King Hussein I of Jordan
Henry A. Kissinger

The meeting was very cordial. The President began the conversation by expressing his great and high regard for the King and expressing his appreciation for the moderation and wisdom that the King had shown. The United States was interested in a just and fair settlement of the Middle East crisis. To this end, the United States had engaged in a more active diplomacy than the preceding Administration in the hope of having the four powers formulate some proposal that the parties might find reasonable. The President added that there were, of course, limits beyond which one could not push the parties and the United States recognized this.

The King replied that he had always attempted to be a force for moderation in the area. He had made great progress in building up his country for fifteen years and then the terrible tragedy of 1967 destroyed this progress. Two-thirds of the population of his country were now refugees. The situation was getting more and more desperate. If there were no solution within six months, he was afraid the extremists would gain the upper hand all over the Arab world. He appreciated the President's interest in a settlement, but it had to be just and honorable. The

---

[1] Source: National Archives, Nixon Presidential Materials, NSC Files, Box 928, VIP Visits, Jordan—Visit of King Hussein, Vol. II. Secret; Nodis. The meeting took place in the Oval Office. King Hussein made an official visit to Washington April 8–10.

Arabs had learned that Israel's right to exist was now unchallenged and they were prepared to accept this. He also was in a position to say on behalf of Nasser that the Arabs were prepared to sign any document with Israel except a formal peace treaty. But the major problem was to get the Arabs somehow to sign. He had tried to be moderate and reasonable with respect to Israel. But, unfortunately, the Israelis had not formulated any concrete proposal that was acceptable.

The President replied that the United States wanted a settlement which both parties could accept so the suffering of all the people in the Middle East would end. He asked the King whether he could formulate his ideas on borders.

The King replied that the Security Council Resolution of 1967 was a good starting point. He could speak for Nasser in expressing their sincere commitment to it. On the various items in the Resolution the King said that the 1967 borders should be re-established, but he recognized that some rectifications might be necessary. He said that if the Israelis were less vague about Gaza, these rectifications could be fairly substantial. The King added that the problem of Jerusalem was very difficult. It was not his to negotiate because it had been Arab for 1200 years and he held it in trust. However, he stated if the Israelis recognized his right in Jerusalem he was prepared to be very flexible in working out complete arrangements and to turn Jerusalem into what it was meant to be: A place of reconciliation for Arabs and Jews instead of a place of conflict. He recognized Israel's security concerns and was willing, in principle, to consider demilitarized zones but there had to be a certain equivalence. Israel, of course, would have free access through the Suez Canal and the Gulf of Aqaba. He repeated that Nasser endorsed these proposals.

The President asked the King to be a little more specific about Nasser. The King said that he and Nasser had always been at opposite poles of the Arab world. However, in recent months their policies had grown identical. Both were under the same pressures from the extremists. Also, the oil producing countries subsidizing them were getting restive. He added that Nasser was eager to re-establish diplomatic relations with the United States.[2] The President said this should be done but without conditions by either side. The King said the conditions would present no difficulties.

The President then spoke of his hope for economic development of the area and his desire to stay in close touch personally with the King.

---

[2] The United Arab Republic formally broke diplomatic relations with the United States on June 6, 1967, citing "US air support for Israel" during the Arab-Israeli war. See *Foreign Relations,* 1964–1968, volume XIX, Arab-Israeli Crisis and War, 1967, Document 178.

At the end of the meeting the President invited the Jordanian Ambassador and the Secretary General of the Royal Court to join the group. He reiterated what he had said during the conversation, that he would ask nothing of Jordan that might undermine the King's position and also his desire for the closest friendship between the two countries.[3]

Henry A. Kissinger

---

[3] Hussein met with Rogers the next day, and both expressed pessimism about the prospects for peace in the Middle East, concluding that the situation had become "dangerous." Rogers noted, however, that the United States believed that the Two- and Four-Power talks offered some hope for progress. He also assured the King that the United States did not agree that Israel should keep West Bank territory, nor did it agree with Israel's assessment that conditions in the region were "not explosive." (Telegram 54258 to Amman, April 9; National Archives, Nixon Presidential Materials, NSC Files, Box 928, VIP Visits, Jordan—Visit of King Hussein, Vol. II) Later that day, the King's delegation met with Laird and other U.S. officials, including Ambassador Symmes, in the Secretary's office at the Pentagon to discuss the possibility of Jordan obtaining additional military equipment from the United States—that is, arms beyond the package already approved but not yet delivered to Amman. To the chagrin of the Jordanians, Symmes argued, and Laird agreed, that it was "preferable" to "sign what [could] be signed" regarding the previously approved package and "leave open the issue of additional items for amendment of sales cases as required." (Memorandum of conversation, April 10; Washington National Records Center, ISA Files: FRC 330–72A–6309, Box 21, Jordan)

---

20. National Security Study Memorandum 40[1]

Washington, April 11, 1969.

TO

    The Secretary of State
    The Secretary of Defense
    The Director of Central Intelligence

SUBJECT

    Israeli Nuclear Weapons Program

The President has directed the preparation of a policy study on the Israeli nuclear weapons program.

---

[1] Source: National Archives, Nixon Presidential Materials, NSC Files, NSC Institutional Files (H-Files), Box H–146, National Security Study Memoranda. Top Secret; Sensitive; Nodis. A copy was sent to the Chairman of the Joint Chiefs of Staff.

As a background for this study, a thorough intelligence study should be provided, describing our best estimate of the current state and future prospects of the Israeli program. The intelligence estimate should be provided on a selected basis to the named individuals of the Ad Hoc Committee of the Review Group and of the National Security Council listed below.

The policy should (a) discuss as specifically as possible the implications of Israel's nuclear weapons program for U.S. objectives in the Middle East, in arms limitation and in non-proliferation of nuclear weapons, and (b) describe the principal policy alternatives for the U.S. and the full range of possible U.S. actions in the situations we are most likely to face. For instance, the paper might consider alternatives (a) in the present situation, (b) in a situation where Israel is known by us but not by the Arabs to have completed a nuclear device, and (c) in a situation where Israel is known by us and by the Arabs to be ready to deploy nuclear weapons. After analyzing alternatives, the paper may state a viewpoint on a preferred course.

The President has directed that this study be prepared by an Ad Hoc Group chaired by a representative of the Secretary of State and including representatives of the Secretary of Defense, the Chairman of the Joint Chiefs of Staff, the Director of Central Intelligence and the Assistant to the President for National Security Affairs.

The paper should be submitted by April 25, 1969, to an Ad Hoc Committee of the NSC Review Group comprised of Elliot L. Richardson, Under Secretary of State; David Packard, Deputy Secretary of Defense; Richard Helms, Director of Central Intelligence; General Earle G. Wheeler, Chairman, Joint Chiefs of Staff, and chaired by the Assistant to the President for National Security Affairs. The special committee of the National Security Council will be comprised of the Secretary of State, the Secretary of Defense, the Director of Central Intelligence and the Assistant to the President for National Security Affairs.[2]

Henry A. Kissinger

---

[2] Because of the "sensitivity of the subject," this study was "not handled by the full NSC mechanism." (Memorandum from Atherton to Barbour, July 30; ibid., RG 59, Lot Files, Bureau of Near Eastern and South Asian Affairs, Office of Israel and Arab-Israel Affairs, 1951–1976, Box 27) See Document 31.

21. Memorandum of Conversation[1]

Washington, April 11, 1969, 3:15 p.m.

PARTICIPANTS

    The President
    Henry A. Kissinger
    Joseph Sisco
    Emil Mosbacher
    Harold H. Saunders

    Dr. Mahmoud Fawzi, Foreign Affairs Assistant to President Nasser
    Mohammad Riad, UAR Foreign Ministry Official
    Ashraf Ghorbal, UAR Minister in Washington

The President opened the meeting by commenting directly to the effect that: We have before us the question of resuming relations. He guesses it comes down to the question of who makes the first move.

The President then broadened his comments to the effect that the United States regrets that it does not have formal relations with a larger number of the Arab people.[2] He said what troubles him most is the fact that our nation is cut off from these people. The time comes when we must forget the recriminations of the past and build a new relationship. This is also true among the peoples of the area.

Dr. Fawzi responded that as long as there is no "implementation of the UN Resolution" there "will be difficulties." He then went on to explain that the UAR's principal concern is to provide better lives for its people. How can the UAR get on with that job while its territory is occupied? The UAR must spend 300 million pounds yearly for arms, a serious drain from the resources available for economic progress. The UAR government hopes to widen and deepen our relations. This is not just a matter of "sentiment," but a matter of mutual interests.

The President agreed that vital interests are involved on both sides. He felt that a new attitude was required on both sides and that nothing could be gained from simply analyzing again and reiterating the attitudes of the past. Speaking specifically of the Arab-Israeli impasse, the President said that the practical problem is how we bridge the gap between the two sides. We believe that it may be possible to narrow that gap but that it will only be possible to bridge the gap if the parties involved want to take serious steps toward each other. We will

---

[1] Source: National Archives, Nixon Presidential Materials, NSC Files, Box 635, Country Files, Middle East, UAR, Vol. II. Secret; Nodis. The meeting took place in the Oval Office. Saunders drafted the memorandum on April 15.

[2] The UAR, Syria, Iraq, Algeria, and the Yemen Arab Republic all severed diplomatic relations with the United States during the Arab-Israeli war of 1967.

do our part in an affirmative way with full respect for the concerns of both sides. The President felt that if our effort cannot be made the beginning of a new relationship, we will have missed an opportunity

Dr. Fawzi said the UAR recalls with deep gratitude the US role in 1956–57.[3] He felt frankly that this time the US is not sufficiently exerting an influence comparable to its interests. He hoped that time would show him to be wrong. The UAR is ready to entertain any suggestion for doing anything it has not done that it might do.

The President asked whether Dr. Fawzi thought an Arab government could survive which made peace with Israel. He recognized that there are practical political problems in the UAR as in Israel—that when governments try to solve these problems they face obstacles which we all recognize.

Dr. Fawzi replied that, for the UAR's part, "we are taking the chance." He said the UAR is ready to assume its responsibility under the UN Security Council Resolution, knowing full well that other Arab governments are not happy with the resolution. Still the UAR is going ahead.

Dr. Fawzi said that the UAR would like the US position to be more clearly defined. Maybe the US does not find this exactly the right time for revealing its position, and that is understandable. But nevertheless the UAR would like to know precisely where the US stands.

The UAR's concept is that Israeli troops must withdraw to June 4 lines. Although it is beyond the scope of the resolution to discuss rectifications in the boundaries and this is more an issue on the Israel-Jordan border, the UAR would not object to changes provided they are genuine rectifications and not "annexations."

The President said we are in a delicate position too. The US Government could come out and say that such-and-such is the way to solve this problem. But we believe this is a way *not* to get the problem settled. The Arab Governments might not like our solution. The Israelis might not like it.

The President conceded that the US has not done as much as it might have until recently but we are going to make a more active effort. He asked Mr. Sisco to comment on the question of our being more specific.

---

[3] Reference is to President Dwight D. Eisenhower's call for British, French, and Israeli forces to withdraw from the Suez Canal Zone after their invasion in October 1956, as well as the success of his administration in compelling them to do so. The invasion was in response to the UAR's nationalization of the Canal on July 26, 1956.

Mr. Sisco said we had tried to be "rather specific" in our recent papers[4] although we have not formulated a blueprint of our own. We believe that a peace settlement requires the full assent and cooperation of both parties. We have tried to indicate a framework within which the parties might find common ground. Our working paper contains a "deliberate vagueness" because we are still working toward that common ground and not trying to dictate it.

Dr. Fawzi reiterated that the UAR hoped we would tell them our position—not necessarily today but "assure us that your position does not allow for the 'acquisition of territory by force.'"

The President said that we have supported the UN Resolution which includes that language.

Mr. Sisco said that a good part of the current problem is that the resolution is differently interpreted. One reason it was unanimously passed was that it allowed for differing interpretations. The UAR believes it calls for withdrawal to pre-war boundaries. Israel points out that it mentions only "secure and recognized boundaries" which it argues must be negotiated between the parties.

The President said he did not believe that there will ever be a precise statement that would satisfy either side. He did feel, however, that with a new relationship between the Arab and American peoples and with a new US administration, the UAR should attach significance to the fact that we want a solution based on the principles spelled out in the UN Resolution.

Having all this in mind, the President said that we still have the very delicate problem of the negotiations and how to bring about a solution in accordance with those principles. This will require trust between the parties. "We do not ask you to buy a pig in a poke."

Dr. Fawzi said again that he understood the US might not wish to reveal its precise position today or tomorrow, but he hoped that it would not be delayed for long. Even more important, when it is revealed he hoped it would be fair.

The President said quickly he could assure Dr. Fawzi of one thing—that our position would be fair. The President realized that unless the solution were fair to the people in the area it would not survive. All sides must accept it.

Dr. Fawzi said that the UAR only wants the US to "use its friendly and firm persuasion with all of us." The UAR could not ask us to support a peace that would not be good for Israel any more than it could ask us to support a peace that would not be good for the Arabs. Forcing Israel on the Arab world would not assure peace, but if the US tells the

---

[4] See, for example, the working paper, Document 17.

UAR that it will pursue further effort toward a fair peace, the UAR will take this seriously.

The President said that he would be presumptuous to get into the details of the settlement himself. But he knew one thing—that no settlement in history has lasted unless it is based not on sentiment but on the vital interests of the parties involved and unless it has contained an element of fairness to both sides. Perhaps sometimes a party outside the conflict can be more objective than those involved about what is "fair." A lasting peace must have that self-enforcing quality that grows only from the conviction that it was the fairest settlement possible under the circumstances.

The President said that we are not tied to any preconceived notions about the nature of the settlement. We have differences upon specific aspects of it within our own house. The position which the President wants the US to take is not to be on either side. We are, he said, only on the side of peaceful settlement with justice.

Dr. Fawzi said, "That's fair enough for us." The President in the preceding exchange had mentioned the refugee problem, and Dr. Fawzi said he especially appreciated the President's concern for the refugees.

The President said he has a strong feeling about their problem. This is not only a matter of great humanitarian concern, but he realized there could not be a lasting peace unless an effective move was made to solve that problem. If it is left unresolved it will be a poison in the atmosphere that undermines the peace. But he emphasized that even without that factor, we have a strong humanitarian concern for helping these people.

Dr. Fawzi hoped that we would get over this hump soon and not waste any more time

The President noted that Dr. Fawzi had earlier mentioned our efforts in 1956 but had been kind enough not to mention the Aswan Dam.[5]

Dr. Fawzi, with a twinkle in his eye, said, "Well, it's a nice day."

The President felt that the Dam is a great human achievement and he personally wished that we had played a part in it.

The President went on to say that the important job now is to build a peace for a later day. There are many problems to be solved. He had told King Hussein that this is one area where the American people

---

[5] In response to Nasser's overtures to the Soviet Union to provide arms to Egypt and fund the Aswan High Dam project, the Eisenhower administration withdrew its loan offer for the project in mid-July 1956, provoking Egyptian nationalization of the Suez Canal the following week.

would, he felt, look with favor on being of assistance. There are lots of things there to be done.

Dr. Fawzi said he had seen Mr. McNamara at the World Bank.[6] He had not asked Mr. McNamara for anything, but Mr. McNamara himself had laid out the great potential for progress in the UAR. Dr. Fawzi said there are "fantastic possibilities"—oil in the Western Desert is almost as great as that in Libya and there are possibilities for other development.

The President said that he shares Mr. McNamara's dream for the future. One of his greatest frustrations about the present situation is that it does not allow us to get on with that future. If we are to do so, we shall all have to take major steps. We shall all have to stick our necks out but it will be worth it.

The President then walked Dr. Fawzi out to his car at the foot of the path behind the Oval Office.

Harold H. Saunders[7]

[6] Robert S. McNamara, Secretary of Defense, January 1961-February 1968; President of the World Bank, April 1968-June 1981.

[7] Printed from a copy that bears Saunders's typed signature.

---

22. Telegram From the Department of State to the Embassy in the Soviet Union and the Mission to the United Nations[1]

Washington, April 18, 1969, 1725Z.

59898. Subject: April 17 Sisco-Dobrynin Meeting on Middle East.

Summary: Dobrynin changed character April 17 bilateral discussion of Middle East by dropping point-by-point review of November 1967 resolution and presenting written replies under instructions to several earlier US questions. Soviet replies, like Dobrynin's verbal presentation made also under instructions, indicate decision which Dobrynin said had been made at highest level in Moscow to try accelerate pace of US-Soviet deliberations on Middle East.

Three principal points emerged: (a) Moscow believes Sisco-Dobrynin talks have drawn US–USSR views QUOTE somewhat nearer

[1] Source: National Archives, Nixon Presidential Materials, NSC Files, Box 648, Country Files, Middle East Negotiations. Secret; Priority; Nodis. Drafted by Walter B. Smith (INR/RSE), cleared in EUR and IO, and approved by Sisco. Repeated Priority to Amman, London, Paris, Tel Aviv, and Cairo. All brackets are in the original except "[sic]", added for clarity.

UNQUOTE; (b) Moscow prepared to try to work out a specific joint US-Soviet proposal in form of a QUOTE preliminary agreement UNQUOTE; and (c) for first time, Soviets have suggested possibility that agreement should be explicitly QUOTE between the parties UNQUOTE and that it might be reflected in a single document of a bilateral nature, rather than separate declarations. Latter shift could be significant because if carried to its logical conclusion, could mean a document signed by UAR and Israel and another signed by Jordan and Israel

Meaningfulness of Soviet shift on nature of peace agreement, however, is still unclear in view of continued Soviet insistence on final act after Israeli withdrawal, such as Security Council decision or signing of multilateral document to put previously signed agreements in final force. Dobrynin also continued at this session to discount possibility any direct talks between parties and insisted demilitarized zones would have to be on both sides of border and in equal depth. End summary.

1. Sisco and Dobrynin held sixth regular session of bilateral talks on Middle East April 17. Toon, Atherton, Smith, Mikhailov, and Semyochkin present. Ambassador Dobrynin opened by presenting written responses under instructions to six questions posed by US side March 24. (Note: US questions were given in writing to Soviet Embassy after Sisco-Dobrynin meeting March 24 in amplification of discussions during meeting.) Dobrynin under instructions then transmitted five written Soviet questions. Texts US questions, Soviet replies and Soviet questions being sent septel.[2]

2. FYI: Soviet replies which being studied by Dept appear intended to suggest slight shifts in Soviet position. For example, replies refer to

---

[2] Telegram 59897 to Moscow, April 18, included the six questions: "(a) Soviet note of December 30 refers to a 'just peace settlement.' Does this mean the 'just and lasting peace' called for by Resolution 242? How does Soviet Union define 'peace' between Israel and the Arabs? In other words, what conditions would be brought about by a just peace settlement? (b) Soviet note of December 30 refers to 'agreement' and 'agreed plan.' Does Soviet Union mean that such 'agreement' involves each side assuming obligations directly to the other so that such obligations are mutually binding between them? (c) Could USSR clarify procedure it has in mind? For example, will documents deposited on day withdrawal begins reflect agreement of the parties and how will that agreement be recorded? Why should a document not be signed and be binding at beginning rather than end of process, and implementation start only after signature? (d) What specifically would be content of the multilateral document and what is its contractual nature? (e) What is Soviet position regarding demilitarized zones? What should be their location and size? What is Soviet concept of demilitarization? (f) Parties are exchanging views indirectly under Jarring's auspices. Does Soviet Union agree that at some appropriate stage it will be necessary for parties to have direct talks before a final peace agreement can be achieved? If so, at what stage would this occur?" (Ibid., Box 725, Country Files, Europe. USSR, Sisco-Dobrynin Talks, Vol. I) Sisco also gave Dobrynin the U.S. working paper (see Document 17) at their March 24 meeting. (Telegram 46143 to Moscow, March 25; National Archives, Nixon Presidential Materials, NSC Files, Box 654, Country Files, Middle East, Sisco Middle East Talks)

need to resolve all questions connected with complete cessation of state of war, vaguely implying Soviet recognition such matters as blockades and boycotts cannot be ignored. Replies contain first Soviet written reference to QUOTE accord between parties, UNQUOTE although term used (QUOTE dogovorennost UNQUOTE) does not necessarily mean a written agreement. According to these Soviet replies, documents to be deposited by parties with UN before withdrawal under Soviet December 30 plan are to be signed by parties and may be single document, implying possible signing by parties of same piece of paper. (In aside to Deptoff after meeting, Semyochkin volunteered significant comment that there actually will have to be more than one document QUOTE because there will be UAR-Israeli document and Jordanian-Israeli document UNQUOTE.) However, hardening of Soviet explicit views on DMZs and direct talks also revealed in replies. Replies state that (as did Malik at April 15 four power meeting)[3] DMZs must be of equal depth on both sides, and also, that raising question of direct talks would only complicate achieving settlement. *End FYI.*

3. After reading Soviet replies and Soviet questions, Dobrynin made following presentation under instructions. Soviet and US sides agreed at last meeting that US side would give Soviets in two or three weeks a draft of a preliminary agreement. Soviets hope this document will take into account provisions of Soviet plan as well as clarifications made by Soviets in course of these meetings.[4] In order to make Soviet position more precise on some major issues of settlement, Soviet side giving today written answers to six questions presented by US side March 24. Soviet side would also like to express wish that this draft preliminary agreement be balanced, that is, taking equally into consideration interests of both parties to conflict and thus being not of one-sided nature. In this case it could serve as basis for working out joint preliminary agreement. It would also be advisable that draft of preliminary agreement approach in its contents as much as possible the final documents on a settlement, giving answers to such basic questions as withdrawal, boundaries, demilitarized zones, and so on.

4. Careful study of US working paper of March 24 and analysis of the exchange of views at past meetings allow Soviet side to conclude that points of view of USSR and US QUOTE have drawn somewhat nearer UNQUOTE concerning questions of ways and means of implementing Security Council Resolution of November 22, 1967. (Dobrynin stressed this a governmental view.) At same time, Soviet side notes that some provisions of US paper do not take equally into account interests

---

[3] The UN Permanent Representatives of the Four Powers were meeting in New York. See Document 23.

[4] See Document 28.

of both sides to conflict, but reflect stand of Israel. At last meeting Soviet and US sides came to understanding in New York talks that SC resolution should be carried out by sides to conflict in all its provisions without any limitations. However, this was not clearly stated in US working paper. Soviets hope it will be clearly stated in draft of a preliminary agreement now being prepared by US side.

6. [sic] Soviet side wishes stress once more that wording of Paragraph Five of the US paper, QUOTE a just and lasting peace will require the withdrawal of Israeli forces to secure and recognized boundaries, UNQUOTE is at variance with provisions of SC resolution, which called for QUOTE withdrawal of Israeli armed forces from territories occupied in the recent conflict, UNQUOTE that is, to the lines held before June 5, 1967. Soviets consider that the issue of Israeli withdrawal to lines which they held before June 5, 1967 is a question of principle, in accordance with provisions of SC resolution on inadmissibility of acquisition of territory by war. US working paper mentions Israeli withdrawal, but it does not contain precise definition concerning obligation to carry out this important element of a Middle East settlement.

7. Sisco thanked Dobrynin for his remarks and Soviet replies and said we shared Soviet Govt assessment that our views have QUOTE drawn somewhat nearer. UNQUOTE.

8. Sisco said we will take into account in any further document which we produce Soviet plan, US paper, and clarifications that Dobrynin had given in past meetings and at today's session. We take seriously Dobrynin statement that interests and views of both sides must be taken into account. A practical reality for achieving peace is that both parties have a veto over situation. US and USSR cannot help promote agreement unless whatever is put forward meets the minimum requirements of both sides. We assume that neither side will be entirely satisfied with substance of any settlement or any US-Soviet paper that might be developed in future.

9. We understand fully and appreciate Soviet Govt's emphasis on withdrawal. We also understand need for specificity in this regard. For same reason we have emphasized need for specificity on permanent peace and a binding agreement between parties in which obligations are undertaken directly one to the other. Obviously all provisions of SC resolution must be agreed on and carried out. In our view, three principal prongs of a settlement are peace, agreement, and withdrawal.

10. Sisco assured Dobrynin that if we are in a position to suggest a further piece of paper at a later stage, USSR views expressed today and previously would be taken into account. Sisco welcomed USSR readiness to see if a joint provisional agreement can be drawn up. Sisco suggested another meeting next week at which time we would respond specifically to questions posed. Sisco stressed no final decisions

have been taken in the USG on whether further piece of paper will be developed.

11. Dobrynin commented that responses given at this meeting to Sisco reflected decision at highest level of Soviet Government. Soviet comments had been carefully worded after governmental decision had been taken.

12. At Dobrynin's suggestion, it was agreed to hold next meeting at 10:30 a.m., Tuesday, April 22.[5]

Rogers

---

[5] Most of the April 22 meeting, which was reported in telegram 62563 to Moscow, April 23, was spent discussing replies to Dobrynin's questions at the April 17 session. (National Archives, Nixon Presidential Materials, NSC Files, Box 725, Country Files, Europe, USSR, Sisco-Dobrynin Talks, Vol. I) In an April 23 memorandum to Kissinger, Saunders described it as "probably the least productive of the series," primarily because Sisco and Dobrynin were waiting for the United States to provide specific formulations that would help resolve Arab-Israeli differences as well as for a decision on whether or not the United States would pursue a joint U.S.-Soviet paper. Saunders concluded: "We have exhausted the Sisco-Dobrynin channel unless we can come up with something more specific to say to the Soviets." (*Foreign Relations,* 1969–1976, volume XII, Soviet Union, January 1969–October 1970, Tab K to Document 38)

---

23. Telegram From the Mission to the United Nations to the Department of State[1]

New York, April 22, 1969, 2331Z.

1181. Dept pass White House for the President and the Secretary. After five meetings of the UN reps of our Four Powers on the Middle East,[2] it seems time to submit a brief assessment of progress and prospects.

My judgment continues to be that all Four, including the Soviets, wish to promote a package settlement leading to a durable peace in the Middle East. While significant differences remain, it is not my impression that any of them are irreconcilable as far as the Four themselves are concerned. If the decision rested solely with them, they could probably come to agreement rather rapidly. The problem is to formulate pro-

---

[1] Source: National Archives, Nixon Presidential Materials, NSC Files, Box 649, Country Files, Middle East, Middle East Negotiations. Secret; Nodis.

[2] The Four-Power meetings were held in New York April 3, 8, 14, 17, and 21.

posals which have a reasonable prospect of being accepted by the parties. Even in this respect, significant progress has been registered both in the Four Powers talks and particularly in the US-Soviet bilaterals in Washington.

There seems to be agreement among the Four that (1) their aim is a just and lasting peace, not another armistice, (2) their recommendations should be based on the UN Security Council Resolution of November 1967 and should be submitted to the parties by Ambassador Jarring for final negotiation and implementation, (3) all terms of settlement would have to be agreed upon by the parties and not be imposed by the Four, (4) all the terms are closely interconnected and would have to be agreed as a package before any part could be implemented, (5) the terms would have to be embodied in an internationally binding document or documents which would commit the parties to each other and to the international community and which would be comprehensive and irrevocable, (6) the political independence and territorial inviolability of all states in the area, including Israel, is recognized and should be guaranteed in various ways by the international community, (7) each state in the area is entitled to secure and recognized boundaries which could be those of June 4, 1967, or could involve rectification in the interest of mutual security accepted by both sides, (the USSR has not yet formally agreed to the rectification for security concept but seems likely to do so), (8) Israeli forces should, when binding commitments to peace have been undertaken, withdraw from occupied territories to the lines of June 1967 or to new agreed lines, (9) freedom of navigation for Israel through the Suez Canal and the Strait of Tiran should be guaranteed, (10) there should be a final settlement of the refugee problem involving, in some form acceptable to the parties, free choice for the refugees between repatriation or resettlement with compensation, (11) there will probably have to be demilitarized zones and some form of UN presence along some of the frontiers.

Major unresolved points are the following: (1) Rectifications in the June 1967 boundaries: the British and French have emphasized that these should be minor, the Soviets very minor. We have simply stressed that they must be for mutual security and must be agreed, though in fact we also feel there need be no changes in the Israeli-UAR line and that changes on the Israel-Jordan line to the benefit of Israel might be compensated by the transfer of Gaza to Jordan. (2) There has been no real discussion of Jerusalem which all clearly feel might be the hardest problem to resolve. (3) Demilitarized zones: the Israelis would probably wish the whole West Bank and the whole Sinai demilitarized. The Soviets have countered with the proposal the zones should be of equal extent on both sides of the boundary. In fact, Jordan would probably agree to demilitarization of the West Bank but there would have to be some compromise on Sinai. (4) UN presence: this has not been discussed in depth but we see no major difficulties in agreeing on some such presence and on its withdrawal being subject to SC approval. This would be particularly necessary at Sharm el Sheik. (5) The means of limiting repatriation of refugees to Israel to an acceptable number may present difficulties. (6) The character of international guarantees has been only briefly touched on, but would presumably be in the SC framework. (7) The exact character of the document or documents embodying the agreed package of binding commitments has not been spelled out, but I anticipate no insuperable difficulties here.

Perhaps the major procedural obstacle to settlement is the Israeli insistence on face-to-face negotiation. Though the Israelis have no doubt conceived of this in some measure as a device to force Arab concessions, it nevertheless has great and real psychological significance for them. Unfortunately it appears to the Arabs as a means of dramatizing their humiliation and imposing Israeli terms, and hence has equal but negative psychological significance for them. It would be a tragedy for the parties and an unacceptable hazard to world peace if a settlement were permitted to break down over this essentially symbolic issue.

In my view the US should work toward a final face-to-face negotiation at the end of the road but until that time should leave Jarring discretion to stage manage as he sees fit the necessary exchanges between the parties. For us to insist on face-to-face negotiations now or in the next stage would almost certainly be unsuccessful and would risk aborting on a non-essential issue the whole effort at peacemaking in the Middle East which this administration has so wisely undertaken. The security of Israel is of great importance to us but this can be assured, if agreement can be achieved, by the legal and substantive safeguards we contemplate. Israel should not expect us to risk the serious US national interests we have at stake in defense of a demand which is not essential to their security, whatever its psychological significance may be.

A related but more substantive issue is how much of the package should be worked out between the US and the USSR or among the Four, and how much should be left to Jarring and the parties to settle. This can be handled to some extent by ear but it would be my judgment, on the basis of the past 18 months' experience, that the parties are unlikely to settle any of the really tough issues without more help than Jarring can provide, and that the Two and the Four Powers will have to remain seized of the problem until it is settled.

I do not underestimate the difficulty of persuading the Israelis to accept even what we would consider a just, durable and internationally binding peace. I can only urge that we continue to formulate the terms of such a peace in closest consultation with them and that we endeavor persistently to convince them and their friends in the US that such a settlement would offer them far more security than has their present military posture.

I personally do not think that Hussein was exaggerating when he argued that the next few months may offer the last chance for peace in the Middle East, at least for a long time to come. The complexion of the Arab world, particularly the states adjacent to Israel, is changing, the prolonged occupation is producing not accommodation but rising passion, the youth are being radicalized, the Palestinians are acquiring a deepened sense of national identity and purpose. It may not be long, if there is no settlement, before Hussein and Nasser lose control of events, are swept along or replaced, and radicals committed to a solution far more dangerous to Israel take over. In that case war might not come soon but it would be infinitely more difficult to avoid eventually.

Yost

24. Memorandum From the President's Assistant for National Security Affairs (Kissinger) to President Nixon[1]

Washington, April 23, 1969.

SUBJECT

Additional Arms for Hussein

You should be aware that Hussein, before leaving the US, has made a final plea for the military equipment he mentioned to you at his final meeting.[2] He made this pitch to Yost in New York and asked that it be passed to you so he can have an answer before he returns to Amman next week (Tab A). Dick Helms reports that one of his senior officers [*less than 1 line not declassified*] believes the King is seriously concerned about getting this equipment in order to convince his military that he is providing what they need to defend themselves (Tab B).

At the same time, Ambassador Barbour in Tel Aviv points out the probable sharp Israeli (and hence Congressional) reaction to the sale of

---

[1] Source: National Archives, Nixon Presidential Materials, NSC Files, Box 615, Country Files, Middle East, Jordan, Vol. I. Secret; Nodis. Sent for action. Tabs A–C are attached but not printed. All brackets are in the original except those indicating text that remains classified.

[2] See footnote 3, Document 19.

artillery to Jordan. What bothers Israel most today is the shelling of its settlements along the Jordan River (Tab C).

Hussein has asked for three things in addition to the package he has received: (a) 80 M–42 self-propelled anti-aircraft guns; (b) 60 more 106 mm. recoilless rifles (55 are already in the package); (c) 8″ Howitzers (he asked for 40 and got none).

Secretaries Rogers and Laird are taking another look. However, State's recommendations to Rogers are:

—That Defense provide just 10 more of the AA guns since these have to come out of our Vietnam inventory. The purpose of providing a token is to prove that we are not refusing on political grounds.

—That Defense not sell additional recoilless rifles (although they could be provided by taking them out of the Turkish program) because the additional are for new units of the Jordan Army. The Jordanians had previously undertaken to develop their forces at present levels to avoid committing themselves to an excessive defense budget.

—That we not provide any more Howitzers because of the extreme Israeli sensitivity.

Secretary Laird's staff is recommending about the same, though it is canvassing to develop a more precise picture of the impact on our Vietnam program. They are used to hard Jordanian bargaining and honestly feel they have gone a long way to meet Hussein's requirements, especially those for early delivery of many of the items in his package.

Ambassador Symmes feels the present package is adequate.

The choice is a purely political one:

1. *Stick to present package.* Ambassador Symmes and Secretary Laird's staff believe that we have made a significant effort to produce this package and there is no serious requirement to go beyond it. Besides, we reduce our credibility by admitting that our past answers were not firm.

2. *Make a token response—the 10 guns State is recommending.* The argument for this approach is to show that we are not holding out on these items for political reasons, since Hussein just does not believe us when we say things are not available. It would make us appear responsive while recognizing that what we do diplomatically is what will really determine Hussein's course. [This is the State recommendation.]

3. *A slightly larger token response.* It is possible to argue that 10 guns do not make much sense and that we should add a few more plus some of the recoilless rifles to make a real show of trying. [This would be my recommendation.]

4. *Agree in principle to most of what he asked for but delay delivery.* We could say we will do what we can but caution that we can make no

promises on delivery. The argument for this approach is that all Hussein really needs is to say we are supporting him all the way. [Some in CIA favor this, but I doubt the wisdom of making commitments we are not sure we can keep.]

Recommendation. I personally lean toward option 2. Since this is the direction in which Secretaries Laird and Rogers are already heading. I propose to stand aside unless you feel strongly otherwise.[3]

---

[3] Nixon approved this recommendation.

---

25. Memorandum From the President's Assistant for National Security Affairs (Kissinger) to President Nixon[1]

Washington, April 24, 1969.

SUBJECT

Summary of Secretary Rogers's Memo and the Issues It Raises for Decision

As you consider Secretary Rogers's recommendation that we now put forward specific proposals on a UAR-Israel settlement,[2] you will want to think about the possible pitfalls in this course:

—One argument underlying this proposal is that we will be charged with undercutting the four-power talks if we do not advance specific proposals now. But we may just as likely end up blocking four-power accord later over specifics as we are to stymie progress now by refusing to discuss specifics.

—Another assumption is that we will improve our position by advancing a specific proposal. But any fair proposal will be equally unpalatable to both the Arabs and Israelis, and we are likely to get most of the blame from both sides. Even if we are able to maneuver the USSR into sharing the blame, we have to assume that our influence with the Arabs will improve only after a settlement and not through a settlement.

---

[1] Source: National Archives, Nixon Presidential Materials, NSC Files, Box 634, Country Files, Middle East. UAR, Vol. I. Secret; Exdis. Printed from an uninitialed copy. All brackets are in the original.

[2] Rogers sent the memorandum with his recommendation to Nixon on April 23. (Ibid., Box 644, Country Files, Middle East, Middle East—General, Vol. I)

—A third assumption is that the best chance of winning Israeli cooperation and generating movement toward a settlement is advancing a draft UAR-Israel agreement that would have Israel accept less than its current minimum position at the outset. But it is more likely that the Israelis will reject our proposal outright and that we will be left with a choice between (a) negotiating the terms of a settlement with the USSR, France and UK knowing Israel will not consider them and (b) being isolated from the other three because we hold out for Israel's maximum terms.

I do not advance these necessarily as arguments against proceeding. However, they do highlight the dangers which you will wish to explore in the NSC discussion. The following analysis discusses these points in greater detail.

I. *Summary of Secretary Rogers's Recommendation—The Options*

The Secretary's memo judges that our efforts to help move the Near East closer to an Arab-Israeli settlement have reached a point where we must either become more specific about the substantive elements of a settlement or accept an early impasse.

It poses a *choice among three courses:*

A. We can go on avoiding entirely putting forward specific substantive positions because we do not believe we can persuade Israelis to reveal their positions except to the Arabs in face-to-face negotiations. [This would bring the US–USSR and four-power talks to an early impasse with us taking the blame for failure and being further isolated with Israel. Almost no one seems to argue following this course, but given the dangers in putting forward a specific proposal, we ought to think twice before abandoning this position.]

B. We can try to reach big-power agreement on the substance of a settlement without limiting ourselves to what Israel will accept on the theory that this would at least improve our position vis-à-vis the Arabs. [This would cause a major blow-up with the Israelis without bringing a settlement closer. But it can be argued that, if our chances of winning Israeli-Arab agreement to specific proposals are slim, this is the cheapest way of building a more defensible U.S. position to stand on in the prolonged absence of a settlement.]

C. We can put forward specific proposals designed if possible to engage Israeli and Arab Governments in negotiations but at a minimum to put us in an improved and more defensible posture even if we fail. [This would still cause a confrontation with the Israelis, though our position in its effort to be fair would be equally unpalatable to both sides. If we took positions that could be defended on their merits, we would stand some chance of pressing the USSR to support fair terms of bringing the Israelis along and of at least stepping out of our role as Israel's sole champion. But there are the dangers outlined above and below.]

The memo recommends the third of these courses on grounds that we will never know whether a settlement is possible until we can probe Soviet, Egyptian and Israeli positions by putting to each a specific and realistic proposition to accept, reject or bargain over. It appends a proposal for a UAR-Israel agreement, saying that we may wish to follow soon with a proposal for a Jordan-Israel agreement.

II. *The First Issue—Whether to Put Forward Specific U.S. Proposals*

The first issue is whether we should put forward a provisional agreement between the UAR and Israel that has enough in it to encourage Israeli cooperation. We have until now taken refuge behind our (Israel's) demand that the Arabs renounce their objective of destroying Israel and commit themselves to sign an agreement directly with Israel before anyone will discuss the specifics of a settlement. But now that the USSR is getting increasingly specific and closer to meeting our (and Israel's) requirements, it is becoming more difficult to stand credibly on our very general position.

The *principal dangers* in surfacing our own proposal are:

—We could end up isolated in the four-power talks supporting Israeli demands (direct negotiations as one evidence of a firm commitment to live at peace) which no one else considers attainable, or even reasonable. We could end up breaking up the peace negotiations over "direct negotiations" and commitment to a vaguely defined "peace" which everyone else regards as utopian. The Russians may very well be maneuvering us cynically into just that position.

—We could end up, instead of improving our position in the Near East, being blamed by both sides for undercutting peace efforts. The Israelis will say we have undercut their negotiating position by doing the Arabs' negotiating for them. The Arabs will say the concessions we ask of them just prove we support Israel's unjust demands.

—The Israelis and their friends will accuse us of playing the Russian's game and saving Nasser from the consequences of his own folly. They will say we have panicked and are acting to save our worst enemy in the Mid-East who will just turn around and resume his vigorously anti-U.S. policy.

—Although we say we are simply trying to get a UAR-Israel negotiation started, we will end up negotiating most of the details ourselves. The best we are likely to get for Israel, if that, is an Arab agreement to sign the final agreement in the presence of Israeli representatives. That does not meet Israel's desire to bargain its territorial conquests into the best deal it can get because we would end up taking away most of its leverage.

The major *arguments for* advancing a specific proposal are:

—Neither the US–USSR nor the four-power talks will go much farther unless we do. If we let them founder now, we shall take full blame for the failure.

—We may have a better chance of moving the others toward our positions by talking in terms of specifics than in terms of general principles as we are now.

—We may even be able to maneuver the USSR into sharing some of the blame for unpalatable proposals by putting them in the position of having to deliver Egyptian concessions.

—We can improve our position provided we demonstrate that we are for a fair settlement and maneuver ourselves into standing on defensible positions.

—Just because we get specific does not mean we are compromising Israel's position or ours. The point is that we will not know Israel's real position—or Nasser's—until we put a specific proposition to them. And until we strip away their bargaining positions and their covers for stalling, we risk basing our own position on bogus—and therefore indefensible—issues.

Recommendation: That you approve our putting forward a specific proposal on the terms of a settlement.

III. *The Second Issue—Whether to Consult Israel First*

The second issue is whether we should try our proposal out on the Israelis first or whether we should see how much Soviet consent we can get before we take it to the Israelis.

The *argument for going to the USSR first* is mainly that we stand a better chance of selling our proposal to Israel if we can say the USSR will deliver Arab consent.

The *arguments for going to Israel first are:*

—Our talks with Dobrynin give us a pretty good feel for the Soviet position now.

—If the Israelis thought we were bargaining away their future with the USSR, an already strained U.S.-Israeli relationship could reach the point where constructive discussion would no longer be possible.

—We must know before we take any proposal to the Russians what positions are crucial to Israel and where we can negotiate.

—Consulting with Israel need not give Israel a veto.

—Consulting may force the Israeli Cabinet to take a precise position for the first time.

—Unless we bring Israel along, we are not advancing the settlement process.

Recommendation: That we consult with Israel first but agree now that we will present our proposal to the Russians regardless of Israel's reaction (though we would ask State to give you an analysis of Israel's reaction before it proceeds further).

IV. *The Third Issue—Whether a Jordan or a UAR Settlement First*

The third issue is whether—if we decide that the time has come to put forward a specific proposal—the best chance of success lies in trying specific proposals first on a UAR-Israel settlement, first on a Jordan-Israel agreement or on both fronts simultaneously. [The Secretary's memo recommends UAR-Israel first but says it will be appropriate to try something with Jordan and Israel soon.]

The arguments for the UAR-Israel approach first are:

—Territorially it is the easier.

—It is easier for Hussein to follow Nasser than to precede.

—Hussein is ready for peace and the Israelis know it, so the real bottleneck to break is Nasser.

—We can involve the Russians in urging Arab concessions on this front. We do not want to involve them on the Jordanian front. It is overloading the circuit to try both approaches on Israel at once.

The arguments for the Jordan-Israel approach first are:

—Hussein is ready for peace and we have little clear evidence that Nasser is, so let's try for a breakthrough where it seems possible.

—The Palestine problem is a Jordan-Israel not a UAR-Israel problem.

—Any breakthrough might bring Nasser along. If it struck at the heart of the refugee problem, it could change the complexion of the whole Palestine issue, encourage the oil-rich moderates to back Hussein and press Nasser (whom they are subsidizing) to reach agreement.

—We have influence in both Jordan and Israel but little on Nasser.

—We have an interest in Hussein's survival but little in Nasser's.

The arguments for at least preparing both simultaneously are:

—Nasser is committed before the other Arabs to not making peace ahead of Hussein. The two must go hand-in-hand.

—Both Nasser and the Russians will quickly ask us whether the principle of full Israeli withdrawal applies to the West Bank as well as to the Sinai.

—The Israelis might be less reluctant to accept full withdrawal in the Sinai if they knew we did not intend to hold them to the same principle on the West Bank.

—While it is important to bring Nasser along in order to win broad acceptance in the Arab world, the support of the moderate Arabs for a settlement depends on what happens to Jerusalem and the refugees. The moderates are our friends.

Recommendation: That you request a specific proposal for a Jordan-Israel settlement with recommendations on phasing the two approaches. They will be handled on quite different tracks, and State will argue for going ahead with the UAR proposal since it is ready. But I believe you should see where you are going on the Jordan front before we get too far down the track with the UAR. This need not lose us much time.

V. *The Fourth Issue—Whether the Terms Proposed Are Defensible*

The final set of issues is whether the terms of a settlement outlined in Secretary Rogers' memo will stand on their merits so that, simply by advancing them, we will put ourselves in a more defensible position.

In general, the main measure of defensibility is that we not get stuck holding out for a nebulous concept of "peace" or for direct negotiations, except in exchange for a concrete Israeli commitment to withdrawal. It is inherent in the situation that the Israelis will be asked to do something concrete—withdraw their troops—in return for paper commitments. But in attempting to elicit a straight-forward Arab commitment to live at peace—with willingness to talk directly with Israel as a sign of good faith—we must have an equally straight-forward Israeli position on where its "secure and recognized borders" will be. If we cannot get that Israeli commitment, then we may wish to reconsider our holding out for direct talks, which no one else accepts as necessary.

The proposal outlined in the Secretary's memo would permit us to say: The UAR will get Israel's promise to withdraw from the Sinai provided it agrees to meet under Ambassador Jarring's auspices to work out an accord with Israel that would spell out the detailed forms and conditions of peace. In other words, the UAR can have its territory back if it will signify its readiness for peace by meeting with Israeli representatives. That seems a defensible position *provided* the Israelis assure us they will take a reasonable position in those talks by agreeing to withdraw to what the Arabs will regard as reasonable boundaries.

To take each of the specific issues in turn:

A. *Is it reasonable in this initial proposal to try to commit the Israelis in advance of negotiations to full withdrawal from the Sinai* as a quid pro quo for drawing the UAR into direct talks under Jarring? Or should the proposal contain a vaguer formulation of the commitment to withdraw?

The *arguments for* seeking commitment to full withdrawal are:

—The UAR will not consider anything less worth making concessions for, and it will regard us as simply playing Israel's game if we try to extract concessions for less.

—We are on solid ground saying that we do not believe Israel needs territory in the Sinai and that its security there can be protected in other ways.

The arguments for a vaguer commitment are:

—The Israelis will probably refuse a firm commitment in advance because (we believe) they want to bargain their withdrawal directly with the UAR for a position at Sharm al-Shaykh and a corridor to it. They may even be holding out for direct talks because they believe the UAR will refuse and leave them on the Suez Canal.

—The Israelis are most adamant on this point, and it is the issue on which they are most likely to part company with us.

Recommendation: That we hold out for an Israeli commitment to full withdrawal from the Sinai but that you request State to come up with a reasonable plan for policing demilitarized zones and guaranteeing free navigation through the Straits of Tiran and Suez Canal.

B. *Is it sensible for us to hold out for a UAR commitment to a direct meeting with Israeli representatives under Jarring's auspices?* Or by wedding ourselves to this point are we putting ourselves in the potentially untenable position of arguing that direct negotiations are a sine qua non of peace?

The *arguments for* doing this are:

—A direct meeting is a small price for retrieving the Sinai.

—It is not all that unreasonable to expect adversaries to sit down after a war and work out peace terms.

—The Israelis, whether sensibly or not, seem to have made direct talks a quid pro quo for revealing their terms for a settlement, though they may also be using this as a cover for their failure to make governmental decisions on the terms they will accept.

The *arguments against* are:

—Russians, French and probably the British will say that terms could be worked out through third parties and ask whether it is reasonable to let the whole peace effort founder over lack of a direct meeting.

—The Arabs are adamant in refusing talks. To them, such talks are a sign of surrender, though there are some indications that they would be less adamant if Israel were committed in advance to withdraw.

Recommendation: That we tell the Israelis we are prepared to hold out for direct talks if they assure us by committing themselves to withdraw that they will make the Egyptians a reasonable offer in such a meeting.

C. *Should we start out asking for the demilitarization of the entire Sinai?* Or should we start bargaining with the Israelis for a smaller area such as the Russians propose?

The *arguments for* trying for full demilitarization are:

—We should leave ourselves some bargaining room with the Russians.

—If we are going to ask the Israelis to pull all the way back to the pre-war border, we must offer them maximum demilitarization in return.

The argument against is that the Russians (and Egyptians) seem to be firmly resisting large demilitarized zones, and we should begin bargaining, with Israel at least, from a smaller base.

Recommendation: That we go to the Israelis with a proposal for demilitarization of the entire Sinai but that we make clear we regard this position as negotiable, if adequate alternative security arrangements are proposed.

Conclusions: After working through this analysis, I conclude that we should state explicitly for our own internal guidance the following minimum objectives in this exercise:

A. To conduct our discussions with the Israelis so as to determine what are genuine Israeli requirements—as contrasted to bargaining positions and positions taken to cover unwillingness to take precise positions—so that we may be certain we are taking our stand on meaningful issues.

B. To conduct our negotiations with the USSR so as to engage them in extracting concessions from the UAR and to put them in a position of sharing the blame for the unpalatable elements in any proposed settlement.

C. To seek to develop a position in the four-power talks that will be defensible enough that the governments who reject it and not we will be blamed for any impasse that develops.

26. Minutes of a National Security Council Meeting[1]

Washington, April 25, 1969, 10–11:15 a.m.

PARTICIPANTS

The President
The Vice President
The Secretary of State, William P. Rogers
The Secretary of Defense, Melvin R. Laird
Chief of Staff, Army, General Westmoreland
Director, Office of Emergency Preparedness, General George A. Lincoln
US Ambassador to the UN, Charles Yost
The Director of Central Intelligence, Richard M. Helms
Under Secretary of State, Elliot L. Richardson
Assistant Secretary of State, Joseph J. Sisco
Dr. Henry A. Kissinger
Colonel Alexander Haig
Harold H. Saunders
Alfred L. Atherton

President: Do we take a position.

Do we peddle it with Israel first?[2] Israel sort of like South Vietnam. Difficult make peace with Israel. Impossible to make peace without.

Do we go to UAR or Jordan first?

Rogers: I promised Eban we'd go to Israel first.[3]

President: I understand. It's a lot better to try to bring the Israelis along with us.

Rogers: Meetings with Jewish leaders show they more rigid than Eban.

President: Eban reasonable but has to represent his hawks.

Rogers: We're discussing problem in several ways:

—Four power talks. Yost will talk.
—Soviet talks. Sisco will report.
—Problem is how to mesh these.

President: What concerned me is Soviet requirement for equal-sized DMZ's.[4] Of course that could be bargaining position.

---

[1] Source: National Archives, Nixon Presidential Materials, NSC Files, NSC Institutional Files (H-Files), Box H–109, NSC Meeting Minutes, NSC Minutes Originals 1969. Top Secret; Nodis. According to the President's Daily Diary, the meeting was held in the Cabinet Room from 10:05 to 11:25 a.m. (Ibid., White House Central Files)

[2] Reference is to the peace plan that Sisco presented to Dobrynin in piecemeal fashion during the second week of May. See Document 28.

[3] Not further identified; presumably during Rogers's meetings with Eban March 12 or 13. See Document 13 and footnote 8 thereto.

[4] See Document 23.

Sisco: *Soviets are talking about* peace and not patchwork, though we recognize "peace" means different things. Soviets agree that whatever framework we evolve will be presented to Jarring so won't be "imposed." Soviets agree all terms must be agreed in advance. This different from French and step forward in Soviet position.

Agree on some kind of international document. Soviets, if Eban objects to Soviet guarantee, say they have no interest in being guarantor.

Dobrynin says he just deferring to US. Soviets have no problem on free navigation.

President: Israeli position quite interesting. Back through the years, *Israeli attitude toward USSR* ambivalent. Eshkol and others tried to see USSR in best possible light. Is there still division on this point?

Sisco: I have feeling still some division but official position is much more categorical.

President: "Is this bargaining or belief?"

Sisco: Some bargaining.

Helms: Israelis want to in-gather exiles so that is the one soft-spot in Israel's position. Otherwise, they take anti-Communist line for US benefit and see mainly the threat of Soviet help for the Arabs.

Kissinger: Not so much anti-Soviet as against Soviet support of Arabs. I don't take Israeli anti-Communism too seriously.

Sisco: *Soviets* push Israeli withdrawal to June 4 lines. We have stuck to our general position. Dobrynin has been trying to divide us from Israelis. Soviets do allow for minor border rectifications. Soviets want DMZ's of equal width. Soviets will object to Israeli requirement for positions at Sharm al-Shaikh.

President: Asked for positions on map.

Lincoln: Would Israelis insist on position at Sharm al-Shaikh if Sinai were demilitarized?

Rogers: Israel doesn't trust UN forces.

Sisco: UAR doesn't like demilitarize whole Sinai. But maybe Aqaba Gulf side of it. *Refugees:* repatriation and compensation.

President: 50,000 go back?

Sisco: At most 100,000.

Rogers: Fawzi claims that if refugees had choice only few would want to go back.

President: Hussein says same.

Why not combine the principle with that fact? People wouldn't want to go back to an unfriendly land.

Sisco: Arab governments could push decision of refugees either way.

Yost: If offered opportunity for resettlement.

President: US effort here if part of peace package, we should go very far—not limited by budget. Poisonous element. We have to go further than we have.

Yost: Agree. Main source of Arab resentment for twenty years.

Sisco: We have told USSR there will have to be *face-to-face negotiations* at some point:

—Israelis feel it sine qua non of recognition.
—Practically necessary to hammer out details.

Russians say Arabs won't buy it.

Generally, USSR wants limited accommodation but whether they will pay price we don't know.

President: *Hussein wants peace. Does Nasser?*

Sisco: Probably not or yes on his own terms.

Yost: Yes, because of his precarious position. We don't know whether he will pay price.

President: *Why does USSR want settlement?*

Sisco Limited settlement they want would leave Soviets a free hand to support Arabs, but give them a string to maintain control. Settlement does not preclude their pursuing political objective. They want good relations with us.

Rogers: Strong feeling they are very worried. Their prestige on the line. Hussein says Arabs will be clobbered, if war breaks out again. They would lose all over Arab world.

Helms: Agree with both Rogers and Sisco.

President: Are Soviets using this for negotiating purposes?

Helms: Soviets have not done well on communications of Mid-East. They could work better in less confused situation. Even they do not profit from a situation "where fellows are throwing bombs around."

President: June war a help to USSR—influence in Mediterranean. There is their desire to cool things with us—e.g., Korean crisis.[5] If there is a chance of a break through, we should go ahead. But it all boils down to who goes first, who sticks neck out.

Yost: Big areas of Arab soil occupied but "big brother can't do anything." If Arabs start something, Soviets will be called on to make good on their promises.

---

[5] Reference is to Soviet actions in the aftermath of the North Korean attack on a U S. Navy EC-121 aircraft on April 14. Following the incident, the Soviets dispatched vessels to the Sea of Japan to search for possible survivors of the U.S. aircraft. See *Foreign Relations*, 1969–1976, volume XII, Soviet Union, January 1969–October 1970, Document 59.

President: Could they be concerned about Israeli nuclear capability? No disagreement.

Kissinger: There will be enough tensions between Arabs and Israelis after a settlement for USSR to exploit. They are asking us to restore their client's (Nasser's) losses so he can go on with his pro-Soviet policy.

Plan we are offering asks intangibles of the Arabs.

Our question is, whether it might not be in our interest as well as theirs to have a settlement. One interest is not having them drawn into a fight on Arab side.

Settlement which is painful to both sides and Soviets sell to UAR would be in our interest. From point of view of our overall relationship, we want a settlement that is unpalatable to UAR and Soviets have paid the price of selling it. We don't want Soviet client to come out ahead of Hussein.

Richardson: This most concrete subject we dealing with USSR on. It is the best way of testing their intent.

President: *USSR may need this more than we do.* While their position hard, our bargaining position may be better than we think. They may be willing to go further than we think.

Rogers: Maybe we psychoanalyze Soviets too much. They don't have a clear policy. Let's assume they negotiating in the same spirit we are. They're assuming, as we are, that the other fellow is trying to get the most he can. Thing we have to do is to get down to specifics.

On *direct negotiations,* Israel wants; US Jewish community wants; Arabs don't. Not necessary. In a divorce case, a lawyer would get nowhere if he forced both parties to sit down and work things out at the beginning. But if he works out a settlement that both sides can discuss concretely, he can negotiate a solution.

Eventually necessary, but though the odds are probably against us, maybe we can work something out.

Yost: Set of *pressures on us*—deterioration in area and what is likely to happen to Hussein. If no settlement, fedayeen get stronger, e.g., what happening in Lebanon now.[6] Israelis making false analysis of their security interests.

---

[6] Clashes between the Lebanese army and fedayeen and pro-fedayeen refugees and students beginning on April 23 led to the resignation of Lebanon's Prime Minister Rashid Karame on April 25 and created a political crisis. (Intelligence Note 309, April 24; National Archives, RG 59, Central Files 1967–69, POL 23–8 LEB and telegram 3451 from Beirut, April 25; ibid., Nixon Presidential Materials, NSC Files, Box 5, Presidential Daily Briefings) President Charles Helou, who imposed a state of emergency in Lebanon until midnight on April 27, hoped to reconstitute a civilian government under Karame, but Karame had said that he would not participate in such a government unless it defined a

President: An *overall settlement may take years. Is it possible to "slice off any part of it?"* I know Arabs and Israelis both demand whole package. I feel some progress would help.

Sisco: (1) Agreement between Arabs and Israelis on package idea. (2) The guts of this proposal are: Israeli commitment to full withdrawal. Alternative: Israel withdraw to "secure and recognized boundaries." The dilemma is that if the commitment is general, Arabs won't buy. Why do we include everything in this document? Finely balanced to leave Israelis leeway to negotiate. To my mind, *direct negotiations are important to Israel.*

Laird: It seems to me it is *important to generalize that point. Israel is* the strong military power. USSR wants us to deliver Israel and not deliver Arabs. Delivering Israel difficult.

Rogers: We conscious of delivering Israel. But our idea is to *discuss paper first with Israel.*

President: Use specific, hard paragraph with Israel?

Rogers: Yes.

Sisco: We have not decided to go ahead with Soviets before talking with Israel.

President: Where do we do this?

Sisco: In Israel, Barbour-Eban.

Rusk outlined eight-point position with Riad.[7] We have never reaffirmed that position. We have kept that option open.

President: If you take it to Eban—not Rabin—

Rogers: What I'd like to find out *whether UAR or Jordan paper first?*

President: *Barbour must not leave Israelis under impression they can do anything they want.* While we're for Israel, what they hear from their friends in the US is not true. American people oppose intervention. Barbour must not give Eban a veto—he must give Eban some sense of our determination to go ahead and do what we can for a settlement. Israel cannot count on us to be with it no matter what it does.

Richardson: A paper might emerge which four powers think is pretty reasonable but both sides object to.

President: *Many believe we should have laid back and let parties get together*—simply because problem too difficult to survive. But maybe this

---

policy toward the fedayeen. (Telegram 3451 from Beirut, April 25, and telegram 3512 from Beirut, April 28; ibid.) A proponent of taking a tough stand against fedayeen operations from Lebanese territory, Helou failed to advance a policy that garnered popular support and was unable to form a regular cabinet. Instead, he established a caretaker government with Karame as Premier-designate, who resigned six months later when the next fedayeen-related crisis occurred. See footnote 2, Document 60.

[7] See footnote 3, Document 1.

is one area for concrete US–USSR agreement. I think we must assume the leadership here—subtly. Any settlement will have to be imposed—without calling it that. Overhanging this is US–USSR relations.

Yost: Absolutely right. Damaging events in area. Will improve our position in whole Arab world.

President: Is there *anything we can do for Israel?*

Yost: This paper gives Israel much of what it wants.

President: On refugees, American commitment—"whatever it costs." On Israeli side?

Sisco: A number of small arms requests.

Vice President: How about desalinization?

President: Too far away.

On both sides, just putting something on the plate. Refugees may be a phony issue. But we must feel we think it's worth a great deal to us to bring parties along.

Yost: Israelis may not be able to hold their own in fedayeen situation.

Lincoln: Wouldn't controlling fedayeen be one.

Laird: Soviets will take over fedayeen and use them against pro-US Arab countries.

Sisco: Present conditions working to advantage of USSR. Moderate governments will be toppling.

Rogers: We have to assume our interest is to have a settlement.

Westmoreland: We have some leverage with Israelis. F–4s begin delivery in September. A–4s, 40 of 100 delivered. Tank engines. Have asked for more A–4s and now A–6s.

President: If a settlement, our interest to see that Israel continues to maintain its edge.

Sisco: *Jordanian side first?* My own feeling is to proceed with what we have here. Recommend against doing both at once with Israel. Address after UAR—leave Israel-Jordan to secret contacts.

President: Jordan before UAR?

Sisco: Go ahead with UAR. Then over 3–4 weeks talk about Jordan.

Rogers: UAR plan is place to start.

Richardson: Jordan asking for more weapons.

Rogers: Leave aside.

Yost: Follow with Jordan paper soon. Interrelated.

President: OK.

Helms: US position eroded since June war. Soviets want tension beneath surface. But unless they make USSR run with us, we will give USSR a second victory.

Rogers: We conscious of that.

President: June war netted out as great help to USSR.

Rogers: Greatest USSR victory would be radical takeover in Jordan, UAR even Lebanon.

President: Got to go forward to build our strength back with moderates.

Yost: As long as Israel in occupation.

27. Memorandum From the President's Assistant for National Security Affairs (Kissinger) to President Nixon[1]

Washington, May 3, 1969.

SUBJECT

Next Step in Our Mid-East Peace Effort—Revised Version

State has reflected on the April 25 NSC discussion,[2] heard your subsequent views and consulted with Ambassador Barbour in Tel Aviv. The result is the attached revision[3] in the course they proposed at the NSC.

The principal changes are:

1. We would not surface a complete American document on the terms of a UAR-Israel settlement now. That would make too big a target for the Israelis to shoot at. Instead, we would deal with the elements of the package piece-meal.

2. We would not, therefore, have one big consultation with Israel before giving our ideas to Dobrynin. Instead, Sisco would try pieces of our proposal out on Dobrynin first, and then—hopefully after negotiating the best possible Soviet response—he would bring Rabin up to date. This would give us a chance of avoiding one sharp Israeli reaction, while still keeping our promise to consult with them.

---

[1] Source: National Archives, Nixon Presidential Materials, NSC Files, Box 1170, Saunders Files, Middle East Negotiations Files, Middle East Settlement—US–USSR Talks. Secret; Nodis. A stamped notation on the memorandum indicates the President saw it.

[2] See Document 26.

[3] Attached but not printed is a May 1 memorandum from Rogers to Nixon.

3. We would not initially commit ourselves to Israel's full withdrawal from the Sinai. Instead, we would start with a vaguer formulation on the final border and see what price the USSR is willing to pay for a more precise commitment.

This seems to me to come much closer than the original proposal[4] to meeting our objectives. It leaves the burden on the USSR and UAR to make the first concession and defers a confrontation with the Israelis until, if ever, we have serious Soviet-Arab concessions from them to consider.

Recommendation

That you authorize me to tell Secretary Rogers you are willing to have him proceed on this basis.[5]

---

[4] See Document 25.
[5] Nixon approved this recommendation. Underneath Nixon's approval, Jeanne Davis wrote: "State (S/S—Walsh) notified 5/8, 10:30 am. JWD."

---

28. **Editorial Note**

Assistant Secretary of State Joseph Sisco met with Soviet Ambassador Anatoly Dobrynin on May 6, 8, and 12, 1969, to present—in a "piecemeal fashion"—elements of a "joint preliminary document" that the United States and the Soviet Union could offer to the United Arab Republic and Israel to use as the basis for a new round of negotiations under Gunnar Jarring. At the May 6 meeting, Sisco unveiled points 1, 2, 3, 6, and 7 of the proposed document, which covered peace and the end of belligerency, the obligations that both sides needed to undertake to resolve future disputes peacefully, and the responsibility of the Arab states to control Palestinian guerrillas. While Sisco invited comments and contributions, both written and oral, Dobrynin said that he would wait for Moscow's reaction before he delivered the official Soviet response. He added that the Soviet leadership would not offer much of substance until Sisco revealed the remainder of the U.S. proposal. (Telegram 71012 to Moscow and USUN, May 7; National Archives, Nixon Presidential Materials, NSC Files, Box 653, Country Files, Middle East, Sisco Middle East Talks) At their May 8 session, Sisco discussed points 8, 9, 11, 12, and 13, which dealt with refugees, the parties' acknowledgement of each other's sovereignty, the guarantees of each other's territorial integrity, reciprocal assurances on freedom of navigation, and implementation of the final accord. The Assistant Secretary also stressed "several times" that the success or failure of their efforts would "depend in large measure" on the Soviet Union's willingness to obtain concessions from the United Arab Republic. (Telegram 72809 to Moscow and USUN, May 8; ibid.) Sisco finished unveiling the draft proposal on May 12, presenting points 4, 5, 10, and the preamble, which covered some of the thorniest issues, including boundaries, the status of Gaza, withdrawal, demilitarization, and the inadmissibility of the acquisition of territory by war. (Telegram 75822 to Moscow and USUN, May 13; ibid.)

Sisco and Dobrynin had two follow-up meetings on May 19 and 21 to clarify what had been discussed previously. On May 19, Dobrynin called on Sisco to ask how the United States planned to handle the Jordanian aspect of an overall settlement, given that their talks had focused only on the United Arab Republic. The Assistant Secretary responded that the United States believed that progress on the UAR side could have a positive influence on the Jordanian side, understanding that implementation of an agreement between Israel and the United Arab Republic depended on an Israel's reaching an agreement with Jordan. Dobrynin also asked about the Nixon administration's departure from positions taken by previous Secretary of State Dean Rusk in his meetings with Soviet Foreign Minister Andrei Gromyko. Sisco replied that he would have to review the record of the Rusk-Gromyko conversation. (Telegram 79805 to Moscow, May 20; ibid.) Two days later, Dobrynin raised the issue of the Rusk-Gromyko dialogue again and said that the current U.S. proposal "fell short" of what had been discussed in 1968, including: 1) that Israel should withdraw to the internationally recognized boundary between it and the United Arab Republic; 2) that both sides of the border should be demilitarized—which meant that the demilitarization of the Negev was a possibility, rather than the whole of the Sinai alone; 3) that Sharm el-Sheikh would contain a UN presence, not an Israeli one; and 4) that the signing procedure would involve Jarring taking the final agreement to one party and then the other for signature. Sisco remarked that after having quickly reviewed the record of Rusk-Gromyko conversation, he "found no deviation in principle between 'proposals' currently discussed and 'views,' which may have been discussed generally in various conversations." He then explained, point-by-point, why this was the case. They both agreed that neither the United States nor the Soviet Union should be "caught in a box" or "inhibited" by their "respective clients." While Sisco pressed Dobrynin to elicit a response from Moscow as soon as possible, Dobrynin said that "consultations would take time." (Telegram 80620 to Moscow; ibid.) The record of Gromyko's meeting with Rusk on October 6, 1968, in New York is printed in *Foreign Relations,*

1964–1968, volume XX, Arab-Israeli Dispute, 1967–1968, Document 274.

A copy of the U.S. draft proposal is attached as Tab B to a memorandum from Saunders to Kissinger, December 31. (National Archives, Nixon Presidential Materials, Box 710, Country Files, Europe, USSR, Vol. VI) The final version of the proposal, which Sisco presented to Dobrynin in Washington on October 28—and which became known as the Rogers Plan—is printed as Document 58.

29. Telegram From the Department of State to the Embassy in Israel[1]

Washington, May 10, 1969, 0018Z.

73819. Ref: Tel Aviv 1735.[2] For Ambassador from the Secretary.

1. Ambassador Rabin delivered to Sisco morning May 9 message from Eban referred to para 1 reftel (text by septel).[3] We believe interim oral message to Eban might be helpful to him and to other moderates before normal Sunday Cabinet meeting at which time we assume possible communication from Prime Minister to President will be considered. Purpose of this message is to make clear our intention to continue our discussions in two and four power context while at same time providing assurances we not intending to give away any vital Israeli interests. In short, we believe Israelis ought to hold their fire to give us an opportunity to do what we are trying to do: to probe directly Soviet in-

---

[1] Source: National Archives, Nixon Presidential Materials, NSC Files, Box 653, Country Files, Middle East, Sisco Middle East Talks. Secret; Immediate; Nodis. Drafted by Sisco, cleared by De Palma and Walsh, and approved by Rogers (per Walsh).

[2] In telegram 1735 from Tel Aviv, May 9, the Embassy reported that Rabin had been instructed by his government to request that the Sisco-Dobrynin talks be interrupted to permit Israel time to prepare and send a letter to Nixon explaining its "negative views." (Ibid., Box 649, Country Files, Middle East, Middle East Negotiations)

[3] In his message, Eban described Sisco's initial formulations for a joint U.S.-Soviet document on the Arab-Israeli dispute as a "retreat by the United States from the principle of a binding reciprocal contractual agreement establishing peace." He also protested that the formulations would "prejudice Israel's vital interests" and argued that the United States should not formally present them to the Soviet Union. (Telegram 73744 to Tel Aviv, May 9; ibid., Box 653, Country Files, Middle East, Sisco Middle East Talks) Eban's message was prompted by Sisco's May 7 briefing of Yitzhak Rabin on his meetings with Dobrynin. (Telegram 71862 to Tel Aviv, May 8; ibid.)

tentions as to whether they want peace in the area and of equal importance whether they are willing to press Nasser to this end. As a major power, and in light of conditions in the area which continue to deteriorate, we have a responsibility in our own national interest to do everything in our power to try to achieve peace in the Middle East. We feel strongly that we would be abdicating our responsibility if we did not persevere in our present efforts. It is self evident another renewal of hostilities in the area carries risk of possible US–USSR confrontation. We are not saying renewed general hostilities are imminent, but we believe early movement toward peace is imperative if situation in area is not to develop in direction which will make eventual hostilities unavoidable.

2. Following is the oral message from me to Eban:

QTE Ambassador Rabin has delivered your message, and I have read Ambassador Barbour's report requesting that US–USSR talks be interrupted to permit GOI time to prepare and send letter to President explaining its views.

QTE We feel that your comments on specific language we have been discussing with Dobrynin reflects misunderstanding of the effort we are making. We do not accept the view that our formulations indicate a retreat by the United States from the principle of binding reciprocal contractual agreement establishing peace and that they simply reflect the juridical doctrine of the 1949 Armistice Agreements. Our formulations on a permanent peace, based on a binding agreement between the parties, would require the UAR to undertake positive obligations which go far beyond the Armistice Agreements in the very fundamental sense that they relate in specific terms to a state of peace, not a state of armistice.

QTE We have made no conclusive judgment as to whether Soviets are prepared to apply the necessary influence on Nasser which would meet both the Israeli and the US requirements for a permanent peace. We are not asking Israel at this juncture to agree to any of the formulations which we are discussing with the Soviet Union. We have never expected and do not now expect Israel to withdraw its forces except in the context of a binding reciprocal contractual agreement establishing peace.

QTE. We are trying to find common ground on a framework which will afford Ambassador Jarring an opportunity to renew discussions with the principal parties concerned. We are not trying to write a detailed blueprint because a number of critical elements of a permanent peace can only be agreed to and worked out by the parties themselves. In this connection, in our next meeting with the Soviets on Monday,

May 12th,[4] we intend to submit a proposal making clear the view which I expressed to the Foreign Minister during his Washington trip that in our judgment no final peace is possible unless the UAR commits itself to enter into direct negotiations at some stage with Israel.

QTE. We are probing the Soviets to see whether they are prepared to support an unequivocal commitment to a reciprocally binding peace through agreement between Israel and the UAR and are able to deliver the UAR on such a commitment. If they are not, it is important both to your interests and to our own for us to know this.

QTE. One final point: Israel and the US enjoy a special relationship. We cherish and attach great importance to this special relationship. We appreciate fully that the vital interests of Israel are involved. The reason we have made every effort to keep in step with Israel, to consult you all the way along, and to invite your specific comments on a day-by-day basis, is that we would like to move together towards a permanent peace in the area. We believe that the record of the last twenty years fully justifies greater faith in the constancy of our support for Israel's vital interests than present GOI criticism of our policy indicates. END QUOTE.[5]

3. Ambassador may use his own discretion in fortifying the above with such arguments as he deems appropriate. He might also reiterate to Eban with reference to para. 1 of Eban's message sent septel that there is no USG "paper." Our hope is that the above interim reply will either deflect GOI from sending any high-level letter or at a minimum help moderate its contents.

Rogers

---

[4] See Document 28.

[5] Barbour passed Rogers's message to Eban during a meeting with him on May 10. (Telegram 1745 from Tel Aviv, May 10; National Archives, Nixon Presidential Materials, NSC Files, Box 604, Country Files, Middle East, Israel, Vol. I)

30. Telegram From the Embassy in Jordan to the Department of State[1]

Amman, May 28, 1969, 1059Z.

2474. Department pass USUN, USINT Cairo, Tel Aviv. Ref: Amman 2464.[2] Subj: Direct Israeli-Jordanian Peace Negotiations.

Summary: Zaid Rifai, on May 27, told us that King Hussein would be willing to send a Jordanian emissary to conduct direct negotiations with the Israelis independently of UAR, provided that Israel assured Jordan it was willing in principle to withdraw from most Jordanian territories, including Arab Jerusalem. Rifai claimed that Nasser would, if necessary, give public blessing to Jordanian initiative. Rifai also indicated he probably would be Jordanian negotiator. Rifai said King still believed that Israeli leaders at bottom wanted a real peace, their harsh public statements notwithstanding, and would be willing to make the few concessions necessary for settlement with Jordan. If not, US should compel them. Rifai said Jordanians did not expect Israeli invasion of Irbid Heights. *End summary.*

1. During May 27 conversation with Embassy officer reported reftel, Zaid Rifai, the King's private secretary and confidant, declared that King Hussein would be willing to send an emissary to conduct direct, face-to-face negotiations with the Israelis independently of UAR. Rifai then went on to develop the theme that Nasser was completely dependent on Hussein to resolve the Palestinian and Jerusalem elements of a general settlement. In fact, he said, Nasser was more sticky as regards Jerusalem than was Hussein himself, adding that Muslims generally, whether in Turkey or Indonesia, held a stricter position as regards Jerusalem than did the Jordanians. Nasser could do almost anything except risk being accused of selling the Arab birthright in Jerusalem or giving up on the refugees. Although Nasser was critically dependent on Hussein, the reverse was not true.

2. When EmbOff questioned whether Nasser could be trusted not to undercut Hussein, Zaid Rifai claimed that Jordanians could secure a public blessing from Nasser in addition to the private go-ahead he had long ago given. Rifai said that concern about Nasser's attitude had never been critically important to Hussein, even in late June of 1967 when he had wanted to enter negotiations. The real problem then, as now, was the absence of satisfactory Israeli assurances that withdrawal

---

[1] Source: National Archives, Nixon Presidential Materials, NSC Files, Box 619, Country Files, Middle East, Jordan Nodis/Sandstorm. Secret; Nodis.

[2] Not found.

from quote most unquote Jordanian territories, including Arab Jerusalem, was acceptable in principle. Only with such assurances or, alternatively, a USG commitment that it would compel the Israelis to negotiate a settlement within such a framework, could Hussein step forward (reftel). When EmbOff commented that Israel might not be attracted to negotiations in which a major party, the UAR, was absent, Rifai said that Israel should be willing to take some chances for sake of peace.

3. He then added that Jordanians had been discouraged by the recent hard Israeli line pursued by PriMin Meir. She was worse than Eshkol. Nevertheless, he said Hussein sensed that at bottom most Israelis wanted a real peace, faced with the prospect of unending war with the Arabs—a prospect becoming more likely every day—the Israelis would make quote the few concessions unquote that Hussein needed. It was this assumption that continued to sustain the King's hopes.

4. Warming to this theme, Rifai said he personally was confident that the underlying common sense would deter the Israelis from a military move against Jordan that would foreclose for all time the prospects of a settlement. He said most top Jordanians, with few exceptions, did not rpt not expect the often predicted Israeli invasion of the Irbid Heights this summer. Although they were prepared for it. If the unlikely occurred, however, Rifai said the Jordanians would put up a much stiffer fight than the Israelis expected. It was possible, Rifai admitted, that the Israelis could badly hurt Jordan by means short of invasion, but, again, he felt Israelis would not want to destroy for all time chances of a settlement. He said he could promise that Jordan would hit back effectively, destroying Eilat and the Israeli factories below the Dead Sea, and shelling Beisan and Tiberias. He said he was now rpt now able to take more initiatives and quote Israelis now know we are here unquote.

5. *Comment:* Foregoing comments were generated after Zaid Rifai had relayed King's views that Israeli-Jordanian aspects of settlement were much more important than UAR-Israeli angles, and US–USSR discussions should not ignore this fact. While Rifai has taken similar line about direct GOJ–GOI negotiations in past, on this occasion he strongly implied that active consideration currently was being given to idea, and reinforced this impression by frequently referring to himself as the probable Jordanian negotiator. In our opinion, Rifai is reflecting the King's very considerable faith that the big power discussions are going to produce a break-through. Interestingly, the same day, the British DCM asked us whether we thought the King's optimism about

the big power talks had reached the point where he might consider risking a confrontation with the fedayeen.

Symmes

---

31. **Memorandum From the Chairman of the Ad Hoc Group on the Israeli Nuclear Weapons Program (Davies) to the President's Assistant for National Security Affairs (Kissinger) and Acting Secretary of State Richardson**[1]

Washington, undated.

SUBJECT

Israeli Nuclear Weapons Program—Issues and Courses of Action

Attached here is a policy study on the Israeli nuclear weapons program as requested in NSSM 40.[2]

The following major issues emerged during meetings of the Ad Hoc Group.

1. *Israel's Nuclear Capabilities and Intentions*

[4½ lines not declassified]. We know that Israel is in the process of deploying a nuclear-capable surface-to-surface missile system (range of about 300 miles); there is circumstantial evidence indicating Israel has acquired fissionable material; there are unconfirmed reports that Israel has begun to construct nuclear weapons. [2½ lines not declassified] Department of State representatives believe more evidence is necessary [less than 1 line not declassified] and that Israel [less than 1 line not declassified] is aware that actual production and deployment of nuclear weapons could place severe strains on US–Israel relations.

2. *Israel's Assurances on Nuclear Weapons and Relation to Delivery of F–4 "Phantom" Aircraft to Israel*

Quite aside from the question of whether the U.S. should impose or threaten to impose this sanction in an attempt to limit Israel's nuclear

---

[1] Source: Washington National Records Center, OSD Files: FRC 330–75–0103, Box 12, Israel. Top Secret; Nodis. Drafted on May 29 in the State and Defense Departments.

[2] Attached but not printed is the study, which was transmitted by John P. Walsh, Executive Secretary of the Department of State, to Kissinger, Laird, Helms, and Wheeler on May 30. NSSM 40 is Document 20.

weapons program, we must face the sensitive issue of carrying forward on deliveries [2 *lines not declassified*]. Providing an aircraft which could serve as a nuclear delivery system [2 *lines not declassified*] might have to be defended in Congress and publicly.

Israel has committed to us that it will not be "the first to introduce nuclear weapons into the area," but there are grounds for believing that Israel does not construe production of a weapon to constitute "introduction." During negotiations in November, 1968 for the sale of the "Phantom" F–4 aircraft to Israel, Ambassador Rabin expressed the view that introduction would require testing and making public the fact of possession of a nuclear weapon.[3] In accepting as condition for the sale Israel's reaffirmation that it would not be the first to introduce nuclear weapons in the Middle East and agreement that it would not use any aircraft supplied by the United States as a nuclear weapons carrier, our reply stated:

"In this connection, I have made clear the position of the United States Government that the physical possession and control of nuclear arms by a Middle East power would be deemed to constitute the introduction of nuclear weapons."[4]

Inasmuch as our reply also made clear that we consider that "unusual and compelling circumstances" requiring cancellation of the F–4 agreement would exist in the event of "action inconsistent with your policy and agreement as set forth in your letter," the door was left open to suspend or cancel the deliveries of the aircraft if Israel by our definition "introduced" nuclear weapons into the area.

3. *Will Raising this Issue with Israel now Complement or Undercut our Diplomatic Effort to Achieve an Arab-Israel Peace Settlement?*

Since we are already having a crisis of confidence with Israel over our peace efforts, will the renewal of the dialogue on the nuclear issue cause the Israelis to dig in even harder on their peace terms? It can be argued that the nuclear issue is overriding and that in any event a settlement is unlikely. On the other hand, progress toward peace would probably be the single most decisive factor making the nuclear issue easier to handle.

In defining options, the NSSM 40 study covers a range of pressures that the U.S. might apply to Israel—for any purpose. If we choose to use the maximum option on the nuclear issue, we may not have the necessary leverage left for helping along the peace negotiations. We are

---

[3] See *Foreign Relations, 1964–1968*, volume XX, Arab-Israeli Dispute, 1967–1968, Documents 306, 308, 309, 311, 317, 330, and 332.

[4] This paragraph is in a letter from Assistant Secretary of Defense for International Security Affairs Paul C. Warnke to Rabin, November 27. See ibid., Document 333.

proceeding with our bilateral exchanges with the Soviets on the nature of a settlement with the expectation that Israel will find the outcome difficult but not impossible to accept and that some pressure will be necessary to bring Israel into line. If there is a real possibility that pressure will be needed, these would not differ substantially from those in the study. Use of leverage on the NPT/nuclear issue may seriously detract from our capability to influence Israel on the settlement issue. On the other hand, if we decide to defer using pressure on the nuclear question so as to preserve leverage on a possible peace settlement, we must ask how long we are prepared to do this in the face of Israel's rapidly advancing program, and the knowledge that, the longer we put off making Israel feel the seriousness of our purpose, the harder it will be to arrest Israel's program.

4. *Should We Move Directly into a Confrontation with Israel on the NPT/Nuclear Weapon Issue on the basis of Supply of F–4s and other pending Arms Deliveries or Should we Follow a Graduated Approach Relying Primarily on Political Suasion but Maintaining the Flexibility to Move to more Coercive Policies if Israel is Unresponsive*

The Department of State believes that a policy of pressure has a fundamental built-in contradiction and involves difficulties for the U S. that should be carefully examined. A threat to cut off Israel's supply of conventional arms could build military and psychological pressures within Israel to move rapidly to the very sophisticated weaponry we are trying to avoid. Moreover, to deny Israel arms needed for its defense would be most difficult to justify in the face of continuing Arab threats and commando attacks. Israel would see from the outset that we would be under considerable pressures not to sustain this position and we would have expended much leverage and good will needlessly.

State believes that for the present we should continue the course of using political argumentation, leaving implicit and for future decision possible sanctions if Israel does not respond to our initial representations and proceeds with its weapons program.[5] Our actions on the nuclear issue should be timed so as to complement or at least not undercut our diplomatic efforts to achieve a peace settlement. Our objective would be Israeli signature of the NPT with (a) the tacit understanding that as long as Israel did not complete manufacture of nuclear explosive devices, we would regard this as being within the terms of the Treaty and, (b) a commitment that Israel would negotiate the IAEA safeguards agreement, and (c) an understanding that we will support the Israelis in a reasonable interpretation of Article III consistent with

---

[5] J/PM differs with this view: see footnote on page 6. [Footnote in the original. The reference is to footnote 6 below.]

the difference we have drawn between *maintaining* and *exercising* the option to manufacture nuclear explosives, provided Israel assures us it will not produce weapons and will consult with us to define this concept in detail.

The Department of Defense (ISA and the Joint Staff) believes that pressures can be applied by the threat to cut off conventional weapons supply and assurances from Israel received with a reasonably good chance (say 75%) of avoiding a public confrontation. Important groups in Israel surely will want to avoid such a confrontation, and the military certainly will not wish to exchange assured conventional weapons supply from this highly preferred source for nuclear-armed missiles. Moreover, it will be difficult, to put it mildly, for Israel publicly to challenge our position on this issue—for our position can be easily and clearly presented as acting in the U.S. interest without jeopardizing Israel's security. (This would not be the case if, for example, we attempted to withhold arms supplies to achieve Israeli concessions to Arabs; our position would be more difficult to defend and sustain publicly in that instance.)

Defense believes that it is important, if we are to stop Israel from going ahead with missiles and nuclear weapons, to demonstrate to the Israelis the seriousness of our purpose so that Israel itself can see the desirability of avoiding confrontation. Israel will surely not stop its long range-nuclear weapons and missile program unless it is made to feel that the United States is truly prepared to adopt policies which would adversely effect Israel's security with respect to more immediate threats. Moreover, the speed with which Israel is proceeding dictates that we must take steps very soon if we are to stop Israel's nuclear and missile activity before it's publicly known.

Defense recognizes that we cannot obtain absolute guarantees that Israel will forego strategic missiles and nuclear weapons over the long-run; we can, however, make it more likely that missiles and nuclear weapons will not be used by stopping their production now and by creating a political obstacle—the necessity to renounce agreements and risk confrontation with the United States—to their later use.

5. *Should we Attempt to Obtain Israeli Assurances that it will Halt its Strategic Missile as well as Nuclear Weapons Program?*

Defense believes that in addition to signature of the NPT and assurances of nuclear weapons restraint, we should seek Israeli assurances that it will not produce, further acquire, or deploy strategic missiles. They argue that since the present Israeli "Jericho" missile is not militarily cost effective as a means of delivering a high explosive warhead, the assumption will be made that they are designed for nuclear warheads, and the practical result may be the same whether or not the nuclear weapons actually exist.

The Department of State, on the other hand, believes that getting the Israelis to abandon their SSM program will be very difficult to achieve, given the program's already advanced stage. Trying to obtain assurances on missiles would therefore seriously compound the difficulty of obtaining assurances on what must be our main objective—the non-production and non-deployment of nuclear weapons.

6. *Courses of Action*

A. The Department of State holds the following view:

1. A dialogue with Israel on the nuclear question can and should be initiated immediately. We believe this will not affect adversely our current efforts to achieve a peace settlement. We should move to reaffirm our opposition to proliferation as soon as possible preferably at the Ambassadorial level both here and in Jerusalem and underscore that the U.S. Government considers it has a firm commitment in this respect from Israel. We believe strongly that we should not at this juncture link this approach to a suspension or slowing down of shipments of conventional weapons to Israel.[6] This possibility should be reviewed prior to September in the light of Israel's response and further intelligence on the progress of Israel's program.

2. At an early occasion a high-ranking U.S. official—preferably the Secretary of State or Secretary of Defense—should make a public statement on our global non-proliferation objectives and, in particular, our hope that nuclear weapons can be kept out of sensitive areas such as the Middle East. Such a statement should note Israel's assurances to us that it would not be the first to introduce nuclear weapons into the area and urge Israel to sign the NPT.

B. The Department of Defense holds the following view:

1. There should be an early meeting with Ambassador Rabin of Israel for the purpose of conveying to Israel (a) the seriousness with which the U.S. views Israel's missile and nuclear developments, and (b) specific U.S. demands that Israel stop certain of its activities and give us assurances to this effect.

2. The assurances we require from Israel are: (a) private assurances (with inspection rights) that Israel will cease and desist from development or acquisition of nuclear weapons and strategic missiles, and (b) public assurances in the form of a NPT signature and ratification.

---

[6] J/PM, while in general agreement with the other formulations identified as the State position in this paper, differs with NEA on this point. J/PM believes a) The implications of Israel's possession of nuclear weapons are serious enough for U.S. interests to warrant reminding the Israelis at the outset of the terms of the Warnke letter, and informing them of the possibility that we might not be able to carry through with deliveries of the F–4 and other aircraft if Israel pursues its weapons program; b) Unless this warning is conveyed, the Israelis are not likely to pay much attention to our representations. [Footnote in the original.]

3. We should reiterate, on behalf of this Administration, that the American definition of "introduction" applies (e.g., the State of Israel will not physically possess nuclear weapons, including the components of nuclear weapons that will explode).

4. Rabin should be called in by the President, or by the Secretaries of State and Defense. Although the negotiations with Israel will be especially difficult, they will be less difficult if our demands for assurances are unequivocal and made at the highest level.

32. Telegram From the Embassy in Jordan to the Department of State[1]

Amman, June 9, 1969, 0844Z.

2710. Ref: Amman 2534, State 085782.[2] Subj: Jordanian-Israeli Contacts: Reiterated Need for Active US Mediation. For Sisco Personal from Ambassador.

1. On June 7, Zaid Rifai told me he had been instructed to convey King Hussein's deep concern that detailed information about secret Jordanian-Israeli contacts which had been passed by Zaid to you in Tehran[3] should be carefully controlled in USG. Rifai said that he had passed this highly sensitive information to you personally, on King's authorization, because King feared that Israeli might be misleading you and other high-level USG officials as to true state of affairs in these talks. Specifically, by going into details, he wanted you to know that these contacts had made almost no progress whatsoever.

2. Rifai said King was worried lest this detailed information be treated in routine fashion, and might be further distributed within USG. He wondered particularly if US reps in Cairo and Tel Aviv would

---

[1] Source: National Archives, Nixon Presidential Materials, NSC Files, Box 619, Country Files, Middle East, Jordan Nodis/Sandstorm. Secret; Priority; Nodis; Sandstorm.

[2] In telegram 2534 from Amman, May 31, Symmes reported that he had assured Rifai that he need not worry that any details he had provided on secret contacts with Israel had been improperly disclosed. "We had always kept this knowledge restricted to very small [circle] within the US Govt." (Ibid.) In telegram 85782 to Amman, Tel Aviv, and USUN, May 28, Rogers informed Symmes that Hussein had instructed Rifai to give Sisco a full account of the secret contacts between Jordan and Israel that had occurred over the previous year, writing: "Rifai was very detailed and what came out was that none of Israeli proposals are starters." (Ibid.)

[3] Not further identified, but see Document 30.

be informed. As he continued, it became clear that what truly was bothering him was the possibility that the names of the parties involved, the dates, the places of meetings, etc. (referred to in para four of your message in State 85782) might have more widely circulated within the USG.

3. I then assured Zaid that my reference to the qte quite full unqte report I had received from you on the meeting had not included the details such as those to which he was referring. I said you had simply noted the fact that contacts had continued but had not resulted in substantive progress. I emphasized that the meat of your report was Rifai's plea that the US somehow intervene to break the logjam. Further explained in detail the extraordinary precautions we have taken in regard to Sandstorm matters, both in the Embassy and in the Department. I pointed out that we handled the occasional messages exchanged between Israelis and Jordanians on other matters with the same sensitivity. I added that the extent of my personal knowledge of the contacts was confined almost exclusively to what the King himself had told me; and I reminded Zaid that we had carefully refrained from probing, even when such reference as qte the Hamadiyah region unqte in the recent Meir-Hussein exchange[4] had aroused understandable curiosity. Embassy officer Draper, who had accompanied me to this meeting with Zaid, said he had normally typed himself the messages to and from Israelis, for example.

4. Rifai was clearly relieved and indicated he was completely satisfied with my explanation. I told him that he could assure King Hussein that details of the special confidences that had been relayed to you had gone no further, even to me. I stressed that we had always been exceptionally careful not to compromise the King or Rifai in any way, and that our record had been good in this respect. The important thing, I reiterated, was that the Jordanian plea for US intervention in this

---

[4] The exchanges occurred over a three-day period, beginning with a May 29 letter from Meir to Hussein in which she raised the issue of what she described as the "very serious deterioration" that had been taking place on the cease-fire and frontier lines between Jordan and Israel. (Telegram 2046 from Tel Aviv, May 30; ibid., Box 613, Country Files, Middle East, Jordan, Vol. I) On May 31, Hussein replied: "I have received your message of May 29, 1969, and I wish to assure you that all possible measures are being taken as a result of my clear and definite instructions to the chief of staff of our armed forces to insure that Jordanian armed forces pay particular attention and a maximum endeavor to insure that settlements in the north of the valley as well as those by the Dead Sea works south the Dead Sea and the works themselves as well as the Rilat area are not subjected to firing from across the border or cease fire positions. The armed forces will only return fire if subject to it and to its sources only or otherwise if civilian targets are subjected to Israeli fire." (Telegram 2521 from Amman, May 31; ibid.) Meir concluded the exchange on June 1, writing: "Tranquility on the borders and ceasefire lines and the maintenance of the ceasefire arrangements will contribute to the achievement of the permanent peace which is our common objective." (Telegram 2066 from Tel Aviv, June 1; ibid., Box 1237, Saunders Files, Israel)

matter had been communicated in a thoroughly clear manner. It was being given the most serious consideration and complete protection.

5. Rifai then redescribed the Jordanian view that the moment was ripe for US intervention. He did not think that the Israelis would budge without such pressure from the US, which he said should include, if necessary, suspension of Phantom deliveries, etc. He stressed that Jordan had done all it possibly could to narrow the gap between their position and the Israeli, but it was as wide as ever on Jerusalem and withdrawal generally. He claimed that the Israelis were going right ahead with the Allon Plan.[5]

6. Rifai stressed again, incidentally, that under no circumstances should Sandstorm matters be discussed or even alluded to with GOJ Ambassador Sharaf in Washington or, for that matter, with anyone other than himself or King Hussein. Beyond Sandstorm, he noted that exchanges with Israelis are not known by or discussed with anyone outside the palace.

Symmes

---

[5] See footnote 8, Document 4 and *Foreign Relations,* 1964–1968, volume XX, Arab-Israeli Dispute, 1967–1968, Documents 186 and 213.

---

33. Telegram From the Department of State to the Embassy in Israel[1]

Washington, June 19, 1969, 0151Z.

99793. 1. Please deliver following letter from President to Prime Minister Meir. QUOTE:

Dear Madam Prime Minister:

Thank you for your letter of May 14.[2] I greatly appreciate your trouble and care in setting before me your government's views on the

---

[1] Source: National Archives, Nixon Presidential Materials, NSC Files, Box 756, Presidential Correspondence 1969–1974, Israel Prime Minister Golda Meir, 1969. Secret; Nodis. Drafted on June 17 by Sterner; cleared by Atherton, Davies, and Saunders; and approved by Sisco.

[2] In the letter, which Rabin delivered to Rogers on May 14, Meir expressed her displeasure with both the Two- and Four-Power talks, especially the former. She wrote: "Our fears have been confirmed. They have been made particularly acute by the latest document submitted to the USSR." She continued: "Instead of leaving the parties free to

difficult issue of building toward peace in the Middle East. Your letter clearly conveys the understandable depth of Israel's conviction and feeling on this subject.

I agree with much of what you say. To the extent that there may be differences between us, I believe they derive from our necessarily different perspectives and not from different understandings of fundamental principles, on which I am convinced we are one.

To avoid any possible misunderstanding of our purposes, I am asking Ambassador Barbour now to discuss my thoughts with you. I would then hope that you might find it possible to come to Washington next month for a fuller and more personal exchange of views. Sincerely, Richard Nixon UNQUOTE.

2. In presenting letter Ambassador should make following points orally on behalf of President.

3. As President has indicated in his letter we are convinced US and Israel do not differ on fundamental principles.

4. We believe that a lasting peace can only be achieved through mutual agreement among the belligerents themselves. We had hoped that the November 22, 1967, UN Security Council resolution would get negotiations underway looking toward such agreement. Had there been progress, we would have continued to stand aside.

5. But clearly the Jarring mission had reached an impasse. The problem is how to get negotiations under way.

6. It is difficult for us to accept the thesis that the passage of time alone would bring the UAR around to a more amenable position. It seems vital to make another effort to get negotiations started.

7. In entering the four-power and Soviet talks, it is not our intention to take negotiations out of Israeli and Arab hands. Our purpose is to test the USSR's intentions and its willingness and capacity to induce the UAR to enter into a real commitment to negotiate a peace settlement. To do this, we are attempting in our talks with the USSR to reduce to writing the areas where our views coincide. We see no way to move forward without going at least this far.

8. The President fully understands your concern that Israel's negotiating position not be prejudiced. We will make every effort to see that our talks do not have this effect.

---

reach their own unfettered agreements, the document under consideration prejudices negotiations before they begin. It essentially predetermines the results of the negotiations on the main matters at issue, including the problems of boundaries, refugees and the nature of peace, setting forth for agreement with the Soviet Union positions which Israel is known to oppose." (Ibid.) Meir was referring to the U.S. plan discussed with Dobrynin in May. See Document 28.

9. We believe that it is essential, if negotiations are to begin, to confirm for both sides that a realistic negotiation is possible. The formulations we have given the Soviets are an effort to define the outer limits of realistic negotiating positions on both sides.

10. We understand the emotions of your people and agree that imperfect remedies cannot be a substitute for peace. At the same time, we hope Israel recognizes that no peace or security is perfect.

11. To attain peace will require a spirit of compromise. You have indicated your willingness to be forthcoming. We honestly do not know whether the UAR and Soviets are or not, and that is the purpose of our probe, even though we share your skepticism.

12. We ask no more of Israel than that it accompany us on an exploration of Soviet and UAR intentions.[3]

13. *FYI.* Dates on which Mrs. Meir will be invited to visit US have been fixed for July 17–18. Instructions on extending invitation follow.[4] *End FYI.*

Rogers

---

[3] Barbour presented Nixon's letter to Meir on June 19 and reported on his conversation with her in telegram 2360 from Tel Aviv, June 19. (National Archives, Nixon Presidential Materials, NSC Files, Box 604, Country Files, Middle East, Israel, Vol. II)

[4] In telegram 100333 to Tel Aviv, June 19. (Ibid.) In telegram 2351 from Tel Aviv, June 19, Barbour reported that Meir had "gladly accepted" Nixon's invitation to visit the United States, but that she could not do so July 17–18. The Prime Minister explained that she had to stay in Israel during the days leading up to the Labor Party convention, scheduled for July 20–22, when "fundamental decisions" would be made. (Ibid.)

34. Memorandum From Secretary of State Rogers to President Nixon[1]

Washington, June 20, 1969.

SUBJECT

Soviet Counterproposal on Arab-Israeli Dispute

The Soviets submitted to us on June 17 a written counterproposal (TAB A)[2] and explanatory "oral comments" (TAB B)[3] for a settlement of the Arab-Israeli dispute following Foreign Minister Gromyko's visit to Cairo.[4] It moves in our direction beyond previous Soviet positions by introducing new elements and omitting certain objectionable points contained in the December 30th Soviet plan, although a number of our fundamental requirements are not met. A detailed analysis of the Soviet plan is attached (TAB C).[5]

The plan we submitted to the Soviets (TAB D)[6] envisaged: (a) an acceptance of the principle of withdrawal by Israel from the UAR to a final border to be worked out by the parties, in exchange for (b) an Arab commitment to a contractual peace and a willingness to negotiate di-

---

[1] Source: National Archives, Nixon Presidential Materials, NSC Files, Box 651, Country Files, Middle East, Middle East (1969). Secret; Nodis.

[2] Attached but not printed at Tab A is telegram 101232 to Tel Aviv, June 20. In telegram 99315 to Moscow, June 18, the Embassy reported Tcherniakov's presentation to Rogers and the Secretary's response, including the comment that the Soviet plan represented "very little movement" and consisted "largely of recasting" of the December 30 Soviet plan "plus some modifications given to Sisco orally by Dobrynin." Tcherniakov also told Rogers that he had been instructed to propose that the U.S.-Soviet talks be moved to Moscow. (Ibid., Box 649, Country Files, Middle East, Middle East Negotiations) Telegram 99315 is printed in *Foreign Relations, 1969–1976*, volume XII, Soviet Union, January 1969–October 1970, Document 58.

[3] Attached but not printed at Tab B is the undated "Oral Comments on 'Basic Provisions' of a Middle East Settlement."

[4] Gromyko visited Cairo beginning on June 10. Director of the Bureau of Intelligence and Research Thomas L. Hughes informed Secretary Rogers on June 11 that a Soviet Embassy source in Washington had intimated that Gromyko's visit to Cairo was "connected with the Sisco-Dobrynin discussions on the Arab-Israeli settlement problem and that it will enable the Soviets to make a new presentation to the US in the near future. There is other good evidence as well that this is the main purpose of Gromyko's trip. Although the evidence is sketchy regarding the extent of Moscow's optimism, it seems likely that Moscow in sending Gromyko was confident that the consultations would produce a useful position which the Soviets could take in Washington, and that the trip does not signify Soviet consternation over a totally negative UAR attitude toward further Soviet settlement talks with the West." (Ibid., Document 54)

[5] Attached but not printed at Tab C is the undated "Detailed Analysis of the Soviet Plan of June 17, 1969. For the December 30 plan, see Document 1.

[6] Attached but not printed at Tab D is the U.S. plan, which Sisco presented to Dobrynin in "piecemeal fashion" on May 6, 8, and 12, as described in Document 28.

rectly at some stage under Jarring's auspices. In our plan the possibility was left open, but not made explicit, that the final border between the UAR and Israel would be the former international frontier which existed before the June war, and the parties would themselves be expected to work out the practical security arrangements in Sharm al-Shaykh and Gaza. Our whole strategy was based on the assumption that if we could tie down both the Soviets and the Arabs to a contractual and negotiated peace, we would have some leverage with the Israelis to encourage them to withdraw from UAR territory.

The new Soviet plan moves in this direction. Like our own, it is a negotiating document. It adopts the concept of a reciprocally binding agreement between the parties, as a package, and signed by the parties. It is insufficiently explicit, and the Israelis will certainly think so, on the binding commitment to a state of peace, and this is one matter on which we feel we are in a position to press the Soviets further in subsequent discussions. The Soviet plan also fails to accept our proposal for direct negotiations under Jarring's auspices, but interestingly enough, leaves open this possibility. We feel that this point also can be pressed further with the Soviets.

Our conclusion is there is sufficient in the Soviet document, perhaps more implicitly than explicitly, for us to develop a further counter document which would take into account some of the Soviet views.[7] I do not wish to give you the impression that these are the only serious problems that remain. There are others as our attached detailed analysis indicates. However, our judgment is that as a minimum the Soviet reply reflects a desire to continue the dialogue with us. This is consistent with the hints Ambassador Dobrynin has given to Assistant Secretary Sisco that the Soviets see value in discussions with us as an element of restraint in the Middle East and as an important ingredient in overall US–USSR relations.

In addition, we feel there are other important reasons to continue the Soviet-American dialogue: we have greater control in the bilateral context than in the Four Power discussions; as long as we and the Soviets continue consultations, the risk of a direct military confrontation between us is diminished; a general renewal of hostilities between the Arabs and the Israelis is less likely; the possibility is enhanced that the present "no war, no peace" situation will not escalate beyond the present pattern of incidents, retaliation, and controlled tension.

We will undoubtedly have great difficulty with the Israelis since they will take the most pessimistic interpretation of the Soviet reply and contend that this confirms their strongly held judgment that nei-

---

[7] See footnote 4, Document 39.

ther the Soviets nor the UAR want the kind of peace they require. They will make a further all-out effort to use this reply to get us to kill the Two Power and the Four Power talks. We must resist this.

The latest Soviet plan contains a number of elements that are difficult for the Arabs, and particularly for the Israelis. While it has major deficiencies and no doubt will be unacceptable to Israel, it will appear reasonable in many respects to others. For example, the substantial UN role envisaged will be attractive to many who feel that a continuing Israeli presence in the occupied territories is expansionist and unrealistic. The public relations aspect is another reason why we believe it is necessary for us to prepare a counterproposal of our own.

The Soviets have also proposed that we move our talks to Moscow. You will recall that we left this possibility open when we insisted at the outset that the talks begin in Washington. Our tentative thinking is that Assistant Secretary Sisco would present any counterproposal, with full explanation of our approach, to the Soviets in Moscow,[8] remain a very brief period of time, and we would await their further reply and discuss it either in Moscow or Washington or both, depending on the timing of Dobrynin's return.

We will be developing a counterproposal at an early date and will submit it to you for your approval.

William P. Rogers

---

[8] Sisco visited Moscow July 14–18. See Document 39.

35. Memorandum for the Record[1]

Washington, June 20, 1969.

SUBJECT

NSC Ad Hoc Review Group Meeting, Friday, June 20, 1969, on NSSM 40—Israeli Nuclear Program[2]

PARTICIPANTS

Henry A. Kissinger, Chairman
Elliot Richardson, Under Secretary of State
David Packard, Deputy Secretary of Defense
General Earle Wheeler, Chairman, Joint Chiefs of Staff
Richard Helms, Director, Central Intelligence
Rodger Davies, Deputy Assistant Secretary of State
Harold H. Saunders, NSC Staff

[1 line not declassified][3] Dr. Kissinger suggested that the group might best get at the problem by talking first about what we are trying to accomplish.

Mr. Richardson outlined the following objectives:

1. We want to do what we can to prevent Israel from going further with its nuclear weapons program—[1 line not declassified].

2. We want to have a record of having tried to do this—for later use if and when [less than 1 line not declassified].

3. We have another objective which could be affected by our pursuit of the above two objectives—the diplomatic effort to achieve an Arab-Israeli political settlement.

Commenting on the above objectives, Mr. Richardson stated that deployment of nuclear weapons in the Middle East carries serious risks. Our main diplomatic effort since January 20 has been predicated on concern over the risk of a US–USSR confrontation in the Middle East. Knowledge by the Arabs [less than 1 line not declassified] would seem to increase the likelihood of a local confrontation—increasing possibility of eventual involvement of the US and USSR.

General Wheeler interjected that if the Israelis deploy their surface-to-surface missiles—[less than 1 line not declassified]—the Arabs might well conclude that the Israelis have nuclear warheads on them. By any

---

[1] Source: National Archives, Nixon Presidential Materials, NSC Files, NSC Institutional Files (H-Files), Box H–038, Senior Review Group Meetings, Review Group NSSM 40—Israel 6/20/69. Top Secret; Nodis; Sensitive. Drafted by Saunders on June 24. All brackets are in the original except those indicating text that remains classified.

[2] Document 20.

[3] [text not declassified]

rational military or economic calculation, there is no justification [2 lines not declassified]. When Dr. Kissinger asked how large a conventional warhead they might carry, General Wheeler said he was not sure but guessed it might be about 2000 lbs.—perhaps about the size of the German V–2 rockets in 1945.

Dr. Kissinger responded that there are two possible comments on General Wheeler's points:

1. The Arabs just don't think that precisely. Because they might not calculate their own cost-benefit ratios that rationally, they would not expect the Israelis to.

2. Even if they suspected strongly that the Israelis had nuclear warheads, they might decide to live with that fact as long as it did not become an announced fact of international life.

Dr. Kissinger continued that if the Israelis did indeed have nuclear warheads we might have two possible approaches to the problem:

1. to stop or reverse their deployment;

2. to keep the fact of their existence below the level of public acknowledgment.

Mr. Richardson returned to his discussion of the dangers of the existence of nuclear weapons in the Middle East. He noted as the most likely Soviet response a Soviet announcement that they were targeting a number of their own missiles on Israel and that any use by Israel of nuclear weapons against the Arabs could bring Soviet retaliation.

Mr. Richardson noted that he had said to Ambassador Rabin and General Yariv, the chief of Israeli military intelligence, that the reason we could not agree to their political strategy of standing pat in the current impasse is that we see the situation deteriorating in ways that could lead to a US-Soviet confrontation, as well as to the deterioration of the US position elsewhere in the area. As part of his description of that deterioration, Mr. Richardson said he had described as one possibility the introduction of nuclear weapons by Israel, and Soviet targeting of its own missiles on Israel with the threat of a US-Soviet confrontation becoming consequently worse. He said that neither Rabin nor Yariv "batted an eye or made any effort to rebut." If pushed they would probably say they do [less than 1 line not declassified] are only seeking a deterrent. In 1967 they saw their conventional superiority fail as a deterrent, and he believed that they had made up their minds then [less than 1 line not declassified]. From the US viewpoint, Mr. Richardson concluded, the risk of a US-Soviet confrontation is clearly raised [less than 1 line not declassified].

Dr. Kissinger asked whether we should push on this issue rather than for a political settlement. Mr. Richardson replied that he felt we should push on both, even though pressure on the nuclear issue might marginally prejudice diplomatic movement. However, he did not take this argument too seriously. He felt that the Israelis will arrive at a political settlement if it is in their interest—if it is not in their interest, as they see it, they will not. The degree to which we irritate them will not be a significant factor in their decision.

Mr. Packard asked whether it was possible to get a political settlement without settling the nuclear issue.

Dr. Kissinger replied to both of the last two points with the following analysis: If we can ever get the current debate over a settlement down to the reality of specific borders, any conceivable geographical settlement would reduce Israel's security. What Israel may gain in goodwill and tentative Arab willingness to live in peace, Israel will lose in conventional security. [*less than 1 line not declassified*] they may provide an added incentive for them to hold on to territory. It seems axiomatic that a nation of three million people confronted by 100 million with any technological capacity at all would not over an historical period have a chance of surviving. But if there is any chance at all, it would come from having the most advantageous possible lines of defense. If the Israelis give up the conventional security which advantageous borders provide, they might want nuclear weapons to offset what they are giving up.

In short, Dr. Kissinger concluded the curious point about nuclear weapons for the Israelis is that—despite our interests in having them forego those weapons—we might find it easier to persuade the Israelis to give up territory if we ease along with them [*1 line not declassified*]. For a nation like Israel, losing one conventional war is as bad as losing a nuclear war. The disturbing feature in Israel's present frame of mind is that [*less than 1 line not declassified*].

Mr. Richardson concurred in Dr. Kissinger's analysis but suggested that perhaps different time frames were involved. If Israel held conventional superiority for ten years, [*less than 1 line not declassified*]. Beyond ten years—or some such period—Israel's conventional margin of superiority might be eroded, but it is very difficult to look that far into the future, because we do not know what other factors will be introduced—on the non-proliferation and other fronts.

Dr. Kissinger felt that the Israelis do not want nuclear weapons just against the Arab nations per se, but rather against the possibility of a defeat in conventional war. Returning to Mr. Packard's question, Dr. Kissinger said it is hard to imagine how we could work toward a settlement without relating these two issues. The problem as Dr. Kissinger saw it is that the relationship between these two issues might work in inverse proportion. He repeated that the Israelis might [*less than 1 line not declassified*] or vice versa, but he found it hard to believe that they would give up both.

General Wheeler felt that it is very important for the US to avoid any degree of [1 line not declassified] the President should be in a position to say that he tried everything possible [less than 1 line not declassified]. General Wheeler had little doubt that the Israelis might analyze the situation in the same way as Dr. Kissinger had. However, General Wheeler doubted that the Israelis would have achieved any real addition to their security if the Soviets respond as Mr. Richardson suggested they might. In fact, in the short term, the Arabs might even go to war to try to prevent Israel from achieving full nuclear capability, while the Soviets "rattled their own rockets in the background." In short, [less than 1 line not declassified] could trigger the very war they are trying to avoid.

Mr. Packard stated that our objective should be to [1½ lines not declassified]. We would need some system of inspection to assure Israeli compliance.

Dr. Kissinger asked, "Inspection of what?" Mr. Packard responded that we would have to "get in there and cover the country."

General Wheeler returned to the idea that we would have to be concerned with [3 lines not declassified].

Dr. Kissinger asked whether we might state our choice of objectives as the following:

1. That the Israelis not deploy missiles.
2. [less than 1 line not declassified].
3. Both of the above.

Dr. Kissinger asked how it would ever be possible to monitor any assurances the Israelis might give. General Wheeler said we could do this only with very close inspection of Israel's military facilities. Dr. Kissinger recalled that he had been shown in Israel how the Israelis had manufactured weapons right under the eyes of the British when the British had all of the power to inspect that comes from comprehensive police power.

General Wheeler returned to the importance of avoiding the appearance of American complicity. If we were inspecting—even if we were not inspecting the right things—we would have made a better record for ourselves.

Dr. Kissinger said that we seemed to have two choices:

1. We could raise the nuclear issue with the Israelis, make our case and then stop.

2. Or we could link this issue to the question of a peace settlement, and see if there is any trade-off between them in Israeli minds.

Dr. Kissinger asked what we are talking about when we talk about applying pressure to persuade the Israelis to [less than 1 line not declassified]. General Wheeler responded that we could withhold the remainder of the A–4 Skyhawks and not begin delivery of the F–4 Phantom aircraft.[4]

Mr. Richardson stated that it might help at this point in the discussion to lay out some of the steps we might take. These were described on pages 6 and 7 of the issues paper.[5] Mr. Richardson then turned immediately to look at the Defense Department proposal on page 7, rather than the State Department's proposal on page 6. Dr. Kissinger noted that Mr. Richardson seemed to be speaking more along the lines of the Defense Department proposal, and Mr. Richardson smiled and said, "As usual, you have very keen powers of discernment."

Mr. Packard interjected it was time for us to take a strong stand while we still have some leverage in holding up the F–4s.

Dr. Kissinger said if we were to hold up the F–4 deliveries we would have to do it quietly. Suppose we did, he said. The Jewish community in the United States would run amok and make a public confrontation. General Wheeler doubted that the Israelis would make it public because they would not be in a very good position on the nuclear issue.

Mr. Richardson suggested that, instead of talking about the pressure we could apply, we ought to start at the other end and think what we could ask the Israelis to do. If we reached the stage of confrontation over delivery or non-delivery of the aircraft, he felt that we would have failed.

He noted further that this was one case where getting the results we wanted and making a record might be in conflict. He felt the question was this: If we go and ask the Israelis to sign the NPT and halt the deployment of missiles [*less than 1 line not declassified*] would they agree if they knew we would refuse to deliver the aircraft?

Dr. Kissinger said that the Israelis might just tell us to go to hell if they felt: (1) that they could withstand whatever sanctions we might apply, or (2) if they thought we would not apply those sanctions.

Dr. Kissinger asked whether everybody agreed that we should at least call Israeli attention to the extraordinary seriousness with which we viewed [*less than 1 line not declassified*] and perhaps suggest that we might not deliver the F–4s.

Mr. Richardson stated that we should not imply that we would not deliver the aircraft unless we were absolutely clear in our own minds in advance that we were prepared to follow through on that threat.

---

[4] Sixty A–4s remained to be delivered. The United States shipped the first four Phantoms on September 5 and the second four on October 20. A total of 100 A–4 Skyhawks and 50 F–4 Phantoms had been approved for sale to Israel. See *Foreign Relations, 1964–1968*, volume XX, Arab-Israeli Dispute, 1967–1968, Document 333.

[5] See Document 31.

Dr. Kissinger reiterated that at a minimum the group seemed to agree that we should call Israel's attention to the seriousness we attach [*less than 1 line not declassified*].

Dr. Kissinger went on to ask whether we should seek from the Israelis the following:

1. that they not deploy missiles;
2. that they not announce [*less than 1 line not declassified*];
3. that they not [*less than 1 line not declassified*];
4. that they sign the NPT.

The tough question, he said, is whether we are prepared to impose sanctions and, if so, what sanctions. He felt that withholding the F–4s carried with it the disadvantage of maximum publicity.

Mr. Richardson pointed out that the negotiations which concluded in the F–4 sale last November included an exchange between Ambassador Rabin and Paul Warnke to the effect that the Israelis promised not to be the first to introduce nuclear weapons into the Middle East and the US stated that, if Israel did, we would consider it grounds for cancelling the contract.[6]

Dr. Kissinger returned to the problem of publicity which would be created by our withholding delivery of the Phantom. This would probably bring out into the open [*less than 1 line not declassified*]. He emphasized that, rather than domestic politics—he said the President was prepared to take the pressure from the Jewish community—the real problem lies in making a public issue out of [*less than 1 line not declassified*].

Mr. Richardson said we were not asking the Israelis to [*less than 1 line not declassified*]. They were in a position where they could [*less than 1 line not declassified*]. If we are just asking them to [*1 line not declassified*]. He posed the question whether we could be satisfied with [*1 line not declassified*]. It might be that we could get Israeli agreement [*1½ lines not declassified*].

Mr. Packard felt that we would need some way to enforce our agreement by inspection. General Wheeler said that it was one reason why we wanted the Israelis not to deploy their missiles. It is easier for us to monitor missile deployment. Mr. Packard said that we needed some way to monitor [*less than 1 line not declassified*] as well.

Dr. Kissinger asked, "How?" He felt that Israeli ingenuity would make it impossible. He said he had had occasion to study French efforts to inspect in Germany after World War I and had concluded that if a

---

[6] See *Foreign Relations, 1964–1968,* volume XX, Arab-Israeli Dispute, 1967–1968, Document 306.

country totally opposes you, you just have no chance of making inspection work.

Mr. Richardson asked whether we might want to settle for an inspection that we knew was inefficient primarily for the purpose of making a record and washing our own hands of responsibility, as much as we could.

Dr. Kissinger said that his main concern was that our mere act of trying to do something might bring on the consequences that we worst feared and most wanted to avoid. We all agree that we should tell Israel that we take this development gravely.

General Wheeler noted that if we tried to inspect the Israeli program, we assumed responsibility before the international community. If on the other hand, we pressed the Israelis to sign the NPT, then inspection becomes the responsibility of an international body.

General Wheeler added that our objective should be to stop missile production—not just deployment—and to have the missiles already produced stored. Dr. Kissinger agreed that it seemed impossible to expect the Israelis to [*less than 1 line not declassified*].

Dr. Kissinger continued that, having isolated the proposal that we make some representation to the Israelis, it is important now to decide what our next steps might be and what steps are attainable and what the consequences of those steps might be. Mr. Richardson said he would restate where the group have come out as follows:

1. We need to distinguish between asking the Israelis [*1 line not declassified*] recognizing that "deployment" may be an artificial proposition because the Israelis might [*1½ lines not declassified*].

2. We need to decide whether to pose some form of inspection other than the inspection of future production facilities which would go with signing of the NPT.

3. We need to decide whether to ask the Israelis to stop further missile production and whether to ask them to dismantle what they have.

Dr. Kissinger asked whether we could list what we might get without sanctions. He doubted that bilateral inspection would be possible without some penalty or some reward.

Dr. Kissinger asked if another paper could be written that would include the following:[7]

1. List a hierarchy of steps that we might ask the Israelis to take;

2. List a hierarchy of sanctions that we might apply.

---

[7] The paper is attached to a June 26 memorandum from Halperin and Saunders to Kissinger. (National Archives, Nixon Presidential Materials, NSC Files, NSC Institutional Files (H-Files), Box H–038, Senior Review Group Meetings, Review Group NSSM 40—Israel 6/20/69)

3. Discuss the consequences of applying sanctions for each of the following:

a. achieving our objective;
b. preventing escalation of the whole issue.

Mr. Richardson said there was one more question—the level through which we should do these things. With Prime Minister Meir coming,[8] the question arises whether or not the President should do this. Dr. Kissinger replied that, if this development is as grave as we see it, it is hard to see how the President could fail to involve himself.

In adjourning, Dr. Kissinger suggested that a new paper be prepared by Mr. Davies and that the group meet a week from June 20.[9]

Harold H. Saunders

---

[8] Meir was in the United States from September 24 to October 6.

[9] The Review Group met on June 26. A memorandum of the meeting is in the National Archives, RG 59, Central Files 1967–69, DEF 12 ISR. It is published in National Security Archive Electronic Briefing Book No. 189, Document 9.

---

36. Memorandum of Conversation[1]

Washington, June 20, 1969.

PARTICIPANTS

Yitzhak Rabin, Ambassador of Israel
Harold H. Saunders

Caution: The conversation recounted below was labelled by Rabin as strictly personal. Therefore, no distribution of this memcon should be made beyond those with an immediate interest, and in no case, should Rabin or any other Israeli be confronted with the substance of the Ambassador's remarks.

---

[1] Source: National Archives, Nixon Presidential Materials, NSC Files, Box 604, Country Files, Middle East, Israel, Vol. II. Secret; Nodis. Drafted by Saunders on June 25. The conversation occurred on the evening of June 20 at Sisco's home. Saunders attached his record of this conversation to a July 1 "eyes only" memorandum for Kissinger noting: "There are no immediate operational conclusions to be drawn from this, except to be wary of Eban's vague statements." Saunders explained that because of the "extremely personal nature of Rabin's talk," he would not distribute the memorandum "through the system." (Ibid.)

Background. As background to this conversation, two points need to be made:

1. On May 13, while waiting with Rabin, Bitan and Argov for Dr. Kissinger to see them,[2] I had remarked in the course of our conversation that it was very difficult for us to know exactly what Israel's position on a territorial settlement is. Ambassador Rabin said he could not understand my remark since Foreign Minister Eban last November had told Secretary Rusk very specifically that Israel, in a settlement with the UAR, would require an Israeli position at Sharm el-Sheikh and land access to it.[3] I recalled that comment but noted that always when we had heard such remarks from Israeli officials, they had been couched as "illustrative" rather than as firm Israeli government positions. In fact, we had been repeatedly told right up to the present that the Israeli Cabinet would not take a firm position on a territorial settlement until the Arabs presented themselves for direct negotiations. Prime Minister Eshkol, and other Israeli officials quoting him, had repeatedly said that they would not have a Cabinet crisis over a hypothesis.

2. On the afternoon of June 20, during the call of Rafael, Rabin and Argov on Dr. Kissinger,[4] Dr. Kissinger had commented that the time was coming when he felt it would be to Israel's advantage to state more precisely its territorial requirements and to come out from behind the screen of "sacramental words—'just and lasting peace' and 'secure and recognized boundaries.'" Ambassador Rabin had taken exception to that remark, saying that Foreign Minister Eban last November had told Secretary Rusk specifically that Israel required an Israeli position at Sharm el-Sheikh and land access to it. When Dr. Kissinger asked my reaction, Rabin stepped right in and, smiling, told Dr. Kissinger that I would say that the remarks by Israeli officials had been "illustrative." I then went on to add that we had repeatedly been told by Israeli officials that the Israeli Cabinet would take no position until the Arabs sat down to negotiate with them. After another comment by Dr. Kissinger, Rafael spoke up and said that the Israeli government would not take a firm position until the Arabs sat down and negotiated with them. Ambassador Rabin looked about as angry and disgusted as I have ever seen him look.

Conversation. Walking downstairs beside Ambassador Rabin after dinner at the Siscos' that evening, I asked Rabin whether he blamed me for being confused. When he asked what I meant, I recalled that after-

---

[2] Memorandum of conversation, May 13. (Ibid.)

[3] See *Foreign Relations,* 1964–1968, volume XX, Arab-Israeli Dispute, 1967–1968, Document 303.

[4] Memorandum of conversation, June 20. (National Archives, Nixon Presidential Materials, NSC Files, Box 1319, Unfiled Material)

noon in Dr. Kissinger's office when I had seen demonstrated right before my eyes within about 75 seconds precisely the contradiction which I had been talking about. He paused for a moment and then said, "No, I don't blame you for being confused."

He said that when he had been in Israel he had, in his private conversation with Prime Minister Meir, explained that the Israeli Government position is not firmly understood in Washington. He recommended to her that she come to Washington and explain to the President exactly what positions the Israeli Cabinet has taken. He said he had told her that he did not believe she would return home with any "political victory" but that she did not badly need this and it was far more important that the President of the United States understand clearly Israel's position.

He then motioned me to a chair and proceeded to explain the Israeli Cabinet decisions on this subject in the following general way:

When Eban had made his comment to Rusk in November 1968 about Israeli desire for a position in Sharm el-Sheikh and land access to it, Eban was speaking from a firm Cabinet decision. Recalling the Israeli scurrying to ready a position vis-à-vis Jordan before the UNGA session, I asked whether that decision had been made in August or September. He said that it had been taken in December 1967. He added that he, as then Chief of Staff, had not been told of the decision at that time. He had only learned of it as he prepared in May 1968 to come to Washington as Ambassador. He said he asked for and got the record of the Cabinet meeting. When he had learned of it, he had told the General Staff of the Israeli Defense Forces, and Prime Minister Eshkol had been "very angry" at Rabin for telling them. He had then gone to Dayan who had been surprised that the US had not been told. Rabin then summarized the position the Cabinet had taken on its four fronts as follows:

1. On the UAR front, the Cabinet had made a definite decision to require an Israeli position at Sharm el-Sheikh and land access to it.

2. On the West Bank, the Israelis had needed a position to ready for the Jordanians and there was "an 80–85% consensus" in the Cabinet for the Allon plan.[5] At one time, Dayan had suggested an alternative of fortifying the heights, but no one pressed that plan now.

3. On Syria, the Cabinet had decided not to decide.

4. On Lebanon, there is no territorial issue.

I asked him whether he did not feel that the Israeli position on Sharm el-Sheikh would rule out the peace settlement with the UAR. I said I realized that the Israelis may judge that such a settlement is impossible now anyway and that this would not disturb them.

---

[5] See footnote 8, Document 4.

He made two points in reply:

1. If the Egyptians unexpectedly show themselves to want peace, the Cabinet could always revise its own decision.

2. More realistically, Rabin—emphasizing that he was speaking strictly personally—said that responsible Israelis fully realize that peace can not come about all at once. He therefore thought the objective was to create a situation which would gradually reverse hostility and create a situation in which Arabs and Israelis could learn to live together. He thought, for instance, that it might be possible to agree that the Israelis would occupy Sharm el-Sheikh for a period of five–ten years with the possibility of review at the end of that period. If at that time it appeared that there had been substantial progress toward living together in peace, then the Israelis might as well decide that they could return that position.

When I asked what evidence the Israelis would consider adequate manifestation of Egyptian desire for peace, he repeated the familiar position that Nasser's willingness to negotiate directly with the Israelis—"under Jarring, of course"—would be the first step.

I said that if this were the case, I could not see why the Israelis objected so strongly to our current diplomatic exercise if we were simply trying to find out whether the Russians could deliver the Egyptians for direct negotiations, and, what I felt was even more important, deliver an Arab willingness to recognize the political independence, the territorial integrity and inviolability of Israel and renounce the use of force or threat of force against Israel. Rabin replied that these would be very important for Israel, but that our document had not supplied that kind of recognition for Israel.

He volunteered that when he had last been in Israel, he had been asked at the Cabinet to explain U.S. intentions in this diplomatic exercise with the Soviet Union. Rabin said that he personally felt that the US without committing itself to the principle of withdrawal, had been trying to probe how far the Soviet Union and the UAR were willing to commit themselves to peace.

I said we had developed our position in June 1967 on the assumption—confirmed by Israeli statements—that Israel had no territorial aspirations. Rabin replied, "You were justified."

Comments:

1. The nuance which is not clear is whether Rabin is referring to a firm but secret Cabinet decision or to a consensus, such as Eban refers to. While there may be a technical difference to cover Eban, Rabin's blunt characterization may be more accurate in describing the net effect of the Cabinet action.

2. Rabin himself noted that the Cabinet could reverse itself, but he clearly sharply disagrees with the Eban-Rafael formulation that the Cabinet will make a decision only when the Arabs negotiate. Whatever the technicality, Rabin states firmly that the Cabinet has made up its mind as far as its UAR border is concerned, and Eban-Rafael continue to suggest that the Cabinet has yet to commit itself. Rabin seems to believe that the "politicians"—to his dismay—have misled us and feels strongly they should now state their position forthrightly.

3. Going back to re-read the report of the November 3, 1968, Rusk-Eban conversation, I am struck by the careful way both Eban and Rabin seem to be avoiding stating that Israel wants permanent annexation of Sharm el-Sheikh. They seem to be talking carefully about "a position" and not "sovereignty."

Harold H. Saunders[6]

---

[6] Saunders initialed "H.H.S." above his typed signature.

---

37. Paper Prepared by the Ad Hoc Special Review Group on the Israeli Nuclear Weapons Program[1]

Washington, undated.

SCENARIO FOR DISCUSSIONS WITH ISRAELIS ON THEIR NUCLEAR PROGRAM

A. *US Objectives*

1. Our objectives are to persuade Israel to:

a) Sign the NPT at an early date (by the end of this year) and ratify it soon thereafter.

b) Reaffirm to the US in writing the assurance that Israel will not be the first to introduce nuclear weapons into the Near East, specify-

---

[1] Source: Washington National Records Center, OSD Files: FRC 330–75–0103, Box 12, Israel. Top Secret; Nodis. The paper is attached to a July 12 memorandum from NSC Staff Secretary Jeanne W. Davis to Rogers, Laird, Wheeler, Richardson, and Helms. All brackets are in the original except those indicating text that remains classified. It was supposed to serve as the basis of a July 16 meeting of the special committee of the NSC, which the President cancelled after he approved a July 19 memorandum that outlined guidance for Richardson and Packard in their meeting with Rabin on the nuclear weapons issue. See Documents 38 and 41.

ing that "introduction" shall mean possession of nuclear explosive devices.[2]

c) Give us assurances in writing that it will stop production and will not deploy "Jericho" missiles or any other nuclear-capable strategic missile.

2. Early signature and ratification of the NPT must be our minimum objective. The NPT provides the best basis for international confidence in Israel's intentions.

Bilateral assurances are equally important. They are also a desirable adjunct to the NPT because of the time factor. The Treaty does not enter into force until the three nuclear signatories and 40 others sign and ratify (present score is one nuclear and about 20 others) and this may take another six months to a year. Even after the Treaty is in force it gives a signatory six months to enter negotiations with the IAEA for a safeguards arrangement, and it gives the signatory an additional 18 months to conclude those negotiations. We need the bilateral assurances to cover the interim and we should do our best to get them.

Israeli agreement to stop production and not to deploy strategic missiles is important because the deployment of a delivery system that is militarily cost effective only as a nuclear weapons carrier would seriously vitiate confidence in Israel's adherence to the NPT. We should therefore make a determined effort, at least initially, to achieve this objective. However, if the Israelis show a disposition to meet us on the nuclear issue but are adamant on the Jericho missiles, we can drop back to a position of insisting on non-deployment of missiles and an undertaking by the Israelis to keep any further production secret.

B. *Scenario*

1. *General Approach.* The venue for our negotiations with the Israelis should be kept in Washington. Ambassador Barbour in Tel Aviv would be kept informed in detail of the negotiations as they proceed and would be asked to reinforce our representations to Rabin whenever this appeared desirable.

2. *First Meeting.* Ambassador Rabin would be asked to call upon Under Secretaries Richardson and Packard meeting jointly. The Under Secretaries would say that in connection with Israel's request to advance the delivery date for the first Phantoms to August, we wish to tie up loose ends left after the Warnke–Rabin negotiations in October,

---

[2] In presenting our requirements to the Israelis, we would not go beyond this formulation. For our own internal purposes, we would decide that [*less than 1 line not declassified*]. [Footnote in the original.]

1968, which led to our agreement to sell the aircraft.[3] Accordingly, we would like to open discussions in Washington on Israel's adherence to the NPT and related questions concerning Israel's intentions with respect to nuclear weapons.

The Under Secretaries would stress the importance the US attaches to Israel's adherence to the NPT. Israel told us last December it was studying the implications of adherence to the NPT;[4] we would be interested to hear what conclusions the GOI has reached. The Under Secretaries would also refer to the Warnke-Rabin exchanges last November and say we feel there are some unanswered questions concerning Israel's assurances to us on nuclear weapon forebearance. Specifically, we would wish to have Israel's confirmation that *possession* of nuclear weapons as well as testing and deployment would constitute "introduction" of nuclear weapons. We would also like to pursue the question of the purpose of Israel developing and deploying a nuclear weapons delivery system—the "Jericho" missile—which can only cast doubt on its nuclear assurances.

At the first meeting with Rabin the US side would not explicitly link deliveries of the F–4s to the Israeli response on the nuclear question, but our reference to the request for early deliveries and the Warnke-Rabin talks would clearly convey the direction of our thinking. Rabin's tactic will probably be to test how serious we are by refusing initially to go beyond the line Israel has taken with us in past meetings: that the GOI has not made up its mind about the NPT; that it has already given us assurances that it will not be the first to introduce nuclear weapons into the area, and nothing further is required. If he is unresponsive in this fashion, the Under Secretaries would make clear their dissatisfaction and ask Rabin to call again in five or six days time to continue the dialogue.

3. *Second Meeting.* If Rabin tries to stonewall us at the second meeting the US side would tell him that Israel's uncommunicativeness on the nuclear question does not strike us as consistent with the high level of cooperation which Israel expects of us in support of its security. Israel's [*less than 1 line not declassified*] also impinges directly on US worldwide security concerns and responsibilities. By the end of the meeting we should lay before Rabin precisely what we need, as outlined in section A above. We would make it clear to Rabin that a lack of response on Israel's part raises a question regarding our ability to continue meeting Israel's arms requests.

---

[3] The negotiations occurred in November 1968. See *Foreign Relations,* 1964–1968, volume XX, Arab-Israeli Dispute, 1967–1968, Documents 306, 308, 309, 317, 330, and 333.

[4] See ibid., Documents 349 and 360.

4. *Subsequent.* Having presented our needs, we would let the GOI formulate its response in its own time, allowing the approaching date for delivery of the F–4s to produce its own pressure on the GOI. Whenever and wherever the Israelis raised the subject of the F–4s, the response would be that, given the terms of the sales agreement and the uncertainties surrounding Israel's nuclear intentions, there are serious doubts about our ability to proceed with deliveries of the F–4s so long as the matters under discussion with Under Secretaries Richardson and Packard remain unresolved.

This would have the effect of turning down the Israeli request for advancing delivery to August. However, no decision would be taken to alter the scheduled September delivery of the F–4s until we get an initial reading on Israeli attitudes and intentions.

5. *Mrs. Meir's Visit.* When Prime Minister Meir gets here the President and other senior US officials would bear down on this subject, stressing that Israel's decisions in the [*less than 1 line not declassified*] field have an important bearing on US security and global interests, and reinforcing our objectives as they have evolved in the meetings between Rabin and the Under Secretaries. The possibility should also be kept in mind that Mrs. Meir may make a special appeal to the President, saying that it is impossible for her government to sign the NPT or give us a bilateral commitment on non-possession of nuclear weapons until after the elections in Israel this October, and that in the meantime non-delivery of F–4s in September would hurt the Labor Alignment's chances. Our response to such an appeal would have to be decided in the light of the way the earlier negotiations had gone with the Israelis.

6. *Public Confrontation.* The USG would take no initiative to make this a public issue. In the event that the Israelis maintain an unresponsive line with us and show signs of going to Congress in an attempt to undermine our position on deliveries of the F–4s, we should have ready a range of actions that the Administration might take to counter this move.

38. Memorandum From the President's Assistant for National Security Affairs (Kissinger) to President Nixon[1]

Washington, July 19, 1969.

SUBJECT

Israel Nuclear Program

You will recall that you created a special group—because of the sensitivity of the issue—to consider the status of the Israeli nuclear program and our possible responses to it. We have met twice at the top level (Packard, Richardson, Helms, Wheeler, Kissinger) to consider analyses drawn up by a small working group under us.

The paper at Tab A is my summary of the situation as our group sees it after reviewing the intelligence and of our discussion of the issues which that situation raises. This is long, but I believe you will want to read through it because this is a complex problem.

The Situation

[*2 lines not declassified*] We judge that the introduction of nuclear weapons into the Near East would increase the dangers in an already dangerous situation and therefore not be in our interest.

Israel has 12 surface-to-surface missiles delivered from France. It has set up a production line and plans by the end of 1970 to have a total force of 24–30, ten of which are programmed for nuclear warheads.

When the Israelis signed the contract buying the Phantom aircraft last November, they committed themselves "not to be the first to *introduce* nuclear weapons into the Near East." But it was plain from the discussion that they interpreted that to mean they could possess nuclear weapons as long as they did not test, deploy, or make them public. In signing the contract, we wrote Rabin saying that we believe mere "possession" constitutes "introduction" and that Israel's introduction of nuclear weapons by our definition would be cause for us to cancel the contract.

Delivery of the Phantoms is scheduled to begin in September. But some of the aircraft will be ready at the factory in August, and the Israelis have asked to begin taking delivery then.

---

[1] Source: National Archives, Nixon Presidential Materials, NSC Files, Box 337, Subject Files. Top Secret; Nodis; Sensitive. Sent for action. Tabs A–E are attached. Tabs A and C–E are not printed. Tab B is printed as Document 37. All brackets are in the original except those indicating text that remains classified.

What We Want

There was general agreement in our group that we must recognize one *important distinction* to begin with:

1. Israel's secret possession of nuclear weapons would increase the potential danger in the Middle East, and we do not desire complicity in it.

2. In this case, public knowledge is almost as dangerous as possession itself. This is what might spark a Soviet nuclear guarantee for the Arabs, tighten the Soviet hold on the Arabs and increase the danger of our involvement. Indeed, the Soviets might have an incentive not to know.

What this means is that, while we might ideally like to halt actual Israeli possession, what we really want at a minimum may be just to keep Israeli possession from becoming an established international fact.

In our discussions, the following positions were taken:

1. Everyone agreed that, as a minimum, we want Israel to sign the NPT. This is not because signing will make any difference in Israel's actual nuclear program because Israel could produce warheads clandestinely. Israel's signature would, however, give us a publicly feasible issue to raise with the Israeli government—a way of opening the discussion. It would also publicly commit Israel not to acquire nuclear weapons.

2. Everyone agreed that, in addition, we should try to get from Israel a bilateral understanding on Israel's nuclear intentions because the NPT is not precise enough and because the Phantom aircraft are potential nuclear weapons carriers.

3. Opinion was divided on the nature of the assurances we should seek and on the tactics of seeking them:

—*The JCS* felt that if Israel's program becomes known, we should be in a position to say we did everything in our power to prevent Israel from going nuclear. JCS felt that we should try to stop Israel's missile production and use the Phantoms as leverage.

—*Defense* felt that we could live with the existence of Israeli nuclear weapons provided they were not deployed. Defense agreed that we should try to stop missile production and that we should use the Phantoms as leverage to get the assurances we want.

—*State* believed that we should try to keep Israel from going any further with its nuclear weapons program—it may be so close to completion that Israel would be willing—and make a record for ourselves of having tried. State has joined in suggesting asking the Israelis to halt production of the missiles. State would not threaten to withhold the Phantoms in the first approach to the Israelis but would be prepared to imply that threat if they were unresponsive to our first approach.

At the end of our discussions, State, Defense, and JCS agreed to describe a course of action which represented as nearly as possible the consensus of our group. Despite the different shades of opinion expressed in our discussions, the State, Defense and JCS members have concurred in the paper at Tab B which proposes asking the Israelis to:

1. Sign the NPT at an early date (by the end of this year) and ratify it soon thereafter.

2. Reaffirm to the US in writing the assurance that Israel will not be the first to introduce nuclear weapons into the Near East, specifying that "introduction" shall mean possession of nuclear explosive devices. [For our own internal purposes, we would decide that we could tolerate Israeli activity short of assembly of a completed nuclear device.]

3. Give us assurances in writing that it will stop production and will not deploy "Jericho" missiles or any other nuclear-capable strategic missile. [NOTE: I do not believe we can ask Israel not to produce missiles. Israel is sovereign in this decision, and I do not see how we can ask it not to produce a weapon just because we do not see it as an effective weapon without nuclear warheads. We might persuade them not to deploy what they produce on grounds that the rest of the world will believe that the missiles must have nuclear warheads.]

This paper recommends approaching the Israelis in two steps:

1. First step. Richardson and Packard call in Rabin and say that, in connection with Israel's request to advance the delivery date for the first Phantoms to August, we want to tie up loose ends left by the exchange of letters surrounding that contract (i.e., the difference over what would constitute "introduction" of nuclear weapons). They would stress the importance of Israel's signature of the NPT and ask for Israel's confirmation that "possession" of nuclear weapons as well as testing and deployment would constitute "introduction". They would also say that Israel's development and deployment of missiles—a nuclear weapons delivery system—would cast doubt on its nuclear assurances. They would not in this first meeting explicitly link delivery of the Phantoms with Israel's response.

2. Second step. If Rabin tried to stonewall, Richardson and Packard would state exactly what we want and make clear that Israeli unresponsiveness would raise a question about our ability to continue meeting Israel's arms request.

The Dilemma We Face

Our problem is that Israel will not take us seriously on the nuclear issue unless they believe we are prepared to withhold something they very much need—the Phantoms or, even more, their whole military supply relationship with us.

On the other hand, if we withhold the Phantoms and they make this fact public in the United States, enormous political pressure will be mounted on us. We will be in an indefensible position if we cannot state why we are withholding the planes. Yet if we explain our position publicly, we will be the ones to make Israel's possession of nuclear weapons public with all the international consequences this entails.

The Options

In the end, we have these broad options:

1. Initiate discussion now and try to reach an understanding before delivery of the Phantoms becomes an active issue in September.

2. Initiate discussion of the nuclear issue in September when Mrs. Meir comes, letting delivery of the Phantoms begin.

3. Initiate discussion of the issue in September and not let delivery begin until we have a satisfactory response to our request for assurances.

4. Not raise the issue.

I recommend the first.[2] I would propose that:

1. Richardson and Packard call in Rabin and go through the first step as outlined in their paper—express our desire to tie up loose ends on Israel's nuclear assurances to us but *not* explicitly link delivery of the Phantoms to their reply.

2. If Rabin's reaction is negative, I call Rabin in and stress your concern that they sign the NPT, confirm that they will not "introduce" (defined as "possess") nuclear weapons, and agree not to deploy their missiles.

3. We then take stock before committing ourselves on withholding the Phantoms.

The rationale for this approach is that:

1. It raises the question with the Israelis before delivery of the Phantoms becomes an active issue. We shall have to find an excuse for not delivering in August, but the scheduled delivery would begin in September. By raising the question now, we at least have a chance to keep the Phantom delivery from becoming an issue.

2. By relating our discussion to the contract, it implies—without committing us—that we are questioning the Phantom delivery and thereby encourage the Israelis to take us seriously.

3. It maintains your control over the point at which we do or do not introduce the threat of withholding the Phantoms.

---

[2] Nixon initialed his approval of this option.

I recommend that you read through the papers that follow before you decide, because this is a complex issue. They are written to help you work your way in more detail through the pros and cons of the major issues (Tab A), to enable you to see how the consensus of the group would play itself out in a course of action (Tab B), and to present to you systematically the principal issues for decision (Tab C). The two remaining papers are background: at Tab D, the exchange of letters consummating the Phantom sale for your reference; at Tab E, the basic working group papers that our group started from.

39. Memorandum From the Assistant Secretary of State for Near Eastern and South Asian Affairs (Sisco) to President Nixon and Secretary of State Rogers[1]

Washington, July 21, 1969.

SUBJECT

Report on Moscow Talks on Middle East, July 14–18, 1969

From two meetings with Foreign Minister Gromyko and three sessions with a delegation headed by Deputy Foreign Minister Vinogradov, I return with the following reflections and judgments:[2]

1. *First, the Soviets want the bilaterals to continue for both Middle East and overall US–USSR reasons.* They are using the talks at least in part as a demonstration to the Arabs that their efforts to get Israel out of the occupied territories continue unabated, and they see utility in them in discouraging or, failing that, in insulating the escalation of violence in the area against major power involvement. More broadly, it is clear from Gromyko's remarks, they consider the bilateral talks as respon-

---

[1] Source: National Archives, Nixon Presidential Materials, NSC Files, Box 650, Country Files, Middle East. Middle East Negotiations. Secret; Nodis. Sisco's memorandum is attached to a July 23 memorandum from Kissinger to Nixon, which is stamped: "The President has seen." Kissinger wrote that Sisco's "most interesting reflections" were that: 1) Soviet officials judged that they could "live with the present situation in the Near East"; and 2) the United States could "get through the next six weeks with the British and French," but they would "become restless" if no progress was made by the time the UN General Assembly opened on September 16.

[2] The undated memorandum from Kissinger to Nixon that approved Sisco's trip to Moscow is printed in *Foreign Relations,* 1969–1976, volume XII, Soviet Union, January 1969–October 1970, Document 63. See also ibid., Documents 67 and 69, for additional accounts of Sisco's discussions in Moscow.

sive, in the context of our overall relations, to the President's desire to find areas of agreement of mutual benefit and to move toward an era of negotiation, not confrontation. From our point of view, the bilaterals are an element of restraint in the area, they provide the means to keep the heat on the Soviets, and are more manageable than the four power talks.

2. *Second,* the Soviets would like a political settlement which would get the Israelis out of the occupied territories, but more significantly, *they gave no serious signs of concern over the present status quo in the area and seemed prepared to live with it as manageable.* While attacking Israeli "stubbornness," they made no pronouncements that the area was moving towards general war. Gromyko continued to condition talks on Middle East conventional arms limitation on prior Israeli withdrawal, and he did not even mention to me his July 10 speech proposal of a Middle Eastern nuclear free zone which presumably is intended to get at the Israeli nuclear option.[3]

3. *Third,* they face something of a quandary about how to handle the UAR since, to get a settlement which will restore occupied Arab territory and bring greater stability to the area thus reducing the risks to them of further Arab military setbacks, they will need to press Nasser to take steps which could undermine him politically. *I found no evidence that the Soviets are prepared to press Nasser on the key points of peace and negotiations.* I believe they have concluded that Nasser must continue to be their primary tool in the Middle East, that they must continue to support him politically and materially (thus no present interest in Middle East conventional arms limitation), and that they believe Nasser is in more danger of being ousted if he agrees to negotiate peace with Israel than in the present no-peace-no-war circumstances. This is borne out by Syrian President Atassi's remarks to French Ambassador

---

[3] The text of Gromyko's speech is in *The Current Digest of the Soviet Press,* vol. 21, August 6, 1969, pp. 6–10. In a July 10 memorandum to Nixon, Kissinger described Gromyko's language as "temperate and on the whole positive as regards relations with the US . . . All told, in my judgment, this speech leaves Soviet policy where it has been; but the temperate tone on relations with us and, especially, on arms talks will probably be cited—as the Soviets undoubtedly intended it to be—by Administration opponents as justifying 'restraint' on our part." (*Foreign Relations, 1969–1976,* volume XII, Soviet Union, January 1969–October 1970, Document 65) DCI Helms informed Rogers on July 14 that with regard to the Middle East, Gromyko's speech offered "nothing new, and stresses again Moscow's position that Israeli occupation of Arab territory is the obstacle to a political settlement. Nevertheless, Gromyko does not indicate any extreme concern about the Arab-Israeli situation and—unlike last year—he does not threaten Israel with the consequences of failure to fulfill the Security Council resolution of November, 1967. Moreover, Gromyko notes that Israeli withdrawal must be accompanied by Arab recognition of Israel's right to exist, thus publicly recording a recent change in the Soviet position. Less authoritative spokesmen often continue to support withdrawal as a unilateral first step toward a settlement." (Memorandum from Helms to Rogers, July 14; ibid., Document 66)

Seydoux in Moscow that the Soviets have taken a decision not to press Nasser for the time being to make concessions.

4. *Fourth, their strategy will be to try to chip away at the US position*, using the four power mechanism, the UN corridors, and the public forum of the UN Security Council and General Assembly this fall to put pressure on us to press the Israelis to withdraw, or at least to isolate us to the degree possible by portraying American policy as pro-Israeli. They have already informed us of their intention to pursue bilateral talks with the UK and France over the next few weeks.

In these circumstances, I believe our strategy and tactics for the next two months should be:

First, play it cool. We have put forward a proposal which will satisfy neither the Arabs nor the Israelis but which protects Israel's basic interests, our own negotiating position and the fundamental principles we consider essential to any settlement.[4] In brief, our counterproposal (a) adheres to the concept that Israeli withdrawal must be in the context of a contractual peace agreement arrived at by direct talks "at some stage;"[5] (b) would resolve the refugee problem on the basis of equity to both sides; and (c) leaves it to the parties to work out borders and practical security arrangements.

We are in a sound public posture. Having presented a balanced counterproposal in Moscow, we have put the ball in the Soviet court and they are obviously uncomfortable about how to return it.

Second, we should insist on a specific and an overall Soviet reaction to the proposal I left in Moscow and not permit them to nibble at the edges on a piecemeal basis.[6] Gromyko knows that greater specificity by us on withdrawal requires greater specificity on *peace* and *negotiations* on their part. They should fully understand what is fundamental to us and where our negotiating position could be flexible if they are able to deliver Nasser. Throughout I tried to convey our sense of confidence that we speak from a position of strength, and while we do not like the present situation in the area, we can live with it if necessary rather than concede on fundamentals.

We got four signs of how the Soviets will play it over the coming weeks:

---

[4] The U.S. counterproposal that Sisco presented in Moscow is in telegram 3485 from Moscow, July 15. (National Archives, Nixon Presidential Materials, NSC Files, Box 649, Country Files, Middle East, Middle East Negotiations)

[5] Nixon underlined point a.

[6] Nixon underlined this sentence and wrote "yes" in the margin.

1. They want to do more business on the Middle East in Moscow as a show to the Arabs that we are going after them, not vice versa.[7] Just as the Israelis fear we will make them sacrificial lambs for overall US–USSR reasons, so apparently the Arabs needed assurance that Soviet concern over Communist China would not tempt them to make concessions to us which the Arabs would find extremely difficult to swallow. We should continue to insist that Moscow not become the venue of our talks, but carry on our business with minimal fanfare in both capitals as desirable and necessary.[8]

2. Rather than exchanging further documents, they want to engage in a process of point-by-point negotiation based on their June 17 draft[9] and our counterproposal.[10] I agree we should avoid further exchanges of documents. However, the procedure suggested by the Soviets is premature at best, given the substantial gaps between our positions. We should insist on a full response to our total proposal.[11]

3. They will try to concentrate their fire on withdrawal, demilitarization, and borders while marking time on other points we consider equally fundamental.[12] It should not be difficult to avoid concentration on these aspects to the exclusion of others.

4. They will try to get us to spell out specifically our views on a Jordanian settlement, particularly on the territorial question, since Nasser has linked this with the UAR settlement. While this is no doubt a real problem for Nasser, the UAR-Jordanian linkage also relieves the UAR of making the tough decisions on peace and negotiations.[13] In my response to Gromyko, I said that we agreed with the basic concept that a package settlement must include both the UAR and Jordanian aspect, and possibly even Syria if it ever changes its tune. I did not, therefore, preclude a general discussion of the Jordanian aspect with the Soviets at some later stage. However, I reserved our position by insisting on prior progress on the UAR aspect of the settlement before serious thought could be given to such a general exchange.[14] (I got some intimation that the Soviets for the first time have become aware of direct Israeli-Jordanian contacts and their desire to engage us on this aspect not only meets Nasser's requirements to delay difficult decisions but

---

[7] Nixon underlined this sentence.
[8] Nixon underlined this sentence and wrote "good" in the margin.
[9] See Document 34.
[10] Nixon underlined most of this sentence.
[11] Nixon underlined this sentence and wrote "good" in the margin.
[12] Nixon underlined "fire on withdrawal, demilitarization, and borders."
[13] Nixon underlined the last phrase of this sentence.
[14] Nixon underlined most of this sentence.

could reflect some Soviet concern over a separate settlement by Hussein, leaving Nasser to stew in his own juice.)[15]

Third, while the two power efforts go forward we should continue close bilateral consultations with the UK and France. From my talks with Stewart and Schumann, it is clear that they have acquiesced, however reluctantly, to the major focus being on the US–USSR talks. However, there are real difficulties ahead with them if, as is likely, no major progress is made by early September. Stewart told me he is under pressure to get the Suez Canal open, and he feels their interests in the Arab states require a UK initiative in the fall. Schumann, while less doctrinaire than ultra-Gaullist Debre, shares the latter's view that the Four Power mechanism is a useful instrument for pursuing French interests and prestige in the Arab world. I see no decisive change in French Middle East policy in the foreseeable future vis-à-vis Israel, only a softened and surface change of style.

On substance, the UK, and to a greater extent the French, are more disposed to favor arrangements devised by the major powers with prime reliance on a long time UN presence rather than the directly negotiated peace and security arrangements which the Israelis are insisting upon. There is considerable parallelism of UK, French, and USSR interests in the Arab world which will continue to plague us in the days ahead. *In my judgment we might well begin to look for ways to disengage from the automatic assumption being made by our allies on the longevity of the four power talks.* They should not become an end in themselves. When the President agreed to four power talks it was in the framework of prior progress in bilateral discussions. We have given the four power talks a good try; for the foreseeable future *we might well return to the original conception of preconditioning further formal four power meetings on progress in the bilateral context with the UK, France and the USSR.*[16]

Fourth, we have begun to lay the groundwork for bilateral discussions between the numerous Foreign Ministers who will be present during the opening two weeks of the UN General Assembly in the last half of September. Israel will wish to mark time during the election period which is likely to become more complicated. They will, at least for the record, contend unjustifiably that the document we left in Moscow last week is a further erosion. We can nevertheless demonstrate clearly to the Israelis, even though they will not grant us this point, that we have held firmly on fundamentals. In any event, it is salutary for the Israelis to know our determination to act independently of them when we judge this is nec-

---

[15] Nixon underlined "separate settlement by Hussein, leaving Nasser to stew in his own juice."

[16] Nixon highlighted this sentence in the margin.

essary in our own national interest. Moreover, the Moscow trip, as part of the balancing act we are in, should help keep up Hussein's morale in the short run.

The present Israeli position is unrealistic: they simply want Jarring to call the UAR to a meeting with them on the basis of an oft-repeated promise they will be flexible in such talks. Jarring, whom I briefed in Stockholm, responded favorably to my suggestion that he plan to be available during the early days of the Assembly. However, he made clear he needs a common document as a fresh substantive framework in order to renew his efforts with the parties. After reading our latest proposal and comparing it with the Soviet document of June 17, he said we are still far apart.

Fifth, we must, of course, remain ready to respond affirmatively if the unexpected occurs: a genuine Soviet move in our direction. At present, we and the Soviets are essentially agreed on the principle that withdrawal can only take place in the context of a contractual peace agreement. If the Soviets should in fact move further toward our position, my own judgment is that neither the form of a commitment to peace, nor navigation rights, nor refugees, nor withdrawal and borders on the UAR side of the settlement will become major sticking points. In addition to the need for progress on the Jordanian side, the major substantive sticking points are likely to relate to the kind of practical security arrangements on the ground which should be part of the settlement. I do not believe this aspect can be satisfactorily resolved by major powers in either the bilateral or multilateral context. With this and related problems in mind, I suggested to the Soviets that we should consider the possibility that we will not succeed in reaching agreement on all issues and that rather than permit our efforts to abort, we should develop a common document for Jarring recording agreement on as many points as possible and formulating points on which we do not agree in neutral language not prejudging either side's position. They seem tempted. With such a document Jarring could renew his efforts with the parties with continuing US and USSR support.

Sixth, we will want to keep in mind the forthcoming visit of Prime Minister Meir in late September which, if an unexpected narrowing of the US–USSR gap should occur, *could provide an opportunity for a major effort with the Israelis.* We are, as you know, ahead of the Israelis in the substantive positions taken, even though we have protected their vital interests and negotiating position. If the Soviets should surprisingly decide to get out ahead of the UAR, or even more surprising, should move Nasser forward on the fundamental elements of settlement, the President will be faced with some hard decisions with respect to US–Israeli relations and a peace settlement in the Middle East.

Finally, from a *public relations* point of view we should continue to portray our efforts as a continuing process in pursuit of a permanent peace with the Moscow interlude *neither a breakthrough nor a breakdown.*[17] We need to continue to avoid in present circumstances the twin dangers of stimulating unfounded expectations or overdrawn characterizations of failure

The above thoughts, of course, are not recommendations, which must await the Soviet response to our counterproposal. However, they do reflect the thrust of my present thinking in the light of the Moscow talks.

I will be joining the President for the last half of his trip,[18] and I will be available if the President desires to discuss the matter further. There will be considerable interest in the Middle East in Delhi, Bucharest and London.

Joseph J. Sisco

---

[17] Nixon circled "neither a breakthrough nor a breakdown."

[18] Nixon was in Southeast Asia, South Asia, and Romania July 23–August 3.

---

40. Memorandum From the President's Assistant for National Security Affairs (Kissinger) to Acting Secretary of State Richardson[1]

Washington, July 22, 1969.

SUBJECT

U.S. Action in Regard to Israel: Nuclear Program

The President has reviewed the record of our discussions and the studies produced in response to NSSM 40.[2] Prior to his departure,[3] the President:

---

[1] Source: National Archives, Nixon Presidential Materials, NSC Files, Box 337, Subject Files. Top Secret; Nodis; Sensitive. Drafted by Saunders.

[2] See Document 31.

[3] According to the President's Daily Diary, President Nixon departed Andrews Air Force Base aboard Air Force One at 10:05 p.m. on July 22. (National Archives, Nixon Presidential Materials, White House Central Files) The President was headed to the mid-Pacific to greet the Apollo XI astronauts who were returning from the moon.

1. Approved the action described in paragraph B2 ("First Meeting") of your paper "Scenario for Discussions with Israelis on their Nuclear Program".[4]

2. Instructed that the discussion not be carried beyond that point until he has reviewed the record of your conversations.

3. Specifically withheld authority to link explicitly at this stage the delivery of conventional weapons to the Israeli response on the nuclear question.

4. Instructed that you are the only official authorized at this stage to discuss this subject with the Israelis, although the Under Secretary of Defense should, of course, be present as you have suggested.

5. Requested a full report on your discussions.[5]

---

[4] Document 37.
[5] Printed from a copy that indicates Kissinger signed the original.

---

41. Memorandum of Conversation[1]

Washington, July 29, 1969.

SUBJECT

Israel's Nuclear Weapon and Strategic Missile Policy

PARTICIPANTS

Lieutenant General Yitzhak Rabin, Ambassador of Israel
Shlomo Argov, Minister, Embassy of Israel
Moshe Raviv, Counselor, Embassy of Israel

Elliot L. Richardson, The Acting Secretary
David Packard, Deputy Secretary of Defense
Alfred L. Atherton, Jr., Country Director, Israel and Arab–Israel Affairs

Mr. Richardson said he was aware of Ambassador Rabin's discussions last year with Assistant Secretary of Defense Warnke relating to

---

[1] Source: National Archives, Nixon Presidential Materials, NSC Files, Box 605, Country Files, Middle East, Israel, Vol. III. Top Secret; Nodis. Drafted by Atherton. An unsigned covering memorandum from Richardson to Nixon was drafted by Atherton on July 31. (Ibid., RG 59, Lot Files, Bureau of Near Eastern and South Asian Affairs, Office of Israel and Arab-Israel Affairs, 1951–1976, Box 27) Sisco's July 28 briefing memorandum with talking points for Richardson is ibid., Central Files 1967–69, DEF 12–1 ISR. It is published in National Security Archive Electronic Briefing Book No. 189, Document 13.

the introduction of nuclear weapons in the Middle East.[2] In light of subsequent progress toward ratification of the NPT, we believed it useful to review the status of this question as it was left in the exchange of letters between Rabin and Warnke of November 22 and November 27, respectively, of last year,[3] which had brought out differing US and Israeli interpretations of what was meant by "introduce" nuclear weapons.

Rabin observed there were two problems: (a) nuclear weapons in the Middle East and (b) the NPT. Warnke had not discussed the NPT. Which, he asked, was the subject of today's talk?

Mr. Richardson said we saw the two problems as inseparable. The NPT question had moved forward since that time and we thought both questions should be reviewed together. Mr. Richardson then read the following oral statement:

"We want to discuss today a subject of deep concern to the United States—the possibility that nuclear weapons and nuclear weapons delivery systems will be introduced into the Middle East.

"This would be a development the United States would regard not only as a tragedy for the Middle East but as a direct threat to United States national security. Our efforts to halt the spread of nuclear weapons worldwide would be dealt a severe blow and the possible risk of US-Soviet confrontation would be enhanced.

"For these reasons, Israel's nuclear policy is a subject of great importance to us. It transcends considerations of purely bilateral significance to our two nations.

"We are aware of Israel's assurances—made publicly at the highest level of its government as well as to us privately—that Israel will not be the first area state to introduce nuclear weapons into the Middle East. We attach great weight to these assurances. But with the Nuclear Non-Proliferation Treaty in existence, unilateral assurances are no longer sufficient in themselves to give the world confidence that Israel does not intend to manufacture nuclear weapons.

"We are particularly troubled by Israel's continued delay in signing the NPT because of Israel's potential for nuclear weapons production. Israel is not just another state that for one reason or another is delaying its adherence to the Treaty. The world knows that unlike most other states Israel has the technical capability to build nuclear weapons. It knows that Israel has a 26 megawatt nuclear reactor capable of producing fissionable material in sufficient quantity to build bombs. It is

---

[2] See *Foreign Relations*, 1964–1968, volume XX, Arab-Israeli Dispute, 1967–1968. Documents 306, 308, 309, 317. and 330.

[3] See ibid., Document 333 and footnote 2 thereto.

also becoming aware that Israel has had developed and is acquiring surface-to-surface missiles capable of carrying nuclear warheads.

"Because of this proximity to the nuclear weapons threshold, Israel's attitude toward the NPT is being closely watched by other small and medium-sized states who are waiting to see whether nuclear weapons non-proliferation can be made to prevail as a global principle.

"We therefore attach utmost importance to Israel's early signature and ratification of the NPT. Last December, Prime Minister Eshkol wrote to President Johnson that Israel was studying the implications of Israel's adherence to the NPT.[4] We would welcome the Ambassador's comments concerning the conclusions the Government of Israel has reached.

"Upon reviewing the Ambassador's conversations with Assistant Secretary Warnke last November, we were struck by the evident difference between our two governments over what constitutes "introduction" of nuclear weapons. The Ambassador expressed the view, as we understand it, that a state could possess a nuclear explosive device but so long as that device was "unadvertised" and "untested" it could not be considered as having been "introduced".

"The U.S. Government cannot accept this interpretation of "introduction," as was made clear in Secretary Warnke's letter to the Ambassador concerning the F–4 sale. We would like to have Israel's assurance that when it says it will not be the first to introduce nuclear weapons into the area it means that it will not *possess* nuclear weapons.

"Israel has had developed and tested in France the so-called MD–620 or "Jericho" strategic missile which is capable of carrying a nuclear warhead. Some of the missiles remaining after tests are already in Israel.

"We are disturbed at Israel's acquisition of this missile because it makes sense to us only as a nuclear weapons carrier. We recognize that Israel claims that it can be used with other warheads; this is not, however, the way the world will see it. Whatever assurances Israel extends with respect to nuclear weapons will be seriously weakened by deployment of strategic nuclear-capable missiles.

"For this reason, we hope Israel will agree not to produce or deploy the Jericho missile. There is no sign of an active SSM program in any Arab country and no sign of Soviet interest in providing any of their Arab friends with assistance in either this or the nuclear weapons field."

Mr. Richardson summarized by noting we were asking (a) for the Ambassador's comments on the results of the GOI's study of the NPT

---

[4] See ibid., Document 349.

question, (b) for an assurance that "non-introduction" means "non-possession" of nuclear weapons and (c) for assurances about the production and deployment of the Jericho missile.

Concerning the NPT, Ambassador Rabin said he could only repeat what Prime Minister Eshkol had said in his December 4, 1968 letter to President Johnson—namely that Israel was studying the question of NPT signature. There had been no change in this respect in GOI policy. Rabin said the NPT had many aspects not directly related to the real problems of the Middle East. He had received instructions the previous day to the effect that Israel had not concluded its study and he is not authorized to comment before that study is completed. Deputy Secretary Packard asked if he could estimate when that would be. Rabin noted that there had been a Cabinet change in Israel and that the Government faced other issues which were more pressing and more immediate.

On the question of introducing nuclear weapons, Rabin said parenthetically he interpreted this as meaning introduction by Middle Eastern states, not by major powers which have them there already. First, Rabin continued, he wanted to clarify his November conversation with Warnke. When Warnke asked for an interpretation of "introduce" he (Rabin) had said he was not clear about the question and could not answer officially but would appreciate hearing the US interpretation from Warnke. Emphasizing that he personally had no knowledge of nuclear weapons, he had asked Warnke two questions: (a) Would Warnke consider an untested nuclear weapon to be an effective weapon? This would not be so in the case of conventional weapons. (b) Would Warnke consider a weapon, which had not been advertised and proven, to be a weapon that could be used? In asking these questions Rabin said he was seeking to learn the US interpretation; he was not representing the Israeli position. On the basic question of nuclear weapons in the Middle East, he could now only repeat his government's position that it would not be the first state in the Middle East to introduce such weapons.

Commenting on the Acting Secretary's oral statement, Rabin said he wanted to make clear that he was not accepting the US assumption that Israel has the capability to build nuclear weapons. He could say neither that Israel was capable nor that it was not. He wanted to note, however, that the US has arrangements with Israel of a kind that do not even exist between the US and its allies, and which demonstrate the extent to which Israel has given us the opportunity to have a close look at what Israel is doing in the nuclear field.

Mr. Richardson said that our purpose in raising the interpretation of the word "introduce" was not to reopen the Warnke-Rabin discussion but to note that the question had been left last November with no meeting of minds. This had been made specific when Warnke had agreed to amend the last line of his November 27 letter to Rabin to avoid any implication that Israel accepted the US interpretation. We now want to move beyond that point and are seeking Israel's concurrence in our interpretation. As stated in Warnke's letter, that interpretation is that "The physical possession and control of nuclear arms by a Middle Eastern power would be deemed to constitute the introduction of nuclear weapons." Concerning the NPT we are anxious to learn more about Israel's position. The risks inherent in nuclear proliferation bring the NPT into the foreground at this stage, given the movement toward signature and ratification. We are discussing the matter with the Soviets, Japanese and Germans, hence the timeliness of raising it with Israel also.

Rabin commented that following the President's European trip, Mr. Nixon had said the US would not twist any arms about signing the NPT, and understood the difficulties inherent in asking the West Germans to sign just before their elections.[5] Mr. Richardson said he would not want to engage in a semantic discussion. We have been discussing the matter with the Germans and think we have reasonable assurances that they will sign after their elections. We also think the Japanese will sign. Rabin replied that he was not saying that Israel would not sign but he could not say it would.

Rabin noted that there had been a recent US visit to Dimona[6] and that everything seemed to be working as agreed. The Acting Secretary said he would not wish to record any complaints about the Dimona visit in this conversation. Nevertheless, Dimona visits do not obviate our concern about nuclear weapons, missiles and the NPT. In this connection there were additional considerations to those he had already mentioned: (a) on the proliferation problem, Israel's position was pivotal for other countries; (b) in terms of US national interests, serious consequences were foreseeable if Israel introduced nuclear weapons. Specifically, the Soviets would feel compelled to come to the assistance of the Arabs in some way since the Arabs do not have a nuclear capability. Rabin repeated that Israel had given us assurances about its nuclear intentions. Mr. Richardson replied that, speaking bluntly, those assurances had been hedged. If "non-introduction" means only that the weapons will not be tested and advertised, we are on the brink of a serious situation. If "introduction" is defined in the narrowest possible sense, meaning that all but minimal final steps will have been taken,

---

[5] Nixon made these remarks in a press conference on March 4 after returning from his European trip. See *Public Papers: Nixon, 1969*, pp. 186–187.

[6] A U.S. inspection team visited the Dimona facility July 10–13. (Telegram 102256 to Tel Aviv, June 21; National Archives, Nixon Presidential Materials, NSC Files, Box 604, Country Files, Middle East, Israel, Vol. II)

then the situation is dangerous and potentially destabilizing. We see risks of a US-Soviet confrontation in the existing Middle East situation. Those risks would be increased radically if nuclear weapons were introduced; hence we feel compelled to raise this subject. Stating that he understood the Ambassador would need to consult his government, the Acting Secretary said he wanted to underscore the seriousness with which we view this matter. We would like to go beyond the point reached in the Rabin-Warnke talks.

Rabin concluded that, although the Israeli position is already well known, he would of course convey Mr. Richardson's comments to Jerusalem

42. Telegram From the Embassy in Israel to the Department of State[1]

Tel Aviv, July 31, 1969, 1615Z.

2941. Subj: Dimona Visit. Ref: State 124641.[2]

Summary: Ambassador July 31 told Prime Minister Meir that US team which visited Dimona early July had not been able to make full examination and requested further one-day visit next month. Mrs. Meir replied this impossible, since any departure from established routine would require action by Cabinet and Foreign Affairs Committee of Knesset, which was out of question in period before elections.[3]

1. In order present substance of reftel, Ambassador sought appointment with Prime Minister Meir early this week. Prime Minister could not arrange time until July 31 and meeting was held this afternoon. DCM accompanied Ambassador and DirGen PM's office Yaakov Herzog and Asst DirGen MFA Bitan also present. Conversation took about one hour.

---

[1] Source: National Archives, Nixon Presidential Materials, NSC Files, Box 604, Country Files, Middle East, Israel, Vol. II. Secret; Nodis. All brackets are in the original except those indicating garbled text.

[2] Not found.

[3] U.S. inspections of Dimona, which began in January 1964 under President Johnson, occurred roughly once per year. President Kennedy had insisted that U.S. representatives be allowed to inspect Dimona biannually, but neither he nor Johnson could persuade Prime Minister Eshkol to agree to such a timetable. Before the visit in July, a U.S. team had not inspected the facility since June 1968. (Telegram 36436 to Tel Aviv, March 8; National Archives. Nixon Presidential Materials, NSC Files, Box 604, Country Files, Middle East, Israel, Vol. I)

2. Amb began by reading from reftel at length. He noted especially that he had been connected with visits for some years, knew GOI problems, but felt that fact visits had become routine, perhaps too routine, had interfered with fundamental purpose for which they had been established. He also pointed out matter was one of substance, not hospitality, and team was pleased with cordial personal reception. Mrs. Meir said Israelis had also been well impressed by US team.

3. In reply to Amb's presentation, Mrs. Meir said she had been in on this matter from beginning. She had been at Ben Gurion's house first time he had to make decision to agree to visit,[4] and she knew how difficult it had been for him, first several visits had been made without knowledge rest of Cabinet, until press leak in *New York Times* (Amb interjected this had been from Israeli side) brought matter out and it had to be taken up in Cabinet and Knesset Foreign Affairs Committee, much to discomfiture of then Prime Minister, Eshkol. Since then Cabinet and ForAff Comite have always known about visits. She could not say that everyone had been extremely happy about visits, but what had enabled them to go on was fact that govt action would have had to be taken to stop them, and it had been possible to avoid this. This year US had suggested that visit be somewhat earlier, in view of coming elections, etc., but she had said no, let it go on on schedule, so that there will be no variance from established procedure and so no opportunity for basic decision to be called in question.

4. Now, Mrs. Meir went on, three months before elections, she was asked to go before Cabinet and Foreign Affairs Comite and raise this matter again. There have already been eight visits, since 1961. US naturally has sent whom it chose, they have looked, and nothing has been found. Is problem that they did not see something that was not there? It would be absolutely impossible to go to Cabinet on this now, to call in Foreign Affairs Comite, on eve of elections. It was not reasonable to ask this.

5. Amb replied he knew these domestic problems were serious but he was not sure that GOI realized how seriously USG regards whole nuclear question, not only with Israel but with whole world. Because of grave dangers, there are those in US who feel we must be prepared to believe the worst, in absence of contrary info, not only of Israel but of anyone. Problem boils down to whether Israel feels it important to disabuse doubters in this respect. As to previous visits, we had in each case accepted GOI groundrules but as record would show we had also been instructed each time to state that visit had not gone as well as had

---

[4] Documentation on U.S. concerns about the Dimona facility and Israeli Prime Minister Ben-Gurion's agreement to U.S. inspections is in *Foreign Relations, 1961–1963*, volume XVIII, Middle East, 1962–1963.

been hoped. Prime Minister Eshkol had been asked by President Kennedy for two-day visits every six months; Eshkol had not given written acceptance but had said orally that President's wishes were acceptable, and this had been taken as GOI agreement. Now visits have become so rushed that it is not possible for team to make report which would be in interests of GOI and USG to allay doubts.

6. Mrs. Meir said that she understood, but that it made [garble—her mad?]. A few weeks ago, USG had asked her to cooperate on question of Jordan, and she had gone along. She had been anxious to go along, and she did so. Since then, during July there had been 98 shelling incidents from across Jordan border, some by Jordanian Army but most by Fatah King had promised there would be no shooting, including by Fatah. Now Syrians have moved in six Russian 130 mm guns at Safi (just south of Dead Sea) with a 27 km range. Israel is surrounded on south, east and north. Iraqis and Saudi Arabians already in Jordan, and now Syrians have moved in. She did not know what importance to accord Eastern Command, but fact was Syrians were now there. Then there had been Nasser's speech,[5] and Brezhnev had sent him message saying USSR would supply UAR with everything needed to fight Israelis. But [garble—it?] is we (underline) who are the suspects in US eyes. This made her terribly sad.

7. Amb rejoined he understood her position but in nuclear equation we were talking about another world, completely different factors. It was not same thing. Potential of nuclear weapons was such that we cannot fail to regard them as separate business. This did not mean we did not understand Israel's need for conventional weapons. However, nuclear weapons were something else, and this is why we negotiated NPT and hope our friends will sign it, as some have. (Mrs. Meir interjected at least Israel was in good company, but Amb [garble—retorted?] not in such good company as those who signed.)

8. Prime Minister went on that everyone with any imagination could see horror of nuclear weapons, whether as user or target of them. Israel's problem, however, was how to keep alive in face of conventional weapons, to which every ounce of her energy and know how was devoted. She did not say that US was not justified in doing all it could to see that these horrible weapons should not be spread around world, but why Israel was under suspicion was hard for her to understand.

---

[5] On July 23, the 17th anniversary of the Egyptian Revolution, Nasser delivered a speech to the Arab Socialist Union in Cairo declaring that the United Arab Republic was passing to "the stage of liberation with Israel." He added: "We have to fight and we shall fight for the recovery of our lands . . . Israel is seeking to spread a sense of despair, that whatever we do there is no hope we can recover our rights. . . . Israel Must Be Defeated for the Good of Humanity." (*New York Times*, July 24, 1969, p. 1)

9. Amb replied he did not say any suspicion of Israel was justified but fact was that it existed and it was in interests US and Israel to remove it. Mrs. Meir then said she did not understand reference to statement US desired another visit to Dimona to take place prior to her visit to Washington. Had King Hussein been told he should stop shooting across border before coming to see President? Amb replied we had never said we thought he could do this completely but we welcomed his efforts to do it. Prime Minister rejoined if he cannot keep Syrians out of his country then he is not ruler and there is no reason to accept his word on anything. He has been invaded by three Arab countries and does nothing about it. But he is the best there is in Jordan, Amb interjected. She didn't care who was there, Mrs. Meir said, if he can't keep others out. She had nothing against him personally, but either there was someone in control who could be depended upon or there was nothing. Jordan was not Israel, Amb replied, and she was applying Israeli standards to it. There were many countries in world weak and shaky like Jordan.

10. Herzog then broke in that there had been two specific messages from King that he would insure that there was no firing. Amb rebutted we knew that would not work completely, that he could not carry that out. Can't he keep Syrians out, Mrs. Meir asked? Either they have come in against his will, and he should do something about it, or with his permission. Next he will have Egyptians in Jordan. Herzog said this was first time Syrians had managed to move in on Jordan, and first time since Six Day War that they had even tried. Lebanon can keep Syrians out, Mrs. Meir continued, but Jordan can't. She could understand it was more convenient for King Hussein to keep at peace with Syrians, but not at Israel's expense. Early this year, Herzog said, in Eshkol-Hussein exchange of messages, there had been clear indication that area at south end Dead Sea and Aqaba-Eilat were out of bounds. Safi (where Syrian guns alleged to be) is central to military control of whole Dead Sea area. Hussein had shown he could control them now. Dead Sea installations at Sedom, Prime Minister went on, represented investment 400 million Israeli pounds. (And big US investment, too, Amb noted) One shot at one of several vital points could put whole business out of operation for long, long time, yet there they are at Safi. US ought to have more things to do at such a time than search Israel for atomic bombs.

11. Amb said matter had to be looked at on broader scale. GOI was making problem by being mysterious. Visits had been set up for a purpose and had become so restricted that purpose not being accomplished.

12. DCM then said Prime Minister's feeling that Israel was object of some unique suspicion on part of USG was not justified. Most free world countries active in nuclear research field had reactors, fuel or other nuclear connections with US and in all such instances US insisted

on complete and continuous safeguards that go far beyond one-day-once-a-year visit to Dimona. Mrs. Meir countered that Dimona had not been bought from US and not fueled by US, so US had no reason to talk about safeguards on it. DCM replied he was not talking about applying safeguards to Dimona, but illustrating that suspicion was not unique against Israel but rather that there was no ally or friend so close but what US applies safeguards whenever it deals with them in nuclear field.

12. Herzog said that when Eshkol first went to Cabinet and told them about Dimona visits, he based his decision to carry on with visits on fact that commitment had already been made by Ben Gurion. Mrs. Meir said that if matter were now coming up for first time, she could not even consider asking Cabinet to concur in US visits to Dimona. She was able to carry on only because Eshkol had done it, and Eshkol had been able only because he could put it on Ben Gurion. If she had to go to Cabinet and Foreign Affairs Comite on matter, there would be no change.

13. Amb said he understood Prime Minister's problems but for final time he would say that rather than consider problems she should consider objective. Objective is to be able to have team produce airtight report that will leave no ground for doubt. If this is not done, doubts will remain. Prime Minister Meir replied she was terribly sorry if things had to turn out that way, but it was absolutely unthinkable, just impossible.

14. *Comment*: I pushed Prime Minister as hard as possible on this, especially on theme, which seems to me heart of matter, that purpose of visits is to establish to US satisfaction that nuclear weapons material not being produced at Dimona and that there is strong Israeli interest in seeing to it that this satisfaction is obtained. Domestic political problems which she adduces are real, and I imagine she is right in saying that this program continues only because, in finely balanced Israeli Cabinet, no one has ability to get majority decision to stop it. I would have preferred to separate out, in this message, parts dealing with Jordanian ceasefire and King Hussein, but they have to stay in because Dimona problem must be seen by US in context of overall situation here. Those in Cabinet who opposed Mrs. Meir on giving GOJ chance to control fedayeen (and there certainly must have been some) are same ones who would oppose relaxation on Dimona visits and make political capital in election campaign out of any discussion of this in Cabinet or committee. I therefore reluctantly conclude that we have done all we can at this time, and that there is no realistic possibility of another Dimona visit before Mrs. Meir's visit to Washington or Israeli elections in late October.

Barbour

43. Letter From the Representative to the United Nations (Yost) to the President's Assistant for National Security Affairs (Kissinger)[1]

New York, August 11, 1969.

Dear Henry:

I found your letter of July 22, in response to mine of July 9,[2] awaiting me on my return from Europe. I should hope very much we might get together soon to discuss this problem. Do you expect to be on the West Coast during most of the next month or will you be in Washington?

At this time I shall only comment on the two points you make. I think the difference in our approach may lie in the fact that you quite naturally look on our Middle Eastern negotiations primarily as one of a number of factors in our relations with the Soviets, while I am more concerned at this juncture with their effect on our relations with the Arabs. This is because, as long as we can prevent a direct military confrontation between the Soviets and ourselves in this area—and I am sanguine that we can—developments there will not be decisive in our relations with them. Developments there over the next year could very easily, however, be decisive in our relations with the Arabs, not only with the radicals but also with the moderates from Saudi Arabia through Jordan and Lebanon to Tunisia and Morocco.

If the conflict gradually sharpens over coming months—as it certainly will without a settlement—and if our negotiating position continues to be as one-sided as it has been—insisting on Arab acceptance of legitimate Israeli desiderata without any apparent willingness on our part to support legitimate Arab desiderata—, there are likely to be three consequences. First, the sharpening conflict will move more and

---

[1] Source: National Archives, Nixon Presidential Materials, White House Special Files, Subject Files, Box 5, Confidential Files 1969–74. Secret & Personal.

[2] On July 9, Yost wrote to Kissinger about his disappointment over the instruction that Sisco await further concessions before demonstrating any flexibility in his discussions with Soviet representatives regarding an Arab-Israeli settlement. In his July 22 reply, Kissinger wrote: "The Soviets and their clients bear a substantial responsibility for bringing on the 1967 war, and they lost it. The issue, therefore is: If there is to be a compromise settlement rather than full acquiescence in their demands, should we bear the onus for proposing the specific terms of the compromise or should they? Is it not their job—rather than ours on their behalf—to persuade the Israelis that they are ready to make peace? The other question your letter leaves unanswered is this: While time may not be working in our favor, will our loss from the passage of time compare with the USSR's?" (Both are ibid., NSC Files, Box 1170, Saunders Files, Middle East Negotiations Files, Middle East Settlement—US–USSR Talks, July 16–September 30, 1969)

more of the Arab governments into the radical posture, and threaten the survival of some that don't move.

Second, the already badly impaired U.S. position in the area will be further and heavily eroded. Third, more and more of the Arab governments will turn to the Soviets, as the great power supporting them most firmly and tangibly.

In answer to your specific question, I should therefore say that our loss from the passage of time is likely to be much more serious than that of the Soviets. Indeed the whole balance of power in the Arab world could in a relatively short time shift to our disadvantage.

All of this is without regard to who started the Six Day War and who should suffer for it. My own view is that the Israeli judgment of the best way to maintain their security is sadly mistaken and that in the long run, unless they change their policy, they will suffer more decisively than the Arabs because they cannot afford to suffer as much.

Of course it may well be that they are in no mood to be persuaded of this at the present time, either by us or anyone else. All that I am urging is that we work out rapidly with the Soviets, British and French the main outlines of a fair and reasonable settlement—"a just and durable peace"—and submit them to the parties through Jarring. This was the policy outlined by the President at the first NSC meeting I attended last winter[3] and I am still convinced it is the right one.

I believe moreover that we could complete the negotiation of such an outline with the other three within six weeks if we treated it as a matter of utmost urgency—which I am convinced it is. Whether the parties would thereafter accept it is quite another matter. But at the very least we would have demonstrated our bona fides and our impartiality, and thereby some of the dire consequences I fear flowing from the maintenance of our present immobility would be avoided.[4]

Sincerely yours,

Charles W. Yost[5]

---

[3] See Document 4.

[4] On September 6, Yost wrote a memorandum to Nixon arguing the same point, explaining that if U.S. efforts failed, "the United States would at least have made clear to all concerned that it had joined in presenting and supporting proposals which are fair to all, and its responsibility for failure, if they were rejected would be minimized." He added: "The Soviets would not be, as they are now the sole beneficiaries of the deepening crisis." (National Archives, Nixon Presidential Materials, Box 644, Country Files, Middle East, Middle East—General, Vol. I)

[5] Yost signed "Charlie" above his typed signature.

44. Memorandum for the Record[1]

San Clemente, California, August 25, 1969.

SUBJECT

Washington Special Actions Group Meeting, San Clemente, August 25, 1969

PARTICIPANTS

Dr. Kissinger
U. Alexis Johnson
Admiral Nels Johnson
G. Warren Nutter
John H. Holdridge
Thomas Karamessines

[Omitted here is discussion of Korean contingency plans and contingency plans for a Soviet attack on China.]

Middle East

1. It was agreed that an integrated paper was needed which would consider what to do to deter the Soviets, moving up the various situations from the least bad to the worst, noting that if deterral failed, then we would help the Israelis, and after going after Soviet LOCs, to face the decision of introducing US forces. The second draft of the papers would go through these considerations in detail.

---

[1] Source: Library of Congress, Manuscript Division, Kissinger Papers, Box TS–76, Committees and Panels, Washington Special Actions Group, July–August, 1969. Top Secret; Sensitive; Eyes Only. All brackets are in the original except those indicating text omitted by the editors. At the July 2 WSAG meeting, Kissinger asked Johnson "to see what could be done bureaucratically to set up a Middle East planning element." Johnson replied that he would "look into what has been done in Middle East planning in the recent past and under the former administration." At the August 8 WSAG meeting, the group decided that a Middle East scenario should be conceived "based on Arab attack of Israel, with Soviet military assistance extending beyond the now-existing border between the Arab States and Israel." Minutes of both meetings are ibid.

In National Security Decision Memorandum 19, July 3, Nixon directed that the political-military contingency plans prepared by NSC Interdepartmental Groups be forwarded to the Washington Special Actions Group. (Library of Congress, Manuscript Division, Kissinger Papers, Box CL–314, National Security Memoranda) The WSAG was created on May 16 when the President directed that the Interdepartmental Coordinating Committee on Korea "be constituted on a permanent basis in the event of future similar crises worldwide." Kissinger explained that Nixon "visualizes" that the WSAG would "confine itself to consideration of the policies and plans affecting crises." Furthermore, "implementation of policy decisions and coordination of operations" would be "conducted through the interagency Crisis Task Forces prescribed by the Under Secretaries Committee under the authority of NSDM 8." (Memorandum from Kissinger to Rogers, Laird, and Helms, May 16; ibid.) For NSDM 8, dated March 21, and Kissinger's May 16 memorandum, see *Foreign Relations,* 1969–1976, volume II, Organization and Management of U.S. Foreign Policy, 1969–1972, Documents 31 and 45.

2. Dr. Kissinger felt that the best thing to do might be to make the Soviets fight in the Middle East rather than in Iran or Turkey. Admiral Johnson pointed out that our biggest problem is where we operate from, most advanced bases would be ruled out for one reason or another and we might have to fall back as far as the Azores.

3. Mr. Holdridge left the meeting at this point with Mr. Karamessines in order to make a flight back to Washington from Los Angeles.

John H. Holdridge

45. Memorandum From the President's Assistant for National Security Affairs (Kissinger) to President Nixon[1]

San Clemente, California, August 28, 1969.

SUBJECT

Memorandum from Secretary Laird on the Arab/Israeli conflict

Mel Laird sent me the attached memo (Tab A)[2] on the Arab/Israeli conflict.

The most interesting section of the paper concerns military sales to Israel (Section 5). In summary, it states that:

1. Further sales to Israel will almost certainly be seen as escalating the arms race.

2. US-supplied equipment will be used in retaliatory strikes, including strikes against civilian targets such as the East Ghor Canal.

3. The Israelis will accept no restrictions on the use of the equipment. They have turned down some cluster bombs because we tried to restrict their use.

---

[1] Source: National Archives, Nixon Presidential Materials, NSC Files, Box 654, Country Files, Middle East, UAR, Vol. I. Top Secret; Sensitive. Sent for information. Both Nixon and Kissinger were at the Western White House in San Clemente.

[2] Attached but not printed at Tab A is the August 22 memorandum in which Laird wrote: "The present situation in the Middle East is of grave concern to the Department of Defense. Because of the rather sizeable Middle Eastern involvement of the Department of Defense in matters ranging from U.S. military bases to the sale of arms, we are giving constant attention to the relationship of military to political questions in this region, especially as these matters relate to the Arabi-Israeli dispute. In this connection, I am sending to you a short report, prepared by OSD/ISA, on the nature of the Arab-Israeli conflict and Department of Defense interest in the Middle East." On the memorandum itself, Laird handwrote: "Henry, I do feel this report is well done and wanted you to have it—Mel" The undated report is attached but not printed.

4. The sale of sophisticated equipment carries the implied obligation to continue supply regardless of the Israeli use of the equipment.

5. As we continue to supply nuclear capable equipment (Phantom jet fighters) our leverage on the Israeli nuclear program decreases.

46. Editorial Note

On August 29, 1969, members of the Popular Front for the Liberation of Palestine (PFLP) hijacked a TWA aircraft bound for Athens, Greece and forced it to land in Damascus, Syria. While the Syrian Government permitted TWA, an American-based airline, to take most of the flight's passengers and its crew on to their final destinations and elsewhere, it detained six Israelis, who remained in Damascus with the damaged aircraft and its captain. Because Syria had severed diplomatic relations with the United States during the Arab-Israeli war of 1967, the Department of State relied upon the Government of Italy, which represented U.S. interests in Syria, and other governments and international organizations to help resolve the matter. (Department of State press statement, August 30; Department of State *Bulletin,* September 15, 1969, page 246; telegram 147543 to Tel Aviv, August 31, published in *Foreign Relations,* 1969–1976, volume E–1, Documents on Global Issues, 1969–1972, Document 12)

Assistant Secretary of State Joseph Sisco asked Shlomo Argov, Minister of the Israeli Embassy, if the Government of Israel wanted to delay the delivery of the U.S. Phantoms, due to arrive on September 5, because of the incendiary effect the shipment might have in Syria and what that might mean for the hostages. The Minister responded: "to raise this question with Jerusalem at this time would be QTE like pouring high octane gasoline on a fire, UNQTE" and the delivery proceeded as scheduled. (Telegram 147567 to Tel Aviv, September 1; National Archives, Nixon Presidential Materials, NSC Files, Box 604, Country Files, Middle East, Israel, Vol. II)

Tensions between the Governments of the United States and Israel emerged over the Israeli detainees when the Israeli press quoted Israeli Prime Minister Golda Meir as saying that "it was inconceivable that airline such as TWA would abandon passengers in Syria." (Telegram 3336 from Tel Aviv, August 31; ibid.) In response, Ambassador Walworth Barbour told Israeli representatives to "keep matters in perspective and not get confused as to who was committing crimes and who trying to help situation." (Telegram 3350 from Tel Aviv, September 1; ibid.) By

September 2, U.S. efforts led to the release of all but two male Israeli passengers, over whom negotiations stalled, while the airplane's captain remained in Damascus because TWA and the Nixon administration feared the repercussions of a bitter reaction from Israel to his release alone. (Memorandum from Rogers to Nixon, September 2; *Foreign Relations*, 1969–1976, volume E–1, Documents on Global Issues, 1969–1972, Document 15; telegram 3588 from Tel Aviv, September 18; National Archives, Nixon Presidential Materials, NSC Files, Box 604, Country Files, Middle East, Israel, Vol. II)

Meanwhile, the International Committee of the Red Cross monitored the condition of the hostages, assuring the U.S. Government that they were being treated well, and the Nixon administration worked to keep Israel from taking any action that might inflame the situation. As for the hijackers, they were expected to be tried by the Syrian Government. (Memorandum from Eliot to Kissinger, September 19, published in *Foreign Relations*, 1969–1976, volume E–1, Documents on Global Issues, 1969–1972, Document 22)

On November 6, Director General of Israel's Ministry of Foreign Affairs, Gideon Rafael, informed the Embassy in Tel Aviv that the Government of Israel had decided to pursue an ICRC-engineered, three-cornered, POW exchange with the United Arab Republic to obtain the release of the Israeli hostages. (Telegram 4196 from Tel Aviv, November 6; ibid., Document 32) A "gratified" Department of State offered to facilitate the exchange, which included the United Arab Republic's release of two Israeli pilots and Syria's release of the two remaining TWA passengers in return for Israel's release of one Egyptian pilot, 17 Egyptian POWs from the 1967 war, the crews of two Egyptian fishing vessels captured in Israeli waters, 11 Egyptian civilians kidnapped in raids, and two Syrian pilots held by Israel. (Telegram 189503 to Tel Aviv, November 8; National Archives, Nixon Presidential Materials, NSC Files, Box 605, Country Files, Middle East, Israel, Vol. III; and telegram 194183 to Beirut, November 19; ibid., Box 620, Country Files, Middle East, Lebanon, Vol. I)

By the third week of November, no action had been taken, and the deal appeared to be in jeopardy when the Syrian Government raised the stakes, demanding that 11 additional Syrians detained in Israel be released. (Telegram 4348 from Tel Aviv, November 20, published in *Foreign Relations*, 1969–1976, volume E–1, Documents on Global Issues, 1969–1972, Document 33; telegram 4363 from Tel Aviv, November 24; National Archives, Nixon Presidential Materials, NSC Files, Box 605, Country Files, Middle East, Israel, Vol. III) Israel's delay in providing a written guarantee to the ICRC at the end of November put the deal further at risk, but everything fell into place on December 5, when the hijacked TWA aircraft carrying the two Israelis was allowed to leave, arriving in Athens at 3:35 p.m. local time. (Telegram 199600 to Tel Aviv, November 28, telegram 4480 from Tel Aviv, December 5, and telegram 5378 from Athens; all ibid.)

47. Memorandum From the President's Assistant for National Security Affairs (Kissinger) to President Nixon[1]

Washington, September 10, 1969.

SUBJECT

The Next Step in the Middle East—NSC Meeting Thursday, September 11

The following is an analysis of the major issues which may become obscured amidst all of the negotiating detail you will hear at the NSC meeting. In addition to giving you the basis for a decision, this meeting will also provide guidance for Secretary Rogers in his first talks with Eban, Gromyko and the Arab foreign ministers in New York. Joe Sisco will propose that we tell Gromyko we will take the position that Israel should return to the pre-war boundary with Egypt *provided* Gromyko can commit Nasser to direct negotiations with Israel and firm arrangements for securing that border and Israel's passage through the Tiran Straits and the Suez Canal. Although you approved the draft document which Joe has been negotiating from,[2] you have never had an opportunity to consider the details of an overall settlement.

As I see it, there are four major and one minor considerations:

1. The US cannot proceed on an Israel-UAR settlement alone. If we are going to press for a settlement, it must include Jordan:

—We have a much greater interest in getting our friend Hussein's territory back than Nasser's because of Hussein's moderate and pro-Western position.

—The Soviets and Nasser would not agree to a UAR-Israel settlement alone.

2. If the US is going to take a stand on the elements of a general settlement, we must be prepared to press hard for their acceptance.

---

[1] Source: National Archives, Nixon Presidential Materials, NSC Files, Box 644, Country Files, Middle East, Middle East—General. Secret; Nodis. Printed from an uninitialed copy.

[2] See Documents 37 and 39.

—If we just state our position without following up, we will have alienated Israel and won little favor with the Arabs. They believe we could move Israel if we wanted to, so they would regard any US position as hypocritical if we did not stop backing Israel with arms. In other words, proceeding along the line State proposes would involve a commitment to Israel's pre-war borders (with only minor modifications except on the Syrian Heights) *and* the willingness to stop the sale of arms if necessary. If we are not prepared to impose a settlement, it will not happen.

—Israel will not be satisfied even if we win Nasser's commitment to direct negotiations (the State formula). Israel wants to bargain with Nasser for an Israeli position at Sharm al-Shaikh and with Hussein for a position on the West Bank. Only strong US pressure, if that, has a chance of moving Israel away from that position.

3. If the US believes continuation of the present situation is dangerous and erodes our position in the Mid-East but if we are not prepared to try to impose a settlement, then we must consider whether there is anything we can do in the absence of a settlement to make the situation less dangerous for us. There are several possibilities, none too bright:

—Try for some understanding with the USSR that would limit US–USSR engagement if there is another Arab-Israeli clash.

—Take a strong US stand for a refugee settlement.

—Concentrate on a Palestine settlement, leaving aside the UAR and encouraging an agreement between Israel and the West Bank Palestinians.

4. There is also the Israeli nuclear issue. You have authorized an approach to the Israelis which was designed as a first step toward getting their commitment not to deploy strategic missiles or nuclear warheads.[3] State and Defense believe—though you have not approved this—that we should cut off their arms supply if they do not comply. Rabin stonewalled our first approach, saying in effect that he expected this issue to be on your agenda with Mrs. Meir and that the Israeli government would be unlikely to make any decision before its October 28 election. One of the consequences of pursuing an Arab-Israel settlement that would require Israel to give up the security provided by expanded borders is that we would probably have to relax on the nuclear issue.

The *minor issue* is that your talks with Mrs. Meir will take place September 25–26. I do not see how we could take the step State proposes with Gromyko before you talk with her.

---

[3] See Document 38.

In short, I do not believe the State Department proposal—giving Gromyko our position on boundaries—should be approved until we have studied its consequences and are prepared to deal with them.

The argument in detail for and against stating a precise US position on where the boundaries should be goes as follows:

The *argument for* taking this step includes these points:

1. If we continue on the present diplomatic track, we have almost no chance of movement toward a negotiated settlement.

2. In the continued absence of a settlement, the moderates in the Middle East will be under increasing pressure from the radicals. This does not mean that moderate regimes such as those in Lebanon and Saudi Arabia might be upset solely because of the Arab-Israeli impasse. It does mean, however, that the continued impasse gives the radicals another issue on which to stand in their efforts to weaken those moderate regimes. If the impasse does not cause their downfall, it may speed it. Thus, the US would have to look forward to a gradual erosion of friendly regimes and a gradual broadening of the Soviet influence in the area.

3. The proposal being made perhaps does not even offer a 50–50 chance of success. What it offers is (a) a further test of Soviet willingness to press Nasser toward serious negotiation and (b) in the process an opportunity for the US to state its view on the terms of a fair Arab-Israeli settlement. As part of the diplomatic move being proposed, it would be planned that our suggestion be made known to the Arab regimes involved.

4. In addition to offering the only possible prospect in sight for a breakthrough toward negotiations, we would be in a better position to ride out the protracted absence of an Arab-Israeli settlement in the broader Middle East if we were standing on our own statement of what the terms of a fair settlement would be than we would be if we continued to hold essentially to the Israeli position. To state no precise US position and to maintain that the Middle Easterners themselves must work out the terms of a settlement is to state an essentially Israeli position. In fact, we are telling the Arabs and Israelis that we will not put US influence on the bargaining scales and that we will leave the Israelis free to put the full weight of their territorial conquest and their military power in the scales on the negotiating table.

As I see them, the *consequences of taking this step* would be as follows:

1. Stating a precise US position on the UAR alone and not on Jordan would put us in a position of spending our influence to help Nasser while leaving our friend Hussein with a divided country. We must decide what we are going to do on the Jordan front before we can

decide whether to make this move. The Jordan settlement is even more difficult territorially than the Sinai. It would be very difficult to allow the Arabs back within 12 miles of Tel Aviv and all but impossible for them to give the Arabs a significant role in Jerusalem.

2. The Israelis would probably reject our proposition, even if we won Nasser's commitment to negotiate face to face. The Israelis would argue that by depriving them of their main bargaining counter—that is, by committing them in advance of negotiation to withdraw to the prewar UAR-Israel boundary—we have made negotiations meaningless. They will ask: What is left for them to negotiate?

3. Even if the Israelis were inclined to accept, the Arabs would probably undercut the significance of their agreement to negotiate directly (a) by claiming that they are just meeting to sign an already negotiated document and (b) by taking positions that would deny Israel the security arrangements that would make such a border tenable. We would then have isolated Israel without contributing anything of our own toward a settlement. We would thus have given the Arabs and Soviets what they want—an isolated Israel—and all we would have gained in return is the major political reaction in the US that the Israelis would have stirred up.

4. Even if the Israelis and Arabs were inclined to accept, the Soviets would still be in the driver's seat. A lot would depend on what we assess their motives to be. At the very least, they could take credit for having extracted concessions from us. If they want to, they can outbid us by pressing for total return of all conquered territory, including the Syrian heights.

5. If our move failed to produce negotiation, we would gain little in Arab goodwill. The Israelis want to bargain for the expansion of their territory, and the Arabs refuse to accept peace on those conditions. The problem for Israel is whether to withdraw and gamble on a settlement with Arab governments that may not survive to fulfill their obligations (which at best will be less than perfect even if fulfilled) or whether to hold on to territory as the only means of guaranteeing their own security. The only way, therefore, that we could make a negotiation succeed is to press Israel hard to make its choice in favor of the gamble on withdrawal with security arrangements. If we failed to exert serious pressure on the Israelis—such as threatening to cut its supply of arms or flow of financial support—the Arabs would immediately question the credibility of the position we had stated on the terms of a settlement.

In short, the principal risk of proceeding as State proposes is that we would provoke a major domestic political storm—including increased opposition on Vietnam and on defense—with only a very limited hope of producing movement toward serious Arab-Israeli negotiations in return. Any Arab goodwill we hoped for would be lost if we continued military supply to Israel.

Therefore, I conclude that *our real choice* is between staying on our present course or making an all-out effort now to press Israel to accept what we regard as reasonable terms of a settlement. To make that decision, I believe you should ask State for:

1. the precise terms of an Israel-UAR settlement, including those which would provide reasonable security for Israel;
2. the terms of a Jordan-Israel settlement;
3. a position on Syria.

If you do not have those before authorizing a move, you will not have a chance to see where the move might take us and you will have little chance of keeping our negotiators within the limits of your policy.

The other dimension of this problem is how the Mid-East negotiations fit into our broader relationship with the USSR. I believe the bargaining advantage lies slightly on our side in that Nasser would lose in another war, although we must face the general judgment that our position in the Mid-East gradually becomes more difficult as the present impasse continues.

There are several possible ways to relate this with other issues on the US–USSR agenda:

1. If we were going to press Israel to accept unpalatable measures, we might expect the Soviets to press Nasser to accept some equally unpalatable terms.
2. If the terms are going to be harder for Israel than for the UAR to accept, then we might look to other areas for compensating Soviet pressure on their clients such as the North Vietnamese. Another possibility would be some sort of understanding about the limits of Soviet imperialistic ambitions in the Mid-East, Persian Gulf, Indian Ocean.

Whether the Soviets will respond depends heavily on how they view their situation in the area. It is common for us to assume that time helps them and hurts us, but there are enough disadvantages in this situation and advantages in a settlement to give us some leverage. With a settlement, they could pursue their interests without risk of war, get their fleet into the Indian Ocean and still have enough tension points like the Persian Gulf to exploit. The balance is fine enough however that they might cooperate with us in pressing a reasonable proposal on the Arabs. They apparently judge that pressing our present proposals would cost them too much in Cairo. Given this delicate a balance and our inability to press the Israelis beyond certain limits, it may be that on this issue we are negotiating in a relatively narrow field.

I would recommend that you issue the following instructions in connection with the meeting:

1. Nothing should be done until after Mrs. Meir's visit. Secretary Rogers should be instructed privately to divide his talks in New York into two phases—first, purely exploratory talks before the Meir visit and then perhaps a series of more specific talks afterwards when you have decided what our course should be. (I know Joe Sisco agrees with this.)

2. Well before the Meir visit, the following should be submitted to you: detailed US positions on the terms of Jordan-Israel and UAR-Israel, including adequate security provisions for Israel, and a position on Syria.

3. CIA should provide an assessment of the Soviet's true attitude toward a settlement with Israel.

48. Minutes of a National Security Council Meeting[1]

Washington, September 11, 1969.

MIDDLE EAST

PARTICIPANTS

The President
The Secretary of State, William P. Rogers
The Attorney General, John N. Mitchell
The Chairman, Joint Chiefs of Staff, General Earle G. Wheeler
The Director of Central Intelligence, Richard M. Helms
Dr. Henry A. Kissinger
Under Secretary of State, Elliot L. Richardson
Deputy Secretary of Defense, David Packard
US Ambassador to the UN, Charles Yost
Assistant Secretary of State, Joseph J. Sisco
Director, Office of Emergency Preparedness, General George A. Lincoln
Colonel Alexander Haig
Helmut Sonnenfeldt
Harold H. Saunders
Alfred L. Atherton, Jr., Department of State
Clinton Conger, CIA

---

[1] Source: National Archives, Nixon Presidential Materials, NSC Files, NSC Institutional Files (H-Files), Box H–109, NSC Meeting Minutes, NSC Minutes Originals 1969. Top Secret; Nodis. All brackets are in the original except those indicating text that remains classified. According to the President's Daily Diary, the meeting was held in the Cabinet Room from 10:17 a.m. to 12:24 p.m. (Ibid., White House Central Files)

Helms: Arab-Israeli problem has gotten steadily worse over last two years. Four-Power talks recessed since early July in favor of US–USSR talks. USSR has probably told Nasser some compromise necessary. Al Aqsa Mosque burning increased Arab frustration.[2] Situation compels moderate Arabs to take a more active military posture.

Israel has adopted "no budge" position. Israel's attitude on borders getting progressively harder. May reflect Meir-Dayan deal to keep Dayan in Labor Party.

Intelligence estimate on military balance: Israeli superiority becoming even more pronounced—Jericho missile, Phantom delivery, [*less than 1 line not declassified*]. Retaliatory strikes doing Arabs more damage—deliberately. Raids these days are for keeps—no prisoners.

On the Arab side, governing factor remains military incompetence. Some progress being made—partly to compete with terrorists.

Palestinians have kept Lebanon without a government since April. Not a military threat but getting "deep into the Israeli psyche." Al Fatah increasing operations but main focus on PFLP with about 500 members. Terrorist position: no settlement until Israel driven into the sea. Their position may make it impossible for some Arab leaders to reach settlement.

Rogers: US–USSR talks have concentrated on UAR-Israel settlement to make Jordan settlement easier.

President: When we speak of Soviet client states, are we speaking of UAR, Syria, Iraq. Israel-Jordan US clients. USSR does not have close contact with Jordan?

Rogers: Hussein doesn't feel he is our client now.

Sisco: USSR showing increased interest in getting into Jordanian aspects of a settlement. US under increasing pressure from Hussein to involve itself in Israel-Jordan settlement.

---

[2] On August 21, a fire broke out in Jerusalem's al Aqsa mosque, one of Islam's holiest sites. During the first two weeks of September, representatives of Arab and non-Arab Muslim countries negotiated the text of a resolution for the UN Security Council that both condemned the arson and reiterated Israel's occupier status. On September 12, Pakistan introduced a resolution that satisfied all of the Muslim countries. (Telegram 2885 from USUN, September 5 and telegram 3007 from USUN, September 12; ibid.) Three days later, 11 members of the Security Council voted for Resolution 271 and 4 abstained, the United States, Finland, Colombia, and Paraguay. (Telegram 3031 from USUN, September 15; ibid.) The text of the resolution, which reaffirmed the "established principle that acquisition of territory by military conquest is inadmissible," is in *Yearbook of the United Nations, 1969*, pp. 221. An official Israeli Commission of Inquiry concluded that the Al Aqsa fire was the result of "malicious arson" and was a "grievous insult to religious feeling of entire Moslem community." (Telegram 3658 from Tel Aviv, September 24; National Archives, Nixon Presidential Materials, NSC Files, NSC Institutional Files (H-Files), Box H–109, NSC Meeting Minutes, NSC Minutes Originals 1969)

Rogers: When we talk about face-to-face discussions, no problem with Jordan.

Sisco: I came away from Moscow judging: Soviets want to continue dialogue with US for both Mid-East and general reasons.[3] Question is how Soviets view the area: If area undergoing increasing radicalization, does Moscow view this as in USSR interest.

US–USSR agreement in talks on the following:

—Israel and UAR would sign same agreement.
—Recognition of Israel's right to exist.
—Freedom of passage through Tiran. On Suez, USSR has qualified by reference to Constantinople Convention of 1888.[4]
—Execution of agreement would await agreement on total package—UAR, Israel and possible Jordan.
—We have agreed on the principle of demilitarization.

Soviet plan:

1. Israeli withdrawal 40 miles.
2. Opening Canal.
3. Israeli withdrawal to June 4 lines and Gaza Strip.
4. Demilitarization of Negev-Sinai border. Seem willing to accept only token demilitarization on Israeli side.
5. Irrevocable UN force at Sharm al-Shaikh.

Position US has taken:

1. Within context of agreement, Israeli withdrawal to "secure and recognized border" to be defined by parties. We "do not exclude" prewar border.
2. Demilitarization of entire Sinai.
3. Options for Sharm al-Shaikh. Let parties negotiate Kept open Israeli presence.
4. Ultimately, sovereignty of Gaza would have to be determined by Jordan, UAR, Israel.

President: To what extent does that reflect Israeli views.

Sisco: They have seen our position. Israelis have opposed, but if they got this they would like it.

Kissinger: What makes you think they would like it? No evidence.

Sisco: Subjective judgment.

Rogers: When Israel really opposes something, they "let us have it with 10 barrels," but they haven't. I think Israel would be happy if they got this much.

President: British and French attitude?

---

[3] Sisco was in Moscow for talks July 14–18. See Document 39.

[4] This multilateral treaty guaranteed the right of free passage through the Suez Canal.

Sisco: Total demilitarization unrealistic, ought to be demilitarization on Israeli side. UN presence. French and British want to improve their position with Arabs.

President: Israelis don't trust UN.

Rogers: We're going to be isolated.

Sisco: Operational issue: Rogers will be talking Mid-East with 50 foreign ministers at UN. Question: Do we state our judgment that final border should be pre-war UAR-Israel border, to be agreed in direct negotiations.

Israeli argument: You have given away our counter.

Counter argument: Erosion of US position.

Questions:

1. What would we get in return from USSR.
2. What from Arabs.
3. Israeli reaction.

Problem is whether we could produce the Israelis. Mrs. Meir will object.

Rogers: Say what is our proposal on Tiran.

Sisco: We've let it open. UN presence logical, but Israelis won't buy.

Yost: Device would be UN couldn't be withdrawn without UNSC consent.

Richardson: No settlement if Israelis stay at Sharm al-Shaikh. Israelis determined to stay.

President: "Do you fellows ever talk to the Israelis?"

Kissinger: Israelis want presence at Sharm al-Shaikh with land access to it. If the Israelis accept principle of full withdrawal, it would hurt them more in Jordan.

President: What does USSR want? Leave it like it is?

Sisco: 1. They want to continue talks as a deterrent in the Mid-East.

2. As long as they talk, this is a demonstration to Arabs that they are trying to help.

3. Be responsive to Nixon "era of negotiations."

Rogers: They think they have brought Arabs farther than we have brought Israelis.

President: Don't Soviets know Arabs will be beaten in another war. "If they get screwed again, they won't have another Glassboro[5] to bail them out?"

---

[5] Reference is to the Glassboro Summit between President Johnson and Soviet Chairman Alexei Kosygin that took place in Glassboro, New Jersey, in June 1967, following the 1967 Arab-Israeli war. See *Foreign Relations, 1964–1968*, volume XIV, Soviet Union, Documents 217, 218, 219, 220, 221, 222, 223, 224, 225, 226, 227, 228, 229, 230, 231, 232, 233, 234, 235, 236, 237, and 238.

Helms: They really want to get down to Persian Gulf.

President: In 1967, Soviets looked unready to help Arabs. If this happened again, Soviets don't want to be in that position. Do they really believe—given that fact—that they consider this worth a US–USSR confrontation? Do they think this is about the best they can get now? They want talks to continue, but a settlement?

Sisco: They want settlement on own terms. Soviets want Nasser as their own tool. They haven't wanted to press him.

President: How is USSR doing in Mid-East? Not bad—some weak reeds but still not bad.

Sisco: We have interest in stable peace. Less clear USSR sees this as its interest.

President: USSR can have influence while situation simmers. Does anybody think US as its friend? June war a tremendous victory for Israel and USSR. From their viewpoint why change the situation. Does Moscow think they're going to have confrontation with US over Israel? "You know damn well we're not and they know it." Do you think they want a deal?

Sisco: Not a deal that would cost Moscow much.

President: We're the honest brokers here.

Rogers: Could have a settlement that would continue exploitable tension. Meanwhile, they have isolated us from world community.

President: "Israel's puppet."

Richardson: One aspect in which USSR might want real settlement. Present situation continued strengthens fedayeen, weakens Nasser. Soviets less able to deliver if fedayeen come out on top, Soviets less able to deliver Arab demands which would then be not just return of territory but destruction of Israel.

President: Agree but if fedayeen prevail, they too would keep situation stirred up. Soviets have to have some reason to want to settle; what is it?

Rogers: If war broke out again, their clients would lose. Our hope is that they want to avoid a war.

Helms: USSR wants to open Canal to get into Persian Gulf.

Yost: On balance, USSR wants settlement but not going to jeopardize their influence. They could even shift support to fedayeen and try to ride that wave.

What concerns me is extent to which we are in trouble with moderate Arabs. Soviets without lifting a finger are profiting. Formula asking Arabs at outset to come to direct negotiations is a non-starter.

Situation is weakening moderate regimes and not increasing Israel's security. Even Moroccans and Tunisians getting worried about US position—has not gone very far yet.

Kissinger: Soviets may have interest in Israel-UAR settlement because continued occupation of Sinai demonstrates USSR impotence. They want naval access to Persian Gulf. Plenty of tension will remain. They may see their opportunity in transitional regimes in Arabian Peninsula. I can see Soviet gains from a settlement.

Problem of concentrating on UAR-Israel settlement is that our friend, Hussein, comes off worse than Nasser.

Sisco: We have not presented our Jordan views to USSR. Gromyko wants to talk about Jordan.

Kissinger: We haven't told Israel our views on Jordan?

Sisco: Yes.

President: More on flavor at UN?

Yost: We would improve our position if we put forward fair terms.

Kissinger: If we propose and Israelis refuse, do we then continue Phantom delivery? What do we gain with Arabs then? We won't be accused of hypocrisy?

Yost: Yes but better off than now.

Richardson: We have to put both sides in a position of being responsible for failure.

Kissinger: If we go this route, don't we have to bite the bullet and go all out for a settlement?

Richardson: We do have to face up to situation.

Rogers: This proposal wouldn't be accepted by Arabs right away.

Sisco: Keep our proposal linked to direct negotiations. That would force Soviets to deliver something uncomfortable.

Yost: We could get to direct negotiations but not as a sine qua non.

Sisco: Not sine qua non as start. If the principle is there, that's all we're asking for.

President: Isn't real Israeli position to "keep it like it is?"

Sisco: Agree. They'd like to see us isolated with Israel.

President: Why are we having Mrs. Meir come here?[6]

Lincoln: US going to have to think increasingly about airplanes.

President: We have these visits—Hussein thought we agreed he should have territory back.[7] She just wants to talk to Jewish community—"she doesn't give one damn about us. I don't know. I've never met her." What do we say to her? Keep our position "exploratory" until after she comes. How can Rogers protect our position.

---

[6] Meir was in the United States from September 24 to October 6.
[7] See Document 19.

Rogers: I suggest no decisions this morning. I can stick on two issues in opening talks—peace and Arab obligations and then direct negotiations. Say then we can't go much further if Arabs want to drive Israel into the sea.

Yost: Arabs could say: If we do such and such, what will you do?

President: Those state visits are generally "a waste of time." I'd like to see us make a couple of specific points. Could we discuss specific terms of Israeli settlements with UAR, Jordan and Syria. Doesn't it make sense for us to get down to specifics? We need some positions they ought to accept.

I don't want to save the face of the USSR; they aren't trying to help us anywhere. I don't see why we should help them. That doesn't mean all their interests are different from ours. In developing our position, let's not give them a chance to claim credit for getting everything back for the Arabs. Mistake to "allow them to look too good."

Mitchell: Looking at our domestic interest, if we took away negotiating base of Israelis, it would take away base for your position on Vietnam and a lot of other issues.

Yost: Press reaction now saying US should do more.

Mitchell: No question. But if we undercut Israelis, "we're going to catch hell all over this country." Look at long-term pull: what are we going to get out of the Arabs in the long term?

Rogers: We have a lot of interests there. Arabs think we won't do anything unless Israel agrees.

President: We have a curious thing politically. But in terms of votes, that influences this Administration less than anything that has been here. I got lowest percent of Jewish vote of any candidate, in US history—8%. What we're really talking about is history in Mid-East. Problem is not votes.

Mitchell: Problem is how this affects Vietnam.

Rogers: In this situation, if we had a posture that seemed reasonable . . . we're not going to win either way.

Mitchell: Yes—I prefaced my statement by saying "if we undercut their position."

Yost: Our position in Israel's long-term interest.

President: Keep UN posture as low as possible so as not to preclude serious discussion with Mrs. Meir.

We should know before she comes our position on:

1. UAR-Israel settlement
2. Jordan-Israel settlement
3. Syria-Israel settlement

Rogers: I'll draw Gromyko out in first meeting. Second meeting will be after Meir visit.[8]

President: Let's leave out Jewish community for a moment. Israel's position short range is unassailable, long range disastrous. I don't like just to sit here and go through the motions with Mrs. Meir. Don't go ahead until we talk to her.

Mitchell: Will Israeli position change after election?

Kissinger: Not much. Physical security is very attractive when all we offer in return are agreements with regimes that may not survive. That is Israeli dilemma.

Yost: They don't have security now.

Kissinger: In a historical perspective, no way 3 million people can survive in the midst of 60 million hostile people unless they can change that hostility.

Richardson: Their future depends on help. They can't expect our help when our position deteriorates.

Kissinger: If any terms are fair, we will have to impose them.

President: Yes, but let's do it gradually.

On delivery of jets: Looking at "menacing Soviet naval building in the area" and future Israeli difficulty in beating Arabs, I don't think we should leave the impression that—in the event of a protracted war—the US will help.

If we determine that we want a settlement, we may have to cut off arms supply. But Israel is just about tough enough to say, "So be it." Masada complex.

We must be better prepared for this talk than for any we've had so far. Have an extended talk with Gromyko.

Rogers: We will give you a memo in next three or four days.[9]

President: What about Congress?

Sisco: Balancing act. On whole, reaction good because they think we're trying while protecting Israeli security. Jewish community relatively quiet.

President: Leaving aside the votes or Jewish community, American public is pro-Israeli. Yet the US public would not support US intervention to save Israel.

Rogers: Rabin says: Could handle USSR short of nuclear weapons or land invasions.

---

[8] See Document 53 for a summary of Rogers's meetings with Gromyko in New York.

[9] Not found.

President: Do we have a position on hijacking—international law, etc. Very few of our allies help us. Airlines, other governments not facing up to this sort of thing—Elbrick kidnapping.[10] We may have to do something on our own.

Yost: Finns thinking about bringing issue to UN.

President: Could I say something about general issue at UN? Worldwide problem of violent methods.

Rogers: On the ambassador kidnapping, have follow-up car.

President: Do it.

To Mitchell: We should have for any state visitor federal legislation to keep demonstrators away. Foreign governments go to great lengths when we visit to avoid embarrassment.

Mitchell: There is legislation on domestic demonstrations at White House and Capitol.

President: But foreign visitors. Under Bill of Rights, hard to distinguish. Would you, John, assume responsibility to negotiate arrangements with local police.

---

[10] On September 4 in Rio de Janeiro, members of the Revolutionary Movement 8th October kidnapped at gunpoint C. Burke Elbrick, the Ambassador to Brazil. Elbrick was released after 78 hours in exchange for 15 imprisoned leftists.

---

49. Telegram From the Mission to the United Nations to the Department of State[1]

New York, September 19, 1969, 0151Z.

3084. Dept pass Amman, Cairo, Tel Aviv, London, Paris, Moscow.

1. Sisco met with Dobrynin for three hours afternoon of September 18. Discussion was in many respects frankest since bilateral talks began and focused primarily on exploring and defining key Middle East

---

[1] Source: National Archives, Nixon Presidential Materials, NSC Files, Box 1170, Saunders Files, Middle East Negotiations Files, Middle East Settlement—US–USSR Talks. Secret; Priority; Nodis. Saunders sent this telegram to Kissinger under cover of a September 19 memorandum. (*Foreign Relations,* 1969–1976, volume XII, Soviet Union, January 1969–October 1970, Document 80)

issues for Secretary-Gromyko meeting September 22. Following are summary impressions (detailed report by septel):[2]

A. After Sisco pressed Dobrynin hard and in detail, we believe Soviets are now largely ready to buy our language on commitment to peace and non-belligerency (point 3 of US proposal)[3] with important exception of explicit Arab commitment contained in this paragraph to control fedayeen. They will probably press, however, for some consolidation of language contained in points 3 and 12 of our July counterproposal.

B. On Arab commitment to eventual direct negotiations, Sisco described it in flexible terms. He stressed need for Soviets to accept last preambular para of our proposal. Dobrynin maintained position stated by Gromyko in Moscow—i.e., that this question difficult and should not be raised now. While Dobrynin revealed no give on direct negotiations, we have impression this is not closed question with Soviets.

C. On refugees, Soviets also seem to be leaving room for maneuver with respect to our proposal. Dobrynin specifically asked for indication of numbers US has in mind for repatriation under annual quota.

D. On security arrangements, Sisco explained our attempt to keep all options open for the parties themselves to work out in presence of Jarring. Sisco described present position of parties on security arrangements for Sharm el-Shaikh as irreconcilable. While Dobrynin understood clearly our desire for a neutral formulation which kept all options open, he categorically rejected concept of Israeli presence at Sharm el-Shaikh and stood firmly on Soviet proposal for UN presence. He was more explicit than before, however, in emphasizing that Israeli-UAR agreement could provide that UN force could only be removed within specified time period with approval of Security Council. He was flexible on time period that such force would be expected to stay.

E. On withdrawal and boundaries, Dobrynin made lengthy plea for US to state explicitly that there should be no changes in pre-June 5 UAR-Israeli line. He argued that Soviets had impression this was real US position in any case and US refusal say so explicitly only raised suspicions and made Soviet job of getting UAR agreement on other points more difficult.

2. After getting some flexibility from Dobrynin on peace commitment, Sisco reemphasized that we saw Arab commitment to direct negotiations at some stage as key to further movement, while making clear our formula is designed to give Jarring maximum flexibility in de-

---

[2] Telegram 3090 from USUN, September 19. (National Archives, Nixon Presidential Materials, NSC Files, Box 1170, Saunders Files, Middle East Negotiations Files, Middle East Settlement—US–USSR Talks)

[3] See footnote 4, Document 39.

termining timing and how negotiations conducted. Sisco also stressed our view that Soviets must face up to need to get out in front of Cairo, as we are out in front of Israelis, if our talks are to progress. In this connection, he made point obliquely that he assumed USSR would agree that bilateral talks should continue as long as there is hope for progress, but talk for sake of talk would not facilitate, but might impede future settlement since parties might feel able to avoid facing up to their responsibilities to make tough decisions required for a settlement. Dobrynin agreed.

3. Brief review of situation on ground in Middle East, Sisco said we were counselling restraint on both sides. Nevertheless, objective fact was that Israelis would not be passive in face of UAR war-of-attrition policy, and situation could get out of hand to UAR detriment if that policy not changed.

4. Sisco and Dobrynin tentatively agreed to meet again morning September 22, (Begin underline) inter alia (End underline) for Sisco to provide further responses to some of Semenov's commentary to Ambassador Beam on our July counterproposal, before Secretary-Gromyko meeting.

Yost

50. Memorandum of Conversation[1]

SecDel/MC/2 New York, September 20, 1969, 7:30 p.m.

SUBJECT
   SYG Dinner for Four FonMins and PermReps

PARTICIPANTS

U.S.
Secretary Rogers
Ambassador Yost
Dr. Ralph Bunche

FOREIGN
SYG Thant
Mr. Phillippe de Seynes
Mr. Leonid N. Kutakov
Mr. Andrew Stark
Mr. C.V. Narasimhan
FonMin Schumann
Ambassador Berard
FonMin Gromyko
Ambassador Malik
FonMin Stewart
Lord Caradon

After dinner the SYG suggested there be a discussion of the Middle East. He said the situation is deteriorating seriously. He referred to the responsibilities of the Security Council and particularly the four Permanent Members and asked what could be done.

Mr. Gromyko said that the key to a solution was withdrawal of Israeli forces from all occupied territory. On the other hand, all were agreed that a solution must be a package embracing all parts of the Security Council resolution. Negotiations should go forward in all fora, Two-Power, Four-Power, etc.

Secretary Rogers agreed that the solution must be a package and that negotiations might go forward in all fora. He suggested, however, that the Four await progress in current talks between the Two, perhaps for another ten days or two weeks.

Stewart said duty to find a solution rests with the United Nations, the Security Council and Permanent Members because the parties are so caught up in mutual hate that they can't make peace. Two-Power and Four-Power negotiations can go on concurrently and each can be in touch with the parties. Someone—whether 4, 3, 2 or 1—must define what the terms of the resolution mean. All four must be impartial. The

---

[1] Source: National Archives, Nixon Presidential Materials, NSC Files, Box 1170, Saunders Files, Middle East Negotiation Files, Middle East Settlement—US–USSR Talks. Secret; Exdis. Drafted by Yost on September 23. All brackets are in the original except those indicating text omitted by the editors. The dinner meeting was held in the Secretary General's suite at the United Nations.

parties won't like what they propose but might just accept it as better than the present and prospective situation. If some of the Four won't accept what the Arabs won't, and some won't accept what Israel won't, no progress will be made. Let the US and USSR proceed for the moment with their bilaterals but at some point the UK and France must play a part. There has to be withdrawal and Israel has not yet stated its position on this with sufficient clarity. But the Arabs also must move away from their Khartoum position of no negotiations and no peace treaty.[2]

Schumann said he thought France had been right in proposing Four-Power talks. There is no hope of direct negotiations taking place until an outline of a settlement has been laid out. Bilaterals have been useful and helped bridge the gap but within a reasonable time—say two weeks—the Four should resume. The Four can speak more impartially, be no one's advocate but advocate for all. Direct negotiations can come after the way has been paved. The Four should resume by mid-October.[3]

Secretary Rogers agreed that the Four might resume at that time but pointed out that the Two could also continue, both proceeding simultaneously.

The SYG said it seemed clear there was no disagreement. The Two would continue and the Four would resume about mid-October irrespective of where the Two had got by that time.

He pointed out that the Arab replies to Jarring had superseded the Khartoum declaration.[4] They had recognized Israeli right to exist. He felt Israel should agree to withdraw when the Arabs make a binding commitment to secure and recognized boundaries and to the other provisions of the Security Council Resolution.

He remarked that the world's eyes are on the United Nations and particularly on the Foreign Ministers and it would be reassuring if they would this evening reiterate the substantive parts of the initial April 3 statement of the Four Permanent Representatives.[5] He read the statement and it was briefly discussed.

---

[2] See footnote 4, Document 18.
[3] The Four Powers did not meet until December 2. See Document 72.
[4] See Document 12.
[5] The statement issued at the conclusion of the first meeting on April 3 reads in part: "The Four Powers are agreed that the situation in the Middle East is serious and urgent and must not be permitted to jeopardize international peace and security. They have straight away entered into a discussion on matters of substance and have started defining areas of agreement. There is a common concern to make urgent progress. The Secretary General of the United Nations will be kept fully informed. Active consultations will continue. These consultations will be private and confidential. All appropriate contacts with the parties primarily concerned will be maintained." (Department of State Bulletin, April 21, 1969, p. 337)

Gromyko said all agree that the resolution must be carried out. Seven or eight of its provisions have to be more fully defined. Withdrawal will begin only after full agreement is reached. There must be a durable peace. All states in the area must exist as sovereign, independent states. These are the basic principles.

It was agreed that a statement would be issued based on the April 3 communiqué and reflecting these principles. The SYG suggested referring to resumption of the Four-Power talks, but vaguer wording was preferred. Copy of the statement as released to the press is attached.[6]

[Omitted here is discussion unrelated to the Middle East.]

---

[6] Attached but not printed. The statement in footnote 5 above was published in the *New York Times* on April 4.

---

51. Memorandum From the President's Assistant for National Security Affairs (Kissinger) to President Nixon[1]

Washington, September 25, 1969.

SUBJECT

The Israeli Position [*less than 1 line not declassified*]

[*1 line not declassified*] The Israelis have often used this channel for revealing their real thinking. These are his main points:

1. The Arabs are now waging a war of attrition. Israel's present military strategy is to show Nasser that this will cost Egypt heavily. The latest raids have greatly damaged Nasser's personal prestige.

2. The Israelis think that if they continue their present course of military action, Nasser may well fall. Nasser's fall would open the way for a new play of forces in the area.

3. If Nasser falls, his successor will be less dangerous to Western interests because he will not have Nasser's personal charisma. Moderate Arab leaders will be more free to make peace.

---

[1] Source: National Archives, Nixon Presidential Materials, NSC Files, Box 644, Country Files, Middle East—General. Secret. Sent for information. All brackets are in the original except those indicating text that remains classified. Haig sent Kissinger's memorandum back to him on October 7 to alert him to comments that Nixon wrote on it.

4. The USSR has exploited Arab frustration with Israel's and Egypt's ambition to dominate the Arab world by leading the attack on Israel. The present struggle is above all an Egyptian-Russian struggle against Israel. Israel's very existence prevents total Soviet domination over the region.[2]

5. The Soviet Union, therefore, can have no interest in a real Arab-Israeli peace. With peace, the Arab states would divert their major energies to economic and social development. Soviet capacity to compete with the US in that field is small.

6. The Soviets hope that the war of attrition in the Mid-East will make the US weary of the situation and ready to accept a compromise peace formula.

7. The war of attrition makes heavy demands on Israel's resources. Prime Minister Meir will discuss additional military and economic aid with you. The "identity of interests between the US and Israel" justifies US material support for Israel's strategy.

Comment

This is a forthright statement of Israel's strategy—change the overall situation in the Mid-East by removing Nasser. It is also a clear example of Israel's assumption that our interests and Israel's are identical. The questionable points about this thesis are:

1. The [*less than 1 line not declassified*] himself points out that the USSR profits from tension and the US can outrun the USSR in peaceful competition.

2. Therefore, for us to have an interest in supporting Israel's strategy, that strategy must promise peace.

3. It is not at all certain that Hussein will be any more able to make peace without Nasser than with him. The fedayeen or the radical governments of Syria and Iraq may prove just as much of an inhibition as Nasser.

4. It seems more likely—and some Israelis admit this—that Israel's purpose is to surround itself with weak Arab governments so that it can weather prolonged tension behind its present borders.[3]

---

[2] Nixon highlighted this paragraph, underlined from "Egyptian-Russian struggle" to the end of the paragraph, and wrote "correct" underneath it.

[3] At the bottom of the memorandum, Nixon wrote: "K—Can't C.I.A. handle Nasser?!"

52. Memorandum of Conversation[1]

Washington, September 25, 1969.

PARTICIPANTS

Secretary Rogers
Dr. Henry A. Kissinger
Assistant Secretary Sisco
Ambassador Walworth Barbour
Alfred L. Atherton, Jr.
Harold H. Saunders

Ambassador Yitzhak Rabin
Yaacov Herzog
Moshe Bitan
Simcha Dinitz
Shlomo Argov

While the President and Prime Minister Meir were talking in the President's office,[2] their advisers held the following discussion in the Cabinet Room.

---

[1] Source: National Archives, Nixon Presidential Materials, NSC Files, Box 1237, Saunders Files, Chronological Files, Israel. Secret; Exdis. Drafted by Saunders on September 30. The meeting was held in the Cabinet Room of the White House. All brackets are in the original. "Draft" is written at the top of the first page.

[2] Nixon and Meir met from 10:47 a.m. to 12:40 p.m. but no record of the meeting has been found. (Ibid., White House Central Files, President's Daily Diary) In her memoirs, Meir recalled that she presented Nixon with a "shopping list" of military hardware, including a "specific request" of 25 Phantoms and 80 Skyhawk jets. She also asked Nixon for an annual $200 million low interest loan for five years to help pay for the planes Israel intended to buy. (Meir, *My Life*, pp. 387–391) In a telephone conversation with Kissinger at 5:20 p.m. on September 27, Meir asked for—and received—confirmation that the President put no conditions on his consideration of the Israeli request for aircraft. (National Archives, Nixon Presidential Materials, Henry Kissinger Telephone Conversation Transcripts, Box 2, Chronological File) Kissinger recounted that the President provided Meir with a formula that he would trade "hardware for software." According to Kissinger, "this meant that [Nixon] would be responsive to Israeli requests for armaments if Israel gave us some latitude in negotiations, which he strongly implied he would ensure would not amount to much. It would be too much to claim that Mrs. Meir agreed; more accurate to say she acquiesced in a formulation whose meaning only the future would reveal." (Kissinger, *White House Years*, pp. 370–371)

Nixon and Meir also discussed Israel's nuclear program and the channel of communication between their two governments. In a November 6 memorandum to the President, Kissinger wrote that "As confirmed in your talk with Golda Meir . . . the NPT will be held in abeyance until after the forthcoming elections, that the 'introduction' issues remain somewhat ambiguous and that there will be no operational deployment of nuclear capable missiles for at least three years." (National Archives, Nixon Presidential Materials, NSC Files, Box 605, Country Files, Middle East, Israel, Vol. III). With regard to the channel of communication between the United States and Israel, Rabin recalled that in his talk with Meir, Nixon proposed that "the two of them set up a line for direct communication, and at a further meeting between them the exact channel was marked out: Kissinger, acting on behalf of the President, would approach me, and I would transmit his message directly to Golda's personal assistant, Simcha Dinitz, in Jerusalem. The prime minister would do the same in reverse. At the president's request, Golda approved the suggestion." (Rabin, *The Rabin Memoirs*, p. 154)

Mr. Sisco initiated the substantive part of the conversation by asking the Israeli party to describe the procedures followed during the 1948–49 Arab-Israeli Armistice discussions on Rhodes.[3] Ambassador Rabin described them as follows:

1. Both sides declared the purpose of the negotiations. In that case, the purpose was to negotiate an armistice agreement.

2. There was an opening meeting with both delegations present. Ralph Bunche was elected as the Chairman.

3. A series of meetings of three different kinds followed:

a. The mediator went from one group to the other. The UAR and Israeli delegations were quartered in different rooms in the same hotel.

b. There were informal meetings between the heads of the UAR and the Israeli delegations which took place with the mediator present and sometimes without.

c. There were formal meetings of both delegations together under the Chairmanship of the mediator. Normally, these were to formalize agreement where it had been reached.

Ambassador Rabin said he could recall two or three of these meetings before the signing, although he noted that he had had to leave Rhodes before the signing and therefore might not recall any that took place in the final stage.

Secretary Rogers asked whether that same procedure would meet Israel's requirements. Ambassador Rabin replied that it would.

Secretary Rogers said that UAR Foreign Minister Riad had told him in New York the previous day that the procedures followed at Rhodes would be acceptable. Ambassador Rabin noted that Riad had said, according to press reports, that he could agree to talks along the Rhodes procedures after Israeli withdrawal. Secretary Rogers noted that Riad had said there should be some Israeli renunciation of expansionism. The Secretary then went on to explain that Riad had reaffirmed to the Secretary in the evening that he had indeed told the press that the Rhodes procedures would be acceptable and that he had not denied this later, even though he had said that he was not talking about "direct negotiations."

Mr. Sisco noted that, in the light of Riad's obvious difficulty in describing the Rhodes talks as "direct negotiations," there would be some advantage in avoiding public comment about precisely what the formula at Rhodes was.

---

[3] The Rhodes procedure was used by UN Acting Mediator Ralph Bunche to negotiate the Armistice Agreements signed on the island of Rhodes that ended the first Arab-Israeli war of 1948–1949. The negotiations involved separate meetings by Bunche with each delegation on substantive terms until discussions reached an advanced stage, at which point joint informal meetings were held.

Ambassador Rabin stressed that we should not think of the Rhodes formula just in terms of the procedures followed to organize meetings. We should remember that the negotiations began with a declaration of the purpose of the negotiations. That declaration is all-important because the Arabs so far have not declared it to be their purpose to make peace with Israel.

Dr. Kissinger asked why the UN Security Council Resolution of November 1967 would not give Israel an adequate statement of the purpose of the negotiations. Ambassador Rabin replied that there are different interpretations of the resolution.

Mr. Sisco noted that the document he has been discussing with Ambassador Dobrynin[4] has a far clearer statement of the purpose of the exercise than was made before the Rhodes meetings. Secretary Rogers noted that another possibility was the brief declaration which followed the meeting of the Ambassadors of the Four Powers the previous Saturday night.[5]

Ambassador Rabin noted that even the word "peace" is subject to different definitions. The Russians define it simply as an end to the state of war. The essence of the Israeli requirement is that the Arabs say they are ready to make peace *with Israel.*

Secretary Rogers said it was his impression from the talks he had held in New York during the previous days that all of the Arabs were ready to say that. The Israelis may suspect that the Arabs do not mean it but the purpose of a negotiation would be to determine how serious they are and what specific arrangements they are ready to agree to.

Ambassador Rabin said he had no evidence that, when the Arabs say they want peace, they mean they want peace *with Israel.* They always talk about "peace in the Middle East" and that is very different from "peace with Israel." Secretary Rogers asked who else the Arabs would be making peace with "in the Middle East" and then said, referring to Rabin's comment that the phrase "with Israel" is essential, "we can get them to say that."

Secretary Rogers then asked whether it would be sufficient for Israel's needs if the US could persuade the Arabs to say it is ready to make "peace with Israel." Ambassador Rabin said "fine."

Mr. Sisco said that we could not be absolutely sure what Foreign Minister Riad had meant by his willingness to use the same procedures that had been used at Rhodes. We will have to clarify this point and we cannot be certain until we have just exactly what the Arabs have in mind.

---

[4] See footnote 4, Document 39.
[5] See footnote 5, Document 50.

[GAP: Note-taker called out]

Secretary Rogers assured Ambassador Rabin that there is no doubt in Gromyko's mind that any settlement will have to provide for execution of agreements on all the issues involved. It is absolutely clear from their conversations, that Gromyko understands what the word "package" means.

Ambassador Rabin cautioned that we should not become too deeply involved simply in the mechanics of a possible meeting and that we must keep in mind the fact that a declaration of purpose was part of the Rhodes formula. The Secretary said he hesitated to overstress this point. The Security Council Resolution of November 1967 seemed to him a reasonable starting point. If we start debating the purpose again, we will have to go back through the whole argument over what the Security Council Resolution means. He suggested that we not reopen that issue again but that we get on with the business of figuring out what the parties need now. Apparently Riad would like some sort of renunciation of "Israeli expansionism" and undoubtedly he reads that as complete Israeli withdrawal. That is just one example of the kind of issue we now have to face, but that is the reason for having a negotiation—because there are such areas of disagreement. Debating the purpose of the exercise will not necessarily bring the discussion to the key substantive points, so it would be more desirable to get on with the negotiation as soon as possible.

Dr. Herzog commented that if indeed the Secretary is right and the Arabs do now seem more willing to make peace with Israel, this means that time has not worked against peace. He recalled the lengthy debates between us and the Israelis a year ago over whose side time worked on and simply noted that, if what the Secretary says is true, this is a commentary on that earlier debate over strategy.

Secretary Rogers said that he would not conclude that another two and one half years would improve the situation further. He asked Dr. Herzog whether that was the conclusion he was suggesting. Dr. Herzog replied that he was not. He was simply noting that time had softened the UAR.

Secretary Rogers acknowledged that he did not intend to be over optimistic. There is no question that the Egyptians see negotiations their way.

Dr. Herzog noted that the latest spanner Nasser seemed to have thrown into the works was the notion that Egypt could not speak for the Palestinians. Secretary Rogers noted that Riad had again thrown out the idea of Israel's need to expand. Ambassador Rabin said he could not believe that the Egyptians really believed that point. All they have to do is to look at the land area of Israel to see that Israel has plenty of land now to expand into. The growth of the Israeli state is not a matter of increasing land areas but rather a question of developing industry and water resources.

Mr. Sisco noted that he does not believe the Arabs now have any quarrel with the notion of their recognizing Israel. Ambassador Rabin questioned Mr. Sisco's use of the word "recognition." He noted that the word had not been used in the Security Council Resolution.

Secretary Rogers said that when he had gone to New York he had had doubts about the intentions of the Soviet Union and the Arabs. After talking with both there,[6] he said, "I think I've changed my mind." While the USSR and the UAR may not be ready to make peace entirely on Israel's terms, he believed that they do seriously want a solution. Gromyko had even indicated that the Arabs have no other choice.

Mr. Sisco underscored the last point by emphasizing that the one theme that comes through in all of the conversations in New York is that there is no real alternative to make a political agreement with Israel.

Secretary Rogers noted that Gromyko, while fully appreciating the hard Egyptian position, seemed to indicate some flexibility in the Soviet position. He cited an exchange with Gromyko in which Gromyko had asked whether Secretary Rogers felt a solution was possible with complete Israeli withdrawal from the occupied territories. When Secretary Rogers had replied that he did not, Gromyko had said only that he was disappointed. He felt that any such solution would violate international law. Any solution not involving complete Israeli withdrawal would be hard for the Egyptians to face. Secretary Rogers had recalled that the US and USSR had been allies in World War II, and the political agreements ending that war had involved territorial changes and that had not bothered Moscow. Gromyko had replied only that "parallels don't help." Secretary Rogers concluded by noting that Gromyko was not arguing the substance of the point—only the political implications.

Dr. Kissinger noted that he had seen Gromyko for only five minutes at the President's reception in New York and Gromyko had

---

[6] A summary of the Rogers-Gromyko talks in New York is printed as Document 53. Rogers also met with Meir on September 25 in New York and explained to her that the United States shared Israel's doubts about the Soviet-UAR desire for peace. Furthermore, he assured her that the United States was "not seeking to develop peace terms for imposition on parties but only to reach agreement on as many points as possible" so that the parties "could negotiate remaining differences." But he urged Israel to "drop insistence on face-to-face negotiations at outset and enter negotiations on Rhodes model" of indirect talks under Jarring that would lead to direct talks, if the Arab states said publicly that they would make peace with Israel. Meir responded that Israel would consider such a suggestion "if and when [the Arab states] made simple statement that they were prepared to sign peace agreement with Israel." (Telegram 163837 to Tel Aviv, September 26; National Archives, Nixon Presidential Materials, NSC Files, Box 604, Country Files, Middle East, Israel, Vol. II)

singled out the Middle East as an area where the Soviets want to make progress. He had only complained that "Joe Sisco was too tough."

Dr. Herzog commented that the ups and downs in Cairo have always perplexed Israel. Mr. Sisco noted that we are very cautious about our interpretation of what goes on in Cairo. Ambassador Rabin said that there is no doubt that the Egyptians are pressed and that the Russians are under increasing pressure to show that they can get back Egypt's conquered territories. Mr. Bitan noted that there is internal trouble in the UAR. He felt that one of the most important objectives for the USSR is to keep Nasser alive.

Secretary Rogers cautioned that he did not want to leave the impression with the Israelis that Foreign Minister Riad had said anything to suggest weakness in Egypt's negotiating stance. At the same time, he had very much taken the line that Egypt has no other choice than to press for a political settlement. Secretary Rogers noted that it is always true in a negotiation that both sides are trying to get the best deal they can but he did not feel that should deter negotiations. Surely, the Israelis are smart enough to hold their own in a negotiation.

Mr. Sisco turned attention to Jordan, asking what sense the Israelis have of what is going on there.

Dr. Herzog replied that the King's position is not as endangered as some people think. By any normal measurement, the King should be in a terrible position with a substantial portion of his territory occupied and with Iraqi, Syrian and Saudi troops on his soil as well as Egyptian installations. Despite this, there seems to be no desire by the fedayeen to overthrow the regime. Moreover, the Israelis believe that Nasser has no desire to overthrow Hussein because he wants to keep alive an Arab link to the US. The major elements of the army seem loyal to the monarchy. Orders do not always get carried out but basically loyalty seems to remain.

Dr. Herzog continued that he did not feel Hussein had ever received a complete go-ahead from Nasser to negotiate. The substantive limitations on Nasser's go-ahead had been such as to be a practical red light. Given the pressures on Hussein over the last few months, Hussein seems to have felt that he had to move more on the Cairo axis. For this reason, any separate settlement between Israel and Jordan seems remote—"for all Hussein's desire for peace."

Dr. Herzog summarized by saying that the desire for peace remains, Hussein's survival is not immediately endangered and the attraction of a close relationship with Cairo is deeper than ever. There is no evidence that Hussein is balancing the US against the USSR. He is basically pro-Western and does not seem to be turning to Moscow, despite occasional tactical threats to us to do so.

Mr. Sisco noted that it was interesting in Foreign Minister Riad's speech that he spoke first about Jordan and Jerusalem. Ambassador Rabin read this as a clear warning from Nasser to Jordan not to do anything to move toward a separate settlement with Israel.

Dr. Herzog noted that Hussein probably felt he had made a historic slip to let the fatah get as deeply entrenched in Jordan as they are, though there was little Hussein could do about it now.

The conversation then drifted off to a number of specific items—the current state of US efforts to arrange for delivery of the Phantoms by other than USAF pilots; the latest US efforts to persuade the Syrians to release the Israeli TWA passengers in Damascus; and then general personal recollections of the US landings in Lebanon in 1958.

Harold H. Saunders[7]

---

[7] Printed from a copy that bears his typed signature.

---

53. Memorandum From Harold Saunders of the National Security Council Staff to the President's Assistant for National Security Affairs (Kissinger)[1]

Washington, October 1, 1969.

SUBJECT

US–USSR Middle East Negotiations in New York

Secretary Rogers and Gromyko failed to make progress toward coming up with a common document during their final meeting in New York. The Soviet strategy now appears to be to get a commitment to total Israeli withdrawal from Sinai and Gaza to the pre-war lines in return for their agreeing to Rhodes type negotiations (interpreted the

---

[1] Source: National Archives, Nixon Presidential Materials, NSC Files, Box 650, Country Files, Middle East, Middle East Negotiations, July 1–October 1969. Secret; Nodis. Sent for information. A stamped notation on the first page reads: "HAK has seen." Attached but not printed are telegrams 3324 from USUN, October 1, which reported Rogers's meeting with Gromyko that day, and telegram 3322 from USUN, October 1, which reported Sisco's meeting with Dobrynin on September 29.

Arab way)[2] and peace after Israeli withdrawal has been completed and without an explicit commitment to control the fedayeen. Secretary Rogers does not believe that this is a satisfactory deal and has therefore held basically to our present position and did not put our fallback position on the table. The talks will now shift back to Washington with Joe Sisco and Dobrynin picking them up again next week.[3]

Summarized below is where we stand with the Soviets on the major points after the negotiations in New York:

1. The Soviets will accept the *Rhodes formula* if we will be more specific on the *UAR border.* Secretary Rogers avoided being more specific on the borders because of disagreement on a number of other points in the package. On the Rhodes formula, the Secretary made clear that we are not insisting on a joint meeting of the parties at the outset and that it was advantageous not to be too precise on the details so that both parties can justify it. Gromyko had a different set of facts than ours on the Rhodes formula. While he started out by insisting that there should be an understanding between us on what it means, he seemed to be pressing this less after Secretary Rogers had explained the advantages of ambiguity.

2. We and the Soviets agree on the principle of cessation of war and the establishment of a state of peace. The Soviets, however, continue to insist that a juridical state of peace can come only after all Israeli withdrawals are completed. This is consistent with the longstanding Arab view. The Israelis, on the other hand, refuse to withdraw an inch until peace is established and all elements of the package in force.

3. The Soviets are still also insisting on a reference to the Constantinople Convention with the language concerning freedom of passage through the *Suez Canal.*

4. On *Gaza,* the Soviets want a clear-cut statement of Arab sovereignty, total withdrawal of Israeli forces, the establishment of a UN force, and reinstitution of the UAR administration that existed before the war. We stuck to our position that all options on the ultimate status of Gaza must be kept open, leaving the concerned parties to work out a solution.

5. A preliminary understanding has been reached by Joe Sisco and Dobrynin to drop any reference to *refugees.* The Soviets can not agree

---

[2] See Document 52 and footnote 3 thereto. A difference of opinion arose between Egyptian and Israeli officials as to the meaning of the "Rhodes formula," with the former interpreting it as indirect talks between the parties while the latter believed it suggested preliminary indirect talks that eventually led to direct ones.

[3] Sisco and Dobrynin did not meet until October 28. See *Foreign Relations*, 1969–1976, volume XII, Soviet Union, January 1969–October 1970, Document 98.

that the principle of choice to refugees should be balanced by an annual quota.

6. The Soviets still hold the view that the UN force should be established in *Sharm el-Sheikh.* Secretary Rogers maintained that practical security arrangements in Sharm el-Sheikh, the establishment of demilitarized zones, and the final disposition of Gaza must be negotiated with the parties on the basis of the Rhodes formula.

7. We and the Soviets have been agreed for some time on Arab recognition of Israel's right to live in peace.

Conclusion: The long and short of this is that we may move toward a much shorter document containing only the key elements. That would leave the tough issues for negotiation, which would suit Israel. Our work would be cut out for us, but we would at least be working in a negotiating context.

54. Memorandum From the President's Assistant for National Security Affairs (Kissinger) to President Nixon[1]

Washington, October 2, 1969.

SUBJECT

Middle East Situation

As you requested, I told Len Garment to organize some Jewish Community protests against the State Department's attitude on the Middle East situation and Len has promised to take prompt action. I informed him that we wish to remain clear of the action he was taking.

I also talked to Rabin to tell him that we had an interest in calmer Israeli relations with Jordan and to confirm your understanding on the nuclear issue.

---

[1] Source: National Archives, Nixon Presidential Materials, NSC Files, Box 644, Country Files, Middle East, Middle East—General, Vol. II. Top Secret; Sensitive; Eyes Only. Drafted on October 1 by Kissinger and Haig. Printed from a copy that indicates that Kissinger initialed the original. A note at the top of the page reads: "Hand carried to Ken Cole 10/2/69—Mid East."

55. Memorandum From the President's Assistant for National Security Affairs (Kissinger) to President Nixon[1]

Washington, October 8, 1969.

SUBJECT

Rabin's Proposed Assurances on Israeli Nuclear Policy

Ambassador Rabin has asked whether the following replies to our queries about Israeli nuclear policy[2] would be satisfactory: (1) Israel will not become a "nuclear power"; (2) Israel will not deploy strategic missiles, at least until 1972; (3) the new Israeli government after the October 28 election will consider the NPT. Following are my analysis of the acceptability and my recommendations on each of these points:

I. *Israel will not become a nuclear power.*

A. *Our July request.* The Israelis had promised in signing the Phantom contract "not to be the first to introduce nuclear weapons into the Middle East." Rabin had informally defined "introduce" to mean "not test and not publicize." Elliot Richardson on July 29 asked him to accept our definition of "not introduce" as "not possess." The papers from which you worked in authorizing Elliot's approach[3] defined "possess" for our own internal purposes as "Israeli activity short of assembly of a completed nuclear explosive device." In short, we tried to put ourselves in a position where we could act as if we assumed the Israelis do not have completed weapons while leaving to the Israelis' conscience the stage short of completion where they would stop.

B. *Implications of the Israeli response.* Instead of accepting our words "not possess," Rabin simply says they "prefer" to say they will "not become a nuclear power."

1. *"Nuclear power."* Their phrase suggests the NPT distinction between a "nuclear-weapon State" and a "non-nuclear-weapon State." But it is quite possible they are simply proposing a suitably vague phrase that has no previous record of discussion between us and hence no earlier effort at precise definition.

2. In the context of the NPT, the concept *"non-nuclear-weapon State"* has the following meaning:

---

[1] Source: National Archives, Nixon Presidential Materials, NSC Files, Box 605, Country Files, Middle East, Israel, Vol. III. Top Secret; Nodis; Sensitive. Sent for action. All brackets are in the original.

[2] Reference is to Richardson and Packard's meeting with Rabin on July 29. See Document 41.

[3] Document 38.

a. "... a nuclear-weapon State is one which has manufactured and exploded a nuclear weapon or other nuclear explosive device prior to January 1, 1967."

b. "Each non-nuclear-weapon State ... undertakes ... not to manufacture or otherwise acquire nuclear weapons or other explosive devices...."

c. The treaty leaves deliberately obscure the position of a nation like Israel that might now already have manufactured but not exploded a nuclear device. There is no history of extensive discussion of this issue among the negotiators. Presumably each such nation is left to make its own good-conscience definition of what constitutes "manufacture." Any such nation signing the treaty would presumably be declaring that it is not retaining such devices, though the state of dismantling would again be left to its own good-conscience judgment.

3. The *reason for Rabin's preference* is not clear. When I asked how a state could become a "nuclear power" without "possessing" nuclear weapons, he simply said they "prefer" their formulation. I can only guess that they are trying to break away from discussions last year in which US Defense negotiators interpreted the Israeli assurance about not introducing nuclear weapons to preclude the mere physical presence of weapons. They may figure they are on better ground with a concept that has some internationally recognized meaning but has been left deliberately vague.

C. *Acceptability* of the Israeli formulation.

1. Any of these phrases is vague and leaves definition to the Israelis. It is not practical for us to try to define them restrictively because we could not determine Israeli adherence to our definition. What we have to settle for, I believe, is an Israeli commitment that will prevent Israeli nuclear weapons from becoming a known factor and further complicating the Arab-Israeli situation.

2. Nevertheless, I am wary of accepting their phrase without some notion of what they mean by it.

3. However, if we could tie their phrase to the NPT concept of remaining a "non-nuclear-weapon State," we would at least be working with an internationally accepted concept—albeit one with its own calculated vagueness of definition.

4. The *argument against* giving up insistence on our word "possess" would come from those who believe we should make a maximum effort to keep Israel as far as possible from a real nuclear capability. They might believe the word "possess" carried with it a more restrictive meaning. However, this argument in my mind founders on two points: the obvious Israeli unwillingness to confide the details of their program—as far as I know—and our inability to enforce any agreement we might theoretically reach.

D. *Recommendation*—That I reply to Rabin as follows: Since the Israeli phrase "nuclear power" suggests the concepts of the NPT, you propose that Israel assure us it will remain a "non-nuclear-weapon State," assuming the obligations of such a state as defined by Article II of the NPT. ["... not to receive" and "not to manufacture or otherwise acquire nuclear weapons or other nuclear explosive devices...."] This would in effect ask the Israelis to accept privately the key obligation of the NPT while allowing them more time to sort out their position on more generally unpalatable aspects of the treaty (e.g. safeguards and public renunciation of the nuclear option).[4]

II. *Israel will not deploy strategic missiles at least until 1972.*

A. *Our July request:* Elliot said, "We hope Israel will agree not to produce or deploy the Jericho missile."

B. *Implications of the Israeli response.* I can only guess Israeli motivation. These are possibilities:

1. Rabin's offer not to deploy finesses our request not to manufacture missiles. This would permit them to run them off the production line and then to store them a few hours from launch readiness rather than putting them on the launching pads.

2. Although our intelligence suggests persuasively that the first missiles should be coming off the production line this fall, it might be that there is some complication in the production line or in the availability of a militarily significant number of warheads that would make the Israelis unready to deploy missiles until 1972 anyway.

3. More likely is the possibility that the Israelis estimate that their military superiority—especially if the additional Skyhawks and Phantoms they have requested are delivered in 1971—is almost certainly assured through 1971. That would be quite consistent with our estimates, although the Israelis present a more dangerous picture when making their case for the additional aircraft. They may figure their sacrifice would be marginal beside the risk of antagonizing the US and jeopardizing the added equipment and aid they want.

C. *Acceptability* of the Israeli proposal.

1. There was general agreement during our special Review Group discussions last July that our minimum requirement was for the Israelis not to deploy their missiles.[5] If they were deployed, everyone would assume they had nuclear warheads because they are not accurate enough to be worth their cost just to deliver high explosives. It was my own conclusion that this was all we could expect the Israelis to accept.

---

[4] Nixon approved the recommendation.
[5] See Document 35.

2. The *argument against* asking only for non-deployment came from members of the group, who felt we ought to try to stop manufacture as well if we were going to try to keep Israel as far as possible from an actual nuclear weapons delivery capability.

3. If it is your view that we should not try to affect Israel's actual capability, then Rabin's proposal should be acceptable with one proviso—that your acceptance not be read as assent to deployment in 1972. I do not believe they should be given a blank check.

D. *Recommendation*—That I reply to Rabin as follows: The Israeli proposal is acceptable provided Israel agrees to further discussion of the subject in 1971 or prior to a decision to deploy missiles.[6]

III. *The new Israeli government will consider the NPT.*

A. *Our July request:* Elliot said, "We therefore attach utmost importance to Israel's early signature and ratification of the NPT.... We would welcome the Ambassador's comments on the conclusions the Government of Israel has reached."

B. *Implications of the Israeli response.*

1. Mrs. Meir may have made some commitment to you privately that would give this statement significance.

2. Interpreted in the light of similar Israeli statements in the past, however, this sounds like a dodge. Prime Minister Eshkol assured President Johnson last December that the Israeli government was studying the implications of Israel's adherence to the NPT.[7]

3. There is no special reason to predict a change in post-election policy because an Israeli Cabinet decision to sign and ratify the NPT would still run opposite to predominant Israeli thinking on several counts:

a. The hard-liners want to hold their nuclear option over Arab heads at least until there is a negotiated peace. They believe the Arabs would interpret signature as a sign of weakness.

b. Israelis have the same qualms and political problems with "surrendering" their nuclear option as any of other potential nuclear powers.

c. Israel has serious reservations about accepting the international safeguards the NPT requires.

---

[6] Nixon approved the recommendation.

[7] Prime Minister Eshkol sent the letter to President Johnson on December 4, 1968, in response to Johnson's November 15 letter urging Israel to sign the Nonproliferation Treaty. Eshkol wrote that Israel was still giving careful consideration to the long-term security implications of the treaty and would take into account the considerations advanced in Johnson's letter. See *Foreign Relations,* 1964–1968, volume XX, Arab-Israeli Dispute, 1967–1968, Document 349.

C. *Acceptability* of the Israeli proposal. While recognizing that Mrs. Meir cannot commit a future government, this formulation strikes me as unacceptably weak. It seems to me that signature of the NPT with its loopholes and escape clause would not jeopardize Israel's potential nuclear capability or diminish Arab recognition of its conventional military superiority.

D. *Recommendation*—That I reply to Rabin as follows: You would prefer Prime Minister Meir's agreement to make a vigorous personal effort to win Cabinet approval of Israel's signature and ratification of the NPT.[8]

One general recommendation: On an issue as complex as this one, I believe you should reserve for yourself the opportunity to have second thoughts. Therefore, I would propose prefacing my approach to Rabin by saying (1) that something along the lines of my counterproposals would seem closer to what you had in mind and (2) if these were acceptable to the Israelis you would take another look at them and give him a firm response. At that point you might want me to find a way to get the views of the special group that dealt with this subject last summer.[9]

The record of Elliot Richardson's July 29 conversation with Rabin is attached.[10]

---

[8] Nixon approved the recommendation.

[9] No action on the recommendation is indicated.

[10] On instruction from the Israeli Government, Rabin officially replied to the queries in a meeting with Richardson on October 15. The Israeli Ambassador said: "1. The Government of Israel is in no position to make further clarifications about the NPT until a new government will be formed after the elections. The new government will continue to study this problem, bearing in mind its importance as expressed by the President during his talk with the Prime Minister. 2. It is the view of the Government of Israel that introduction means the transformation from a non-nuclear weapon country into a nuclear weapon country. 3. As a result of the French embargo and other factors there will be no operational deployment of missiles in Israel for at least three years from now." (National Archives, Nixon Presidential Materials, NSC Files, NSC Institutional Files (H-Files), Box H–146, National Security Study Memoranda)

On November 21, Sisco sent a memorandum to Richardson in which he wrote: "NEA has carefully considered the implications of the reworded Israeli statement concerning Israel's nuclear weapons intentions given you on October 15 by Ambassador Rabin, and concludes that it represents a continuation of the evasion which has characterized responses to our previous approaches." (Ibid., RG 59, Lot Files, Bureau of Near Eastern and South Asian Affairs, Office of Israel and Arab-Israel Affairs, 1951–1976, Box 27) Richardson followed up with Rabin on February 13, 1970, asking him if the "new Israeli Government had reached any decisions," to which the Ambassador responded that he had "nothing to add" to what he told Richardson in October. (Memorandum from Richardson to Nixon, February 18, 1970; ibid.) On February 23, 1970, Rabin met with Kissinger to inform him that Israel had "no intention to sign to NPT" and to warn that linking signature of the NPT and arms sales to Israel would be "extremely unfortunate." (Memorandum of conversation, February 23, 1970; ibid., Nixon Presidential Materials, NSC Files, Kissinger Office Files, Box 134, Rabin/Kissinger 1969–1970, Vol. I)

56. Minutes of a Washington Special Actions Group Meeting[1]

Washington, October 21, 1969, 3:28–5:12 p.m.

SUBJECT

Berlin, Sino-Soviet Hostilities, and the Middle East

PARTICIPANTS

Henry A. Kissinger—Chairman

State
U. Alexis Johnson
Martin Hillenbrand
William Cargo
Rodger Davies

Defense
G. Warren Nutter

CIA
Thomas H. Karamessines

JCS
Vice Admiral Nels C. Johnson

NSC Staff
Harold H. Saunders
Helmut Sonnenfeldt
William G. Hyland
Col. Robert M. Behr

[Omitted here are the "Summary of Decisions," discussion of Berlin, and Sino-Soviet hostilities contingency planning.]

Kissinger opened discussion of the Middle East paper[2] by noting that it is conceptually good but confusing in format. He asked for Saunders's view of the paper. Saunders agreed that it is unwieldly and suggested there be developed a "basic issues" paper for each scenario. He asked the Group if the drafters had chosen the most useful scenarios. Secretary Johnson replied that the scenarios were the ones agreed to by

---

[1] Source: Library of Congress, Manuscript Division, Kissinger Papers, Box TS–76, Committees and Panels, Washington Special Actions Group, October 1969. Top Secret; Sensitive; Eyes Only. All brackets are in the original except those indicating text omitted by the editors. The meeting took place in the White House Situation Room.

[2] Saunders summarized the paper, which presented the contingencies for two scenarios, in a September 17 memorandum to Kissinger. The first scenario involved "an increase in tension followed by overt and major involvement of Soviet military forces supporting Arab forces seeking to oust Israel from the occupied territories and to inflict a major defeat." The United States would respond in four phases: 1) *"before open Soviet involvement*, diplomatic efforts to restore cease-fire and deter Soviet involvement"; 2) "efforts to restore cease-fire fail, Israel is being pushed back and Soviet personnel are involved; U.S. decides to *supply additional combat aircraft into Israel*"; 3) "Israel being pushed back; President determines that it is necessary to *halt the flow of Soviet supplies* and personnel to the Mid-East"; 4) "effort to block Soviet lines of communication has failed; Israel is about to be driven back beyond 1967 borders; President decides to *intervene*." The second scenario posited "a situation in which USSR naval units have attacked Israeli targets and the U.S. decides on *retaliatory action* of some sort." (National Archives, Nixon Presidential Materials, NSC Files, NSC Institutional Files (H-Files), Box H–072, Washington Special Actions Group Meetings, WSAG Mtg. 2/9/70 USSR and Egypt)

the WSAG at an earlier meeting[3] and that he considered the paper to be on the right track.

Davies called attention to a section of the paper that disturbed him. At one point in Scenario I there is expressed a time-sequenced need for a "hunter-killer" submarine force in the Mediterranean, yet the paper reveals that it may require eight days to position the force. Kissinger said the submarine force was not the only example of unreality. He noted also the long delays incident to the positioning of ground forces, thus calling into question the basic suitability of the tactic. He wondered whether these actions are operationally sound. Another question relates to the requirement for obtaining the force disposition and operations plans of U.S. allies in the Mediterranean. Don't we have these now? Admiral Johnson said force dispositions are known but not operational plans.

Kissinger then inquired why military alerting actions should be disguised. After considerable discussion the decision of the Group was to use alerting actions as signals of U.S. concern.

Admiral Johnson called for a discussion of base availability, which is a severely limiting factor for U.S. operations in the Middle East. He doubted, for instance, that Spain would be available. Davies agreed, but qualified his agreement with the thought that Spain would become more tractable (as would other friendly Mediterranean powers) if the Soviets became actively involved. Admiral Johnson observed that the nature of the Soviet involvement would be the determinant—if only logistic support were involved allied reluctance to provide base support would remain high; if direct military assistance were the case, the reluctance would soon disappear. With regard to this ambivalence, he remarked that we should continually remind our allies of the increasingly evident Soviet naval activity throughout the Mediterranean.

Kissinger questioned the likelihood that France would deliver Mirage fighters to Israel in the event Israel's existence became jeopardized. Davies replied that the French have indicated they would consider releasing the fighters if a case for dire military necessity could be made.

Kissinger concluded the meeting with an observation that another "Lebanon operation"[4] is not possible. We will have neither the operating bases nor the forewarning. Furthermore the balance of forces in the area has been upset by increased Soviet naval presence. He asked that the remainder of the Middle East paper be addressed at the next meeting.

---

[3] See Document 44.
[4] See footnote 2, Document 4.

Before departing Secretary Johnson inquired whether the Nixon Administration had reviewed the rules of engagement for the area. Admiral Johnson said that the only review he knew of was concerned with Southeast Asia. He will look into the matter and prepare a document on rules of engagement for WSAG review.

The Group adjourned at 5:12 P.M.

---

57. Memorandum From Harold Saunders of the National Security Council Staff to the President's Assistant for National Security Affairs (Kissinger)[1]

Washington, October 22, 1969.

SUBJECT

Where We Stand in the Mid-East

As you and the President ponder Secretary Rogers's memo on Joe Sisco's proposed next step with Dobrynin,[2] I would like to throw out these thoughts. In some ways, I regard this as the most important—though not the clearest—memo that I have written since January 20. This is not because I believe that any one decision or any single diplomatic move like this changes the course of history but because I see a series of decisions being made almost tacitly that could.

I am not sure where the President's thinking stands at this point, so this may not be as pointed as it might be. However, the situation has

---

[1] Source: National Archives, Nixon Presidential Materials, NSC Files, Box 1169, Saunders Files, Middle East Negotiations Files, Middle East Settlement—US–USSR Talks. Secret; Nodis. Sent for action. A typed notation at the top of the page reads: "This is the version that went to Joe Sisco 10/27/69." All brackets are in the original.

[2] In an October 14 memorandum to the President, Rogers wrote that, "taking advantage of the atmosphere created by the recent round of talks in New York," he intended to present the Soviet Union with a UAR-Israeli settlement based on the following: "a) a binding commitment to peace and specific obligations to maintain the peace; b) acceptance of the principle of withdrawal of Israeli forces from UAR territory to the pre-June 5 lines conditioned on UAR willingness to negotiate with Israel," which would include "practical security arrangements" in Sharm el-Sheikh and Gaza, demilitarized zones and freedom of passage through the Strait of Tiran and Suez Canal for all vessels, including Israel, and Israel's right to live in "secure and recognized boundaries." Rogers concluded by saying that "only an unabashed optimist can predict agreement between ourselves and the USSR on the above proposition, let alone agreement of the parties. However, it is clearly in our interests to move to this position whether or not the Soviets buy. It is a position that both sides will criticize, but neither can really assail effectively." (Ibid.)

now reached a point where I feel I owe you the reflections that follow even if they are somewhat wide of the mark.

In short, *I'd like to make two points:*

1. US Mid-East policy is on the verge of shifting from the strategy of the past twenty years—trying to maintain as broadly based a position as possible—to one based centrally on Israel.

2. If I assume correctly that we do not want to make that shift, the main issue we face is not just how to achieve a peace settlement but how to avoid being forced into a change of policy that is not consistent with US interests.

Our Present Policy

For twenty years, the US has attempted to keep a foot in all camps in the Mid-East. We developed our special friends in the moderates—Jordan, Saudi Arabia, Lebanon, Iran, Libya, Tunisia, Morocco. We spent a good deal of effort courting Nasser for better or worse. We stood by Israel.

We have done this because we have interests in oil, encouraging moderate political trends, trying to avoid an exclusive Soviet relationship with the area's chief troublemaker and keeping Israel afloat.

In following that policy, we rejected a strategy promoted by Israel's friends in the US. That strategy was built around the idea that Israel—a "bastion of democracy"—was holding the Mid-East for the Free World against encroaching Communism. We rejected it because it assumed that friendly control of a certain plot of Mid-Eastern ground would some how prevent Communist encroachment. We rejected it because we felt we had to meet a political encroachment in political—not military—terms on the ground where it was gaining. We elected to compete in Cairo, Beirut, Amman, Baghdad. By 1967, we were still holding our own.

Now, however, we seem to be on the verge of adopting the strategy of basing our Mid-East strategy exclusively on Israel. I doubt we are doing this because the President wants to, although I don't know. I assume we are doing it because we cannot see a practical alternative—or because the price of choosing the alternative seems too high.

Whatever the cause, the following steps which Israel and its friends are pressing us to take would commit us to Israel in a way that we have never before accepted:

—Helping Israel to acquire modern weapons and build up its own defense industry to the extent of more than *$3 billion* in purchases of military equipment and other equipment needed for defense production over the next six years.

—Covering a foreign exchange gap of *$1.2 billion* (included in the above) through financial assistance over the next five years. [That's the equivalent of four years of development loans to India—given to a country with a per capita GNP higher than Italy's.]

—Becoming *Israel's sole supplier of military equipment.* (France has stopped sending new end-items, and the UK seems about to drop out.)

—Acquiescing in Israel's possession of a *nuclear deterrent.*

—Acquiescing in Israel's redrawing its map or at least in Israel's strategy of sitting tight until peace comes.

I realize we have not taken all these steps yet. But the pressure is on, and it would take persistent effort on our part not to slip into them as the path of least resistance. If I assume correctly that we do not want to go this route, then the main issue is to find a way to establish a position independent of Israel with minimum damage to the President's policies across the board.

Finding a practical alternative to the course we are on is difficult. We do not want to hurt Israel, and we recognize that Israel has a real security problem with its unpredictable and none-too-trustworthy neighbors. Even if we wanted to press Israel, it is not clear we would succeed. If we tried, the domestic damage to the President's program—and his freedom of maneuver on Vietnam—could be extensive. *The broad choices are:*

1. *Stop where we are,* act as Israel's lawyer and underwrite Israel's stand-fast strategy.

—The arguments for this are that it may best reflect our impotence in breaking the current impasse and it would best assure support of Israel's friends in the US for the President's policies.

—The argument against is that it would increasingly—and in the end exclusively—tie the American position in the Middle East to Israel. This would be a major shift from past US policy not consistent with the present view of US interests. It would tie us to an Israeli strategy which the President has described as "unassailable short range, disastrous long range."

2. State's alternative would be to *adopt a position we regard as balanced and to see how far we can get with it without forcing it on Israel.*

—The argument for doing this is that we would at least be standing on a position consistent with US interests, not just Israel's. There may be an outside chance over time of persuading somebody else to buy it, but in any case it would put us in a position of not backing Israel regardless of what it does.

—The argument against this is that it would carry the continuous risk of angering the Israelis and their US friends while not entirely pleasing the Arabs.

3. *Adopt a balanced position and* then by a combined use of the carrot and stick—the promise of military support and over $1.2 billion in financial help—to *try to bring Israel to a settlement.*

—The argument for this is that only a settlement can create conditions conducive to US interests. We have more leverage with Israel today than at any time in the last decade.

—The strength of the argument against is in direct ratio to the scale of the Israeli counterattack we estimate. It also depends on the extent of the President's promise to Mrs. Meir not to apply pressure.

Each of these approaches has serious disadvantages, so I see our job as picking the least dangerous and then moving ahead with the best safeguards we can build for ourselves at each step.

For me, the first course—stopping where we are—is ruled out because it is potentially the most dangerous both to our interests and in building over the long term a situation where the US and USSR would confront each other over Israel. Stopping where we are would gradually put us in a position of tying our Mid-East policy almost exclusively to Israel. (I am speaking here of US Government policy; US oil interests might survive some time beyond the USG as they are now in Cairo.) Also, this would leave the US as Israel's ultimate defender against more than 60 million Soviet-backed enemies who, as you have said, in any historical period must prevail unless the US is to defend it.

Similarly, any abrupt move in the direction of the third course is probably too dangerous for the President in the absense of a real Arab peace proposal. I would leave open the option of relating our military and economic help to peace moves, recognizing that it is too early to consider this as an active choice. There's no point in having a confrontation over a mirage (no pun).

That leaves us with the problem of how to stake out an independent US position while minimizing Israeli reaction. As I see it, the key to avoiding the worst pitfalls lies in our taking a substantive position that we can say does not hurt Israel.

The question is whether Joe's formula provides that safeguard. What it really does is put us on record as saying that we do not believe Israel should keep any part of the Sinai *provided* the UAR will *negotiate* satisfactory security arrangements for Sharm al-Shaikh and the Sinai along with a final Arab government for Gaza. This may weaken Israel's negotiating position, but the US interest is in Israel's *security, not* its *expansion.* We would be opposing expansion *provided* security can be gained another way.

I see this as a necessary step if we are to move toward a position consistent with US interests—and not move to a position tied exclusively to Israel. I believe, too, that it is a defensible stand to take in this country to say that we will support Israel's *security* wholeheartedly but *not* Israel's *expansion.*

58. Paper Prepared in the Department of State[1]

Washington, undated.

JOINT US–USSR WORKING PAPER
FUNDAMENTAL PRINCIPLES

Israel and the UAR,

In consideration of their obligations under the Charter of the United Nations,

Confirming their obligations under Security Council Resolution 242 of November 22, 1967 and expressing their readiness to implement it in good faith in all of its provisions,

Recognizing the inadmissibility of the acquisition of territory by means of war,

Recognizing also the need to establish a just and lasting peace in the Middle East under the terms of which each State in this area can live in security,

Agree that their representatives under the auspices of Ambassador Jarring will follow the procedures the parties utilized at Rhodes in 1949[2] to work out without delay, starting on the basis of the following provisions, a final and reciprocally binding accord on ways of implementing Security Council Resolution 242 of November 22, 1967 to establish a just and lasting peace.

Point 1

The parties, in reaching a final accord (contained in a final document or documents) on a package settlement on the basis of these Fundamental Principles, would determine a timetable and procedures for withdrawal of Israeli armed forces from UAR territory occupied during the conflict of 1967 to boundaries to be delineated in accordance with Point 3 as well as an agreed plan for interrelated fulfillment of all other provisions of Security Council Resolution 242.

Point 2

The state of war and belligerency between Israel and the UAR would be terminated and a formal state of peace would be established

---

[1] Source: National Archives, Nixon Presidential Materials, NSC Files, Box 650, Country Files, Middle East, Middle East Negotiations. Secret. Attached to a November 16 memorandum from Rogers to Nixon. Sisco presented this paper, which became known as the Rogers Plan, to Dobrynin on October 28. See Document 61.

[2] See Document 52 and footnote 3 thereto.

between them, and both parties would refrain from acts inconsistent with the state of peace and the cessation of the state of war.

In particular:

1. No aggressive action by the armed and other forces—land, sea, or air—of either party would be undertaken or threatened against the people or the armed forces of the other.

2. Both parties would undertake to do all in their power to ensure that acts of hostility and belligerency whether by government agencies, personnel, or private persons or organizations will not originate from and are not committed from within their respective territory.

3. Both parties would refrain from intervening directly or indirectly in each other's domestic affairs for any political, economic, or other reasons.

4. Both parties would confirm that in their relations with each other, they will be guided by the principles contained in Article 2, paragraphs 3 and 4 of the UN Charter.

Point 3

The parties would agree on the location of the secure and recognized boundary between them, which would be shown on a map or maps approved by the parties which would become part of the final accord. In the context of peace, including inter alia agreement between the parties on the establishment of demilitarized zones, on practical security arrangements in the Sharm al-Shaykh area for guaranteeing freedom of navigation through the Strait of Tiran, and on practical security arrangements and final disposition of Gaza, the former international boundary between Egypt and the mandated territory of Palestine would become the secure and recognized boundary between Israel and the UAR

Point 4

For the purpose of ensuring the territorial inviolability of the parties and guaranteeing the security of the recognized boundary, the parties, following the procedures set forth in the last preambular paragraph of this document, would work out an agreement on:

(a) Zones to be demilitarized and procedures for ensuring their demilitarization;

(b) Practical security arrangements in the Sharm al-Shaykh area to assure freedom of navigation through the Strait of Tiran; and

(c) Practical security arrangements for and final disposition of Gaza.

Point 5

The parties would agree and the Security Council would reaffirm:

(a) That the Strait of Tiran is an international waterway; and

(b) That the principle of free navigation for vessels of all countries, including Israel, applies to the Strait of Tiran and the Gulf of Aqaba.

Point 6

The UAR would affirm that, in its exercise of sovereignty over the Suez Canal, the ships of all nations, including Israel, will have the right of freedom of navigation without discrimination or interference.

Point 7

The parties would agree to abide by the terms of a just settlement of the refugee problem as agreed upon in the final accord between Jordan and Israel, and to participate as Ambassador Jarring may deem desirable in working out the terms of said settlement.

It would be understood that the accord between the UAR and Israel would be paralleled by an accord between Jordan and Israel, which would include agreement on a just solution of the refugee problem. Implementation of both accords would begin only after agreement had been achieved on the entire package.

Point 8

The UAR and Israel would mutually agree to respect and acknowledge each other's sovereignty, territorial integrity, inviolability and political independence and each other's right to live in peace within secure and recognized borders free from threats or acts of force.

Point 9

The final accord would be recorded in a document which is to be signed by the parties and immediately deposited with the UN. After the parties have deposited such a document, the Secretary General of the UN would be requested by the parties immediately to inform the Security Council and all UN Member States to that effect.

From the moment of deposit, the document would become binding on the parties and irrevocable, and implementation and observance by the parties of the provisions of the accord would begin. In the implementation of the final accord, it would be understood by the parties that their respective obligations would be reciprocal and interdependent. The final accord would provide that a material breach of that accord by one of the parties shall entitle the other to invoke the breach as a ground for suspending its performance in whole or in part until the breach shall be cured.

Point 10

Both parties would agree that the final accord would be submitted to the Security Council for its endorsement.

It would be understood that France, the United Kingdom, the United States and the Union of Soviet Socialist Republics would submit and support an appropriate Security Council resolution and pledge that they would concert their future efforts to help the parties abide by all of the provisions of the final accord or accords.

59. Memorandum From the President's Assistant for National Security Affairs (Kissinger) to President Nixon[1]

Washington, October 28, 1969.

SUBJECT

Putting Israeli Request in Perspective

Mrs. Meir has left us with two substantial requests—for 75 more jet aircraft (50 A–4s and 25 F–4s) and for help in meeting a projected $1.2 billion balance of payments deficit 1970–1974.

Although I believe you are sympathetic, you will need to know what is involved before you make final decisions. There are budgetary implications in the request for credit on the military sales, which go far beyond the planes—some $500–600 million in total purchases per year are projected for FY 70–74. There may even be some need for legislation in responding to the request for financial assistance. Israel probably even wants to go back on the AID list, so we shall have to look at all our options.

To provide you with the necessary analysis of costs and options, I propose setting up two NSC Ad Hoc Groups to be run in a combined effort by my program analysis and operations staffs with participation by the involved departments.

1. The first study would analyze for you Israel's projected military requirements and U.S. options in helping to meet those requirements.

2. The second would analyze Israel's projected requirements for financial help and U.S. options in responding.

When these studies are completed, Joe Sisco's Interdepartmental Group would prepare a policy paper for you.

---

[1] Source: National Archives, Nixon Presidential Materials, NSC Files, Box 605, Country Files, Middle East, Israel, Vol. III. Secret; Exdis. Sent for action. Printed from a copy that indicates Kissinger signed the original. All brackets are in the original except "[their?]", added for clarity.

Finally, I would suggest telling the Israelis generally what our planned timetable for response is—without committing you on the nature of the response. If we can persuade them that we are not stalling but meeting your [*their*?] legitimate needs and that our timetable will not hurt them, I think we might keep them from turning on the domestic pressure.

Recommendation

That you approve the above procedure as embodied in the two NSSMs attached (Tab A and Tab B).[2]

---

[2] Nixon initialed his approval on November 6. The attached NSSMs were signed by Kissinger; see Documents 62 and 63. A single NSC Ad Hoc Group was established to consider Israeli assistance requests.

---

60. Minutes of a Washington Special Actions Group Meeting[1]

Washington, October 29, 1969, 2:08–3:20 p.m.

SUBJECT

    Lebanon

PARTICIPANTS

    Henry A. Kissinger—Chairman

State
U. Alexis Johnson
Rodger Davies

Defense
G. Warren Nutter

CIA
Thomas H. Karamessines

JCS
Vice Admiral Nels C. Johnson

NSC Staff
Harold H. Saunders
Col. Robert M. Behr

---

[1] Source: National Archives, Nixon Presidential Materials, NSC Files, NSC Institutional Files (H-Files), Box H–114, Washington Special Actions Group, WSAG Minutes (Originals) 1969 and 1970. Top Secret; Sensitive. All brackets are in the original except "[*sic*]", added for clarity. The meeting was held in the White House Situation Room.

SUMMARY OF DECISIONS

1. Incident to Lebanon[2] and the general Arab-Israeli problem, the WSAG will develop for the President a paper on Libya which determines and analyzes alternative pressures that can be brought to bear in an effort to make the radical government more tractable.[3]

2. President Helou will be queried regarding Lebanese arms needs and will be advised of our willingness to assist.

3. Preparations will be made to supply arms (on a covert basis) to the Falange. Implementation will be withheld until the WSAG determines the action to be necessary and in the U.S. interest.

3 [sic]. Interagency evacuation plans for Lebanon will be deposited in the White House Situation Room.

4. Situations II, III and IV will be amended to include greater specificity in military detail. Integrated political-military scenario format will be followed.

5. The issue of Israeli versus U.S. intervention will be brought before the NSC.[4]

The meeting began at 2:08 P.M.

Davies reported the military situation in Lebanon as of early morning, October 29th. GOL regular forces have engaged the fedayeen with considerable success. The only remaining major fedayeen stronghold is in Tripoli. The Lebanese army has been heartened by these operations. Kissinger inquired about the unexpected effectiveness of the GOL forces. Davies attributed their success to the strong leadership of the mostly-Christian Officer Corps.

Kissinger reported his discussion of Lebanon which he had had with the President shortly before the meeting. The President wishes:

1. Formal consideration of a "tough option."

2. Recognition of political trends in the Middle East which, if not checked, will lead to the downfall of the remaining moderate regimes in the area.

---

[2] Beginning on October 15, Lebanon experienced an upsurge of fedayeen activity against the government, including pro-fedayeen military intervention by Syria, which sparked the second major political crisis of the year. (Memorandum from Rogers to Nixon, October 23; ibid., RG 59, Central Files 1967–69, POL 23 LEB; telegram 8896 from Beirut, October 25; ibid.) Prime Minister-designate Rashid Karame resigned over the government's inability to define a fedayeen policy, and President Charles Helou struggled to form a viable cabinet. (Department of State Intelligence Note 763, October 27; ibid., Nixon Presidential Materials, NSC Files, Box 620, Country Files, Middle East, Lebanon, Vol. I)

[3] See *Foreign Relations*, 1969–1976, volume E–5, Part 2, Documents on North Africa, 1969–1972, Document 44.

[4] See Document 74.

3. A determination and analysis of the pressures that can be brought against Libya (e.g., reduced oil draw-down) to make the radical government more tractable.

With regard to Point 1, above, the Group agreed that a "tough option" is already contained in the Lebanon paper[5]—specifically, the U.S. military intervention actions described in Situations III and IV. More work needs to be done in detailing these options.

After a brief discussion of Point 3 (Libya), the Group agreed that the WSAG should develop a paper for NSC consideration. State will chair the interdepartmental working group.

Kissinger then turned to the Lebanon paper, asking Secretary Johnson for his comments. Johnson deferred to Davies for introductory remarks.

Davies reviewed Situation I (a two-part option consisting of providing arms overtly to the Lebanese regular forces and/or covertly to the Falange). State, he said, sees little short term benefit in providing arms to GOL. Even if the requested line items were made immediately available, they would be insufficient to make much of a difference militarily. The action would, however, constitute a morale booster for Helou. Before discussing the option of arms for the Falange irregulars, Davies observed that the descriptor "fascist" is perhaps too harsh a term for these forces. They are more appropriately described as militant, right-wing Christians. State's view of this option is that it should be done only under the circumstances of a collapse of the GOL with ensuing confessional strife—and then it should be done covertly.

Secretary Johnson asked about lead times. Karamessines outlined two methods of delivery:

1. The USG would intercede with a private U.S. firm such as INTERARMCO that maintains stocks of arms in Europe. The Falange would arrange for delivery without involving the USG as transfer agent, but the U.S. would pick up the tab for the arms. This could be done covertly.

2. Large scale air drops of arms and munitions to points specified by the Falange (this probably could not be done without some risk of exposure).

---

[5] Saunders sent a summary of the contingencies to Kissinger on October 27 prior to a November 24 WSAG meeting (see Document 68). (National Archives, Nixon Presidential Materials, NSC Files, NSC Institutional Files (H-Files), Box H–071, Washington Special Actions Group Meeting, WSAG Mtg. 10/29/69 Lebanon) An updated version of the contingency paper is ibid.

Kissinger returned to the first option, that of supplying arms directly to the GOL. Would we do it covertly, and would there be financial or political problems? Davies said the assistance would be openly provided, but more to the point is the apparent lack of urgency in doing it at all. The GOL doesn't need the arms at this juncture. Moreover, the option has to be viewed in the broader context of the overall Arab-Israeli problem. Neither Muslims or Christians in Lebanon can comfortably, at this point in time, accept arms which will be used against the fedayeen to the benefit of the Israelis. Kissinger disagreed. If the U.S. desire is to preserve a moderate government in Lebanon, we should be prepared to send the arms necessary to keep the government in power. He recommended, therefore, that we tell President Helou we are prepared within reason to give him what he wants in the way of arms and to ask if financing will be a problem. The Group agreed with this course of action. Davies was charged with preparing a cable to Ambassador Porter requesting that he communicate with Helou.

Kissinger then outlined the steps that should be taken by the WSAG before arms are sent covertly to the Falange.

1. Define the conditions under which we would give covert assistance.

2. Coordinate with the 303 Committee.

3. Determine when the conditions for shipment have been met.

Nutter inquired why we should not do it now. Secretary Johnson replied that the possibility of embarrassing security leaks seemed to be the main drawback. Kissinger elaborated on the pros and cons of the action saying that, on the one hand, provision of arms to the Falange could make them overly adventuresome, but on the other hand, withholding the arms could encourage the Muslims to greater militancy. On the whole, the best option seems to be arms for GOL forces because they are controlled by officers sympathetic to the Falange. What you have, in effect, is support of the Falange by proxy, while retaining the option of covert support should the GOL show signs of imminent collapse. What we need to do is make the necessary logistic arrangements now, but put a hold on the package until a decision is made that the course of action is appropriate. The Group agreed. Karamessines advised that the airlift would require four C–118s or their equivalents.

Nutter asked if the Russians are supporting the fedayeen. Davies replied affirmatively. The Soviets have strongly supported not only the fedayeen but also the PFLP. At first the support was furnished by the UAR, on a replenishment basis. Now the Soviets appear to be dealing directly with the guerillas. Because this cannot but disturb Nasser, the Russians will have to play it cool. Much depends on the outcome of the talks in Cairo.[6] As far as our interests are concerned, the results will inevitably be bad—it is merely a question of how bad?

Davies then reviewed Situation II, which has to do with evacuation of U.S. personnel from Lebanon. There are, he reported, detailed interdepartmental plans covering this contingency. Kissinger asked for copies of the plans to be kept on file in the White House Situation Room. He then asked about the current location of the forces that could be employed should it become necessary to secure the airfield at Beirut as a part of evacuation. Admiral Johnson advised that a Marine Battalion Landing Team is located at Souda Bay in Crete, about 44 hours out of Beirut. Kissinger wondered if the Marines shouldn't be moved closer. Secretary Johnson thought not. The situation is not that grave.

Admiral Johnson noted an alternative possibility to the use of the Marines. If military airlift from Europe is used, the aircraft could transport a rifle company to Beirut. Secretary Johnson agreed, but observed that such an action might be unnecessary because it is not certain that we will be faced with a totally hostile population.

Kissinger asked that the military aspects of Situation II be expanded to include greater detail on required forces, their places of origin, and the timing incident to their employment. He wondered, moreover, if we need a political scenario to cover evacuation procedures. Davies said we should have no basing problems. Turkey, for instance, would be amenable to staging operations provided evacuation and not military involvement were guaranteed. Secretary Johnson asked about the safety of Americans in other Arab countries. Davies was confident that in a purely evacuation scenario no difficulties would be encountered. The case would be entirely different in the event of U.S. military involvement.

Kissinger said the paper would be improved by developing an integrated political-military scenario for Situation II similar to the Korean paper[7] but not as extensively detailed. *All* agreed it could and should be done.

---

[6] The United Arab Republic offered to mediate the dispute between Lebanon and the fedayeen, prompting representatives of the Lebanese Government and the Palestine Liberation Organization (PLO) to meet in Cairo at the end of October to negotiate a peaceful resolution of the confrontation. (INR Intelligence Note 777, October 31; National Archives, RG 59, Central Files 1967–69, POL 23 LEB; telegram 9012 from Beirut, October 29; ibid.) While the two sides settled on general principles regarding the relationship between the Government of Lebanon and the fedayeen, the so-called "Cairo Agreement" of November 2 contained few details. (Telegram 9178 from Beirut, November 4, and telegram 9582 from Beirut, November 19; both ibid., Nixon Presidential Materials, NSC Files, Box 620, Country Files, Middle East, Lebanon, Vol. I)

[7] See *Foreign Relations*, 1969–1976, volume XIX, Part 1, Korea, 1969–1972, Document 27.

Davies outlined the principal elements of Situation III—U.S. military intervention in response to serious internal disorder in Lebanon. Karamessines cautioned the Group to be careful about the definition of "internal," reporting that the Lebanese had captured 150 "fedayeen" prisoners who turned out to be Syrian regulars. Kissinger pondered the question of whether the U.S. would ever commit forces if the Lebanese problem were strictly internal. The consensus of the Group was generally negative, but *all* agreed that planning for such an event is an imperative. Kissinger asked if the internal disorders in Lebanon could get completely out of hand. Secretary Johnson said they could, and most assuredly would if polarization developed along confessional lines. Kissinger indicated that, if confessional strife developed, our action would be to support the Falange. Saunders noted the possibility of an "in-between" scenario, in which Lebanese internal disorders increase alarmingly and Helou advises U.S. that without help his government is doomed. This prompted Kissinger to ask if Situation II and III could not be complementary, that is, couldn't "evacuation" provide a pretext for "intervention"? The Group mulled over the question before concluding that after the period of time required for evacuation had elapsed (roughly 48 hours), the continued presence of U.S. troops would be a transparent ploy.

Kissinger requested additional detail for Situation III in the form of greater specificity about forces, timing, logistic support, airlift requirements, etc. Again, the re-work should follow the style of earlier integrated political-military scenarios developed for the WSAG but not necessarily in the same detail. The important point which should come through is a clearly revealed statement of actual military needs. Secretary Johnson mentioned overflight rights and basing problems, noting that WSAG Middle East papers[8] contain a useful treatment of these problems. Kissinger inquired about actual air corridors that would be available in the event of U.S. intervention. The Group agreed that European overflight may not be possible and that routing through the Straits of Gibralter may be the only alternative. Kissinger said that we must consider not only the problems in Lebanon but the consequences of our actions in terms of their effects in other Arab states. What other force commitments or evacuation efforts might be required?

Davies remarked that Situation IV—U.S. intervention in response to external aggression—would also present very difficult problems. Secretary Johnson agreed saying there is a great deal of fuzziness between Situations III and IV. In actuality, there could be a combination of both. Kissinger asked what the Israelis would be doing while all of this is going on. Davies remarked on the unfortunate geographical situ-

---

[8] See footnote 2, Document 68.

ation. The Lebanese Muslims and the fedayeen are located in the areas contiguous with Israel, while the Lebanese Christians and the Falange are farther to the north. If they concluded it necessary, the Israelis would strike the territory in Lebanon occupied by the fedayeen. Nutter observed that the Israelis would respond to a Syrian invasion of Lebanon by striking Damascus. Admiral Johnson thought we should develop in Situation III and IV a statement of likely Soviet responses. Although this point was not pursued, the Group agreed that such considerations were absolutely germane to the problem.

Kissinger said the Group should work out intervention scenarios that will show the President the full amplitude of the problem. There is, however, an issue even broader than intervention. If the Israelis are likely to respond positively to a deteriorating situation in Lebanon, why not let them do the job? If we did this, given the unambiguous and seemingly irreversible decline of the GOL, the Israelis might be able to handle the problem while the U.S. attempts to hold off the USSR on the basis of non-intervention by the superpowers. This is a matter, Kissinger said, that should be addressed by the NSC at an early date. He concluded the meeting by asking for a revised paper on Lebanon by Tuesday, November 4th.

Before the Group adjourned at 3:20 P.M. Admiral Johnson distributed a paper on rules of engagement[9] (called for at the WSAG meeting on October 21, 1969).[10]

---

[9] Not found.
[10] See Document 56.

61. Telegram From the Department of State to the Embassies in Jordan, Saudi Arabia, and Israel[1]

Washington, October 29, 1969, 1831Z.

182922. 1. *FYI:* In Sisco-Dobrynin meeting October 28 (septel)[2] Sisco gave Dobrynin our current position on UAR-Israel boundary question as part of package involving (a) withdrawal, (b) peace, and (c) neutral formulations on Sharm al-Shaykh, demilitarized zones and Gaza with details to be worked out by parties in Rhodes type negotiations.[3] Sisco stressed this package represented attempt on our part to find common language for joint US-Soviet document and did not constitute elements of new US document. Pending Soviet reaction, we do not want to get into discussion of specific texts with parties. We have requested Soviets to inform us if they plan to consult UAR, and we said we would similarily inform Soviets if we decided to consult parties.

2. Question arises of how to handle this latest development in US-Soviet talks with Arabs and Israelis. With UAR, we intend to call in Ghorbal about Thursday and fill him in generally. Bergus' further recommendation on how much more we should tell UAR requested.

3. With Hussein and Faisal, we think it would help bolster their confidence for us to give them private indication in general terms of step we have taken. Would appreciate Ambassador Porter's recommendations re possibility of taking similar action with President Helou.

4. With Israelis, we want to avoid this becoming major issue before we have some indication of Soviet reaction. On other hand we feel our credibility requires that we let Israelis know in general terms what we are trying to accomplish with Soviets. *End FYI.*

5. *For Amman and Jidda:* Ambassador should pass following to Hussein for his strictly private and confidential information. Chargé should similarly inform Saqqaf with request info be passed Faisal for his private information. QUOTE In meeting with Ambassador Dobrynin October 28, Assistant Secretary Sisco made major effort to break deadlock on UAR-Israel aspect of a settlement, which we consider key to overall settlement. To that end, he told Dobrynin it is USG position that old in-

---

[1] Source: National Archives, Nixon Presidential Materials, NSC Files, Box 653, Country Files, Middle East. Sisco Middle East Talks, October (1969). Secret; Immediate; Nodis. Drafted by Atherton, cleared by Sisco, and approved by Richardson. Repeated Priority to Beirut, Cairo, London, Paris, Moscow, and USUN. All brackets are in the original except "[7]", added for clarity.

[2] Telegram 182821 to Moscow, October 29. See *Foreign Relations,* 1969–1976, volume XII, Soviet Union, January 1969–October 1970, Document 98.

[3] Document 58.

ternational border between Palestine and Egypt should be the secure and recognized boundary between Israel and Egypt in the context of peace and of agreement worked out by parties under Jarring's auspices for security arrangements at Sharm al-Shaykh, demilitarized zones, and security arrangements for and final disposition of Gaza. We are passing this message to their Majesties for their private information in view of our close relationship with them and request that they do not share it at this time with others. UNQUOTE.

6. *For Tel Aviv:* Ambassador should inform Eban that in Sisco-Dobrynin meeting October 28, we continued effort to find common formulations for inclusion in joint US-Soviet document we are seeking to evolve. We have made clear to Soviets that USG will present no new document and that we are now at stage of seeking joint formulations to express common positions or neutral language where agreement not possible. We have also made clear that purpose remains to help Jarring get negotiating process started between parties under his auspices. General direction of our current efforts is away from specificity to generalized formulations in most respects. We are seeking to maximize areas for negotiation between parties and minimize specificity and detail as Eban indicated at breakfast meeting with Sisco in New York.[4] He should also be aware that we are bearing fully in mind importance of how any document is ultimately transmitted to Jarring, i.e., QUOTE for his guidance with parties UNQUOTE or some other possible non-mandatory formulation. We are standing on specific language on peace and on negotiations according to Rhodes formula. As Sisco foreshadowed to Eban in New York October 2 and Under Secretary Richardson to Rabin October 15,[5] we have moved on a very contingent and tentative basis in direction of specific language on Israel-UAR boundary question—i.e., toward reaffirmation of QUOTE Rusk formula UNQUOTE of November 1968.[6] As Under Secretary made clear to Rabin, we are seeking quid pro quo from Soviets for restating what has in effect been US position all along; such restatement on our part remains contingent upon agreement of USSR to specific commitment to peace and Rhodes type negotiations to work out practical security arrangements and other details of settlement. We are passing this information to Eban in strictest confidence and ask that it be closely held. We are not asking Israel at this time to react in any way, pending reaction of other side. GOI position on this question has been made abun-

---

[4] Sisco's October 2 meeting with Eban was reported in telegram 173876 to Tel Aviv, October 14. (National Archives, RG 59, Central Files 1967–69, POL 27–14 ARAB–ISR)

[5] See footnote 10, Document 55.

[6] See *Foreign Relations*, 1964–1968, volume XX, Arab-Israeli Dispute, 1967–1968, Document 301.

dantly clear to us and we are not seeking its agreement. We will wish to discuss this further with GOI after we receive Soviet reaction.

6 [7]. *For London and Paris:* We will brief UK and French here and report by septels.

Rogers

62. National Security Study Memorandum 82[1]

Washington, November 6, 1969.

TO

    The Secretary of State
    The Secretary of Defense
    The Secretary of the Treasury
    The Secretary of Commerce
    The Secretary of Agriculture
    The Director of the Bureau of the Budget
    The President of the Export-Import Bank
    The Administrator of AID

SUBJECT

    U.S. Economic Assistance Policy Toward Israel

The President has directed that U.S. economic policy toward Israel be evaluated. This study should examine:

—The amount of foreign exchange needed to meet Israel's requirements over the next five years.

—The availability of foreign exchange exclusive of external assistance to finance Israel's defense requirements.

—The alternative levels of U.S. economic assistance, if any, needed to meet Israeli military and non-military objectives.

—The alternative means of financing U.S. economic assistance to Israel.

This study shall be carried out by an NSC Ad Hoc Group chaired by a representative of the Assistant to the President for National Security Affairs. Its other members will be designated by the addressee agencies.

---

[1] Source: National Archives, Nixon Presidential Materials, NSC Files, Box 605, Country Files, Middle East, Israel, Vol. III. Secret; Sensitive.

The study will be submitted by December 19 to the President's Assistant for National Security Affairs and will then be referred to the IG/NEA for review.

Henry A. Kissinger

63. National Security Study Memorandum 81[1]

Washington, November 6, 1969.

TO
> The Secretary of State
> The Secretary of Defense
> The Director of Central Intelligence
> The Director of the Bureau of the Budget

SUBJECT
> U.S. Arms Transfer Policy Toward Israel

The President has directed that U.S. arms transfer policies toward Israel be evaluated. This study should:

—Examine the balance of Arab/Israeli military capabilities given alternative levels of U.S. and Soviet arms transfers over the next five years.

—Analyze Israel's force requirements to meet a variety of alternative defense objectives, including a) deterrence through preemptive attack; b) deterrence of Arab attack through superior force; and c) maintenance of its independence if deterrence fails.

—Determine Israel's technical and economic capacity to produce its arms requirements.

—Formulate alternative U.S. arms transfer policies toward Israel, including specific program levels over the next five years.

This study will be carried out by an NSC Ad Hoc Group chaired by a representative of the Assistant to the President for National Security Affairs. Its other members will be designated by the addressee agencies.

---

[1] Source: National Archives, Nixon Presidential Materials, NSC Files, Box 605, Country Files, Middle East, Israel, Vol. III. Secret; Sensitive. A copy was sent to the Chairman of the Joint Chiefs of Staff.

The study will be submitted by December 12 to the President's Assistant for National Security Affairs and will then be referred to the IG/NEA for review.

Henry A. Kissinger

64. Telegram From the Department of State to the Embassy in Israel[1]

Washington, November 6, 1969, 0055Z.

187681. For Ambassador.

1. We believe reported agreement between Lebanese Government and guerrilla leadership[2] likely to result as a minimum in some greater freedom of action for the fedayeen. This, of course, carries with it risk that Israelis will feel obliged to take early counter measures as warning to Lebanese Government and to guerrillas themselves. We assume you will continue to counsel restraint.

2. We doubt this will be sufficient, however, and believe more drastic effort on our part may be necessary to persuade Israelis to adjust themselves to new situation in Lebanon in ways designed avoid to extent possible further political deterioration there. We have accordingly been giving thought to what further we might say to Israelis with respect to lessons to be drawn from current Lebanese crisis. In this connection, we feel that events have borne out our somber predictions that Israeli policy of large scale military retaliation against two remaining moderate regimes, Jordan and Lebanon, while militarily successful, would be in long run a political disaster. You will have noted that in Richardson-Rabin conversation last Friday,[3] we made point that we thought at the time that Beirut airport attack[4] was a mistake and would be a real beginning of political deterioration in Lebanon. Events since then have, in our judgment, tended to confirm this conclusion. We do not disagree with Rabin's assertion to Under Secretary that fedayeen

---

[1] Source: National Archives, Nixon Presidential Materials, NSC Files, Box 605, Country Files, Middle East, Israel, Vol. III. Secret; Exdis. Drafted by Sisco and Atherton, cleared in NEA/ARN, and approved by Rogers. Repeated to Amman, Beirut, Cairo, Jidda, London, Moscow, Paris, Jerusalem, and USUN.

[2] See footnote 6, Document 60.

[3] October 31. No record was found.

[4] See footnote 6, Document 1.

would have become increasing problem in Lebanon even in absence Beirut raid. This misses point, however, that Beirut raid in our view gave fedayeen boost and seriously hampered GOL's ability to cope politically with fedayeen problem when it subsequently began assume major proportions.

3. We believe principal lessons to be drawn from current Lebanese crisis are two-fold: (A) that U.S. must continue to make major efforts to try to achieve a political settlement despite continued expressed opposition of Israelis; and (B) that, as was indicated to Rabin, Israelis must do some hard thinking and reassess their policy of the past months of quote seven-fold unquote retaliation on Jordanian and Lebanese soil. It may be that guerrilla movement has picked up such steam politically and militarily that trend will not be reversible. We are struck by the fact, however, that neither UAR nor Soviets seem interested in pushing present crisis to ultimate challenge. We feel, therefore, that there may still be room to maneuver in this situation.

4. We would like to have any thoughts that you may have regarding the above as well as your judgment regarding USG approach to GOI along following lines:

A. For some time we have expressed grave doubts to GOI about wisdom of its policy of large scale retaliation in response to fedayeen activities mounted from Lebanon and Jordan. We believe that latest political crisis in Lebanon has demonstrated that such policy can only contribute to political chain reaction threatening very existence of moderate regimes and thereby over long run US as well as Israeli interests.

B. Hard reality is that, in absence of political settlement, moderate regimes have no alternative to tolerating certain level of fedayeen activity from their territory if they are to survive. In our view, agreement between Lebanese Government and fedayeen is irreversible and only question is extent to which GOI can counter and limit fedayeen activities, not whether it can prevent them entirely.

C. In interest of preserving regimes with whom Israel can eventually make peace when opportunity presents itself, we believe GOI must make fundamental reassessment of its entire doctrine of how to deal with this problem as it relates to Lebanon and Jordan. We urge Israelis in particular to reassess political implications of their actions, giving greater weight to these than has been case in past where they have tended to concentrate on military success or failure of a given action.

D. We appreciate fully that Israel cannot remain passive and react in no way to fedayeen attacks across its borders, particularly when they take toll of innocent civilian lives. What we are urging, however, is that Israelis adopt new doctrine based on premise they must live with certain level of fedayeen attacks from Lebanon and Jordan and that, so far as these 2 countries are concerned, they limit their military response first to defensive actions to reduce infiltration and secondly to responding in kind and only in a measured way. In other words, we urge that they adopt self-denying doctrine to extent of avoiding escalating counter actions and cross border initiatives in the form of air and commando strikes, which have been successful militarily but have resulted in strengthening fedayeen politically at expense of both Jordanian and Lebanese Governmental leadership.

E. We think Israelis should make conscious revision of their retaliation doctrine along foregoing lines and should so advise Hussein and Helou through contacts available to them, making clear that while they understand that fedayeen activities cannot be stopped completely and will have to be countered from time to time, they will exercise extra measure of restraint so long as Hussein and Helou reciprocate by pursuing vigorously efforts to limit fedayeen operations from their territory to maximum extent possible.[5]

Rogers

---

[5] In telegram 4202 from Tel Aviv, November 7, Barbour replied: "Appreciate Department's concern about the undesirable consequences of Israeli military responses to fedayeen across ceasefire (or armistice) line attacks. I believe however that a generalized approach such as that suggested in reftel [telegram 187681 to Tel Aviv] is not likely to have more effect than the continued reiteration of counsels of restraint by us at all levels both here and in Washington." The Ambassador concluded: "In sum, I think it is a misnomer to speak of general Israeli policy of retaliation or to tailor our démarches to the GOI as if such a policy did exist. Our approaches had better be particular ones designed for the particular circumstances. For present, therefore, I believe our best chance to promote Israeli restraint will be for us to keep in close touch with GOI and exchange with them to fullest extent possible information and opinions on situation in Lebanon." (National Archives, Nixon Presidential Materials, NSC Files, Box 604, Country Files, Middle East, Israel, Vol. II)

65. Memorandum From the President's Assistant for National Security Affairs (Kissinger) to President Nixon[1]

Washington, November 10, 1969.

SUBJECT

New Soviet Doctrine on the Middle East

The recent official Soviet statement[2] has disturbing implications beyond the particular problem of Lebanon with which it ostensibly dealt. It said:

"The firm belief is expressed in Soviet leading circles that not a single foreign power should encroach on the sovereignty of Lebanon and its right to settle its internal affairs and *must not interfere in matters within the competence of the Arab states themselves.*"

This is reminiscent of the Brezhnev doctrine of limited sovereignty for Eastern Europe, which asserted that a threat to the security of a socialist state was a "common" problem and a "concern" for all socialist states.

In effect, the statement

—sets up the USSR as the arbiter of what constitutes a matter within the sole "competence" of the Arab states, and

—asserts the principle that the internal affairs of Lebanon or any other country in the area should be decided by the "Arab states themselves."

One can be fairly certain that the Soviets will take credit for forestalling a US intervention as the Soviet press is now claiming. And there is no doubt that the Soviets have strengthened their hand in the area by their maneuver.

Left unchallenged, the Soviet statement puts the USSR in the position of placing a protective umbrella over radical Arab intervention in other Arab states.[3]

---

[1] Source: National Archives, Nixon Presidential Materials, NSC Files, Box 644, Country Files, Middle East, Middle East—General, Vol. II. Confidential. Sent for information.

[2] Sonnenfeldt sent a memorandum about the statement, which was released in Moscow on October 25, to Kissinger on October 29. (Ibid., Box 710, Country Files, Europe, USSR, Vol. VI)

[3] Nixon underlined this sentence and wrote: "*I agree.* What is Sisco's reaction & recommendation?"

66. Memorandum From the President's Assistant for National Security Affairs (Kissinger) to President Nixon[1]

Washington, November 11, 1969.

SUBJECT

The Middle East—Where We Stand

As we wait for the Soviet response to Sisco's latest formulation of our position on a UAR-Israel settlement,[2] I want to put down some general reflections on where we stand in the Mid-East. When we have that response, it would be a logical time for another NSC session to take stock.

The arguments for going ahead with the Sisco initiative were that:

—It is essential to the US position in the Mid-East to take a position more consistent with US interests. We have been too much Israel's lawyer. As a result, we are on the verge of a major policy shift—by force of circumstances, not by design. For twenty years, we have tried to maintain a broadly based position in the area. Now we are looked on as basing our position exclusively on Israel.

—The new formula would position us where we ought to be— holding out for Israel's *security* but not for Israel's *expansion*. Until now, we have seemed to be holding out for Israel's freedom to negotiate for major changes in its borders.

—The overriding US interest is in a peace settlement. If the Soviets responded positively, we might just have some chance of getting a negotiation started. If they responded negatively, we would have a clearer measure of their intent. The alternative was the certainty of a continued impasse.

—While the Israelis would not like this move, we would still be in a defensible position domestically as long as we held out for Israeli security. Israel's expansion is not one of our interests if security can be provided otherwise. Israel's long-term security depends in part on a US position in the Mid-East to hold off the USSR, but Israel's present strategy of standing fast is creating conditions which hasten the erosion of our position.

My reservations on the Sisco initiative are as follows:

---

[1] Source: National Archives, Nixon Presidential Materials, NSC Files, Box 651, Country Files, Middle East, Middle East through December 1969. Secret; Nodis. Sent for action.

[2] See Documents 58 and 61.

—I am not sure that a diplomatic move like this can any longer affect the deep-rooted forces at work in the area. It seems to me that the fedayeen movements have now become an almost autonomous force which the moderate governments will no longer be able to control. It has already become an explicit point in the US–USSR negotiations that the UAR cannot (or will not) commit itself to clamp down on the fedayeen. What I am saying is that (a) we should not be overoptimistic about our ability to bring about a peace settlement but (b) we should not allow ourselves to think that even a peace settlement would set things right for us in the Mid-East. The fedayeen would still be there working—if not to undercut the settlement—against moderate interests.

—But even if continued Israeli occupation of Arab territory—and not the fedayeen—is still the main cause of pressure on governments friendly to US interests, I believe we are off on a wrong tangent in concentrating on a UAR-Israel settlement. We have a much greater interest in Hussein than in Nasser and—what is even more important—the real issues in resolving the Palestine problem are on the Jordanian side. The West Bank is part of Palestine; there will be no solution without a refugee settlement; the refugees are a Jordanian not an Egyptian problem; Jerusalem is an issue for the entire Moslem world but is part of a Jordan settlement. We have focused on a UAR settlement first on the theory that Nasser's agreement would make Hussein's easier, but I have long felt that we should shift focus. While I hesitate to say this because of the complications it raises, there will be no settlement until Syria comes into the process. In essence, the roots of the 1967 war lay in Syrian support for fedayeen attacks on Israel. There is no reason not to expect that to continue.

—I am afraid the step we have taken, even if we make our position known, will gain us little in the Arab world if we then go on supporting Israel with arms and money after it rejects our position. At the same time, the Israelis will dissociate themselves from it.

What we are doing, I fear, is helping to build a case for greater Arab militancy—since we have backed slightly away from Israel—and making it more likely that Israel will rely more heavily than ever on its military strategy. We are doing too little to have a chance of success but enough to divert indigenous forces from reaching their own decision.

I see three choices:

1. Get out of the way and take no position (as Acheson recommended).[3]

---

[3] In an October 27 meeting with Nixon at the White House, former Secretary of State Dean Acheson recommended that the United States "should not intervene either di-

This would have the advantage of recognizing the situation as it is—that peace is unlikely and the US is unable to force it—and disengaging from responsibility for forces beyond US control.

The counter argument is that it may not be possible. First, the only way to do this and preserve an independent position would be to take our distance from Israel. In effect, a passive US policy favors Israel. We would have to cease our support for Israel if we were really going to dissociate ourselves. Second, we would be virtually disengaging and leaving our friends—including large private US investors—and the field to the USSR. Whether the US likes it or not, it is held responsible for Israel's existence. Whatever the US might do, it will be associated with the Israeli issue as long as it persists.

2. We could pursue what we are doing now with whatever modifications the evolving situation suggests.

The argument for doing this is that doing nothing leaves no likelihood of a settlement, while our present course at least keeps alive the possibility of constructing a diplomatic alternative to the present military course. As in any other difficult negotiating situation, there is something to be said for third-party efforts to give the contestants an honorable way out. As long as the diplomacy is not completely sterile, there is an argument for continuing to chip away at the problem.

The arguments against are those I have noted above.

3. We could come down hard on Israel and try to squeeze her back to pre-war borders if we once had a viable peace proposition with Arab backing.

The first argument for is that there probably will be no peace settlement without this kind of pressure in the end. The more basic argument is that Israeli strategy and peace terms now are inconsistent with US interests. We have come to the point where Israel would be content to see US Mid-East policy tied exclusively to Israel, reversing twenty years of US effort to maintain a broadly based policy. Israel is following a strategy detrimental to our interest—and, as you have said, to their own in the long run. Unless the US takes an independent stand, its options in the Mid-East will be increasingly narrowed.

The argument against includes jeopardizing the headway we have made with the Jewish community on Vietnam. But the principal ques-

---

rectly or by supplying military items to such a conflict." Acheson was "sure that the Government could find ways of letting the Russians know that our purpose was not to be involved and would be greatly facilitated by their adopting a similar course." He concluded by telling Nixon that he "saw the only hope of being a willingness of both Arabs and Jews to accept a more live-and-let-live policy as a result of a sharp and painful experience." (Memorandum of conversation with the President, October 27; Yale University, Sterling Memorial Library, Acheson Papers, Group 1087, Record Group IV, Box 68, Folder 173)

tion is whether the US could win in this sort of confrontation. This is not only a matter of whether we could follow through in any persistent application of pressure in the face of strong domestic reaction. Success would depend on Nasser and Hussein standing by a reasonable position. It would not be reasonable for us to try to force on the Israelis a settlement that lacked a fair chance of providing security for Israel.

If we were going to try the third, I would consider trying it initially at least as part of a global deal with the USSR on Vietnam.

The reasons why the Soviets might be interested are their inability to get their friends' land back, their own concern about radicalization of the area and their interest in getting Suez open. While they may prefer riding out the present situation a while longer to pressing Nasser hard, they are less than completely comfortable and see serious risks for themselves.

There are two questions in this approach: (1) Do the Soviets feel they are in a worse position in the Mid-East than the US is in the Mid-East? (2) Do they feel they are in as difficult a position in the Mid-East as the US is in Vietnam?

They would certainly like us to force Israel to give Nasser back his territory. On the other hand, while they are in a difficult position as long as we refuse, they can see US options continually narrowing in the area. The US position is not improving relative to theirs. At the same time, they may feel the US is far more seriously weakened by its involvement in Vietnam than the USSR is in the Mid-East.

The alternative to a global deal with the USSR is a straight Mid-East deal in which we would press Israel if Moscow pressed Nasser. This, of course, is implicit in our current course. My reservation with this, as I have said, is that we will end up pressing Israel on behalf of the Soviet client when our interest is really in settling the Palestine question—in contrast to the UAR-Israel geopolitical contest—which is a Jordanian issue.

Recommendation: That as soon as we have had a chance to evaluate Moscow's reply to the Sisco formulation, an NSC meeting be scheduled to discuss where we stand and next steps.[4]

---

[4] Nixon approved the recommendation on November 15.

67. Memorandum From Secretary of State Rogers to President Nixon[1]

Washington, November 16, 1969.

SUBJECT

Middle East Settlement Efforts

I want to review the current state of our efforts to achieve a Middle East settlement, the immediate decisions we face, and the courses of action for the future which we recommend for your approval.

Politically, the situation in the area has become more difficult for us and our friends. While the Lebanese crisis has temporarily abated, the basic aims of the Palestinian militants and of the Lebanese Government remain incompatible and the situation is therefore extremely fragile. In addition, the meeting of Arab Foreign and Defense Ministers,[2] which has just ended, highlighted and gave further emphasis to the strong anti-U.S. currents in the Arab world. It also further crystallized Arab frustrations at the lack of progress toward a political settlement, reflected the increasingly fatalistic attitude that another war is inevitable and strengthened the hand of the Palestinian militants and their supporters such as Syria. The summit conference of Arab Chiefs of State now scheduled to open in Rabat December 20[3] will give impetus to these trends if they are not reversed, will lock the Arabs further into postures making the chances for a peaceful settlement even slimmer and could bring a formal Arab renunciation of peace efforts based on the November 22, 1967 Security Council Resolution. In this atmosphere the remaining moderate Arab governments feel increasingly beleaguered, the most dramatic example being that Hussein has put out strong feelers to the Soviets for meeting certain needs for arms.

On the Israeli side, the Government of Israel has staked out its firm opposition to the positions we have taken in the major power talks. This opposition is likely to increase in the days ahead, and criticism from the Jewish community in the U.S. is likely to grow, particularly if we go much beyond our present position. In Israel, as the maneuvering for the formation of a new Government goes forward, Prime Minister

---

[1] Source: National Archives, Nixon Presidential Materials, NSC Files, Box 650, Country Files, Middle East, Middle East Negotiations. Secret; Nodis.

[2] The Arab League's Joint Defense Council met in Cairo November 8–10.

[3] The Arab League summit was held in Rabat December 21–23. Sisco summarized the results of the summit in an information memorandum to Rogers, January 6, 1970, printed in *Foreign Relations,* 1969–1976, volume XXIV, Middle East Region and Arabian Peninsula, 1969–1972; Jordan, September 1970, Document 18.

Meir is seeking to retain elbow room to negotiate a settlement with the Arabs if Israel's minimum condition is met—i.e., an Arab willingness to sit down and negotiate peace with Israel.

In our bilateral talks with the Soviets, we have made a major effort to reach agreement with them on a package framework for an Israeli-UAR settlement based on the trade-off of: (a) an Israeli commitment to withdraw to the former international frontier with Egypt; and (b) a UAR commitment to peace, including control of guerrilla activity, and to negotiate detailed security arrangements and related matters with Israel according to the flexible negotiating procedures followed by the parties at Rhodes in 1949.

While recognizing that prospects were slim, our objective has been to achieve an agreed US-Soviet document along these lines that could be turned over to the Four Powers and then to Ambassador Jarring to help him renew the dialogue among the parties. It now appears that the reaction to our efforts on an Israeli-UAR document will lead to further protracted discussion. The initial UAR reaction is negative, largely on the grounds that the document we have been developing with the Soviets leaves the question of a Jordanian settlement (including particularly the territorial aspects) untouched and requires the parties themselves to work out such issues as Sharm al-Shaykh and Gaza instead of providing a complete blueprint which would exclude Israel from any say in these questions vital to its security. We expect that the Soviets will neither accept nor reject our latest effort but rather will seek to negotiate it into a document conforming more closely to what the UAR desires. The British are wobbly, and the French are likely to be unhelpful.

This will give us great difficulties which arise largely because, as the other major powers spell out the terms of a settlement, we will be pressed to take positions on which we cannot produce Israel, given its strong feeling that the settlement terms should be negotiated directly between it and the Arabs.

Against the foregoing background, we face two urgent decisions:

1. Do we return to the Four Power forum or disengage; the British, French and Soviets are pressing for an early resumption. The Soviets have probably concluded we will go no further in the bilateral context than our present proposals which are, in our judgment, balanced, fair to both sides, and defensible to public opinion at home and abroad.

2. What to do about the Jordanian aspect of a settlement, which involves not only many of the same issues as a UAR settlement but the more complicated questions of refugees, Jerusalem and the West Bank border between Israel and Jordan within the former Palestine mandate area where no recognized international boundary has ever existed.

Four Power Talks: Do We Resume Or Do We Disengage?

The signs are clear that the French will not stand with us. They are willing to go beyond our position substantively for two principal reasons: they properly assess the chances for a settlement as slim and therefore want to be sure the positions they adopt will help to bolster and bulwark their position primarily in the Arab world; and their approach to achieving a settlement is different than ours. They lay greater store than we do on the possibility of the weight of a Four Power consensus on the parties, and more particularly its effect on Israel. A failure to convince Israel would be our failure and not theirs; therefore, they have a relatively free ride in the Four Power context. The foregoing pressures also operate on the British, and their firm support is not assured; they are inclined more than the French to avoid a break with us.

There is a case to be made for the U.S. to refuse to agree to resumed Four Power meetings as long as we and the Soviets remain unagreed on the Israeli-UAR Joint Working Document (TAB A).[4] Submitting the joint US–USSR document without Soviet agreement will inevitably invite U.K. and French whittling away and lead to digging ourselves deeply into a substantive position on which there will be no real hope of producing Israel. It can also be argued that while Nasser's reaction is unpredictable, U.S. unwillingness to engage in Four Power talks would be a clear signal that the Four Powers are unable to produce for him the Israeli withdrawal from the occupied, territories. As long as there was serious hope of a common US–USSR position, the Israeli argument that the Four Power forum provided Nasser an instrument to escape his responsibilities was open to serious doubt. There is more substance to this argument today.

On the other hand, such a move would appear to the world that the U.S. was giving up and, therefore, blocking further peace efforts; our position in the Arab world would further deteriorate even to the point where American lives and property could be put into jeopardy; the pressures on Lebanon and Saudi Arabia would continue to increase; and this would be a strong blow to King Hussein, whose continuing desire to make peace needs all the moral and political support we can muster. In these circumstances, we could expect that the December 20th Arab summit meeting would decide formally to close the door on a political solution. I reluctantly conclude therefore, with all of the difficulties that I foresee, that we should agree to renewal of the Four Power meetings beginning on November 21.

---

[4] Attached at Tab A is the "U.S.–USSR Joint Working Paper on Israel-UAR Settlement." It is printed as Document 58.

The question will immediately arise: what should the Four Powers focus on? The Soviets will probably press for an across-the-board approach dealing with the entire problem in all its aspects and especially with the question of total Israeli withdrawal everywhere including Syria and Jerusalem as well as Sinai and the West Bank. We cannot support such a position because we could not produce Israel. From our viewpoint, one possible counter to so unproductive an approach would be to table the paper we have developed for an Israel-UAR settlement. We may want to table it in the Four Power forum at some point, but I would not want to do this unless the French and the British are first firmly tied down. We have in mind the possibility of personal messages from you to Wilson and Pompidou at an appropriate stage. In the unlikely event the Soviets accept the bulk of the joint US–USSR document, or if necessary to pin down the UK and French, there are only two additional changes in the paper on an Israel-UAR settlement which we should be prepared to make: (a) a cosmetic change in the paragraph dealing with the Israeli-UAR border (Point 3) which would improve its presentational form from the Arab point of view; and (b) an addition to Point 4 to clarify that neither Israel nor the UAR would lay claim to Gaza.

These two changes will add to Israel's concern over the proposed document on an Israel-UAR settlement. They are, however, consistent with the basic principles guiding our approach to a settlement and fully protect Israel's interests by providing for Israeli participation in negotiating security arrangements on the ground. I do not believe we should go any further than this in modifying our position on an Israel-UAR settlement as reflected in the current U.S.–USSR Working Paper. Furthermore, I believe we must make clear to the British and French that we will not discuss that paper in the Four, and will reconsider the whole question of our continued participation in that forum, unless they commit themselves not to seek to whittle away our position, particularly as it relates to the concept of neutral formulations for the parties to negotiate: (a) practical security arrangements for Sharm al-Shaykh and Gaza; and (b) areas to be demilitarized. If the Four Powers pronounce themselves on these, what chance we have of producing Israel will be doomed. Israel will say, with some validity, what is there left to negotiate on the UAR-Israeli aspect? We will be pressed by the other three to "impose" this on Israel; it is naive for Foreign Minister Stewart to say that no nation can long refuse a solution agreed upon by the Four Powers and backed by the weight of world opinion. No nation other than Israel, that is. I doubt we can defend such a line here at home without jeopardizing support from certain elements of public opinion of our stance on Vietnam.

If we do not begin with a UAR-Israel settlement in the Four Power forum, the alternative—and the one I recommend—is that we agree that the Four Powers resume and propose that they consider the Israeli-Jordanian aspect of a settlement. The British and French are anxious for us to join them in calling an early meeting of the Four Powers, and we propose to use the leverage this gives us to seek to line up as much of their support as possible in advance for steering the Four Power talks in this direction.

Jordanian Part of Settlement

Neither the Soviets nor the Egyptians are likely to make final commitments on the UAR-Israeli part of the settlement until they know more about the shape of the Jordanian settlement. Hussein himself is very anxious for the U.S. to become more directly involved on the Jordanian part. He does not want, nor do we want, a Soviet broker. We believe, therefore, that in the days ahead we should concentrate on this part of the settlement in two ways: (a) Ambassador Yost would engage in discussions on this aspect in the Four Power context; (b) we will raise with Israel and Jordan at an early date whether they would agree to the U.S. playing a singular middle man role between them while the Four Power talks are going on to see whether there is some common ground that can be developed between them.

We have given considerable thought to both the tactics and the substance of the U.S. position on the Jordanian aspect in the Four Power forum. We have concluded that tactically there is merit in letting the British and French take the lead on the Jordanian aspect and for us to try to assume a lower silhouette in the Four Power forum. Substantively we believe Ambassador Yost should stay within the confines of the document setting forth the framework for an Israeli-Jordanian settlement which I sent you on October 10. I now recommend that Ambassador Yost be authorized to use this document (TAB B)[5] as guidance for the position he would take in reacting to proposals by others in the Four Power discussions; he would not table this paper and would ask for further instructions on any proposals that go beyond it.

Policy Statement

While the foregoing moves are in train, we also want to take steps to get the elements of our position on an overall Arab-Israeli settlement on the public record in an effort to make clear that it is basically a balanced position and not simply a carbon copy of Israeli views. Israel is already criticizing our position publicly, and such an effort on our part is not likely to come as a surprise to them even though they would clearly prefer that we not make this effort. Such an effort will not satisfy

---

[5] Attached but not printed at Tab B is the paper "Fundamental Principles for Israel-Jordan Settlement."

the Arab extremists, but it will be difficult for either side or world opinion to criticize objectively and will be of some help to our beleaguered friends in the Arab world. I will be sending you shortly for your review the text of a speech I propose to make very soon outlining the elements of our Middle East policy.

William P. Rogers[6]

---

[6] Rogers initialed "WPR" above his typed signature.

---

68. Minutes of a Washington Special Actions Group Meeting[1]

Washington, November 24, 1969, 3:03–5:18 p.m.

SUBJECT

Libya and Lebanon

PARTICIPANTS

Henry A. Kissinger—Chairman

State
U. Alexis Johnson
David Newsom (Libya only)
Rodger Davies

Defense
G. Warren Nutter

CIA
Thomas H. Karamessines

JCS
Vice Admiral Nels C. Johnson

NSC Staff
Harold H. Saunders
Col. Robert M. Behr
Keith Guthrie

SUMMARY OF DECISIONS

[Omitted here are the decisions related to Libya.]

---

[1] Source: National Archives, Nixon Presidential Materials, NSC Files, NSC Institutional Files (H-Files), Box H–114, Washington Special Actions Group, WSAG Minutes (Originals) 1969 and 1970. Top Secret; Sensitive. All brackets are in the original except those indicating text omitted by the editors. The meeting was held in the White House Situation Room.

2. *Lebanon*

a. The following revisions are to be made in the Lebanon contingency paper:[2]

(1) The analysis of base availability in the Eastern Mediterranean will be given greater prominence. This analysis will be expanded to include not only the extreme possibilities (all bases available vs. no bases available) but also an intermediate contingency such as the availability of a single base at Athens.

(2) A discussion will be included concerning the possible consequences that U.S. military intervention in Lebanon may have in terms of violence against U.S. communities in other Arab countries.

(3) The option of a naval and air blockade is to be deleted.

b. Presidential approval will be sought for the U.S. to offer to equip the Lebanese Army with M–14 rifles.[3] If the President approves, details of price, quantity, and funding will be worked out by the State and Defense Departments and CIA. Also, if supply of M–14s to the Lebanese Army is authorized, preparations to furnish arms to the Falange will be discontinued.

c. The WSAG agreed that the U.S. should not encourage an Israeli invasion of Lebanon.

[Omitted here is the discussion of Libya and Lebanon.]

---

[2] The paper, November 17, is ibid., Box H–071, Washington Special Actions Group Meetings, WSAG Mtg. 11/24/69 Libya and Lebanon. A revised paper was not found.

[3] Not found.

69. Memorandum From Secretary of State Rogers to President Nixon[1]

Washington, November 26, 1969.

SUBJECT

Possible Move By King Hussein To Acquire Soviet Arms

The following memorandum is a status report for information only and will be followed in due course by a memorandum which contains recommendations for action.[2]

King Hussein of Jordan is awaiting a Soviet reply to his recent query regarding the availability of Soviet arms assistance.[3] The King is looking for anti-aircraft artillery and field artillery, particularly the former in order that Jordan may better cope with the quickening pace of Israeli air attacks. The King states that he has turned to the Soviets because of our past inability to meet his needs fully. In this connection, you will recall that when the King was here in April we were unable to sell him everything he wanted because of non-availability.[4]

The King tells us that even though he has sounded out the Soviets, he would prefer to continue to buy American arms if they should become available. As evidence of this the Jordanian Commander-in-Chief has presented us with a list of arms requirements similar to that presented to the Soviets. The King indicates that he might be prepared to settle for less than the total amount of equipment requested. Our military people in Amman confirm Jordan's defensive need for most of the equipment requested, particularly the anti-aircraft guns.

It is important to note that the King's contemplated move toward the Soviets is evidently intended to be an arms transaction only. The King assures us that any such move would represent no shift whatsoever in Jordanian policy. Jordan would continue to maintain close ties

---

[1] Source: National Archives, Nixon Presidential Materials, NSC Files, Box 613, Country Files, Middle East, Jordan, Vol. II. Secret; Exdis.

[2] Not found.

[3] According to telegram 5294 from Amman, November 1, Hussein confirmed for Ambassador Symmes that he had "asked for Soviet assistance in furnishing Jordan with heavy, medium, and anti-aircraft artillery," and that the request was made "some time ago." (National Archives, Nixon Presidential Materials, NSC Files, Box 613, Country Files, Middle East, Jordan, Vol. III) Telegram 438 from Amman, January 29, 1970, reported a favorable response from the Soviet Union to Jordan's request as well as Hussein's desire to refuse the Soviet offer if the United States would "come through" with its own package in a timely manner. The King emphasized the "urgency of a favorable US response." (Ibid., Box 614, Country Files, Middle East, Jordan, Vol. III)

[4] See Documents 19 and 24.

with the West and to seek a peace settlement in accordance with the Security Council Resolution of November 1967.

A check of our military stocks indicates that in order to meet the King's requirements we would have to make a decision to divert them from our Army units. For planning purposes, the Defense Department is preparing a report on the impact such a diversion would have on our forces.[5] We are also in the process of checking other free world sources.

A decision by the King to buy arms from the Soviets would cause problems in that it: (a) could provoke a sharp Israeli response both militarily and politically, and thus make our peace efforts that much more difficult; (b) could make Israel even less responsive to our counsels of restraint toward Jordan; (c) could be an irretrievable first step which, despite the King's best intentions, might lead eventually to a shift of Jordanian policy in the direction of the Soviets; (d) could make it difficult for us to obtain Congressional approval to continue existing military and economic aid programs and thus could undermine the King's policy of maintaining close relations with the West; and (e) could be interpreted as a blow to United States Government prestige and thus, in a psychological sense, could strengthen the hands of the Arab radicals while weakening the moderate regimes.

On the other hand, we are reluctant to contribute further to the arms race in the Middle East. Also it might be argued that since we are unlikely to achieve a peace settlement, the trend toward radicalization in Jordan may well be ineluctable, i.e., the Hashemite regime in Jordan will probably gradually have to develop closer relations with the USSR as time goes on if it is to survive or at least to survive longer.

Our Ambassador in Amman has recommended that we should respond to this new development with equanimity and should avoid giving the impression of being in a hurry to preempt the Soviets. He suggests that we treat the Jordanian request for more arms as a function of our annual review of Jordanian arms requirements. In this connection, he recommends that we send military representatives to Jordan to consult with the Jordanian military for the purpose of developing a firm request for artillery that we can consider. We are in the process of reviewing these proposals.

Even if we were to decide to sell the King more arms, we might not be able to meet the King's requirements sufficiently to preclude his going to the Soviets. If he did go the Soviet route, we would have legal problems. Our obligations under our present defense assistance agreement with Jordan are conditioned upon Jordan's secret undertaking "that it will not purchase major items of military equipment, either

---

[5] Not found.

ground or air, from other than United States sources without United States approval." We consider the artillery requested from the Soviets to be in the category of major items of military equipment and, accordingly, if purchased (rather than given) without our approval, we would be legally justified in suspending our defense assistance obligations to Jordan.

Penalizing the King in this manner could well be counterproductive, however, in that it would probably weaken the constructive influence which we would otherwise continue to exercise in Jordan. Therefore, in circumstances in which the King turned to the Soviets we might wish to consider ignoring Jordan's breach of its arms agreement with us or, conceivably, grant approval if it is requested. Any such decision on our part would have to flow from the assumption that Jordan's basic policy orientation would remain unchanged and that United States Government punitive action would tend to reverse this policy orientation.

I plan to be in touch with you further on this matter once we have collected more information and have crystallized our views.

William P. Rogers[6]

---

[6] Rogers initialed "WPR" above his typed signature.

70. Memorandum From Secretary of State Rogers to President Nixon[1]

Washington, November 26, 1969.

SUBJECT

Four Power Talks on the Middle East

In my memorandum of November 15th,[2] I recommended that we agree to an early resumption of the Four Power meetings on the Middle East. We have reassessed this recommendation in light of the following developments: (a) the temporizing Egyptian position of not responding substantively to the latest formulations in the US–USSR talks on the grounds that they are "incomplete" until positions on other aspects of the settlement are clearer; (b) the absence of any concrete Soviet reaction to the latest formulations; (c) the continued strong feelings of Hussein, Faisal and Helou that the Four Power talks resume; (d) the scheduled Arab Summit Meeting of December 20th at which Nasser can be expected to make a major effort to mobilize all possible resources on his behalf; and (e) Israel's request of November 25 that we refrain from resuming the Four Power talks and particularly from discussing an Israeli-Jordanian settlement until Eban has an opportunity to discuss their views with me on December 9.[3]

Our conclusion continues to be that we resume the Four Power meetings immediately, remaining available to continue the US–USSR bilateral talks if and when the Soviets respond concretely to the October 28th working paper formulations.[4] We suggest the Four Power talks resume on December 2.

In brief, the reasons for this recommendation are: (a) If we decline to resume the talks in New York, we will be taking on the onus for blocking further peace efforts, our position in the Arab world will continue to deteriorate even more rapidly, moderate Arab regimes will be

---

[1] Source: National Archives, Nixon Presidential Materials, NSC Files, Box 650, Country Files, Middle East, Middle East Negotiations. Secret; Nodis. Attached to a November 28 memorandum from Haig to Saunders that reads: "To keep our bureaucratic skirts clean, we ought to send an info memo to the President on where the subject now stands, with the Secretary's memorandum to him tabbed in." On Haig's memorandum, Saunders wrote by hand: "This was later handled orally with President. No further action."

[2] Rogers's memorandum of November 16 is Document 67.

[3] Eban did not meet with Rogers until December 16, after a meeting that day with Kissinger. See Document 77 and footnote 2 thereto. Richardson also discussed the proposal for a Jordanian settlement and the Rogers Plan with Rabin on December 19; see Document 78.

[4] Document 58.

further disillusioned and be more vulnerable to radical pressure, and the risk will be greater that the Arab summit will close the door to a political solution. (b) We have been committed to Four Power talks since February, they were interrupted in July at our initiative, and we agreed to their resumption in principle in September. The British and French have been patient largely because of our on-going efforts with the Soviet Union. In light of the present impasse between the US and the USSR, we no longer have a strong argument against early resumption of the Four. (c) The on-going Four Power meetings, even if the Four cannot agree on recommendations to Jarring, will give us a further opportunity to help improve our general position in the area. We would anticipate that the Four Powers would focus in the first instance principally on the Jordanian aspect and this would be welcomed by Hussein. We realize we will have to exert great efforts to avoid the twin pitfalls of either being isolated in the Four or being pressured to go along with a proposition on which we could not produce Israel; but the disadvantages of blocking Four Power talks are even greater.

We would also inform the Israelis that we are willing to talk about the substance of the Jordanian-Israeli aspect of the settlement or any other aspects of our Middle East policy either with Ambassador Rabin right away and/or with Eban when he arrives in the United States on the 9th of December. In order to assure them that we will take into account fully their substantive views, we will indicate our intention not to submit any substantive American proposals on the Jordanian-Israeli aspect until I have had my conversation with Eban. Moreover, we will want also to consult fully with Hussein who has long been anxious for the United States to play a leading role on the Jordanian-Israeli aspect along the lines of your discussions with him in April.

William P. Rogers[5]

---

[5] Rogers initialed "WPR" above his typed signature.

71. Telegram From the Department of State to the Mission to the United Nations[1]

Washington, December 2, 1969, 0232Z.

200463. Subject: Four Power Meeting on Middle East.

1. As you know from your conversations here, we have agreed to resume Four Power talks on December 2 on understanding that: (a) We will not wish to put forward any new proposals before Secretary has had opportunity to consult with Eban on Dec. 16;[2] and (b) in first instance focus will be on Jordanian aspect, pending receipt of a reply from Soviets on UAR part of settlement. We will also be consulting Jordanians fully before you get deeply into substance.

2. We know you are fully aware of difficult situation we face in Four Power context and our desire to avoid twin dangers of being committed to formulations on which we cannot produce Israel or being isolated from other three. Moreover, since initially you will be dealing primarily with Jordanian aspect our position will be under particular scrutiny from both our friends, Israel and Jordan. In general, we suggest you be guided in Four Power talks by following:

(a) There are three key features to our position: *negotiations*, *peace*, and *withdrawal*. We believe major emphasis should be on equating specific commitments to peace and withdrawal and on Rhodes type negotiations between parties on detailed elements of a settlement, including security arrangements, demilitarized zones, refugees and Jerusalem.

(b) Every formulation on Jordanian aspect is inextricably bound with UAR aspect. Therefore no formulations should be accepted which go beyond or would have effect of undermining October 28th UAR-Israeli working paper formulations,[3] on which we intend to stand firm in belief that we could not produce Israel on anything going beyond them.

(c) Throughout the exercise each proposal must be evaluated in terms of whether it will be possible to produce the parties. In particular, since we will be expected to produce Israel, you should make clear we consider it essential to have regular consultations with Israelis and Arabs on formulations as they are put forward. We realize French and

---

[1] Source: National Archives, RG 59, Central Files 1967–69, POL 27–14 ARAB–ISR. Secret; Priority; Exdis. Drafted by Sisco, Atherton, and Betty J. Jones (IO/UNP); cleared in IO; and approved by Richardson. Repeated to Amman, Beirut, Jidda, Kuwait, London, Moscow, Paris, Tel Aviv, Cairo, and Bucharest.

[2] See footnote 3, Document 70.

[3] Document 58.

to lesser extent British will be very reluctant to proceed in this way, but we consider it important that in event of failure to make progress as much onus as possible rest on the parties rather than US.

(d) You should make major effort to keep formulations general; we continue to feel that major powers cannot write blueprint and largest possible area must remain for parties to negotiate on basis Rhodes formula.

(e) While we agree fully with sense of urgency which UK in particular feels, you should bear in mind our judgment that there will be no positive indications from Arabs before December 20th Arab Summit.

(f) Finally, Dec. 2 and subsequent Four Power meetings provide opportunity, which should be fully exploited, to develop pressure on Soviets to respond to Oct. 28 formulations.[4]

3. We agreeable to UK suggestion that opening meeting deal with US and Soviet report on status of bilaterals. (Guidance by septel).[5] At first meeting suggest you make clear that at least until we receive Soviet response to document discussed at October 28 Sisco-Dobrynin meeting,[6] we would expect UAR aspect of settlement to continue to be dealt with in two-power context while four powers concentrate on Jordanian aspect. How we play UAR aspect after receiving Soviet response will depend in large measure on nature of that response.

4. We anticipate that UK will plan to put forward Israeli-Jordanian boundary language at early stage. We are now reviewing UK formulation and will have further comment for you on it.[7] Since we are expected to produce Israelis, we will be consulting with British re consultations with Israelis on UK formulation or such alternative as we may suggest and seeking Israeli reaction though not necessarily approval. Our hope would be that this would put some pressure on GOI to be more forthcoming re Jordanian aspect. At such time as British submit boundary language, we would want you to table for inclusion in Jordanian-Israeli document language calling for Rhodes-type negotiations and on peace taken from UAR-Israeli document i.e., preamble and Point 2. All that is required is substitution of word "Jordan" for "UAR" in appropriate places.

5. Your major problem is likely to be French desire to put forward much more detailed proposals, particularly on UAR aspect, than we believe traffic will bear. We are prepared to weigh in at any appropriate level in Paris as four power discussions evolve.

---

[4] The Soviets did not respond until December 23. See Document 80.
[5] Not found.
[6] See Document 61.
[7] Not found.

6. Additional problem is that Soviets may well seek to generalize discussions to deal with settlement in overall terms, along lines of their December and June proposals.[8] If they do, suggest you make point that this is retrogressive and raises question whether they more interested in making propaganda or progress. We all recognize that settlement must cover all Arab states who have accepted SC Resolution before it can be put into effect—i.e., it must be horizontal as well as vertical package, as Gromyko put it to Sisco in July.[9] We all recognize also that certain elements will be common to both UAR and Jordanian aspects. Discussions over past eight months have made clear, however, that each aspect has its unique problems as well, which must be dealt with on a country-by-country basis. We see this as only responsible and businesslike way to proceed.

7. We expect a propaganda statement by Soviets; you are requested to rebut fully.

Rogers

---

[8] See Documents 1 and 34.
[9] See Document 39.

---

72. Editorial Note

The Four Powers resumed their discussions in New York on December 2, 1969. At the first meeting, the four UN Permanent Representatives issued a communiqué announcing the resumption of the talks. (Department of State *Bulletin*, December 29, 1969, page 630) Ambassadors Charles Yost, Yakov Malik, and Lord Caradon agreed on the urgency of providing recommendations to UN Special Representative Gunnar Jarring, while Ambassador Armand Bérard hoped that the U.S.-Soviet talks would produce an Israeli-UAR agreement for the group's review. Both Bérard and Malik expressed concern over increasing hostilities in the Middle East, with Malik blaming Israel for the region's instability. (Telegram 4391 from USUN, December 3; National Archives, RG 59, Central Files 1967–69, POL 27–14 ARAB–ISR) Malik tabled draft language on the issues of Israeli withdrawal, boundaries, and demilitarized zones, all of which were drawn from the Soviet counterproposal presented to the United States on June 17 (see Document 34).

At the end of the meeting, Yost responded to Malik's argument that the Four Powers should strive to achieve a comprehensive agreement between Israel and its Arab neighbors rather than consider one country at a time by saying that Dobrynin, in his conversations with Sisco, had never objected to discussing the United Arab Republic separately. Caradon and Bérard agreed with Yost that without a Soviet response to the October 28 proposal from the United States (Document 58) the Four should begin discussing the outlines of an Israel-Jordan settlement at the next meeting. (Telegram 4390 from USUN, December 3; National Archives, RG 59, Central Files 1967–69, POL 27–14 ARAB–ISR)

At the December 6 session, Bérard, Caradon, and especially Yost again pressured Malik for an early Soviet reply to the U.S. proposal on a settlement between Israel and the UAR. Meanwhile, Bérard said that he expected to present concrete proposals for an Israel-Jordan agreement at the next meeting, which would occur on December 9. (Telegram 4460 from USUN, December 6; ibid.)

73. Editorial Note

On December 9, 1969, Secretary of State William Rogers delivered a speech to the Galaxy Conference on Adult Education in Washington, in which he publicly unveiled the Department of State's plan for an Arab-Israeli peace settlement that had been in the works with the Soviet Union since the beginning of the Two-Power talks in March. Rogers declared that the United States had adopted a "balanced and fair" policy in the Middle East consistent with UN Security Council Resolution 242. He argued that the Arabs must accept a "permanent peace" with Israel based on a "binding agreement" and maintained that any settlement between Israel and the Arabs must contain a "just settlement" of the Palestinian refugee question that took into consideration "the desires and aspirations of the refugees and the legitimate concerns of the governments in the area." Regarding Jerusalem, Rogers stated that it should be a "unified city within which there would no longer be restrictions on the movement of persons and goods. There should be open access to the unified city for persons of all faiths and nationalities."

Perhaps the most important part of the speech, however, had to do with the future borders between Israel and its Arab neighbors. Rogers put the United States firmly on record as supporting Israel's withdrawal from Arab territories occupied in the 1967 Arab-Israeli war in exchange for security arrangements that would include demilitarized zones. "We believe that while recognized political boundaries must be established and agreed upon by the parties, any change in the pre-existing lines should not reflect the weight of conquest and should be confined to insubstantial alterations required for mutual security. We do not support expansionism. We believe troops must be withdrawn." The full text of the speech is in the Department of State *Bulletin*, January 5, 1970, pages 7–11. It was also published in the *New York Times*, December 10, 1969, page 8.

Although the details of the speech were largely a reflection of the October 28 "Joint US–USSR Working Paper" (Document 58), and were known to the Soviets, Egyptians, and Israelis, Rogers went forward with the speech at the urging of Assistant Secretary of State for Near Eastern and South Asian Affairs Joseph Sisco. In a November 6 memorandum to Rogers, Sisco argued that "the principal purpose of the speech would be to expose some of the substantive positions that we have taken during the past months, which are much more balanced than the impression the world has of them." From a public point of view, Sisco added, "we have suffered in the area generally because we have not revealed more of the substance, while the Soviets have pegged out the most extreme position publicly—total withdrawal of Israeli forces from all the occupied territories to the pre-June 5 lines. We can never hope to beat this in the Arab world from a propaganda point of view, but exposing more of our substantive positions, and in particular placing on record our views on the question of withdrawal, should help to ease some of the increasing pressures in the Arab world and take a little sting out of the emotionalism." Sisco concluded by explaining to Rogers that "the speech is both necessary and desirable whether or not the U.S. and the USSR find common ground on a document. It will not satisfy the Arabs and will draw some flak from Israel, but it cannot be objectively attacked from either side. It gives us a solid basis to stand on for some time to come." (Memorandum from Sisco to Rogers, November 6; National Archives, RG 59, Records of Joseph J. Sisco, Lot Files 74 D 131 and 76 D 251, Box 27, Two Power Talks, 10/28/69 Démarche)

The following month, during a December 4 telephone conversation with the President's Assistant for National Security Affairs Henry Kissinger, Sisco again reiterated the need for the speech. The transcript of their conversation reads in part:

"K said what is the advantage of giving it [the speech]? S said it's geared to upcoming summit meeting. S said it's within the framework of our present policy. K said assuming what the P doesn't yet accept ... that we have to keep pushing negotiations. S said the speech goes down in whatever foreseeable purpose we could have in the future. S said we haven't said anything substantive since March; we haven't taken a balanced stand in the discussions; we think it will bolster the Jordanians, Moroccans and Libyans; it makes our position reasonably clear in circumstances where we are not likely to get a political settlement.

"K said he is not at all sure from talking with the P that he believes we are on the right track. K said the P wants to reserve judgment until the NSC meeting. [See Document 74.] S said it's a statement of policy on what we've done. K said he has passed it on. S said he thought this was based on the assumption that the NSC meeting would be today. K said the more he thought about it he thought to make a major policy decision without the Secretary of State present . . . If it were arms supply for Pakistan or something . . .

"S said he has come to two conclusions: 1) we've got to operate on the assumption that we are not going to get a consensus; 2) as long as we're not going to get a consensus, it's better in the area having the disagreement part of the overall disagreement in a four power context rather than we being pushed into a corner where it's 3 against 1 and we can't produce the Israelis. K said I don't understand. S said he is going to try to get this down on paper. S said on the Jordan aspect, we ought to decide what the outer perimeter of what our views are on the Jordan settlement: hope to maintain a toehold on Hussein; consistent with Jordanian security. S said secondly, if Charlie [Yost] is armed with that—can say that's our position—it's unlikely to get a Russian agreement. If that's the case we can stand firm on the October 28 document. We can say we think it's a reasonable and fair proposal. We say these proposals stand; there's no purpose in talking further until a closer meeting of the minds can be achieved. K said are you doing this as a formal proposal or personal. S said he can't do it as formal. S said he talked with Elliot [Richardson]. K said Elliot agrees with you. K said do you mind if I show it to the President? S said he's only going to make it personal first; only going to give to Elliot and K. S said what he would do for example: the assistant to the King wants to talk with S—just a friendly chat on December 12; the Secretary is going to talk to Eban on the 16th. S said it's an opportunity to consult generally along these lines. Say this is fair; as far as we are going to go. It's not the Russians playing lawyer for the Egyptians and we for the Israelis. S said we've got to get something if we're not going to let Hussein go down the drain. K said he's just concerned about letting the Russians in on [omission in the original]. S said the opening meeting of the four powers indicates that they've pegged out their most extreme position; paper asked for total withdrawal of Israeli forces from all occupied territory. K said including Syria? S said yes, on Syria the President spoke to Golda Meir in a way that would make it tough. K said yes he remembered." (Transcript of telephone conversation; National Archives, Nixon Presidential Materials, NSC Files, Kissinger Telephone Conversation Transcripts, Box 3, Chronological File)

74. Minutes of a National Security Council Meeting[1]

Washington, December 10, 1969, 10 a.m.

The Middle East

PARTICIPANTS

The President
The Vice President
The Secretary of State, William P. Rogers
The Secretary of Defense, Melvin R. Laird
The Chairman, Joint Chiefs of Staff, General Earle G. Wheeler
Director of Central Intelligence, Richard M. Helms
Director, Office of Emergency Preparedness, General George A. Lincoln
Under Secretary of State, Elliot L. Richardson
Ambassador Charles Yost
Henry A. Kissinger, Assistant to the President
Assistant Secretary Joseph J. Sisco
Alfred L. Atherton, Jr., Department of State
William Watts, NSC Staff
Harold H. Saunders, NSC Staff
Pat Conger, CIA

President: Let's limit discussion to the Mid-East. It would be useful at a later time to review Lebanese contingency planning—to know that the U.S. has less flexibility today than in 1958.[2] We could not order today the kind of landings that had been mounted then. Also, let's put the Libyan issue aside until later and concentrate on the Mid-East.

But first, let's hear report from Secretaries Rogers and Laird on trip to Europe.[3] [This briefing followed and will be covered in Mr. Watts' notes: "On Mid-East, Schumann may be a bit of a problem."]

---

[1] Source: National Archives, Nixon Presidential Materials, NSC Files, NSC Institutional Files (H-Files), Box H–109, NSC Meeting Minutes, NSC Minutes Originals 1969. Top Secret; Nodis. Drafted by Saunders. All brackets are in the original.

[2] See footnote 2, Document 4.

[3] Rogers led the U.S. delegation to the Ministerial meeting of NATO in Brussels December 3–5. Laird and Secretary of the Treasury David M. Kennedy, among others, accompanied him.

Let's turn to the Mid-East. In the last two weeks, the pressures to see me on the Mid-East have been mounting. Oil people were in yesterday; the Israeli group in Congress is ready to jump down our throats.

Helms: [Text will be provided.][4]

Deterioration has continued. Chances for violence have increased:

—UAR forces remain impotent.
—Lebanese front opened.
—Hussein almost powerless to control fedayeen. Almost an autonomous Palestinian state within Jordan.

New Israeli cabinet will have to cope with new financial problem. Problem arises from military purchases. With or without help, government will have to control spending strictly. Electorate endorsed government position on peace conditions. Only argument is over what exactly to do with occupied territories—assimilate or not. Israeli settlements increasing on Golan Heights, West Bank, north Sinai coast, Sharm al-Shaykh. Military objectives: (1) deter UAR; (2) if possible, topple Nasser. Israel could be considering a penetration in force into the UAR; an Israeli attack across canal could incur substantial casualties. We think Israelis feel they can bring Nasser down.

Arab leaders know they cannot defeat Israel. They want outsiders to bail them out. Attitude is one of "monumental frustration." Ideal goal: make Israelis consider whether better to return occupied territories rather than go on sustaining casualties. Nasser's November 6 speech—"mostly sound and fury";[5] same may well be outcome of December 20 Arab summit meeting.

Israel remains militarily superior. Soviets appear to be just about replacing Arab losses.

Since September, violence has increased on all fronts but Lebanon. That appears likely to become more active now. Israeli policy—community responsibility—on West Bank a response to greater fedayeen activity. Hussein looking for more equipment.

Fedayeen movements (8,000 guerrillas) do not pose a serious military threat but can be disruptive. Moscow may begin supplying fedayeen directly. Shelepin statement October 20.[6]

---

[4] Not found.

[5] In his speech to the National Assembly, Nasser rejected the October 28 peace proposals and accused the United States of taking the position of Israel, the UAR's "enemy." He also repeated Arab demands for complete Israeli withdrawal from the occupied territories. (*New York Times,* November 7, 1969, p. 1)

[6] Presumably a reference to a speech in Budapest by Aleksandr Shelepin, a Politburo member, that expressed support for the Palestinian guerrillas. (Ibid., October 30, 1969, p. A15)

President: Will Dr. Kissinger now brief on the issues.

Dr. Kissinger: We have discussed negotiating positions before in the NSC. What I want to do here is to discuss some of the basic premises which underlie them, leaving negotiating positions to the negotiators.

I would sum up the issues in the following way:

1. The first issue is whether it is possible to improve the U.S. position in the Arab world by dissociating ourselves from Israel's positions. If so, how permanent would that improvement be? What does it mean to dissociate ourselves?

—Those who favor dissociation argue that our problem in the moderate Arab world is that we seem to be Israel's lawyer.

—Others argue that the objective of the Arab radicals is to do away with Israel, not just to do away with Israel's conquests. A second issue is not just our negotiating position but whether we are willing to see sanctions imposed on Israel for not withdrawing.

2. A second issue is: Assuming we have decided to continue working for an Arab-Israeli settlement no matter how hard to achieve, what is the best strategy for achieving this? There are two schools of thought:

a. Let local forces assume responsibility for the terms of a settlement, leaving to outsiders the problem of bringing the parties together and guaranteeing those terms once agreed. (Our position right now is part way between this and the second.)

—Those who favor this approach believe that the problem is probably insoluble. The more we get into the issue, the more we will be pressed to impose sanctions on Israel. Our most useful role is simply to try to promote Rhodes-type talks.

—Those who oppose say that: This is the strategy tried from November 1967 to January 1969, which we abandoned last February. This assumes that the Arabs can contain their frustration and channel it into negotiations. It also assumes that Israel can remain militarily superior and deter UAR attack.

b. Generate international pressures for the terms of a settlement.

—Those who favor this approach argue: We cannot just sit back. The Near Easterners are too suspicious of each other to initiate negotiations unless outsiders frame the terms of negotiation.

—Those who oppose feel that we might end up with the worst of everything. International diplomatic action has raised Arab hopes too high without being able to produce results and diverted the Arabs from coming to terms with Israel. If international pressure is generated, the U.S. will be expected to come up with all the ideas and impose terms unilaterally on Israel.

3. The third issue: Assuming the U.S. has an interest in generating whatever international pressure may be possible, how do we go about it? We have two broad choices:

—Continue the present talks, try to achieve consensus on the terms of a settlement and then press Israel to accept (the USSR pressing the UAR).

—Break off the talks now—or let them peter out—to cut our losses but also to generate pressure on the USSR and the Arabs to face up to the necessity to discuss reasonable terms.

I have already outlined the arguments for and against each of these.

4. The next issue is: If the U.S. wishes to continue negotiations what is the best forum? The three options reviewed last February remain the logical choices:[7]

a. Four Power talks. We confront all the problems of whether we should be specific about the terms of a settlement or stick to the broad negotiating framework.

—Those who have argued for this course started with the fact that last January–February the U.S. was under heavy international—and special French—pressure to join in Four Power talks. There was strong sentiment at that time for taking a more active role to see whether outsiders could help the belligerents formulate at least a framework to get negotiations started. If we reached consensus, it seemed desirable to diffuse the onus.

—Those who have worried about these talks have argued that:

—This is the forum in which the U.S. is most likely to be pressed to move away from a position that has any chance of acceptance in Israel.
—The other three disagree with us on procedure and substance.
—This brings the USSR into the Jordan talks.

b. US–USSR talks have been confined to the UAR because the issues seemed more tractable, because a UAR settlement would facilitate a Jordan settlement and because we thought the USSR might press the UAR.

—Those who argued for entering these talks did so on three grounds:

(1) For global reasons, the U.S. had an interest in seeing whether it could negotiate seriously on a range of important issues.

(2) The USSR's persistent requests since September 1968 to talk about a Mid-East settlement suggested that Moscow might be uncomfortable in the Mid-East and might participate seriously in trying to

---

[7] See Document 5.

work out a reasonable arrangement. While we maintained a proper skepticism, it made sense to probe far enough to see what was possible.

(3) The USSR should pay at least as much of the price for a settlement as the U.S. in expanding its influence with its clients.

—Those who opposed this course argued mainly that the USSR did not want a real peace; it simply wanted to persuade us to press Israel to give back the territory of Moscow's clients. Since the USSR was not likely to act seriously, it did not make sense to formalize the USSR's role in the Mid-East by giving it a place at the peace table.

c. U.S. mediation not heretofore explored in detail.

—Those who argued for felt in general that:

—The U.S. should exploit its exclusive ability to move Israel and not share credit for a settlement, if any. The others only make our job more difficult.

—Nasser really wanted peace but that he could not say so publicly so he would welcome a private U.S. mediation effort.

—It made no sense to involve the USSR in any exchange on a Jordan-Israel settlement.

—Those who argued against argued that we have an interest in diffusing responsibility.

President: It has been one of our assumptions in the U.S.–Soviet talks that we could get the Soviet Union to help bring the UAR around. Mr. McCloy yesterday hit hard on the following point: Nasser tells him and other American businessmen that the Egyptians don't want to be exclusively in Soviet clutches. They would like the opportunity for direct communication with the U.S.[8]

The oil people all seem to feel that we are making a mistake not to have a direct channel of communications with the Egyptians.

Secretary Rogers: We do have direct channels of communication with the Egyptians. It is interesting to note that when I sent my letter to Foreign Minister Riad,[9] Ambassador Dobrynin came in and told me

---

[8] Nixon met with John J. McCloy, David Rockefeller, and U.S. oil executives on December 8. See *Foreign Relations, 1969–1976*, volume XXXVI, Energy Crisis, 1969–1974, Document 24.

[9] On November 8, Rogers wrote to Riad: "I am sending this brief message to you in the spirit of the frank conversation which the two of us had in New York. I felt that there was a good deal of understanding between us during that talk, particularly regarding the difficulties that both our Governments confront in the search for peace in the Middle East. If all of us grasp present opportunities, I am confident that progress can be made in the interest of all of the peoples of the Middle East. I hope, too, that it will be possible in the days ahead for better relations to evolve between our two Governments. I urge therefore that your Government give the draft US–USSR working paper the most careful and sympathetic consideration. It represents a balanced effort to try to meet the principal concerns on both sides." (National Archives, Nixon Presidential Materials, NSC Files, Box 1186, Saunders Files, Middle East Negotiations Files, Middle East—US–USSR Talks)

that Foreign Minister Gromyko had been embarrassed by what I had said in my letter. Riad had turned over a copy of my letter to Gromyko. Here was an opportunity given to the Egyptians to communicate with the U.S. and not to involve the Russians, and the first thing they did was to turn over the communication to the Russians. Also, we have a man in Cairo.

Mr. Sisco: We have had a considerable degree of direct contact with the Egyptians all along. My own feeling is that if we tried unilaterally to work out a plan with them, they would reject it, accusing us of trying to drive a wedge between them and Jordan.

The question is different on the Jordanian side. King Hussein wants us to be directly involved.

Dr. Kissinger: To sum up, we have three broad choices:

1. Let the talks peter out. Two sub-options:

—Stick to present position even if Israel rejects it.

Some argue that this is the course most likely to isolate us. It would put us in a position where we would be pressed to continue military and economic support for Israel while Israel rejects the U.S. concept of what would constitute a fair settlement.

Others argue that this is the only position that would avoid a confrontation with Israel. It would enable us to stand on a position we regard as fair. We could blame failure on all sides and maintain that we are only providing enough aid to maintain Israeli security.

—Stick to present position, pressing Israel to accept it.

Some argue that this would be the best possible position to be in if possible short of a negotiated settlement. We would have produced Israeli agreement to a position we regard as fair.

Others argue that since Israeli agreement is unlikely, this course is really the same as the first with all its disadvantages. We might use a good deal of influence with Israel—possibly eroding its position—and yet not have produced an Arab offer of peace.

2. Press the talks to fruition.

—Achieve big-power consensus but not impose on Israel.

Some argue that it would improve our position with the Arabs just to take a position closer to theirs than our present one. Also this would diffuse responsibility.

Others argue that the Arabs would judge us not on our position but on what we did with Israel. If we refused to press it on Israel—and it would be more difficult than our present position to sell to Israel—we would be called hypocritical.

—Achieve big-power consensus and try to impose it.

Some argue that this is the only way a settlement could be achieved because imposition is necessary and it is essential to have at least the USSR aboard for imposition on the UAR.

Others argue that the process of achieving consensus would dilute the substance of the consensus to the point where it would be all but impossible to impose it on Israel.

3. Develop an untried combination of negotiations.

The choice among these must be made in the light of four conflicting U.S. interests:

1. Arab-Israeli settlement. This may be unattainable.

2. Not worsening relations with the Arabs, hopefully improving them. U.S. investment in oil is heavy and Western Europe and Japan depend on Mid-East oil supply.

3. Israel's survival. We are committed to Israel's survival, though not necessarily in its present expanded borders.

4. Avoiding a confrontation with the USSR. The Soviets would find it hard to stand by and accept the humiliation of its clients again.

I have presented a list of perplexities—choices, not answers.

President: It seems to me as we look back over the 11 months since we took office, this area is the one where we have gone backward, not forward. I do not say this in any critical way, but I believe it is the case.

—The Soviet position in the Mediterranean seems stronger.

—Our position with the moderate Arab states seems weaker.

—The danger of war seems greater.

I do not mean to say that we have not done all we could do.

I would like to ask Mr. Helms a question. Just as an aside, I recall being briefed in the spring of 1967 by Eugene Rostow before the June war. He told me then, undoubtedly with the best will in the world, that there would not be a war. I repeated this in some of my public comments and then of course the war broke and my visits to all countries but Morocco and Israel had to be cancelled. Now, I do not want to put Mr. Helms on the spot and I will not hold him to his answer to this question, but I would like to ask: What do you think about the prospects for another war? Is the outbreak of war likely?

Mr. Helms: The most likely trend is a "continuing bleeding process." I come down on the side that there will not be a major conflict. I say this because I think the 1967 war taught the UAR and the Soviets a lesson in what not to do in creating a situation where Israel believes that its survival is at stake.

President: You see nothing, then, that the UAR could do to give Israel the excuse I think it is looking for to "bang them."

Mr. Helms: Farther down the track, if the moderates are driven into the radical camp, the Saudis, for instance, might try to close the Straits of Tiran. But predicting for the foreseeable future, I do not see this kind of development.

You may recall, Mr. President, that you asked me a similar question at the dinner you held last spring for King Hussein. The scenario that I foresaw then seems to be playing itself out—a steadily rising level of violence but not another full-scale war.

President: The Soviet attitude in SALT seems more responsible and more reasonable than could have been predicted. This does not indicate that we have any easy bargain ahead of us but it does indicate that there is a chance that the USSR wants to make a deal.

One could make the same sort of deduction about the recent moves with Germany, although at the same time one could posit a Soviet objective fragmenting the Western alliance.

On the Middle East, however, is it fair to say that Soviet interests can only be served by tension. I know it is sometimes said that the Soviets are uncomfortable in the present situation. But I sometimes have trouble understanding why.

Mr. Helms: I think they want the situation to stay the way it is.

Secretary Rogers: I am not so sure of that. I believe they are quite concerned about the consequences of the kind of explosion Israel could provoke.

Dr. Kissinger: The longer Israel holds its conquered Arab territory, the longer the Soviets cannot deliver what the Arabs want. As that time drags on, the Arabs must begin to conclude that friendship with the Soviet Union is not very helpful—that it led to two defeats, one of which the U.S. rescued the Arabs from, and to continued impotence in regaining what they have lost.

Secretary Rogers: The Soviets have some of the same problems with the UAR that we have with Israel. They cannot just walk in to Nasser's office and gain his acceptance of any proposition they may put to him. They must consider the fact that the more radical Arab elements like the fedayeen are going to blame the Soviets for not producing what the Arabs want.

President: Then it is possible to argue, is it not, that if we want the Soviets to help, Israel is producing that result by scaring them. Why should it not be our policy to let Israel scare them a little bit more?

Secretary Rogers: I think our position is pretty well spelled out now as a result of my speech last night.[10] The position I elaborated on there is thoroughly consistent with the UN Security Council resolution.

---

[10] See Document 73.

President: I have one question about what we should be doing in the next couple of weeks. At my meeting yesterday with Mr. McCloy and others, the American businessmen there were very much concerned that the pressures for a united Arab front at the Arab summit on December 20 would be too great for our moderate friends to resist. They felt that we needed some gesture before then in order to help the moderates. Is the Secretary's speech enough? They suggested that a Presidential emissary be sent to some of the moderates before December 20.

Dr. Kissinger: I think the speech does all that we can now do.

President: The speech will probably enrage Israel, but does it give the moderate Arabs enough? Is there no other gesture that we should be making?

Mr. Sisco: We have done three things in relation to the summit:

—In advancing the October 28 formula with the USSR, we stated a position that is fair and balanced.[11] This has not really been rejected by the UAR. All the UAR has said is that it wants to see what the Jordanian side of a settlement would look like before passing its judgement.

—In the speech last night, Israel should find a good many things that it likes. Israel will be critical,—but probably not enraged. Israel will feel that the Secretary was too specific, but the Arabs will also object that the Secretary did not call for total Israeli withdrawal from Arab territory. It should be helpful to the moderates, although they will not be able publicly to recognize it as such. Nasser at the summit wants to mobilize Arab opinion behind him, and there is not much we can do to temper that process. But intelligence indicates that some travel is taking place among the moderates, and we do not believe the summit will lead to the dire consequences that someone like David Rockefeller has projected—a break in relations or extreme measures against our oil companies.

—With all the reservations that all of us have about the Four Power talks, the fact that the talks have resumed leaves open the possibility of a political settlement, and there will be pressures on the Arabs not to foreclose that possibility.

The business people I have talked to have suggested an emissary. I must say in all candor that many such emissaries have not been entirely helpful. Any man who goes must be familiar with the nuts and bolts of the dialogue. Nasser would use such a visit to build himself up, and the moderates would not see this as helpful. Anyone who went would not have much to add to what has already been said unless he were able to take with him some new concessions.

---

[11] See Documents 58 and 61.

President: Forget about Nasser for a moment. If we are interested to avoid a united Arab front, what about sending someone to the moderates?

I know Elliot Richardson has to leave soon. Perhaps we should hear his comments now.

Mr. Richardson: A good place to start, Mr. President, is the evolution that you have traced since January. It seems true that our situation relative to that of the USSR has deteriorated on balance in the short run and that the Soviets have gained proportionately. Why is that so? I see two reasons:

—Among the Four Powers, the U.S. is the only one capable of exerting effective influence on Israel. So the U.S. is blamed for the continuing impasse.

—This negotiation is possibly unique in that Israel puts a high premium not only on the results of the negotiation but on the procedure by which those results are achieved. They will make concrete concessions to get from the Arabs a recognition that Arab willingness to sit down and talk would signify.

So we cannot talk simply about the terms of a settlement in an even-handed way. Israel doesn't care how reasonable the terms are as long as it does not have a part in their formulation.

It follows, therefore, that if we go farther down the track toward specifying the terms of a settlement, it will be increasingly difficult for the U.S. to deliver Israel. If we are brought along this route into defining the details of a settlement, all eyes will turn to us to deliver Israel and yet the very fact of our having specified the details of a settlement would make it less likely that we could deliver Israel.

If that is a fair analysis, the question is: How do we get out of this? I conclude that it is highly important to break away from this trend toward involving ourselves more and more in the details of a settlement.

President: You say it is important to get out. Let me understand your reasoning. Is it because you see this as a dead end street? Is it because we would be making a deal and then not being able to deliver on it?

Mr. Richardson: As Dr. Kissinger described the options, one of them is to press the current talks to fruition. Within that option there are two sub-options:

—We could press for a big-power consensus but then not impose it on Israel. If that is the result, the U.S. will appear to the rest of the world as unwilling to support the consensus because it refused to deliver Israel.

—We would press for consensus and then try to impose it on Israel. The result again would be failure to deliver Israel because we will have gone into so much detail that we will not be able to persuade the Israelis to accept the consensus.

My point is that any effort to get into the formulation of the details of a settlement is a dead end street.

The question that I have posed: How to avoid that.

In answering that question, I would prefer to think not in terms of letting present talks peter out or breaking them off. I would prefer to focus attention on Israel's requirements for negotiation of the specific terms of a settlement among the parties. I would like to see us hammer on the Rhodes formula talks as the only way to achieve a settlement. If we could get the other three powers to agree that this is the only reasonable route to a settlement, then if the parties will not get together, or if they do get together and cannot agree, the onus for failure is shifted to them.

What I am suggesting is that we should put ourselves in a position so that, if there is no settlement, we will avoid to the extent we can the question why the U.S. is not delivering Israel.

Another way of stating this issue is to say that the strategy we adopt as we proceed in the Four Power talks boils down to the question of how hard we resist British and French efforts to hammer out a detailed position.

Secretary Rogers: This has been and is our policy. It is the policy I announced in my speech last night.

We should not delude ourselves. We are not forced to deliver Israel simply because of our negotiating position. We have been in this situation one way or another for 20 years. We are not going to escape from that position simply by getting out of the talks. The question will come up in the UN Security Council or in some other forum. Getting out of the talks will not relieve us of that problem.

I think perhaps we are putting too much emphasis on the forms here. Our position has deteriorated because we are seen as the principal supporters of Israel. We send planes and economic aid. Unless we want to change that policy, our position is going to deteriorate.

I might say that I have never heard a discussion of the Middle East—and you know, Mr. President, that I have sat through a lot of them beginning in the mid-1950s—where it was not said that our position is worse now than it was a little while ago.

As far as the Four Power talks are concerned, I do not know what we can do except to have a fair policy and to stand by it. That is why I believe we should emphasize Rhodes type talks.

But we are never going to escape from this problem unless we discontinue our support for Israel.

Ambassador Yost: I would like to endorse Secretary Rogers' main point. Our deteriorating position is inherent in the situation. Israel is depending on us and is pursuing a policy that most of the world considers unreasonable. Even if we pulled out of the talks, people would still look to us to deliver Israel. We would, in fact, be even more isolated than we are now, because we would have created the impression that we do not care.

If the Four Power talks fail, the issue will be thrust into the UN Security Council. If that happens, we at least want to be in a position where we, the British and French agree and where we are not alone.

The British and French do not differ with our position on substance; they differ on tactics.

If the U.S. puts forward a paper on a Jordan-Israel settlement analogous to the paper that Mr. Sisco has been discussing with Ambassador Dobrynin on a UAR-Israel settlement, there is a fair chance that we might bring the French and British along. If we did, we would have to exert pressure on Israel to get Israel to the table on that basis, just as we would expect that the UAR would come to the table only under Soviet pressure.

I believe we should continue on this road.

President: I think it is a mistake to have the USSR messing around on a Jordan settlement. We should be able to do anything that is necessary on that front. I just think that side of the problem should be sorted out in a different way. I hope we could stand as Jordan's friend as much as we are Israel's friend. We cannot have it said that Jordan was saved by the USSR.

Secretary Rogers: That is one thing to say, another to avoid. It is the situation—not the talks that isolates us. The Soviets will go on championing Arab causes no matter what the forum.

Ambassador Yost: Our position has been that a settlement must be a package, so we have to talk at some point about the Jordanian side of a settlement. At the same time, behind the scenes, we can work closely by ourselves with the Jordanians and the Israelis.

Mr. Sisco: I will be seeing Zaid Rifai in London tomorrow.

President: What will you talk about?

Mr. Sisco: I will do more listening than talking. We have no position right now that we can be concrete about. However, I will try to leave an impression about how far it might be possible to go. In any case, the process of consultation is important in itself.

President: Let's be sure we understand that the Soviets should not be involved on the Jordan front.

Secretary Laird: One of the things that will be raised in any talks with Jordan is the military shopping list.

Mr. Sisco: I doubt that we will get into that. This particular individual is not concerned about that problem.

President: A response to the Jordanians would be sensible as a parallel to whatever we have to do with the Israelis.

Mr. Richardson: Have we had an indication of the Soviet response to the Jordanian request for arms?

Mr. Sisco: No we have not heard.

Mr. President, if I may, I would like to say a word about how I would suggest proceeding.

I believe that we are limited in what we can achieve. I am skeptical that we can achieve a Four Power consensus or common ground among the parties in the area.

I do, however, have some thoughts about a way to proceed that might ameliorate the situation.

We have put to the USSR our fundamental position on a UAR-Israel settlement. It is my personal view that if we ever get a Soviet-Arab agreement to that formulation, Israel would accept it.

We now have drafted an analogous document on a Jordan-Israel settlement.[12]

It is my own feeling that this document should be given to Ambassador Yost to submit early in the Four Power talks. This would accomplish the following:

—It would demonstrate that we are taking the initiative on a Jordan settlement and not leaving Jordan to the USSR.

—The position in that document is consistent with what Israel has said to us in the past about its position on a Jordan settlement.

—In its emphasis on Rhodes type talks, it leaves the details of a settlement to negotiation between the parties.

I believe it would help tactically to preempt the talks by putting our position on the table early. If there is no Four Power consensus, then, we will have pegged out a fair and balanced position.

One of the basic weaknesses in the U.S. position now is that Israel does not accept our approach. Israel has taken the onus for failure to achieve a settlement. I believe we should take the position that if Israel could accept our position, we would be in a better position to justify helping Israel. If Israel accepted our approach, the onus for the continued impasse would shift partly to the other side.

---

[12] See footnote 5, Document 67.

President: You are talking now about the Jordan settlement?

Mr. Sisco: Yes. I would leave the formula on the UAR-Israel settlement just as we last gave it to the USSR. I would not budge an inch from that position.

Secretary Rogers: I might report that our friends in NATO feel that Israel has not been forthcoming. We are saddled with backing the party that, in their view, is responsible for blocking success.

President: Coming back to Mr. Richardson's point, how do you see us coming out of these talks? If after we go through the procedure Mr. Sisco has outlined and we fail, how can we disengage? Are you suggesting disengagement?

Mr. Richardson: My suggestion has to be seen in the context of the options laid out in the paper Dr. Kissinger has circulated and from which he has briefed.[13] I addressed myself to the three choices which he laid out:

—Let the talks peter out.
—Press for a big-power consensus with two sub-options of either not imposing it on Israel or of trying to impose it.
—Seeking a new combination of talks.

I do not believe we can undertake either of the last two.

We will proceed on the present course, and we will not succeed. Then we will have to consider how we achieve a posture that we can stand on to put ourselves in the best possible position.

I do not disagree with the desirability of continuing along the lines that Mr. Sisco has outlined.

I would, however, argue against allowing the other three powers to make our UAR document more specific. I believe it is important to leave details to the parties. It is important to keep the emphasis on Rhodes formula talks.

If we can do that, we would be in a fair position but not expected to exert pressure to achieve a settlement. The onus for that would rest on the parties.

Dr. Kissinger: I do not disagree with that assessment. But I believe we must face the consequences of that course.

—On the side of a UAR-Israel settlement, I agree that Israel might well yield, but we will pay a price for making them accept that formulation.

---

[13] The paper's options were included in a memorandum that Kissinger sent to Nixon the previous day regarding Rogers's recommendations for a Four-Power talks strategy. (National Archives, Nixon Presidential Materials, NSC Files, Box 644, Country Files, Middle East, Middle East—General, Vol. II) A copy of Rogers's December 9 memorandum to the President with his recommendations is also attached to Kissinger's December 17 memorandum to the President, Document 76. See also Document 70.

—On the Jordanian side, however, I see two prospects:

(1) The other three powers will go farther than we want and that will make it more difficult to impose a settlement on Israel.

(2) I cannot see Israel accepting our provisions on the Jordanian settlement.

I am concerned that putting forward a specific Jordan plan will slide us down the slippery slope toward the difficult question: Are we willing to proceed toward some form of pressure on Israel? If we are not, advancing a specific proposal in the Four Power talks will buy us no more than two or three weeks.

President: Do you agree?

Mr. Sisco: I agree that provisions on a Jordanian settlement may be even more difficult for Israel to accept than the provisions on a UAR settlement. But also, I doubt that the Arabs will accept. Our proposal would fall far short of Arab expectations on Jerusalem and on the refugee settlement.

I believe we should put ourselves in a posture that this is the framework within which we believe the parties should get together.

The leverage we have with Israel is the following: As long as they appear to be the main obstruction to peace, our job is more difficult in supplying them with the economic and military help they need. We recognize that we have to help Israel, but they have to help us if we are going to be able to help them.

Mr. Richardson: We have to think what we mean when we say that Israel will accept "it." The proposal we are talking about leaves all of the tough questions for negotiation between the parties. Acceptance would involve acceptance of some procedure for negotiation.

That is why the issue is whether or not we fill in the details of a settlement. If we go down that road, it is dangerous because we are even more exposed than now.

President: Secretary Laird knows a lot about the domestic pressures on this issue. What do you think?

Secretary Laird: Exerting pressure on Israel would make life politically difficult for us "for a little while." But I believe that Israel will go along—they do not have anyone else to turn to. They have fewer friends in Europe and certainly none in Eastern Europe or the Soviet Union. Israel is isolated and is going to have to make some sort of settlement.

Vice President: I concur.

As I travel around, the heat from the supporters of Israel is couched in general terms. There is a feeling in the community that supports Israel of disenchantment with the Administration.

I do not see how we can fail to pay attention to the European feelings that Secretary Rogers has expressed.

President: Assume for the sake of discussion that there is no domestic political pressure and that there is no moral question of continuing support involved, would the U.S. foreign policy interests be served by dumping Israel?

General Lincoln: I have thought a lot about this. I would lean in the direction of dumping Israel but keeping something there—something less than we have.

Secretary Rogers: What would be left?

General Lincoln: Israel is now the strongest power in the Middle East militarily—though not economically except as supported by the U.S.

Israel's being there has helped to make the Soviets a stronger influence in the Middle East.

President: Looking at this from the Soviet viewpoint, if we save the UAR's bacon, the Soviets would gain by our act. In my view, Soviet-U.S. relations are the overriding concern. Therefore, the overriding question is: Who gains?

General Lincoln: If there were a settlement and if the Arabs were no longer dependent on the Soviet Union, they might be less hostile to the U.S. If some such miracle took place, they might even be grateful for our role in helping to get their territory back.

President: When we came into office, there was pleasure in Cairo because I had not received a large number of Jewish votes and the Israelis knew it. We will put that fact aside but we do have to note that the situation has now changed and Israel sees us as their only hope—not because of trust or affection—and the Arabs say that we have turned to Israel's support.

Politics aside, the talks in which we are engaged put up a facade of reasonableness and trying.

But I am concerned that we avoid what Dr. Kissinger called "the slippery slope."

I have a feeling that there isn't a thing we can do about "that place." I think anything that we do will fail. But before we go into the specifics of a settlement, if we are going to squeeze Israel, then I think we must expect the Soviets to squeeze the UAR.

Vice President: Before we leave domestic political concerns, I think we have not exploited through our own political avenues the possibility of bringing Israel to realize that it must help us in Asia.

President: General Wheeler, what do you think?

General Wheeler: I do not think these proposals will be blessed with any desirable outcome. They are doomed to failure. I do think, however, we must make the effort in order to achieve a more detached position. We are regarded now as being Israel's supporters and the prime offenders against the Arab world. I am not optimistic.

Mr. Helms: Here, here!

Secretary Rogers: Each time we have one of these meetings we all state the problem. Our relations with the Arabs will continue to deteriorate. If we are going to change that, we have to take positions that we would hate to take.

You, Mr. President, should realize, that we have done all we can think of doing. It is sort of like the situation in Vietnam. What we do in the Middle East probably will not work. But there is nothing anyone else can think of doing.

Theoretically, we could stop talking to anyone but that is unrealistic. The issue would end up back in the UN Security Council, and we would have to deal with it there in a much less advantageous forum.

President: I am not always one in favor of talking for the sake of talking, and I am concerned about the "slippery slope" that Henry talks about. But it is a point that if the talks break down we will have to deal with this problem in a much more difficult situation.

Ambassador Yost: If they do break down, it is important that we have the British and French with us agreeing that they have broken down for reasonable causes.

Mr. Helms: At the risk of stating the obvious, I think we must do what we can to bolster the spirit of the Arab moderates.

President: With reference to the moderate Arabs, we should bolster their spirits as we can—but without letting the Soviet Union take credit for it.

Secretary Rogers: Secretary Laird has given us some additional wherewithal for bolstering the spirits of one moderate Arab in agreeing to provide military equipment for Jordan.

President: Why not do this before December 20?

Secretary Laird: We have been trying to wait for the Congress in order to be assured that we would have the necessary appropriations.

President: What do you think, Henry?

Dr. Kissinger: I believe that you should look at the Jordan package before it is presented in the Four Power talks.

I agree that we should probably go ahead with the present talks in a general way and not break the Four Power talks now.

We will have to face the problem, however, that we will be faced at some point with the following argument: Whatever we do will require pressure on Israel. If we do not get a consensus in the Four Power talks, we will be told that the issue will be thrown into the Security Council and that we should therefore attempt to press Israel to accept our position in order to go into the Security Council in a better posture. If we do get a consensus, we will be told that we must press Israel to accept the consensus in order to avoid going into the UN Security Council in the position of not having done all we could to enforce an international consensus.

President: Henry has put his finger on the heart of the problem. Whether we succeed or fail we face a question of pressing Israel. If we fail, we will face the question of whether we should go on supporting Israel or squeeze Israel to accept our position. If we succeed in the Four Power talks, we will be faced with the question of what we are going to do to make the Israelis accept the consensus.

The basic point is whether we are going to put the squeeze on Israel.

If we are going to have to do that, we ought to get as much as possible in return for it. The Soviets should not come out ahead. The Arabs played a substantial part in bringing on the war, and the Soviets should pay some price for picking up the pieces.

Mr. Sisco: What the present proposal does is simply to ask Israel to accept our formulation as the basis of negotiations. It does not press Israel to withdraw as in 1957. If we are going to disengage, I think we should do this after having shifted the onus to the Arab side in order to justify our continuing help for Israel.

I believe Secretary Rogers should tell Foreign Minister Eban that Israel must help the U.S. if the U.S. is to help Israel.

President: Eban needs to know that world support is eroding.

The businessmen I talked to yesterday emphasized the importance of doing something on the refugee question. Is there anything we can do?

Secretary Rogers: This was in the speech I gave last night. I believe this is as far as we can go.

I would like to know what you mean by squeezing the USSR.

President: The question is what the UAR pays for its role in bringing on the war. If the UAR comes out of a settlement whole and gives only vague obligations to peace in return, the Soviets come out looking good and Israel has little in return.

Secretary Rogers: That also cuts the other way. The harder we squeeze the Arabs and the Soviets, the more our position in the area deteriorates.

President: I am thinking mainly here of distinguishing between the UAR and Jordan. I think perhaps we might squeeze Israel for a Jordan settlement.

Ambassador Yost: If the Arabs undertook the commitments to peace that are in the document that Mr. Sisco has been discussing with Ambassador Dobrynin, the UAR would have conceded what Israel has sought for 20 years.

Mr. Richardson: The problem is that the Arabs want territory and Israel wants a commitment to peace. If Israel got what it wanted, it would have only intangibles.

Dr. Kissinger: If Israel got a settlement this would simply bring Israel to the point where other countries begin their foreign policy. In most instances in history, wars have started between nations that have theretofore been at peace.

Harold H. Saunders[14]

---

[14] Printed from a copy that bears Saunders's typed signature with an indication that he signed the original on December 17.

---

75. Editorial Note

The UN Permanent Representatives of the Four Powers met on December 9, 1969, to discuss France's proposals on Jordan, which Ambassador Armand Bérard introduced orally. Ambassador Charles Yost responded to the presentation with the remark that the group should try to avoid giving recommendations to UN Special Representative Gunnar Jarring that contained excessive detail for fear that they might hinder his efforts. Bérard maintained that they must decide upon a "'delicate mixture' between enough precision and 'substituting selves for parties' in determining what guidelines to provide Jarring." (Telegram 4503 from USUN, December 10; National Archives, RG 59, Central Files 1967–69, POL 27–14 ARAB–ISR) Ambassador Yakov Malik tabled draft language on the cessation of the state of war in the Middle East, which represented a further unveiling of the June 17 Soviet counterproposal that he had begun on December 2. (Telegram 4502 from USUN, December 10; ibid.)

The next meeting was held on December 12, at which time Bérard and Ambassador Lord Caradon praised the major policy speech on the Middle East that Secretary Rogers had given three days earlier (see Document 73). Malik did not approve or criticize the speech but believed that it would have "repercussions around the world." He agreed with Bérard that the Jarring Mission should possibly be re-launched without providing Jarring with full guidelines on every issue. None of the four commented further on the French or Soviet proposals presented at the previous meetings, nor did they recommend anything new, but they all agreed once again on the importance of re-establishing Jarring's mission. The session closed with the agreement that the Four Powers would meet on December 18. (Telegram 4546 from USUN, December 13; National Archives, RG 59, Central Files 1967–69, POL 27–14 ARAB–ISR)

76. Memorandum From the President's Assistant for National Security Affairs (Kissinger) to President Nixon[1]

Washington, December 17, 1969.

SUBJECT

Whether to Present a Jordan Paper in Four Power Talks

I sent to you before last Wednesday's NSC meeting Secretary Rogers' memo proposing a strategy in the Four Power talks (attached).[2] This is essentially what you heard Assistant Secretary Sisco describe at the NSC. It was agreed there that you should have a close look at it before we go ahead.

The Secretary proposes that our prime objective be "as much improvement as possible in our overall position and image in the area against the contingency that the Four Power talks reach an impasse and we conclude it is desirable to disengage." To accomplish that, he proposes that we:

1. Stick to our present negotiating position—that outsiders should concentrate on developing a framework within which the belligerents can get together to negotiate and not try to spell out the details of a settlement.

2. Advance in the Four Power talks a document on a Jordan-Israel settlement parallel to the document on a UAR-Israel settlement that Sisco and Dobrynin have been discussing.[3]

---

[1] Source: Library of Congress, Manuscript Division, Kissinger Papers, Box CL–178, Geopolitical File, ME, Chronological File. Secret; Nodis. Sent for action.

[2] Dated December 9; attached but not printed. The NSC meeting was held December 10. See Document 74.

[3] See Documents 58 and 61.

3. After playing out this line, if it does not achieve consensus on our terms, disengage from the Four Power talks and seek another device for carrying forward the settlement effort.

The Presidential issue here is not the details of the document we would put forward such as where the border should be (though these are included with the Secretary's memo). It is not clear whether the Arabs agree that this would constitute a fair basis for negotiation. Their judgment will depend in large part whether we are going to press Israel to accept it and whether we are going to go on delivering military assistance if Israel refuses.

The key issue, thus, is not how to handle negotiations but whether to squeeze Israel. If we are willing to do so I see two courses of action:

1. Condition our future military and economic assistance to Israel on their acceptance of our position. This could be put positively as a promise of future support over a period of five years or so rather than as a threat. But whatever form the condition takes, the best situation would be one in which we are dealing exclusively with Israel on the basis of our position, not one diluted by the French, British or Soviets who have nothing to contribute. If we bear the burden, we might as well take whatever credit might come from success.

2. Offer a package deal to the USSR through which we would agree to press Israel provided Moscow either delivered Egyptian agreement on our proposals or provided significant help on Vietnam.

If you are prepared to impose a settlement on Israel, I lean toward the first course. The Israelis have asked us for massive aid. I shall have for you within a week a thorough analysis of the implications of the Israeli requests.[4]

Once this issue is understood, the rest is tactics. I would be inclined to let Ambassador Yost play out the present course, but after that State should be prohibited from taking any new initiatives.[5] If we are willing to impose a settlement, we do not need the Soviets' pressures on the Jordanian side. If we are unwilling, negotiations will only isolate us.

However, we should recognize: (1) we are leading into a confrontation with Israel; the Jewish community reaction already to Secretary Rogers' speech is just an indication of what may come; (2) if Israel were to conclude it is cut off from its only remaining source of major outside support, the likelihood that it will strike again to topple Nasser will increase.

---

[4] See Document 79.

[5] Yost introduced the U.S. proposal for a Jordan-Israel settlement at the Four-Power meeting the following day, December 18. See Document 78. Rogers sent the proposal to Nixon attached to his November 16 memorandum, Document 67.

Recommendation

That you authorize advancing this document on a Jordan-Israel settlement, but prohibit any other Middle East initiatives until we have carefully reviewed the courses of action open to us on the fundamental question of our handling of Israel.[6]

---

[6] Nixon approved the recommendation on December 23.

---

77. Memorandum From the President's Assistant for National Security Affairs (Kissinger) to President Nixon[1]

Washington, December 18, 1969.

SUBJECT

    My Talk with Foreign Minister Eban

Foreign Minister Eban came in to see me the morning of December 16 before his afternoon talk with Secretary Rogers.[2] He said that Prime Minister Meir is disturbed by a "sharp atmospheric change" since her visit[3] evinced in the resumption of Four Power talks,[4] the Secretary's policy statement[5] and the "cancellation" of the desalting project.[6] [I hope I laid this last to rest by stressing that they had over-read our position on the desalting project and that, to the contrary, you had just approved going ahead with the test module.]

I assured him that there had been no change in attitude toward Israel and that your objective remains the enhancement of Israel's long-term security. I explained exactly where we stand in our analysis of

---

[1] Source: National Archives, Nixon Presidential Materials, NSC Files, Box 605, Country Files, Middle East, Israel, Vol. III. Secret; Nodis. Sent for information. All brackets are in the original.

[2] Reported in telegram 209262 to Tel Aviv, December 18. (Ibid.)

[3] The Prime Minister was in the United States September 24 to October 6. See Document 52.

[4] See Documents 72 and 75.

[5] See Document 73.

[6] On November 21, Saunders asked Leonard Garment to inform the Government of Israel that the November 20 "cancellation" of the desalting project did not "close the door" on it. (Memorandum from Saunders to Garment, November 21; National Archives, Nixon Presidential Materials, NSC Files, Box 1238, Saunders Files) For U.S. policy on the desalting project, see *Foreign Relations,* 1969–1976, volume XXIV, Middle East Region and Arabian Peninsula, 1969–1972; Jordan, September 1970, Documents 4, 5, 9, 12, and 14.

their substantial aid requests and said we would be replying within a reasonable period.

Eban's main concerns were:

1. *Borders.* By getting into the issue of where the UAR–Israel border should be, he felt the US had hampered Israel's freedom to negotiate a position at Sharm al-Shaikh. I told him that it might have been better if Israel had confided that objective to us a long time ago because most of the US Government had long labored under the misunderstanding that Israel put more stock in Arab recognition than in territory. He conceded that it had taken time for Israeli thinking to evolve but insisted that Israel must have a position at Sharm al-Shaikh.

2. *Tactics.* He repeated several times the advice to "let the other side sweat a little." His main point seemed to be that resumption of the Four Power talks let the USSR off the hook too soon and that we should have held up resumption until Moscow had responded to the October 28 US position paper.[7] While he objected to the US formulation, he acted almost as if that were now taken for granted and that the US should have been content to stand on it.

3. *Jordan-Israel.* He particularly did not like involvement of the Soviets or the Four Powers in this aspect of a settlement. I told him that we fully appreciated this concern and that if they felt the US could be useful as a mediator we would much prefer this role to either the US–USSR or the Four Power talks. He replied only that the problem with Jordan was not communication but whether Hussein could make an agreement and keep it.

4. *US–USSR dialogue.* He felt that we should limit ourselves to (a) discussing how to prevent war (Soviet agreement to non-intervention and maintenance of Israeli strength) and (b) bringing the belligerents to the negotiating table. He repeated several times that we should confine the big-power talks to the questions of how, where and under what conditions the belligerents should begin negotiation.

In short, he recalled his talk with you last March[8] and your statement that we had to try consultations with other major powers to see what could be achieved.[9] With ten months of experience behind us, he

---

[7] See Document 58.

[8] See Document 14.

[9] An apparent reference to Nixon's March 4 press conference, at which he said: "from the four-power conference can come an absolute essential to any kind of peaceful settlement in the Mideast, and that is a major-power guarantee of the settlement, because we cannot expect the Nation of Israel or the other nations in the area who think their major interests might be involved—we cannot expect them to agree to a settlement unless they think there is a better chance that it will be guaranteed in the future than has been the case in the past. On this score, then, we think we have made considerable progress during the past week. We are cautiously hopeful that we can make more progress and move to the four-power talks very soon." (*Public Papers: Nixon, 1969*, p. 185)

felt it was time to stand back from that experience to see what lessons it taught. This sort of joint stock-taking was the purpose of his visit.

78. Telegram From the Department of State to the Embassy in Israel[1]

Washington, December 19, 1969, 2013Z.

210193. Subject: Under Secretary's Meeting with Israeli Ambassador on US Proposal in Four-Power Talks for Jordanian Settlement. Reference: State 209946.[2]

Following is based on uncleared memcon, Noforn and FYI, subject to revision upon review.

Summary: Following tabling in Four Powers yesterday of our proposal for Jordanian aspect of an Arab-Israel settlement,[3] Under Secretary Richardson called in Israeli Ambassador Rabin to hand him copy of proposal and to review for him its essential elements and our reasons for tabling it. Under Secretary stressed that absence of any indications of movement between Israel and Jordan in our talks with Eban, and need to preempt other initiatives, to strengthen Hussein and to dilute Soviet involvement all led us to conclude that we had no alternative to moving ahead in Four Powers. Under Secretary also emphasized that we believe our proposal fully protects Israel's security, its basic goal of peace and principle of negotiations. Rabin's reaction was strongly negative. Without entering into detailed discussion prior to referring our proposal and Under Secretary's comments to his Government, Rabin said he could state that proposal would be "totally unacceptable" to Israel. *End summary.*

---

[1] Source: National Archives, Nixon Presidential Materials, NSC Files, Box 650, Country Files, Middle East, Middle East Negotiations. Secret; Priority; Nodis. Drafted by Atherton, cleared in U, and approved by Sisco. Repeated to Amman, Beirut, Cairo, Jidda, Kuwait, London, Moscow, Paris, and USUN.

[2] Telegram 209946 to Tel Aviv, December 19, authorized Barbour to provide the Government of Israel with the text of the U.S. proposal on the fundamental principles of a settlement between Israel and Jordan that Charles Yost presented in the Four-Power meeting at the UN the previous day. The telegram also included oral comments for the Ambassador to make as he delivered the proposal to Israeli representatives. (Ibid., Box 605, Country Files, Middle East, Israel, Vol. III)

[3] Reported in telegram 4583 from USUN, December 19. (Ibid., RG 59, Central Files 1967–69, POL 27–14 ARAB–ISR)

1. Under Secretary Richardson provided Israeli Ambassador Rabin copy of US proposal on Jordanian aspect of settlement afternoon Dec. 18 and conveyed to Rabin points in para. 2 reftel. Minister Argov and Asst. Sec. Sisco also participated.

2. After reading proposal, Rabin said he saw two turning points in US approach to Arab-Israel settlement: (a) decision to enter Four-Power talks in March, which undermines goal of agreement between parties and which Israel opposed and continues to oppose; and (b) Oct. 28 formulations on UAR[4] aspect which specifically defined secure and recognized boundary; Israel believes this should be left to parties.

3. Re US-Jordanian proposal, Rabin said its submission to Four Powers had further aggravated situation. There would be great concern and disappointment in Israel that USG is discussing details of Israel-Jordan settlement in Four Powers. He would refer document to his government and was meanwhile not in position to discuss it in detail but could say that it was "totally unacceptable." Rabin added that he was sure our proposal was prepared prior to Eban's visit[5] and he could not understand why it had not been shown to Eban before we submitted it in New York.

4. Under Secretary replied that we had not submitted document first to Eban because discussion of document between us would have obliged US and Israel to say that they had consulted on document in advance. As things now stand, we can say that document reflects our position and represents our best judgment on how to reach settlement. Israel free to take its own position.

5. Re Rabin's characterization of turning points in US policy, Under Secretary said we have evolved a position which we think is more secure today than when we started. We now have position we can stand on. Israeli position, on other hand, is not secure internationally. We think it a mistake that Israel will not be more forthcoming about its terms for a settlement. We and Israel therefore have difference of judgment. We want to support Israel's security but cannot confuse Israeli and US interests. We think Israel's security rests on its occupation of territory which it is not obliged to give up except in conditions of peace and security.

6. Under Secretary continued that US wants a settlement but recognizes there is substantial chance we may not get one. Meanwhile we are in dynamic international situation affecting our overall position. Given situation in Four-Power talks and our position generally, we think our proposals, which are a blend of the general and the specific, offer best

---

[4] See Document 58.
[5] See Document 77.

chance of getting negotiations started. Our objective is to keep Four Powers from turning toward greater specificity on terms of settlement.

7. Rabin replied that failure to reach Israel-Jordan settlement not due to lack of communications but to fact that Jordan cannot be first Arab country to reach settlement. US has created situation permitting Soviets to champion Jordanian interests.

8. End result of US proposals, Rabin said, would be to undermine Israeli security. No Israeli government will take position under which (a) Jerusalem would not be under Israeli control except for special provisions for holy places as explained by Eban and (b) Jordan River would not be Israel's security border.

9. Rabin reiterated that he not in position to give detailed, authorized GOI reaction to US proposal. In any case, there no use in doing so since US has now submitted proposal and is committed to it.

10. Sisco asked that Rabin specifically report to his government that our proposal leaves question of control and sovereignty over Jerusalem for Israel and Jordan to negotiate. Rabin said he would do so but considered that our Jerusalem formulation represented further erosion of US position. In May paper US had said that Jordan should have civic, economic and religious role in Jerusalem.[6] Now we said both Israel and Jordan should have such role, thereby putting Jordan and Israel on equal basis. Sisco reiterated that we had not addressed question of sovereignty. Under Secretary asked whether our present formulation might not be considered an improvement rather than an erosion since previously we had not mentioned Israeli role. Rabin said it was definitely an erosion given fact that larger part of Jerusalem had always belonged to Israel and all of Jerusalem was now in Israeli hands.

11. During conversation Rabin also focused briefly on two other points in US proposal: (a) Point 10 re deposit of final accord with UN after signature, and (b) addendum re Four Power action in Security Council in support of settlement. Re (a), Rabin asked why emphasis is on action vis-à-vis UN rather than on agreement between parties. Sisco stressed that proposal calls for signature by parties and makes clear parties must undertake obligations to each other; deposit with UN has added advantage of giving agreement the aspect of a treaty. Re (b), Rabin asked what purpose is of language on Four Power action in Security Council. He was told this was simply way of expressing concept

---

[6] An apparent reference to the U.S. working paper that Charles Yost presented to the Four Powers in March. See Document 17.

which has always been inherent in major power discussion of settlement, of associating Security Council with final settlement.[7]

Rogers

---

[7] In an interview in Jerusalem on December 22, Meir expressed her anger at both the U.S. proposal for an Israeli-Jordanian settlement and the Rogers Plan. (*New York Times*, December 23, 1969, p. 1) Earlier that day, the Knesset released a statement rejecting the Rogers Plan, asserting that the "proposals submitted by the US cannot but be construed by the aggressive Arab rulers as an attempt to appease them, at Israel's espense." For the full text of the statement, see *Israel's Foreign Policy: Historical Documents*, volumes 1–2, 1947–1974, Chapter XII, The War of Attrition and the Cease Fire, Document 10.

---

79. **Memorandum From the President's Assistant for National Security Affairs (Kissinger) to President Nixon**[1]

Washington, December 23, 1969.

SUBJECT

Where We Stand on Israeli Aid Requests

We have completed the analysis of Israel's military and economic assistance requests and our technically possible options in response.[2] We are now ready to move into the policy phase. In view of your promise to Mrs. Meir to give these requests sympathetic and prompt study, I want to check our next step with you before I proceed.

Mrs. Meir left the U.S. on October 6. CIA, DIA and State had already begun analysis of the intelligence and economic data the Israelis gave us to explain their requests. This included seeking clarification on some points through normal working-level contacts.

Experience in the Johnson Administration with the first Phantom requests apparently taught those involved that it is essential to get a fair analysis of Israel's requirements *before* turning the bureaucracy loose on the issue of whether or not we should meet those requirements. In order to avoid having that argument color the basic analysis, I

---

[1] Source: National Archives, Nixon Presidential Materials, NSC Files, NSC Institutional Files (H-Files), Box H–166, National Security Study Memoranda. Secret. Sent for action. Kissinger's handwritten note to Haig on the first page reads: "Al—Pres, Laird, and I decided to handle in the same group that dealt with Israeli nuclear program, the all-purpose undersecretaries group."

[2] In response to Documents 62 and 63.

proposed setting up an NSC Ad Hoc Group to provide that analysis. You approved this procedure on November 6.

I now have in hand that Group's paper.[3] It has succeeded in rigorously avoiding policy questions. It has broken significant new analytical ground in identifying our options on both the military and economic questions. For the first time, a President will be able to make his political decisions on Israeli aid requests with a clear view of their military and economic consequences. It also describes for the first time Israel's substantial efforts to develop its own capacity to produce jet planes and tanks by 1974, and this is where the military and economic requests become closely interrelated.

The next step is to put the technically possible options identified in this paper into political context. You will want a paper outlining your political options and their consequences. The procedure for getting that is what I wish to discuss here. There are two main choices:

1. Ask Assistant Secretary Sisco's NSC Interdepartmental Group to produce a paper on the political options and send it up to the NSC through the *usual machinery*. Allowing time for the inevitable debate in that group, for Review Group deliberation and for scheduling in the NSC, it might be as late as March before we reached a decision.

2. The alternative would be to ask Sisco to produce the paper with whatever interdepartmental working participation is necessary but then to bring his *paper directly into the Review Group*. This would save one step in the bureaucratic process. The important bureaucratic point here is to be sure each department involved has a fair hearing for its viewpoint. Since they are all represented on the Review Group, we should be able to accomplish this with a little care. This should permit us to bring the issue into the NSC by early February.

I think it would be wiser to try for the earliest possible consideration. You will want to be in a position to respond to Mrs. Meir as soon as possible. It is also possible that some of the general budget decisions will have affected the Skyhawk production line and make an early February decision necessary if the Israelis are to add new requirements to the end of their present line.

Recommendation: That we try for the earliest possible consideration in the Review Group, by-passing the Interdepartmental Group if I judge it necessary after talking with Assistant Secretary Sisco.[4]

---

[3] A summary of a later draft of the paper is Document 93.
[4] Nixon approved this recommendation on December 29.

80. Telegram From the Department of State to Certain Diplomatic Posts[1]

Washington, December 24, 1969, 0043Z.

211998. 1. Dobrynin conveyed Soviet response to October 28 Middle Eastern formulations in meeting with Secretary today at which Sisco also present.[2] Response was in form of oral commentary, text of which Dobrynin then left with us. On basis preliminary study, reply, while indicating desire to continue both bilateral and quadrilateral talks, is not constructive, and does not move matters forward, and is retrogressive in some respects. It adheres closely to positions taken in the Soviet June document[3] and is propagandistic in a number of respects.

2. Secretary made clear that US feels it has gone as far as it can in October 28 UAR-Israeli document and December 18 Jordanian-Israeli document.[4] We indicated that careful study will be given to Soviet reply and judgment will be made whether reply justifies continuation of major power talks. Text of Soviet reply will be sent septel[5] as well as full report of Secretary's conversation with Dobrynin. Soviet reply should be tightly held, pending determination of how we wish to proceed. In reply to press queries, we are merely acknowledging that reply received and saying a) we are giving it careful study and b) preliminary review indicates it is not constructive.

3. Principal points of Soviet reply are as follows:

A. US October 28 document is one-sided and pro-Israeli and Quote cannot facilitate finding ways of settlement in the Middle East Unquote.

B. Soviets have backed off from Rhodes formula. Stress is on major powers working out principles of settlement, and then in Soviet view Quote it could be possible to find a proper form of intermediary ac-

---

[1] Source: National Archives, Nixon Presidential Materials, NSC Files, Box 1169, Saunders Files, Middle East Negotiations Files, Middle East Settlement—US–USSR Talks. Secret, Exdis. Drafted by Sisco and Atherton and approved by Sisco. Sent to Amman, Beirut, Cairo, Jidda, Kuwait, Tel Aviv, London, Paris, Moscow, USUN, Bucharest, and Rabat.

[2] For the October 28 proposal, see Document 58. A report on this December 23 meeting between Dobrynin and Rogers was sent to the same addresses in telegram 211994, December 24, printed in *Foreign Relations, 1969–1976*, volume XII, Soviet Union, January 1969–October 1970, Document 109.

[3] See Document 34.

[4] See footnote 2, Document 78.

[5] Telegram 212662, December 26, transmitted an official translation of the Soviet reply. (National Archives, Nixon Presidential Materials, NSC Files, Box 711, Country Files, Europe, USSR, Vol. VI)

tivity for Ambassador Jarring, providing he will discuss questions of settlement separately with each side . . . Unquote

C. Coupled with Dobrynin's supplementary remarks, reply makes clear Soviets favor more detailed treatment of certain points though at same time Dobrynin indicated their desire to find a Quote more neutral formula Unquote to express negotiating procedure under Jarring.

D. It calls for specific statement on withdrawal from Gaza and says there is no justification for Israeli participation in determining future of Gaza.

E. It implies that Syria must be included in any major power agreement.

F. While mentioning Quote a settlement which would ensure a lasting peace in the Middle East rather than restore the situation of an unstable armistice Unquote, it links in several places withdrawal of troops only with Quote cessation of state of war Unquote. Nowhere does it talk in terms of establishment of a binding peace between the parties and nowhere is there positive reaction to specific elements in the October 28 formulations designed to give content to peace, which are in fact implicitly rejected.

G. It retains previous Soviet concept of DMZs on both sides of the borders.

H. It once again stays with the June position that all that is required to solve the refugee question is for Israel to fulfill previous UN resolutions. It is unresponsive on the question of safeguards for Israel re the number of refugees to be repatriated.

I. Soviets continue to insist that reference to the Constantinople Convention of 1888 must be made in connection with freedom of navigation in the Suez Canal.

J. Soviet reply does not, on other hand, include any reference to UN peacekeeping forces which were prominent features of their June plan, though this concept seems implicit in reference to need for major powers to development detailed proposals in lieu of neutral formulations for parties to work out. In general, Soviet reply strongly emphasizes major power role and virtually eliminates role of parties in working out settlement.

K. Only bow in direction of October 28 formulations is statement that our language on boundaries represents "certain progress," coupled however with caveat that any joint US-Soviet document must explicitly provide for UAR sovereignty at Sharm al-Shaykh.

L. Finally, Soviet reply asserts that October 28 proposal departs from positions taken earlier by U.S., ignoring fact that this was done in effort develop neutral language to overcome irreconcilable differences in our positions on such matters as DMZs.

Rogers

81. Memorandum From the President's Assistant for National Security Affairs (Kissinger) to President Nixon[1]

Washington, December 30, 1969.

SUBJECT

Middle East

Attached are some interesting comments by Joe Sisco on the U.S. approach to the Middle East Four-Power talks and on the domestic problem with the Jewish community.[2]

Concerning the U.S. position on Four-Power talks, Sisco feels:

—We now have put forward two documents covering both the UAR and the Jordanian aspects of the settlement on which we *must* stand firm. Further concessions might weaken the "safety catch of our position," the principle of negotiations between parties.

—Yost should be told he is not authorized to go beyond the documents already submitted on UAR and Jordanian settlements.[3]

—Failure of the Four-Power talks is preferable to concessions that are unacceptable to Israel.

Concerning the domestic problem, Sisco believes:

—Three little-known background facts might help in preventing our present position from becoming a partisan issue, since they can help demonstrate that our position on the Jordan-Israel side is basically the same as that taken by the Johnson Administration.

1) In making a similar proposal to the U.A.R. on Israeli withdrawal, Rusk went further than our present position by favoring an international presence at Sharm al-Shaykh. (It should be noted, however,

---

[1] Source: National Archives, Nixon Presidential Materials, NSC Files, Box 664, Country Files, Middle East, Middle East—General, Vol. II. Secret; Nodis.

[2] Undated; attached but not printed.

[3] Nixon underlined this recommendation and wrote *"right"* in the left-hand margin.

that Rusk's offer was not, like ours, made to the Soviet Union. In Israel's view, Rusk's offer had lapsed when rejected by Egypt.)

2) Goldberg[4] assured Hussein we would support return of the West Bank with minor rectifications and we would use our influence to obtain for Jordan a role in Jerusalem. These same assurances have been reaffirmed by the Secretary of State during the past year.

3) Israel indicated in July 1968 that a real peace settlement would result in return of most of the West Bank.

—Unlike 1957, we are not asking Israel to withdraw under conditions which others work out but only under safeguards which Israel considers adequate.

—Much concern would be dispelled by an early and positive decision on the assistance package.[5]

---

[4] Arthur J. Goldberg, U.S. Permanent Representative to the United Nations until June 1968.

[5] Nixon circled this sentence and wrote: "K, *I agree*—Let's discuss this with Mel and Bill soon."

The Cease-Fire Agreement

82. Telegram From the Department of State to the Embassy in Jordan[1]

Washington, January 9, 1970, 2310Z.

3992 Subject: Letter from President to King Hussein. Ref: London 10351.[2]

1. Embassy requested deliver following oral message from President to King Hussein:

2. QUOTE Your Majesty:

In response to your message, I want to assure you of our readiness to do what we can to keep this situation from deteriorating and I have asked Secretary Rogers to keep in close touch with your government. We have over the past few months tried to impress on all parties in the area the need for restraint. We realize that your government is making great efforts to contain the situation. In this connection, I have asked that the Israeli Government be informed that you have repeated your strict orders that no shelling be permitted across the Jordan River, whether by fedayeen or regular forces. As you know, the Israelis have reported and have expressed deep concern over shellings of their civilian settlements.

I appreciate your comment regarding the efforts we are making to achieve peace and justice for the Near East. We believe a stable peace would be in the interest of all concerned in the area.

---

[1] Source: National Archives, Nixon Presidential Materials, NSC Files, Box 797, Presidential Correspondence. Secret; Priority; Nodis. Drafted on December 30, 1969, by Thomas J. Scotes (NEA/ARN); cleared in NEA, NEA/ARN, NEA/IAI, and the White House; and approved by Richardson and Sisco. Repeated Priority to London.

[2] Telegram 10351 from London, December 29, 1969, transmitted a message from King Hussein to Nixon in which the King sought to draw the President's attention "to the recent and currently deteriorating situation" in the Middle East. He attributed the deterioration to the "very high limit" that "Israel's belligerency has reached," citing air and artillery attacks against Jordanian cities, villages, and "other civilian targets," which he described as the "one-sided war" that Israel was waging against his country. (Ibid., Box 614, Country Files, Middle East, Jordan, Vol. III)

As the New Year begins, may I extend to you my personal best wishes as you endeavor to serve the cause of your people as well as that of world peace.

Sincerely yours,

Richard Nixon END QUOTE[3]

Rogers

---

[3] In telegram 145 from Amman, January 12, the Embassy reported Symmes's delivery of Nixon's message to Rifai and Hussein, who thanked the Ambassador but made no comments. (Ibid.)

83. Telegram From the Department of State to the Mission to the United Nations[1]

Washington, January 13, 1970, 0412Z.

4992. Personal for Ambassador Yost from Secretary.

1. I am convinced that, as a result of position taken in December 9 policy statement[2] and October 28 and December 18 guideline documents,[3] we are now in strongest possible position to stand firmly. We have adopted a position which meets legitimate concerns of both sides, and beyond which we cannot go in any substantial way.

2. I appreciate tactical difficulties which confront you in Four Power talks. I am sure you would agree that tactical difficulties that confront us in Four Powers should not in any way cause us to alter course laid down in October 28th and December 18th documents. It is now up to Soviets and Nasser to decide whether they wish to grasp opportunity which this U.S. position affords.

3. I have given very considerable thought and have discussed with President how we wish you to proceed in Four Power talks as you personally renew your efforts on Tuesday.[4] We note that our UK friends

---

[1] Source: National Archives, RG 59, Central Files 1970–73, POL 27–14 ARAB–ISR. Secret; Nodis. Drafted on January 9 by Sisco, cleared by De Palma and Kissinger, and approved by Rogers.

[2] See Document 73.

[3] Document 58 and footnote 5, Document 76.

[4] January 13.

seem to be all right for time being and are willing to stay with us on basis of our documents at least until Wilson has had a talk with President later this month.[5] We note also continuing unwillingness of French to stand with us and Soviet strategy has now become clear; namely, to fall in with French proposals[6] and thereby attempt to chip away at U.S. position. We cannot agree with Soviet-French approach which leads immediately to process of marrying various proposals.

4. Fact that at one time or another all of parties in area and major powers have agreed to Rhodes formula[7] provides us with opportunity to prevent this risky Soviet-French gambit from succeeding. At your Tuesday meeting, therefore, I wish you to make clear and to insist that there be agreement in first instance on Rhodes formula. You should make clear that our substantive views regarding framework for Jarring's guidance are laid down in October 28th–December 18th documents, and we cannot agree to any substantial alteration. We would like you also to get across the idea that unless early agreement on Rhodes procedure and specific elements of our peace language can be achieved, it is difficult to see how progress can be made towards a Four Power consensus that will start negotiating process between parties. Gromyko agreed to this proposal in his talks with me at UN;[8] I do not believe we should let Russians or Egyptians get off hook.

5. I realize that position you are being asked to take in Four Powers causes some tactical difficulties; however, alternative is moving down slippery slope which Soviet and French are pursuing which would very soon face us with agreeing to propositions on which there is absolutely no chance of getting Israeli acquiescence. Despite present strong Israeli opposition, we do not preclude possibility Israel can be brought to engage in Rhodes-type discussions on basis our two documents; anything beyond this would be impossible for them.

6. If Four Powers are to reach an impasse, as is probable in our judgment, it is better from point of view of our overall interests for impasse to be on basis of forthcoming, constructive and positive position that is reflected in October 28th, December 9th, and December 18th US statements rather than in circumstances where other three had reached near agreement on alternative proposal.[9]

7. I have cleared this message with President.

Rogers

---

[5] The President met with Harold Wilson and others in both the Oval Office and the Cabinet Room on January 27 and 28. See footnote 3, Document 89.

[6] See Document 75.

[7] See footnote 3, Document 52.

[8] See Document 53.

[9] At the Four-Power meeting on January 13, Yost made a "strong and lengthy presentation" based on Rogers's instructions. During the meeting, the French Representative presented a nine-point plan to produce guidelines to aid Jarring in his effort to negotiate a settlement between Israel and Egypt and Jordan. (Telegram 51 from USUN, January 15; National Archives, RG 59, Central Files 1970–73, POL 27–14 ARAB–ISR)

84. Telegram From the Department of State to the Embassy in Israel[1]

Washington, January 22, 1970, 0224Z.

10153. For Ambassador Barbour from Secretary. Please deliver following oral message from me to Foreign Minister Eban:

QUOTE 1. In the light of developments since our conversation of December 16[2] I want to share my thoughts with you on the current status of our proposals and our peace efforts as a whole.

2. As you know, we have received an oral reply from the Soviet Union to our formulations of October 28, a copy of which was provided to Minister Argov here on December 26.[3] We do not consider the Soviet answer constructive or responsive. This will be communicated to the Soviet Union officially at an early date.[4] I have asked that a copy of our reply be given to Ambassador Rabin.

3. The substance of our proposals on both the UAR and Jordanian aspects of a Middle East settlement are now widely known. We believe they fully protect Israel's security interests and negotiating position. I regret that your Government has interpreted our proposals differently. I hope the Government of Israel will come to appreciate in time the strength and inherent soundness of our position for it reflects our common interests in a binding, contractual peace between the parties. Our proposals are firmly rooted in the principle of negotiations between the parties, on the need for which we are in full agreement. They are also firmly rooted in Security Council Resolution 242 which in our view sets the pre-conditions within which negotiations should take place.

4. With regard to our diplomatic efforts, we have sought to keep your Government fully advised of our position and the steps we were taking, and to exchange views with you. Regarding in particular our recent proposal on Jordan, I believed I had made clear to you on December 16 that we would probably go ahead in the Four Power talks on the basis of positions already well known to you, a step we had delayed

---

[1] Source: National Archives, Nixon Presidential Materials, NSC Files, Box 605, Country Files, Middle East, Israel, Vol. III. Secret; Nodis. Drafted on January 9 by Sisco and Atherton, cleared by Kissinger, and approved by Rogers. Repeated to USUN.

[2] See footnote 2, Document 77.

[3] See footnote 5, Document 80.

[4] See Document 85. Nixon approved the communications to both Israel and the Soviet Union on an undated memorandum from Kissinger. (National Archives, Nixon Presidential Materials, NSC Files, Box 644, Country Files, Middle East, Middle East—General, Vol. II)

until there had been opportunity to exchange views with you. You should know that no decision had been taken at the time of our talk, since I had hoped that you might be able to give me some indication of progress on the Jordanian side which would make our initiative unnecessary. I also raised with you, unfortunately without success, the possibility of the United States singularly undertaking a helpful role on the Jordanian-Israeli aspect of the settlement. After assessing the views of the Israeli Government following our talks on December 16, we concluded it was desirable to move quickly in the Four Power meeting scheduled for December 18.[5]

5. We believe we can stand substantially on the proposals we have made. They maintain the essential position that peace must be based on agreement between the parties arrived at through negotiations. With particular regard to the views on Ambassador Jarring's Mission which Ambassador Tekoah conveyed to Ambassador Yost January 20,[6] I would hope that your Government can see its way clear to maintaining its freedom of action with respect to any negotiating opportunities that may arise in the future and in particular that you will weigh carefully the suggestions I made during our recent meeting with respect to Israel's posture toward a peace settlement.

6. I also hope this message will help clear up any misunderstandings which have developed in recent days. The commitment of the United States to Israel's future is firm and steadfast. We are two friends with parallel interests and should so appear in the eyes of the world. CLOSE QUOTE

Rogers

---

[5] See footnote 5, Document 76.

[6] According to telegram 81 from USUN, January 20, Tekoah, reading from instructions from his government, said: "We received Jarring on the basis of his mandate to promote agreement and in view of the fact that his terms of reference did not include anything prejudicial on such questions as refugees, Jerusalem, the establishment of boundaries, etc. Consequently, should he be provided with guidelines divergent from these essentials, Israel's consent given on the basis of his original mandate will lapse." (National Archives, RG 59, Central Files 1970–73, POL 27–14 ARAB–ISR)

85. Telegram From the Department of State to the Embassy in the Soviet Union[1]

Washington, January 23, 1970, 0117Z.

10865. Subject: US Reply to Soviet Statement of December 23 on Middle East.[2]

1. Text of oral statement made on Jan 22 by Assistant Secretary Sisco to Soviet Ambassador Dobrynin follows. British, French, and Israeli Embassies provided with Sisco's oral statement January 22 (septels). Jordanian Amb will be briefed Monday pm.

2. *Begin text.*

Oral reply to Soviet oral comment of December 23, 1969

The US Government has studied carefully the oral statement delivered by Ambassador Dobrynin to the Secretary of State on December 23, 1969.

As the Soviet Government is aware, the proposals we developed and suggested to Soviet representatives over a period of many weeks, most recently on October 28, 1969,[3] were designed to provide a framework for Ambassador Jarring's guidance with respect to the UAR-Israeli aspect of a settlement, to be paralleled by proposals for the Jordanian-Israeli aspect which we subsequently submitted in the Four Power talks in New York on December 18, 1969.[4] The formulations of October 28, in the form of a proposed joint US–USSR working paper, drew upon elements of both the Soviet document of June 17, 1969 and the US document of July 15, 1969 and were intended to reflect common positions.[5] As such, they represented a serious attempt on our part to meet both Soviet and US views on certain fundamental issues. We reject the Soviet allegation that our position as reflected in the proposed October 28 joint US–USSR working paper is one-sided. It is a fair and balanced document which meets the legitimate concerns of both sides.

There is need for negotiations between the parties to begin promptly under Jarring's auspices. The October 28 and December 18

---

[1] Source: National Archives, Nixon Presidential Materials, NSC Files, Box 1186, Saunders Files, Middle East Negotiations Files, Middle East Settlement—US–USSR Talks. Secret; Exdis; Priority. Drafted by Walter B. Smith (NEA/IAI), cleared in EUR/SOV, and approved by Sisco. Repeated to Amman, Cairo, Beirut, London, Paris, Tel Aviv, USUN, Kuwait, Jidda, Nicosia, Belgrade, Algiers, Khartoum, Rabat, Tripoli, and Tunis.

[2] See Document 80.

[3] See Document 61.

[4] See footnote 5, Document 76.

[5] Regarding the June 17 and July 15 papers, see Document 34 and footnote 4, Document 39, respectively.

documents deal with the key issues of pace, withdrawal and negotiations to reach the agreement called for in the UN Security Council resolution of November 1967. These two documents provide an equitable framework which would enable Ambassador Jarring to convene the parties immediately and get on with his task of promoting the just and lasting peace called for by the Security Council resolution. In this connection, the Soviet contention that the US has now proposed to limit itself to "neutral formulas alone" is without foundation.

The Soviet oral response of December 23 and the position being taken by the Soviet representative in the Four Power talks on the Jordanian-Israeli aspect are not constructive, are delaying the prompt resumption of the Jarring mission and have raised doubt in this government as to the Soviet desire for a stable and durable peace in the Middle East. We see no significant difference between the present Soviet position and the position stated in the Soviet proposals of December 1968[6] and June 1969.

We do not believe it is useful to comment on every point in the Soviet response of December 23 since the US position and the reasons for it have been fully explained to Soviet representatives on many occasions in the past. We do wish, however, to draw to the attention of the Soviet Government the following:

We note that the Soviet Government no longer supports the provision for negotiations between the parties under Ambassador Jarring's auspices according to the procedures the parties utilized at Rhodes in 1949. This retrogression in the Soviet position is particularly regrettable, since the formulation on this point contained in the October 28 wording was worked out jointly by Asst. Secy. Sisco and Ambassador Dobrynin following the understanding reached by Secretary of State Rogers and Foreign Minister Gromyko during their talks at the UN.[7] Resolution 242 calls upon Ambassador Jarring to promote agreement. In the context of the resolution this clearly means agreement between the parties concerned which can only be achieved through a process of negotiations—a view which the Soviet Government indicated it shared in accepting on a contingent basis the Rhodes negotiating procedure in the proposed October 28 joint document.

The Soviet response of December 23 misrepresents the US position on the question of withdrawal of Israeli armed forces from UAR occupied territory, implying that our position does not envisage such withdrawal when in fact our proposal makes clear that withdrawal should be to the former international boundary once the parties have agreed

---

[6] See Document 1.
[7] See Document 53.

upon their commitments to a contractual peace and have negotiated between them under Jarring's auspices the practical arrangements to make that peace secure.

The Soviet reply is completely unresponsive to our suggestions, on which we have placed particular stress from the start, for language to give specific content to the parties' commitments to the just and lasting peace. We note, in particular, that the Soviets have linked withdrawal not with the establishment of peace between the parties but with "cessation of the state of war." The USSR will recall that the Security Council resolution is very specific: its principal objective is the establishment of a just and lasting peace between the parties. Does the Soviet Union agree with the specific formulations on peace contained in the suggested October 28 joint paper? A clear, and not evasive, response is required.

The US Government believes the Soviet Union should reconsider its views in light of these observations. *End text.*

Rogers

86. Memorandum for the Record[1]

Washington, January 26, 1970.

SUBJECT

Meeting of Special NSC Review Group on Israeli Assistance Requests

PARTICIPANTS

Henry A. Kissinger
Elliot Richardson
David Packard
Earle Wheeler
Richard Helms
Joseph Sisco
Harold Saunders
Robert Munn

---

[1] Source: National Archives, Nixon Presidential Materials, NSC Files, NSC Institutional Files (H-Files), Box H–111, Senior Review Group, SRG Minutes Originals 1970. Top Secret. Drafted by Saunders. All brackets are in the original.

Dr. Kissinger opened the meeting by saying that he wanted to mention two factors in addition to those highlighted in the papers[2] that had been circulated:

—When the President had talked with Israeli Prime Minister Meir last September,[3] he had indicated without committing himself to any specific numbers that, while the U.S. could not always be helpful on "software," we would help on "hardware."

—In December when Ambassador Rabin had been in seeing Dr. Kissinger, the President had called Dr. Kissinger to his office and, learning that Rabin was there, asked him to bring the Ambassador along. In the presence of Secretary Laird, the President had indicated that we would look at Israel's assistance requests with a sympathetic attitude.[4]

While the President did not specify any particular aid levels with either Mrs. Meir or Ambassador Rabin and the group was not bound to any particular level, it had to keep in mind this part of the picture.

Mr. Richardson asked how Dr. Kissinger conceived the responsibilities of this group.

Dr. Kissinger said he thought the group should put to the President a paper which covers the following points:

—How the Israeli request bears on the President's general approach to the Middle East.

—The implications of various levels of assistance.

—If the group can come to a recommendation, it should give the President one taking account of the above two points.

---

[2] "U.S. Options on Assistance to Israel," January 14. (Ibid., Box 605, Country Files, Middle East, Israel, Vol. III) The second paper was not identified.

[3] See footnote 2, Document 52.

[4] No record of Nixon's meeting with Kissinger and Rabin on December 26, 1969, has been found. A transcript of Nixon's telephone conversation with Kissinger is in the National Archives, Nixon Presidential Materials, NSC Files, Henry Kissinger Telephone Conversation Transcripts, Box 3, Chronological File. In his memoirs, Rabin recalled that he had requested an "urgent" meeting with Kissinger to deliver a "personal letter" from Prime Minister Meir to President Nixon. Rabin told Kissinger that "Mrs. Meir still continued to believe that President Nixon was Israel's friend. But she did not understand how this friendship could be reconciled with the recent American steps culminating in the two documents on the Egyptian and Jordanian questions." Rabin then told Kissinger: "Let me tell you in complete frankness, you are making a bad mistake . . . In taking discussion of a peace settlement out of the hands of the parties and transferring it to the powers, you are fostering an imposed solution that Israel will resist with all her might. I personally shall do everything within the bounds of American law to arouse public opinion against the administration's moves!" Regarding his impromptu meeting with Nixon, which was also attended by Secretary of Defense Laird and Kissinger, Rabin wrote that the "strange encounter" lasted no more than seven or eight minutes, and focused heavily on pending Israeli arms requests. (Rabin, *The Rabin Memoirs*, pp. 161–163)

Mr. Richardson entered the proviso that he was not sure that Secretary Rogers at this stage was prepared to enter into a joint recommendation. He was sure the Secretary would want to have a hand in the recommendation.

Dr. Kissinger asked whether that meant that the Secretary would want an NSC meeting.

Mr. Sisco said that he thought perhaps a smaller group would be adequate, especially if we ended up taking a series of diffuse actions rather than an overall decision on the total Israeli requests.

Mr. Richardson concurred that a smaller meeting might be perfectly adequate; he was not talking about the forum but simply about the fact that the Secretary would want to have a hand in this.

Mr. Sisco felt that the Secretary was prepared to look at a narrowed range of possibilities and would not insist on reviewing the total range of options that had been laid out in the papers.

Dr. Kissinger suggested that the group see whether it could reduce the range of options to a narrow list.

Mr. Packard said that he felt that the papers had not properly covered all of the issues that need to go into a decision. For instance, he did not feel that the paper adequately discussed the question of whether we should try to get something from the Israelis in return for our aid. Nor did he feel that broader U.S. interests in the Middle East were adequately covered in the paper. He was also concerned about the issue of building Israel's capability and about the nuclear question.

Dr. Kissinger suggested that there are two aspects of Mr. Packard's first point:

—The extent to which granting or withholding aid can be used to influence future Israeli political decisions.

—Whether or not, having made an agreement to give some assistance, we could hold up on delivery as a means of influencing later Israeli decisions.

Mr. Sisco said that any linkage between aid and political conditions could be done at whatever crucial time might develop later. If hypothetically at some future point Nasser appeared ready to enter negotiations, we might want to use aid as leverage if we have kept the option open by our present decisions. On the other hand, he is convinced that the amount of leverage we have over Israel is not as great as is sometimes thought.

Dr. Kissinger asked whether it would be greater if we withheld aid now.

Mr. Sisco replied that this would not be the case in the absence of a serious Arab proposal now.

Mr. Richardson asked what we should do about the NPT.

Mr. Sisco replied that it would be desirable to make a follow-up approach to the Israelis urging them to sign. But he did not feel we should tie that approach to our aid decision.

When Mr. Packard asked why not, Mr. Sisco replied that he felt what we decide to do on military assistance should be based on the political and psychological requirements of the U.S.-Israeli relationship. He felt that the signing of the NPT was not an issue which is crucial in governing Israeli policy toward peace-making.

Mr. Packard pointed out that it would help our position if we could be the government responsible for producing an Israeli signature.

Mr. Richardson felt that the hardest question was not the problem of what level of assistance to provide Israel but how to handle this level in connection with other things. There is a variety of other issues ranging from Israeli oil drilling in the Gulf of Suez to Israeli relations with Lebanon and Jordan.

Mr. Sisco said his difficulty lies in the general question of tying aid to Israeli policy decisions. He has no objection to pressing Israel at the same time we are making our aid decisions, but he does not see how we could work out an appropriate specific linkage.

Mr. Richardson said that going ahead with positive decisions on Israel's aid requests now would risk our seeming to bluster about the NPT, missiles, drilling for oil in the Gulf while not really appearing serious about any of these things.

Mr. Packard agreed that the Israelis only listen to actions.

Mr. Richardson pointed out that deliveries only come much later, and the Israelis will hear our words now without thinking very much about the possibility of our exercising future pressure by withholding deliveries.

In response to a question from Dr. Kissinger, Mr. Sisco said that he felt there are some things the U.S. would want to do for Israel in any circumstance. Mr. Sisco said he would fall short of taking a position of "sign or else."

In response to Dr. Kissinger's question about his views, Mr. Helms said that he had not seen any disposition on the part of the U.S. to stick to one of these linkages on previous occasions.

Dr. Kissinger said he thought the President would be inclined to do something. The President had not made any linkage in talking to Mrs. Meir.

Mr. Richardson said there is a whole range of ways of linking—from explicit linkage to simply dealing with subjects concurrently with only implied linkage.

Mr. Packard noted that there are some things that could be done that would not amount to major decisions such as making up losses and helping with basic ordnance and spare parts.

Dr. Kissinger asked whether, if we use our leverage on the NPT, can we use it again on the terms of peace.

Mr. Sisco replied that, since we have limited leverage, he would prefer to reserve what we have for later.

Mr. Richardson commented that we could use the same thing more than once if we were willing to use it first in connection with our decision and then later in connection with delivery.

Mr. Richardson said that he agreed with Mr. Packard on the question of linkage and on the implications of developing Israeli self-sufficiency. He felt that there was a third heading of issues that needed to be discussed. This was the fact that we do not have enough information on the economic side.

[At this point Dr. Kissinger was called out.]

Mr. Packard pointed out that one of the implications of helping Israel become self-sufficient in the production of arms was that Israel would become an arms exporter.

Mr. Richardson noted the advantages of self-sufficiency in that we would be less tagged as being Israel's supporter. What we are trying to do here, he said, is to square a circle—we are trying to provide Israel with the means of survival but the more visible we are in doing it the more we hurt our other interests in the area.

Mr. Richardson, General Wheeler and Mr. Helms all noted the fact that the analysis of Israel's requests seemed to indicate that Israel's needs were not large. Mr. Sisco noted that there were several things that could be decided on now like the P.L. 480 request and the $119 million in additional military credit.

Mr. Richardson asked Mr. Sisco how he would assess the Israeli reaction to a U.S. policy of dribbling out our aid. Would the Israelis get hysterical or would they stick with us through a process of consultation that might lead to more aid.

[Dr. Kissinger returned.]

Mr. Sisco felt that it would be desirable to give the Israelis an early signal that the pressure campaign they have mounted against the Administration in favor of a big assistance package makes it harder for the President to make a decision. He reiterated his view of the desirable package as above plus replacing Israeli losses of airplanes and committing ourselves to keep flowing the less dramatic items now in the pipeline. Then he would opt for one of the modest options as a hedge against some of the unpredictables in the situation such as the possibility that the Mirage aircraft recently sold to Libya would end up in the UAR.[5]

Mr. Packard asked how we would handle the Jordanian side of this picture, and Mr. Sisco noted that a new squadron of F–104s is under consideration for Jordan.[6]

Mr. Richardson asked what assumption we should make about publicity on any decision. Would the Israelis cooperate in keeping it secret? And would that be possible? If possible, he felt that it would be in our interest to lower the visibility of this decision. Mr. Richardson did not feel we could assume that Israel and the U.S. shared the same interests.

Dr. Kissinger said that it was clear to him that the Israelis did not want to withdraw.

Mr. Richardson felt that the Israelis were split internally but as far as our role is concerned, we have an interest in Israel's saying that it would be willing to withdraw from occupied territory if the Arabs would negotiate.

In response to Dr. Kissinger's question about his view, General Wheeler said that we ought to push the NPT urgently. He said, however, he did not feel that we have any leverage to speak of in our arms supply. He doubted that linking the NPT signature to arms supply would have much effect. He would recommend pushing for signature simply on its merits. As far as Israel's armaments industry is concerned, he felt the decision was a narrow one since the U.S. is already indicted in Arab eyes as Israel's main supporter.

Dr. Kissinger said he did not feel that he understood the degree of self-sufficiency that Israel might achieve. He noted the attraction of being able to say to Israel that from "now on, it is your baby."

General Wheeler said he completely disagreed with Israel's position on negotiations but he did not feel we had enough leverage to change it.

Mr. Packard said that on the question of developing Israel's arms industry one issue is that we will make Israel an exporter.

Dr. Kissinger asked why we care, since somebody is going to sell arms to these people.

Mr. Richardson said he did not object to selling arms but he felt that having more salesmen in the business stimulated the acquisition of arms in the underdeveloped countries unnecessarily.

---

[5] At the end of November 1969, France reached a $400 million arms deal with Libya, agreeing to sell it 50 Mirage jets and 200 heavy tanks, among other weapons. (*New York Times*, December 19, 1969, p. 1) See also *Foreign Relations, 1969–1976*, volume XLI, Western Europe; NATO, 1969–1972, Documents 135, 136, and 137.

[6] See Document 87.

[Dr. Kissinger was called out.]

Mr. Richardson raised the question of whether there was anything we could do to keep Israel from achieving self-sufficiency in arms production.

Mr. Sisco said that he felt the Israelis would absorb the costs of doing this in some way because of their psychosis that they cannot rely on others.

Mr. Packard noted that withholding financial support is the only way we could possibly control this. Mr. Saunders pointed out there was also the question of export licenses. Mr. Richardson said that before we talked to the Israelis about this subject we should know on the whole whether we want them to get into the production or not.

[Dr. Kissinger returned.]

Mr. Richardson suggested reviewing for a moment. The papers that have been prepared are excellent. Now we need a paper further developing the picture of how we might proceed. It is difficult to extricate how we approach the Israelis from the substance of our approach, but we need a paper with this focus. Further, we need a fuller study of the implications of Israel's own arms production. Under the procedural heading, we have to consider how to talk to the Israelis about where their economic figures come from and to decide on steps for finding out how those figures were produced.

Mr. Packard said that we have to be responsive to what the President has already said and to the political facts of life. Perhaps in the short term we should do something like what Mr. Sisco underlined. This would not look as if we were pressuring Israel. Beyond that, it is difficult to figure out what trade-offs we should try to achieve but it is desirable. In short, we come down to a paper describing our short-term moves and then one on those subjects requiring more study.

Dr. Kissinger said that he saw these questions:

—Whether we give any military assistance or not. He assumed that we would give some.

—If so, at what level, what should we do in the short run to take the pressure off and what should we do in the longer term? Then these same two questions should be applied to the economic issues.

Mr. Packard raised a question of whether we could do anything for Jordan to look more even-handed.

Mr. Sisco replied that we already had programs in the works for Jordan, Lebanon, Saudi Arabia and Kuwait.[7]

---

[7] For Lebanon, see Document 98. For Saudi Arabia and Kuwait, see *Foreign Relations, 1969–1976*, volume XXIV, Middle East Region and Arabian Peninsula, 1969–1972; Jordan, September 1970, Documents 133 and 82, respectively.

Dr. Kissinger said he felt we needed a paper on what is immediately feasible. Mr. Sisco interjected that the question is how we go about proceeding with this package and what linkage we may want to establish. Dr. Kissinger said that we should put together a "stop-gap" package to give us breathing space, expecting that this would not give us very much leverage.

Mr. Richardson said he felt we should establish whether we can go any further with our own economic analysis without talking to the Israelis.

Dr. Kissinger said he felt we needed a scenario on how to discuss our aid package with the Israelis, including whatever linkage we decide to make.

Mr. Richardson said he felt we needed to carry further our thinking about Israel's self-sufficiency in arms production. Dr. Kissinger asked Mr. Saunders to expand the pros and cons of Israeli self-sufficiency and to produce a paper explaining more fully what is involved.

Mr. Packard raised the question of whether now is the time to try another approach on arms limitation. Mr. Sisco noted that the President had authorized him to raise this subject with Gromyko in July.[8] Secretary Rogers had raised it with Gromyko at the UN General Assembly,[9] and Sisco had mentioned it to Dobrynin. There is no problem in raising it again.

Dr. Kissinger said he felt sure the President would endorse that.

Dr. Kissinger concluded the meeting by saying that we would have a paper on interim steps within two weeks.[10] Then the NSC might consider in early March[11] the larger issue of further aid to Israel. The special Review Group might get together once more to review these papers.

Harold H. Saunders[12]

---

[8] See Document 39.

[9] See Document 53.

[10] Three papers, "Responses to Israel's Arms and Economic Assistance Requests," "Israel: Development of Military Industries," and "U.S. Arms Supply Policy toward Israel: Options Paper," a Defense options paper, were discussed at the February 25 Special Review Group meeting. (National Archives, Nixon Presidential Materials, NSC Files, NSC Institutional Files (H-Files), Box H-166, National Security Study Memoranda; Washington National Records Center, OSD Files: FRC 330-76-0076, Box 8, Israel) See Documents 93 and 94.

[11] The NSC did not meet on this issue.

[12] Saunders initialed "H.S." above his typed signature.

87. Telegram From the Department of State to the Embassy in Jordan[1]

Washington, January 30, 1970, 2019Z.

14726. Subject: Jordanian Request for Additional F–104s. Ref: State 5624, Amman 265 and State 11160.[2] Joint State-Defense Message.

1. *FYI* We reluctant to sell Jordan additional military aircraft because any such transaction contributes to escalation arms race in Near East—at least in psychological sense—and because current squadron of F–104 aircraft still not rpt not operational. We recognize, however, that King Hussein has legitimate defense requirements and that both internal and inter-Arab considerations require him to maintain a ready military posture. Moreover, Soviet offer[3] makes prompt positive US response essential. At same time we shall continue to endeavor to restrain GOJ appetite for weapons and, as in the past, meet only those needs we consider wholly justifiable. In case of additional F–104 aircraft we have already agreed in principle to sell additional squadron. Our tactics have been to delay sale as long as possible, using argument that preferable hold up pending clarification GOJ absorptive capacity. King's request we now carry out our undertaking (Amman 5460),[4] together with Rifai follow-up (Amman 265), necessitates our now moving ahead. We are, nevertheless, puzzled as to how GOJ intends to pay for aircraft, particularly in light of fact GOJ plans purchase more artillery. We definitely do not rpt not intend in any event to make FMS credit available for this transaction. *End FYI.*

2. You therefore authorized to inform GOJ that we are agreeable to providing eight additional F–104 aircraft in accordance following commitments:

---

[1] Source: National Archives, Nixon Presidential Materials, NSC Files, Box 614, Country Files, Middle East, Jordan, Vol. III. Secret; Nodis; Immediate. Drafted by Seelye; cleared by Sisco and in OSD/ISA, NEA, NEA/RA, and PM; and approved by Richardson. Repeated to Tel Aviv.

[2] Telegram 5624 to Amman, January 14, transmitted the Department's approval of the Embassy's suggestions of how to respond to Jordan's request for F–104 aircraft. In telegram 265 from Amman, January 19, the Embassy reported a conversation between Symmes and Rifai during which the Foreign Minister asked if the Department had replied to Jordan's request for the aircraft. In telegram 11160 to Amman, January 23, the Department responded with the message: "This matter is receiving our urgent attention and we plan to have a reply for you early next week." (All ibid., RG 59, Central Files 1970–73, DEF 12–5 JORDAN)

[3] See footnote 3, Document 69.

[4] In telegram 5460 from Amman, November 10, 1969, the Embassy reported a message from Rifai informing Symmes of Jordan's decision to exercise its option to purchase a second squadron of 18 F–104 aircraft. (National Archives, Nixon Presidential Materials, NSC Files, Box 613, Country Files, Middle East, Jordan, Vol. II)

A. In March 1968, when agreement for first squadron was signed,[5] we informed GOJ that we would be prepared to consider supply of second squadron at some future date.

B. On April 2, 1969, in response to King Hussein's expression of desire to exercise GOJ option re acquiring second squadron, Secretary Rogers informed Hussein that USG agreed in principle to sell Jordan 18 additional F–104 aircraft with delivery to be mutually agreed upon.[6]

3. You should make clear in context foregoing that we consider eight F–104 aircraft requested to be part of option for second squadron and not rpt not additional thereto. You may state that we are earmarking eight F–104 aircraft for sale to Jordan and as soon as GOJ makes official request to us in writing we will begin processing. Because of necessary modifications in bringing aircraft up to latest standards we estimate lead time of approximately one year between signing of letter and delivery of aircraft. More precise info will be provided later. If appropriate at this time, you may state that transaction will be strictly on cash basis. You might also inquire as to how GOJ intends pay for aircraft in view other pressing requirements. *FYI* Aircraft, which are models F–104 A and B, must be reconfigured to take larger engine in order to conform with F–104 models now on hand in Jordan. Current strike at GE plant may delay J–79 engine production and further extend lead time. *End FYI.*

Rogers

---

[5] See *Foreign Relations,* 1964–1968, volume XX, Arab-Israeli Dispute, 1967–1968, Documents 95, 107, and 111.

[6] See Document 24. A record of Rogers's response to Hussein has not been found.

---

88. Editorial Note

In late January 1970, Israel began a campaign of bombing attacks and commando strikes across the border into Egypt, including an attack on a UAR army camp close to Cairo. On January 28, the Department of State released a statement calling for restoration of the cease-fire in the Middle East. (*New York Times,* Janaury 29, 1970, page 8) On January 31, Chairman of the Soviet Council of Ministers Alexei Kosygin sent President Richard Nixon a letter complaining that Israel had "resumed anew military actions against the Arab states" that targeted both military installations and civilian populations. He argued that Israeli leaders were "evidently proceeding from the assumption that the US will go on supporting Israel," regardless of its actions, and cautioned that the violence would "only widen and deepen the conflict" and "perpetuate tension in one of the most important areas of the world." Kosygin also warned that if Israel "continues its adventurism," the Soviet Union "would be forced to see to it that the Arab states have means at their disposal" to "rebuff" their "arrogant aggressor." He concluded by suggesting that the bilateral and Four-Power talks be energized to ensure the "speediest withdrawal of Israeli forces from all the occupied Arab territories" and asked that Nixon "appraise the situation from the viewpoint of special responsibility for the maintenance of peace which lies on our countries." (*Foreign Relations*, 1969–1976, volume XII, Soviet Union, January 1969–October 1970, Document 121)

Secretary of State William Rogers sent Nixon a suggested response to Kosygin's letter on February 2, explaining that "a prompt reply would have the advantage of informing Kosygin of the current efforts we started on our own several days ago to help bring about restoration of the UAR-Israeli cease fire." (Ibid., Document 125) In his February 3 covering memorandum to Rogers's suggested response, President's Assistant for National Security Affairs Henry Kissinger wrote to Nixon that he agreed with the Secretary that an early reply to Kosygin best served U.S. interests in that to "stand back and let pressure on the UAR and the USSR mount further" carried "an element of risk" by putting pressure on the Soviet Union to "do something visible to reverse the present trend." He added that the "onus for delay" should not be placed on the United States. (National Archives, Nixon Presidential Materials, NSC Files, Box 340, Subject Files, Dobrynin/Kissinger) On February 4, Kissinger sent Nixon a memorandum that conveyed his further reflections on Kosygin's letter, which he described as an "inept performance" and "disturbing," intended presumably to "get the Israelis to desist" as well as to "keep their [Soviet] reputation as an effective protecting power of the Arabs alive." He concluded that it was "unlikely to produce a cease-fire, except under conditions little short of humiliating for Nasser," emphasizing again that it only served to put further pressure on the Soviet Union "to make good on their threat." (*Foreign Relations*, 1969–1976, volume XII, Soviet Union, January 1969–October 1970, Document 127)

Nixon responded to Kosygin on February 4: "For its part, the United States intends to continue its efforts to promote a stable peace between the parties in accordance with the UN Security Council Resolution of November 22, 1967 and to encourage the scrupulous adherence by all concerned, not just one side, to the cease-fire resolutions of the United Nations." He added that Kosygin's "attempt to place responsibility on one side" for the increasing level of violence in the

Middle East was "not supported by the facts" and that "any implication that the United States has been a party to or has encouraged violations of the cease-fire is without foundation." Regarding Kosygin's threat "to see to it that the Arab states have means at their disposal," Nixon wrote: "The United States has always opposed steps which could have the effect of drawing the major powers more deeply into the Middle East conflict," but continued, "While preferring restraint, ... the United States is watching carefully the relative balance in the Middle East and we will not hesitate to provide arms to friendly states as the need arises." The President also argued that the United States' October 28 and December 18, 1969, proposals met "the legitimate concerns of both sides on all key questions, including withdrawal," and provided "reasonable guidelines" for Special Representative Gunnar Jarring to begin negotiations under his auspices. (Ibid., Document 126)

On February 6, Kissinger sent Nixon a memorandum with further background on the Kosygin letter. Kissinger concluded that "Brezhnev was obviously bitter about the Israeli raids, and especially the accuracy of the strike on the house of the Soviet advisers, which he implied was deliberate." Kissinger added that "the Soviets seem to be responding emotionally to the killing of Soviet advisers and out of frustration over their inability to do much about the entire state of affairs. This, of course, could have some ominous implications for future moves, since as I noted in my earlier memorandum, the Middle East was a source of internal tensions within the Soviet leadership at the time of the June war. Brezhnev may be worried that his own position is vulnerable to charges of softness, and the letter could have been for the record to protect himself against any new Kremlin debate over Middle East policy." (Ibid., Document 128)

89. Memorandum From the President's Assistant for National Security Affairs (Kissinger) to President Nixon[1]

Washington, February 6, 1970.

SUBJECT

Status of the Four Power Talks

Since pressure is building for a new departure in the Four Power talks[2] and as an outgrowth of your talk with Prime Minister Wilson,[3] I thought you might find useful a brief analysis of the situation.

The tactical situation is that we have stood firm on our December 18 formulations for an Israel-Jordan settlement.[4] The British have given us strong support on all of the major issues and have refrained from presenting any specific ideas of their own. The pressure arises from the fact that the French, who were earlier helpful in keeping the pressure on the Soviets to respond to our proposals for an Israel-UAR settlement, have now tabled their own proposals on the Jordan aspect[5] and most recently have launched an energetic effort to have the Four draft a paper reflecting the "common ground" achieved in the talks. The Soviets, having taken a flat stand against our position[6] but feeling some compulsion not to be completely negative, have moved almost entirely to the original French proposals.[7] These are unacceptable to us and, even more important, to the Israelis.

The major substantive issues which the Four have concentrated on concern Israel's withdrawal from the West Bank, rectification of boundaries, the nature of the negotiations to be held between the parties, the

---

[1] Source: National Archives, Nixon Presidential Materials, NSC Files, Box 650, Country Files, Middle East, Middle East Negotiations. Secret. Sent for information.

[2] The UN Permanent Representatives of the Four Powers met on January 23 and February 2, as reported in telegram 107 from USUN, January 24, and telegram 162 from USUN, February 3. (Both ibid., RG 59, Central Files 1970–73, POL 27–14 ARAB–ISR)

[3] President Nixon met with Prime Minister Wilson at the White House January 27–28. Regarding Arab-Israeli issues, the President stressed "the imperative need of sticking together on the Middle East." Wilson replied that it was not their position to "outflank" the United States with concessions. "Britian may have to restate its view in slightly different language, but since Israel has already described the U.S. plan as a sellout, there's no sense in going further." (Memorandum of conversations, January 27–28, 1970; *Foreign Relations*, 1969–1976, volume XLI, Western Europe; NATO, 1969–1972, Document 320) Kissinger discussed the Nixon–Wilson meeting in *White House Years*, pp. 416–417.

[4] See footnote 5, Document 76.

[5] See Document 75.

[6] See Document 80.

[7] Nixon underlined "Soviets" and "have moved almost entirely to the original French proposals" in this sentence.

obligations of a binding peace and the Palestinian refugee problem. Much of the recent discussion of these issues has been in working meetings of the deputy permanent representatives rather than of the permanent representatives themselves, and that may account for some of the flexibility. Nevertheless, on the issues of withdrawal, boundaries and refugees all four positions seem close enough to give hope that, if everyone negotiated in good faith and with some flexibility, mutually acceptable language might be found, though there are still some minor differences to be resolved.

More important, however, the Soviets remain adamant on the two most important issues for us—the obligations which each side would have to assume in committing themselves to coexist peacefully and negotiating procedures. Specifically:

Peace. We have made virtually no progress with the Soviets on the commitments that would be undertaken in a state of peace. The basic disagreement is on how specific the Four Powers should be in spelling out the obligations that the parties would assume. The British have supported our position that the obligations of peace, especially regarding control of the fedayeen, must be specified. The Soviets, reflecting the Arab desire not to be made responsible for future fedayeen actions, continue to resist on the grounds that this is unnecessary since the fedayeen will fade away after a peace settlement. They show no inclination to take as much distance from the Arabs on this key issue as we have taken from the Israelis on withdrawal and boundaries. The French have recently tried to shift tactically in our direction, but their proposal seems a non-starter.[8] Their idea is that Israeli withdrawal would come in two phases. The Arab armies would end hostilities as withdrawal began, but the Arab governments would not assume responsibility for controlling the fedayeen until the Israelis had withdrawn part way. This in effect would legalize fedayeen attacks while inhibiting Israeli retaliation.

Negotiating Procedures. The basic problem here is to find a formula that leaves open the interpretation that there will be direct contacts at some stage. For us this is a key issue since unless the Israelis believe that there will be direct talks—preferably at the beginning—there is no chance of getting any kind of negotiations underway. For lack of anything better we are still pushing the Rhodes formula. The Soviets have so far been most unhelpful on this issue, refusing to consider it of sub-

---

[8] In telegram 162 from USUN, the Mission reported that the French Representative advanced what he described as "new information on peace," focusing on the issue of Israeli withdrawal from territories occupied during the 1967 war, in the hope of breaking the "deadlock" in the Four-Power forum. (National Archives, RG 59, Central Files 1970–73, POL 27–14 ARAB–ISR)

stantive importance. The British have supported our position and the French are searching—so far without success—for new language that everyone can accept.

Conclusion. For all practical purposes the Four Power talks are deadlocked on the most important issues—specifying the obligations of peace and negotiating procedures. Our December 18 proposals made substantial concessions to the Soviets on the issues that they and the Arabs see as most important (Israeli withdrawal and boundary rectification) but they have not budged on the issues most vital to us and the Israelis. The British have provided useful support, although if the impasse continues they will most likely feel compelled to present their own ideas which could further complicate the situation. The French appear to be moving closer to us on some questions, but their tactic of searching for the common ground has provided the Soviets with a convenient way to ignore our proposals by supporting French positions rather than discussing ours.

The new front that presents itself is Jordan's desire—with Nasser's concurrence—to talk with us directly about our documents. This could open the theoretical possibility of trying to win Jordanian and Egyptian acceptance of our formulations directly, although on balance it seems unlikely that Nasser will feel able to go along.

At Tab A I am attaching a State Department analysis which explains the differences in the various positions point by point.[9]

---

[9] Attached but not printed.

90. Minutes of a Washington Special Actions Group Meeting[1]

Washington, February 9, 1970, 10:21–11:02 a.m.

SUBJECT

Possible Soviet Moves in Egypt

PARTICIPATION

Chairman—Henry A. Kissinger

State
Mr. Rodger Davies

Defense
Mr. Richard Ware
Mr. Robert Pranger

JCS
Lt. Gen. John W. Vogt

CIA
Mr. Thomas H. Karamessines

NSC Staff
Mr. Harold Saunders
Col. Robert Behr
Mr. Keith Guthrie

SUMMARY OF CONCLUSIONS

1. A US position for dealing with possible Soviet moves in Egypt must be ready within one week. The WSAG will meet on the afternoon of Wednesday, February 11[2] to draw up an initial position and will meet again Monday, February 16[3] to give the problem further consideration.

2. In connection with preparation of the US position the following papers should be prepared:

a. Assistant Secretary Sisco should submit on February 9 proposals for intensifying our diplomatic efforts to bring about a cease fire and, in this context, to warn the Soviets against further intervention in Egypt. These proposals should take into account the possible usefulness of a renewed cease-fire effort in dealing with public opinion pressures, staving off a further Israeli request for aid, and placing the onus on the Soviets for escalating the Arab-Israeli conflict.

b. For WSAG consideration at its February 11 and 16 meetings the military situation in the Middle East and the options open to the United

---

[1] Source: National Archives, Nixon Presidential Materials, NSC Files, NSC Institutional Files (H-Files), Box H-114, Washington Special Actions Group, WSAG Minutes (Originals) 1969 and 1970. Secret; Nodis. All brackets are in the original except those indicating text omitted by the editors. The meeting was held in the White House Situation Room.

[2] See Document 91.

[3] This meeting did not take place.

States should be reviewed. This review should be related to the existing contingency plans, particularly Tab H (action by Soviet naval forces) and Tab D (responses to Soviet overt intervention in renewed Arab-Israeli hostilities) of the WSAG contingency plan of October 1969.[4]

The analysis should take into account the overall power situation in the Middle East and not just the Arab-Israeli dispute. State and CIA should coordinate in preparing this aspect of the study.

c. The ad hoc Under Secretaries group is to meet Monday, February 16 to consider the paper that has been prepared on aid to Israel.[5] This paper must be coordinated with current contingency planning and should discuss what aid levels to Israel are appropriate in the light of foreseeable Soviet moves. It should also consider tacit US Government facilitation of Israeli military purchases in the US.

[Omitted here are the minutes, which are printed in *Foreign Relations, 1969–1976*, volume XII, Soviet Union, January 1969–October 1970, Document 130.]

---

[4] See Document 57 and footnote 2 thereto.
[5] Summarized in Document 93.

91. Minutes of a Washington Special Actions Group Meeting[1]

Washington, February 11, 1970, 4:25–5:27 p.m.

SUBJECT

Possible Soviet Moves in Egypt

PARTICIPATION

Chairman—Henry A. Kissinger

State
Mr. U. Alexis Johnson
Mr. Rodger Davies

Defense
Mr. Richard Ware
Mr. Robert Pranger

JCS
Lt. Gen. John W. Vogt

CIA
Mr. Thomas H. Karamessines

NSC Staff
Mr. Harold Saunders
Col. Robert Behr
Mr. Keith Guthrie

SUMMARY OF CONCLUSIONS

1. The WSAG working group paper should be refined to categorize possible Soviet actions to strengthen Egyptian defenses and identify US options in response.[2] The paper should discuss the issues raised by these options, make clear relative US and Soviet military capabilities in the Middle East, and consider the impact which Soviet actions could have on the overall balance in the Middle East.

2. An analysis should be prepared of what would be involved if the Soviets were to install an effective air defense for Egypt. This should include information on likely types of equipment, numbers of personnel, lead time, and means of transporting to the UAR.

3. Existing Middle East contingency plans should be reviewed to determine their applicability to the present situation.

---

[1] Source: National Archives, Nixon Presidential Materials, NSC Files, NSC Institutional Files (H-Files), Box H–114, Washington Special Actions Group, WSAG Minutes (Originals) 1969 and 1970. Top Secret; Nodis. All brackets are in the original except those indicating text omitted by the editors. The meeting was held in the White House Situation Room.

[2] A paper entitled "Increased Soviet Involvement in UAR Military Effort—Contingencies and Options," was drafted by Saunders and Rodger Davies for consideration by the WSAG working group. (Ibid.) In a February 10 memorandum to Nixon, Kissinger informed the President of intelligence reports that the Soviet Union was planning to give the UAR "some sort of 'system'" to counter Israeli air operations. (*Foreign Relations, 1969–1976*, volume XII, Soviet Union, January 1969–October 1970, Document 132)

4. CIA should prepare an analysis of possible Soviet intent in diverting an intelligence collection ship to a location south of Cyprus.

5. The WSAG will meet on February 16[3] for further consideration of Middle East contingency planning.

6. The results of the WSAG studies will be made available to the Ad Hoc Group on aid to Israel. The Ad Hoc Group will meet February 17 or 18[4] to consider pending proposals on supplying military equipment to Israel. It will meet later to consider overall US strategy in dealing with the Middle East situation.

7. Proposals on all available intelligence capabilities covering possible Soviet moves in Egypt should be prepared for discussion by the 303 Committee on February 17.[5] These proposals should take into account possible means of improving Israeli reconnaissance.

[Omitted here are the minutes, which are printed in *Foreign Relations, 1969–1976*, volume XII, Soviet Union, 1969–October 1970, Document 134.]

---

[3] This meeting did not occur.

[4] The Special NSC Review Group met on February 25; see Document 94.

[5] The minutes of the February 17 meeting of the 303 Committee, which coordinated covert action, have not been found. The President changed the 303 Committee's name to the 40 Committee on February 17, when he signed and issued National Security Decision Memorandum 40. (*Foreign Relations*, 1969–1976, volume II, Organization and Management of U.S. Foreign Policy, 1969–1972, Document 203) The 40 Committee met on February 25, but did not discuss Soviet moves in Egypt. (National Security Council Archives, Box 1007, 40 Committee Meetings, Minutes, 1970, RMN)

92. Telegram From the Embassy in Jordan to the Department of State[1]

Amman, February 12, 1970, 1645Z.

677. Subject: Possible Arms for Israel.

1. I am certain the Dept is aware from field reporting that the President's Jan 30 statement regarding a decision on arms for Israel[2] has stimulated renewed anti-American feeling and suspicion among the Arabs. The Cairo communiqué[3] was a mild version of the kinds of criticisms we are hearing about US policy motives. To be sure, in an area of almost entirely venal newspapers and state-controlled radio and TV, we can discount much of what we see and hear in the local media. The manic depressive and ephemeral qualities of Arab attitudes are also well known.

2. Bearing the foregoing in mind, I wish to register my own conviction that the Arab interpretations of the Jan 30 statement, as seen by them against the background of the deep Israeli air penetrations into the UAR, have brought about a new and significant dimension of bitterness and suspicion within the Jordanian establishment. I would draw a sharp distinction between these deep feelings on the part of the Jordanian establishment and the reactions of the Arab communications media. Both may be unrealistic and in some ways shortsighted, but I would emphasize we have a real problem when our friends here reach the stage of desperation about our policies that I now observe.

3. I want to be sure the Dept understands what is bothering the Jordanians. As they see it, the USG is now holding a thirty-day deadline,

---

[1] Source: National Archives, Nixon Presidential Materials, NSC Files, Box 614, Country Files, Middle East, Jordan, Vol. III. Secret; Priority; Exdis. Repeated to Beirut, Cairo, Jidda, Tel Aviv, and USUN.

[2] In response to a question on U.S. arms sales to the Middle East at his press conference on January 30, the President said: "We are neither pro-Arab nor pro-Israel. We are pro-peace. We are for security for all the nations in that area. As we look at this situation, we will consider the Israeli arms request based on the threats to them from states in the area and we will honor those requests to the extent that we see—we determine that they need additional arms in order to meet that threat. That decision will be made within the next 30 days." A transcript of the entire press conference is printed in *Public Papers: Nixon, 1970*, pp. 36–44.

[3] Issued on February 9 at the close of the conference of Arab "confrontation countries" in Cairo, the communiqué in part criticized the United States, proclaiming: "Israel would not have gone that far in her aggression and recklessness with regard to all human values and principles and would not have defied world public opinion and violated the United Nations Charter and the United Nations resolution as she does, had it not been for her constant reliance on United States support and supplies of arms and aircraft and had it not been for the United States' allowing its citizens to serve in the Israeli armed forces and for the United States' political support in the international field." The complete text of a translation of the communiqué is printed in the *New York Times*, February 10, 1970, p. 3.

even a threat, over the Arab head, and they are almost fatalistically convinced the end result will be more Phantoms for Israel. Yet, the Jordanians stress, in this same time-frame Israeli aircraft are bombing the outskirts of Cairo and other places in the UAR with virtual impunity, and with the barely veiled objective of bringing down Nasser. The government directing this apparently overwhelming military power occupies Arab territories taken by outright "aggression" and launches its attacks from those territories. This same government, in their view, has not only refused to accept formally and unconditionally SC Resolution 242 but has also publicly and harshly rejected US proposals for a peaceful settlement. The Jordanians thus find it inconceivable that in such circumstances the USG could even consider supplying more arms to Israel. They believe in effect our posture justifies an Israeli policy of intransigence and implies approval of Israeli hopes of causing Nasser's fall.

4. Certainly the problem is not as simple as the Jordanians put it. In fact, we have never hesitated in talks with Jordanian leaders emphasize that the USG cannot stand aside to watch the development of an arms imbalance that could lead anyone to consider renewed general hostilities as an alternative to a peaceful settlement. Nevertheless, given the Jordanian views I have summarized above, I must emphasize that the chances of positive Jordanian (let alone UAR) consideration of our settlement proposals become increasingly dim. Moreover, I do not consider it at all unlikely that the Jordanians might feel forced to reconsider the outstanding Soviet arms offer[4] if we respond favorably to the Israeli arms request. I am convinced we must find a way out of this situation of distrust and suspicion if we are going to have any hope of pursuing successfully our peace efforts.

5. I believe disclosure at this time of a US decision to supply Israel with additional aircraft will risk ruining chances of playing out our hand on peace. I am strongly attracted to a number of ideas for getting around this problem, including the interesting proposal of Minister Bergus (Cairo 260).[5] We also have been giving further thought to the implications for the US position in Jordan of a unilateral US arms embargo. As soon as we can refine our ideas further, we will forward some specific suggestions.

Symmes

---

[4] See footnote 3, Document 69.

[5] Bergus wrote: "Could not our decision on Israel request for more aircraft be an assurance that we closely watching situation and if imbalance actually develops we prepared release aircraft from Defense Department's own inventories on, say, sixty days' notice?" (Telegram 260 from Cairo, February 4; National Archives, Nixon Presidential Materials, NSC Files, Box 635, Country Files, Middle East, UAR, Vol. III)

93. Paper Prepared by the National Security Council Staff[1]

Washington, February 23, 1970.

ANALYTICAL SUMMARY

ASSISTANCE TO ISRAEL: OPTIONS AND ISSUES

I. *The Decisions To Be Made*

A. *The context.* Israel's requests fall into two groups: *First*, Israel seeks answer within U.S. FY 1970 on four major requests. *Second*, Israel has put these requests in the context of a projected $1.2 billion balance of payments deficit, 1970–1974. Israel has not made specific requests for the longer period but has implied that U.S. support will be expected. The point relevant to the present decision is that the objectives underlying the five-year projections partly determine the size of this year's financial requests.

B. *The specific requests requiring decision this year* are for:

1. Agreement to sell *25 F–4 Phantom* and *100 A–4 Skyhawk* aircraft for delivery in 1971–1972. Cost would be about $270 million, and the Israelis wish to discuss credit.

2. *$119 million in additional military sales credit* to finance that remaining portion of the 1968 Phantom sale for which Israel originally contracted to pay cash.

3. *$54 million in P.L. 480 purchases.*

4. *$50 million in AID loans.*

5. *Lesser requests for specific items* are in normal channels: 250 M–60 tanks; 20,000 bombs; 500 armored personnel carriers; patrol boats; ground and air launched tactical missiles; special status for access to excess U.S. military equipment from vehicles to jet engines.

C. The implied *longer range requests* do not require specific decision now. They do, however, *require a decision to enter consultation with the Israelis on their longer range projections.* These projections include imports of a magnitude much greater than U.S. analysts have been able to explain, even taking into account high military imports, construction of a domestic arms industry and enough civilian imports to maintain an 8% economic growth rate. They also suggest a possible option of supporting Israel's own arms production as an alternative to direct U S.

---

[1] Source: National Archives, Nixon Presidential Materials, NSC Files, NSC Institutional Files (H-Files), Box H–043, Senior Review Group Meetings, Review Group Israel 2/25/70. Top Secret; Nodis. All brackets are in the original. For the titles of the papers on which this paper is based, see footnote 10, Document 86.

supply. But before decisions can be made, more data will be needed from Israel.

D. The following, therefore, are *the operational decisions to be made:*

1. What decision are we going to make on this year's Israeli requests? And shall we enter consultations on the longer-range requests?

2. What are we going to tell the Israelis?

3. What position are we going to take publicly?

E. What follows is an effort to lay out:

1. the major military, economic and political considerations that bear on this decision;

2. the major issues in making a decision on the aircraft requests;

3. the principal options for response to Israel; and

4. the main options in presenting our decision to Israel and publicly.

II. *The Setting for Decision*

The setting in which the Israeli requests are being considered has become much more complicated in recent weeks. Intensive analysis of the Arab-Israeli military balance and of Israel's economic situation within the U.S. Government since last September as well as recent intelligence and diplomatic reporting indicate that these are the main elements of that setting:

A. *Military.*

1. Our technical studies of the military balance show that, although Israel is outnumbered 2–5:1 in the principal categories of equipment, *Israel can maintain clear military superiority during 1971–1972—the period covered by its specific requests—with little equipment beyond that now scheduled for delivery.* This is true because the effective military balance is not just determined by amounts of equipment but by ability to use it. This point is best illustrated by the fact that, while the Arabs outnumber Israel 681–224 in jet aircraft, Israel outnumbers the Arabs 450–375 in numbers of combat-qualified pilots to fly those aircraft. Since human training is involved, that ratio will change only slowly.

2. These projections have not assumed direct *Soviet involvement*— the only development that could have significant effect on the present balance relatively soon. Deliberations of the Washington Special Actions Group have concluded that the most likely Soviet move would be direct involvement to improve the UAR's air defense. This *could in time result in higher Israeli aircraft losses if Israel continues its present raids into the Nile Valley.*

3. The *conclusion* from these studies has been that there is *no military need for committing ourselves at this time to a higher level of Israeli air strength than it will enjoy upon completion of deliveries under the present A–4*

and F–4 contracts. If Israel continues its present pattern of raids and if the Soviets improve UAR air defenses, *Israel might need replacement* of some aircraft in 1970–1971 to maintain its strength roughly at the level foreseen when the current contracts were concluded.

4. This analysis suggests that, other than providing for possible replacement of losses and unforeseen contingencies, *our decision can be made primarily in the political context.*

B. *Political.*

1. *Israel's deep penetration raids* on the Nile Valley have not only dramatized Israel's clear military superiority but have generated heavy *pressure on Nasser and then on the Soviets* to end those raids. The recent mistaken Israeli bombing of a civilian factory with F–4 aircraft has charged the political atmosphere and focussed attention on the U.S. decision.

2. *The Kosygin letter*[2] tends to cast the U.S. decision as a response to a Soviet challenge. This is the case not only because the USSR has threatened to supply the Arabs with additional arms but also because Moscow has failed to respond to U.S. proposals for return to observance of the cease-fire, arms limitation or a more positive response to U.S. peace proposals.

3. A number of Arab friends in Tunisia, Morocco, Lebanon, Saudi Arabia, Kuwait and Jordan have told us that a decision to supply additional aircraft will virtually put an end to any diplomatic effort to achieve a *political settlement* on the basis of the U.S. peace proposals. If the U.S. in Arab eyes backs Israel's current strategy, the Arabs say they will not be able to regard U.S. peace proposals as sincere.

4. Israel has also encouraged casting our decision in the context of a response to a Soviet challenge. More than that, Israel has made the U.S. decision on arms *a test of U.S.-Israeli relations.*

5. In *summary,* two different sets of considerations will affect our decision: The first relates to Mid-Eastern issues—efforts to promote a peace settlement and U.S. relations with Israel and the Arabs. The second relates to the political implications of our decision to the U.S.-Soviet balance in the Mid-East.

C. *Economic*

1. U.S. analysis of Israel's balance of payments projections reveals a very *ambitious Israeli program of expenditures, 1970–1974.* In attempting to understand Israel's planned expenditures, U.S. analysts have determined that Israeli projections include import of substantial amounts of

---

[2] See Document 88.

military equipment; imports of enough equipment and matériel to develop an Israeli arms industry so as to produce before 1974 its own Mirage-type combat jet aircraft, tanks, armored personnel carriers, artillery and naval patrol boats; increase of foreign exchange reserves by $300 million; *and* civilian imports sufficient to maintain an optimum economic growth rate of at least 8%. After identifying all of these elements, U.S. analysts still find *an unexplained requirement* of some $900 million, which together with the $300 million increase in reserves is *about equivalent to the $1.1 billion in aid Israel is seeking 1970–1974.*

2. Israel's foreign exchange reserves now are falling at the rate of $1 million a day and, at this rate, would be almost totally exhausted by the end of 1970. *Israel's recently proposed budget* for its 1970–1971 fiscal year which begins April 1 indicates that its leaders do not intend to slow losses in foreign exchange through an austerity program. Instead they are pushing ahead with their programs of civilian and military expansion. Following a 12% increase in real GNP in 1969, the new budget *projects a 9–9.5% GNP increase in 1970.* This budget indicates that Israel still is depending on record contributions from World Jewry and substantial credit assistance from other governments, particularly the U.S., to halt further deterioration in its foreign exchange reserves. *Israel's projections assume some $200 million in U.S. aid in 1970.* If assistance from either the U.S. Government or from World Jewry—and projections in this category seem highly optimistic—fall short, Israel will have to slow the growth of its economy below 9.5% and therefore reduce civilian imports or substantially reduce military imports.

3. The *conclusion* from U.S. analysis has been that Israel could meet most of its financial requirements from its own resources without added U.S. aid if it were prepared to accept a lower growth rate of, say, 6%. This would still permit Israel to achieve all the other objectives described above, including developing its own arms industry.

4. U.S. analysts are quick to point out that *more complete data are required from Israel* on its plans for 1971–1974 before the U.S. analysis can be treated as a basis for definitive U.S. decisions. They have, therefore, recommended detailed consultations with Israel on its economic projections before the U.S. commits itself beyond U.S. FY 1970. These consultations would also surface more information on Israel's plans for further developing its own arms industry to determine whether supporting Israeli production would constitute an alternative to direct supply by the U.S.

III. *The Economic Options*

Since the U.S. response to Israel's economic requests in FY 1970 has proved relatively uncontroversial in the course of this review, it seems appropriate to get this part of the problem out of the way before dealing with the much more difficult decision on supply of aircraft.

A. The *broad options* can be judged against the Israeli estimates that $200 million in additional capital imports will be needed in 1970 and that this need will rise toward $300 million after 1971. The main options fall into these general ranges:

1. *Provide no further economic aid.* The rationale for this approach would be either to apply political pressure or to press Israel to make its own decisions on economic priorities before asking the U.S. taxpayer to support both "guns and butter" in Israel.

2. *Continue in the range of recent aid levels, $50–150 million yearly.* This would meet the political requirement of doing something and provide assistance that could support close to an 8% growth rate in Israel and military imports if the Israeli Government took reasonable austerity measures.

3. *Meet the full Israeli requests of about $200 million in 1970.* According to Israeli budget estimates just published, this would support all planned military imports, an active program for building its own arms industry and a 9.5% growth rate in 1970. This budget includes no austerity measures.

B. *Possible Elements of an Economic Package in U.S. FY 1970.* It is generally agreed up through the level of the Special Review Group that one part of the U.S. response to Israel's requests should be these two points: (1) the U.S. will need more data on Israel's long-range plans before talking about longer term assistance; therefore, (2) the U.S. would like to send a small group of economic experts to Israel to consult. Short of that, however, a package for this year can be put together from the following elements:

1. *$119 million additional military sales credit* to cover Israel's remaining payments under the current F–4 Phantom contract. This request could be met totally or in part as follows:

a. *Promise the entire $119 million now.* In practice we would have to fund this from the appropriations of two fiscal years—FY 1970 and FY 1971—and could not formally complete the transaction until Congress passes the Foreign Military Sales Act (probably mid-April). But enough money has been included in the requested appropriation and could be promised now to meet Israel's 1970 needs.

b. *Allocate $52 million now,* withholding the balance of $67 million. This balance is the amount Israel has on deposit in France, and Defense questions whether the U.S. should pay the price for the impasse created by France's embargo.[3]

2. *The $54 million P.L. 480 request* could also be met at one of three levels.

---

[3] France imposed an arms embargo on Israel after the 1967 war.

a. Approve the *entire $54 million*. The main complication in this is that $22 million would involve feasible but somewhat out-of-the-ordinary procedures for Agriculture (extending P.L. 480 terms to what would normally be Israeli commercial purchases here required by law) when Agriculture has not established the need. Including the extra $22 million would force the overall P.L. 480 program above our budget ceiling.

b. Approve the *$32 million* Israel originally requested before seeking the special arrangement for the added $22 million noted above. This would keep the program within the budget ceiling.

c. Approve an *intermediate level of say $40 million*. This could probably be worked out by adjustments within the present budget ceiling.

C. In *summary:* Adding to the above $30 million in this year's military sales credit already committed under the 1968 Phantom contract, these options would give us a range of $114–203 million in economic assistance for U.S. FY 1970. This would be measured against projected Israeli need of $200 million from the U.S. The question of AID assistance—not possible under present AID criteria though legally possible—would be deferred this year on grounds that conventional programs and possible Israeli austerity measures should be exhausted before the U.S. considers reversing AID criteria with an extensive legislative history.

IV. *Arms Supply—The Issues for Decision*

A. *U.S. interests.* The central question to be answered is: *What decision will best serve the long-term national interest of the U.S.?* The main U.S. interests in the Middle East are:

1. *That this area not become the arena or the trigger for a U.S.-Soviet confrontation.* The most obvious course in pursuit of this interest is to promote a solution of the Arab-Israeli conflict, which threatens to draw in the U.S. and USSR. Failing a settlement, the next course for the U.S. is to avoid steps which would force deeper U.S. or Soviet involvement.

2. *That this area not fall under Soviet predominance.* It seems unlikely that the USSR intends to move quickly to establish the kind of influence it achieved in Eastern Europe after 1945. But there is no question that the Soviet objective is to undercut U.S. influence in the Middle East and to become the major outside influence. While the Middle East itself is not literally vital to the U.S., it is more nearly so to Western Europe, and the extension of Soviet predominance into a new area would have global implications.

3. *That Israel survive.* The U.S. has rightly or wrongly undertaken a non-legal national commitment to assure Israel's survival. In the military context, this commitment has taken the form of assuring Israel's capacity to defeat any possible Arab threat to its existence. Israel's

ability to defend itself is also important in avoiding direct U.S. involvement in a Mid-Eastern war.

4. *That the Arab nations continue to welcome an American presence.* This is relevant to the U.S. effort to prevent Soviet predominance. But it is also related to protecting the investments of private Americans as well as some $1.5 billion in national income credited yearly to the U.S. balance of payments. Finally, it is related to the obligation of the U.S. Government to protect American citizens (well over 10,000) working and living in this area.

B. The important question, therefore, is *what effect a decision to supply Israel with additional arms now would have on each of these interests.*

1. Given the analysis of the present military balance above (para II. A, page 3), it seems fair to conclude that the U.S. obligation to contribute to *Israel's chances of survival* could be fulfilled without any commitment right now to increase further Israel's aircraft inventory. Therefore, the governing judgments in this decision will be those related to the remaining U.S. interests in the area. These are discussed in the following paragraphs.

2. *Would a publicly declared decision within the next few weeks to supply additional aircraft to Israel lessen the likelihood of U.S.-Soviet confrontation in the Mid-East?*

Pro.

—Since a major Arab-Israeli clash is most likely when Israel feels threatened, one could argue that a strong Israel is more likely to calibrate its military pressure on the UAR so as to fall short of a level that would force the USSR into open defense of the UAR and pose to the U.S. the question of direct response.

—While the Israeli leadership at present seems uninclined to reduce its military pressure on the UAR (and USSR), a positive decision would make it possible for the U.S. to urge Israel to ease off its attacks at least on populated areas in the Nile Valley. A negative decision or delay would decrease Israeli receptivity to such an approach.

—The likelihood of U.S.-Soviet confrontation is increased when the USSR believes the U.S. lacks resolution. The only way to encourage the USSR to turn toward serious efforts to achieve a political settlement is to make clear that Moscow can get what it wants—Nasser's survival without undue Soviet involvement—only by promoting a negotiated settlement.

—It is in the U.S. interest to be sure *before* the USSR involves itself further that Israel is promised the means to defend itself. It is potentially less inflammatory for the U.S. to move now than for the U.S. to move in direct response to an open Soviet move, even though the Soviets might use the U.S. move as an excuse for its own.

Con.

—A U.S. decision now, in the wake of Kosygin's warning[4] and Nasser's pressure on Moscow, could force a major change in the quality of the Soviet presence in the Mid-East. It would force the USSR to assume greater responsibility for the defense of the UAR.

—Open assumption by the USSR for UAR defense would face the U.S. with the difficult question of whether to make a direct response of its own. Such a response would change the Arab-Israeli conflict into a direct US–USSR contest. To date, the U.S. and USSR have been content to keep their contest for influence in the Mid-East on the political level.

—Backing Israeli strategy whether we agree with it or not would represent diminution of great power control over their role in the situation. The Israeli strategy of bombing the Nile Valley, a strategy in which the U.S. has little interest, has generated present pressure on the USSR to move more directly to the UAR's defense. If the U.S. moved to back that Israeli strategy, it would in effect be joining a confrontation with the USSR on Israel's terms. If each great power begins moving in support of its client the likelihood is increased that either Arab or Israeli acts could force them into moves vis-à-vis each other that neither has an interest in taking.

—In short, the U.S. has no interest in seeing the USSR pressed so hard that it feels compelled to escalate its own direct involvement. The most dangerous situation that could be created is one in which the USSR feels it is faced with humiliation and has no way out.

Summary of the Issue

Recent Israeli bombing has forced Moscow closer to assuming responsibility for UAR defense—a step which could elevate the Arab-Israeli conflict to a U.S.-Soviet contest. A U.S. decision which seems to back the Israeli strategy that achieves this result would appear to enhance Israel's voice in setting the terms of the U.S.-Soviet contest. Yet U.S. firmness in the face of Soviet pressure is important in deterring a confrontation.

3. *Would a publicly declared decision in the next few weeks to supply additional aircraft to Israel impede Soviet efforts to achieve predominance in the Mid-East?*

Pro.

—Israeli power is a threat to Soviet prestige because it alone can periodically defeat and weaken pro-Soviet governments. This is all the U.S. has to depend on. Given the political forces at work in the Mid-

---

[4] In his January 31 letter; see Document 88.

East, it is unlikely that the U.S. can win the more prominent Arab regimes from the radical camp. If the U.S. cannot win them politically, the only alternative is to keep them weak.

—Soviet prestige will gradually be eroded by Soviet inability to regain the Arabs' lost territories from Israel.

—As Soviet impotence is demonstrated, the Arabs will realize that the U.S. is the power they have to deal with.

Con.

—An open U.S. move would increase Soviet influence in the UAR. It would almost certainly compel increased Soviet involvement in the UAR's air defense. To do anything effective, the USSR would have to involve its own technicians and maybe even pilots in considerable numbers, perhaps 10–15,000. With an increase of this magnitude would come greater Soviet influence, at least in the UAR military and perhaps even over political policy.

—If the USSR openly assumed responsibility for UAR air defense, this would be the first major extension of that kind of Soviet political relationship in the Middle East and, except for Cuba, the first such Soviet venture globally beyond the lines of 1948.

—If the USSR extended its protective mantle over the UAR, this would increase pressure on the U.S. to stand even more openly behind Israel. The USSR would then have maneuvered itself formally into the position of the sole champion of the Arab cause, leaving even the moderate regimes little choice of maintaining a close countering relationship with the U.S.

Summary of the Issue.

The basic fact of Israel's military superiority strengthens the U.S. bargaining position. However, excessive use of Israeli power could drive the USSR into open assumption of responsibility for UAR defense—a step which would enhance the Soviet position in the Mid-East.

4. *Will a publicly declared decision within the next few weeks enhance or at least not worsen the U.S. position in the Arab nations?*

Pro.

—The moderate Arab regimes have an interest in continuing their relationship with the U.S. because a relationship with the USSR is incompatible.

—The Arabs respect power. Even though they may react emotionally to a U.S. decision in the short term, they will in the long run recognize that the U.S. (with Israel) is the only effective power in the area.

Con.

—An open U.S. move would weaken U.S. relationships even with moderate regimes. It would be conclusive proof even to Arab friends of the U.S. that the U.S. will give Israel unlimited backing regardless of its policy. This even closer U.S. identification with Israel would make it more difficult for moderate regimes to sustain politically a close relationship with the U.S. It would increase the pressure on them from their own radicals.

—Senior U.S. diplomatic representatives in four Eastern Arab capitals have reported their concern over the likelihood of Arab attacks on American citizens (more than 10,000) and property if a decision to supply more aircraft to Israel is announced.

Summary of the Issue

The Arabs have talked themselves into a state of mind where they would regard a U.S. announcement of further aircraft shipments to Israel now as a sign of complete U.S. backing for present Israeli strategy. Yet the U.S. cannot allow its decisions to be governed by Arab emotions.

V. *Arms Supply—the Range of Options*

A. *The broader context.* U.S. technical analysis of the Arab-Israeli military balance as it may evolve 1970–1974 has identified the following general ranges of possible U.S. supply of aircraft to Israel *over the next five years:*

1. *20 more Phantoms and up to 20 more Skyhawks delivered by 1974* would be necessary to meet Israel's minimum security needs. This would enable Israel to win another war like that in 1967 when it concentrated on defeating one enemy at a time.

2. *20 more Phantoms and up to 45 more Skyhawks delivered by 1974* would enable Israel to defeat a coordinated attack by the UAR, Jordan, Syria and Iraq (which U.S. intelligence now estimates as unlikely in any militarily effective form).

3. *25 more Phantoms and 100 more Skyhawks delivered by 1974* (Israel has requested them in 1971–1972) would enable Israel to defeat an effectively coordinated attack by 14 Arab states.

B. *Options for the FY 1970 decision.* The Israeli request was for delivery in 1971–1972. Israeli Ambassador Rabin has said Israel would regard anything meeting from 60–100% of Israel's requests as a positive U.S. response. The Israelis have also been pressing Defense for a U.S. agreement to make up losses from its present inventory of Phantoms and Skyhawks. Against that background, the U.S. has *the following choices in making its present decision:*

Option 1: Negative decision. A decision could be made not to provide Israel with additional aircraft, at least this year.

Option 2: Postponement of a decision. It could be announced that, given Israel's present clear superiority and the high state of tension in the area, a decision is being postponed for the time being. To meet possible contingencies, the USAF would prepare on a standby basis to provide aircraft out of its inventory.

Option 3: A small number of aircraft for replacement. If it is judged that Israel will have the power it needs provided it maintains the aircraft level now envisioned when the present Skyhawk and Phantom deliveries are completed later this year, the U.S. could commit itself to maintain that level by replacing losses. There are *two possible variants* for handling this option:

a. *Three-year replacement contract.* Present Skyhawk and Phantom contracts would be amended to include replacement up to a specified number of Israeli losses (with Skyhawks replacing Mirages). Based on 1969 losses, we would agree to reserve *8 Phantoms and 18 Skyhawks for replacement of losses in 1969, 1970, 1971.* We would agree to joint review of this level if actual losses ran higher. We would make public only the principle of controlled replacement.

b. *Standby reserve for replacement.* Without making a contract new, we could make arrangements to earmark and have available on an immediate standby basis for formal sale to Israel on short notice.

Option 4: A three-year replacement contract as above with added agreement in principle now to provide, subject to review in early 1971, an additional squadron of 16 Phantoms. The combination of these agreements would make a potential *total of 24 Phantoms and 18 Skyhawks* with Israel's total inventory being increased by 16 Phantoms. [A variation of this would be to raise the number of Skyhawks slightly.]

Option 5: A one-time sale of 16 Phantoms and 24 Skyhawks now. This would provide for anticipated losses as now estimated and provide a modest increase in Israel's inventory but would not commit the U.S. for the future.

Option 6: Meet all of Israel's requests for a short-term period. Israel has requested 25 Phantoms and 100 Skyhawks by the end of 1972. Therefore, a decision now for delivery of about half that amount in 1971 should be regarded as positive. This would mean another *15 Phantoms and 50–60 Skyhawks.*

C. *The Argument.* Rather than restate the arguments made on the principal issues under IV above or risk redundancy by arguing each of the options, it seems sensible to repeat here only the main elements that bear on choice among these options:

1. The Israelis regard this decision as a test of this Administration's support for Israel. This makes it difficult to do nothing.

2. The USSR has warned against a positive decision. It would be difficult to do nothing if that would make the U.S. appear to have been intimidated.

3. The military balance right now does not require us to increase Israel's aircraft inventory, though it may make replacement of losses desirable.

4. An open U.S. decision could force the USSR into assumption of responsibility for UAR air defense.

5. The Arabs will read a positive decision as U.S. support for Israel's raids in the Nile Valley.

D. *What do we tell Israel?* Any response to Israel if it is to preserve a close U.S.-Israeli relationship must assure Israel of U.S. intent to see that Israel retains its position of military superiority as well as the economic base to support that position. The key to making any response short of total acquiescence in all of Israel's requests politically acceptable to Israel will be that assurance *plus* the promise of continuing consultation on Israel's needs. Within that framework, we will have to tell Israel exactly what we intend to do. It has been possible in the past to maintain the secrecy of exact numbers of aircraft.

E. *What is said publicly* will depend on the decision. Two general options are available:

1. State that a decision has been made but there will be no detailed comment.

2. Describe the general nature of the decision and emphasize continued interest in arms limitation.

3. State vaguely what we intend to do with restatement of basic objectives: meet military needs of friends, arms limitation, peace.

4. Let the thirty-day deadline pass without comment to allow pressure to die down before dealing with the problem publicly.

F. *Formula for public announcement.* What is said will depend on the decision. But for the sake of illustration, if the decision were a relatively inconspicuous replacement of Israeli losses plus a slight addition to inventory, the question would arise what formula might be found that would make us appear firm and yet sensitive to the situation. Such a formula might include points like the following:

1. The U.S. will maintain the strength of its friends by whatever means it considers appropriate [e.g., replacement of losses].

2. The U.S. does not believe that force alone can resolve the Arab-Israeli conflict. Therefore, the U.S. will not fuel an arms race. The U.S. will continue to act with restraint and to press other suppliers to discuss arms limitation.

3. At the same time, the U.S. will renew its efforts to restore the cease-fire and to help start negotiation of the terms of a peace settlement.

94. Memorandum for the Record[1]

Washington, February 25, 1970.

SUBJECT

Meeting of Special NSC Review Group on Israeli Assistance Requests

PARTICIPANTS

Henry A. Kissinger
Elliot Richardson
David Packard
F.T. Unger
Richard Helms
Joseph Sisco
Harold H. Saunders
Alfred L. Atherton, Jr.

Dr. Kissinger opened the meeting by saying that he felt that he should acquaint the Group with the President's views insofar as he knew them. He noted that Prime Minister Meir would not have been mistaken if she thought she had been promised something. Although Dr. Kissinger had not been present at all of the conversations, he had heard the President in several ways indicate that though the U.S. might not be able to please Israel on "software," the U.S. would make it up to Israel on "hardware." As far as Dr. Kissinger knew, the President had never talked specific numbers of airplanes or specific levels of economic aid.

Mr. Packard asked whether the President had said anything in that context that had indicated that the U.S. would not require anything in return for any aid it might give.

Dr. Kissinger replied that we can do anything we want. It would be logical for Mrs. Meir to assume, however, that the trade-off had already been made in that the U.S. had gone ahead with its unpalatable peace proposals.

Dr. Kissinger continued by recalling that on December 26, 1969, Ambassador Rabin had been in his office when the President had called for him.[2] The President had asked Dr. Kissinger to bring the Ambassador over briefly. Secretary Laird had been present. The President had said that he realized the Israelis were unhappy but that the U.S. would make it up to Israel in hardware.

---

[1] Source: National Archives, Nixon Presidential Materials, NSC Files, NSC Institutional Files (H-Files), Box H–111, Senior Review Group, SRG Minutes Originals 1970. Top Secret. Drafted by Saunders on February 28. All brackets are in the original. The meeting was held in the White House Situation Room.

[2] See footnote 2, Document 52.

Dr. Kissinger, noting that he would not cite various public statements by the President on the question of arms supply, completed his list by noting to the group that he had on February 18 sent to the President a compilation of the reports from U.S. diplomatic posts in the Middle East describing their estimates of Arab reaction to a sale of more planes to Israel. [Note: This was in the daily brief of February 18.][3] The President had written in the margin, "We must do this regardless of political reaction."

Dr. Kissinger concluded these comments by saying that the Group should still state its views to the President. But he wanted to note for the Group these previous expressions of the Presidential viewpoint so that the Group could operate realistically in the knowledge of what the President may feel is a commitment, albeit vaguely defined.

Mr. Packard asked whether Dr. Kissinger felt that what he had said ruled out asking the Israelis for something in return for whatever we give. Dr. Kissinger replied in the negative.

Mr. Richardson said that he would prefer to think of the question in terms of how little we can do and how long the decision might be deferred. He also thought we should consider what we could do by earmarking aircraft to be available to Israel in an emergency as distinguished from making an announcement in the near future about a new sale. He suggested that there may be ways of delivering on our assurance of Israel's basic security that would not necessarily arouse a strong Arab reaction.

Mr. Richardson continued saying that he did not feel that the U.S. ambassadors had exaggerated in predicting a sharp Arab reaction. He had the same impression from talking to Messrs. McCloy,[4] Eugene Black[5] and others who have recently traveled in the area. He felt that Israel has no right to expect the U.S. to destroy its position in the Middle East. Israel has no security interest in doing this.

Mr. Richardson concluded by noting the fact that we face a dilemma in that trying to find a formula that would provide least visibility would make it difficult to extricate concessions from the Israelis. By its very nature, the kind of package that would provoke little Arab reaction would not be big enough to make the Israelis willing to concede anything.

---

[3] President's Daily Brief, February 18. (National Archives, Nixon Presidential Materials, NSC Files, Box 1, President's Daily Briefings)

[4] John J. McCloy was Chairman of the Advisory Committee on Disarmament and Arms Control.

[5] Eugene Black was Chairman of the Overseas Development Council, an international policy research institution.

Mr. Packard emphasized that it would be possible to take certain actions to assure that we could meet any legitimate Israeli needs in an emergency. Mr. Richardson seconded this by noting that a number of planes could be set aside in the United States for delivery under certain circumstances.

Mr. Richardson noted that Mr. Packard had asked whether it would be consistent with the President's commitments to attach conditions to a sale. He said that he would pose a different question: Would the President consider it within the range of what he had promised if we were to work out an arrangement for meeting Israel's basic needs without actually promising now to deliver more aircraft.

Dr. Kissinger said that he did not want to be in the position of interpreting the President's views. He would prefer to stop at simply having passed on those expressions of Presidential viewpoint which he could pass on as things that the President had actually said. However, if he had to guess, he would suppose that the President would lean more toward the Richardson proposal than toward the Packard proposal. [The "Packard proposal" referred to a paper that Mr. Packard had circulated to the members shortly before the meeting.[6] Each member had a copy of it there. When Mr. Packard had asked his questions about attaching conditions to the sale, he had indicated that such conditions would be those like the ones outlined in his paper—restoring the cease-fire, signing the NPT, etc.]

Dr. Kissinger continued saying that the Richardson position was more easily defensible. The problem is that the closer one gets to attaching conditions to a package, the larger the package needs to be.

Dr. Kissinger continued by summarizing as follows: There are two approaches to the decision. One is to attach specific conditions. If this approach is taken, there are two ways of doing it—attaching conditions to the agreement or attaching conditions to the actual delivery. The second approach is that suggested by Mr. Richardson which would offer Israel basic assurance while permitting us to continue a dialogue on the whole range of issues before us, not necessarily linking them to sale of weapons.

Dr. Kissinger felt that Israel would be so disappointed if the U S. offered any of the smaller options that attaching conditions would just be rubbing salt in an open wound.

Dr. Kissinger summarized by saying that the first decision before the President is whether to go the Packard route of attaching conditions to whatever package may be decided on or to go the Richardson route

---

[6] See footnote 10, Document 86.

of trying to achieve low visibility but without much prospect of attaching conditions.

Mr. Packard noted that the Richardson route would be "a little more troublesome" to handle in the U.S. It would be so refined that it would be difficult to explain.

Dr. Kissinger said, "Suppose we gave the full package that the Israelis had requested but attached conditions, wouldn't the Arabs regard the conditions as phony?" Mr. Sisco said he was sure they would regard the conditions as phony.

Dr. Kissinger asked whether it was the judgment of the Group that if the U.S. were to meet Israel's complete requests, it would "blow the place apart." He then asked each member of the Group in turn for his judgment on this point, and each member stated his unqualified judgment that such a decision would "blow the place apart." Mr. Sisco noted that Ambassador Rabin, in talking with Mr. Richardson, had defined a positive U.S. response to the Israeli requests as meeting at least 60% of them.

Mr. Richardson then turned to an option described in detail in a memo of February 18 which he had privately passed to Dr. Kissinger on February 20.[7] [This memorandum entitled "Israel's Requests for Arms and Economic Assistance," is a memorandum from Sisco to the Under Secretary and the Secretary and was included in Dr. Kissinger's briefing book under the Tab "Sisco Memo." The option to which Mr. Richardson here referred is Option 4–2 which is described beginning on page 9 of that memo.] Mr. Richardson read from his paper describing his option as follows: "Without making a contract now with Israel, we could make arrangements to earmark and have available on an immediate stand-by basis for formal sale to Israel on short notice a number of aircraft for replacement purposes (1971–1972) perhaps a bit above the present anticipated replacement need (e.g., 16 F–4s and 24 A–4s, the latter to be used also to replace Mirages)." Mr. Richardson felt that this might be the best way to deal with the problem.

Dr. Kissinger said that he doubted that the President would feel that this would be enough to meet his commitment.

Mr. Richardson said that he would like to inject another element—somewhat along the lines of that described in Mr. Packard's paper—which had come out of a meeting with Secretary Rogers that morning. This proposal is that the President use the occasion of an announcement of his decision to make a dramatic appeal for resolution of the Arab-Israeli problem. It is hard to think of anything concrete that

---

[7] The memorandum is in the National Archives, Nixon Presidential Materials, NSC Files, Box 605, Country Files, Middle East, Israel, Vol. III.

would offer something dramatically new to be introduced into the situation. But the problem is that there is nowhere near the public understanding of the Middle East problem which exists on Vietnam. The Administration could make a pretty good public case on what it has done to try to restore a cease-fire, what it has done to try to begin negotiations, what it has done to assure Israel's security, and what it has done to try to achieve arms limitation. It might put the Administration in a stronger position if the President were to make a full TV speech explaining the elements of the problem.

Mr. Packard proposed that one thing the President could do in this context would be to declare a moratorium on decisions on new arms agreements to continue while the U.S. made a dramatic new effort to achieve a peace settlement. [His paper called for the U.S. virtually to undertake a unilateral mediation effort.]

Mr. Sisco said he felt that a unilateral self-denying decision is not a good idea. Following the French jet deal with Libya[8] and following the President's offer of three reasonable political options to Kosygin[9] with no Russian response, the U.S. would appear to have given in to unreasonable pressures if it then announced that it was not going to make a positive decision.

Mr. Richardson felt that there are two distinguishable elements in his proposal: First, there would be a Presidential statement on the components of the problem. Second would be the question of how to handle Israel's requests. On the second, he was inclined to be against a moratorium, but it would be possible to say that a decision was being postponed for the moment and a definitive response would depend on the response of others.

General Unger noted that such an approach would be compatible with the President's statement at his January 30 press conference when he said that we would analyze the situation and make our decision in the light of it.[10] Any Presidential statement now could report the conclusions of such analysis, stating that Israel is in no immediate danger.

Dr. Kissinger said that, as a realistic matter, he doubted that the President could do that. He could imagine the President slipping the 30 day deadline but he found it difficult to visualize the President making a decision to do nothing now.

Dr. Kissinger noted that Congressman Celler had been in to see the President a few days previously.[11] If he had walked out thinking that

---

[8] See footnote 5, Document 86.
[9] See Document 88.
[10] See footnote 2, Document 92.
[11] Nixon met with Congressman Emanuel Celler (D–NY) on February 19 from 10:51 to 11:21 a.m. (National Archives, Nixon Presidential Materials, White House Central Files, President's Daily Diary)

the President would do something for Israel, "he would not be lying." In Dr. Kissinger's view, the President has to do something for Israel.

Dr. Kissinger felt that the options have probably been narrowed by this discussion to "the two Richardson packages" [the one described above and a contract to replace Israeli aircraft losses up to specified numbers, 1969–71—Option 4–1 on page 9 of the Sisco memorandum] plus one package a little bit larger than either of those. In addition, the President would have the choice of accepting the suggestion Secretary Rogers had made of a major presentation to the American people.

Dr. Kissinger noted that one reason the Administration had not put across its Mid-East policy is that it does not have internally as clear a conception of its objectives as it has evolved on Vietnam. A Presidential speech might be a good device to focus on in this regard.

Mr. Sisco said that the next paper[12] should include attachments on precisely what we tell Israel and what we say publicly. Two courses could be presented: First, there is an argument for a big Presidential announcement. Second, there is an argument for the lowest key handling possible.

Mr. Helms noted that one of the most difficult aspects of the problem is that the American public just does not realize how much Israel has and how much Israel is already getting. There is no understanding of the degree of Israeli wealth and military superiority. Mr. Helms read from a recent Agency memo on the new Israeli budget[13] [included in Dr. Kissinger's briefing book under the Tab "Israeli Budget"] to note how well Israel is doing and how much it is doing with still apparently a substantial economic cushion. Mr. Sisco noted that Israel was undoubtedly stockpiling in all categories of equipment.

Dr. Kissinger, picking up this discussion of Israeli economic performance, said that one of the most interesting questions raised in his mind as he had read through the material for the meeting was the Agency analysis of Israel's ability to develop its own independent arms industry. Dr. Kissinger asked why it is not in the U.S. interest to help Israel develop such an industry.

Mr. Sisco noted that Israel is well on its way. He said he felt it is in the U.S. interest since it is the U.S. interest to help Israel preserve its security. Mr. Sisco said that he would encourage Israeli development of this capacity.

---

[12] The paper is attached as Tab A to the memorandum from Kissinger to Nixon, Document 95.

[13] The intelligence memorandum, "Israel: Development of Military Industries," February 1970, is in the National Archives, Nixon Presidential Materials, NSC Files, NSC Institutional Files (H-Files), Box H–043, Senior Review Group Meetings, Review Group Israel 2/25/70.

Mr. Packard said that he would not disagree if there were no other solution. But he would hate to see Israel exporting arms. He would also hate to see Israel devoting so much of its resources to this purpose.

Mr. Sisco said he worried about that problem less in this case because the Israelis are relatively sensible in sorting out their own economic priorities. This is not the case of an underdeveloped country without much thought about its rational economic planning.

Dr. Kissinger noted that Israel might have just as much need for an armaments industry if it made peace as it would if the war continued. If there were peace, Israel would still have to be an armed camp. Israel would be no more secure than, say, France was after the Franco-German peace treaty of 1871.

General Unger felt that the U.S. could give Israel licensing privileges for the J–79 engine and that this would be better than giving them completed planes.

Mr. Helms returned to the theme that the public just does not understand how advanced Israel is in all of these respects. Therefore, the pressure on the Administration to provide arms is perhaps greater than it would be if the Administration could openly make the case that Israel is in no danger.

Dr. Kissinger asked the tactical question whether there was anything the Administration could do to get through this election year.

Mr. Sisco said that an announcement could be made along the following lines:

1. We have analyzed the situation carefully. In the foreseeable future, we judge that Israel has enough to protect itself.

2. We have assured Israel that, if there is any development between now and the end of the year which alters that assessment, we are prepared to provide the necessary equipment.

3. We have decided to postpone any decision for additional aircraft on the understanding that if there is any attrition replacements will be provided.

4. For the foreseeable future, we will redouble our efforts in restoring a cease-fire, pressing for a political settlement and attempting to achieve arms limitation.

5. We will go ahead with the predominant elements in the economic package.

Mr. Sisco summarized by saying that this would tell the American people that Israel has what it needs now. It would assure the American people and the Israelis that we will not stand by and see the situation turn against Israel. It would be a sign to the Soviets that we intend to act with restraint. It would, however, leave the situation open for later U.S. decision if the situation required.

Mr. Helms suggested that if we were to go this route, we should "nail the Soviets to the wall" by saying that our position would have to be reviewed if the Soviets sent "one new weapon" to the UAR.

Dr. Kissinger said that we have to move quickly now to a point where the President can look at his choices. He felt that these consisted of the following:

1. A low option such as that described by Mr. Sisco. In connection with this we could, of course, say privately that the pipeline of basic supply items would continue to flow and that would amount to a lot of equipment.

2. The Richardson proposal for having ready on a stand-by basis the aircraft Israel might need in an emergency. Perhaps at this level the variant of signing a contract to replace Israel's losses could be considered.

3. A minimum package of aircraft now large enough to consider trying to extract concessions.

One way of putting this decision into the larger context would be to try now to look five years down the road to see what situations we would like to avoid, to state a U.S. policy for this area.

Dr. Kissinger assumed that this decision would have to go to the NSC.

Mr. Richardson suggested that the analysis could distinguish among the following elements:

1. The various packages that might be possible.

2. What conditions or Israeli actions might be attached. These would increase in ratio to the size of the package.

3. The possible contexts in which the President would make this decision known, ranging from a quiet communication to the Israelis up to a fifteen minute address to the nation on TV.

Mr. Richardson expressed his preference for a minimum package with no conditions and a major statement on policy.

Mr. Packard acknowledged that whatever we do would provide the occasion at least for informal discussions with the Israelis. Mr. Sisco said that it was not clear to him what concessions Mr. Packard had in mind. Mr. Packard cited the ending of raids in the Nile Valley, signing the NPT, a more flexible position on peace terms, ending oil drilling in the Gulf of Suez.

Mr. Sisco questioned how far we could go in taxing the Israelis for continuing their raids. They have already agreed to abide by a mutual cease-fire.

Mr. Richardson reflected that the U.S. position in the Arab countries has deteriorated because the U.S. has not wanted to exert pressure on Israel to do things it does not think Israel will do. From that viewpoint, the conditions suggested would not be worth much to the Arabs because they would not address the issues which the Arabs are most concerned about. This is the route, Mr. Richardson said, by which he comes out to a minimal package. He said he was not even sure he would lean on Israel to end the deep penetration raids.

Dr. Kissinger said that it would be necessary to have a paper quickly. The ingredients are now available. He did not feel that it would be good procedure to try to define a minimum package to which we could attach conditions. He was inclined to feel that conditions would simply infuriate both sides.

Mr. Packard suggested that perhaps the possible conditions could be delineated separately.

Dr. Kissinger said he could see Mr. Richardson's point on the Israeli raids. At some point, it will become apparent that time is not working for the Soviets. If they cannot get Arab territory back, the Arabs may well come to us. That would be the time to lean on Israel. However, we probably cannot calibrate that sequence of events finely.

Mr. Sisco noted that it would be important, whatever decision we make, for the President to get across his assurance to Israel that we would not allow the balance to shift against Israel. He felt it is also important that we not put ourselves in a position where the Soviets can claim credit for having forced the U.S. to back down.

Mr. Richardson suggested that if the President made a statement, he would have to say that if the Soviets escalate, all bets are off.

Mr. Sisco said he could have a paper ready for a Tuesday (March 3) meeting.[14]

Dr. Kissinger asked Mr. Saunders to collaborate on this paper.

Dr. Kissinger asked what views are on the economic issues. Mr. Sisco said that he had taken for granted the $30 million in military credit already granted, the $119 million in additional military credit which Israel had asked for, something like $40 million in P.L. 480 sales, continuation of the pipeline of basic military supplies and consultation with Israel on its projected economic problems.

Dr. Kissinger said he was inclined to see the merits of some sort of Presidential statement on TV as the only way to pre-empt the inevitable domestic outburst on almost any decision.

Mr. Richardson agreed that the President has to pre-empt the domestic reaction.

---

[14] This meeting did not take place. The paper, attached as Tab A to Document 95, is not printed.

Mr. Helms said that he had one intelligence note which he would like to bring to the Group's attention before adjournment. He had a report to the effect that an Iraqi contact had been told by an official of the Arab Socialist Union in Egypt that the Soviet desk officer on Israeli affairs in the Communist Party of the Soviet Union in Moscow had said that the Soviet Union judges that Israel has five atomic bombs.

Dr. Kissinger said this was just another indication that the Soviets are trying to keep the Arabs edgy.

Harold H. Saunders[15]

---

[15] Saunders initialed "H.H.S." above his typed signature.

---

95. Memorandum From the President's Assistant for National Security Affairs (Kissinger) to President Nixon[1]

Washington, undated.

SUBJECT

Economic and Military Assistance to Israel

—At Tab A is a statement announcing your decision on the Israeli arms request which has been worked up by a member of my staff with Joe Sisco.

—At Tab B is a game plan prepared by the Department of State for carrying out your wish to postpone providing additional aircraft for Israel.

This will have profound consequences domestically and abroad. The domestic implications are apparent. Abroad, the appearance of bowing to Soviet pressure cannot be disposed of by simple denial. I have these suggestions:

First, the announcement should be made by the State Department, not the White House.[2]

---

[1] Source: National Archives, Nixon Presidential Materials, NSC Files, Box 606, Country Files, Middle East, Israel, Vol. IV. Top Secret; Nodis. Sent for action. A handwritten comment in the upper right-hand corner of the page reads: "Probably handed to the President on Mar 6, 1970 at K.B. [Key Biscayne]." Tabs A and B, both dated March 5, are attached but not printed.

[2] Nixon wrote "OK" next to this paragraph in the left-hand margin.

Second, it might be possible to make a minimal response to Israel that would provoke a somewhat less sharp Israeli reaction by some combination of the following:

1. The past Skyhawk and Phantom contracts could be amended without fanfare to include U.S. agreement to replace actual Israeli aircraft losses 1969–1971 up to a specific number. This number, based on the actual rate of attrition in 1969, would be up to 8 Phantoms and 18–20 Skyhawks (with Skyhawks replacing Mirages). This would essentially be a U.S. commitment to maintain the level of Israeli superiority which would exist at the end of present Phantom and Skyhawk shipments later this year. But it would not be a decision to increase Israel's aircraft inventory.[3]

2. As a variant of the above, without amending contracts, arrangements could be made by Defense to have manufactured to Israel's specifications and earmarked a number of aircraft—for instance, 16 Phantoms and 24 Skyhawks—for delivery on short notice should the situation require. Israel could be told of this arrangement.[4]

3. A combination of these approaches would be possible—providing replacements and at the same time creating a small additional reserve to fall back on should the need arise.

4. Israel could be told that the normal pipeline of support equipment will continue to flow and P.L. 480 sales (about $40 million) and additional military sales credit ($119 million applied to the 1968 Phantom contract) will be negotiated. Together with $30 million in military credit committed under the 1968 Phantom contract, this would make an economic package of $189 million, almost the complete $200 million annual rate Israel has projected from U.S. aid.[5]

Assistant Secretary Sisco agrees privately that some combination of these steps should be taken.

I will be writing you a separate memo on our strategy in the Middle East[6] which as you know has been a matter of great concern to me.

If you approve going ahead with announcement of a program with some combination of the above, the game plan recommended by Secretary Rogers would include the following steps:

---

[3] Nixon wrote "OK" next to this paragraph in the left-hand margin.
[4] Nixon wrote "no" next to this paragraph in the left-hand margin.
[5] Nixon wrote "OK" next to this paragraph in the left-hand margin.
[6] Sonnenfeldt prepared a memorandum for Kissinger to send to the President on "Our Middle East Policy." (National Archives, Nixon Presidential Materials, NSC Files, Box 652, Country Files, Middle East, Middle East, Vol. I)

1. Prior to the announcement:

—Brief Congressional leadership. (One possibility is a breakfast meeting.)
—Brief Jewish leaders (via Leonard Garment, Max Fisher).
—Instruct Ambassador Barbour to inform Mrs. Meir. Follow up with Ambassador Rabin here.
—Inform British and French just before announcement.

2. After the announcement:[7]

—Call in Ambassador Dobrynin to emphasize the need for a constructive Soviet response.
—Instruct our ambassadors in Arab capitals to seize the opportunity to move toward a peace settlement.

RECOMMENDATIONS:[8]

With respect to the statement at Tab A:

Approve _____

Disapprove _____

With respect to aircraft deliveries for the Israelis:

Variant (1) would replace losses. (Up to 8 Phantoms and 18–20 Skyhawks)

Variant (2) would earmark a certain number of aircraft for emergency requirements. (16 Phantoms and 24 Skyhawks)

Variant (3) would be the combination of both (1) and (2).

I want:

(1) _____

(2) _____

(3) _____

With respect to economic aid package:

Approve _____

Disapprove _____

---

[7] Nixon highlighted both points 1 and 2 and wrote "OK" next to them.
[8] Nixon did not initial any of the recommendations.

With respect to game plan (Tab B):

Approve _____

Disapprove _____

---

96. Transcript of a Telephone Conversation Between President Nixon and the President's Assistant for National Security Affairs (Kissinger)[1]

Washington, March 10, 1970, 10:40 a.m.

P: I can't get into this Israeli thing. I have a (education) group meeting coming up. I don't quite understand State's position and what we favor here. I want economic assistance and taking care of their losses and then the game plan—with increased Soviet movement we will move in amount (dictated). What basically is different?

K: State sent over a transigient [sic] statement.[2] Bill will agree after I work it over.

P: So the statement is put on guidance. We will provide economic assistance up to 7 million dollars; and provide for losses[3] but we're not going beyond that point.

K: There seems to be some discussion over who will make the announcement. State thinks it's going to be made over here.

P: They will make the announcement. That's an order.

K: My concern is Jewish control of the press and Rabin's request to see me with a message from Meir. I should tell Rabin that we will replace their losses and let the good news come out of here and the bad news from State.[4]

---

[1] Source: National Archives, Nixon Presidential Materials, Henry Kissinger Telephone Conversation Transcripts, Box 4, Chronological File. No classification marking. All brackets are in the original except those indicating text omitted in the original and "[sic]", added for clarity.

[2] Likely a reference to the Department's plan, attached as Tab B to Kissinger's memorandum to Nixon, Document 95.

[3] Of Phantom jet aircraft.

[4] Kissinger met with Rabin on March 12. See Document 99.

P: Call Rabin in Thursday and tell him the good news—economic up to whatever it is.

K: Close to 8 mill. dollars.

P: Replace losses and Third, we will re-evaluate if there is a change.

K: Sisco recommends that they keep production at such a level we can get planes to them.

P: I recommended no on the memo[5] because I didn't want anything announced. I don't want it to seem we are giving the Israelis everything they want.

K: We have to get across to the Israelis that this is a tactical move.

P: Tell Rogers that this is a diplomatic move and I want them to use it as a move with the Soviets on this.

K: If the Soviets stop moving arms, then we move right on this. We will change if the Soviets keep sending arms.

P: This is not the time to do it. We have problems in this country, even from those they think they have support from.

K: [omission in the original] Media will go for this even more. That's my concern.

P: Rabin couldn't control them against Pompidou[6] and I'm not sure he can control the intellectuals. Rabin should know this is policy.

K: The danger is that if we kick them in the teeth they might start a war.

P: We aren't. We field the losses—put this in a peaceful context. We will be of assistance there then put it to the Soviets. We are not going along on a massive Israeli request. It would force the Soviets into a massive reaction including men into the UAR.

K: They have held back and now we must see what they are doing.

P: You decide whether you want to tell Dobrynin.

---

[5] See footnote 4, Document 95.

[6] Roughly 10,000 demonstrators led by American Jewish organizations jeered French President Georges Pompidou as he and his wife arrived in Chicago for a dinner sponsored by the Chicago Council on Foreign Relations. The demonstrators were protesting France's decision not to sell arms to Israel. (*New York Times,* March 1, 1970, p. 9) Haldeman recorded in his diary on March 1 that Nixon received news of the protests from Protocol Chief Emil Mosbacher. "P[resident] furious. Will announce cancellation of Israel arms tomorrow, wants legislation to provide protection for foreign visitors, and he will go to New York dinner tomorrow night to add an extra touch. Really disturbed because Mrs. Pompidou has decided to go home tonight, wants to try and stop her. So we swing into immediate action this afternoon and have all the wheels grinding. Fun to have a crisis, if only a little one." (*Haldeman Diaries: Multimedia Edition,* March, 1, 1970)

K: I'm seeing him today on SALT.[7]

P: But I don't think this soon. Let Rogers tell him. And State is to make the announcement.

K: I will get that set this afternoon and they will make the announcement Friday.

P: You prepare the papers. I will be tied up until [omission in the original].

K: There's another issue—My Lai. That general is going to find disciplinary problems and I think you should stay out of that.[8]

P: That should be done at the Laird level.

---

[7] For the memorandum of conversation of Kissinger's March 10 meeting with Dobrynin, see *Foreign Relations, 1969–1976*, volume XII, Soviet Union, January 1969–October 1970, Document 140.

[8] Reference is to the U.S. attack on unarmed Vietnamese civilians in the village of My Lai on March 16, 1968. Following public disclosure of the killings by investigative journalist Seymour M. Hersh in November 1969, Secretary of the Army Stanley R. Resor and Army Chief of Staff General William C. Westmoreland appointed Lieutenant General William R. Peers to conduct a thorough review of the events. Peers concluded in a March 17, 1970, report that a "tragedy of major proportions" occurred at My Lai, which prompted action against 14 officers, including the commanding officer of the American Division, Major General Samuel W. Koster, by then Superintendent of West Point. The officers were accused of dereliction of duty and supression of evidence. Platoon commander Lt. William L. Calley was found guilty of murder but was freed in 1974 after three years confinement at Fort Benning, Georgia. The others were acquitted or never tried. (*New York Times*, April 9, 1984)

---

97. Memorandum From Secretary of State Rogers to President Nixon[1]

Washington, March 12, 1970.

SUBJECT

Ambassador Dobrynin's Call on the Middle East

Soviet Ambassador Dobrynin called on me yesterday[2] at his request to discuss the Middle East. He proposed a resumption of bilateral

---

[1] Source: National Archives, Nixon Presidential Materials, NSC Files, Box 652, Country Files, Middle East, Middle East, Vol. I. Secret; Nodis. A copy was sent to Haig.

[2] Telegram 36337 to Moscow, March 12, reported their discussion. See *Foreign Relations, 1969–1976*, volume XII, Soviet Union, January 1969–October 1970, Document 141.

talks[3] and indicated Soviet willingness to consider a more precise formulation on peace provided that we would indicate a willingness to consider their position that Sharm al-Shaikh would return to UAR sovereignty, that an irrevocable UN presence would be stationed there to assure freedom of passage through the Gulf of Aqaba, and that we would be willing to extend our proposal for withdrawal of Israeli forces to include Gaza.

I responded that we would study both the suggestion to resume bilateral discussions and the substantive Soviet proposals. I made it clear, however, that if we should agree to resume bilateral talks[4] there would have to be an understanding of what the resumption of those talks signifies. Our willingness to resume talks could not be interpreted to mean an acceptance of the Soviet proposals or that we were willing to make concessions going beyond our present position as reflected in the October 28th and December 18th documents.[5]

For the time being at least, we are limiting press comment merely to confirming, in response to any inquiries, that Dobrynin called on me and that the subject discussed was the Middle East.

William P. Rogers[6]

---

[3] In a March 10 meeting with Kissinger, Dobrynin told him "in confidence that he had been instructed to call on Secretary Rogers" to offer the continuation of bilateral discussions; see ibid., Document 140. Kissinger's analysis of the Soviet offer, sent to Nixon in a memorandum of March 13, is ibid., Document 143.

[4] Bilateral talks resumed on March 25; see footnote 5, Document 105.

[5] Documents 58 and 78.

[6] Rogers initialed "WPR" above his typed signature.

98. Telegram From the Department of State to the Embassy in Lebanon[1]

Washington, March 12, 1970, 0149Z.

36213. Subject: USG Assistance to Lebanon. Ref: Beirut 1809.[2]

1. We have read with interest report of Ambassador's March 5 meeting with President Helou (reftel). Ambassador may assure Helou that there is clear understanding in USG of his dilemma regarding fedayeen. We fully appreciate constraints under which Helou operates in dealing with fedayeen and that GOL in no position use large-scale force against fedayeen. We have said as much to Israelis and have urged them to raise their level of tolerance. We will indeed continue to Quote exercise our influence to be sure it (Israeli attack) doesn't start Unquote (last para reftel), but our ability to restrain Israelis in face repeated fedayeen attacks is limited. We trust that Lebanese army will continue do its best to prevent and, at minimum, limit such attacks.

2. President's comment (para six reftel) to effect USG Quote seemed reluctant Unquote to provide Lebanon with arms suggests he may have overlooked our past offers in this regard. While it is true that we have been unable provide GOL with grant aid, we have attempted be responsive as possible to GOL's arms request. Might be useful to recapitulate what we have undertaken to do on Lebanon's behalf over past few years in addition to routine sales: (A) In 1967 we offered sell Lebanon arms package including 20 M–41 tanks. Sale was never concluded. (B) In January 1969 we offered special airlift of military equipment which we understood Lebanese needed urgently (State 7234). GOL unable accept offer. (C) In August 1969 40 quarter ton trucks were expeditiously made available for sale to army. (D) In November 1969 we authorized sale of 5,000 M–14 rifles to GOL. This authorization required highest level USG approval. GOL, however, decided against purchase these weapons. (E) In December 1969 we provided price and availability data on number items equipment including CH46F and CH47C helicopters, 106mm recoilless rifles mounted on jeeps, 66mm rockets, M–14 and M–16 rifles, M–55 quad 50AA, M42A1 40mm AA and spare parts for M–41 tanks. (F) Pursuant to General Nujaim's re-

---

[1] Source: National Archives, Nixon Presidential Materials, NSC Files, Box 614, Country Files, Middle East, Jordan, Vol. III. Secret; Exdis. Drafted by Bryan H. Baas (NEA/ARN) and Seelye; cleared in NEA, NEA/RA, and PM/MAS; and approved by Sisco. Repeated to Amman, Jidda, London, Paris, Tel Aviv, and USUN.

[2] In telegram 1809 from Beirut, March 6, Porter reported on his March 5 meeting with Helou, which dealt chiefly with the issue of fedayeen attacks and Israeli reprisals across the Lebanese-Israeli border. (Ibid., RG 59, Central Files 1970–73, POL 23–8 LEB)

quest, we are looking into availability M–41 tanks and are preparing price and availability data on other items mentioned Beirut 1372.

3. Foregoing not exhaustive list of offers USG has made but it could be cited as reminder to GOL that we have stood ready to meet legitimate Lebanese military equipment requirements.

4. We hope also that President Helou is aware of special effort expended in arranging our current P.L.–480 undertaking to Lebanon. We have succeeded in initiating this program for Lebanon in view of over-riding political considerations which Helou has touched on in reftel.

5. We have noted Helou's suggestion (para 7 reftel) that the USG make public statement designed to demonstrate support for GOL. We are sympathetic to this proposal, but in view distortion by radical press of Sisco statement last October,[3] we concerned that public statement at time of fast breaking developments might again be counter productive. We therefore concur with your judgment that we do nothing at moment (Beirut 1876).[4]

Rogers

---

[3] Sisco's statement that the United States would view a threat to Lebanon's integrity with "greatest concern" was distributed on October 14, 1969, by USIA to Lebanese newspapers. (*New York Times,* October 15, 1969, p. 5) In telegram 180293 to Beirut, October 24, 1969, the Department reported a conversation between Sisco and British Ambassador John Freeman during which the Assistant Secretary said: "US official statements have been grossly distorted in emotional atmosphere of Middle East. He specifically noted how President's use of word 'substantial' in address to UNGA had been twisted. Sisco's statement of our support for Lebanese independence and integrity also being misinterpreted in some quarters. In this connection, Sisco informed Freeman our statement made at Helou's behest." (National Archives, Nixon Presidential Materials, NSC Files, Box 1239, Saunders Files, Lebanon 1/20/69–10/27/69) In his address to the UN General Assembly on September 18, 1969, Nixon declared: "We seek a settlement [in the Middle East] based on respect for the sovereign right of each nation in the area to exist within secure and recognized boundries. We are convinced that peace cannot be achieved on the basis of substantial alterations in the map of the Middle East. And we are equally convinced that peace cannot be achieved on the basis of anything less than a binding, irrevocable commitment by the parties to live together in peace." For the text of his address, see *Public Papers: Nixon, 1969,* pp. 724–731.

[4] In telegram 1876 from Beirut, March 10, the Embassy reported how the Lebanese press covered Porter's meeting with Helou, including a misleading story that the Ambassador "gave assurances that Israel would not attack Lebanon." (National Archives, RG 59, Central Files 1970–73, POL LEB–US)

99. Memorandum of Conversation[1]

Washington, March 12, 1970, 11:15 a.m.

PARTICIPANTS

Dr. Henry Kissinger
Ambassador Yitzhak Rabin, of Israel
Brig. General A.M. Haig, Military Assistant to Dr. Kissinger

Dr. Kissinger opened the discussion by referring to the exchange of notes between Soviet Premier Kosygin and President Nixon during the first week of February.[2] He recalled the report he received several days after the exchange of letters to the effect that the Soviets were concerned that President Nixon did not appreciate the seriousness of Premier Kosygin's letter and that they were contemplating the introduction of Soviet military personnel into the UAR.[3] Dr. Kissinger stated that we had received this report both through intelligence channels and as a result of statements by junior Soviet Embassy personnel to a member of the U.S. press corps. Dr. Kissinger stated that as a result of these reports he called in Soviet Ambassador Dobrynin and confronted him with these reports, discounted the methods which the Soviets had employed to circulate them, and strongly warned Ambassador Dobrynin that the United States would view with the greatest concern the introduction of Soviet combat personnel into the Middle East.[4] The U.S., he said, was choosing this method of communication with the Soviets rather than making a formal declaration. At the same time we want to make sure that the Soviet leaders would be under no illusion about the possibility of grave consequences. (Dr. Kissinger showed Ambassador Rabin the summary sheet (Tab A) which included the specific points he covered with Dobrynin.)

Dr. Kissinger continued that he saw Ambassador Dobrynin again this week on a routine matter involving the Strategic Arms Limitation Talks, but that it was obvious that Dobrynin was primarily interested in discussing the Middle East. During the meeting Ambassador Dobrynin read a prepared written reply to some points that Dr. Kissinger had

---

[1] Source: National Archives, Nixon Presidential Materials, NSC Files, Box 612, Country Files, Middle East, Israeli Aid. Top Secret; Nodis. The conversation was held in the East Wing of the White House in the Military Aide's office. Tabs A–D are attached but not printed.

[2] See Document 88.

[3] See *Foreign Relations,* 1969–1976, volume XII, Soviet Union, January 1969–October 1970, Document 132.

[4] For the memorandum of conversation of Kissinger's February 10 meeting with Dobrynin, see ibid., Document 131.

raised at their earlier meeting. The statement in effect proposed a de facto cease-fire between Israel and the UAR.[5] Dr. Kissinger allowed Ambassador Rabin to read the text of a portion of the message read by Ambassador Dobrynin at this meeting, attached (Tab B).

Dr. Kissinger stated that the White House shares the Israeli analysis of recent events in the Middle East, but emphasized that these events confirm that some movement can occur. Dr. Kissinger said it is our judgment that the USSR made a commitment to Nasser in January, during his visit to Moscow,[6] and that during the next few months this will be manifested by additional Soviet arms shipments to the UAR. Dr. Kissinger added that it was President Nixon's view that a U.S. decision to provide arms to Israel should be accomplished on the basis of a response to stepped-up Soviet shipments and that while this was the President's view it was not necessarily shared by others in the U.S. bureaucracy. He pointed out that with respect to assistance to Israel the President hoped to break out immediate action from the longer term action. In other words, to treat both separately.

Dr. Kissinger stated that he could forsee no problems with respect to economic assistance to Israel and showed Ambassador Rabin the summary of proposed economic assistance (Tab C).

Concerning military hardware, Dr. Kissinger stated that with respect to immediate action the U.S. government would replace actual Israeli aircraft losses during the period 1969–71, up to 8 Phantoms and 20 Sky Hawks. On the longer term, the U.S. would supply the major part of the Israeli hardware request if more significant USSR arms shipments into the UAR take place. Dr. Kissinger then handed Ambassador Rabin a draft Aide-Mémoire which affirmed this commitment (Tab D). Dr. Kissinger emphasized that we considered that the phraseology of the Aide-Mémoire which reads "the significant introduction of Soviet arms into the UAR as endangering the military balance" to be negotiable language. It would be extended to include arms shipments to other countries and from other sources. He then added that the President recognizes his commitment to Prime Minister Meir and emphasized again that President Nixon prefers to furnish assistance to Israel in response to Soviet arms shipments to the UAR, and confirmed the U.S. intention of amending the contract on the Phantoms and pro-

---

[5] For the memorandum of conversation of Kissinger's March 10 meeting with Dobrynin, see ibid., Document 140.

[6] In a memorandum to Nixon on February 1, Kissinger wrote: "There is a strong likelihood that Nasser made a secret visit to Moscow January 22–27." (Ibid., Document 123) Hyland informed Kissinger on June 8: "We have the hardest possible intelligence that the decisions leading to the present situation were approved by Brezhnev on January 28–29, in the wake of Nasser's secret visit to Moscow. The Soviets had no choice but to support Nasser, and strong moves were obviously called for." (Ibid., Document 163)

viding for some standby production capability if this can be done secretly. He emphasized that the Aide-Mémoire was not written in diplomatic language because it was prepared unilaterally in the White House and was not being presented on a take-it-or-leave-it basis. Referring to the final portions of the Aide-Mémoire, Dr. Kissinger stated that President Nixon is requesting also that the Israeli government stop bombing the UAR, providing the UAR in turn ceases its military action against Israel. He pointed out that the Aide-Mémoire restated President Nixon's commitment but added the request for a de facto cease-fire. The Aide-Mémoire, Mr. Kissinger stated, would be signed by President Nixon if it were satisfactory to the Israeli Government.

Dr. Kissinger then turned to a proposed U.S. public announcement concerning military assistance to Israel. He stated that the language of this announcement went far beyond the consensus of the U.S. bureaucracy on this issue. It will be made by the Department of State sometime next week[7] after it has been shown to Ambassador Rabin by the Secretary of State. It was our hope that the Israelis would agree to an Aide-Mémoire along the lines of that being given to Ambassador Rabin prior to the public announcement. Dr. Kissinger again emphasized that the President hoped to be in a posture which would enable him to respond tp the Israeli arms request as a result of additional Soviet shipments and that this would facilitate his handling of the issue both domestically and bureaucratically.

Ambassador Rabin expressed his concern that the U.S. and the Israelis would share different opinions as to whether or not the Soviets had in fact introduced a significant amount of Soviet arms. He stated that the U.S. Government would continually delay in accepting the justification for a decision to proceed with shipments to Israel under the conditions proposed in the Aide-Mémoire. He recounted his experience in recent months and the difficulty he had with the U.S. intelligence community in arriving at an agreed assessment on the level of Soviet arms supplies to Egypt. He pointed out that, for example, since July 1969 Israeli intelligence concluded that Egypt had received 130 planes and that the Arabs as a whole had received 254 planes. The U.S. intelligence community did not agree with this figure.

Dr. Kissinger stated that we would check these figures and added that perhaps the Israelis would prefer to establish a combined U.S.-Israeli framework for making these assessments. Rabin replied that no

---

[7] The announcement was made by Secretary Rogers on March 23. The text of the announcement and the transcript of the news conference that followed are printed in the Department of State *Bulletin*, April 13, 1970, pp. 477–484. Nixon discussed Rogers's upcoming statement in his press conference on March 21. See *Public Papers: Nixon, 1970*, pp. 288–298.

matter what is concluded the Soviets will deny that they made such shipments.

Mr. Kissinger stated that recent events had had a serious impact on the U.S. attitude on the subject and that the Israelis' friends here had done great damage to their interests. Dr. Kissinger recommended that the Israelis make some proposal on how we could arrive at an agreed position on facts from which a decision could be made. He asked that Ambassador Rabin advise him before Tuesday (March 17) and expressed sympathy for the Ambassador's concerns.

Ambassador Rabin stated that this morning Israel penetrated 60 miles west of the Canal and struck some bunkers that appear to have been configured for SAM III weapons. They observed no missiles but the bunkers which have been constructed by over 100 workers on an urgent basis were definitely of a distinctive type. Dr. Kissinger noted that the Israelis had hit a facility in the UAR containing Soviet personnel and asked if this had been a deliberate strike. Rabin replied that they were aware that this was a main training center but inferred that the strike was not specifically targeted against the Soviets although they knew that many Soviet personnel had been killed and wounded. Rabin then stated that he believed the Russian threat to introduce their armed forces into the UAR was a trick.

Referring to the Aide-Mémoire, Ambassador Rabin stated that he is convinced that President Nixon is sincere but that he felt the importance of this matter required that he speak to his Prime Minister. It was agreed that Ambassador Rabin would fly to Israel tonight and return sometime Sunday after consultations with Prime Minister Golda Meir.[8] Then Dr. Kissinger and Ambassador Rabin would meet sometime Tuesday.[9] Dr. Kissinger asked Ambassador Rabin to inform Assistant Secretary Sisco this afternoon that he had been called home. Rabin replied that this would make some sense since speculation to this effect had already been rampant in the Israeli press. Dr. Kissinger cautioned him that nothing of their conversation should appear in the Israeli press as a result of his visit, emphasizing that Ambassador Rabin had more information than anyone in the U.S. Government with the exception of the President, himself, and General Haig.

Dr. Kissinger emphasized that the U.S. Aide-Mémoire was a unilateral document but that he believed the following portions of it were negotiable:

1. The Israelis might elaborate on the conditions for determining a disruption in the arms balance in the Middle East.

---

[8] In his memoirs, Rabin recalled that "the reaction in Jerusalem was indignant, and I relayed that response to Kissinger upon my return." (*The Rabin Memoirs,* p. 170)

[9] March 17. See Document 103.

2. Some flexibility for the period of the undeclared cease-fire appears possible.

Rabin replied that the main problem with this sequence of events would be the reaction of the Israeli Cabinet to the U.S. public announcement. Pressure would immediately develop to incease military activity, not to stop it. Dr. Kissinger cautioned that the Israelis must have discipline on this issue and Rabin countered that this is a problem of emotion, not logic. The U.S. public announcement will encourage the Arabs. Experience has shown that the only way to cool them down was the kind of military action which has been employed by Israel recently. Dr. Kissinger stated that from the viewpoint of Israeli security, if they can obtain a de facto cease-fire which the other side breaks, no one here in the United States would object to strong counter-action. Ambassador Rabin did not contest this logic and added that if the Prime Minister could announce such a decision at the Israeli Cabinet meeting on Sunday and if we held up briefly on our public announcement this sequence might suceed. He pointed out that if the Israeli Cabinet accepts the decision it would of course not be announced publicly but merely implemented. Dr. Kissinger added that the Israelis should inform us however Ambassador Rabin then questioned whether or not the Soviets were talking about deep penetration raids or all kinds of air raids against the UAR. Dr. Kissinger stated that he had asked Dobrynin the same question and did not really get a reply. Rabin stated that they really worry about the deep raids. Dr. Kissinger asked what the purpose of the shallow raids was and Rabin replied that they are designed to prevent any SAMs from being installed. He added that since the Israelis have received the Phantom fighters they are able to stand-off above the more dangerous ack-ack which is effective at lower altitudes and deliver ordnance in relative safety. Dr. Kissinger asked Ambassador Rabin if the story about the two Egyptian pilots who bailed out after one of their planes was hit by their own SAM was correct. Ambassador Rabin confirmed that this was so and that it had occurred about six months ago, adding that unfortunately the Israelis had done the same thing with a Hawk missile which shot down an Israeli light aircraft. Dr. Kissinger stated that he felt the President would be very interested in a cessation involving only deep penetrations for a period of perhaps sixty or 45 days. The U.S. could then tell the Soviets that Israel has demonstrated restraint and that they in turn will have to prohibit the UAR from taking advantage of this by building additional SAM sites. The U.S. would also warn the Soviets that additional arms shipments to the UAR would trigger a new round in the arms race. This in effect would tend to put the Soviets on the defensive.

Dr. Kissinger asked Ambassador Rabin to develop the proposed rules of engagement for a de facto cease-fire and recapped the discussion with respect to the coordination of the Aide-Mémoire with Prime Minister Meir. Ambassador Rabin then inquired about the nature of the U.S. public announcement. Dr. Kissinger showed him a copy of the current version of the announcement. After reading the announcement several times Ambassador Rabin stated that it made him very unhappy. Dr. Kissinger acknowledged that the U.S. recognized this but that the document was actually far less negative than the versions originally prepared within the bureaucracy, adding that the Aide-Mémoire went way beyond anything recommended and that the President had prepared it strictly on his own initiative. For this reason if it were compromised the most serious consequences would develop. Ambassador Rabin asked for a copy of the proposed press announcement and Dr. Kissinger agreed to have one prepared for him this afternoon which could be picked up by a messenger.

The meeting concluded at 12:25 p.m.

100. Telegram From the Embassy in Lebanon to the Department of State[1]

Beirut, March 13, 1970, 1410Z.

1989. Ref: State 35651.[2]

1. Last fall during the Lebanese-fedayeen war[3] this Embassy was asked to suggest possible measures for assisting Lebanon. Today, almost five months later, the U.S. has done nothing except to approve in principle a small P.L.–480 program. The Lebanese request for arms assistance and the similar recommendations of this Embassy have either been turned down or are in bureaucratic limbo. Perhaps there are

---

[1] Source: National Archives, Nixon Presidential Materials, NSC Files, Box 621, Country Files, Middle East, Lebanon, Vol. II. Secret; Exdis. At the top of the page a handwritten notation in an unknown hand reads: "A strong but valid message. I hope that Al Haig and Hal Saunders see this." Attached is a note from Haig to Kissinger, March 16, that reads: "Henry, The attached cable dealing with the Lebanese situation suggests that we may have some problems which are minimal to remedy."

[2] In telegram 35651 to Beirut, March 11, the Department informed the Embassy that it was "looking into availability of M–41 tanks pursuant to General Noujaim's request" but asked that the Embassy "point out to Lebanese that this tank was phased out of US Army approximately 15 years ago." "Thus," the Department wrote, "all M–41s in US stocks are in used condition and would need rehabilitation before they could be sold," which meant that delivery could take up to 18 months. (Ibid., RG 59, Central Files 1970–73, DEF 12–5 LEB)

[3] See Document 61.

valid legal or practical reasons for this inactivity, but the result is the same—inactivity.

2. There is either a serious misunderstanding between the Dept and myself on the urgency of the situation in Lebanon or perhaps we have failed to make the point with enough clarity. May I now state as clearly as I can that I think we are in for real trouble in Lebanon within the next few months, if not sooner.

I think it is almost inevitable that there will be a serious confrontation between the Palestinians and the Lebanese. The alternative will be that the Lebanese will cave in to the fedayeen. Equally predictable result will then be a severe Israeli response. American interests will suffer generally and specifically in this process, and we cannot rule out violent action against our presence here.

3. The only instrument which might bring a measure of stability to the internal situation in Lebanon is a strengthened army. The Lebanese took a long time to make up their minds to tell us what kind of arms they wanted. They were without a government and, when they formed one,[4] Pres Helou had to get rid of his incompetent CIC.[5] The new CIC, Noujaim,[6] after carefully reviewing his needs and his country's finances, approached us on Feb 19 with a modest requirement for some WWII tanks and AA machine guns—used equipment which the Lebanese hoped would be on our surplus list, and therefore available for little or nothing. The Lebanese, with an empty treasury, were forced to beg, but their request was indeed modest, considering the threat which they are trying urgently to meet.

4. To recapitulate from our earlier messages: (A) Helou wants to strengthen his army now—for a fedayeen challenge which he thinks may occur no later than May; (B) GOL cannot pay going prices, even for reconditioned equipment; (C) GOL cannot at moment legally accept USG credits, even if we have them to offer; (D) Lebanon has no chance to get subsidies from other Arab states; (E) Helou desperately wants to continue to get arms in West, to avoid accepting proferred Soviet "gift."

5. On March 12, we received USG's first response to GOL's request. It said: (A) 18 months delivery time for U.S.-owned M–41's; (B) No other tanks available from U.S. sources; (C) Lebanese might wish try buy their M–41's on open market from "Levy Bros"; (D) If they do, USG will tell them later whether or not we will veto the purchase. There is no hope in this reply which I can use to buck up Helou's and Noujaim's morale.

---

[4] See footnote 6, Document 26.

[5] Commander in Chief of the Lebanese Armed Forces, General Emil Boustany.

[6] General Jean Noujaim replaced Boustany on January 7.

6. I am led to conclude that the USG cannot respond either to the urgent nature of the Lebanese request for arms, or to the request for concessional prices. If this is the case, I believe it is essential that I so frankly inform Pres Helou. At this point Helou is relying on the hope that a friendly USG, whose interests he feels are identical with his, will respond to his urgent pleas for help. (He indeed has nowhere else to turn, unless he accepts the recent Soviet offers.) We cannot, in all fairness, allow him to plan on false premises. He must know where he stands and what his assets are or may be, and make his decisions accordingly.

7. I do not want to appear to be tilting my lance in this message, but I see no ray of hope in any of Dept's messages that USG is considering any course of action that responds to Helou's requests or to the realities of the problem. If I am wrong, please tell me.

8. Also, valid as the facts may be, I cannot satisfy Helou, provide him solace, or assist in easing the situation here by repeating the history of our past efforts to help Lebanon (para 2, State 36213).[7] Helou is just as aware as I of the inadequacies and mistakes of his former CIC—the man who helped create this sorry history. It was, after all, Helou who fired him, and perhaps above all because he was aware of the facts which the Dept has enumerated, and which he and I have often discussed in the past.[8]

Porter

---

[7] See Document 98.

[8] On April 6, Nixon sent a letter to Helou in which he wrote: "It remains a matter of deep concern to me and my government that Lebanon's stability and independence be preserved and that Lebanon be enabled to pursue its democratic way of life without outside interference. My government will continue to do what it can to facilitate this objective. Many of the problems facing Lebanon today are a direct result of the Arab Israel confrontation. Recognizing this, we are vigorously pursuing our efforts to find a way of achieving lasting peace in the Middle East." (Telegram 49939 to Beirut, April 6; National Archives, Nixon Presidential Materials, NSC Files, Box 621, Country Files, Middle East, Lebanon, Vol. II)

101. Letter From President Nixon to Israeli Prime Minister Meir[1]

Washington, undated.

Dear Madame Prime Minister:

Ambassador Barbour will be informing you of the results of our review of your government's financial and military needs, particularly with respect to aircraft, which you and I discussed last September. He will also convey to you the announcement on these matters which we shall be making shortly.[2]

I fully understand your deep sense of personal responsibility for the security of your country and the survival of your people. I carry a similar burden and can appreciate the sense of concern and urgency in the message you sent me through Ambassador Rabin last week.[3] To be isolated in the world and deprived of the means of defense would indeed be tragic for your people, who have endured so much and struggled so valiantly. The response we are conveying to you is intended to make clear to the world that Israel is not alone.

I know you would have preferred a more definitive decision now on your request for additional aircraft. Weighing all factors, I have concluded that such a decision at this time would not serve the cause of peace in the Middle East—the common goal which is essential to the long term interests of both our countries. The achievement of this goal requires both strength and restraint. I say this to emphasize the difference between restraint and weakness.

Our present response takes into account that in the absence of peace, Israel's margin of safety and security must be maintained. The

---

[1] National Archives, Nixon Presidential Materials, NSC Files, Box 606, Country Files, Middle East, Israel, Vol. IV. No classification marking. The letter is attached to a March 14 memorandum to Nixon, in which Kissinger wrote: "In view of Mrs. Meir's direct personal appeal to you on the aircraft decision, a personal response would seem desirable in connection with our telling her of the decision. The main purpose of such a note would not be to convey the details of the decision or to argue the case but to reassure her that Israel is not being cut off."

[2] See Document 106.

[3] Meir's March 8 letter to Nixon was delivered to Kissinger by Ambassador Rabin during their meeting at the White House on March 12 (see Document 99). Meir wrote: "Lately some rumors have reached me that your decision [on arms requests] may be negative or at best postponed. I absolutely refuse to believe it . . . To envisage such a blow to my people is more than the courage I have to believe. If, God forbid, this were true, then we would feel really forsaken. Our enemies, including the Russians, would, for the first time, really believe that we are at their mercy . . . The encouragement to the Arabs that we have been abandoned by our best friend while their supplies pour in, spells not only a security danger but a psychological shock for our people. The effect of this shock cannot be overestimated . . . Mr. President, we are alone! Again, I say to myself and to you, I do not believe it." (National Archives, Nixon Presidential Materials, NSC Files, Box 612, Country Files, Middle East, Israeli Aid)

provision for maintaining Israel's strength in the face of attrition is designed to express our continuing support for Israel's security. This point will not, I am convinced, be lost on any who may harbor hopes of reversing the military balance in the area.

The relationship between our two countries is based in the final analysis on mutual confidence in each other's fundamental intentions. I want to reaffirm to you that, for our part, these remain as steadfast and firm as they have been during all the years of Israel's nationhood.

Sincerely,[4]

---

[4] Printed from an unsigned copy.

---

102. Memorandum From President Nixon to the President's Assistant for National Security Affairs (Kissinger)[1]

Washington, March 17, 1970.

In your talk with Rabin[2] and also in your further talk with Mrs. Meir if you have it I think it is important that you lay it on the line with regard to Israel's interest going far beyond the present conflict.

Israel is relying on the peace at any price Democrats, Mansfield, Fulbright, Symington et al, and on some Republicans like Goodell and Scott[3] to come through for them in the event we come to a crunch, not just in aid but in case Israel is threatened directly by Soviet power.

What they must realize is that these people are very weak reeds. They will give Israel a lot of lip service but they are peace at any price people. When the chips are down they will cut and run, not only as they are presently cutting and running in Vietnam but also when any conflict in the Mideast stares them straight in the face.

On the other hand, their real friends (to their great surprise) are people like Goldwater, Buckley,[4] RN et al who are considered to be

---

[1] Source: National Archives, Nixon Presidential Materials, NSC Files, Box 652, Country Files, Middle East, Middle East, Vol. I. Confidential.

[2] See Document 104.

[3] Senators Mike Mansfield (D–MT), J. William Fulbright (D–AR), Stuart Symington (D–MO), Charles Goodell (R–NY), Hugh Scott, Jr. (R–PA).

[4] Senator Barry Goldwater (R–AZ) and William F. Buckley, nationally-syndicated columnist and founder of *National Review* magazine.

hawks on Vietnam but who in the broader aspects are basically not cut and run people whether it is in Vietnam, the Mideast, Korea or any place else in the world. They may be concerned, for example, that Buckley wrote a column indicating displeasure that the Jewish community demonstrated against Pompidou and didn't demonstrate against Kosygin. This, however, is the most fundamental point of all. They must recognize that our interests are basically pro-freedom and not just pro-Israel because of the Jewish vote. We are *for* Israel because Israel in our view is the only state in the Mideast which is *pro* freedom and an effective opponent to Soviet expansion. We will oppose a cut and run policy either in Vietnam or Cuba or the Mideast or NATO or any place else in the world. This is the kind of friend that Israel needs and will continue to need, particularly when the going gets very tough in the next five years.

It is time for Israel (and I don't think it will do any good to suggest this to the American Jewish community) to face up to the fact that their only reliable friends are the hawks in this country—those that are hawks in the best sense when it comes to Soviet expansionism any place in the world, not just Soviet expansionism in the Mideast.

They think, for example, that in the event some move is made in the Mideast that what really counts is to have Lindsay,[5] Goodell or Scott to come out for more arms to Israel. Lindsay, Goodell and Scott can deliver only their own votes despite the fact that Manny Celler[6] got 200 names on a Congressional petition which was presented to me (incidentally, a very stupid move on their part since it was so unnecessary and so obvious a move).

What they must understand is that people like Goodell, Scott and Lindsay have no character and that when the crunch comes they will cave. What they must also realize is that people like RN, Buckley, Goldwater et al will stand up for them when the crunch comes basically because we admire them for their character and their strength and because we see in Israel the only state in that part of the world which will not become an abject tool of Soviet policy the moment the Soviet begins to flex its missiles.

What all this adds up to is that Mrs. Meir, Rabin et al must trust RN completely. He does not want to see Israel go down the drain and makes an absolute commitment that he will see to it that Israel always has "an edge." On the other hand, he must carry with him not just the Jewish constituency in New York and Pennsylvania and California and possibly Illinois which voted 95 percent against him, but he must carry

---

[5] John Lindsay, Mayor of New York City.
[6] Congressman Emanuel Celler (D–NY).

with him the 60 percent of the American people who are in what is called the silent majority and who must be depended upon in the event that we have to take a strong stand against Soviet expansionism in the Mideast. Only when the Israeli leaders realize this fact are they going to have any kind of security which will be reliable.

This is tough talk for them to hear because they read the Jewish press, the *New York Times,* the *Washington Post* and also listen to the media and get the impression that because they have so much clout with some of those people that they will get their way. They must realize that that group has lost its credibility with the American people and that they are *not* going to get their way with a majority of Americans when the chips are really down.

In this connection, they must realize that one of their best friends also is Agnew. Agnew will stand up and be counted in the event there is a Soviet expansionist move in the Mideast. On the other hand, he will not stand just as I will not stand for a double standard. We are going to stand up in Vietnam and in NATO and in the Mideast, but it is a question of all or none. This is it cold turkey and it is time that our friends in Israel understood this.

We are going to be in power for at least the next three years and this is going to be the policy of this country. Unless they understand it and act as if they understood it beginning now they are down the tubes.

---

103. Aide-Mémoire From President Nixon to the Government of Israel[1]

Washington, March 17, 1970.

Reaffirming the discussion of September 26, 1969 with Prime Minister Golda Meir,[2] I hereby confirm that the United States Government will continue its commitment to the military security of Israel by the provision of hardware required to maintain the military balance in the Middle East. We would construe any significant introduction of Soviet

---

[1] Source: National Archives, Nixon Presidential Materials, NSC Files, Box 652, Country Files, Middle East, Middle East, Vol. I. No classification marking. The aide-mémoire, originally prepared by Nixon, was re-written by Kissinger at 5 p.m. on March 17 after a meeting with Rabin that morning (see Document 104). Rabin saw a draft of the aide-mémoire on March 12. See Document 99.

[2] Nixon and Meir discussed arms for Israel on September 25. See footnote 2, Document 52.

or other arms into the Middle East as endangering the military balance. In these circumstances my Government would provide a substantial majority of the military assistance requested by your Government. At the same time, I want to reaffirm our intention to pursue a policy of seeking a negotiated settlement of the situation in the Middle East. As I stated on September 26, 1969, we expect the Government of Israel to adopt an understanding attitude with respect to our efforts. Finally, I would like to request that the Government of Israel terminate for a period of 60 days its air and other attacks against the UAR providing a complete cease-fire is observed by the other side and recognizing that there would be no official statements to this effect by either side. Any relative disadvantage suffered by Israel as a result of these restraints—for example, through the unimpeded building up of SAM sites—will be taken into account in replacement decisions for 1971.

104. Editorial Note

Over the course of the day on March 17, 1970, Assistant to the President for National Security Affairs Henry Kissinger and Israeli Ambassador Yitzhak Rabin held several conversations to discuss future U.S. economic and military assistance to Israel, a proposed cease-fire agreement between Israel and the UAR, and the discovery of Soviet personnel and new air defense systems inside Egypt. The first meeting took place at 10:15 a.m. and was held in the library of the White House residence. According to the memorandum of conversation, Rabin stated he would like to review the Israeli estimate of the "entire situation" of the Arab-Israeli conflict and reaffirmed that Kissinger was the only U.S. Government official to whom this information was being given. Rabin continued:

"As a result of the continued violations of the cease-fire, Israel had concluded that deep air attacks were the only way to prevent further escalation and to control Nasser's armed forces. Ambassador Rabin stated that the Israelis consider that the Soviet and Egyptian problem is not the fact that Egypt does not have a sufficient number of offensive aircraft or the equipment necessary to develop an efficient air defense capability. Also, both Egypt and the USSR recognize that the problem involves the inability of the Egyptians to operate the equipment.

"Ambassador Rabin continued that all the Israeli air attacks with a single accidental exception had been against Egyptian military targets and that these attacks had been extremely effective and caused great turbulence in Egypt. For example, Egyptian pilots have been sent to Syria to train, seven Egyptian Divisions along the Canal were pulled back resulting in severe confusion and disruption of Egypt's overall training plans. As a result of this, Nasser visited Moscow during the end of January to present the criticality of their situation to the Soviets. Apparently, the Soviets tried to handle the problem through the release of some public assurances and a decision to develop a more sophisticated air defense capability for Egypt. This was evidenced by mid-January when the Israelis noticed the beginning of 15 new air defense sites with unique and elaborate facilities (Ambassador Rabin showed Dr. Kissinger a schematic drawing of the T-type missile bunkers which were made of concrete and were 300 meters in length, 60 meters in width and 5 meters in height).

"Ambassador Rabin continued that initially the Israelis did not know what this new facility was and suspected that it was a new ground-to-ground missile site. Subsequently, they noticed the construction of a site in the area of the Aswan Dam and concluded that it had to be air defense because of the remoteness of the location. Since Israel concluded that these were new and sophisticated air defense facilities, they determined to concentrate their air effort against them in order to prevent their completion. Israel now believes that the sites have been prepared for SA–3 missiles despite the fact that the U.S. intelligence has described them as far more sophisticated than the SA–3 sites that have been observed in East Germany. Initial Egyptian reaction to the concentrated Israeli attacks was to bring their conventional antiaircraft artillery back from the Canal to provide greater protection in depth. They also tried to intercept with Egyptian aircraft but after several losses declined further air combat. The pattern of the new Egyptian sites appears to be designed to provide maximum protection over the Canal itself. This permits in-depth displacements since the SA–3 has a range of approximately 22 miles. Dr. Kissinger commented that this was a low-level missile. Ambassador Rabin confirmed this. Ambassador Rabin then concluded that if the Egyptians succeed in emplacing an SA–3 missile system of this sophistication, the Israelis will suffer an increase in both air losses and human casualties.

"Ambassador Rabin continued that because the Israeli attacks against the missile sites had been so effective, the Egyptians decided to seek another solution—one which might enable them to achieve a lull for two or three months, and one which would enable them to complete the sites and then resume the war of attrition. Rabin said they had hard evidence from one highly reliable source that this plan had been worked out with the Soviets over the period of 3 to 5 March and that it had been decided that they would concede on two of their five points and would permit the Soviets to start negotiations again within the two or four-power framework. There other conditions would remain firm:

"1. Insistence on total withdrawal, including Jerusalem.

"2. No face-to-face negotiations with Israel.

"3. Solution to the refugee program on the basis of the 1948 United Nations Resolution.

"Ambassador Rabin emphasized that Prime Minister Meir had concluded that this would be suicide for Israel. Mrs. Meir also expressed severe reservations about the feasibility of an undeclared cease-fire under these conditions for it would, in effect, permit Egypt to complete the sites and to gain time without a public commitment. This would thereby preserve their option to continue the war of attrition as soon as they considered themselves properly postured. Israel had concluded that the Soviets' objective is to attain these temporary conditions for Egypt, thus enabling Egypt to continue the war of attrition and also to deflect an affirmative decision by the U.S. on the Israeli plane request. Further, this strategy, Rabin added, would permit the continued erosion of the U.S. position with respect to Israel and the Middle East as a whole which had started with our more recent declarations of October 28, 1969 and December 9, 1969. In view of the preceding estimate, the President's proposal with respect to both the public statement and the private assurances on replacement aircraft was a cause of major concern.

"Mrs. Meir sees great danger in the U.S. position. The public statement would have incalculable impact not only on the Middle East but elsewhere and she, therefore, was making the following request:

"1. Modify the public announcement to make it more positive with the view not towards committing the U.S. to providing more planes but to more positively guarantee a preservation of current Israeli air capability.

"2. Concerning the political language in the public announcement, some insertion should be made reaffirming the U.S. determination to maintain the balance of power in the Middle East . . .

"3. In addition, Ambassador Rabin stated that Prime Minister Meir asks that the U.S. reconsider its position on the practical matter of providing replacement aircraft and that we also provide some positive public expression in our public statement.

"4. Finally, with respect to the cease-fire, Ambassador Rabin stated that Mrs. Meir had considered the issue in great depth and had come to the conclusion that she could accept the undeclared cease-fire under the conditions that there would be no public statement and that it constituted a complete cessation of military activity along the Canal.

"To implement the cease-fire, Mrs. Meir proposed the following conditions:

"1. Elimination of the 60 or 90 day restriction and substitute therefor a period of 3 to 5 days in which Israel would refrain from in-depth air attacks against Egypt. During this period, however, if the Egyptians violated the cease-fire by rifle or artillery fire, for example, Israel would respond in kind, i.e., with an identical response.

"—After the three or five day modified moratorium, if Egypt continued to violate the cease-fire, then Israel would not feel constrained to respond in like manner but would not be limited in their retaliation by either type or distance of penetration.

"—Israel would require one day's notice in order to implement the three to five day moratorium.

"Dr. Kissinger asked what would be Israel's attitude if the Soviets and Egypt agree to these conditions but in doing so continue to complete the SA–3 sites. Ambassador Rabin replied that Israel will have to accept this risk, providing they abide by the total cease-fire.

"Ambassador Rabin then commented that even though Golda Meir would accept the foregoing conditions, she was actually furious that she was being forced to do so but, on balance, considered that Israel could accept these conditions in order to avoid higher costs. In accepting these conditions, however, Mrs. Meir felt that the U.S. should double the number of planes to be provided under the replacement formula, i.e., the U.S. should agree to deliver up to 8 Phantoms and 20 Skyhawks by the end of CY 1970 and that an identical number should be provided by the middle of CY 71. Ambassador Rabin then complained that U.S. calculations of attrition differ from Israel's. He pointed out the U.S. seems to consider only the loss of U.S.-provided planes while, in fact, Israel must consider overall inventory, regardless of source."

After Rabin summarized Prime Minister Meir's position and discussed further discrepancies in U.S. and Israeli intelligence estimates, Kissinger explained that the U.S. estimate of the cease-fire proposal, which was only known to the President, General Haig, and himself, was that it would help Israel by providing the United States an additional leverage on the Soviets. He added that President Nixon was "Israel's best friend," and wanted to do "everything possible" to resolve the situation. He then told Rabin:

"The President had asked him to assure the Ambassador that he would like to satisfy the whole Israeli arms request . . . [and] stated that the President was anxious to maintain Israel's current advantage, that he has given Dr. Kissinger full power of attorney on this matter but that unfortunately the realities of the situation prevent him from utilizing it. . . .

"Dr. Kissinger stated that he has no intention of deceiving Israel, stating 'it would be a simple matter under these conditions to get Israel to accept the cease-fire on a shallow promise but the U.S. has no interest in doing so.'" (National Archives, Nixon Presidential Materials, NSC Files, Box 612, Country Files, Middle East, Israeli Aid)

In a memorandum to President Nixon the following day, March 18, Kissinger summarized Rabin's position:

"At the first meeting at 10:15 a.m. he said Israel was accepting your proposition [see Document 103] with the following provisos:

"1. That the Egyptian ceasefire be total and not confined to air activity and that your Aide-Mémoire be changed accordingly;

"2. That the public announcement of our decision state that we were replacing Israeli losses;

"3. That we commit ourselves to 8 Phantoms and 20 Skyhawks to replace Israeli losses this year and that a similar number would be required in 1971, especially in light of the SA–3s becoming operational and increasing the rate of attrition." (Ibid., Box 652, Country Files, Middle East, Middle East, Vol. I)

Kissinger saw Rabin again at 4 p.m. in the afternoon of March 17. Rabin handed Kissinger a piece of paper that outlined the actions Israel was prepared to take under a cease-fire and indicated that he would be prepared to sign this on behalf of his government. Kissinger thereupon informed the Ambassador that the United States Government could not change the announcement and would not commit to a flat replacement figure. Rabin took the view that the combination of these decisions "condemned Israel to the same haggling with respect to replacements that they had already experienced with respect to new planes; in short that our commitment was not a commitment." Kissinger replied that he would arrange an appointment with the President the next day to set his mind at ease. (Ibid.)

Later that evening, Kissinger discussed the Israeli arms request over the telephone with President Nixon. A portion of their conversation reads:

"P: On this Israeli thing, I think you should play it that this is a damn good deal and we will play ours to the hilt and we want them to play theirs. I will re-assure them.

"K: If they don't get reassurances on the 8 [Phantoms] & 20 [Skyhawks] they will kick over the whole deal.

"P: I will assure them of the 8 & 20.

"K: They don't want to be in an endless negotiation. That's my guess. I put it to Rabin very strongly after our talk at lunch and he seemed extremely disturbed.

"P: The 8 & 20—I will back it up to the bureaucracy. Let him play our game. It's very important.

"K: Right." (Transcript of a telephone conversation between Nixon and Kissinger, March 17, 1970, 8:07 p.m.; ibid., Henry Kissinger Telephone Conversation Transcripts Box 4, Chronological File)

Before President Nixon had the opportunity to reassure the Israelis of the deal, however, the Defense Intelligence Agency confirmed reports of Soviet SA–3 sites manned by Soviet personnel in Egypt. Upon learning the news, Rabin called Kissinger at 10:10 p.m. to inform him that he was cancelling the agreement:

"R: About 2 hours ago the DIA informed our military attaché that they have got information that 10 sites of SA–3, including a considerable number of Russian experts—that their estimation will be 1500 experts and they are foreign, that is to say Russian. We got this information from them two hours ago. In light of this information, I feel that it's my obligation to inform the Prime Minister that we have this information and as a result that all that I have told you will have changed.

"K: I understand.

"R: I am sorry but in light of such vital information I feel that it is my duty to tell my government and it may decide to change it on the basis of this information.

"K: When you saw the sites, what did you think?

"R: There's a difference between thinking and knowing. Third, I am sure that the U.S. Government should also re-consider this decision in light of this information if its message to Congress is to be taken seriously. I cannot find words to explain and to say what would be the meaning and interpretation of the decision by your government in light of the new development. As a result, I must await instructions from my government and I would like as a result not to have the meeting tomorrow.

"K: All right.

"R: I hope you understand.

"K: I understand." (Transcript of a telephone conversation between Kissinger and Rabin, March 17, 10:10 p.m.; ibid.)

In his March 18 memorandum to Nixon summarizing the day's events and offering his assessment of the options now available to the President, Kissinger wrote:

"I believe that State's inability to change the announcement and my inability to guarantee a flat replacement figure convinced the Israelis that they were getting nothing for the ceasefire except a written for an oral promise. My views are as follows:

"1. The Israelis are getting desperate. Convinced that they have nothing to lose, they may well attack. Indeed, had we followed the original scenario and made the original announcement when it was scheduled last week, the situation would probably be out of control.

"2. I would be remiss in my duty if I did not tell you that our course involves the most serious dangers of a Middle East war and of a profound misunderstanding by the Soviets.

"3. You have two choices:

"a. To proceed on our course and make the announcement but use the SA–3 evidence to make a flat promise to Israel of 8 Phantoms and 20 Skyhawks for each of the next two years in return for a ceasefire.
"b. To use the SA–3 evidence to order a complete restudy in the bureaucracy of the issue of hardware to Israel coupled with an appeal to the Soviets to stop the introduction of Soviet combat personnel into Egypt. At this stage I lean toward the second." (Ibid., NSC Files, Box 652, Country Files, Middle East, Middle East, Vol. I)

While Nixon decided to defer any commitment to provide Israel with additional aircraft (see Document 105), he nonetheless ordered a restudy of the issue in National Security Study Memorandum 93 (Document 108) in light of Israel's evidence regarding Soviet-manned SA–3s in Egypt. He also met with Rabin on March 18 to discuss the arms request and Soviet involvement in the Middle East. The meeting was held in the President's private office in the Executive Office Building. The President's Daily Diary makes no mention of any meeting with Rabin on March 18, but Kissinger later prepared a record of the conversation that reads as follows:

"The President said he wanted to see Rabin to tell him one thing—that the line of communication to the President was via me [Kissinger]. He knew that the Israelis had legitimate concerns about their security and that they had some doubts on whether we would not nitpick them to death, if they felt their security was in danger. He therefore wanted to tell Rabin to let Kissinger know if the balance of power was in danger. We have great difficulty looking at the problem massively but if you put it to us in an informal way, we will find our way to solve the problem. Quite apart from helping Israel which means a lot to us, we don't want the power balance to change. Within our bureaucracy, there are many who don't agree. They think our real interests in the Middle East lie with the Arabs but those others don't have my power. I am aware of the introduction of Soviet SA–3s and I hope you knock them out. You can't let them build up.

"Rabin said I know I am speaking to the most powerful man of the most powerful country in the world. I must tell you that the public announcement which you will make produces great concern. It will give great encouragement to the Arabs because they believe Israel has been left alone to defend itself by its oldest friend. It will give great encouragement to the Soviets because it shows them that they are free to do what they want and it will lead them into greater intransigence towards the Arabs. It will have great consequence for the other states in the Middle East, going as far as the Persian Gulf who will draw the conclusion that you have been forced off your course by the Soviets. We Israelis have no one to turn to except to you the President of the United States. We believe in freedom and human dignity and we will defend ourselves but we are only 2.5 million [people]. We would like to knock out the SAMs but we now know that if we knock out the SAM sites we will face the Soviet Union alone. I am in no position to disbelieve the President of the United States but our survival is at stake and I am deeply worried.

"The President replied, when you see that the need exists, convey it to us. What this means is what my letter [Document 101] says.

"Rabin said the need exists now. What is the balance of power in the world today? Egypt has 160 supersonic planes. Syria has 100 supersonic planes. We have less than 90. We are brave but we can't be superhuman. We will do what I can but the Arabs don't need more arms. And as soon as they get greater competence, we will be in mortal danger.

"The President [said] when you are in danger, let Kissinger know. We will get it done." (Record of conversation between President Nixon and Israeli Ambassador Rabin; National Archives, Nixon Presidential Materials, NSC Files, Box 612, Country Files, Middle East, Israeli Aid)

In his memoirs, Rabin recalled that during his conversation with Nixon, he (Rabin) launched into "an emotional charged speech about the perils of a small nation fighting for her life." Rabin added:

"Whenever the U.S. is believed to be reducing her support for Israel, the Arabs revive their old hope of overcoming us by force. And the longer the war of attrition goes on, the more the Soviets will flaunt their insolence. They will interpret the United States' decision on arms as a sign of weakness. And if the Russians can station SAM–3s and man them with their own technicians while America continues to deprive Israel of arms, they will take it to mean they can go even further! Once again, Mr. President, I appeal to you as the only man in whose sympathy and understand we have trust: Give us the arms we need!

"I was a bit startled at myself—and all the more at the total silence that ensued. Evidently my emotion had been infectious. The pause went on for a minute or so—to me it seemed like an eternity—as the president sat mute with his eyes averted. Finally he said, 'Thank you for putting it that way, Mr. Ambassador. I understand you, and I understand Israel's situation. You can be sure that you'll get your arms. I only want to go about it in a different way.' He paused again, and when he continued speaking I thought I could detect a strange glint in his eye. 'Do you have any more information about the SAM–3s? How do you feel about those missiles being manned by the Russians? Have you considered attacking them?'

"Totally flabbergasted, I blurted out: 'Attack the Russian?' Strange, I thought to myself, how complex are the motives of a great power. Was the president suggesting that for fear that we would attack the Russian missiles, with all the attendant risks, the United States would avoid strengthening Israel? Or was it conceivable that he meant precisely the opposite? Could it be that the president of the United States was intimating his interest in our attacking the missiles and their Russian crews? And if he knew that Israel intended to do so, would he provide us with all the planes we had requested—and perhaps even more?

"The president did not reply further to my outburst, and, frankly, I didn't want him to elaborate on the subject. If he had said, 'Yes, go ahead and attack,' it was doubtful that Israel would have been able or willing to. If he said, 'No, do not attack them under any circumstances!' and developments later made it imperative for Israel to destroy the missiles, she would run the risk of defying the president of the United States and disrupting relations with her strongest ally." (*The Rabin Memoirs*, pages 171–173)

105. Telegram From the Department of State to Certain Diplomatic Posts[1]

Washington, March 21, 1970, 0050Z.

41693. Subject: USG Decision on Israeli Aircraft Request.

1. Septel forwards text announcement which Secretary plans make at press conference noon, Monday, March 23 re Israeli aircraft request.[2] In essence, announcement says USG is deferring for now any commitment to provide Israel additional aircraft, since (a) we have identified no present military need, and (b) we believe restraint on part all concerned is required if dangerous trend toward higher levels of military confrontation is to be reversed and atmosphere created in which opportunities for peaceful settlement can be more fruitfully explored. At same time announcement makes clear that deferral of decision will be reconsidered if action by Soviets or others upsets military balance or if

---

[1] Source: National Archives, Nixon Presidential Materials, NSC Files, Box 606, Country Files, Middle East, Israel, Vol. IV. Secret; Priority; Nodis; Noforn Until Acted Upon. Drafted on March 19 by William D. Brewer (NEA/ARP); cleared by Sisco and Kissinger and in AF, EUR, and NEA; and approved by Rogers. Sent to London, Paris, Rome, Bonn, Jidda, Amman, Beirut, Kuwait, Rabat, Tunis, Tripoli, Cairo, Algiers, and Khartoum. Repeated to Tel Aviv, Jerusalem, Dhahran, Moscow, Belgrade, Bucharest, USUN, Ankara, Tehran, New Delhi, and Rawalpindi.

[2] The text of the statement and the transcript of the news conference that followed are printed in the Department of State *Bulletin*, April 13, 1970, pp. 477–484.

we believe political developments warrant. Action addressees instructed inform host government of this decision at highest possible level at or about noon Washington time on March 23 and provide them copy of announcement. This message being sent now to facilitate arranging appointments which should be made for as close to noon Washington time on Monday as local circumstances make feasible. Posts are to adhere strictly to this guidance; if there are questions which you cannot answer, request you report them without offering prior comments to Government to which you are accredited.

2. *For Arab Capitals:* In conveying foregoing, you should stress following:

(a) In taking this step, USG has taken into account urgings our Arab friends. We see it as positive contribution to improve atmosphere for progress towards peaceful settlement Arab/Israeli impasse. Our decision reflects constant USG policy to do all we can to achieve peace in Mideast in accordance with Security Council Resolution 242. It was taken despite strong Israeli desire for positive decision now and such recent developments as French Mirage deal with Libya. This in itself should sufficiently demonstrate our determination do all we can facilitate relaxation present tensions and progress towards peaceful settlement.

(b) In USG view, only lasting security for all parties to current dispute lies in peace, and we believe restraint will contribute to that goal. In taking its decision, USG believes it is acting with restraint and thus serving the cause of peace. But clapping cannot be done with one hand. Others must also exercise restraint and show themselves willing cooperate in genuine efforts resolve present impasse if settlement is to be attained.

(c) On December 9, 1969, the Secretary of State outlined publicly our views as to what framework for a settlement should look like.[3] Those views are spelled out in proposals submitted in major power talks, which have been developed in consultation with the parties and other interested states. So far, there has regrettably been little positive reaction, particularly from Cairo. Our present decision reflects what the Secretary then said—that our policy is balanced and fair. We earnestly hope that those concerned will now take a constructive view of principles we have set forth, which we think provide fair basis for moving forward.

(d) Specifically, USG decision offers Soviets and parties themselves major opportunity find alternatives to further sterile military escalation. Arabs have not always taken advantage of such constructive

---

[3] See Document 73.

opportunities. There have been too many missed opportunities in past; our arms decision offers a further opportunity. Now is time to examine with renewed seriousness and sense of purpose all possible avenues to a settlement. There will be no settlement without compromise on both sides.

3. *For Cairo and Amman:* You should make a major pitch for a positive reaction to October 28 and December 18 proposals.[4] Nasser remains key and cannot get a settlement by standing aloof and uncommitted in relationship to these proposals.

4. *For Moscow:* We will be calling in Dobrynin to put case to Soviets in strongest possible terms that we expect corresponding restraint and constructive effort or peace front from them.[5] You should take no repeat no action in Moscow at this time.

5. *For Western Eur Capitals:* In conveying our decision, you should inform host govts of pitch we are making in support of it per paras 2 and 3 above and emphasize our conviction that USG restraint now provides Soviets and UAR, in particular, with major opportunity for forward movement out of present impasse. We hope host governments will support us on political front in order to keep up pressure.

6. *For all addressees: FYI.* Press in Israel and UAR has already been speculating that no public US commitment on aircraft can be expected but that secret commitments have been or will be made. If this question comes up, you may say that we have made no secret deal to provide additional aircraft to Israel. As for future, we cannot say what we may do or how we may do it since this depends on how military and political situation develops. *End FYI.*

Rogers

---

[4] See Documents 58 and 78.

[5] Rogers met with Dobrynin on March 25, as reported in telegram 44153 to Moscow, March 26. (National Archives, Nixon Presidential Materials, NSC Files, Box 725, Country Files, Europe, USSR) The text of Rogers's oral statement to Dobrynin was transmitted in telegram 44154 to Moscow, March 28, printed in *Foreign Relations,* 1969–1976, volume XII, Soviet Union, January 1969–October 1970, Document 148. See also ibid., Document 151.

106. Telegram From the Embassy in Israel to the Department of State[1]

Tel Aviv, March 23, 1970, 1630Z.

1502. Subj: Decision on Aircraft and Economic Aid for Israel. Ref: State 41927.[2]

1. Ambassador, accompanied by DCM, called on Prime Minister Meir at 1030 a.m. March 23, handed her copy of text of Secretary's announcement on Israel's military and economic requests (State 41924)[3] and briefed her on President's decision in accordance State 41921 and previous.[4] Mrs. Meir was accompanied by Foreign Minister Eban, her Special Assistants Herzog and Dinitz and Acting Assistant Director General MFA Elizur.[5]

2. Mrs. Meir said that she valued immensely President Nixon's personal message.[6] Regarding final sentence of last additional point made by Ambassador, to effect that for U.S. part confidence in Israel's fundamental intentions remain as steadfast and firm as they have during all the years of Israel's nationhood, she said that this was true on Israel's part as well for the U.S. She said that she would study announcement and Ambassador's presentation, but from having heard oral presentation she could say that she would not lose sight of positive elements she had heard. Facts that decision was held in abeyance, and was on interim basis, and that U.S. would replace and add on aircraft were fundamentally positive and she was glad to take note of them. On economic aid, Finance Minister Sapir (whom she described as "split personality", meaning he wants both aircraft and to save money)

---

[1] Source: National Archives, Nixon Presidential Materials, NSC Files, Box 612, Country Files, Middle East, Israeli Aid. Secret; Immediate; Nodis. The telegram is attached to a March 23 memorandum to Kissinger in which Eliot wrote: "The attached telegram from Tel Aviv sets forth the Israeli response to our decision on aircraft and economic aid for Israel. In view of its sensitivity I would be grateful if you would limit its distribution in the White House to as few as possible."

[2] Dated March 23. (Ibid., RG 59, Central Files 1970–73, POL ISR–US)

[3] Telegram 41924 to Tel Aviv, March 23, transmitted the text of the Secretary's announcement. (Ibid.) See footnote 2, Document 105.

[4] Telegram 41921 to Tel Aviv, March 23, was a correction to telegram 41705 to Tel Aviv, March 21, which provided guidance to Barbour on briefing Meir on the U.S. decision regarding military and economic assistance to Israel. Rogers also briefed Rabin that morning in Washington, as reported in telegram 42545 to Tel Aviv, March 24. (All in National Archives, Nixon Presidential Materials, NSC Files, Box 606, Country Files, Middle East, Israel, Vol. IV)

[5] Elizur was also Director of North American Affairs, Israeli Ministry of Foreign Affairs.

[6] Document 101.

would find this gratifying. It was especially important that USG was prepared to deal with long-term needs, and not only on one-year basis.

3. On question of aircraft and balance of power, Mrs. Meir continued, there had been some discussions between intelligence services and military concerning considerable discrepancy between Israel's estimates and those of U.S. GOI convinced its figures right and hopes this will rapidly be cleared up. She wished Israeli figures were not right but this is not simply case of winning an argument. A week or ten days ago she would only have said that she was "concerned about rumors" regarding SA–3 missiles in Egypt, but now everyone knows that they are there. Ambassador agreed evidence points in that direction. Mrs. Meir said she was convinced of it. With missiles come Soviet personnel and number of Russians in Egypt is growing.

4. Question is, said Prime Minister, what elements are taken into account in deciding balance of power. It cannot be denied SA–2 and SA–3 are defensive. If we lose sight of other elements, we can say answer to SA–3s is to keep out of Egypt and SA–3 will not then operate. But we know this implies that Israeli men on Suez Canal are to be objects of immense UAR artillery (and no one says there is balance of power on artillery alone) and only way to overcome this is to use aircraft in which Israel is superior not in numbers but in men. In this context, SA–3 becomes a deadly weapon in that it prevents Israel from using weapons in which it is superior. She was not a military person but did not need to be to understand this. All of this means that if Israel does not consent to sit and take a beating on Canal, it will have to consider if it can afford to use planes and men. This is extremely serious matter for Israel. This connection between so-called defensive weapons and Israel's use of planes should be understood.

5. Mrs. Meir continued that there was no doubt Kurdish agreement would make it possible for Iraq to send more troops to Jordan.[7] Ambassador replied this might be true if agreement works. As friend of Kurds, Mrs. Meir said, she hoped that it would. One might even say, she went on, that at this moment Israel was not in such a critical position, which is right. But when the month comes when the last four Phantoms arrive, the end of this position is in sight. Ambassador Barbour noted USG was prepared to discuss further aircraft on short notice if need arises. What Israel needs, Mrs. Meir said, was certainty, but it would appear that Israel still has long negotiations ahead. She wanted to be able to infer that it means a lot to be told that USG will

---

[7] Signed March 11, the agreement provided for Kurdish autonomy within Iraq, which allowed the Iraqi Government to move troops elsewhere that had been fighting Kurds in the northern part of the country. (*New York Times*, March 13, 1970, p. 10)

grant additional and replacement aircraft promptly. Will it be possible, she asked, to come to agreement promptly that this is the moment?

6. Ambassador said he would like to break in here to comment. It would appear that we have sufficient contacts to be able continuously to reassess situation and reconcile differences regarding facts. He did not see need to open new channel for this purpose.

7. Prime Minister continued saying that one more element of situation, not concerned with missiles or bombs but extremely important in Israel's situation, was mental attitude of Israel's neighbors. Positive elements of U.S. reply cannot be made public (Ambassador interjected positive elements were in Secretary's public announcement) and question is how decision will be interpreted by Israel's neighbors and USSR. They will read, listen, and reach own conclusion: Israel is not getting planes now. They will include word "now" but will not emphasize it. From radio, TV and newspapers everyone will learn that Israel received negative answer from only supplier available. This will certainly not put them in mood that President, Secretary of State and Israelis want, to make even a modest step towards peace or even cease-fire. This certainly not intended by USG to be reaction but will be.

8. Ambassador said this was question of assessment. U.S. would not rule out Prime Minister's assessment, but feels our decision puts Soviets and Egypt on spot and if they do not make moves towards peace in reasonable time we will know decision has not had political and psychological effects we wanted.

9. Mrs. Meir said that what Soviets were doing in Egypt they were doing in face of President's having taken time to appraise situation seriously. If Soviets had least intention to take some kind of token step towards peace or cease-fire they would have done so, but they have not. The audacity of what they had been doing while President was weighing his decision! Certainly no one can deny that this creates a new situation.

10. Question was, Ambassador said, what created this situation? Why did Soviets bring in SA–3? Our feeling is that this was because Phantoms were getting through in deep penetration raids. Sure, answered Mrs. Meir, but why were deep penetration raids necessary? Because of shooting on Canal!

There should not be any difference between US and Israel on this. GOI had given long consideration before beginning raids but could not just see boys falling on Canal because Israel did not have artillery. Egyptians want to stop Israel and to prevent its self-defense. Israel is not trying to occupy Cairo and is willing to stop when they stop. Let Nasser argue from a position of strength, say that he is now ready to stop. But he will not do so. Delivery of SA–3s and US decision against planes for Israel will just encourage him to go on. What this does to Israeli people, she said, she did not need to explain to Ambassador. She must say something that is neither political nor military: she is sorry for Israeli people for having to be disappointed in this way. This is a burden they do not deserve. Israelis are literate people, they will read and listen. What will remain to them will be negative answer from USG. Some will make a fair analysis of US announcement, but negative aspects will stand out.

11. Ambassador replied it would be unfortunate if GOI does not play up positive factors, especially that USG is prepared replace attrition losses and provide additional aircraft if situation changes. Mrs. Meir replied government could not go to people and say there is nothing to worry about. She did not want to be misunderstood, she appreciated that decision was only being held in abeyance. However, it was too much to expect government to say Quote never mind Unquote to people because she did not say this to herself. If she had been asked two weeks ago, she would have been sure decision was going to be positive. She had been sure because it was so evident that Israel needs aircraft, and that Russians carrying out anti-Israel propaganda more viciously than ever before.

12. What you are saying, Ambassador told Prime Minister, is that GOI would take agreement by USG to start negotiating now for 25 Phantoms and 100 Skyhawks as more valuable for Israel's security than all the firm and broad commitments which USG says must be matter of confidence between governments. Eban replied that affirmative answer on aircraft would have caused increase in this mutual confidence. What divides us, he said, is effect of Secretary's statement: whether it is enough for Arabs to know Israel will not get aircraft now, or whether it would be better for them to know with certainty that Israel will get them in future. USG has decided not to give them this certainty. It is enormously important that they know Israel's capacity for future. As US doctrine itself holds, deterrence is most important. What people think about future determines how they act now. US decision has in effect been known for a week and one can test response already. Soviet attitude in Four Power talks is almost an insult to USG and GOI. Eban could not see what value US attaches to this uncertainty.

13. US had had opportunity, Eban continued, which it has passed over, to give Nasser and Russians clear picture that no future attack on Israel can succeed. He could not see reason for not giving both Israel and Arabs this certainty.

14. Ambassador told Mrs. Meir that American Embassies in Moscow and Arab capitals would be making point that we expect Soviets and UAR to react productively to our decision and to make sure that they realize that USG is not weakening its position.

15. Referring to Ambassador's remark concerning how GOI should treat announcement, Eban said that GOI would not be able to play up points like USG willingness to provide replacements for lost aircraft. USG could do this better (Embassy note: there has not been any public announcement of any Phantom loss).

16. Mrs. Meir continued that getting replacements presents a serious matter but it should also be understood that something has happened in Egypt that changes situation entirely. Ambassador replied that President recognizes that. Eban said he hoped reappraisal could begin right away and Mrs. Meir joined in to say that should be done Quote almost immediately Unquote.

17. On economic matters, Ambassador said, we would envisage discussions between experts here on long-term matters. If GOI agreed we could work out question of who and when. Mrs. Meir said it was extremely important that door had been left open on long-term economic aid.

18. Meeting concluded with Eban saying that statement to be issued by GOI this evening after Secretary's announcement would include all elements that Prime Minister had indicated.[8] It would express disappointment but also point out things to which Israel attaches importance. For own good, Mrs. Meir concluded, GOI would not leave out any positive element.

19. *Comment:* Meeting took place at rest home near Jerusalem where Mrs. Meir is spending brief period. Since elements of US decision anticipated by GOI, there were no surprises in our statement or presentation, but affirmative elements therein were well received by Prime Minister. Principal point of difference remains, we believe, that Israelis have no hope whatsoever that reasonable US attitude will produce any forthcoming reaction from Arabs or Russians but rather are strongly convinced that only complete certainty of Israeli invulnerability will deter UAR from false hopes of military victory. While Mrs. Meir was calm and unemotional during meeting, it is clear that she feels deep disappointment that affirmative decision on aircraft was not given at this time. We can expect early Israeli request for reassessment of situation in light of discrepancies revealed between US and Israeli estimates of present Arab military strength and evidence of introduction of SA–3 missiles and Soviet personnel to man them.

Barbour

---

[8] Eban's statement on the evening of March 23 expressed "disappointment and concern" and pointed to the "interim" nature of the U.S. position. (*New York Times*, March 24, 1970, p. A12) The next day, Rabin also gave Rogers a talking paper, which provided further detail on the official Israeli response to the U.S. decision, as reported in telegram 42624 to Tel Aviv, March 24. (National Archives, Nixon Presidential Materials, NSC Files, Box 606, Country Files, Middle East, Israel, Vol. IV)

107. Telegram From the Department of State to the Embassy in the Soviet Union[1]

Washington, April 2, 1970, 0115Z.

47932. 1. At working lunch April 1, Dobrynin and Sisco agreed that in this first follow-up meeting after Dobrynin's session with Secretary March 25[2] it would be well to examine as precisely as possible where we are and to try to determine what possibilities of agreement were. Principal results of meeting were:

(a) Soviets continue unwilling to join appeal to parties to restore ceasefire, but propose as alternative that US and USSR work quietly with Cairo and Tel Aviv to achieve an informal understanding on de facto ceasefire;

(b) Soviets continue adamant against arms limitation talks on ground Arabs feel this would only result in freezing a military balance clearly favorable to Israel;

(c) Soviets are willing to consider a formulation on peace along lines proposed by US to include explicitly obligation that there be QUOTE a cessation of war and establishment of peace UNQUOTE provided we are willing to commit ourselves to total withdrawal. Dobrynin explicitly specified this included Israeli withdrawal from Sharm al-Shaykh and Gaza, with latter to be explicitly designated as an Arab territory.

(d) Soviets propose a slight variant of past USSR proposal on relationship between timing of withdrawal of Israeli forces and entry into effect of peace obligations. Variant was described by Dobrynin as follows: (1) Once agreed document was deposited with UN, both sides would be obligated not to take any actions contrary to agreement; (2) Withdrawal would proceed by stages, and UN forces would be introduced at the end of the first stage during which UAR personnel would be limited to clearing Suez Canal rather than be introduced in area initially evacuated by Israeli forces. (3) At the end of the first stage there would be a de jure acceptance by UAR of both cessation of war and the state of peace. (4) With the understanding that the second stage of withdrawal would not be a long one (a month or two), UN forces would occupy the additional territories evacuated in that stage, and UAR forces would return to the Sinai with a UN buffer retained be-

---

[1] Source: National Archives, Nixon Presidential Materials, NSC Files, Box 1186, Saunders Files, Middle East Negotiations Files, Middle East Settlement—US–USSR Talks. Secret; Nodis. Drafted on April 1 by Sisco, cleared by Adolph Dubs (EUR/SOV), and approved by Sisco. Repeated to USUN.

[2] See footnote 5, Document 105.

tween the opposing sides. Dobrynin refused to be drawn out on the area of demilitarization or on whether UN buffer was to be on one side or on both sides of the border.

(e) Dobrynin refused to agree to the formulation on peace contained in Point 2 of the October 28th document[3] but insisted that the formulation USSR has in mind is close to that of the US. When asked whether he agreed to US formulation as it related to the fedayeen, he did not accept this formulation but maintained Soviets had language in mind that might approximate this.

(f) On the question of negotiations, Dobrynin said Soviets no longer can accept present formulation on Rhodes formula, reiterating argument made previously that interpretation given to it by the parties has made this unacceptable.[4] When pressed by Sisco for an alternative formula, Dobrynin said something roughly along the following lines: The parties will have contact between themselves through Jarring with the understanding he could use various forms.

(g) On Sharm al-Shaykh, Dobrynin insisted that there be explicit reference to UN force, its removal being subject to major power veto, and indicated willingness to suggest that UN Secretary General consult with the parties on question of composition and command of that force. He categorically precluded any Soviet troops being involved in such a UN force.

2. Sisco pressed Dobrynin on two procedural points without success: (a) Sisco suggested that while Dobrynin exposition was useful and helpful in understanding Soviet position, best vehicle for making progress would be for Dobrynin to offer specific new language as emendation to October 28th document which we consider to be a joint US–USSR effort and not solely an American product; and (b) Sisco suggested that in next session, which now set for afternoon April 6,[5] he and Dobrynin discuss all other points in order to be sure that there are not other significant areas of disagreement. With respect to first point, Dobrynin insisted that he was under instructions to talk in terms of emendation of the Soviet June 1969 paper.[6] Re (b), Dobrynin refused to focus on these other points unless and until US reacted to latest concrete Soviet suggestions. Sisco pointed out these gave rise to difficulties since (1) there were a number of points of difference between June and Oc-

---

[3] Document 58.

[4] See footnote 2, Document 53.

[5] Sisco and Dobrynin met on April 6, as reported in telegram 50459 to Moscow, April 8. (National Archives, Nixon Presidential Materials, NSC Files, Box 340, Subject Files, Dobrynin/Kissinger) For Saunders's summary and analysis of the dialogue among Dobrynin, Rogers, and Sisco during March and the first week of April, see *Foreign Relations, 1969–1976*, volume XII, Soviet Union, January 1969–October 1970, Document 151.

[6] See Document 34.

tober documents, (2) October document was based on a precise format in which obligations were undertaken between parties in relationship to one another, whereas Soviet June document was considerably less so, and (3) Soviets were asking us to react and to make concession on concrete points of particular interest to them in circumstances where US did not even know whether common ground could be found on these decisive points or just where we stood on other matters such as freedom of passage through Suez Canal, Straits of Tiran, refugee question, etc.

3. During meeting, Sisco also said he wished to raise one broad question which he thought more fundamental than any other in determining whether common ground can be achieved: Would Soviets be willing to agree to guidelines for Jarring based on assumption of other than total withdrawal? Dobrynin said he could not reply to this question and suggested he and Sisco concentrate on concrete points they have been discussing.

Comment: Above exposition by Dobrynin represents no appreciable advance in Soviet position.[7] It does contain appearance of greater oral flexibility and a few additional enticements (e.g., timing of peace, possible new formulation on negotiating procedures). Our inclination is to continue efforts smoke Dobrynin out and press for written counter language from Soviets, and, meanwhile, to show no signs of give in our position. Would appreciate Ambassador Beam's comment on this tactic.

Rogers

---

[7] According to the memorandum of conversation of Kissinger's meeting with Dobrynin on April 7, the Soviet Ambassador said that he "had come to the conclusion that talking to Sisco was getting to be a waste of time" and added that "it would be good if I [Kissinger] intervened." See *Foreign Relations, 1969–1976,* volume XII, January 1969–October 1970, Document 150.

108. National Security Study Memorandum 93[1]

Washington, April 13, 1970.

TO
- The Secretary of State
- The Secretary of Defense
- The Director of Central Intelligence

SUBJECT
- The Arab-Israeli Military Balance

The President has directed that, as a follow-up to the study produced in response to NSSM 81[2] and in the light of recent exchanges with Israeli intelligence representatives,[3] further studies be prepared which will provide the following:

—Present intelligence estimates of Israeli and Arab air order of battle. The study should (1) identify U.S. and Israeli estimates and (2) where there are significant differences explain the reasons for the differences as specifically as possible.

—Present detailed intelligence assessments of the principal indicators of Arab air capability. The study should (1) identify U.S. and Israeli assessments and (2) where there are significant differences explain the reasons for the differences insofar as possible.

—An assessment of the present effective Arab-Israeli military balance. This study should present a refinement of the analysis in the NSSM 81 paper in the light of any revision in estimates of quantitative and qualitative factors and in the light of any improvement in analytical technique.

---

[1] Source: National Archives, Nixon Presidential Materials, NSC Files, NSC Institutional Files (H-Files), Box H–171, National Security Study Memoranda. Secret; Sensitive. A copy was sent to the Chairman of the Joint Chiefs of Staff.

[2] NSSM 81 is Document 63. For a summary of the study, see Document 93.

[3] Led by Major General Aaharon Yariv, Israeli intelligence officials met with U.S. officials between April 5 and 9, including sessions with Sisco and Saunders, to present Israel's case for further shipments of U.S. aircraft based, in part, on the participation of Soviet pilots in operational flights in Egypt. (Memorandum from Saunders to Kissinger, April 6; National Archives, Nixon Presidential Materials, NSC Files, Box 606, Country Files, Middle East, Israel, Vol. IV, and memorandum from Saunders to Kissinger, April 9; ibid., NSC Institutional Files (H-Files), Box H–171, National Security Study Memoranda) Regarding the new level of Soviet military involvement in the United Arab Republic, Meir wrote to Nixon on April 7: "It is inevitable that these developments will before long become public knowledge. I am convinced, however, that an extremely grave situation would arise if the publication of this new phase in Soviet involvement were not followed urgently and immediately by a clear and vigorous American public reaction on the highest level of authority." (Ibid., Box 1155, Saunders Files, Middle East Negotiations Files)

The NSC Ad Hoc Group created by NSSM 81 will be reactivated for the purpose of assembling this study.[4] The study will be submitted by May 15 to the President's Assistant for National Security Affairs for reference to the Special Review Group.[5]

Henry A. Kissinger

[4] See Document 112 and footnote 2 thereto.

[5] The Ad Hoc Special Review Group met on May 21 and May 28, the minutes of which are printed as Documents 117 and 119.

109. Telegram From the Embassy in Israel to the Department of State[1]

Tel Aviv, April 17, 1970, 1130Z.

1976. For President and Secretary from Sisco.

1. A few impressions of my two-hour meeting with PM Golda Meir[2] and some related reflections on trip so far may be of interest.

2. I found her disappointed over arms decision, but reflecting deep and genuine confidence in President and affection for him and ready promptly to proceed quietly and discreetly with US officials in future discussions on basis small packages not large publicized shopping bags.

3. In Cairo I found Nasser[3] resigned to reliance on Soviets and with a fixation on Quote Phantoms Unquote. Equally, Mrs. Meir came back time again to Quote additional aircraft Unquote pleading Quote give us benefit of doubt Unquote as to our needs since for Israel Quote it is to be or not to be Unquote.

4. As expected, neither in Cairo nor in Tel Aviv did I detect any prospect of changes in their respective maximum positions or of their moving toward acceptance of October and December proposals as

[1] Source: National Archives, Nixon Presidential Materials, NSC Files, Box 606, Country Files, Middle East, Israel, Vol. IV. Secret; Priority; Nodis.

[2] Sisco visited Israeli and Arab capitals April 8–24. He met with Meir on the afternoon of April 16. The full report of their discussion is in telegram 1963 from Tel Aviv, April 16. (Ibid.)

[3] Sisco met with Nasser on the evening of April 12. The full report of their discussion is in telegram 794 from Cairo, April 12. (Ibid., Box 635, Country Files, Middle East, UAR, Vol. III)

basis for negotiations. Although both continue say they seek peaceful settlement, chasm between their respective positions remains wide for now at least. I can, however, report one very modest gain here. After I explained at length to Mrs. Meir the benefits that would accrue to Israel from a systematic series of Israeli political peace initiatives, Mrs. Meir is now expected to appoint a small committee to develop such a program for her consideration. There is, of course, no commitment that any of the painful decisions which would result in a bit more flexibility in the Israeli position will be taken, but this is a start.

5. Mrs. Meir and top officials are greatly preoccupied with and concerned over increased Soviet direct involvement in Egypt. Without being specific, she stressed the need for the US to be Quote firm Unquote with the Soviets since otherwise the Russians may be tempted to broaden even further the parameters of brinksmanship in Middle East in belief we are so preoccupied with Viet Nam we will not react. But there is every sign Israelis will be prudent and selective militarily in Egypt, without however denying selves right to continue deep penetration raids if they deem military situation makes necessary. For time being, at least, they have no intention to hit Russian-manned SA–3s in Cairo, West Alexandria or Aswan. They will, however, maintain intensive air attacks near Suez Canal frontline positions to prevent installation of either SA–2s or SA–3s.

6. Finally, I am grateful that the attacks on our installations in Amman resulted in no loss or injuries to American lives. Since focus of extreme PLP fedayeen attacks and demonstration used as their principal thrust that Quote Sisco was carrying political settlements in his bag, Unquote and since I had nothing new to give to Hussein, I cancelled.[4] It was not worth risking American lives in Amman; neither Symmes nor I had any confidence that Hussein would act resolutely. Symmes and I agreed that main goal of fedayeen in their recent demonstrations was to make it impossible for Hussein to continue his dedication to idea of political settlement with Israel which they, of course, reject. If Hussein is unable to sustain a 24-hour visit of a US Assistant Secretary of State and does not even feel himself strong enough to ex-

---

[4] The American Cultural Center and the Embassy in Amman were attacked on April 15 by Palestinian demonstrators. Despite King Hussein's assurances to Symmes that Sisco would be safe, Symmes recommended that the Assistant Secretary not visit Jordan. He wrote: "I have not doubted Jordanian good intentions with respect to assuring safety of the Sisco mission but I continue to believe that there is a considerable gap between their good intentions and the ability to control the actions of others." (Telegram 1630 from Amman, April 16; ibid., Box 614, Country Files, Middle East, Jordan, Vol. IV) Zaid Rifai informed Symmes that Hussein considered Sisco's cancellation a "personal offense" and that the Ambassador should be transferred to another post because he had not encouraged the Assistant Secretary to visit Jordan. (Telegram 1635 from Amman, April 16; ibid.)

press publicly regret over these unfortunate developments, it raises fundamental question of whether he is a wasting asset. Hussein is going to have to make up his mind whether he or fedayeen are running his country. Recent events in Jordan require some sober thought by all of us in the days ahead.

7. With all other Americans, we are praying for the safe return of our astronauts.[5]

Barbour

---

[5] Reference is to the Apollo 13 astronauts, Jim Lovell, Jack Swigert, and Fred Haise. While en route to the moon beginning on April 11, an oxygen tank exploded aboard their aircraft, forcing an immediate abort of the moon landing mission. The astronauts returned to earth safely on April 17.

---

110. Memorandum of Conversation[1]

Washington, April 24, 1970, 6 p.m.

PARTICIPANTS

Yitzak Rabin, Ambassador of Israel
Shlomo Argov, Minister, Israeli Embassy
Henry A. Kissinger, Assistant to the President
Harold H. Saunders, NSC Staff

Ambassador Rabin began by saying that, since April 18, there is a new phenomenon in the Middle East. Soviet pilots have taken an active role by participating in the air defense of Egypt.

In response to Dr. Kissinger's question, the Ambassador said that Israel estimates there are fifty Soviet pilots involved; Israel does not know how many aircraft are involved. They fly from three bases, two southwest of Cairo and one (Djankialis) near Alexandria. The last has been involved in only two incidents where planes were scrambled. Most of the activity has been from the two southern bases.

Dr. Kissinger asked whether Soviet pilots have engaged Israeli aircraft. The Ambassador replied, "Almost," on April 18 over the Nile. The Ambassador described the new pattern of Soviet activity as

---

[1] Source: National Archives, Nixon Presidential Materials, NSC Files, Box 606, Country Files, Middle East, Israel, Vol. IV. Secret. Sent for information. Drafted by Saunders on April 25. The meeting was held in Kissinger's office.

follows: Soviet-piloted aircraft operate south of an east-west line from Cairo to Suez. For the time being, they are not interfering with Israeli attacks in the Suez Canal Sector. Israel does not yet know whether they will expand their operations into that area.

Over the past week, the number of Soviet responses has grown rapidly. Whenever Israeli planes approach, Soviet planes are scrambled. As a normal thing, they have not tried to interfere directly with attacking Israeli planes, even in one instance when Israeli planes were attacking a target on the west shore of the Gulf of Suez south of the Cairo-Suez line.

The corollary to this move in Egyptian actions has been greater aggressiveness in Egyptian air attacks on Israeli positions in the Sinai. Since the Egyptians feel that their hinterland is defended by SA–3 missiles (there are now ten operational sites—four around Alexandria, six around Cairo), they have mounted more sorties themselves.

The Ambassador concluded his presentation by stating emphatically and with some emotion that this is no longer a question of a UAR-Israeli military balance. Now there is a new dimension. Israel wants more planes.

Dr. Kissinger asked how many. Rabin initially replied, "at least as many as when the Prime Minister was here," but Argov later called Saunders to ask that a correction in the record be made to show the Ambassador's reply as reading, "The number submitted when General Yariv made his intelligence presentation here."[2]

In the conversation that followed, there was a series of brief exchanges between Dr. Kissinger and the Ambassador with the following points made:

—The Ambassador asked how the U.S. would respond to this Soviet move. Dr. Kissinger indicated that we would have to look at this new intelligence and consider the new elements in the situation, but "we will not tolerate their using military force against you."

—Rabin implied that the Soviet decision was brought about by the U.S. decision not to provide Israel with aircraft now.[3] He also felt that perhaps the Israeli decision not to attack Soviet-manned SA–3 positions in the Nile Valley had contributed to the Soviet decision. The Soviets will fill a vacuum whenever they feel one exists.

---

[2] See footnote 3, Document 108. In a meeting with Kissinger and Saunders on April 9, Yariv submitted charts that showed past attrition rates of Israeli aircraft and forecasted attrition rates for the next two years. He wanted replacements based on the loss of 152 aircraft from 1967 to 1971. (Memorandum of conversation, April 9; National Archives, Nixon Presidential Materials, NSC Files, Box 606, Country Files, Middle East, Israel, Vol. IV)

[3] See Document 105.

—Making clear that he was asking the question only to improve his own understanding of Israeli thinking, Dr. Kissinger asked whether Israel would attack the bases from which Soviet pilots are operating. Ambassador Rabin replied, "What would that do?" The U.S. would come to Israel and urge it not to further involve the Soviets. Assistant Secretary Sisco had made clear in Jerusalem[4] that the U.S. believes that SA–3 missiles are now in the UAR because of the Israeli deep penetration raids. Dr. Kissinger asked, "Is that wrong?" Rabin said, "No. That is why there is no good reason for Israel to attack the Soviet-manned air bases."

—Rabin said that the Israelis did not think the Soviets would feel "so much freedom to involve themselves to back the Egyptian war of attrition." Israel was on the verge of forcing Nasser to accept a cease-fire. Israel had not backed the Soviets against the wall; Israel had given them a "political out" in the proposal to accept a cease-fire.

The conversation concluded with Dr. Kissinger saying simply that he would of course report the Ambassador's approach to the President and we would review our position.

Harold H. Saunders[5]

---

[4] See Document 109.
[5] Saunders initialed "H.H.S." above his typed signature.

111. Telegram From the Department of State to the Embassy in the Soviet Union and the Mission to the United Nations[1]

Washington, May 1, 1970, 0302Z.

65851. Ref: Moscow 2099 and 2114.[2]

1. Further direct involvement of Soviets with pilots flying operational missions for UAR injects new element into question of how we should proceed in bilateral talks on Middle East with Soviets. Following are relevant considerations as we see them:

(A) Soviets, as you point out, seem unwilling or unable to make any meaningful concessions on settlement proposals at this stage. As result of steps they have taken to strengthen UAR air defenses and cautious Israeli reaction to date, they probably feel they have bought some time in terms of their relations with Nasser and of stabilizing military situation. It would appear reasonable to assume that they now want to see whether this development will have any effect on US and Israeli positions and that they meanwhile feel under no immediate pressure on diplomatic front.

(B) Sisco's discussions in Middle East[3] make it increasingly clear that two power exercise in some ways plays into Soviet hands in Arab world, since Soviets benefit not only from taking inflexible positions as protector of Arab rights, but also from distorting and using against us positions we take in bilateral talks in order to maintain firm negotiating stance vis-à-vis USSR.

(C) Above considerations suggest it would be undesirable at this stage for us to appear eager to increase pace or visibility of bilaterals. Present publicity re Soviet pilots reenforces this conclusion,[4] since we

---

[1] Source: National Archives, Nixon Presidential Materials, NSC Files, Box 712, Country Files, Europe, USSR, Vol. VIII. Secret; Priority; Nodis. Drafted on April 29 by Atherton, cleared by Sisco and Richardson and in IO and EUR, and approved by Rogers.

[2] In telegram 2099 from Moscow, April 27, Beam reported his conversation with Vinogradov, whom he described as "amiable and non-polemic." Analyzing Vinogradov's comments, Beam wrote: "I am not sanguine that the Soviets are ready to make concessions at this time, since their propaganda indicates they feel situation has stabilized following US arms decision and SA–3 delivery. Nevertheless I think it worthwhile to push them to produce the flexibility they have hinted at on peace and negotiations." (Ibid., Box 711, Country Files, Europe, USSR, Vol. VII) Telegram 2114 from Moscow, April 27, reported the conversation in further detail; see *Foreign Relations, 1969–1976*, volume XII, Soviet Union, January 1969–October 1970, Document 154.

[3] See Document 109.

[4] The Israeli Government issued a statement on April 29 asserting the presence of Soviet pilots flying operational missions in Egypt, concluding: "Israel will continue to defend itself against all aggression which violates the ceasefire arrangements and which aims at renewal of war in the area. In all its struggles Israel drew strength from its unity and from the justice of its cause. Israel will continue in its firm stand and in its quest for

would not want to create impression either publicly or vis-à-vis Soviets that we feel under pressure as result of this development to consider negotiating changes in our position in absence of prior concrete responses from Soviets on peace and negotiations language which we have told them we expect.

(D) For above reasons as well as ones you cite, we agree it would not be desirable for Sisco to go to Moscow. Furthermore, we would not want to send NEA expert since this could signal to Soviets that we are prepared to enter new phase in bilateral talks. On other hand, we do not want to give impression we are breaking off or suspending bilaterals. We believe we should, however, make clear we continue to feel that next move is up to Soviets. We must also make clear that their increasing military involvement is new factor in situation which cannot help but influence our judgment re their intentions on diplomatic front.

2. In light of foregoing considerations, you should seek early appointment with Vinogradov to make following points:

(A) We remain prepared to continue bilateral talks. We do not think, however, that question of where they are conducted or by whom is main issue at this time. So long as Dobrynin is away from Washington, you are available in Moscow. We can also talk to Vorontsov as necessary.

(B) As we have repeatedly said, we consider position reflected in October 28 and December 18 documents represent fair middle ground and are not prepared to depart from principles contained therein.[5] While precise language in those documents is not immutable, we need to know where Soviets agree with it and where they do not. We particularly need to know if they accept preambular language on negotiations plus language on peace commitments. If they do not, then we need from them alternative language which we could consider. Precise responses from Soviets on these points would help us decide how we might most usefully proceed in bilaterals. We do not rule out procedure Vinogradov suggests at appropriate stage. Sisco tried to get Dobrynin to in effect do this in last two meetings by asking Dobrynin whether there were any other points in October 28 document to which Soviets objected. Sisco said it important to know what remaining points of difference there might be. Dobrynin refused to be drawn out.[6] We are becoming increasingly concerned over Dobrynin's lack of authority to go beyond a narrow brief. Meanwhile, so far as identifying points of

---

true and lasting peace." For the text of the statement, see *Israel's Foreign Policy: Historical Documents,* volumes 1–2, 1947–1974, Chapter XII, The War of Attrition and the Cease Fire, Document 14. It was also published in the *New York Times,* April 30, 1970, p. 8.

[5] See Documents 58 and 78.

[6] See Document 107.

agreement and disagreement is concerned, four power deputies in New York are now doing precisely that, and position being taken by Soviets far from encouraging.

(C) You should also make clear we will not agree to go back to June 69 document as basis.[7] October 28 document is composite of June 69 Soviet document and US July 69 document[8] and intended to reflect common positions. For example, Soviets have teased us with saying "agree to total withdrawal including Gaza and Jerusalem, and we will consider more detailed language on peace." We heard that several times before from Dobrynin without result. Now in four power talks Soviets, even for description purposes alone, are not willing to accept a British/French formulation[9] which falls short of our present point 2 formulation in October 28 document. This causes us to view with great doubt Soviet willingness to move towards us in a serious way on points dealing with peace and negotiations. Either they accept present formulation in October 28 document or provide us with alternative language to consider.[10]

(D) At same time we must make clear to Soviet Government that their operational involvement in military role in UAR has injected new element into situation. Secretary already stressed this point to Ambassador Dobrynin following introduction of SA–3s and Soviet personnel.[11] Introduction of Soviet pilots flying operational missions

---

[7] See Document 34.

[8] See footnote 4, Document 39.

[9] The British-French approach, as reported in telegram 637 from USUN, April 8, involved the Four Power Deputy Representatives producing a memorandum for Jarring (see Document 98) that developed "concrete formulations, rather general in nature and designed to encompass existing positions, of 'common denominators' on maximum points of agreement reached to date with statement of points on which disagreement remains included in separate section or sections." (National Archives, RG 59, Central Files 1970–73, POL 27–14 ARAB–ISR) The Soviet problems with this approach were reported in telegram 677 from USUN, April 16. (Ibid.) As of May 26, the Four-Power deputies had met 13 times "pursuant to their mandate," but had "not yet completed work," and, as a result, the Department concluded that absent a "major change in Soviet attitude," any report that the deputies produced would be unlikely contain "anything very useful to Jarring attainable in foreseeable future." (Telegram 1050 from USUN, May 26, and telegram 80274 to USUN, May 25; both ibid.)

[10] Beam met with Vinogradov on May 5, as reported in telegram 2288 from Moscow, May 5, and made the points requested by the Department, "sticking closely to Dept's language." The Deputy Foreign Minister responded that Beam's comments "reflected great misinterpretation of events in ME" and that the "warnings" in his statement were "unnecessary and not at all justified." He added that the blame that the United States had placed on the Soviet Union and the Arab states for the "continuation of unfortunate events" in the Middle East should be directed at the "Israeli aggressor" which was "unwilling to withdraw troops, implement SC res, or listen to any proposal which would lead to peaceful settlement." (Ibid., Nixon Presidential Materials, NSC Files, Box 712, Country Files, Europe, USSR, Vol. VIII)

[11] Rogers made this point to Dobrynin during a meeting on March 25. See footnote 5, Document 105.

makes this development even more serious and potentially dangerous. We hope Soviets have not misinterpreted our restraint in deferring decision on more aircraft for Israel.[12] We regret they have not matched our restraint. We want again to make clear that we will do what is necessary to see that the military balance is not tipped against Israel.

(E) We realize that Soviets say their military actions in UAR are purely defensive. In our view, however, it is not possible to draw so clear a distinction between defensive and offensive actions. Fact is that what Soviets are doing facilitates more offensive UAR military action. We consider recent Soviet steps as serious move constituting deeper involvement and in direct opposition to USG efforts to promote peace settlement through limitation on arms shipments to the area and through observance of ceasefire. Among other things, they raise question whether Soviets have now reached limit of their involvement. To avoid any miscalculation, we consider it important to have an indication of Soviet intentions in this regard.

Rogers

---

[12] See Document 105.

---

112. Paper Prepared by the National Security Council Staff[1]

Washington, May 7, 1970.

ANALYTICAL SUMMARY

DIPLOMATIC OPTIONS—ARAB-ISRAELI IMPASSE

Introductory note: A previous paper deals with how the U.S. should respond to Soviet pilots in the UAR, particularly in considering its response to Israel's further aircraft requests.[2] At the same time recent political developments, including the Soviet initiative, make it necessary to reappraise overall U.S. strategy toward the Arab-Israeli impasse.

---

[1] Source: National Archives, Nixon Presidential Materials, NSC Files, NSC Institutional Files (H-Files), Box H–044, Senior Review Group Meetings, Review Group Soviet Pilots in Egypt 5/8/70. Secret; Nodis. All brackets are in the original.

[2] The paper, "Reassessment of Current Arab-Israel Situation and Possible US Courses of Action," undated, as well as the other papers for the May 8 Review Group meeting, are ibid.

Diplomatic options were included in a general way in the previous paper, but that viewed the problem mainly as one of U.S. response to the USSR. The purpose of this paper is to focus on the diplomatic options. [The State discussion papers under this memo recommend one course of action. The purpose of this memo is to suggest a wider framework of options.]

I. *The Situation*

A. *Soviet assumption of a greater role in the defense of Egypt—whatever its ultimate degree—has changed the political-military balance.* The U.S. (and Israeli) assumption has been that the USSR might rather press Nasser toward a more reasonable negotiating position than risk greater Soviet military commitment. What now seems clear is that the USSR would rather risk that commitment than press the Arabs to give up territory in a settlement. What is not clear is how concrete the USSR will press Nasser to be on measures to enforce a settlement if he gets his territory back and the Palestinians get a fair settlement.

B. *Nasser has posed the issue sharply to the U.S. in his appeal to President Nixon:*[3] Does the U.S. support enlargement of Israel's boundaries and denial of restitution to the Palestinians? Right or wrong, he has now put the issue so that the Arabs must read provision of further U.S. aid to Israel as an affirmative answer to that question. In other words, it will become increasingly costly to negotiate from the strength of Israel's occupation of Arab territory without at the same time making clear that we do not believe Israel should keep any of that territory in a peace settlement. Nasser has put himself in a position to say that he has offered to make peace with a Jewish state in Palestine but the U.S. in return is not prepared to press Israel to withdraw. As the issue is now posed, if the U.S. confronts the USSR it will be over Israel's enlarged boundaries, not over Israel's survival. It is in the Soviet interest to have the issue posed this way: If the U.S. confronts the USSR, it loses in the Arab world; if the U.S. tries to shift the issue, it makes a negotiating concession.

C. *Israel has posed the issue equally sharply: Will the U.S. back down in the face of a Soviet threat by refusing to provide Israel with the arms it needs?* Israel is attempting to bargain for enlargement of its borders. It has therefore refused to say that it is prepared to withdraw from occupied territories as part of a settlement. Israel has repudiated the U.S. suggestion that it move a step at a time toward negotiation by accepting the principle of withdrawal if the Arabs accept some concrete obligations involved in making peace. The Israeli position is that Nasser will not

---

[3] See Document 115.

make peace and that any sign of flexibility by Israel or the U.S. will be read as backing down in the face of a Soviet threat.

D. *The advent of the Palestinians as a quasi-independent force with a veto over Jordanian—and perhaps Lebanese—policy raises the question whether the Palestinian movement can be dealt with still just as a refugee problem.* To date, the U.S. has assumed that their movement could be defused by (a) providing a generous refugee settlement and (b) leaving it to King Hussein to provide the Palestinians with whatever degree of autonomy after Israel withdraws from the West Bank. So far, it has been unthinkable to consider a settlement directly between Israel and the Palestinians (perhaps with U.S. involvement) because (a) this would mean writing off King Hussein and (b) the Palestinian movement is still so fragmented that it is difficult to know who might speak for it in a negotiation. But now if the Palestinians hold the upper hand in Jordan, we have to consider whether to try some sort of negotiation on this front as a possible means of circumventing Nasser.

E. *The major power talks have not worked, and the option of a direct U.S. effort with Nasser is re-opened.* Nasser has said that he does not wish to discuss the terms of a settlement directly with the U.S. But the USSR has not pressed Nasser to change his position materially, and Nasser knows the U.S. alone—if anyone—has the influence to move Israel. Since Nasser has made an open appeal direct to President Nixon, it is at least an issue to be considered whether the U.S. should now go straight to Nasser to try to reach an understanding.

F. *In the perspective of a year, the position of governments friendly to the U.S. has worsened.* Specifically: The Libyan coup last September. The fedayeen position in Lebanon in October; King Hussein's compromise with the fedayeen in February;[4] the plot against Faisal last fall. In each case, radical forces have capitalized on the moderate regime's relationship with the U.S. and the U.S. position on Israel to the disadvantage of the regime.

II. *Summary of State Suggestion*

For the sake of convenience, the course of action described in the following paper for the purpose of discussion consists of the following steps:

A. In response to Nasser's peace appeal propose to him that the UAR and Israel:

1. subscribe formally and publicly to restoration of the ceasefire;

---

[4] On February 12, King Hussein reached an agreement with guerrilla representatives to rescind security measures that the Palestinian commandos viewed as curbs on their military strikes against Israel. (*New York Times*, February 14, 1970, p. 5, and February 15, 1970, p. 19)

2. begin discussions under Jarring, according to whatever procedures he recommends on the basis of statements by both sides that they accept the UN Resolution (242) and agree that the purpose of the discussions is the establishment of peace between them, recognition of Israel's right to exist and the withdrawal of forces in accordance with the resolution;

3. tell Nasser that, if he accepts this proposition, we will undertake to obtain Israeli acceptance and meanwhile will continue to defer a decision on additional aircraft for Israel, limiting ourselves for now to replacement of Israeli losses.

B. Tell Israel in advance that:

1. We are going to make such an approach to Nasser.

2. If Nasser is responsive, we would expect a flexible and positive response from Israel. Failing that, we would have to reconsider our position of standing firm on our October and December documents and not negotiating more detailed proposals in the Two and Four Power talks.

3. We expect Israel to refrain from resuming deep penetration raids.

4. As an interim measure, we are prepared immediately to amend present contracts to provide replacement for present and projected aircraft losses through 1970, thus assuring continuation of deliveries when those already contracted are completed (perhaps 8 Phantoms and 18–20 Skyhawks).

C. *The tactical alternative* within this option—not mentioned in the State paper—would be to try to pin down an Israeli position before going to Nasser.

III. *The Range of Diplomatic Options*

A. Proceed within the framework established by the diplomatic moves of 1969—Four Power and US–USSR talks and U.S. documents—to try to re-establish the cease-fire and launch negotiations under Jarring.

Option 1: Major-power effort. Move in the Four Power and U.S.-Soviet talks to fill in the gaps in our proposals on Sharm al-Shaikh, Gaza, DMZ's and UN forces which are now left for the parties to negotiate.

Pro.

—Further Soviet military involvement in the UAR has sharply increased the dangers in the present situation, and it is important to work out directly with the USSR just exactly what the Soviets will settle for politically in limiting their military involvement.

—The U.S. must at least clarify its position on these points anyway to the extent of leaving no doubt that we expect the Israelis to retain possession. While such a move could look like a concession to Soviet pressure, it is a move that we must make to base our position on the right issue—protecting Israel's survival not conquests—whatever we do.

Con.

—This would look too much like giving in to Soviet pressure without a compensating move from the Soviets on issues of interest to us.

—The Soviets have shown little apparent inclination to press the Egyptians to make concessions, so we should regard the experiment to enlist their help as having been unsuccessful and deal directly with Nasser ourselves.

Option 2: Bilateral. Go directly to Israel and the UAR, trying to persuade them to begin negotiations on the basis of the U.S. October 28 document.[5] In some respects the arguments are simply the obverse of those above but the refinements are these:

Pro.

—The major-power talks have not produced results, so the U.S. should go directly to the parties.

—The October 28 formulation represents as balanced a set of principles as are likely to be put together as a prelude to negotiation. Apart from wording, they combine the essentials for getting a negotiation started—an Israeli commitment to withdraw and Arab agreement to specific obligations for enforcing the peace.

Con.

—The Israelis have already rejected this document, so tactically this would make it unnecessarily difficult to bring them along.

—The U.S. documents have aroused enough suspicion on both sides that it would be well to drop them.

Comment: The broad arguments for and against both of these options include those that have been repeated for the past year on whether the U.S. should try to work out with other major powers semi-detailed guidelines for Jarring. Even though the second option above is a partial break with this approach, the October 28 document is still the product of it and therefore subject to many of its disadvantages, even though the bilateral approach might overcome some of them.

B. Step aside from the 1969 tack and try to re-establish the cease-fire launch negotiations by some simpler formula.

---

[5] See Document 58.

Option 3: UAR-Israel. Try to persuade Israel and the UAR to re-establish the cease-fire and to start negotiating indirectly on the basis of a simple commitment by both sides that the purpose of the negotiation is to establish a state of peace with Israel, based on recognizing Israel's existence and Israeli withdrawal. Ambassador Jarring tried—and nearly succeeded in spring, 1968—to launch talks on the basis of a simple formula like this. [This is the State suggestion described in II above. State factors in the arms decision.]

Pro.

—Some initiative is required to contain the dangers created by recent Soviet moves. Taking this new tack would permit the U.S. to make a move that does not require us to make concessions in the context of the U.S.-Soviet discussions of the past year. It would also get away from many of the suspicions.

—Nasser's May Day appeal to President Nixon has provided an opening for a direct response.

—While this would require the Israelis to state their willingness to withdraw if there is peace and start talking without an open Arab commitment to direct negotiation, it would preserve a negotiating process, on which Israel insists.

Con.

—This seems unlikely to work unless it is possible to clarify precisely beforehand that the Israelis will not try to bargain for major territorial changes and that Nasser is willing to coexist peacefully with a Jewish state and control the Palestinians. This approach does not really clarify the calculated ambiguity on that point in the UN resolution. Unless the U.S. is willing to come down hard on those points, the effort is a half-measure hardly worth the effort.

—If the U.S. is going to do anything, it should go all the way and attempt to work out an Israel-UAR agreement without leaving this to a vague negotiating process that is bound to fail.

Option 4: Jordan-Israel. Try again to launch a Jordan-Israel negotiation, this time seeking a way to involve the Palestinians and thereby perhaps free Hussein of Nasser's restraint.

Pro.

—This course has been rejected previously mainly because it was judged, apparently correctly, that Hussein could not negotiate a settlement on his own if Nasser disagreed. Now, however, the increased strength of the Palestinians at least raises the question whether there is an opportunity for an Israeli settlement with the Palestinians using Hussein as a figurehead.

—If this were a possibility (and the Israelis would have to take the lead), it might offer a way of circumventing Nasser and the Soviets. Nasser would have difficulty opposing a settlement to which a substantial group of Palestinians agreed.

—The Palestinian movement must be taken into account if a settlement is to be realistic.

Con.

—The Palestinian movement is not sufficiently coherent yet to present a united negotiating front. It may in time, but that time is not yet.

—Any premature move in the direction of the Palestinians risks building them up without assurance that they can produce a unified position or that such a position will be sufficiently moderate and constructive that the Israelis can live with it.

C. By-pass Jarring and make a unilateral effort at a settlement.

Option 5: Work out bilaterally with Nasser the arrangements for enforcing a peace settlement that he would agree to provided the U.S. could force Israel to withdraw then press this on Israel along with a pledge of long-term economic and military assistance and perhaps a U.S. security guarantee.

Pro.

—Only action this decisive, if any, is likely to produce a political settlement. The alternative is accepting the deterioration in U.S.-Arab relations and the U.S.-Soviet confrontation that are likely if present trends take their course.

—Continued U.S. support for Israel can be sustained only if there is a political settlement based on virtually complete withdrawal. The present course of events is likely to lead to an Israeli-Soviet clash. The U.S. does not have an interest in a confrontation with the USSR over Israel's right to hold occupied Arab territory. Therefore, unless Israel withdraws, any U.S. Administration is unlikely to find domestic political support for confronting the USSR in present circumstances. The result will be an even more humiliating back-down in the face of dramatic Soviet pressure than would be the case if the U.S. made changes in its position now.

—Nasser has opened the door to this kind of effort in his peace appeal to President Nixon.

Con.

—The U.S. is unlikely to be able to bring enough pressure to bear on Israel to make Israel withdraw to virtually pre-war borders. Whether this is desirable or not, it just will not work.

—Nasser is unlikely to agree to any terms in advance of an Israeli commitment to withdraw with sufficient precision to permit us even to make a good case to the Israelis.

—The threat of such a squeeze would create a national crisis in Israel which could well lead to a decision for early pre-emptive military action of some sort on grounds that success is more likely before the Soviets are completely entrenched.

—Going to Nasser would look like U.S. capitulation.

Option 6: Have a complete sorting out with Israel of the extent of U.S. support against the Arabs and against the USSR, making clear that U.S. support is contingent on withdrawal. On the basis of an Israeli commitment to withdraw attempt to work out an Israel-UAR agreement with Nasser.

Pro.

—A commitment of substantial U.S. support for the future coupled with a clear understanding of its limits is the only way we could begin to persuade Israel to cut back its present demands.

—Unless the U.S. begins thinking in these terms, it will be drawn into a confrontation with the USSR by Israel on the issue of protecting Israel's conquests.

—Israel is expecting massive economic and military support from the U.S. It is fairer to both Israel and the U.S. to reach an understanding now than to let Israel proceed on what could prove false expectations.

—A substantial U.S. commitment to Israel in the context of withdrawal and peace would be tolerable to the Arabs.

Con.

—The Israelis will not withdraw under any circumstances. The U.S. will be faced with the choice between backing down and sharply cutting back its aid. This would be domestically unsupportable, especially in the present atmosphere.

—The U.S. cannot in good conscience squeeze the Israelis until it has confidence in Nasser's willingness to make peace and live up to his commitments.

—Putting this choice to the Israelis would create a national crisis that could well result in a pre-emptive attack of some sort.

113. Memorandum From the President's Assistant for National Security Affairs (Kissinger) to President Nixon[1]

Washington, May 11, 1970.

SUBJECT

Arms Supply to Jordan

Background

At the time of King Hussein's talks with you last April,[2] it was agreed to meet some of Jordan's more pressing military equipment needs. With your approval, Secretary Rogers told the King then that we would sell some ground equipment and a second squadron of F–104 aircraft if requested, as had been agreed in 1968.[3] As the package was finally worked out, it contained less artillery than Jordan wanted.[4]

The question of artillery became active again last summer when Hussein asked the Soviets what they might be able to supply him. They delayed for six months and then came up with an offer to deliver 90% of everything the King wants this year.[5] You may recall that this was mentioned at the NSC meeting on December 10 and you encouraged Secretary Laird to do what could be done before the Rabat Arab summit conference.[6] A U.S. military team went to Jordan and put together a package designed to meet Jordan's minimum needs.

The package which Secretary Rogers now recommends you approve [memo attached][7] consists of enough artillery to provide minimum support for Jordan's 9 infantry brigades and 1 armored division which are presently deployed in defensive positions along a line in the heights 3–5 miles from the Jordan River. Although the proposed U.S.

---

[1] Source: National Archives, Nixon Presidential Materials, NSC Files, Box 614, Country Files, Middle East, Jordan, Vol. IV. Secret; Nodis. Sent for action. Printed from an uninitialed copy. Attached to a memorandum from Haig to Saunders on May 12 asking him to prepare a National Security Decision Memorandum reflecting the President's decision. The brackets are in the original.

[2] See Document 19.

[3] See footnote 3, Document 19.

[4] See *Foreign Relations*, 1964–1968, volume XX, Arab-Israeli Dispute, 1967–1968, Documents 95, 107, and 111.

[5] See footnote 3, Document 69.

[6] See Document 74. The Rabat summit conference was held December 21–23, 1969.

[7] Attached but not printed. The details of the package are included in attachments to a memorandum that Warren Nutter sent to Laird on April 15. (Washington National Records Center, OSD Files: FRC 330–76–0067, Box 75, Jordan) In a telephone conversation on May 1 at 11:25 a.m., Sisco told Kissinger that the arms package was "peanuts" compared to what the Soviet Union was "not selling but giving" to Jordan. (National Archives, Nixon Presidential Materials, NSC Files, Henry Kissinger Telephone Conversation Transcripts, Box 5, Chronological File)

package is not insignificant, the Soviets have offered a more substantial package to Jordan. For example, only medium range weapons are included, whereas the Soviet package includes weapons with a range to reach Jerusalem. Fifteen million dollars in sales credit have been earmarked from FY 1970 funds, and another $15 million could be made available from FY 1971 funds if necessary.

Issues

The first issue arises from the fact that one purpose of this package would be to pre-empt a Soviet arms offer.

If we provide no artillery or a smaller package than the one proposed (which has been considerably reduced below what Hussein requested), or if we delay further giving Hussein an answer, he will almost certainly go the Soviet route for arms. He could do so in a matter of weeks or even days, if his special emissary who is arriving in Washington Monday carries back a negative or temporizing response from us.

If the Soviets take this first step toward establishing a foothold in Jordan, it would probably be the irreversible beginning of a reorientation of Jordan away from the U.S. toward Moscow. U.S. influence would begin to decline, and over time the Soviets might achieve a position in Jordan comparable to that which they have established in the UAR.

The second issue is whether this package would seriously affect the Jordan-Israel balance.

The proposal would provide a significant increase in Jordan's artillery, but there are some limits. It would not give the Jordanian army the capability to cross the Jordan River against Israel, and the Jordanian army would remain inadequate against the Israeli ground threat. The main point, however, is that a safe military balance as the Israelis see it includes the capability to mount a sharp decisive strike. Moreover, the Israelis are less concerned about the Jordanian offensive threat than they are about Jordan's capability to conduct a war of attrition. The proposed package would significantly enhance Jordan's capability in this respect.

The other side of this point is that while the Israelis would prefer no weapons in Jordan, they have generally agreed that if Jordan is armed Israel would prefer a U.S. to a Soviet military presence. Israel is nervous about the Soviet role in the UAR, and may well see the importance of keeping the Soviets out of Jordan. The choice for them is between a smaller U.S. package and a larger Soviet one. But Tel Aviv would in any case use whatever we do in Jordan as one further argument in support of additional military assistance for Israel.

The third issue, closely related, is how Israel's view of the overall military balance will be affected if the Israelis see some decrease in their ability to mount a pre-emptive strike in Jordan as well as in the UAR.

The problem is more acute with respect to the Israeli air balance with the UAR. The combination of the new missile system (SA–3) provided by the Soviets and more active participation of Soviet pilots in the UAR air force presents Israel with a serious threat. Since the Israelis measure the balance of power, both on the ground and in the air, in terms of a long war of attrition, the cumulative impact of a shift on the Jordanian front coupled with significantly increased Soviet aid to Egypt is likely to appear most ominous to Israel.

The fourth issue is the question of domestic reaction at a time when some segments of the public are already aroused because of our action in Cambodia.[8] The degree of domestic criticism would depend to a large extent on whether Israel is persuaded that U.S. aid to Jordan is the lesser of two evils. But even if Israel could be convinced, pressure would increase for a positive response to Tel Aviv's requests for U.S. assistance. The Israelis know we are discussing an arms package for Jordan and would be informed of its magnitude.

Although the decision on the arms package could have been delayed at least a week, State's agreement to see King Hussein's emissary on Monday has forced our hand and we should be prepared to discuss the Jordanian request at that time.

Recommendation

On balance, I recommend that you approve the proposed arms package for Jordan provided that you make it clear:

—That approval is based on the premise that it is an alternative which will hinder Soviet entry into Jordan;

—That approval is linked with a decision on your part to provide additional hardware support to meet the increased threat posed to Israel by the combination of this action and substantially increased Soviet aid to Egypt;

—That you require a recommendation as to the level of additional aid for Israel by June 15, 1970.[9]

---

[8] The United States began bombing North Vietnamese sanctuaries in Cambodia in April.

[9] Nixon approved Kissinger's recommendation, and Kissinger sent it to Rogers and Laird as NSDM 61, May 19, which reads: "The President has approved the arms package for Jordan," adding that "if Jordan accepts this package, it does so with the understanding that it will not accept Soviet arms" and "that this decision is linked with the decision to provide additional equipment to Israel." (National Archives, Nixon Presidential Materials, NSC Files, NSC Institutional Files (H-Files), Box H–216, National Security Decision Memoranda) But King Hussein had already rejected the arms package, a decision that Zaid Rifai conveyed to Sisco on May 13. Hussein informed Rifai: "I could not justify to myself or the Armed Forces, who are aware of our needs, accepting an offer short of what the Untied States Armed Forces Team recommended as the bare minimum required with total deliveries this year." He concluded: "In short if your list as stated is the final offer, thanks but no thanks." (Telegram 73228 to Amman, May 13; ibid., RG 59, Central Files 1970–73, DEF 15–2 JORDAN)

114. Memorandum From the President's Assistant for National Security Affairs (Kissinger) to President Nixon[1]

Washington, May 12, 1970.

SUBJECT

Sisco Reflections After Mid-East Trip

Secretary Rogers personally asked that you receive Assistant Secretary Sisco's characterization of the situation in the Near East as he saw it during his recent trip and his reflections on some of the basic assumptions we have been working from.[2]

In short: Nasser believes he can outwait the Israelis, and Mrs. Meir believes no peace is possible with Nasser. Neither side believes the other has in good faith accepted the UN resolution as the basis for a settlement.

Mr. Sisco in stating his conclusions suggests that it is time to review certain of our working premises:

1. Whereas we have assumed that major power talks might break the impasse between the parties, they have not brought any of the parties to modify their positions in any significant way.

2. Whereas we have assumed that the Soviets, in order to defuse the situation and limit Soviet involvement in the UAR, might have an interest in pressing Nasser to adopt a more positive attitude toward negotiation, the Soviets to the contrary have deepened their military commitment to him.

3. Whereas we have assumed Israel might in the end go along with a properly guarded U.S. position, the Israelis have flatly rejected our position while asking us to support theirs militarily and economically.

4. Whereas we have assumed that the Palestinians can be dealt with in a settlement purely as a refugee problem, they have become a quasi-independent force with a veto over policy in Jordan and, soon, in Lebanon.

Conclusion: Perhaps it is time to shift our attention from the two-power and four-power exercises to direct action vis-à-vis the principal actors—Israel, the Palestinians and the UAR. An options paper is being prepared.[3]

---

[1] Source: National Archives, Nixon Presidential Materials, NSC Files, Box 645, Country Files, Middle East, Middle East—General, Vol. III. Secret; Nodis. Sent for information. A notation on the memorandum indicates the President saw it.

[2] Saunders sent Sisco's report of April 28 to Kissinger on May 7. (Ibid.) Sisco toured the Middle East April 8–24. See Document 109.

[3] A summary of the paper is Document 116. The paper was discussed at a meeting of the NSC Ad Hoc Special Review Group on the Middle East on May 21; see Document 117.

115. Memorandum From the President's Assistant for National Security Affairs (Kissinger) to President Nixon[1]

Washington, May 12, 1970.

SUBJECT

Nasser's "Appeal" to You—A New Diplomatic Initiative

As you know, Nasser inserted an unusual open message to you into his annual May Day speech (Tab A).[2] The first two-thirds of the speech was a simplistic and dreary review of the last 23 years of the Arab-Israeli problem. The last third of the speech was a direct "appeal" to you to help restore peace in the Middle East, albeit on Egyptian terms. This came a day after an interview with *US News and World Report* in which Nasser dwelt on his willingness to make peace with a Jewish state. (Tab B)[3]

Nasser's "Appeal"

Nasser said specifically to you that, despite all that has happened, he has not completely closed the door to the U.S. He warned, however, that if the U.S. takes "another step toward confirming Israel's military superiority" it would "affect all U.S. relations with the Arab nations for several decades and perhaps for centuries." Then he launched his "appeal" to you. He asked two things:

—"If the United States wishes peace, it must order Israel to withdraw from the occupied Arab territories."

—If the U.S. does not have this capability, then he "requests" that the U.S. "refrain from giving any new support to Israel as long as it occupies Arab territories—be it political, military or economic support."

If the U.S. does neither, Nasser said, "the Arabs must come to the inevitable conclusion that the U.S. wants Israel to continue to occupy our territories so as to dictate the terms of surrender. This—and I am still addressing myself to President Nixon in a last attempt—will not happen."

This, Nasser continued, is "a decisive moment in Arab-American relations" that will determine whether "we will declare estrangement forever" or if "there will be a new serious and definite start." All this he was saying to you because "the situation is delicate and because the

---

[1] Source: National Archives, Nixon Presidential Materials, NSC Files, Box 636, Country Files, Middle East. UAR, Vol. IV. Secret. Sent for information.

[2] Attached but not printed at Tab A is an extract of the speech.

[3] Attached but not printed at Tab B is the article in the May 2 *U.S. News and World Report*.

consequences are extremely dangerous." Yet "nothing can prevent us from making another and final appeal for the sake of peace in the Middle East."

Diplomatic Initiatives

The Egyptians have followed up Nasser's speech with diplomatic moves apparently intended to emphasize that it is a serious initiative. The following day UAR Foreign Minister Riad called in the head of our Interests Section to tell him he hoped that we would take the speech seriously as an appeal for peace rather than to interpret it as propaganda or a threat. He said that Nasser hoped that you would respond in a positive manner. Riad also told the British ambassador in Cairo the same thing and asked specifically for British support. At the U.N., the Egyptian ambassador has asked for U Thant's support and requested that he circulate the speech as a U.N. document. The UAR is also sending special representatives to the other Arab states to explain the statement that the UAR desires a political solution and to stress the seriousness of Nasser's appeal to you. Cairo has asked African governments to press the appeal with the U.S.

As if to complement this diplomatic offensive, Nasser just prior to his May Day speech gave an interview to a correspondent of *US News and World Report* in which he said, among other things, that the UAR agreed to accept the existence of a Jewish state in Palestine and would guarantee free Israeli passage through both Suez and the Gulf of Aqaba. He emphasized his desire for peace but made clear that it must be on the basis of complete Israeli withdrawal. He has also unexpectedly volunteered another interview to an American for use on National Educational Television.

What Does It Mean?

It seems clear that Nasser has embarked on a peace offensive and is taking steps to project to the U.S. the image of someone sincerely interested in a peaceful settlement. It is not as clear, however, what are his intentions in doing this at this time.

The most obvious explanation is that Nasser is trying to head off a hasty U.S. commitment to provide more aircraft to Israel in the wake of the Israeli public allegations that Soviet pilots are flying operational missions in the UAR.[4] On the other hand, Nasser gave the impression that he felt he was talking from a position of strength. Having stepped up his military activities along the Canal and with Soviet help having strengthened his air defense system, Nasser may think he is now in a stronger political position to talk more openly about peace. He may

---

[4] See footnote 4, Document 111.

even think that he can now put increasing military and political pressure on the Israelis and on us. In any case, he might feel in a better public posture to justify further military activity if he can say the U.S. rejected his appeal for peace. Alternatively, we may be seeing a genuine appeal from a man who feels he is increasingly coming under the control of the Soviets but cannot begin to pull away from their grasp until he can show some tangible progress toward regaining the occupied territories.

Conclusion:

Nasser's appeal comes at a time when the increased Soviet commitment in Egypt as well as recent developments in Jordan warrant a new overall look at our strategy in the Mid-East. The staff work is being prepared for such a review.[5]

---

[5] See Document 116.

---

116. Paper Prepared by the National Security Council Staff[1]

Washington, May 20, 1970.

U.S. POLICY OPTIONS IN THE MIDDLE EAST

SUMMARY

I. *The Issues*

The basic issue is how to strengthen the US position vis-à-vis the Soviets. Two broad strategies are possible.

A. Rely primarily on strengthening the military counterweights to the Soviets and their clients, making Israel our military proxy in the area but with at least the implication of U.S. readiness to back Israel more directly if necessary.

B. Rely primarily on political efforts to strengthen the US position, seeking to force an Arab-Israeli political settlement involving almost

---

[1] Source: National Archives, Nixon Presidential Materials, NSC Files, NSC Institutional Files (H-Files), Box H–044, Senior Review Group Meetings, Review Group Middle East 5/21/70. Secret; Nodis. The undated Department of State paper that this paper summarizes, entitled "U.S. Policy Options in the Middle East," is attached. All brackets are in the original.

total Israeli withdrawal in return for Arab acceptance of a Jewish state in Palestine. This might require a formal US defense commitment to Israel.

A choice on strategy has been sharpened by two recent developments: (1) The new Soviet role in the air defense of the UAR (which has intensified pressure on us to provide more aircraft to Israel; and (2) Nasser's May Day "peace appeal"[2] (which relates to our relations with the Mid-East in regard to future sales to Israel and our position on a peace settlement, especially on withdrawal).

These developments require that we make early decisions on two operational issues:

(1) What moves, if any, should we make with respect to a peace settlement?

(2) How should we respond to Israel's request for additional aircraft?

Decisions on these issues will be determined by—or will determine—which of the two broad strategies we pursue in dealing with the general Soviet challenge in the area and will provide an answer to a third: How to respond to Nasser's peace appeal.

II. *The Political-Military Framework—Basic Factors*

(1) The parties disagree on interpreting the purpose of UN Security Council Resolution 242.

(2) The parties disagree on the propriety of "imposing" a settlement.

(3) A qualitatively new—and we assume irreversible—factor has entered the situation: The Soviet commitment to the air defense of the UAR. A signal to the Russians from the US might not only require additional aircraft for Israel but also signs of our willingness to get involved on the Israeli side. This prompts the question of whether we get involved to defend the big Israel or the little one.

(4) Following Nasser's peace appeal, there is now the clear implication that if the US continues to supply Israel militarily, there will be a sharp decline in our relations with the Mid-East, presumably encouraged by Nasser. It is assumed that this would be an irreversible deterioration in our ties with the area.

(5) The Israelis are now reading events in the Mid-East as a Soviet challenge to the US which therefore would require a positive response to Israel's military requests. [We cannot be sure that such a positive response would increase Israeli flexibility on a settlement or ultimately avoid an Israeli-Soviet confrontation.]

---

[2] See Document 115.

Conclusions:

—There are two fixed factors in our relations with the Mid-East: (1) We are committed to keeping Israel in existence and thus to keeping the military balance in her favor. (2) We cannot abandon the Mid-East to the Soviets without losing important US financial, economic and strategic interests there. However, to provide Israel now with additional aircraft would accelerate the movement of the Arab world into the Soviet camp.

—An Arab-Israeli settlement would best resolve these conflicting factors. In moving toward this, we could consider deferring decision on Israel's requests without endangering her security; we might give some ground to the Soviets and the UAR on a political settlement. These two moves would protect our overriding interests in Israel's existence and in maintaining a role in the Arab world.

—Our influence on both sides is limited: On the Israeli side, we supply arms but are limited by the fact that we cannot allow the military balance to shift against them. On the Arab side, there is a desire not to see the US excluded from the area and the fact that Israeli withdrawal cannot be achieved without US help.

—With these considerations in mind, the following policy options are open to the US:

III. *Policy Options*

On a settlement:

(1) Stand fast on present proposals, encourage cease-fire, seek continuation of present Soviet-Israel military stand-off but prepare to confront the USSR militarily (via Israel in the first instance) through a prolonged conflict. [While this is a non-compromising position for the U.S., it might lead to endless escalation and not necessarily result in negotiations.]

(2) Take new initiatives to get negotiations started: (a) Get both sides to accept our proposals [Both sides have rejected them; a pre-negotiating process would be necessary, while withholding aircraft in the interim.]; or (b) begin negotiations under Jarring using a simple formula: both sides would agree to Resolution 242 and both sides would give assurances to the other on its fulfillment (the Arabs would agree to live at peace with Israel; the Israelis would say they were prepared to withdraw). [This might be the inducement for both sides to enter negotiations; however, it might involve continuing US pressure on Israel or encourage the Arabs to stiffen their position.]

(3) Become more specific on our proposals in the two and four power talks. [We would have trouble getting Israel to accept a detailed settlement; without any movement toward a cease-fire, the war of attri-

tion would continue and the pressure on us to provide additional aircraft would intensify.]

(4) Abandon the Jarring Mission and invite the parties to participate in the Four Power talks to work out agreement on implementing Resolution 242. [This might be the way to break the impasse; it might also isolate us with the Israeli position.]

On Israel's Aircraft Request [These options correlate roughly with numbered options above.]

(1) Meet the full request. [Further escalation might increase the chances for US involvement and decrease the chances for political settlement in the near future.]

(2) Defer on the Phantoms, provided limited number of aircraft for interceptor role (F–5s) and additional Hawk missiles. [This would strengthen Israel's air defense capability while limiting its forward air strategy; however, introduction of the F–5 would confuse the Israeli inventory and (though less than the F–4) be seen by the Arabs as a significant strengthening of the IAF.]

(3) Defer on full requests and sell only add-ons (i.e. replacement of losses or continuation of F–4 and A–4 deliveries for limited periods). [If this were a secret deal, it would constitute indirect pressure by the US on Israel to review its position; leaked, the US would appear to have backed down under Soviet/UAR pressure and strains in US-Israeli relations would not be relieved.]

(4) Defer on everything. [This would be the best atmosphere for new political initiatives; however, adverse Israeli reaction might lead to desperate military moves and give the impression that the US had backed off under Soviet/UAR pressure.]

117. Memorandum for the Record[1]

Washington, May 21, 1970.

SUBJECT

Meeting of the NSC Special Review Group on the Middle East

PARTICIPANTS

Elliot Richardson—Under Secretary of State
David Packard—Deputy Secretary of Defense
Lt. General John McPherson—JCS
Richard Helms—Director, CIA
Dr. Henry Kissinger
Joseph Sisco—Assistant Secretary of State
Warren Nutter—Assistant Secretary of Defense
A.L. Atherton, Jr.—Deputy Assistant Secretary of State
Robert Pranger—Deputy Assistant Secretary of Defense
Helmut Sonnenfeldt—NSC Staff
Harold Saunders—NSC Staff

Dr. Kissinger noted that this review was triggered by the President's commitment to Prime Minister Meir and to Ambassador Rabin that if the military balance in the Middle East changed the US would supply aircraft to Israel.[2] There are three questions:

1. Has the balance changed in such a way as to require stop-gap measures?

2. What could be our long-range policy on military supply?

3. Where are we trying to go?

Mr. Packard felt that we should get away from the question of aircraft for a moment and talk about the larger problem of where we are trying to go.

Dr. Kissinger agreed that that might be the case today except for one preliminary question: Is there some need before the President sees Foreign Minister Eban[3] to agree to make a token commitment to Israel to supply 6–8 aircraft now to take the heat off while we made more basic decisions.

Mr. Sisco said he felt that we should try to find a course of action that: (a) does not look weak to the USSR and does not provoke the

---

[1] Source: National Archives, Nixon Presidential Materials, NSC Files, NSC Institutional Files (H-Files), Box H–111, Senior Review Group, SRG Minutes Originals 1970. Secret; Nodis. Drafted by Saunders. The meeting was held in the White House Situation Room.

[2] See Document 101.

[3] See Document 118.

USSR and (b) provides a minimal reassurance to Israel. He felt that we needed to move simultaneously on the political and military tracks. On the political front, he would propose to Cairo a public declaration of ceasefire and commitment to make peace with Israel in exchange for an Israeli commitment in principle to withdraw. On the security front, we should inform Israel secretly that we would supply additional aircraft for two more months after the present deliveries run out—that is, in August and September—and that we would earmark an additional number of Phantoms and Skyhawks with the final decision to be made in the light of Israel's response to our diplomatic initiative. Meanwhile, we would respond quickly on Israel's basic logistical needs.

We would tell Nasser that we saw this as a non-escalatory step.

Mr. Richardson acknowledged that it would be difficult for the President to say that we are still thinking about this problem. But the problem was to say anything about the kinds of political steps we are thinking about until we have sorted ourselves out. Therefore he thought the proper line to take with Eban is to say that it is important for the US and Israel to reach some consensus on where we are going together.

Mr. Richardson continued that, developing this line, we might say that the US has a number of interests in the Middle East: maintaining the military balance because we will not abandon Israel; not turning the Arabs over to Soviet domination; preventing a continuing deterioration of the US position in the Middle East.

He felt that we could not simply batten down the hatches and ride out the present situation indefinitely. We have to have a settlement. There is no other way of solving the problem.

Dr. Kissinger said that question was still at issue.

Mr. Richardson replied that he felt we need a settlement even if we have to squeeze Israel and even if this looked like a concession to the USSR. We cannot stand an extrapolation of present trends. A decision to provide large numbers of new aircraft to Israel could blow up our position in the Middle East.

As we look to other parts of the Middle East, Mr. Richardson noted, we see other Soviet objectives such as the Persian Gulf. We have already concluded that cooperation between the Shah and King Faisal is essential for stability in that area. For the US to destroy its relationship with Saudi Arabia over additional aircraft for Israel would upset any contribution we might make to stability in the Gulf.

Mr. Richardson felt that if one adds all this up, the President at least needs to signal to Foreign Minister Eban that some movement on Israel's side—such as saying the word "withdrawal"—is essential to our ability to help Israel.

Mr. Packard said he felt strongly that we have to move toward a political settlement; we have to do this now, or it will be too late. He said he did not feel that we could do this with any delivery of aircraft to Israel in the next couple of months. We could, however, assure Israel in general terms that we will not allow it to become defenseless.

Dr. Kissinger asked Mr. Sisco whether he believed that verbal assurances would do any good.

Mr. Sisco said that he disagreed with Mr. Packard. He felt that the proposal he was making would be a major concession to the Arabs and therefore deliveries of aircraft to Israel were essential to balance this.

Mr. Helms asked if we are creeping over our original contract for 50 Phantoms.

Mr. Sisco replied that three Phantoms had been lost, so three of the new planes could be justified as "replacements."

Dr. Kissinger did not see how we could avoid publicity on this move. He did not see how we could expect Egyptian acquiescence. Of course, the Egyptians will mind if its enemy gets more weapons.

Mr. Sisco said he felt it was possible to hope that we might persuade Israel to talk about accepting the principle of withdrawal and beginning negotiations. In response to a comment from Mr. Packard, he said he did not believe we could realistically talk about symbolic Israeli withdrawal until after a peace agreement had been signed.

Mr. Helms said he did not think Israel wanted a cease-fire along the Suez Canal. That would simply give the Egyptians and the Soviets a chance to move SA–3 sites up to the Canal.

Mr. Sisco replied that any agreement to cease-fire would have to be coupled with an agreement that troops would observe a stand-still wherever they are.

Mr. Packard said he thought we should be thinking about trying to open the Suez Canal.

Dr. Kissinger asked Mr. Sisco if, in accepting the principle of withdrawal, Israel would be asked to include the Golan Heights.

Mr. Packard felt that all we could do at this point would be to try to get negotiations started.

Mr. Richardson said the issue is: What does "withdrawal" mean? We have emphasized the word "secure" in the phrase "secure and recognized boundaries." The purpose of the negotiation is to determine what constitutes "secure".

Dr. Kissinger said he felt we needed a strategy. We had had a year and a half of gimmicks. What if this proposal is not accepted?

Mr. Richardson agreed that we had to keep considering our strategy.

Mr. Sisco said that this strategy is different from past efforts in two ways. First, this by-passes the major power talks of 1969. The strategy here is to go to both parties direct. He felt that getting negotiations started is more important than doing something like a symbolic withdrawal on the ground. Second, the strategy of the past year has been to acquiesce in the Israeli strategy of letting the Arabs come to Israel. Since the Israelis may be now beginning to think that they need a settlement, it may make some sense to try to get negotiations started by direct US intervention.

Dr. Kissinger said that Israel may prefer to fight from its present boundaries. What are we going to do about arms supply?

Mr. Richardson replied that he would give Israel as much as the traffic would bear and a lot more if Israel would go back to its pre-war boundaries.

Mr. Nutter asked whether we should take Nasser's peace appeal[4] seriously.

Mr. Sisco replied that basically it was an appeal for the miracle that Nasser has been hoping for—someone to press Israel to withdraw completely from the territories it occupied in 1967. The more important aspect of the "appeal" is the statement that in the absence of Israeli withdrawal the US cannot continue to support Israel economically, militarily or politically because Nasser had made this a test of US-Arab relations. We could not ignore the aspects of a threat in this statement.

Mr. Richardson said that his own version of the scenario would go as follows: He would tell Israel that we would extend existing contracts and earmark additional aircraft for Israel but this must remain secret. It could remain secret only if Prime Minister Meir were in a position to say publicly simply that she is satisfied with contingency arrangements that have been made. Then we would tell Nasser that he should not worry, we have completed our review. We remain committed to maintain the military balance. But the question of our ultimate response short of interim steps is being held in abeyance. The question in this approach is whether or not the Israelis are politically required to say that they have assurances of additional aircraft.

Dr. Kissinger said he saw at least two problems. The scenario seemed to be based on an assumption that may not be true—that a settlement will resolve the Middle East problem. One could assume that, if we respond to Nasser's peace appeal by a diplomatic initiative, then any later deliveries or prospect of deliveries would evoke some kind of similar blackmail.

---

[4] See Document 115.

Dr. Kissinger noted also that Israel may prefer to have its Armageddon now rather than wait until later.

The problem, as he saw it, is that we had to find a way of saying nothing to Eban that would foreclose the Sisco option. He asked Mr. Sisco to provide talking points that do not commit us but do not foreclose the option. The other question is what to say about the replacement of aircraft lost. To say nothing may be impossible in the President's judgment.

Mr. Sisco said that he felt that his proposal would keep the lid on domestic Jewish community reaction.

Dr. Kissinger said that one of the assumptions that seems to underlie Mr. Sisco's proposal was that the way to get a settlement is to give Nasser what he wants.

Dr. Kissinger continued by saying that he felt it would be desirable to present to the NSC the assumptions and the courses of action envisaged in the Sisco policy and then in addition the assumptions and course of action in a counter model.

Mr. Richardson said it was important to get straight the fact that any public response to Israel's request would trigger a sharp Arab reaction.

Mr. Helms said that there is no question that Mr. Richardson is right.

Mr. Richardson said we could move the whole Middle East to the Soviets in a matter of months.

Mr. Packard suggested that we try to give Israel defensive equipment in the interim. There were other types of aircraft that we might provide such as F104s or F5s.

Mr. Sisco said that this was to suggest something that Israel has no interest in.

Dr. Kissinger said that this might be possible in the context of a big long-term arms package, but it hardly met the needs of the interim problem.

Mr. Sisco said he felt that Israel has to think in terms of offensive weapons.

Mr. Packard said that, if they only do this, they may not now have a feasible strategy.

Mr. Helms noted that if it developed that the Soviets pushed their aircraft up to the Suez Canal that could change the whole situation.

Mr. Packard said that is why we have to move now.

Mr. Sisco said that it would be important in any effort to achieve a cease-fire to include a stand-still that would keep planes out of the Suez Canal area.

In concluding the meeting, Dr. Kissinger asked Mr. Sisco to send talking points for the President's meeting with Foreign Minister Eban. He said he would try to arrange an NSC meeting for the week after next which could discuss alternative approaches.

Mr. Sisco asked whether we would not need another meeting at this level.

Dr. Kissinger replied that there would be another meeting the middle of the following week to discuss the two alternative courses.

Mr. Richardson said that the line he would suggest taking with Eban would be as follows: We are both embarked on a bleak course in the Middle East; the US and Israel must review its positions from the ground up. The main question is how we can work out together a strategy that will meet our separate interests.

Harold H. Saunders[5]

---

[5] Saunders initialed "H.S." above his typed signature.

---

118. Editorial Note

On May 22, 1970, President Nixon met with Israeli Foreign Minister Abba Eban in the Oval Office from 11:31 a.m. to 12:19 p.m. Also present were Assistant to the President for National Security Affairs Henry Kissinger, Assistant Secretary of State for Near Eastern and South Asian Affairs Joseph Sisco, Israeli Ambassador Yitzhak Rabin, and Israeli Minister Shlomo Argov. (National Archives, Nixon Presidential Materials, White House Central Files, President's Daily Diary) According to a record of the conversation prepared by Argov, Nixon began the meeting by expressing his "sorrow and condolences" over the attack on an Israeli school bus earlier in the morning, describing the perpetrators as "savages" who were "out of control." Nixon then moved the discussion to the issue of arms supplies and said: "The Prime Minister wrote me a letter some time ago [see footnote 3, Document 101] and we have very much in mind the Prime Minister's concern. I spoke to Rogers about it and we have a clear understanding of the matter. We have it under consideration and are studying intensively the intelligence reports. We, and I personally, will do what is necessary. The immediate thing is to get the 'stuff' over there." The important thing is the planes; and you will get them without fanfare."

After a further exchange with Eban about the delivery of planes and tanks to Israel, Nixon asked about the Soviet Union's military involvement in the Sinai Peninsula. Rabin replied: "The situation facing us was a very difficult one, the Russians had effectively driven us out of Egypt. We stand on the Canal and will defend it no matter what. We have to stand and the Russians are probing us to see if we will. They are making an attempt to push us by introducing SA–II and SA–III missiles in the area. We are anxious not to engage the Russians. Therefore we are trying to prevent installation of these missiles by not allowing them to complete any construction. We know that once they begin to doubt our resolution to stand on the Canal they will try to push us out. They have already tried to reach the Suez Canal twice. We should make clear to them that here we stay. It is therefore essential to make sure first of all that we have the tools to make them realize that we mean it . . . They must know that if they come we will defend ourselves."

Nixon responded by telling Rabin: "I told you before to give it to them and to hit them as hard as you can. Every time I hear that you go at them, penetrate into their territory, I am delighted. As far as they are concerned, go ahead and hit them. The trouble is the rest of the Arabs. I very strongly believe that you are right, they are testing both you and us and we have to enable you to deter them. We can also talk directly to the Russians. It has been some time since we did so. They are testing us, no doubt, but we ought to play it so we don't lose everything (in M.E.)." He went on to say: "We want to help you without hurting ourselves. The hell with oil! We can get it from somewhere else. We have to retain the other decent people in the Middle East."

The President concluded the meeting with an appeal to the Israelis to begin political discussions with the Arabs. "We can't go down the road of inevitable military escalation," he said. "We have to have your assurances on the political initiatives which we shall take. We have a problem here in terms of public opinion which won't accept just mindless escalation." He went on to say: "We have to show the efforts we are making and we have to have your commitment. We are not conditioning anything, we only need your assistance in order to overcome the difficulties that may arise when we go to Congress for support and the money . . . It isn't a question of resources or Soviets. We need to work on both fronts and have to show that we are doing so." Nixon added that he knew that certain people were describing Nasser's May 1 speech as "conciliatory" but commented, "Hell, no!" The fact remains, Nixon explained, that "there was the need to satisfy people's sensitivities and public opinion." (Israel State Archive, Ministry of Foreign Affairs, 6720/11)

119. Memorandum for the Record[1]

Washington, May 28, 1970.

SUBJECT
    Meeting of the NSC Special Review Group on the Middle East

PARTICIPANTS
    Under Secretary Elliot Richardson
    Deputy Secretary David Packard
    Director Richard Helms
    Dr. Henry A. Kissinger
    General Earle G. Wheeler
    General F.T. Unger
    Assistant Secretary Joseph J. Sisco
    Assistant Secretary Warren Nutter
    Deputy Assistant Secretary Alfred L. Atherton, Jr.
    Deputy Assistant Secretary Robert Pranger
    Harold H. Saunders

Dr. Kissinger opened the meeting by noting that the Group had before it a State Department paper[2] outlining two basic strategies—one for confronting the USSR and another geared more to political initiatives. He noted that the two are not exclusive. For instance, even if the second strategy were chosen, there might be a problem of putting some restraints on the USSR or demonstrating to it that, if it did not go along with a political strategy, it might have to face unpleasant consequences. Continuing, Dr. Kissinger noted that in addition there is a short-term problem of what interim response to give to Israel on its aircraft requests while we develop a broader political strategy. The purpose of the meeting was to formulate these strategies in such a way that they could be put before an NSC meeting.[3]

At Dr. Kissinger's request, Mr. Sisco explained the strategies outlined in the State Department Strategies paper. In beginning to discuss Strategy 1—after outlining some of the assumptions in the paper—he made two points: (a) We have to be keenly aware of the political and economic costs of adopting this strategy; (b) this course of action might move us closer faster to a confrontation with the USSR.

---

[1] Source: National Archives, Nixon Presidential Materials, NSC Files, NSC Institutional Files (H-Files), Box H–111, Senior Review Group, SRG Minutes Originals 1970. Secret; Nodis. Drafted by Saunders. The meeting was held in the White House Situation Room.

[2] For a summary, see Document 116.

[3] See Document 124.

Dr. Kissinger interrupted to ask about the counter to that point, namely that this would be a way to avoid confrontation with the USSR by giving support to Israel and making clear that the Soviets could not gain their ends by military action and by warning the Soviets clearly early in the game that they would face us if they tried to press Israel militarily. It is entirely possible, he said, that the second strategy—attempting to break the political impasse and start negotiations—would bring confrontation sooner by making the Israelis feel desperate and under pressure to lash out.

Mr. Sisco replied that the argument is not demonstrable either way. He felt that we would end up with an amalgam of Strategies 1 and 2. For Strategy 2 to be effective, it would have to be made credible by some elements of Strategy 1. If Soviet brinksmanship were to succeed, the price of peace would be too high for us.

Mr. Richardson pointed out that we have to be careful not to kick out the window a chance for negotiations at the outset. Waiting for the Arabs to get tired of Soviet efforts to get their territory back—as would be the case under Strategy 1—might take five-ten years.

Mr. Packard felt that we should not speak of Soviet brinksmanship but of Israeli brinksmanship. He felt the Soviets had no other recourse in the face of Israel's deep penetration raids except to come to Nasser's defense.

Mr. Sisco replied that one's view on this point depends on where one begins. Nasser last year declared a war of attrition, and one could just as well argue that Israel's moves were a response to Nasser's provocation.

Dr. Kissinger said that, however the USSR got there, their presence is a geo-political fact of considerable consequences. Ten years ago almost anybody would have considered this move a casus belli.

Mr. Sisco, responding again to Mr. Packard, said he felt the Soviets had gone farther than they need to have done. They could have limited their moves to installing surface-to-air missiles.

Mr. Packard said that the trouble with Strategy 1 was that it would preclude negotiations. Dr. Kissinger replied that it is not axiomatic that the application of force does not provide a way to get to negotiations. It is not absurd to think that the Arabs might lose hope in the face of superior force and turn to negotiations.

Mr. Sisco said that he felt that we should try Strategy 2. The likelihood of its working is not great. If it fails, then we would have to consider elements of Strategy 1. He also felt that we would have to consider breaking off the two power and the Four Power talks because the longer they continue, the longer they relieve Nasser of responsibility for facing up to the necessity to come to terms with Israel.

Mr. Sisco felt further that we have played the new Soviet decision in relatively low key. He felt that our posture had reflected prudence—not weakness. He felt that we ought to react both politically and militarily. The strategy outlined in the State Department paper was a very restrained reaction.

Mr. Packard felt that we could afford to be restrained while trying Strategy 2. We still have time to return to Strategy 1 later on.

Mr. Sisco returned to Dr. Kissinger's earlier point—that perhaps the application of force is the fastest way to reach negotiations. He said he is not certain which is the faster road to negotiations. We have been trying Strategy 2 for fifteen months and have not succeeded.

Mr. Richardson noted that Strategy 2 does not impose short-run costs. Dr. Kissinger said, "Except another war if Israel is convinced that they are getting into a hopeless position." Mr. Richardson replied that this would depend on convincing them that our diplomatic route was a route worth trying.

Mr. Packard noted that if the Soviets moved to the Suez Canal, then it would be a new ballgame. He felt that now we still have a chance to "make a run for it."

Dr. Kissinger said that in many of the papers that had been written, the point had been made that the military balance had not been significantly affected. He felt, however, that any move that enhances the chances for a strategy of attrition is Israel's death warrant.

Mr. Richardson said that Israel has two ways of achieving security: (1) achieving or maintaining a military position including advantageous territorial lines; (2) a U.S. commitment of some kind. He did not feel that the Soviets would be impressed by arms deliveries to Israel as such. He felt that we should consider what more to say to the Soviets and to Israel about the nature of the U.S. commitment.

Dr. Kissinger said that he felt that Israeli policy since 1967 had been disastrous. However, he could understand their dilemma of being asked to trade physical security for something highly problematical. He felt that even a U.S. commitment would be highly doubtful given the current mood of the United States.

Mr. Nutter asked how Israel could maintain its superiority in the present situation. Dr. Kissinger replied that Israel would strike out before it goes back to its pre-war boundaries. As they see it, they are confronted by hostile Arabs and face a major almost insoluble problem. The domestic dynamics of the Arab countries are becoming incompatible with the existence of Israel.

Dr. Kissinger said he did not feel that the negotiation Mr. Sisco had proposed in Strategy 2 was going to get off the ground.

Dr. Kissinger noted again that the presence of Soviet forces in the UAR is a geo-political fact of the greatest consequence. The Soviet Union might be able to use its military position in the UAR against the U.S. in the Eastern Mediterranean. In any case, Israel would look around and see the Mirages in Libya which would have to find their way to the UAR, new U.S. weapons in Jordan, and they would see the noose tightening. Then they would strike.

Mr. Richardson asked what striking would do for Israel. In 1967 they could improve their geographical position but not now.

Dr. Kissinger replied that they might destroy the Arab forces in one of these countries.

Mr. Sisco said that territory would not be their objective this time. But they would seek to destroy the air power and the economic capacity of their enemy. He felt that an extensive attack would permit them to come back to defend their present lines better than they can now or could in an extended war of attrition. They cannot take a strategy of attrition.

Mr. Nutter said he did not see how any U.S. policy would deter Israel—even giving them airplanes.

Dr. Kissinger said he felt that talking about a U.S. commitment to Israel was a waste of time. A defense treaty with Israel would call on us to pay too high a political price in the Arab countries. The Israelis would be "crazy" to believe that we could make good on such a commitment. Mr. Sisco said that he was not even sure that the U.S. could sign such a commitment given our present domestic mood.

Mr. Richardson said that we have to communicate to the Soviets a more direct sense that we will oppose them and we would by giving Israel more planes. Some of the moves against the USSR might hurt us with the Arabs. It seemed to him that the only way to get tough with the Russians is to convey the idea that if they go too far the U.S. will involve U.S. personnel.

Mr. Sisco said he did not feel that threat could be made credible. If the USSR moves its pilots to the Suez Canal, U.S. action would have to include a combination of political and military moves such as the following: breaking off all Middle East negotiations; supplying additional substantial assistance to Israel; setting up a mechanism for continuous consultation with Israel in order to project an image of military coordination; and discussion of overall U.S.-Israeli relations in order to imply the possibility of a security treaty. The danger of these moves is that they go down the polarization track and it is hard to turn back. This becomes a confrontation of prestige by both the Great Powers.

Mr. Nutter asked, "What do you accomplish by this?"

Mr. Sisco said that the Arabs might realize that they cannot get their territory back on a basis other than negotiation. He felt that we would have to pursue Strategy 2 first but might have to move into Strategy 1 at some time later.

Mr. Richardson said he wanted to emphasize the fact that the only card the U.S. holds against the Soviet Union is the risk of confrontation.

Dr. Kissinger asked Mr. Nutter what his strategy is. Mr. Nutter replied that it seems to have been ruled out that approaching the Arabs could launch negotiations. He said he would move directly with the Egyptians and Israelis to try to get a cease-fire in exchange for a partial Israeli withdrawal from the Suez Canal. He did not feel that Strategy 2 in the State Department paper offered enough of a change from past diplomatic approaches.

Mr. Sisco replied emphatically that Strategy 2 was quite different in that it proposes that the U.S. go directly to the Arabs and to the Israelis, asking Israel to commit itself to the principle of withdrawal and asking the Arabs to commit themselves to negotiations of some sort and to peace.

Mr. Nutter asked, "In exchange for eight airplanes?"

Dr. Kissinger said that the President felt committed to provide additional aircraft to Israel. Mr. Nutter asked whether the President felt committed to respond with the F–4. If so, then the Group was wasting its time.

Mr. Pranger noted that we could promise Israel quick re-supply rather than giving them aircraft right now. We could tell them that we are ready to earmark new production for them in order to be able to supply them with emergency aircraft on short notice.

Mr. Nutter said that he did not feel that we could give Israel planes secretly. "Why do the Israelis want planes unless others know they have them?"

General Wheeler, returning to an earlier point, said that the primary risk in providing a security guarantee for Israel is that it brings the U.S. back to Strategy 1 which "has no attraction for me *at all.*"

Mr. Helms seconded General Wheeler's point by noting that anyone who had lived through 1967 never wants to hear the word "guarantee" again.

Mr. Packard asked Mr. Sisco just exactly what Strategy 2 comprised. Mr. Sisco outlined the strategy in detail as described in the State Department paper. He said that it was very much the same as Mr. Nutter's strategy until it came to the question of whether or not to provide airplanes to Israel and the question of whether to try for some sort of physical movement of forces in withdrawal in the early stages of such a program. On the question of planes, he felt there were two choices: (1) There is Mr. Nutter's idea of earmarking planes but not delivering them. (2) There was the possibility of continuing to deliver planes under present contracts for another two months, three each month. Since only 44 of an original contract for 50 would be delivered this year, we could still deliver 6 more without having anyone know that we had exceeded our original plan since 6 Phantoms in a reconnaissance configuration are not scheduled for delivery until 1971 anyway. On the point of partial Israeli withdrawal, he did not feel that Israel would move an inch. He was aware of Mr. Pranger's discussion with the Israeli defense attaché,[4] but he did not feel this was Israeli policy. However, he did not want to debate that point since anyone at the table could confirm it by picking up the phone and calling Ambassador Rabin. If the Israelis were willing to agree to it, we would all be very happy.

Mr. Richardson said he wanted to introduce another element: How to make the conditions under which we would be confronted if we went down the Strategy 1 route more tolerable. Should we be holding out the prospect of a Palestine-Israel federation? Should we be more forthcoming in our position on the status of Jerusalem?

Dr. Kissinger noted that this is the carrot in the policy, but we also need a stick. What will discourage the Soviets is fear of confrontation with us. We have to have thought of how to convey that idea to them. He felt that the only thing that would make Strategy 2 work would be fear that if Strategy 2 fails, there is something worse. We need to devise the maximum stick to introduce into Strategy 2.

Someone asked what kinds of things we could do, and Mr. Sisco replied that one thing we should *not* do is to cut back the Sixth Fleet.

Dr. Kissinger closed the meeting by summarizing as follows:

1. He thought it was a fair consensus that Strategy 1 by itself was not favored by the Group.

2. He felt that Strategy 2 represented a fair consensus except on the question of aircraft deliveries. He felt the President should not be asked to sign off on the question of whether to try for partial Israeli withdrawal from the Suez Canal. If we could get that, it would be desirable, but if we cannot then we would have to do something else. This is more a question of feasibility than of policy.

3. There should be some analysis of where we go from here. If Strategy 2 does not work, should we move to an effort to work out a Palestinian solution or should we think more about how to make the "stick" more credible.

Harold H. Saunders[5]

---

[4] Not further indentified.
[5] Saunders initialed "H.H.S." above his typed signature.

120. Memorandum of Conversation[1]

Washington, June 2, 1970, 3 p.m.

SUBJECT

Middle East

PARTICIPANTS

The Secretary
Assistant Secretary Sisco
Mr. Dubs, EUR/SOV

Ambassador Dobrynin
Yuli Vorontsov, Minister-Counselor, Soviet Embassy

At the outset of the meeting, the Secretary asked about Dobrynin's health. The Ambassador said he felt good.

Dobrynin said he understood that the meeting this afternoon would focus on the Middle East. Nevertheless, he was prepared to discuss other matters, such as European affairs and SALT, in the future at the Secretary's convenience.

Dobrynin said that he had been authorized during his recent consultation in Moscow to inform the U.S. Government that he was prepared to continue discussions on the Middle East with Mr. Sisco. He hoped that mutual efforts would lead to a solution. The Soviet Government was also interested in finding guidelines which Ambassador Jarring could use in the search for a settlement on the Middle East.

Dobrynin then referred to his conversations with Mr. Sisco prior to the latter's trip to the Middle East.[2] Dobrynin noted that the U.S. side had expressed an interest during those talks in obtaining more detailed formulations on the nature of peace and the obligations which the sides would undertake. At the same time, the Soviet side had indicated an interest in more precise language from the U.S. on the question of withdrawal and other matters. Dobrynin said he was instructed to present formulations on the two points mentioned and that he hoped these points would meet the wishes of the U.S. Dobrynin then handed the Secretary two papers with the following formulations[3] (NOTE: these

---

[1] Source: National Archives, Nixon Presidential Materials, NSC Files, Box 1159, Saunders Files, Middle East Negotiations Files, Middle East Settlement—US–USSR Talks. Secret; Nodis. Drafted on June 3 by Adolph Dubs. The conversation took place in the Secretary's office. The memorandum is Part I of III; Parts II (NATO) and III (SALT) are attached. All three parts are printed in *Foreign Relations, 1969–1976*, volume XII, Soviet Union, January 1969–October 1970, Document 159. Saunders summarized the meeting for Kissinger in a June 8 memorandum; see ibid., Document 162.

[2] See Document 107. On Sisco's trip to the Middle East, see Documents 109 and 114.

[3] The Soviet Union presented these formulations at the June 24 Four-Power meeting. (Telegram 1315 from USUN, June 25; National Archives, RG 59, Central Files 1970–73, POL 27–14 ARAB–ISR)

actually are extensions or modifications of points 3 and 11 of Section II of the Soviet paper of June 17, 1969):[4]

"Point 3, Section II

From the moment of deposit with the UN of the concluding document or documents the parties shall refrain from acts contradicting the cessation of the state of war and the establishment of the state of peace, in accordance with paragraphs 10 and 11, with the understanding that, juridically, cessation of the state of war and establishment of the state of peace will begin at the same time of the completion of the first stage of the withdrawal of Israeli troops from the territories occupied during the conflict of 1967."

"Point 11, Section IX

The Arab countries, parties to the settlement, and Israel mutually agree

—to respect and recognize the sovereignty, territorial integrity, inviolability and political independence of each other and their mutual right to live in peace in secure and recognized borders without being subjected to threats or use of force;

—to undertake everything that is necessary so that any military or hostile acts, with the threat or use of force against the other side will not originate from and are not committed from within their respective territories:

—refrain from intervening directly or indirectly in each other's domestic affairs for any political, economic or other reasons."

Dobrynin commented that these two formulations along with others they had presented to Sisco previously would stand or fall together. In any event, he expressed the hope that they would remain confidential. The Soviet side looks forward toward movement from the U.S.

Commenting that we would look at the two formulations carefully, the Secretary then recalled his conversation with Dobrynin of March 25,[5] at which time he had noted that the U.S. found the operational involvement of Soviet military personnel in the UAR defenses to be serious and potentially dangerous. The Secretary noted that in reply Dobrynin had expressed the view that Soviet actions were of a defensive nature and that Dobrynin had expressed the hope that the U.S. would be of some assistance in getting the Israelis to desist from deep-penetration raids. Since that conversation, the Secretary noted Israel

---

[4] See Document 34.
[5] See footnote 5, Document 105.

has halted the deep-penetration raids and Israeli representatives have publicly stated that Israel would observe a cease-fire. In addition, Prime Minister Meir has publicly accepted, during a speech in the Knesset, Security Council Resolution 242.[6] The Secretary said that Israel's position on deep-penetration raids was announced by Israeli Defense Minister Dayan on May 4. Subsequently, on May 26, Dayan went further by indicating that Israeli air activity was being limited to an area 30 kilometers west of the Canal. These moves on the part of Israel represented real progress, and we feel that we have been helpful in this context by urging Israel to cease its deep-penetration raids. Furthermore, in our view, Prime Minister Meir's acceptance of Security Council Resolution 242 provides a basis for negotiations.

The Secretary then said that the U.S. remained deeply concerned over the increased military involvement of the Soviet Union in the UAR. In view of this concern he wished to convey a statement, the text of which would be provided to the Ambassador after the meeting. The statement, which he wished to convey to the Soviet Government, reads as follows:

"The USSR has indicated that Soviet military activities in the UAR will remain defensive. We want to make clear that we would not view the introduction of Soviet personnel, by air or on the ground, in the Canal combat zone as defensive since such action could only be in support of the announced UAR policy of violating the cease-fire resolutions of the Security Council. We believe that introduction of Soviet military personnel into the delicate Suez Canal combat zone could lead to serious escalation with unpredictable consequences to which the U.S. could not remain indifferent. In this connection, we believe, and I am sure you do, it is neither in the interest of the Soviet Union nor the United States for the Middle East to become an area of confrontation between us."[7]

The Secretary then noted that the Soviet Union had at one point indicated an interest in a cease-fire in the area. The U.S. side would like to renew discussions on this subject with Dobrynin as well as on the general matter of a Middle East settlement. With respect to the continuation of the talks between the Ambassador and Mr. Sisco, we believe this

---

[6] The text of Meir's May 26 speech to the Knesset is in *Israel's Foreign Policy: Historical Documents*, volumes 1–2: 1947–1974, Chapter XII, The War of Attrition and the Cease Fire, Document 15.

[7] In his memoirs, Kissinger described this statement as "extraordinary" since he believed that it gave the Soviet Union a "blank check" by "acquiesc[ing] in the Soviet combat presence in Egypt except in the immediate vicinity of the Suez Canal." Kissinger also complained that Rogers informed neither him nor Nixon, at least as far as he knew, that the Secretary was going to read such a statement. (*White House Years*, pp. 574–575)

very desirable. We welcome the written formulations provided by the Ambassador and are willing to resume bilateral discussions very soon.

Mr. Sisco noted that the U.S. side would wish a bit of time to review the new formulations and to consider them in the light of papers that had been exchanged previously.

Dobrynin emphasized that the formula on mutual obligations should be kept very confidential. He had no particular problem regarding publicity surrounding meetings but did hope that the substance of the proposals advanced during conversations would not be revealed publicly. Dobrynin noted further that he had no objections to having the fact revealed that new proposals were advanced, so long as the substance was not disclosed. He warned that if the proposals were leaked, the Soviets would not feel bound by them. Mr. Sisco suggested that any public disclosure that new formulations had been advanced would only arouse curiosity and could lead to unwarranted speculation. Mr. Sisco, therefore, suggested that nothing be said publicly on this score. Dobrynin agreed.

The Secretary then asked Dobrynin whether he could provide any clarification regarding the Soviet Union's intentions with respect to Soviet personnel and military equipment in the UAR. Dobrynin replied that he was not qualified to discuss "military details." He referred to the Dayan statements regarding penetration raids and wondered whether these represented personal comments or whether they were sanctioned by the Government of Israel.

Alluding to the Secretary's remarks, Dobrynin said that the only thing that has happened in the Middle East is that deep-penetration into UAR air space and bombardment of heavily populated Egyptian areas by Israel have ceased. This is the only thing which has really changed in the Middle East. He added that the outlook for the Middle East was not very hopeful if U.S. policy was aimed at maintaining Israel's military superiority and Israel's policy of dealing from a position of strength. If, on the other hand, the U.S. wants to find a solution that would be fair to both Israel and the Arab countries, the Soviet Union would be willing to cooperate. Frankly, Dobrynin said, maybe the situation now is a little more equal in the military sense. Perhaps this provides a good opportunity to advance toward a settlement. The Soviet Union feels that the time may be ripe. Dobrynin stressed that the Soviet Union does not feel that anything has happened in the way of a developing confrontation between the Soviet Union and the U.S. He wanted to assure the Secretary that the Soviet Union does not want such a confrontation, even though he claimed that some forces in the world and pro-Zionist forces in the U.S. would like this to happen. Dobrynin proceeded to repeat that nothing has changed drastically in the situation, looking at it coolly and realistically. A possibility for a peaceful settlement still exists, and there is no doubt from the Soviet side with respect to not wanting a confrontation.

In reply to Dobrynin, the Secretary said there should be no doubt that the U.S. wanted a fair and equitable solution. Our formulations of December 9 indicated that.[8] These proposals were unacceptable to Israel, and the UAR had not accepted the proposals either. With respect to other comments by Dobrynin, the Secretary said that we felt strongly that a shift in the military situation had taken place. It is conceivable that the Arabs, having felt deeply humiliated in the past, may be in a better frame of mind now. The basic question, however, is whether the Soviet Union and the Arabs really want a peaceful settlement. We feel that we should actively pursue a political solution. The Secretary underlined that any additional actions by the Soviet Union, especially toward the Suez Canal, could be highly explosive and that is why we felt it necessary to make the statement that we did. We believe that the time is ripe to work toward a peaceful settlement and we will work actively toward this end. The Secretary said that he could not think of anything that would be more helpful in improving the world atmosphere at the moment than a peaceful settlement in the Middle East. He reminded Dobrynin that Israel's actions and statements over the past weeks were not totally apart from what we have done in urging Israel to be more flexible in its positions. In addition to the statements and actions he had already referred to, the Secretary cited Foreign Minister Eban's comment that the world would be surprised at the concessions that Israel would make once genuine negotiations got underway. We have not seen anything similarly forthcoming from Nasser's side, however. The Secretary said that he hoped the Soviet Union would impress upon the Arabs the importance of a settlement. Otherwise, it can be seen that the fedayeen would become more and more a factor in the situation and unlikely to be subject to the influence of others.

In response to Dobrynin's request, Mr. Sisco said his office would provide Mr. Vorontsov with the text of the statement made by the Secretary as well as information bearing on the statements of Defense Minister Dayan and Prime Minister Meir to which the Secretary had referred.

---

[8] See Document 73.

121. Memorandum From Secretary of Defense Laird to President Nixon[1]

Washington, June 5, 1970.

SUBJECT

Proposed US Peace Initiative in the Middle East

In my discussion with Dr. Kissinger at breakfast on 4 June, he suggested I provide you with my views on the present Middle East crisis. The following comments are provided in response to this suggestion, and for use in connection with the NSC review scheduled for next week.[2]

The Department of Defense has participated fully and most urgently in the recent review of Middle East policy, and specifically the question of further aircraft for Israel. The crucial issue confronting us in this review is how to resolve the conflict between our support for Israel, and our desire both to preserve our own interest and influence in the Arab world and to prevent the further spread of Soviet influence. The fact of Israel's creation, survival and growth has largely determined political attitudes and shaped political strategy in the Middle East. About it almost all other issues and events revolve, including the relative influence and prestige of the United States and the Soviet Union in the Middle East.

Our dilemma lies in the fact that the conflicting aspects of our policy in the Middle East are fully reconcilable only during periods of lessening tension. However, recent actions by the Soviets, the Arabs and Israelis have served to raise rather than lower the level of tension and hostilities. Both the UAR and Israel have undertaken new military initiatives, and the Soviets have involved their own forces to an unprecedented degree. In the present context of increasing violence, the Israelis are pressing us for an enlarged commitment, including some $2.5 billion in arms ($1.6 billion on credit) over five years, and for firm US actions aimed at limiting the Soviet role in the area. In effect, we are being asked to guarantee the continued existence of Israel with whatever means and policies are required, regardless of Israel's own actions, and with the implicit expectation that unilateral employment of US forces may be necessary at some future time if there is no other alterna-

---

[1] Source: National Archives, Nixon Presidential Materials, NSC Files, Box 654, Country Files, Middle East, Middle East—Recent Actions. Keep File Intact. Top Secret; Eyes Only. All brackets are in the original except those indicating text that remains classified.

[2] See Document 124.

tive to ensure Israel's survival. On the other hand, the Arabs press us to abandon our special relationship with Israel, and tell us that further escalation of our support to that country will destroy the US position in the Arab world for the foreseeable future. In these circumstances, the central question facing us is whether it still is possible or desirable to pursue a policy based on limited support of Israel, at the same time attempting the preservation of our interests and influence in the Arab world. It is the purpose of this memorandum to outline a number of considerations which lead us to believe that we can in fact pursue such a policy, but to do so successfully will be difficult and will require major new US initiatives. To abandon this policy will mean compromising basic US national security interests.

A Policy of New Initiatives and Limited Commitment

This option is still open but requires US initiatives. There is substantial evidence that both sides still want peace, but find themselves so locked into public positions that they cannot or will not undertake, on their own, the new peace initiatives needed to break the stalemate. Instead, they attempt new and escalatory military initiatives, and seek the support of the great powers in doing so. The Soviets have demonstrated at least a degree of restraint (their moves in the UAR appear to result from Israeli actions), but are unwilling to advance beyond the Arab position. Thus, if there is to be an escape from the present vicious cycle of military action–military response, it is the US which must provide it with new and meaningful peace initiatives. These initiatives must emphasize the still substantial common interests of all the parties, and take advantage of the private and more reasonable positions of both the Arabs and Israelis. With the Soviets we must make the most of our common interest in avoiding a nuclear confrontation and preventing nuclear proliferation in the Middle East. We can and should seek to enlist the support and assistance of the many other nations with an interest in settlement.

This option also requires US restraint and Israeli cooperation. We must not permit ourselves to be pressured into actions which will weaken our initiatives. In particular, we must not sell, at this time, additional attack aircraft to Israel. We are looking for long-term solutions, and sleight of hand maneuvers to meet short-term Israeli aircraft requests pose too great a risk to be acceptable. In the long run they will become known, and their adverse impact will be the greater for having been hidden. Further, Israel, which already has a very substantial bombing superiority over its combined Arab foes, has no immediate need for such aircraft: against the Arabs they are unnecessary, and against the Soviets they would be insufficient. For the most part, future Israeli aircraft requirements can be met with air defense fighters, such as the F–5, the F–8, or the F–104, all of which are available. In the interim, should an urgent need arise you will recall that we do have contingency plans to provide attack aircraft promptly. The Israelis have been reassured in this regard on several occasions, and we are prepared to repeat these assurances as necessary. By the same token, we must have Israeli cooperation in taking a major "first step for peace": it is the probability that we can get Israeli concessions which makes our approach to the Arabs credible, and it is Israeli agreement which must act to unstop the bottle. An Israeli concession in the form of agreement to a phased and conditional withdrawal, would be contingent on reciprocal Arab moves, but it is indispensable for any forward movement.

Both indigenous and external powers must assume some portion of the tasks necessary to success. There must be movement by the UAR and Israel, followed by other Arab powers, to stop their open warfare so that they can prepare for peace. Moves on all sides should take place simultaneously in order to avoid embarrassing situations where one party must "lose face" by moving first. Also, public disclosure of detailed plans should be kept at a bare minimum, since it is essential that old rhetorical symbols be jettisoned for minimal gains instead of maximal demands. The critical first step of a de facto cease-fire would be followed by other phases:

—progressive demilitarization of the occupied territories, with simultaneous efforts to control terrorist activities;

—reopening of the Suez Canal to all nations, special attention to points of international sensitivity (Straits of Tiran, Jerusalem, nuclear weapons) and formal peace negotiations as inducements for progressive Israeli withdrawal under conditions of maximum security;

—UN action on the status of the West Bank of the Jordan and the position of the Palestinians in international society;

—Arab recognition of Israel, leading to a formal peace treaty.

—Soviet withdrawal of combat forces from the UAR.

During the de facto cease-fire phase, and thereafter, the US would work through its own good offices in political/military channels; through third countries (with minimum reliance on USSR); through interested and reliable private individuals and groups; and through the UN. It may be necessary, for example, to provide Israel with an arms package of APCs, tanks, and self-propelled artillery to enhance its ability to react to UAR violations of the agreement.

A more detailed outline of a possible new approach will be made available for consideration by the NSC. The critical decision does not depend on details, however, but on a US determination to take the initiative, to insist on Israeli cooperation, and to be fully flexible in our approach.

Security Considerations

In evaluating the proposal for a new US initiative, it is of the greatest importance that you consider the implications for our national security of the alternatives. Realistically, the only alternatives are (a) to make a full commitment to Israel, or (b) to continue to add to our present commitment, in the hope that somehow complete polarization can be avoided. The effects of these alternatives on our position in the Arab world would be largely the same, and the chances are very great that even if we sought to avoid it, we would shortly find ourselves pushed into a full commitment posture. The implications of such a posture are extremely serious.

First, we have concluded that *there is no acceptable military solution to the present impasse.* This impasse has its roots in a number of basic human problems, which are not susceptible of military solution. Nothing we provide to Israel in the way of equipment or financial support can enable that small country to prevent casualties, to halt the war of attrition, to end terrorist activity, or to assure perpetual control of a captive and restive Arab population. The Arabs, even with defensive support by the Soviets, are incapable of mounting more than harassing raids into Israeli-held territory. They can inflict significant, but not decisive losses over time by attrition.

Second, *the sale at this time of additional F–4s will contribute to further Soviet success in the Arab world.* The F–4s have become the outstanding symbol of Israeli power, and their use as attack bombers has come to be identified in Arab eyes with the US, which has supplied these aircraft to Israel. We have an important security interest in countering Soviet penetration in this vital area, and the sale of additional attack aircraft at this time can only worsen our own image and present the Soviets with new opportunities. The consequences of the sale could, indeed, be made even worse should Israel use these additional aircraft, as they have previous ones, for expanded attack purposes. We have no assurance that provision of additional attack aircraft to Israel at this time will act as a restraining influence on their military strategy or moderate their political stance.

Third, expanding our commitment to Israel, *by promising or implying that US forces would be used directly to support Israel under any circumstances, is unacceptable.* We cannot overstate the importance of this reservation. Israel's current military development certainly includes a major effort [1½ *lines not declassified*]. Israel has refused to sign the NPT, despite repeated US efforts in that direction. [2½ *lines not declassified*] This consideration reinforces our strong conviction that there is inherent in the present Arab-Israeli conflict a very real potential for a US-Soviet nuclear confrontation. We consider it imperative that the US avoid such a confrontation, and avoid undertaking any additional commitments to Israel which would increase that danger.

Conclusions

Our basic interests require that we avoid nuclear war with the Soviets, or a direct confrontation wherein the threat of nuclear war is possible. A corollary interest is to prevent nuclear weapons from coming into the hands of Middle Eastern states. Our interests also require that we prevent the further spread of Soviet influence, and preserve and strengthen the US position in the area vis-à-vis the Soviets. The critical consideration is one of our basic national security and in our considered judgment an expansion of US commitments to Israel, including a decision to supply additional attack aircraft to Israel at this time, would constitute a significant and dangerous threat to our security interests.

The most sensible move, in my judgment, is to undertake new US initiatives aimed at working toward achieving a phased peace in the area. Should Israel cooperate, but not the Arabs, further aid to Israel can be justified and Arab reaction attenuated, without enlarging our commitment to Israel. Should the Arabs (specifically the UAR) be agreeable, but not Israel, the Israelis would be put on notice that our heretofore implicit guarantee of their security is contingent upon Israeli actions being consistent with US national interests. If Soviet reaction is not in favor, this would give us the opportunity to mobilize world (and particularly European) opinion against them. It would also lessen the adverse effects of further aid to Israel, and give us a lever for use against the Soviets in the Arab world.

Recommendation

I recommend that this memorandum be considered as the basis for the discussion at the NSC meeting on the Middle East.

General Wheeler concurs with the views expressed in this paper.

Melvin R. Laird

---

122. Editorial Note

On the evening of June 8, 1970, Secretary of State William Rogers invited Soviet Ambassador Anatoly Dobrynin to his home in the Washington suburbs for a "secret unofficial conversation." No U.S. record of the conversation has been found, but according to a record of the conversation prepared by Dobrynin, and provided to the Department of

State by the Russian Ministry of Foreign Affairs, the conversation lasted nearly 3 hours and focused primarily on the Middle East. A portion of the record of the conversation follows:

"*The Near East:* This question took up the main part of the conversation. Rogers began the conversation by noting that, with the direct involvement of President Nixon, they are now completing a multi-faceted analysis of the current situation in the region and the development of possible further steps for the USA in that regard. Assuring that they 'aim for peace and a lessening of tensions in the existing dangerous Near-East conflict,' and complaining about the 'excessive difficulty of problems,' with which they meet now, in developing a 'reasonable course,' Rogers said that in their opinion, the Soviet military presence, in part in the UAR, would have very important effect on the situation in the Near East.

"Rogers asked if the Soviet Union is planning to increase its presence. This is not indifferent to us—now and in the future—especially if Soviet pilots appear in the region of the Suez Canal, the Secretary of State forcefully underlined.

"I said that such a formulation of the question is unclear to say the least. If one follows the logic suggested by the Americans, then it seems the Soviet Union is the main reason for the current dangerous and tense situation in the Near East, although the whole world knows that this is not the case. The Soviet military presence is just the consequence of an openly aggressive course taken by Israel, supported by the USA, directed at a continuation of the occupation of Arab lands, at the undermining of disagreeable governments of Arab countries—victims of Israeli aggression. The Soviet Union has given and will continue to give aid to these Arab countries, but is not a supporter of any military confrontation, does not follow any selfish goals, but aims at a just peaceful settlement. Only recently the Secretary of State had been provided additional proposals by the Soviet side [see Document 120] to which it had not received any response. In general there is an impression that the American side is not in a hurry to continue serious Soviet-American talks on peaceful settlement, but prefers instead to look at further military aspects of aid to Israel. This course can only intensify the situation, I told the Secretary of State.

"Rogers started to advance a thought that in Moscow, apparently, they don't imagine what kind of pressure the government of Golda Meir is putting on them in connection with the appearance of Soviet pilots in the UAR. The Israelis tell us, the Americans, that these are not instructors, but military pilots ready to fight. The Israeli pilots can tell immediately when Soviet pilots go into the air. This is clear by the 'pilots signature' as well as the decisiveness with which they intercept Israeli pilots when they cross over deep into the territory of the UAR.

The Egyptian pilots never go directly into battle unless they have significant advantage in numbers.

"I told Rogers that it is unlikely that the point of our conversation is to discuss the Israelis' impressions. But from what he said regarding the Israeli flights *deep* into Egyptian territory, it then follows who is the initiator of provocative acts. In connection with this it is strange that the USA stands as a defender of such acts.

"Rogers started to justify himself. He entered into a diffuse discussion of American 'peaceful efforts' on settlement, starting with 1967, to show that the Nixon administration 'always aims for peace.' Rogers' statements had a very unsystematic character, he jumped from one thought to another, not really saying anything new.

"Keeping in mind Rogers' well known manner of speaking rather diffusely and not clearly enough, at the end of the discussion I put before him a question in a direct form: 'What can I tell the Soviet government regarding the position of the USA regarding a settlement in the Near East? What does it intend to do? Can I get, in a more concrete form, an explanation of what he himself meant when he, the Secretary of State, gave a television interview on Sunday, June 7, when he said that the USA in the coming weeks will begin a new diplomatic initiative?' (Department of State *Bulletin,* June 29, 1970, pages 785–792)

"Rogers thought for some time. Then he once again began to diffusely set forth the US position, although in a more precise manner. However even here I had to ask him specific questions. His statements, if one were to sum them up, amount to the following:

"The Government of the USA is currently completing its assessment of the general situation in the Near East. It is worried that, speaking frankly, the current state of mind in the Israeli government where there is a new intensification of the divide between 'hawks' and 'doves.' But as part of pressure on the Soviet side, he, Rogers, can unofficially say that in Washington they are afraid lest 'hot heads' in Tel Aviv decide to deliver a strong blow to the Arab countries, first of all the UAR, 'which would be a suicidal step,' at least from the point of view of future prospects, for Israel. The situation is made more difficult by the fact that Golda Meir is completely convinced, although this is not the case, especially under President Nixon, who came to power without the Jewish vote and in fact despite it, that she can always force the government of the USA, using the Jewish influence here, to follow and support Israel regardless of what it does. Right now Golda Meir has also become convinced that the Soviet Union has decided to go on the path of a military blow to Israel, by participating directly in military activity, in part through its flights. Because of this conviction the premier of Israel is currently bombarding Nixon with calls to give Israel 'firm assurances' that the USA will not leave it 'one-on-one against the

Soviet Union.' It is in this context that Golda Meir puts the question of selling Israel a new set of American planes.

"The Government of the USA, Rogers went on to say, is currently, in a private manner, putting serious pressure on the government of Israel, directly warning against any reckless military activity. In Washington this is based on a belief that this would cause an essential effect. But at the same time the government of the USA would like to give Israel some new assurances that it would 'not leave it.' Besides the public announcements already made on this score by various American officials and representatives, the Nixon administration is looking at the question—precisely in connection with this—of new deliveries of airplanes to Israel.

"Although it has in principle been decided beforehand that, towards the goals outlined above, Israel will be given a promise to satisfy its request, it has however not been decided to this day on what scale it should be done and how such a decision should be made public.

"The main [issue] here—is the unwillingness of the administration to further worsen its relations with the Arab world. This is the second main direction, which the government of the USA is now strenuously thinking.

"The third course being discussed in Washington is the question of how to more quickly make the 'Jarring mechanism' start working so that both sides could, finally, renew contacts.

"Here, in connection with what was said by Rogers on the last question, one situation calls for attention. Judging by his initial comments one gets the impression that in the administration there is currently a discussion regarding possible further actions within the framework of Soviet-American contacts, and the following possibility: concentrate all efforts of American diplomacy first of all on bringing the Arab world and Israel under Jarring's aegis, possibly bypassing bilateral talks for the time being or a further development of the questions of settlement in the framework of talks—'this could be continued parallel to the resumption of the Jarring mission,' the Secretary of State said. At the same time one cannot exclude the possibility that the Americans are hoping right now to convince Israel, in exchange for a deal on planes, to take a more flexible position on questions of a peaceful settlement, specifically: to more precisely announce about the readiness to accept the Security Council resolution (Golda Meir has already started making gestures in this direction) and to agree for direct talks with the Arabs through Jarring.

"In connection with this Rogers' comment that the overall situation in the Near East is such that it is necessary to immediately resume Jarring's mission 'even before the General Assembly session approaches' is notable. In response to a question regarding what sort of contacts, in the Secretary's opinion, would exist between the Arabs and Israel, Rogers immediately said 'Not direct ones, of course, but indirect, through Jarring—in one city, or maybe in one building—otherwise the Arabs won't go.'

"It is not impossible that the Americans are counting on convincing Nasser to agree to a renewal of the Jarring mission (it is possible that this is implied by the 'new American initiative').

"Rogers also noted the possibility that the 'important question' of a ceasefire could have a more serious decision during Jarring's mission, even as a temporary measure for the time being, for the period of talks, as a good-will gesture by both sides, which would have an 'enormous psychological effect' on the whole territory of the Near East.

"To repeat—Rogers himself did not divulge in any detail or precision the intentions of the American side noted above. He also completely avoided specifying, what exactly is meant when he speaks of an American initiative being proposed. However his individual statements give a known basis for considering such a course by the Americans possible.

"In connection with this it should be noted that when I asked him what he thinks about the situation with our bilateral talks he did not give an immediate clear answer. At first he said that the most important thing is 'launching the Jarring mission,' and the USSR and USA could at the same time 'continue parallel discussions, helping Jarring and the sides themselves.' Then, in connection with my question, he corrected himself, saying that it seems that our two sides need to speed up the development of recommendations to Jarring which, however, do not necessarily have to have a very specific character, but it is necessary to fix the primary principles on the more important points of settlement. When I reminded him our strong point of view on this score (in part, in our response to the previous American plan 'with neutral formulations' on points of contention) he did not enter into a discussion saying that 'you and Sisco know the details better' and all of this can be discussed in greater detail when our discussions with Sisco resume, which, apparently, will be in the near future. In connection with this Rogers avoided a detailed discussion of the points regarding peaceful settlement, although we did exchange opinions on the main points (the Secretary of State did not say anything new, pointed out that they did not finish looking at all of the related questions, including our latest position).

"*The overall impression* of the conversation with Rogers regarding the Near East amounts, in short, to the following. The Nixon government, for the first time in many months, has started a serious review of its policy in the region in light of events currently taking place there. It seems that the most serious impulse for this was our military presence in the UAR, in the first place of Soviet pilots and missiles. They are particularly worried about the lack of clarity, for Washington, regarding our further intentions, whether we will significantly increase our military presence in the UAR and whether Soviet pilots and missiles will cover the Suez Canal zone where the likelihood of our collision with Israelis would increase. The Americans would clearly like to achieve some mutual understanding with us regarding whether we will move right up to Suez. At the same time they have to resign themselves quietly to our military presence and air defense of population centers in the UAR deep in its territory.

"In a political sense the Nixon administration, worried about developments in the general situation in the Near East, which are unfavorable to the USA, judging by a host of signs, would like to convince the Israeli government to take a more flexible line. If the Americans are successful at this (the question of supplying aircraft to Israel plays the role of a sort of exchange coin here), then they have two paths open before them to a quick resumption of the Jarring mission.

"One, within the framework of the current Soviet-American talks. The second (attractive for Washington and, apparently, also being discussed in the administration) is to try to 'sell' possible Israeli concessions, if they are offered, directly to the Arabs, Nasser first and foremost, as a purely American achievement. If the 'direct bridge' with the Arabs (Nasser) does not work, then the center of gravity will again be shifted to our bilateral discussions.

"It seems that related discussions in the White House (and talks with Israel) are not yet finished. Therefore the Americans are currently maintaining a known tactic of delaying concrete discussions, wishing at the same time to keep open for itself a path to talks with us.

"I conducted the discussions with Rogers on Near Eastern affairs in a calm but firm manner so that the Nixon administration would not have any doubts that while we are not aiming for any military confrontation, at the same time we will decisively defend the interests of the Arab countries which are victims of aggression, and our interests in the Near East in the framework of an overall peaceful settlement which will be the only possible path to solving the current acute and dangerous conflict situation in the region." (Archive of Foreign Policy, Russian Federation, f. 0129, op. 54, p. 405, d. 5, 1. 230–240)

123. Memorandum From Secretary of State Rogers to President Nixon[1]

Washington, June 9, 1970.

SUBJECT
    Next Steps in the Middle East

We have conflicting objectives in the Middle East, the achievement of which poses dilemmas for the US at this present juncture. Our purpose is to find a course of action which: (a) stops the fighting on the principal fronts, or at least reduces the likelihood of confrontation between Israel and the USSR which would increase the possibility of a more direct US-Soviet confrontation; (b) offers a fresh and new approach to get negotiations started between the parties; (c) provides Israel with sufficient assurance regarding military assistance as an inducement towards military prudence and political flexibility, without causing a major break with the non-radical Arab regimes and jeopardizing the chances for success on the political front; and (d) neither reflects weakness to nor provokes undue escalation from Moscow.

To this end, the following courses of action are recommended as a "stop shooting, start talking" American initiative.

1. *Ceasefire.* We would propose to Israel and the UAR, and subsequently to as many other Arab frontline states as possible, agreement on a publicly declared ceasefire for a limited period from July 1 to September 15, the opening day of the UNGA, during which time major efforts will be made to get the parties to start talks on a political solution. Under such a ceasefire, Israel would continue to refrain from deep penetration raids. The UAR (USSR) would have to refrain from changing the military status quo (by emplacing SAMs or any other new installations) in a 25-mile zone on either side of the Suez Canal ceasefire line, and Israel would be required to observe a standstill on new installations on the East Bank of the Canal. While concentrating in the first instance on a UAR-Israeli aspect, we would also seek to broaden the limited ceasefire to include other fronts as well. However, the proposal described below to get talks started between the parties under Jarring's auspices, while linked to the ceasefire, can stand on its own. If Nasser agrees to get talks started on the basis we are suggesting, we should not permit the proposal to fall on the ground that the ceasefire has not been accepted. We should make this very clear to the Israelis when our entire proposal is explained.

---

[1] Source: National Archives, Nixon Presidential Materials, NSC Files, Box 645, Country Files, Middle East, Middle East—General, Vol. IV. Secret; Nodis.

2. *Negotiations on a Political Solution.* We would make another attempt to start the negotiating process by means of a new, fresh approach directly with the parties rather than through either the two- or four-power mechanism. We would propose to Israel and the UAR (Jordan) that indirect negotiations under Jarring's auspices begin promptly, in accordance with procedures determined by him, on the basis of the following agreed framework: (a) that they both accept the UNSC Resolution of November 1967 in all its parts and will seek to reach agreement on ways of carrying it out; and (b) that the UAR (Jordan) accept the principle of a just and lasting peace with Israel, including recognition on their part of Israel's right to exist and that Israel accept the principle of withdrawal from occupied territories in accordance with the SC resolution of November 22, 1967.

3. *Military Assistance for Israel.* Your decision in March to hold in abeyance Israel's request for additional aircraft was based on the judgment that Israel's qualitative superiority compensated amply for its numerical inferiority in planes. The direct Soviet involvement in an operational role has injected a new qualitative capacity and a reinforced quantitative capacity on the UAR side.

Our intelligence evaluations conclude that the new Soviet involvement has affected the military balance, though how much presently and in the future is not entirely clear. As a minimum, the Soviet presence has reduced the Israeli qualitative superiority, which in turn connotes a new Arab-Soviet ability to exhaust the Israelis through attrition. More importantly, the Soviet presence probably has rendered Israel's preferred strategy of preemptive attacks too costly to be tolerable. If the present standoff is maintained (i.e., Israel staying away from UAR rear areas and the Soviets keeping out of the Canal combat zone), the result will be to restrict Israel's freedom of action in the air without, however, losing its air superiority over the Suez sector. If the Soviets decide to challenge the Israelis in the Suez sector, Israel's air power would be quickly worn down. Our intelligence prediction is that Israel, faced with prolonged attrition, would be forced either to abandon the Canal line or attempt major preemptive strikes.

In short, the intelligence evaluations indicate that the weight of the Soviet presence has already reduced the material and psychological advantages previously enjoyed by the Israelis. Fundamentally, the Arab-Israeli military balance now depends on Soviet actions and decisions which have already created a situation in which Israel's air superiority could be rapidly neutralized.

In the light of the foregoing and your public and private statements regarding possible additional assistance to Israel if a change in the balance required, we recommend Israel be informed quietly and discreetly of the following.

(a) By the end of June, 44 Phantoms of the 50 will have been delivered. The other six, which are to be special reconnaissance models, have not been promised for delivery until early 1971. We, therefore, will (1) sell and deliver three additional Phantoms to Israel in July and three in August bringing the total to 50 (which Soviet and UAR intelligence will interpret as completion of the 1968 Phantom deal; only 88 Skyhawks have been delivered of the 100 committed in past contracts. The 12 remaining will be delivered over the next few months); (2) as replacements for past and future projected losses, earmark four Phantoms per month and four additional Skyhawks per month out of future production for delivery starting in September through the end of the year. This would be subject to review, only if negotiations between parties under Jarring's auspices had started and showed signs of success; and (3) make contingency plans for immediate delivery of F–4s and A–4s to Israel out of USAF inventories if there should be a dramatic shift in the balance.

(b) As part of your decision which I announced on March 23,[2] we would also inform Israel of our intention to continue to respond affirmatively to other Israeli military requests in order to maintain the logistic pipeline. We would respond affirmatively to most items in their latest request—i.e., Hawk ground-to-air missiles, bombs, tanks, radar, acceleration of spare parts deliveries for F–4s and A–4s.

(c) A low key announcement would be made which made clear: (1) that for the next two months, during which we would make new efforts to launch a "stop fighting, start talking" proposal, the deliveries of aircraft by the U.S. to Israel would not bring them beyond levels committed on the basis of past contracts (not over 50 Phantoms and 100 Skyhawks); and (2) that we have made contingent provision for immediate delivery of additional or replacement aircraft to Israel if the need arises. As a condition, Israel must agree to affirm publicly that it is satisfied with the contingent arrangements made by the U.S., otherwise there is apt to be a strong reaction in the Congress. The announcement would be made shortly after we have launched our political initiative through diplomatic channels (see Scenario attached).[3] We would insist on full cooperation from Israel with respect to our political proposal.

(d) We would inform Nasser that we are limiting ourselves for the time being not to go beyond the 50 Phantom and 100 Skyhawk level committed in the 1968 and 1966 contracts, but that further deferral of sale of additional aircraft is only feasible in circumstances of a ceasefire and his agreement to enter discussions under Jarring on the basis of the new American proposal.

---

[2] See Document 106.
[3] The undated scenario is attached but not printed.

4. *U.S. Resolve Vis-à-Vis the USSR.* One of our most serious problems is to reflect resolve and firmness to the USSR. The diplomatic efforts we have made with them, to underscore how seriously and how potentially dangerous their decision is to commit operational personnel in Egypt, have elicited no visible reaction or clarifications from the Soviets. There are increasing signs that the Soviets are prepared to live with and derive the political benefits from turmoil in the Middle East, and that they are operating on the assumption that they can press for unilateral political advantage while we are heavily involved in Southeast Asia. We believe more must be done privately in the area, and publicly over the coming weeks to reflect our resolve to the USSR. I recommend that you direct Secretary Laird and me to make a high priority study of this aspect immediately covering the whole range of our relations with the USSR. Both political and contingent military steps should be studied. What do we do if the Soviets challenge the Israelis in the Suez area? All of us are agreed this means a "new ballgame," but precisely what are the options open to us? If Cairo and Moscow refuse to accept our proposals for a ceasefire or for the start of negotiations between the parties, what political and military steps should we take? Should we break off the Two and Four Power talks rather than continue giving the present impression that the door to a political solution is still open? Should we slow down our efforts to achieve understandings on certain bilateral matters? In addition to giving Israel more military help, which in itself is unlikely to deter the Soviets, can we dramatize efforts to make the Sixth Fleet more modern and effective, or can we fly routine patrols between Sixth Fleet carriers and Israel? Are such steps possible given the atmosphere on the Hill? How do we begin to educate the American people that the Middle East is a principal test between the US and USSR over the next few years?

In the meantime, we are limited largely to diplomatic efforts which are not apt to make much impact on the USSR.

Enclosed is a brief scenario and detailed instructions required to carry out the recommendations contained in this paper.

William P. Rogers

124. Memorandum for the Record[1]

Washington, June 10, 1970.

SUBJECT

NSC Meeting, Wednesday, June 10, 1970—Middle East

PARTICIPANTS

The President
The Vice President
William P. Rogers, Secretary of State
Elliot Richardson, Under Secretary of State
David Packard, Deputy Secretary of Defense
Admiral Thomas Moorer, JCS
Attorney General John M. Mitchell
Richard Helms, Director, Central Intelligence Agency
General George A. Lincoln, Director, OEP
Charles Yost, U.S. Ambassador to the UN
Joseph Sisco, Assistant Secretary of State
A.L. Atherton, Jr., Deputy Assistant Secretary of State
[*name not declassified*], CIA
Alexander Haig, NSC
Harold H. Saunders, NSC
Henry A. Kissinger, Assistant to the President

The President opened the meeting by noting that it would be the last meeting for Under Secretary Richardson.[2] He then turned to Mr. Helms for a briefing on the situation in the Middle East.

Mr. Helms began by noting that the new Soviet presence required careful evaluation. Israel retained military superiority, but the elements of the Soviet presence are under careful study.

The Soviets have 4–5 regiments of SA–3 missiles in the UAR and 3–5 squadrons of Soviet-piloted MIG 21 aircraft.

The President interjected: "Are you stating that as a fact? Are we now convinced?"

Mr. Helms replied that we feel no doubt that these forces are there. The debate within the intelligence community is over how they have been used. We have intelligence on the forces themselves [2 *lines not declassified*]. On the basis of intelligence from all these sources, the pres-

---

[1] Source: National Archives, Nixon Presidential Materials, NSC Files, NSC Institutional Files (H-Files), H–109, NSC Meeting Minutes, NSC Minutes, Originals 1970. Top Secret; Nodis. All brackets are in the original except those indicating text that remains classified. The meeting was held in the Cabinet Room from 9:36 to 11:24 a.m. (Ibid., White House Central Files, President's Daily Diary)

[2] On June 6, Nixon nominated Richardson Secretary of the Department of Health, Education and Welfare. The post of Under Secretary of State remained vacant until the Senate confirmed the appointment of John N. Irwin II on September 18.

ence of the missiles and the pilots is unquestioned. The big issue is how the Soviets intend to use them.

The President asked what the number of Russians in Egypt other than diplomats is. Mr. Helms replied that it is in the neighborhood of 10,000. It has doubled in the last six months.

Mr. Helms continued, saying that the Soviet forces are located mainly in the Nile valley. The Israelis have confined their recent attacks to the area adjacent to the Suez Canal. The question now is whether the Soviets will refrain from moving their missiles and pilots into that area near the Canal and whether the Israelis will refrain from challenging the Soviet pilots.

Intelligence confirms 13 sites of SA–3 missiles. These are manned by 2600–3700 Soviet personnel. There are probably 6–7 other sites under construction. These are located in the Nile Delta north of Cairo, west of Cairo, south of Cairo in connection with a Soviet-manned airfield and at Aswan. The Israelis have unconfirmed reports of SA–3 sites—but not equipment—along the Canal.

This equipment arrived in March and April. Three squadrons of Soviet-piloted aircraft are flying from three bases—15 aircraft in each squadron with about 90 pilots by present count. The pilots arrived in February and March. These were originally reported [*1 line not declassified*].

As a rule, the Soviets stay clear of the Suez Canal. The one major exception noted to date was on May 14, [*less than 1 line not declassified*] a Soviet pilot had apparently pursued an Israeli attack aircraft. Even in this instance, however, the intent to engage cannot be confirmed. The MIG was unable to gain on the retreating Israeli plane.

Israel has publicly stated that it would avoid the Nile valley but would maintain supremacy over the Canal. Israel has said it would bomb anything along the Canal. They have been bombing heavily bunkers they maintain are being built to house equipment related to the SA–3 missile. U.S. intelligence analysts are inclined to think that these sites are for the SA–2 missile, but they have been so heavily bombed that we may never know what they were intended for.

On the ground, the Israelis only have some 5–700 men along the Bar Lev line[3] on their side of the Canal. There are some 93,000 Egyptians on the other side of the Canal altogether. Dayan says that the main Israeli objective is to keep these Egyptians from massing for a cross-Canal attack.

---

[3] The Bar-Lev Line, named for Israeli Chief of Staff Haim Bar-Lev, was a chain of fortifications that Israel built along the eastern coast of the Suez Canal after it captured the Sinai Peninsula from Egypt during the 1967 war.

As far as the Arab-Israeli military balance is concerned, the UAR has some 210–250 aircraft in 20 squadrons. But it does not have enough qualified pilots. Israel has 81 supersonic aircraft and 121 subsonic aircraft and 500 jet pilots. Israel's superiority rests on pilot quality. We assume that Israeli pilots are the equal of ours. Israel keeps 85% of its aircraft flying, while the Egyptians keep only about 75% in the air. The Israelis are able to mount 5 sorties per aircraft per day, while the Arabs can only manage 2. Israeli aircraft have superior performance characteristics. The addition of some Soviet pilots will improve the UAR ability to intercept Israeli attackers if the Soviets engage. Soviet pilots are probably more capable than the Egyptian pilots. But they lack combat experience.

The new factor in the situation is the potential for attrition of Israeli aircraft in a prolonged contest with the Soviets. They could exhaust the Israelis in both aircraft and pilots. Israel could at some point come to consider losses intolerable. The present Israeli losses are somewhat less than the annual traffic toll. In terms of economics or demography Israel could stand such levels of losses. But Israel takes losses hard and any level of losses creates a psychological factor on which the Israeli level of tolerance is relatively low.

This is why Israeli strategy is based on the pre-emptive strike to keep the enemy from bringing its numbers to bear against Israel. This strategy now seems unworkable. It has for some time because of the dispersal of Arab aircraft and the hardening of protective hangars on Arab airfields. Now there is the additional factor that the presence of Soviet pilots could bring on a U.S.-Soviet clash. With the strategy of pre-emption perhaps lost to Israel, the Israelis have more reason than ever to try to control the area along the Suez Canal. The Israelis believe that unless they sustain their present level of attacks or increase it, the Arabs will be so emboldened as to step up the war of attrition.

Israel's ability to maintain air superiority seems to depend on what the Soviets do. The indicators of Soviet intention are the fact that one Soviet pilot on May 14 did pursue an Israeli aircraft and the photographs which indicate the possibility that the Soviets are moving SA–3 missile sites up to the Canal. On the other hand, since May 14, there has been no identified incidents of Soviet pilot pursuit. If the Soviet pilots are ordered to keep their present pattern this situation could go on for some time. If they move up to the Canal, Israel could be quickly worn down. Even at that, the impact of such a Soviet move might be more important psychologically than militarily.

At the least, the Soviet presence has probably already emboldened the Arabs. At most, a situation has been created in which the balance could be altered to Israel's disadvantage. Again, the real effect on the balance will depend on what the Soviets decide to do.

U.S. assistance to date is as follows: 40 Phantoms have been delivered and 3 have been lost; 10 remain to be delivered. Eighty-eight Skyhawks have been delivered with 12 remaining.

On the economic side, an earlier study of the Israeli economy[4] revealed only U.S. confusion about Israel's projection of its economic needs. A recent team visit to Israel, however, revealed that the Israelis are expecting to buy far more in the way of military equipment than we had anticipated in last fall's study. They don't necessarily plan to produce their own fighters and tanks but they do plan to produce armed personnel carriers, jet engines and naval patrol craft. In short, Israel's economic needs depend very much on whether or not there is a political settlement.

[1 paragraph (7 lines) not declassified]

The President asked how many Russians are in Syria. Mr. Helms said he did not know the exact number but it was small.

[1 paragraph (3 lines) not declassified]

The President said that he wanted to be sure he understood one point: Is it true that, since World War II, the Soviets have not lost any men in non-Communist countries in combat situations? Mr. Helms replied that Soviet officers have been lost in Egypt in the last year. They may also have lost a few in Korea which we never identified—some Soviet pilots.

The President said this fact underscored for him the enormous significance of this recent Soviet step. It involves Soviet personnel in becoming casualties in a combat situation outside a Communist country. To them, this poses a very serious problem. [2 lines not declassified]

Mr. Helms replied [1½ lines not declassified]. The judgment which he had described was not just a casual one.

The President asked what the Soviets say about the fact that they have generally had a free ride for the last 25 years, using proxies to do their work for them.

Secretary Rogers said the Soviets do not talk about numbers of combat personnel. They do not deny or admit that they have combat personnel or pilots in the UAR. They say that the reason the Soviets are training Egyptian forces is that the Israeli deep penetration raids in January made this necessary. Whatever the Soviets are doing, the Soviets say has a purely defensive role. They say that they have to back up Nasser. The Secretary concluded that, as long as the deep penetration raids do not continue, the present posture will probably be maintained.

---

[4] Not found.

The Vice President asked about the relationship of the SA–3 missile system to the missile system that we have heard about recently as being converted to an ABM. Mr. Helms said that that was another system. The SA–3 is simply an extension of the SA–2 system which is improved to handle low-flying aircraft. It is designed to force the Israeli aircraft higher into the range where they can be hit by SA–2s or by interceptors. The system the Vice President was asking about is the SA–5.

Secretary Rogers said he did not think the U.S. had any alternative to providing planes to Israel. It is consistent with our policy that we have to continue to supply them. The problem is how to do this.

Secretary Rogers continued that this is a good time to try to get negotiations started. The parties have never really negotiated with each other. This is a good time. Israel is concerned about its future. Nasser is concerned about the Soviet presence. The Soviets are possibly willing to help with a political settlement, though maybe this possibility is remote. But for the first time the Soviets seem to be talking in more serious terms.

The Secretary proposed that the U.S. use the next three months to try to get negotiations started. He felt that we should continue to sell planes to Israel at about the same rate as in the recent past. At the same time we should make a major effort in New York under Ambassador Jarring to get negotiations started. "We think there is a good chance Israel will go along now." The Secretary said his plan is to have a low-key announcement in about a week.[5] He thought there was a possibility to get negotiations started. Until we do, there is no possibility of a settlement. He repeated that he felt the Israelis and the Soviets are interested.

The President turned to Dr. Kissinger to brief on the issues involved.

Dr. Kissinger said he had intended to draw together some of the issues which had been raised in the Special Review Group meetings on this subject,[6] but he would like to go back a half a step to start with.

The immediate issue is aircraft for Israel. The State Department view has been as Secretary Rogers outlined it—that we should continue some shipments of aircraft to Israel while we launch a diplomatic initiative.[7] The Defense Department view has been that we should provide no planes now because deliveries would inflame the Arab world.[8]

---

[5] Rogers made the announcement at a news conference on June 25. His statement and the question-and-answer session that followed are printed in the Department of State Bulletin, July 13, 1970, pp. 25–33.

[6] See Documents 117 and 119.

[7] See Document 123.

[8] See Document 121.

Dr. Kissinger continued that discussion of some of the issues underlies any decision we may make on aircraft. For instance, although the facts of Soviet intervention in the UAR are pretty agreed, there are different views of Soviet purpose and of the significance of the Soviet move:

—One view is that the Soviet move is entirely defensive, that the Soviets had no choice but to make this move in response to Israel's deep penetration raids and that the significance of the move is therefore limited.

—Another view is that, whatever Soviet intentions are, we are confronted with certain results. The Soviet move does free the UAR to be more belligerent. Even if there is an Arab-Israeli settlement, if the Soviet forces remain in Egypt, the UAR will feel stronger in whatever adventures it decides to pursue. Britain did not want an empire; it simply acquired one in the course of seeking coaling stations on the commercial route to the Far East. The practical consequence of a Soviet presence in the UAR is that it is a major geopolitical fact with which we have to deal. The consequences cannot be judged by Soviet intent.

Secretary Rogers asked what difference it makes which view one takes. Dr. Kissinger replied that the view one takes makes some difference on whether the USSR is confronted now or not. The President said there was a question of whether the USSR should be confronted on a broader front. Dr. Kissinger pointed out that even if the Arab-Israeli dispute is settled, that still leaves a problem for the U.S. in that the Soviet Union can work behind the radical Arabs in further eroding U.S. influence in the area.

The President asked whether it is in the Soviet interest to see an Arab-Israeli settlement. The USSR may not want to see Israel "go down the tube." It may well be that the Soviets have an interest in having Israel there as a "burr under the U.S. saddle." The President said he questioned whether the Soviets have an interest in a real settlement; he could understand their interest in a truce or a cooling of the situation but had more question about a full settlement. He felt that Dr. Kissinger's point is relevant and that it is not right for the US to look at what the Soviets are doing in the UAR as an isolated problem.

Secretary Rogers said he thought everyone could agree to that.

Mr. Packard noted one Soviet interest that had not been mentioned: The Soviets want the Suez Canal open.

The President noted that if the UAR were freed of pressure from Israel, it could concentrate on the Persian Gulf.

Dr. Kissinger continued, saying that he was not trying to argue a case but simply to report all the views that had been discussed in the Review Group and to relate them to the decisions before the NSC.

He noted that a number of views had been expressed about the situation

1. The Israeli view is that if Israel and the U.S. will only stand fast, the USSR and the Arabs will decide to negotiate. This means that the U.S. must give Israel all the equipment it needs and make no concessions to the USSR. The consequence of this is that it may be feasible for Israel, but U.S. and Israeli interests diverge. Israel cannot pursue that strategy without U.S. support, but U.S. support for that strategy has consequences which everyone agrees the U.S. cannot accept.

2. A second view is that we should re-examine whether the U.S. can risk any involvement in this area for any issue at all. It can be said about this point of view that if we take the position that we have no interest in the area, it would seem impossible to get the Soviets to back off their course. Also, it would seem almost impossible to persuade Israel to withdraw if we at the same time told the Israelis that they could not count on the U.S. to take action in protecting Israel.

3. It is also argued that the U.S. should separate Israel conquests from Israel existence and to try to convince Israel to gain security in more restricted boundaries via Arab recognition and a U.S. commitment at least to supply necessary military equipment.

In formulating a U.S. strategy it is necessary to bring into balance the conflicting problems we face:

1. The Israeli quest for security. Military balance in the present situation would lead to a war of attrition that Israel could not take. For Israel to continue to exist, Israel requires some margin of military superiority. The problem is to provide enough of a margin but not so much as to permit them to ride out the present situation on the Canal for an extended period.

2. On the Arab side, the U.S. has an interest in the moderate Arabs and has to make sure that no settlement could strengthen the radical Arabs.

The President indicated his understanding that Arabs and Israelis are always going to hate each other—that we are talking about a political settlement and not reconciliation. Dr. Kissinger noted that an Egypt protected by Soviet power after a settlement would be strengthened in its efforts to produce pressures in the Persian Gulf.

The President asked how the UAR is getting along. Mr. Helms replied that the UAR is totally dependent on the subsidies from Kuwait, Saudi Arabia and Libya. The UAR is an economic mess. The UAR's oil income is not yet significant. Without subsidies, the UAR would be bankrupt.

Dr. Kissinger returned to the thread of his briefing, noting that the third element that must be dealt with in any strategy is the USSR. The normal pattern of Soviet activity is to begin with a relatively modest step and then to inch forward testing the ground as they go.

The President interjected by asking how the Soviets proceeded in Cuba. The replies were vague, and Dr. Kissinger continued briefing.

Dr. Kissinger said that the problem with the USSR is to convince them that their present course has incalculable risks. But at the same time we do not want to engage Soviet prestige and leave the Soviets no escape. The choice for the U.S. is not whether to try for a settlement or to confront the USSR. The choice is how to do both in order to achieve a settlement.

Dr. Kissinger concluded by saying that there is one other question: Whether it is conceivable to get an Arab-Israeli settlement that is not imposed. It could be argued that it is necessary to try to achieve understanding on both sides so that a genuine accommodation can be reached. On the other hand, it is clear that without some pressure no such agreement is likely to be reached. The problem is not that the two sides fail to understand each other's interests but that they understand them too well. If this is true, then it remains for outsiders to devise a situation in which there are incentives for each side to accept imposed terms.

Secretary Rogers said he did not feel this was a case of our doing one thing or the other. What we want to do is to get the parties into a negotiating posture and then to force them to accept a settlement. But to exert that kind of pressure behind the scenes we have to begin negotiations. Then at that point we will have to figure out whether, if we cannot get a settlement, we just quit.

The President said there is no question that there will be no settlement unless it is imposed. It is not useful for the U.S. to talk that way publicly, but there should be no misunderstanding about this fact around the NSC table. The question is whether there is enough in a settlement for the USSR to participate in imposing it.

Secretary Rogers replied that the UAR could not accept a settlement without USSR support.

The President said that the U.S. would have to use a big stick with Israel. In good conscience we cannot use that stick with Israel unless we are as sure as we can be that the other side is going to do its part in making a settlement stick.

The President asked whether Defense holds different views from those expressed by State. Mr. Packard replied that there is "general agreement" with State. Defense starts from the premise that it is hard to see a military solution to this problem in any context, whether it be the supply of arms to Israel or U.S. confrontation of the Soviet Union. Defense takes the question a step further and asks whether the U.S. would even be in a position to intervene. The Middle East is an awkward place for the U.S. to operate militarily; there is a long supply line and probably there would be little support from Europe. The President said we would probably be supported by Greece.

Mr. Packard continued, saying that in the final analysis we would have to rely on our nuclear power, and that is the last thing we want to fall back on. Defense agrees that this is the time to try to start negotiations and feels that it may be our last chance. The main difference between the Defense viewpoint and State's is that Defense feels the U.S. ought to take a totally new approach instead of going back to the UN and Ambassador Jarring. We ought to consider a direct approach to the UAR in the form perhaps of a Presidential envoy.

The President said he didn't feel that the State proposal would rule that out. Mr. Sisco said that the State proposal does differ from old approaches in precisely the way that Mr. Packard had mentioned. This is not the old way. State is proposing going directly to the parties.

Secretary Rogers said that we cannot get away from the UN resolution.[9]

Mr. Packard said he felt that we should go straight to the UAR and find out exactly what they want. The UAR and the Soviets would benefit from having the Suez Canal open. Perhaps we could use the Panama Canal as a lever. However that may be, there is very likely a legitimate interest in the UAR in minimizing the Soviet presence. We are going to have to impose a settlement and use leverage on Israel. We should therefore try to develop a position which is in everybody's interest. We are not going to get much from Israel for a few airplanes; we are going to have to lay down the law to Israel.

Mr. Packard concluded that Defense is not too far from State's general appreciation of the situation. Whether to sell airplanes before or after approaching Israel for a settlement is a matter of judgment. Defense simply believes that progress in negotiations is so important that we should not do anything to jeopardize it.

Mr. Sisco said that he wanted to explain the State Department proposal on planes. By the end of June under past contracts 44 Phantoms will be delivered. There are 6 others covered by this contract which are not scheduled to be delivered until 1971 because they are of a special reconnaissance configuration. That means that we could deliver 3 planes in July and 3 in August without going beyond the initial contract total of 50. Then, we could earmark 4 Phantoms and 4 Skyhawks per month with delivery beginning in September and continuing through December. We would assume that these deliveries would be made unless

---

[9] UN Security Council Resolution 242.

negotiations are so successful that we conclude that delivery might jeopardize them. We would take a decision now, however, on these additional planes for delivery in September and only withhold delivery in the unlikely event that delivery would be badly timed in relation to negotiations.

Secretary Rogers said that these aircraft would be referred to as "replacements." Mr. Sisco said that by this definition "replacement" means covering past losses, probable future losses and obsolescence. The President wondered whether this would not be just enough to irritate the Arabs and yet not enough to provide real stroke with Israel. Mr. Sisco replied that it is possible that even a minimal number of airplanes would cause an explosion in the Arab countries if Nasser decides he wants an explosion. There is even a greater possibility if the PFLP decides it wants an explosion. The President asked what about Morocco, Jordan, Tunisia and Saudi Arabia. Secretary Rogers replied that they are braced for the U.S. decision to provide replacements. The Russians also expect this. Such a move would not be escalatory. It would be escalatory if we sold the whole 125 airplanes that the Israelis had asked for.

The President asked what it was the 73 Senators had been pressing for.[10] Secretary Rogers replied that they had been pressing for the whole 125 beyond the replacement concept.

The Vice President said that he would like to move back a step and ask whether we are certain that a settlement is in the U.S. interest. With the Fedayeen and the Soviet abilities enhanced and the history of insurgency as we have seen it, would Israel be able to cope with the Palestinians? Secretary Rogers replied that that would depend on the kind of settlement that comes about. We do not have to decide this now because the settlement itself is still remote.

Mr. Richardson said he agreed that settlement would take a while. He felt that we need to address ourselves to the question of what the U.S. can do to achieve a position to keep the balance from shifting radically versus the U.S. and Israel if agitators upset prospects for a settlement. We really do need some position toward the Palestinians. We may have missed the boat earlier in thinking only of the Palestinians as refugees. If we can take a posture of some sympathy toward the Palestinians, we might ride out the protracted absence of a settlement. On the other hand, if we move closer to a settlement we might be able to get a better settlement for having taken the interests of the Palestinians into account.

Mr. Richardson said that this is really a question of whether we make public a sympathetic position on such issues as a Jerusalem set-

---

[10] On June 4, 73 U.S. Senators sent a letter to Nixon asking him to meet Israel's request for additional aircraft. (*New York Times*, June 6, 1970, p. 22)

tlement and the formation of a Palestinian state. This is a dimension of the problem that has not been sufficiently addressed. It would also help us in the Muslim world outside the area of conflict. For instance, the Indonesian Foreign Minister had said that this would be very helpful in his part of the world; it might also be helpful in Saudi Arabia.

Ambassador Yost said he was glad that the Palestinian angle had been brought out.

Ambassador Yost continued, saying he felt that we must push very hard for a settlement. He is not as pessimistic as Secretary Rogers. The only way of assuring Israeli security is a settlement. If the war of attrition goes on, Israel will be in serious jeopardy. The situation in Jordan and Lebanon will get worse.

While the UAR may be prepared to recognize Israel, Ambassador Yost continued, the Palestinians may not be. We must be in some way in a position to take account of their real interests.

Ambassador Yost felt that the first increment of aircraft in the summer would be wise. He was doubtful, however, about Mr. Sisco's formulation for continuing shipments in the fall unless negotiations are succeeding. It would seem that, under this formula, Israel would have an incentive to make the negotiations fail.

Secretary Rogers said that we have done some thinking about the Palestinians. His last statement included a sentence on them.[11] The real problem is how to deal with them. In Jordan, they are against King Hussein, and they have no leader who speaks for them.

The President said that one of the mistakes since 1948 has been failure to give full attention to the refugee problem. He said he is aware of all the arguments, but this is a terrific irritant. Secretary Rogers asked whether the President felt that the 1956 decision[12] was right. The President replied, "No." The problem with it was that it came at the wrong time. The invasion of Egypt was badly executed by the British and French, and the crisis in Hungary[13] was simultaneous with it. The British and French did not need to be involved. Israel could have done the job alone. In the United States the whole issue came right at the end of an election campaign.

The President felt that the great tragedy of 1956 was that it finished the British as a world power. The French really didn't care, but the British began their course of getting out of involvement all around the

---

[11] Not found.

[12] Reference is to President Dwight D. Eisenhower's decision to call for British, French, and Israeli forces to withdraw from the Suez Canal Zone after their invasion in October 1956. The invasion was in response to Egypt's nationalization of the Canal on July 26, 1956.

[13] The Soviet invasion of Hungary in November 1956.

world at that point. It is not a healthy thing for the world for the U.S. to be the only major power in Asia or the Middle East. The French are out of the Far East, and the Dutch are out of Indonesia. Britain's withdrawal is a great tragedy. While French withdrawal did not make much difference, the British have great brains and sophistication. To have them out of Asia is a very sad situation. After the British election, it may be important to try to keep them in Singapore.

Mr. Packard said he wished to return to one detail about aircraft deliveries. It is one thing to say that we are simply delivering 6 more airplanes within the total number of aircraft originally contracted for. It is quite another if we recognize that we are replacing 6 reconnaissance aircraft with 6 attack aircraft. The Sisco proposal is to increase Israeli attack capability when it does not need enhancement. Mr. Sisco said that it is a combination of replacement for 3 airplanes lost plus 3 new ones.

The President asked what the Israelis would think of this. Would they think that it is nothing? Will we get another letter from the Senators? Mr. Sisco said that they would have to look carefully at the earmarking promised. He felt that the domestic problem was containable if the Israelis would just say that the earmarking arrangement is "satisfactory."

Mr. Helms said he felt that it was important to maintain the numbers of 50 Phantoms and 100 Skyhawks that were known in the Arab world. If there were any way to stay within those numbers we could possibly avoid an explosion in the Arab world.

Mr. Richardson said he strongly supported the general Sisco approach. But in a short time we will know whether it will or will not work. We should tell the Israelis that our interests and theirs do coincide in the field of launching negotiations. If we cannot start a negotiation both of our interests will suffer. The Israelis will face a long war of attrition. Hopefully, the Israelis would see their interests in cooperating. We should be able to explain to the Israelis that they have an interest in playing this low-key and that it is contrary to their interests to have a big announcement which would kill all chances for negotiation.

Secretary Rogers said that the Israelis do not have much hope of negotiations. He did not feel they were going to be as reasonable as Mr. Richardson hoped.

The President asked whether this was enough to push the Israelis with. Attorney General Mitchell said that if we talked to the Israelis first this should take the heat out of the domestic reaction. Mr. Sisco said it would be important how we phrased our statement on earmarking.

Mr. Sisco continued, saying that we would be asking the Israelis to engage in indirect negotiations on the basis of the UAR's acknowledgement of Israel's right to exist. We would also be asking for Israeli acceptance of the principle of withdrawal. Secretary Rogers said that we would be asking two concessions from Israel—indirect negotiation and acceptance of the principle of withdrawal. The President asked whether that could be bought for 6 airplanes. Secretary Rogers said it would not be easy to persuade them.

General Lincoln said that he simply wanted to report that the Western Europeans with whom he has had contact are deeply concerned about Middle East oil supplies. The OECD is actively discussing the problem.

The President said he would want to consider the State Department proposal further. He said he realized that while people were hopeful something could be done there was also a good deal of skepticism.

The President said he still came back to a basic point that militates against a settlement: What is in it for the Soviets? The present situation is costing them some money. They may be concerned about a possible confrontation with the U.S. But if they look at that proposition coldly, they know as well as we know around the NSC table that the likelihood of U.S. action directly against them is "in doubt." It did not use to be in doubt. That was what the Lebanon invasion of 1958[14] was about.

Again looking at the Soviets: they have made noises that they would like to see a settlement. They have a muscle-bound bureaucracy and have trouble seeing things in gradations. It may be that as far as the Soviets are concerned our job is to get them to play a role in imposing a settlement. The ingredient that is missing and has to be supplied in some way is the incentive to them to play that role.

Secretary Rogers noted that the Soviets are concerned about the Chinese and about the Fedayeen. Soviet officials often allude to those problems. Nasser is concerned about what has happened in Jordan and that he may be in some danger.

Ambassador Yost said that the Soviets do not call the tune in Cairo. If a settlement in Arab interests emerges, he did not believe that the Soviets could prevent it.

Mr. Sisco said that, while he agreed about the Fedayeen and the Chinese, he put greater weight on what the Soviets think of American will. The real leverage on the USSR is fear of a confrontation with the U.S. We ought to be looking at the 6th Fleet to see whether it is pro-

---

[14] In response to Lebanese President Camille Chamoun's call for help to quash a rebellion against his government that had widened into a civil war, President Eisenhower sent 14,000 U.S. troops to Lebanon on July 15, 1958. The presence of U.S. forces helped to resolve the crisis, which ended with the election of a compromise candidate, General Fuad Chehab, as President on July 31, and the troops were eventually withdrawn by October 25.

jecting American power to the maximum extent. His conclusion, he said, is that the Soviets feel now that they can broaden the conflict. We are essentially up against a Soviet political strategy, but at the end of the line they must feel that they could run into a confrontation with the U.S.

Mr. Richardson indicated his agreement. He felt that we need to find a way to use the only lever that we really have—the Soviet fear of confrontation.

Mr. Packard said that this is a matter of timing. He said we have to move ahead soon. We should avoid moving planes. He liked the idea of having a pool of aircraft perhaps in Texas as a reserve for Israel which would not be moved to Israel unless the situation required.

The President concluded the meeting by saying that he would look at all of this.

---

125. Minutes of a Washington Special Actions Group Meeting[1]

Washington, June 11, 1970, 2:53–3:40 p.m.

SUBJECT

Jordan

PARTICIPATION

Chairman—Henry A. Kissinger

State
Mr. U. Alexis Johnson
Mr. Joseph J. Sisco
Amb. Harrison Symmes

Defense
Mr. David Packard
Mr. Robert Pranger

JCS
Adm. Thomas H. Moorer
Col. Marvin C. Kettlehut

CIA
Mr. Richard Helms
Mr. David Blee

NSC Staff
Mr. Harold Saunders
Gen. Alexander Haig
Mr. D. Keith Guthrie

---

[1] Source: National Archives, Nixon Presidential Materials, NSC Files, NSC Institutional Files (H-Files), Box H–114, Washington Special Actions Group, WSAG Minutes (Originals) 1969 and 1970. Top Secret; Nodis. All brackets are in the original except those indicating text omitted by the editors. The meeting was held in the White House Situation Room.

SUMMARY OF CONCLUSIONS

The WSAG received a report of action taken to evacuate American nationals from Jordan and agreed that first priority should be given to arranging evacuation under the auspices of the International Red Cross (ICRC). Admiral Moorer outlined planning for possible military action to support an evacuation if the international effort fails or if order in Amman breaks down completely. Two scenarios are to be drawn up covering possible military action (1) to support an evacuation or (2) to intervene in Jordan in response to a request from King Hussein for help against outside intervention. The scenarios will specify troop requirements and the likely duration of the military operations and will include a full discussion of relevant political factors. The State Department will submit immediately a memorandum listing steps taken and planned to protect American citizens in Jordan.

[Omitted here are the minutes of the meeting.]

126. Minutes of a Washington Special Actions Group Meeting[1]

Washington, June 12, 1970, 2:35–2:50 p.m.

SUBJECT

Jordan

PARTICIPATION

Chairman—Henry A. Kissinger

State
U. Alexis Johnson
Rodger Davies
Amb. Harrison Symmes

Defense
Richard A. Ware
Dennis J. Doolin

JCS
Adm. Thomas H. Moorer
Brig. Gen. Jacob E. Glick

CIA
Gen. Robert E. Cushman, Jr.
Thomas Karamessines
David Blee

NSC Staff
Harold H. Saunders
D. Keith Guthrie

---

[1] Source: National Archives, Nixon Presidential Materials, NSC Files, NSC Institutional Files (H-Files), Box H–114, Washington Special Actions Group, WSAG Meetings Minutes (Originals) 1969 and 1970. Top Secret; Nodis. All brackets are in the original except those indicating text omitted by the editors. The meeting was held in the White House Situation Room.

SUMMARY OF CONCLUSIONS

The WSAG received a status report on the evacuation of U.S. and other foreign nationals from Amman[2] and reviewed progress on contingency planning for possible military action in Jordan. The contingency plan for military action in response to a request from King Hussein for support against outside intervention[3] is to be completed no later than June 17. The WSAG also noted that there was a possibility that an evacuation from Beirut might have to be undertaken and that there were existing WSAG-approved plans to cover this contingency.[4]

[Omitted here are the minutes of the meeting.]

---

[2] The report has not been found. The contingency plan for "Military-Supported Evacuation of U.S. Citizens from Jordan," undated, is ibid., Box H–075, Washington Special Actions Group Meetings, WSAG Meeting Jordan and Cambodia.

[3] These contingencies were discussed at the June 22 WSAG meeting; see Document 131.

[4] A summary of the Lebanon evacuation plan, June 11, is in the National Archives, Nixon Presidential Materials, NSC Files, NSC Institutional Files (H-Files), Box H–075, Washington Special Actions Group Meetings, WSAG Meeting Jordan 6/11/70.

---

127. Memorandum From the President's Assistant for National Security Affairs (Kissinger) to President Nixon[1]

Washington, June 16, 1970.

SUBJECT

The Middle East

I have been generally restrained on Middle East issues for obvious reasons. To date, I have confined myself to pointing out pitfalls of recommended policies, making tactical suggestions, and on several occasions helping to modify recommendations which I considered would have had disastrous consequences. For example, if we had not at the last moment altered the State Department approach of a flat turndown on aircraft this past March, our announcement could have had serious domestic effects, especially since it would have surfaced simulta-

---

[1] Source: National Archives, Nixon Presidential Materials, NSC Files, Box 645, Country Files, Middle East, Middle East—General, Vol. VI. Secret; Nodis.

neously with the disclosure that the Soviets had just drastically escalated their role in Egypt's defense.[2]

Since the situation in the area continues to deteriorate and you are now at still another important tactical crossroads, I believe I must emphatically point out the dangers if we continue on our projected course.

Our Policy to Date

We have three principal objectives in the Middle East:

—To prevent Soviet dominance in the area;

—To prevent the spread of Arab radicalism which could pose a threat to Western interests;

—To honor the commitment we have to the survival of Israel.

On all three counts, we have seen our position eroded since January 1969. The Soviets have greatly increased their influence in the region. The moderate Arab states, and even the more radical ones, are increasingly subject to Fedayeen pressures. The Fedayeen have become a powerful separate force which may already make it impossible for the Arab governments to accept or enforce any settlement that we could sell to Israel. Israel is becoming increasingly desperate and sees her future survival at stake, with its preemptive capability as its sole remaining asset.

From the beginning, our policy has rested on some basic assumptions:

—That the root problem in the Middle East is the Arab/Israeli conflict over territory;

—That once we settle this dispute by negotiation, the influence of the radical Arabs will dwindle;

—That the Soviet influence in the Middle East can be seen largely in terms of this conflict.

These basic assumptions are all open to question. Even if the Arab/Israeli territorial dispute is solved by negotiation, we will still face the fundamental problems of thriving Arab radicalism and Soviet influence.

Arab radicalism has five components: (1) the Israeli conquests of territory; (2) the very existence of Israel; (3) social and economic objectives; (4) opposition to Western interests; and (5) opposition to Arab moderates. Only the first of these components would be affected by a settlement. The others will remain, maintaining Arab radicalism as an independent force. Israel will still be there for the radicals to erase—it is precisely because for much of the Arab world the issue is its existence,

---

[2] For the March 23 announcement, see Document 106.

and not its particular frontiers, that Israel has scant confidence in Arab promises and sees little to gain in a settlement. The causes of social and economic unrest will persist. Western oil and Arab moderates will be prime targets. For example, the recent upheavals in Libya and the Sudan, and the possible coming turmoil in Saudi Arabia are little related to the Arab/Israeli question and would thus be little affected by a settlement. In fact, an Egypt free of its Sinai obsession could then focus on moderate Arab regimes.

Similarly, the expanding Soviet beachhead poses a growing challenge irrespective of the Arab/Israeli dispute. One of our major problems is that the Soviets may emerge as the strongest military power in the region, directly responsible for the protection of Egypt. In fact, the Soviets have much more to gain through a settlement than we—return of the lands to the Arabs, the opening of the Canal for Soviet ships to operate in the Persian Gulf and Red Sea, and the prospect of Arab radicals freed for concentration against Western interests and Arab moderates.

You inherited a very dangerous situation and faced a painful dilemma. In this complex situation, we have gone down the single track of technical negotiations on the specifics of a peace plan, always outdistanced by events and without a clear strategic conception. Our policy has been punctuated by tactical decisions under largely self-imposed time deadlines. It has consisted of almost compulsive stabs at tactical negotiating initiatives which have been just enough to sweep us up in a negotiating process but not enough to bring about a fundamental change in the situation.

While events have become more dangerous, we have paid a price with each of the three major audiences. We have strained our relations with Israel by moving further and further from her positions; she, in turn, has increasingly relied on military moves to preserve her security. On the other hand, we have not given enough to the Arabs, partially because of our reliance on the formal aspect of the negotiating process. This has made us fall between two stools. The fact of our intervening displeased the Israelis and its formal nature infuriated the Arabs. Finally, our whole approach with the Soviets has been uncertain: rather than making it clear to them that their actions pose a direct threat to *our* interests, we have always made our representations on Israel's behalf. This was illustrated once again by Secretary Rogers' June 2 meeting with Dobrynin where he told the Soviets only to stay away from the Canal area, in effect acquiescing in the massive Soviet presence already in Egypt.[3]

---

[3] See Document 120.

To understand where we are today, it is useful to recall briefly how we got here. The following review includes first some of the decisions and then some of the major concerns I expressed in memoranda at each of the decision milestones. While I would not normally burden you with this record, I do so in this case to emphasize that my concern is over the fundamental philosophic approach of our Mideast policy rather than any individual tactical decision.

Since January 1969, we have moved from a position of no direct involvement in seeking a Middle East settlement, to exploratory talks among the four powers looking toward a set of general principles, to bilateral discussions with the Soviets and presenting of specific American proposals on the terms of UAR/Israel and Jordan/Israel border agreements.

In *February 1969*, we decided to take the initiative in finding a settlement, changing our previous policy of letting the local forces play themselves out.[4] We entered into exploratory four-power talks to work toward a set of general principles. At the time I emphasized the principal issue: whether by going all out for a general settlement—which might be impossible—we would cripple our ability to contain the conflict in the absence of a settlement. We must be sure a settlement was possible *before* we began negotiating and using up our political capital. Persuading Israel to accept any political arrangement would require a combination of pressure and the enticement of sound U.S. or international guarantees.

In April, we decided to present our positions on specific terms of a UAR-Israel settlement other than borders. The argument was made that the talks, which had concentrated on trying to establish a framework for a UAR-Israel settlement, would reach an impasse unless discussions could become more specific.[5]

At the time I highlighted certain pitfalls in putting forward specific proposals. A proposal that Israel could accept could be countered by more lenient proposals by the other powers which we would have to oppose, and thus be charged with breaking up the talks. A fair proposal would be equally unpalatable to the Arabs and Israelis and we were likely to get the blame from both sides. A proposal that was less than Israel's minimum position would probably be rejected by her—leaving us the choice of negotiating without Israeli assent or being isolated by holding out for Israeli terms. The first course might tempt Israeli preemption; the second would produce Arab frustrations directed against the U.S.

---

[4] See Document 8.
[5] See Documents 25 and 26.

In October, we put forward in the US–USSR talks our position on the UAR-Israel borders,[6] which we had considered our fallback until then. We were told that this would emphasize to the Soviets that Israel could be pressed to withdraw only if the UAR were pressed to accept arrangements that Israel would regard as giving her security comparable to the present ceasefire lines.

I doubted at the time that a diplomatic move could any longer affect the deep-rooted forces at work in the area, especially the uncontrollable Fedayeen. The Jordanian and Syrian aspects needed to be addressed along with the UAR-Israel problem. The Arab world would not judge us by proposals, only by results. I saw little gain for us in the Arab world if we continued supplying arms and money to Israel after she rejected our position. We were helping to build a case for greater Arab militancy without getting close to a settlement. At the same time we were making it more likely that Israel would rely more heavily than ever on its military strategy. We were doing too little to have a chance of success but enough to divert indigenous forces from reaching their own decisions.

In December, we advanced a proposal on a Jordan-Israel settlement in the four-power talks.[7] The real issue, I pointed out, was not these negotiating tactics but whether we were willing to squeeze Israel. If you were prepared to impose a settlement, I leaned toward conditioning future military and economic deliveries to Israel on their acceptance of our position—we should do so not by cutting off aid but by promising a generous aid package regulating deliveries by Israel's agreement to a negotiating scenario. My concern was that we were heading for a confrontation with Israel and the American Jewish Community and that if Israel thought it were cut off from outside support, she was likely to strike again to topple Nasser.

In March, as I mentioned earlier, we barely avoided disastrous consequences by our last-minute sweetening of our announcement denying Israel her basic request for aircraft.

If we continue this process, we will wind up being responsible for all the formulas and principles of a Middle East settlement and all the failures, with Israel hysterical, the Arabs belligerent and the USSR contemptuous.

Current Decision

You are now faced with yet another tactical decision on the Middle East under time pressure from the bureaucracy.

---

[6] See Document 58.
[7] See Document 78.

Last fall I said that for us to formulate specific negotiating proposals could bring Israeli escalation and push us to the edge of war. This is exactly what has happened. Our October 28 and December 18 proposals were accepted by no one. They emboldened the Arabs who stepped up their border pressures. Israel began making deep penetration raids which, in turn, caused Nasser to allow a massive influx of Soviet personnel and influence. Israel's preemptive raids are now inhibited by Soviet pilots and air defenses; and she faces the prospect of slow attrition.

I believe the proposal that the State Department has suggested[8] at this juncture would continue to take us down the same path and would not produce a settlement. The State plan involves a limited commitment of six Phantoms now, pending outcome of a new effort to get a ceasefire and negotiations, coupled with a clearly implied promise of 16 Phantoms and 16 Skyhawks to be shipped during the fall. (At Tab A is a detailed look at the State scenario.)[9]

I don't believe this combination of a minimal commitment at this time and an ambivalent earmarking of additional planes for the future will work to produce the ceasefire and settlement it seeks. In order to sell the overall proposal to Israel, she would have to feel practically certain that she will get the 32 additional planes. The Arabs, on the other hand, would find the proposal palatable only if they were convinced that Israel would not get more than the six planes. Unless there were a major breakthrough by September, we are bound to disappoint one of the two sides at the time.

Furthermore, we would send the wrong signals to each of our three audiences. For Israel the aircraft earmarking suggestion will not induce her to negotiate, whether or not she interprets it as a firm commitment. If Israel does not believe that she will get the follow-on planes in the fall, she will take our decision as giving her only six planes, or only three more than was already promised her in March. It is absurd to think that on this basis she would yield her total position on boundaries that she has maintained for three years. The Israelis will not contemplate withdrawals unless they are assured of the equipment necessary for their security behind less defensible borders than they have now.

The State approach would have us force the Israelis back to the pre-war borders while they get no further planes after the summer. They would be asked to give up both elements of their security at the same time—their territorial buffers and the prospect of more aircraft.

---

[8] See Document 123.
[9] Attached but not printed at Tab A is the undated scenario.

As peace with more vulnerable frontiers approached, their aircraft inventory would drop.

If, on the other hand, Israel believes that she will get the larger aircraft package if negotiations are going badly, she will have no incentive to make negotiations go well. She would prefer the planes to the promise of a settlement which can only be negotiated at the expense of the assets which the territories represent.

The ceasefire element in the package is another disincentive for Israel. Once she has obtained a halt to all Arab military pressures, she can sit securely on her captured territories, blunt negotiating progress and look forward to 32 more planes.

The response of the *Arabs* turns on the position of Nasser. His actions depend on how decisive we are and how serious he thinks we are in squeezing Israel back to her former borders, the one incentive for him to negotiate. Nasser would interpret our action as a halfway move. He would seriously doubt that we could really press Israel to withdraw on the basis of six aircraft and perhaps others later on. He would think that only a threat of a cut-off or the promise of substantial support after withdrawal would be sufficient to move Israel. For him, the prospect of Israel's having six more aircraft and staying along the Canal is more uninviting than Israel's getting a greater number of planes and withdrawing to her former borders. He would be asked to negotiate more or less directly with Israel in exchange for her commitment only to the "principle of withdrawal," not interpreted as complete withdrawal. Since he would have no reason to think we would succeed in moving Israel back, Nasser will pursue his tactical moves and the other Arabs will follow suit.

To the *Soviets*, the State Department proposal would be a weak gesture in the face of their continued expansion of influence. Our formula would be of too little military consequence and too hesitant to convince them that we are prepared to match their escalation in the area. They considered our March announcement uncertain; they will read this one the same way. Moreover, this course rests on direct U.S. approaches to the parties, principally Nasser, which the Soviets might read as attempting to squeeze them out of Egypt as well as the negotiations.

Thus, I believe that the State Department proposal will only serve to accentuate present dangerous trends. Israel, particularly if she thinks she is only getting the six aircraft, will border on hysteria, in light of continuing American hesitation, growing Soviet involvement, and increasing Arab pressures. We will face the likely radicalization of the American Jewish community and the loss of their support—or at least restraint—on our Southeast Asian policies. At best, the Arab reaction will be to continue their current policies. And the Soviets can only be induced to become more bellicose and inch closer toward the Canal.

Even if we reach a settlement, we would have demonstrated that threats against the United States and blackmail against our oil interests pay off.

I should point out again that a settlement would hardly erase our problems in the region. Arab radicalism is not just a product of the Arab-Israeli impasse. It has its own ideological roots and will still be present to attack Western interests after a settlement. The Suez Canal will be opened for the Soviet fleet to operate in the Persian Gulf and Egyptian forces will be free to move against friendly Arab states like Saudi Arabia. Radical Arab nationalists will still be prone to attack our oil interests.

If you choose to accept the State Department plan, the only palliatives that I can suggest would be the following:

—Deliver the six aircraft plus replace the three that the Israelis have lost, making for a total of nine through this summer.

—Make our commitment for the other 32 as clear as possible. The two-stage formula of the State Department proposal is a tricky course to navigate and could get us into trouble in September.

A More Promising Course

Rather than the State Department approach, I believe a more promising course would be the one that I outlined as the third option in my June 9 memorandum to you.[10]

We would offer a larger number of aircraft to Israel (25 Phantoms and a substantial number of its requested Skyhawks over 12 months) with the thought of withholding delivery unless Israel cooperates in a diplomatic approach We would require Israel's assurance that it would return essentially to her prewar borders, in exchange for Arab commitments and an enforceable peace. We would tell both the Soviets and Nasser that Soviet combat personnel would have to be withdrawn after an agreement. We would go to Nasser and state that we would do everything in our power to get Israel back to her former borders if he will cooperate in the negotiations. We would make clear to Nasser that we are the only government that can get Israel to withdraw and that he cannot expect us to squeeze Israel and withhold aid at the same time. If

---

[10] The "third option" was set forth in an attachment to a June 9 memorandum from Kissinger to Nixon, which discussed the Middle East issues to be covered at the NSC meeting the next day. (National Archives, Nixon Presidential Materials, NSC Files, Box 645, Country Files, Middle East, Middle East—General, Vol. IV) The memorandum is printed in *Foreign Relations, 1969–1976*, volume XII, Soviet Union, January 1969–October 1970, Document 65.

he uses the provision of aircraft to Israel as the pretext for encouraging attacks on American installations elsewhere, then we will give the planes to Israel without pressing her to withdraw. (A fuller description of this proposal is at Tab B.)[11]

This approach recognizes that the only way we can produce a settlement is to combine great pressure on Israel to withdraw with great reassurance that we will supply her the means for her security. We would combine the sticks of diplomatic pressure and withholding aircraft deliveries with the carrot of a large number of planes as a settlement is reached. The *Arabs* themselves should understand that only such reassurance to Israel will cause her to withdraw.

This could be a decisive move for all three of our audiences. It would give Israel an incentive to negotiate while making clear that we will not back a strategy which could lead to US–USSR confrontation. It would show Nasser and the Arabs that we are determined to move toward a settlement and give promise of pressures on Israel to withdraw. And it would be a firm move versus the Soviets who would see both that we are prepared to match their escalation with a well-supplied Israel and we are ready to move toward the escape hatch of a settlement acceptable to their Arab clients.

It thus could weave together the three essential strands of a Mideast settlement. The large number of aircraft would meet *Israeli security concerns* (whereas State's few planes would aggravate these concerns)—she might then opt for negotiation. Our decisive move and our clear commitment to pressure Israel would hold out for the *Arabs* a good prospect of regaining their *territories* (whereas the State proposal won't convince them we can move Israel)—they might agree to negotiations. And our proposal would give the *Soviets* both a sense of danger and an escape route which should give back to the Arabs their territories (whereas the State scenario would seem indecisive to them)—they might support negotiations.

There are, of course, serious risks in this course as in any other for the Middle East. The promise of this large aircraft package for Israel could hardly be kept secret for long. No matter how the deliveries are conditioned on Israeli performance on withdrawal, a violent reaction in the Arab world is conceivable. The Arabs might see our formula as merely emboldening Israel and doubt our willingness to withhold delivery of the planes if Israel does not move on withdrawals. We will face sticky timing decisions on aircraft deliveries as negotiations proceed. Engineering the removal of Soviet combat personnel from Egypt will be especially difficult. And even if a settlement is achieved, we will

---

[11] Undated; attached but not printed.

be back to the 1967 situation, with both sides militarily stronger and the Fedayeen a new disruptive factor.

Despite these problems, I believe this course holds out better hope for a settlement than the one proposed by State. It would, of course, have to be carefully managed and I would envisage that we would go with our proposal to Israel, the Soviets and Nasser in that order.

Conclusion

This approach, with all its inherent risks, is the most likely way to halt a deteriorating situation. But it would require a disciplined effort by us, bureaucratically as well as diplomatically. I frankly do not believe that we have the kind of governmental framework necessary to do the job. Shortly after our Cambodian experience, you would have to override the recommendations of your top Cabinet advisers, and impose a wholly different policy upon a very reluctant bureaucracy, which would then be charged with implementing it.

The only alternative would be (1) to shift control of the negotiations out of State to the White House, or (2) to let State go with its approach, while I dealt with Dobrynin, telling him that we were just marking time. Either of these alternatives, of course, raises tremendous problems.

There is the further factor that Secretary Rogers has almost certainly laid out the State Department proposal to Dobrynin. Joe Sisco, in his June 12 talk with Dobrynin,[12] further locked us in by indicating that our general strategy would follow this line.

In these circumstances and given the existing bureaucratic framework, I believe that you have little choice but to pursue the State Department route,[13] perhaps cutting the risks somewhat with the modifications I have suggested.

---

[12] In telegram 92515 to Amman, Beirut, Cairo, Jidda, Kuwait, Tel Aviv, London, Moscow, Paris, USUN, Algiers, Khartoum, Rabat, Tunis, Tripoli, Belgrade, Bucharest, Nicosia, Rome, and USNATO, June 12, the Department reported Sisco's 1½-hour meeting with Dobrynin in Washington that day. (National Archives, Nixon Presidential Materials, NSC Files, Box 614, Country Files, Middle East, Jordan, Vol. IV)

[13] See Document 128

128. National Security Decision Memorandum 66[1]

Washington, June 18, 1970.

TO
    The Secretary of State
    The Secretary of Defense

SUBJECT
    Next Steps in the Middle East

Based on discussion in the NSC meeting of June 10,[2] the President has approved the steps recommended in the Secretary of State's memorandum of June 9,[3] subject to the following:

1. He wishes to increase the number of earmarked Phantoms for the months of September and October from four to five.

2. He wishes to make clear that Israel should be informed that we are making a commitment to deliver the earmarked planes starting in September unless such deliveries at that time would seriously jeopardize any ongoing negotiations between the parties which may be in process. It is not contemplated that there would be a need for further internal review at that time of the arms delivery question unless some new dramatic development were to occur. Neither would there be need for a further publicized request by Israel.

3. In addition, the President believes it is important that in the discussions between Israeli representatives and our Pentagon officials we respond both affirmatively and promptly to the ongoing requests which Israel has made for various items of logistic support. These include the items listed in your memorandum, i.e., Hawk ground-to-air missiles, bombs, tanks, radar and acceleration of spare parts deliveries for F–4s and A–4s.

                                                       Henry A. Kissinger

---

[1] Source: National Archives, Nixon Presidential Materials, NSC Files, NSC Institutional Files (H-Files), Box H–217, National Security Decision Memoranda. Secret; Nodis; Exclusively Eyes Only. A copy was sent to the Chairman of the Joint Chiefs of Staff.

[2] See Document 124.

[3] See Document 123.

129. Telegram From the Department of State to Certain Diplomatic Posts[1]

Washington, June 19, 1970, 0134Z.

96540. For Ambassador or Chief of Mission From the Secretary.

1. President has approved major new USG initiative on M.E. Problem[2] consisting of following elements:

A. Approach directly to Israel, UAR and Jordan designed to get negotiations started under Jarring's auspices on basis of short formula spelled out below. We would seek agreement on 90 day ceasefire as part of this package but would not make it a sine qua non.

B. Approach to USSR designed (1) to elicit its cooperation in foregoing proposal on understanding two power talks would proceed in parallel once negotiations between parties were launched, and (2) to make clear to Soviets that likely alternative is heightened Israel-UAR military conflict with risk of US-Soviet confrontation.

C. Approach to UK and France designed (1) to reassure them we envisage utilizing four power talks on continuing basis as mechanism for feeding ideas to Jarring to help keep parties negotiating once they have started and (2) to elicit their support of our initiative with the parties.

D. Briefing of U Thant and Jarring on our initiative.

E. Response to Israel's request for military assistance designed (1) to keep general logistical supply pipeline open, and (2) to reassure Israelis that we have made contingency arrangements for quick delivery of further F–4 and A–4 aircraft as replacements for attrition if situation so requires, while (3) not delivering aircraft to Israel beyond numbers committed in existing (1966 and 1968) contracts so long as our efforts for political settlement are actively in train.

2. Political initiative we envisage will require, as precondition for negotiations, concession by UAR on principle of accepting and agreeing live in peace with Israel (and perhaps on ceasefire), and by Israel on form of initial negotiating procedures and principle of withdrawal. We recognize these are concessions neither side has previously been pre-

---

[1] Source: National Archives, Nixon Presidential Materials, NSC Files, Box 1155, Saunders Files, Middle East Negotiations Files, U.S. Peace Initiative For the Middle East. Secret; Priority; Noforn; Nodis. Drafted on June 17 by Atherton, cleared by Rogers in substance, and approved by Sisco. Sent Priority to Amman, Cairo, London, Moscow, Paris, USUN, Beirut, Jidda, Kuwait, Algiers, Rabat, Tunis, Bonn, Tripoli, Khartoum, Ankara, Tehran, New Delhi, Rawalpindi, Belgrade, Bucharest, Nicosia, Rome, Tel Aviv, Dhahran, and Jerusalem.

[2] See Document 128.

pared to make but think UAR, Jordan, Israel and USSR may be sufficiently nervous about risks of present military situation to give initiative along these lines some chance of getting off the ground in present changed circumstance.

3. Our proposed timing is (a) to inform Israelis in advance in detail of our proposals but not ask their formal acceptance pending Arab and Soviet reactions, (b) to approach UAR, Jordan, USSR, UK and French about 24 hours later, and (c) to make general public announcement re our political initiative and interim aircraft decision a few days after that.[3]

4. To launch foregoing initiative, Ambassador Barbour will see Prime Minister Meir and I will see Ambassador Rabin Friday, June 19.

5. Following FYI is summary of talking points being used in presentation to Israelis:

A. Political and military situation in area has reached such critical point that only new and intensive efforts, by those of us whose long term interests require peaceful settlement, can have any hope of reversing present trend toward long, costly and dead-end war of attrition. Pressures are mounting on UAR and Jordan to abandon SC Resolution 242, which is only common framework for peaceful settlement. Immediate implications for Lebanon, and longer term implications for such other moderate governments as Saudi Arabia, Kuwait, Morocco, and Tunisia, are dangerous in the extreme. At same time, Soviet military involvement in UAR has injected qualitatively new and potentially open-ended element into military balance.

B. Israel has asked us to make clear to Soviets that we will not tolerate their conspiring in threat to Israeli security and existence. We have made this clear, and will continue to do so. We will continue, of course, to support Israel's survival. There should be no doubts about the constancy of our support in this regard.

C. However, it is also in our national interest to preserve US position in moderate Arab world and in checking further Soviet gains in area as a whole.

D. We therefore need a strong political as well as a firm military strategy. Soviet thrust is as much political as military, and can only be countered by comparable two-pronged approach by us.

E. On political side, there is urgent need to launch genuine negotiating process between parties. The key to getting negotiating process started is to test commitment of parties to principles of RES 242, and in

---

[3] Rogers made the announcement at a news conference on June 25. His statement and the question-and-answer session that followed are printed in the Department of State *Bulletin,* July 13, 1970, pp. 25–33.

particular (1) the UAR's commitment to the principle of acceptance of and peaceful coexistence with Israel, and (2) Israel's commitment to the principle of withdrawal, both in accordance with the SC Resolution.

F. Three recent developments offer an opportunity to test Nasser's commitment to peace: (1) his May 1 speech[4] which provides us an opening to put his intentions directly to the test; (2) Nasser's NET TV interview, including statement of willingness to observe ceasefire for specified period; and (3) recent indications in our bilateral talks with the Soviets[5] that they are now prepared to move toward our formulations on the specific obligations of peace.

G. We therefore intend to approach Cairo (and Amman simultaneously) with the proposal that Nasser (and Hussein) subscribe to the following formula, which would be in the form of a public report from Jarring to the UNSYG, as the basis for beginning negotiations—indirect in the first instance—under Jarring's auspices:

BEGIN TEXT.

The UAR (Jordan) and Israel advise me that they agree:

(a) that having accepted and indicated their willingness to carry out Resolution 242 in all its parts, they will designate representatives to discussions to be held under my auspices, according to such procedure and at such places and times as I may recommend, taking into account as appropriate each side's preference as to method of procedure and previous experience between the parties.

(b) that the purpose of the aforementioned discussions is to reach agreement on the establishment of a just and lasting peace between them based on (1) mutual acknowledgment by the UAR (Jordan) and Israel of each other's sovereignty, territorial integrity and political independence, and (2) Israeli withdrawal from territories occupied in the 1967 conflict, both in accordance with Resolution 242.

(c) that, to facilitate my task of promoting agreement as set forth in Resolution 242, the parties will strictly observe, effective July 1 at least until October 1, the ceasefire resolutions of the Security Council. END TEXT.

H. Ceasefire to be effective would have to include understanding that (1) both sides would stop all incursions and all firing, on the ground and in the air, across the ceasefire lines, (2) UAR and USSR would refrain from changing military status quo (by emplacing SAMs or other new installations in an agreed zone west of Suez Canal cease-

---

[4] For Kissinger's description and analysis of this speech, see Document 115.

[5] Rogers and Dobrynin had most recently met on June 8. See Document 122. Kissinger and Dobrynin met on June 10. See *Foreign Relations,* 1969–1976, volume XII, Soviet Union, January 1969–October 1970, Document 168.

fire line), and (3) Israel would observe similar standstill on new installations in similar zone east of Canal.

I. We will simultaneously inform Jarring, U Thant, the British and the French of this initiative with Nasser and Hussein. We will also seek to enlist support of Soviets to influence Cairo. In doing so, we will tell Soviets (1) we see continuing useful role for our joint efforts only in circumstances where there is genuine negotiation in process between parties, and (2) alternative to genuine Soviet cooperation is continuation of military conflict in which not only will we assure maintenance of Israel's military strength, but also further Soviet military involvement risks more direct confrontation with U.S.[6]

J. Pending UAR response to foregoing approach, we are not asking Israel to react. While we will press Nasser hard on ceasefire, we do not intend to make this a breaking point. However, if UAR responds positively to negotiating aspect of our proposal (i.e., subparas (a) and (b) of above formula), we will expect equally positive GOI response. We recognize that this will require serious and difficult political decision by GOI. We have never concealed from GOI, however, that we do not agree with its formula of "direct negotiations without preconditions." We have consistently held to view, which we understood was also Israel's position in June, 1967, that when Israel won war which was thrust upon it in 1967, its overriding goal should be peace substantially within its 1949–67 borders. Given risks GOI is asking us to undertake in its interest in area, we believe political risks we are asking of GOI are reasonable—the more so since they are based on solid assurance of our support for Israel's survival.

K. On military side, we will continue to make our resolve clear to Soviets. So far as military assistance to Israel is concerned, we will continue to be responsive to Israel's requests in keeping open the normal logistical supply line for equipment, spare parts, expendable supplies and production technology.

L. On aircraft, pending the outcome of these political initiatives, as an interim measure we are prepared (a) to continue Phantom and Skyhawk deliveries through summer up to but not beyond numbers provided for in existing contracts, and (b) to work out contingency plans which put us in position to deliver replacement aircraft rapidly to Israel if the situation should require it.

M. We expect that Israel will continue to refrain from resuming deep penetration raids over Egypt whether or not a ceasefire is achieved. We expect Israel to damp down public discussion of the air-

---

[6] Rogers and Sisco met with Dobrynin on June 20 to present the new peace initiative. See *Foreign Relations,* 1969–1976, volume XII, Soviet Union, January 1969–October 1970, Document 170.

craft issue by making clear it is prepared to enter into meaningful negotiations and that it is satisfied with the contingency arrangements which have been made. We count on Israel's cooperation with respect to publicity and to our negotiating proposals in the spirit of the request conveyed to FonMin Eban during his recent visit.[7]

N. It is essential to maintain a calm and restrained public atmosphere while our negotiating initiatives are being tested. We, therefore, intend to make a public statement along the following lines within the next week. (*FYI*—In making following statement available to Israelis, they should understand it is subject to change. *END FYI*.)

BEGIN TEXT

In view of the serious nature of developments in the Middle East in recent weeks, we have undertaken a thorough review of all aspects of the problem. We have concluded that the most immediate and compelling need in the area is for the parties to stop fighting and start talking in accordance with the resolutions of the UN Security Council. We are currently taking a number of steps to this end.

We have also weighed carefully Israel's most recent request for the sale of additional aircraft. We have come to a judgment on this matter in light of four principal considerations: (a) that the overriding objective is fresh efforts to achieve a stable peace in the Middle East through negotiations under Jarring's auspices; (b) that US support of Israel's existence and security remains firm; (c) that there is an urgent need in the area in the days ahead for prudence on the ground by all concerned; (d) that the USSR has installed SA–3s in the UAR and is operating them with its own personnel, and its pilots are flying operational missions in the UAR; and (e) that the United States strongly desires to maintain its friendship with all countries in the area who desire our friendship.

In light of these considerations, we have decided that for the period of time during which the efforts to get the parties to stop shooting and start talking will be pursued, deliveries of aircraft to Israel will be limited and not go beyond the total number contemplated under previous contracts. At the same time, we have also made contingent arrangements which will put us in a position in the future to provide Israel with replacements of aircraft if the situation so requires. *END TEXT*.

O. We are informing Israel now of our moves in the straightforward spirit we believe should characterize our relations. We cannot overstress the importance we attach to discretion in this matter and to avoiding any actions which could prejudice Nasser's reaction. If Israel should take any action jeopardizing our peace efforts, this will require a

---

[7] See Document 118.

reassessment of our position re arms assistance. There must be an opportunity for movement by both sides without the glare of publicity. Pending Nasser's reaction, we urge Mrs. Meir to hold it within the circle of her closest advisers and particularly not to make it a matter for full Cabinet consideration until we have had reactions from Cairo and Amman and have had the opportunity for a further discussion with her.[8]

6. Foregoing is NOFORN for all addressees except Tel Aviv until instructed otherwise.

Rogers

---

[8] Barbour met with Meir and Eban on June 19. He reported in telegram 3200 from Tel Aviv, June 19: "Mrs. Meir's reaction was strongly adverse, on basis Israel was being asked to accept weakening of IDF as price for negotiations while U.A.R. would remain free to carry on war of attrition, receive unlimited military supplies from U.S.S.R., and continue negotiations indefinitely without concessions." (National Archives, Nixon Presidential Materials, NSC Files, Box 423, Backchannel) Rogers and Sisco also met with Rabin on June 19. Rabin took "vigorous exception to our making supply of aircraft September–December (as he put it) 'subject to political developments.'" (Telegram 97690 to Tel Aviv, June 20; ibid., Box 1155, Saunders Files, Middle East Negotiations Files)

---

130. Telegram From the Department of State to the Embassy in Israel[1]

Washington, June 20, 1970, 2185Z.

97781. For Ambassador. Following is revised draft letter approved by the President. You should deliver it promptly to Prime Minister Meir.[2] Previous text prepositioned with you can be drawn upon by you to make additional points contained in it orally.[3]

---

[1] Source: National Archives, Nixon Presidential Materials, NSC Files, Box 756, Presidential Correspondence 1969–1974, Israel Prime Minister Golda Meir 1970. Secret; Flash; Nodis. Drafted and approved by Sisco.

[2] Barbour reported that the Israeli Foreign Ministry delivered the letter to Meir "first thing" in the morning, June 21. (Telegram 3203 from Tel Aviv, June 21; ibid., Box 1155, Saunders Files, Middle East Negotiations Files)

[3] Reference is to Barbour's talking points regarding Nixon's decision on the supply of U.S. aircraft to Israel (see Document 129) which were contained in telegram 96573 to Tel Aviv, June 19. (National Archives, RG 59, Central Files 1970–73, DEF 12–5 ISR)

QUOTE: Dear Madam Prime Minister:

Ambassador Barbour's report of his conversation with you yesterday reached me this morning.

From his report and that of Ambassador Rabin's talk with Secretary Rogers,[4] I am concerned that you are interpreting our decision on aircraft as having an element of conditionality prejudicial to Israel's security needs. I want to assure you categorically this is not the case. There is no relationship in our decision between the question of negotiations and the supply of aircraft. What we have said is simply that a situation might arise where timing would be important to both of us in the course of an effort designed to move the Middle East from a state of ever more dangerous hostilities to a state of peace.

I can assure you that we in no way under-estimate the weight of your concerns. I ask, however, that you study our decision and proposals with deliberation and avoid taking any irreversible action. I would hope that you could adopt a positive public posture toward our efforts. If that is not possible, however, it is my hope that you will reserve judgment and not respond until the other side has reacted. For Israel to take on the onus for the failure of the new effort to get negotiations started between the parties would be a major setback both for Israel and the United States.[5]

Sincerely,

Richard Nixon END QUOTE

Rogers

---

[4] See footnote 8, Document 129.

[5] Nixon received a reply from Meir on July 2. She thanked him "warmly" for taking the time to send her a personal note, commenting that it in itself was evidence that he appreciated how "vital" the aircraft decision was to Israel and that he understood the "gravity" of Israel's situation. She continued: "But we are convinced that the possibility of peace with our neighbors will not be furthered by a weakened Israel. Therefore, we could not understand why any developments in peace negotiations should affect the delivery of aircraft to us. We, of course, all know that whatever negotiations take place, the continuous supply of Russian arms, and probably personnel, will not be affected. For this reason I particularly welcome your assurance that there is no relationship between the question of negotiations and the supply of aircraft, and I venture to hope that the question of timing will not arise." (National Archives, Nixon Presidential Materials, NSC Files, Box 607, Country Files, Middle East, Israel, Vol. V)

131. Minutes of a Washington Special Actions Group Meeting[1]

Washington, June 22, 1970, 3:10–4:04 p.m.

SUBJECT

Middle East

PARTICIPATION

Chairman—Henry A. Kissinger

State
Mr. U. Alexis Johnson
Mr. Rodger Davies

Defense
Mr. G. Warren Nutter
Mr. Robert Pranger

JCS
Adm. Thomas H. Moorer
Col. Frank W. Rhea

CIA
Gen. Robert E. Cushman, Jr.
Mr. Thomas Karamessines

NSC Staff
Col. Richard T. Kennedy
Mr. Harold Saunders
Mr. Keith Guthrie

SUMMARY OF CONCLUSIONS

The WSAG reviewed the status of contingency planning for military-supported evacuation from Arab nations and for military intervention in response to possible requests for assistance from friendly Arab governments threatened with overthrow by outside and/or indigenous forces. The objective is to be able to provide the NSC a complete analysis of alternatives and implications in the event the NSC is faced with a decision on whether to take military action to meet a crisis in one or more Arab countries.

The WSAG Middle East Working Group will prepare a study setting forth the pros and cons of military intervention at the invitation of a friendly Arab government.[2] The study will be a general one dealing with all countries in which the United States might be asked to take military action in support of friendly governments (including Lebanon, Jordan, Kuwait, and Saudi Arabia). However, the study will identify special factors applicable only to individual countries. It should specify what the US can reasonably expect to accomplish within a given time-

---

[1] Source: National Archives, Nixon Presidential Materials, NSC Files, NSC Institutional Files (H-Files), Box H–114, Washington Special Actions Group, WSAG Minutes (Originals) 1969 and 1970. Secret; Nodis. All brackets are in the original except those indicating text omitted by the editors. The meeting was held in the White House Situation Room.

[2] The study, "U.S. Response to an Appeal for Support by King Hussein of Jordan," undated, is ibid., Box H–078, Washington Special Actions Group Meetings, WSAG Meeting Jordan & Israel 6/22/70.

frame. The study will be submitted for consideration at an early meeting of the Special Review Group.[3]

For Libya and Kuwait the WSAG Middle East Working Group will prepare a chronological listing of steps to be taken and assignment of responsibilities for action in the event of a crisis. In addition, the Working Group will insure that the contingency plan for each country includes an annex specifying the number and location of US nationals in that country. The JCS will prepare a listing of various alternative routes for staging troops to the Middle East, with information about the time factors involved.

The WSAG agreed that it would be desirable to hold advance consultations with the UK to see if British bases on Cyprus might be available for staging US troops. The State Department is to look further into the possibility of consulting with the British.

In connection with possible use of Greek facilities, the WSAG agreed that it was important that the studies and plans being prepared contain a full assessment of the availability of Greek bases under various contingencies.

[Omitted here are the minutes.]

---

[3] The next Ad Hoc Special Review Group meeting was held on July 9; see Document 133.

132. Memorandum From the Assistant Secretary of Defense for International Security Affairs (Nutter) to the Deputy Secretary of Defense (Packard)[1]

Washington, July 8, 1970.

SUBJECT

Israeli Arms Requests

We understand (from Hal Saunders on the NSC staff) that Dr. Kissinger plans—as a result of a call by Ambassador Rabin last night[2]—to raise the subject of Israel's "want" lists of military hardware. Significantly, Ambassador Rabin has again turned to the White House, despite our request to the Attaché that these requests be handled through channels. The GOI is now beginning to make a practice of threatening "to go to the White House" if we are slow in responding to their requests.

Needless to say, it is highly irregular to handle military requests in an Ambassador-to-White House channel, leaving out both State and Defense. There are good reasons for following authorized channels: US decisions on arms requests must take into account the political impact of the sale, the military requirement to be met (and we do not simply take the word of the customer), equipment availability, and overall military impact of the sale. These judgments require expert knowledge and professional judgment, which is available only in the DoD and State. For NSC staff members (including Dr. Kissinger) to make commitments of US military assets, without consulting DoD and State is dangerous, seriously degrades the role of both State and Defense, and risks compromising US security by giving away secret information or critical assets.

---

[1] Source: Washington National Records Center, OSD Files: FRC 330–76–0067, Box 73, Israel. Secret. A stamped notation indicates that Packard saw it.

[2] No record of Rabin's July 7 conversation with Kissinger has been found. In a July 8 memorandum to Laird, Moorer, and the Acting Secretary of State, Kissinger wrote that Rabin had requested an "urgent appointment" with him (Kissinger) on the morning of July 8 to discuss recent changes in the Middle East situation. The three most urgent problems raised by Rabin involved: "Assembly now and possible modification of A–4 aircraft to reduce a three to four months leadtime in the event a decision is made to proceed with the provision of additional aircraft to Israel commencing in September 1970; provision of improved ordinance to Israel; and provision of additional credit to Israel." Kissinger added that "an additional and perhaps more serious implication of the discussion with Ambassador Rabin is the possibility that the Israelis may initiate air strikes against the SA–3 sites in the UAR which are reportedly located 22 to 25 miles from the Suez Canal. Should these attacks be undertaken and Soviet aircraft respond, this could have the most grave implications for the U.S. government." (National Archives, Nixon Presidential Materials, NSC Files, Box 607, Country Files, Middle East, Israel, Vol. V.) A memorandum of conversation between Kissinger and Rabin is ibid.

If this subject is raised, we recommend you respond by (1) noting that we have received and are studying these requests, as a matter of urgency, (2) that OSD is establishing a special committee to review the ECM and advanced weapons requests, and has already sent a team of experts to Israel to assist in our review; (3) that the US response must be based on careful State-Defense study, given the very serious security implications involved, and (4) that you avoid any discussion of details on particular items of equipment at this time (Mr. Pranger will be available to comment on the individual items if this should be necessary).

On A–4s, you should know that we are staffing the A–4 "earmarking" problem, and will have a detailed position by Friday. The simple fact is, however, that we are not prepared to begin aircraft modification and rehabilitation unless and until a contract has been signed, and the Presidential decision on aircraft excluded such a contract until September.

Finally, you should know that this insistence by Ambassador Rabin on "going to the White House" has become a matter of the greatest concern both here and in State. The basic rationale of these two departments is to provide the expertise needed for just such matters as this, and if the NSC staff is to make all arms decisions, our role ceases to exist. We consider it of the greatest importance that DoD's position not be compromised on this subject.[3]

G Warren Nutter

---

[3] On July 9, Nutter wrote in an attached note: "Since this memo was written, the Secretary has spoken to Kissinger on the phone about some of these problems. I still feel it is useful for you to have our views before you in preparation for the meeting this afternoon." Reference is to the Ad Hoc Special Review Group meeting; see Document 133.

133. Minutes of an Ad Hoc Special Review Group Meeting[1]

Washington, July 9, 1970, 2:35–3:50 p.m.

SUBJECT

The Middle East

PARTICIPATION

Chairman—Henry A. Kissinger

State
U. Alexis Johnson
Joseph Sisco
Alfred L. Atherton, Jr.

Defense
David Packard
G. Warren Nutter
Robert Pranger

CIA
Richard Helms

JCS
Adm. Thomas H. Moorer

NSC Staff
Harold H. Saunders
Richard T. Kennedy
Jeanne W. Davis

SUMMARY OF DECISIONS

It was agreed that:

a. State and Defense would clarify the question of the lists of equipment for Israel approved by the President[2] and delivery would proceed without delay;

b. the new list received by Defense from Amb. Rabin[3] would be circulated and staffed for decision—by the President if necessary;

c. diplomatic and military scenarios would be prepared[4] for various possible responses to our initiative;[5]

d. Navy would be instructed to place a contract with McDonnell-Douglas for the reconfiguration of the A–4s for Israel;

e. we should proceed with the Jordanians on delivery of the agreed arms package,[6] allowing the Jordanian team to come to the US, signing the letters of intent and giving them delivery dates for the F–104s.

---

[1] Source: National Archives, Nixon Presidential Materials, NSC Files, NSC Institutional Files (H-Files), Box H–111, Senior Review Group, SRG Minutes Originals 1970. Top Secret; Nodis. The meeting was held in the White House Situation Room.

[2] Not found.

[3] The list is attached to a July 9 memorandum from Nutter to Laird. (Washington National Records Center, OSD Files: FRC 330–76–0076, Box 9, Middle East)

[4] The undated paper, "Possible Steps to Underline U.S. Determination to Limit Further Soviet Military Involvement in the Near East," is in the National Archives, Nixon Presidential Materials, NSC Files, NSC Institutional Files (H-Files), Box H–046, Senior Review Group Meetings, Senior Review Group—Middle East 7/9/70.

[5] See Document 129.

[6] See Document 113.

f. the Special Review Group will meet next week[7] to consider the diplomatic and military scenarios, review contingency plans and sharpen the issues for a possible NSC meeting.

Mr. Kissinger suggested that the group review the state of play in our diplomatic initiative; consider what next steps might be appropriate; and possibly review contingency preparations. It might also review the delivery schedule for the arms to Jordan.

Mr. Sisco said we had received no considered reply to our initiative, but that we might expect one in about a week, after the Egyptians leave Moscow and have time to concert with Jordan. It would be interesting to see if we get our response direct from the Egyptians or through the Soviets or both. He and Mr. Helms confirmed that Nasser was still in Moscow for medical treatment.[8] He saw two diplomatic possibilities: (1) an inconclusive response amounting to a rejection, or (2) a response through which the Soviets and Egyptians would attempt to push the US back into the four-power context. He noted that they had consistently preferred to handle the issue in the two or four-power framework rather than address themselves to proposals to get the two parties talking.

Mr. Kissinger asked for Sisco's definition of a flat turndown—would this be a demand that we spell out the details of our proposal before they would agree to talk?

Mr. Sisco said yes, or a rephrasing of our proposal which could call for an Israeli withdrawal to the pre-June 1967 lines. On the political level he saw two alternative US responses: (1) that we fall in with the strategy and make substantive countermoves in either the two or four-power framework, building on the Soviet formulation involving a commitment to peace and a promise to deal with the fedayeen; or (2) that we institute a pause, suspend our participation in the two or four-power discussions for a period of time, during which we could take some interim steps, with a view to a possible political move in the context of the opening of the UN General Assembly in mid-September. During the interim period we could consider: (1) whether to stick with Israel militarily along the line of the decisions already taken; (2) whether to increase our support of Israel quietly or publicly; or (3) what steps, if any, we might take to give concrete meaning to the

---

[7] The Ad Hoc Special Review Group met on July 20. According to the "Summary of Decisions," it was decided that: "The WSAG contingency plans would be updated; State and Defense would meet to consider Israel's financial problems with regard to arms deliveries; JCS would do a scenario on putting together a sizeable package to augment our forces in the Mediterranean." The minutes of the meeting are in the National Archives, Nixon Presidential Materials, NSC Files, NSC Institutional Files (H-Files), Box H–111, Senior Review Group, SRG Minutes Originals 1970.

[8] Nasser was in Moscow June 29–July 17.

President's words, both his public statements and what we have been saying to the Soviets over the past weeks. He thought we might be able to interpret such a response one of two ways. If we interpret it as a turndown, we could apply a certain degree of shock treatment to prepare the way for a new effort. If we interpret it as leaving the door open, we could continue to do what we are doing with Israel and meanwhile decide what to do about the Soviets.

Mr. Packard asked what we have told the Egyptians.

Mr. Sisco replied that we have given our political initiative in writing to the Egyptians and Jordanians, and have informed the Russians, British and French. Nasser was now considering with the Soviets how to answer. He thought it unlikely that they would "kick it out of the park," both because they would be concerned about the political repercussions and because they would be worried over possible US and Israeli military moves.

Mr. Kissinger asked if it was correct to say that, while we don't expect them to accept our initiative, they could fudge their response by demanding that unless we move into the two or four-power context and there spell out the terms of reference for Jarring, there would be nothing to talk about.

Mr. Sisco added that they could confirm their acceptance of the Security Council resolution, accept the proposition of talks under Jarring, but claim that the basis for the mandate to Jarring was insufficient. They could say that we should continue the useful discussions in the two or four-power groups and that they would cooperate, provided we spelled out the mandate in more detail.

Mr. Kissinger asked how we could refuse to talk in the two or four-power groups, particularly since they would be accepting some of our proposals.

Mr. Sisco agreed it would be hard.

Mr. Kissinger asked, if the Egyptians handle their response skillfully, and the President wants to administer some shock treatment, how would we go about it?

Mr. Sisco said we could take the position that the US has put forward a proposal that they stop shooting and start talking, which involves a minimal commitment from the other side. Since they appear unwilling to move, we believe that a pause and a reassessment of the situation are in order.

Mr. Johnson asked what if the response was more forthcoming. What would Israel accept?

Mr. Sisco agreed that if we can interpret the Egyptian answer as an acceptance, we would have to twist Israel's arm.

Mr. Kissinger asked what would constitute a response that was not a flat acceptance but that we could interpret as an acceptance.

Mr. Sisco replied that they could say they are ready to start talks on the basis proposed by the US. However, we must change our general statement on withdrawal to a specific commitment of Israeli withdrawal to the pre-June 5 lines. He reviewed the history of the language of the Security Council resolution on Israeli withdrawal, saying that the language finally agreed on allowed everyone to interpret its meaning in his own way. Accordingly, the problem was turned over to Jarring, which everyone wanted, on the basis of two varying interpretations of the meaning of the resolution.

Mr. Packard asked if we had an adequate definition of cease-fire.

Mr. Sisco thought we did.

Mr. Kissinger noted that Israel was arguing that a 90-day cease-fire would abrogate the various UN resolutions on the subject.

Mr. Sisco said that Israelis use two arguments against a cease-fire: (1) that it might provide a cover for increased or accelerated SAM development; and (2) the specious argument that agreement to a 90-day cease-fire would abrogate the UN resolutions, which is not correct.

Mr. Kissinger agreed that Israel could not say it would withdraw for 90 days then go back at the end of 90 days.

Mr. Sisco commented that if we received a flat rejection, our response should be stiff. We should get out of the two or four-power talks for six weeks and continue our military support of Israel.

Mr. Kissinger said in the case of a modified rejection, we could play tough as described or we could counter either by re-raising the question of a cease-fire or by going back with a more detailed formulation. He asked what we get out of the four-power talks? Are we not better off in two-power talks?

All agreed.

Mr. Sisco said we could keep the four-power talks limping along in a meaningless dialogue if we wished to, particularly if they were aware that something was going on in the two-power talks. He said we would, of course, have trouble with the French whose behaviour in the four-power talks he described as shameful.

Mr. Kissinger said we always have trouble with the French and attempting to butter them up has not helped. He commented the difference between a modified acceptance and a modified rejection was not so great.

Mr. Helms asked why we considered some of the moves discussed to be tough. Tough on whom?

Mr. Sisco replied tough on the Arabs, the Russians and the French. The Russians and the Arabs want to continue the talks in the four-power context where they could put maximum pressure on the US. He said Gromyko was advising his people to take their time and wear the US down in these talks.

Mr. Helms said he had no objection to calling off our participation in the talks but he didn't think it would help.

Mr. Sisco outlined an illustrative scenario for a tough line. We could say, in view of the rejection of our proposal, we see no possibility of progress in the two-power or four-power talks. Therefore, we will give an X amount of military assistance to Israel and, in addition, will take steps A and B. Maintaining this posture for a while might create a climate in which the other side would develop some flexibility on the political side. Of the specific actions we might take, he suggested putting a US carrier into the port of Haifa and giving the crew a three-day leave, or putting a hunter-killer ASW group into the Mediterranean.

Mr. Packard agreed it might come to that.

Mr. Johnson commented that we should look further down the line and ask then what?

Mr. Kissinger thought we should consider ways to galvanize the negotiations. How we should play the response to our initiative is a tactical problem. We should focus on what the answer means. Does it mean Nasser is heading toward negotiations? Or does it mean he is stalling to allow time for more Soviet support to come in. If the former, we should go back to them. If the latter, it would be better to convey some warning.

Mr. Sisco commented that we could not disregard the Israeli reaction.

Mr. Kissinger asked if the Israelis might get desperate and pull the trigger.

Mr. Sisco doubted this, saying they could not reproduce the 6-day war in present conditions.

Mr. Packard thought we should do anything we could to press on in the interim. He suggested we might hold back on the supply of some arms to Israel.

Mr. Sisco said that was the wrong target.

Mr. Packard thought such a move would indicate to the Arabs that we were serious about a ceasefire. He also thought proceeding with the package for Jordan would indicate that we are serious. He considered it inconsistent, at least in the short term, to build up Israel while we talk about a ceasefire.

Mr. Johnson said no one was suggesting additional aircraft deliveries to Israel.

Mr. Packard replied that there was a good deal "on the deck" and some delay would show some good faith to the Arabs.

Mr. Sisco asked if Mr. Packard was suggesting that we reopen the decision on the things we are now delivering to Israel, in a situation where the Arab response to our initiative was not entirely satisfactory and in the circumstances of a creeping increase in Soviet involvement.

Mr. Packard said he was talking about the list of Israeli requests they had received.

Dr. Kissinger said this was a separate problem that had not yet been addressed. He asked if Mr. Packard was suggesting reopening the list of items that the President had already agreed to or was referring to a new list.

(It was determined after some confusion that Mr. Packard was referring to a new list delivered to Defense by Ambassador Rabin after his July 8 conversation with Dr. Kissinger,[9] which list had not yet been seen by the other agencies.)

Dr. Kissinger said he had circulated the memorandum of his conversation with Rabin purely for information, with no intention that it was to be considered as a directive of any kind.

Mr. Sisco reviewed the two decisions that had been made: 1) the list of items approved by the President in the context of the NSC meeting some weeks ago;[10] and 2) the list of electronic equipment and other items which had been approved by the President over the July 4 weekend.

Mr. Pranger agreed that Defense was now talking about a new list, not previously considered, but said he had been in telephone touch with State on drones and some of the other equipment on the new list. He noted that Israel had some $577 million in debits since the decision on the jets and was moving toward $1 billion.

Dr. Kissinger replied that we could not discuss the issue on that basis. He reviewed the developments of the July 4 weekend, saying the President's original inclination had been to replace all Israeli planes that had been shot down. He had reconsidered and had approved the list of electronic equipment and other items contained in the Defense Department cable sent to San Clemente on Friday, July 3.[11] He said we could not reopen the decisions on this list unless the Israelis did something inconsistent with our peace approach.

---

[9] See footnote 2, Document 132.
[10] See Documents 124 and 128.
[11] The list is contained in an undated memorandum from Nutter to Laird which bears the stamped notation "Sec Def Has Seen, July 6, 1970." A note attached to the memorandum reads: "Attached memo forwarded to White House West for BG Haig was received at 2026 hours EDT, 3 July." (Washington National Records Center, OSD Files: FRC 330–76–0076. Box 74, Israel)

Mr. Packard said he thought we should look at the total amount of equipment to be delivered to Israel in a given time period to be sure we aren't doing the wrong thing.

Dr. Kissinger said any requests received after the Presidential approvals must of course be looked at, but nothing that had been approved can be held up.

Mr. Packard reiterated that he thought we should look at the total list. Admiral Moorer added that we can't decide on the list of equipment until we decide what we want Israel to do: whether we want them to continue to suffer attrition in the course of our diplomatic initiative, or whether we want to stop the attrition so they can hold their own.

Dr. Kissinger said he must protect the President's decisions. They must be carried out. Any new list of requests should be staffed and considered on its merits. He said the present list of deliveries had been approved on the basis that the Israelis would not undertake further deep penetration. Nothing beyond that had been approved.

Mr. Pranger and Mr. Nutter noted that there had been no itemized list prepared in connection with the NSDM on the subject.[12]

Dr. Kissinger said there had been a clear Presidential understanding that we would hold back on the aircraft but would meet the other requirements. The list considered at the NSC meeting and the July 4 electronic equipment list had been approved. Drones and any other items on a new list had not been considered and were not approved.

Mr. Nutter reiterated that there was no list of items attached to the NSDM, and Mr. Sisco said he would provide one to the Defense Department.

Mr. Pranger acknowledged that Defense had the list which had been circulated by State but said they were not sure that the NSDM meant that list. He said they have moved on the tanks and other items, but some of the items, including Red Eyes, cause difficulties in Defense.

Dr. Kissinger reiterated the President's clear understanding that the non-aircraft items had been approved and would be delivered. We cannot hold up delivery on items already decided upon. If there is a new list, we will look at it. He asked Mr. Sisco to straighten out the confusion with Defense, and asked that the new list be circulated and the items staffed. He said if there were items on the new list which were duplicates of requests on other lists or which asked for expansion or acceleration of delivery of previously approved items, we should take these out and circulate them for consideration.

---

[12] See Document 128.

Mr. Packard reiterated his desire for a review of the entire list, but agreed to get together with State and straighten out any confusion.

Dr. Kissinger said in the event we received a qualified acceptance of our proposal which required going back to the two-power group with detailed guidance, should we not prepare a diplomatic track for such a contingency.

Mr. Sisco said he was already preparing counter-formulations in the context of two-power talks.

Dr. Kissinger asked what we might do if we received a qualified or total rejection of our proposal with a continued Soviet buildup.

Mr. Sisco replied that State had been considering what signaling steps the US might take without any real idea of what kinds of things would be feasible militarily.

Mr. Johnson added that, on the basis of previous contingency planning, they could suggest either a carrier visit to the port of Haifa or some increased ASW capability in the Mediterranean. In the latter connection, there is a hunter-killer ASW group on the east coast which could be in the Mediterranean in two weeks. This would be a strong demonstration of our determination. He thought we should, however, consider the next steps. A carrier visit to Haifa would result in the closing of all Arab ports to the 6th Fleet but, as a practical matter, these ports were already closed.

Dr. Kissinger asked what this would achieve.

Mr. Johnson replied a show of force.

Dr. Kissinger asked about a movement in the Eastern Mediterranean.

Mr. Johnson replied it would not be as good demonstrably.

Admiral Moorer commented that we have moved into the Eastern Mediterranean in force before but we have never entered an Israeli port. He noted we could move the hunter-killer group with a Task Force. In response to Dr. Kissinger's question, he said the Soviets would undoubtedly read such a move as stepped-up readiness on our part.

Dr. Kissinger asked if we were trying to confront the Soviets or put ourselves behind Israel. If we were trying to confront the Soviets, there were other ways besides support for Israel. He thought the hunter-killer ASW group was a better signal of increased readiness than a port call at Haifa.

Admiral Moorer commented that the Navy did not like to put a carrier into a port.

Dr. Kissinger remarked that the Soviets would know of such a development before the Arabs did. He asked the composition of the hunter-killer group.

Admiral Moorer replied that it consisted of a helicopter carrier with a few fixed-wing aircraft, and six destroyers. He said there were four such groups in existence.

Dr. Kissinger asked how far the 6th Fleet is from the potential area of operation in the Mediterranean.

Admiral Moorer replied two days, commenting that they could move the group to the vicinity of Cyprus.

Mr. Packard asked if we could increase our ASW activities from the land.

Admiral Moorer replied we would do this as a matter of course if we moved the carrier to the East.

Mr. Johnson remarked that this would not be as demonstrable as the hunter-killer group.

Dr. Kissinger said we would need another meeting of the Special Review Group next week by which time we may know more about the responses to our initiative, to go through the military and diplomatic scenario, we should sort out the possible diplomatic responses in foreseeable contingencies. We could also sort out possible military measures and what we would put into the two-power or four-power context. We could also review the contingency plans developed last year. He thought the NSC would have to consider the strategic decision on how we might most likely move to a political resolution, including how and when we would need to the pressure the Israelis and how to put pressure on the Arabs. Next week's Special Review Group meeting could sharpen the issues.

Mr. Johnson asked about Rabin's three requests in his conversation with Dr. Kissinger.

Mr. Pranger said the A–4Es he is requesting are being configured specifically to meet Israeli needs. These aircraft are earmarked, but no contract has been let to McDonnell-Douglas who will do the work, and the work cannot proceed without a contract. He thought there would be a 3–4 month delay until the aircraft were available.

Admiral Moorer said they could accelerate the work as soon as they could sign a contract, but they had no money for a contract and no authority to do more than earmark the aircraft to be reconfigured.

Mr. Sisco reviewed the President's decision on aircraft which called for the delivery of 5 Phantoms in September, 5 in October, and 4 in November and 4 in December. It also called for the delivery of 4 A–4s in each of the four months. This decision could be reopened only if we achieve a ceasefire, or if talks are underway between the two parties under Jarring's auspices and it was felt that delivery of the aircraft would jeopardize the progress of the talks. He said Defense should do whatever was necessary to deliver the aircraft.

Mr. Pranger and Mr. Nutter said they had checked with State and had not received the impression that they were to proceed on the A-4s.

Dr. Kissinger asked if this had been covered in the President's letter to Mrs. Meir.[13]

Mr. Sisco replied only in a general way, but it had been included in the NSDM that was sent to State and Defense.

Mr. Packard said they would instruct Navy to place the contract.

Dr. Kissinger remarked that there is nothing to prevent cancellation under the conditions noted by Mr. Sisco.

Dr. Kissinger asked if Rabin had submitted to Defense the request for improved air ordnance.

Admiral Moorer said it was included in the new Israeli list.

Mr. Pranger said that a Defense Review Committee composed of representatives of OSD and the services was processing the individual items on the list.

Dr. Kissinger said, if the new list raises controversial items, we should get them to the President showing agency positions.

Mr. Pranger replied that many of the technical items can be handled routinely in Defense.

Dr. Kissinger reiterated that his circulation of the memorandum of his conversation with Rabin did not constitute a Presidential instruction. He thought the Rabin visit was primarily to call the President's attention to Israel's needs.

Mr. Pranger said the Defense Department Review Committee was meeting on Friday. They would circulate the new Israeli list, then circulate the committee's proposals.

Dr. Kissinger asked Mr. Packard to separate out the new items on the list and circulate them. He thought there might be some repeats or a request for a speed-up of old items.

He asked if the group could turn to a discussion of Jordan.

He said the Jordanian arms package had been approved on the assumption that it would strengthen the King and help maintain a moderate regime in the country. If the radical element in Jordan should gain the upper hand, we might find ourselves making significant arms shipments to a radical regime. It was thought wise to get the judgment of this group as to whether the original assumptions under which the arms package was approved were still valid.

Mr. Packard said Defense had no problem with proceeding with delivery of the material.

---

[13] See Document 130.

Mr. Sisco agreed with Mr. Packard. He thought the situation was a little more tenuous, but noted that the Army had remained loyal to the King. The King was, however, in a weaker political position, with a new Cabinet with a substantial Palestinian representation. He thought, however, we should let the Jordanian team come over and sign the letters of offer, continuing to emphasize to the King that we are doing so on the assumption that he does not go to the Russians as a source for additional arms. We could review the situation carefully before actual deliveries take place. He noted that it would be five months before deliveries commenced.

Mr. Helms agreed with Mr. Sisco's appraisal.

All others agreed.

Mr. Saunders asked if we could now give delivery dates on the F–104s and it was agreed to do so.

134. Memorandum From the President's Assistant for National Security Affairs (Kissinger) to President Nixon[1]

Washington, July 15, 1970.

SUBJECT

Middle East Problem

Having observed press speculation[2] over the two weeks since your television interview[3] and my San Clemente press backgrounders, you

---

[1] Source: National Archives, Nixon Presidential Materials, NSC Files, Box 646, Country Files, Middle East, Middle East—General, Vol. V. Secret. Sent for information. Kissinger initialed this memorandum at the top right-hand corner and wrote, "OBE." Beneath the note the date July 17, 1970, is stamped.

[2] In the week before the date of this memorandum, the press speculated about a division between the Department of State and the White House on Middle East issues. On July 9, Kissinger sent a message to Rogers, while the Secretary was in Japan, that begins: "In your absence, a mischievous press campaign has developed which suggests a sharp policy disagreement between the White House and the Department of State on the Middle East initiative. I wanted you to know that from the White House perspective, these allegations are completely without basis in fact." He also wrote: "I wish to assure you that the President and I are completely behind the Middle East initiative which, as you know, was the result of thoroughly coordinated State-White House action." (Telegram 109223 to Tokyo; ibid., Box 1155, Saunders Files, Middle East Negotiations Files)

[3] In a July 1 televised interview, Nixon addressed the Middle East situation: "Now what should U.S. policy be? I'll summarize it in a word. One, our interest is peace and the integrity of every country in the area. Two, we recognize that Israel is not desirous of

can best judge for yourself the manner in which the bureaucracy is treating this issue. However, the attached cable from Chargé Bergus in Cairo[4] suggests to what an absurd degree the lack of discipline has reached.

In summary Bergus states:

—The U.S. may become a prisoner of a small power (Israel).

—The U.S. is unwittingly being buffeted toward a new confrontation with the Soviet Union over a line which is to be established west of Cairo.

—He is unconvinced that the Soviets are creeping west and infers that we are being influenced by Israeli estimates.

—No major Ally will support us in the event of a confrontation with the Soviets on this issue.

—We have placed the issue of confrontation in the hands of the Israelis rather than controlling it ourselves.

The facts are:

(1) That the line to which Mr. Bergus refers is a line actually established by his own Secretary of State during his June 2 meeting with Ambassador Dobrynin when he said: "The USSR has indicated that Soviet military activities in the UAR will remain defensive. We want to make clear that we would not view the introduction of Soviet personnel, by air or on the ground, in the Canal combat zone as defensive since such action could only be in support of the announced UAR policy of violating the ceasefire resolutions of the Security Council. We believe that introduction of Soviet military personnel into the delicate Suez Canal combat zone could lead to serious escalation with unpredictable consequences to which we could not remain indifferent. In this connection, we believe, and I am sure you do, it is neither in the interest of the Soviet Union nor the United States for the Middle East to become an area of confrontation between us."[5]

(2) The reference by the Secretary to a "combat zone" was further defined by the Secretary when at the same meeting he handed Ambas-

---

driving any of the other countries into the sea. The other countries do want to drive Israel into the sea. Three, then, once the balance of power shifts where Israel is weaker than its neighbors, there will be a war. Therefore, it is in U.S. interests to maintain the balance of power, and we will maintain that balance of power. That is why as the Soviet Union moves in to support the U.A.R., it makes it necessary for the United States to evaluate what the Soviet Union does, and once that balance of power is upset, we will do what is necessary to maintain Israel's strength vis-à-vis its neighbors, not because we want Israel to be in a position to wage war—that is not it—but because that is what will deter its neighbors from attacking it." The complete transcript of the interview is printed in *Public Papers: Nixon, 1970*, pp. 543–559.

[4] Telegram 1539 from Cairo, July 14, is attached but not printed.

[5] See Document 120.

sador Dobrynin a summary of Israeli press reports quoting Dayan's May 26 statement that Israel was currently limiting itself to bombing up to 30 km inside Egypt.

(3) Subsequently, the Israelis registered concern that the Secretary's statement and his use of the Dayan statements might mislead the Soviets into thinking they could place installations right up to the 30 km line to take advantage of expected Israeli forebearance. This the Soviets have apparently done.

(4) Neither you nor I have made any public reference to the Soviets moving forward.

(5) Mr. Bergus' use of the word "confrontation" is a direct challenge to you and your choice of phrases at the West Coast press conference. It is inconceivable that a Chargé would send such a message unless he felt he had at least tacit sympathy at the highest levels within the Department of State.

135. Editorial Note

On July 16, 1970, Assistant to the President for National Security Affairs Kissinger sent President Nixon the records of his three most recent conversations with Soviet Ambassador Anatoly Dobrynin, which took place on June 23, July 7, and July 9. The memoranda of conversation are printed in *Foreign Relations, 1969–1976*, volume XII, Soviet Union, January 1969–October 1970, Documents 171, 177, and 179. In a covering memorandum to President Nixon, Kissinger offered some "highlights" of the conversations:

"*Change in Tone*. On June 23, shortly after the launching of our Middle East initiative, Ambassador Dobrynin was evasive and uncooperative. In our July 7 and 9 conversations, after our ten days in San Clemente, he presented a sharp contrast, being both conciliatory and effusive about the Soviet desire to reach understandings.

"*Middle East*. Dobrynin moved from his June 23 statement that the Soviets were temporarily absolved of any responsibility for a settlement because of our direct approach to the regional parties to his July 7/9 underlining of Soviet anxiousness for a settlement. He emphasized that the Soviets did not seek a confrontation with us, that it was essential to come to an agreement and that he was fully authorized to deal with me to conclude an agreement. He indicated, although ambiguously, that the Soviets would consider withdrawing their troops from Egypt once they knew what a political settlement would look like. I bore down very hard on the Soviet presence in the Mideast and, in response to a question, acknowledged that it appeared we were on a collision course." (National Archives, Nixon Presidential Materials, NSC Files, Box 712, Country Files, Europe, USSR, Vol. VIII)

"Following Kissinger's July 9 conversation with Dobrynin, Assistant Secretary of State Joseph Sisco met with the Soviet Ambassador on July 13 to discuss the recent cease-fire initiative proposed by Secretary Rogers on June 19 (see Document 129). Telegram 111425 to Moscow, July 13, reporting the conversation is in the National Archives, Nixon Presidential Materials, NSC Files, Box 490, President's Trip Files, Dobrynin/Kissinger, 1970, Vol. 3. The same day, Sisco sent a memorandum to Kissinger informing him of some "strictly personal" impressions he gave Dobrynin regarding the Soviet Union's continued military involvement in the UAR:

"I wrote a very brief telegram covering my last conversation with Dobrynin. What is not contained in the telegram is that I gave the Ambassador some personal impressions—strictly personal—of the atmosphere which the continuing increased Soviet military involvement in the UAR is creating which increases the risks of possible confrontation with us. I said that it would be well for Dobrynin to reflect that the President at the outset of his Administration had declared an era of negotiations. For seventeen months we had negotiated in good faith, and we feel that the Soviets have not come half the way; and that our restraint on the military side has not been met by restraint but rather by a fundamental decision on the part of the Soviet Union to involve its personnel in an operational capacity. This is a most serious decision for the Soviets to have taken, and our concern has increased not only because of the creeping process in recent weeks, but also because of Soviet unwillingness to tell us quietly and confidentially what their intentions are and what the outer limits of their involvement may be as they see it.

"I said I had watched our President for months and felt that he had offered political proposal after political proposal, and political option after political option in the context of the United States exercising great restraint in the face of pressures for providing Israel with substantial numbers of additional aircraft. I hoped that Dobrynin was not reporting to Moscow that our involvement in Vietnam reflected any lack of resolve in the Middle East. The President was a man of peace, a man who wanted a negotiated settlement, but also a man of firmness and toughness, which it would be well for the Soviet Union to take fully into account as it develops Middle East policy. He would not be pushed around in the Middle East or anywhere else. These were only personal judgments I was expressing; but I would advise Dobrynin to take very, very seriously the words expressed by the President some months ago that the United States would view with deep concern any attempt by the Soviet Union to dominate the Middle East.

"Dobrynin responded critically to the recent 'tough talk' which he said would not force the Soviet Union to make decisions of the kind it would not wish to make. He remonstrated several times that the emphasis on the Soviet role was creating a crisis atmosphere, and that it was not making it easier for Moscow to take constructive initiatives during the current discussions with Cairo. At the same time, he was quick to say, these were personal remarks and we would be receiving the replies to our political initiative at an early date." (Memorandum from Sisco to Kissinger, July 13; ibid., Box 340, Subject Files, Dobrynin/Kissinger) Sisco's memorandum is printed in *Foreign Relations, 1969–1976,* volume XII, Soviet Union, January 1969–October 1970, Document 181.

136. **Telegram From the Department of State to the Embassy in Israel**[1]

Washington, July 23, 1970, 2020Z.

118300. For Ambassador. Following is letter from President for Prime Minister Meir. You should deliver it promptly to Mrs. Meir. Instructions follow septel.[2]

QUOTE:

Dear Madame Prime Minister:

I am writing to inform you that we have received the following oral message from the Foreign Minister of the UAR:

INTERIOR QUOTE: The Government of the UAR accepts the proposal of Mr. Rogers contained in his message of June 19.[3] We are ready to subscribe to the statement as it is written in this message that is in the

---

[1] Source: National Archives, Nixon Presidential Materials, NSC Files, Box 654, Country Files, Middle East, Middle East—Recent Actions. Secret; Immediate; Nodis. Drafted and approved by Sisco on July 22.

[2] Telegram 118301 to Tel Aviv, July 23. (Ibid., Box 607, Country Files, Middle East, Israel, Vol. VI)

[3] Rogers's message to Mahmoud Riad is in telegram 96867 to Cairo, June 19. (Ibid., Box 636, Country Files, Middle East, UAR, Vol. IV)

form of a report from Ambassador Jarring to the Secretary General of the United Nations.[4] END INTERIOR QUOTE.

In our prior confidential discussions regarding this proposal, we asked that the Government of Israel refrain from taking a public position pending receipt of the Egyptian reply. As you know, we made this suggestion in the belief that it would not have served our mutual interests for Israel to have assumed the responsibility for rejecting a proposal whose aim is to stop the fighting and to begin negotiations under the auspices of Ambassador Jarring.

I am fully aware, Madame Prime Minister, of your Government's strong objections regarding this proposal. In light of the Egyptian acceptance, I ask you and your government to review this matter in hopes that a prompt affirmative reply from the Government of Israel will lead to an early stop of hostilities and bloodshed on both sides and to serious talks between the parties conducted by Ambassador Jarring within the framework of the UN Security Council resolution of November 22, 1967.[5]

The Egyptians have informed us their acceptance is unconditional. On the basis of additional views conveyed to us in writing by the UAR, we expect that in the negotiations it will continue to press two principal objectives: total Israeli withdrawal from the territories occupied in the 1967 conflict to the pre-June 5 lines; and a refugee solution based exclusively on the strict application of paragraph 11 of UN General Assembly resolution 194 (III).[6] I want to assure you that we will not press Israel to accept the aforementioned positions of the UAR. Our position on withdrawal is that the final borders must be agreed between the parties by means of negotiations under the aegis of Ambassador Jarring. Moreover, we will not press Israel to accept a refugee solution which would alter fundamentally the Jewish character of the state of Israel or jeopardize your security. We will also adhere strictly and firmly to the fundamental principle that there must be a peace agreement in which each of the parties undertakes reciprocal obligations to the other and that no Israeli soldier should be withdrawn from the occupied territories until a binding contractual peace agreement satisfactory to you has been achieved.

---

[4] The UAR's acceptance of the U.S. peace initiative (see Document 129) was reported in telegram 1614 from Cairo, July 22. (National Archives, Nixon Presidential Materials, NSC Files, Box 1155, Saunders Files, Middle East Negotiations Files)

[5] Israel responded positively to the U.S. peace initiative on August 4. See Document 140.

[6] Paragraph 11 of UN General Assembly Resolution 194, adopted on December 11, 1948, called for the return of the refugees to their homes and payment of compensation to those who did not wish to return. It directed the UN Conciliation Commission to facilitate the process. For more on the resolution, see *Foreign Relations, 1948, The Near East, South Asia, and Africa,* volume V, part 2, Document 806.

Finally, and most important of all, I am sure that you noted my recent public comments and nationally televised conference of July 1 in which I made clear the strong and unequivocal support of the United States for the state of Israel and its security.[7] Furthermore, I want again to assure you, as I have previously done in our personal talks, of my support for Israel's existence and security and my intention to continue to provide Israel with the necessary assistance to assure that the balance of power will not be altered to the detriment of Israel.

I hope, Madame Prime Minister, that you will receive my views in the spirit of mutual friendship and interest that has characterized the close relations between our two countries. I am certain, too, you will appreciate the weight of responsibility which I bear to exhaust every effort to achieve a stable and durable peace in the Middle East. I am confident that together we can move towards that goal.[8]

Sincerely,
Richard Nixon
ENDQUOTE.

Rogers

---

[7] See footnote 3, Document 134.

[8] Barbour delivered the letter to Meir on July 24 and then had a 1½-hour meeting with her and Eban, as reported in telegram 3931 from Tel Aviv, July 24. According to Barbour, he told the Prime Minister that "he felt as seriously as he had at any time in nine years" that he had dealt with her that they "might now be on threshold of turning from hostilities to negotiations." Meir responded that she was certain that he did not expect an immediate answer from her and proceeded to discuss her concern over Soviet activity in Egypt. She also expressed "deep appreciation" for the military equipment the United States had supplied to Israel in the previous several weeks, and she wanted to know if the flow of arms would stop once Israel accepted the U.S. peace initiative. (National Archives, Nixon Presidential Materials, NSC Files, Box 1155, Saunders Files, Middle East Negotiations Files)

137. Telegram From the Department of State to Certain Diplomatic Posts[1]

Washington, July 23, 1970, 2236Z.

118624. 1. Secretary, with Sisco and Dubs present, saw Dobrynin at latter's initiative to receive following oral statement, text of which left in writing by Dobrynin. Statement is Soviet acceptance of US peace proposal.[2]

QTE The Soviet Union, as the Government of the United States is well aware, from the very start of the Arab-Israeli conflict in the Middle East has consistently sought a settlement of this conflict through political means on the basis of the UN Security Council Resolution of November 22, 1967. With this aim in mind the Soviet Union repeatedly introduced proposals directed towards practical implementation of this Resolution.[3]

QTE The U.S. Government declares now that it agrees to a resumption of the mission of Ambassador Jarring, Special Representative of the UN Secretary General in the Middle East. It is well known that the Soviet Government has always insisted on the necessity of carrying out the mission entrusted with Ambassador Jarring, that it put forward appropriate proposals to this end and made efforts so that his mission be effective enough.

QTE That is why the Soviet side not only holds no objections to this effect but, on the contrary, it reiterates its position with regard to the necessity of resumption by Ambassador Jarring of his mission. Positively evaluating the possibilities in Ambassador Jarring's mission, we are ready to go on making our contribution in the future as well so that contacts between the sides through Jarring which could be resumed in the nearest future could produce positive results.

QTE As we know, the Governments of the UAR and Jordan have expressed their readiness to cease fire for a definite period of time if Israel also takes upon herself the same obligation. The Soviet Government's attitude to this is positive.

---

[1] Source: National Archives, Nixon Presidential Materials, NSC Files, Box 1155, Saunders Files, Middle East Negotiations Files, U.S. Peace Initiative For the Middle East Vol. I. Secret; Priority; Nodis. Drafted and approved by Sisco. Sent to Amman, Beirut, Cairo, Jidda, Tel Aviv, London, Moscow, Paris, and USUN.

[2] A memorandum of conversation of this meeting is printed in *Foreign Relations, 1969–1976*, volume XII, Soviet Union, January 1969–October 1970, Document 184.

[3] The Soviet Union introduced its most recent formulations at the Four-Power meeting on June 24. Dobrynin first introduced the text of these formulations in confidence at a June 2 meeting with Rogers and Sisco; see Document 120.

QTE Undoubtedly, the success of Ambassador Jarring's activities requires that both sides unequivocally declare their readiness to implement the above mentioned Resolution of the Security Council in all its parts. The Soviet side hopes that the American side is being guided by the same motivations. The Governments of the UAR and Jordan have repeatedly stated and are confirming now that they are ready to implement the Resolution in all its parts. Therefore it is necessary that Israel should also clearly state her readiness to implement this Resolution. Otherwise the sides would find themselves in an unequal position: one of them does recognize the November Resolution of the Security Council and expresses its readiness to implement it while the other side ignores it.

QTE At the same time in the interests of success of Jarring's mission it is important that he should have a definite enough understanding as to the basis upon which contacts should take place between the sides in search of ways to implement the Resolution of the Security Council. For the success of Jarring's mission first of all a direction is required on the main questions of settlement—the withdrawal by Israel from the Arab territories occupied during the conflict of 1967, including the question of secure and recognized boundaries along the lines which existed prior to the conflict in June 1967, and the simultaneous establishment of a just and stable peace in the Middle East. The U.S. Government, on its part, has also repeatedly emphasized the utmost importance of the above-mentioned questions. Both of these questions are organically connected with each other and should be considered jointly. Appropriate proposals to this effect have been put forward by the Soviet Government in the course of Soviet-American exchange of opinion on June 2 and also at the four-sided consultations in New York. The American side has not given so far its reply to the above mentioned proposals—neither in the course of bilateral exchange of opinion nor at the four-sided consultations. Yet these proposals are in complete conformity with the Security Council Resolution and the Soviet Government is expecting a reply from the U.S. Government.

QTE Parallel to the resumption of activities by Jarring and the initiation through him of contacts between the parties the four-sided consultations in New York should be made more active to work out agreed guidelines for Jarring. The Soviet Government on its part will be doing its best to facilitate it. END QTE.

2. After reading above QTE Oral Statement UNQTE Dobrynin made following additional points:

A. USSR statement has been made in expectation US will make necessary efforts towards achieving a just political settlement of Middle East problem and will exert its influence upon Israel.

B. Soviets have taken into consideration US clarifications that with Jarring's activities resumed, US–USSR bilateral consultations on Middle East will continue and US will show active and constructive approach both in Four and Two Power talks.

2 [sic]. After thanking Dobrynin, Secretary recalled one of important considerations in our proposal regarding ceasefire was that each side would commit itself not to improve its military position. Secretary said we assume that a military standstill as part of the ceasefire is also acceptable to the Soviet Union. Dobrynin responded affirmatively adding QTE Yes, of course UNQTE; it was his understanding that Foreign Minister Riad's statement to the Secretary covered this point.

3. Secretary asked whether Soviet side saw any objections to releasing Arab response to our initiative.[4] Dobrynin replied it was his understanding that UAR did not intend to publicize its response; in any event, he suggested this matter be raised with the Egyptians. Secretary said it would be helpful from our standpoint to make public simple UAR acceptance of our proposal. He understood Dobrynin's remarks to mean that publicizing response would be acceptable to the USSR if this matter could be worked out with the UAR. Dobrynin said that he did not anticipate any objections from the Soviet side. Secretary added that US would do its part in support of Jarring to bring about a settlement, and he indicated our willingness to continue Two and Four Power talks. Secretary said that he viewed Soviets response as indication USSR was interested in a peaceful settlement; such a settlement would be in mutual US–USSR interest and in interest of world community.

4. Dobrynin stressed USSR has no objections whatsoever to having Jarring resume his mission in few days. He wanted to be sure that US understood that comment in Oral Statement referring to absence of US reply to Soviet June 2nd proposals was not meant to be a Soviet precondition for resumption of Jarring's Mission. Dobrynin asked whether US Government had had any reply from Israel; Secretary indicated we would inform Dobrynin as soon as we could regarding this question.

Rogers

---

[4] See footnote 4, Document 136. Jordan accepted in a letter to Rogers on July 26, which was transmitted in telegram 3533 from Amman, July 26. (National Archives, Nixon Presidential Materials, NSC Files, Box 1155, Saunders Files, Middle East Negotiations Files, U.S. Peace Initiative For the Middle East Vol. I)

138. Telegram From the Department of State to Certain Diplomatic Posts[1]

Washington, July 24, 1970, 2336Z.

119651. Over the next 48 hours, our principal effort will be directed toward securing Israeli acceptance of US peace proposal. On the assumption that we can get all of the parties, we have been doing some tentative planning as to how we would proceed in getting Jarring into play. Following are some thoughts which we wish USUN to explore with Bunche confidentially in first instance. Other posts may wish comment.

1. While Jarring is acceptable to both sides, we are concerned that he has up to now failed to exercise any real initiative. If he does not grasp nettle and apply maximum imagination in getting parties together and keeping dialogue rolling, progress that we may have made could be irrevocably lost. Therefore, wish you to explore with Bunche desirability of getting Jarring to take on intermediate level assistant who can help him in negotiations, who would be imaginative in developing proposals, and who would establish kind of relationship with Jarring that would nudge him along at key points. In reviewing some possibilities, we believe best man would be Mr. Ilkka Pastinen, Finnish Deputy Representative. Finns prepared to make him available and he definitely our preference. Other possibilities are: Robert Furlonger, former Minister of Australian Embassy in Washington, now assigned Canberra, Geoffrey Murray, Canada, Thorsten Orn (Sweden), Michael Cork (Australia), Jonkeer Von Ufford (Netherlands). In discussing this matter with Bunche it is important that he understand we not be faced with fait accompli with naming of an individual by SYG who in long run would prove to be unhelpful in situation.

2. In this connection, Gromyko statement to Beam just reported signals possible fundamental difficulty.[2] If Soviets have in mind that Four Powers must meet and first develop detailed guidelines before restarting Jarring, then this is a condition which likely to delay start of any talks between parties for indefinite period. You should make clear

---

[1] Source: National Archives, Nixon Presidential Materials, NSC Files, Box 1155, Saunders Files, Middle East Negotiations Files, U.S. Peace Initiative For the Middle East Vol. I. Secret; Priority; Nodis. Drafted by Sisco, cleared in IO, and approved by Sisco. Sent to USUN, London, Paris, Cairo, Amman, Beirut, Nicosia, Stockholm, Moscow, Jidda, and Tel Aviv. A note at the end of the telegram indicates it was also sent to the White House.

[2] An informal Embassy translation of the statement is printed in *Foreign Relations, 1969–1976*, volume XII, Soviet Union, January 1969–October 1970, Document 187.

to Bunche, and we intend to make clear to Gromyko, that procedure we have in mind, and we made this very clear to Dobrynin here in our previous discussions, is for Jarring to start process promptly upon receipt US proposal. For our part, we will insist that Jarring process not await further refinement of mandate by Four; talks should get started on basis US proposal. Two and Four Power meetings could be pursued simultaneously with Jarring talks. If any difficulties arise with respect to prompt transmission of US proposal (without any changes in text), we would be prepared to transmit this to SYG on our own since it is an American proposal which presumably all of the parties would have accepted.

3. There is a slight technical problem on which your views are requested. Proposal is put in the form of a Jarring report to SYG. Given SYG's sensitivities, we are willing for it to be transmitted in any way he deems appropriate. Important thing is that SYG then would put out Jarring report reflecting acceptance of parties. Hope that UN would not get itself involved, as it has in the past, with long independent checking with parties. For this reason, we are suggesting to Egyptians that they make available informally and promptly appropriate documents confirming their acceptance of US proposal, to SYG.

4. Would hope also that any such SYG announcement would indicate that parties had been invited to send representatives to meet with Jarring promptly at agreed site. We understand that SYG and Jarring have had in mind New York or Nicosia. We believe it would be desirable for SYG to begin process now of checking what would be an acceptable site for parties. On the whole, we would prefer Nicosia as conducive to a more businesslike atmosphere and closer to area and more convenient for representatives. We believe SYG and Jarring should urge that three governments send their Foreign Ministers rather than to start talks at lower levels. Assuming Israeli acceptance, we in turn intend to encourage Israelis to designate Foreign Minister Eban.

5. Simultaneously with political talks on a settlement which Jarring would be conducting with the parties, we envisage that SYG would ask UNTSO Chief of Staff to establish contact with appropriate military liaison officials in the area to work out details of limited ceasefire, including military standstill. Originally our proposal provided for a July 1 beginning on the ceasefire. Because of time needed to develop Moscow-Cairo response, this date obviously out of the question. Believe objective should be early August for beginning of fully agreed limited ceasefire, including military standstill. We will wish to brief Thant and Jarring fully on the details of standstill as we have communicated them to parties in the area and the other major powers. You will wish to note in this connection that Dobrynin July 23 informed Secre-

tary of acceptance of concept of standstill as part of limited ceasefire; Bergus believes that UAR has also accepted.[3]

6. In short, what we have in mind are simultaneous talks on the political side between parties under Jarring and on the military side with the Chief of Staff directly involved with technical, military liaison representatives. Reason why we believe tandem operation of this kind ought to be conducted is that if any wrinkle should develop regarding ceasefire, political talks under Jarring's auspices would be put in train. We wish to avoid a situation where all of details of the ceasefire have to be buttoned down before the parties get involved in a dialogue on the elements of a settlement; establishment of a ceasefire and standstill should not be condition precedent to starting political talks.

7. Believe you should suggest to Bunche that Jarring ought to be alerted as to the desirability of an early trip to New York to be fully briefed.[4]

8. Above are all tentative, since we will be guided by views of parties.

9. Fuller cable being sent on our further ideas.[5]

Rogers

---

[3] See Document 137 and footnote 4, Document 136.

[4] Buffum met with Bunche on July 27 for a "hair-down session" at which they discussed the future resumption of the Jarring Mission. Buffum expressed concern that "Jarring seems so worried about maintaining good relations with both sides that he may be reluctant to show necessary forcefulness in moving negotiating process ahead." Bunche agreed with "this analysis of Jarring's character" and explained that he had already spoken to U Thant, "warning him" that if Jarring "[did] not succeed in this round, entire problem will be dropped in SYG's lap and instead of Jarring's becoming expendable SYG will become expendable." (Telegram 1560 from USUN, July 27; National Archives, Nixon Presidential Materials, NSC Files, Box 1155, Saunders Files, Middle East Negotiations Files, U.S. Peace Initiative For the Middle East Vol. I)

[5] Not found.

139. Telegram From the Department of State to All Diplomatic Posts[1]

Washington, July 29, 1970, 1720Z.

121639. Subject: US Initiative on Middle East.

1. Following is for posts' information and guidance in confidential discussions at Ambassador's discretion with host governments.

2. We have now received positive replies to our initiative from UAR and Jordan.[2] We expect Israeli reply shortly[3] and are strongly urging that it be equally positive.

3. We do not underestimate difficulties that lie ahead. Neither side has given any indication of real movement from substantive positions long adhered to. Achievement of workable ceasefire poses highly complicated problems. Radical Arab and fedayeen opposition to ceasefire and resumption talks rapidly crystallizing. Military conflict unabated. These imposing obstacles, however, should not obscure fundamental fact that principal parties to dispute may now apparently be ready to give diplomacy a chance and are not making prior acceptance of their positions on terms and nature of settlement a precondition for beginning negotiating process under Jarring.

4. If positive Israeli reply forthcoming we envisage following steps: we will present our proposal formally in Four-Power meeting[4] for quick transmittal by Four to SYG and Ambassador Jarring. (When we refer to US proposal we are referring to text of proposed Jarring to SYG report contained in Secretary's letter to UAR FonMin Riad carried in Wireless File MEF 59, July 22).[5] We believe our formula as accepted by parties after careful deliberation should not rpt not be subject to amendment on its way to Jarring. Our objective is to see parties en-

---

[1] Source: National Archives, Nixon Presidential Materials, NSC Files, Box 1155, Saunders Files, Middle East Negotiations Files, June Initiative Vol. II, July 24–August 8, 1970. Secret; Limdis. Drafted by Stephanie C. Perry (NEA/PRO) and approved by Thomas D. Boyatt (NEA).

[2] See footnote 4, Document 136 and footnote 4, Document 137.

[3] See Document 140.

[4] See footnote 1, Document 145.

[5] The letter to Riad containing the U.S. proposal (see Document 129), dated June 19, was made available to the press by the Department of State on July 22 and is printed in the Department of State *Bulletin*, August 10, 1970, pp. 178–179. The proposed report from Jarring to the UN Secretary-General is in telegram 127711 to Tel Aviv, August 7. (National Archives, RG 59, Central Files 1970–73, POL 27–14 ARAB–ISR) In the end, Secretary-General Thant sent a note on August 7 to the Security Council stating that he and Jarring believed there was a reasonable basis to reactivate the Jarring Mission and that Jarring had invited the parties to meet in New York on August 25. See *Yearbook of the United Nations, 1970*, pp 253–254. See also Document 133.

gaged in negotiating process under Jarring as soon as possible, according to procedures and at time and place he recommends, so that positive momentum so lately acquired will not be lost. At same time as Jarring getting negotiation process started, we would hope steps could be taken simultaneously to arrange between parties details and modalities of ceasefire and standstill on new military installations. We do not believe completion of arrangements for a ceasefire and standstill in combat zones should be a condition precedent for starting political talks. Keys to achievement and maintenance of ceasefire are adherence to principle of military standstill and readiness to accept effective, equitable verification procedures.

5. Once negotiating process started, US intends continue play active role directly with parties, and in Two-Power and Four-Power forums, providing counsel and cooperating in efforts help Jarring Mission succeed.

6. Alternative to success of current diplomatic steps is further deterioration of military situation in area. Given Soviet operational involvement in UAR and our own determination to prevent shift in area military balance, this could have gravest implications not only for interests of states and peoples directly involved but wider repercussions as well. It is therefore incumbent on world community to lend support to current peace efforts, which will require both sides to relax their maximum positions as negotiations proceed if those efforts are to succeed. While we have provided initial momentum, we see this as effort requiring widest possible support and cooperation to which we will continue to contribute our part.

Rogers

140. Telegram From the Department of State to the Embassy in Israel[1]

Washington, August 4, 1970, 2009Z.

125220. Subject: Israel Reply to US Peace Proposal.

1. Amb Rabin, accompanied by Minister Argov and First Secy Ben Aharon delivered GOI's reply to US peace proposal to Asst Secy Sisco August 4. (Text in Para 4 below.)

2. Sisco perused it quickly. Rabin commented that USG now had got GOI to use word QUOTE withdrawal UNQUOTE. Rabin explained his understanding that shortly would follow letters from FonMin Eban to the Secretary and from PM Meir to President.[2] Sisco noted that this means to USG Israel's acceptance. We have informed UN of Israel's acceptance and Yost is in touch with Tekoah about informing Jarring of GOI detailed reply. Rabin did not react one way or another to this latter observation.

3. Sisco said next steps relating to principal elements of ceasefire/standstill are being worked on, and hopefully will be drafted today. Before discussing our proposals with UAR and Soviets, we want to check them with GOI; we shall be sending them to Amb Barbour. We have in mind suggesting ceasefire take effect Friday, August 7. Rabin offered personal opinion Aug 7 was too early, in light unresolved questions re supervision and verification.

4. Text detailed reply addressed Secretary Rogers follows:

---

[1] Source: National Archives, Nixon Presidential Materials, NSC Files, Box 1155, Saunders Files, Middle East Negotiations Files, U.S. Peace Initiative For the Middle East Vol. II. Secret; Priority; Nodis. Drafted on August 4 by Lissfelt (NEA/IAI); cleared by Atherton, Stackhouse (NEA/IAI), and Eliot; and approved by Sisco. Repeated Priority to Amman, Beirut, Cairo, Jidda, London, Moscow, USUN, and Paris.

[2] Meir's letter to Nixon has not been found. Eban wrote to Rogers on August 19 with "a more detailed summary of our positions on some of the questions mentioned in our August 4 communication." Eban stated that Israel accepted UN Security Council Resolution 242 and would cooperate with the Jarring Mission so long as "the Four-Power Group should not seek to prejudice the conduct of the mission by submitting their own views on the matters at issue between the parties." Regarding future boundaries, Eban wrote that "Israeli forces will not be moved from any of these cease-fire lines, until a binding, contractual reciprocal peace agreement which we believe satisfactory to us has been achieved." Finally, addressing refugees, Eban stated that Israel "would make a contribution in appropriate form, but refused to acknowledge "a prior right of choice inherent in Arabs outside of Israel to enter Israel. Our position is that the principle of sovereign equality of States gives Israel the right and duty to determine its contribution to this international and regional problem as a voluntary sovereign act, taking full account of its security and national character." (Israel State Archives, Ministry of Foreign Affairs, 6854/8)

BEGIN TEXT

4 August 1970

Dear Mr. Secretary:

I have the honour to inform you that my Government's position on the latest United States peace initiative is as follows:

Having considered President Nixon's message of 24 July 1970, basing itself on its contents and in strict adherence to its policy principles and authoritative statements, the Government of Israel has decided to reply affirmatively to the latest United States peace initiative, and to inform the United States that it may convey to Ambassador Jarring that:

1) Israel is prepared in due time to designate a representative to discussions to be held under Ambassador Jarring's auspices with the UAR (Jordan), according to such procedure and at such places and times as he may recommend, taking into account each side's attitude as to method of procedure and previous experience of discussions between the parties.

2) Israel's position in favor of a cease-fire on a basis of reciprocity on all fronts, including the Egyptian front, in accordance with the Security Council's cease-fire resolution, remains unchanged. On the basis of clarifications given by the United States Government, Israel is prepared to reply affirmatively to the United States proposal for a cease fire (for at least three months) on the Egyptian front.

3) The discussions under Ambassador Jarring's auspices shall be held within the framework of the Security Council Resolution (242) on the basis of the expression of readiness by the parties to carry out the Security Council Resolution (242) in all its parts, in order to achieve an agreed and binding contractual peace agreement between the parties which will ensure:

a) Termination by Egypt (Jordan) and Israel of all claims or states of belligerency and respect and acknowledgment of the sovereignty, territorial integrity and political independence of each other and their right to live in peace within secure and recognized boundaries free from threats or acts of force, each of the parties will be responsible within its territory for the prevention of all hostile acts by regular military forces or para-military forces, including irregular forces, against the armed forces or against civilians living in the territory of the other party.

b) Withdrawal of Israeli armed forces from territories occupied in the 1967 conflict to secure, recognized and agreed boundaries to be determined in the peace agreements.

4) Israel will participate in these discussions without any prior conditions. Israel will not claim the prior acceptance by the other party

of her positions, as Israel does not accept in advance the positions of the other parties as communicated publicly or otherwise. Each party will be free to present its proposals on the matters under discussion.

Please accept the assurances of my highest consideration.

Sincerely yours,

Y. Rabin, Lt. Gen. (Res.)

Ambassador END TEXT

Rogers

141. Transcript of a Telephone Conversation Between the President's Assistant for National Security Affairs (Kissinger) and the Assistant Secretary of State for Near Eastern and South Asian Affairs (Sisco)[1]

Washington, August 5, 1970, 3:40 p.m.

S: I am trying to get the cease-fire proposal into effect, but it's very complicated Henry.

K: I can imagine.

S: I just did a cable which I am going to take to the Secretary. It is a definitive proposal for a cease-fire standstill.[2] We want to put it to the Israelis first. But I am recommending to the Secretary that it be cleared with you. I would be much more comfortable if it goes through you first.

K: Isn't it a policy matter? So it has to be cleared with me?

S: Well I think it is. Secondly, I wanted to report to you where we stand on the question of military assistance which Israel has requested. They want as a matter of priority four things: 1) Helicopter standoff equipment to help jam SAM electrical equipment, 2) Shrikes, 3) CBUs (to attack SAM sites), 4) Pods—electrical equipment. I have had two good talks with Packard. He will, by tomorrow morning, see what is possible to present to the Israelis. But there needs to be a discussion with our Secretary of State and I think this is a matter of interest to the White House as well. The Secretary believes that the over-riding objec-

---

[1] Source: National Archives, Nixon Presidential Materials, NSC Files, Henry Kissinger Telephone Conversation Transcripts, Box 6, Chronological File. No classification marking. All brackets are in the original except "[submit]", added for clarity.

[2] See footnote 7, Document 142.

tive should be to get the cease-fire working immediately. If there is any further delay there may be incidents and also a loss of momentum. When the package is gotten together the Secretary wants to know whether and how we should tell the Israelis. Let me give you the Secretary's thinking on this: If the Israelis are the cause of any delay in the establishment of a cease-fire, we shouldn't provide the equipment. If, however, the Egyptians cause a delay and in a manner which would improve their situation, then we should study the whole thing further. In other words, the Secretary wants to look at the existing situation before we go ahead. Rabin has informed the Pentagon (either on a tactical basis or under instructions, I don't know) that unless they get the four items and get the opportunity to hit the SAM sites, there may be a delay on the cease-fire. This is a form of pressure that didn't go well with the Secretary. We took the view that the compelling need is to get on with the cease-fire and that it is just as much in the interest of the Israelis to do so as the others involved, if not more so. But the problem is that if you have a cease-fire and then the Israelis make a dramatic attack, the other side will feel the need to restore the balance and then you might as well not have a cease-fire.

K: If there is a cease-fire will they get the equipment?

S: Yes, the Secretary feels that we should give them the equipment and Dave Packard agrees, if there is a cease-fire.

K: So we can tell them that if there is a cease-fire they will get the equipment?

S: Yes.

K: Do you agree with this?

S: Yes, generally. The Secretary and I agree that the overriding consideration is to get the cease-fire as quickly as possible.

K: When these things are discussed where is Saunders? Do I have a man in there?

S: No the reason is that these discussions go on in the Pentagon. The only discussion we've had with Packard are two brief telephone conversations. On this organizational thing, I'll be taking care of that once we get over the hump on the cease-fire; it's tough Henry.

K: How does the cease-fire look to you?

S: There's a real hope. My only worry is that the Israelis will be insistent about getting the equipment and hitting the SAM sites before it. One other thing Rabin said to me and you may hear it from him ...

K: He's coming over this afternoon.[3]

---

[3] See Document 142.

S: I didn't know that, but you should know one other thing he said was—last night he said to me that his government would in the cease-fire and standstill [submit] a political proposal for a rollback. I said that would be knocked out by the other side and that it changes our proposal. Then he said well at least give us the means immediately. I told him it is being looked at and that within 48 hours there will be some kind of judgment. But I would leave that very neutral; we'll have to weigh these considerations. Their argument is "Never mind a perfect package: if you think we are wrong let us have the chance to prove it—just give us the wherewithal." But the problem is if this were to go it would take days and we want the cease-fire in three or four days. I said there's no way which, by a major attack, you can get this balance when they've got mobile SAMs; so the best thing for you to do is to get a cease-fire right away.

K: Good, that's the line I will take. You have been very helpful.

S: It's been very difficult—but who thought it was going to be easy?

K: Without your eternal optimism we'd be dead.

S: We've got to pull this off for the President.

142. Memorandum of Conversation[1]

Washington, August 5, 1970, 5:30 p.m.

PARTICIPANTS

    Ambassador Rabin
    Minister Argov
    Mr. Kissinger
    General Haig

Ambassador Rabin opened the meeting by stating that he wished to summarize events that had occurred over the extended period since he had last talked to Dr. Kissinger. He stated that Israel had decided to accept the U.S. initiative in the terms by which they had responded for-

---

[1] Source: National Archives, Nixon Presidential Materials, NSC Files, Box 1157, Saunders Files, Middle East Negotiations Files, June Initiative (Memos Only), June 9–September 1, 1970. Top Secret; Sensitive. The meeting took place in the White House Map Room.

mally to the Department of State.[2] Israel had decided to respond positively, although with great skepticism and with the full realization that their positive response would incur very real political and even more serious military risks. Without President Nixon's letter to Prime Minister Golda Meir,[3] Israel's reply would most certainly have been negative. Israel's skepticism is justified since the major issues of difference between Israel and the Soviets and the Egyptians have still not been resolved by the U.S. initiative and there is no indication of a willingness to compromise, especially on the following issues:

1. Concerning the form of the talks on which Israel's position is well known, the U.S. has made no effort to ask for direct talks.

2. The Soviet/Egyptian and other Arab states' demands for total withdrawal are upheld under the U.S. plan.

3. A U.S. demand for the solution of the Palestinian refugee problem under the formula of free choice, without any other preconditions is called for.

On July 17, at the conclusion of Nasser's Moscow visit, the USSR/Egyptian communiqué, which was essentially negative on the major points at issue, was released.[4] Knowing this, the Israelis have great difficulty in seeing what can be achieved through the initiative just launched by the U.S. In essence, the USSR/Egyptian position has not changed. It is the same as it has been within the two- and four-power forum for an extended period. The other side has rejected even the U.S. position, not just the long established Israeli positions.

Israel believes the Soviets accepted the U.S. initiative because their creeping involvement in military operations brought a sharp U.S. reaction as manifested by the President's television interview.[5] The Soviets felt a crisis was developing and they decided to try the diplomatic route

---

[2] See Document 140.

[3] See Document 136.

[4] Nasser was in Moscow June 29 through July 17. The joint communiqué included this statement: "the two sides confirmed their desire go on expanding and strengthening the sincere cooperation between the United Arab Republic and the Soviet Union in the political, economic and defense fields in the interests of the peoples of both states." In the document, the UAR and the Soviet Union placed sole blame on Israel for the "continuing grave crisis situation," which they argued had resulted from the country's "aggression against the U.A.R. and other Arab states," and proclaimed that "Israel would not have been able to persist in this aggressive and expansionist policy were it not for the continuing support it receives from the imperialist circles and specifically the United States." The communiqué did not include a reply to the U.S. cease-fire proposal. (*Washington Post*, July 18, 1970, p. A1) In a memorandum to President Nixon, Kissinger noted that the communiqué gave "almost no hint of conclusions reached and the U.S. initiative is not even mentioned." (*Foreign Relations*, 1969–1976, volume XII, Soviet Union, January 1969–October 1970, Document 182)

[5] See footnote 3, Document 134.

in order to reduce tensions and to project a better international image for the Soviet Union.

From the Israeli perspective, once the talks start, both sides will present their positions to Jarring who will go from place to place without there being direct contact between the parties concerned. He will learn that there is no give and will then make a report to the Secretary General of the United Nations. The situation will be the same as during the last round of peace efforts.

Dr. Kissinger pointed out that this time at least the world press was conveying that a new atmosphere had developed.

Ambassador Rabin stated neither of the parties most directly concerned will gain by the new round of negotiations but only the Soviets. The most serious consequence that has resulted from the U.S. initiative is that the Soviets have been able, under the cover of the U.S. initiative, to take two fundamental military steps:

1. On the night of June 29–30, they moved a system of ground-to-air missiles to a line 40 to 60 kilometers from the Canal. Israel was compelled to attack these sites, destroying between eight and ten, with a loss of five airplanes. The Soviets then gave a positive response to the U.S. initiative and at the same time realized that the Israelis were still operating as far as 15 kilometers east of the Canal since the SA–2 missiles were at the limit of their range in this defense configuration and thus, Israel could still silence some of the Egyptian artillery along the Canal.

2. On July 26 Soviet piloted MIG–21s attempted to intercept Israeli aircraft, firing some seven air-to-air missiles.

On the 27th, they gave air-to-air cover to Egyptian strike aircraft hitting Israeli emplacements on the East side of the Canal. In this effort, Egyptian pilots operated east of the Canal, while Soviet cover aircraft remained west of the Canal. In this action, the Israelis pursued the Egyptian piloted MIGs some 80 kilometers west of the Canal. The Soviet piloted MIGs could not intercept because of the low altitude at which the Israeli fighters were operating. However, on the 30th of July, Soviet piloted MIG aircraft did intercept Israeli fighters along the Egyptian bank of the Gulf of Suez. During this engagement, the Israelis shot down four Soviet piloted MIGs. It is Israel's view that the Commander of the Soviet Air Force traveled to the UAR, as a result of these losses, to make an on-site decision as to what steps would be taken next. It is Rabin's personal view that the Soviets have decided to avoid air-to-air combat with Israel for the time being.

Dr. Kissinger asked for the Israeli appraisal of the Soviet pilots' capability. Ambassador Rabin replied that while they were reported by Israeli pilots to be more aggressive than the Egyptians, their skills were considered limited. The kills were accomplished by U.S. air-to-air missiles (Sparrows and Sidewinders). Subsequent to this action, on August 3, the Soviets moved a missile ambush to within 15–20 kilometers of the Canal. Israel estimates four sites were established—three SA–2s and one SA–3. These sites provide the Soviets the ability to engage Israeli aircraft some 15 to 20 kilometers east of the Canal. The next day this ambush cost Israel one Phantom shot down and one damaged. As a result of the second series of escalatory steps, Israel now faces a new and more serious problem along the Canal.

With respect to the U.S. ceasefire proposal, it is the Israeli position that it is unacceptable if the USSR is allowed to put in place SA–2s and SA–3s closer than the 40–60 kilometer limit that existed prior to the Israeli acceptance of the U.S. position last Friday, July 31. If the missiles remain at their new locations, Israel will retaliate: (1) by striking them as soon as possible or (2) by hitting Egypt in areas where they are less immune to attacks.

Ambassador Rabin reported that he had talked to Pentagon officials (Deputy Secretary of Defense Packard and Mr. Pranger) and Assistant Secretary Sisco at State about the urgent need for additional military equipment.

Dr. Kissinger stated that he understood that Israel could not use the Shrike missiles that they had asked for earlier. Ambassador Rabin replied that if the U.S. will provide the missiles we will all find out what their utility is. Ambassador Rabin stated that since his negotiations on additional military equipment had begun, very little beyond electronic equipment had been provided. Israel had recently received approval for additional Phantom reconnaissance and fighter/bomber aircraft[6] but had received no answer to their request for drones and Shrike missiles and have been told instead that the U.S. had not completed its studies. Ambassador Rabin emphasized that it is essential that Israel have the necessary equipment needed to cope with the new threat. For this reason, they have need of four specific items:

1. Standoff electronic jamming equipment for E and C band radars.
2. C band radar canisters in pods.
3. CBU bomblets, which Israel guarantees will not be used against civilian targets.
4. Shrike missiles.

Dr. Kissinger then asked if we were to deliver this equipment, would the Israelis use it against the forward SAM sites before agreeing

---

[6] In a July 29 memorandum from Nutter to Laird, the Secretary approved Israel's purchase and the immediate delivery of two RF–4C aircraft, also known as the Phantom II, on July 30. (Washington National Records Center, OSD Files: FRC 330–76–0076, Box 74, Israel) In an August 1 memorandum from Nutter to Laird, Laird approved the sale of one EC–97G ELINT reconnaissance aircraft on August 3. (Ibid.)

to the implementation of the ceasefire. Ambassador Rabin replied that Israel will not implement the ceasefire until they remove the forward sites or the United States is able to bring the Soviets to redeploy these sites to the 40 to 60 kilometers area. Ambassador Rabin added that Israel has not made public the Soviet escalation or the fact that they had successfully shot down Soviet piloted MIG–21s, at the request of the United States and in order not to engage the Soviets' prestige. He continued that Israel now needs the four items just mentioned or they will be required to take action without this equipment. Ambassador Rabin reported that he had spoken to the Prime Minister and was informed that Israel would hit the Egyptians in various forms and at various places in a manner convenient to Israel.

Dr. Kissinger stated that he would pass this information on to the President. Ambassador Rabin reiterated that Israel would move with or without U.S. help, emphasizing that the new sites closer to the Canal could be destroyed with less losses if the United States would provide the equipment requested. Dr. Kissinger asked if Israel would agree to accept the ceasefire if we made a commitment to provide the equipment but with delivery still pending. Ambassador Rabin responded that this would serve no useful purpose and that what was needed was to prevent a Soviet fait accompli in the form of an air defense capability at the Canal itself and even beyond. Ambassador Rabin stated that Israel has seven divisions, 700 tanks and 1,000 guns just 50 kilometers from the Canal and that the implications of this new Soviet-Egyptian aerial capability were unacceptable.

Dr. Kissinger stated the U.S. Government is most concerned that a ceasefire be obtained as soon as possible[7] and asked whether Rabin had informed the Department of State that a ceasefire is unacceptable in the light of new conditions. Ambassador Rabin stated that he had informed Assistant Secretary Sisco of this fact yesterday, August 4. At the same time, Ambassador Rabin said he wished to insure that the President and Dr. Kissinger had the Israeli position first hand, which is that Israel will not accept a ceasefire until they have attacked the new forward air defense system. Ambassador Rabin emphasized that Israel needed the four equipment items to assist in this operation.

Dr. Kissinger asked Ambassador Rabin to reiterate in detail to General Haig the specifics of the various escalatory Soviet moves after the U.S. launched its peace initiative. He added that he considers this a

---

[7] On the morning of August 6, Rogers sent a telegram to the Embassy in Tel Aviv instructing the Ambassador to seek immediately Israeli views on the precise terms of the cease-fire, which were included in the telegram, so that the Department could discuss them with the Soviet Union and the United Arab Republic. (Telegram 126601 to Tel Aviv, August 6; National Archives, Nixon Presidential Materials, NSC Files, Box 655, Country Files, Middle East, Ceasefire Mideast Vol. I)

personal communication from the Prime Minister to the President and informed Ambassador Rabin that he would send copies of the memcon of this discussion to the Departments of State and Defense.

Ambassador Rabin then stated that Israel had other problems which they hoped the United States would express its view on. These include a response to Israel's request for additional credits and the means of getting the latest model A–4D aircraft since Defense had not been responsive to his request in this regard.

Dr. Kissinger then reiterated that he would provide all concerned copies of the memcon of this conversation. Ambassador Rabin stated that the Department of State was aware of the content of this conversation with the exception of the message that he had just gotten from the Prime Minister with respect to Israeli attacks against Egypt which would be conducted at a time and place of their own choosing.

Dr. Kissinger stated that while he could not speak formally he was certain such a step at this time would be considered contrary to the spirit of the U.S. peace initiative.[8]

Attached is a summary[9] of the Soviet escalatory steps provided by Ambassador Rabin to General Haig following his meeting with Dr. Kissinger.[10]

---

[8] Later that evening, Rabin repeated to Sisco the gist of the message that he had delivered to Kissinger, as reported in telegram 126614 to Tel Aviv, August 6. (Ibid.)

[9] Attached but not printed.

[10] At 10:18 p.m. on August 5, Kissinger telephoned the President to report that Rabin had called him three hours after their meeting to withdraw Israel's conditions for accepting a cease-fire agreement, while still reserving Israel's right to "take out" the Soviet SAM sites in the United Arab Republic "by direct or indirect means" before signing such an agreement. Kissinger said that he believed that Israeli officials were "approaching again a state of extreme agitation" and added: "I would guess that the Israelis, if they don't hit tonight, will strike within the next 48 hours. Rabin does not talk idly. I think they have decided to move." Nixon replied: "I would do that." (National Archives, Nixon Presidential Materials, NSC Files, Henry Kissinger Telephone Conversation Transcripts, Box 6, Chronological File) Kissinger then telephoned Rabin at 11:10 and said: "May I make a suggestion? If you are planning to do something I think it would be in everyone's interests if the President did not read about it in the newspapers first. If you could give us a few hours warning." Rabin responded: "I would like to make it clear. I don't know any specifics." (Ibid.)

---

143. Editorial Note

Late on August 5, 1970, strong disagreement emerged between the United States and Israel over the operating text of the cease-fire agreement. The Israelis took exception to the fact that Gunnar Jarring, in his letter to UN Secretary General U Thant announcing the acceptance by the parties of the U.S. initiative, adhered strictly to the original text Secretary of State William Rogers proposed on June 19 (see Document 129), ignoring Israel's own letter of acceptance provided by Israeli Ambassador Yitzhak Rabin to Rogers on August 4 (see Document 140) and announced by Prime Minister Golda Meir to the Israeli Knesset the same day. Although the differences were minor, Rabin's letter contained statements not included in the original text, including the need for discussions to take place "in order to achieve an agreed and binding contractual peace agreement between the parties," as well as Israel's "right to live in peace within secure and recognized boundaries free from threats or acts of force." Meir asked for a private meeting with Ambassador to Israel Walworth Barbour on the evening of August 5 to discuss the discrepancies. Following the meeting Barbour sent a report of his conversation with the Prime Minister to the Department of State:

"She noted that language of Israeli reply as presented in Rabin's letter to Secretary and repeated in her speech to Knesset had been negotiated with her Cabinet colleagues with extreme difficulty and that the wording contained therein which constituted additions to the text of the original US proposal was extremely important to one or more of the remaining colleagues in her government. She said categorically that Israeli endorsement of the original three paragraphs in US statement would result in further departures from the government, including perhaps that of herself and that for that reason US statement as such not acceptable. She had no difficulty with the first paragaph nor the language on the ceasefire but the additions to the second paragaph describing the purposes of the contemplated discussions were absolutely essential . . . My strenuous and I hope forceful argument that this language is all included in the US initiative 'in accordance with Resolution 242' fell on deaf ears." (Telegram 4175 from Tel Aviv, August 5; National Archives, Nixon Presidential Materials, NSC Files, Box 1155, Saunders Files, Middle East Negotiations Files, U.S. Peace Initiative For the Middle East Vol. II)

The following day, August 6, when the text of the agreement still had not been changed to meet Israeli requests, Meir instructed Rabin to deliver the following statement to Assistant Secretary of State for Near Eastern and South Asian Affairs Joseph Sisco:

"I have just spoken to the Prime Minister. She has instructed me to say that she is dismayed over the latest development. She is shocked at the behaviour of the United States placing before Israel a fait accompli. The issue of the initiative has been completely overshadowed by the manner you have acted. The Prime Minister has told me to tell you that the conduct of the US Government is an insult to Israel—its Government and people. You have taken upon yourselves to place words in the mouth of the Government of Israel which we have never agreed to say. This attitude bears the mark of dictation—not consultation. Your whole approach has the gravest implications as to the relations between our two governments. Your conduct seriously questions how we can embark on the process of negotiation. My government will be meeting either tomorrow evening or Sunday and I have been called to Jerusalem for urgent consultations. End Statement." (Israel State Archive, Ministry of Foreign Affairs, 6854/8)

Sisco replied that he would report the message to his superiors immediately, but felt that Meir's characterization of the actions, intent, and motivations of the U.S. Government was "unjustified." He hoped that after the passage of some time "a more considered and a more balanced judgement in terms of what our actions have been over the weeks will be reached." (Ibid.) Still, Meir remained upset over the text of the cease-fire agreement and telephoned Sisco at the State Department on the evening of August 6 to discuss the matter. No record of the conversation has been found. But Rabin, who listened in on the telephone call in Sisco's office, recounted the conversation in his memoirs:

"Golda said that the United States had practically forged Israel's signature. No more and no less. Sisco was astounded: 'What do you mean "forged"?

"'You notified Jarring that we had accepted the initiative before we accepted it!' the prime minister barked. 'That's what I mean by "forged." I reached an agreement with Barbour, and the United States now denies that agreement. You can't formulate answers on our behalf. We have our reservations about the text of Jarring's letter . . .'

"Sisco was astonished by Golda's complaint: 'You received the text of our initiative weeks ago. One page, one paper—that's the whole initiative. Did you accept it or didn't you?'

"Golda could not understand his exasperation. 'What do you mean did we accept the initiative? Do we have to accept your formulation? We have a formulation of our own!'" (Rabin, *The Rabin Memoirs*, pages 180–181)

Rabin described the "tragic" telephone conversation between Meir and Sisco as "a dialogue of the deaf." Sisco, he wrote, "did not understand what the Israeli formulation was. Golda did not understand why Sisco was getting tough." Rabin telephoned Meir afer the "abortive conversation," at which time she instructed him to seek an immediate meeting with Henry Kissinger to discuss redrafting the text of the cease-fire agreement. "I can't go back to the cabinet with a formulation unlike the one it adopted," she told Rabin. (Ibid.)

Acting on his instructions, Rabin and Minister Shlomo Argov met with Kissinger at the White House at 10 p.m. on August 6. According to a memorandum of conversation, Rabin opened by saying that Prime Minister Meir had personally asked him to come and see Kissinger and that she was concerned that "we were approaching one of the most critical moments in United States-Israeli relations as the result of some misunderstanding and that a serious problem existed." Meir believed that the Israeli response to the U.S. peace initiative was clear in regard to what was meant by its acceptance. Israel had accepted all of the basic principles set forth in the text of the report which Jarring was to deliver to the Secretary-General and provided Kissinger with the text that they wanted forwarded. Kissinger stated that while he had not been following all the details closely he was under the impression from the cables that "all was in order," and added that "it was hard to explain why they objected to the Jarring report when there was no substantive difference." Kissinger said that "he just did not understand the differences" and then asked Ambassador Rabin and Minister Argov to sit down with his secretary and dictate the "specific operational instances" in which the texts differed. (Memorandum of conversation, August 6; National Archives, Nixon Presidential Materials, NSC Files, Box 654, Country Files, Middle East, Middle East—Recent Actions Keep File Intact)

While Kissinger waited for the Israelis to compose their response, he placed a telephone call to Deputy Assistant Secretary of State for Near Eastern and South Asian Affairs Alfred L. Atherton. A portion of the transcript of their conversation follows:

"K: Do you know about this Israeli blow up? . . .

"A: It came to a head this afternoon. It came in a phone call from Israel this afternoon.

"K: I have them [Rabin and Argov] in a separate room. I have asked them to tell me the difference between the two versions. They claim that the Jarring message wasn't to be surfaced.

"A: That's not plausible. Their reply was understood in the same light as from Riad and the Jordanians.

"K: They said their government will disintegrate if they do.

"A: That's what Meir said.

"K: Do I get the President in?

"A: We are trying to get up some gimmicks which Jarring and U Thant can use . . .

"K: What happens now if the Egyptians accept tomorrow morning and the Isrealis don't? . . .

"A: If they get wind of the waffling it may blow up." (Transcript of a telephone conversation, August 6, 10:30 p.m.; ibid., Henry Kissinger Telephone Conversation Transcripts, Box 6, Chronological File)

Kissinger returned to his meeting with the Israelis, but after 15 minutes of consulting, Rabin and Argov informed Kissinger that they did not want to put the differences down on paper because it might in some way "bind them." Rabin stressed that the problem was with the Cabinet. "The Cabinet has assumed that since there was no reaction when their substitute text was submitted that it was accepted." Argov interjected that if the Jarring text were made public tomorrow the Prime Minster would have to stand up in the Knesset and reject it. "In essence," Argov said, "the Prime Minister wants to be safeguarded by her substitute statement." Kissinger replied that "the best Israel could achieve would be a statement of its interpretation, but the U.S. would not accept its interpretation." Kissinger ended the meeting by saying that "this seemed to be a lesser case than others they had made in the last couple of days and lived with." (Memorandum of conversation, August 6; ibid., Box 654, Country Files, Middle East, Middle East—Recent Actions Keep File Intact)

Following his meeting with the Israelis, Kissinger called Sisco to discuss the consequences of the disagreement with the Israelis:

"K: What's going to happen?

"S: I don't know. Give me a couple of hours. I will think of something or another formula. I want you, the Secy. and the President to know where we stand. I will try in the morning. But I will be here. Let's not give up. It's too close.

"K: What can I tell Rabin?

"S: I didn't want to talk to Golda. They put her on to calling me because they gave up with her and they thought I could convince her. They went out of this office with their tails between their legs.

"K: I told them—do you want me to talk to the President? They said yes. I said, I want to know, then, what's wrong with the statement except that you don't like it . . .

"S: If the President calls me tomorrow morning and asks me to explain the problem, I am not sure I can explain it easily. When two bright people like Joseph Sisco and Henry [Kissinger] cannot explain the problem, maybe there's no problem.

"K: We have to convince Golda Meir.

"S: I failed. " (Transcript of a telephone conversation, August 6, 11:30 p.m.; ibid., Henry Kissinger Telephone Conversation Transcripts, Box 6, Chronological File)

The next morning, Kissinger informed Nixon over the telephone of the previous day's events, explaining that while the Egyptians had accepted the cease-fire, the Israeli position had come "unstuck " again. He added: "It's some shell game between Rabin and Sisco with both trying to sneak texts past each other. It has to do with Jarring's presentation to the Secretary General. Israel feels that the text we gave Jarring constricts their negotiating position. Anyway, both sides were not making their differences explicit, hoping to sneak versions by each other. " (Transcript of a telephone conversation, August 7, 8:35 a.m.; ibid.)

144. Transcript of a Telephone Conversation Between Secretary of State Rogers and the President's Assistant for National Security Affairs (Kissinger)[1]

Washington, August 7, 1970, 12:30 p.m.

R: I have had McCloskey go in[2] and he won't refer to this.

K: We can't do anything about it now anyway. What the President wants is to give the announcement here and give the backgrounding to you.

R: What is the announcement? I understand "Godspeed" is in there.

K: We got the lines from you.

R: But if the thing falls through, which it might, and they had the statement from the President he'd have egg on his face. I am willing to take some risks, but I'm not sure the President should.

K: When should it be done?

R: Well, we said 12:00. It's now 12:30. But if you announce it you are going to get a million questions that can't be answered.[3]

K: The UAR hasn't agreed to it yet.

R: We were going to say that there are rules, but we're not releasing them now. We may now have ruined the thing.

---

[1] Source: National Archives, Nixon Presidential Materials, NSC Files, Henry Kissinger Telephone Conversation Transcripts, Box 6, Chronological File. No classification marking.

[2] Department of State Spokesman Robert J. McCloskey. Reference is to the Department of State noon press briefing.

[3] McCloskey made the announcement at 1:45 p.m. EST in the name of the Secretary of State: "We have just been informed by the Governments of the United Arab Republic and Israel of their acceptance of the United States proposal for a standstill ceasefire to come into effect at 2200 Greenwich Mean Time today, Friday, August 7. We welcome this statesmanlike action taken by the leaders of the governments concerned. We hope this important decision will advance the prospects for a just and lasting peace in the Middle East." (Department of State *Bulletin,* August 31, 1970, p. 244)

K: Not me because you haven't been talking to me.

R: These things are operational and I think I should take the lead. This meeting last night[4] screwed it up so badly ...

K: Don't be ridiculous.

R: I'm not being ridiculous.

K: You are being absurd. The thing was totally screwed up and everything I did was checked with Sisco. He said Mrs. Meir was about to resign ...

R: You either have somebody running the operation or you don't.

K: If you have a complaint, talk to the President. I am sick and tired of this. If he has a message for the President he isn't going to give it to you. I was at a dinner last night. I had an urgent call. I came back to my office. As soon as I came in I called Sisco and Atherton for instructions.

R: He didn't have a message for the President; he wanted to talk with you. When you have an audience with him they think they have two ways to play it. I don't think it's a good procedure. I am not saying you shouldn't be involved ...

K: I don't want to be involved. I said I noted what he said and they would hear their answer from Sisco.

R: Well, you and I don't see alike on these things. They need to have the idea that when we are acting we act pursuant to the President. If they have a feeling that there are two channels to the President they will use them differently.

K: I didn't take it to the President. He doesn't even know about it yet.

R: But they think you did. It would be helpful to me if, when all it is is carrying out orders, you would not take part in the discussions. When they have a message that's different, but when they have a complaint about something they did with us, you should refer them to me or Sisco. I don't think when you have such a critical matter they should have a feeling that they have got two ways to play it. They should think when we speak that we speak for the President.

K: There is no separate channel. Every conversation I have had I have sent you a memcon and I have checked every comment with Sisco and I have been told the fact that I backed Sisco has helped.

R: Why do you think they go to you?

K: To try to end run and get the President to overrule you.

R: That's right.

K: But that has never happened.

---

[4] Reference is to Kissinger's 10 p.m. meeting on August 6 with Rabin and Argov concerning the cease-fire agreement. See Document 143.

R: But why give them the impression that it might.

K: I thought they were going to tell me that they had attacked the SAM sites across the Canal.

R: I'm not making any headway. I think this is operational—I don't think you should see these people. Anyway, let me know what the President wants. When is Ron[5] going to do it?

K: When we get word from you that we can.[6]

---

[5] White House Press Secretary Ronald Ziegler.

[6] Referring to the disputes between Rogers and Kissinger over Middle East policy, Haldeman wrote that during a "long talk" about the issue with the President, Nixon said that Kissinger was "too self-concerned and inclined to overdramatize." He also said that Kissinger was "overly concerned about anything that affects Israel," but that the larger problem was that neither Rogers nor Kissinger would "really admit the other might be right." (*Haldeman Diaries: Multimedia Edition*, July 16, 1970) A month later, Haldeman wrote that Kissinger's admitted paranoia about "the State Department's maneuvering" worried the President. Nixon commented that it "creates doubts about K[issinger]'s reliability on other recommendations, and gets in the way of his doing his work." He added that Kissinger was "basically jealous of any idea not his own, and he just can't swallow the apparent early success of the Middle East plan because it is Rogers' In fact, he's probably actually trying to make it fail for just this reason. Of all people, he has to keep his mind clean and clear, and instead he's obsessed with these weird persecution delusions." (Ibid., August 17, 1970)

---

145. Cease-Fire Agreement Between Israel and the United Arab Republic[1]

Undated.

A. Israel and the UAR will observe cease-fire effective at 2200 GMT Friday, August 7.

---

[1] Source: National Archives, Nixon Presidential Materials, NSC Files, Box 1157, Saunders Files, Middle East Negotiations Files, June Initiative (Memos Only), June 9–September 1, 1970. Secret; Nodis. A notation at the bottom of the page reads: "Copied from State Telegram 8/21/70." This copy of the agreement is attached to a memorandum from Hoskinson to Kissinger, August 21. On August 5, the Representatives of the Four Powers agreed to send a message to U Thant stating: "A) agreement to text of US proposal and subscription to it by UAR, Jordan and Israel; B) that circumstances are favorable for resumption of Jarring Mission and to this end work of Four becomes even more valuable; and C) SYG should communicate these developments to SC members in a [note]." (Telegram 1603 from USUN, August 6; ibid., Box 654, Country Files, Middle East, Middle East—Recent Actions Keep File Intact) For the Secretary-General's note to the Security Council, released on August 7, see footnote 5, Document 139 On August 7 in Washington, Secretary Rogers announced the 90-day cease-fire, which was to take effect at midnight Israeli time and last until November 5. The texts of his statement and statements by Thant, Meir, and the UAR Foreign Ministry were published in the *New York Times*, August 8, 1970, p. 2.

B. Both sides will stop all incursions and all firing, on the ground and in the air, across the cease-fire line.

C. Both sides will refrain from changing the military status quo within zones extending 50 kilometers to the east and the west of the cease-fire line. Neither side will introduce or construct any new military installations in these zones. Activities within the zones will be limited to the maintenance of existing installations at their present sites and positions and to the rotation and supply of forces presently within the zones.

D. For purposes of verifying observance of the cease-fire, each side will rely on its own national means, including reconnaissance aircraft, which will be free to operate without interference up to 10 kilometers from cease-fire line on its own side of that line.

E. Each side may avail itself as appropriate of all UN machinery in reporting alleged violations to each other of the cease-fire and of the military standstill.

F. Both sides will abide by the Geneva Convention of 1949 relative to the treatment of prisoners of war and will accept the assistance of the ICRC (International Committee of the Red Cross) in carrying out their obligations under that Convention.

146. Telegram From the Department of State to the Embassies in Turkey, Greece, and Italy[1]

Washington, August 8, 1970, 0100Z.

128496. Deliver Opening of Business Saturday, August 8.

FYI—In support of UAR-Israeli ceasefire and military standstill, which USG has just successfully negotiated, we have told Israelis we will provide high level aerial reconnaissance by U–2 aircraft to supplement their surveillance of ceasefire zone west of Suez Canal to help assure them military standstill being observed.[2] Only a U–2 with oblique

---

[1] Source: National Archives, Nixon Presidential Materials, NSC Files, Box 1155, Saunders Files, Middle East Negotiations Files, June Initiative Vol. II, July 24–August 8, 1970. Secret; Immediate; Nodis. Drafted on August 7 by Atherton, cleared in draft in EUR, and approved by Johnson. Repeated to Cairo, Tel Aviv, Moscow, and London.

[2] In telegram 128782 to Tel Aviv, August 10, the Department instructed Barbour to tell Israeli General Aaharon Yariv that the United States assumed a "common GOI–US intelligence objective" and wished to "work closely" with Israel on the U–2 missions, also known as Operation Even-Steven. In support of this objective, the United States would:

cameras can give coverage of entire ceasefire zone without overflight of UAR. This will be discreet but not repeat not covert activity.[3] Even though no overflight of UAR involved, we have advised UAR of our intention and we shall shortly be advising Soviets. UAR reaction was that they do not much like idea and will QUOTE ignore it completely UNQUOTE. We take this as minimum Egyptians could say and relatively positive in circumstances. We are now urgently in process of arranging logistics of this operation, including specifically question of where U–2 aircraft will be based. Two U–2s are proceeding to Western European point tonight. *END FYI.*

1. At level Ambassador or Chargé deems likely to prove most effective, Embassy should urgently approach host government asking for basing and refueling facilities or, in event USAF facility used, agreement for U–2 aircraft to be used for surveillance from Israeli-controlled territory on east side Suez Canal. You may say this is part of operation to supplement Israeli means of ensuring against violations by UAR of ceasefire and standstill agreement and is known to governments of UAR and Israel. If queried re UAR reaction you may draw on FYI section above. You may also say we assume Soviets may want to do same for UAR. We view this as constructive effort in support of current moves toward peace in Middle East, and as operation with which we would hope other governments would be pleased to be associated. We will, of course, seek avoid publicity but cannot guarantee there will be no publicity, in which case we will acknowledge activity while seeking to protect country providing base facility.

2. Since Greek facilities would be of particular use, request Ambassador Tasca personally explain to GOG importance this project, which is important adjunct to assuring both sides that neither being placed at military disadvantage and contributing to atmosphere conducive to successful negotiations.

---

1) provide information on each flight a minimum of four hours before launching; 2) provide the times when the flights entered, turned-around in, and exited from the Sinai; and 3) process photographs "as quickly as possible" and make them available to a "designated representative" of the Israeli Embassy in Washington. (Ibid., Box 1156, Saunders Files, Middle East Negotiations Files, June Initiative Volume III, August 8–27, 1970)

[3] Shortly before the cease-fire took effect, Rogers sent Bergus a telegram instructing him to tell Mohamed Riad that they would have to expect that the U–2 flights would eventually become public knowledge. The Secretary explained that, if they did, the U.S. Government would make this statement: "The United States, having taken the lead in proposing a standstill ceasefire and in working out details of this agreement, feels an obligation to assist in seeing that the terms of this agreement are fully carried out. We are from time to time conducting high level reconnaissance flights to help verify observance of the ceasefire. These flights are entirely limited to the zone east of the Suez Canal ceasefire line." (Telegram 128247 to Cairo, August 7; ibid., Box 655, Country Files, Middle East, Ceasefire Mideast Vol. I)

3. We would hope to deploy to base selected not later than Sunday, August 9.[4]

4. *FOR ANKARA*: We would hope to use Incirlik.

5. *FOR ATHENS*: We would hope to use Thessalonika.

6. *FOR ROME*: We would hope to use Aviano or Sigonella.

Rogers

---

[4] In cooperation with the British Government, the U–2s were based in Cyprus. The first two flights, which had not been coordinated with Israel, occurred on August 9 and 10. General Yariv protested these "surprises" and asked that future flights be postponed until the two governments could complete the work necessary to coordinate the missions. (Telegram 4285 from Tel Aviv, August 11; ibid., Box 1156, Saunders Files, Middle East Negotiations Files, June Initiative Vol. III, August 8–27, 1970)

---

147. Telegram From the Department of State to the Embassy in Israel[1]

Washington, August 9, 1970, 0157Z.

128626. Deliver to Ambassador 0700 Sunday.

1. Please convey following message from Secretary to Prime Minister Meir:

2. QUOTE I have been informed by Assistant Secretary Sisco of your telephone conversation with him August 6 and of the feelings you expressed in the message conveyed by Ambassador Rabin the evening of August 7.[2]

3. It is a matter of deep regret to me that any difficulty has arisen between us since over the weeks and months we have been working so closely together as good friends should. All of our efforts have been devoted to the task of bringing about a secure ceasefire which we hope will stop the needless bloodshed and of getting negotiations started between you and your neighbors. We have pursued this difficult course in the conviction that it offers the only hope of moving toward that secure peace which is your highest aspiration as it is ours.

---

[1] Source: National Archives, Nixon Presidential Materials, NSC Files, Box 655, Country Files, Middle East, Ceasefire Mideast Vol. I. Secret; Immediate. Drafted on August 8 by Atherton, cleared in draft by Sisco, and approved by Rogers.

[2] See Document 143.

4. We shall remain firm in support of the principles we share. We are determined to continue to move forward in a spirit of cooperation and friendship to our common goal of a just and lasting peace. I want to assure you, Madame Prime Minister, of my full respect and support. UNQUOTE

Rogers

148. National Security Study Memorandum 98[1]

Washington, August 10, 1970.

TO

The Secretary of State
The Secretary of Defense
The Director of Central Intelligence

SUBJECT

Further Review of Israeli Arms Requests

As a follow-on to the procedures for initial review of Israeli requests for military equipment established by the Secretary of Defense, the President has requested that a study be prepared quickly outlining the principal Israeli strategies that could be supported against the Soviet and Egyptian missile defense complex west of the Suez Canal, their technical feasibility and their relation to political courses of action.

This study should include a range of options such as the following:

—a major effort to destroy the defense installations west of the Canal;

—a strategy for suppressing the effectiveness of the missile defense system and freeing the airspace for attack on front-line positions;

—a strategy for using means other than air attack for suppressing artillery fire and disrupting any effort to mass for attack on the west bank;

—a program for erecting an Israeli air-defense system on the east side of the Canal.

---

[1] Source: National Archives, Nixon Presidential Materials, NSC Files, NSC Institutional Files (H-Files), Box H–173, National Security Study Memoranda. Secret; Nodis. A copy was sent to the Chairman of the Joint Chiefs of Staff.

Each of the strategies outlined should be related to a specific list of equipment required.

For the sake of comparison, a list of all current Israeli requests should be provided with a rationale for those major items not included in one of the packages.

Because of the close relationship between the provision of arms and U.S. diplomatic strategy the NSC Interdepartmental Group for Near East is charged with the preparation of this study and with the formulation of policy options in responding to Israeli requests. This and any following similar studies will incorporate the technical conclusions of the task force established by the Secretary of Defense.[2]

This study should be forwarded for consideration in the NSC through the NSC Special Review Group no later than the opening of business August 17.[3]

Henry A. Kissinger

---

[2] An analytical summary of the study is Document 152.

[3] The Ad Hoc Special Review Group meeting was held on August 19; see Document 153.

---

149. **Telegram From the Department of State to the Embassies in Israel, Egypt, and Jordan and the Mission to the United Nations**[1]

Washington, August 11, 1970, 0033Z.

129334. 1. We realize Israelis do not appear to be in any mood at moment to begin to discuss with us what their plans are once Jarring begins process of discussions on substance.[2] On the other hand, it is important that after they have had a few days to cool off, there be full consultations between us regarding upcoming discussions between parties under Jarring's auspices.

---

[1] Source: National Archives, Nixon Presidential Materials, NSC Files, Box 655, Country Files, Middle East, Ceasefire Mideast Vol. I. Secret; Priority. Drafted on August 10 by Sisco; cleared by Atherton, Stackhouse, and Sterner; and approved by Sisco. Repeated to London, Paris, and Moscow.

[2] According to Barbour, Dayan notified him on the morning of August 10 that Israel believed that the United Arab Republic had violated the conditions of the cease-fire by moving military equipment forward in the standstill zone as the cease-fire was going into effect. (Telegram 4259 from Tel Aviv, August 10; ibid., Box 1157, Saunders Files, Middle East Negotiations Files, June Initiative (Memos Only), June 9–September 1, 1970)

2. Our principal short-range objective is to try to encourage the two key countries in the area—Israel and the UAR—to engage in serious negotiations while they maintain the ceasefire. In our judgment, this means that each must be encouraged to make sufficiently forthcoming substantive proposals at outset so that a genuine negotiating engagement takes place. From then on in, our objective should be to make it as impossible as possible for the parties to disengage from negotiations. All have some vested interest to make talks succeed.

3. We are struck with the fact that the QUOTE stop shooting and start talking UNQUOTE proposal has had a wide measure of support among the peoples of the area, both in Israel and the Arab world. This seems to suggest that people may well be ahead of governments with respect to their desire for a peaceful settlement. While we may still remain skeptical in view of past disappointments with Nasser, we nevertheless feel that the UAR has been forthcoming both on question of ceasefire and talks over the past weeks and this attitude must be tested in a serious way in concrete discussions under Jarring's auspices. Insofar as Israel is concerned, the grudging manner in which they have come along with our proposal, and the Prime Minister's continuing propensity for looking backward rather than forward, is creating some doubt on whether, if Jarring is able to engage the parties in a serious negotiation, the present Israeli Government is willing to face up to the hard and necessary decisions to achieve a sensible and reasonable compromise. We say this in full appreciation that GOI has had to take some painful decisions and survive a governmental crisis in order to respond positively to US initiative.[3]

4. We realize it will be very difficult to convince Cairo and Jerusalem of the need to begin thinking in terms of a settlement on a basis less than their maximum positions. Over this next week, Jarring will sort out the problem of time, place, and level of discussions. We will continue to press him to take greater initiative in the discussions than he has in the past. However, both Cairo and Jerusalem must be encouraged to put forward concrete substantive proposals on which actual discussions can begin. For example, if Israel were willing to put forth a proposal in negotiations along the lines of the March 1969 US working paper,[4] this could be a good starting point. As for Cairo, we realize their main thrust will be to get Jarring to draw up a QUOTE timetable for withdrawal UNQUOTE. This might be feasible at later stage of discus-

---

[3] Following Israel's acceptance of the U.S. peace initiative on August 4, Prime Minister Meir's Government of National Unity broke up when six members of the Gahal faction, a coalition group led by Menachem Begin, withdrew in protest of the Cabinet's decision to participate in the cease-fire with the UAR and Jordan. (*New York Times,* August 4, 1970, p. 9)

[4] See Document 17.

sions, but likely to abort Jarring's efforts in early days if UAR insists. Moreover, we hope that we are over hurdle of UAR emphasis on QUOTE acceptance of Security Council Resolution UNQUOTE which became the standard answer in the early 1968 round between them when Israel began to ask the other side some specific substantive questions. UAR should be encouraged to put forward initially a fuller, concrete proposal with principles stated in US proposal as main core.

5. Above are tentative thoughts on which Department would appreciate prompt reaction of Tel Aviv, Cairo, Amman, and USUN. Pending receipt your reactions, no actions should be taken.

Rogers

150. Minutes of an Ad Hoc Special Review Group Meeting[1]

Washington, August 12, 1970, 11:35 a.m.–12:25 p.m.

SUBJECT

Middle East

PARTICIPATION

Chairman—Henry A. Kissinger

State
U. Alexis Johnson
Joseph J. Sisco
Alfred L. Atherton, Jr.

Defense
David Packard
Robert J. Pranger

CIA
Richard Helms
David H. Blee

JCS
Adm. Thomas H. Moorer
LTG Richard T. Knowles

NSC Staff
Harold H. Saunders
Jeanne W. Davis

SUMMARY OF DECISIONS

It was decided:

1. to proceed with delivery of the weapons promised Israel before the ceasefire as quickly as possible;

---

[1] Source: National Archives, Nixon Presidential Materials, NSC Files, NSC Institutional Files (H-Files), Box H–111, Senior Review Group, SRG Minutes Originals 1970. Secret; Nodis. All brackets are in the original except those indicating text omitted by the editors. The meeting was held in the White House Situation Room.

2. to undertake a study of the objectives of the equipment Israel is requesting and what we are prepared to support;[2]

3. to consider any new Israeli requests in the framework of these objectives, subjecting them to technical evaluation by Defense, integrating the political factors in the IG and resolving any differences in the Special Review Group, if necessary;

4. to investigate the possibility of linking military assistance for Cambodia, and possibly Korea, with Israel in presentation to the Congress;

5. State to prepare a rough scenario for the Jarring negotiations,[3] if possible before the President leaves for San Clemente;

6. to meet next week[4] to consider the financial issues and the question of the strategy we should be prepared to support for the Israelis.

[Omitted here are the minutes of the meeting.]

---

[2] The Department of Defense study, "Options for U.S. Arms Assistance to Israel," in response to NSSM 98, is ibid., Box H–173, National Security Study Memoranda. NSSM 98 is printed as Document 148.

[3] The options paper "Next Steps on the Middle East," is in the National Archives, Nixon Presidential Materials, NSC Files, NSC Institutional Files (H-Files), Box H–047, Senior Review Group Meetings, Senior Review Group—Middle East 8/12/70.

[4] See Document 153.

---

151. Memorandum of Conversation[1]

Washington, August 17, 1970, 9:05 a.m.

PARTICIPANTS

The President
Ambassador Rabin (Israel)
General Alexander M. Haig

After Ambassador Rabin and General Haig were situated in the Map Room, the President entered. Ambassador Rabin opened the meeting by stating that he had been asked by Prime Minister Golda

---

[1] Source: National Archives, Nixon Presidential Materials, NSC Files, Kissinger Office Files, Box 134, Country Files, Middle East, Rabin-Kissinger. Top Secret; Sensitive; Eyes Only. The conversation was held in the Map Room of the White House. Rabin described his August 17 meeting with President Nixon in *The Rabin Memoirs*, pp. 184–185.

Meir to convey a message to President Nixon in lieu of an immediate visit from her.[2] Rabin continued by remarking that Israel had only accepted the United States peace offer,[3] after having originally rejected it, because of the President's personal letter to Prime Minister Golda Meir.[4] He stated that Israel has expressed a willingness to negotiate only because of this letter and did so with the gravest doubt as to the wisdom of this course of action because of both the military and the political risks involved for Israel.

Rabin stated that in Israel's view the key problem was the Soviet threat and that they had no illusions with respect to Soviet motives. He added that in the case of the Soviet Union Israel was convinced that Soviet acceptance of the US proposal[5] was predicated not on the proposal itself but rather on the strong threat made by President Nixon during his television interview on the West Coast in early July.[6]

Rabin then stated that since accepting the US peace initiative Israel's confidence had been badly shaken by two events. The first was the political misunderstanding involving the Jarring Report's submission to the United Nations[7] and the second was the violation of the ceasefire by the Soviet Union and Egypt which, according to Rabin, was confirmed by positive evidence in the hands of the Israeli Government.[8] Rabin continued by asserting that this ceasefire violation had

---

[2] In his memoirs, Rabin wrote that after Israeli intelligence discovered Egyptian violations of the cease-fire agreement during the second week of August, he asked Kissinger to arrange for a meeting between Meir and Nixon "for an overall discussion of the post-ceasefire situation, but he put me off by claiming that the time was 'not ripe' for such a meeting. A few days later, when I pressed him again, he proposed that I meet with the President. I felt uneasy about the idea, for I could not be regarded as a proxy for the prime minister and I had grounds to assume that such a substitution would thoroughly irritate Golda." (Ibid., p. 184)

[3] See Document 140.

[4] See Document 136.

[5] See Document 137.

[6] See footnote 3, Document 134.

[7] See Document 143.

[8] Rabin told Kissinger during an August 15 meeting at the White House that "on the nights of 29 and 30 July the Soviets and Egyptians had moved forward massively with their ground-to-air missiles, and during the first half of August, they had continued this movement from their earlier position of 40–60 kilometers from the Canal." He added that on the night of August 7 and 8, there was additional movement of missiles toward the Suez Canal. "Israel had both ComInt and photos," he said. "The Soviets and Egyptians deployed 14 sites forward." (Memorandum of conversation, August 15; National Archives, Nixon Presidential Materials, NSC Files, Kissinger Office Files, Box 134, Country Files, Middle East, Rabin-Kissinger) In an August 15 memorandum to Rogers, Sisco reported that U.S. intelligence "clearly showed there was a buildup of SAM installations in an area 15 to 35 kilometers west of the ceasefire line between the end of July and August 10. The Israelis say this began in the hours before the ceasefire went into effect (midnight August 7 Israeli time) and continued at least through the next day. If the Israeli contention as to timing is correct, this missile deployment would constitute a violation of the standstill provision of the Israeli-UAR ceasefire agreement." Sisco added that "because

fundamentally altered the military balance in the Middle East because sufficient air-to-ground missiles had been moved forward to permit the Soviets and the Egyptians to exact a severe toll on Israeli aircraft which were conducting suppressive missions against Egyptian artillery spread across the entire breadth of the Canal. Rabin further stated that there were some 1,000 artillery pieces backed up by seven Egyptian divisions which could now be employed with the full cognizance that ground-to-air defenses would render Israeli counter action prohibitive.

Rabin then commented that Mrs. Meir and the entire Israeli Government were very unsettled by United States unwillingness to accept the evidence offered by Israel establishing the fact that a ceasefire violation had occurred. He also remarked that public statements countering the Israeli assessment added further to the difficulties.

Ambassador Rabin continued by asserting that the simple fact now existed that the military balance has been substantially altered by the Soviet action in moving missile defenses forward along the Canal. He stated that Israel was very conscious of the Soviet action and had anticipated that it would occur. Soviet objectives were obvious from the outset since they had started creeping forward before the ceasefire was to take effect. Initially, they established defenses along the rear areas of Egypt. The Soviets then moved forward to the 50 kilometer line. Then, once the US peace initiative was announced and even for the two-day period after the ceasefire, the Soviets proceeded to move the missiles forward to within 10 to 15 kilometers from the Canal. Today 10 to 14 new sites existed along the Canal itself. Rabin insisted that they had proof positive of this infraction. Israel had flown missions against these sites and reconnaissance missions every day for 72 consecutive days and was in no doubt that an infraction had occurred. He added that they also had communications and electronic intelligence which confirmed the movement of missile battalions after the ceasefire from Cairo itself.

Rabin continued by commenting that whether one accepts that the movement was made before or after the formal ceasefire, the intent of the Soviet Union was obvious and that this, after all, was the only important fact. He stated that since the military balance had been changed it was now a matter of how long it would be before the Egyptians violated the ceasefire and how, therefore, Israel would be able to counter the new threat. He added that Israel had been prepared and willing to

---

we lack a data base of our own for August 7, our evidence on the question of timing (but not on the buildup itself) is and will remain inconclusive. When evidence the Israelis have provided us is taken into account, there is a reasonable presumption that a violation occurred." (Ibid., RG 59, Central Files 1970–73, POL 27–14 ARAB–ISR) See also footnote 2, Document 149.

strike the forward missile complexes but when they had attempted to do so, they found that the attrition on the attacking aircraft was very high. It was therefore necessary for them to acquire some additional technical means, electronic countermeasures and standoff shrike missiles as well as CBU ordnance. Ambassador Rabin also added that having requested this from the United States, they had yet to receive the assistance they had hoped for.

Rabin stated that he was scheduled to meet with Defense officials today to ascertain whether or not this equipment, especially the shrike missile, would be available. President Nixon stated that he had approved the delivery of shrike missiles some three weeks earlier and asked General Haig the reason for the delay. Ambassador Rabin interjected that the delays resulted from some technical misunderstandings. General Haig agreed that this was correct and commented that there was some question initially as to whether or not the shrike missile could be delivered from the aircraft available to the Israelis. The President instructed General Haig to insure that this matter was resolved promptly.

President Nixon then stated that Israel must understand that he too understood the Soviet motives, perhaps better than Israel itself; we had launched our initiative with no preconceived notions as to Soviet goodwill. On the other hand, he commented, it was important that the initiative proceed and that a conscious and overt effort be made by the United States at this time to achieve peace in the Middle East. The President then remarked that Rabin must be conscious of the problem and the attitude existing in the United States at this time. This was an attitude which affected not only the situation in the Middle East but the conduct of US affairs in Southeast Asia, Cambodia and South Vietnam. President Nixon told Rabin that he must be conscious of the difficulties caused by certain of our congressional leaders such as Senator Fulbright, Senator McGovern and Senator Hatfield.[9]

The President continued by stating that the American people and indeed the world at large were very much impressed by the progress made thus far within the US peace initiative. The world was especially pleased that both sides had agreed to a ceasefire. Thus, it was important that we continue on with the negotiations. It was also important, the President added, that no one attribute to Israel the fault for a fracturing of the ceasefire. If the US peace initiative were to fail, everyone should recognize who was at fault. Certainly he, the President, hoped that it would be the other side and not Israel who must share the blame.

---

[9] Senator George S. McGovern (D–SD) and Senator Mark O. Hatfield (R–OR).

The President then stated that he agreed fully with Ambassador Rabin's assessment that the Soviet Union was indeed the main cause of Middle East tensions and that if the Soviet Union were removed from the situation Israel would certainly be able to handle matters without difficulty. Ambassador Rabin reaffirmed that this was the case. President Nixon commented that he would not discuss this with even his closest advisors but that he wanted it understood that he would raise the issue of Soviet involvement through special channels. It was obvious to all that the Soviet Union had problems of its own. Therefore, if there were to be a Summit, as some have surmised, the departure of the Soviets from the Middle East certainly would be the first item on the agenda of such a meeting.

President Nixon then stated that he would, of course, be willing and delighted to receive Prime Minister Golda Meir but he did not feel that now was the time for such a visit. A visit at this time would be misunderstood since the peace effort had just gotten underway. He hoped that the Prime Minister would recognize this fact and be willing to come at a later date,[10] perhaps in connection with the anniversary of the United Nations.

President Nixon also stated that these were most difficult times for Israel and that it would be necessary for Israel to demonstrate a maximum degree of self-restraint. Certainly this was expected not only by the American people and the Jewish community in America but by world public opinion as well. Before we could anticipate acceptance of a violation of the ceasefire by Israel or the rectification of whatever violations might have occurred thus far, it was essential that public opinion be prepared for such a problem.

Finally, the President noted that we have now taken steps to assure that future violations are picked up without any equivocation and asked Ambassador Rabin to furnish to General Haig any intelligence which Israel may develop that is not held by us and to raise any additional question about military matters that may be disturbing the Government of Israel. The President concluded the meeting by asking Ambassador Rabin to keep General Haig and Dr. Kissinger informed of any changes in the military situation.

---

[10] Meir met with Nixon at the White House on September 18. See Document 162.

152. Paper Prepared by the National Security Council Staff[1]

Washington, August 18, 1970.

ANALYTICAL SUMMARY

U.S. ARMS ASSISTANCE TO ISRAEL

Military and Diplomatic Options

I. *What the Paper Represents*

The paper at the next tab ["IG Paper"] was written in the following way:

—A Defense Department task force, which has been working with the Israeli weapons problem for the past seven weeks, identified a series of Israeli strategy options for defending the Suez cease-fire line.

—At Assistant Secretary Sisco's request, Hal Saunders put these options in policy context in the cover memo at the next tab. This memo (1) states the pros and cons of each military option, (2) identifies the next steps in a military assistance scenario from now to November and (3) makes a preliminary effort to relate those steps to the next steps in the diplomatic scenario.

—Defense and State both made refinements and the full Defense study[2] is attached to the policy paper.

—Sisco's Interdepartmental Group endorsed the paper Monday.[3]

II. *A Preview of the Decisions Required*

It would be *desirable to reach conclusions on a general framework within which our military assistance relationship with Israel can proceed.* These conclusions can be reported to the President for decision after the meeting since major dissent does not seem likely. *Three major points should be addressed:*

A. *What range of Israeli military strategies for defending the Suez cease-fire line is the U.S. prepared to support if the cease-fire breaks down?*

The options are ranged in the next section of this summary with a view to setting aside those which seem infeasible or undesirable. This

---

[1] Source: National Archives, Nixon Presidential Materials, NSC Files, NSC Institutional Files (H-Files), Box H–047, Senior Review Group Meetings, Senior Review Group—Military Assistance to Israel—Chile (97) 8/19/70. Secret; Nodis. The paper prepared by the NSC Interdepartmental Group for the Near East, "U.S. Arms Assistance to Israel: Military and Diplomatic Options," undated, which is summarized here, is attached. A cover memorandum by Saunders is attached but not printed. All brackets are in the original.

[2] See footnote 2, Document 150.

[3] August 17.

process of elimination leaves a range of options which *could* be discussed with the Israelis if we wish for political reasons to invite them into consultations on strategy. They *should* be discussed if any precise strategy is to be chosen because there are questions which only the Israelis can answer.

B. *Shall we invite Israeli military planners to consult with us on a sensible equipment package within the range of strategies the U.S. is prepared to support?*

The basic answer is really stated above—YES. The issue is what limits to place. Defense is wary of anything that smacks of formal joint planning but would go along with some fairly detailed talks with Israeli military officials on the reasoning behind the various options we have identified. Sisco wants such detailed talks as a means of bringing the Israelis to face the financial and military realities of their present situation as well as to provide the general assurance of cooperation the Israelis need. A decision is required on the limits to be imposed on these talks.

C. *How should this invitation be timed to relate to the diplomatic scenario?*

This is least clear because it is still uncertain how the diplomatic scenario will play itself out. The invitation to discuss strategies should be issued fairly soon so it is important to identify what we should seek in connection with it since this is the main "carrot" we will have to offer in the next few weeks.

III. *The Military Options*

For the sake of simplifying, the options are grouped below to facilitate the process of narrowing and focusing. For the same reason, they are dealt with here in reverse order.

—The *options are described* fully in the attached paper at pp. II:3–7. A small tab marked "Options" identifies these pages.

—An *equipment package for each* option is in the annex paper at a small tab marked "Packages." You do not need to get into the packages, but you may wish to take a quick look to see what is involved.

—A full statement of *pros and cons* appears in Section III of the IG paper at the next tab; it is marked with a tab, "Pros and Cons."

A. *Options Most Quickly Set Aside*

Alternative 6: Prepare for full-scale U.S. intervention. This option is included by Defense "only to show that beyond a certain point in the Israeli capabilities described below U.S. involvement is probably the next step."

Alternative 5: Provide a surge capability for pre-emptive strikes against deep Egyptian targets as a possible prelude to ground invasion. The Israeli need to administer a serious blow is recognized, and some would make the argument that the U.S. has an interest in showing the USSR's vulnerability. But no one-time Israeli strike seems likely to be decisive in the longer perspective if the USSR is committed to get Egyptian territory back, and the risk of Soviet retaliation would be serious.

Alternative 4–B: Provide continuous forward SAM-attrition capability. This was the Israeli strategy before the cease-fire of seeking capability to *attack the missile sites themselves.* It is the judgment of the Pentagon task force that this is militarily infeasible for these reasons:

—The Soviet-UAR missile defense is denser, more sophisticated and better manned than anything the USAF flew against in North Vietnam, and the USAF adopted a strategy of not attacking the sites but of trying to suppress them while attacking other targets.

—The Soviet capacity to replace sites is probably greater than Israeli capacity to destroy them.

—Israel probably cannot afford this strategy. Pentagon gaming suggests this strategy would cost Israel $100 million a month. That would include losses of 12 Phantoms and 16 Skyhawks a month.

NOTE: There is very little feeling in the Pentagon that this is even a feasible strategy for Israel to consider. However, *the following question should be asked: Is this strategy infeasible only because the U.S. is not prepared to supply its most advanced munitions for stand-off pinpoint bombing?* [There are a few weapons specialists who feel that this strategy might become feasible if the U.S. were prepared to give Israel such things as laser bombs. The argument for using this technology would be to demonstrate U.S. superiority.]

B. *Options to be Most Seriously Argued*

The strategies outlined below are not necessarily mutually exclusive, and the answer may be some combination of them. However, there does seem to be a special choice between 3–B and some combination of the rest. The question is whether the Israelis need the capability to attack Egyptian artillery sites badly enough to warrant the cost.

Alternative 3–B: Provide continuous gun-attrition capability. This would—by heavy jamming—permit continuous Israeli attacks on front-line artillery positions in a 5–10 mile zone west of the Canal. The main argument for this approach is that the Israelis have maintained they could not sustain the losses from Egyptian artillery barrages. This is why they began their steady air raids in July 1969. However, the Pentagon estimates this strategy might cost the Israelis $70 million a month in munitions and lost aircraft alone. Moreover, some in the Pentagon feel that Israel could hold its position on the Suez cease-fire line with a much less costly strategy (see Alternatives 1 and 2 below).

Alternatives 3–A and 4–A: Provide a one-time surge capability to silence guns (3–A) and forward SAM sites (4–A) on the west bank to defeat a canal-crossing build-up. These two alternatives differ more in numbers than in types of equipment. The equipment involved would cost just under $15 million. These strategies by themselves would probably not be sufficient because they do not provide means for coping with day-to-day Egyptian firing across the Canal.

Alternatives 1 and 2: Provide additional equipment for better air defense and for defeating an armored invasion into the Sinai (2) and equipment for infiltration control (1). This package would include more armor and anti-aircraft weapons to a one-time total of about $95 million for the heavy equipment and another $15 million for intelligence and anti-infiltration equipment. Some of the tanks are already being provided.

NOTE: The *question to be asked* about this alternative is whether the Israelis could stay on the Canal without some capacity to bomb steadily across the Canal. Some Pentagon answers are that the Israelis could further reduce the number of men on the Canal and rely on sensors to identify raiding parties. A mobile force could then be moved rapidly to meet any such group. Others in the Pentagon, however, feel that some Israeli capacity to bomb Egyptian gun positions across the Canal (Alternative 3–B above) would remain necessary.

C. *Issues in Devising a Combination of Strategies*

1. *Minimum.* If deep raids and continuous attacks on the SAM's are ruled out, Alternatives 1, 2 and 3–A—4–A would seem to be a minimum. This would give the Israelis the capability to defend the Sinai with insurance in a one-strike capability to defeat a build-up on the west bank for a canal-crossing. This could all be done for about $125 million.

2. *The issue* is whether Alternative 3–B—the ability to bomb the gun positions continuously is necessary. This is where costs mount—to $70 million a month in expendable items alone. The decision depends on:

—Whether the Israelis feel they can give up cross-Canal bombing *and*

—Whether it is in the U.S. interest to let the USSR establish the fact that its defense of the UAR is invulnerable.

IV. *The Central Political-Military Issue*

One of the central conclusions of the Pentagon study is that the military situation across the Canal may finally have reached one of rear balance—or stand-off. The Egyptians still are unable to cross the Canal without direct Soviet involvement. The Israelis are unable to fly across the Canal steadily without incurring expensive losses which only the U.S. can replace or to cross the Canal in force without risking Soviet retaliation.

In some ways the situation has become more unstable because the Israelis in increasing desperation may launch a ground attack against the Soviet system.

In other ways, by strengthening Israel's defensive position it is possible to demonstrate to the USSR that only its own direct involvement in a cross-canal attack will make such a crossing possible. In other words, a stable, long-term stand-off might still be possible if the Israelis could see their way clear to adopt it.

The central military issue, therefore, is whether the Israelis could and would be willing to adopt a strategy that would not require them to cross the Canal on a regular basis.

Ideally, the U.S. could have reason for wanting to see the continuing ineffectiveness of the Soviet SAM system demonstrated. However, a cost of $70 million monthly and up, may outweigh any advantage.

However, only the Israelis can factor out the relative costs and advantages in this choice. That is why consultation is necessary to determine whether Alternative 3–B should be added to Alternatives 1, 2 and 3–A—4–A.

V. *Should We Consult With Israel?*

For the reason described in the last section—we do not know all the factors involved in Israel's selection of strategy—and for the sake of giving Israel the reassurance of continuing consultation, consultation on these strategy choices seems necessary:

—first, to establish with Israel that attacking the SAM sites (Alternative 4–B) is too costly;

—second, to develop a combination of the remaining lesser options.

The *main issue* is to determine a format that would avoid the over-commitment of formal joint planning and yet provide the framework for necessary consultation. Defense should be asked for a scenario.

VI. *Diplomatic Scenario*

Assistant Secretary Sisco should be asked to discuss this in greater detail. However, in very general terms, it seems helpful to consider the military assistance and diplomatic scenarios in three phases:

A. Phase I—between now and late September when the foreign ministers gather in New York.[4]

1. The main *military* move would be to offer full consultations on strategy.

2. The main *diplomatic* move would be to persuade the Israelis to advance negotiable positions in the early stages of the Jarring talks.

B. *Phase II*—mid-September to November 5 when the cease-fire expires.

1. The main *military* move would be U.S. approval for some combination of Israeli strategies for defending the Suez cease-fire line if the cease-fire breaks down or expires. The first deliveries of earmarked aircraft are also due in this period.

2. The main *diplomatic* move is difficult to foresee. However, while we might try to avoid a major crunch with Israel over withdrawal in this period, we will have to produce enough Israeli movement to persuade the Arabs that it is worthwhile renewing the cease-fire.

C. *Phase III*—after November 5.

1. The main *military* move would be approval of (a) some $500 million in financial assistance and (b) a package that might make Israeli withdrawal possible. [This should be the subject of the next phase of in-house planning.]

2. The main diplomatic move—should we be so lucky—would be an effort to gain Israeli acceptance of the final peace agreement.

---

[4] At the 25th session of the UN General Assembly, which convened on September 15.

153. Minutes of an Ad Hoc Special Review Group Meeting[1]

Washington, August 19, 1970, 4:10–5 p.m.

SUBJECT

U.S. Military Assistance to Israel

PARTICIPANTS

Chairman—Henry A. Kissinger

State
Joseph J. Sisco
Mr. Alfred L. Atherton

Defense
David Packard
Brig. Gen. John W. Baer

CIA
Richard Helms
[*name not declassified*]

JCS
Adm. Thomas H. Moorer
R. Adm. W.R. St. George

NSC Staff
Harold H. Saunders
Richard T. Kennedy
Jeanne W. Davis

SUMMARY OF DECISIONS

1. Defense will put together a package to support a strategy which would contain hostilities at the Canal (i.e., what Israel would need to discourage Egyptian crossing of the Canal), with the costs involved.[2]

2. We will meet informally with Israeli military officials to discuss strategy;[3] this is not to be considered as "joint planning."

3. State will prepare an analysis of what we could offer Israel in exchange for their agreement to return to mutually-accepted borders.[4]

[Omitted here are the minutes of the meeting.]

---

[1] Source: National Archives, Nixon Presidential Materials, NSC Files, NSC Institutional Files (H-Files), Box H–111, Senior Review Group, SRG Minutes Originals 1970. Secret; Nodis. All brackets are in the original except those indicating text omitted by the editors or that remains classified. The meeting was held in the White House Situation Room.

[2] Laird sent the study on the equipment package, "Further Response to N.S.S.M. 98," to Kissinger on August 29, writing in the covering memorandum: "I recommend that N.S.S.M. 98 should be considered as a standby U.S. EYES ONLY document for use in case the cease-fire breaks down. As an alternative, I would recommend that any military discussions with the Israelis be directed toward their defense requirements following signature of a peace treaty and that in such discussions we be as forthcoming as possible. With this in mind, I have directed DOD planners, as a matter of urgency, to consider equipment packages which might be appropriate for Israel under the terms of a peace treaty calling for withdrawal to roughly the pre-1967 boundaries." (Ibid., NSC Files, Box 607, Country Files, Middle East, Israel, Vol. VI)

[3] See Document 163.

[4] The paper, "U.S. Arms Assistance to Israel: Military and Diplomatic Options," undated, is in the National Archives, Nixon Presidential Materials, NSC Files, NSC Institutional Files (H-Files), Box H–047, Senior Review Group Meetings, Senior Review Group—Middle East 8/12/70.

154. Telegram From the Department of State to the Interests Section in the United Arab Republic, the Embassy in Israel, and the White House[1]

Washington, August 25, 1970, 0058Z.

138163. White House please pass San Clemente for Assistant Secretary Sisco. Ref: Cairo 1911.[2]

1. *FOR CAIRO*. You should seek appointment as soon as possible with Foreign Minister or if he is not available Muhammad Riad to say that we have studied FonMin's presentation to you and in reply we wish convey following.

2. USG cannot agree with interpretation that ceasefire/standstill agreement[3] permits relocation of missile batteries from one location to another within ceasefire zone. This is explicitly precluded by para C of agreement which stipulates inter alia: "Activities within the zones will be limited to the maintenance of existing installations *at their present sites and positions* and to the rotation and supply of forces presently within the zones." In light of language just preceding it, word "rotation" cannot be taken to mean relocation of missile batteries from one site to another. Beyond this explicit language, it appears to us self-evident that movement of missile sites from one position to another is inconsistent with concept of military status quo. Unless there were some military advantage to be gained, why would UAR want to move missile batteries? Any forward movement within zone obviously confers military advantage, but even lateral movement, possibly from site to another more advantageous, could also be held to do so. USG must insist that paragraph C explicitly does not permit relocation of missile batteries within zone and that continued relocations by GUAR will place whole ceasefire/standstill agreement in grave jeopardy.

---

[1] Source: National Archives, Nixon Presidential Materials, NSC Files, Box 1156, Saunders Files, Middle East Negotiations Files, June Initiative Vol. III, August 8–27, 1970. Secret; Priority; Nodis. Drafted by Sterner on August 24 and approved by Atherton. Repeated to Amman, London, Moscow, Paris, and USUN.

[2] In telegram 1911 from Cairo, August 24, the Section reported Bergus's conversation with Foreign Minister Mahmoud Riad regarding U.S. accusations that the United Arab Republic violated the cease-fire agreement with Israel. (Ibid.) On August 19, the Department of State had released this statement on the issue: "We have concluded that there was some forward deployment of surface-to-air missiles into and within the zone west of the Suez Canal around the time the ceasefire went into effect; there is some evidence that this continued beyond the ceasefire deadline, although our evidence of this is not conclusive. With respect to additional information which the Israeli Government has brought to our attention concerning possible violations of the ceasefire, we will examine it and be in touch with Israel through diplomatic channels. We do not now anticipate making further public statements on this matter." (Department of State *Bulletin,* September 7, 1970, p. 278)

[3] Document 145.

3. "Rotation and supply of forces" in paragraph C of agreement clearly refers to rotation and supply within levels and types existing at time of ceasefire and cannot be construed to permit improvement or change in military dispositions. This would rule out, for example, conversion of dummy missile site into operational site, or replacement of SA–2 site with SA–3 site.

4. We also have serious problem with FonMin's assertion that provision for maintenance in agreement would allow UAR to improve "weak" installation or to repair "destroyed" installation. Status quo means exactly what it says and precludes any action that improves military position of either side over that obtaining at time ceasefire/standstill went into effect. This precludes new construction at existing sites as well as construction of new sites.

5. We welcome FonMin's categorical statement that UAR would not establish any new installations or sites in zone and that it is not constructing new sites. We hope that clarifications in preceding paragraphs which are based on clear and precise language of agreement itself, will remove any misunderstandings and that adherence to that agreement will enable us to close this chapter and devote our full attention to talks now opening in New York.

6. With respect to FonMin's allegations of Israeli violations of standstill, you may reiterate to GUAR that we have already taken up question overflights and GOI has promised investigate and give us report. On other charges leveled by FonMin, we will proceed immediately to raise them with GOI. If they turn out to be well-founded, we will take same serious view that we have of UAR activity. We will inform GUAR of results of our inquiry.[4]

7. *FOR TEL AVIV.* You should tell GOI we have received response from UAR FonMin to our approaches on standstill violations. You should say that FonMin states categorically that UAR has not (sic) and will not introduce any new missiles or construct any new sites within 50 kilometer zone. However, GUAR claims it has right under agreement to relocate missile sites within 50 kilometer zone. USG does not agree and we are making this clear in immediate return approach. We are also informing GUAR of our firm view re limitations inherent in provisions for "maintenance" and "rotation of forces." We are saying this cannot include such activity as converting dummy site into operational battery, or replacing SA–2 battery with SA–3.

---

[4] On August 26, Bergus wrote: "I conveyed substance paras 2 through 6 of State 138163 to Mahmoud Riad at 1100 local this morning. He promised to pass our views along to highest authority soonest." (Telegram 1927 from Cairo; National Archives, RG 59, Central Files 1970–73, POL 27–14 ARAB–ISR) The next day, Bergus had another meeting with Riad, at which the Foreign Minister assured him that his presentation from the previous day "was before UAR military command where it was receiving intensive study." (Telegram 1940 from Cairo, August 27; ibid.)

8. You should also raise with GOI UAR assertions of Israeli stand-still violations in para 5 reftel. You should say sooner we deal with these charges and, hopefully, lay them to rest, more effectively we will be able to urge points in preceding paras upon GUAR. Since we are not photographing Israeli side of ceasefire line, we request that USDAO be allowed to visit precise locations specified by GUAR to look into GUAR charges.[5]

9. FYI. We see no useful purpose in prolonging debate about provision of military equipment to Israel and prefer to let this matter rest on points you made (para 13 reftel). If Riad presses this question, however, and you feel you must respond, point you should get across is that we are continuing to exercise restraint. It is unrealistic, however to expect that moves or activities to gain military advantage can be one-sided. This is essence of problem of escalation and is why we have so consistently favored talks on arms limitation. END FYI.

Johnson

---

[5] The Deputy Chief of Mission presented the points in paragraphs 7 and 8 to Gazit on August 26. He suggested that the information from the second of the two paragraphs "be passed to military authorities for their consideration and possible action." (Telegram 4619 from Tel Aviv, August 26; ibid., Box 1156, Saunders Files, Middle East Negotiations Files, June Initiative Vol. III, August 8–27, 1970) On the evening of August 28, Barbour met with Meir, Eban, and other Israeli officials at the Prime Minister's invitation. She expressed her dissatisfaction with the cease-fire agreement due to violations by the United Arab Republic and asked the Ambassador what the U.S. Government was doing to address the issue. Barbour replied that it was doing everything it could "to get other side to live up to agreement," but Meir remained pessimistic, confessing that she "could not see a rosy road ahead." (Telegram 4692 from Tel Aviv, August 29; ibid.)

---

155. Telegram From the Department of State to the White House[1]

Washington, August 31, 1970, 2328Z.

142479. White House pass San Clemente for Secretary Rogers and Assistant Secretary Sisco. For Secretary Rogers from Cline. Subject: INR

---

[1] Source: National Archives, Nixon Presidential Materials, NSC Files, Box 1156, Saunders Files, Middle East Negotiations Files, June Initiative Vol. IV, August 28–November 15, 1970. Secret; Exdis. Drafted by Robert Baraz (INR/RSE) and cleared and approved by David Mark (INR/DRR). All brackets are in the original except "[and]", added for clarity.

Briefing Note: "Middle East: Soviets Seek Negotiating Advantage from Military Moves."

1. Following is text of INR Intelligence Brief analyzing current Soviet tactics in their missile build-up in the Suez Canal ceasefire zone and considering possible political implications. Sisco carried an earlier version of this paper to San Clemente today.

Begin text: Moscow's objection to U–2 reconnaissance of the cease-fire is a significant development, not because an aircraft might be shot down, but because of what the Soviet statement of August 28 adds to a picture of deepening Soviet commitment to pressure tactics in the peace negotiations.[2]

Not interdiction but intimidation. In our view the oral statement to Embassy Moscow signals no effort by the Soviets or the Egyptians to try to shoot down a U–2. Moscow would appear to have nothing to gain from such an action, which would seriously strain its relations with the US. The Soviets could not expect to keep the US from finding out what was happening in the UAR, even if a U–2 were shot down. (The only purpose to be served by delaying American information would be in the event that a sudden tactical move such as a cross Canal attack were contemplated, and there is nothing to indicate that any such move is in prospect. Indeed, there are good reasons against it at this time.)

The purpose of the Soviet statement appears, rather, to be an effort to discourage the US from making an issue of ceasefire violations. Warnings of "possible consequences" and "special surprises" which U–2s might elicit, coupled with the argument that U–2 flights are not "national means" and thus violate the American terms for its own ceasefire, seem designed to persuade the US that all it can get by raising the matter of ceasefire violations is acrimony from Moscow.

Timing may be significant. The timing of the belated protest against the flights which Moscow had previously tolerated may be interpreted as no more than a gesture of solidarity with the UAR, which objected to the U–2s shortly after they were told that the U–2s had collected evidence of violation of the standstill. There is some ground, however, to support a hypothesis of a more immediate tactical purpose in the protest.

Just before the Soviet oral statement, there were American press reports of new techniques to be employed in the American reconnais-

---

[2] On August 28, Vinogradov called Beam to the Ministry of Foreign Affairs and read an oral statement in response to Beam's August 8 approach regarding the U.S. reconnaissance flights near the UAR-Israeli cease-fire line. In the statement, the Soviet Union said that it expected the United States to discontinue the reconnaissance flights and to take "full responsibility for possible consequences of such flights" if they did continue. (Telegram 4950 from Moscow, August 28; ibid.)

sance effort. Even if Moscow was able to sort out the technical inaccuracies in these stories, it would still have been likely to see them as officially inspired. Moreover, on the morning of the day before the oral statement, the Soviets would have known of the flight, for the first time, of a double U–2 mission. Moscow may have calculated that the US was preparing new disclosures about continuing violations and made its statement in an effort to discourage them.

Negotiations—having one's cake. The oral statement made no reference to the peace negotiations, for which Brezhnev's speech of the same day expressed continued support.[3] Moscow evidently hopes to enjoy both the prospect of success in the negotiations and the tactical military advantages of having vitiated the standstill provision of the ceasefire.

In accepting the peace initiative, the Soviets understood the purpose and importance of the standstill provision. Whatever room for arguments over details there may be, American diplomatic conversations even before the peace initiative was launched, the terms of the initiative, and the record of Israeli bombing in the Canal zone made it quite clear what the overall purpose of the standstill idea was. Moscow evidently concluded that it would be possible both to launch peace talks and to complete earlier plans to strengthen air defenses in the Canal area.

Risks involved. Soviet behavior with regard to the ceasefire has been something out of the ordinary in Moscow's dealings with the US. The Soviets have as a rule avoided putting themselves in a position where they could be taxed with breaking their word. In deciding to concert with the Egyptians to move the missiles forward, the Soviets evidently decided that two kinds of risks were manageable. First was the possible damage to relations with the US not only with respect to the Middle East but also in terms of wider implications for other issues such as SALT and other disarmament topics. Second was the chance that the Israelis—even in the face of American opposition—might take matters into their own hands and attack the new deployments.

Decision reflects attitude toward talks. That Moscow opted as it did shows an extremely confident attitude about the strength of its position in the peace talks. The Soviets evidently were prepared to jeopardize the talks rather than forgo improvement of the Soviet-UAR military position, but they must have thought the risk to be small. Presumably they believe Washington to be bereft of satisfactory alter-

---

[3] In a nationally-televised address on August 28, Brezhnev asked for "an honest observance" of the cease-fire agreement, declaring: "It is our profound conviction that an end to the conflict in the Middle East would meet the vital interests of both the Arab countries and of Israel." (*New York Times*, August 29, 1970, p. 1)

natives to the pursuit of its peace efforts as long as Moscow continues to favor negotiations. The Soviets evidently hoped that, if their maneuver worked, they might be able to bring about a situation in which Israel, in a weakened psychological position, would be obliged to continue the talks under increasingly unfavorable circumstances.

If the August 28 oral statement was a reflection of Soviet concern that the US was about to turn increased attention, unwanted by the USSR, to ceasefire violations, then its thrust must have been an effort to deflect the US from that course and to return the focus to the negotiations. The Soviets must also have hoped that the experience would put political pressure on both Americans [and] Israelis, by reminding the Americans that they must now press Israel on to a settlement agreeable to Moscow and Cairo, and by reminding the Israelis that they must cease their resistance to such an outcome, since resuming the cross-Canal raids would be increasingly costly to the Israeli air forces. *End text.*

Samuels

156. Editorial Note

The National Security Council held a meeting, the minutes of which have not been found, on September 1, 1970, from 10 to 11:47 a.m. at the Western White House in San Clemente, California, which in part concerned the Middle East. (National Archives, Nixon Presidential Materials, White House Central Files, President's Daily Diary) On August 31, in preparation for the meeting, Assistant Secretary of State for Near Eastern and South Asian Affairs Joseph Sisco sent Secretary of State William Rogers a paper outlining three options for how the United States could proceed following the violations of the August 7 cease-fire agreement for presentation at the NSC meeting. The options included:

"1. *We can continue to support the ceasefire and Jarring talks, pressing the Soviets and UAR to stop their violations but in effect acquiescing in them at the same time pressing Israel to continue to observe the ceasefire.* This would be the first time we would be charging the Soviets directly with ceasefire-standstill violations. The emphasis could be on stopping any further violations rather than on a rollback. This would assuage the Israelis somewhat, but would leave them dissatisfied to a substantial degree. At a minimum, we would need to step up military supply to Israel as compensation for what the Soviets and UAR are doing on the West Bank of the Canal. This would probably mean that in addition to the scheduled delivery of the September-December F–4s and A–4s, we would provide a considerably expanded anti-SAM package. There is further risk that, by acquiescing in violations which improve the UAR-Soviet military position, we will be increasingly on the defensive as political talks progress in circumstances where our credibility and influence with the Israelis will have been further undermined. If a larger anti-SAM package is provided, it would have to be on the same conditions as the previous package, that Israel would not use the equipment to break the ceasefire. A suggested letter to Gromyko carrying out this option is attached.

"2. *We could continue to support the ceasefire and urge Israel to observe it but tell the Soviets we would support Israel in suspending participation in the Jarring discussions until the UAR and Soviets removed the missiles introduced during the ceasefire period and ceased all further violations.* The Soviets and UAR would probably react to this approach by stepping up their military activities in the ceasefire zone, combined with a campaign to put the blame on the US and Israel for suspending the peace talks. Our principal leverage in seeking to forestall this would be to tell the Soviets that we are prepared to charge them and the Egyptians publicly with violating the ceasefire and to document our charges. It is doubtful at best whether this would be enough to get them to back down, and peace talks therefore would be at an indefinite impasse. Furthermore, under this option, the risk would remain high that Israel would strike militarily despite our urgings to the contrary.

"3. *We could tell the Soviets that we will no longer cooperate in pursuing the peace talks or in the continuation of the ceasefire and would support Israel in a return to the military and political situation pre-August 7 unless the violations are corrected and no further violations occur.* This would constitute a major test of whether the Soviets attach as much importance as we do to the success of the current settlement efforts. If they are prepared to see those efforts break down rather than suspend their strategy of putting increasing military pressure on Israel, it is perhaps better to find this out sooner rather than later. If we choose this option, we must be prepared to risk the collapse of our whole initiative. This is thus the option of maximum risk. On the other hand, it is also the option under which we have maximum leverage, since (a) we could make a good public case of Soviet-UAR responsibility for the breakdown of the ceasefire and (b) a return to the pre-August 7 situation and military risks which they presumably accepted our initiative to avoid." (Telegram 141836 to the White House, August 31; National Archives, RG 59, Central Files 1970–73, POL 27–14 ARAB-ISR)

In an August 31 memorandum to the President, Henry Kissinger explained that, when discussion at the NSC meeting turned to the Middle East, "particular emphasis" would "be placed on future U.S. actions in the face of further evidence of violations of the standstill cease-fire." (Ibid., Nixon Presidential Materials, NSC Files, NSC Institutional Files (H-Files), Box H–029, National Security Council Meetings, NSC Meeting—Middle East 9/1/70) Kissinger addressed the meeting in his memoirs, writing that Nixon "directed that a very strong protest be made in both Cairo and Moscow" about UAR violations and that Israel "be asked to send a representative to the Jarring talks in New York." (*White House Years,* page 591) According to Haldeman's September 1 account of what Nixon told him about the NSC meeting, Kissinger and the President "went at it pretty hard," which Haldeman wrote in the context of the "several long talks" that he and Nixon had that day about "the K[issinger] problem." Nixon told Haldeman to speak with Kissinger and Haig to "get K off of Middle East" and have him "concentrate on Vietnam and Russia." While Haldeman "got a little way with Al," he got "nowhere with Henry." (*Haldeman Diaries: Multimedia Edition,* September 1, 1970) Haldeman recorded in his diaries that "the K problem" stemmed from his ongoing rivalry with Rogers. "He's just obsessed with conviction Rogers is out to get him and to sabotage all our systems and our foreign policy." (Ibid., August 6, 1970) Haldeman added that "K is uptight about the Middle East and is imagining things ... All this really worries P[resident] because it creates doubt about K's reliability on other recommendations, and gets in the way of doing his work. P realizes K's basically jealous of any idea not his own, and he just can't swallow the apparent early success of the Middle East plan because it is Rogers's. In fact, he's probably actually trying to make it fail for just this reason." (Ibid., August 16 and 17, 1970)

157. **Telegram From the Department of State to the Interests Section in the United Arab Republic, the Embassies in the Soviet Union and Israel, and the Mission to the United Nations**[1]

Washington, September 3, 1970, 0309Z.

144257. Watch Officer please convey this message to Chargé Tel Aviv no later than 7 a.m. Tel Aviv time.

---

[1] Source: National Archives, Nixon Presidential Materials, NSC Files, Box 655, Country Files, Middle East, Ceasefire Mideast Vol. I. Secret; Immediate; Nodis. Drafted on September 2 by Sisco, Sterner, and Theodore A. Wahl (NEA/IAI); cleared in INR, J, EUR, the White House, and the Defense Department; and approved by Rogers. Repeated to London, Paris, Beirut, Jidda, Kuwait, and Amman.

1. We now have completed a careful and systematic evaluation of all evidence based on our own means and have concluded that since August 10 (date on which we have reasonable base of evidence from which to operate) there have been violations in the fifty kilometers zone west of the Suez Canal, continuance of which likely to jeopardize ceasefire-standstill and delay indefinitely talks between parties under Jarring's auspices. In these circumstances, we have decided that a strong démarche must be made immediately both to UAR and USSR to bring continuing violations to an immediate halt.

2. Israelis are pressing us to insist on a rollback, which we in turn do not feel is achievable. Nevertheless, in making approach to UAR and USSR we are putting it in terms of rectification of situation, without indicating explicitly how, while at same time making clear that principal objective is to get UAR to stop immediately any further violations.

3. We feel our approaches in Cairo and Moscow would be more effective if for time being, no public confirmation of UAR ceasefire-standstill violations are made. However, in view press reports already out confirming UAR violations, *(Washington Post, New York Times)*, and some editorializing that Administration is in effect covering up violations it may be essential that some brief, low key public statement be made in day or so. We will keep this under active review.

For Tel Aviv:

4. In private discussion Monday,[2] Rabin told Sisco he felt that most helpful thing US could do at this juncture would be to QUOTE clear the air with Israelis UNQUOTE by telling them what our judgment is regarding their charges of violations of the ceasefire-standstill, and what we proposed to do about it. Rabin called again early Wednesday a.m. September 2 to say he very anxious to get results of San Clemente meeting,[3] since if Sisco could give indications of US conclusions and steps being taken, it would be most helpful to PM Meir in getting decision at Thursday Cabinet meeting to send Tekoah back to New York and to proceed with talks.

5. Sisco is conveying following to Rabin today[4] which Chargé is instructed similarly to convey to Foreign Minister Eban immediately:

A. We are satisfied based on all available evidence that UAR has committed since August 10 a number of violations of ceasefire-

---

[2] August 31.

[3] Presumably the September 1 NSC meeting; see Document 156.

[4] Sisco and Rabin met at 10 p.m. on September 2. A report of the meeting is in telegram 144262 to Tel Aviv, September 3. (National Archives, Nixon Presidential Materials, NSC Files, Box 655, Country Files, Mideast, Ceasefire Mideast Vol. I)

standstill agreement. Violations have been of following character: (1) There has been construction between August 10 and 27 that has increased the total number of sites; (2) There have been a number of SA–2 sites which on August 10 were unoccupied which since then have been occupied; and (3) There has been some movement of equipment within the zone.

6. We view these continuing violations most seriously and President has directed that a strong démarche and protest be made to both UAR and USSR with a view to securing immediate stoppage of continuing violations. We will also press for a rectification of the situation, but wish to repeat again candidly and honestly to Israelis that our continuing judgment is we unlikely to be able to achieve a rollback.

7. Our view regarding effect of these violations is that Israel has been put to some disadvantage. We recognize that as a result of these violations Israel's air maneuverability has been restricted, though we hope Israel will recognize that appreciable restriction had already taken place prior to ceasefire when Israeli attempts to suppress certain sites proved unduly costly. Our assessment continues to be that GOI can defeat any combination of Arab forces, and that UAR not in position to mount and maintain sustained attack across Canal permitting it to retake part of Sinai.

8. In order to assure that Israel will not be at any serious disadvantage in event ceasefire-standstill should break down, we are proceeding expeditiously with delivery of anti-SAM package. Moreover, delivery of five Phantoms in September will proceed. We will be in a position to give GOI a specific delivery date in September in next few days. We are ready to proceed on delivery of four A–4's in September as previously scheduled. However, our understanding is that GOI prefers to have us make modifications rather than take the four scheduled for delivery in September unmodified. On this basis, two modified A–4's would be delivered by end of October or early November and five every thirty days thereafter until sixteen are delivered. These deliveries, of course, must continue to be kept in strictest confidence between us.

9. With adoption of Jackson Amendment by Senate,[5] we hope to be able to proceed in firming up details regarding GOI credit needs without too much further delay as we foresee no serious difficulties in House-Senate conference.

10. We feel approaches to UAR and USSR should be more effective if for at least time being no public statement is made regarding our

---

[5] Senator Henry M. Jackson (D–WA) inserted an amendment into a Defense procurement bill, which passed the Senate on September 1, authorizing an unlimited arms-buying credit to Israel. (*Washington Post*, September 2, 1970, p. A1)

judgment that UAR is in violation of ceasefire-standstill. We urge GOI to cooperate to this end.

11. Finally, we hope that GOI will find itself in a position to send Tekoah back to New York and to resume discussions under Jarring's auspices immediately. We feel that such move is in GOI interest since talks are further way to test UAR intentions. In any event, if GOI view that UAR is not interested in proceeding in a serious way in peace talks is confirmed, GOI willingness to explore all possibilities under Jarring's aegis would help place onus on Cairo rather than on Tel Aviv.

12. We want GOI to know that any hesitation on our part in making judgments re violations in days immediately after ceasefire was based not on any doubts of our Israeli friends but rather on our strong desire to draw conclusions based on our own evidence. US hopes that any feelings that have developed that we have doubted Israeli credibility can be made a thing of the past. It only became clear after ceasefire that we were operating from a different intelligence base. Now as a result of close cooperation in surveillance, there is less possibility of any misunderstandings. It was unfortunate, too, that any differences or misunderstandings have been aired publicly. We continue to believe that both of us can work more closely and more cooperatively by concerting together in first instance through diplomatic channels. Finally, regardless of Israeli doubts, and we can fully understand and appreciate difficulties that face Israelis on the firing line. Israel can be assured that US is the one friend in whom it can have continuing confidence. We cannot promise miracles; but we can promise that we will do everything possible through diplomatic channels to stop violations. If results are less than one would hope, we are guarding against that by providing necessary wherewithal, as indicated above.

13. We doing this, of course, on assumption Israel would not itself unilaterally break ceasefire which we would view most seriously.[6]

14. *FOR CAIRO:* You should immediately seek appointment with Foreign Minister Riad to convey following message.

---

[6] Zurhellen met with Eban on September 3 at 9:45 a.m. to convey the information in paragraphs 5A through 13. (Telegram 4801 from Tel Aviv, September 3; National Archives, Nixon Presidential Materials, NSC Files, Box 1156, Saunders Files, Middle East Negotiations Files, June Initiative Vol. IV, August 28–November 15, 1970) On September 6, Eban responded to the U.S. presentations in an "oral paper" to Rogers, in which he said that Israel looked to the United States "as the initiator of the ceasefire and the new stage of the Jarring Mission to use its full influence to secure the restoration of the position as it was when the ceasefire came into force." He also expressed Israel's appreciation for the Nixon administration's expressed intention to deliver an anti-SAM package and fighter jets to Israel. (Telegram 147014 from Tel Aviv, September 9; ibid., Box 655, Country Files, Middle East, Ceasefire Mideast Vol. I)

15. We have not yet received explanation from GUAR concerning specific missile-related activities raised in our August 19 and August 22 approaches.[7]

16. In addition to violations raised on those occasions our evidence on subsequent dates reveals following changes. We are presenting here confirmed information and are leaving out number of sites at which there are suspected activities but which so far have not been confirmed.

17. To recapitulate, following changes have occurred August 10 through 27:

a.	New SA–2 sites constructed:	2
b.	SA–2 sites on which construction continued:	6
c.	SA–2 sites occupied:	12
d.	SA–2 battalions that have been field deployed:	2
e.	SA–3 battalions that have been field deployed:	2

18. In presenting this information you should say this does not include any of the activity claimed by Israel to have taken place August 7–10 period.

19. You should tell Foreign Minister this pattern of activity is matter of serious concern to USG. We must say in all frankness that we are at loss to understand this activity which is at such variance with role his government has played in our joint effort to help Ambassador Jarring promote agreement between the parties on terms of just and lasting peace in Middle East. What possible gain can there be for UAR? GUAR has repeatedly urged that Jarring talks get under way as soon as possible, yet it is clear that principal impediment to this very goal has become UAR's continuing military activities in ceasefire zone. UAR has invested much in success of talks and now is in process of taking onus for jeopardizing both ceasefire-standstill and talks.

20. You should say USG recognized, as we are sure Foreign Minister did, grave risks inherent in continuation of situation prevailing before ceasefire and beginning of Ambassador Jarring's present efforts. Were the ceasefire to fail and those efforts to come to halt, risks would be even greater than before because chances of again achieving whatever has been accomplished in past month would be greatly reduced. Government of United States would not be able to continue to support Jarring discussions and ceasefire, and would see no alternative but to return to conditions prevailing before August 7, unless ceasefire-standstill is strictly observed and continuing violations stopped immediately. These violations greatly restrict our ability to play constructive role in support of settlement since it was clearly understood that nei-

---

[7] See footnote 2, Document 158.

ther side would seek military advantage of any kind in ceasefire-standstill zones while agreement was in effect. Standstill means standstill.

21. You should tell Foreign Minister that you personally reported his view that terms of agreement give UAR right to move missile battalions from one location to another within zone, so long as no new missiles are introduced into zone. Careful reading of text of agreement makes it impossible for us to support such interpretation. Indeed we think it obvious that such movements are contrary to and in violation of military standstill. Moreover, UAR activity is contrary to his assurance that UAR would not construct new sites or introduce any new missiles in 50 km zone.

22. You should tell Foreign Minister that we are raising this serious matter in confidence with him in earnest hope that appropriate action to rectify situation will be taken promptly and we be given full assurance that all violations will stop immediately. In this way, it would become possible for all concerned to devote full attention to peacemaking efforts currently in progress under Ambassador Jarring's auspices.

23. If Riad raises question of UAR charges of Israeli violations, you should say we have raised this with Israeli Government and they assure us that their activity has been limited entirely to maintenance. As we are now raising these matters of violations with the UAR, we will continue doing same on Israeli side.

24. If Foreign Minister again raises question US arms for Israel, you should say US policy continues to be one of restraint. However, we cannot disregard violations of ceasefire/standstill or continuing Soviet supply of arms to the UAR.[8]

25. *FOR MOSCOW:* You should transmit following oral statement to highest possible level Soviet Foreign Ministry September 3.

26. The US Government wishes to raise with the Soviet Government a matter of deep concern. We now have incontrovertible evidence of continuing significant changes in the disposition of missile installations in the ceasefire zone west of the Suez Canal. Not only has there been construction continuing on a number of missile sites, but also construction of new sites where none existed at time of ceasefire. Moreover, a number of SA–2 and SA–3 missiles have been installed since the ceasefire went into effect. These are clearcut violations of ceasefire-

---

[8] Telegram 1859 from Cairo, August 20, reported Bergus's August 19 conversation with Mahmoud Riad, during which the latter said that he did not want to comment on Bergus's presentation until he had an opportunity to study it carefully. (National Archives, Nixon Presidential Materials, NSC Files, Box 1156, Saunders Files, Middle East Negotiations Files, June Initiative Vol. III, August 8–27, 1970) Telegram 1889 from Cairo, August 22, reported Bergus's second approach to Riad, a "firm presentation." (Ibid., RG 59, Central Files 1970–73, POL 27–14 ARAB–ISR)

standstill agreement; they are contrary to Brezhnev's statement re need for honest observance of agreement.[9]

27. The US Government is at a loss to understand this activity, which is at such variance with the role that the Soviet Government has played in our joint effort to help Ambassador Jarring promote agreement between the parties on the terms of a just and lasting peace in Middle East.

28. The US Government recognized, as undoubtedly the Soviet Government did, the risks inherent in a continuation of the situation prevailing before the ceasefire and the beginning of Ambassador Jarring's present efforts. Were the ceasefire to fail and those efforts to come to a halt, the risks would be even greater than before because the chances of again achieving what has been accomplished in the past month would be greatly reduced. The UAR and USSR will have borne the onus for ending the ceasefire and aborting the talks between parties.

29. The Government of the United States must make it clear to the Soviet Government that it may no longer be able to continue to support the Jarring discussions and the ceasefire, unless the ceasefire-standstill is strictly observed and continuing activity stopped immediately. These activities have already seriously undermined our ability to play a constructive role in support of a settlement since, as the USSR knows, it was clearly understood that neither side would seek military advantage of any kind in the ceasefire/standstill zones while the agreement was in effect. Prompt rectification of this situation is essential. Any continuation of these activities will place on the Soviet Union and the UAR the responsibility for a possible resumption of the fighting.

30. *FYI.* Although not part of the above message, you should find way to get across personal suggestion that most useful thing Soviets could do would be to have several sites representing most clear-cut violations moved from zone. We have no desire to take advantage of any such move in public but would find great value in repairing damage to U.S. ability to bring Israelis along in negotiation. In addition, try get across idea that Soviet credibility in Washington also heavily involved in this issue. *END FYI.*[10]

---

[9] See footnote 3, Document 155.

[10] Beam carried out his instructions on the late afternoon of September 3, making his oral presentation to Vinogradov. Beam reported that the Deputy Foreign Minister responded with a "lengthy, repetitive, and largely unyielding reply," but that he said his remarks were "preliminary in nature" and that Beam's statement "would be studied." (Telegram 5076 from Moscow, September 3; National Archives, Nixon Presidential Materials, NSC Files, Box 1156, Saunders Files, Middle East Negotiations Files, June Initiative Vol. IV, August 28–November 15, 1970; printed in *Foreign Relations, 1969–1976*, volume XII, Soviet Union, January 1969–October 1970, Document 201)

31. *FOR USUN:* You should inform Jarring as follows:

A. We are satisfied on basis of our own evidence that there have been numerous violations by UAR of standstill-ceasefire agreement.

B. At same time, we are drawing Israelis attention to great emphasis we place on getting negotiating process started. Accordingly, we are strongly urging Israelis to instruct Tekoah to return forthwith to New York, we hope before upcoming Labor Day weekend.[11]

Johnson

---

[11] Yost met with Jarring on the morning of September 3, after which he wrote that the Special Representative "expressed considerable doubt that, despite our urging, GOI would send Tekoah back to NY before Eban," who had planned to come later that month. If Israel did send him back. Jarring added, he doubted that Tekoah "would be authorized to do more than engage in probing action" until after Eban's arrival. (National Archives, RG 59, Central Files 1970–73, POL 27–14 ARAB–ISR)

---

158. Telegram From the Interests Section in the United Arab Republic to the Department of State[1]

Cairo, September 4, 1970, 1725Z.

2017 1. Here are first personal impressions of hour's conversation Wiley and I had with FonMin Riad tonight. Subsequent telegrams report conversation in detail.[2]

---

[1] Source: National Archives, Nixon Presidential Materials, NSC Files, Box 1156, Saunders Files, Middle East Negotiations Files, June Initiative Vol. IV, August 28–November 15, 1970. Secret; Immediate; Nodis. A note at the end of the telegram indicates it was passed to the White House. All brackets are in the original except "[sure]", added for clarity.

[2] Telegram 2018 from Cairo, September 4, reported that Riad stated that the United Arab Republic was "entitled" to move surface-to-air missiles "from one place to another inside the zone and to replace these missiles with others from outside the zone." Riad also said that U.S. information that the United Arab Republic had violated the cease-fire was incorrect, that it had not "introduced new missiles to the specified zone" and "all existing missiles have been present on the day the cease-fire came into effect." He explained that current UAR activities in the zone represented "maintenance measures" that were "essential for the safety and security of our personnel." (Ibid.) Telegram 2019 from Cairo, September 4, reported Bergus and Wiley's conversation with Riad in detail. (Ibid.)

2. FonMin almost totally repudiated factual data I gave GUAR on September 3.[3] He associated Nasser and General Fawzi with this repudiation.

3. Egyptians extremely agitated by yesterday's statement issued by McCloskey.[4] FonMin said more than once that McCloskey statement was equal to a certificate authorizing Israelis to attack Egypt. FonMin recalled "collusion" of June 5, 1967,[5] and said GUAR confidence in USG which had recently risen to ten percent had now fallen back to zero.

4. I believe Egyptians have been severely shaken by this latest démarche. Mohamed told me that President had been "preoccupied" all night with our charges.

5. Egyptians probably felt only feasible alternative open to them was to deny USG evidence as blandly as possible. They did the best they could, which was not too good.

6. I believe Egyptians (and Russians) have an obsession over danger of another surprise attack from Israel.[6] There was consistent note of fear in FonMin's presentation. My guess would be that they are now in final stages of disposing their defenses in Canal Zone against this contingency.

7. This development imposes cruel necessity on us make some very crucial decisions. I told FonMin that we would not have taken serious step of transmitting to him detailed facts of Egyptian violations unless we were [sure] of our ground. But let us run another check even though we are certain our margin of error could not be more than say 5

---

[3] Telegram 2007 from Cairo, September 3, reported Bergus's conversation with Riad after the former's presentation. (Ibid.)

[4] On September 3, McCloskey read this statement: "Our latest evidence confirms that there have been violations of the cease-fire standstill agreement. We are not going into details. We are taking up this matter with both the U.A.R. and the U.S.S.R. through diplomatic channels. We are continuing to watch the balance closely and, as we have said previously, have no intention of permitting Israel's security to be adversely affected. In the meantime, we believe it is of utmost importance that the talks between the parties under Ambassador Jarring's [U.N. Special Representative Gunnar Jarring] auspices proceed forthwith." (Department of State *Bulletin*, September 21, 1970, p. 326; brackets are in the original)

[5] Reference is to the belief among Arab states that the United States provided air support to Israel during the 1967 war.

[6] On September 5, Soviet officials in Moscow delivered an oral statement to U.S. Embassy officials regarding what they believed was a pending Israeli attack on Egypt: "According to information received by the Soviet Government, the Israeli Air Force intends to carry out on Sunday, September 6, bombings of a number of regions of the UAR in the zone of the Suez Canal beyond the ceasefire line . . . The Soviet Government expects that the Government of the USA will urgently undertake the necessary steps to restrain Israel from the dangerous actions it is planning, the entire responsibility for the consequences of which, under whatever pretexts they might be carried, would fully fall on Israel and the United States." For the full text of the Soviet statement, see *Foreign Relations, 1969–1976*, volume XII, Soviet Union, January 1969–October 1970, Document 202.

percent, and go back to GUAR. Let us maintain and intensify surveillance of UAR territory, and let Egyptians know we doing so.

8. Above all, our overriding interest is peace in this area and it just can't be built without Egypt. UN Res 242 and Jarring Mission are only feasible bases for peace.

Bergus

159. Memorandum From Harold Saunders and Samuel Hoskinson of the National Security Council Staff to the President's Assistant for National Security Affairs (Kissinger)[1]

Washington, September 8, 1970.

SUBJECT

Intelligence on Egyptian and Soviet Cease-Fire Violations

You may well have had enough of the numbers game on Egyptian and Soviet violations of the military standstill. However, we have been making a major effort to reduce this complex intelligence problem to some simple propositions the policy-maker can work from without at the same time losing sight of the limitations involved. The following analysis includes the latest intelligence on the SAMs but it does not reveal the response on the ground to our more recent démarches in Cairo and Moscow. In other words, this memo brings the situation up to the day on which those démarches were made and tries to bridge the gap between the analysts' problems and the policy-maker's needs.

Intelligence Problems

First of all, it is important to note the limitations and problems associated with our intelligence on possible cease-fire violations.

Photographic intelligence can tell us a great deal but, despite all the technical sophistication that goes into this kind of analysis, it is far from being a highly developed art and has some important limitations. There are two main types of problems:

---

[1] Source: National Archives, Nixon Presidential Materials, NSC Files, Box 656, Country Files, Middle East, Mideast Ceasefire, Vol. II. Top Secret; Sensitive. Sent for information. It was sent back to Saunders to answer Kissinger's query; see footnote 2 below. All brackets are in the original except those indicating text that remains classified.

1. To cover adequately the Egyptian cease-fire zone it is necessary to have photography taken with both high and low resolution cameras. The low resolution photography is necessary to cover the whole area but it can only identify the more general features of suspected SAM sites and usually not the more specific details which reveal such important facts as status (i.e. operational or not) and type of occupancy. High resolution photography is therefore taken to make up for these inadequacies, but it covers a much smaller area.

2. Most of our photography is low resolution and taken at a wide angle from the U–2s. In addition to the resolution limitation, the obliqueness of the U–2 coverage is another limitation since the farther away the target is the less detail we are able to identify and even then not all the area can be adequately covered in each flight. We can monitor most developments fairly well up to about 10 miles from the canal but beyond that the quality begins to taper off significantly. We have begun using a new higher resolution camera with the U–2s but again this presents the dilemma of being able to identify more detail but covering less area. Many gaps can be at least partially filled by using a combination of regular high and low resolution U–2 coverage supplemented by periodic high and low resolution satellite coverage.

3. There are a variety of other technical problems. These include such things as weather near the ground, upper atmospheric conditions, terrain features and the condition of the film and its development. The human analytical factor also plays a big role since many of these points are highly debatable even for highly trained photo interpreters.

Our main source of information on the SAMs is photography, but [*less than 1 line not declassified*] also play a role. So far, because of our [*2 lines not declassified*]. This appears to stem as much from budgetary and bureaucratic reasons as from the state of the art and an effort is being made to increase somewhat [*4 lines not declassified*]. As you know, however, [*2½ lines not declassified*].

Conventional clandestinely collected intelligence has so far played a very limited role in detecting possible Egyptian and Soviet cease-fire violations. It could, however, at some future point prove to be important for confirming evidence from other sources and for revealing Egyptian motives and intentions.

There is *one major gap in our intelligence* which prevents us from being able to document all the violations since the cease-fire went in effect on August 7. As you know, we can not be sure of what exactly happened within the Egyptian cease-fire zone in the week or so before and in the two days immediately after the cease-fire went into effect. We know that there was a substantial movement of SAMs toward the canal during this period, but because of the periodicity of our satellite missions we can not prove—even with the evidence supplied by the Israelis—that there were substantial violations. Therefore, for our own working purposes, we have used the results of low resolution U–2 flights (August 9 and 11) plus good quality low resolution satellite photography on August 10 to establish a data base against which we can measure violations since then.

What this adds up to is in substantive terms:

1. Our evidence is best in documenting *construction of new SAM sites*. It is now possible to say that there are some sites on ground where there was no sign of activity at all before the ceasefire.[2]

2. It is harder to identify the *status of completed sites*—whether they are occupied or unoccupied or whether they are occupied by dummy, SA–2 or SA–3 equipment. This means, for instance, that, even though we have recently discovered SA–3 equipment in several SA–2 sites, we cannot say for sure that this equipment was not at these sites on August 10.

3. It is even more difficult to document the *net increase* of [*less than 1 line not declassified*] SAM battalions (particularly SA–2s). This means that it is so far not possible to prove that the Egyptians have done more than rotating units within the standstill zone without increasing their overall equipment strength, although there are fairly good circumstantial indications they have done more than this.

Intelligence Results

One major source of considerable confusion since we began trying to identify Egyptian and Soviet violations of the military standstill has been the *difference between when we have discovered possible violations and when they have actually occurred*. This arises essentially from the technical problem of differing quality and type of photographic coverage and the delay required for careful analysis and re-evaluation of information. Sometimes identification of activity in high resolution photographs of a given site makes it possible to look back at earlier low resolution photos and "see" evidence of activity that had not been noted in the earlier photos. What is most important for diplomatic purposes is when possible violations actually occurred—not when we discovered them. Therefore what follows is an effort to construct a "real time" analysis under the five main categories that were used in making our presentation to the Egyptians.[3] This will be a "real time" picture of the situation the day we made that presentation worked out from the photos taken that day:

---

[2] In the margin, Kissinger wrote: "How many?"

[3] Presumably Bergus's presentation of "factual data" on September 3. See Document 158 and footnote 3 thereto.

1. *SA–2 sites built before the ceasefire but not occupied on August 10.* Counting from August 10 (our reliable data base), it appears that—through September 3—13 or 14 SA–2 missile sites built before the cease-fire were occupied. Two of these sites, however, were evacuated during this period so there has only been a net increase of 11 or 12 pre-cease-fire sites occupied with SA–2 equipment. We do not know how many of these occupied sites are truly [*less than 1 line not declassified*] and high resolution photography of these sites have been inadequate to settle that point. We also do not have sufficient [*less than 1 line not declassified*] whether there has been a net addition to the number of Egyptian SA–2 battalions within the cease-fire zone since the military standstill went into effect, as would be necessary if all the additionally occupied sites had become [*less than 1 line not declassified*]. Our intelligence analysts, however, based on their estimate of the amount of SA–2 equipment presently visible within the cease-fire zone, believe that some of it must have been brought in since August 10 since we do not know of any storage depots for SA–2 equipment within the zone. It is conceded, of course, that some of the newly occupied sites may, as the Egyptians claim, be filled with equipment relocated from previously occupied sites or from unidentified excess equipment stocks, but since only two occupied sites have been evacuated such relocation cannot account for the equipment visible at many of the 13 or 14 newly occupied SA–2 sites. That is difficult to prove, however.

2. *SA–2 sites which did not exist on August 10 and have since been constructed and sites partly built by August 10 on which significant construction has continued since.* The Egyptians have also been constructing and occupying new SA–2 sites within the cease-fire zone. We have clear evidence of Egyptian construction work on twelve SA–2 sites. Work began on six of these sites after August 10 (four since August 27), and, although construction had begun on the other six sites apparently before the cease-fire, they have been finished or nearly finished since August 10. Three of these sites have been occupied.

3. *SA–2 battalions field deployed since August 10.* Two battalions have been field deployed.

4. *SA–3 battalions field deployed since August 10.* As you know, the Soviets are also involved in possible cease-fire violations. As of August 10 we were able to identify five Soviet-manned and occupied SA–3 sites within the cease-fire zone. We suspect that some or all of these may only have been occupied after the cease-fire went into effect (on August 8 and 9) but we cannot prove this. In addition to these suspected Soviet violations, we have evidence of the deployment of two additional SA–3 units in what appears to be a field unit configuration. Both of the deployments were completed after the cease-fire (by August 18), although one of the deployments may have been partially completed by

August 10 and we cannot be sure whether this was actually begun before the cease-fire.

We have also identified four SA–3 units occupying SA–2 configured sites. The SA–3 equipment was only discovered in high resolution photography in late August and the sites were previously identified on the basis of low resolution photography as occupied SA–2s. The SA–3 equipment may, however, have been in the sites since the military standstill went into effect. At least we cannot prove otherwise.

Standstill Violations

As you know, there are considerably different Egyptian (and by inference Soviet) and Israeli/U.S. interpretations of the military standstill provisions of the cease-fire agreement. The official UAR position is that they (and by inference, the Soviet forces in Egypt too) are permitted to rotate and relocate SAM missiles and equipment from site to site, as well as complete the construction of sites where work was initiated prior to the cease-fire. We and the Israelis do not accept this loose interpretation of the terms of the cease-fire and our views were clearly placed on the record shortly after the cease-fire in both Cairo and Moscow. The Israelis, of course, have pinned us down to a very strict interpretation of the standstill.

Most of the evidence of violations that we have acquired relates to the area of difference between the Egyptian/Soviet and Israeli/U.S. interpretations. In fact, *in only six instances do we have evidence of brand new post-August 10 construction starts, all SA–2s. In addition, we have one instance of the field deployment begun and completed since August 10 of an SA–3 unit—an apparent Soviet violation.* Presumably, this Egyptian and Soviet activity would be a violation even by their definitions.

The case against the Egyptians and Soviets is much more impressive, of course, when viewed from our strict interpretation of the cease-fire agreement and based on circumstantial evidence. But we cannot prove all of it sufficiently to make a strong case on the specifics in Cairo and Moscow. All we can really use against the Egyptian and Soviets, even using our interpretation of the cease-fire agreement, are the following violations:

—The Egyptian construction of twelve SA–2 sites, three of which have been occupied. Six of these are the sites started since the cease-fire (three of which have also been occupied) which are violations even by the Egyptian definition. The other six were all begun before the cease-fire but construction had been stopped probably because of Israeli bombing. The present construction on these sites involves substantial improvements and clearly represents an Egyptian effort to take advantage of the cease-fire.

—Both of the Soviet field deployments of SA–3 units can be proved to be violations. As mentioned above, one is even a violation in Egyptian/Soviet terms. The other unit appears to have been partially deployed as of August 10 and then finished by August 18.

Conclusion

Our information ideally could be better, but it seems very clear that the Soviets and Egyptians have continued to erect their missile complex within the cease-fire zone along the Egyptian side of the Canal. This is apparently a continuation, albeit at much less intensity, of the big movement of the SAMs toward the Canal in the days immediately before the cease-fire. We cannot document all of the moves precisely but we have a very good idea, in gross terms, what has happened.

There are limitations to our intelligence but these are not likely to be resolved by the information the Israelis pick up with their almost daily overflights of the Egyptian cease-fire zone [*less than 1 line not declassified*]. The people at DIA, who have worked most closely with the Israelis, have found that their intelligence has not turned up anything important that we have not identified ourselves. In fact, so far as we can determine, we have discovered more possible violations than they have, especially concerning the Soviet-manned SA–3s. Our photography is more precise than theirs.

Because of the nature of this kind of intelligence, we can expect continuing clarifications. This will be especially true when good quality high resolution photography is acquired from satellite coverage. This means that the numbers game will continue as we refine our knowledge of what has happened. We know enough already, however, to be reasonably confident in our protests to the Egyptians and Soviets. Our main interest now is in their response on the ground to our démarches. Intelligence on this aspect should be available later this week. U–2 missions were flown on September 6 and 8 and together—all other things being equal—these may provide us with our first good indications of how the Egyptians and Soviets are reacting. Because of the limitations in this kind of intelligence, it may—if there are more violations of standstill—be a while before we can construct a case good enough to call them on.

160. Minutes of an Ad Hoc Special Review Group Meeting[1]

Washington, September 8, 1970, 3:45–4:25 p.m.

SUBJECT

Middle East

PARTICIPANTS

Chairman—Henry A. Kissinger

State
U. Alexis Johnson
Rodger P. Davies
Joseph J. Sisco

Defense
David Packard
Robert Pranger

CIA
Richard Helms
Thomas Karamessines
David Blee

JCS
Adm. Thomas H. Moorer
LTG John W. Vogt

Attorney General John N. Mitchell

NSC Staff
Harold H. Saunders
Col. Richard T. Kennedy
Jeanne W. Davis

SUMMARY OF DECISIONS

The Defense Department would:

1. provide a delivery schedule for the August 14 package of arms and equipment for Israel;[2] and

2. put together an additional package of equipment for Israel, in response to the President's request of September 4[3] with a brief statement of what it could accomplish, with the understanding that we may decide to recommend against such a package.

Mr. Kissinger: Can we review the non-hijacking aspects of the present situation,[4] particularly two issues: (1) our choices with regard to various combinations of peace talks and a standstill cease-fire; and (2) the President's request, made on Friday, that we prepare an immediate additional arms package for the Israelis. He had wanted to pro-

---

[1] Source: National Archives, Nixon Presidential Materials, NSC Files, NSC Institutional Files (H-Files), Box H–111, Senior Review Group, SRG Minutes Originals 1970. Top Secret; Nodis. The meeting was held in the White House Situation Room.

[2] Israeli and U.S. officials, including Rabin and Packard, discussed the details of the arms package at an August 14 meeting in the Deputy Secretary's office. (Washington National Records Center, ISA Files: FRC 330–75A–1975, Box 20, Israel) The package was approved at the August 12 SRG meeting; see Document 150. The delivery schedule was not found.

[3] Not found.

[4] On September 6, members of the Popular Front for the Liberation of Palestine hijacked the first of four aircraft; see Document 161.

ceed immediately with a new package on Friday, but I suggested we put it through the SRG mechanism and get the views of some of his other advisers. However, we do owe the President a new package. We can put a negative recommendation on top of it if we wish, but we will have to say what we could do if the President should decide he wants to proceed with additional help to Israel.

Mr. Johnson: I assume this would be a larger package than the one already in train.

Mr. Kissinger: This is not completely clear. The President's first reaction was to double the number of aircraft. I suggested that this might not be the thing that was needed and said we would see what kind of package would make sense in the circumstances. We owe him a package, although we can say what we like about the wisdom of it. We cannot *not* give him a package. It might be wise to return to the question of what strategy we are trying to implement rather than merely supply an indiscriminate list of items. The strategy approach might be a good vehicle in which to present the package and our recommendations to the President. (to Sisco) what do you think?

Mr. Sisco: The opening of the GA will give us an opportunity to talk to both the Egyptian and the Israeli Foreign Ministers. We have to try to make the standstill effective. This will involve what amounts to a renegotiation of the standstill cease-fire without characterizing it as such. This renegotiation will have to contain some if not all of the following elements: as a minimum, what the Israelis would consider at least a partial roll-back of the missile advance.

Mr. Kissinger: What does the U–2 photography this weekend show?

Mr. Sisco: It shows a tapering off but continued construction at five sites.

Mr. Helms: We believe the total number of sites has jumped from 106 to 111.

Mr. Saunders: But these photographs were taken before our démarche of last Thursday.[5]

Mr. Helms: Yes, these are Thursday's photographs. We don't yet have a read-out on this week's photos.

Mr. Johnson: Construction at additional sites doesn't necessarily mean additional missiles.

Mr. Helms: Let me give you the exact language because there are so many qualifications. (Reading)

---

[5] September 3; see Document 158 and footnote 2 thereto.

(We are getting the item so as to quote it exactly.)[6]

Mr. Mitchell: Do the Israelis have this information?

Mr. Sisco: No.

Mr. Kissinger: Am I right in reading this as a minimum increase of 13?

Mr. Helms: That is a fair estimate, although we won't know for certain until we see the results of the latest photography.

Mr. Johnson: Is it fair to say that the September 3 photography showed, in gross terms, a leveling off in activity?

Adm. Moorer: We are talking about two different things. The Egyptians are talking about the number of missiles. We are talking about the number of sites. We will never agree on this basis. There is no question that they have increased their capability although, in strict terms, they may not have actually increased the number of missiles. They have certainly violated the spirit of the agreement if not the letter.

Mr. Kissinger: Is it correct to say that there has been an increase in occupied sites in a range between 7 and 20, and probably between 13 and 20?

Mr. Helms: Yes.

Mr. Sisco: The Egyptians say they have not brought in any additional missiles after the cease-fire began. While they could have done it in the first few hours after the cease-fire, it is possible that they already had some missiles somewhere nearby, possibly in storage, or at least not in these positions. We are in a bad position to disprove the Egyptian contention that they did not bring any missiles into the zone after the cease-fire. There is no question, however, that they have improved their position and increased their capability.

Mr. Mitchell: Wasn't this the point of the agreement?

Mr. Kissinger: Under that interpretation, they could be building 50 new sites. We have no way to disprove their contention that they didn't have to move them into the zone.

Mr. Sisco: I see three elements as a basis for renegotiation: (1) a partial roll-back of missiles; (2) a new categorical assurance from the Egyptians that they have not and will not introduce new missiles into the zone; (3) a commitment from the Egyptians that there will not be any movement of missiles within the zone.

The Chief of Israeli Intelligence, General Yariv, believes the Russians and Egyptians probably had a definite plan to distribute these missiles throughout the area by a creeping process. The cease-fire caught them on a short time fuse. You recall they asked for a 24-hour

---

[6] No quote was inserted in the minutes.

delay. The Israelis believe they had not completed their plan and needed a few more hours or days to put it into effect. Interestingly enough, they do not consider that Nasser went into the agreement in bad faith. If there is some roll-back and Nasser gives the two assurances concerning introduction of new missiles and movement of missiles within the zone, Nasser will probably ask for some assurance that the missiles will not be clobbered by the Israelis in a surprise attack. The US cannot guarantee the action of either side, but we can make it clear that there must be an agreement on a standstill if we are to have an agreement on a cease-fire. Both sides could then reaffirm their agreement. At the risk of seeming too optimistic, I think this is do-able over the next two weeks, since I am convinced no one wants the situation to blow up.

Mr. Packard: I agree with this reasoning.

Mr. Johnson: Dayan has invited this kind of approach.

Mr. Sisco: Referring to the proposed package on page 9 of the assistance paper,[7] we cannot give the Israelis full satisfaction since we are not entirely sure what was there at the time of the cease-fire. We could tell them, however, that while we can only get this much of what they want, here is an additional arms package as compensation. This package does not leave them at any disadvantage. It is a very considerable compensation.

Mr. Packard: All evidence indicates that the missile movement was underway before the cease-fire. In present circumstances, the Israelis are better off now with the August 14 arms package.

Mr. Kissinger: But we have sold them that package three times.

Adm. Moorer: They should realize, also, that even if the missiles are withdrawn, it only takes a few hours to restore them.

Mr. Sisco: We must recognize, however, that this is a serious internal political problem for the Israelis.

Mr. Kissinger: Where does the August 14 package stand? Are the items moving?

Mr. Packard: All items are available within 90 days. They are moving.

Mr. Pranger: The contracts have just been signed, but there have been no deliveries as yet.

Mr. Johnson: But we are going ahead on the September planes.

Mr. Pranger: We will begin airshipping the material now that the contracts have been signed.

---

[7] See footnote 4, Document 153.

Mr. Kissinger: In July, the President and the Secretary of State agreed to do something about getting Shrikes to the Israelis.[8] During his recent conversation with Rabin, the President asked General Haig to make sure that the equipment moves.[9]

Mr. Packard: There are some problems, however—for example, they don't have enough aircraft to deliver the Shrikes.

Mr. Kissinger: Could you give us a delivery schedule?

Mr. Mitchell: Have the Israelis complained about deliveries?

Mr. Sisco: Yes.

Mr. Pranger: There was no Defense Department commitment until the end of August.

Mr. Packard: We moved on the package the week after my August 14 discussion with Rabin.

Mr. Kissinger: But the President thinks he ordered it in early July. We do need a delivery schedule.

Mr. Packard: We are moving as fast as possible. You can't just pull these items off the shelf.

Mr. Kissinger: Can we get a recommendation on any additional package? We can, of course, make a negative recommendation.

Mr. Packard: This package (the one attached to the Assistance paper in the book) might be enough. The limiting factors are the numbers of CBU-24s and Shrikes. We have given them 150 CBU-24s. Figuring conservatively, they may use four per site, thus enabling them to take out some 37 sites. Do we want to give them more CBUs? As many as would be required to take out 100 sites? There is another alternative—to give them some 175mm artillery which has a 32-kilometer range. This would give them superiority in artillery across the Canal which they could use to neutralize the nearer sites. Other than that, there isn't much we can do.

Mr. Mitchell: Do we know what they have asked for?

Mr. Kissinger: Friday afternoon the President asked me to call Secretary Laird and tell him to double the package for Israel. I suggested he put the issue into this group.

Mr. Johnson: This could be a part of the philosophy to deter them from further moves in the zone.

Mr. Kissinger: It would both compensate Israel and warn the Egyptians that this is a losing game.

---

[8] Not found.
[9] See Document 151.

Mr. Johnson: If the Egyptians level off their activity, and the present arms package leaves the Israelis in a favorable position, is there a need for an additional package?

Mr. Kissinger: I am prepared to put these considerations in a cover memorandum to the President, but we do owe him a package.

Mr. Packard: I don't think we want to go all the way with Walleyes, etc. We could, however, double the number of missile sites they could handle for about $2 million.

Mr. Sisco: This would be Option 1 on page 5 of the paper. I had understood the number of weapons in the anti-SAM package was minimal in their capacity to suppress missile sites.

Mr. Saunders: They could suppress from 6–10 sites.

Mr. Kissinger: What good are 6–10 sites?

Mr. Packard: That package contains enough ammunition for 35–70 sites, depending on how many are used per site.

Mr. Kissinger: Do you mean 6–10 sites at one time?

Mr. Packard: I mean the number of sites that could be suppressed while you are attacking them. They wouldn't take on 100 sites at once. It would be 6–10 sites in one successful mission.

Adm. Moorer: They would need more for a continuous attrition operation.

Mr. Sisco: If they could take out 6 on one mission, a capacity for one mission is not enough. How much more would they have?

Mr. Packard: Assuming it takes 4 CBUs per site, they would have enough for 37 sites.

Mr. Pranger: The 6–10 figure was used originally because the Israelis said they wanted a one-time capability to suppress the sites around Ismailia. The number was decided on the basis of a one-time strike on sites within the normal bombing range. Now the Israelis do not think this is sufficient.

Mr. Packard: The current package contains many more CBU's than they would need for one strike.

(Mr. Kissinger left the room)

Mr. Pranger: We were very generous for a one-time strike. To double the amounts would give them more than double the capacity.

Mr. Packard: That would be awfully generous.

Mr. Johnson: We are talking about what they could do in one operation.

Mr. Pranger: The figures taken for the planning factor were well above what they would need for 6–10 strikes.

Mr. Packard: (to Mr. Johnson) Let me draw you a picture of the way they could use the elements in the special equipment package and the way in which it would provide them with additional capability. (In an across-the-table conversation with Mr. Johnson, Mr. Packard drew a diagram and described the sequence of an attack. The description was too cryptic to follow without the diagram.)

(Mr. Kissinger returned)

Mr. Packard: The number of sites that could be suppressed is determined by the number of missions flown. They don't have enough planes to attack 100 sites at one time. If we double the number of CBU's and Shrikes, that should be all they need.

Mr. Kissinger: Could we have a package by tomorrow morning, with a brief statement of what it would accomplish. We will then move it to the President.

Mr. Sisco: We should understand the political and psychological aspects of this package—it would be compensation to Israel in a situation where we cannot fulfill the standstill requirement adequately from the Israeli point of view.

Mr. Kissinger: We should meet again tomorrow[10] on this subject— we can tack the discussion onto the next meeting of this group.

---

[10] The Ad Hoc Special Review Group did not meet on September 9.

---

161. Editorial Note

On September 6, 1970, Israel announced it would withdraw from talks under UN Special Representative Gunnar Jarring's supervision due to what an Israeli communiqué described as grave and continuing violations of the cease-fire agreement. (Telegram 1845 from USUN, September 9; National Archives, Nixon Presidential Materials, NSC Files, Box 1156, Saunders Files, Middle East Negotiations Files, June Initiative Vol. IV, August 28–November 15, 1970) Little more than two weeks earlier, on August 24, Jarring had announced at the United Nations that the Governments of Israel, Jordan, and the United Arab Republic had appointed representatives for discussions that were intended to reach an "agreement on the establishment of a just and lasting peace in the Middle East." (Telegram 1734 from USUN, August 24; ibid.) Israel's September 8 communiqué explained: "The strictest observance of the ceasefire-standstill agreement is one of the central elements of the American peace initiative and of the talks under the auspices of Amb Jarring. Therefore, so long as the ceasefire-standstill agreement is not observed in its entirety, and the original situation restored, Israel will not be able to participate in these talks."

In Jordan, the government and the fedayeen were approaching open conflict. On September 2, Kissinger sent a memorandum to Nixon informing him that "Fedayeen-controlled Palestine Liberation Army units attached to the Iraqi Army, the Al Qadissiya Forces" had moved into Amman that day and that regular Iraqi units had "moved into positions alongside Fedayeen units." Jordanian and fedayeen forces had already begun to exchange fire, and the Embassies in Amman and Beirut reported that King Hussein was considering a declaration of martial law. (Ibid., Box 615, Country Files, Jordan, Vol. V) The crisis escalated September 6 to 9 when the Popular Front for the Liberation of Palestine hijacked four airplanes and forced three of them to land at Dawson's Field, an airport 20 miles from King Hussein's palace. By September 16, a full-scale civil war was underway, attracting other regional actors, including Syria, which positioned troops along its border for a possible invasion of Jordan in defense of the Palestinian guerrillas, and Israel, which was ready to support Hussein's regime by force if necessary. The episode ended on September 25 with the government's suppression and dispersal of the fedayeen, an event commonly referred to as "Black September" by Palestinians and other Arabs. Extensive documentation on the Nixon administration's response to the Jordan crisis is printed in *Foreign Relations, 1969–1976,* volume XXIV, Middle East Region and Arabian Peninsula, 1969–1972; Jordan, September 1970.

162. Memorandum of Conversation[1]

Washington, September 18, 1970, 11 a.m.

PARTICIPANTS

U.S. Side
President Nixon
Assistant Secretary of State Joseph Sisco
Brigadier General Alexander M. Haig, Deputy Assistant to the President for National Security Affairs

Israeli Side
Prime Minister Golda Meir
Ambassador Rabin
Political Adviser Simcha Dinitz

Following photographs, President Nixon opened the meeting by stating to the Prime Minister that he was conscious of the difficulties that cease-fire violations had caused Israel. He was not naive, he said, about Soviet motives and actions with respect to the Middle East situation. He pointed out that he had been following the Egyptian–Soviet violations closely, and that when the violations first surfaced he had had General Haig call Ambassador Rabin from San Clemente to inform him that the United States would, in response, increase the military assistance package that we had provided to Israel to combat the new missile threat.

The Prime Minister responded that, in her view, the U.S. response to the Israeli reports of cease-fire cheating was slow, and our initial acquiescence encouraged additional violations. Ambassador Rabin added that while the U.S. had indicated that it would provide additional anti-SAM equipment, the U.S. side had continually reduced the size of the aid package prepared in response to Israeli requests. The

---

[1] Source: National Archives, Nixon Presidential Materials, White House Special Files, President's Office Files, Box 82, Presidential Meetings. Top Secret; Sensitive. The meeting took place in the Oval Office and lasted until 12:32 p.m. (Ibid., White House Central Files, President's Daily Diary) Nixon approved the meeting with Meir on an August 18 memorandum from Kissinger. (Ibid., NSC Files, Box 607, Country Files, Israel, Vol. VI) According to an August 17 memorandum from Kissinger to Nixon, Meir was unwilling to begin negotiations on Middle East peace until she met personally with the President and established a "clear understanding" with him on "1) boundaries; 2) future actions with respect to the Soviets; and 3) future U.S. arms decisions." Apparently, she told Rabin: "It is time for a moment of truth between our governments." (Ibid., White House Special Files, President's Office Files, Box 82, Presidential Meetings) Haldeman wrote that Kissinger "pled" with him to keep Rogers out of the meeting with Meir "on grounds he's most hated man in Israel and would be a disaster." Kissinger offered to "stay out ' if it meant that Rogers would also not attend the meeting, and when Haldeman raised the issue with Nixon, "he agreed." (*Haldeman Diaries, Multimedia Edition*, September 10, 1970)

package on SHRIKE missiles, for example, was cut from the 100 requested down to 40, and the package on CBUs was also reduced.

The President then asked General Haig if this was true. General Haig replied that it was correct that we arrived at a figure of 40 SHRIKE missiles, and that the new anti-SAM package which the U.S. had decided to provide subsequent to the cease-fire amounted essentially to a doubling of the first anti-SAM package.

Ambassador Rabin stated that this new package was still qualitatively and quantitatively inadequate, especially since the Soviets had now introduced a new type of SAM–2 against which the current model of the SHRIKE was ineffective. The Prime Minister added that Israel was aware of a newer production model SHRIKE which would be more effective and which they urgently required.

The President thereupon instructed General Haig to take immediate action to insure that the entire issue was carefully reviewed on a priority basis jointly between the Israelis and U.S. representatives, so that a more responsive package could be developed.[2]

Assistant Secretary Sisco commented that the problem involved not only quantities of weapons, but also the kinds of military assistance that should be given and the strategy which Israel should adopt to best meet the changing threat.

The President then asked about the follow-on military requirements for 1971. Both sides, he said, should work together to develop an appropriate military program for Israel. He instructed General Haig to insure that this was done on a priority basis.

After expressing Israel's gratitude for all the assistance and support which the United States has provided, the Prime Minister described the circumstances under which Israel had accepted the U.S. initiative. The Israeli Cabinet had been split on the acceptability of the U.S. initiative, she noted. In fact, they had decided not to accept the proposal because the U.S. initiative appeared to embrace the so-called "Rogers Plan." But after this decision to reject the U.S. initiative was made, President Nixon's letter arrived urging Israel to accept.[3] On the basis of the President's letter, the Prime Minister was able to assemble a majority of votes; only then did Israel accept the U.S. proposal. As a result of these Cabinet deliberations, the six members of the Gahal Party resigned from the Government. While this was not a critical event, in her view, it was a reflection of the difficult internal situation she faced.

No sooner had Israel accepted the U.S. initiative, the Prime Minister continued, than the other side undertook to violate the provisions

---

[2] See Document 163.
[3] See Document 136.

of the cease-fire by the forward movement of SAM missiles into the cease-fire zone.

The Prime Minister then asked Ambassador Rabin to explain to President Nixon the specific violations which Israel had uncovered. Ambassador Rabin spread three maps on the rug before the President. Using the first of these, he pointed out the situation as Israeli intelligence carried it on August 11. At this time, according to Ambassador Rabin, there were only six SA–2s and two SA–3s in the cease-fire zone. On the next map, which depicted the situation six days later, he pointed out eight SA–2s. Finally, turning to the third map, depicting the situation on September 13, Ambassador Rabin pointed to nine SA–2s within the 30 kilometer zone and 22 more SA–2s within the 50 kilometer zone. He added that there were no additional SA–3s within the 50 kilometer zone, three of which were within the 30 kilometer zone.

Ambassador Rabin stated there were 129 sites now constructed within the cease-fire zone, of which 27 contained units and 27 were dummy positions. The Prime Minister explained that the Soviet-Egyptian tactics involved the constant shifting of missiles between sites.

The Prime Minister then stated that there was strong opposition in Israel to the so-called "Rogers Plan" and the specific border changes which that plan visualized.

President Nixon replied that there was no "Rogers Plan" as such. Prime Minister Meir stated that the real point of contention involved Israel's borders. Israel accepted the formulation that the President himself had stated when he referred to a return to "defensible borders." Anyone who had seen the Golan Heights, she continued, could not expect Israel to relinquish them to the Arabs. She stated that the real difficulty developed in Israel when the preamble of the U.S. initiative was finalized. Israel's problems were not a result of the Arabs but due entirely to the Soviet Union. Russia, she stated, was not concerned with the interests of either the Arabs or the Israelis but only her own interests in expanding Red influence in the Middle East. It was Soviet military equipment and Soviet presence which had charged the situation. Egyptians cannot operate SA–3 missiles. Soviet personnel were interspersed at all levels of decision within the Egyptian military and Soviet pilots had been active over the Canal. In fact, she stated, Israeli pilots had met the Soviets in air-to-air combat, and while she was pleased with the outcome of these engagements, Israel did not welcome confrontations with the Soviet Union.

Ambassador Rabin added that the Soviets had now provided new 8-inch type artillery with greater destruction capability, as well as longer range 152mm guns. The missile complex which had been installed during the cease-fire now extends beyond the East Bank, and the military situation has been drastically changed.

The Prime Minister stated that the strategic situation had changed during the period of the cease-fire. She mentioned that Defense Minister Moshe Dayan, who so many think of as a Hawk, had been at the East Bank several days ago and had told her how wonderful it was to have the guns silenced. It was the Soviet action that caused the problem and not a lack of Israeli goodwill. While the Israelis favor peace in the area, they cannot accept the situation as it now stands nor can they enter into negotiations with a Russian pistol in the form of SAM missiles at their head. The Prime Minister stated that the U.S. did not seem to be as concerned as it should be about the violations, at least initially, and that, in her opinion, the U.S. should now go to the Soviets directly and demand an adjustment of the situation if the negotiations are to continue.

President Nixon pointed out that indeed we had already, quietly through diplomatic channels, made strong démarches to the Soviets.[4] He wanted Mrs. Meir to understand five principal points:

1. The United States Government is under no illusions as to Soviet intent and involvement in the Middle East. He referred the Prime Minister to his statements of September 17 in Chicago in which he clearly recognized Soviet culpability.[5]

2. The U.S. recognized that there had to be some rectification with respect to the forward movement of the Egyptian-Soviet missiles.

3. He wished to reaffirm the U.S. intent not to permit the military balance in the Middle East to be disturbed.

4. The U.S. was prepared to work jointly with Israel in developing an appropriate military package for 1971 which would include aircraft and other military equipment, whether it might be tanks or artillery or whatever was appropriate for the strategy which Israel should adopt.

5. The U.S. recognized Israel's economic problem and their need for additional credits.

The President asked Assistant Secretary Sisco where this particular item stood. Assistant Secretary Sisco replied that the recent passage of

---

[4] See footnote 10, Document 157.

[5] In his memoirs, Kissinger recounted that while speaking at an off-the-record meeting with the editors of the *Chicago Sun-Times* on September 17, Nixon stated that he would respond to Soviet adventures along the Suez Canal. "We will intervene if the situation is such that our intervention will make a difference." Kissinger added: "It was too much to expect that such sensational news could be kept off the record. The *Sun-Times* ran the exact quote in an early edition. Though it was then withdrawn when Ziegler insisted on the off-the-record rule, this only heightened its foreign policy impact." (*White House Years*, pp. 614–615)

the Jackson Amendment[6] would now enable the U.S. to come up with a specific figure and program in Israel's support. He expected to have an overall dollar figure for the President's approval very shortly.

In conclusion, the President stated that the Prime Minister can be assured that all of Israel's requirements would receive "sympathetic consideration." The President then asked Prime Minister Meir what Israel's thinking was on the Jordan situation,[7] saying that he hoped Israel would do nothing precipitously, since it was important that both the U.S. and Israel do nothing which would make King Hussein's position untenable in the Arab world.

The Prime Minister replied that Israel would not move precipitously with respect to the Jordanian situation and preferred to have the King solve the problem himself. Israel had no intention of breaking the cease-fire, she said. The cease-fire would be adhered to by Israel unless it were broken by the other side. She stated, however, that if the Egyptians and Soviets started to move their artillery forward along the Canal under the umbrella of their new missile defense, Israel would move—emphasizing that she wanted the President to be completely apprised of Israel's intentions in this regard. Israel cannot talk now, however, she added; the missile situation had to be corrected.

The President replied that this will take time and that Israel should be willing to discuss the situation.

The Prime Minister stated that the border settlement as formulated by the U.S. was most difficult. Defensible borders had to be the criteria. However, negotiations cannot be conducted with a pistol at Israel's head, and negotiations can only be carried out by equals. This was not true in view of the current Soviet involvement.

The President then asked the Prime Minister to remain with him briefly while the remainder of the party proceeded through the West Portico. The President and the Prime Minister remained in private conversation for approximately 15 minutes.[8]

---

[6] See footnote 5, Document 157.
[7] See Document 161.
[8] No record of this private conversation has been found.

163. Memorandum From President Nixon to Secretary of State Rogers and Secretary of Defense Laird[1]

Washington, September 23, 1970.

SUBJECT

Follow-up Actions with Israel

As a follow-up to my conversation with Prime Minister Meir,[2] will you please assure that discussions take place promptly with Israeli representatives to develop (a) a suitable further package of military equipment to offset the military advantages gained by the UAR in violations of the military standstill and (b) recommendations for Israel's longer term equipment needs in US FY 1971 and 1972. In these discussions, sympathetic attention should be given to Israel's requirements.[3]

A first set of discussions, to be held this week if at all possible under the aegis of the Deputy Secretary of Defense, should be arranged to develop an anti-missile package. The following should be covered in these discussions:

1. The equipment provided to date for use against the surface-to-air missile complex in the UAR should be reviewed as to quantity and quality and possible additions should be identified.

2. Complementary or alternative Israeli strategies for defending the Suez cease-fire line until it is replaced with permanent borders should be discussed (a) in relation to the anti-missile package and (b) with a view to establishing a framework for determining what other additional equipment Israel may need (e.g. artillery, aircraft, armor) over the longer term.

A recommendation on this package with alternatives should be submitted by October 2.[4] Although the contents may overlap, development of this package should not delay immediate preparation of the contingency package in connection with WSAG planning on the current Jordan crisis.

A subsequent meeting should be called to hear a presentation of Israel's longer term equipment requirements. The interagency group that has been used for this purpose in the past, chaired by the Assistant Secretary of State for Near Eastern and South Asian Affairs, should be convened for this presentation.

---

[1] Source: Washington National Records Center, OSD Files: FRC 330–76–0076, Box 8, Israel. Top Secret; Nodis. Copies were sent to Helms and Moorer.

[2] See Document 162.

[3] See Document 167.

[4] See Document 166.

A recommendation on this package with alternatives should be submitted by October 23.

Memoranda containing these recommendations should be forwarded through the NSC Interdepartmental Group for Near East to the Chairman, NSC Senior Review Group by the dates specified.

Richard Nixon

164. National Security Study Memorandum 103[1]

Washington, September 26, 1970.

TO

The Secretary of State
The Secretary of Defense
The Director of Central Intelligence

SUBJECT

Future Options in the Middle East

The President has directed that a review of our options in the Middle East be conducted quickly before resumption of any significant diplomatic activity in connection with efforts to produce a diplomatic settlement.

This review should take into account violations of the military standstill agreement, recent developments in Jordan and Soviet actions.

The President has directed that a memorandum containing the results of this review be submitted to the Senior Review Group by October 8, 1970, through the NSC–IG–Near East.[2]

Henry A. Kissinger

---

[1] Source: National Archives, Nixon Presidential Materials, NSC Files, NSC Institutional Files (H-Files), Box H–175, National Security Study Memoranda. Secret; Nodis. A copy was sent to the Chairman of the Joint Chiefs of Staff. On November 13, Kissinger issued NSSM 105, an addendum to NSSM 103, which asked that a paper be prepared on the status of the U.S. response to a list of Israeli requests for economic assistance. (Library of Congress, Manuscript Division, Kissinger Papers, Box CL–316, National Security Council, National Security Study Memoranda)

[2] An analytical summary of the memorandum is Document 170. The Senior Review Group and the Washington Special Actions Group met in a combined session to discuss the Middle East on October 9; see Document 168.

The Interim Settlement Proposal

165. Editorial Note

United Arab Republic President Gamal Abdel Nasser died of a heart attack on September 28, 1970, at age 52. His Vice President, Anwar al-Sadat, immediately took over as interim ruler, and began sending signals to U.S. officials that he wanted to improve U.S.–UAR relations. During Nasser's funeral on October 1, Sadat met privately with Secretary of Health, Education and Welfare Elliot Richardson, the highest-ranking American official in attendance, and told him that under his direction Egypt planned to become much more closely aligned to the West. (Telegram 2262 from Cairo, October 3; National Archives, Nixon Presidential Materials, NSC Files, Box 637, Country Files, Middle East, UAR) Two days later, in a meeting with Donald Bergus, Chargé d'Affaires in Cairo, Sadat reiterated that he wanted a friendly relationship with Washington. Following his meeting with Sadat, Bergus reported to the Department of State that he "found it hard to believe that this was the same man who had indulged in so much plain anti-American rabble-rousing in public meetings throughout Egypt during the first six months of this year," adding that Sadat stressed his and Egypt's "feeling of friendship" for the United States (Beattie, *Egypt During the Sadat Years,* page 53)

Nixon administration officials questioned whether Sadat would be around long enough to see these promises through. On September 28, Harold Saunders of the National Security Council Staff wrote in a memorandum to Kissinger that while the constitutional successor was Vice President Sadat, "it seems likely that some sort of collective leadership would take over while potential leaders jockey for control." Even more likely, Saunders added, was that "some other military leader would eventually assume the real power since it seems unlikely that a purely civilian leader alone could consolidate control." (National Archives, Nixon Presidential Materials, NSC Files, Box 636, Country Files, Middle East, UAR) On October 12, after the Egyptian National Assembly officially nominated Sadat as President, Kissinger sent a memorandum to Nixon offering his assessment of the new Egyptian President:

"*Why Sadat?*

"As a member of Nasser's original revolutionary group, and because Nasser named him Vice President in December 1969, Sadat brings an aura of legitimacy and continuity to the succession and to the presidency. He lacks, however, Nasser's charisma and as a perennial figurehead in the government with a lackluster record of public service he also lacks widespread respect and authority. Sadat's greatest claim to leadership would seem to rest on his extreme nationalism, his long record of loyal, if unspectacular service to Nasser and to the apparent fact that he is acceptable to both pro-Soviet and more moderate factions.

"Given Sadat's character and background it is unlikely that he achieved ASU endorsement on his own. He fits the general qualifications acceptable to the senior military officers—that the new president be a member of Nasser's original revolutionary group—but there is no evidence that he is the army's man. We do not yet know who specifically backed Sadat but it seems likely that his selection rests upon the support of other influential Egyptian political figures. There are indications that former Vice President and Soviet supporter Ali Sabri may have figured heavily in Sadat's selection as well as the powerful Interior Minister Sharawi Jumah. They may have found Sadat's selection the most convenient way of blocking selection of a stronger rival like the more moderate Zakaria Muhiedin. Others among the top leadership who may have played important roles in the succession struggle include Nasser's shadowy intelligence adviser Sami Sharaf, propaganda chief Haykal, War Minister Fawzi and Foreign Minister Riad.

"Sadat's Supporters

"It is, of course, impossible to determine at this point specifically who will ultimately hold the reins of power in Egypt. So far the military appears to have remained on the sidelines in terms of actually running the government, but it will exert considerable influence, if not a de facto veto, on decisions directly affecting its interests. Sadat may turn out to be more than a front man and as a probable compromise choice will still have some important influence, but the men around him will undoubtedly be more influential than those Nasser kept around." (Memorandum from Kissinger to Nixon, October 12; ibid.)

President Nixon sent Sadat a letter on October 14, writing: "As a leader, President Nasser did much to shape the destiny of his nation and the history of his era. It is significant to us that in his final days, he looked toward the prospects for peace as offered in the United States proposal for a limited cease-fire and for talks between the parties to the Arab-Israeli conflict. We are encouraged by that constructive choice and by your assurances to Secretary Richardson that under your leadership, the United Arab Republic will continue to pursue these goals. The achievement of those goals is among the highest hopes of my country as well." (Ibid., Box 763, Presidential Correspondence 1969–1974, UAR President Anwar Sadat, Vol. I)

166. Memorandum From the President's Assistant for National Security Affairs (Kissinger) to President Nixon[1]

Washington, October 9, 1970.

SUBJECT

Financial Assistance for Israel

You will recall from your talk with her that Prime Minister Meir has requested $500–600 million in financial assistance.[2] Ambassador Rabin has since written to Secretary Laird [Tab C] pinpointing that figure at $519 million in FY 1971 (including $119 million that seems to be dying with the Foreign Military Sales Act).[3]

In purely economic terms, there is room for some argument over whether that much assistance from the U.S. is justified at a time when you are making an extraordinary effort to hold our budget deficit down. The Israeli economy continues to grow at a rate in excess of 12%, and the corrective fiscal policy measures taken by the Israeli government have been unsuccessful in coping with the widening foreign exchange gap. Therefore, while the main Israeli financial problem is caused by defense purchases, civilian imports continue unchecked.

On the political side, however, there is of course strong argument for meeting a substantial portion of Israel's requirement. The main point is the need to maintain continuing support for Israel's military position if Israel is to be in a position of strength from which to negotiate.

There have been *two issues*—the exact level of assistance and the terms on which it should be offered.

There are two recommendations on the *level of assistance:*

1. *$400 million* is the figure that can be fully justified as covering all equipment the U.S. has committed to date. Mr. *Weinberger* recommends this figure [Tab B]. He feels that letting Israel pay cash for purchases beyond this level would put the Administration in a position to argue with the Congress that Israel would be tightening its own belt at the same time. Israel with its 12% growth rate and rising civilian imports has not done this. If more were needed for purchases later this year an additional appropriation could be requested. The *Treasury Department* concurs in recommending this $400 million option. In terms of bud-

---

[1] Source: National Archives, Nixon Presidential Materials, NSC Files, NSC Institutional Files (H-Files), Box H–219, National Security Decision Memoranda. Secret. Sent for action. Tabs A–C are not attached. All brackets are in the original.

[2] See Document 162.

[3] The law, passed in 1968, separated foreign military sales from the Foreign Assistance Act of 1961.

getary impact, this option would produce an estimated $130 million increase in FY 1971 outlays.

2. *$500 million* is the figure recommended by Secretary *Rogers* and concurred in by Secretary *Laird* [Tab A].[4] Their arguments are:

—It will be better to cover all Israel's probable needs for this year in one appropriation request. The Israelis will see it as ungrudging support. It is better to take the heat in the Arab world just once, and now is as good a time as any with the UAR on the defensive as a result of standstill violations.

—Israel will need the full $500 million and probably more. If the limit is set at that figure now, we can insist that Israel cover the rest as its austerity measure.

—This is the right time tactically to put this to the Congress.

The budgetary impact of this option would be to produce an estimated $150 million in FY 1971 outlays.

There are two recommendations on the *terms of assistance:*

1. *7½%, 20-year repayment, 5-year grace period.* The interest rate—essentially the same as offered under the Foreign Military Sales Act—would avoid setting the precedent of a concessionary rate for a country with a per capita GNP higher than Italy's. The long repayment period and the grace period would recognize Israel's balance of payments problem. This is *Mr. Weinberger's recommendation.*

2. Provide the *first $350 million at 3%, 5-year grace period and 20-year repayment;* provide the *remaining $150 million at 7½% with 10-year repayment* (Foreign Military Sales Act terms). This is the recommendation of Secretaries *Rogers and Laird.*

Whichever level and whatever terms you approve, the decision would be communicated to the Congress as an appropriations request under the Jackson Amendment to the Defense Procurement Act.[5] Since this comes out of a different series of committees from the military assistance appropriations, Secretary Rogers proposes moving this request before Congress recesses for the pre-election period. It is important to Israel to have this appropriation because some $200 million in payments fall due before the end of the year.

Recommendation: That you authorize an appropriations request for $500 million on the concessionary terms recommended by Secretaries Rogers and Laird.[6]

---

[4] A copy of Rogers's September 26 memorandum, entitled "U.S. Financial Assistance to Israel," is in the Washington National Records Center, OSD Files: FRC 330–76–0076, Box 8, Israel. Laird concurred on that memorandum.

[5] See footnote 5, Document 157.

[6] Nixon approved the recommendation. See Document 171.

167. Memorandum From the President's Assistant for National Security Affairs (Kissinger) to President Nixon[1]

Washington, October 9, 1970.

SUBJECT

Anti-SAM Package for Israel

Following up your instructions,[2] Mr. Packard, General Ryan and their specialists met with the chief of Israel's air force and General Dayan's deputy September 28–30 to discuss the equipment Israel had requested for possible use against the missile complex in the UAR.

The result of these discussions was the package described below (and in detail in Mr. Packard's memo at Tab A).[3] The anti-missile equipment would total $55 million. Four C–130 transport aircraft would add $20 million, and reconnaissance drones—if technical arrangements could be worked out—would add $15 million more.

Ambassador Rabin has expressed general satisfaction with the package that Mr. Packard has recommended.[4] He seems satisfied that where Israel was not given all it asked for it is because the U.S. has legitimate requirements of its own that must be met first or because equipment to provide the capability Israel requested is still in the research and development stage.

Before you review the details, there is one broad issue that you will want to be aware of. It is not an argument against approving the package; it is a point which should be understood about its limits.

The judgment of most of our weapons specialists is that this package—which includes almost all of our most sophisticated equip-

---

[1] Source: National Archives, Nixon Presidential Materials, NSC Files, NSC Institutional Files (H-Files), Box H–219, National Security Decision Memoranda. Top Secret; Nodis. Sent for action. All brackets are in the original.

[2] See Document 163.

[3] Packard's October 3 memorandum to Nixon (Tab A) is attached but not printed. Entitled "Follow-up Actions with Israel," it recommended that the United States furnish Israel with the most effective equipment available and included a list of weapons that could and should be provided and a list of those that could not and should not be provided.

[4] In an October 5 memorandum to Kissinger, Haig wrote: "I have spoken to Ambassador Rabin and got the distinct impression that the Israelis are delighted with the outcome, although they would like to have the two tankers mentioned in Packard's memorandum as well as one or two other pieces of electronic gear. On balance, however, it is obvious that the Defense response has been forthcoming and constructive and one which should go a long way to alleviate residual problems with Israel." (National Archives, Nixon Presidential Materials, NSC Files, Box 608, Country Files, Middle East, Israel, Vol. VII)

ment—will not prevent losses which would be significant to Israel's limited supply of pilots and planes and will therefore not enable the Israeli Air Force to attack continuously across the Canal in the missile zone. These judgments have been discussed openly with the Israelis. The Israelis discount them, perhaps because they have not had experience with this equipment. There remains the danger, therefore, that they may be drawn into attacks on the basis of loss estimates which may be over-optimistic.

There is little more to do now than to note this problem. In the slightly longer run, however, some limited research and development work could produce an improved capability for our forces and theirs. Mr. Packard is exploring these possibilities.

The Package

Mr. Packard has divided the list of Israeli requests into the following categories in making his recommendations:

1. *Items which he recommends should be approved in principle and provided in the full quantities requested by Israel or (in a few instances) in the numbers available.* [Tab B of Mr. Packard's memo.]

a. Those items *for approval in the quantities requested* include cluster bombs, SHRIKES for use against the old SA-2, WALLEYE munition providing pinpoint accuracy from standoff position), a variety of bombs and mines, air-to-air missiles, some jamming equipment.

b. Those items *for approval in less than the quantities requested* include mainly four types of very sophisticated jamming equipment. Mr. Packard says that providing more than he recommends would delay equipping of USAF aircraft. There is one other item in this category—an advanced version of the SHRIKE usable against the new SA-2. Mr. Packard says providing more than recommended (20 of 100 requested) would draw U.S. supply below an acceptable level.

2. *Items requested which Mr. Packard recommends not be provided for special reasons.* These include:

a. Two kinds of bombs that could be launched from stand-off positions. Mr. Packard has approved the WALLEYE which has this capability but recommends against these two principally because the USAF is short of them in Southeast Asia.

b. An advanced SHRIKE for use against the newest SA-2. This is just now entering the USAF inventory.

c. One new jammer which the USAF has only in limited quantity represents our most advanced technology which Defense recommends not be subjected to compromise.

d. REDEYE missiles. These are man-carried air defense missiles. Defense is much concerned that our introducing them in Israel could induce the USSR to introduce their comparable weapon in Southeast Asia against our helicopters. They also argue that Israel's problem now is not air defense.

e. RB–57 aircraft is not recommended because it would be too vulnerable in the dense UAR/USSR missile complex.

3. *Items on the Israeli list which are still in research and development and not in production.* Four jammers fall in this category.

4. *One item which is not recommended for political reasons* is the lease of 2 KC–97 L tankers for air-to-air refueling. This would give Israel the capacity for extensive deep penetration raids. It is not needed for raids in the Canal missile zone. Defense recommends holding this request in abeyance for the time being.

The above has been described in some detail to give you a concrete sense of what has gone into this package. Most of those in State and Defense and on my staff who have been involved—as well as Ambassador Rabin—feel this is a responsive package that would serve the political purpose of compensating Israel for the UAR gains as a result of the standstill violations.

Political Considerations

In reviewing this package, you should be aware of these political points in Mr. Packard's cover memorandum:

1. Mr. Packard says it was clear in his discussions with the Israelis that the military representatives at least do not favor beginning peace talks without a SAM rollback. The new UAR leadership seems unwilling to draw back any of its missiles or to extend the cease-fire indefinitely without some talks. If an impasse develops, Israel has made clear its intention to attack all the missile sites across the Canal whether or not the U.S. approves. Defense doubts Israel could succeed in forcing a Soviet pullback and points out the danger of Soviet escalation. Mr. Packard's specialists suggested other strategies but the Israelis were not overly interested.

2. Mr. Packard recommends:

a. That the same conditions be attached to this as to the first antimissile package (i.e. Israel would not unilaterally break the cease-fire with this equipment or use it beyond a 50 km. zone across the Canal.)

b. That Israel agree to begin peace talks without a total missile rollback.

The State Department agrees with Mr. Packard's recommendations on the equipment package but not with his recommendations for political conditions. State would not recommend coupling this package with a request to Israel that it drop its insistence on a missile rollback and agree to begin participation in the Jarring talks. As State sees it, the purpose of this package is to fulfill our past assurance that we would do what we could to see that Israel did not suffer a military disadvantage as a result of its agreement to the cease-fire under the June peace initiative.

State earlier concurred in the condition that this equipment not be used to break the cease-fire.

Recommendations[5]

1. That you approve the equipment package Mr. Packard recommends as described above and in his memo [Tab A].

2. That no new political conditions be attached and that the question of conditions for beginning the talks be dealt with in the NSC system in the context of the review of future options already ordered.

3. That earlier conditions on use of the equipment—not to be used in breaking the cease-fire unilaterally and not to be used beyond the 50 km. zone—be applied to this package.

---

[5] Nixon approved all three recommendations.

168. Minutes of a Combined Senior Review Group and Washington Special Actions Group Meeting[1]

Washington, October 9, 1970, 2:40–3:10 p.m.

SUBJECT

　Jordan

PARTICIPANTS

　Chairman—Henry A. Kissinger

　State
　U. Alexis Johnson
　Talcott Seelye

　Defense
　David Packard
　G. Warren Nutter
　James H. Noyes

　CIA
　Lt. Gen. Robert E. Cushman
　David H. Blee

　JCS
　Gen. William Westmoreland
　Lt. Gen. John Vogt

　NSC Staff
　Col. Richard Kennedy
　Harold Saunders
　Jeanne W. Davis

SUMMARY OF DECISIONS

It was agreed to:

1. transfer responsibility for consideration of longer-term economic assistance to the Under Secretaries Committee;[2]

2. send a survey team to Amman[3] to discuss with the King the organization of his military forces, and reexamine the two military assistance packages (the $40 million and $23 million) in the light of these discussions;

3. instruct Ambassador Brown[4] to discuss with the King certain financial questions particularly with regard to payment for additional military assistance;

4. ask Brown for his estimate[5] of King's ability to preserve a peace settlement;

---

[1] Source: National Archives, Nixon Presidential Materials, NSC Files, NSC Institutional Files (H-Files), Box H–114, Washington Special Actions Group, WASG Minutes (Originals) 1969 and 1970. Top Secret; Nodis. The meeting was held in the White House Situation Room.

[2] NSC working group of Cabinet Under Secretaries that produced studies for and made recommendations to the National Security Council.

[3] See footnote 4, Document 191.

[4] In telegram 167542 to Amman, October 10. (National Archives, Nixon Presidential Materials, NSC Files, Box 616, Country Files, Middle East, Jordan, Vol. VI)

[5] Not found.

5. ask Brown to estimate the longevity of the King in connection with the arms package and the impact of the package on the preservation of a moderate government.

Mr. Kissinger: I thought we might have a rundown on Jordan—where we go from here on. (to Gen. Cushman) Could you give us a report on the situation?

Gen. Cushman: The King and the Army appear to be ahead, at least for the short term. They have made a dent in the Fedayeen capability to take over the Government, but not necessarily in their capability for terrorist or guerrilla activities. The Arab Commission[6] has had considerable success in getting the Fedayeen out of the cities.

Mr. Kissinger: Is that a result of the Commission's talking or the weakness of the Fedayeen?

Gen. Cushman: Both.

Mr. Kissinger: If it is not a result of Fedayeen weakness, why would they move out?

Mr. Seelye: Partly the effect of the Arab meeting. Fatah is committed to the cease-fire because of the Nasser mediation.[7]

Gen Cushman: They are still operating under the Nasser influence. Also, Arafat gained recognition by the Arab countries as the head of the Fedayeen movement. The more radical Fedayeen, of course, will not like this. However, in the short term, the King is in a better position than he was before the troubles. There is some question of the loyalty of the Palestinians, given the reports of high casualties, but we think they will probably cool down.

Mr. Johnson: We are getting good stories from Amman that the casualties were not as high as originally thought.

Mr. Kissinger: Do we have an estimate?

Mr. Seelye: About 4500 all together, with 500–1000 killed.

Mr. Kissinger: How many of these were guerrillas?

Mr. Seelye: We don't know; some civilians got caught in between.

Mr. Kissinger: The artillery can't be very good since they were reported to be firing directly into the refugee camps.

Gen. Cushman: But they were all dug in.

Mr. Kissinger: They were expecting it?

---

[6] The inter-Arab body that oversaw adherence to the provisions of the Cairo Agreement that ended the conflict between Jordan and the fedayeen at the end of September.

[7] A summit meeting of Arab leaders in Cairo, hosted by Nasser, negotiated the September 27 cease-fire that ended the Jordan crisis. See *Foreign Relations*, 1969–1976, volume XXIV, Middle East Region and Arabian Peninsula, 1969–1972; Jordan, September 1970, Document 303, footnote 2, and Document 330.

Mr. Seelye: Yes. Many of them had evacuated in expectation of trouble.

Gen. Cushman: There is no complacency, but the King is in a better position than when he started.

Mr. Johnson: We agree.

Mr. Kissinger: Is there any estimate that the cease-fire might break down in the medium-term future?

Mr. Seelye: Yes, I think there is a good possibility that it will break down once the peace team leaves in two or three weeks. It is particularly likely if the Fedayeen are not withdrawn from all cities. They are still in two or three of the northern cities.

Mr. Kissinger: What do they do with them—put them in camps?

Mr. Seelye: Yes, the Jordanians plan to deploy them to the west in camps.

Mr. Johnson: They would be sandwiched between Jordanian units.

Mr. Kissinger: How will they react to this as an indefinite future?

Mr. Seelye: They won't like it.

Gen. Cushman: It is hard to say whether the Fedayeen will turn their attention to Israel or will continue to fight the Jordanian Army. The more radical elements may continue to fight the Army.

Mr. Kissinger: Will they be permitted to turn to Israel?

Gen. Cushman: That is part of the agreement.

Mr. Packard: The key question is whether there are any viable solutions to the Palestinian question.

Mr. Kissinger: I agree absolutely—this is the key question. The President has issued a NSSM calling for a strategy paper.[8]

Mr. Saunders: The IG is meeting on this paper this afternoon.[9]

Mr. Seelye: The King is now talking in these terms.

Mr. Kissinger: The problem of the Palestinian identity, and how to use it, must be addressed.

Mr. Packard: A lot of work has been done on it, but it has not been brought into focus.

Mr. Johnson: We are doing that in this paper.

Mr. Kissinger: Is it our estimate that the King is in a position to make an agreement which he can enforce?

---

[8] Document 164. For an analytical summary of the paper, see Document 170. For an analytical summary of the paper that deals entirely with the Palestinian question, see Document 176. For the Review Group meeting that considered the Palestinian question, see Document 177.

[9] No record of this meeting has been found.

Mr. Seelye: We have passed the buck to Ambassador Brown on that and have asked for his estimate.

Gen. Cushman: We believe that for the next month or so the King could defeat the Fedayeen if they resorted to force to stop the cease-fire.

Mr. Kissinger: What if they simply violate the cease-fire? Will the King be able to force his will on the Fedayeen if, by doing so, he will be protecting Israel?

Gen. Cushman: Yes, over the next month or two. Many Palestinians are fed up with the Fedayeen and will not support them if they break the cease-fire.

Mr. Kissinger: I doubt if even Joe Sisco can get an agreement in a month.

Mr. Seelye: I think the King might well continue on the path of negotiations if the "silent majority" of Palestinians continue to support him. We had a definite indication earlier that the majority of the Palestinians wanted a peace settlement. It depends on how many of the Palestinians still favor a settlement.

Gen Cushman: If the cease-fire holds for a month or two, there is a question of the degree to which the Fedayeen could rebuild their strength through help from Syria and Iraq.

Mr. Kissinger: But aren't they being moved away from Syria and Iraq.

Mr. Seelye: Supposedly.

Mr. Kissinger: I saw a cable on the trip that indicated the U.S. and the British were assessing the situation differently.

Mr. Seelye: The British have changed their original position. They are now talking in terms of the King's survival, even about the possibility of providing military assistance, which they have never done before.

Mr. Johnson: (to Mr. Kissinger) I think that is the result of your visit.[10]

Mr. Kissinger: It was partly the conversations with Home, but was also the fact that he was greatly impressed by Hussein at Nasser's funeral.

Gen. Cushman: Nasser, of course, was on the side of the King in a peace settlement. The absence of Nasser now creates another unknown factor.

---

[10] Nixon and Kissinger met with Prime Minister Edward Heath at Chequers in England on October 3. The record of their conversation is printed in *Foreign Relations, 1969–1976*, volume XLI, Western Europe; NATO, 1969–1972, Document 329.

Mr. Kissinger: We have also the operational issues with regard to military assistance, relief, and longer-term economic assistance. What is the military assistance situation?

Mr. Packard: We have authorized 20 airlift sorties of ammunition from their priority list. We have two flights a day going into Dawson Field.[11] We have two problems when we consider the next step: what the Jordanians really need, and how it will be paid for. We can work out the rest of equipment, but the financing is another question. We are asking for $30 million in the supplemental. We can sell for cash for 120 days and then overlook non-payment for awhile, but not indefinitely. Someone should talk to the King and find out what he can do in this regard.

Mr. Kissinger: We have two separate packages: the $40 million artillery package plus an additional $23 million for post-crisis assistance.

Mr. Packard: $3 million worth of the $40 million package has already been shipped. The $22.8 million is a new request.

Mr. Kissinger: Is this essentially the contingency package we put together during the crisis week?[12]

Mr. Saunders: It goes beyond that. The contingency package is closer to the 20 airlift sorties of ammunition.

Mr. Packard: The King wants more mobility. He wants tanks and armored personnel carriers.

Gen. Westmoreland: The $23 million package includes $8 million in ammunition, howitzers, trucks, 44 APC's, 26 tanks, and half a million in small arms, and $1 million in small arms ammunition. We have no problems in supply. The more fundamental question is whether this package provides for the type of force the King needs in the present circumstances. In the $40 million package, he had asked for 100 automated AA weapons and 248 artillery pieces. This is far more artillery than he needs under present circumstances.

Mr. Packard: I think that we should discuss this with the King before we make final deliveries on the $40 million package in view of the change in circumstances.

Mr. Johnson: I agree.

Mr. Saunders: Only $3 million of the $40 million package has been shipped.

Mr. Kissinger: Who put together the $23 million package?

---

[11] An airport in northern Jordan, 20 miles from King Hussein's palace.

[12] See *Foreign Relations,* 1969–1976, volume XXIV, Middle East Region and Arabian Peninsula, 1969–1972; Jordan, September 1970, Document 303.

Mr. Seelye: The Jordanians requested it in several batches through the Defense Attaché.

Gen. Westmoreland: There is a ship at sea now with 12 8-inch howitzers and 155 tubes on board. We had planned to send 155 SPC's by water in November. Very little of the $40 million package is enroute.

Mr. Kissinger: Are you suggesting that we go ahead with the $23 million package and reexamine the $40 million package?

Gen. Westmoreland: No, we should look at both.

Mr. Kissinger: Would this be acceptable to the King?

Gen. Westmoreland: The King has asked for a survey team to look into his needs. He is having second thoughts about the $40 million package.

Mr. Seelye: He was worried about Israeli air raids when he asked for the $40 million package. Now he wants equipment to make him more effective against the Fedayeen and against Syria and Iraq.

Mr. Johnson: The King is taking a new look at the kind of force he needs. Sending the survey team would be a logical next step. We also have to talk to him on finances. The King could help out, given his strong reserves position. If he could supply $11 million by January 1, this would carry us until we can, hopefully, get a supplemental. This should be feasible for the King. We have the draft telegrams instructing Brown to offer the survey team and to talk to the King on financing.

Mr. Packard: We could continue the ammunition shipments which would give him some replenishment.

Mr. Kissinger: Is the survey team necessary? Couldn't we analyze the problem here and put together a package just as well?

Gen. Westmoreland: I don't think that would be psychologically sound or practical. The Jordanian Army has good officers. They would take exception to our telling them what they need without consultation.

Mr. Kissinger: While we are getting the answer from Ambassador Brown on the King's ability to enforce peace, let's also get his estimate on the longevity of the King in connection with the arms package. We don't want to find ourselves arming the Fedayeen if they should take over the Jordanian Army. While we are quite receptive to the King's request, our receptivity must be affected by an estimate of his longevity. I understand, of course, that his longevity will be affected by size and type of our assistance package.

Mr. Seelye: If the King goes, it does not necessarily mean the Palestinians will take over.

Mr. Kissinger: When I referred to the King I meant the moderate government structure.

On the relief operation, are we all agreed with the relief phase should end toward the end of October? Otherwise, relief seems to be in good shape.

All agreed.

Mr. Kissinger: What about long-term economic assistance? (to Mr. Johnson) I would propose we shift some of these operational items to the Under Secretaries Committee.

Mr. Johnson: The King's long-term economic needs depend heavily on the degree to which the Libyan and Kuwaiti subsidies[13] are restored.

Mr. Seelye: The Libyans probably will not restore their $25 million subsidy, but we hope the Kuwaiti will restore their $40 million subsidy. The Saudi Arabian subsidy is still okay.

Mr. Kissinger: If the Kuwaiti are forthcoming, will there be a $25 million gap or have new gaps developed?

Mr. Seelye: The existing subsidies are based on a normal situation. The reconstruction period will bring new needs. We are thinking about the IBRD and using some PL–480 funds.

Mr. Kissinger: We need a coherent program.

Mr. Seelye: We are working on it.

Mr. Kissinger: This is not a crisis situation and I think we should shift responsibility to the Under Secretaries Committee. (to Mr. Saunders and Col. Kennedy) Let's get a piece of paper which transfers long-term economic assistance to the Under Secretaries Committee. We will get the estimate from Brown about the impact of the operation on the ability of a moderate Jordanian government to preserve the peace; also an estimate of the impact of the arms package on a moderate government. We should also send the telegrams on the survey team and on the financial discussions with the King.

Mr. Johnson: We will get them out right away.

---

[13] Libya, Kuwait, and Saudi Arabia established a fund in 1967 after the Arab-Israeli war to assist in the economic recovery of the United Arab Republic and Jordan. Kuwait and Libya suspended their annual subsidies to that fund in protest of the Jordanian Army's treatment of the fedayeen during the crisis in September.

169. Memorandum From the President's Assistant for National Security Affairs (Kissinger) to President Nixon[1]

Washington, October 11, 1970.

SUBJECT

U.S. Position on Mid-East Standstill violations this week

I understand that the State Department is considering taking a position in Secretary Rogers' talks with Eban,[2] Riad[3] and Gromyko[4] this

---

[1] Source: National Archives, Nixon Presidential Materials, NSC Files, Box 656, Country Files, Middle East, Ceasefire Mideast Vol. II. Secret; Nodis. Sent for action.

[2] Rogers met with Eban on October 13 for about an hour. The Secretary asked Eban what kind of rectification of the cease-fire violations he thought could be achieved since "total rectification standstill violations did not seem possible." Eban responded: "we will look at what they suggest and then we will see," adding that "what was necessary was that US and Israel press for rectification." Rogers also asked Eban whether he thought that Israel should invest its energy in reaching a peace settlement with the United Arab Republic or simply keep the cease-fire status quo while waiting for "something to happen in long run." Eban chose the latter but "reiterated Israel wanted keep ceasefire, keep its options open, clarify principles of settlement, and try not to go back and lose ground." (Telegram 169237 to Tel Aviv, October 14; ibid., Box 1156, Saunders Files, Middle East Negotiations Files, June Initiative Vol. IV, August 28–November 15, 1970)

[3] On October 15, Rogers met with Foreign Minister Mahmoud Riad for almost two hours at the Waldorf-Astoria in New York, with other U.S. and UAR officials present. In response to accusations of cease-fire violations, Riad said that "no one in his country is prepared to remove any missiles from zone." He added that his government would even add missiles—what he described as defensive weapons—to the area because it was within his country's right to defend itself. He also commented that he would "raise whole question" in the UN General Assembly "because for three years Arabs had been trying to get SC Resolution 242 implemented without any success." Rogers described the conversation as "cordial and restrained," with neither side proposing solutions to overcome the cease-fire impasse. (Telegram 2504 from USUN, October 16; ibid.) According to telegram 2686 from USUN, October 24, Rogers and Riad met again on the morning of October 23 for a follow-up discussion. (Ibid.)

[4] Rogers met with Gromyko on October 16 and discussed the Middle East for a "full hour, with no give on either side." The Soviet Foreign Minister argued that since the Soviet Union was not party to the cease-fire agreement, it was not responsible for violations. Rogers countered that the United States held the Soviet Union responsible for the violations along with the United Arab Republic because they "could not have taken place without knowledge and complicity and probable participation of Soviet Union." In response to Gromyko's proposal of *"washing out past difficulties,"* that the cease-fire be extended for a *"limited period,"* and that Jarring, bilateral, and Four Power talks be resumed or continued, Rogers said that the United States could not move forward *"without some rectification* of the situation that has resulted from violations of the ceasefire standstill." (Telegram Secto 15, October 16) Rogers and Gromyko met again on October 19, but ended the meeting with the Secretary's conclusion that no compromise between the United States and the Soviet Union was possible at the time and that the next step was the Soviet-UAR pursuit of the issue in the UN General Assembly. (Telegram Secto 33. October 19) Both telegrams are attached to an October 20 memorandum from Kissinger to Nixon summarizing the meetings, printed in *Foreign Relations*, 1969–1976, volume XIII, Soviet Union, October 1970–October 1971, Document 19.

week that would begin exploration of a plan for partial rectification of the standstill violations in the UAR. Secretary Rogers has not agreed to this yet, but he sees Eban Tuesday morning and I felt you should have a chance to make your views known before then.

The idea being discussed in State is that Secretary Rogers would explore (not propose) with Eban and Riad the following plan: The UAR would remove missiles (but not raze sites) from a zone 20 kilometers west of the Suez Canal cease-fire line but be allowed to redeploy them to sites elsewhere in the 50 kilometer standstill zone. This would permit Israel some rollback. (As of the last firm readout of photography there were 23 operationally equipped SAM sites within 25 kilometers of the Canal, 14 of them SA–3, at least half of the 23 were within 20 kilometers of the Canal.) But it would also permit the UAR to say that it had removed "not one missile" from the standstill zone.

The argument being made for at least exploring an approach like this tentatively is based on some reports that Israel would settle for a face-saving way to put the standstill violations behind them and get on with the talks. The argument further holds that this moment with the foreign ministers in New York must be seized to get the talks started or the cease-fire will gradually deteriorate and hostilities will begin again at a much more sophisticated level with the USSR more heavily involved than ever. The momentum gained over the summer will be completely lost.

The argument against this approach, however, seems compelling. The central point is that it would put us—the aggrieved party—in the position of seeking a way to cover up for the transgressors. The U.S. would be suggesting a way to cover up Soviet and Egyptian violations of their understanding with us on the standstill. As Aron and others pointed out to me in Paris,[5] the hesitant way we dealt with the initial violations in August probably gave the USSR an unintended signal that the U.S. was prepared to close its eyes to violations and, in effect, encouraged them to continue their expansion of the missile complex. To try now to find a cover-up would be to repeat that signal. It would also undercut the stronger position we have gained in the Jordan crisis and by our further arms shipments to Israel.

The alternative to the above approach is to ask Riad and Gromyko—as well as Eban in a lower key—for their proposals for getting the talks started now that part of the original basis for them has been

---

[5] Reference is presumably to French philosopher Raymond Aron. No record of Kissinger's conversation with Aron in Paris has been found. In a February 6 telephone conversation with Milton Viorst, Kissinger said: "I think highly of Aron and he has the best analytical mind I know." (National Archives, Nixon Presidential Materials, NSC Files, Henry Kissinger Telephone Conversation Transcripts, Box 4, Chronological File)

undercut. Although there is room for doubt that either the UAR or Israel really wants talks under present conditions, it is still possible to negotiate a new standstill arrangement on which talks could be based.

The advantage of this approach is that it would leave the initiative in the hands of those who broke the agreement or (though unlikely) in the hands of the Israelis if they wanted talks badly enough to suggest their own compromise. It would avoid our appearing to be looking for a cover-up.

You will recall that, before departing on the Mediterranean trip, you ordered that no new significant diplomatic steps be taken until we had a chance to reassess the situation in the wake of the Jordan crisis and the standstill violations.[6] Nasser's death later made that reassessment all the more necessary. It is in progress, and a Senior Review Group is scheduled Thursday on this subject.[7] It would seem logical for Secretary Rogers to use his sessions Tuesday with Eban and Friday with Riad and Gromyko to hear their proposals for getting talks started.

Recommendation: That you authorize me to inform Secretary Rogers that in his discussions this week on the Middle East standstill violations and negotiations he should merely listen to the views of others and *not* put forward any U.S. suggestions pending interdepartmental review of next measures.[8]

---

[6] See Document 164. The trip, which included visits to Italy, Yugoslavia, Spain, the United Kingdom, and Ireland, lasted from September 27 to October 5.

[7] See Document 172.

[8] Nixon did not approve Kissinger's recommendation but, rather, wrote: "This is too dogmatic—present our views but *not* as a proposal—& listen to theirs."

170. Paper Prepared by the National Security Council Staff[1]

Washington, October 14, 1970.

ANALYTICAL SUMMARY

Mid-East Options

Introduction

The Interdepartmental Group paper at the next tab consists of three parts:

—A good collection of thumbnail sketches of the *policy situation* in the UAR, Jordan, Israel, the USSR and among the Palestinians. These do not, however, analyze why each side has acted as it has toward the U.S. peace initiative. This analytical summary attempts to fill that gap.

—The general *options for extending the cease-fire* are described. These are summarized and elaborated below.

—The range of *options for launching* talks is described with pros and cons. These are summarized and elaborated below.

In short, the IG paper can serve as a framework for discussion, but you will want to narrow the discussion very quickly to focus on central issues. What should come from the meeting[2] is guidance for a second paper laying out precise courses of action from which to choose.

I. *The Situation*

A. The IG paper identifies these as the *practical problems the U.S. faces:*

—at a minimum, how to keep the cease-fire going;

—beyond that or in combination with it, how to move the situation toward negotiation. [In dealing with this question it concentrates more on the diplomacy of dealing with conditions in the Near East than on the broader global framework for any negotiations.]

B. The *key questions* to pin down in analyzing the present positions of the parties seem to be these:

—Whose interests are served by continuation of the cease-fire?

---

[1] Source: National Archives, Nixon Presidential Materials, NSC Files, NSC Institutional Files (H-Files), Box H-048, Senior Review Group Meetings, Senior Review Group—Middle East (NSSM 103) 10/15/70. Secret; Nodis. The IG–NEA paper on which this summary is based, "Middle East Policy Options" (in response to NSSM 103), is ibid., Box H-176, National Security Study Memoranda. All brackets are in the original. NSSM 103 is Document 164.

[2] See Document 172.

—How have shifts in the military balance affected readiness for negotiations? This is a question not only of the Israel-UAR balance but of the US–USSR balance as affected by the wider US-Soviet relationship and by US actions during the Jordan crisis.

—How have developments in Jordan affected prospects for an Israel-Jordan settlement? What political process might be devised for drawing responsible Palestinians into a settlement?

—Whose interests would be served by talks now?

C. Since the IG paper presents a static picture of the new *Policy situation* in the UAR, Israel, Jordan and the USSR, a brief statement on each is appended at the end of this summary.[3] The important point is what conclusions are drawn from that analysis. *The following are stated as hypotheses that need to be tested as a basis for policy decisions:*

—Both sides probably have an interest in extending the *cease-fire* beyond November 5 with these qualifications:

—Israel's interest in the cease-fire will begin to run out when it believes that the UAR is preparing actively for resumption of offensive activity, either artillery attacks or actual efforts to cross the Canal. Israelis know resumption of attacks will be costly for them.

—The UAR's interest will begin to run out when it feels that there is no near prospect of negotiations and that the great powers are slipping into a frame of mind that would permit the Suez cease-fire line to solidify into an accepted fact of international life. The UAR's military preparations are less costly while there is a cease-fire.

—The *standstill* arrangement as conceived on August 7 is probably dead. Another way of putting this is that the present military situation in the Canal area is probably not reversible (except for our additional assistance to Israel).

—The UAR makes little attempt to hide what it has done (although it is trying to throw the responsibility on the U.S. and Israel). The new government seems adamant on not removing a single missile.

—Israel says the situation must be restored as of August 7, although Eban hinted that Israel would listen to proposals for getting the talks started.

—Given those postures, it would be surprising if either party volunteered a compromise sufficient to get talks started on the basis of the U.S. initiative as originally formulated. Yet the U.S. cannot be in a position of sweeping Soviet/UAR violations under the rug and has generally paralleled Israel's insistence on rectification. The U.S. would be in-

---

[3] Not printed.

terested in a compromise solution but not at the expense of appearing to cover up Soviet sins.

—*King Hussein* does not seem to have come out of the September crisis with the ability by himself—i.e. without a political process for involving the Palestinians—to commit Jordan to an enforceable settlement with Israel.

—The *UAR* seems still tentatively willing to enter *talks* on the terms suggested by the U.S. in June and accepted by the UAR in July[4] but on the basis of the present military balance. *Israel* remains reluctant to enter talks on any political basis—like the U.S. formula of June–July—that would limit the range of discussions. Israel may probe quietly the Palestinians, Hussein and the new leadership in Cairo to see whether private unconditional talks are possible, but even that would cause serious debate in Israel.

—The *USSR* seems unlikely to press the UAR or take any serious initiative to alter its missile defense complex significantly for the sake of getting talks started.

[You will not find all of these conclusions stated as such in the IG paper. The statements that the standstill is dead and that King Hussein alone is unable to commit Jordan to go beyond what is said in the IG paper, although it explicitly does not rule out the possibility of a separate Jordan-Israel settlement if the terms are reasonable from Hussein's viewpoint. The conclusions above on the UAR and Israeli attitudes toward talks and on the Soviet position are consistent with views stated in the IG paper.]

II. *Options.*

The IG paper deals separately with the questions of (a) how to arrange extension of the cease-fire which expires November 5 and (b) what actions, if any, to take with regard to peace talks. Two comments must be made about this portion of the paper:

—The options in both sections are sweeping. More detailed courses of action will be necessary for eventual decision. The broad options are summarized below, but some suggestions for more specific courses are also included [and identified as such].

—When it comes to defining precise courses of action, both the cease-fire and the talks will probably have to be dealt with as parts of the same course of action rather than separately. But for your convenience, this summary follows the outline of the IG paper.

---

[4] See Documents 127, 129, and 136. The June initiative led to the August 7 agreement, Document 145.

A. *Options for extending the cease-fire.*

The IG Paper identifies three broad options:

1. A *unilateral U.S. initiative* with Israel and the UAR proposing extension of the cease-fire.

—*Pro.* The U.S. should take no chance that the cease-fire breaks down just because no one takes the lead in assuring its renewal. The U.S. was the original negotiator and is probably the only reliable re-negotiator.

—*Con.* We should not seek to do this too elaborately. Both parties have already said they are willing at least to avoid being the first to shoot.

2. *An initiative by Jarring.*

—*Pro.* This would keep Jarring engaged with the parties and give him an opening to explore ways of getting the talks started.

—*Con.* Jarring is too formal a negotiator and might make the job more complicated than it really is.

3. *Extension by tacit agreement* rather than by explicit commitment.[5]

—*Pro.* Both sides have said they will not be the first to shoot. The uncertainty thus introduced might cause the UAR to be a little more careful with its forward deployments lest the Israelis attack, undeterred by any agreement not to.

—*Con.* This is too risky. The parties probably will not shoot, but so much is at stake that it is safer to be more certain.

[The principal *refinements of the above not included in the IG paper* include:

—Stimulating U Thant to note the statements by both sides that they will not be the first to shoot and to make a statement (after consultation) that these had been conveyed to him as statements of policy.

—Try to use the UNGA resolution the UAR may promote as a general reaffirmation of the cease-fire. It is conceivable (though difficult to achieve) that there might be a resolution that both the UAR and Israel could vote for.

—Couple renewal of the cease-fire with some of the efforts described below to get talks started.

What is needed on this question is a more precise statement than in the IG paper of several specific scenarios including extension of the cease-fire as well as a posture on beginning talks.]

---

[5] Above this sentence, Kissinger wrote in the margin: "Why not U S.-Soviet?"

B. *Options for furthering a settlement.*

The IG paper lists six theoretically possible options. Two of these can be laid aside: #2 in the IG paper is to press Israel to resume talks; #3 in the IG paper is to resume two-power or four-power negotiations. A third—suspending participation in the Four Power talks (#6 in the IG paper)—is a tactical move that could be taken to reinforce other possible moves described below.

Therefore, the main options are the four described below. The first three of these appear in the IG paper; the fourth below, not included in the IG paper, seems the area that ought to be explored if the hypotheses stated in paragraph I C above are judged valid and a course of action is to be built on them.

1. *Partial rectification of standstill violations.* [This is option #1 on p. 13 of the IG paper.] This would be a course like that discussed over the past weekend—enough missile rollback to give symbolic satisfaction to Israel with enough redeployment in the zone to save face for the UAR.

—*Pro.* If both sides really wanted talks to start, they might be satisfied with such an approach.

—*Con.* While the U.S. should not stand in the way if Israel wanted talks badly enough to accept such a proposal, that is not the case. This would put the U.S. in the impossible position of covering up Soviet violations.

2. *Leave the UAR front alone for a time and turn to a Jordan-Israel settlement, exploring especially the "Palestinian option."* [This is option #4 on p. 17 of the IG paper.] *State should be asked to prepare a paper on the Palestinian aspects of a settlement in any case.* The issue here is whether Nasser's death and Hussein's renewed determination offer opportunity for movement on a Jordan settlement that might induce Egyptian movement over time in fear of being left out.

—*Pro.* The Palestine question can only be settled with the Palestinians. The UAR-Israel confrontation is a geopolitical one of a different order. While Hussein might not be able to blaze a trail to the end on his own, just the appearance of his starting could make the UAR somewhat more interested in negotiating.

—*Con.* While this should be explored the complications are such that only Hussein and the Israelis can set the pace. It is not an option for the U.S. Hussein, in any case, cannot go too far on his own—either ahead of the Egyptians or ahead of the Palestinian guerrillas. He did not emerge strong enough from the September crisis to move on his own, and he has not yet found a way of bringing a significant number of Palestinians with him.

3. *Mark time on all fronts while the dust settles on the new situation; concentrate only on extending the cease-fire for the time being.* [This is option #5 on p. 19 of the IG paper.] This would be an interim strategy, not precluding others later. It could also, however, be prelude to return to the pre-1969 policy of letting pressures build on the parties.

—*Pro.* This may be the only realistic choice given the uncertainty of King Hussein's authority and the likely inability of the new Egyptian leadership to make any of the decisions that would be essential to a serious compromise.

—*Con.* This course risks that, as time passes, radical forces in the area will begin to consolidate their forces and the more moderate ones who took the risk of accepting the U.S. peace initiative will be undercut. Also, the judgment made in February 1969 is still valid—that it is too dangerous to let local forces play themselves out without restraint.

4. *Establish a new base—other than the U.S. June initiative—for getting the Jarring talks started.* [This is the option to which analysis of the situation leads but which is not included in the IG paper.] The standstill agreement has been killed, but there is an inclination on both sides to continue the cease-fire. It might be possible for both sides to refuse formal extension of the cease-fire (thereby gaining the political advantage of dissociating themselves from an agreement which did not work) but to say they will not be the first to shoot. They would tacitly accept the new military situation—the UAR buildup and Israel's additional assistance from the US. The question then is whether Israel would be prepared to enter talks on this basis.

—*Pro.* Continuation of the cease-fire is more in Israel's interest than in the UAR's since Israel has an interest in the status-quo. Israeli opponents of talks could use UAR violation of the standstill as an excuse for avoiding talks, but at the same time there would be the same pressures to talk that existed in July and Israel would have received some compensation (military package plus $500 million in financial assistance) for the UAR buildup. The UAR buildup is probably irreversible, and Israel cannot forever use that as a reason for not negotiating. The U.S. by decoupling the resumption of Jarring talks from the June initiative would have withdrawn the incentives it offered the Arabs in June (restraint on assistance to Israel) as the penalty for the standstill violations. The political situation would have been restored to the more general one existing before the U.S. initiative—the three-year effort to get talks started—and Israel could say it remains ready to talk to Jarring as it has for the past three years.

—*Con.* Israel on balance would probably prefer not to risk talks. There would not be enough positive in this proposal to permit Israel to back away from its position that it would not talk until the UAR rolled back its missiles. It would be difficult to persuade Israelis that this is anything but a disguised effort to get them into talks without a UAR rollback.

This approach will be unpopular internally because it would declare the June initiative at least half-dead. That, of course, does little more than recognize the facts and start from where we are. It removes the temptation to toy with ideas of partial rectification. It leaves us with a cease-fire and tacitly with the replies of July to the U.S. political formula.[6] The Israelis could insist that theirs is nullified by breach of the standstill arrangement, but that remains a question. More work would be required to flesh out details since this is essentially a back-to-the-drawing-boards approach. But it seems the only one that clears the air, recognizes the situation as it is and could be a starting point for plotting several realistic courses of action.

[6] For the Israeli reply, see Document 140.

171. National Security Decision Memorandum 87[1]

Washington, October 15, 1970.

TO

The Secretary of State
The Secretary of Defense

SUBJECT

Military and Financial Assistance to Israel

The Deputy Secretary of Defense on October 3 sent to the President a memorandum entitled "Follow-up Actions with Israel." The Secretary of State with concurrence of the Secretary of Defense on September 26 sent to the President a memorandum entitled "U.S. Financial Assistance to Israel, FY 1971."[2]

In response to these memoranda, the President has made the following decisions:

[1] Source: National Archives, Nixon Presidential Materials, NSC Files, NSC Institutional Files (H-Files), Box H–219, National Security Decision Memoranda. Secret; Nodis. A copy was sent to the Director of the Office of Management and Budget, the Director of Central Intelligence, and the Chairman of the Joint Chiefs of Staff.

[2] Kissinger sent the memoranda to President Nixon in separate memoranda on October 9; see Documents 166 and 167.

1. The list of military equipment at Tab B under the memorandum from the Deputy Secretary of Defense is approved as described. This equipment should be provided to Israel promptly. No political conditions are to be attached; options for trying to launch Arab-Israeli negotiations will be dealt with in the NSC system in connection with NSSM 103.[3] The conditions on use of this equipment applied to the August 14 equipment package[4] (i.e. Israel would not unilaterally break the cease-fire using this equipment or use it beyond a 50 kilometer zone across the Suez Canal) should also be applied to this package.

2. The substance of the recommendation for $500 million in financial assistance to Israel in FY 1971 is approved as described in the memorandum of the Secretary of State. The timing of the presentation of this appropriations request to the Congress is to be dealt with in a separate memorandum[5] and is to be held until that decision is made.

Henry A. Kissinger

---

[3] Document 164.
[4] See footnote 2, Document 160.
[5] Not found.

172. Minutes of a Combined Senior Review Group and Washington Special Actions Group Meeting[1]

Washington, October 15, 1970, 3:25–4:15 p.m.

SUBJECT

    Middle East

PARTICIPANTS

    Chairman—Henry A. Kissinger

State
U. Alexis Johnson
Roy Atherton
Arthur Hartman

Defense
David Packard
G. Warren Nutter
James Noyes

CIA
Lt. Gen. Robert Cushman
David H. Blee

JCS
Adm. Thomas Moorer
Adm. Mason B. Freeman

NSC Staff
Harold Saunders
Col. Richard Kennedy
Jeanne W. Davis

SUMMARY OF DECISIONS

It was agreed that:

—a continuation of a de facto cease-fire would not be unfavorable;

—State should begin work on a new formula for getting talks started, not necessarily linked to the June proposal or to the cease-fire;[2]

—the NSC Staff, in consultation with State, should prepare a paper on a Palestinian solution with our options, and the implications for Jordan and King Hussein.[3]

Mr. Kissinger: We have three areas for consideration: an assessment of the situation; possible extension of the cease-fire; and how to move toward peace. This paper, which is very good, identifies the practical problems of how to keep the cease-fire going and how to move the situation toward negotiations.[4] How do we assess the situation in relation to the stand-still violations and the events of the last few weeks? How have these affected the cease-fire?

---

[1] Source: National Archives, Nixon Presidential Materials, NSC Files, NSC Institutional Files (H-Files), Box H–111, Senior Review Group, SRG Minutes Originals 1970. Secret; Nodis. The meeting was held in the White House Situation Room.

[2] See Document 175.

[3] See Document 176.

[4] See Document 170.

Mr. Johnson: The Secretary and Joe Sisco are seeing Riad at 5:00 p.m. today and we will know better after that conversation.[5] We seem now to be moving toward a de facto extension of the cease-fire which is not entirely unfavorable. It gives us an indefinite situation rather than the announced 90-day limitation. It seems easy to slide from the standstill into a de facto situation.

Mr. Kissinger: Is it our judgment that neither side wants to resume hostilities?

Mr. Johnson: Yes.

Mr. Kissinger: This would take off the inhibitions of a cease-fire but would not remove the political restraints. From the Israeli point of view the most desirable situation would be a cease-fire without talks.

Mr. Johnson: In his talks with the Secretary, Eban has indicated they would be quite content with this.[6]

Mr. Kissinger: Israel has come out very well. A cease-fire without progress toward peace confirms their situation. How long can the Arabs maintain a cease-fire under these conditions?

Mr. Atherton: For some months, I think.

Mr. Johnson: We haven't detected any Egyptian desire to renew the fighting—quite the opposite.

Mr. Packard: It is the Palestinians or the Fedayeen who will start the trouble.

Mr. Kissinger: There are no restraints on them—they are not affected by the cease-fire.

Mr. Johnson: We are all agreed that more work is needed on the Palestinian question. We have these two interesting intelligence reports this morning,[7] indicating that the Fedayeen are setting up a Liberation Organization comparable to the Algerian Liberation Organization and that they are getting in shape to negotiate. Their program calls for recognition of the existence of the State of Israel and creation of a Palestinian State covering both banks of the Jordan.

A senior member of the Fatah has indicated that Fatah is forming a national front similar to the Algerian Organization on the grounds that the present Palestine Liberation Organization is unworkable. They plan to call a conference after Ramadan (October 31–November 29) announcing its formation.[8] Other Fedayeen groups will be asked to join

---

[5] See footnote 3, Document 169.
[6] See footnote 2, Document 169.
[7] Neither has been found.
[8] Palestinian guerrilla groups met during the second week of December in an attempt to harmonize their individual efforts to re-establish a Palestinian homeland in area occupied by Israel. They formed a single secretariat to oversee their movement and established a unified information office. (*New York Times*, December 13, 1970. p. 12)

and put themselves under Fatah orders. This group would be the sole agent of the Palestinians and would undertake contacts with other governments. The Lebanese have agreed to recognize Fatah as their spokesman. Iraq is said to be the only country which has not accepted the proposal. They see the emergence of a new Palestinian State including the West Bank of the Jordan, Jerusalem, the East Bank west of a line through the major cities, and the Gaza Strip. Some areas would be demilitarized. They apparently do not seek the elimination of Israel—only a reduction in its size.

Mr. Kissinger: What size?

Mr. Johnson: This is ambiguous. If this report is valid, it is the first time a Palestinian organization has been willing to accept the existence of the state of Israel and to organize itself for negotiations.

Mr. Atherton: This would leave Israel with a lot of desert.

Mr. Kissinger: On the first issue, is it our judgment that the cease-fire could best be extended in a de facto manner?

Mr. Johnson: Not necessarily "best," but the trend seems to be in that direction and it is not necessarily unfavorable.

Mr. Atherton: Israel would not agree to an extension of the cease-fire without rectification of the missile movement. They would prefer to let it lapse and base its observation on the UN resolution. The Egyptians would agree to an extension of the cease-fire only on the condition that the Israelis agree to resume the talks.

Mr. Johnson: Riad has said this explicitly. The reason for the Secretary seeing him today was that Riad is speaking tomorrow morning in the General Assembly and we expect he will introduce a resolution of some kind. The Secretary had hoped to exert some influence. We expect Riad to repeat the line that if there are no negotiations, there will be no formal extension of the cease-fire.

Mr. Kissinger: Is it our view that there is no need to request an extension of the cease-fire?

Mr. Johnson: We wouldn't go that far—we don't know enough.

Mr. Kissinger: Let's leave the tactics of extension of a cease-fire until after the Secretary has spoken to Riad and Gromyko.[9] We can be prepared to let the November 5 slip and move into a de facto extension.

The IG paper identifies three possible options for extending the cease-fire: a unilateral US initiative, a Jarring initiative, and extension by tacit agreement. Why not a US-Soviet initiative?

Mr. Atherton: That would raise the question of the stand-still violations and would drive Israel up the wall.

---

[9] See footnote 4, Document 169.

Mr. Kissinger: They would be up the wall anyhow with extension of the cease-fire without rectification. Adding the USSR to the initiative would be no worse. I have been wondering what made the Soviets and Egyptians violate the stand-still so crudely. Could it be that this was a unilateral US initiative and they felt that we would have to take the blame for what happened afterwards? It seemed so unreasonable. Anyone could have predicted that the talks would deadlock. It would have made sense for them to violate the stand-still during a deadlock. Why did they move in at midnight on August 7? I could understand such movement in the first week following the standstill, but why did it continue and escalate?

Mr. Johnson: I agree. It looked for a while as though they were slowing down, but it built back up again.

Admiral Moorer: I still think they have just followed their original plan to set up a missile pattern.

Mr. Kissinger: What if Israel had continued bombing? How much would this have slowed them up?

Admiral Moorer: It would have slowed them up but Israel would have suffered significant losses.

Mr. Packard: It is a lot more effective for them to build additional sites than it is to move in additional equipment. They can then move their missiles around

Mr. Johnson: This is their formal position of course.

Mr. Kissinger: But we have identified 30-odd entirely new sites with equipment.

Admiral Moorer: They argue that the equipment was already in storage inside the stand-still zone.

Mr. Packard: And we can't prove that they brought in new equipment.

Mr. Johnson: The terms of the agreement were very explicit though.

Admiral Moorer: They claim they didn't move new missiles into the zone.

Mr. Johnson: The agreement didn't refer to missiles—it referred to new military installations.

Mr. Kissinger: The language of the cease-fire agreement was explicit and the intent was obvious.

Mr. Johnson: And they had our additional explanation.[10]

---

[10] Beam discussed the cease-fire agreement with Gromyko on June 29 in an hour-long meeting; see *Foreign Relations, 1969–1976*, volume XII, Soviet Union, January 1969–October 1970, Document 187.

Mr. Kissinger: So you don't think a joint US-Soviet initiative would be good?

Mr. Atherton: No, I would have reservations.

Mr. Packard: If we could get a de facto cease-fire, we then might get some talks underway.

Admiral Moorer: Egypt can't organize itself to the point of initiating a break in the cease-fire at this time.

Mr. Johnson: No, we see no signs of an Egyptian offensive.

Mr. Kissinger: On the main problem of a strategy for furthering a settlement, the paper identifies six options.

Mr. Johnson: We are on the fifth option today—marking time on all fronts. We are in a holding action.

Mr. Kissinger: Leaving aside the question of timing, we have option 1—partial rectification; option 2—press Israel to talk without rectification; option 3—resume the two-power or four-power talks; option 4—turn to a Palestine solution; option 5—a holding action; and option 6—the opposite of option 3—suspend US participation in four-power talks. I do not find these mutually exclusive. We can still explore a Palestinian solution while some other things are going on. One point has not been raised. The IG paper assumes continuation of negotiations in the June frame-work. Is it conceivable that we would say at some point that the June basis for an agreement had been overtaken by events and we should look for a new basis and find a new formula for getting talks started?

Mr. Johnson: We could move into that if we move into a de facto cease-fire.

Mr. Kissinger: Should we rule out doing something of this sort at an appropriate time after November 5?

Mr. Johnson: No, not at all.

Mr. Packard: I think this is a likely course.

Mr. Kissinger: What sort of proposal could we make? Could we do some work on such a proposal? As long as a settlement is linked to a cease-fire Israel will demand total rectification which is absurd. What do we mean by partial rectification? A 20-kilometer zone would be a phony. It would be too tight for Israel and would just lead to endless discussion.

Mr. Saunders: At one time we talked about 23 sites within 25 kilometers of the zone, with half of them within 20 kilometers. This meant 15 sites occupied and operational.

Mr. Atherton: We have 34 sites now, with 25 occupied.

Mr. Kissinger: I am not opposed to partial rectification but does it get us anywhere?

Admiral Moorer: The arguments will never be settled.

Gen. Cushman: This just increases the problems of verification.

Mr. Nutter: How about a proposal to demilitarize 25 kilometers on both sides of the Canal.

Mr. Johnson: Why would Israel take that?

Mr. Kissinger: Israel killed the idea of a 25-kilometer zone.

Mr. Nutter: We have indications from the Israeli military that they might consider it.

Mr. Kissinger: I don't believe Israel would accept it.

Mr. Nutter: We have indications that if there were an attack, Israel might withdraw its outposts anyway. They might be willing to demilitarize now.

Mr. Johnson: If Egypt accepts that, the game's over—they would have no hope of getting back. This would open the Canal.

Mr. Nutter: That would depend on what the Egyptians really want. They may want a way out.

Mr. Kissinger: I doubt Israel would accept. They already have the stand-still zone. They would be getting half of the present zone, and withdrawing as well.

Mr. Nutter: It would get the missiles out.

Mr. Kissinger: But they shouldn't have been there in the first place. The stand-still was sold on the basis of only 3 missile sites and none within 25 kilometers. Israel doesn't object to a cease-fire without negotiations. Why should Israel pay a price to get negotiations started? They think they should be paid a price. Their first price is rectification. If they are offered rectification, they will find another price. They don't see themselves doing anything to get negotiations started. They are in the best possible situation with a cease-fire and no negotiations.

Mr. Nutter: This would be one way of getting a more satisfactory cease-fire.

Mr. Saunders: The Egyptians might object even more than the Israelis.

Mr. Kissinger: The Egyptians might take it as a way into negotiations, but Israel would have no reason to take it. If rectification is dropped, we would need a new basis for negotiations. What would be a new basis? Unconditional negotiations?

Mr. Atherton: That would be ideal. Or negotiations without necessarily being linked to the US initiative.

(Mr. Packard left the meeting)

Mr. Atherton: If Israel were released from the limited cease-fire, they would retain more military flexibility, particularly if it were not linked to the Jarring mission or to the formal commitments under the June proposal.

Mr. Saunders: We could start from scratch. What incentive would Israel have to go into new talks unless they really want talks? They couldn't do it without a major fight within Israel. Also, given Nasser's death and the situation in Jordan, they would have no one solid to talk to.

Mr. Kissinger: One way to get to this may be the de facto cease-fire. Would we then give up any linkage between the cease-fire and negotiations, and then propose new negotiations.

Mr. Atherton: Yes.

Mr. Kissinger: Tsarapkin took the view that they had never agreed to any cease-fire therefore they couldn't violate it. We could claim that we were not linking negotiations to a cease-fire. Would it be appropriate to advance that theory at some point?

Mr. Saunders: After November 5.

Mr. Kissinger: If we press for a formal extension of the cease-fire, Israel will insist on rectification and the Arabs will insist on talks. This is a prescription for an impasse. If we continue a de facto cease-fire without a formal linkage, we can propose talks on their merits. What would be wrong with that?

Mr. Saunders: What incentive would Israel have to volunteer for this process?

Mr. Kissinger: Under this procedure, the terms of reference would be defined by our side. Unless something different emerges from the Secretary's talk with Gromyko it may be in our interest to play this in a low key. That is the Secretary's inclination. We can probably get a de facto extension of the cease-fire. Neither side would resist particularly if the US and the Soviet both indicated they wanted it extended.

Mr. Atherton: And we could, over time, press toward talks.

Mr. Nutter: What will the Egyptians be doing in the meantime?

Mr. Johnson: They will continue to strengthen their position.

Mr. Saunders: We have a month before these pressures would become too great, given Ramadan and the GA debate. We would be okay for a month.

Mr. Kissinger: The advantage to Israel would be that they would be released from the June formula. The advantage to the Arabs would be that they would not have to agree to a formal cease-fire. The pressures on Israel would be that if they don't agree to talk, they would give up their already waning international support.

Mr. Atherton: They would also run the risk that the shooting will start again.

Mr. Kissinger: Yes, the Arabs cannot accept a permanent cease-fire. What about Option 1 (partial rectification)?

Mr. Johnson: This is a non-starter. I assume the Secretary will take this position this afternoon with Riad although he will make no specific proposal.

Mr. Atherton: No, the Secretary will say to Riad "you created this problem—what do you offer as a means of solving it?" He will probe for any ideas.

Mr. Kissinger: Option 2 (pressing Israel to begin talks without rectification) would be possible only under conditions of a de facto cease-fire.

Mr. Johnson: I agree.

Mr. Kissinger: What about resumption of the two-power or four-power negotiations?

Mr. Johnson: That would be a subsidiary development.

Mr. Kissinger: One thing which has not been addressed is the Palestinian solution. Can we get a paper indicating what we mean by this?

Mr. Johnson: We recognize the need for such a study.

Mr. Kissinger: Assuming we have a de facto cease-fire, and assuming King Hussein and the Egyptians are not strong enough to make a settlement—would the Palestinians be strong enough to make a settlement?

Mr. Johnson: That implies the Palestinians would be willing to discuss a settlement.

Mr. Atherton: We have three new factors: the death of Nasser, the alienation of the Palestinians from Hussein and the involvement of Tunisia and others in the Palestinian problem in the context of the Arab conference.[11] They have become involved in this for the first time; they are beginning to see it as a political problem, not an abstraction.

Mr. Kissinger: What does their identity as Palestinians entail? How would we establish contact with them? What would be the implications? Would this be seen as a way of scuttling Hussein?

Mr. Atherton: It would probably lead to partition if not the disappearance of Jordan.

Mr. Kissinger: And that is what we went to the brink to avoid.

Mr. Saunders: It's not that clear-cut. Israel may be happy to turn over the West Bank to this group.

Mr. Kissinger: This group has the minimum incentive to settle and the maximum potential to upset King Hussein.

---

[11] See footnote 7, Document 168.

Mr. Atherton: The Palestinians are in considerable confusion—they had lost their bearings. This may crystallize their loyalty and sense of identity.

Mr. Saunders: They didn't have all that many collective bearings to lose—they were never clear as to their objective.

Mr. Atherton: The Arabs would be glad to accept part of Palestine at the expense of part of Jordan.

Mr. Kissinger: We need a Palestinian paper with the options. (to Saunders) Let's get on paper the tentative conclusions of this discussion. We can wait until we hear the outcome of the Secretary's talks with Riad and Gromyko and then consult with State.

173. Memorandum of Conversation[1]

Washington, October 22, 1970, 11 a.m.–1:30 p.m.

PARTICIPANTS

US
The President
William P. Rogers, Secretary of State
Henry A. Kissinger, Assistant to the President for National Security Affairs
William D. Krimer, Interpreter, Department of State

USSR
A.A. Gromyko, Soviet Foreign Minister
A.F. Dobrynin, Soviet Ambassador
Viktor Sukhodrev, Interpreter, Soviet Ministry of Foreign Affairs

The President welcomed Foreign Minister Gromyko to Washington and said that he appreciated the opportunity to have a talk with him. He had been informed that Mr. Rogers and Mr. Gromyko had held useful conversations in New York.[2] It would be helpful if today they could discuss the questions of the general relationship between their two countries. The President said he was prepared to take up any items that the Minister wanted to bring up. Specific problem areas, in

---

[1] Source: National Archives, Nixon Presidential Materials, NSC Files, Box 71, Kissinger Office Files, Country Files, Europe, U.S.S.R. Top Secret; Sensitive. All brackets are in the original except those indicating text omitted by the editors. The meeting took place in the Oval Office. For the full text of the memorandum of conversation, see *Foreign Relations*, 1969–1976, volume XIII, Soviet Union, October 1970–October 1971, Document 23.

[2] See footnote 4, Document 169.

his view, which could be usefully discussed concern the Middle East, the Berlin negotiations between the Four Powers, SALT, a most important issue, Western Hemisphere problems, specifically Cuba, and problems in Asia, specifically Vietnam.

Mr. Gromyko suggested that each problem be discussed in turn and as one was finished the next problem be taken up. This procedure was agreeable to the President.

[Omitted here is discussion unrelated to the Middle East.]

Middle East

Foreign Minister Gromyko said that he had had a good exchange of views with Secretary Rogers in New York on the subject of the Middle East. To restate the Soviet position briefly, the Soviets were for peace in the Middle East. They would not like to see a new military clash in this area. The independent existence of all states needed to be assured and secured, and saying this, he included the existence of Israel as a sovereign independent state. If someone ever told the President that the Soviet Union had some other objective in the Middle East, or if it was alleged that it had some idea of subverting the independent existence of Israel, the President should not believe any such allegations. What was required today was a withdrawal of Israeli forces from the Arab territories they were occupying and a formal, detailed agreement insuring a stable peace in this area. To accomplish these purposes, the role of the two great powers was far from being the least important. It was the Soviet position that peace in this area should be secured by a most solemn act, if necessary involving the participation of the UN Security Council, an act stating that troops are to be withdrawn, that peace is established, and that no one needs to be apprehensive for the security of any of the independent states of the Middle East.

It would be good if some work could be performed in the direction of a solution now. It was important that these efforts not be discontinued at the present time. As to the Soviet view of what needed to be done now, he had already told Secretary Rogers that the first thing required was a resumption of the Jarring mission. Let there be exchanges of views between the Israelis and the Arab states. Such exchanges could certainly not be harmful to any of the parties involved. Secondly, agreement must be reached on extending the ceasefire. The present situation must be formalized in the form of an appropriate agreement to the effect that firing between the sides will not be resumed and this was to be without any preconditions. Attempts to impose conditions on the extension of the ceasefire could only complicate the situation. After all, a ceasefire was a ceasefire, meaning that the two opposing sides had agreed not to shoot at each other.

Third, the bilateral contacts between the Soviet Union and the United States on this question should perhaps be renewed. They had been suspended for some time now and should be reactivated. It would be good to resume these contacts, and not only from the point of view of attempting to facilitate a solution for the Middle East. So far, the American side had not yet responded to the Soviet proposal on the substance of the matter even though that proposal had been submitted in response to the expressed wishes of the American side.[3] Fourth, Four Power consultations should be continued. This would be a step creating more favorable conditions for consideration of various possibilities to solve the problem.

As for Israel, Mr. Gromyko said that the Soviet Union was prepared to give the most solemn guarantees of its existence.

Secretary Rogers said that he and Mr. Gromyko had discussed this question at some length in New York and seemed to agree on many aspects of the problem, but differed on how to get started. He asked Mr. Gromyko if, assuming that agreement would be reached, the Soviet Union would be willing to undertake peacekeeping activities together with the United States, specifically whether the Soviet Union was prepared to send troops for that purpose.

Mr. Gromyko inquired what the Secretary meant by peacekeeping activities. In the Soviet proposal they also mentioned the use of United Nations guarantees and personnel. He had thought this discussion was procedural; peacekeeping should be kept for substantive meetings. When would negotiations on substance begin, however? In his view the matter was pressing and this should be the first order of business. The four points he had just made were intended as steps to be taken at the present time.

Secretary Rogers said that the reason he had asked the question was that it affected the security of the parties involved.

President Nixon remarked that Israel no longer had any confidence in the ability of the United Nations to keep the peace.

Mr. Gromyko replied that what he was proposing was procedural in nature. These were the first steps to be taken and he realized that they were procedural rather than substantive. However, Secretary Rogers' idea was not excluded.

Secretary Rogers inquired what steps the UAR intended to undertake in regard to a UN resolution on the Middle East.

Mr. Gromyko replied that they had this idea because there had been no forward movement toward a solution of the problem. Should the situation change, should the Jarring mission be resumed and the ceasefire continued, he thought the Arab position might change as well. Since he had not received an answer from the United States, he had not

---

[3] See Document 120.

as yet contacted the Arabs in this regard. Secretary Rogers remarked that Mr. Gromyko should certainly be able to influence the Arabs.

President Nixon said that the Secretary had reported to him the conversations he had held with Mr. Gromyko about the Middle East. He was aware of the concern Mr. Gromyko had expressed regarding what he believed were misunderstandings which occurred at the time the ceasefire first went into effect. He was aware of Mr. Gromyko's position that (1) the Soviet Union had not been a party to the ceasefire agreement, and (2) it was unfair to say the Soviet Union had collaborated in violations of that agreement.[4] He did not want to go into this question in detail, but as practical men we had to recognize that a problem did indeed exist. In fact, this was our problem with the Israelis and affected our ability to influence them.

Mr. Kissinger recapitulated the procedural steps mentioned by Mr. Gromyko, namely, (1) resumption of the Jarring mission, (2) resumption of bilateral contacts, and (3) resumption of Four Power contacts. He asked whether they could be separated or whether Mr. Gromyko was proposing a package.

Secretary Rogers remarked that it would be a mistake to go into bilateral and Four Power meetings prior to reactivating the Jarring mission. Mr. Gromyko agreed, but added that purely bilateral contacts could take place at any time.

The President remarked that in the Middle East our respective interests differed considerably and that it was logical for great powers to compete with each other in this area. It was in the paramount interest of both sides, however, to secure the peace in this area since we would be very foolish to allow conflicts between minor powers to lead to a collision between us.

Mr. Gromyko agreed that the President was right and said we should stress what unites us rather than what divides us.

[Omitted here is discussion unrelated to the Middle East.]

---

[4] This view was also expressed in a Soviet "private note" for Nixon that Dobrynin handed to Kissinger in a meeting with him on October 9. (Memorandum from Kissinger to Nixon, October 15; National Archives, Nixon Presidential Materials, NSC Files, Box 71, Kissinger Office Files, Country Files, Europe, U.S.S.R.) Kissinger's summary of his four meetings with Dobrynin from September 25 to October 9 is printed in *Foreign Relations, 1969–1976*, volume XIII, Soviet Union, October 1970–October 1971, Document 6.

174. Memorandum From Director of Central Intelligence Helms to the President's Assistant for National Security Affairs (Kissinger)[1]

Washington, October 23, 1970.

SUBJECT

Fatah Request for Contact with U.S. Officials

1. In the course of operations directed at the leadership of the Palestinian guerrilla movement, this Agency has established clandestine contact with a senior official of "Fatah". Through other independent assets we have confirmed his claim that he is [*1 line not declassified*] one of the top Fatah leaders.

2. On 19 October 1970 this Fatah official, [*1 line not declassified*] advised that, with the approval of Fatah leader Yasir Arafat, Fatah proposed a "confidential" meeting in the immediate future somewhere in Europe between senior Fatah officials and one or more senior U.S. Government officials. [*name not declassified*] listed six items which Fatah wished to discuss, and asked that the U.S. side limit itself to no more than ten principal policy or political matters which it wished on the agenda. The six items set forth by Fatah are:

    a. The U.S.G. position on the establishment of a Palestinian state on the basis of the 1947 UN resolution on the partition of Palestine.[2]

    b. The U.S.G. definition of the term "rights of the Palestinian people," which it has used on occasion in official statements.

    c. The U.S.G. understanding of the term "Palestinian entity."

    d. The U.S.G. position vis-à-vis Jordan as it is presently constituted; i.e., boundaries, etc.

---

[1] Source: National Archives, Nixon Presidential Materials, NSC Files, NSC Institutional Files (H-Files), Box H–048, Senior Review Group Meetings, Senior Review Group—Future Mid-East Options 10/26/70. Secret; Sensitive. All brackets are in the original except those indicating text that remains classified.

[2] An October 20 CIA Intelligence Information Report described the October 19 meetng with a Palestinian with access to senior Fatah officials. He revealed that the U.S. position on the creation of a Palestinian state as part of a broader Middle East settlement, which the Department of State had announced on October 15, was "well received" by those officials, including Yasir Arafat. According to this source, Fatah officials "noted that the Soviet Union has never mentioned the possibility of creating a Palestinian state and, in fact, has been against the establishment of such a state." (Ibid., Box 636, Country Files, Middle East, UAR) The statement about the emergence of a Palestinian state was made by a Department of State press officer on October 15. (*New York Times*, October 16, 1970, p. 1) UN General Assembly Resolution 181, adopted November 29, 1947, recommended a plan to partition the territory of western Palestine between Arabs and Jews with Jerusalem as an international city. The text of the resolution is printed in the *Yearbook of the United Nations, 1947–1948*, pp. 247–256.

e. Does the U.S.G. believe that King Husayn offers the best possibility for normalizing the situation and creating stability in Jordan in the future? On what basis?

f. Will the U.S.G. be prepared to give immediate, meaningful aid and assistance on creation of a Palestinian State? How about prior to its actual creation?

3. We believe that this request by Fatah is bona fide and that the Palestinians who would attend such a meeting would represent the Fatah leadership.

4. The contents of this memorandum have not been disseminated to any other agency. I would appreciate guidance regarding any further dissemination and also on the nature of the reply we should give to the request for a meeting. We should give at least a tentative reply within the next few days.[3]

Richard Helms[4]

---

[3] No reply was found, and no meeting was held. See Document 180.
[4] Helms signed "Dick" above his typed signature.

---

175. Paper Prepared by the National Security Council Staff[1]

Washington, October 24, 1970.

ANALYTICAL SUMMARY

Mid-East Policy Options

Attached is a policy options paper which focuses more narrowly than that considered at the last meeting[2] (at last tab, "NSSM 103 Op-

---

[1] Source: National Archives, Nixon Presidential Materials, NSC Files, NSC Institutional Files (H-Files), Box H–048, Senior Review Group Meetings, Senior Review Group—Future Mid-East Options 10/26/70. Secret; Nodis. All brackets are in the original. The undated paper that this paper summarizes, "Addendum to Middle East Policy Options Paper," is attached. At an October 26 NSC Senior Staff meeting, Kissinger commented that the paper was "loaded" and complained that "the option to carry out the existing Presidential commitment was not included." He remarked further that the paper was "sloppy not only in its analysis but in its statement of alternative remedies" and "wondered if would not have been just as easy to draft a poor paper biased in one direction as in another." (Memorandum for the record, October 26; Library of Congress, Manuscript Division, Kissinger Papers, Box CL–314, NSC Meetings)
[2] See Document 172.

tions Paper")[3] on the present situation. The main new element is the UAR request for General Assembly debate on the Mid-East which begins October 26.

Recapitulation of Discussion at Last Meeting

Discussion at the SRG meeting October 15, you will recall, seemed to lead to a consensus that there would be some advantage in *not* negotiating an extension of the cease-fire beyond November 5, but simply letting the date pass with statements of intent from both sides not to resume the shooting. The main points were:

—Israel probably would not agree to an extension of the cease-fire without some rectification of the standstill violations. That is a prescription for an impasse.

—If there were a de facto cease-fire without formal linkage to negotiations, talks could be proposed on their own merits. Israel, at least, would be willing to base its observance on the June 1967 ceasefire resolutions.

—The advantage to Israel is that it would be released from the June formula and would increase its military flexibility. The advantage to the Arabs is that they would not have to agree to a formal cease-fire.[4] The danger is that the shooting would start again. The Arabs cannot accept a permanent cease-fire.

The Immediate Problem—Strategy in the UNGA

It is not clear what the UAR's objective is. In general, it probably wants to apply pressure on the U.S. to get talks started right away without rectification and would like to find a face-saving formula for extending the cease-fire. But the UAR does not appear to have thought through the kind of resolution it wants.

There are some indications it wants a resolution limited to reaffirmation of Resolution 242, a call for resumption of the Jarring talks and extension of the ceasefire for a specified period. Pressures may mount, however, for language on withdrawal or the Palestinians that goes beyond Resolution 242. According to Mrs. Meir, Israel would resist even the former if the breach in the standstill agreement is permitted to stand.

The options paper outlines two possible broad strategies:

1. Work with others—particularly UAR and USSR—in an effort to contain the UNGA debate and produce a resolution which avoids undercutting the delicate balance in Resolution 242.

---

[3] The paper is summarized in Document 170.
[4] Kissinger wrote in the margin next to this sentence: "How?"

Pro. This is probably the minimum foreseeable outcome and could provide part of a basis for beginning talks as well as continuing the ceasefire.

Con. We could not expect a resolution which referred to the standstill violations. Without that, we would in voting for such a resolution expose ourselves to Israeli and probably domestic criticism for acquiescing in a Soviet-UAR breach of agreement. Moreover, cooperating with the USSR in the wake of the violations would weaken our position.

2. Adhere firmly to the position that any GA action must take account of the standstill violations and the need for rectification.

Pro. This would put us in a position after the debate to tell Israel we had made an all-out effort on the violations but now it is time to put this effort behind us and get on with peace talks.

Con. This could produce Arab counter-reaction and a more pro-Arab resolution and also make it more difficult for us to get off the rectification hook afterwards.[5]

Comment: Some combination of the above is probably the most likely approach. The paper suggests, for example: Tell the UAR and Soviets that we cannot go along with a resolution that ignores the violations issue but if the final outcome is a resolution or consensus that does not destroy the balance of Resolution 242 we would engage ourselves to start the Jarring talks. A variation of this course might be to imply this but not promise it.

A harder *alternative* in this vein would be to make clear to the USSR that the U.S. will have nothing to do with launching negotiations if Resolution 242 is undercut. We would offer nothing.

The real issue, however, would seem to be whether there is any advantage in the UNGA in having the U.S. peace initiative, laudable as it was, declared ended or transformed to a new stage. This might be one way of acknowledging the standstill violations.[6]

The Problem of Getting Talks Started

The problem will be how to bring Israel along. It has painted itself into a corner (perhaps deliberately) on the rectification issue.

Since the ceasefire/standstill will not be renewed in its present form after November 5, a new phase of peacemaking will have begun.

One issue which the options paper hints at but does not really address is: *Is there any special advantage in signaling the end of our peace initia-*

---

[5] Kissinger wrote in the margin next to this paragraph: "How?"

[6] Kissinger wrote in the margin next to this paragraph: "We could have neutral resolution reaffirming all previous ones."

tive? The paper suggests ending our U–2 flights. Although Secretary Rogers has dismissed the idea of announcing the end of our initiative, that is also a possibility.

—*Pro.* While someone in Israel would have to take the trouble to make this argument work, ending our peace initiative with more aircraft, electronic equipment and $500 million in financial assistance could permit Israel to say it is beginning talks on the basis of its long term commitment to cooperate with Jarring. It might help if talks could begin at the Foreign Minister level.

—*Con.* This would probably cost us Israel's commitment to the U.S. formula which was to have been the basis for talks even if it worked. More important, though, it seems unlikely that anyone in Israel would really want talks badly enough to want to make this work.

The options paper ends at this point, saying it will be necessary to explore these and other ways to persuade Israel to negotiate.

The issue stated above—exploring whether there is some advantage in ending the 90-day period of the U.S. initiative in some semi-formal way— needs to be further explored. We would not have to declare it dead. We might simply declare it transformed. The points in such a transfiguration might look something like the following:

—The U.S. launched an initiative in June to enable the belligerents to "stop shooting and start talking."

—Everyone has gained from the fact that the ceasefire has held.

—Part of the understanding reached during the first stage of that initiative was that talks would be based on a military standstill. That part of the agreement has been undercut. There have been two consequences of this:

—Good faith for talks has been undercut.

—The military balance from which talks were to have started has been changed.

—It remains urgent to get talks started. There seems to be no way of repairing the damage done to good faith. That is history now. There are ways of restoring the military balance, and these have been attended to.

—The UN Security Council resolutions of 1967 (ceasefire and settlement) are still the basis for talks.[7] We believe [and some arrangements have been made] that the General Assembly debate should now be followed by talks at the Foreign Minister level while the ministers are in New York.

---

[7] Reference is to UN Security Resolutions 233, which called for an immediate cease-fire, and 242.

176. Paper Prepared by the National Security Council Staff[1]

Washington, October 24, 1970.

ANALYTICAL SUMMARY

U.S. Policy Toward the Palestinians

The State paper begins (Pages 1–3) by explaining why we are now showing *renewed concern for the Palestinians*—their ability to affect chances for a settlement affects U.S. interest, including a settlement and the stability of friendly Near Eastern states.

The paper notes (pages 4–5) but does not describe in detail the *idea of a "Palestinian entity"*—ranging from local autonomy on the West Bank or a Palestinian-dominated East Bank in the absence of peace and from a new Palestinian West Bank state on the West Bank or a Palestinian dominated Jordan (and maybe Gaza) in connection with a peace settlement.

The paper describes (page 6) the *problems of dealing with the Palestinians*—principally their uncertain leadership and our lack of something precise to say to them.

It outlines but in this draft does not try to resolve (pages 7–9) *several policy questions:*

1. Do we still believe that Hussein is the force most likely to bring peace to the Jordan-Israel front, or do we now believe that the Palestinians must be given a stronger or perhaps dominant voice?

2. Is continued commitment to the integrity of Jordan as now constituted an overriding U.S. interest, or are we prepared to expose Hussein and Jordan to considerable danger as part of the price for dealing with the Palestinians?

3. Are we prepared to press Israel to help in the creation of a Palestinian state?

4. Would a Palestinian state contribute to peace and stability or be irredentist, militant and destabilizing?

5. Is there in fact a "moderate" Palestinian majority that can be mobilized for a settlement?

The paper then notes (pages 10–12) a range of approaches which could be followed separately or in combination. These begin from a

---

[1] Source: National Archives, Nixon Presidential Materials, NSC Files, NSC Institutional Files (H-Files), Box H–048, Senior Review Group Meetings, Senior Review Group—Future Mid-East Options 10/26/70. Secret; Nodis. The paper on which this summary is based, "U.S. Policy Toward the Palestinians," October 22, is ibid.

base of continuing present policy of working through Hussein but with slight expansion of informal contacts with the Palestinians and move toward trying to deal separately and officially with the Palestinians. The range includes:

1. Try to involve Palestinians in the peacemaking process by expanding Jarring's mandate to include contacts with Palestinians.

2. Encourage representatives of Palestinian organizations to become actively engaged in functional UN activities (UNRWA, UNDP, WHO, ILO) relating to Palestinian interests.

3. Let Palestinians know the U.S. is interested in contact with Palestinian leaders who could speak for Palestinian interests in an international dialogue.

4. Same as 3 but achieved through Arab governments like Tunisia, Libya, Morocco, Kuwait.

5. Choose a Palestinian leader or organization for direct contact.

6. Same as 5 with West Bank Palestinian leaders.

7. Make a public statement specifically recognizing the legitimate aspirations of the Palestinian people.

Critique: This is really just an outline so far. The point to emphasize in the next draft is discussion of how U.S. interests would be affected by various Palestinian solutions. Until we know where we want to go, the question of increased contacts does not arise in any serious way.

You will receive separately a Saunders memo going into the issues in much greater detail.[2] At this meeting, the purpose is to show interest in the basic issues to make them the main focus for the next draft of the paper.

---

[2] Not found.

177. Minutes of a Senior Review Group Meeting[1]

Washington, October 26, 1970, 3:40–4:18 p.m.

SUBJECT

Middle East (NSSM 103)[2]

PARTICIPATION

Chairman—Henry A. Kissinger

State
Mr. U. Alexis Johnson
Mr. Joseph J. Sisco
Mr. Alfred L. Atherton

Defense
Mr. David Packard
Mr. G. Warren Nutter
Mr. James Noyes

CIA
Mr. Richard Helms
Mr. William Parmenter

JCS
Gen. Richard T. Knowles
Adm. William St. George

NSC Staff
Mr. Harold H. Saunders
Col. Richard T. Kennedy
Mr. D. Keith Guthrie

SUMMARY OF CONCLUSIONS

1. The State Department would provide before day's end a draft resolution for possible use in the UN General Assembly.[3]

2. The State Department will submit by October 30 a memorandum on the prospects for the General Assembly debate on the Middle East, the kind of resolution likely to emerge and the issues which the United States will face in voting on a resolution.[4]

Dr. Kissinger: We have two problems on the agenda today. We need to discuss our immediate tactics in the UN General Assembly debate on the Middle East and to consider how we might go about dealing with the Palestinians. There is one other item I would like to discuss with only the principals plus Joe Sisco.

Mr. Johnson: (handing Dr. Kissinger a draft cable)[5] Here is the answer on tactics. The [NSSM 103] options paper[6] is considerably outdated.

---

[1] Source: National Archives, Nixon Presidential Materials, NSC Files, NSC Institutional Files (H-Files), Box H–111, Senior Review Group, SRG Minutes Originals 1970. Secret; Nodis. The meeting was held in the White House Situation Room. All brackets are in the original.

[2] See Document 164.

[3] A U.S.-backed "Latin American" draft resolution was rejected on November 4 by a roll-call vote of 45 in favor, 49 against, with 27 abstentions. The text of the resolution is printed in Department of State *Bulletin*, November 23, 1970, p. 663. The General Assembly debate on the Middle East began on October 26.

[4] Not found.

[5] Not found.

[6] See Document 175.

Dr. Kissinger: What did Riad have to say this morning?[7]

Mr. Johnson: Perhaps it would be a good idea to have Joe [Sisco] give us a rundown on where we stand on the whole question at the moment.

Mr. Sisco: As a result of the consultations we have been conducting in New York during the last ten days, two or three conclusions have become obvious. First, no possible formula can be found to break the impasse on standstill violations. For that reason we have not put forward any formula of our own. Second, it is clear the Egyptians have decided they need a show. The show began this morning in the form of the General Assembly debate. We have to look toward a damage control operation in the General Assembly with the objective of ending up in the best possible position to exert influence after the debate—particularly on our Israeli friends. We have to realize that we have little leverage on the outcome of the debate. To the extent we adopt a reasonably helpful posture toward the Israelis during the debate, this will give us a leg up in dealing with them afterward.

The Egyptians want a resolution extending the cease-fire for sixty days and calling for the resumption of talks on the basis of the US proposal—but without reference to rectification. They want to use the debate to put pressure on the United States to write off the standstill violations. They have linked the beginning of talks under Jarring's auspices with the extension of the ceasefire although the *Al Ahram* article indicates there may be some softening of their position in this regard.

Dr. Kissinger: What is the *Al Ahram* article?

Mr. Sisco: It indicates that the linkage the Egyptians are making between starting the Jarring talks and extending the ceasefire may not be as strong as had been indicated earlier.

If the General Assembly adopts a resolution along the lines the Egyptians desire, then the U.A.R. will buy a ceasefire. The Israelis will refuse to accept the resolution and ceasefire but will declare that they won't shoot first. Thus, there will be a sort of de facto ceasefire.

As to how to play the issue in the General Assembly, it appears that the Africans and the Egyptians may introduce a more extreme resolution which would undermine the 1967 Security Council resolution,

---

[7] Speaking at the United Nations on October 26, Egyptian Foreign Minister Mahmoud Riad accused Israel of adopting a policy of territorial expansion since its establishment as a state in 1948. He also said that the United States, by providing Israel with weapons during its occupation of Arab territory, had become an accomplice in Israel's "aggression." (*New York Times*, October 27, 1970, p. 1)

include a number of pro-Arab provisions, and be critical of the Israelis. Israel has asked us to put forward another resolution as a counterpoise. This would be our maximum position. It would provide for extension of the ceasefire, call for resumption of talks on the basis of the US proposal, and say something about rectification. I think it would be a good idea to go along with the Israelis on this. It would put us in a good position later on to deal with them.

Dr. Kissinger: They got in touch with me yesterday. They said they wanted to resume talks on the basis of all previous resolutions and the US peace proposal. I talked to the Secretary [of State] about this.

Mr. Sisco: Our proposal does what the Israelis desire.

Dr. Kissinger: Do you mean that the Israelis don't know their own desires? What they were saying to me doesn't indicate what they want?

Mr. Sisco: What I am saying is that they may have phrased it differently when talking to you but that our proposal is in line with what they want.

We need to do a paper for you on how we vote when we come out with the expected resolution in the General Assembly.

Mr. Johnson: Are there not some signs that the Egyptians are amenable to some modification of their resolution? They are anxious to have us along on it.

Dr. Kissinger: If the final resolution provides for a sixty-day ceasefire and resumption of the Jarring talks but makes no mention of rectification, we will have spent much of our capital with the Israelis.

Mr. Sisco: That's right. What we will work for is a resolution that is absolutely neutral on the question of rectification and violations. This would call for "all parties" to cooperate in creating the conditions that would permit resumption of talks.[8]

---

[8] On November 4, the UN General Assembly adopted Resolution 2628, "deploring the continued occupation of the Arab territories since June 5, 1967." It reaffirmed the principles of Security Council Resolution 242 and urged the "speedy implementation" of that resolution. It also called for the resumption of peace talks under Jarring and recommended that the cease-fire between Israel and the United Arab Republic be extended for another three months. Among the 57 countries that voted for the resolution were the front-line Arab states, some of the Arab states of the Middle East and North Africa that did not border Israel, the Soviet Union, and France. Among the 16 that voted against it were the United States and Israel, while the United Kingdom and 38 others abstained. States that did not register a vote at all included Algeria, Iraq, Yemen, South Yemen. Kuwait, Saudi Arabia, and Syria. The complete text of the resolution as well as the list of countries present for the roll-call vote is printed in *Yearbook of the United Nations, 1970*, p. 261.

Dr. Kissinger: Is the General Assembly debate the place to spend our capital with the Israelis? Would it not be better to try to earn some capital there?

Mr. Sisco: I agree.

Dr. Kissinger: If forced to make a choice, one could make a case for the proposition that the best way to get Israel to resume negotiations is not to line up against them in the General Assembly. Then we could put pressure on them to negotiate afterwards.

Mr. Sisco: That is our approach.

Mr. Packard: We have allowed the Israelis to make more of the violations than is justified. We don't really know whether there are more missiles in the ceasefire zone than there were on August 10. We know that a lot of sand has been bulldozed. Besides, we have given the Israelis a great deal of equipment to help them out.

We got in this box. I don't know if we can back out now. But if we can make the violations seem less troublesome, it would make things easier.

Dr. Kissinger: Is it in fact true that we don't know that there are more missiles than before?

Mr. Packard: We can't prove it absolutely. There were 53 sites on August 10; I think there are 61 today. However, we don't know whether they actually brought in more missiles.

Mr. Johnson: We know that there are missiles ready to fire that were not there in August. As for SA–3s, there were five and there are now twenty-one.

Mr. Packard: There is no doubt there have been changes. But our data is not good enough to draw precise conclusions.

Dr. Kissinger: (to Helms) This is a factual question. What do you think about it?

Mr. Helms: Secretary Laird also mentioned this to me. We are making a study of the balance of forces, but that will not really answer the question, which is how many missiles were in the ceasefire zone before but hidden under tarpaulins or buried in sand. We know that there are now more missiles ready to fire.

Dr. Kissinger: We would be in a weak position if we were to end up arguing with ourselves that something which happened didn't happen.

Mr. Packard: I am not saying there were no violations. But we should take into account that Israel is now better off as a result of the equipment we have provided them.

Dr. Kissinger: I can see how we might come to the view that no matter what happened the talks will resume. We should not say that because there were violations, the talks will end for all eternity. As for the aid we have furnished Israel since the ceasefire, we would have provided some of this in any event.

Mr. Sisco: What about the psychological-political situation? We have to remember that an understanding between the US and the USSR is involved, and also one with the U.A.R.

Mr. Packard: We don't have to say that there were no violations. We can say that the violations were not significant enough to require rectification.

Dr. Kissinger: I think that might be a dangerous thing to say. We are likely to end up trying to arrange a settlement that involves having Israel give up territory in return for promises by the US, the USSR, and the Arabs. To the extent that the value of such promises is depreciated, we are going to make such a settlement more difficult to attain.

I believe that everyone agrees it is desirable to resume the negotiations. We have to consider how we are more likely to be able to do so—by taking an anti-Israeli position in the General Assembly or by avoiding doing so.

Mr. Packard: We could take a more moderate position. We could say, "Yes, there have been violations, but they can't be rectified. Now we have to have an arrangement to insure that there will be no violations in the future."

Dr. Kissinger: What do you mean—that we say, "You get one violation free?"

Mr. Packard: We could try to get better inspection arrangements. We have got to set this up so that it can be better verified.

Mr. Johnson: What do you propose to do?

Mr. Packard: We could try on-site inspection.

Dr. Kissinger and Mr. Johnson: What would that tell us that we don't already know?

Mr. Johnson: What we have to do is build a bridge between the positions of the two sides. Egypt refuses to extend the ceasefire unless the Israelis start talks, and Israel says there can be no talks unless there is rectification.

Mr. Packard: What do you mean by rectification? If the Egyptians move back, then there would be some reason for us to move back in terms of what we have supplied to the Israelis.

Dr. Kissinger: The two things are not equivalent. We never promised not to deliver equipment to Israel.

Mr. Packard: Our position should be that there have been violations and that we have to fix things so that there are no more violations in the future.

Dr. Kissinger: There are two separate questions. What do we say once negotiations are started again? (That could be along the lines of what you have just been saying.) What do we say publicly at this time in order to get through the General Assembly debate? The issue is whether we can adopt a position in the debate such that we do not adversely affect what happens afterward.

Mr. Johnson: The Israelis want us to say something about rectification, but we are not proposing to do that. (to Packard) I don't think our positions are too far apart.

This draft cable states what we are proposing. It states that the parties will exert their best efforts to generate conditions that will lead to a resumption of negotiations.

Mr. Sisco: This is our first or maximum position.

Dr. Kissinger: What do we retreat to?

Mr. Sisco: To a formula that is neutral on violations. It would avoid a direct call to resume negotiations. This would be left till after the General Assembly concludes its debate.

Dr. Kissinger: How does this differ from your first position?

Mr. Sisco: Let's not get into this now. To do this you have got to read the precise language, and this is not the place to discuss wording.

Dr. Kissinger: When in hell are we going to get into it?

Mr. Sisco: This is not the right place to work out the language.

Dr. Kissinger: Then what are we talking about?

Mr. Sisco: It would be all right to try to define the subject matter of our resolution, but we should not seek to establish the precise language here.

Dr. Kissinger: But what do we talk about then?

Mr. Johnson: The issue is our general position in the General Assembly debate and whether we should try to build up some capital with Israel during the debate.

Mr. Packard: We ought to consider whether we should build up some capital with the rest of the world.

Mr. Johnson: The Israelis are the ones we have to bring to the table, and the Israelis have no desire to go to the table.

Mr. Packard: They are making hay. They are taking advantage of us.

Mr. Johnson: What do you propose that we do?

Mr. Packard: Just not come down so hard in support of the Israeli position. We need to figure out where we are going to come out on this.

Mr. Sisco: That is what we have been doing. We want to get in a position to achieve what we want after the debate.

Mr. Packard: Then let's not talk about building up capital with the Israelis. Instead, we should be building up our capital with the rest of the world.

Mr. Johnson: What you want to end up with is not much different from what we are seeking.

Mr. Packard: I think we should soften our support for the Israelis.

Mr. Kissinger: We had a major crisis in September. As long as I am going to be in this, we are not going to slide into another crisis. We have to get the facts and make sure that everyone is singing from the same sheet. What we do about it is another matter, but we need an agreed statement on what has happened.

Mr. Packard: The difficulty is that we didn't have a good enough data base to begin with.

Dr. Kissinger: We had some good data during the first week.

Mr. Sisco: We should review the US Government's public record on this. The Secretary of State said in a press conference that the violations are conclusive.[9]

Dr. Kissinger: He also said so privately on a number of occasions.

Mr. Sisco: We have also said that some rectification is required. The Secretary left the definition of rectification ambiguous and referred only to "what the parties can agree to." That leaves open whether there should be total, partial, or no rollback. The Secretary went further and stated that there had been three kinds of violations. There were new sites where none had been before. Positions previously initiated had been completed. Missile equipment had been brought in, and there had been forward movement within the ceasefire zone. That is the policy of the United States as stated by the Secretary of State.

What Dave [Packard] is referring to is that we stated on August 19 that in the period around the start of the ceasefire something happened but our evidence on violations was not conclusive.[10]

Mr. Packard: What I am talking about is what I saw last week—the change in sites from 53 to 61.

Mr. Johnson: The Secretary [of State] spent three hours going over the data. He wouldn't accept what Joe [Sisco], Dave [Packard], Dick [Helms], or Ray Cline said.

---

[9] At an October 9 press conference, Rogers responded to a question about U.S. evidence regarding missiles in the cease-fire zone saying: "Yes, we have evidence that they have moved missiles in. And the evidence is conclusive that they have moved missiles in. When I say 'they,' I mean there have been SA–3 sites constructed since the day of the cease-fire, and we are convinced, I think beyond a doubt, that the Soviet personnel are there to assist in the construction and manning of those sites." (Department of State Bulletin, October 26, 1970, p. 474)

[10] See footnote 2, Document 154.

Mr. Packard: I am just saying that we don't know how serious the violations are.[11]

Dr. Kissinger: This is important also in terms of our relations with the Soviet Union. They have to make a big decision on how they are going to deal with us on the big questions including the Middle East. They will have to choose between adopting a hard line and waiting for us to shift our position, or making some movement themselves in order to reach an agreement. I believe that they are at least considering making a few concessions with a view to seeking bilateral agreement rather than relying on unilateral action.[12] However, if we adopt the wrong posture on the ceasefire violations, they might conclude that there is no need for them to make any shifts and that they are home free.

Mr. Sisco: We have three options in the General Assembly. We can agree to the Egyptian position. We can hold to our position. Or we can try for something in between that doesn't prejudice our position that there have been violations and doesn't wash out the question of rectification. I believe that there *is* a two-thirds vote in favor of washing out rectification. In the event it turns out that this is the case, we will have to decide how we are to vote and that will be a very difficult decision.

Dr. Kissinger: Can we have a memorandum by Friday on this?

Mr. Sisco: We would like to see how the debate evolves.

Dr. Kissinger: Even if we take an extreme position in favor of rectification as a negotiating gambit, that would not mean that we would take the same position after the General Assembly debate is over. My guess is that as an ultimate position we will wind up very close to

---

[11] Rogers telephoned Kissinger at 12:16 p.m. on October 27 and said, "I was amazed to hear that the Defense Department says that they are not sure that the missile violations amounted to much," to which Kissinger responded, "It's outrageous." Later in the conversation Rogers remarked: "If we have a story that leaks out that we don't know what we are talking about, it will kill us with the world," and then added that the President would "go through the roof." (National Archives, Nixon Presidential Materials, NSC Files, Henry Kissinger Telephone Conversation Transcripts, Box 7, Chronological File) Kissinger raised the issue with Laird in a telephone conversation at "1:45 pm-ish," noting that if Packard's argument leaked, "it could be disastrous." Laird replied that there was "no question of violations," but that analysts could not prove, based on aerial photos of the Sinai, that missiles had been moved into the new sites that they had counted, and, thus, he had asked for a paper accounting for any missile increases in the cease-fire zone. (Ibid.) Kissinger telephoned Rogers at 5:15 p.m. to report his conversation with Laird and said that there was "no sense in arguing with" the Defense Secretary and that "the only thing to do" was to "get an agreed intelligence statement. And then have no one deviate from the guidance." Rogers agreed. (Ibid.)

[12] Kissinger and Dobrynin discussed negotiations on October 23. See *Foreign Relations, 1969–1976*, volume XIII, Soviet Union, October 1970–October 1971, Document 29.

where Dave [Packard] wants to go, that is, trying to get the Israelis to negotiate without rectification.

Mr. Sisco: The best way to get there is not to say now that the violations are not important.

Dr. Kissinger: We have two problems—the public record, and the effect on our relations with the Soviets. There has been a considerable change from August to September in the tenor of US-Soviet relations. We don't want to bring the Soviets back to their August mentality.

Mr. Packard: What I am saying is that the data on the violations is somewhat imprecise. Over the last two readings, the description of some missiles was changed from "operational" to "probably operational".

Dr. Kissinger: (to Helms) Can you give us a conclusive reading?

Mr. Sisco: It is true that the estimates do change.

Dr. Kissinger: We still have the Palestinian paper to consider.[13] However, I have a matter that I want to discuss with only the principals.

(At this point the Senior Review Group went into restricted session with only Mr. Kissinger, Mr. Packard, Mr. Johnson, Mr. Helms, Mr. Sisco, General Knowles, and Colonel Kennedy present.)[14]

---

[13] See Document 176.
[14] No record of the meeting has been found.

178. Minutes of a Senior Review Group Meeting[1]

Washington, October 29, 1970, 9:30–10:10 a.m.

SUBJECT

Middle East

PARTICIPANTS

Chairman—Henry A. Kissinger

State
U. Alexis Johnson
Joseph J. Sisco
Alfred L. Atherton
Ray Cline

Defense
David Packard
Armistead I. Selden
James S. Noyes

CIA
Richard Helms

JCS
Lt. Gen. Richard Knowles
Lt. Gen. Donald Bennett

NSC Staff
Col. Richard Kennedy
Harold Saunders
Jeanne W. Davis

SUMMARY OF DECISIONS

It was agreed to:

1. prepare a statement including:

... the difference between the number of occupied sites as of August 10 and today;

... the difference between the number of operational sites on August 10 and today;

... the differences between the number of SAM–3 sites on August 22 and today;

... a general statement on the degree to which the system has been moved forward;

... our best judgment as to how the new equipment was probably introduced.

2. circulate the statement for clearance

3. issue the statement *for internal use only* as an agreed Government position to be followed by all concerned.[2]

---

[1] Source: National Archives, Nixon Presidential Materials, NSC Files, NSC Institutional Files (H-Files), Box H–111, Senior Review Group, SRG Minutes Originals 1970. Top Secret; Codeword. The meeting was held in the White House Situation Room.

[2] No statement was found.

Mr. Kissinger: We want to look at the missile situation in the standstill zone and get a government-wide position in language which is not subject to Talmudic interpretation. This is a factual matter. We need to get our intelligence into a position where it guides and does not follow policy.

Mr. Helms read the briefing (text attached),[3] referring to the bar graph and map.

Mr. Johnson: Is firing position a new term? Are these what we have been referring to as sites?

Mr. Helms: Yes.

Mr. Kissinger: When you speak of the forward deployment of the sites creating some threat to Israeli aircraft operating on their side of the Canal, how far could the missiles penetrate?

Mr. Helms: Ten to twelve kilometers.

Mr. Kissinger: I have a paper here which indicates that the maximum range of the SAM envelop east of the Canal had not changed significantly since the cease-fire. What does that mean? Does it mean that they could reach across the Canal before the cease-fire?

General Bennett: Yes.

Mr. Kissinger: How many missiles could reach across and how deep could they penetrate?

General Bennett: We don't really know.

Mr. Kissinger: If the envelop itself hasn't changed, then they must have shortened their range, if we can now say that there is no significant change even though so many more missiles are now in forward positions.

General Bennett: They had some on the Canal on August 7.

Mr. Packard: Also, the SAM–3 range is shorter than the SAM–2. The SAM–2 range is 30 miles and the SAM–3 is 12 miles.

Mr. Kissinger: I remember a briefing by Ray Cline before the cease-fire which indicated that the sites along the Canal were probably not operational.

Mr. Packard: On August 22, they had eight sites that could reach across the Canal.

Mr. Sisco: The Israelis told us on August 8 that none could reach across the Canal.

General Bennett: (Showing a map to Mr. Kissinger) You can see the envelop and the precise location of the sites better here.

---

[3] Attached but not printed.

Mr. Kissinger: In early August we were told that these sites were not operational. However, if we are now saying that the envelop had not significantly changed, we must assume that they were operational.

General Bennett: What we are saying is that the Egyptians now have the same capability in the area.

Mr. Cline: There is no question that there are now many more missiles able to fire in the envelop so that there has been a definite change in the intensity of the coverage. What Mr. Kissinger remembers is that the Israelis had told us they thought the missile sites along the Canal were dummies since they had flown directly over them and had never been fired upon. Also, the Israeli photos suggested that there were eleven dummy sites in the forward zone. We carried these as occupied sites, however.

Mr. Kissinger: If the envelop hasn't changed, the coverage within that envelop has intensified. Can we all agree on this?

All agreed.

Mr. Packard: There is no question that there are many new firing positions. However, we had only low resolution photography before August 10, and this was not good enough to fix the status with certainty. It was just not possible to tie these things down with absolute certainty.

Mr. Kissinger: We have two problems—what we tell ourselves and what we tell others. We must be sure that we are telling ourselves the truth.

Mr. Cline: There were no SAM–3s operational in the zone before the cease-fire. The interlocking of the SAM–2s and 3s in the zone has made it very tough.

Mr. Kissinger: Secretary Rogers has made a statement that the forward movement of the SAM–3s was not considered by the U.S. to be a defensive move.[4] For a time the Soviets seem to have respected this and were hugging the 30 kilometer line with their missiles. Now their installations are well inside. They were, of course, not legally bound by the Secretary's statement.

Mr. Packard: (to Mr. Helms) You mentioned the arrival of Soviet cargo ships in Alexandria. When did those ships come in?

Mr. Helms: Some time in August—I can get you the precise date.

Mr. Packard: I think that is a significant piece of information.

Mr. Kissinger: Does anyone disagree with Mr. Helms' statement of the facts in his briefing?

---

[4] See footnote 9, Document 177.

General Bennett: We have a minor difference relating to the number of sites on August 10. CIA uses a figure of 97 with 53 of these equipped. We classify 3 of those 97 as field deployed sites, and think the figure was really 94.

Mr. Sisco: Those 3 sites are crystal clear in the photographs however.

Mr. Packard: How many were occupied as of the cease-fire date?

General Bennett: As of August 10, we show 94 sites plus three field sites, with 56 occupied. CIA shows 97 sites with 53 occupied.

Mr. Cline: There is no disagreement on the facts, but we are using slightly different definitions of the categories.

Mr. Packard: There were 56 sites occupied on the cease-fire date. Now there are 55 to 65 sites occupied?

General Bennett: No, these are not in the same category. We are talking about the occupied and operational sites. There are now 108 sites, meaning sites with some missile-related equipment.

Mr. Sisco: We are relating 56 occupied sites on the cease-fire date to 108 occupied sites now. We are not relating 56 sites to 55 sites.

Mr. Packard: On August 10, there were 56 sites occupied, but not necessarily operational? Now there are 108 sites occupied?

General Bennett: We are all agreed on the 108 figure.

Mr. Packard: How many sites were operational on August 10?

Mr. Johnson: 15 to 25.

Mr. Sisco: And it is now 55 to 65.

General Bennett: We would go up to 69.

Mr. Kissinger: Am I correct that there were no SAM–3 sites operational on August 10 and that the largest increase has been in SAM–3 sites?

Mr. Packard: How hard is our evidence that there were no SAM–3 sites operational at the time of the cease-fire?

Mr. Cline: There were none operational a few days before the cease-fire. There may have been some units in place by August 10—possibly two. We tentatively identified five SAM–3 sites on August 10 which were occupied. As of now, there are 32 occupied SAM–3 sites. On August 10 somewhat less than those 5, possibly 2, were operational.

Mr. Kissinger: I remember the discussion at San Clemente as to how two operational sites could affect the strategic balance.[5]

Mr. Packard: What are our figures on operational SAM–3's now?

---

[5] Reference is presumably to the NSC meeting on the Middle East at San Clemente on September 1. See Document 156.

General Bennett: We say 15 to 31.

Mr. Helms: We are using 25 to 30.

General Knowles: The lower figure—the 15—are fully operational with 4 missiles to each site. The higher level—the 31—are somewhat less fully equipped possibly with one to three missiles. Fully equipped means that all essential elements are in place—radar, at least one launcher, etc.

Mr. Helms: A more significant time period might be from late August to late September, which was the period of our better photography. In late August, there were two operational SAM–3 units. In late September, there were 25 to 30.

Mr. Sisco: It would be even more significant if we went back to July.

General Bennett: As of July 28, there were five unoccupied SAM–3 sites but none were occupied.

Mr. Packard: What kind of missile was involved in the shoot-down of the four Israeli aircraft?

General Bennett: Probably SAM–2s.

Mr. Kissinger: Have the SAM–3s ever brought one down?

Mr. Sisco: The Israelis think there is a possibility that one was a SAM–3 but the other three were SAM–2s.

General Bennett: Both 2s and 3s were operational in the area at the time.

Mr. Kissinger: The Secretary of State has said publicly that there are sites in existence now where none were before; that there is missile equipment in the sites where no such equipment was before; and that there are operational missiles now in sites where no missiles were before. Is that an accurate reflection of the Secretary's statement?

Mr. Sisco: The Secretary has said four things: (1) there are a number of instances where there had been nothing there and now new sites have been built; (2) there are a number of instances where our photography at the time of the cease-fire showed positions were in the process of construction, and these have now been completed; (3) there were a number of positions which had no missile equipment at the time of the cease-fire and now contain such equipment; and (4) there has been a general forward movement of SAMs closer to the Canal.

Mr. Kissinger: Does anyone disagree with these statements of the Secretary's?

No one disagreed.

Mr. Kissinger: You can tell from the map that there has been an increase in SAM–3 sites. Also, the SAM–2 sites have increased and have been moved forward.

All agreed.

Mr. Irwin: In the meeting between the Secretary and Riad in New York[6] Riad used a date, acknowledging that after that date the Egyptians had gone full-speed ahead. He claimed that Israel had already violated the agreement and that the United States had said we were going to assist Israel, and that, therefore, after that time the Egyptians had moved ahead.

Mr. Sisco: Riad said this was September 3.

Mr. Irwin: Do any of our figures work between August 10 and September 3? Do we have a clear case of violation even if we should accept Riad's statement as being true?

Mr. Cline: Yes. Between August 10 and August 27, three sites were built from scratch. By September 3, 14 additional sites had been started. In other words, there were about 15 sites built from scratch by September 3.

Mr. Kissinger: So we are talking about an increase in operational sites of 50, which means 200–300 missiles, assuming there are six missiles in a SAM–2 site and four in a SAM–3 site. Is it possible that they could have hidden 200–300 missiles plus the necessary supporting equipment in the standstill zone? We are agreed that no one saw them move, but could they have been moved at night? Even if they had been hidden in the zone, there would still be a violation of the cease-fire. Is this the only unsettled issue?

Mr. Cline: We did not make the question of movement part of our violation charge—we spoke only of new sites. I believe the CIA evidence, some of which is new, is fairly conclusive.

Mr. Sisco: We must distinguish between what we think and what we said. Does anyone here doubt that some missiles were moved into the zone after the cease-fire?

Mr. Packard: Have we carefully examined all the pictures for evidence of any hiding place in the zone?

Mr. Helms, Mr. Cline and General Bennett: Yes we have.

Mr. Cline: I think the better question is whether the Egyptian Army is up to moving that much equipment in 48 hours.

Mr. Sisco: I think Riad's talk with the Secretary was significant. In the first place he said he was out of town and that when he returned and read the agreement, he considered it unfair. He claimed he would not have accepted the agreement had he been in town. He also claimed they hadn't violated the agreement, but, even if they had, they had a right to do so to protect themselves. I consider his statement that they

---

[6] See footnote 3, Document 169.

had a right to violate the agreement as an indirect acknowledgment that they did.

Mr. Kissinger: Let us get a statement of our agreement which will include: (1) the difference between the number of occupied sites as of August 10 and today; (2) the difference between the number of operational sites on August 10 and today; (3) the difference between the number of SAM–3 sites on August 22 and today; (4) a general statement on the degree to which the system has been moved forward; (5) our best judgment as to how the new equipment was probably introduced. This will be used for internal guidance only. I see no reason to call Riad a liar or to engage in any public confrontation with the Arabs. Let's get this statement drafted and I will circulate it to all of you to be sure that it is an accurate reflection of your judgments. Then we can issue this as a Government position and ask everyone to follow this line.

179. Memorandum From the President's Assistant for National Security Affairs (Kissinger) to President Nixon[1]

Washington, November 1, 1970.

SUBJECT

Status of SAM Sites in the Egyptian Standstill Zone

A new inter-agency task force under the chairmanship of CIA has been formed to improve the quality and usefulness of intelligence reporting on the Egyptian-Soviet missile complex within the Egyptian standstill zone. The first product of this group is a graphic description of the development of the missile complex accompanied by an explanatory narrative (attached).[2] Better quality photography and the gradual development of improved and more sophisticated analytical techniques has recently made it possible to refine our judgments on the operational status of the "occupied" SAM sites. This analysis will be updated as new information becomes available.

---

[1] Source: National Archives, Nixon Presidential Materials, NSC Files, Box 656, Country Files, Middle East, Ceasefire, Mideast Vol. I. Top Secret; Sensitive. Sent for information. A notation on the memorandum indicates the President saw it.

[2] Attached but not printed is the October 21 "Status of SAM Sites in the Egyptian Standstill Zone."

You may wish to study this memorandum yourself, but the following are a few of what seem to be the more important points:

—The number of sites which probably were operationally equipped on September 3 (17 to 23, including two sites with the Soviet-operated SA–3 equipment) was close to the number estimated to be in the area immediately after the cease-fire/standstill went in effect (15 to 25, including up to five SA–3's). As you know there was a big Soviet and Egyptian push to move SAMs toward the Suez Canal in the weeks immediately preceding the cease-fire/standstill agreement on August 7. After the standstill went into effect and up to early September the rise in the number of total sites was relatively small and was accomplished largely through modifications and improvements in previously existing facilities.

—There appears to have been a substantial increase in SAM site construction between late August and mid-September as well as some increase in the number of operational sites. It is especially important to note that Soviet-operated SA–3 equipment accounted for most of the increase in operational sites during this period.

—After mid-September the construction of new sites began to slow down and level off, but if anything, the push to occupy and turn operational the already constructed sites increased for awhile. Thus, for instance, during the week of September 13–21 the number of operational SA–3 sites doubled to a total of 28, while the comparable total of SA–2 sites increased by one-fourth to 30.

—Since late September there appears to have been a general leveling off of all missile-related activity in the standstill zone, but a longer time period and more information is probably necessary before such a judgment can be made with a high degree of confidence. As of early October, however, the number of sites which were probably operational had stabilized at around 58 to 61. Of these, it is estimated that between 25 and 29 are the Soviet-operated SA–3s and the remainder are SA–2s. Preliminary analysis of subsequent U–2 missions had not revealed any new SAM sites up to October 18.

Several important conclusions seem possible from this analysis.

—In the first two weeks of the cease-fire period, the Egyptians seem to have been doing about what they said they were doing—hardening sand sites there before the cease-fire and maybe moving some missiles around.

—The Soviets and Egyptians appear to have answered our strong protests on September 3 against standstill violations[3] with not only a continuation of the activity we objected to but with an increase in both

---

[3] See Document 157.

the construction of new sites and especially the deployment of equipment to turn them operational.

—The Soviets cannot legitimately claim, as they are trying, that they are uninvolved and not responsible for whatever happened in the standstill zone. We know that the number of operational sites has more than doubled since the cease-fire/standstill went into effect. The Soviets, of course, supplied the equipment and the Egyptians would simply not have been able to plan and execute such a massive buildup. Moreover, the increase in Soviet-operated SA–3s is even more dramatic, with perhaps half of the some 25–29 operational units having been introduced between late August and mid-September, and the remainder since that time.

—It is too early to know for sure, but it is possible that the Soviets and Egyptians are in the process of completing the buildup of the missile complex. They have already constructed the densest and most sophisticated barrier-air-defense system ever erected and there are early indications that SAM-related activity is leveling off within the standstill zone.

180. Memorandum From Director of Central Intelligence Helms to the President's Assistant for National Security Affairs (Kissinger)[1]

Washington, November 5, 1970.

SUBJECT

Fatah Request for Contact with U.S. Officials

Further to my memorandum of 29 October 1970, concerning the Fatah request for policy talks,[2] [2 lines not declassified]. He commented as follows:

1) Although seriously disappointed by the U.S. Government's failure to send a representative [less than 1 line not declassified] can un-

---

[1] Source: National Archives, Nixon Presidential Materials, NSC Files, NSC Institutional Files (H-Files), Box H–049, Senior Review Group Meetings, Senior Review Group—Middle East 11–13–70. Secret; Sensitive. All brackets are in the original except those indicating text that remains classified. A copy was sent to the Under Secretary of State for Political Affairs.

[2] Not found. Helms sent his first memorandum to Kissinger on the subject of Fatah's request for contact with U.S. officials on October 23; see Document 174.

derstand and, in fact, objectively accept, our factual explanation that a variety of practical factors prevented a speedy response to Fatah's proposal to establish a dialogue, but many other Fatah leaders might not be able to do so. As a major world power and one with important interests in the Middle East, the U.S. Government must be prepared to go more than half way to understand and accommodate the legitimate interests and even the "fixations" of the Palestinian people.

2) Fatah is extremely aware of the imperative need, in the interest of its survival, to keep its contact with the U.S. Government absolutely secret. [*name not declassified*] noted that if his own role in the current contact were ever to become known or widely suspected, he would be branded as an "American Agent" and might even be liquidated under such circumstances.

3) Fatah's interest in honest, secret dialogue with the U.S. Government at this time is the product of many considerations, such as: (A) Its recognition that the United States is a key power factor in the area, especially vis-à-vis Israel; (B) Its sensing, from recent statements by senior U.S. Officials, that the U.S. Government has finally come to realize that no lasting peaceful settlement is possible without the consent and active participation of the Palestinian people and its leadership (and Fatah is confident that it alone can provide that leadership); (C) Fatah's present readiness to accept the establishment of a Palestine entity (and in fact to furnish the government of such an entity) and the pragmatic necessity for this entity to live in peace with and indeed to enter into cooperative relations with Israel; and, (D) Its realistic recognition that to become viable economically, a Palestine entity will require sizable foreign aid, especially from the United States.

4) [*name not declassified*] argued that the U.S. Government, in order to understand the milieu in which it must act regarding the Palestinian problem, has to recognize as a practical factor the emotional imperative of the younger Palestinian generation to assert itself combatively, even at mortal cost. In effect, resistance has finally restored the essential degree of national pride to the younger Palestinian generation, and if this pride is not permitted to channel itself into constructive effort (for example, within the context of a Palestine entity), it will vent itself violently and destructively against all foes, real or imagined.

Richard Helms[3]

---

[3] Helms signed "Dick" above his typed signature.

181. Paper Prepared by the National Security Council Staff[1]

Washington, November 9, 1970.

ANALYTICAL SUMMARY

Options for Moving Toward a Mid-East Settlement

Introduction

Attached is Sisco's paper, "Middle East—Where Do We Go From Here?"[2] This suggests mainly trying to develop a joint strategy with Israel for trying to get talks started on the basis of some UAR political concessions (e.g., agreement to a POW exchange or to Jarring talks at the Foreign Minister level, which Israel wants). This considers none of the other options which have been suggested. These are detailed below for the sake of establishing a broader framework for discussion.

Inventory of Steps that Could Be Taken

Listed as major headings below are the broad options described in the IG paper. Under them are noted the principal operational proposals related to each one. These are proposals from all quarters; the IG paper does not go into this much operational detail. They are included here as a step toward looking at exactly what steps are available in the present situation. The arguments on these options are deferred to the next section of this summary.

1. *We can make a specific proposal to the UAR and Soviets for rectification of the standstill violations, and to Israel to resume talks under Jarring once such rectifications have taken place.*

—We could suggest UAR redeployment of missiles (without razing sites) outside a 20 km. zone next to the Canal but within the 50 km. zone.

—There has been a proposal for mutual withdrawal of all forces on both sides of the Canal to lines 25 km. back. This has sometimes been coupled with a proposal to begin clearing the Canal.

2. *We could press Israel to resume talks under Jarring's auspices without rectification of the violations.*

---

[1] Source: National Archives, Nixon Presidential Materials, NSC Files, NSC Institutional Files (H-Files), Box H–049, Senior Review Group Meetings, Senior Review Group—Middle East 11–13–70 (1 of 2). Secret; Nodis. All brackets are in the original.

[2] Undated; attached but not printed.

—We could take the line that any shifts in the military balance as a result of the violations has been redressed by subsequent U.S. military assistance to Israel. We could also mention:

—$500 million in military assistance.
—New aircraft and other military equipment for delivery in 1971.

—We could promise Israel that we would not press the U.S. formulations put forward by Secretary Rogers on December 9, 1969,[3] and in the U.S.–USSR talks in any negotiation that might begin.

—We could try to negotiate some new standstill agreement.

—Jarring could call for talks on this subject just to get the parties engaged.
—The U.S. and USSR could attempt to work out a new agreement.

—Jarring could be urged to issue an invitation to talks at the Foreign Minister level (which Israel wants) and we, in connection with new arms aid, could let Israel know that we expected it to find a way to accept.

—We could try to get outside the Jarring framework and stimulate a call for a peace conference. One suggestion has been to have this a meeting with the permanent representatives of the UN Security Council (the Four Powers under their formal UN hats).

3. *We could resume active substantive negotiations in the two and four power talks.*

—While there is little pressure for this in U.S. councils, it could perhaps be envisioned in connection with one of the steps listed above. There is Malik's informal suggestion of talks on US–USSR guarantees (rather than on settlement terms).[4]

4. *While continuing to hold out for rectification and against shifting the negotiations to the four powers, we could explore a "Palestinian option"—i e., the possibility of an Israeli-Jordanian-Palestinian settlement.* [The operational suggestions for this option are dealt with more fully under the analytical summary of the Palestinian background paper.[5] The thoughts below are in addition to those described there.]

—Jarring could be asked to invite Jordanian and Israeli (and perhaps Palestinian) representatives to begin talks on the foundation that the standstill violations do not apply to Jordan.

---

[3] See Document 73.
[4] Not further identified, but on October 30, Malik addressed the UN General Assembly and called for the immediate resumption of Arab-Israeli peace talks. (*New York Times,* October 31, 1970, p. 1)
[5] See Document 182.

—An economic program could be launched involving the Palestinians as a possible prelude to their greater involvement in peace talks. For example, there might be a refugee commission to begin arranging the details of compensation; Israel might make an offer in this connection; the U.S. might relate its economic rehabilitation program in Jordan to phasing UNRWA functions into Jordanian and Palestinian hands.

5. *While taking a number of interim steps and holding out for rectification, we could in effect mark time on all fronts with respect to a peace settlement until the forces set in motion by recent events in the area have become clearer and the parties have adjusted themselves to this new situation.* This would presumably require some steps that would permit the UAR to justify continuing the ceasefire past the present extension.

—The U.S. or Jarring might start circulation of working drafts of portions of a final settlement on their own. This could be called preliminary work while the standstill was being renegotiated, for instance.

—An effort could be made to arrange secret UAR-Israel contacts which could then be merged into Jarring talks. This might be enough to encourage Israel to find a formula for resuming talks under Jarring.

—Steps on the refugees described above could be taken with a possible Israel offer of some controlled program for permitting those who left the West Bank in 1967 to return to their homes. This might be characterized in some way so as to relate it to eventual West Bank freedom.

—Two power talks would be resumed to discuss U.S.-Soviet modalities for avoiding confrontation rather than for an Arab-Israeli settlement.

—An Israeli withdrawal of occupation forces from the populated areas of the West Bank (while maintaining security positions along the Jordan River) if connected with other moves toward the Palestinians might provide a sense of movement on that front. A related move would be arrangement for freer flow of people and commerce, especially to Jerusalem. Israel might even turn over to West Bank Muslim authority control of the Islamic holy places.

Issues for Discussion

The above operational possibilities raise the issues below. The major arguments presented in the IG paper for and against each option are reflected below.

1. *Should the U.S. press to get Jarring talks started soon?* The alternative is marking time either until the new situation in the area is clearer or at least until Israel makes up its own mind to begin talks as a means of keeping the ceasefire going.

Pro. The main argument for our pressing to start talks now are (1) that the U.S. does have an interest in not completely losing the momentum of the summer initiative and (2) that some movement in peace talks is necessary if the UAR is to continue the ceasefire after the present extension.[6] Behind these arguments is the feeling that we should capitalize on the fluidity in the present situation in Cairo.

Con. The main longer term arguments for moving more slowly are that neither Sadat nor Hussein is now strong enough to deliver his country to a compromise settlement and that the U.S. must allow some time to pass in order that the USSR and UAR can demonstrate their intention to be constructive. It is difficult to imagine any other "rectification" of the situation arising from the standstill violations. The more immediate argument for standing back is that the Israelis must recognize that the UAR cannot continue the ceasefire indefinitely without talks. It would be better for Israel to start talks for its own reasons than for us to press.

2. *If the U.S. chooses or is forced by circumstances to mark time, are there realistic interim steps that could be taken that would permit the ceasefire to continue?*

Pro. A variety of steps is described in paragraphs 3–5 of the previous section. A major argument for moving ahead with some kind of Jordan-Israel talks, for instance, would be to ignore the UAR because of the standstill violations and yet put pressure on them by moving ahead with talks that might command some Palestinian support and therefore make it difficult for the UAR to disrupt. One could even argue that movement on the Palestinian front would hold greater promise of success, if constructive, than immediate resumption of Jarring talks.

Con. Any interim steps except those that can pass as an honest effort at negotiation will be regarded in the Arab countries as stalling tactics. They would, in fact, run more parallel to Israeli than to Arab interests.

3. *If the U.S. decided to press for Jarring talks, should those talks be the only focus of our efforts to achieve a settlement?* The alternative would be to let the talks proceed but to supplement them in ways that may have more chance of success.

Pro. Both sides have accepted a basis for talks after three years, and we cannot afford to throw that away. Eban has reconfirmed Israel's acceptance of that basis in the recent UNGA debate. Everybody seems to recognize that the standstill provision of that agreement is dead. Time will take us past the rectification problem, so there is no good reason

---

[6] UN General Assembly Resolution 2628 extended the cease-fire for 3 months beginning on November 6; see footnote 8, Document 177.

for giving up what has been gained. We can be as active as necessary behind the scenes.

Con. The passage of November 5 provides an opening for unhooking us from the precise arrangements of the standstill agreement. Some people would like to get rid of Jarring, and now might make a logical time. While we do not want to throw away the advantages gained this summer, it is not in the U.S. interest to have prospects for peace completely tied to a process of formal talks that is likely to stall. We need more strings to our bow, even if we choose to maintain the Jarring framework as an umbrella. Principally, the Palestinian-Jordanian-Israeli settlement is so complex that Jarring is not likely to make a dent in it. Therefore, it would make sense to tackle this problem separately. If progress were made, it could be brought into the Jarring framework if that seemed useful, either for the sake of appearances or to bring a UAR arrangement into tandem.

One Conclusion

Without attempting to load the argument, it may be useful to state one general conclusion from the above as a focus for further discussion:

The Jarring talks by themselves do not seem likely to produce a settlement. There are some crucial issues that will have to be dealt with outside that framework. Two of these are: (1) the role of the U.S. and USSR in guaranteeing a settlement and (2) the role of the Palestinians.

If one agrees with this proposition, then one might conclude that the June initiative and the Jarring talks are not sufficient by themselves—that they need the support of complementary tracks. Specifically, it might be regarded as essential now to:

—develop a complementary but separate negotiating strategy for an Israel-Jordan settlement;

—develop a plan for movement on the refugee question in support of the above;

—develop options for U.S.-Soviet, Four Power or other international guarantees for a settlement.

What at root is questioned here is the viability of the 18-month-old strategy of seeking a UAR settlement first and letting the Jordan-Israel settlement follow. The fact is that Sadat is not likely to sign an agreement before the Palestinians are satisfied. A UAR-Israel agreement on boundaries and peace would not by themselves bring a settlement, though it might pave the way. Besides, the U.S. should have more interest in getting a settlement for Hussein than for Sadat. Therefore, it seems essential now to turn our attention to a Jordan-Israel settlement while pursuing Jarring talks between Israel and the UAR.

182. Paper Prepared by the National Security Council Staff[1]

Washington, November 13, 1970.

ANALYTICAL SUMMARY

Palestine Options

Introduction

At the next sub-tab are:

—A long State Department background paper[2] on the Palestinian problem—the principal options and the broad issues they raise for U.S. policy and interests. It does not make recommendations. Its purpose is to lay out the problem that has been overshadowing peace efforts for two decades and has achieved a new prominence since June 1967, and, as such, to serve as a basis for discussion of U.S. policy.

—A short State Department paper [on top][3] drawing from the longer one certain working hypothesis and recommendations for policy.

These papers in addition to the earlier Saunders memo[4] comprise a first effort to put out on the table in a policy context the problem of satisfying Palestinian aspirations in the course of moving toward a Jordan-Israel settlement—which in this context can be read as the final partition of Palestine. After going back and forth over the issues, one finds it helpful to begin putting on paper some general policy guidelines for testing in discussion. What follows is an effort to put the judgments in the shorter State paper into perspective for discussion.

A Prefatory Note: The Broader Policy Context

Elements of an Arab-Israeli settlement as the United States has officially viewed them are embodied in Secretary Rogers' speech of December 9, 1969,[5] and in the document on an Israel-Jordan settlement

---

[1] Source: National Archives, Nixon Presidential Materials, NSC Files, NSC Institutional Files (H-Files), Box H–049, Senior Review Group Meetings. Senior Review Group—Middle East 11–13–70. Secret. All brackets are in the original.

[2] Attached but not printed is the undated paper, "The Palestinian Problem: Options in an Arab-Israeli Settlement."

[3] Attached but not printed is the November 9 paper, "Palestinians: Working Hypotheses and Recommendations for Action."

[4] The memorandum, "Analytical Summary: Palestinian Options," November 6, is in the National Archives, Nixon Presidential Materials, NSC Files, NSC Institutional Files (H-Files), Box H–049, Senior Review Group Meetings, Senior Review Group—Middle East 11–13–70.

[5] See Document 73.

submitted in the Four Power meeting of December 23.[6] With regard to the Palestinians, those formulations go only so far as to note the grievances of the Palestinians and to promise their resolution in a refugee settlement.

Much of the present discussion essentially contests the validity of that approach toward the Palestinians as being comprehensive enough. It raises the question of going beyond that stance and formulating a more definitive posture in light of the rising tide of Palestinian nationalism. In so doing, some key issues of the Palestinian problem must be borne in mind. Detailed in the longer State paper and in the Saunders memo, they are briefly as follows:

—We do not have a clear picture of who really speaks for the 2.6 million Palestinians. Do the fedayeen reflect the sentiments of the majority of Palestinians or do they speak only for themselves? How real is the gap between the thinking of West Bank notables and the fedayeen?

—We do not have a clear picture of what the Palestinians really want, both with regard to the degree of political freedom they would desire [what kind of entity] and with regard to their intentions in exercising that freedom [do they want to destroy Israel].

—The U.S. must consider what would happen to King Hussein. It would seem that any discussion of trying to meet legitimate Palestinian aspirations beyond what is already envisaged would have implications for the future of the Hashemite dynasty. How would U.S. interests be affected?

—What can realistically be expected of the Israelis? Even in the refugee context, they are adamant against an influx of Palestinians which might threaten their internal security. Beyond that, the Allon Plan[7] for a settlement is an Israeli military strategy which, although it would provide greater local autonomy for West Bank Palestinians, would make any Palestinian entity essentially a captive of Israel. How would U.S. interests be affected vis-à-vis Israel were we to move beyond our present position on the Palestinian question?

—Finally, given the hostility surrounding the newly emerging Palestinian movement, does the U.S. want to get involved in endorsing this kind of resistance? Would this set a bad precedent for U.S. policy elsewhere? Would it be as helpful to moderate Arab governments as they have been suggesting? On the other hand, can we escape this new phenomenon in the Arab world by sticking to our present policy which could be read as ignoring Palestinian political aspirations?[8]

---

[6] See Document 78.

[7] See footnote 8, Document 4.

[8] A handwritten note under this paragraph reads: "HAK comments: 1. Isn't this the end of Jordan? 2. The most anti-Israeli element."

A Tentative Base for Policy

The most practical way to deal with the issues raised in the longer State paper is to try to develop some working hypotheses from its discussion. This is what the shorter State paper attempts to do. Since the shorter State paper jumbles judgments together, the most economical procedure—followed below—is to state a generalization with the State Department position noted beneath it followed by comment.

You might use the following for talking points at the SRG meeting:[9]

1. *A first generalization that seems to emerge from the two papers is this: There is increasing evidence that the problem of the Palestinians is no longer just a problem of refugee compensation and resettlement.* It is also a problem of providing a means for the Palestinians to play a greater political role (a) in the process of a settlement between Israel and Jordan and (b) in a governmental structure thereafter, with the likely possibility being the West Bank.

State's shorter paper (page 1, paragraph #2) says: "There appears to be a growing need to meet a Palestinian desire for some sort of identifiable political personality. Such a personality could be created in the form of a semi-autonomous unit, i.e. the West Bank and Gaza linked to the East Bank and under the overall direction of the central government in Amman."

The Issues

Does everyone agree that the Palestinians can no longer be treated as a refugee problem?

There are two contradictory tendencies in the papers that have been written:

—On the one hand, the case is made that nothing short of a seat at the peace table and a semi-autonomous political unit alone can hope to meet Palestinian aspirations. It is said that they will not be content again to be treated just as refugees.

—On the other hand, the case is made that their aspirations can be met only part way. Hussein can serve as their spokesman and they can live under the direction of Amman.

A devil's advocate might say it seems possible that once we start avowedly seeking a distinct political role for the Palestinians, we will turn loose something that cannot be stopped. Consider these questions:

—Going beyond our present position and getting into devising a proper political role for the Palestinians could take years. Do we want

---

[9] An unknown hand circled "talking points."

to delay a final Palestine settlement for that if there is a chance of something sooner?

—Are we turning loose forces that will spell an end to the Hashemite monarchy?

—Is it possible that there is nothing wrong with our present position except that we have not made the most of it? Perhaps a dramatic offer on a refugee settlement with appropriate political gloss could revitalize chances of making our present political position tenable. Then we could leave the political problem to Hussein.

The other side of the question is whether it is now possible to stop what has already been turned loose.

—Is it fair to say that Hussein cannot deliver Jordan to a peace settlement without Palestinian participation?

—If Hussein's days are numbered, should not the U.S. come to terms early with the Palestinian nationalists?

One possible conclusion is: The main U.S. interest is in a Palestine settlement. The U.S. interest, therefore, dictates the minimum moves necessary to assure Palestinian support for a settlement. At this point—knowing as little as we do about Palestinian intentions—it seems premature to talk about a separate Palestinian state. However, the U.S. is far from having done all that might be done to meet Palestinian concerns, even within this present limited policy constraints. The question is how far the U.S. can go within limits imposed by other U.S. interests.

2. *A second generalization* one might state is: *Palestinian political aspirations might be met by recognizing several different forms of Palestinian entity. It is too soon for the U.S. to endorse or reject any.*

State's short paper (page 1, paragraph #1) concludes: "The concept of a separate and distinct Palestinian state is unrealistic to consider except in the context of a peace settlement and unless a part of Jerusalem is included. Even then, since such a state would presumably have to be limited to the West Bank and Gaza, it would probably not be economically viable without the injection of large-scale outside financial assistance. Its political viability is also doubtful, since a large number of Palestinians would remain outside its borders and it would tend to be dominated by a larger and more powerful Israel." State, therefore, concludes that a semi-autonomous unit on the West Bank under Amman is the best way to articulate Palestinian nationalism.[10]

The issue is whether U.S. interests would be served by the existence of some separate Palestinian entity as contrasted to a Palestinian prov-

---

[10] Kissinger highlighted this paragraph and wrote in the right margin: "Part of Jerusalem."

ince under Hussein. The State Department paper would limit the U.S. now to working with Hussein. Do we want to cross that bridge now?

On the one hand, the most desirable government in Jordan from the viewpoint of U.S. interests is the one that has the best chance of delivering Jordan to a peace agreement with Israel and enforcing it over time. This so far has been the main argument for continuing to work through Hussein. The U.S. does not to date have convincing evidence of Palestinian leadership that is (a) acceptable to most Palestinians or (b) willing to make and enforce peace with Israel.[11]

On the other hand, there is reason for not putting all our bets on Hussein. Both Israelis and Arabs have said that there will be no Arab-Israeli settlement until the Palestinians and Israelis come to terms with each other. If they did in a way the Palestinian leadership seemed prepared to enforce, it is difficult to argue that the U.S. would not find an interest in such a settlement regardless of its implications for the Hashemite monarchy.

One possible conclusion is: The U.S. interest is less in the Palestinian or non-Palestinian complexion of the political unit to Israel's east than it is that its leadership effectively control it and commit itself to peace with Israel. Therefore, while we may wish to work through Hussein for the time being, it seems premature to dismiss the idea of a separate Palestinian state either on the West Bank or in all of Jordan. It might be more sensible, in fact, for the U.S. to think in terms of how an orderly evolution to Palestinian domination of Jordan could take place.

3. A *third generalization* is: *If a separate Palestinian entity were to be established, the U.S. interest in its boundaries would depend to a large extent on the nature of its leadership.*

State's papers come out against any separate entity and therefore do not express a preference for a particular entity. State at most thinks in terms of a semi-autonomous West Bank under Hussein.

The issue is that to think in terms of any Palestinian entity is to think in terms of at least partitioning Jordan and at most supplanting Jordan with Palestine.

If there were responsible Palestinian leadership, it would make more economic sense to have both banks together. To be economically viable in the near term both East and West banks must at least have access to each other's markets and to substantial earnings from tourism in Jerusalem as well—which would require Israeli cooperation. This could be accomplished by federation. The sharing of revenues might be difficult under any arrangement that created more distinct political entities.

---

[11] A handwritten note next to this sentence reads: "HAK comment: and on what terms?"

If Palestinian leadership were less responsible, there might be some value in preserving a bedouin East Bank as an insulator between the Palestinians and Iraq, Syria and Saudi Arabia. Also, two weaker units might be more inclined to fall into Israel's economic orbit and under Israel's protective military umbrella. This, of course, would depend on Palestinian willingness (perhaps unlikely) to settle for such an arrangement. Additionally, Israeli pre-eminence might create more problems than now exist.

One possible conclusion is that it is too soon to close the door on the idea that Jordan may one day become Palestine. The nature of the Palestinian leadership is the key to what will serve U.S. interests.

What seems desirable now are (a) reformulation of these guidelines in light of SRG discussion and (b) a scenario describing exactly how the U.S. might go about increasing attention to the Palestinians without closing the door on any future options.

TALKING POINTS END HERE

The Real Choice for the U.S.

The overriding issue, therefore, would seem to boil down to *what degree the Palestinians might be given a political role*. The choice is between two broad attitudes which the U.S. could assume:

Choice 1: Identifying the Palestinians as a relevant political voice [which we have not done before], but operative *only* through the established governments of Israel and Jordan. Any promise of self-determination would be worked out within that context. In this approach, we would *press Hussein* to go as far as he felt he could with the Palestinians.

This is the course recommended by the State Department. The United States could pursue a course which would attempt to enhance the Palestinian role within the existing framework of Israel and Jordan governments. The departure from pre-existing policy would be that the U.S. would publicly identify as favoring enhanced Palestinian representation in peace negotiations, albeit within the present Jarring context. Apart from that, such a policy would really amount to encouragement of talk both in Israel and in Jordan of folding the Palestinians more directly into the peace efforts and of thinking about some measure of self-determination for them after a settlement. Flowing from that are State's recommendations on tactics and on a possible semi-autonomous unit for the Palestinians under Jordanian control.

Choice 2: Identifying the Palestinians as a distinct and relevant political voice, perhaps operative through their own representation in negotiations—or perhaps through Israel and Jordan—but nevertheless deserving a separate political entity in the final outcome. In this approach, we would stake out a position of our own in favor of a Palestine entity and *force Hussein* toward it simply by stating it.

This alternative is one step beyond Choice 1. The U.S. could pursue a course designed to identify the Palestinians as a separate group which could speak for itself and could be granted some separate entity. This would involve actions—contacts with Palestinians, public endorsement of a separate state—meant to catalyze Palestinian political organization. The departure from present policy is that we would in effect be recognizing a new political entity. Instead of gently prodding Hussein and the Israelis to include the Palestinians, we would be forcing them.

These two postures must be viewed in their broadest sense. They seem to reflect what would be the difference in the U.S. setting in motion various actions: those that would confine the Palestinian political problem to the present context—prodding Hussein and the Israelis to produce a more realistic Palestinian voice—and those that would not confine the problem to the present governmental structure but would aim for a distinct Palestinian voice and entity—such as unilateral U.S. contacts or statements vis-à-vis the fedayeen.

Picking Choice 1 above would not preclude moving to Choice 2 later, but choosing Choice 2 now would prevent us from returning to Choice 1 later. Operational proposals for the pursuit of both are elaborated in the following section.

Current Operational Proposals

Choice 1—Enhance a Palestinian Role Within Existing Framework

This is the State Department framework with which I (Saunders) generally agree except that no State Department proposal yet suggests a broad enough range of action within this framework to make a realistic course of action.

1. *Press Hussein to a course that would involve some Palestinians in negotiations with Israel.* This would probably involve Hussein's commitment to some more precise arrangements for self-determination for the Palestinians after a settlement—such as State's view of a semi-autonomous unit. Coupled with it might be a fairly dynamic program for shifting UNRWA functions to combined Jordanian-Palestinian control. [The Under Secretaries Committee should—but has not yet—addressed this last point.]

2. *Press the Israelis—as the other proprietor of Palestinians—into bringing the West Bankers, as potential Palestinian leadership, into the settlement process.* [State did not include this.]

3. *In general, look for ways in which the peace initiative could be viewed as taking into account the legitimate concerns of the Palestinians.* State would include the U.S. establishing its own contacts with the Palestinians, looking for ways to bring them into the peace negotiations

and becoming specific—in connection with discussion of self-determination on the West Bank—on the need for a Jordanian-Palestinian political status in Arab Jerusalem. [This last point seems inconsistent with the State approach in that it would seem to promise more to the Palestinians than can be delivered.]

Pro.

—On balance, this would be the best way of trying to do something for the Palestinians without wrecking the established governments. Both Israel and Jordan have talked about bringing the Palestinians closer to the settlement process and about some future political voice for them. We would not have to commit ourselves to a Palestinian entity or to one Palestinian group but would rely on the long-established and better known relations between Israel and its Palestinian population and Jordan and its Palestinian population.

—We would not have to confront the issue of creating a new political entity nor put ourselves in a position where we might be compromising Jordan and Hussein. We do have a heavy commitment to King Hussein. Writing him off would have some effect in Saudi Arabia.

—Encouraging the Israelis to engage the West Bank leaders would capitalize both on their interest in doing something for them and on the relations that have built up between occupier and occupied. Additionally, they have often been viewed as the natural nucleus of some form of West Bank Palestinian leadership.

Con.

—The militant fedayeen would not be satisfied unless Hussein went a long way to reflect their sentiments. If he did, Israel would object, and Hussein might jeopardize his own control.

—The U.S. should not engage in any unilateral actions involving the fedayeen if we are intent on keeping Israel-Jordan context alive. Such action would amount to Choice 2 with all the implications of letting the Palestinians establish an independent relationship with us. It would undercut Hussein's efforts. If our strategy is to devote our energies to promoting the Israelis and Jordanians to take the problem more seriously, them we should avoid direct contact.

—Jerusalem is too sensitive and should be set aside. If there is anything that will lose the Israelis, it is the issue of Jerusalem. To raise that issue now would be to lose any momentum we might have toward bringing the Palestinians into a settlement.

Choice 2—Encourage the Palestinians to Come Forward as a Legitimate Party to the Dispute

The long and short of this strategy would be that by creating the political opportunity, we might stimulate political responsibility on the part of the Palestinians which has been so noticeably diffuse over the years. There are very few advocates of this course in the government—many outside.

1. *Make a U.S. statement that the Palestinians must have a role in the settlement process and then wait to see what Palestinian actions that provckes.* [Unlike Choice 1, our public declaration would make clear that the Palestinians would have their own voice.]

2. *Broaden official contacts with Palestinian organizations.*

3. *Broaden Jarring's mandate to include contacts with Palestinians.*

Pro.

—This would project the U.S. image as responsive to the Palestinians without explicitly committing the U.S. to one solution or another, although internally we would have made the decision to look for a separate Palestinian political force. It would place some of the burden on the Palestinians and might promote political jockeying within the fedayeen movement leading towards the formulation of a representative group to talk with us.

—It would permit us to learn more about the Palestinian movement directly. This is the only way of finding out what they represent and what they will really settle for. It could also win some Palestinian cooperation with U.S. positions.

—It would probably improve our image with some of the Arab states.

—It would give us the option of favoring the moderate Palestinians as the potential leadership.

Con.

—The U.S. has almost done this in Ambassador Yost's speech to the General Assembly.[12] There is not much advantage in more talk until we see Palestinian leadership coalescing.

---

[12] On October 29, Yost addressed a plenary session of the UN General Assembly during the debate on the Arab-Israeli dispute and said: "During this debate we have heard quite a bit of discussion of the question of the Palestine Arabs. The United States agrees with the conclusion of several speakers that if any peace is going to come to the Middle East it has to take into account the legitimate concerns and aspirations of the Palestinians. We do not have, however, any preconceived ideas about what form Palestinian participation in a settlement would take. It is not now clear what peaceful goals Palestinians set for themselves, who speaks for them, what their relationship is to established Arab governments, or if there is any consensus on the Palestinian role in a peaceful settlement. The answers to these questions need to be clarified. We think this is primarily a matter for the Palestinians themselves to work out in conjunction with established Arab governments." The entire address is printed in the Department of State *Bulletin*, November 23, 1970, pp. 656–661.

—If the U.S. were to take any of these actions, it might be difficult to back off if we decided we could not work with the leadership that emerged. If we entered an official relationship with them, not only would we undercut whatever hopes we had for Israel and Jordan coming to terms with them but also might find ourselves in the position of in-fighting between the groups and of being denounced if we did not produce what the militants were looking for.

—Any official contact, therefore, would play into their hands before the U.S. is clear about the ultimate objectives of the Palestinian fedayeen and before we can have any confidence that their success is in U.S. interests.

—If the U.S. wants to set limits to the Palestinian role and to try to relate it to Hussein for as long as is reasonable, the last thing we want to do is to task an agent beyond our control with relating them to the settlement.

—The Israelis would choke.

—Working with a national liberation movement would have precedents elsewhere.

—This might mean the end of Hussein. We would have to make some serious judgments on where our interests lie, unless we could insure that any contact we would have with the fedayeen was only for informational purposes.

—Broadening the Jarring mandate might disrupt the tenuous base on which it already rests. Israel might withdraw even further.

183. Minutes of a Senior Review Group Meeting[1]

Washington, November 13, 1970, 3:45–5:20 p.m.

SUBJECT

　Middle East

PARTICIPATION

　Chairman—Henry A. Kissinger

State
U. Alexis Johnson
Joseph J. Sisco
Haywood Stackhouse
Thomas Thornton
Ray Cline

Defense
G. Warren Nutter
James H. Noyes
Armistead I. Selden
Lt. Gen. Donald Bennett

CIA
Richard Helms
David H. Blee

JCS
Lt. Gen. Richard Knowles
Rear Adm. William St. George

NSC Staff
Col. Richard Kennedy
Harold Saunders
Jeanne W. Davis

SUMMARY OF DECISIONS

It was agreed that:

1) Palestinian participation in a peace settlement in some form would be important at some stage;

2) State would prepare a telegram of instruction for a discussion with King Hussein on a possible approach to the Palestinians;[2]

3) after we had the King's reaction, we would decide on the next step;

4) Mr. Saunders and Mr. Sisco would prepare a new strategy paper;[3]

5) The IG would put together a proposed aid package for Israel covering the next two years, with a clear statement of the opposing State and Defense views;[4]

---

[1] Source: National Archives, Nixon Presidential Materials, NSC Files, NSC Institutional Files (H-Files), Box H–111, Senior Review Group, Meetings Minutes Originals 1970. Top Secret; Codeword. All brackets are in the original except those indicating text that remains classified. The meeting was held in the White House Situation Room.

[2] See Document 185.

[3] Saunders's analytical summary of the new strategy papers on the Middle East is printed as Document 198.

[4] See Document 194.

6) the statement on stand-still violations would be distributed to agencies as an agreed statement of the factual situation;[5]

7) CIA would submit proposals for a higher budget for satellite photography.[6]

Mr. Kissinger: We have three problems to consider: The general Middle East situation including the Palestine option, where we go from here, and the question of U–2 flights, which I think are on the track now. I would like to spend ten minutes on the intelligence problem since I intend to get an agreed statement on this. Since this is a factual matter, it has to be possible for us to get an agreed description of what we believe. Following the Middle East discussion, we will have a report from Charlie Meyer on Chile and then I have one item for the 40 Committee.

Let us go first to the Palestinian option. This is a very good State Department paper[7] but it raises a number of basic questions. Essentially, the question is what kind of Palestinian outcome would be in our interest. This raises various issues which are probably best explored in the State Department paper on Working Hypotheses and Recommendations for a Palestinian Solution. I refer you to page 1, paragraph 2 of this paper which, along with other statements in the paper, makes it clear that Palestine can no longer be treated as a refugee problem. I note, however, two contradictory tendencies in the paper: (1) that nothing short of a seat at the peace table can meet Palestinian aspirations; and (2) that these aspirations can probably be met only part way and that this will probably have to be done through King Hussein. I wonder whether it is possible to stop part way. Once we recognize the fedayeen as a semi-autonomous political entity are events still under our control? Can we stop short of independence or political autonomy? Of course, we may want that. But do we really believe that a semi-autonomous status can be maintained?

Mr. Sisco: I recognize the risk you cite, but I believe the prospect of its being manageable depends on the manner in which it is done. If we work through Hussein, with the King taking the lead, and leaving open further steps toward self-determination in an unspecified future, I believe there is a hope and indeed a possibility that it can be done in some limited form. If Hussein can make some proposal to the Palestinians, saying "here's the deal" and then organize it in some form, it may stick. The situation, of course, will never be completely stable. The option to break away from any kind of federation would always be there for the

---

[5] See Document 178. No statement was found.
[6] Not found.
[7] See Document 182.

fedayeen. Its success would depend on Hussein's conditions, on the mutuality of interests between the East and West Bank, on the degree of freedom of movement, etc. If there were freedom of exchange leading to a degree of economic viability the two banks might be better off together. The possibility of an overall Jordanian state depends on whether Hussein can take the lead and can deal with a fedayeen leadership that is able to consider a limited approach. Such an agreement might stick for five years, then who knows?

Mr. Kissinger: Would we ask Hussein if he minds if we deal with the fedayeen? This is like a wife asking her husband if he minds if she commits adultery. Would our very asking of the question be enough to shake Hussein's confidence?

Mr. Sisco: That depends on how we ask the question. I agree there is some danger that the question itself would be prejudicial. But I think we could put it to Hussein along the following lines: (1) We have come to the conclusion, and we think you have too, that we must take the Palestinians into account; (2) you have begun to put a government together with some Palestinian representation; (3) you have indicated that you are willing to give some self-determination once a settlement has been reached. We must convince Hussein that any discussions with Arafat or another fedayeen leader would be in the context of complementary US efforts toward common objectives. It would be a delicate operation. We don't want to give Hussein a veto, but if we do not move in concert with the King, even an initial contact with the fedayeen could be undermining.

Mr. Kissinger: Granted that we believe a Palestinian entity is desirable and that we should talk to the King, should we also talk to the Palestinians? Is the King likely to take the position that how he arranges his country is his business? How would he look on our political contact with the faction that led an insurrection against him with its implication of a relationship to a group which was subversive to his authority? Could we accept Joe's (Sisco) idea but without any mention of talking to Arafat or any other fedayeen representative?

Mr. Sisco: Unless we are ready to go all out with the Palestinians, and to see the King go down the drain, we should not contact Arafat if the King is not sold on the idea that it is complementary to his own actions.

Mr. Kissinger: I don't know how the Arabs react but I do think they can be pretty devious. Suppose the King acquiesces in our suggestions but then draws his own conclusions as to our real intent?

Mr. Johnson: We shouldn't decide on talking with Arafat until we have talked with the King.

Mr. Helms: I agree—we should take one step at a time.

Mr. Sisco: Our next step should be to talk to Hussein, keeping under review the possibility of talking to Arafat.

Mr. Kissinger: Are we agreed then that we should open the possibility of talking to Hussein about a Palestinian entity in the context of a settlement?

Mr. Johnson: The entity could be either geographic or political.

Mr. Kissinger: By political, you mean representation at the peace settlement?

Mr. Nutter: If consideration of a Palestinian entity is important, we can't possibly keep it away from the King. We couldn't proceed without his knowing about it.

Mr. Kissinger: Trying to proceed without his knowledge would be the worst thing we could do unless we should decide that we don't care what happens. We could, of course, conclude that the Palestinians have to be brought in but that we should not play a dominant active role in bringing this about. This has been our strategy up to now—we have left it to the Jordanians.

Mr. Nutter: This runs the risk that it won't come up otherwise.

Mr. Kissinger: One argument for a particular Palestinian entity is that they are the best group to guarantee a settlement involving the greatest number of Arabs. The problems of the Egyptian border are easier than those of the Palestine border. On the other hand, they are also the group which has the greatest interest in the destruction of Israel since more of the territory belongs to them than to any others.

Mr. Sisco: The Fedayeen have adopted this posture. However, I think the Palestinians—not necessarily the Fedayeen—can be brought around in the hope that there is light at the end of the tunnel.

Mr. Noyes: I feel the same way. Our sympathetic approach to the Palestinian problem could undercut Fedayeen influence and could offer an opportunity for the more moderate Palestinians.

Mr. Kissinger: What sort of boundaries would the moderate Palestinians have in mind?

Mr. Sisco: The Arabs will certainly think of a Palestinian entity as including some piece of what was Arab Jerusalem. This is a very tough problem. We have revised our paper in this regard, and will do a telegram on this for all of you to look at.

Mr. Johnson: I think there is a growing sense of realism and a desire for peace among the Palestinians.

Mr. Kissinger: Will Israel accept the 1967 borders? Will the Palestinians accept the 1967 borders or will they insist on the 1947 borders?

Mr. Sisco: We can't operate on the assumption of the '47 borders—this would be no deal. It might be possible, however, to develop some leadership on the basis of a Palestinian entity based on the '67 borders, minus Jerusalem. This would be a feasible objective; indeed no other objective makes sense. We will have trouble convincing Israel to go with the '67 borders. They certainly wouldn't buy the '47 borders.

Mr. Helms: I agree.

Mr. Kissinger: So we are agreed to work for a Palestinian entity in some form.

Mr. Helms: Either political or geographic.

General Knowles: I agree, provided we take one step at a time, starting with an approach to King Hussein. Of course, it would be better if he suggested it.

Mr. Kissinger: May I sum up my understanding of the situation. We are agreed that Palestinian participation in a peace settlement in some form would be important at some stage. We don't have to decide now what that entity should be. It might be the political participation of the Palestinians in the peace negotiations. The first step would be to put the question to King Hussein in the terms outlined by Joe Sisco. We could ask for his reaction and how we might be helpful. Depending on his reaction, we could then consider the next step.

Mr. Sisco: There is one related development. The new Jordanian government is giving some thought to the refugee question. The King's brother has asked us to set up a small working group with them to see what might be done. This is the first realistic indication that the Jordan Government is trying to organize itself to get at the problem. Such a Jordanian initiative would fit in with such a proposal.

Mr. Helms: I think we should go ahead.

Mr. Kissinger: (to Mr. Sisco) You draft a telegram outlining an approach to the King for us to look at. After we have an answer from the King, we can decide on the next step.

(to Mr. Sisco) Will you sum up where we stand diplomatically? Both the President and the Secretary have said publicly that we want to try to get the negotiations started again. I have the feeling that Israel is not fighting for rectification of the standstill violations with the same intensity as before.

Mr. Sisco: The General Assembly consideration of the question concluded with considerably less damage than we had feared, due largely to our damage-control operation.[8] In my judgment, the talks will start in a few weeks. I base this on three factors: 1) the Israelis have

---

[8] The General Assembly debate on the Middle East and especially the cease-fire violations took place in plenary meetings from October 26 to November 4, culminating in the adoption of Resolution 2628. See footnote 8, Document 177. For a summary of the debate, see *Yearbook of the United Nations, 1970*, pp. 254–260.

now come to the conclusion that the time is propitious to resume the talks; 2) they have concluded that rectification of the standstill violations is not possible; and 3) the statements by Moshe Dayan[9] reflect a change in the Israeli attitude.

Mr. Kissinger: I don't believe Dayan's statements are as unguided as they appear to be.

Mr. Sisco: I think they indicate the general thrust of the Israeli Cabinet. The Secretary's conversation with Eban makes clear their strategy.[10] Their Parliamentary debate opens Monday and will continue for several days. Following the debate there will be further internal conversations. Then Israel will come to us and say that they are prepared to get the talks started, and they are grateful for our military assistance and our support in the GA debate. They have submitted a specific request for additional military assistance over the next 18 months which is now being considered in the IG. It is a substantial request, but there is evidence that the financial people in Israel have gotten to the military on the request. I think they will make three proposals: 1) that the US indicate that we are prepared to make a positive response to their military assistance request; 2) that we do what we can for them in terms of credit; and 3) that we give them some assurances that we will give them reasonable freedom of movement.

Mr. Kissinger: After we give them that assurance we can still regulate deliveries of the material.

Mr. Sisco: There is no question that our leverage will be needed in the context of the negotiations and the deliveries are our leverage. I believe, however, that we can get further with the Israelis in the context of confidence than by threatening to withhold their equipment.

Mr. Kissinger: (to Mr. Helms) What do you think of that?

Mr. Helms: I have no comment on Joe's presentation.

Mr. Kissinger: Do you agree on the strategy?

Mr. Helms: I think it's the only one available to us.

Mr. Kissinger: We could say they won't get anything more from us until they start negotiations, then dole it out to them two months at a time.

Mr. Helms: I think if we want to get on with the talks, we should get on with everything.

Mr. Nutter: It amounts to 150 planes.

---

[9] On November 6, Dayan announced that Israel no longer had to adhere to commitments associated with the U.S. peace initiative.

[10] See footnote 2, Document 169.

Mr. Sisco: Fifty-four Phantoms and 120 others, also certain supporting equipment and some other things they have asked for such as personnel carriers, it amounts to $600 [million] over the next 18 months. That is in addition to the current $500 million request. This would take us to June 1972.

Mr. Helms: I didn't understand that this was in addition to the $500 million already requested.

Mr. Johnson: What if peace breaks out in the next 18 months.

Mr. Sisco: We will say we would look at the situation.

Mr. Kissinger: Any new frontiers might be more bearable to the Israelis if they have this package.

Mr. Sisco: The Arabs don't care about what equipment Israel gets if a settlement is achieved. The next 18 months will be a no-peace situation; we can't plan any other way.

Mr. Kissinger: So Joe (Sisco) believes we can get more from the Israelis by confidence; and we can get more from the Russians by convincing them that no matter what they pour in, they will not get a military advantage. On the other hand, DOD believes that if we give Israel these weapons, they will not have the incentive to negotiate, and we should keep them on leaner rations with no long-term committment.

Mr. Nutter: Paying them $600 million to get them to the table gives them a free hand. If the talks bog down, what next?

Mr. Kissinger: We can regulate deliveries.

Mr. Sisco: I meant a free hand in the early stages of the talks. The US must play a pressure role at some stage.

Mr. Kissinger: Neither side is in a position domestically to make peace. They will both need pressure. Could we make the term of the package a little longer? Having it end in the middle of an election campaign is not an ideal situation.

Mr. Sisco: Would it help if we stretched it from 18 to 24 months? I recognize that the IG meeting exposed a gulf between the thinking of State and Defense; I understand there are real problems.

Mr. Kissinger: I think the worst possible way of giving aid is the way in which we have done it over the last three months. By being forced to consider a new request every month or so we ended by giving more than if we had agreed on a sizeable package in April or in June.

Mr. Sisco: I agree. Let's try to put together a package for decision by the President that can carry us for the next two years.

Mr. Kissinger: Yes. Let's make it possible for the President to say "I have done this and I won't talk to any other group about this question." If we do it, we should do something to tie the package to the negotiations so that we could use it as leverage.

Mr. Sisco: We must make this crystal clear to the Israelis.

Mr. Kissinger: Let's get the issue defined so as to get it to the President so we can then authorize an integrated approach to the Israelis.

Mr. Nutter: It is very important that we stretch the time to 24 months.

Mr. Johnson: That is reasonable.

Mr. Kissinger: I just invented the 24 month period, but I would hate to see it end in June of 1972.

Mr. Sisco: This makes a lot of sense.

Mr. Noyes: I will be discussing this Wednesday with the second man in the Israeli Air Force.

Mr. Kissinger: Let's get a statement of the views from the IG.

Mr. Sisco: We will try to put down the two approaches to the problem in the fairest possible way.

Mr. Kissinger: I would like to raise a question on the strategy of the Jarring talks.

Mr. Sisco: We must be careful not to fall into the Soviet trap. They are circulating in New York the idea that we should start talking about guarantees. Any substantive discussion in either the two-power or four-power forum before negotiations between the two parties begin is a diversion and would be bound to make the Israelis nervous. I have sent a cable to Yost indicating that we would have no problem talking about guarantees at the right time.

Mr. Kissinger: Why is this Soviet trap? Don't they want to get the talks started?

Mr. Sisco: They want to get on with the four-power discussions and mobilize the other powers to isolate the U.S. The French position is even worse than it was before, and the UK is very wishy-washy. Golda Meir's talks in London were a disaster.[11] There has been a marked deterioration in both the French and British positions, which means even greater danger in the four-power context.

---

[11] Meir met with British Prime Minister Edward Heath and British Foreign Secretary Sir Alec Douglas-Home on November 4 and 5. According to a November 4 record of their conversation, Meir made a "plea" to Heath to reject the "Arab" resolution in the UN General Assembly "deploring the continued occupation of the Arab territories since June 5, 1967." (Resolution 2628, adopted November 4) Meir insisted if the UN adopted the resolution, "as far as Israel was concerned Security Council Resolution 242 was dead, and Israel would have nothing more to do with that resolution or with the Jarring Mission." She also said she was "shocked" at the Foreign Secretary's recent Harrogate speech, objecting to his reference to Israel's future frontiers with the UAR, Jordan, and Syria. Meir went on to criticize the term "formal state of peace," a Soviet term in her view, and also the reference in the speech to the "political aspirations of the Palestinians." (The National Archives (United Kingdom), PREM 15/540, The Middle East, 1970–1971)

Mr. Kissinger: Even if the discussions were on a subject the Israelis should like, it would set the precedent of confronting them with four-power negotiations on the subject.

Mr. Sisco: Let's wait until talks start between the two parties; then we could consider the strategy of marking time in the four-power talks. We certainly should not renew the U.S.-Soviet talks.

Mr. Kissinger: We must first establish that the principal parties are talking.

Mr. Sisco: Jarring will certainly need help right away. He will probably put together some formulation in two or three weeks. We will all have to focus on this formulation; then we should talk to the Russians about it in concrete terms.

Mr. Nutter: I agree. The first talks should be between the Israelis and the Arabs.

Mr. Kissinger: Our June proposals and much of our strategy since has been on the basis that a settlement with Egypt was a pre-condition to a settlement with anyone else. Should we look at this again? We are certainly not less interested in an Egyptian settlement, but should we give equal priority to a Jordanian settlement? The Soviets will get the credit for an Egyptian settlement.

If it were possible to get a Jordanian settlement either before or at the same time as an Egyptian settlement, it would mean that our friends—and a more moderate regime—would be helped first. With the death of Nasser, Jordan may not still be that dependent on Egyptian approval. Should we give more emphasis to the Jordanian part of the settlement?

Mr. Sisco: I don't think Hussein wants to get out in front, even now. I think both settlements have to move together. Jordanians would prefer that the principal focus in the talks be on Egypt. In time, if the situation in Jordan continues to improve, we may then give them equal treatment. For now, however, we should focus on Egypt, although not exclusively. Jarring will certainly consider both.

Mr. Johnson: An Egyptian settlement is easier than a Jordanian settlement.

Mr. Helms: That was our reason for doing it this way in the first place.

Mr. Kissinger: (to Mr. Sisco) Joe will you and Hal Saunders work together on a paper that ties this strategy together? We can then give it to the President for information and decision. It should of course, be consistent with what the President and the Secretary have said publicly. [*1 line not declassified*]

Mr. Johnson: [*5½ lines not declassified*]

Mr. Helms: [*2½ lines not declassified*]

Mr. Sisco: [1 line not declassified]
Mr. Kissinger: [1 line not declassified]
General Knowles: [1 line not declassified]
Mr. Kissinger: [1 line not declassified]
Mr. Helms: [3½ lines not declassified]
Mr. Kissinger: [7 lines not declassified]
Mr. Helms: [2½ lines not declassified]
(4:40 p.m.—Mr. Cline and General Bennett joined the group)

Mr. Kissinger: Can we turn once more to the question of standstill violations? If our principals are to make meaningful judgments, based on our intelligence, we should be sure that our intelligence reflects the facts and is not a tool to be used in fighting the policy argument. I am trying to get a statement of the standstill issues. It is now a moot point of course, but both the President and the Secretary have made public statements. The paper left the implication that a large number of missiles could have been hidden in the zone before the violations occurred. The violations would have been no less real, of course, since the agreement barred such placement. Whether they were hidden or not is immaterial. In addition, we have the situation where no one saw any missiles move in. We can't prove that they were moved in after or that they were not moved in before. You can't prove why something hasn't happened. I have had some systems analysis done on this. The amount of sand that would have to have been moved to conceal the equipment for 45 SAM batteries would have left a hole big enough to put the White House and the Executive Office Building in together. We saw no such engineering equipment in the standstill zone. Also, we have checked the cubic feet of all the hangars in the standstill zone and it is simply not enough to hide 45 batteries. In addition, why would they have hidden weapons in a standstill zone that didn't exist when it was permitted to do so, and take them out and put them in place when it was prohibited? How can we explain the ships and the flatcars loaded with SAM equipment? I have asked Mr. Helms to do another memo, so now we have two papers to consider; the joint statement on which all were agreed, and a new CIA paper which covers the question of where the missiles came from.[12] Can we look at the new CIA paper. If we agree this is a fair statement, we will send it out as an agreed position.

Mr. Sisco: (referring to the CIA memorandum of November 12) I think the first paragraph is very good. Also, with regard to point 5, I think the evidence on the timing is even stronger. Riad told the Secre-

---

[12] The paper, "SAM Equipment in the Egyptian Ceasefire Zone," is in the National Archives, Nixon Presidential Materials, NSC Files, NSC Institutional Files (H-Files), Box H–049, Senior Review Group Meetings, Senior Review Group—Middle East 11–13–70.

tary that he was out of town when the agreement was presented and, when he returned and read the agreement he thought it was unfair. He also indicated that they had expected that the material would be turned over to Jarring and that they would negotiate for three to four weeks.[13] They were surprised to be presented with an agreement the next day. They obviously expected three or four weeks to give them an opportunity to do what they wanted to do in the standstill zone.

Mr. Helms: Do we have this in writing?

Mr. Sisco: If we don't, I will put it in writing.

Mr. Kissinger: The statement that he would not have agreed to the agreement was in an outgoing cable, but I have not seen in writing the statement about negotiating for three or four weeks. (to General Bennett) Is this statement all right with you?

General Bennett: We have tried to challenge it in every possible way and I believe it is a logical presentation.

Mr. Kissinger: Is there any other presentation of the issue? I want to be sure we have a fair statement of the issues.

General Bennett: I agree with the statement in paragraph 1 that we have found no evidence to support the claim that the SAM equipment was present in the zone before August 7.

Mr. Cline: I agree with the CIA paper. It is true that we can't prove beyond any doubt that the missiles weren't there. You can't prove a negative. But given all of the evidence, it defies reasonable expectations. I am convinced that they carried out their original plan over a period of several weeks.

General Knowles: How would this paper be used?

Mr. Kissinger: We would circulate it and say that this is an agreed estimate on the basis of which each department will operate.

General Bennett: We might point out that the lower figures used in discussing the number of SAM sites are those which were fully operational. We should footnote this point.

Mr. Kissinger: Let's do it and distribute the paper.

Mr. Cline: I have one nitpick: In paragraph two of the agreed statement [*less than 1 line not declassified*] you speak of a net increase of 55 and then mention two-thirds of the sites. Do you mean two-thirds of the increase?

Mr. Helms: Yes.

---

[13] See footnote 3, Document 169.

184. Memorandum From Secretary of State Rogers to President Nixon[1]

Washington, November 19, 1970.

SUBJECT

An Analysis of Latest Events in Syria

We should not attach undue importance to the recent power play in Syria in which the military faction of the ruling Baath Party has apparently forced the civilian wing of the Party into submission. While the military group under Minister of Defense Hafiz el Asad has reportedly seized control of all government institutions and has arrested the top leaders of the civilian wing of the Party, including the leading party ideologue, Saleh al Jadid, this could well be a temporary rupture between the two rival factions who have been jockeying for position for several years.

From the standpoint of USG policy interests, the emergence of the military faction as undisputed leaders of Syria would be advantageous. This faction is more pragmatic and less doctrinaire than the civilian wing. It is disposed to expand and improve its relations with other countries and to rely less exclusively on the Soviets for outside support. It favors relaxing the strict government controls over the economy and has even talked about setting up a Parliament and a Constitution. It would probably be willing to consider seriously accepting the Security Council Resolution of November 22, 1967 in certain circumstances.

However, the point is that the military faction will probably not remain in undisputed control of the regime and will probably not be able—or willing—to change Syrian policy in any major way. The reason for this is that the military Baathists are to a great extent beholden to the civilian wing since there are two overriding considerations which must continue to influence their actions:

(1) their desire to perpetuate Baathist supremacy in Syria, and

(2) their desire to keep the Alawites in control of the Government.

Both the Baathists and the Alawites are a minority in Syria. The former represent a tightly-knit, highly organized Arab socialist-nationalist party which advocates the union of all Arab states under a socialist system. While the Party has branches in all Arab countries, it has a narrow power base in Syria. To maintain clearcut Baathist su-

---

[1] Source: National Archives, Nixon Presidential Materials, NSC Files, Box 631, Country Files, Middle East, Syria, Vol. I. Secret.

premacy the two factions must stick together or at least not oppose each other.

The Alawites, who represent 12 percent of the population and are a splinter Moslem group, have long been the underdogs in Syria. Asad is an Alawite as is Saleh al Jadid, his adversary. They and their Alawite compatriots in both factions have used the Army and the Baathist Party apparatus as a springboard to power. Accordingly, an irreparable split between the two Party factions would weaken Alawite control and threaten their dominant position in the regime.

Therefore, we do not expect any important foreign policy changes to flow from the recent Syrian developments because if this happened the civilian Party wing would probably be alienated from the military faction and, as a result, both the Baath Party as a whole and the Alawites who run it would probably suffer an eclipse. The one modification in Syrian policy which might nevertheless evolve from the current events is a more forthcoming Syrian posture toward other Arab states as a substitute for Syria's erstwhile isolation. This much Asad might succeed in achieving as a result of his power play without the risk of losing Baathist civilian cooperation. He could sell this policy as a necessary step toward seeking to fill the vacuum created by Nasser's death.

It is too early to predict whether there will be a change in Syria's policy of support for the fedayeen and of opposition to the Jordan Government. The military faction has been suspicious of Saiqa, the fedayeen instrumentality of the Baath civilian wing, because of the fear that Saiqa was being developed as a counterpoise to the Army. But this does not necessarily mean the Asad group opposes fedayeen action per se or will seek to place obstacles in the way of the fedayeen movement. Regarding Jordan, we can probably assume that for a number of reasons, Syria will be unlikely to intervene again for some time to come.

William P. Rogers

185. Telegram From the Department of State to the Embassy in Jordan[1]

Washington, November 20, 1970, 1646Z.

190308. Eyes Only for Ambassador.

1. We have recently made a thorough review of the Palestinian question[2] since the GOJ–fedayeen confrontation of some weeks ago. In recent weeks, you undoubtedly have noted that various U.S. spokesmen have made statements indicating our general sympathy for the Palestinians.[3] It is our belief that it likely to be desirable that Palestinians at some appropriate stage become participants in the negotiating process as well as partners in any peace settlement if that peace settlement is to stick. We have noted also that many Palestinians have focused on some form of entity. Nevertheless, the present Palestinian leadership is fragmented and divided, the question of who speaks for the Palestinians is no clearer today than it has been in months past, and what the majority of the Palestinians would consider a satisfactory resolution of the problem is very unclear, to say the least. As a result of our review, we have decided that for at least the time being, we should continue to operate on the assumption that the Palestinian objective can best be met through negotiations by the principal parties concerned (UAR and Jordan) with Israel under the aegis of Ambassador Jarring[4] in accordance with Security Council Resolution 242.

2. At the same time we believe that increasing attention to the Palestinian factor will be required since if we were to disregard it, this would tend to dash hopes of those whom we believe hold moderate views and could eventually be brought around to a policy of seeking a

---

[1] Source: National Archives, Nixon Presidential Materials, NSC Files, Box 616, Country Files, Middle East, Jordan. Secret; Nodis. Drafted by Sisco; cleared by Kissinger, Johnson, and Helms; and approved by Rogers. All brackets are in the original except those indicating text that remains classified.

[2] See Documents 182 and 183.

[3] See footnote 2, Document 174 and footnote 12, Document 182.

[4] On November 18, U Thant announced through his spokesman that, until the talks with Jarring could be resumed, there was "little more" that the Special Representative could do at UN Headquarters in New York. As a result, he was "well advised" to return to his post as Swedish Ambassador to the Soviet Union in Moscow. (Telegram 3244 from USUN, November 18; National Archives, Nixon Presidential Materials, NSC Files, Box 1157, Saunders Files, Middle East Negotiations Files, June Initiative Volume V) Jarring had confided in Yost that he had been "growing increasingly fed up with his long and useless vigil in New York," adding that Israel's refusal to "call and talk with him" had "aggravated his bitterness." He characterized Meir's November 16 Knesset speech (quoted at great length in telegram 6323 from Tel Aviv, November 16; ibid.), in which the Prime Minister declared that Israel would not return to talks under Jarring until the United Arab Republic rectified its cease-fire violations, as the "last straw." (Telegram 3184 from USUN, November 16; ibid.)

political solution based on coexistence with rather than destruction of the state of Israel.

3. There is an immediate operational question with which we must deal. Through other channels a representative of Fatah whom we consider to be bona fide, proposed recently on behalf of Arafat that a confidential meeting somewhere in Europe be held between senior Fatah officials and one or more senior U.S. Government officials. The Fatah official listed a number of items which the Fatah wished to discuss with us. [1½ lines not declassified] We made contact through other channels with this individual, keeping the channel open but indicating that practical factors prevented a speedy response to Fatah's proposal to establish a dialogue, and no such meeting has taken place.[5]

4. We therefore request that you have a very confidential conversation with King Hussein, purpose being exchange assessments as to how he sees the Palestinian factor in the future, how he intends to deal with it, and whether there are ways in which we can be helpful. You should level with him and indicate that Arafat has sought a direct meeting for some of his colleagues with U.S. officials. You should indicate to Hussein that we, of course, have not agreed to any such meeting and that we would wish to receive his views as to how we could be helpful, if at all, at this juncture in dealing with the Palestinians. You should, of course, avoid giving any impression that this approach to him reflects any loss of confidence on our part in him or the leadership of his government.

5. We obviously do not want to do anything that would undermine King Hussein and until we know how Hussein plans to deal with the Palestinians we do not wish to press the question of separate U.S. contacts. If after hearing his reply, we decided contact would serve our interest, we would propose your sounding him out at next discussion of the subject. If he felt, for example, that contact at that juncture with Fatah (we would if we went ahead have in mind some individual who was not an official of the government in the first instance and who could be disavowed if necessary) would undermine him and be unhelpful we obviously would take this fully into account (without necessarily giving him a veto over such a decision).

6. In short, we are asking you to undertake for the first time a serious dialogue with King Hussein with respect to the Palestinian factor which we are convinced must be taken more fully into account in weeks and months ahead. Here are some things which we think you can raise:

A. Are there ways for King Hussein to make more explicit and to define in more detail for benefit of the Palestinians his ideas regarding

---

[5] See Documents 174 and 180.

the future political role of the Palestinians? What are his views in this regard?

B. Is there something more that we can do to demonstrate that the US has very much in mind the interests of the Palestinians in any negotiation and in any settlement?

C. If negotiations under Ambassador Jarring's auspices get started, which we hope can be the case in the next few weeks, does the King feel that it is desirable, and at what stage, to bring in Palestinians in the negotiating process or does he feel that taking such a step would tend to enhance one faction as against another?

D. Most fundamentally, does he feel that the bulk of Palestinians in Jordan in particular can be brought to the fundamental notion of a political solution based on co-existence with Israel and how can we best contribute to that particular process?

E. Does he feel that we should begin to broaden our contacts with Palestinians in various capitals in the Arab world?

7. Above questions are only illustrative. They are intended to provide you with some thoughts to explore, though there are obviously a good many others. Principal purpose of this talk is to let the King know that we have been approached, to give him confidence that we are consulting him fully before making any decisions and to get him thinking more in terms of what kind of a strategy has to be pursued vis-à-vis the Palestinians, and what sort of a role we could play complementary to his that would be helpful. He should know that we have not taken any position re the idea of a Palestinian entity and we believe that this is matter between King and the Palestinians. However, your talk with King will offer you the opportunity to explore what precisely King may have in mind when he says that in a post-settlement situation the West Bank of Jordan would be given self-determination.[6]

Rogers

---

[6] In telegram 6712 from Amman, November 23, Brown reported that he had had an "exploratory talk" with Hussein on the morning of November 22, during which he broached the subject of the Palestinian question, as instructed by the Department. Brown described the discussion as "long and complicated," reporting that the King would have been "delighted" to find a Palestinian entity to which he could turn. Hussein also commented that he had "no real objection" to the United States initiating limited and guarded contacts with Fatah representatives, although he decided that he wanted to "think it through" and discuss the matter again later. He mentioned that he knew that U.S. officials were meeting with Palestinians in Amman and Beirut, had "no objection" to it, and was interested to know what these officials believed the Palestinians were thinking. The King also wanted to see "Palestinianism" defined further, having not yet decided when and if Palestinians should be brought into the Jarring talks. Finally, he said that he would be "expanding on his ideas for self-determination" in the West Bank when he visited the United States. (National Archives, Nixon Presidential Materials, NSC Files, Box 616, Country Files, Middle East, Jordan)

186. Memorandum From Director of Central Intelligence Helms to the President's Assistant for National Security Affairs (Kissinger)[1]

Washington, November 24, 1970.

SUBJECT

Fatah Request for Contact with U.S. Officials

1. Further to my memorandum of 5 November 1970[2] concerning our contact [2 lines not declassified] in our most recent meeting with [less than 1 line not declassified] he reported that Fatah has now completed preliminary plans for the creation of a Palestine State. According to [name not declassified] Fatah Chief Yasir Arafat's recent trip to Syria, Iraq, Saudi Arabia and North Africa covered one purpose only: the creation of this Palestine State.

2. [name not declassified] stated that all Arab States with the exception of Jordan have now agreed on Arafat's decision and method of establishing a State of Palestine having full sovereignty and independence, and to include the territories of the West Bank of Jordan, the Gaza Strip—with unimpeded access between the West Bank and the Gaza Strip—certain (unstated) portions of the East Bank of Jordan, and internationalization of the Old City of Jerusalem. [name not declassified] said that Arafat "has this in his hand right now." (Comment: Earlier in CSDB–312/02905–70 dated 14 October 1970,[3] we reported Fatah's plans to create a National Front, from which they envisage the emergence of a Palestine State similar to the above, with the added specific notation that the East Bank territory to be included in this State would be the East Bank of Jordan west of the Ramtha-Amman-Ma'an line.)

3. According to [name not declassified] all Arab States except Jordan have now accepted Fatah's position as the only sure way to bring lasting peace to the area. Fatah's point to the Arab rulers was simply that once all displaced Palestinians were in one place, the other Arab States would no longer have to worry about Israeli retaliation, and the Palestinians themselves would never venture attacks against Israel because Israel could easily destroy them since the Palestinians would possess no conventional military capability. [name not declassified] said that King Husayn was now trying to set up an Arab Summit Conference to discuss a "Palestinian Entity" but this will come to nothing be-

---

[1] Source: National Archives, Nixon Presidential Materials, NSC Files, Box 208, Agency Files. CIA. Secret; Sensitive. All brackets are in the original except those indicating text that remains classified. A copy was sent to the Under Secretary of State for Political Affairs.

[2] Document 180.

[3] Not found.

cause the issue is already settled: all Arab States except Jordan have already agreed to Fatah's plans for creating a Palestinian State. [*name not declassified*] said that Fatah had learned that King Husayn had received a "deputation" from the West Bank, the members of which stated that they wanted to remain with Jordan and that King Husayn would present this as "evidence" at his proposed Arab Summit Conference. However, according to [*name not declassified*] such a presentation will be meaningless as the issue has already been resolved.

4. Continuing, [*name not declassified*] said that with the agreement of all Arab States (except Jordan) to the establishment of this Palestine State, the key to the whole situation now is the United States Government, and this is a matter of extreme urgency. [*name not declassified*] asserted that the USG and Fatah must sit down at a senior level within the next week to ten days in order to review each others' positions "before it is too late." Once the decision on creation of a Palestinian State becomes open knowledge, either at the Arab Summit or at a time of Fatah's choosing, then the USG will be obliged to indicate its position openly regarding annexation to the Palestine State of some regions of present-day Jordan. It would be wise, [*name not declassified*] said, to discuss the Fatah position now, so that understanding could guide the actions of USG officials. [*name not declassified*] said that if the USG tries to oppose annexation of those Jordanian territories demanded by Fatah and agreed to by the other Arab States (except Jordan), Fatah and the Arab States "would respond harshly." Speaking dramatically but not threateningly, [*name not declassified*] said that if the USG tries to stop this, "we will look at each other through a wall of flames." [*name not declassified*] said that the USG must understand the absolute and utter frustration of the Palestinian people, and that while he fully realized that Palestinian fighters would end up the ultimate losers in a head-on confrontation with the United States on this subject, the loss of life and property which could be avoided by a simple and timely exchange of ideas between Fatah and the USG required that he present Fatah's case in the most vivid manner possible.[4]

Richard Helms[5]

---

[4] In his January 7, 1971, memorandum to Kissinger, Helms reported that the CIA had maintained "discreet contact" with [*name not declassified*] since November 24, including a meeting with him on [*text not declassified*]. At the meeting, [*name not declassified*] asked that "the political attitude of the U.S. Government toward the Palestinian movement be clarified before any further meeting takes place, and that this clarification must be in the form of an official agenda of topics to be discussed at this next meeting." Helms wrote: "It is possible he means what he has said and that he will refuse further meetings without the promise of some substantive discussion of U.S. policy on the Palestine question. We shall endeavor, however, to induce him to continue to maintain at least occasional contact with us for 'the informal exchange of views.'" (Central Intelligence Agency, ODCI Files, Job 80B01086A)

[5] Helms signed "Dick" above his typed signature.

187. Letter From President Nixon to Israeli Prime Minister Meir[1]

Washington, December 3, 1970.

Dear Madam Prime Minister:

Your letter of December 1, written in the spirit of the close friendship and understanding which exists between us, our governments, and our people, has been most helpful in clarifying your present views and concerns.[2]

I am responding to you immediately since I sense that you share our view of the importance of resuming the Jarring talks at an early date. As you know, we believe present circumstances are particularly favorable for this. There have been profound changes in the Arab world since September, whose implications can only be tested in negotiations. In addition, both our governments have by our actions clearly demonstrated that the violation of agreements is not without its political and military costs to those who seek to win unilateral advantage in this way. It seems to me that a move now by Israel into negotiations would be a move from a position of strength and would be clearly perceived as such by others.

The concern of your government to maintain that position of strength as the negotiating process goes forward is one which we fully understand and appreciate in light of our own national experience in difficult negotiating situations. I want to assure you, Madam Prime Minister, we will be responsive to your needs and we will continue to take into full account Soviet support—military, economic, and political—of the UAR as specific decisions are taken by us.

With respect to your long-term military equipment needs, including aircraft in particular, I believe the principle of a continuing military supply relationship between our two governments has been firmly established. Given the requirements of our own services and our many obligations around the world, the process of working out in specific terms what is possible in response to your long term requests will

---

[1] Source: National Archives, Nixon Presidential Materials, NSC Files, Box 756, Presidential Correspondence 1969–1974, Israel Prime Minister Golda Meir 1970. Secret; Nodis. Copies were sent to Haig, Kennedy, Sonnenfeldt, and Saunders. Telegram 197609 to Tel Aviv, December 4, instructed Barbour to deliver the letter promptly to Meir. (Ibid.)

[2] The letter, written on November 29, was delivered to Sisco by Rabin on December 1. In it, Meir addressed Israel's desire to: 1) receive further arms shipments from the United States; 2) enter into territorial negotiations without being tied to the proposals that the United States advanced in the fall of 1969; 3) have the United States "communicate to the Soviet Union the full weight of its commitment to the survival and security of Israel;" and 4) clarify the framework of the cease-fire agreement with "concrete arrangements." (Text in telegram 197609 to Tel Aviv, December 4; ibid.)

require additional time. I have asked that your requests receive priority and sympathetic consideration,[3] and the additional information recently received from your representatives will help expedite our examination. Meanwhile, I can assure you that the question is not whether we will maintain the supply and financing relationship already established but simply how to do so most rationally and effectively. The fact that, of the total supplemental appropriation for military assistance worldwide which I have requested from the Congress, almost one half is for Israel,[4] should leave no doubt about the importance we attach to your needs.

As for the course of the negotiations under Ambassador Jarring's auspices, I want to reiterate what I said to you in my message of July 23:[5] We will not press Israel to accept the positions of the UAR that there must be total Israeli withdrawal from the territories occupied in the 1967 conflict to the pre-June 5 lines or that there must be a refugee solution based exclusively on the strict application of paragraph 11 of United Nations General Assembly Resolution 194 (III).[6] Our position on withdrawal is that the final borders must be agreed between the parties by means of negotiations under the aegis of Ambassador Jarring. Moreover, we will not press Israel to accept a refugee solution which would alter fundamentally the Jewish character of the State of Israel or jeopardize your security. We will also adhere strictly and firmly to the fundamental principle that there must be a peace agreement in which each of the parties undertakes reciprocal obligations to the other and that no Israeli soldier should be withdrawn from the occupied territories until a binding contractual peace agreement satisfactory to you has been achieved.

It is true, as you point out, that our perceptions differ as to what may be possible in a final settlement. I believe our relationship is based on such a degree of mutual respect and confidence, however, that it can accommodate differences of judgment. The point I want to stress is that, in our view, the primary focus of the Jarring talks must be on the negotiating positions of the parties directly concerned. We believe those negotiations must be given every reasonable opportunity to proceed without outside interference. We will act in this spirit.

---

[3] Military assistance to Israel was discussed at the December 3 Senior Review Group meeting and then again at the January 11, 1971, Senior Review Group meeting; see Documents 188 and 195.

[4] The President earmarked $500 million for Israel in the $1.03 billion supplemental foreign aid package that he sent to Congress on November 18. (*New York Times*, November 19, 1970, p. 11) For the text of his message transmitting the proposal to Congress, see *Public Papers: Nixon, 1970*, pp. 1074–1079.

[5] See Document 136.

[6] See footnote 6, Document 136.

It follows from the foregoing that we could not be a party to an attempt by the Security Council to substitute its judgment for that of the parties with respect to the territorial and other detailed aspects of a settlement.

You have also raised the question of what this government would do in the event of direct Soviet military intervention should the UAR resume large scale hostilities against Israel. The United States under a series of Administrations has made clear in word and deed the importance it attaches to the security and survival of Israel. I believe the Soviet Union fully understands this. However, we will take an early occasion to make certain the Soviet Union is under no misapprehension in this regard.

Finally, Madam Prime Minister, I want to thank you for suggesting that it would be useful for us to exchange views with your Minister of Defense. I personally look forward to meeting with General Dayan, as do Secretaries Rogers and Laird, when he comes to Washington next week.[7]

It is our desire and intention to stay in close consultation with you and your government as the difficult process of negotiations under the aegis of Ambassador Jarring goes forward in the days and weeks ahead. As Secretary Rogers conveyed to Foreign Minister Eban on my behalf,[8] I hope the talks will begin promptly.[9] I cannot emphasize too strongly my conviction that the present moment is one of opportunity in our continuing search for a binding peace agreement based on reciprocal commitments between the parties.

Sincerely,

Richard Nixon

---

[7] See footnote 9, Document 188.

[8] According to telegram 190011 to Tel Aviv, November 19, Rogers conveyed the President's message during a 45-minute meeting with Eban in Washington on the afternoon of November 18. (National Archives, Nixon Presidential Materials, NSC Files, Box 1158, Saunders Files, Middle East Negotiations Files, June Initiative (Memos Only))

[9] After discussing the President's letter at a December 6 Cabinet meeting, Israel decided to defer its decision to return to the Jarring talks for two weeks. Israeli newspapers reported that the government would probably participate in the talks in January, following further "clarifications" between Israel and the United States. (Telegram 6696 from Tel Aviv, December 7; ibid., Box 1157, Saunders Files, Middle East Negotiations Files, June Initiative Volume V) Meir informed Barbour of the decision during a meeting on December 7 at which she also "expressed appreciation for spirit of friendship and understanding expressed in President's letter." Regarding the Jarring talks, the Prime Minister stressed Israel's "need for assurance" that the United States would support Israel during "sensitive points" of the negotiation process, given the Soviet Union's support of the United Arab Republic. Furthermore, while she found Nixon's letter "reassuring in tone on military supplies," she "needed to know Israel would be receiving steady deliveries of Phantoms and Skyhawks after January 1." (Telegram 6726 from Tel Aviv, December 8; ibid.)

188. Minutes of a Senior Review Group Meeting[1]

Washington, December 3, 1970, 11:30 a.m.–12:20 p.m.

SUBJECT

Middle East

PARTICIPANTS

Chairman—Henry Kissinger

State
U. Alexis Johnson
Joseph J. Sisco
Alfred L. Atherton
Talcott Seelye

Defense
David Packard
James S. Noyes
Gen. Devol Brett

CIA
Thomas Karamessines
David Blee

JCS
Gen. Richard Knowles
Adm. William St. George

NSC Staff
Col. Richard Kennedy
Harold Saunders
Jeanne W. Davis

SUMMARY OF DECISIONS

... The options paper on military assistance to Israel[2] should include the tactical question of whether to offer the package before or after the Arab-Israeli talks have started.

... The request for December 4 U–2 flights would be withdrawn; but, if arrangements can be made for training flights and aircraft maintenance, we should keep the U–2s on Cyprus, raising the matter with Prime Minister Heath, if necessary.[3]

... The package on military assistance to Jordan should be processed in the same way as the Israeli package—i.e. an options paper to be considered by the SRG and presented to the President for decision.[4]

---

[1] Source: National Archives, Nixon Presidential Materials, NSC Files, NSC Institutional Files (H-Files), Box H–111, Senior Review Group, Meeting Minutes Originals 1970. Top Secret; Nodis. All brackets are in the original except those indicating text that remains classified. The meeting was held in the White House Situation Room.

[2] An analytical summary of the paper is Document 194.

[3] Nixon met with Heath on December 17 and 18 one week after the administration had decided to withdraw the U–2s from Cyprus, as reported in telegram 202028 to London, December 11. (National Archives, Nixon Presidential Materials, NSC Files, Box 1157, Saunders Files, Middle East Negotiations Files, June Initiative Volume V) Thus, the U–2 issue was not addressed in their conversations; see *Foreign Relations, 1969–1976*, volume XLI, Western Europe; NATO, 1969–1972, Documents 334 and 335. [*Text not declassified*]

[4] An analytical summary of the paper is Document 191.

Mr. Kissinger: This was intended to be a relatively brief meeting to bring ourselves up to date before the decisions have to be made over the next few weeks. (to Mr. Sisco) Can you run down some of the problems?

Military Assistance for Israel

Mr. Sisco: Our principal objective is still to try to get the Israeli-Arab talks started. The President has received a letter from Golda Meir[5] expressing two concerns: (1) the look of the future as it relates to US military and financial support for Israel; and (2) some assurance that they will be left free to take a reasonable approach to the negotiations. They were, of course, deeply concerned over the US plan developed in the October-December 1969 period, at least as it involved the border with Egypt. We do not interpret this letter as laying down conditions for resumption of the talks. It expresses Israeli concerns and appears to be aimed at developing a general understanding between the US and Israel. We believe it should receive a prompt reply so as to give the Israeli Cabinet a chance to consider it at their meeting on Sunday.[6] Secretary Rogers believes that the reply should be somewhat general in nature, with no specific commitment.

With regard to the work on our recommendations for providing Israel with the equipment she has requested, the Defense Department has completed a good technical options paper.[7] We are beginning to look at it, and will put together two or three possibilities, taking the political factors into account, for submission to the SRG. We can look at these options and, hopefully over the next few weeks, shape them so they can be presented to the President for decision. We believe we should make no specific commitment to the Israelis prior to the beginning of the talks. Following that, we should try to be reasonably responsive.

Mr. Kissinger: I have a tactical question. Let's leave aside what we should do, assuming we should do something for Israel and that whatever we do will give us trouble with the Arabs. Would it be tactically better to give Israel something before the talks commence and then present it as a quid pro quo for Israeli agreement to enter the talks? If we give them equipment while the talks are going on, we might be criticized for introducing an arms package into the talks. Or, we might give Israel an excuse to say that, because of the talks, she has an even greater need. I was troubled by the June formula which had us telling the Israelis that if it appeared that the talks were not getting anywhere, then

---

[5] See footnote 2, Document 187.
[6] See Document 187. The Cabinet met on Sunday, December 6.
[7] An analytical summary of the paper is Document 194.

we would give them arms. This would have given the Israelis an incentive to stall in the talks. Tactically, wouldn't it be wiser to put ourselves in a position to claim that the arms package was a way of getting them to talk?

Mr. Sisco: You can make a case that a prior commitment would be an inducement. I'm aware that the kind of general response, short of a commitment, we are suggesting may not do the job. I think we should try, however.

Mr. Kissinger: The reply to Mrs. Meir's letter is a different problem. If we reply in the way you suggest, do you think their response will be to enter the talks?

Mr. Sisco: Not necessarily.

Mr. Packard: I am troubled by how much we have had to do to get the Israelis to talk. We have already done a good deal for them.

Mr. Kissinger: I agree. But if we are going to give them arms anyway, wouldn't it be tactically wise to give them before the talks and then present the act as a quid pro quo for their entering the talks, even if it was not. I'm worried about the Arabs.

Mr. Sisco: I see your point, but I think presenting the arms package during the talks would be manageable because: 1) the Arabs are more concerned about the use of the arms than about the fact that Israel is getting them; and 2) the arms package could still be related to the stand-still violations and to the ongoing effort by the USSR for Egypt. The Arabs will be concerned but it will be manageable. If we can come up with reasonable arms packages, somewhat extended in terms of time and money, we would have established an ongoing military relationship with Israel in a reasonably quiet way.

Mr. Johnson: This is based on the assumption that the Soviets will continue to support Egypt. What the US is doing for Israel would be part of the response to Soviet help for Egypt.

Mr. Sisco: Yes, although I don't entirely accept the Israeli theory of an open-ended relationship between the USSR and Egypt.

Mr. Kissinger: Have there been substantial Soviet deliveries?

Mr. Sisco: Not recently. There were two periods of intensive supply in April and August of this year.

Mr. Packard: We should also watch what kinds of things the Russians are supplying Egypt. Are they supplying air defense equipment or equipment which will enable them to cross the Canal and mount an attack. We should consider what they are getting as well as how much?

Mr. Johnson: If the Soviets put a ceiling on what they are supplying Egypt, we would certainly take this into account.

Mr. Kissinger: We would have to.

Mr. Sisco: A general response to Mrs. Meir's letter may not do the job. However, I think the Israelis have made a decision to resume the talks shortly before the Jarring report is due on January 5. I don't think the Israelis really expect an explicit commitment from us. We should try to get the talks resumed without a commitment. If we can't, we may have to link our arms package with the talks.

Mr. Packard: We should see how far we can get with them before using the arms package.

Mr. Kissinger: This has nothing to do with the Meir letter, since we cannot include a commitment on military assistance in the President's reply. We are talking now about our general posture and whether to make the material available before the talks or after they have started. This is independent of the Israeli decision unless it becomes necessary to use the arms package to get them to the talks.

Mr. Packard: There's also the question of how much we should give them. This will vary according to what the Soviets do.

Mr. Sisco: We are putting together an options paper on the variables, based on the very good Defense paper. There are three options: do nothing; do something; and give them everything they want over an extended period. Secretary Rogers generally agrees with a formula that would meet their requests in a substantial way, but extend the response over some period of time.

Dayan Proposal[8]

Mr. Kissinger: I have two questions on the Dayan visit.[9] Do we believe the Israelis will reach a decision before Dayan returns?

Mr. Sisco: We're not sure. They may try to reach a decision at Sunday's Cabinet meeting, before Dayan returns. This is what Golda should do. If a decision is postponed until after Dayan returns, he will get the credit for it.

---

[8] In a November 22 Israeli Cabinet meeting, Dayan outlined a plan for a long-term cease-fire agreement with the United Arab Republic based on a thinning out of forces along the Suez Canal, but encountered strong opposition among the other Ministers. (*New York Times*, November 23, 1970, p. 7) Four days later, he discussed this idea, along with the equally controversial notion that the United Arab Republic could be encouraged to open the Suez Canal before a peace agreement was reached, in an interview on Israeli television. (Ibid., November 27, 1970, p. 9) One observer described the Defense Minister's "thinking out loud" over the last few weeks of November as "shattering the political calm and seeming immobility of the Israeli government" and sending "respected political commentators, diplomats, and even Cabinet ministers scurrying around to figure out what he is up to." (Ibid., November 29, 1970, p. 196)

[9] Dayan met with Nixon on December 11; see Document 190. He also met with Rogers and Laird that day, as reported in telegram 202635 to Tel Aviv, December 13. (National Archives, Nixon Presidential Materials, NSC Files, Box 1158, Saunders Files, Middle East Negotiations Files, June Initiative (Memos Only))

Mr. Kissinger: Assuming you would get any credit for this in Israel.

Mr. Sisco: You would. I believe Dayan's statements are closer to the pulse of Israeli sentiment than Golda's. There is strong feeling among the Israeli people that they must get on with the discussions. Dayan's statements are based on a more accurate reading of Israeli public opinion than Golda's are.

Mr. Karamessines: [1 *line not declassified*]

Mr. Kissinger: I just don't know. Perhaps Dayan is positioning himself to appear more reasonable—which brings me to my second question: is Dayan saying that the standstill has to be renegotiated in terms of his demilitarized zone proposal?

Mr. Sisco: We must be very careful about this. Mrs. Meir's letter indicated Dayan wants to talk about a new agreement on a cease-fire, assuming adequate machinery can be developed. The President must be very careful. He should say "yes we will talk about this, but we believe the Israeli-Arab talks must begin." Otherwise, Israel will say they will sit tight until we can achieve a new cease-fire agreement. And I am convinced that no new cease-fire agreement can be negotiated. We will have to be completely frank with Dayan—tell him that a new standstill agreement is not possible. Dayan will suggest that a thinning out of forces on either side of the Canal would be part of a cease-fire agreement. We should reply that the idea is worth exploring, but it should be done in the Israeli-Arab negotiations as part of a political settlement. It should not be a condition for the negotiations.

Mr. Kissinger: Is Dayan serious about his proposal?

Mr. Sisco: Yes, but he has no support in the Israeli Cabinet. Most Israelis feel very strongly that there should be no movement from the cease-fire lines until a peace settlement has been achieved. The Israelis have told Dayan that if he wants to discuss this idea with anyone, to discuss it with the Americans. The Egyptians would never agree to a thinning out of forces. They don't mind Dayan's discussing it with us, since everyone is convinced that someone else will knock the idea out.

Mr. Kissinger: At one point, when there was some press talk about a 30-mile demilitarized zone on either side of the Canal, Don Bergus came back with a telegram saying "make it 15 miles and you have a deal." This was presented as an alternate to a cease-fire, I believe.

Mr. Sisco: Egypt has already taken a public position against this.

Mr. Kissinger: There are two questions: 1) is it a good idea, and 2) what forum should be used? State's recommendation is not to tie Dayan's proposal to the beginning of the negotiations. If it is a good idea, it should be discussed in the Jarring talks. We don't have to take a position now. I can see where the idea might have some attraction for the Russians if it opens the Suez Canal. If it does not, I don't see any attraction for anyone.

Mr. Sisco: If Israel should pull its forces back 20 or 30 kilometers, Allon says they would have to increase the strength of their positions beyond the zone in Sinai, and that they could not do this without partial mobilization.

Mr. Packard: They have no good defensive line there now.

Mr. Kissinger: If neither Israel nor Egypt wants this, it would be very hard for us to do anything about it.

Mr. Sisco: Dayan should return from his talks in the US saying he didn't find much enthusiasm for the idea here.

Military Assistance for Israel

Mr. Kissinger: Could we review the status of military assistance for Israel. You have completed your technical studies. Then it goes through the IG, which makes its recommendations to the SRG,[10] including the question of tactics as to whether to offer the package before or after the talks have started assuming, of course, that the talks have not already started.

[Omitted here is discussion of the U–2 flights that monitored the cease-fire zone.]

Assistance for Jordan

Mr. Kissinger: May we now turn to the question of assistance for Jordan.

Mr. Sisco: I think State and Defense are generally together on the package. All we need is money.

Mr. Seelye: We are preparing a joint memorandum to the President from the Secretaries of State and Defense which will enable him to decide in principle, subject to the availability of funds, on a package, along the lines the Jordanians have requested and that our survey team agrees is sound for the new mission of the Jordanian Army.[11]

Mr. Kissinger: What is that new mission?

Mr. Seelye: Before the civil war, the King had thought more in terms of defense—anti-aircraft, etc. Now, following the Syrian intervention, the King believes he needs a more mobile force and his priorities have changed—in the direction of tanks, for example. The problem is money, and this can't be resolved before the King comes here.[12] An

---

[10] The Senior Review Group next held a meeting to discuss this issue on January 11, 1971; see Document 195.

[11] The memorandum is attached to and summarized in Document 191.

[12] Hussein met with Nixon on December 8. See Document 189.

attachment to the State-Defense memo will indicate our thinking on what we might do in the next two years to help in the financing. We have $30 million in MAP included in the supplemental. This is inadequate for the package the King is talking about, which is around $186.6 million. We could of course, pare this down, phase it over two or three years, and subject it to annual review so that we are not providing equipment at a time when it should not be provided. We could offer the King something as a first slice while he is here, but he is talking about a 6–9 month time frame.

Mr. Kissinger: Where is the money coming from?

Mr. Seelye: We have the $30 million in the supplemental. I believe we should consider reinstituting our program of budgetary support to Jordan. Until 1967, we were supplying $30 million annually in budgetary support. We discontinued it because our general aid philosophy moved away from the idea of budgetary support and because the Arab countries agreed to provide Jordan with regular subsidies. We are still not completely satisfied that we have a true picture of Jordan's economic and financial situation and its needs. In the next two weeks, we will sit down with Jordanian financial experts to see what the situation is and what they could do to tighten their belts. We will have a better idea of exactly what gap we have to plug after we see how much Jordan can do.

Mr. Sisco: The President can tell the King we will do the best we can for him but that we have a funding problem.

Mr. Kissinger: We should put the Jordan package through the same process as the Israeli package. We can tell the King the same thing we are telling Mrs. Meir—a general expression of sympathy, and we will see what we can do. Then we can put the requests through our machinery and come up with a recommended package.

Mr. Noyes: The President is committed publicly to make good Jordan's losses.

Mr. Kissinger: That is no problem. I am talking about the larger two or three year package which should be put through the machinery.

Mr. Seelye: Jordan still needs $9.8 million for replacement of their losses. They will tell us they don't have it.

Mr. Kissinger: Doesn't that come out of the $30 million?

Mr. Sisco: No, this is beyond that.

General Knowles: They could give up something out of the $30 million package.

Mr. Kissinger: There would be no policy objection to taking it out of the $30 million.

Mr. Noyes: But the President would be going back on his word.

Mr. Kissinger: Then find the money.

Mr. Sisco: It may have to come from some future increment. We could commit ourselves to X amount.

Mr. Kissinger: I agree. We will tell the King he will get something. We can give him the $9 million which he needs now. By the time the $30 million is being spent, we will have a slice of the larger amount. We won't have to face the issue.

General Knowles: By that time we will be in a new fiscal year.

Mr. Seelye: The King wants the equipment in 6–9 months time.

Mr. Kissinger: Where the money comes from is our internal bookkeeping problem.

Mr. Noyes: The King was going to give us cash for some of this but then his country blew up. We have already spent some of the $30 million making up his losses.

Mr. Kissinger: There is no policy issue here. Either find the $9 million or juggle the books.

Palestine

Mr. Sisco: We will have another thorough discussion with the King on Palestine next week. We don't need anything more on this until after that discussion.

Mr. Karamessines: I would like to call your attention to a series of reports over the last two or three weeks, and particularly some in the last two or three days. Rifai is now acting as political adviser to Fatah. There are indications that the Palestinians are planning to announce formation of a Palestinian entity, independent of the State of Jordan, and request the stationing of Iraqi troops. They would take over the East Bank "by popular acclaim." In other words, they would kick the King out and take over. Fatah will initially denounce formation of the entity, but once it is established, they will move in and take control. We have summarized these reports and I wanted to focus your attention on them. (Handed the attached summary paper around the table.)[13] You will note the King's suspicion of the UAR.

Mr. Kissinger: We will have a separate meeting on the Palestinian question.[14]

---

[13] "Summary of Significant Reporting on Jordan," undated, covers the period October 14–December 2 and includes the subheadings: "I. Creation of a Palestine Entity," "II. Jordan-UAR Relations," "III. Relations with Other Arab States: Views on a Peaceful Middle East Solution and Khartoum Payments," and "IV. Iraqi Troops in Jordan." (National Archives, Nixon Presidential Materials, NSC Files, Box 1260, Saunders Files, Subject Files)

[14] The Senior Review Group discussed the Palestinian question on December 17; see Document 192.

189. Memorandum of Conversation[1]

Washington, December 8, 1970, 11 a.m.

PARTICIPANTS

Jordan
His Majesty King Hussein Bin Talal
His Excellency Abdul Hamid Sharaf, Ambassador
His Excellency Zaid Rifai, Ambassador to London

United States
The President
Mr. Henry Kissinger, Assistant to the President for National Security Affairs
Mr. Joseph J. Sisco, Assistant Secretary of State for Near Eastern and South Asian Affairs
Ambassador to Jordan, L. Dean Brown

The President congratulated the King on the successful outcome to Jordan's grave problems of September. Central to the solution of the Middle East's problems is the survival of a strong and independent Jordan. Jordan's survival is, in turn, dependent on the King's survival.

The King thanked the President warmly, saying that Jordan could not have gotten through its difficult days without the support and interest of the United States. He and Jordan are proud of the close and excellent relations between the two countries and two peoples. He stressed his conviction that the U.S. and Jordan share the same views and principles. Stresses and strains have increased in the Middle East since 1967. The number of extremists has grown: There is greater disunity among the Arabs as evidenced by the recent UN vote when Arabs split seven-and-seven.[2] Extremism among the Arab states seems to grow in relation to the distance from the problem. He has feared that the Middle East is changing from one of Arab-Israeli involvement to one of major power involvement. There are those in the area who want to see that sort of confrontation. The situation in Jordan has improved: the task now is to rebuild. Since 1967 Jordan has been trying to find a just and lasting solution to the Middle East problem. It is now trying to consolidate the unity of the country and to make itself an area of sta-

---

[1] Source: National Archives, Nixon Presidential Materials, NSC Files, Box 616, Country Files, Middle East, Jordan, Vol. VI. Secret; Exdis. Drafted by Brown and approved by Sisco and Kissinger. The meeting took place in the Oval Office from 11:06 to 11:48 a.m. (Ibid., White House Central Files, President's Daily Diary) The King was in Washington December 8–10. Later in the day on December 8, he met with Laird. A memorandum of conversation is in the Washington National Records Center, OSD Files: FRC 330–76–0067, Box 74, Jordan. He met with Agnew on December 10. A memorandum of conversation is in the National Archives, Nixon Presidential Materials, NSC Files, Box 616, Country Files, Middle East, Jordan, Vol. VI.

[2] Reference is to General Assembly Resolution 2628; see footnote 8, Document 177.

bility. It will not be easy. Jordan is the target of extremists, both from Arab and Israeli quarters.

The President commented that Jordan is getting it from both sides. Jordan really is in the middle.

The King went on to say that Jordan wants to play a constructive role. It wants to build and get its young people back from abroad to take part in this new effort. He had just visited Saudi Arabia and the UAR where he found many cross-currents on the Palestine issue. The Cairo atmosphere is more relaxed: There is decentralization of authority. For the first time he had heard differing views as to what to do, but there was deep concern as to what would happen when the cease-fire comes to an end. Egyptians are worried by the lack of progress towards talks and wanted him to tell the President of their fears. They say there could be disaster if nothing substantial is initiated before the expiration of the 90-day period. The new government is under greater pressure than that of Nasser and less sure of itself or its ability to meet internal pressures. The Egyptians fear Israel will agree to talks just a few days before the cease-fire ends and then procrastinate again. He thinks this might lead to another explosion.

The King said in accordance with the commitment he made in Cairo, he wanted to bring up another UAR idea which had already been broached with the Soviets. Could there be concentration now on guarantees? These could be worked out by US and USSR or perhaps by the Big Four. The guarantees essentially would be aimed at settling the question of security once Security Council Resolution 242 was implemented. The UAR had told him that peace achieved this way could lead to disbandment of the UAR armed forces. He had committed himself to bring this up. He was not prepared to move farther along this path until he has further discussion with the Egyptians. He expects to see them again soon. He believes, however, that there is no solution except an imposed one. Jarring will probably not get anywhere. In any case Resolution 242 is not clear to all concerned.

The President replied that this is a very delicate problem. We want to get the parties together and not separate them. Imposition requires finding parties who are ready to have solutions imposed upon them. This is just not the case. The US recognizes that Jordan's security must be adequate. We will look at what we can do as sympathetically as possible, given the limitations we have. The President stated that he has already asked Congress for funds to start this assistance.[3] As for the cease-fire, its continuation is in the interest of all. It would solve

---

[3] The President earmarked $30 million for Jordan in the $1.03 billion supplemental foreign aid package that he sent to Congress on November 18. See footnote 4, Document 187.

nothing to resume hostilities. People in the area are tired of fighting. As for negotiations, candidly there is no guarantee that if talks were to begin we would get the results we hope for, but continuing as we are will get us nowhere.

The President said the King is surrounded by problems: Palestinians, radical neighbors, and Israel. That he has survived is both a modern miracle and a key to a solution. He then asked Mr. Sisco to talk about an imposed settlement and solution.

Mr. Sisco said that we are trying to get negotiations started and expect that this will happen by a reasonably early date. Even if negotiations start, we do not intend to stand aside. Jarring has no divisions to back him up.

The President noted that Jarring has no more than the Pope, maybe less. Mr. Sisco said we intend to be active in the context of the Jarring talks. He cannot do it alone. The President said this was correct.

Mr. Sisco said he would like to discuss the question of guarantees and the role of the big powers, noting that it is a problem for the U.S. and is delicate since it could involve commitments.

The President said we have to think about this problem of guarantees and in this connection, what those in the area think about them. Mr. Sisco said the primary basis of security has to be a peace agreement based on reciprocal commitments between the parties. What the major powers then did would be complementary and additive. If there is a peace agreement between those involved, major powers could endorse them within the context of the Security Council.

Ambassador Sharaf said he thought that the King wants to see guarantees springing from Israeli withdrawal from occupied Jordanian territories. The Arabs have played their part: they have accepted Israel as a state and it is now Israel's turn to withdraw. The Arabs are ready to entertain any sort of international guarantee which brings about withdrawal and peace. Jordan cannot just go into talks with Jarring without some sort of goal: that goal must be withdrawal and peace.

The President said he would be discussing the Israeli position with Dayan on Friday.[4] To be fair, Israelis have a point when they say that written guarantees are not enough. They need to have the ability to defend their security if guarantees break down. The world has, indeed, changed since 1967. Arab states are now ready to do what they were not prepared to do then. They now accept Israel as an independent state with secure borders. We want to look carefully at both sides and see where we can be helpful in between. Israel cannot accept faith

---

[4] See Document 190.

alone. Somewhere guarantees will need to be fitted in. Jordan needs these too. It also has enemies in the area.

Mr. Sisco said that international guarantees can provide an additional and complementary psychological basis for confidence. In addition, there need to be commitments between two sides and practical security agreements on the ground. He noted that violations of the standstill have undermined the weight Israel would attach to international guarantees.

The President said that we have to face up to the fact that Israel has such views. Wars occur in peacetime and often between states which have non-aggression pacts. De Gaulle thought this way, believing that France needed a minimal ability to defend itself; if there is no defense, treaties are meaningless. Sophisticated government leaders always look to the future, asking what next the government will do. Great powers may have a role as a result of this.

Ambassador Rifai said he was skeptical. He just does not know what the Israelis want. The King interjected that maybe they do not either. Ambassador Rifai said the Israelis want peace but as they see it and this will be at Jordan's expense. Jordan paid the price of defeat of 1967. It recognized Israel. Peace also has its price. This is for Israel to pay and it requires withdrawal.

The President said this is preceptive thought: Defeat has a price and peace has a price. The Government of Jordan is the most responsible government in the area. We admire and respect the King for this. Jordan has earned the right to survive. We will keep in mind the thoughts the King has expressed.

The advisors then left and the President and the King had a brief private talk.[5]

---

[5] No record of the private talk has been found. That evening, the President held a working dinner for King Hussein in the State Dining Room, attended by Rogers, Laird, Sisco, Kissinger, Helms, Moorer, Shakespeare, Hannah, Mosbacher, Brown, Atherton, Saunders, Seelye, and Jordanians including Salah, Sharaf, and Zaid Rifai. They discussed Jordan's success in putting down the fedayeen uprising in September, the Palestinian question, the Jarring talks, the possibilities presented by new leadership in Cairo, and Soviet intentions in the Middle East, while the King expressed particular concern over growing "extremism" in the region. (Memorandum of conversation, December 8; National Archives, Nixon Presidential Materials, NSC Files, Box 616, Country Files, Middle East, Jordan, Vol. VI)

190. Memorandum of Conversation[1]

Washington, December 11, 1970, 3:30 p.m.

PARTICIPANTS

The President
Israeli Defense Minister Moshe Dayan
Israeli Ambassador Rabin
Secretary of Defense Laird
General Haig

Following greetings, Defense Minister Dayan stated that he was giving a speech in New York tomorrow which would be in an open forum and that he would like to have the President's permission to state to the members of the American Jewish Community, who would be in the audience, that Prime Minister Golda Meir had told him that President Nixon had always been true to his word and that he had given her many good words. The President agreed.[2]

The meeting was then delayed for press photography. Following the departure of the press, President Nixon said that he had great admiration for the people of Israel and had been tremendously impressed primarily by their spirit during his visit to Israel in 1967.

Defense Minister Dayan stated that it was conceivable that in the spring the Egyptians would be reinforced by Soviet aircraft and would feel capable of trying to cross the Canal. He wanted the President to know that Israeli forces would not turn their back but would fight and that the spirit of Israel was still strong and aggressive even if the Soviets provided air superiority to the UAR.

Defense Minister Dayan added that the Israeli air battle of last summer with the Soviets[3] was a calculated decision on the part of his government and one which was taken alone without consultation with any other Government, with the full realization of the implications of the engagement.

President Nixon stated that his policy had been, from the outset, to counterbalance Soviet power in the Middle East. He was confident that

---

[1] Source: National Archives, Nixon Presidential Materials, NSC Files, Box 608, Country Files, Middle East, Israel, Vol. VIII. Top Secret; Sensitive. The meeting took place in the Oval Office. Printed from an unsigned copy.

[2] In his speech to the United Jewish Appeal on December 12, Dayan asserted that while President Nixon "has kept every word" to Israel concerning its military needs since his election, "we do not want to find ourselves in a position where only the other parties have military supplies, soldiers, and missiles." He added: "We do not want to sit down at a table with a gun being pointed at us." (*New York Times,* December 13, 1970, p. 11)

[3] Rabin described Israel's July 30, 1970, air battle with the Soviets to Kissinger; see Document 142.

the Arabs alone would be no match for Israel's military. For this reason, it was his concern that the Soviets recognize that the U.S. would guarantee Israel's survival. He had followed this policy since the first days of his Administration, both in public and in private contacts with the Soviets.

The President added that U.S. actions during the Jordan crisis were designed to demonstrate this point. The movement of the Sixth Fleet was ordered to convey to the Soviet Union that the U.S. would not stand idly by in this situation. The President also complimented the Israeli Government for the readiness measures which they took and which were also an operative factor in de-escalating the situation.

Secretary Laird added that it was especially significant that Israel had moved in concert with Jordan and enabled the King of Jordan to strip his border with Israel and concentrate his forces against the Syrians.

The President noted that the magnificent performance of the Jordanian armored forces was also a key factor. The President stated that it would be difficult for him to foresee the Egyptians crossing the Canal alone without suffering a catastrophe.

Minister Dayan stated that it would be unlikely that the Egyptians would move unless they had a guarantee of air superiority through the provision of large numbers of Soviet aircraft but even in this instance he believed that Israeli armor utilized properly in the desert would be ultimately decisive.

President Nixon stated that he would never mislead the Prime Minister or the people of Israel. He intended to be forthright and honest and make no promises that he would not deliver or provide any assurances that he would not keep. He stated that from time to time friends would disagree on particulars but that the essence of international friendship was mutual trust. He trusted Prime Minister Meir and anticipated that she shared this trust in him.

The President added that it was quite evident to him that the American people anticipated that Israel would move to the conference table under the auspices of Jarring. He pointed out that this was expected in light of the $500 million assistance being provided by this government which he hoped would soon be approved by the Congress.[4] He stated that it was important that the youth of Israel be permitted to apply their great talents, ingenuity and industry to peaceful pursuits and that for this reason the time was right to enter into the talks. He pointed out further that Israel at this time could move with an air of confidence since the military balance would be re-

---

[4] Congress passed the supplemental foreign aid package on December 22.

established through the current aid package and since the overall international environment dictated such a move. He emphasized that all responsible U.S. officials were of one mind on this.

Defense Minister Dayan replied that Israel wanted to negotiate and that last year one of the elements of their Government resigned on this issue[5] but the consensus was in favor of negotiation and it still is. He pointed out, however, that the standstill violations posed a most serious complication for Israel. To proceed now in the face of these violations would be almost impossible. He added that if the U.S. could make some commitment with respect to Israel's future military needs, he was confident that the talks could proceed, emphasizing however that he was not authorized by his government to discuss these issues.

Minister Dayan stated that he was concerned about the status of Israel's air inventory since they had lost 8 Phantoms and since the Prime Minister had requested in September a flow of 6 Phantoms and 6 Skyhawks per month, starting in January of 1971[6] but that no word had been received from the U.S. side as to whether or not this request would be satisfied.

President Nixon asked Secretary Laird and General Haig where this issue stood. General Haig stated that the Israeli arms request for 1971 was being considered at interdepartmental level.[7] Secretary Laird stated that it would be very difficult for the U.S. to meet the request for aircraft since it would be necessary for us to enter our own inventory to do so. Production lines would take over a year to provide the aircraft directly from the manufacturers.

Secretary Laird also pointed out that Israel's main requirement was for ground control equipment and that the Department of Defense was working on a package to alleviate Israel's problem in this respect.

Minister Dayan again emphasized that Israel's air inventory was not adequate in the light of the heavy weight of air assets controlled by the enemy. He knew that without some U.S. commitments and a steady flow of replacement aircraft it would be difficult to expect Israel to proceed with the talks under Jarring.

President Nixon stated that this posed complex problems for us, that he was not familiar with the details but that Israel must understand that the U.S., on occasion, could not meet all of Israel's requirements. Israel would have to rely on our assurances and good faith which have never been found lacking.

---

[5] See footnote 3, Document 149.

[6] See Document 162.

[7] The Senior Review Group next considered military assistance to Israel at its meeting on January 11, 1971; see Document 195.

Ambassador Rabin stated that previous Israeli requests had sometimes run into great difficulty in that decisions were made at the last minute and only after crises had developed and, therefore, it was next to impossible for Israel to plan properly and to train adequately for and maintain, as well as modify surge shipments of equipment. It was therefore important for a steady pipeline of material to be provided and with sufficient notification so that past turbulence could be eliminated.

President Nixon restated that the U.S. had no intention of permitting Israel to fall and that he personally, with the full weight of this government, was fully committed to its survival.

Meeting was adjourned at 4:45 p.m.

---

191. Paper Prepared by the National Security Council Staff[1]

Washington, December 16, 1970.

ANALYTICAL SUMMARY

MILITARY ASSISTANCE TO JORDAN

U.S. Options

The attached State Department draft memo (reviewed but not formally cleared through Deputy Assistant Secretary Noyes in Defense)[2] outlines as one course of action these two steps:

—Approving in principle and subject to an annual US-Jordanian review the provision over a three-year period of military equipment to Jordan as recommended by the military survey team to facilitate the reorganization of the Jordanian armed forces. The total value of this equipment would amount to about $130 million roughly prorated over four years, FY71 through FY74.

—Replacing U.S.-manufactured equipment lost during the September civil war and not covered in Secretary Laird's letter of December 10[3] [see previous sub-tab].

---

[1] Source: National Archives, Nixon Presidential Materials, NSC Files, NSC Institutional Files (H-Files), Box H–050, Senior Review Group Meetings, SRG Meeting—Jordan 12–17–70. Secret. All brackets are in the original.

[2] Attached but not printed is the undated memorandum from Sisco to Kissinger.

[3] Attached but not printed.

If this course of action were approved, King Hussein would be informed now of the above.

Mr. Sisco in his covering memo to you outlines two other possible courses:

—Stalling Hussein for the time being by telling him that we are studying the survey team's report[4] urgently and will discuss additional requirements in the near future.

—Telling Hussein that, because of lack of funds, we cannot be responsive to his requests for more arms beyond the Laird commitment until we have obtained Congressional approval for financing.

These are tactical means for delaying a decision or a reply. They are not real alternatives. The real alternative would be to decide that we are not going to commit ourselves now to a three-year program for Jordan and promise Hussein something less, if anything at all. To promise something less, we would simply move down the four increments recommended by the military survey team from the full program to, say, the first full increment. (The Laird letter of December 10—the "impact package" offered to Hussein—promised part of the survey team's first increment.)

In order to describe how selecting a smaller package would work, the survey team's options are laid out below.

The Survey Team's Options

All options which the Survey Team developed contain two constant components:

—$9.1 million in replenishment of battle losses.

—$30.7 million for the revised FY70 artillery and air defense package. [This figure is down from the original $42 million approved last spring.[5] The revision results from the fact that the proposed reorganization of the Jordanian forces replaces some of the earlier requirements met in that package with new ones.]

On top of that $39.8 million minimum, the team developed four alternatives to the Jordanian request. These options, which build from a minimum response up to the full Jordanian request (described below) can be sketched as follows:

---

[4] According to the December 7 report of the Department of Defense Military Survey Team, the group went to Jordan at the King's request, after the fedayeen uprising in September, to "assess Jordanian military needs resulting from a planned reorganization of the Jordanian Arab Army, and to consider the financial implications of that reorganization for the governments of Jordan and the United States." (Washington National Records Center, ISA Files: FRC 330–73A–1975, Box 20, Jordan)

[5] See Document 113.

Alternative IV—$42.6 million: This is essentially a package for providing equipment in the next 6–9 months to meet the modernization needs of the Jordanian forces in being. [The major items would be 33 APC's; 50 tanks; 40 self-propelled 155 mm. howitzers; 15,000 M–16 rifles; 500 grenade launchers; 275 Sidewinder missiles, a ground control radar, spares and ground equipment for the present F–104 squadron. The Laird package of December 10 provided some of these items: 57 APC's; 14 M–60 A1 tanks; no longer range guns but 42 106 mm. recoilless rifles; 16,000 M–16 rifles; 500 grenade launchers; 80 machine guns (50 cal. and 30 cal.); promise of a later answer on more tanks and on radar. The cost of the Laird package is about $26 million.]

Alternative III—$81.5 million: This includes the equipment under the above alternative and adds to the above the equipment necessary to equip new units, particularly mechanized infantry battalions and another brigade in the mechanized division. [In addition to equipment under alternative IV, there would be 125 more APC's; 50 more tanks; 20 self-propelled 105 mm. howitzers.]

Alternative II—$117 million: This would add to both of the above one squadron (24 aircraft) of close support/intercept aircraft (the F–5).

Alternative I—$146.7 million: This represents a paring down of the Jordanian request to represent a reasonable long range capability objective for the Jordanian Armed Forces. The plan would be to reach this goal in increments over a three to four year period, starting with Alternative IV above as the first increment. Incremental increases could follow periodic review of absorptive capability, the threat and financial availabilities. [This would involve, including the above increments, the following total of major items: 288 APC's; 100 tanks; 20 105 mm. self-propelled howitzers; 45,000 M–16 rifles; 1500 grenade launchers; 24 F–5 aircraft; 2 C–130 aircraft.]

The Jordanian Request—$186.6 million. In addition to the equipment listed under Alternative I above, this list includes among major items: 156 more APC's; 50 more tanks; 20 more 105 mm. self-propelled howitzers; 23,000 more rifles; and additional quantities of ammunition.

The Issues

The provision of any equipment beyond that already committed presents two key problems:

1. *Financial.* The supplemental appropriation if passed by Congress[6] would provide $30 million—just enough to cover a good part of the December 10 package and replenishment of September. Jordan still needs another $30 million (roughly the cost of last spring's artillery

---

[6] See footnote 4, Document 190.

package) in FY 71. This may require a special FY 71 supplemental bill for Jordan requesting a combination of military assistance grant and supporting assistance. If this is not possible, the President could approve under Section 506 of the Foreign Assistance Act furnishing the equipment on a grant basis from Defense stocks. [He would have to make a determination that such action is "vital to the security of the U.S." This would be subject to reimbursement from subsequent military assistance appropriations.]

2. *Political.* With growing fedayeen thought about taking over Jordan rather than destroying Israel, the longer term commitment to Hussein would make sense mainly if it is in the context of a major effort (a) to achieve an Israel-Jordan settlement and (b) to settle the Palestinian problem by working through Hussein. [This issue is discussed in connection with the Palestinian option.]

The principal issue therefore is whether the U.S. believes now is the time to make a major long-term commitment to Hussein. The *conclusion* of the attached memo is that we should make such a commitment—but in a very guarded way by subjecting it to annual review. The approach recommended is to establish the framework of a three-year program but to hold an annual review of Jordanian needs and available financing.

The *argument for* this approach is that it has the element of supporting the one element in Jordan that seems committed to a settlement with Israel while still giving the U.S. an escape if the situation in Jordan changes.

The *argument against* is that such a commitment would take the U.S. one step closer to precluding any serious ties with a Palestinian government in Jordan.

192. Minutes of a Senior Review Group Meeting[1]

Washington, December 17, 1970, 3:15–3:55 p.m.

SUBJECT

JORDAN

PARTICIPATION

Chairman—Henry A. Kissinger

State
Joseph J. Sisco
Talcott Seelye
Thomas Thornton
William Lewis

Defense
David Packard
G. Warren Nutter
James S. Noyes

CIA
Richard Helms
David H. Blee

JCS
Adm. Thomas H. Moorer
Rear Adm. William P. St. George

NSC
Harold H. Saunders
Jeanne W. Davis

SUMMARY OF DECISIONS

It was agreed that the NSC staff, working with State and Defense would prepare a compilation of all our obligations to Jordan and the status of their implementation.[2]

Mr. Kissinger: We have two problems today: the Palestinian options and the question of arms to Jordan. The state of play of the Palestinian question is that we have raised it with King Hussein who said he would think it over. Were there any discussions of this when he was here?[3]

Mr. Sisco: Only of a very general nature. The Secretary told him that: 1) we had made no policy decision favoring a separate Palestinian entity; 2) both we and, we believe, he himself recognize that the Pales-

---

[1] Source: National Archives, Nixon Presidential Materials, NSC Files, NSC Institutional Files (H-Files), Box H–111, Senior Review Group, SRG Minutes Originals 1970. Secret. All brackets are in the original except "[*Palestinian*?]", added for clarity. The meeting was held in the White House Situation Room.

[2] The compilation took the form of a January 18, 1971, memorandum from Rogers to Nixon, "Recommendations and Options Re Jordan Arms Requests," plus annexes, which Kissinger forwarded to the President on February 19. On March 1, Nixon initialed his approval of the recommendations. National Security Decision Memorandum 100, issued by Kissinger to Rogers, Laird, and Helms on March 1, provided for $141.8 million in arms to Jordan over the next three fiscal years, plus $9.7 million to replenish battle losses. (Ibid., Box 616, Country Files, Middle East, Jordan, Vol. VII)

[3] See Document 189.

tinians must be taken into account in any permanent settlement; and 3) that we would do nothing to undermine the King—that we would take his views into account and would work through him. I interpret this to mean that we are keeping everything on ice. We will keep the door open without pushing ahead.

Mr. Kissinger: Can we do this?

Mr. Sisco: I hope so.

Mr. Helms: The disarray among the Palestinians is even worse than when we talked about this earlier. It makes all the more sense to move cautiously.

Mr. Kissinger: Apart from the operational problem of what to do in response to Palestinian overtures, the real problem from a policy point of view is whether or not we have reached the point where we now consider that the Palestinian issue is no longer a refugee problem.

Mr. Sisco: I think we have reached this judgment. I think the King has also. We think we know what the King is prepared to offer at the end of line: very considerable autonomy to a Palestinian state or entity focussed primarily on the West Bank and Gaza, provided it is done in association with Jordan, under the umbrella of the Hashemite Kingdom, worked out in the context of the state of Jordan rather than at the expense of Jordan.

Mr. Kissinger: Would this be a totally independent Palestinian state?

Mr. Sisco: This is what Arafat wants—including probably eventually part of the East Bank.

Mr. Packard: Dayan would concur in this.

Mr. Sisco: This is one time when Jordan and Israel would be in agreement.

Mr. Packard: The problems arise in trying to move from here to there.

Mr. Kissinger: If we agree that such a state should be established at the end of the line, and that it should be done through the King, aren't we precluded from developing a line on what we might do?

Mr. Sisco: We are committed to doing it through him but we haven't given him a veto.

Mr. Kissinger: If we have agreed to work through him, we have given him a veto.

Mr. Sisco: Not necessarily. The Secretary was very careful. He said we would be guided by his views but stopped short of giving him a total veto.

Mr. Packard: We would have some leverage.

Mr. Sisco: If a new development should occur which would make it desirable for us to respond to a Palestinian contact, we could go to the King and say "here's what we want to do."

Mr. Kissinger: He could say no.

Mr. Sisco: He could, but he probably wouldn't.

Mr. Kissinger: So you interpret our commitment as merely to inform him first.

Mr. Sisco: No. We are committed to genuine consultation, but without giving him a veto.

Mr. Kissinger: How can we go about deciding for ourselves what is a desirable position for us to take, rather than waiting for a tactical situation to develop to trigger us into a decision on how to respond? Should we not decide what degree of Palestinian entity is in our interest?

Mr. Packard: We need a more specific idea of where we're going.

Mr. Kissinger: (to Hal Saunders) What is the status of the Palestinian paper?[4] It is a good paper.

Mr. Saunders: It has been distributed to everyone here.

Mr. Sisco: We think the discussion in that paper presents the most feasible and reasonable objective: i.e., some form of Palestinian entity focused primarily on the West Bank and Gaza, in association with the King, under the Hashemite umbrella and in the framework of the Jordanian state. The King's views are similar to those in the paper. The question is how to get there. Jordan and Israel will have to work out the various alternatives in the course of negotiations. Our presumption is that Israel would have to agree to a West Bank border approximating the 1967 border.

Mr. Kissinger: Why do we have to depend on that? They could state that, whatever border is finally established, the West Bank could be automatically linked with Gaza.

Mr. Sisco: Theoretically yes. But the only other theoretical possibility is the Allon Line[5] which runs roughly along the Jordan River. I can't see setting up border posts on the Jordan River and still approximate a Palestinian entity.

Mr. Packard: We should be careful about being too specific on boundaries. Our objective is to get a Palestinian state in association with the King. An independent state separate from the King is not our objective.

---

[4] See Document 182.
[5] See footnote 8, Document 4.

Mr. Sisco: I agree.

Mr. Kissinger: Suppose the King should accept the Allon Line? This is not our problem. It is part of the negotiating scenario between the Palestinians and Jordan.

Mr. Sisco: This is why we like the formulation "based on whatever border that can be agreed."

Mr. Packard: We should look at all the things that might give some flexibility on the borders.

Mr. Kissinger: The idea of Jordanian [*Palestinian*?] sovereignty has its intriguing aspects. From the Israeli point of view, a sovereign Palestinian state would be the most worrisome. Also, the King might have a greater interest in demilitarization of an autonomous West Bank than of an independent West Bank. He could finesse the demilitarization aspect through autonomy. This formula has many attractive features. The only drawback is that it may not work.

Mr. Packard: Yes, but you can say where you want to go and then try to get there.

Mr. Sisco: I think the next stage of our discussion in this group should be on guarantees. We are preparing papers on this which we will suggest be discussed in the SRG.

Mr. Packard: What guarantees to whom?

Mr. Sisco: On the whole peace settlement.

Mr. Kissinger: If you're talking about the whole question of guarantees—US, Soviet, international—we should be very sure of what we mean by guarantees.

Mr. Sisco: That is why I think it should be discussed in this forum.

Mr. Kissinger: (to Hal Saunders) You wrote a very good paper on this. Would you like to address any additional issues?

Mr. Saunders: Only that the bridging question to the arms packages is how much we should put into the Jordanian regime.

Mr. Kissinger: To summarize, the basic Sisco formulation is for a Palestinian entity, autonomous but linked to the Hashemite Kingdom under general Jordanian jurisdiction, including Gaza, the West Bank and whatever frontiers might be agreed. Are we agreed that this is reasonable objective?

All agreed.

Mr. Kissinger: So the question is how to get there?

Mr. Sisco: One of the next papers which should be addressed here is the overall strategy—how we should act on the assumption that the talks get started in earnest after January 1. We can talk about this on

Monday,[5] but we would prefer a little more time so as to finish work on the papers.

Mr. Kissinger: We will keep in touch on this. I see no particular sense in having a meeting on Monday if the papers aren't ready and we can probably delay it. We will talk to you about it. If we are realistic in looking ahead, is it not probable that an autonomous Palestine unit would become independent?

Mr. Sisco: Yes, in time. There will certainly be heavy pressure in this direction. It is a calculated risk that in four or five years it could go further. They might start with the West Bank and Gaza, with an autonomous state linked to the King. But unless the settlement is holding and things have improved economically and they have got on with some development program, there is the latent danger of Palestine irridentism with regard to the East Bank. Any Palestine entity on the West Bank would have a flypaper attraction to some people on the East Bank, although the bedouins and the Palestinians on the East Bank as a whole are oriented toward moderation. No one can guarantee this. We must consider whether or not it is a good bet. Should we commit ourselves to the King on an arms program over a two to three year period? My judgment is yes—that this is the best alternative. The King is in a better position today than he was X months ago. I think it is a good calculated risk, particularly if we can get on with the settlement. A continued impasse would have a great impact on the King. I think it desirable to make the commitment.

Mr. Packard: What would be wrong with it? It certainly wouldn't do any harm for the King to be strong.

Mr. Kissinger: If we talk about what might be wrong with it, let me be the devil's advocate. What would be the impact on the military balance in the Middle East? No matter what we do, nothing seems to affect the military balance in the area.

Mr. Sisco: It wouldn't upset the military balance as long as we provide Israel with the wherewithal. When Argov was told that Secretary Laird had committed us to a short-range provision of arms to Jordan and that we were looking at a longer range commitment, he replied that that was interesting, that he thought that was the right thing to do, and that Israel wanted to keep the King as a neighbor. He said they understood that these arms might be used against them, but they thought we had no alternative but to help the King.

Mr. Helms: Also, with Nasser's death, there is very little strength in the area. We need to have someone strong who can hold his own and make any agreement stick.

---

[6] December 21. The next SRG meeting was held on January 11, 1971; see Document 195.

Mr. Kissinger: Another argument is that the Palestinians are apt to be irridentist. If they take over completely, which seems to be Arafat's objective, we would be faced with an irridentist Jordan, armed with the equipment we had provided.

Mr. Packard: Also, the King might lose control of the Army to a radical group.

Mr. Kissinger: That is a third possibility.

Mr. Sisco: The risk is there.

Mr. Kissinger: Are you all in favor of the $120 million arm package?

Mr. Sisco: It is $130 million for three years.

Mr. Seelye: Between $120 and $130 million.

Mr. Sisco: This package reflects a considerable amount of close careful coordination between State and Defense and there is real unity of view. We operated on your expressed conclusion that there was no real policy problem and that it was a question of the availability of funds.

Mr. Kissinger: What is the advantage of a three-year program over a year at a time?

Mr. Sisco: We would have an annual review. The King is looking for some assurance. He is trying to reorganize his Army so as to meet both the internal and external threat. He wants a one-bite commitment to reorganize over an 18-month period. We have three reasons for prefering the three-year program: 1) it gives a general commitment in principle to the King and is reassuring and psychologically beneficial; 2) the one year review permits a reexamination of the program in the light of the existing situation; 3) it cuts down the amount of money we would have to spend at one time. The King has asked for $186 million over 18 months. We have proposed $120–130 million over three years. It cuts the amount, provides for the annual review, and gives the King a general psychological commitment.

Mr. Kissinger: What exactly is he getting from a military point of view? Are the prices realistic?

Mr. Packard: They are pretty good.

Mr. Kissinger: What is he getting?

Adm. Moorer: He is getting increased mobility, an improved tank capability, and better internal security equipment.

Mr. Kissinger: Is there a list of weapons?

Mr. Sisco: Annex 2 of the paper.[7]

---

[7] The annex to the paper summarized in Document 191.

Mr. Kissinger: How does this compare with what he already has—in tanks, for example?

Mr. Packard: It upgrades his tank capability. Also, it provides him with armored personnel carriers which are particularly useful for internal security.

Mr. Kissinger: How many tanks does he have now?

Mr. Noyes: About 100. Many of them have gasoline engines, though.

Mr. Kissinger: So it doubles his tank capacity.

Adm. Moorer: It gives him better capability: longer range, better fire-control equipment, larger guns.

Mr. Kissinger: How many tanks does Israel have?

Mr. Sisco: About 1200.

Mr. Packard: We wouldn't be giving him a lot of tanks.

Adm. Moorer: But he could move from Amman to the northern border without having to stop to refuel.

Mr. Kissinger: Would we have to compensate Israel? They would know immediately.

Mr. Sisco: We will tell them what we are doing. We told them about the $30 million package in Annex I.[8] We won't get any outcry.

Adm. Moorer: We needn't worry about the Israeli reaction.

Mr. Kissinger: This $30 million is in addition to the $120 million?

Mr. Seelye: Not entirely. The King asked for $186 million. We cut that to $140 plus $10 million for replenishment of their losses, bringing it to $150 million. Secretary Laird promised him a $30 million package immediately. That brings it to $120 million.

Mr. Kissinger: We are giving them $10 million to replace their losses? Is the $30 million on top of this?

Mr. Seelye: No, some of the replenishment is included in the $30 million.

Mr. Kissinger: How much?

Mr. Seelye: I can't tell exactly. The important thing is that we have cut his $186 million to $140 million for FY 1971 equipment. If we add the $10 million replenishment, subtract the Laird $30 million commitment, we arrive at $120 million in addition to what we are already committed to send them.

---

[8] "Survey Team's Proposed USG Arms Package FY 71–FY 74," undated; attached to the paper summarized in Document 191. A copy is attached to Rogers's January 11 memorandum to Nixon; see footnote 2 above.

Mr. Kissinger: Can't we break down the $30 million between replenishment and other equipment?

Mr. Noyes: We can, but not at the moment. It is roughly 50–50.

Mr. Packard: For example, of the 14 tanks, 11 are replacements.

Mr. Kissinger: The annual review would give us some flexibility if there should be a dramatic change in the situation.

Mr. Sisco: It also lets us regulate deliveries.

Mr. Packard: And such things as training.

Mr. Sisco: We would have to try to do this with minimum American presence. The political repercussions of a lot of Americans to do things on the ground would be very difficult for the King.

Mr. Kissinger: How can we pay for this?

Mr. Packard: It would come out of next year's budget. We are getting $30 million from the MAP supplemental.

Mr. Seelye: We need an additional $30 million to finish off the requirements for FY 1971. We could go for an additional supplemental for Jordan, a combination of MAP grant and supporting assistance, or work through Section 506 of the Foreign Assistance Act, taking the equipment from Defense stocks on a grant basis. Or we could steal MAP assistance from some other country. There is still another increment of the 1970 package that we haven't talked about yet. Much of this is already being delivered and the King has paid us only $2 million.

Mr. Helms: We did a good piece recently on the Jordan economy—it explains their predicament.

Mr. Sisco: We are trying to meet a liquidity problem.

Mr. Kissinger: (to Hal Saunders) Will you put together a paper on all our obligations to Jordan—what we are shipping under what categories. The next step will be to get a proposal which we can consider and then move forward to the President.

193. Telegram From the Department of State to the Embassy in the Soviet Union[1]

Washington, December 24, 1970, 2046Z.

209304. We suggest that you see Jarring and make following points:

1. We continue to expect a favorable decision from GOI to resume talks.[2] Our hope is that Jarring can get started early January.

2. We understand that he must prepare SYG report to SC. You should make clear to Jarring that in our view he should resist the temptation to be critical in his report over the Israeli delay to resume talks.[3] Such a judgment would necessarily be taken as one-sided. While Jarring or the UN admittedly had no responsibility for negotiating cease-fire/standstill, delay in resumption of the talks, regrettable as we feel it is, cannot be unrelated to violations of the cease-fire/standstill. We assume Jarring would not want to get into this, and therefore, we urge him to submit briefest kind of report saying that he intends to get on with job of negotiations between the parties.

3. You should explore with Jarring the desirability of an early move (if not immediately at outset) on his part to have these talks resume at his headquarters in Cyprus, at the Foreign Minister level. We

---

[1] Source: National Archives, Nixon Presidential Materials, NSC Files, Box 714, Country Files, Europe, U.S.S.R., Vol. XI. Secret; Priority; Nodis. Drafted by Sisco, cleared by Armitage and Atherton, and approved by Sisco. Repeated Priority to USUN and to Cairo, Tel Aviv, Amman, and Nicosia. Kissinger wrote the following note on the telegram: "Why didn't we clear this? If Saunders can't do it, we'll get somebody who will. HK."

[2] On December 28, the Israeli Cabinet issued a communiqué announcing Israel's decision to resume participation in the Jarring talks. It reads: "The Government decided today that the present political and military conditions enable and justify the termination of the suspension of Israel's participation in talks under the auspices of Ambassador Jarring. The Government decided to authorize the Minister for Foreign Affairs to inform those concerned of the readiness of the Government of Israel to resume its participation in the Jarring talks, in accordance with the basic principles of the Government's policy and on the basis of its resolutions of 31 July and 4 August 1970, as approved by the Knesset, concerning Israel's affirmative reply to the American peace initiative." (*Israel's Foreign Policy. Historical Documents*, volumes 1–2, 1947–1974, Chapter XII, The War of Attrition and the Cease Fire, Document 25) The Embassy transmitted the text of the communiqué in telegram 7063 from Tel Aviv, December 28. (National Archives, Nixon Presidential Materials, Box 1157, Saunders Files, Middle East Negotiations Files, June Initiative Vol. V)

[3] Beam reported in telegram 7655 from Moscow, December 23, that Jarring had "expressed disappointment that his report will have to be negative toward Israel because of its continued failure to respond" to him on the issue of resuming peace talks. (Ibid., Box 714, Country Files, Europe, U.S.S.R., Vol. XI) The Secretary-General's report was released on January 4. For the text, see *Israel's Foreign Policy: Historical Documents*, volumes 1–2, 1947–1974, Chapter XII, The War of Attrition and the Cease Fire, Document 27.

believe this would constitute a much more serious beginning than an exchange at the UN Representatives level.

4. We will want to discuss this idea further with him and will have some concrete suggestions after his arrival in New York as to how we believe he should proceed. You should say to him that we are prepared to play an active role diplomatically in support of him. You should indicate to him our feeling that we have reached the stage where he as the UN Representative will have to take considerable initiative in assuring that there is a serious engagement between the parties. This means formulating Qte contingent ideas Unqte, trying them out on the parties, and insisting on specific reactions to specific ideas. Under US June proposal Jarring has maximum latitude as to procedure he employs.

5. He should know that we consider the commitments made by both sides in the August 7th US proposal stand. This means (A) that UAR and Jordan are committed to the principle of recognizing Israel's right to exist as a state and to live in peace within secure and recognized borders, and (B) that Israel has committed itself to the principle of withdrawal in accordance with Security Council Resolution 242.

6. He could start initially developing areas of agreement. We believe much of the specific phraseology contained in October and December 1969 US proposals[4] will prove to be useful to Jarring. For example, formulation on peace falls short of what Israelis want but our judgment is that it would satisfy them. Equally, while peace language goes slightly beyond where UAR has been willing to go, we believe based on Soviet response of last June,[5] that UAR would buy peace formulation contained in those documents. Jordan has already given positive indication to it. Also there should be no serious problem re freedom of passage.

7. Jarring should know that we intend to discuss the idea of guarantees in the Four Powers after his talks begin.[6] Our objective in these

---

[4] See Documents 58 and 78.

[5] See Document 34.

[6] Yost read a statement in the January 18, 1971, Four-Power meeting that addressed the issue of guarantees: "As I have previously informed the other members of the group, the US believes that it would be useful for the Four to discuss the general question of supplementary guarantees. We strongly believe that the question of guarantees cannot be a substitute for either serious negotiations between the parties under Ambassador Jarring's auspices or a binding, contractual peace agreement containing reciprocal commitments between the parties. I am authorized to inform you that we are prepared to begin these discussions in the Four as soon as we are satisfied that substantive talks under Ambassador Jarring will continue and that the parties will concentrate upon these quiet, diplomatic efforts to reach a settlement rather than resort to the Security Council or other forms of public propaganda." (Telegram 8169 to USUN, January 17; National Archives, Nixon Presidential Materials, NSC Files, Box 1158, Saunders Files, Middle East Negotiations Files, Middle East Negotiations—Four Power Talks, August 13, 1970–November 15, 1971) A summary of the meeting is in telegram 147 from USUN, January 19. (Ibid.)

talks will be to provide qte a series of options unqte for Jarring to try out on the parties. We are against the idea of a formulation which would appear to be a Four Power imposed conclusion and judgment. None of the major powers is in a position to foist upon any of the parties either practical security arrangements or supplementary international guarantees which they might not want.

8. You should indicate to Jarring in clearest terms that we feel next six months are critical; that we are sure he would agree with us that after the long period of waiting a tremendous amount of imagination and initiative is going to be required by him on the assumption that he is expendable if need be. Jarring will not misunderstand what we mean by this. We know in the past Israelis have felt that Jarring's putting forward ideas is contrary to his mandate. We believe he must do this and it can be done in such a way that it will avoid giving GOI valid grounds for saying that he is going beyond his mandate by putting forward formal proposals. This is another reason for establishing identifiable negotiating format by convening delegations on Cyprus; since in such circumstances it would be much more difficult for Israelis to explain suspending participation and their cooperation with him that it would be if they could simply follow device of recalling their UN PermRep for consultations.[7]

9. Anything you can elicit from Jarring on his talk with UAR Foreign Minister would obviously be helpful.

Rogers

---

[7] In telegram 7702 from Moscow, December 26, the Embassy reported Beam's conversation with Jarring that morning, during which the Special Representative said that he would consider the Department's recommendation that the Arab-Israeli talks be quickly moved to Cyprus upon their resumption. Thinking aloud, Jarring "enumerated" the disadvantages and advantages of such a move: the disadvantages being a lack of security and the possibility that the United Arab Republic and Jordan would regard the change of venue as an "Israeli maneuver to delay serious discussion and device to engage them in direct talks" and the advantages being a "permanent negotiating format" with special delegations and "minimal press interference." (Ibid., Box 714, Country Files, Europe, U.S.S.R., Vol. XI) Jarring opened indirect talks with Israeli, Jordanian, and UAR representatives in New York on January 5. (*New York Times*, January 6, 1971, p. 1)

194. Paper Prepared by the National Security Council Staff[1]

Washington, January 8, 1971.

ANALYTICAL SUMMARY
Strategy for Relating Assistance to Israel to
Mid-East Peace Negotiations

At the immediately following sub-tabs are two papers:[2]

—The second ("Technical Options") is a Defense Task Force study of the technically feasible options in supplying aircraft to Israel.

—The first ("State Paper") deals mainly with the considerations and strategy in relating any decision on those options to negotiating strategy.

What follows is a summary of (1) the technical options and considerations (because they do provide some argument in selecting the options) and (2) the political options in relating these to negotiations.

I. *U.S. Supply Options*

The Israelis have requested:

—54 F–4 Phantoms delivered at the rate of 3 per month January 1971 through June 1972.

—120 A–4 Skyhawks as follows: *20* of the modified *A–4E* (similar to the 16 now being diverted to Israel) and *16 A–4M* models to be diverted from the initial production run of 44 aircraft ordered by the U.S. Marines. Israel asks for delivery of these 36 planes in *CY 1971.* The *balance of 84 A–4Ms* are requested to be delivered as follows: *36 in 1972, 36 in 1973, 12 in 1974.*

The U.S. *decision in December* was to supply 12 Phantoms and 20 A–4Es, thus reducing the above requests and the numbers in the options below by those amounts. The options below are not reduced because they still provide a sensible technical framework for decision.

Phantoms

Technical considerations. Production time is approximately 22 months, so any deliveries to Israel within the next 22 months will re-

---

[1] Source: National Archives, Nixon Presidential Materials, NSC Files, NSC Institutional Files (H-Files), Box H–050, Senior Review Group Meetings, SRG Meeting—Middle East 1–11–71. Secret; Nodis. All brackets are in the original.

[2] The undated papers are attached but not printed.

quire diversion from presently planned production for the USAF or other buyers. There is also a long lead time on the ground support equipment which is necessary if Israel plans to disperse these aircraft to several bases. The USAF now has only 80% of its requirements.

Options.

1. Provide the *full number* Israel has requested, either on Israel's schedule or over a longer period.

  a. Provide 54 F–4 Phantoms by June 1972 (cost $243 million). All would have to be diverted from the USAF and other programs.

  b. Provide 54 F–4 Phantoms over a *2½ year period* with delivery of four aircraft per quarter until the third quarter of CY 1972, then 6–8 aircraft per quarter thereafter (cost $243 million). This would soften the impact on the USAF and ease the financial burden on Israel by lengthening the payment period.

  c. Provide 54 Phantoms from new procurement which would mean delivery beginning in 22 months (cost $243 million).

2. Respond positively but with *less than the 54 Phantoms requested.*

  a. Provide 24 additional Phantoms at 4 per quarter, January 1971–June 1972. This would be enough for attrition plus a fourth squadron. (Cost: $108 million.)

  b. Provide some *variation* of the above. Defense suggests, for instance, 16 Phantoms financed by U.S. credit and 16 more if Israel is willing to use $67 million impounded in France for the Mirages.

  c. Agree to replace promptly Israeli aircraft lost through attrition.

3. *Disapprove the request* for additional aircraft but provide attrition aircraft.

Comment: The most promising area for discussion seems to be 1–b above. This meets Israel's overall need but allows for some consideration of the needs of U.S. forces. Stretched over a longer period, deliveries by the quarter might offer greater diplomatic flexibility.

Skyhawks.

Technical considerations are more complex than with the F–4 because of a shift in the models being produced.

The *A–4E* which Israel now has is no longer being produced so providing this model requires taking planes from the U.S. Navy as it replaces them and modifying them for Israel instead of turning them over to Naval Reserve squadrons as now planned. Not turning them over to the Reserve will require replacement of Reserve aircraft with the more expensive ($1 million per plane) A–4M model. [The first 100 Skyhawks sold to the Israelis were the A–4H. The last 16 now being sent are the A–4E modified to be as close to the A–4H as possible.]

The *A–4M* is a brand new aircraft just entering production. Adequate ground support equipment is not likely to become available until after the production line has stabilized. Since the first run is only 44 aircraft for the U.S. Marines, diversion to Israel would delay deployment of this weapons system until after it had been provided to Israeli forces. It costs $1.5 million versus $500,000 (plus modification cost) for the A–4E.

Options

1. Provide the *full number requested*, though perhaps in some other combination of models or on some other schedule.

   a. Provide *20 A–4E* (modified) and *100 A–4M* as requested. (Cost: $254 million.)

   b. Provide *66 A–4E* at four per month from April through December 1971 and three per month January through October 1972; and 54 A–4M at three per month from November 1972 through April 1974. This would meet Israel's requests in terms of total number and delivery time frame, though not in ratio between the models. However, it would involve no disruption of A–4M programming and would be less expensive because of the higher number of A–4Es. Additionally, the A–4M could be configured identically to the A–4H models already in the Israeli inventory. This course would, of course, require taking the A–4E from Reserve squadrons with replacement at higher cost to the U.S.

   c. Provide 20 A–4Es as requested and 12 A–4Ms at two per month starting in July 1972. Provide up to 88 A–4Ms out of FY 72 and FY 73 procurement.

2. Provide 72 A–4 aircraft—enough to replace all older French models on a one-for-one basis. If this number were decided on, Israel would probably want 20 A–4Es in 1971, 16 A–4Ms in 1971, and 36 A–4Ms in 1972. A number of variations for scheduling would be possible.

3. Disapprove additional aircraft but agree to *replace* promptly with A–4Es any *A–4s lost through attrition*. This would mean sale of perhaps 5 A–4Es per year.

Comment: The range for discussion would seem to be in the area of paragraph 1–b above—giving Israel a voice in deciding on the trade-offs between model types and delivery schedules.

II. *Political Options*

The Sisco paper [next tab, "State Paper"] presents four options with the arguments noted below:

Option 1: To say that, in present circumstances, Israel's needs have been generously met by our recent military supply and financial commitments and that we will make no further commitments unless and until Israel adopts positions and a negotiating posture that accord with our own view of what would constitute a reasonable and realistic approach to a settlement—i.e., positions along the lines of our proposals of October and December 1969.[3]

The *argument for* this approach is that giving anything more now than we already have would deprive us of leverage that we will seriously need. This approach would be least abrasive in Arab eyes.

The *arguments against* are that (a) this would create a maximum sense of insecurity in Israel which would strengthen the hand of the hardliners and (b) this would increase the likelihood that most of Israel's energies would be devoted to the military supply question in an atmosphere of increasing tension. Past experience has indicated that we end up giving more than we planned when we finally give in.

Option 2: To commit ourselves now to meet Israel's long-term requests in substantial measure if not totally.

The *arguments for* this approach are that (a) Israel is more likely to be flexible when it feels secure and (b) this would remove most bickering over arms from the U.S.-Israeli relationship and from U.S. politics and permit total concentration on negotiation. We are not likely to buy with a few aircraft Israeli concessions on issues Israel regards as vital to its future. Having committed ourselves to supply Israel's needs, we could then put our diplomatic and military support on the line for major changes in Israel's position. A technical argument for this approach is that it would make for a more orderly supply program in the U.S. and minimize impact on U.S. forces.

One *argument against* is that the Israelis just do not operate this way. They will take what we offer and give as little as possible in return. Those who hold this position argue that the only way to deal with Israelis is to bargain hard and to use leverage. Since Israel itself has linked military supply to its return to the talks, we should accept that linkage. Also, this would cause the sharpest Arab reaction.

Option 3: To demand no specific quid pro quo for a general commitment on the continuity of supply but keep Israel on a relatively short leash by limiting future commitments to short-term periods, e.g. for six months at a time.

The *argument for* this approach is that it would reduce the fears that option 1 would produce and yet preserve an element of uncertainty in Israel about how long and in what degree it can continue to rely on U.S.

---

[3] See Documents 58 and 78.

material support while persisting in policies that the U.S. considers unsatisfactory.

The *argument against* this approach is that it makes a period issue out of arms supply and makes it as likely as not that we will have to deal with this in an atmosphere of tension. We have in the past provided more under these circumstances than we would have otherwise, and the process has been disruptive to our own force supply patterns.

Option 4: To defer decision.

The arguments for and against are essentially the arguments stated above because deferring decision is essentially a decision against option 2, leaving open the choice between options 1 and 3.

---

195. Minutes of a Senior Review Group Meeting[1]

Washington, January 11, 1971, 10:55–11:45 a.m.

SUBJECT

Middle East Negotiations

PARTICIPANTS

Chairman—Henry A. Kissinger

State
John N. Irwin
Joseph Sisco
Alfred Atherton
Thomas Thornton

Defense
David Packard
Armistead Selden
James Noyes

JCS
Lt. Gen. R. Knowles
Adm. William St. George

CIA
Richard Helms
David Blee

NSC Staff
Harold Saunders
Chester Crocker
Jeanne W. Davis

---

[1] Source: National Archives, Nixon Presidential Materials, NSC Files, NSC Institutional Files (H-Files), Box H–112, Senior Review Group, SRG Minutes (Originals) 1971. Secret. The meeting was held in the White House Situation Room.

SUMMARY OF DECISIONS

It was agreed that:

1. State will prepare a paper, in consultation with Defense, assuming the negotiations will break down, assessing the military and political situations, considering our political and military options, with some idea of the type of settlement we might consider acceptable, and what we mean by guarantees, with the pros and cons of various guarantee schemes;[2]

2. the NSC staff will prepare a paper, for Presidential decision, on the advantages and disadvantages of using the Jackson Amendment for provision of assistance to Israel as opposed to the normal foreign military sales legislation;[3]

3. subject to any questions Mr. Sisco might have, Defense could proceed to grant most of the Israeli request for production assistance on a list of items;

4. Defense will examine alternative aircraft production plans so that our ability to deliver aircraft to Israel will not be dictated by our production capabilities.

(Before the meeting began, Mr. Noyes distributed the attached paper: *Questions on U.S. Objectives and Strategy in Mid-East Peace Negotiations)*[4]

Mr. Kissinger: I thought we might have a quick run-through of where we stand on various items. What about our diplomatic situation?

---

[2] For an analytical summary of this paper, see Document 198.

[3] For the Jackson Amendment, see footnote 5, Document 157. The paper was not found, but on January 28, the President directed Laird: "Pursuant to the authority contained in the Supplemental Appropriation Act, 1971, I hereby allocate from the appropriation for 'Military credit sales to Israel' to the Secretary of Defense $500,000,000.00 to be expended by said Secretary to finance the sale of defense articles and services to Israel. I direct that the procedures for interdepartmental consultation and coordination under the Foreign Military Sales Act and Executive Order No. 11501, providing for Administration of Foreign Military Sales, be followed in expending the funds hereby allocated." (National Archives, Nixon Presidential Materials, NSC Files, Box 608, Country Files, Middle East, Israel, Vol. VIII)

[4] Attached but not printed. The questions were: "Should other questions take priority over deciding on further arms commitments to Israel? Would a successful U.S. initiative for full diplomatic relations with UAR help de-polarize the atmosphere, exert pressure on the Soviets, and lend credence to the evenhandedness of the U.S. peace initiative? Would Israel perform better during negotiations if she knows more precisely what the U.S. expects? Should we attach conditions at the time of any further arms commitments rather than rely solely on exerting pressure at some future date?"

Mr. Sisco: The Israelis put forward some concrete suggestions to Jarring during his visit there.[5] Their proposal outlines some of the essential elements, from the Israeli point of view, of a peace settlement. While it obviously falls short of where we would have to be at the end of the line, it is a reasonable opening gambit. Jarring also judges the proposal to be a reasonable beginning. He assured us late last evening that he is approaching the proposal in a positive frame of mind. This is helpful, since if he had decided that the proposal was insufficient—too little and too late—it would have died there. He will put the proposal to the Egyptians this afternoon. I am concerned about the Egyptian reaction. The public statements from Cairo, particularly in the last ten days, have been stronger than normal. Sadat could be digging himself into a hole that he would have difficulty getting out of.

Mr. Kissinger: Why is he getting himself into something that might be hard to get out of?

Mr. Sisco: I don't know if he wants to get out. Their recent public statements might reflect the fact that the Egyptians do not feel themselves strong enough to get into the give and take of negotiations. It raises the question of whether Egypt can get itself in a position to enter negotiations or whether the pressures are such that they would prefer an alternate route. Riad has been talking to the British and French and today the Italians. They are also sending other representatives to other capitals, particularly the African capitals. This looks like they are preparing for a move into the UN Security Council. The Egyptians are emphasizing that either the Four Powers or the Security Council should lay down an explicit view, calling for total Israeli withdrawal, guarantees of a settlement, a solution of the Egyptian border question, etc. If they are saying this privately, on top of their public statements, I wonder what their reaction to the Israeli opening proposal will be. We may be reaching a critical juncture. We may be confronted with increased propaganda and maneuvering in the UN which will set us back.

Mr. Kissinger: Do I understand correctly that Jarring is giving the Israeli proposal to the Egyptians this afternoon, and they will either reject it or offer a counter-proposal?

Mr. Sisco: Jarring will try to get a reaction that will enable them to continue a dialogue. The Egyptians can reject it as an instance of further

---

[5] In telegram 147 from Tel Aviv, January 9, the Embassy reported Jarring's 2½-hour conversation with Meir and Eban the previous day, including the text of the proposal that Israel handed to the Special Representative entitled "Essentials of Peace." (National Archives, Nixon Presidential Materials, NSC Files, Box 1159, Saunders Files, Middle East Negotiations Files, Middle East—Jarring Talks) Israel prepared three versions of the proposal, addressed to the United Arab Republic, Lebanon, and Jordan. (Telegram 152 from Tel Aviv, January 10; ibid.) Jarring was in Israel January 7–10.

Israeli delay and call for a Security Council meeting tomorrow. They can come back with a counter-proposal. They can delay calling a SC meeting, but tell Jarring that the Israeli proposal is not enough and that he should go back and get more. It is in our interest to support Jarring in putting a positive cast on the Israeli proposal. I am seeing the British and French later today and will tell them that we think this is a beginning. I will ask them to encourage Cairo to come back with a counter-proposal so the negotiating process can continue.

Mr. Kissinger: How can the negotiating process continue? Why is it not mathematically certain to deadlock.

Mr. Sisco: The odds are certainly very great that it will deadlock, but I would not say mathematically certain. The odds are strongly against us. But we do have an Israeli proposal in writing and we hope we can get something in writing from the other side. If we assess the situation objectively, we have an Israel which is basically reluctant to proceed with the negotiations. And we have a situation in Cairo where the new group may think it is too weak to come forward with a concrete proposal.

Mr. Kissinger: So what will happen?

Mr. Sisco: I don't think shooting will resume on February 5 when the cease-fire expires. I think the Egyptians will mobilize maximum pressure on us in the context of the UN. The critical juncture will come some time after the deadline—March or so. Resumption of Security Council operations will not be helpful. It will provide Israel with a further pretext (as did the General Assembly debate) for not participating seriously, using the argument that they have put something forward and the other side has not. If the Egyptians move to the UN, it will strengthen the Israeli argument that Cairo is not seriously interested in negotiating and that this is largely a propaganda exercise. This would raise some fundamental questions on the long-range implications on the ground (how long can violence and counter-violence be avoided?) and on the political side. The thrust of the US position has been to try to get the parties to negotiate. If this is not possible, we will have to make some judgement as to who is primarily responsible. We will also have to consider whether the time has come for the US to try to impose something in the Four-Power context; or to decide that negotiations are not possible and to disengage ourselves from the Four-Power context and from further US efforts.

Mr. Kissinger: You are not now thinking of anything in the Two-Power context?

Mr. Sisco: No. The Russian willingness to do something in Cairo will be tested in the current phase. While the US-Soviet alternative may be an option for us, we won't know until after this phase.

Mr. Kissinger: I just want to avoid looking at this option with a six-hour deadline. How can we get this possibility before this group for thorough, systematic consideration? I think we are likely to be heading toward that choice. Even if we should assume that Israel would be willing to go back to its border with Egypt (which I don't think will be true), we know they won't return to their old border with Jordan.

Mr. Sisco: We can prepare a paper with Defense that makes the assumption that the negotiations will break down and assesses the military situation on the Egyptian-Israeli front, the diplomatic situation and our options on the political and military side. I agree that it is about time to think about what to do if and when the negotiations break down.

Mr. Kissinger: You will do the paper?

Mr. Sisco: Yes.

Mr. Kissinger: It is probable that the negotiations will deadlock. We need to know what the issues are.

Mr. Packard: Shouldn't we put some effort into what we might consider acceptable? We should have some idea of what we think.

Mr. Kissinger: I agree. (to Mr. Sisco) Wasn't there an element of that in the papers you did a year ago?

Mr. Sisco: Yes.

Mr. Kissinger: Let's look at it again.

Mr. Packard: We're talking about pressure on Israel, but pressure to do what?

Mr. Sisco: Yes, we will consider that in the context of the new paper.

Mr. Kissinger: In talking about guarantees, I assume we mean what Israel would want as a quid pro quo for withdrawal. But we have never had a systematic examination of the pros and cons of the various guarantee schemes.

Mr. Packard: That's a good idea. These range all the way from a unilateral agreement to supply certain equipment under certain contingencies to a formal alliance of some sort.

Mr. Kissinger: Can we wrap all this together? Not the immediate tactics of the negotiations, but what happens when the negotiations deadlock; what sort of decisions we will face, what we mean by guarantees. This is part of the question of what settlement we might be willing to propose.

Mr. Irwin: We have had a long discussion of guarantees. The question of a real political guarantee—an alliance of some sort—has all sorts of problems.

Mr. Packard: Also, some other alternatives might be more effective than the things we've talked about.

Mr. Irwin: We might ask Dick (Helms) how much farther the Soviets are willing to go in giving military assistance to Egypt.

Mr. Helms: Quite far.

Mr. Packard: The Soviets could get involved in two ways: in advance of an Israeli attack, or they could be pulled in gradually in a war of attrition. I can see some advantage to Israel to get it over with quickly, which might discourage a Soviet response.

Mr. Kissinger: I agree we should have a meeting on all these issues soon. At this meeting I merely wanted to raise the issues of where we are going, the question of guarantees, what sort of settlement we would consider reasonable, what we really want if the thing takes a military course.

Mr. Irwin: Dave (Packard) makes a good point on the possibility of a slow Soviet build up. Also, would the Soviets be prepared to move in quickly on their side before we go in on the side of Israel?

Mr. Kissinger: I didn't understand Dave to say that we would go in on the side of Israel.

Mr. Irwin: I didn't mean that that was what Dave said. However, if Israel believes that, with our military support, they can move quickly, the Soviets might move more quickly to keep us out. I didn't mean to get into this abstraction.

Mr. Helms: It's not all that abstract.

Mr. Packard: We will have to think about this ahead of time.

Mr. Kissinger: That raises the question of the Israeli military requests.

Mr. Sisco: Before we go to that, may I say a little more about guarantees based on our paper. We draw the distinction between international guarantees and bilateral assurances. We have established a general framework on this issue on the basis of the President's and the Secretary's public statements. Assuming the negotiations go on for a while, we have an immediate tactical question: do we discuss the question of international guarantees in the Four-Power context. I think yes. The Secretary has already indicated to the other parties that such discussions would be useful. What are the elements here?

First, on the political side, we have opted for the Israeli view that the principal element of a guarantee is a peace agreement with reciprocal obligations on both sides. Second, our October and December papers indicated that the US would be willing to endorse such an agreement within the meaning of the UN resolution.[6] This adds a political, psychological element, but is clearly of an additive character. And

---

[6] See Documents 58 and 78.

third, the willingness of the US to participate in a UN peacekeeping operation with other UN members. It would be helpful if the Defense Department could look at this in the technical sense. State is already looking at it from a political point of view, but it would be helpful if Defense could look at what would be involved—how many people, etc.

Mr. Kissinger: Have we examined the relative advantages and disadvantages of a Four-Power force as against a neutral force?

Mr. Sisco: Yes, we are examining that in our political paper on the international guarantees. Also there has to be a paper on what assurances the US can provide bilaterally. What inducements can the US provide to persuade Israel to exchange some territory for some international guarantees and bilateral assurances? What sort of long-range military and financial commitment should we make to Israel? There is also a wide range of assurances on the political side of the US attitude in circumstances where Israel might be in jeopardy, ranging from a formal alliance (which the President has set aside) to simple assurance to consult.

Mr. Packard: We should also consider what assurances might be justified in helping achieve a Palestinian solution. Possible inducement to the Palestinians might be an important key.

Mr. Sisco: That is a very sound suggestion.

Mr. Irwin: And we should also consider the effect of Four-Power vs. Two-Power involvement, including the Israeli attitude toward having Soviet troops close to its borders.

Mr. Kissinger: The guarantees have to be something Israeli wants. We can't ram both an unpalatable settlement and unpalatable guarantees down their throats. What do we want the guarantees to do? What do we want them to prevent? What forces are most suitable to achieving our objectives? Let's get some preliminary work done on this and then have another meeting.[7]

On the question of arms supply, the President wants this issue out of the way by summer for a sufficient period so as to avoid endless debate in 1972. He wants it settled in 1971 for a period to go beyond 1972.

Mr. Sisco: That means that between now and the end of June we must make a decision.

Mr. Kissinger: It is not in the national interest to have an escalating debate next year on various packages in which everyone is trying to outdo everyone else in an election year. The President is not necessarily suggesting a high package. He just wants it done by summer. I think this is in the interest of a moderate policy.

---

[7] See Document 199.

Mr. Packard: We should be aware that by not relying on the Jackson Amendment we have constrained our flexibility in 1972.

Mr. Sisco: But we haven't closed any doors, have we?

Mr. Packard: By going the foreign military sales route we avoided trouble with the committees. But the Jackson Amendment would make it possible for us to move more quickly with his support.

Mr. Kissinger: But if we used largely the Jackson Amendment, people will argue that we didn't really need the money for Israel and had tricked them into giving us the money for Cambodia.[8]

Mr. Packard: Yes, the argument was that Israel would help carry the supplemental through. But there will be some changes in the committees this year and we were just lucky in getting it split away from Fulbright. We propose using both—some money for Israel in FMS and some under the Jackson Amendment.

Mr. Irwin: In earlier discussions, Defense had suggested $300 million in Jackson money and $200 million in FMS money. State thought we should go the normal route since we would get into trouble with the Senate Foreign Relations Committee. The White House, specifically OMB, took the position that it should all be done in the normal framework of foreign military sales.

Mr. Kissinger: We can reopen this question. Would this make the Jackson Amendment lapse completely?

Mr. Irwin: It is a question of the attitude of Jackson versus the attitude of the SFRC.

Mr. Packard: Jackson thinks we will be in worse political trouble by not using his amendment than by using it.

Mr. Kissinger: This is a political decision which the President should make.

Mr. Packard: I agree. If the President hasn't looked at it specifically, he should.

Mr. Kissinger: He hasn't since this hasn't been a substantive issue.

Mr. Sisco: If we do go the foreign military sales route, the door should be left open to go the Jackson route.

Mr. Selden: Defense suggested $300 million in the budget, with $100 tied to FMS and $200 tied to the Jackson Amendment.

Mr. Kissinger: I haven't really engaged myself in this issue.

Mr. Packard: If we get hung up on the FMS bill, we may have to do something in a hurry. This will be difficult without the Jackson Amendment.

---

[8] Reference is to the supplemental foreign aid package that the White House sent to Capitol Hill on November 18, 1970, and that Congress passed on December 22.

Mr. Irwin: If the President does opt for the FMS route, what would Jackson's attitude be if we have to go back to his amendment? Would he be annoyed?

Mr. Packard: Jackson says he doesn't care personally, but there is strong sentiment in the Senate for his amendment. There are two sides to this, of course.

Mr. Irwin: I agree it is a political question.

Mr. Kissinger: (to Hal Saunders) Will you do a paper on this right away, with the pros and cons. Check it with State and Defense and get it to San Clemente tomorrow.

Mr. Irwin: Our Congressional Relations people think that if we go essentially the Jackson route, we will have difficult problems in the Foreign Relations Committee, and possibly in the House Foreign Affairs Committee if we give the impression of pulling away from these committees. They also point out that the SFRC went 2–1 against Fulbright for the Administration on the supplemental.

Mr. Kissinger: Would we have the money if we worked through Jackson?

Mr. Selden: We already have the authorization.

Mr. Sisco: Will $300 million be sufficient?

Mr. Packard: Probably not.

Mr. Selden: But we have an open-ended authorization under the Jackson Amendment.

Mr. Kissinger: Would $100 million be enough to keep the Jackson Amendment alive?

Mr. Packard: Anything to give recognition to the possibility of that route. It could even be a statement that this amount might not be adequate and that we might request additional appropriations under the authorization of the Jackson Amendment.

Mr. Kissinger: That's an important element.

Mr. Packard: I would also like to raise the Israeli request for production assistance on spare parts, etc. We would like to go ahead on that. It seems a reasonable request.

Mr. Kissinger: Does anyone oppose?

Mr. Sisco: Do we have a paper that describes this process? This is a long outstanding request and I agree in principle but I would like to see a paper. (Mr. Noyes gave Mr. Sisco and others the last two pages of the Technical Options paper.)[9]

---

[9] Summarized in Document 194.

Mr. Packard: There are some things on there that are very sensitive. They have asked for assistance on some 200 items, and I think we can do most of the 200. Third-country sales by Israel of these items would be prohibited.

Mr. Kissinger: Let's say that you could go ahead subject to any questions Joe (Sisco) might have in the next 48 hours.

Mr. Sisco: It seems a sensible thing to do.

Mr. Irwin: With regard to furnishing aircraft to Israel, my concern is not for or against any scheme of providing aircraft, but that we are sure we are not denigrating our abilities to equip our own forces beyond what Defense really thinks is wise.

Mr. Packard: The question of aircraft availability should be a part of the long-range paper we will be doing.

Mr. Kissinger: I agree it should be part of that paper. The question is how to move this to a decision.

Mr. Sisco: I think Jack (Irwin) is raising a more immediate question. We can say that we need not make a decision right now. But Israel will counter with the argument that, if we do not decide now, given our production priorities, what will happen in July? We can see a reason to decide in the next four or five months. What does Defense have to do with regard to production if we have to deliver these planes? There are certain internal steps we should be taking to avoid having to take these planes out of production for our own forces.

Mr. Packard: We will look at all the alternatives.

Mr. Kissinger: I agree with Joe (Sisco) that we should look at this now so that we're not precluded from taking a decision by summer. We don't want to commit ourselves to any program now, but we want to be sure that we have all our options and that our hands are not tied by our production capabilities. If it is to be done this year, we should be in a position to give some assurances on military deliveries. It might be important for us to be able to move fast. Let's look at this question, but in a way so Israel doesn't get wind of it.

Mr. Packard: We'll do our best.

Mr. Irwin: There could be circumstances where we might unduly draw down our own strength.

Mr. Packard: Some people will think we are doing that whatever we do.

196. Telegram From the Department of State to the Interests Section in the United Arab Republic[1]

Washington, January 14, 1971, 2351Z.

6930. 1. Please deliver the following written message from the Secretary to FonMin Riad, stressing that this is a private communication between them:

Quote

Dear Mr. Minister:

Reflecting on the present situation in the Middle East particularly in the light of Mr. Bergus' report of his talk with you yesterday,[2] it occurred to me that if circumstances only permitted it would be very worthwhile for us to sit down for a thorough and frank discussion. As the next best thing, in the spirit of the warm and personal relationship which has developed between us, I am sending you this private message.

You indicated to Mr. Bergus, after outlining your proposals, that you would welcome any thoughts that I might have on an alternative course of action. I would like, therefore, to respond to this thoughtful suggestion. In doing so, let me again say that our only objective is to assist in any way we can in bringing about a peace in the area that is permanent and to do this in a way which is pursuant to and totally consistent with the Security Council Resolution.

Let me start by saying that I am much concerned from what you said to Mr. Bergus that at the very time when negotiations under Ambassador Jarring's auspices have finally begun and we may be on the threshold of success that a situation is developing which would result in failure. What do I mean by this? For the first time—and many have worked long for this result—the Israeli Government has put forward a proposal in indirect negotiations under Ambassador Jarring's auspices[3] which is substantive in content and carefully avoids setting up procedural roadblocks or difficulties. This is an Israeli proposal which was not rpt not made known to us until after it had been communicated to Ambassador Jarring. Obviously it does not contain—nor could you

---

[1] Source: National Archives, Nixon Presidential Materials, NSC Files, Box 636, Country Files, Middle East, UAR, Vol. V. Secret; Immediate; Nodis. Drafted by Rogers, Sisco, and Atherton and approved by Sisco. Repeated to Amman, Tel Aviv, Beirut, USUN, London, Paris, and Moscow.

[2] The Ambassador's report of his 75-minute conversation with Riad on January 13 is in telegram 64 from Cairo, January 14. (Ibid., Box 637, Country Files, Middle East, UAR, Vol. VI)

[3] See footnote 5, Document 195.

have expected—all you seek in such an initial proposal. But it is a serious beginning. This judgment is shared by Ambassador Jarring Indeed many of the points are within the framework of what we have understood is UAR policy. Certainly it could be the basis for a counterproposal by your government which could lead to further meaningful substantive exchanges and this, of course, we are pledged to support and facilitate.

Without presuming to advise you on how you should reply, I would only suggest that it is important to look not only at what the Israeli proposal says but at what it does not say as well. Viewed in this way, I believe it will be apparent that nothing in the Israeli proposal forecloses the position of your government on any aspect of a settlement. In this connection, I wish to reaffirm to you that the U.S. position remains that contained in the documents of October 28 and December 18, 1969.[4]

A positive reply by the UAR would have many advantages. It would be taken as directly responsive and reflective of a serious intention to negotiate; a move to the Security Council on the other hand will be taken as diversionary—and in fact would be diversionary. It would offer further opportunity to focus in even more specific terms in the immediate and more active next stage of the talks on the key questions of withdrawal, borders, demilitarized zones, and practical security arrangements. It would provide Ambassador Jarring the opportunity to make a brief public report that serious talks were underway, that he believed progress was being made and that the ceasefire should be renewed for an additional period.

I fully understand your view that the ceasefire should not and must not become a basis for an indefinite prolongation of the status quo. However, I see no rpt no better way to move toward a peace settlement which will change the status quo than for you to engage the Israeli Government in a meaningful and substantive negotiating process. I am convinced the opportunity now exists for such negotiations for the first time since the June war. As you know under our initiative Ambassador Jarring is given the authority to hold discussions between the parties under his auspices Innerquote according to such procedure and at such places and times as he may recommend, taking into account as appropriate each side's preference as to method of procedure and previous experience between the parties. End innerquote.[5] Thus, I believe he has considerable freedom of action in formulating the next stage of the negotiating process.

---

[4] See Documents 58 and 78.

[5] The quotation is from the U.S. initiative contained in Document 129.

It would be a tragedy to miss this opportunity. As I understand it, your idea of pressing for action by the Four Powers and the Security Council was developed before Ambassador Jarring's recent discussions with the Israeli Government. I assume that you might have expected that the Israelis would emphasize procedural matters in their talks with Ambassador Jarring. In fact they have not done so, and I firmly believe that to ignore this new factor in the situation and to press for major power intervention or through the Security Council would be a serious setback. Such a course could, in my considered opinion, constitute a fatal blow to our own efforts to help move the situation toward implementation of Security Council Resolution 242.

I appreciate your wish to cooperate with us in the Security Council. I fear, however, that with the best will in the world we would find ourselves in disagreement because of factors inherent in the situation which are well known to both of us. It is not merely a question of how a Security Council debate is managed. The problem is more fundamental than that, since we are persuaded that the whole concept of this approach is the wrong way to go about helping Ambassador Jarring promote agreement between the parties as he has been charged to do in Security Council Resolution 242. Certainly there is nothing that could be said in a public forum that had not been said hundreds of times before or since November 1967.

On the other hand, if negotiations can be pursued privately and quietly under Ambassador Jarring's auspices, I believe we can look forward to the early development of a situation in which not only can my government play an increasingly helpful role but the Four Powers in concert can begin to make a meaningful contribution with particular reference to the question of guarantees and peacekeeping arrangements. I want to assure you that we have noted the new emphasis of your policy on this key aspect of the settlement, to which we also attach high importance.

I have set forth my thoughts, Mr. Minister, in the hope that we can see the present situation in the same light and to persuade you of our determination to move forward quickly along the course charted in the proposal which we made and the late President Nasser so courageously accepted in June.[6] I cannot stress too strongly my conviction that we are at perhaps the most critical and at the same time hopeful point since the passage of Resolution 242—a point where your government's decisions will be a major factor in determining whether 1971

---

[6] See footnote 4, Document 136.

is to be the year in which a just and lasting settlement is achieved or the Middle East set on the path toward a continuing and costly conflict.[7]

Sincerely,

William P. Rogers

End quote.

2. *For Amman:* Would like your judgment as to whether it will be helpful for you to draw upon the above as means to encourage a positive Jordanian reaction to GOI paper. We hope GOJ will see advantage in letting UAR take lead in responding.[8]

3. *For USUN:* You are authorized to show, but do not leave, above letter to Jarring so that he will know precisely what it is we are telling the UAR and will cooperate with us in his report near end of month.

Rogers

---

[7] On the morning of January 15, Bergus, accompanied by Wiley, delivered the message to Mohamed Riad, who said he would call the Foreign Minister at his hotel in Aswan that afternoon to read the message to him. Regardless, Riad said, the Foreign Minister would return to Cairo by 2 p.m. the next day and would be able to give the text his full attention at that time. (Telegram 81 from Cairo, January 15; National Archives, RG 59, Central Files 1970–73, POL 27–14 ARAB–ISR)

[8] In telegram 361 from Amman, January 20, the Embassy reported that the Foreign Minister was "completely in tune with Secretary's thinking" that the time was ripe for "quiet diplomacy." (Ibid.)

197. Telegram From the Department of State to the Interests Section in the United Arab Republic[1]

Washington, January 21, 1971, 2107Z.

10839. Ref Cairo 2802.[2]

1. For two reasons we have felt short hiatus was desirable before responding to Sadat's talk with you December 24.[3] We do not want Sadat to place unreasonable expectations upon summit dialogue as means of solving tough problems we face. Second, we wish to underscore our unhappiness with Sadat's own recent public statements attacking U.S. While we are prepared to tolerate considerable discrepancy between UAR's public and private statements, Sadat overstepped mark in his ASU [Asyut] speeches.[4] At same time, President is appreciative of Sadat's desire to open private dialogue with him, and we do not

---

[1] Source: National Archives, Nixon Presidential Materials, NSC Files, Box 636, Country Files, Middle East, UAR, Vol. V. Secret; Exdis. Drafted by Sterner and W.B. Smitt II (NEA/UAR); cleared by Sisco, De Palma, and Kissinger; and approved by Rogers. All brackets are in the original except "[Asyut]", added for clarity.

[2] Telegram 2802 from Cairo, December 28, 1970, contained Bergus's recommendation that the United States "respond fairly soon" to the oral message that Sadat had conveyed to Nixon on December 24, believing that "it might be useful" for Nixon to "reply on the eve of the actual resumption of the Jarring talks." (Ibid., Box 637, Country Files, Middle East, UAR, Vol. VI) After receiving no indication of a response to Sadat's message, Bergus wrote on January 19: "I urge Department take another, and urgent, look at possibility President Nixon's sending message to Sadat along lines suggested in my 2802 of December 28. I think Sadat's anti-American noises have, for the moment, abated to level where we can, with dignity, resume dialog." (Telegram 103 from Cairo; ibid.)

[3] In his conversation with Bergus, Sadat expressed how "deeply touched" he had been by Nixon's December 21 message to him, as conveyed to him through Fawzi. He then proceeded to list the "many important differences" between the United States and the United Arab Republic, including the notion that the United States believed that the latter wanted to "promote a confrontation between two superpowers in the Middle East" and the idea that Egyptians should have behaved like "defeated people" in the aftermath of the 1967 war. (Telegram 2798 from Cairo, December 24, 1970; ibid. Nixon's letter is discussed in Sadat, In Search of Identity, pp. 277–278.)

[4] As reported in telegram 49 from Cairo, January 11, and the New York Times, January 12, 1971, p. 4, Sadat delivered a series of speeches in the early part of January, at least two of which were given in the Middle Nile town of Asyut. Bergus wrote that Sadat criticized Israeli-American propaganda for trying to portray the United Arab Republic as refusing to accept continuation of the cease-fire after February 5 and claiming that Sadat had "decided to declare war" on that day. Sadat explained that he had merely said that he would "not be bound" to the cease-fire after February 5 and "would not renew it," which he argued was "completely different" from a declaration of war. (National Archives, Nixon Presidential Materials, NSC Files, Box 1159, Saunders Files, Middle East Negotiations Files, Middle East—Jarring Talks Edited) Because of the speeches, Sisco had told Kissinger that the Department was "holding off" on providing a recommended message from Nixon to Sadat. Sisco continued: "We didn't like the President to have to send something when this guy Sadat is hitting us publicly." (Transcript of a telephone conversation, January 13, 12:07 p.m; ibid., Henry Kissinger Telephone Conversation Transcripts, Box 3, Chronological File)

believe we should close door on any channel which might improve US–UAR relations and thus contribute to our efforts to achieve peace settlement. Moreover, Riad's oral reply to Secretary[5] set positive framework for President's reply.

2. At early and appropriate occasion you should answer Sadat orally along following lines:

A. President Nixon is pleased that President Sadat has thought it useful to communicate directly, personally, and so frankly with him. The parties to the Arab-Israel dispute are now engaged in important and complicated negotiations. The U.S. has pledged its willingness to give such help as it can to the parties directly concerned. Moreover, we believe there are other world problems as well as aspects of our bilateral relations which might usefully be discussed at the highest level between the two countries. We would like to assure President Sadat that President Nixon believes this channel to be a useful augmentation of traditional diplomacy. We will give full and earnest consideration to any messages that President Sadat may care to send him. We appreciate President Sadat's readiness to do likewise and hope that the public tone and atmosphere of our relations will make continuation of this dialogue possible. We think it essential that the UAR understand our goals and policies. Noting that President Sadat recently said on American television that he was uncertain about what the U.S. wanted in the Mid-East,[6] we hope through exchanges such as this to make our views clear.

B. President Sadat has spoken frankly of the differences which separate our two govts. Such differences do exist and are real. This does

---

[5] After discussing Rogers's letter with Sadat (see Document 196), Riad replied to Bergus and Wiley on January 19: "Egypt and the United States have the same basic idea" regarding a "peaceful settlement" based on Security Council Resolution 242. Riad continued: "The Secretary thinks the Security Council is now inappropriate and that we finally have a chance to achieve peace. This means he must have something in his mind or must intend to do something. The President and I have, therefore, decided that we can postpone our decision to call for a Security Council meeting." According to Bergus, Riad then said that the United Arab Republic could not extend the cease-fire because, he remarked: "That can be done only on condition that there is a serious move towards peace. We cannot allow an indefinite continuation of the cease-fire. There is, however, a lot of time. The big powers can do something in the next few weeks." (Telegram 109 from Cairo, January 19; National Archives, RG 59, Central Files 1970–73, POL 27–14 ARAB–ISR) In a separate telegram summarizing the meeting, Bergus wrote that the United Arab Republic hoped that, before February 5, Israel would present a "new and substantive response to Jarring" or that the Four Powers would "intensify their efforts and issue public statement covering points of substance." (Telegram 108 from Cairo, January 19; ibid)

[6] Reference is presumably to an interview with Sadat conducted by James Reston of the *New York Times* in Cairo on December 23, 1970. Sadat said, as reported by Reston: "The U.S., believe it or not, I don't know their stand up till now." (*New York Times*, December 28, 1970, p. 1)

not alter the fact that we in the U.S. wish to see a sovereign, stable, and developing Egypt living in peace in the area. We recognize that other Arab countries feel deeply involved in Egypt's destiny, and that Egypt feels involved in the destiny of other Arab states. We are impressed by the dignified and effective manner in which the Egyptian people closed ranks after the sudden death of President Nasser and, in accordance with the constitutional process, chose new leadership. We are following with sympathetic interest the efforts of President Sadat and his new govt to tackle the problems affecting the daily lives of the citizens of the UAR. The U.S. has cooperated with the UAR in economic and social development in the past. The economies of our two nations are supplementary in many respects, and we believe that there are many helpful steps in the reconstruction of Egypt which we could take to our mutual economic advantage.

C. Reconstruction requires peace. We believe that a just and lasting peace is possible. It will not be easy. Resolving problems that have been allowed to fester for over two decades is never easy. One of the hardest things for any nation to do is to put aside the grievances of the past and build for the future. But the promise of peace makes such efforts essential.

D. Talks under Amb Jarring have begun in a positive way. Secretary Rogers has recently written to FonMin Riad at length conveying our views of the present situation, stressing his conviction, which President Nixon shares, that the opening of these talks presents a real opportunity to move toward a settlement.[7] It would be a tragedy, as Secretary Rogers said in his letter, to miss this opportunity. None of us can be sure of being able to control the flow of events if the situation is allowed to return to hostilities, as it almost certainly will at some point if there is not a just and lasting peace settlement.

E. In one important respect President Sadat's comments reflected a misunderstanding which President Nixon hopes he can dispel. The U.S. does not look upon Egyptians as a quote defeated people unquote. The U.S. has great respect for the UAR—a civilization that has been a force in the world for 5,000 years. (You should interject as your personal comment that after carefully checking, Washington is unable to find any statement by a Presidential adviser along the lines alleged by Sadat.) Moreover, President Nixon does not believe that any peace settlement can be enduring if it is based on the humiliation of one side. We do not believe Security Council Resolution 242 treats either side as defeated, and that is why the U.S. supports it. It provides the framework for a settlement that is honorable to both sides and that ensures the es-

---

[7] See Document 196.

sential interests of both sides. We continue to give Resolution 242 our full support and we stand by our past statements of what we believe is entailed in that Resolution.

F. We do not underestimate the difficulties ahead. The critical factor is the spirit which the parties themselves bring to the talks that are now beginning. In a true negotiating atmosphere—one in which each side makes a genuine effort to understand and deal with the concerns of the other side—much can be accomplished. President Nixon wishes to assure President Sadat that the U.S. recognizes its responsibilities if such conditions emerge.

G. At the same time, President Nixon hopes President Sadat will agree that after more than 20 years of conflict the Arab side too has responsibilities. The Security Council Resolution calls for a commitment to live at peace with Israel but leaves much to be spelled out in terms of the practical arrangements that will give assurance the peace will not break down. Given the background of the past two decades, the U.S. believes it is only reasonable for Israel to feel it has the right to hear from the Arab states themselves as to what the specific elements of the peace will be. President Nixon does not see how this requirement can be construed by the Arab states as an attempt to impose humiliating conditions upon them. To the contrary, it is a matter of vital concern to both the Arab states and Israel, and is therefore one of the proper subjects for the talks now in train under Amb Jarring. We believe outside powers can and will at the appropriate time play an important supplementary role in helping the parties reach agreement, but we are persuaded this cannot take the place of reciprocal undertakings worked out by and binding on the parties themselves.

H. President Sadat expressed concern that the US may misunderstand Egypt's reasons for accepting assistance from the USSR and may underestimate the UAR's independence of policy as well as the UAR's desire to have good relations with both the Soviet Union and the US. We share his regret that the Mid-East problem has acquired a US-Soviet aspect. We also share his hope that the UAR's relations with the US can improve. For us, the fact that the UAR has close relations with the Soviets should not necessarily be an impediment to concrete steps to improve US–UAR relations. At the same time President Nixon hopes that the global responsibilities of the US. will be taken into account in Cairo; the United States cannot ignore what the Soviets do, anywhere in the world.

I. In closing President Nixon wishes to say he was heartened by President Nasser's acceptance of our peace initiative last summer. Despite later obstacles, we believed then and still believe that the US and the UAR can work together for peace on a basis of mutual interest and mutual understanding. Washington hopes that Mr. Bergus can be in close touch with Minister Riad to discuss the parties' positions on various substantive issues as they are tabled in the Jarring talks in the coming weeks.[8]

Rogers

[8] Bergus presented Nixon's oral message to Sadat on January 23, as reported in telegram 145 from Cairo, January 23. Sadat first responded: "I believe President Nixon's message leaves us exactly where we are." He further remarked that the United States was the "only power" that could "bring about a peaceful settlement" and that it was "unrealistic to expect the parties to come together in a negotiation." Sadat "would not sit alone at the same table with Israel as long as Israeli occupation continued," he said, explaining that he would only negotiate with Israel "in the presence of the Big Four or the Security Council." Sadat concluded with the comment that the United States Government should not view his statements as a "final answer to President Nixon's message" and affirmed that the direct channel between the two of them "could be very useful." (National Archives, Nixon Presidential Materials, NSC Files, Box 1160, Saunders Files, Middle East Negotiations Files)

198. Paper Prepared by the National Security Council Staff[1]

Washington, January 23, 1971.

ANALYTICAL SUMMARY

Guarantees of an Arab-Israeli Settlement

The Papers

Three papers produced in an interdepartmental working group are at the following tabs:[2]

—"*Guarantees Scenario.*" This is a brief paper on the present tactical situation explaining how commitment this week to discuss the guarantees issue in the Four Power talks relates to Jarring's next step in maintaining momentum in his talks and to the general effort to extend the cease-fire.[3]

[1] Source: National Archives, Nixon Presidential Materials, NSC Files, NSC Institutional Files (H-Files), Box H–051, Senior Review Group Meetings, SRG Meeting—Middle East 1–25–71. Secret; Nodis. All brackets are in the original.

[2] Attached but not printed are the three undated papers prepared by the NSC Interdepartmental Group for Near East Affairs.

[3] On January 23, the Department sent an informational telegram to the Mission to the United Nations outlining a "scenario" that it "envisaged pursuing over the next two weeks or so," including: 1) keeping the "principal focus on negotiations between the

—*"Issues."* This is a discussion of the more important issues that must be looked at very carefully before the U.S. becomes too heavily committed in any direction on participating in guarantees. This is the paper you will want to concentrate on.

—*"Guarantees."* This is a basic study of what kinds of guarantees and inducements are possible. The summary below is enough if you are pressed for time.

In the analytical summary below, the first and last of the papers above are dealt with first since they describe what we are talking about. The latter half of this summary deals with the issues raised.

Scenario

The situation is as you know it from your discussions with Sisco at the end of the week. These are the main elements [see tab marked "Guarantees Scenario" for Sisco paper]:

—*The UAR* has dropped for the moment its plan to call a UN Security Council meeting. Its original intent was to urge the Security Council to take a position favoring total Israeli withdrawal to spur Jarring's effort to achieve a settlement and to give the UAR an excuse to extend the cease-fire on February 5. The UAR suspended its plan on the assumption that Israel would be more forthcoming on withdrawal, if the US planned some move or if the Four Powers would increase their activity as pressure on Israel. The UAR has emphasized the importance to it of big-power guarantees for a settlement.

—*Jarring* is planning to make a report to U Thant, possibly as early as Tuesday. The purpose of this would be to consolidate progress to date, provide a basis for his next round and indirectly give the UAR an excuse for extending the cease-fire. Jarring does not at present plan himself to call for extending the cease-fire, but *U Thant* appears ready to put a cover note on Jarring's report doing so.

—*The Israelis* have not expressed themselves formally on guarantees in the current talks, but their informal thoughts are these: They hope we will not take the pressure off the UAR by giving it reason to believe that the Four will do its work for it—that the UAR can substitute pressure by the Four on Israel for its own negotiating concessions. The Israelis would also object to US–USSR participation in a peacekeeping force (a) because that would put Soviet troops on Israel's borders and (b) the US and USSR would neutralize each other in a crisis

---

parties"; 2) keeping "pressure on Jarring" to maintain momentum in his talks; 3) "joining in a Four Power announcement" after U Thant issued his report on Jarring's recent activities; and 4) sending Yost a draft of a Four-Power announcement as well as "guidance regarding position to be taken on guarantees at subsequent meetings." (Telegram 12157 to USUN, January 23; ibid., Box 1160, Saunders Files, Middle East Negotiations Files, Jarring Talks Edited, January 22–31, 1971)

by wanting to avoid nuclear confrontation. The Israelis want minimal outside involvement in their negotiations.

—*The Four Powers* are the scene of steady pressure to discuss guarantees. The U.S. position for some time has been that the U.S. would be prepared to discuss guarantees only when serious negotiations between the parties were under way. On January 18, the U.S. added the condition (uncleared here) that this discussion would take place if the threat of an early Security Council meeting were removed.[4]

—*In short,* the pace is being set by Jarring's plan to report Tuesday and the scheduled meeting of the Four Wednesday.[5] Sisco's scenario, as you know, is for the Four to respond to Jarring's report by exhorting the parties to serious negotiations, calling for a cease-fire extension and revealing that the Four would discuss guarantees.

Options for Guarantees

The State Department paper with Defense contributions [see tab marked "Guarantees"] examines the role that international guarantees and forces or US assurances might play as an inducement to Israel to give up more territory in a settlement than it now intends. This is thought of as perhaps a margin of difference supplementing an Arab-Israeli agreement in a situation where Israel is faced with a choice between (1) retention of territory without peace and the virtually certain prospect of renewed war and (2) a serious peace agreement involving no major retention of territory.

The precise *purpose* of international guarantees is the first of the issues discussed later in this summary. The State paper describes the general purposes as:

—committing the major powers to desist from any inducement to the primary signatories of an agreement to break their commitments;

—providing inducements for compliance and deterrents to violation;

—generalizing responsibility for observance of the agreement.

No single guarantee is likely to be persuasive to Israel. *A realistic package would have to contain three elements:*

1. The various kinds of *international guarantees* all consist of some kind of association of the international community—particularly the major powers—with the settlement through the UN Security Council

---

[4] See footnote 6, Document 193.

[5] The January 27 Four-Power meeting "produced nothing, despite somewhat proforma efforts by USSR and France to obtain approval for different communiqués," according to Yost. (Telegram 240 from USUN, January 28; National Archives, RG 59, Central Files 1970–73, POL 27–14, ARAB–ISR)

(UNSC), probably including a commitment to action if the agreement is broken:

—UNSC endorsement of the terms of a settlement under Chapter VI of the UN Charter. Unanimous Council action would imply that a significant breach of the settlement would lead to international action to rectify the situation. [Chapter VI simply authorizes the UNSC to involve itself and urge resolution of disputes by peaceful means. This is essentially the UNSC's diplomatic pressure role.]

—UNSC endorsement under Chapter VII. This would simply imply that UNSC action could include sanctions, including the use of military force.

—Four Power commitment to consult. This, comparable to the commitment in connection with the NPT, would simply assure that the major powers would not ignore a violation.

—Four Power commitment to call a UNSC meeting to discuss steps to be taken if there is a breach of settlement.

2. Any of the above would have to be supplemented by *arrangements on the ground. Two broad types* are theoretically possible: (a) a mission with *strictly observer* functions; (b) a larger operation combining observer functions with a *real military* capability. Specifically, these are possible:

—*Joint observer commissions of the parties with UN liaison.* This would be most acceptable to Israel, least acceptable to the Arabs and most feasible as part of a broader arrangement (e.g. at Sharm el-Sheikh, possibly the West Bank.).

—*UN observer commissions with or without liaison representatives of the parties.* The principal weakness would be lack of effective follow-up in event of confirmed violations, as in the past. This is one characteristic Israel has objected to in past UN observer forces. The question of composition raises questions of U.S. and Soviet participation which are dealt with under "issues" in the next section of this summary.

—*Four Power peacekeeping force.* This would combine observer functions with a military capability to prevent attacks across borders, through DMZ's and at other key points by regular or irregular forces. The advantage would be the four-power commitment to enforcement. A major problem would be Israeli rejection of the stationing of Soviet forces on Israeli borders or territory or U.S. disinterest in introducing Soviet forces into Jordan. This would bring U.S. and Soviet forces face to face.[6]

—*UN peacekeeping force* would have the same advantages in enforcement capability as the above but without the disadvantages of the

---

[6] Kissinger placed two checkmarks next to this paragraph.

Soviet presence. The Israelis would not put much faith in third-country contingents which did not commit the U.S. and it might be difficult to find contingents willing to undertake a potential combat role.

—*Mixed arrangements.* Different arrangements could be used in different areas.

—*Transitional administrative commission.* Constructing some such umbrella might provide an opportunity for Israel to leave forces behind in some areas for a time as public security forces over a period of perhaps five years. Since these would be mainly in the present occupied territories, demilitarization and peacekeeping forces could be kept away from Israeli territory for a time.

3. *Unilateral US guarantees and commitments* would seem an indispensable part of any package. What Israel will really want to know—especially if the US presses it to accept a settlement that provides less than total security—is what the US will consider its obligation to be if the peace agreements break down. Possible *elements in a US commitment are:*

—Continued *military support.* This is easy to contemplate, but there could be a contradiction if and when the US and USSR get down to discussing arms limitation.

—*Economic support.*

—*Mutual defense treaty.* Although the Israelis voice skepticism about the US ability to carry out such a commitment, it is difficult to believe that Israel would thoroughly discount a formally ratified US commitment to hold off the USSR. This might find little support in the US today and would tend to formalize polarization of the Mid-East.

—*Bilateral defense consultation* and planning on a regular basis is something the Israelis have long wanted. This would, for instance, set up a joint aircraft control system in case US carrier aircraft were committed in Israeli skies.

—*Congressional resolutions* would strengthen any US participation in UNSC guarantees or any executive reiteration of US support for Israel.

Issues Raised

Choice among the above schemes raises the following key issues: [The State paper at tab marked "Issues" discusses these issues by raising questions. The arguments below cover essentially the same ground but in declarative statements in pro-con format. The "tentative conclusions" are Saunders', formulated to give you something to react to.]

1. *What should be the function of a peacekeeping force?* Should it simply be an observer force, or should it have a combat role using military

force to prevent violations? *The arguments for and against a force with a military function are:*

Pro.

—This would seem more effective in providing security than an observer force serving a trip-wire function.

—A main argument against UN forces in the past has been that they are powerless observers with no capacity to follow up violations with action that could deter future violations.

—It is possible to differentiate between a major military force and a force with police capability. It is also conceivable that a larger force would be desirable during withdrawal than after. Therefore, an argument for a force with military capability during withdrawal need not be extended to the period after withdrawal. A transitional period of some duration might allow time for a new situation after peace to be consolidated.

Con.

—For Israel, the most significant deterrents to Arab breach of the agreement will be Israeli freedom to use their own military forces and assurance that the U.S. would respond to involvement of Soviet forces.

—It is doubtful that any UN force could stop a determined attacker, e.g. a surprise air attack.

—It is doubtful that governments could be found willing to commit forces that could be caught between two superior forces.

—The U.S. would not want to endorse such a role for Soviet forces or be involved (possibly against Israel) in that way itself.

—It seems unlikely that the Israelis would welcome a force most likely to add to Arab military weight (since the Israelis would rely on their own pre-emption rather than the UN force to protect them).

—For Israel, the fact of significant US participation in a real crisis involving the USSR is more important than curbing local threats which they will insist on being in a position to handle.

Some Tentative Conclusions:

—With one possible exception (Golan Heights) it would seem possible to rely on demilitarized buffer zones to keep local forces apart. Observer forces would be sufficient to verify absence of local forces.

—The threat of another war will not come from minor infractions but from major mobilization. In that situation what would be important would be the action to be taken by enforcing powers from outside.

—During withdrawal, some police force would seem necessary for a transitional period.

2. and 3. *Should Soviet forces be involved in a peacekeeping force? Could the US expect straightforward Soviet cooperation in a peacekeeping mission? Would not Soviet participation legitimize permanent Soviet military presence?* A Four Power force would require Soviet participation. *The arguments for and against Soviet participation are:*

Pro.

—Only the US and USSR have the military capacity to stop the threatened outbreak of hostilities by force.

—If the Israelis trust any outsider at all, it will only be the U.S. If the US is involved, the USSR must be.

Con.

—There would be a real possibility of paralysis of the operation through US–USSR differences of view and Soviet veto of even minor decisions.

—Should a crisis arise on which the USSR and US held different views, it could be dangerous to have US and Soviet forces in the field, although this might be minimized by not having those forces next to each other.

—The Israelis would not trust the Soviets and say informally that they do not want either the US or USSR.

—With the achievement of a settlement there would be a good possibility of reduction in the Soviet military role. Participation in a UN force would legitimize this.

Some Tentative Conclusions:

—The dangers and disadvantages of Soviet involvement would seem to outweigh the advantages. This would seem to rule out a Four Power force.

—More important than a permanent peacekeeping force would be some understanding on what international action could be taken in the event of violation that threatened major hostilities.

4. *Should the U.S. participate in a UN peacekeeping force?*

Pro.

—If Israel trusts any outsiders at all, the only presence that Israel will regard as of any value is the American. Israel might consider this as useful, not for the peacekeeping force itself, but as an indication of US commitment to act if Israel is threatened.

Con.

—If faced with a crisis provoked by the UAR backed by Soviet forces, the US could find itself in an extremely risky situation from which it would be difficult to withdraw.

—US participation would require Soviet participation, which Israel would oppose.

—Since the force would be guaranteeing Arab borders, the US could end up in open opposition to Israel.

—US domestic support for such involvement would be questionable.

Some tentative conclusions: The disadvantages of US involvement would seem to outweigh the advantages. US assurance to support Israel could be provided in other ways.

5. *Can the problem of Israeli objection to UN forces be met?* One purpose of guarantees is to induce Israel to withdraw. Yet Israel has no faith in UN forces and is firmly opposed to the demilitarization or stationing of forces on its side of the border. The Arabs insist on demilitarization on both sides of the borders. There is precedent for UN observers and control officers operating in Israel, so some token arrangement might be worked out. There might be a way to avoid the problem altogether by attaching international security forces to the administrative machinery overseeing Israeli withdrawal and allowing it later to assume de facto observer status in evacuated territory.

Some Tentative Overall Conclusions

These are Saunders' propositions set down solely for the sake of discussion:

1. The most practical point to start from is to discuss arrangements for some sort of police force to operate during the transitional phase from Israeli occupation to withdrawal. A medium-sized police force might over time become a small quasi observer force.

2. Separation of local forces, e.g. by demilitarization of large areas like the Sinai, is the best guarantee against accidental war. If there is a major mobilization, it will take more than a small international force of some kind. It will require major international action, if anything. (1967 is an example. No normal UN force in the Sinai could have stopped the war once Egyptian mobilization reached a point where Israel felt it necessary to attack. Perhaps landing the 82nd Airborne Division might have had an impact.) Therefore, what seems important is not so much the force on the ground—except for minimal observation duties—but how the major powers are committed to act in a crisis.

199. Minutes of a Senior Review Group Meeting[1]

Washington, January 25, 1971, 5:12–5:50 p.m.

SUBJECT

Middle East

PARTICIPANTS

Chairman—Henry A. Kissinger

State
John N. Irwin
Joseph J. Sisco
Alfred L. Atherton
Thomas Thornton

Defense
David Packard
G. Warren Nutter
James S. Noyes

CIA
Richard Helms
David H. Blee

JCS
Lt. Gen. Richard Knowles
Adm. William St. George

NSC Staff
Harold Saunders
Jeanne W. Davis

SUMMARY OF DECISIONS

It was agreed that:

—the Defense Department should proceed with its paper on defense production schedules;[2]

—the State Department would prepare by Monday, February 1 a paper on possible courses of action if the Jarring talks deadlock,[3] and the SRG will meet to discuss it on Wednesday or Thursday, February 3 or 4.

Mr. Kissinger: I thought we might get together to let Joe (Sisco) tell us where we stand.

---

[1] Source: National Archives, Nixon Presidential Materials, NSC Files, NSC Institutional Files (H-Files), Box H–112, Senior Review Group, SRG Minutes (Originals) 1971. Secret; Nodis. The meeting was held in the White House Situation Room.

[2] The paper was discussed at the next Senior Review Group meeting, held on February 8; see Document 204.

[3] For an analytical summary, see Document 202.

Mr. Sisco: The negotiating procedure has perhaps begun with the submission of individual papers by Israel, Egypt and Jordan.[4] The Israeli paper is substantive and related to elements of the Security Council resolution. The Egyptian paper is substantive also, but surrounded by polemics in its first version. Jarring had the Egyptians reshape their paper before giving it to the Israelis. Israel is expected to put something further forward tomorrow.[5] Our objective now is to get Jarring to submit a brief report indicating a certain amount of progress. Hopefully, he can engage the parties in the next stage, preferably at the Foreign Minister level, but we think this is doubtful. Also, we would like to see the cease-fire extended. We have preferred a formal extension, with statements by both sides, hopefully for three months. Our choices, however, may be a formal extension of the ceasefire of a shorter duration as against a de facto extension wherein neither side resumes the shooting. Both Israeli and Egypt have agreed there should be no resumption of the fighting. We may be better off with a de facto extension, without a deadline. This would avoid the recreation of a crisis every few weeks.

Mr. Kissinger: Which do you prefer?

Mr. Sisco: Our preference has been for the formal, three-month extension as being most satisfactory to both sides and creating the most stable situation since both sides would be on record. But, if the formal extension can only be achieved for a shorter period—one month, for example—the de facto ceasefire might be better. We have to play it by ear for the moment.

Regarding the papers that have been prepared for this meeting,[6] we believe the Four Powers should now begin to examine the question of international guarantees. We have indicated informally to the Israelis that we consider this a likely development and have asked infor-

---

[4] For the Israeli paper, "Essentials of Peace," see footnote 5, Document 195. The United Arab Republic's paper, a response to Israel's, is in telegram 121 from USUN, January 15. (National Archives, Nixon Presidential Materials, NSC Files, Box 1159, Saunders Files, Middle East Negotiations Files, Middle East—Jarring Talks Edited) The text of the Jordanian paper, also a response to Israel's, in telegram 156 from USUN, January 19, was delivered to Jarring on January 18. (Ibid.)

[5] On January 27, Israel replied to the United Arab Republic's paper, which Jarring had conveyed on the latter's behalf on January 18. The text of the reply is in telegram 237 from USUN, January 27. Israel addressed the points raised by the United Arab Republic in its paper, while commenting that it expected the United Arab Republic to address "at an early stage" the points from the original Israeli paper to which it did not refer. It dealt in various ways with such phrases as "peace in the area," "respect for and acknowledgement of the sovereignty, territorial integrity and political independence of every state in the area," and the "termination of all claims of belligerency," and concluded by taking umbrage with the use of the terms "Israeli aggression" and "policies of territorial expansion." (Ibid., Box 1160, Saunders Files, Middle East Negotiations Files, Middle East—Jarring Talks Edited)

[6] Summarized in Document 198.

mally for their reaction. We haven't presented a U.S. position, as such. We believe that if we can talk about guarantees as supplemental to an actual agreement—not as a substitute for negotiations but as a corollary—this would introduce a greater degree of flexibility into the negotiating process. Our principal problem is with the Israelis. We haven't made any decision in favor of any peacekeeping machinery. There has always been opposition to international guarantees in lieu of a binding peace agreement, but in this case the guarantees would be additive and supplementary.

Mr. Kissinger: What do you mean by a binding peace agreement?

Mr. Sisco: That is a euphemistic expression used instead of "peace treaty" in deference to Arab views. We still need to have a further chat with the Israelis.

Mr. Kissinger: Before the Four Power meeting?

Mr. Sisco: Yes, I hope to do it tomorrow. If we can approach the subject in the Four Power meeting[7] by sketching out the options for consideration by the two parties, we will be less apt to get a strong negative reaction from the Israelis. They will have reservations, of course, but if our objective is to develop options for the negotiators to consider, it might be okay. We would stress that the judgment of the Four Powers would not be conclusive.

Mr. Kissinger: How can the judgment of the Four Powers be anything other than conclusive if one of the parties accepts it?

Mr. Sisco: That depends on what the Four Power paper[8] says. We would take the position that the principal element of guarantee is a

---

[7] See footnote 5, Document 198.

[8] U.S., Soviet, and French draft public statements were discussed at the February 4 Four-Power meeting, but, because the four Representatives could not reach a compromise, they decided not to make any statement at all. According to Yost's report on the meeting, the Soviet and French Representatives viewed the U.S. draft as "unacceptable" since it did not allow for a more active Four-Power role in negotiations. Yost had said that the United States preferred not to make a statement in the first place but could agree to a "nonsubstantive endorsement" of U Thant's February 2 appeal to the parties to continue indirect negotiations under the auspices of Jarring. In deference to the United States, Crowe did not take a position on the differing drafts, nor did he submit a British version. (Telegram 361 from USUN, February 5; National Archives, Nixon Presidential Materials, NSC Files, Box 1158, Saunders Files, Middle East Negotiations Files, Middle East—Jarring Talks Edited) On February 2, just before the expiration of the cease-fire, U Thant issued a statement that commented on Jarring's activities since Jarring's report to the Secretary-General on January 4 and urged the parties to continue the indirect talks: "While recognizing that the resumed discussions are still at an early stage and that much further clarification is required, I find grounds for cautious optimism in the fact that the parties have resumed the talks through Amb Jarring in a serious manner and that there has been some progress in the definition of their positions. Furthermore, the parties, who have already indicated their willingness to carry out Res 242 (1967), are now describing in greater detail their view of their obligations under that resolution." (Telegram 311 from USUN, February 2; ibid., RG 59, Central Files 1970–73, POL 27–14 ARAB–ISR)

binding peace agreement. Political endorsement by the Four Powers in the Security Council should be considered by the parties as additive. The parties should consider some practical security arrangements to help keep the agreement. Here are some alternative possibilities. We should not conclude that a Four-Power peacekeeping force is the way to do it. We would put down a series of alternatives for presentation to Jarring by the Four Powers for consideration by the parties. They would be a series of options, not a conclusive judgment. To answer Henry's question, I think it is possible to have an expression of views by the Four Powers without indicating a conclusive judgment.

Mr. Kissinger: On the assumption that some peacekeeping force will be required, we will be giving them some possible alternatives. Suppose the Egyptians say they want a UN third-country force and the Israelis say they don't want any. What do we do then? When would we go to the Four Powers?

Mr. Sisco: We should consult Israel and await their reaction. We could go into the Four Powers near the end of the month.

Mr. Kissinger: That means before the end of the week. Would you go to the Israelis tomorrow and give them 48 hours to react?

Mr. Sisco: I'd give them a few days. The next Four Power meeting is Wednesday and we can temporize in that meeting. There will be another meeting roughly a week hence.

Can we look at the headings of the Guarantees paper. On page 4, Section III, the Four Powers would set down various alternatives. On page 10 is one alternative that Israeli would probably buy—joint Observer Commissions of the parties with UN liaison. This is one of a half-dozen options, and we would leave it to the parties to argue them out.

Mr. Kissinger: It would make a difference what the forces are supposed to be controlling. If they are to support a settlement with no demilitarized zones there would be one set of problems. If there are demilitarized zones there is an entirely different set of problems.

Mr. Sisco: The options must be options that the parties will consider. Demilitarized zones are a key question.

Mr. Kissinger: Are we for or against demilitarized zones?

Mr. Sisco: In favor. We voted for them in the November 1967 SC resolution. We reaffirmed this in the Secretary's and the President's statements of October and December 1969.[9] We have always held, however, that the location of the zones would have to be approved by the parties. The Four Powers would be presenting possible alternative

---

[9] See Documents 58 and 78.

ways to police the demilitarized zones which had been approved by the parties.

Mr. Kissinger: But it's just not going to go that way. Everyone knows that the parties will deadlock—that they won't reach a settlement and won't come to any conclusions. In these circumstances, the Four Powers will be under increasing pressure to be more specific. I have been trying to get this group to address the real issues—to think about where we want to come out and develop a strategy.

Mr. Packard: I agree.

Mr. Kissinger: This discussion will get us through the next week. But, for example, suppose Egypt agrees to demilitarize all of Sinai—or suppose there are fairly large demilitarized zones only on the Arab side. Sinai would be a fairly simple case. You wouldn't need a large force and probably wouldn't want Four Power involvement. All they would need was to make sure there was no mobilization. On the West Bank the problem would be more difficult because of the fedayeen. If there were demilitarized zones on both sides, assuming Israel would accept this, there would be a difficult problem of supervision. It is very hard to separate the question of guarantees from the nature of the settlement.

Mr. Sisco: You have just made an eloquent plea for the kind of paper that is before you. We have done a series of alternatives based on the likely situations, but they will have to be negotiated by the parties. If they can agree on a settlement, the nature of the agreement will probably make one of the six options more feasible than the others.

Mr. Kissinger: If the parties can agree, this is a piece of cake.

Mr. Sisco: We don't think the Four Powers can make any conclusive judgments. Israel won't buy it. In order to leave Israel and the Arabs with maximum flexibility, the most we can do is present the range of alternative arrangements for the parties to consider.

Mr. Packard: How useful is it to talk about guarantees except to keep the talks going?

Mr. Irwin: That is the reason for doing it.

Mr. Sisco: I agree. At some stage the negotiations will reach an impasse. This paper is intended to keep the talks going. The next paper we do will deal with what to do if the talks deadlock: 1) disengage; 2) try to implement a Four Power consensus; or 3) decide to go on our own with a new U.S. initiative. We will do that paper, but the immediate task is to keep the talks alive. We have to begin talking about guarantees in the Four Powers in a way which will not prejudge the options if we reach an impasse.

Mr. Packard: That is most important—to keep the talks going but not to foreclose the options.

Mr. Helms: We don't know if a Four-Power imposed settlement is the only solution if the talks deadlock. Shouldn't we start addressing the question of what a settlement might actually be?

Mr. Kissinger: This is the point I made at the last meeting.[10] We need a general strategy paper telling us where we think we're going so the President can look at it. Are there any arguments against that?

Mr. Sisco: I have no argument against it. A paper of this kind is sensible and we are prepared to do it and focus exclusively on it at the next meeting.

Mr. Kissinger: Suppose Israel rejects violently any discussion of guarantees by the Four Powers on the grounds that they won't permit the Four to prejudge the negotiations. Would we go ahead anyway?

Mr. Sisco: There will be some measure of disagreement by Israel, but it is likely we would have to go ahead. We would measure the Israeli reaction before making a judgment.

Mr. Packard: It would help if we had a better idea where we want to end up. We would have a better chance of figuring out how to get there.

Mr. Kissinger: Are we proceeding on the assumption that we want to get the Israeli aid request disposed of so as not to be faced with this problem during 1972? We should be shooting for July 1, 1971.

Mr. Irwin: The only question is that of defense production schedules.

Mr. Packard: We may have to make a tentative decision on the A–4s. The simplest thing to do would be to permit the Israelis to talk to McDonnell-Douglas on contract details. Alternatively, we might approve a small number, say 16, predicated on keeping the production line going. Or, we could put in an order, estimating what Israel needs, with the understanding that they would have to forego other toys.

Mr. Kissinger: (to Packard) Let's do a paper on how to keep this option going.

Mr. Saunders: Defense is doing that.

Mr. Sisco: The Israelis have asked Dave (Packard) and me to keep the options open.

Mr. Kissinger: Unilateral American steps would be the most favorable to Israel and these may be the only guarantees Israel is interested in. While there is some advantage in vagueness in the Four Power talks, *we* should know where we're going.

Mr. Irwin: This is sensible.

(5:45 p m.—Mr. Irwin left the meeting)

---

[10] See Document 195.

Mr. Kissinger: Are there any guarantees not indicated in the paper that should be there? What do we tell the Israelis?

Mr. Sisco: That our overall objective is the same as theirs: to encourage negotiations and to do nothing which would divert from the negotiations. We feel the kind of discussion in the Four Powers we have in mind would be helpful to Jarring in the negotiating context. We would make it clear that we don't see it as very useful unless serious talks are in progress and the ceasefire is maintained. Four Power discussion must not be substituted for the negotiating process.

Mr. Kissinger: Will Israel take this?

Mr. Sisco: No, we will have problems. They will be concerned by the possibility of conclusive judgments by the Four Powers or by substitution of the Four for the negotiations. We are trying for a middle ground between the Israeli position of no major power involvement at all and the Arab position of total major power involvement to the exclusion of negotiations. We are trying to carry water on both shoulders and I would welcome any ideas.

Mr. Kissinger: There is no good alternative now. We will schedule a meeting next week on a strategy and the basic issues.

Mr. Sisco: Let's not set a meeting date until we have had the paper in hand for several days.

Mr. Kissinger: Give me a definite date for the paper.

Mr. Sisco: You will have the paper by Monday noon.[11]

Mr. Kissinger: All right; we won't schedule a meeting before Wednesday.

Mr. Packard: Let's give more thought to the specific outcome we want to see.

Mr. Sisco: That will be part of this paper.

Mr. Kissinger: The paper will be here Monday and we will meet again on Wednesday or Thursday. We all recognize that these decisions are really fundamental and are some of the most important the President will face.

---

[11] February 1.

200. Telegram From the Department of State to the Interests Section in the United Arab Republic[1]

Washington, January 27, 1971, 0241Z.

13921. For Bergus.

FYI. 1. We have studied carefully your messages reporting on your conversations with Sadat, FM Riad, and Mohammed Riad.[2] We are not surprised, but are deeply concerned over present UAR approach. For months we have worked long and hard to get negotiating process started. It has begun, admittedly gingerly, preliminarily, haltingly. Parties seem to be speaking in stutters. Nevertheless, a beginning has been made; this is as much as could be expected.

2. But we are deeply concerned that UAR may not have faced up to need for serious negotiations. As you say, UAR is mortally afraid of engaging in any process which would be within our concept of negotiations; but without this central process our chances of influencing Israel are dim indeed. We share also your judgment of unrealism of Riad's belief that Egypt's best course is Quote to put pressure on us Unquote. Various UAR reps have come to you every 48 hours to have us produce commitment of total Israeli withdrawal to pre June 5 lines even in circumstances where had it not been for Jarring's sensible clean-up job, polemical UAR paper might have resulted in an immediate deadlock.[3]

3. UAR concept of negotiation seems to be to pressure us to pressure Israel to give UAR what it wants: total Israeli withdrawal to pre-June 5 lines. There seems increasing evidence that UAR concept of negotiations is of pro forma exchange while Four Powers take on main

---

[1] Source: National Archives, Nixon Presidential Materials, NSC Files, Box 637, Country Files, Middle East, UAR, Vol. VI. Secret; Priority; Exdis. Drafted by Sterner and Sisco, cleared by Atherton, and approved by Rogers. Repeated Priority to Amman and to Beirut, Tel Aviv, USUN, London, Moscow, and Paris.

[2] See footnotes 2 and 7, Document 196 and footnotes 3 and 5, Document 197. On January 25, after reflecting on a week of several high-level conversations with UAR officials, Bergus sent a telegram with some conclusions regarding the United Arab Republic and the peace process. He began by writing that the Egyptians were "mortally afraid of engaging in any process which would be within our [the U.S.] concept of negotiations," which he believed represented a "culture block" between the two countries. He argued that the United States had played all of its "readily available cards with the Egyptians," and that the only person who had "the power to change the present situation" was Jarring, due to the United Arab Republic's fear of losing his "sympathy." Bergus concluded that if Jarring were "willing to take bold risks on the basis of his own expendability," he might succeed in breaking what Bergus believed was an emerging "impasse." (Telegram 150 from Cairo, January 25; National Archives, Nixon Presidential Materials, NSC Files, Box 1160, Saunders Files, Middle East Negotiations Files, Middle East—Jarring Talks Edited, January 22–31, 1971)

[3] See footnotes 4 and 5, Document 199.

task. One side has committed itself to the principle of peace, and the other side has committed itself to the principle of withdrawal; what is required is that specific details of a peace agreement be hammered out in serious discussions between the parties under Jarring's auspices.

4. UAR notion that all that is required is for SC Resolution to be implemented is based on naive assumption that third party entities can do the job for it, the Security Council, or the Four Powers laying down an ukase on peace, withdrawal and guarantees. UAR is apparently still unwilling to accept that best way in which US can exercise quiet influence on Israel is within context of serious negotiations between parties that we have spent a year producing. Four Power imposition exercise would not be effective in producing Israel. We continue to believe deeply that within the context of a serious exchange between the parties, in which Jarring takes, as you suggest, greater initiative, we can on a step-by-step and point-by-point basis best seek to develop kind of flexibility on Israeli side which could in time lead to a peace agreement along lines of the October/December 1969 documents.[4] We agree with Foreign Minister Riad's observation that we are not in fact too far apart on what we consider to be a sensible settlement at end of line. But Riad must understand that we cannot produce such a miracle by some preemptive sweep of hand, that we are committed to the October–December 1969 documents, that full cooperation and detailed participation of UAR is required in central negotiating process if US is to play the kind of positive and constructive role it is committed to in helping bring about a solution. Present UAR attitude seems to be that it has done us a favor by not resorting to Security Council, by accepting US peace initiative of last June, and by continuing ceasefire following General Assembly consideration of the matter last December. This is not the case; all of these steps were essential building blocks toward settlement which UAR must realize it needs more than us.

5. We know also that UAR feels that it has already made principal concessions by recognizing Israel's right to exist. But fact of matter is that other side remains unconvinced that UAR is serious about this as long as it is unwilling to sit down (even indirectly) and to work out on a bilateral basis specifics of peace commitment, final borders, demilitarized zones, and practical security arrangements that would make the difference between a real and a paper peace.

6. Finally, we wonder whether UAR has entirely grasped that we are probably at most critical juncture in peace-making effort since end of June war. If a genuine negotiating process cannot be brought into train, our judgment is that further efforts will not be possible for

---

[4] See Documents 58 and 78.

months if not the next year or two, that what would probably result in such circumstances is another round in which the parties would bash at each other, at minimum leaving question of political settlement in even more elusive stage or deteriorating into something much worse.

7. We wanted share above thoughts and concerns with you as background to oral message from FM Riad as given below which is obviously written in more gentle, diplomatic tones. While we can appreciate sense of frustration and impatience that UAR feels, there is one point that we hope you will continue to stress: we do not view negotiations as a device to perpetuate GOI occupation, but patient, step-by-step negotiations are central in order to permit us to play kind of role which could lead to a solution along the lines of the October/December 1969 documents. We cannot play this role on the basis of falsely created deadlines and under threats not to extend a cease-fire which is in UAR interest. To summarize, the simple fact is that there are 3 courses of action possible and only three: 1) continue the status quo, 2) war or 3) negotiations leading to peace. *End FYI.*

8. At earliest opportunity you should convey following oral message from Secretary to Foreign Minister Riad either directly or through Muhammad Riad.

9. At outset Secretary wishes to clarify report you have received concerning his remarks to King Hussein.[5] Purpose of his conversation at that juncture was to illustrate need for both sides to approach talks under Ambassador Jarring in a spirit of give and take. United States views on peace, withdrawal, boundaries, security arrangements and all other elements of settlement continue to be those expressed in October–December 1969 documents and Secretary's December 9 speech.[6]

10. We share your government's desire for rapid progress toward a peace settlement. We recognize that the status quo cannot and should not last indefinitely. US does not consider that negotiations are a delay device for perpetuating occupation of Arab territory. US is prepared to make an all-out effort to help the parties reach a settlement this year. As Secretary told Ambassador Zayyat when he came to Washington recently, 1971 is a critical year because, first, we sense that both sides are seriously interested for first time in finding an alternative to war and present status quo, and second, because if a peace settlement cannot be achieved this year there is not likely to be as good an opportunity for many years to come.

11. At same time, we do not feel that progress can be made under recurrent short deadlines. Positive US role can only be played in con-

---

[5] Reference is presumably to remarks during the dinner for King Hussein on December 8; see footnote 5, Document 189.

[6] See Document 73.

text of on-going, serious negotiations between parties. This is essential for UAR to understand. With issues as complex as ones parties face, and psychological attitudes of distrust so deeply imbedded, progress is going to have to come step-by-step and obviously this will take some time. We want the negotiations to proceed as rapidly as serious dialogue between the parties on crucial issues will permit. The pace cannot be forced artificially. Continuation of cease-fire is as much in UAR interest as it is in Israel's, and it is more important to both than it is to United States.

12. We believe your government's decision not to call for a Security Council meeting was wise, constructive, and in UAR interest. To have subjected the talks to public discussions could only have been a setback. A start has now been made. We have no desire to try to portray this small first step as more than it is. On other hand, compared with steady drift toward increasingly serious warfare that we witnessed in 1969 and first part of 1970, even small steps, if they are in right direction, should be nurtured and built upon.

13. It is our judgment that Israel has now made decision to negotiate seriously in Jarring talks. Its initial submission to Jarring went directly to substance, did not raise procedural problems, and did not contain polemics. We recognize, of course, that what parties have said thus far in this initial exchange is not everything that other side wants. But we believe progress can be made if both sides proceed seriously to negotiate critical specifics. Such negotiations will not, as your representatives have sometimes put it, qte leave the Arabs alone with Israel unqte. The UAR is not alone in negotiations; it is not negotiating from weakness. Major powers will be following process closely and have a role to play in guaranteeing the peace. Framework for a peace settlement is set forth in the Security Council Resolution and has been further defined by discussions among the powers. In our view that framework offers the Arabs a settlement that is honorable.

14. We are aware of your government's sensitivity on the subject of negotiations. It was in deference to these views and only with a great deal of effort that US succeeded in persuading Israel to drop its insistence on face-to-face negotiations at the outset and proceed in indirect negotiations under Ambassador Jarring. We had always assumed that once this hurdle was overcome your government was willing to engage seriously in negotiations under Jarring.

15. The Secretary does not see that the UARG need feel at a disadvantage in the Jarring negotiations. Both UAR and Israel have the military strength to ensure their nation's survival. On the other hand, neither side has the military strength, nor is it likely to achieve this, to impose its will on the other through military means. In our view this not only testifies to need for negotiations but also confers fundamental

parity in a negotiating situation. We have not given Israelis a veto over settlement; both sides have an effective veto. Moreover, all the parties are agreed that the final settlement must be a package deal. This means that in exploration of what the elements of the package may be, neither side has committed itself, neither side has lost or gained anything, until all the pieces fall into place and are agreed upon by the parties in a final agreement. Concerns of each side can be explored by the parties confidentially and conditionally without prejudice to final position of each government concerned.

16. Foreign Minister has asked where do matters stand? As Secretary wrote recently to FonMin Riad,[7] if negotiations can be pursued privately and quietly under Ambassador Jarring's auspices, we believe we can look forward to early development of situation in which not only can USG play increasingly helpful role but Four Powers in concert can begin to make meaningful contribution on question of guarantees. Our judgment is that some progress has already been made. We hope that Jarring will record progress made thus far in a public report which will permit him in the next stage to concentrate on specifics of peace, withdrawal, borders, and security arrangements. We understand GOJ is putting forward additional substantive ideas. We hope UAR will respond positively as we have indicated.

Rogers

[7] See Document 196.

201. Telegram From the Department of State to the Embassy in Jordan[1]

Washington, January 30, 1971, 2036Z.

16548. For Ambassador Brown from Sisco.

We request you see King Hussein immediately and have a heart-to-heart talk with him regarding the current situation, taking into ac-

[1] National Archives, RG 59, Central Files 1970–73, POL 27–14 ARAB–ISR. Secret; Immediate; Exdis. Drafted and approved by Sisco and cleared by Saunders. Repeated Priority to Kuwait, Jidda, Cairo, Tel Aviv, London, Paris, Moscow, USUN, Beirut, Tunis, Tripoli, Rabat, Algiers, Rome, Belgrade, Bucharest, The Hague, Brussels, and USNATO.

count that we see every sign that the King is as concerned and suspicious over present UAR policy and course of action as we are.

1. You should tell King you have been instructed to see him immediately because we need his wise counsel and advice and help. This is in the nature of a candid and frank discussion between two close friends who share common objectives and in the spirit of our recent talks in Washington.[2]

2. We are frankly puzzled and concerned as to present UAR policy which in our judgment could court disaster. First, after months of arduous efforts on our part we finally got the Israelis to do what the UAR asked us to do: to get a specific Israeli commitment accepting the resolution, a commitment to the principle of withdrawal, to indirect rather than direct negotiations, and a limited rather than open-ended ceasefire. Secondly, the shooting stopped and the talks began only to be broken off as a result of UAR-Soviet violations of the ceasefire-standstill which to this day continue to be inexplicable to us. In addition, contrary to our advice, the UAR embarked upon a General Assembly operation, in favor of propaganda rather than private diplomacy, which further delayed the resumption of talks and weakened our capacity to influence the Israelis. Third, after weeks of further effort we convinced the Israelis to return to talks despite the violations. We had no alternative, albeit reluctantly, but to QUOTE help rectify the situation by additional military assistance. UNQUOTE.

3. All of these efforts have finally brought the parties to a stage of indirect discussions under Ambassador Jarring's auspices. The substantive talks have started. We do not claim any more; they only represent an initial beginning. But it is unrealistic to have expected something more in the first stages. The important point, which Cairo does not seem to realize, is that as a result of developments of past few months there is genuine reassessment of policy going on in Israel which active negotiations will further encourage. We are persuaded that Israelis for first time have made decision to negotiate seriously.

4. We are convinced, as is evidenced by the fact that the Israelis have not thrown up any new procedural proposals and have directed their two papers to the substance straight away without polemics and in terms that do not foreclose any Arab position,[3] that if a serious process of negotiations can in fact proceed, free of threats or use of force, flexibility will develop and the US will be in a position to use its influ-

---

[2] See Document 189.
[3] See footnote 5, Document 195 and footnote 5, Document 199.

ence to help bring about a settlement along the lines of the October–December 1969 documents.[4] In this connection, the King should know that we are standing firmly on the positions about which the US and Jordan have had a very clear understanding.

5. We are now coming very reluctantly to the view that after all of our efforts, on the assumption that it was clearly understood that our influence could only be played in the context of indirect negotiations under the auspices of Ambassador Jarring, that the UAR may not be serious about pursuing this process. Continuously in recent weeks, her principal thrust seems to be in the direction of applying pressure on us either by threatening use of force, a resort to the public forum of the Security Council or a diversionary move to the Four Powers. We cannot and will not exercise effective influence in this context. We can exercise influence, as has been demonstrated in the context of the June initiative of last year, while serious private diplomacy and serious negotiations are going on between the parties. If this process ensues, the Four simultaneously can get at question of guarantees at appropriate early stage.

6. Moreover, there are signs that the UAR does not intend to formally extend the ceasefire but rather will leave the matter in an ambiguous state. This is very dangerous. We have had quiet and intensive discussions with the UAR in recent days and have made the point that the ceasefire is as much in the UAR's interest as it is in Israel's interest, let alone in that of the world community. We would appreciate His Majesty's assessment of current UAR attitude on this coupled with the fact that we have noted in recent days certain UAR actions which in our judgment have been aimed directly at Jordan.

7. The US has only one interest in the area: to bring about a political settlement that meets the legitimate concerns of both sides. The present turmoil serves the interest of the Soviet Union not the US or Jordan, and for this reason it is in our mutual interest to help bring an immediate end to it. But we cannot do this if the UAR seems more intent upon relieving itself of the hard decisions that negotiations require in hopes that some third party entity, the Security Council or the Big Four or both, can do the job for it. We do not believe this is in the UAR interest, and we feel that this course could in the long run be injurious to our good, staunch, and courageous friend King Hussein.

8. Thant and Jarring are ready to put out a report on Monday noting that a bit of progress has been made in the opening substantive

---

[4] See Documents 58 and 78.

exchanges.[5] Thant also is prepared to call for the extension of the ceasefire. We feel that this public report creates the QUOTE new fact UNQUOTE which the UAR can use to justify both a continuation of the substantive talks and the extension of the ceasefire for a reasonable period, not a short, four week artificially created deadline. We hope His Majesty by whatever means, by message or even a possible trip of his own to Cairo, will try to influence our Egyptian friends to this end since we are convinced it is in the UAR interest and it will help create the conditions in which the US can play the kind of positive and helpful role it wants to play in order to bring about a just and lasting solution.

9. We realize the problem in Cairo in part is a lack of trust in us. We note also some genuine anxiety and confusion. But the Arab-Israeli dispute has proved intractable for twenty years. Little progress has been made since the end of the June war. The UAR has much to gain by giving the US a reasonable opportunity to try to help move things forward. Only the US can do this, and we must do it in our own way. UAR should realize that a solution cannot be brought about by some magic wand in a period of a day or two. Only circumstances under which UAR can hope to arrive at settlement within framework of SC Resolution and along lines of our October and December papers is if they are willing to proceed in manner which enables us to use our influence with Israel. This has to be a step-by-step process, and the UAR must engage itself in the indirect negotiation process under Jarring in a specific, point-by-point way. Serious oral exchanges through Jarring are required to supplement exchange of papers.

10. We appreciate fully, too, the UAR's desire to have a categoric commitment from Israel to total Israeli withdrawal to the pre-June 5 lines. We believe the specifics of the GOI position on withdrawal and borders will come in genuine negotiation process under Jarring's auspices; otherwise it will not. We believe that if the step-by-step negotiating process is pursued patiently, the US is in a position to exercise its influence and to encourage Israel towards a solution along the lines of the October-December 1969 documents. We are not sure that the UAR has grasped at what critical juncture matters presently stand. If this opportunity which exists at the present time is lost primarily as a result of UAR unwillingness to engage seriously in the central process of indirect negotiations, it is likely that the opportunity will be lost not just for a week or a month but for a very indefinite period.

11. We hope you can prevail upon the King not only to weigh in with the UAR to this end but also suggest that he send a message to SYG encouraging the SYG to go ahead and issue the kind of report that

---

[5] See footnote 8, Document 199.

he is tentatively planning for Monday. We feel Hussein's quiet encouragement to the SYG in this regard will be helpful.

12. You are also free to brief him on the substance of President Nixon's reply to King Hassan.[6]

Rogers

[6] Brown met with Hussein on January 31 to discuss the issues raised by the Department. As a result, the King "wrote out private, personal message" to Sadat that was supposed to have been sent that evening. While the message did "not relate specifically" to the Department's concerns, which Hussein said that he shared, it was a "warning to Sadat that Jordan unwilling repeat mistakes of past (e.g., war) and that UAR had better re-examine its position." When the meeting ended, the King communicated his and the Department's joint concerns to Jordan's Prime Minister, who began working on his own letter to the United Arab Republic, which he believed "should have some effect." (Telegram 576 from Amman, January 31; National Archives, RG 59, Central Files 1970–73, POL 27–14 ARAB–ISR) The exchange of letters between Nixon and King Hassan of Morocco presumably concerned the recent visit of Robert Murphy to Morocco.

202. Paper Prepared by the National Security Council Staff[1]

Washington, February 3, 1971.

I. DIPLOMATIC OPTIONS IN THE FACE OF A NEGOTIATING DEADLOCK

The Sisco-Atherton paper at the next tab—marked "Diplomatic Options"[2]—is quite good, and you will want to read it through yourself. Therefore, instead of reviewing the background with which you are familiar, the following summary concentrates on those elements of the paper which characterize the possible deadlock and spell out the principal options with arguments for and against each.

The deadlock will have these two principal elements:

1. The UAR and Jordan, while having accepted the general principle of ending belligerency and recognizing Israel's right to sovereign national existence, remain unwilling to discuss in detail the obligations

[1] Source: National Archives, Nixon Presidential Materials, NSC Files, NSC Institutional Files (H-Files), Box H-051, Senior Review Group Meetings, SRG Meeting—Middle East 2–8–71. Secret; Nodis. Drafted by Saunders. All brackets are in the original.

[2] Attached but not printed is the February 1 paper entitled "Policy Options in Event of Deadlock in the Jarring Talks."

which they would accept in a peace settlement until Israel first renounces any claims to territory beyond its 1949–1967 borders.

2. Israel remains unwilling to discuss specific final borders until the UAR and Jordan define those obligations.

While progress must be made in both of these fronts if negotiations are to continue, the territorial question seems the more intractable. [*Saunders comment*. It would seem possible for Jarring (or the U.S.) to consolidate positions in the current exchange of documents and past U.S. and Soviet documents in order to reach agreement on the obligations of peace. If the U.S. were to decide to press Israel to take a more specific position on borders, tactically the first step might well be to take to Cairo a consolidated statement on what obligations the UAR would assume in making "peace with Israel"—the commitment Eban says would open the door to discussion of refugees and borders—and press for a UAR agreement in return for a U.S. promise to take the next step with Israel.]

The Sisco paper recalls that the memos leading up to the U.S. peace initiative last June pointed out that implicit in such an initiative was the willingness to bring Israel along in the context of negotiations on an interpretation of the territorial aspects of a settlement which approximated that of the USSR and the Arabs (Jerusalem being the principal exception). The paper suggests that we may now be approaching the point where it will be necessary to face up to that implication of the strategy adopted in June. It concludes its introductory presentation with the statement: *"If the negotiations deadlock, the basic issue will be the gap between the Arab and the Israeli positions on the territorial aspects of a settlement."* The options presented proceed from the assumption that the deadlock can only be broken by eliminating the issue of territory and final borders (Jerusalem and "insubstantial changes" excepted)—but not the issue of the terms and conditions for withdrawal—from the agenda of issues to be negotiated.

[*Saunders comment*. This assumes, as I have commented above, that it should be possible to get the UAR to make the required commitments on its obligations. That is obviously easier because, as we all know, they are paper commitments while the Israeli concessions on borders would be concrete. State's point, I think, is not that the issue of borders is unrelated to the security arrangements to be negotiated but that the negotiation, if it is to bring the Arabs into it seriously, would have to move to the following plane: If Israel is prepared to withdraw to essentially pre-war borders, what security arrangements would be possible? In other words, if the Arabs could feel they were negotiating the *terms* and timing of withdrawal and *not whether* there would be withdrawal, a realistic negotiation might be possible.

The point I will make in a comment below after summarizing Sisco's options is that it may not be able to persuade the Israelis all in one step to move the negotiations decisively to that plane. To move Israel that far we would have to seek its commitment now (as in Option 2 below) to withdraw essentially to pre-war borders. If it is not possible for Israel to move that far all in one step, then we must look for a shorter step, such as a partial withdrawal in return for an interim Arab commitment to something less than total peace. There are strong arguments against this—continued uncertainty and a built-in deadline that would increase tension later. But it may be better than a total breakdown in negotiations and the consequent increased likelihood of resumed hostilities.]

The paper outlines two basic policy options: (1) disengaging from an active role in pressing negotiations; (2) making a serious effort to break the deadlock by trying to move Israel on the territorial issue.

OPTION 1

We could decide to live with a deadlock and in effect *disengage from the active role we have pursued in the past two years* in an effort to promote progress toward a settlement.

The *disadvantages* in this course would be:

—The Jarring talks would quickly atrophy and soon be suspended.

—The cease-fire might well hold a bit longer, but the risk would progressively increase that the UAR would be compelled to resume the war of attrition with all of the familiar dangers of escalation. The Soviets would be under pressure to raise the level of their involvement.

—A stalemate in the peace talks and resumption of hostilities could embolden the fedayeen to seek to recoup their losses, with an increased threat to the regimes in Jordan and Lebanon.

—Tensions in U.S.-Arab relations would rise, especially if American-supplied Israeli weaponry were being used again against Arab territory. This would carry the risk of violence against American installations.

There are three principal *arguments for* this option:

—It would confront both Arabs and Israelis with the difficult choice between renewed hostilities and modification of their positions on a settlement. It might lead them to reassess their alternatives more realistically. [Given the history of the Arab-Israeli conflict, however, both sides without wanting war could well be unable to make the concessions necessary to avoid it.]

—It would avoid the kind of serious U.S.-Israeli confrontation which would result if we sought to move Israel toward the Arab (or even the U.S.) position on territory. [*Comment:* In Presidential decision-making terms, this is probably the more important consideration, although Sisco insisted on putting the above first.]

—It would avoid putting the U.S. in the position of pressing Israel to accept a settlement in which it had no confidence. It would avoid a situation in which, if the settlement broke down after U.S. insistence that Israel accept it, the U.S. would have incurred serious moral responsibility to uphold the settlement unilaterally.

OPTION 2

We could make a *serious effort to break the deadlock* by steps designed to move Israel on the territorial issue. This would involve *pressing for Israeli agreement that, with limited and specified exceptions, it will withdraw to the pre-war line in return for contractual Arab commitments to peace and agreed guarantees and peace-keeping arrangements*, including security arrangements at Sharm al-Sheikh. The exceptions to total withdrawal would relate primarily to the unfinished business of the partitions of Palestine—the status of Jerusalem, the status of Gaza, and rectifications in the West Bank armistice line as well as in the Golan Heights area of Syria if the latter accepted Resolution 242. *The paper identifies two suboptions.*

OPTION 2A

We could *move in the Four Power talks to begin to work out a detailed blueprint* based on our 1969 documents.[3] We would fill in the gaps in those documents to the extent necessary to obtain agreement with respect to guarantees of free navigation and borders, the DMZs and peace-keeping forces, Gaza, the West Bank armistice line and Jerusalem. [Attached to the State Department paper is a draft which illustrates the general lines of the kind of position we might realistically aim for in this process. This is an amalgam of the UAR-Israel and the Jordan-Israel U.S. documents of October and December 1969 with a few more details than before, but their main outlines are not changed. Mr. Sisco emphasizes this document is strictly a working paper and not even intended by him as a final product.]

The main *argument made for* this approach would be that it would be most acceptable to the Arabs and most likely to elicit the kind of Arab commitments on peace, navigation and refugees that Israel has long sought.

The main *argument against* this approach would be that it would be the most difficult of all on which to deliver Israel, and yet failure to do so would leave us no better and probably worse off in the area than we are now. A second major disadvantage would be that we would be making a judgment, in opposition to Israel's, that the final settlement thus achieved would in fact be viable. If we pressed Israel to accept

---

[3] See Documents 58 and 78.

such a settlement against its will, we would assume a heavy responsibility to assure Israel's security if it broke down. [It must be remembered, however, that we would be involved politically with Israel if *any* settlement broke down.] A side effect could be the end of any hope of persuading Israel to renounce nuclear weaponry.

OPTION 2B

We could undertake *steps on our own with Israel, the Arabs, and Jarring to generate a genuine give-and-take negotiation in the Jarring talks.* The State paper outlines three ways of going about this:

1. *Press the UAR and Jordan* to make the first move by responding positively to the document on "Essentials of Peace" put forward by Israel on January 8.[4] [Sisco is even now—with the Israelis about to surface another Jordan document—considering pressing Hussein to produce a document which includes the commitments Eban wants. He would urge Hussein to take the tack we would like to see the UAR take. This could produce Israeli engagement on the subjects of refugees and Jerusalem.]

2. *Press Israel* to modify its position on the territorial aspect of this settlement as a carrot to the Arabs to be more forthcoming on peace and withdrawal. [This would seem the least attractive course by itself until we get what Eban wants from the Arabs. One tactical variant here is really to make up our minds to press Israel but go first to the Arabs and use our decision to elicit what we need before going to the Israelis.]

3. We could put to Israel and the UAR in the first instance, and discuss with Jarring at the same time, a proposition analogous to our June initiative. By this approach *both sides would be asked simultaneously to accept a formula in identical language* including these three components: (a) both sides would reaffirm their acceptance of Resolution 242; (b) the UAR would accept Israel's "essentials of peace" as a basis for negotiating the detailed conditions for withdrawal; (c) Israel would agree to accept the former international frontier as the final border subject to negotiation of a package settlement.

The first of the preceding courses would be difficult to sell to the Arabs and the second would be hard to sell to Israel. The third has the difficulties inherent in both of the first two, particularly on the Israeli side since it would cause the Israelis to face up to the main territorial issue. It would have the advantages of simultaneity. It would also leave the Israelis free to negotiate the timing and the conditions for their complete withdrawal.

---

[4] See footnote 5, Document 195.

Saunders Comment on Options 2A and 2B

Option 2A—going to the Four to negotiate a blueprint—*should be dropped*. It is totally unpalatable to the Israelis. If we want to go that route, it would have more potential effect to go back to the *US–USSR channel*. This option is not mentioned.

Option 2B raises the question of whether we should try to get an Israeli commitment to near-total withdrawal now out of the present negotiations. The three sub-variants are choices among tactics, and realistically Sisco would probably end up combining all three approaches if he detailed a scenario.

The *key question* is whether we can now imagine any presentation to Israel in which we would be in a reasonable position to press Israel to accept near-total withdrawal. [If we were to make the decision to go ahead on this course, I would recommend going to Sadat first and getting as much as possible from him.]

In terms of our decision-making, therefore, the next step, in my mind, is to spell out in detail—in precise detail even with Congressional consultation behind it—exactly what we would offer Israel in this presentation, as well as what we would seek from Sadat.

As you see, I am suggesting that the time has come—if we are to choose OPTION 2 rather than OPTION 1—for the U.S. to become the broker for a final agreement. This would be done secretly in the first instance and details could be negotiated under the Jarring umbrella. The end-product could be the third tactical choice under OPTION 2B above, but *it would not be just another tactical move*. [Your talking points lead up to a proposal for putting together this package to look at.]

A second question is whether we can expect the Israelis to take the full step to commitment to near-total withdrawal all at one time. There has been enough talk about partial withdrawal schemes from both Israelis (Dayan) and Egyptians (Amin) to make this worth talking about. I do not necessarily advocate this as a first step, but I do think it could offer a serious fallback. This is spelled out in greater detail at the next tab which is marked "Third Option."[5]

---

[5] Attached but not printed is the February 3 memorandum to Kissinger outlining Saunders's third option, an "immediate fallback" position if the second option of "pressing Israel to accept near-total withdrawal" was not successful. This plan encompassed "partial withdrawal in return for something less than full peace."

203. Editorial Note

On February 4, 1971, United Arab Republic President Anwar al-Sadat made a 45-minute speech before the country's National Assembly in which he extended the cease-fire with Israel for 30 days and also proposed an interim settlement that would pave the way for reopening the Suez Canal. (*New York Times*, February 5, 1971, page 3) Regarding the cease-fire, he said: "We accept the appeal of the U.N. Secretary-General and decide to refrain from opening fire for a period which we cannot make extend beyond 30 days, ending on March 7. During this period, the Secretary-General and the entire world community must insure that there is genuine progress regarding the heart of the problem and not in its outward manifestations." While the announcement about the cease-fire's continuation was expected after Thant's appeal, the proposal for reopening the Suez Canal came as a surprise. The UAR President declared: "During this period in which we will refrain from opening fire, we demand that a partial withdrawal of Israeli forces on the Eastern bank of the Suez Canal be realized as a first stage of a timetable which will be prepared later to implement the other provisions of the Security Council Resolution. If this is realized within this period, we will be prepared to begin immediately to clear the Suez Canal course and reopen it for international navigation to serve the world economy." (Foreign Broadcast Information Service 72, February 5; National Archives, Nixon Presidential Materials, NSC Files, Box 1160, Saunders Files, Middle East Negotiations Files, Middle East—Jarring Talks Edited and Indexed, February 1–7, 1971)

Israeli Prime Minister Golda Meir's public reaction emphasized the "gravity and danger" of Sadat's proposal. In a statement to the Knesset on February 9, she said, concerning a cease-fire: "to my great regret I must state the grave truth: that the announcement of abstention from shooting for not more than 30 days is equivalent to a threat to renew the war on 7 March 1971. We are invited to continue with talks in an eve-of-war atmosphere, in the shadow of an ultimatum, and on the basis of the unrealistic claim that agreement can be reached on such a complex subject in such a brief period." As for opening the Suez Canal, she said that Sadat's "proposal, as presented in his speech, tries to achieve a strategic advantage by the withdrawal of Israel's forces without actual progress towards peace. To me, it seems strange to propose the withdrawal of our forces from the Canal outside a framework of agreed arrangements for the absolute termination of the war." For the full text of her statement, see *Israel's Foreign Policy: Historical Documents*, volumes 1–2, 1947–1974, Chapter XII, The War of Attrition and the Cease Fire, Document 29.

204. Minutes of a Senior Review Group Meeting[1]

Washington, February 8, 1971, 5–5:18 p.m.

SUBJECT

Middle East

PARTICIPATION

Chairman—Henry A. Kissinger

State
U. Alexis Johnson
Alfred L. Atherton
Thomas Thornton

Defense
David Packard
G. Warren Nutter
James S. Noyes

CIA
Richard Helms
William Parmenter

JCS
Adm. Thomas H. Moorer
Adm. William St. George

NSC Staff
Harold Saunders
Col. Richard Kennedy
Jeanne W. Davis

SUMMARY OF DECISIONS

It was agreed:

—that Israel should be allowed to commence negotiations for the sale of 18 A–4s;

—that the State Department would prepare a paper on the combination of pressures and promises that would be required to get Israel to withdraw close to the 1967 borders.[2]

Amb. Johnson: We have a new message, as you know, and Joe Sisco is with the Secretary discussing it. Rabin is coming in at 5:45.[3] This

---

[1] Source: National Archives, Nixon Presidential Materials, NSC Files, NSC Institutional Files (H-Files), Box H–112, Senior Review Group, SRG Minutes (Originals) 1971. Top Secret. The meeting was held in the White House Situation Room.

[2] For an analytical summary, see Document 207.

[3] During Rabin's February 8 meeting at the State Department, Sisco informed the Israeli Ambassador that the United States had received a message from Sadat delivered by an "impeccable source" in the UAR Government. The source reported that Sadat was concerned at the "absence of USG reaction" to his proposal on partial withdrawal and the reopening of the Suez Canal. (See Document 203) The source added that Sadat believed his proposal "could take the danger out of this present situation" and wanted to assure officials in Washington that "the proposal was not a Cold War exercise. There was no Soviet pressure on him to make this proposal." Sadat asked the United States to "exercise influence" on Israel to consider his proposal, insisting that this was "a matter of substance." Sisco asked Rabin that Israel provide a "constructive, positive reaction" to Sadat's proposal. (Telegram from Rabin to the Ministry of Foreign Affairs, February 8; Israel State Archive, Ministry of Foreign Affairs, 6810/8)

situation is moving so fast and in so many different directions that these papers[4] are really overtaken.

Mr. Kissinger: They are good papers, but one problem is that this new overture[5] may become the dominant factor. The first option of disengagement seems purely theoretical at this point. And the option of moving into the Four-Power context also seems highly unrealistic.

Amb. Johnson: I agree.

Mr. Kissinger: This leaves us with Option 2B[6] which is basically what Jarring is doing now.

Mr. Atherton: It's really 2B3.

Mr. Kissinger: (to Amb. Johnson) Alex, what do you recommend? I hate to be in a position where we are proceeding on purely tactical grounds without knowing what we want to accomplish.

Mr. Packard: We have a different situation here. There is no longer the solidarity among the Arabs that formerly existed. We might try to get Israel to deal with the UAR and keep the issue related to Syria completely separate. Also, the Jordanians have done a good job, and we might try to isolate that aspect of the problem. We could try to move with the UAR on the Canal first.

Amb. Johnson: You're not suggesting we deal with Hussein ahead of the UAR?

Mr. Packard: No, we should move first toward some pull-back to reopen the Canal. Let the Palestinian issue sit for a while, then work on it independently. Also, the Golan Heights problem is almost a separate issue.

Amb. Johnson: I agree. This is just about what we are doing.

Mr. Kissinger: I had intended to steer this meeting in the direction of the paper which, as I read it, sees the options as total Israeli withdrawal with a total Arab commitment to full peace, or disengagement. Prior to the Sadat overture, I was going to ask if it wouldn't be better to try for partial Israeli withdrawal and a partial Arab commitment. The Sadat speech gives us the opportunity to explore exactly that.

(Mr. Kissinger was called from the room)

---

[4] The three papers were the Department of State's "Diplomatic Options" (see Document 202), Saunders's "Partial Withdrawal Options," and the Department of Defense's "U.S. Options in Preserving/Restoring Ceasefire," which are in the National Archives, Nixon Presidential Materials, NSC Files, NSC Institutional Files (H-Files), Box H–051, Senior Review Group Meetings, SRG Meeting—Middle East 2–8–71.

[5] Reference is to Sadat's speech before the UAR National Assembly on February 4; see Document 203.

[6] Reference is to Option 2B in the Department of State paper summarized in Document 202.

Amb. Johnson: (to Mr. Packard) We have no differences with you. The Sadat proposal gives us an opportunity. The Egyptians really seem serious about this.

Mr. Atherton: It certainly needs exploring, but we will have to look at the fine print.

(Mr. Kissinger returned)

Mr. Kissinger: What you want from Rabin today is to keep Israel from slamming the door?

Amb. Johnson: Yes.

Mr. Kissinger: I think any formulation under Option 2 is doomed to failure. I'm sympathetic to what we're doing now which, of course, wasn't available when the paper was written. If we are agreed that this is the right strategy, let's see what develops. We might also reflect on what other partial schemes we might see, now that the door is open.

We also have the paper on the aircraft issue.[7]

Amb. Johnson: May I ask a question about this? (to Mr. Packard) Your paper indicates a need for various amounts of money. Is there a problem of funding?

Mr. Packard: I don't think so. We can let Israel go ahead and negotiate the sale of 18 A–4s which would keep the production line going. Israel will buy these planes.

Mr. Atherton: You propose to let them negotiate for the sale of 18 of the 100 planes they have requested—in other words, a partial go-ahead.

Mr. Packard: We can figure out the funding. You may assume we can handle it.

Mr. Kissinger: (to Mr. Packard) You are recommending we agree on 18?

Mr. Packard: Yes, I think we should give Israel the go-ahead to start negotiations now. Essentially, this is a commitment to let them buy A–4s.

Mr. Atherton: It still leaves open the question of the other 82 A–4s.

Mr. Packard: Yes. We will need another decision in 6 to 9 months to keep the line going.

Mr. Kissinger: We want to make our decision by July anyhow. We certainly won't turn down the whole package.

Mr. Atherton: Why did you decide on 18?

---

[7] The attached paper presented options for meeting Israel's outstanding request for 100 A–4M Skyhawk jets and 42 F–4E Phantom jets in such a way that minimized their procurement by Israel, thereby giving the President flexibility in timing his decisions without delaying their delivery.

Mr. Packard: It was an arbitrary number.

Mr. Noyes: That is one squadron.

Mr. Packard: On the F–4s, we have various alternatives in case of a crisis. We could divert them from our own inventory, so it would be basically a problem of internal counting in the Air Force. There is money in the '72 budget for F–4s.

Mr. Kissinger: Are we all agreed to let them go ahead on the 18 A–4s?

All agreed.

Mr. Packard: The F–4s are more of an internal Air Force problem. We will initiate long lead-time procurement and be prepared for the number of F–4s they will need.

Mr. Kissinger: Isn't Jarring really going ahead with Option 2B3?

Mr. Atherton: He is agonizing over it.

Mr. Kissinger: Should we try to get him to hold off?

Mr. Atherton: The two things aren't mutually exclusive. The danger in the partial approach is that Israel may see it as taking pressure off them, while Sadat may have conceived it as a way of putting pressure on Israel. If Jarring goes ahead with his proposal, the partial approach might look good to the Israelis.

Mr. Kissinger: If Option 2B3 is somewhere down the road anyway, what inducements or pressures would be needed to get both sides, particularly the Israelis, to that point. The negotiating process won't do it.

Mr. Packard: We'd just have to tell them.

Mr. Kissinger: When, and tell them what? That we would continue to supply them? That we would give them certain guarantees? Let's have State do a scenario. When we reach the point of making recommendations to Israel, what exactly would the Secretary say to Eban.

Mr. Atherton: In other words, write the talking points now.

Mr. Kissinger: Let's lay out the combination of promises and pressures that would be needed to get Israel back close to the 1967 borders.

Mr. Packard: You don't say how close.

Mr. Kissinger: We can assume that any settlement which is acceptable to the Arabs would push Israel back further than they want to go. A partial withdrawal could happen without or with very little American pressure. I'm thinking of the next phase—a permanent settlement. What combination of pressures and promises would that require?

Mr. Packard: That depends on what we mean by a final solution. There are some other things that might be viable. If there is a partial settlement and the UAR is happy, they might not be so worried about Jordan. There might be a little flexibility and things wouldn't have to move so far so soon.

Mr. Atherton: At least not so soon. It would certainly create a delay which would provide time for a reappraisal.

205. Telegram From the Embassy in Israel to the Department of State[1]

Tel Aviv, February 12, 1971, 1129Z.

856. Department Pass USUN. Deliver to Action Office Opening of Business.

1. Mrs. Meir and Eban called in Ambassador, accompanied by DCM, morning February 12. Mrs. Meir said she was shocked and worried about Jarring initiative[2] and deeply concerned because she thought difficulty lay with State Department rather than simply with Jarring. As GOI had now learned from summary of exchange of messages with UAR, USG had reiterated its continued support for "Rogers plans" of 1969. Mrs. Meir felt this was contrary to assurances given her, most recently in President's message of December 4, 1970,[3] that USG would leave negotiations to parties and not intervene. Moreover, while she did not know whether US–UAR messages had been made available to Jarring by USG or Egyptians, or whether Jarring had consulted USG about his proposed initiative, it seemed clear to her that he would never have taken initiative except for knowledge that USG stood by 1969 plans and that Egyptians were counting on that.

2. Ambassador took strong exception and pointed out USG had continuously reiterated to all concerned that its policy remained as out-

---

[1] Source: National Archives, Nixon Presidential Materials, NSC Files, Box 1160, Saunders Files, Middle East Negotiations Files, Middle East—Jarring Talks Edited and Indexed, February 12–18, 1971. Secret; Immediate; Nodis. Repeated Immediate to Cairo.

[2] On February 8, Jarring handed identical aides-mémoire to Israeli and UAR representatives in New York in which the Special Representative sought to "make clear" his views on what he believed to be "the necessary steps to be taken in order to achieve a peaceful and accepted settlement in accordance with the provisions and principles of Security Council Resolution 242 (1967), which the parties have agreed to carry out in all its parts." He continued: "I have come to the conclusion that the only possibility of breaking the imminent deadlock arising from the differing views of Israel and the United Arab Republic as to the priority to be given to commitments and undertaking—which seems to be the real cause for the present immobility—is for me to seek from each side the parallel and simultaneous commitments which seem to be inevitable prerequisites of an eventual peace settlement between them." (Ibid.) For the text of Jarring's aide-mémoire, see *Israel's Foreign Policy: Historical Documents*, volumes 1–2, 1947–1974, Chapter XII, The War of Attrition and the Cease Fire, Document 28.

[3] Document 187.

lined in 1969 papers and we had given no commitment either to change fundamental position or to refrain from stating that it still valid. Pointed out we supported idea that negotiations must be between parties but had not tied our hands or hidden belief that we would continue to be of assistance to parties as negotiations proceeded. Stated he did not know whether USG had apprised Jarring of exchanges with Egyptians or whether Jarring had consulted or informed anyone in advance of his proposed paper to parties, but doubted that USG had had any foreknowledge. Called on Mrs. Meir to continue smoking out Egyptians and not to make any negative reply to Jarring paper.

3. Mrs. Meir said GOI position was that it still awaiting simple reply from UAR to simple question of whether, under any circumstances, UAR prepared to make binding peace with Israel. In absence such reply from UAR, she said, GOI would not "take even one more step" and would not take any action on Jarring paper.

4. Mrs. Meir also raised discussion of guarantees and reiterated strong Israeli opposition.[4]

5. Details by septel.[5]

Barbour

---

[4] After reading Meir s complaints regarding Jarring's initiative, Yost wrote: "I am afraid that, if we wish to preserve the negotiating process under Jarring as the main vehicle for a ME political settlement, as the GOI has so long desired, we must speak urgently and very frankly indeed to Mrs. Meir and Eban. The conversation reported reftel [telegram 877 from Tel Aviv; see footnote 5 below] reflects such a preoccupation with their own grievances and such an absence of perception of the true situation that I despair of keeping negotiations going more than few more weeks unless there is a fundamental change in the GOI approach." (Telegram 446 from USUN, February 13; National Archives, Nixon Presidential Materials, NSC Files, Box 1160, Saunders Files, Middle East Negotiations Files, Middle East—Jarring Talks Edited and Indexed, February 12–18, 1971)

[5] Telegram 877 from Tel Aviv, February 12. (Ibid., RG 59, Central Files 1970–73, POL 27–14 ARAB–ISR)

206. Telegram From the Department of State to the Interests Section in the United Arab Republic[1]

Washington, February 20, 1971, 2003Z.

29195. 1. We believe Cairo is sophisticated enough in its knowledge of Israeli political processes to realize that GOI is now faced with very difficult decisions which will have serious domestic political repercussions.[2] Knowing this, UARG is probably prepared give Israelis certain amount of time to come to their decision. Nevertheless, it may at this point be useful to pass low-key message to Egyptians to reassure them of significance we attach to UAR response to Jarring and of our continuing close engagement in efforts to encourage Israel to come up with positive reply that Jarring can build on.

2. You should therefore see Mohammed Riad at early opportunity and give him following message:

A. We have carefully studied UAR reply to Jarring and consider it serious move forward.[3] We believe it merits very close and constructive consideration by Israel.

B. We are encouraged by recent indications that Israeli Government is also viewing UAR response in this light. Special Cabinet meeting was held February 18 to discuss UAR reply and regular Cabinet meeting on Sunday, which Ambassador Rabin has flown home to attend, will continue discussion.[4] GOI is now faced with making very

---

[1] Source: National Archives, Nixon Presidential Materials, NSC Files, Box 1161, Saunders Files, Middle East Negotiations Files, Jarring Talks Edited and Indexed, February 19–26, 1971. Secret; Nodis. Drafted by Sterner, cleared by Atherton and Stackhouse, and approved by Sisco. Repeated to Tel Aviv and USUN.

[2] Reference is to the international expectation of an Israeli response to Jarring's February 8 aides-mémoire to Israel and the United Arab Republic. (See footnote 2, Document 205.) The United Arab Republic sent its reply to Jarring on February 15, the text of which is in telegram 328 from Cairo, accepting many of the aide-mémoire's key elements. (National Archives, Nixon Presidential Materials, NSC Files, Box 637, Country Files, Middle East, UAR, Vol. VI)

[3] On February 20 at 10:07 a.m., Sisco telephoned Kissinger and said: "I want to give you my reading on this Egyptian proposal. It's very good and positive. That's the first time I've ever said that. It meets the principal Israeli private and public conditions that the Egyptians are directly responsive to whether they are or are not willing to make a peace agreement and it gets into specifics for the first time in a clear-cut way. It's the first serious intention to get on with this thing. I think now the Israelis will have to face the tough decisions." (Ibid., Henry Kissinger Telephone Conversation Transcripts, Box 4, Chronological File) The UAR Government released the text of its response on March 10; see *Israel's Foreign Policy: Historical Documents*, volumes 1–2: 1947–1974, Chapter XII, The War of Attrition and the Cease Fire, Document 28.

[4] Rabin wrote in his memoirs that during his short visit to Israel for consultations, the Cabinet adopted a resolution expressing "a favorable view" of the UAR readiness to enter into "meaningful negotiations on all matters connected with peace between the two countries." (Rabin, *The Rabin Memoirs*, p. 193)

important decisions with major domestic political implications involving reconsideration of policy positions that will require basic Cabinet and parliamentary review. This may take some time, but we believe it will be most productive in long run if Israelis are given opportunity to sort out these issues they are faced with according to their internal processes and without public pressure.

C. We have made it clear to Israelis that USG considers UAR reply serious forward step and that we have urged Israel to come forward with positive and constructive reply that advances matters equally on their side. As Sisco emphasized on "Face the Nation" program last Sunday, USG considers that Jarring's initiative is clearly within his mandate under SC Res 242 and that time has come for hard decisions by all concerned.[5]

Rogers

---

[5] Expecting to meet with Mohammed Riad on February 22, Bergus was instead received by Foreign Minister Mahmoud Riad, who wanted to know what the U.S. Government's next move would be, given what he described as Israel's "refusal" of Jarring's aide-mémoire by refusing to withdraw to the June 5 borders. Bergus told him that he "should be in no doubt as to the seriousness and value which we attached to the UAR reply to Jarring" and then proceeded to read paragraphs 2A and 2C of the telegram. The Ambassador concluded by telling Riad that he had "put an important and serious matter" before the U.S. Government and Rogers and that he would "communicate it to Washington as soon as possible." He also said that the U.S. Government would "not be interested in guaranteeing peace agreement that was not inherently viable." (Telegram 379 from Cairo, February 22; National Archives, Nixon Presidential Materials, NSC Files, Box 1161, Saunders Files, Middle East Negotiations Files, Jarring Talks Edited and Indexed, February 19–26, 1971)

207. Paper Prepared by the National Security Council Staff[1]

Washington, February 22, 1971.

ANALYTICAL SUMMARY

Options Vis-à-vis Israel

The Sisco Paper

At the next tab is the Sisco paper entitled, "Scenarios for Seeking to Obtain Modification of Israel's Position on Withdrawal and Borders."[2] This is a summary of that paper and its arguments plus Saunders' discussion at the end of the issues it omits.

You should read the Sisco paper in the following sequence:

1. the first page and a half which sets the stage;

2. go to the last three lines on page 10 and read to the end because this describes the probable political process in Israel;

3. then return to the middle of page 2 and begin reading the scenarios.

The reason for this reading is that the three scenarios describe the elements in three different postures toward Israel. They do not describe a sequence of approaches to Israel. Hence it is more realistic to think about them first as elements of a posture to be displayed in the course of an ongoing political process in Israel. Then a second decision would relate to the tactics of how this posture is revealed to Israel.

If our general posture toward Israel can be set, then we will have a framework within which we can be flexible. We will get away from the simplistic notion that we should cut off military supply if Israel does not swallow the Jarring formula[3] all in one bite.

The Situation

The situation described in the paper has three familiar elements:

1. Israel is now faced with a Jarring memo which seeks Israeli commitment to withdraw to the pre-war international boundary between the UAR and Israel, subject to agreement between the two sides on security arrangements. [Text of Jarring memo is attached at end of Sisco memo.]

---

[1] Source: National Archives, Nixon Presidential Materials, NSC Files, NSC Institutional Files (H-Files), Box H–052, Senior Review Group Meetings, SRG Meeting—Middle East/Chile 2/25/71 (1 of 2). Secret; Nodis. All brackets are in the original.

[2] Undated; attached but not printed.

[3] See footnote 2, Document 205.

2. No quick Israeli decision can be expected. Even if Israel made a positive decision on this issue and negotiations continued, we would still be faced with the problem of bringing Israel along on a whole series of follow-on issues—Jerusalem, Gaza, West Bank boundary, refugee repatriation, DMZs, peacekeeping arrangements (including at Sharm al-Shaikh), to say nothing of the Golan Heights. We cannot "shoot our wad" with Israel at the outset, yet there must be enough Israeli movement to keep the peace talks going.

3. The proposals for partial withdrawal from the Suez cease-fire line offer the prospect of buying needed time. In fact, Israel itself may well attempt to shift the focus from the Jarring talks to this issue. An interim agreement, of course, would not remove basic pressures for further Israeli withdrawal.

Three Possible Approaches to Israel

The Sisco paper is written to address a situation in which for the purpose of presentation it is assumed that Israel seems about to reply negatively to the Jarring proposal and conventional diplomatic representations show no signs of persuading the Israelis to change their minds. The paper groups possible US postures ("scenarios") under three headings: inducive, inducive/coercive, and coercive. They are elaborated as follows:

1. *Inducive.*

Reliance under this approach would fall primarily on diplomatic argument, responsiveness to Israel's present material and financial requirements and readiness to commit the US to long-term support of Israel's security.

The US would tell Israel that if Israel agreed to the Jarring memo the US would take the position that:

—The parties should now be given a free hand and reasonable opportunity to come to grips themselves with security arrangements and DMZs.

—No option should be excluded from negotiation, including proposals for demilitarizing the entire Sinai, including Israeli representatives in any verification system, continued Israeli presence at Sharm al-Shaikh in a manner not transferring sovereignty.

—The US would be prepared to include a US contingent in any force at Sharm al-Shaikh and to insist that termination of that force should be barred for a specified period (5–10 years).

—Supported Israeli passage through the Canal.

—Allowed return of refugees only in numbers satisfactory to Israel.

—Barred return of Gaza to UAR control and introduction of any Arab military forces.

The US would continue military support on concessional financial terms and offer to discuss with Israel possible executive and Congressional declarations in support of Israel's security, formalization of bilateral defense consultations, contribution to refugee resettlement and to conversion of the Israeli economy to peacetime lines.

The main *argument for the inducive approach* is conviction that an Israel confident in itself and in US support is more likely to be flexible than an Israel made uncertain by US efforts to exert pressure. A case can be made that Israel's acceptance of the US initiative last summer was a partial demonstration of the effectiveness of this approach, although the pressure generated by the Soviet military presence played an important role. This approach is also attractive because it would avoid a difficult confrontation with Israel.

The main *argument against* this approach is that it is questionable whether mere inducement is sufficient to persuade Israel to give up what it regards as central to its negotiating position—freedom to trade one part of the Sinai for other parts it regards essential to its security. The possible inefficacy of inducements is compounded by the fact that we have already provided substantial inducements for marginal Israeli moves that their effect tends to be blunted. They may well feel, too, that they can get these things from us whatever they do.

Comment: No single inducement—aircraft, financial assistance, a diplomatic position—is likely to "buy" an Israeli change of position on an issue Israel regards as literally vital to its survival. However, the sum of these—the whole US-Israeli relationship—is very important to Israel, and the US as a deterrent to Soviet attack on Israel is vital. While this is connoted in the Sisco paper's allusion to further US executive and Congressional declarations in support, it seems to me *the key question to be addressed with some degree of decisiveness is what the US is now prepared to promise Israel in regard to standing off Soviet collaboration in a future Arab attack* if a peace agreement is reached and then breaks down.

There is an argument which states that if we are going to rely on inducements to produce a major Israeli step, we have to make major decisions now on our future security relationship with Israel. We may not want ever to have a closer relationship, but if we are prepared to, now may be the time for that decision—at least perhaps to explore a tentative decision with key Congressional leaders. Otherwise we may be asking too much from Israel for too little.

2. *Inducive/Coercive.*

Under this approach we would offer the positive undertakings described above. But we would make clear to Israel that Israeli unwillingness to compromise would lead to US re-examination of certain aspects of our relationship. The US would keep the Congress informed of its view that the Israeli position is now the major stumbling block to a settlement.

Specifically, the USG would brief Congress and the press; solicit support from the US Jewish community; slow down arms shipments and be unreceptive to new requests without actually rejecting them; retain a public posture of basic support for Israel's security.

The main arguments for this approach are that it would underscore the seriousness of the USG position in taking some domestic political risk and raise questions in the Israeli mind as to whether US support can be taken for granted regardless of Israel's position. At the same time, it avoids the risks of full confrontation.

The *main arguments against* this approach are: It might strengthen the hands of the Israeli hawks by arousing latent fears that ultimately Israel must stand alone. The Arabs might be encouraged to greater belligerence if they thought the US was deserting Israel. The Soviets might be encouraged to be more venturesome. Yet Israel might not be intimidated at all.

Comment: It may be premature to think of open confrontation with Israel or slowing down arms shipments as the State Department paper proposes. The point might best be made by offering such key inducements as a commitment vis-à-vis the USSR and then making clear that such support will not be possible if Israel insists on holding territory because the likelihood of breakdown in the agreement would be too great.

3. *Coercive.*

Under this approach all the elements of the inducive/coercive option would be exhausted and then arms shipments would be halted or drastically curtailed; discussion of arms and credits would be halted; steps would be taken to halt the transfer of funds to Israel; the President would explain these steps to the public.

Comment: It seems (a) too early in the game to think in these terms and (b) unrealistic in any case to assume that the US can virtually break the US-Israeli relationship.

The Issues

The Sisco paper ends at this point. However, it seems worth continuing here to suggest that it is important now to be as precise as we can be in our own minds about the answers to these two questions:

—What is the most we are prepared to offer Israel concurrent with a peace agreement as a bilateral assurance of US support for Israeli security? The promise of continued military supply and financial assistance seems almost a foregone conclusion. But can we promise that US forces will react directly if the Arabs with the support of Soviet combat forces attack Israel? If so, should we be prepared to formalize this in some sort of arrangement with Senate concurrence?

—What is the farthest we are prepared to go in reducing US support for Israel as a means of pressing Israel to accept an agreement that we think would be viable?

When we think in these terms, it becomes apparent that the Sisco paper before us today is not subtle enough or precise enough in addressing the key questions:

—a specific proposal to be made to Israel on the nature of the US-Israeli security relationship that would exist if there is a peace agreement with the pre-war Israel-UAR border;

—a specific proposal for (or against) participation of US forces in a peacekeeping force;

—specific talking points to be used with Mrs. Meir in offering the above and in making clear that the US offer vis-à-vis the USSR would not be available if Israel retains territory.

[NOTE: All of the above is written in the context of the Jarring negotiations. It is fully recognized—as has been presented in other memos—that the partial withdrawal proposal remains a means of avoiding total settlement of the boundary issue all in one step now.]

208. Minutes of a Senior Review Group Meeting[1]

Washington, February 25, 1971, 2:36–3:50 p.m.

SUBJECT

Middle East, Chile

PARTICIPATION

Chairman—Henry A. Kissinger

State
Under Secretary John N. Irwin
Mr. Joseph J. Sisco
Mr. Alfred L. Atherton
Mr. Thomas Thornton

Defense
Mr. David Packard
Mr. Armistead I. Selden
Mr. James S. Noyes

CIA
Mr. Richard Helms
Mr. David H. Blee

JCS
Adm. Thomas H. Moorer
Adm. Elmo R. Zumwalt, Jr.*
R/Adm. Wm. R. St. George

NSC Staff
Col. Richard T. Kennedy
Mr. Harold H. Saunders
Mr. Arnold Nachmanoff*
Mr. D. Keith Guthrie

*Present for Chile discussion only.

SUMMARY OF CONCLUSIONS

1. *Strategy toward Israel.* The IG/NEA will prepare a scenario for a US strategy toward Israel in the event that the Israeli reply to the Jarring proposal is not sufficiently forthcoming on boundaries.[2] The scenario should set forth measures which the United States might use to move Israel toward productive negotiations and should analyze the consequences of each measure. The scenario should be focused on the forthcoming three weeks and should outline anticipated developments during that period.

[Omitted here is discussion of Chile.]

Middle East

Dr. Kissinger: (to Sisco) Can you sum up where you think we stand right now in the Middle East? I want to be sure that the next time I see Ambassador Rabin at a dinner party I will know what is going on.

---

[1] Source: National Archives, Nixon Presidential Materials, NSC Files, NSC Institutional Files (H-Files), Box H–112, Senior Review Group, SRG Minutes (Originals) 1971. Secret; Nodis. The meeting was held in the White House Situation Room. All brackets are in the original except those indicating text omitted by the editors.

[2] See Document 214.

Mr. Sisco: We have been pursuing three tracks. The first relates to the negotiations under Jarring's auspices. You have all seen the latest UAR reply to Jarring's questions.[3] Jarring formulated on a contingency basis the kind of peace commitments heretofore sought by Israel and put to the Israelis the specific question whether Israel is willing to withdraw from UAR territory to the previous international boundary provided satisfactory arrangements can be made on Sharm-al-Shaykh and demilitarized zones in the Sinai. He made no mention of Gaza or of the principle of total Israeli withdrawal to the pre-June 1967 lines.

The Egyptian response is the first serious indication that they will say explicitly that they are willing to enter into a peace agreement with Israel if there are satisfactory security arrangements. The Egyptians have called on Israel to get out of both Sinai and Gaza.

The Israelis are considering the situation. They are having a cabinet meeting Sunday.[4]

Ambassador Rabin said he expected that Israel would acknowledge privately and publicly that the Egyptian position represents a step forward and would recognize the principle of withdrawal to secure, recognized boundaries. He thought the Israelis would express a willingness to negotiate but would categorically bar total withdrawal to the armistice lines.[5]

In our judgment this evades Jarring's key point, which was to invite a clear Israeli position on borders. All Israel will be doing is to come back with a negative statement.

---

[3] See Document 206.

[4] February 28.

[5] Rabin met with Sisco on February 23 to discuss Israel's imminent reply to Jarring's aide-mémoire, as reported in telegram 30820 to Tel Aviv, February 24. (National Archives, Nixon Presidential Materials, NSC Files, Box 1161, Saunders Files, Middle East Negotiations Files, Middle East—Jarring Talks Edited and Indexed, February 19–26, 1971) He also met with Rogers the following day to discuss the matter further. (Telegram 31741 to Tel Aviv, February 25; ibid.) According to the Israeli record of their conversation, Rogers emphasized that it is now time for the Israelis to "face up to the decisions" of responding positively to Sadat's overtures and to Jarring's memorandum. "It is only a matter of time before your hand will be disclosed. Sooner or later you will have to face up to it," he said. Rogers added that if Israel responded negatively to Jarring's memorandum "everyone will say that you did it to evade a decision. If you say yes we are willing to withdraw and now wish to negotiate, then you have said nothing new. They have said a lot. Unless you indicate what you are speaking sbout you are not saying anything. It is going to put us in a terrrible spot. We feel very strongly your answer should be positive to Jarring. They will laugh us out of the room in the Sec[urity] Council if you are only going to say that which you have indicated. You must have a position of your own, not just quote no unquote. We are concerned because we made progress. We are most concerned because it all might be lost." (Israel State Archive, Previously Classified Material, 7021/4)

Dr. Kissinger: Let me make sure I understand what you take to be the Israeli position. They are barring total withdrawal to the 1967 boundaries but not withdrawal to one of the 1967 borders. Their position is not inconsistent with withdrawal to the previous boundary with Egypt. The Egyptian line per se is not unacceptable.

Mr. Sisco: That's what we don't know. Rabin was not very explicit about this. I asked him if he was barring the 1967 boundaries in every instance and he replied: "Yes, insofar as it relates to the peoples we are fighting." I then asked him: "If you don't want the 1967 line, then what is the line you want? This is what Jarring wants to know." Rabin replied only that "we are willing to negotiate."

We have to recognize that the Israelis have serious internal political problems. They can only agree on what they are against. They can't even define the concept of total withdrawal against which they are expressing themselves. They are not able to put forward anything concrete or formal. The Secretary made all the points I have mentioned, and we know that Rabin sent back a further strong message to Jerusalem.

Dr. Kissinger: Was he asking for a change in their position?

Mr. Sisco: He was asking them to be more precise. In his press briefing before leaving for Israel, he said in effect that the only position for Israel is the Rogers position. However, we have to remember that he is not Golda Meir or Moshe Dayan. Dayan's statement the other day is a very bad way to present the Israeli position.[6]

The Israelis are on the defensive at the moment. Golda Meir told Wally Barbour the other day that "if the Egyptians say they are in favor of a peace agreement, Israel will have to face up to the territorial problem."[7] The Israelis recognize that this is where there are serious differences between Israel and the United States.

Dr. Kissinger: Maybe she did [face up to the problem].

Mr. Sisco: We have never pressed the Israelis on this. Now we can't evade the border question. The other side has met the principal Israeli concerns in the most explicit terms. Now we are in great danger of losing what it has taken us one year to put together: a cease-fire, continuation of the negotiations, and exercise of control over the four-power talks. We are in for serious difficulties unless we can bring the Israelis around. The moment of truth has arrived. We are trying to get our

---

[6] According to the *New York Times*, at a private dinner, Dayan said that "given the choice between a peace treaty and an Israeli presence at Sharm el Sheik to ensure passage through the Strait of Tiran, he would prefer the presence at Sharm el Sheik." (February 19, 1971, p. 1)

[7] Meir and Barbour met on February 12, but the comments that Sisco ascribed to her were not included in the record of that meeting; see Document 205.

points across to the Israelis. We are not trying to draw the President in; we want to save him for the crucial time.

Dr. Kissinger: There will be a briefing on the Middle East on the NSC agenda tomorrow,[8] but no decisions. At that meeting you can tell the NSC members what might be coming up soon.

Mr. Sisco: If there are positive elements in the Israeli reply, we can emphasize these in an effort to get things moving. But if the reply, as seems likely, is negative, there is likely to be a Security Council meeting and there will be no alternative but for the US to join with other Security Council members in saying that the Israeli response is inadequate and that something further is required from the Israelis. We will also be under increased pressure in the four-power talks. We have taken the position that the four powers should make no conclusive judgments until it is known exactly what we are talking about.[9] The other three are willing to hold the line as long as there are serious indications that negotiations will take place.

Dr. Kissinger: What do we want from the Israelis?

Mr. Sisco: We want a reply to Jarring that says "Yes, we are willing to withdraw to the boundary you specified provided we are satisfied on Sharm-al-Shaykh and demilitarized zones. We are sending our foreign minister to negotiate."

Mr. Irwin: It would be all right even if they don't go that far but just say that they will withdraw and mention Sharm-al-Shaykh and the demilitarized zones. The point is that they give some specifics.

Dr. Kissinger: I remember that some Israeli (I think it was Rabin) told me once that they wanted a line straight north from Sharm-al-Shaykh. Were they to say that, we would still be in the Security Council wouldn't we?

Mr. Sisco: We would at least for the first time be moving on negotiations on the concrete question of where the border is to be located. [Mr. Sisco indicated on a map the two possible alignments mentioned by Israel for tracing the boundary north from Sharm-al-Shaykh.]

Dr. Kissinger: Let's take the case where the Israelis say: "This is our notion of a line." The question then goes to the Security Council, and we vote that the Israeli proposal is not satisfactory.

Mr. Sisco: We have got to see the actual Israeli reply before discussing this.

---

[8] See Document 209.

[9] In telegram 23650 to USUN, February 11, the Department provided "broad guidelines for carrying out our strategy in dealing with supplementary guarantees question in Four Power talks." (National Archives, Nixon Presidential Materials, NSC Files, Box 1158, Saunders Files, Middle East Negotiations Files, Middle East Negotiations—Four Power Talks, August 13, 1970–November 15, 1971)

Dr. Kissinger: But suppose the Israelis make a conciliatory reply except on the question of borders.

Mr. Sisco: That would not be satisfactory.

Dr. Kissinger: This is getting us to the position where the only acceptable Israeli reply is to accept the 1967 borders. The Security Council would be judging the situation, and we would be edging toward an imposed solution. Anything else [i.e., besides the 1967 borders] will elicit a Security Council condemnation. If things develop that way, we will have a hell of a time getting any support.

If we feel we may have to support the Israelis, we have to consider what is going to happen in the Security Council. If we vote against Israel in the Security Council and a war starts and we have to support the Israelis ...

Mr. Sisco: First of all, the Security Council is not about to get into precise judgments of that sort. If Israel does not express itself concretely on the subject of boundaries, our strategy in the Security Council should be to limit any action to the general thrust of exhortation. Our position would still be that it is still for the parties to sort out the dispute and that we should not have the Security Council making a substantive judgment of the situation. This would be a bad precedent for resolving other elements of the dispute.

Dr. Kissinger: Isn't that what is going to happen?

Mr. Packard: You may have it developing that way. The trouble is that we are awfully close to attaining the goal we have been seeking if we can just go the distance that remains. We will get more credit if we keep the matter in our ball park rather than the Security Council. Besides, we will also have more influence with the Israelis that way, and our relations with the Arabs will be better.

Mr. Sisco: I recognize Henry's [Kissinger's] point. Anything substantive the Security Council says will be unacceptable to the Israelis. Our position is that the best thing for the Security Council to do is to encourage the negotiating process rather than itself to make substantive judgments.

Mr. Irwin: There are several possibilities. The Israelis may come back with the answer Joe [Sisco] says we want to have; that is, they may match the forthcoming attitude of the Egyptians. From everything we hear, we don't expect that to happen. The Israelis may also come back with a specific boundary proposal. This would be an advance, and we could treat it as a negotiating position. We would then be better able to withstand pressure in the Security Council.

Dr. Kissinger: The Israelis have said they favor withdrawal to secure boundaries. That sort of a reply won't advance the negotiations much. If the negotiations blow up, the Egyptians will be under great pressure to re-start the war.

Mr. Sisco: Our own judgment is that in this kind of a situation the Soviets *are* a restraining influence. The Egyptians are not likely to start shooting in a serious sort of way.

If they move into the Security Council, they will not make an all-out effort to direct the Security Council. This is a political process the Egyptians will feel they need to pursue. One thing a Security Council resolution might contain would be a call for an extension of the ceasefire. It could note the Israeli position, as for continued negotiations, and call for an extension of the ceasefire.

I mentioned earlier we were pursuing three tracks. The second is to pursue the Suez Canal proposal further, and the third has to do with four-power discussion of guarantees. The Suez Canal proposal could provide a short-run show of progress. Sadat made this proposal over the objections of his advisers. We have offered to provide assistance to both sides, and both have indicated that they wanted us to serve as middleman. Sadat talked about opening the Canal, and Golda Meir referred to military deescalation in the canal area. We have a good idea what the Israelis might bite on, but we have held back because of not wishing to encourage the forces in Israel that prefer to go the partial route in order to relieve pressure to face up to the boundaries problem.

There is going to have to be some public US dissociation from Israel if the Israeli reply is negative.

Dr. Kissinger: But there will be no short fuse on this.

Mr. Sisco: Yes, there will.

Dr. Kissinger: Joe [Sisco] has stated the issues well. The question is how we are going to move the Israelis. The President is going to have to take the heat on this. I think we are going to be heading toward a greater or lesser confrontation with Israel. My instinct says the Israelis are not going to accept the 1967 boundaries easily.

Mr. Sisco: I agree regarding the Egyptian front.

Dr. Kissinger: The question is how we are going to get them there. We need to know what the consequences of alternative forms of dissociation are. What if the war does start again, the Israelis clobber the Egyptians, and the Russians come in—not massively, but with active military forces?

Mr. Packard: We are faced with the problem of getting the cattle through the gate. If we don't do it now, it will take three weeks. They are almost there.

Dr. Kissinger: The question is how to do it and what the consequences will be.

Mr. Packard: I think we ought to push pretty hard.

Dr. Kissinger: That is one proposal we have had. We need to consider what measures will move the Israelis. We had a paper here that set forth inducive and coercive tracks.[10]

Mr. Sisco: Yes, the questions posed are addressed in this paper. However, it is premature to decide these things now. The paper you asked for made the following assumptions. It says: "The scenarios in this paper rest on the following assumptions: (1) we have word from Jarring that the UAR has accepted the terms of his Aide Mémoire without reservation as a basis for continuing negotiations or the UAR-Israeli aspect of a settlement, and (2) Israel has either declined to reply or indicated it intends to reply negatively or with major reservations to the Jarring proposal." The three tracks are inducive, inducive-coercive, and coercive.

Dr. Kissinger: I have the impression you favor Option 2—inducive-coercive.

Mr. Sisco: I have not opted for any of them. We have got to proceed carefully on a step-by-step basis in putting pressure on Israel. We want to keep the pressure as much as possible in the private domain. We could make a major quiet effort after the Security Council. There may have to be some public dissociation from Israel. We have to say frankly if the Israeli position is not acceptable in terms of our approach.

Mr. Packard: When do you expect an answer?

Mr. Sisco: We had thought we would have something tomorrow. But I think it will be delayed.

Dr. Kissinger: It will be a week at the latest.

Mr. Sisco: Yes.

Mr. Packard: Have we ever said to them that if they accept one of the lines, we won't push on the others. That is an approach that might help.

Mr. Sisco: We have spelled this out in the Rogers proposal by saying that we agree there should be a united Jerusalem and that there should be "insubstantial" adjustments in the border along the Jordan River.

Mr. Packard: What about the Golan Heights?

Mr. Sisco: We have said nothing because Syria is not involved in these negotiations. Syria does not accept the Security Council resolution.

Mr. Kissinger: We are all agreed that we will have to apply pressure of one sort or another. We need a scenario showing how this is going to evolve so we are not asked to make one decision after an-

---

[10] See Document 207.

other—a note now, a letter later, etc. The scenario should set forth the full combination of pressures that might be used. For example, it might include Dave Packard's proposal that we indicate that acceptance of the pre-1967 Egyptian frontier would not be a precedent for all other frontiers. We would ask the President to consider a scenario that would spell out how we see things evolving over two or three weeks. It would explain how we get the cattle through the gate.

Mr. Helms: We have information that the Israelis are already getting ready to respond to what they think will be our position. They are collecting statements and quotes to use. This is all the more reason why we should decide what we want to do.

Mr. Kissinger: (to Irwin and Sisco) Would you have the IG put together a proposal such as you have described covering the next three weeks? That way the President will have an idea of the sort of decisions that might come up. We will not have to develop our strategy one cable at a time.

Mr. Packard: But Joe (Sisco) is going to need some flexibility.

Mr. Irwin: He will need a lot of flexibility.

Mr. Kissinger: I have noted that Joe doesn't seem to feel restrained whenever he feels something should be done. We could put in the document that it is always possible to make new proposals.

Mr. Sisco: I think it is only fair to say that many people are beginning to believe that the cupboard is bare insofar as any new proposals are concerned.

Mr. Kissinger: We are coming to a confrontation.

Mr. Sisco: We are arriving at the point we have been aiming at for eighteen months.

Mr. Kissinger: This is all the more reason for us to see how the situation is going to evolve. We never had any illusions that Israel would go back of its own volition. We knew that pressure would be needed. Can you get this paper prepared by next week?

Mr. Irwin: The President is going to be personally involved to a considerable extent.

[Omitted here is further discussion of Chile]

209. Memorandum of Conversation of a National Security Council Meeting[1]

Washington, February 26, 1971, 11:45 a.m.

PARTICIPANTS

    President Nixon
    Vice President Agnew
    Secretary of State William P. Rogers
    Secretary of Defense Melvin Laird
    Director of Central Intelligence Richard Helms
    Chairman, Joint Chiefs of Staff, Admiral Thomas H. Moorer
    Under Secretary of State John N. Irwin II
    Assistant to the President Henry A. Kissinger
    Ambassador George Bush, U.S. Representative to the UN
    Under Secretary of State for Political Affairs U. Alexis Johnson
    Director, U.S. Information Agency, Frank Shakespeare
    Joseph J. Sisco, Assistant Secretary of State for Near Eastern and South Asian Affairs
    Alfred L. Atherton, Jr., Deputy Assistant Secretary of State for Near Eastern and South Asian Affairs
    General Alexander M. Haig, Deputy Assistant to the President for National Security Affairs
    Harold H. Saunders, NSC Staff
    Colonel Richard Kennedy, NSC Staff

SUBJECT

    National Security Council Meeting: The Middle East

[As the discussion turned from Laos to the Middle East, Mr. Sisco, Mr. Atherton and Mr. Saunders entered the room.]

The President: Perhaps the group should delay discussion of the Middle East until later, because I have to go on to a 12:00 noon appointment.

Laird: [leaning over to the President]: The problem is we have to move quickly. The next few days will be very important—if it gets into the Security Council. Perhaps the subject should at least be discussed.

The President: All right. We'll take a few minutes on the Middle East. Joe, would you brief?

---

[1] Source: National Archives, Nixon Presidential Materials, NSC Files, NSC Institutional Files (H-Files), Box H–110, NSC Meeting Minutes, NSC Meetings Minutes Originals 1971 thru 6–20–74. Secret. The meeting was held in the Cabinet Room of the White House. According to the President's Daily Diary, the meeting lasted from 10:40 a.m. until 12:35 p.m. (Ibid., White House Central Files) A tape recording of this meeting is ibid., White House Tapes, Cabinet Room, Conversation No. 48–4. All brackets are in the original.

Mr. Sisco: The present situation can be described as operating on three different tracks. The first two can be dismissed very quickly; the third—the Jarring talks—is the most important:

—In the Four Power talks, the supplementary guarantees are the issue. So far we have been successful in keeping this from becoming very substantive, but if there is not progress soon in the Jarring talks we will have our hands full in containing this discussion further. The pressure from the British, French, and Soviets will mount on us to proceed with a substantive discussion with a view to producing Four-Power agreement on guarantees for a settlement.

—On the proposal for partial withdrawal from the Suez cease-fire line, there is unlikely to be movement in the short term until the UAR has a good look at the Israeli reply to the current Jarring proposal. State feels that President Sadat is "somewhat desperate" to show progress toward Israeli withdrawal. State feels that Sadat made the proposal for partial withdrawal from the Suez Canal contrary to the advice of a number of his advisors. This is an ongoing issue, but for the moment it would seem to be in suspense pending clarification of the state of the dialogue through Jarring.

—Both sides want us to play a middleman role.

Secretary Rogers: At the moment—this week—we do not think we should tackle this subject. It is something for discussion a little farther down the track. We do not mean at all to rule it out. We are only saying that in this period of a few days, the Jarring exchange is center stage.

Mr. Sisco: The most important of the three tracks is the exchange through Ambassador Jarring. In the four to six weeks since the start of these exchanges in early January, the Israeli positions were serious and the UAR positions were polemical and did not lend themselves to real negotiations. In the new phase which has begun recently, the UAR has now come forward with concrete positions. It has said it would be willing to join in a peace agreement with Israel. Prime Minister Meir explicitly stated to Ambassador Barbour that if the U.S. could get a specific UAR commitment to make a peace agreement with Israel, she would face up to the difficult issues raised by the differences between the U.S. and Israeli views of what final borders should be in a peace agreement.[2]

It should be clearly understood what Ambassador Jarring has asked Israel to commit itself to. The Israelis are "throwing up a smoke screen" by claiming Jarring has proposed that Israel commit itself to total withdrawal. Jarring has not asked that of Israel. He has asked that the Israelis agree to withdraw to the international border with Egypt

---

[2] See footnote 7, Document 208.

provided there is satisfactory agreement on demilitarized zones and on security arrangements at Sharm el-Sheikh. Gaza is not mentioned at all.

The Israeli response to Jarring will probably not answer this question directly. Israel will probably welcome the UAR move, say it is ready to negotiate, perhaps even suggest negotiation on subjects other than borders and state that it will not return to the pre-1967 borders. The Israeli cabinet is divided. It has only been able to agree on what it is against. It has not been able to agree on a specific negotiating position to advance as the next stage in the Jarring talks.

If this does turn out to be the Israeli response, Ambassador Jarring will have to say that it is not responsive to his question. If this is Jarring's judgment, this raises concern over the future of the negotiations and the cease-fire. Even more important, a breakdown in both would give the Soviets a handle for further inroads in the area.

Secretary Rogers: We are at a critical juncture. The UAR has accepted all that Israel has said it wants. If the UAR had said in 1967 what it has now in effect said in response to Jarring's memorandum, Israel would have been delighted. Now, however, Israel is unwilling to make a decision of any kind. Israel is going to say simply that it is ready to negotiate. That is not enough. They have to lay their cards out now. I told Ambassador Rabin Wednesday that Israel has to say what its position is.[3] The negotiation is already going on. We will be in a difficult position if they do this.

The President: What do they want? We have provided the aircraft and the financial assistance. What more are they asking for?

Secretary Rogers: They won't make up their minds. The Cabinet has discussed this subject and has been unable to decide exactly what borders Israel should ask for in a peace agreement. At the same time, the record shows that Foreign Minister Eban in June 1967 told Secretary Rusk in connection with Israel's views toward an Egyptian-Israeli settlement that Israel would go back to the pre-war boundary if there was a security arrangement for Sharm el-Sheikh, and that Israel did not seek territory, only security. [The record which Mr. Sisco had in hand to document this comment is attached.][4] The U.S. cannot support Israel in the UN Security Council if, now that a negotiation has been launched, Israel refuses to advance a negotiating position. This is where we stand today.

The President: Let me understand what you are saying about the second track you describe. What is it you are saying about the scheme

---

[3] See footnote 5, Document 208.

[4] Attachment not found; see *Foreign Relations,* 1964–1968, volume XIX, Arab-Israeli Crisis and War, 1967, Document 314.

for opening the Suez Canal? I had thought from the briefing papers I had read that perhaps this offered an alternative for buying some time.

Secretary Rogers: All we are saying is that, right now, it is not "talkable." If we were to raise this with the Egyptians as long as the Israelis had not replied constructively to Ambassador Jarring, the Egyptians would regard the proposal as an effort by the U.S. to help Israel evade answering Jarring's questions. If, on the other hand, the Israelis give Jarring a reasonable reply, then it is quite possible for this course to be discussed.

The President: In those circumstances, then, opening the Canal would be regarded as a step in the negotiations—a step toward a final settlement?

Secretary Rogers: Yes, if Israel gives a positive answer to Jarring, we could say to the UAR that the continued negotiation of final positions on borders, refugees, and the other issues is going to take time. For the purpose of creating an appropriate atmosphere for those negotiations, a partial withdrawal from the Canal might be a valuable interim step.

The President: If the Israelis are going to take the position you predict, why do we provide arms, then? I have taken a strong position in support of Israel—perhaps as strong as any President. I have assured Mrs. Meir of my strong support for the survival of Israel.[5] She knows this. I have taken a strong position with respect to the Soviet position in the Middle East.

There is no denying that there is a political campaign coming in this country in 1972. A number of politicians are already making it plain that they will make political capital out of their support for Israel. Senator Jackson is already making noises of this kind.

We will provide arms, long-range agreements with Israel, and guarantees. Also, as far as borders are concerned, I have said repeatedly that they must be "defensible borders."

But if any Israeli leader feels that Israel by taking advantage of internal U.S. politics can have both arms and that kind of support from the U.S. and then refuse to act—even to discuss—then he is mistaken.

Secretary Rogers: I have no confidence in the Soviets or in the UAR. I have a little respect for King Hussein.[6]

There is just not going to be any American political pressure on this score despite the fact that there is an American political campaign. "To hell with that."

---

[5] See Document 136.

[6] An examination of the tape recording clearly indicates that the statement was made by President Nixon, not Secretary Rogers. (National Archives, Nixon Presidential Materials, White House Tapes, Cabinet Room, Conversation No. 48–4)

Some people talk about imposing a settlement. We are not trying to impose anything. But Israel just can't say it won't talk. Israel cannot count on being able to evade talking because Congress says it would support Israel and because I have said we would support Israel. They can't say they won't talk.

We have got everything Israel wanted. Prime Minister Meir told Ambassador Barbour that if we got the UAR commitment to make a peace agreement with Israel then Israel would face up to the tough question of borders. Foreign Minister Eban in talking with Secretary Rusk back in 1967 said that Israel would withdraw to the old international border and did not seek territory from Egypt if the UAR would commit itself to make peace with security. That understanding was the basis for the U.S. position throughout 1967, and that is why we voted for the 1967 UN Security Council resolution.

The President: What is going to happen on March 6? I read in my briefings and news summaries that the Arabs may break the cease-fire. Who will start the shooting?

Mr. Sisco: I doubt the Arabs will resume the shooting. But there would not be a formal cease-fire framework.

Secretary Rogers: Neither is likely, but you never know what will happen. Somebody might just start shooting at any time.

The President: They can do crazy things. One other way something could start is that the Arabs would "start huffing and puffing" and the Israelis would strike back forcefully.

We will go all the way with Israel in maintaining the military balance in its favor. But Israel has to know that if Israel starts a conflict where it has been responsible for the breakdown in the peace talks, it cannot count on U.S. support. I realize what the attitudes in Congress will be, but Israeli leaders just have to understand this.

Secretary Laird: We have a few more days before this issue gets into the public arena, for instance, in the UN Security Council. When this gets into the public arena, it will be much more difficult to handle.

The President: People don't do things unless they are denied or given what they want. What is it that the Israelis want? Arms?

Mr. Sisco: Our present arms commitments will continue deliveries of aircraft through June. But you, Mr. President, have not yet made the big decision on Israeli aircraft requests for this year. I believe we should withhold this until we see how the Israeli position develops.

The President: They know I will lean as far as I can in being generous with them. But I cannot continue to say that Israel can have all it wants and have them do nothing in return. This is highly confidential information, but within this room this must be understood.

Ambassador Bush: *The New York Times* has had several understanding editorials in recent days, suggesting that it is now time for the Israelis to be more forthcoming.

Secretary Rogers: They're embarrassed.

The President: Henry put them up to that.

Secretary Rogers: We are not in a bad position. We do not have to be apologetic about our position.

Ambassador Bush: That is what I am saying. We might get a little less flak just because of the position that *The New York Times* has taken.

Secretary Rogers: We are not saying that we should decide now to withhold military equipment at the moment. We should make no threats now.

The President: That's right, we should use no clubs now. However, there must be no assumption here that we will help Israel regardless of what Israel does. We sure as hell will not.

Secretary Laird: Bill Rogers did a good job with Ambassador Rabin the other day. He made the point perfectly clear that it is time for Israel to take a position without really making any threats.

Secretary Rogers: Rabin knows he does not have a good position to argue.

The President: The Israelis seem to think they are in a pretty good position. They assume that the U.S. will see them through regardless of what they do. This is not true. But in this period we want to be very careful about how we deal with them.

The main thing is the "dilatory tactic." We want to get the cease-fire extended.

Secretary Rogers: That is certainly true, but we may be almost at the end of the line on what we can achieve. We have delayed and delayed. The time is now coming where we have to show some movement or it will be difficult for us to hold out any longer.

[The meeting adjourned.]

---

210. Editorial Note

On February 27, 1971, President Richard Nixon held a meeting with President's Assistant for National Security Affairs Henry Kissinger from 9:47 to 11:57 a.m. in the Oval Office. At 10:06 a.m., they were joined by Secretary of Defense Melvin Laird, Director of Central Intelligence Richard Helms, Assistant Secretary of State for Near Eastern and

South Asian Affairs Joseph Sisco, and President's Deputy Assistant for National Security Affairs Alexander Haig. (National Archives, Nixon Presidential Materials, White House Central Files, President's Daily Diary) Although not listed in the Daily Diary, Secretary of State William Rogers is on a tape recording of the conversation. One topic of discussion was how the United States would approach Israel's imminent response to UN Special Representative Gunnar Jarring's most recent efforts to restart talks between the parties. Referring to Israel in the private conversation before the meeting began, Kissinger told the President: "At some point, there has to be, there has to be some pressure on them. There's, there's no doubt about that. But, it has to be done, it seems to me, as part of a, of a scheme which avoids, on the one hand, giving them a veto over our action and letting them drag us into, into their concerns. On the other, avoid a situation where the Russians and Arabs think they can, think they can get a big shot at them." After Nixon said "Um-hmm," Kissinger continued: "And that's—those are the two extremes between which we have to navigate this crisis." Turning to Sisco's activities, Kissinger said, "I happen to like Sisco very much," but added: "He's got to be reined in a little bit, because he's so impetuous, and he's got such a tendency for tactics that he—that almost everybody—I don't know about the Arabs—but I know both Dobrynin and the Israelis have no confidence in him. And—the Arabs I have no judgment on. But the major thing is to get some game plan and then, and then carry it out."

After the others arrived, the question of how to handle Israel continued to dominate the discussion. Nixon asked if the United States had any "stroke" with the Israelis and later described a hypothetical conversation with Israeli officials in which the United States offered a long-term military commitment if they would demonstrate flexibility in negotiations. Rogers countered, "I don't want to do it now. I don't think we're at that stage," adding that Israel should first respond positively to Jarring's overtures, to which Nixon remarked: "You have to give them some reason to do it, Bill." Much later in the conversation, Kissinger reaffirmed Rogers's point, reiterating what he told Nixon privately: "I think, Mr. President, the Israelis cannot simply ask for a blank check." Nixon agreed, and Kissinger added: "We have to be in a position to say when they're unreasonable."

The group discussed using the Four Powers to pressure Israel if it did not present something substantive to Jarring. Rogers explained that such a prospect would be "very troublesome for Israel" because the United States would "have to vote with the others" who would demand that Israel respond to Jarring. "That is exactly what Israel does not want," he added. Laird commented that Israel "ought to know that, that we're going to have to go the Four-Power route fairly soon." Sisco weighed the advantages and disadvantages of going to either the Four Powers or the UN Security Council, neither of which he considered good options. Regarding the Four Powers, the Assistant Secretary presumed that France and the Soviet Union would "press" Israel to "go well beyond the simple proposition" of reconsidering its original response to Jarring. On the other hand, he said, the Four Powers could "work out some communiqué with less public debate." As for the Security Council, he argued that it offered little more than "an open debate with everybody shouting at one another." But he also believed that such a scenario would prove more amenable to Israel because a stalemate in the Security Council would be less troublesome than any kind of Four-Power action, given that the latter was "the meat and potato group," steeped in the fundamental issues. Kissinger agreed, arguing that Israel would "under all circumstances refuse whatever" the Four Powers proposed.

On three separate occasions during the conversation, Nixon commented on territorial issues. Referring to Israel he said, "Hell, they can have a strip down there if they can work it out. They can have the West Bank; and they can have Jerusalem; they can have the Golan Heights. I don't know. I don't know. Whatever is that's worked out. They just can't take the position that we're just going to continue to wait and wait, delay and delay, just assuming that American political forces will develop in their favor. That's the thing that I'm concerned about. I— you see, I don't give—I don't go for the idea that you could just say, 'Well, they agreed in '67 to do this and that. They're gonna do what they did in pre-'67.' That will not happen. The word 'secure' has got to be expanded. That definitely must happen now because of the Soviet presence." Later he said, "From a military standpoint, I concede the West Bank. I concede Jerusalem for other reasons, and the rest." And, finally, once again referring to the Golan Heights, he said, "forget it," Israel's "got that," adding that "everybody thinks they ought to have the Golan Heights, anyway," and that "the Syrians won't need anything." The meeting produced no major conclusions, but Rogers ended it with this remark regarding Israel: "Could I say, Henry? Listen, we have told them this time and time again. They know exactly." (National Archives, Nixon Presidential Materials, White House Tapes, Oval Office, Conversation No. 459–2) The editors transcribed the portions of the tape recording printed here specifically for this volume.

211. Telegram From the Department of State to the Embassy in Israel[1]

Washington, February 27, 1971, 0304Z.

33688. Subj: Preliminary US Comment on Israeli Reply to Jarring.

Summary: Sisco Feb 26 received from Israeli Amb Rabin text of Israel's reply to Jarring (text septel).[2] Sisco gave personal and preliminary comment that Israeli reply is inadequate and unresponsive to the positive step taken by the UAR; that it does not address itself specifically to question put by Jarring; that it will prejudice extension of cease-fire; will stalemate negotiations; cause difficulties for US in Four-Power talks; result in Security Council meeting in which US would find it difficult to support Israel; and will facilitate Soviet expansion in M.E. Sisco reviewed accomplishments USG and Israel had achieved during past year and then asked what USG and Israel can do further together to help GOI overcome reluctance to face needed hard decisions on territory. Rabin repeated principal arguments he made to Secretary Feb 24 (State 31741).[3] *End summary.*

1. In call on Asst Secy Sisco late afternoon Feb 26 Israeli Amb Rabin gave copy of Israeli paper earlier handed Jarring in New York. Asked if Rabin had comment to make, Amb pointed out UAR had not given precise, clear-cut response to Jarring paper and said that just as Israel does not consider UAR position as precondition for Israel, neither does Israel expect UAR to consider Israeli position as precondition. In his view there are enough points for Jarring to continue discussions; there is

---

[1] Source: National Archives, Nixon Presidential Materials, NSC Files, Box 609, Country Files, Middle East, Israel, Vol. IX. Secret; Priority; Nodis; Cedar. Drafted by Theodore A. Wahl (NEA/IAI) and approved by Sisco. In a February 26 telegram, Rogers explained that the "Nodis/Cedar" and "Nodis/Cedar Plus" classifications were created to protect the "most sensitive traffic on the current peace negotiations on the Middle East" and that they would "receive extremely limited distribution in Washington within the Department and the White House and to principal officers of other agencies involved in NSC discussions of subject matter." Nodis/Cedar Plus messages would "be distributed only to White House and within Department on strict need-to-know basis" and that officials in Tel Aviv, Cairo, and New York should give such telegrams "similarly restricted distribution." (Telegram 32414 to USUN, Tel Aviv, and Cairo; ibid., RG 59, Central Files 1970–73, POL 27–14 ARAB–ISR)

[2] Telegram 33689 to Tel Aviv, February 27. (Ibid., Box 1161, Saunders Files, Middle East Negotiations Files, Middle East—Jarring Talks Edited and Indexed, February 27–28, 1971) The reply was handed to Jarring on February 26 and made public by the Israeli Government on March 8. For the text, see *Israel's Foreign Policy: Historical Documents,* volumes 1–2, 1947–1974, Chapter XII, The War of Attrition and the Cease Fire, Document 28.

[3] The telegram is in the National Archives, RG 59, Central Files 1970–73, POL 27–14 ARAB–ISR.

no reason why meaningful talks between parties should stop. As he had noted to Secretary, Israel wishes start from lowest common denominator.

2. After reading Israeli paper, Sisco said its nature and contents do not come as any surprise since Israel's position was forecast clearly in earlier meetings with both Sisco and Secretary.[4] He said text of Israeli paper will be communicated promptly to Secretary and President, and we will give GOI our considered judgment later. Comments Sisco will now make are preliminary and personal.

3. While he is in no position to commit President and Secretary, Sisco continued, his preliminary reaction will be against background of full review of Israeli position at NSC meeting this morning.[5] What he will say will be more in sorrow than in anger and will come from a friend who has believed very deeply in Israel's expressions of desire for peace. Israeli paper is, of course, for Jarring, and we will not seek to influence Jarring's judgment. However, he would be greatly surprised if Jarring's views differed from what he is about to say preliminarily.

4. Sisco then made following points re Israeli paper:

A. Israeli reply in his view is inadequate and unresponsive to the positive step taken by UAR. It does not address itself concretely and specifically to question put in Jarring paper. In his question, Jarring did not seek commitment to total withdrawal from all occupied territories to the pre-June 5 lines but asked whether Israel would give commitment to withdraw to former international boundary provided satisfactory arrangements are made for establishing DMZs and practical security arrangements at Sharm al-Sheikh.

B. Reply does not do what Prime Minister Meir indicated to Amb Barbour Israel prepared to do; i.e., if Egypt is willing to sign a peace agreement, Israel would face up to the question of territory.

C. Reply will come as deep disappointment to all concerned in US and world generally. He expressed fear that Israel will be held responsible for not having grasped this best opportunity for peace since creation of state of Israel.

D. Sisco said he believed Israeli action will set matters back seriously: it will jeopardize extension of cease-fire; will stalemate negotiations and result in early meeting of Security Council in which it very difficult to see how US could support Israel.

E. He said reply will cause major difficulties in Four Power talks where we have been able to manage situation satisfactorily from US

---

[4] See footnote 5, Document 208.
[5] See Document 209.

and Israeli point of view as long as we could demonstrate serious process of negotiations was in train.

F. More fundamentally, he noted, Israeli reply will provide Soviet Union with precisely the instrument it needs to make further inroads in the area contrary to interests of both US and Israel. We have tried to make clear we consider our vital interests involved in the area and consider our interests directly involved in Israeli response.

G. In our judgment Israeli reply will weaken forces in Cairo and Amman favoring political solution. It will be broadly interpreted in the world as evasion of Israel's responsibility to face up to hard decisions now needed.

5. Sisco then reviewed developments of past year in which USG, with Israeli cooperation, had made extraordinary efforts: we helped bring about cease-fire, negotiations, commitment from UAR to recognize and make peace agreement with Israel and to spell out specific reciprocal undertakings. Furthermore for two years, in view of Israel's reservations, no action has been taken in Four Power talks to which Israel could take exception.

6. Sisco continued he wished to put serious question to Rabin and GOI: what is it we and you together can do to help Israeli Government get over its reluctance and face up to hard decisions now required? Obviously there are differences between us but we have important mutual interests. USG wants to help. We understand Israel's need for security and have said privately we would be willing put American boys under UN umbrella in order to meet Israeli concerns. This is most serious undertaking. Rabin should also note sentence in President's state of world message that US willing play a major role in providing supplementary guarantees.[6] Sisco repeated question what more can we do to help Israel face up to what we consider is reality of situation?

7. In response Rabin noted that during past year Israel had agreed to accept most of US advice re procedures and other matters. Rabin also reiterated GOI position as endorsed by President Nixon that question of defensible boundaries should be negotiated between the parties. Israel has tried to start such negotiations but cannot accept conditions demanded by Egypt.

8. Sisco interjected to remind Rabin of precise question put by Jarring, and asked if Israeli leaders are aware that we are not pressing

---

[6] Reference is to the part of Nixon's "Second Annual Report to the Congress on United States Foreign Policy," delivered on February 25, in which he said: "The lack of mutual confidence between Israel and the Arab countries is so deep that supplementary major power guarantees could add an element of assurance. Such guarantees, coupled in time with a reduction of the armed strength of both sides, can give the agreement permanence." (*Public Papers: Nixon, 1971*, p. 289)

them to commit themselves to total withdrawal from all occupied territories to the pre-June 5, 1967 lines.

9. Rabin then read from Egyptian paper, pointing out that Egypt wants Israel to give commitment to implement all conditions of Res 242 and withdraw from all of Sinai and Gaza Strip. Rabin said Israel had not hidden from USG its firm position that it would not accept as a condition Israeli withdrawal to former international boundary.

10. Sisco recalled Secretary's comment that Israel's position states what it is against and not what it is willing to do on question of borders. Rabin responded this would come in give-and-take of real negotiations.

11. Sisco reiterated USG fully appreciates difficulties GOI faces. We have great understanding and sympathy for Israel and recognize there are differing views within GOI. However, we feel time has come for Israel to face up to decision which we consider inescapable. Sisco continued that our heart aches that for twenty years Israel has never known peace. If present trend continues it will never know peace. Arab-Israel conflict is history of lost opportunities. This is now a critical opportunity.

Rogers

212. Transcript of a Telephone Conversation Between President Nixon and the President's Assistant for National Security Affairs (Kissinger)[1]

Washington, February 28, 1971, 11:30 a.m.

K: State wants to send out a cable[2] which I believe will be the first step in a confrontation with Israel.

P: Did you discuss it with Sisco?

K: Yes it has been discussed. We gave him some word changes designed to soften it to the degree possible and they have accepted them,

---

[1] Source: National Archives, Nixon Presidential Materials, NSC Files, Henry Kissinger Telephone Conversation Transcripts, Box 4, Chronological File. No classification marking. All brackets are in the original except those indicating text omitted by the editors.

[2] Document 213.

but the basic problem remains one of strategy.[3] I am afraid that time will force us to let them go but if we had known it was developing this way earlier we could have perhaps worked bilaterally with the Soviets and gotten a great deal more for what we are going to have to do to Israel—perhaps even the Summit. Now it appears we will have to go with the cable but we should try to slow State down.

P: How can we do that?

K: First, to soften the cable. Secondly, to avoid launching into the four-power forum. Explore the issue with the Egyptians, thus buying some time. And perhaps agree to go to the four-power in return for an extension of the ceasefire by the Egyptians.

P: Stay on top of this Henry. Determine where we are going and check with the Soviets. See what we can get from them.

K: At this point I think we are bound to get a brutal public confrontation with Israel. If they cave we will pay a price for nothing. I only wish we had moved with the Soviets and gotten something for it.

P: Is this still possible?

K: In my private discussions they have certainly offered.[4]

P: Should we let the cable go?

K: I am afraid our only alternative is to do that. But someone else should be put in charge. It's moving too fast this weekend. Laird and Rogers are locked together. Therefore, I think for now it is best to let the cable go with the changes I have suggested to State plus a bid to get something from the Egyptians. The important thing is to slow the process down for now.

---

[3] On February 27 at 5:05 p.m., Kissinger telephoned Sisco about the cable, which the Assistant Secretary had sent to the White House for clearance earlier that day. Although he had not yet seen the telegram, Kissinger remarked that the Israelis "will not change their position." Sisco replied: "In this cable I have laid down a little scenario and I think we should go to both Tel Aviv and Cairo and get their views over the weekend." Kissinger answered: "I can give you what Cairo will say. I could write the response. Look, I have no overwhelming desire to get stuck with it," and then later explained, "What I am trying to get for the President is what comes afterwards—where will we go. You know that the next tactical move may lead next to six moves." (National Archives, Nixon Presidential Materials, NSC Files, Henry Kissinger Telephone Conversation Transcripts, Box 4, Chronological File)

[4] During two meetings with Kissinger near the end of January, Dobrynin stated that the Soviet Union was prepared to make a "realistic agreement" on the Middle East. Dobrynin asked whether the President was prepared to resume bilateral talks on the Middle East, insisting that the current Arab-Israeli negotiations "aren't going to go anywhere. They are at a deadlock. I hope you do not think you can settle this without us or, even less, that you can settle it against us." (Memoranda of conversation, January 23 and 28; *Foreign Relations,* 1969–1976, volume XIII, Soviet Union, October 1970–October 1971, Documents 103 and 105)

P: All right Henry. Clear the cable but tell Sisco I don't wish this to move to a blow-up with Israel. Tell him to delay and filibuster to the extent possible. We must be in a position to see what we can get. We should not be polemic or abrasive. It cannot be helpful at this time to put pressure on Israel. Can you talk to Sisco in this way?[5]

K: We have no personal problem, just one of temperament.

P: What about the Soviets?

K: I think we should watch the four-power process.

P: Then go to the Israelis, let them know my position on the Golan Heights and assure them I will support them.[6]

K: That is where yesterday's meeting[7] was not exactly candid. State has told the Jordanians the territorial changes will be very minor. We will have to reverse this.

P: Obviously we will have to handle the Jordanians in order to get a settlement.

K: The four-power process must be slowed down.

P: How?

K: I will talk to Sisco.

[Omitted here is discussion unrelated to the Middle East.]

---

[5] Kissinger called Sisco at noon on February 28 and told him that he had just spoken with the President. He reported to him that Nixon was willing to approve the cable, but that he did not want "an all out confrontation" with Israel, and that he wanted the Department of State to "cool the tone a little bit." Sisco replied: "That is just what we are trying to do." Kissinger eventually made further suggestions regarding changes in the telegram's language—which Sisco did not accept—prompting Kissinger to remark: "This is a head on confrontation. Joe could you explain one thing to me? You know this will lead to imposed settlement. Let's not kid ourselves." (National Archives, Nixon Presidential Materials, NSC Files, Henry Kissinger Telephone Conversation Transcripts, Box 4, Chronological File) When they spoke again on the telephone at 3:26 that afternoon, Kissinger asked: "Why do we have to put out this cable?" Sisco responded: "We want to preempt the Soviets, control reactions and reassure Egyptians. I have sent the cable. I can tell you that. I think it is the right move." (Ibid.)

[6] Kissinger telephoned Rabin at 3:20 p.m. on February 28 and told him that the President had asked him to tell him that: "he [Nixon] is doing what he can to ameliorate the excesses of some of the things that are being proposed to you. It is very difficult for him but any reaction you should keep in mind this fact. I am not saying you will particularly like the reaction." Rabin replied: "I know. Jarring is going to talk this afternoon to Sadat. I do not know in what way Jarring will present our position to Sadat. I see no need for you to take a position before you know what the Egyptians are going to do. I may be completely off base but Egypt is looking for a way out and we have given them a way to get out of it—I am not convinced that they will turn this down. But the United States should not make a statement before they do know what Egypt's reaction will be." (Ibid.)

[7] See Document 210.

P: Going back to the Middle East, be sure and sit on this problem. Tell Sisco to go slow and talk to Dobrynin at the right moment. Tell Sisco to buy time. He should reassure the Israelis on the Heights and we will have to push the King right to the brink. With the Egyptians we will have to put in our weight against the Soviets. Get everyone talking this way. I am convinced that State knows they are at a deadend. You tell Rabin I am watching. That I will not hurt Israel. I am their friend. I will be the buffer for them. Tell them about the Heights. Do not allow State to do anything precipitous.

K: Mutual confidence is the issue.

P: I will get them the arms but only if they are reasonable.

213. Telegram From the Department of State to the Interests Section in the United Arab Republic, the Mission to the United Nations, and the Embassy in Israel[1]

Washington, February 28, 1971, 1738Z.

33796. 1. You will have seen the Israeli reply and our preliminary reaction that it is unresponsive and unsatisfactory.[2] Jarring's reaction has been equally negative, and he has asked the Israelis to reconsider their reply, particularly para 4,[3] since he feels Israelis have not responded specifically to principal question put to them re borders. We understand Jarring is holding off giving the Israeli reply to the UAR for the weekend pending Israeli reconsideration. He informed Israelis that if he transmits Israeli reply to UAR in its present form this will create major impasse, place in jeopardy his entire mission, and probably lead to an early SC meeting. After a high-level review here this morning, we called the Israelis and urged reconsideration as requested by Jarring. Rabin has made it clear that it is unlikely that any change in Israeli position will be forthcoming at present time.

---

[1] Source: National Archives, Nixon Presidential Materials, NSC Files, Kissinger Office Files, Box 129, Country Files, Middle East. Secret; Immediate; Nodis, Cedar. Drafted by Sisco, cleared by Kissinger, and approved by Rogers. Repeated Immediate to Amman and to Beirut, London, Moscow, and Paris.

[2] See Document 211.

[3] Paragraph 4 reads: "Withdrawal of Israel armed forces from the Israel-U.A.R. cease-fire line to the secure, recognized and agreed boundaries to be established in the peace agreement. Israel will not withdraw to the pre-June 5, 1967 lines." See footnote 2, Document 211.

2. In light foregoing, our principal objective is to:

(A) Take such interim steps that might help in achieving an extension of the cease-fire; and (B) keep UAR reaction within manageable proportions while we continue efforts at a subsequent stage to secure a more forthcoming Israeli position. Cairo will undoubtedly need something in order to keep matters within reasonable confines and provide rationale for extension of cease-fire.

3. We have in mind the following scenario on which we request comments of addressees soonest:

A. We have weighed relative utility of SC and use of Four Powers and find choice between the two relatively evenly balanced. On one hand even though Israelis will not like it, SC would probably give them less concern than Four Powers since they would view Four Power communiqué as first step towards imposed settlement. On other hand, SC debate would force parties to make statements which would tend to rigidify their positions, particularly with Syria as member of SC, and could lead to a longer hiatus in Jarring Mission. While we are sure French and Soviets will give us plenty of trouble in Four, we feel that it may prove more manageable than SC if we go to UAR in first instance and see whether we can develop agreement on parameters of a possible Four Power statement. If we find that this is not possible, we would have to fall back to SC and do best we can in keeping resolution reasonable.

B. On the assumption GOI reply remains as it is, Jarring can be expected to give it to UAR on Monday. We therefore would discuss with UAR on Monday a possible short-term course which offers some hope of extending the cease-fire and keeping open avenue of negotiations. Bergus would be instructed to convey following oral message from Secretary to FM Riad some time on Monday:

(1) We have examined Israeli reply and we find Israel has not responded to specific critical question posed by Jarring on question of borders. We intend to discuss this matter further with Israel.

(2) We feel that latest UAR position is positive and regret that Israeli reply has not advanced matters. We feel it is all important, however, if we are to proceed further and if our on-going efforts are to be effective no precipitate action be taken by UAR which could exacerbate situation, increase tension and foreclose possibility of further progress.

(3) We appreciate fully difficult position which Cairo finds itself in at present time. We wish to discuss with them what we can do to help maintain a reasonably favorable climate which will provide basis for an extension of a cease-fire while our further efforts continue.

(4) We are prepared to support a Four Power statement[4] along the following lines as a follow up to a report by Secretary General on the current state of Jarring's efforts.[5] Statement follows:

The Permanent Representatives of France, the USSR, the U.S., and the U.K. met on March 4, 1971.

They noted with satisfaction the initiative undertaken on February 8 by the Special Representative of the Secretary General, an initiative which they consider to be fully in accord with his mission under Security Council Resolution 242.

They reaffirmed their support for Security Council Resolution 242 and the efforts of the Special Representative and expressed the view that the parties should cooperate with and respond positively to him.

They welcomed the positive UAR reply to the Special Representative and expressed the hope that Israel will soon make a similar positive reply.

They agreed to continue their preliminary examination of various possible supplementary guarantees. They expressed their willingness to play a responsible and cooperative role in keeping the peace arrived at through negotiation between the parties.

They expressed the hope that in order to facilitate the mission of the Special Representative the parties will continue to withhold fire, ex-

---

[4] According to Bush, U Thant, Jarring, the Soviet Union, and France had urged the Four Powers to meet as early as March 1 or 2 to discuss and release a communiqué before the Secretary General published his report on Jarring's recent activity, but the United States resisted, refusing to be "stampeded" into advancing the meeting and thereby "take the lead away" from U Thant. (Telegram 627 from USUN, March 6; National Archives, Nixon Presidential Materials, NSC Files, Box 656, Country Files, Middle East, Middle East Nodis/Cedar/Plus, Vol. I) The Four Powers eventually met to discuss the communiqué on March 4, but the conversation stalled over the Soviet Union's refusal to include direct or indirect reference to an extension of the cease-fire, as reported by Bush. (Telegram 616 from USUN, March 4; ibid.) They met again on March 5 but made no further progress, prompting the Department to write to the Mission: "We assume question of communiqué is dead. If raised please indicate matter has been overtaken by events and US no longer prepared to participate in any further effort to issue communiqué." (Telegram 40734 to USUN, March 11; ibid., Box 1158, Saunders Files, Middle East Negotiations Files, Middle East Negotiations—Four Power Talks)

[5] The Secretary General submitted his report on March 5, the conclusion of which began: "Ambassador Jarring has been very active over the past month and some further progress has been made towards a peaceful solution of the Middle East question. The problems to be settled have been more clearly identified and on some there is general agreement. I wish moreover to note with satisfaction the positive reply given by the UAR to Ambassador Jarring's initiative. However, the Israeli Government has so far not responded to the request of Ambassador Jarring that it should give a commitment on withdrawal to the international boundary of the United Arab Republic. I therefore appeal to Israel to respond positively to Ambassador Jarring's initiative." He concluded with an "appeal to the parties to withhold fire, to exercise military restraint and to maintain the quiet which has prevailed in the area since August 1970." (Telegram 614 from USUN, March 4; ibid., Box 656, Country Files, Middle East, Middle East Nodis/Cedar/Plus, Vol. I)

ercise military restraint, and maintain the quiet which has prevailed in the area since August 1970. End statement.[6]

4. If we can achieve common ground with UAR and others along above lines, we would wish to consider whether time ripe to try out separate Suez Canal proposal within framework of Sadat-Meir public statements.

5. In order to minimize any misunderstanding with Israelis, we would inform them we believe above course best designed to provide basis for extension of cease-fire and keep door open for further negotiations at next stage.

6. We will undoubtedly be bombarded on Monday by press and are developing appropriate press line. We are also planning on steps to begin to keep key members of Congress fully informed.

7. Request addressees comments.[7] No action should be taken with government to which you accredited without further department instructions.

Rogers

---

[6] Bergus delivered Rogers's oral message to Riad on March 1 and met with him for 70 minutes. Much of their meeting was taken up by the Foreign Minister's "lengthy statement" in which he said that the United States had to "face facts" regarding Israel's commitment to expansion rather than peace, as demonstrated by its "flat rejection of withdrawal as a matter of principle" in its response to Jarring. He added that there was "no doubt in Cairo and in all other world capitals" that if the United States wanted to "persuade" Israel to withdraw from the Sinai Peninsula for peace with the United Arab Republic it could "easily be done." Regarding Rogers's message, Riad remarked that "there was little new" in it, and, as for the Four-Power communiqué that the United States was prepared to support, he said that it was "not helpful." Continuing, he told Bergus that his government could not "accept the proposition that it should extend ceasefire and then wait and see what Israelis will do," although he clarified that "this did not necessarily mean Egyptians would start shooting." Finally, he concluded that he would "accept guarantees only for June 4 borders, not rpt not for anything else" and reserved the right to "withdraw his support for concept at some future time" given the opposition he faced to the issue of guarantees. (Telegrams 422 and 423 from Cairo, March 1; ibid., Kissinger Office Files, Box 129, Country Files, Middle East)

[7] Comments are in telegram 1198 from Tel Aviv, February 28 (ibid., RG 59, Central Files 1970–73, POL 27–14 ARAB–ISR); telegram 1070 from Amman, March 1 (ibid., Nixon Presidential Materials, NSC Files, Kissinger Office Files, Box 129, Country Files, Middle East—Nodis/Cedar/Plus); telegram 1613 from Beirut, March 1 (ibid.); and telegram 1245 from Moscow, March 1 (ibid.).

214. Paper Prepared by the National Security Council Staff[1]

Washington, March 2, 1971.

OPTIONS IN BREAKING THE IMPASSE

The present situation[2] is well known to you. There is no point in describing it.

For the purpose of focusing discussion on central issues, *the two main issues are:*

—what approach to make to Israel in the light of its response to Jarring *and*

—how to posture ourselves toward the USSR, not only in response to Kosygin's letter[3] but more fundamentally toward Soviet involvement in the peacemaking process and the Soviet combat presence in the UAR.

These issues are related in two ways:

—The Israelis will regard the Soviet strength that remains after any settlement as the most serious threat to Israeli security.

—If the US is to get the Soviet combat presence removed from the UAR, Israeli withdrawal from the Sinai is its principal bargaining card.

Below are discussed the principal options in dealing with each of these issues and the arguments for and against them.

---

[1] Source: National Archives, Nixon Presidential Materials, NSC Files, Box 1161, Saunders Files, Middle East Negotiations Files, Jarring Talks Edited and Indexed, March 1–4, 1971. Secret; Nodis. Drafted by Saunders. All brackets are in the original.

[2] Reference is to the general dismay, especially within the Department of State and the United Nations and in the Middle East, to Israel's response to Jarring that it would not withdraw to pre-June 5, 1967, borders.

[3] In his February 26 letter to Nixon, Kosygin wrote that over the previous few weeks "one was getting the impression that in the matter of political settlement in the Middle East a certain breakthrough was about to emerge towards solution of that problem." He further commented that the breakthrough "was the result of a constructive position of the United Arab Republic whose government had displayed high responsibility" by taking a position conducive to reaching an agreement. The Soviet Premier then expressed disappointment over Israel's "defiant statement declaring its refusal to withdraw troops from the occupied territory of the UAR," given previous assurances from U.S. officials that the United States "stood for the withdrawal of Israeli troops." Thus, because of the U.S. Government's "more than adequate means of influence" over Israeli policy, he concluded that it was "impossible even to imagine that Israel could take such an obstructionist, bluntly expansionist position if that were in contradiction to the true aims of American policy." (National Archives, Nixon Presidential Materials, NSC Files, Box 490, President's Trip Files, Dobrynin/Kissinger Vol. 4) For Kissinger's summary and analysis of the letter, see *Foreign Relations, 1969–1976*, volume XIII, Soviet Union, October 1970–October 1971, Document 130.

Possible Approaches to Israel

1. *Comprehensive approach.* In Rogers-Rabin and Barbour-Eban (or Meir) talks, this US position would be taken:

—The US position since 1967 has been based on the assumption that Israel's main objective has been security, not territory per se. The US has held out for a loophole in Resolution 242 language—on withdrawal—to "secure and recognized borders"—primarily because of Jerusalem, Golan Heights and the need for some modifications in the Israel-Jordan lines. But apart from special security arrangements in Gaza and at Sharm al-Shaikh, the US never envisioned major territorial acquisition, and this view was based on US-Israeli exchanges in June 1967.[4]

—For a peace agreement built on that kind of map, the US would be prepared to offer the following: assurance of long-term military supply and financial support; US troops as part of a peacekeeping force at Sharm al-Shaikh (as a substitute for Israeli forces); formal provision for bilateral consultation on defense of Israel.

—The US asks Israel to take a position that will permit this kind of settlement. The US recognizes that this will require a fundamental change in Israeli government policy—a return to its policy of June 1967. But in the interests of peace, the US asks Israel to make that change. Once the change is made, the US is willing to work closely on a diplomatic strategy for getting the best possible agreement in return.

—The implication would be delicately left that if Israel did not make that change in policy, the nature of continuing US support would be left in doubt.

The arguments for this approach are:

—If we try to deal with the situation tactically, we will always come back to the major obstacle that Israel is really negotiating for territory.

—US policy since 1967 has been based on the assumption that, in return for the right peace and security commitments, Israel would go back to something approximating pre-war borders. If that is an erroneous assumption, this should be clarified. A direct approach is the only way to get this out into the open.

—A precise description of what the US is prepared to offer in the long run could help increase the flexibility of the Israeli position, especially if tacitly juxtaposed to the possibility that US support might be minimized.

---

[4] For example, see ibid., 1964–1968, volume XIX, Arab-Israeli Crisis and War, 1967, Documents 227, 263, and 290.

—The US has never believed that peace would be possible if Israel sought territory. Allowing major border changes, even if they were possible, would just sow the seeds of the next war.

—While a heart-to-heart talk of this kind could produce a major Israeli confrontation, this may be the last good chance for peace in some time.

The arguments against this approach are:

—This is too much for the Israelis to swallow all at once. We should do everything possible to help the Israelis deal with this problem a step at a time.

—If we lose this confrontation with the Israelis where are we? Can we really afford to give the UAR and USSR the satisfaction of seeing Israel divided from its main source of support?

—Since the Israelis are unlikely to move all the way at once and are likely to counter with some tactical move at best, we should start on a tactical track and avoid a confrontation.

2. *Tactical approach.* The US could stop short of asking Israel now to give up its aspiration to major border changes and urge Israel to make some tactical move to advance negotiations another step.

—Israel might tell Jarring that it is prepared to take a specific position on borders and security arrangements in the Sinai and will send Foreign Minister Eban to New York for this purpose. The US might promise only that it would urge the UAR to respond by attempting to narrow any gap on security arrangements. The US would reserve its present position on borders but accept an Israeli strategy, for a time, of taking a hard stand on borders to elicit the best possible UAR position on security arrangements.

—It might also be possible in this connection to try to activate the scheme for the partial withdrawal from the Suez Canal, although the Arabs might reject that as diversionary.

—It might be possible to stretch out phasing of the implementation of a settlement so that the Israelis would have some evidence of Arab performance before they had to withdraw to borders that would be difficult for them to agree on.

The arguments for this approach are:

—We must find a way to turn this into a step-by-step process for Israel. If there is any chance at all of Israeli withdrawal, it is in a gradual process over time in which the Arabs have a chance to persuade the Israelis of their good faith.

—The Israelis themselves, even apart from their efforts to negotiate border changes, must be working with some sort of strategy in mind for getting the UAR to stop imposing short cease-fire deadlines and for trying to get the best possible trade for what territory they give up. Rather than have a confrontation, we ought to tune ourselves to Israeli tactics insofar as possible.

The arguments against this approach are:

—The Arabs would have great difficulty accepting either the idea of negotiating with Eban for their territory or of drawing out withdrawal over too long a period.

—The US would still be in a position of trying to build a settlement on an unreal assumption (that Israel is prepared to pull back to pre-war lines).

3. *Compromising with Israeli strategy.* It would be possible to tell the Israelis that we want to work closely with them but to do so we will have to know what their real objectives are. This approach could lead in one or both of two directions:

—It could produce an essentially US-Israeli negotiation on the terms of a settlement.

—It could lead to a change in the US position on the terms of a settlement the US would support.

This is already being discussed in our own councils in the following way: If we were to tell the Israelis that we will not hold them to near-total withdrawal from the West Bank provided they accept the international border with Egypt, that would amount to a fundamental change in previously stated US policy.

The *argument for* this approach is that it may be the only realistic way to move toward a settlement. It is possible that, if we knew the full Israeli position, there are elements in the US position that might reasonably be changed.

The *argument against* this approach is that the weight of public positions taken—including the US position in voting for Resolution 242—and the weight of what seems necessary for peace make it very difficult to change the US position on the territorial settlement.

Possible Stances Toward the USSR

1. *Comprehensive approach.* In responding to Chairman Kosygin's letter and in a Rogers-Dobrynin conversation, the US would make clear that the introduction of Soviet combat forces into the UAR has created a major obstacle to Israeli withdrawal from the Sinai and that assurance on the withdrawal of those combat forces is essential to a settlement. [The objective would be to add whatever we were able to get to the list of inducements offered to Israel.]

The general *argument for* some such approach is that the USSR is taking a free propaganda ride at the moment and should not be allowed to get completely off the defensive. The fact remains that the Soviet combat presence in the area is still the issue of paramount concern to us.

The argument for this specific approach now is that a strong US position on this subject will be necessary providing Israel with maximum inducement to cooperate with us.

The *argument against* such an approach is that it implies that Israel might be persuaded to withdraw from all of the Sinai if the Soviets made such a commitment. It is a toss-up which side is less likely to take such a step, but it would be dangerous for the US to put itself in a position of implying Israeli withdrawal before we know whether it is possible.

2. *Approach for the record.* If it is going too far at this stage to press for Soviet assurance on reduction of combat forces, then a minimal approach—if this subject is to be dealt with at all—would be to reply to Kosygin noting the responsibility of the USSR for complicating negotiations between the parties by introducing Soviet combat forces.

The *argument for* this approach is that we should at least begin building a record on this subject. It is important to us. Several Presidential statements have mentioned it. It is time to introduce it into the negotiations.

The *argument against* is that it will be difficult enough to negotiate an Arab-Israeli settlement without introducing this US-Soviet issue. It would be better to concentrate on a settlement and let this follow.

3. *Leave the issue aside.* A third approach would be to concentrate on an Egyptian-Israeli settlement in the conviction that the Egyptians themselves will ease the Soviet combat forces out as soon as possible after a settlement.

The *argument for* this approach is that an Arab-Israeli settlement would permit the UAR to ease the Soviets out over time. The Egyptians themselves are prepared to do this, but they need an Israeli settlement first. That should be our overriding concern.

The *argument against* is that the Egyptians have some gratitude for Soviet support and are unlikely to deprive the USSR of anything it really wants, e.g., an air squadron for surveillance of the Sixth Fleet

215. Telegram From the Department of State to the Interests Section in the United Arab Republic[1]

Washington, March 7, 1971, 0521Z.

38131. For Bergus.

1. We request you see Heikal promptly before Sadat makes his speech on Sunday.[2] We feel that Sadat, as a result of his trip to Moscow,[3] has made up his mind in concert with USSR to go ahead along the lines indicated and nothing short of our being able to deliver a categoric Israeli yes answer to the latest Jarring initiative would result in any change in his position for the time being. We feel, however, that a brief interim hand-holding sort of message might help in a very marginal sort of way.

2. As we analyze the Sadat letter,[4] we believe it is a manifestation of his present ambivalence; regardless of his close ties to the Soviets, he does not feel that the Soviets can produce Israeli withdrawal. On the other hand, we have indicated to him that we are going to continue our efforts with both sides to try to achieve progress, but he knows we have not been able to produce Israel thus far and cannot be expected to produce results on the basis of Sadat's self-created deadlines. His ambiva-

---

[1] Source: National Archives, Nixon Presidential Materials, NSC Files, Box 656, Country Files, Middle East, Middle East Nodis/Cedar/Plus, Vol. I. Secret; Flash; Nodis; Cedar Plus. Repeated Priority to Tel Aviv and to USUN.

[2] In his March 7 speech, which was broadcast over UAR radio and television, Sadat declared that he would not extend the cease-fire along the Suez Canal, which would expire that evening. He said that the United Arab Republic would nonetheless continue to participate in ongoing diplomatic efforts to achieve a settlement with Israel. (*New York Times*, March 8, 1971, p. 1)

[3] According to telegram 477 from Cairo, March 6, Sadat was in Moscow from March 1 to 2, where he had "intensive talks with Soviet leaders." (National Archives, Nixon Presidential Materials, NSC Files, Box 1161, Saunders Files, Middle East Negotiations Files, Middle East—Jarring Talks Edited and Indexed, March 5–11, 1971)

[4] Sadat's letter, written in response to Bergus's presentation to Heikal on March 4 (as reported in telegram 454 from Cairo, March 4; ibid., Kissinger Office Files, Box 129, Country Files, Middle East, Middle East—Nodis/Cedar/Plus), was handed to the Ambassador in Cairo shortly before midnight on March 5. As instructed by Sisco in telegram 36085 to Cairo, March 3, Bergus had relayed the message that the United States intended to continue its efforts "to bring about a peaceful settlement" in the Middle East but that the United Arab Republic should understand that it would "take time for Israeli leadership and the Israeli people to fully fathom and comprehend the significance of the positive move" that it had made. (Ibid., Box 1161, Saunders Files, Middle East Negotiations Files, Middle East—Jarring Talks Edited and Indexed, March 1–4, 1971) In his March 5 letter, Sadat wrote that it was shocking that the United States, "as it appeared to us from this message, is waiting for the Israeli statesmen and the Israeli people to understand our constructive stand, but they do not adequately assess, we feel, the explosive psychological burden which our people bear as a result of their territory's continuing under the yoke of occupation." (Telegram 478 from Cairo, March 6; ibid., Box 656, Country Files, Middle East, Middle East Nodis/Cedar/Plus, Vol. I)

lence is also reflected in tough talk on the one hand and yet an almost plaintive plea to the U.S. indicating an unwillingness to close any doors with us.

3. Though we obviously do not agree, we know reasoning behind UAR and USSR decision for a non-extension of the ceasefire. Foreign Minister Riad has said time and time again that the only thing that will work with the U.S. is pressure applied in circumstances where the tensions are high and where U.S. fears renewal of hostilities. Sadat knows that general view of the world, and in particular ours, has been that he has no desire to resume the shooting. He undoubtedly realizes that threat to renew fighting over past months has not been a very credible one, and posture of non-extension is an attempt to recreate that as more credible option and to concert with USSR on increased pressure on U.S. in climate of a threat to open hostilities.

4. All of the above is by way of background, but we want you to have the benefit of our thinking in this regard. We feel that you should see Heikal immediately and make the following points orally (do not leave any paper), which we hope will as a minimum underscore to Sadat our continuing desire to play a constructive role which he acknowledges as a fact.

A. You should tell Heikal that President Sadat's message is being given the most careful study and consideration. We appreciate fully the sense of urgency which President Sadat feels since we recognize that the positive move made by the UAR recently has provided a new opportunity for progress. We regret, however, that President Sadat will not find it possible to extend the ceasefire, for we continue to feel that the efforts to achieve a peaceful settlement can best go forward without deadlines. In any event, we hope he would make his intention clear to heed SYG's appeal to Quote withhold fire, to exercise military restraint, and to maintain the quiet which has prevailed in the area since August 1970 Unquote.[5] All the broad support which the recent UAR move has generated in the world would be dispelled if UAR resumes shooting.

B. We intend to continue our efforts with both sides to help achieve a peace agreement because this is in our mutual interest.

C. You should point out that we are fully aware of the importance which the UAR attaches to the question of guarantees and for this reason we agreed to start talks in the Four and to continue to develop our ideas in this regard.

D. Finally, we note that President Sadat has said that the door is open with respect to Suez Canal proposal. You should first recall to

---

[5] The quote is from the Secretary General's official report on Jarring's activities. See footnote 5, Document 213.

Heikal that on February 13 we conveyed an Israeli message to the UAR.[6] We had hoped and expected a reply from the UAR and when no such further indications had come we had thought UAR had lost interest. You should tell Heikal that we welcome indication that this avenue is still open and as a result we are examining what may be possible in this regard and would also welcome UAR views.[7]

Rogers

---

[6] The message, which was conveyed to Sisco by Rabin during a meeting at the State Department on February 12, stated: "We are willing to discuss with Egypt arrangements for the opening of the Canal, even as a subject to be treated separately from other issues. The unknown elements in Sadat's proposal are more than those specified, and we welcome the readiness of the US as expressed by Mr. Sisco in the conversation of February 8 that the US is ready to use its good offices for a detailed clarification of the subject. We have taken that President Sadat, too, wishes to engage in a clarification process. USG is requested to transmit this, our position to President Sadat." (Israel State Archive, Ministry of Foreign Affairs, 5252/7)

[7] Bergus met with Heikal on the morning of March 7 and delivered orally points A–D. When the Ambassador recalled a previous remark by Mahmoud Riad that the end of the cease-fire "did not necessarily mean that GUAR would stop shooting," Heikal responded that, while it "would not start shooting right away," he "doubted this position could be held for very long." Heikal also said that, if Nixon could give Sadat a "firm pledge that USG would support Jarring's request that Israel withdraw from Gaza and Sinai," Nixon could prevent Sadat from being "increasingly isolated and overcome by Egyptian hawks." (Telegram 490 from Cairo, March 7; National Archives, Nixon Presidential Materials, NSC Files, Box 1161, Saunders Files, Middle East Negotiations Files, Middle East Edited and Indexed, March 5–11, 1971) In a follow-up telegram sent that afternoon, Bergus reported Sadat's reaction, as presented by Heikal, to the Ambassador's comments that morning: Sadat wanted the United States to know that "he still considers his initiative on the Suez Canal to be valid," that it would "offer the necessary formula for the United Arab Republic, the United States, 'and others' to move out of the present impasse," and that it would also be "a test of all three parties' intentions." (Telegram 491 from Cairo, March 7; ibid.)

216. Memorandum From the President's Assistant for National Security Affairs (Kissinger) to President Nixon[1]

Washington, March 9, 1971.

SUBJECT
State Department Game Plan on the Middle East

Here is the State Department's game plan which we requested for trying to break the Arab-Israeli impasse.[2]

The details of the proposal are in the attached summary. The essence of the proposal is an approach to the Israelis asking them to make a fundamental change in their policy to accept the 1969 US position on boundaries in return for substantial and concrete assurances of continuing US support.

The procedure for approaching the Israelis would be for Secretary Rogers first to call in Ambassador Rabin and for Ambassador Barbour then to follow up with a parallel presentation to Foreign Minister Eban. Neither you nor Prime Minister Meir would be directly involved at this first stage.

The *advantages* of this paper are:

—It is a game plan for one possible course of action which has often been advocated. It enables you to see what an all-out effort to move Israel would look like and to assess its chances of success.

—The proposed approach would let the Israelis know what the US is for, not just what we are against. The Israelis seem unlikely to make piecemeal concessions in the absence of understanding what Israel can count on from the US in return. Getting all the cards on the table could help them develop a total position that could be presented in Israel as a package to assure Israel's security and US support.

—It contains a substantial carrot in the form of security assurances the US would offer Israel in a settlement. There is the implication of the stick in the probability that we would not provide them if Israel failed

---

[1] Source: National Archives, Nixon Presidential Materials, NSC Files, Kissinger Office Files, Box 129, Country Files, Middle East. Secret; Nodis; Cedar. Sent for information. A stamped notation on the memorandum indicates the President saw it.

[2] According to Haldeman, Kissinger and Haig called him on March 6 and 7, respectively, "worried about the developing situation vis-à-vis Rogers again." He wrote in his diary: "Apparently, he's [Rogers] moving to take some unilateral action on the Middle East that Henry feels would be disastrous, and that the P[resident] has ordered covered by a senior review group which Rogers is going to bypass, apparently. Haig suggested we try to outfox Rogers' maneuver by putting a special meeting on this right at the tail end of the NSC tomorrow, which I told him to go ahead and try to set up " (*Haldeman Diaries: Multimedia Edition*, March 7, 1971)

to change its policy as we requested. However, the carrot is more prominent.

The *disadvantages* of this plan are:

—This procedure would result in a major approach to the Israelis that they have almost no choice but to reject. It would ask them to accept US positions which they have already rejected. You will recall the violent Israeli reaction of January 1970 against the US positions of the previous October and December.[3]

—The US-Israeli confrontation that would result would make achieving a settlement even more difficult than it already is. It might provoke such a negative Israeli reaction and stalemate in the Jarring talks that the ceasefire would be jeopardized in a short time. If Israel remained adamant in resisting the US approach, the US choice would be to back down or to show the USSR/UAR that we were separating ourselves from Israel. Chances of reducing the Soviet presence would be reduced.

—The implications of this approach are that the changes in the West Bank border and in the Golan Heights border would be minimal.

An alternative to this approach would be to press the partial withdrawal from the Suez Canal in order to buy time. This might permit the Israelis to establish direct contact with the UAR, which they want. This would give them a chance to test UAR intentions. Meanwhile, it would give us a way of avoiding confrontation, restoring Israeli confidence in us and then exploring with them quietly positions that might be negotiable on some of the other issues.

I personally feel that a confrontation with Israel now would virtually end chances of any negotiated Arab-Israeli arrangement for the next year or so.[4] I share the view expressed in the State Department paper that we do not want to lose the opportunity of the present mo-

---

[3] See Documents 58 and 78. For the Israeli reaction, see footnote 6, Document 84.

[4] At 5 p.m. on March 9, Rogers held a meeting in his office with Laird, Sisco, Kissinger, Helms, and Moorer to discuss this issue. Moorer drafted a memorandum of the conversation, but because he arrived a half hour late his record is incomplete. (National Archives, Nixon Presidential Materials, NSC Files, Box 647, Country Files, Middle East, Middle East (General)) In a memorandum to the President, March 10, Kissinger wrote: "The meeting went just about as expected. Secretary Rogers, supported by Secretary Laird, pushed hard for its approval, with the full realization that the scheme means a total confrontation with Israel. This outcome was understood by all of the attendees." (Ibid., Kissinger Office Files, Box 129, Country Files, Middle East) On March 8, Kissinger had told Haldeman that he did not want to attend the meeting "because if he ends up in agreement with Rogers' position, then he and Rogers will confront the P[resident] with a lack of options, and he'll [Kissinger] have to go along even if he has a different view." Kissinger further explained that "if he disagrees with Rogers, he'll then be in a position of having to force the P[resident], or try to, to his position." (*Haldeman Diaries: Multimedia Edition*, March 8, 1971)

ment. I fear the approach to Israel described in the game plan would produce the result no one here wants.[5]

Whether or not this alternative could succeed would depend on whether it is correct to judge that Sadat can work with anything less than an Israeli commitment now to total withdrawal. Given uncertainty on that point, the only way to find out is to test his position by having a specific Israeli proposal put to him. Given the certainty of Israeli reaction to a major effort to change Israel's position, such an approach to the UAR would seem a worthwhile risk.

Attachment

SUMMARY

Following are the two main elements in the State Department proposal:

1. *Israel would be urged to accept the following positions:*

—*Sharm al-Shaikh.* An Israeli presence at Sharm al-Shaikh will be unacceptable to the UAR. Israel's security concerns there can be fully met by American military participation in a UN presence there. Termination of that force should be barred for a specific period (e.g., five years) and subject thereafter to approval of the Security Council. We would not exclude using our veto to prevent such termination.

—*Security arrangements and DMZ's.* The parties should be given a free hand and a reasonable opportunity to come to grips themselves in the Jarring talks with the problems of security arrangements and DMZ's. No reasonable option should be excluded from discussion, including: demilitarization of most of Sinai and inclusion of Israeli and UAR representatives under a UN umbrella in any system for verification. An effective mechanism could be devised which would engage the major powers and at the same time avoid placing Soviet forces on Israel's borders. We would envision an overall UN peacekeeping

---

[5] In a conversation with the President in the Oval Office that afternoon, Kissinger told Nixon: "My view is that I just can't go on under these conditions. You will just lose control. And the next issue is going to be as hard as this one, so I might as well draw the line now." He continued: "But the really basic point, Mr. President, is that I feel that if a Presidential assistant, for whatever reason, becomes himself such a controversial figure, and if the bureaucracy continually challenges him even if he's totally right, I think then one should seriously consider leaving. This has nothing to do with right or wrong, but I think the necessity of Presidential assistants is that they have to speak for the President without challenge." Later he added: "And that doesn't mean it's anybody's fault. I understand Rogers's view, and I know he's got proud people at State, and I have as much ego as anybody else, but I really believe that it might be in the interest of everybody if we began to think of a terminal date for my stay here." (National Archives, Nixon Presidential Materials, White House Tapes, Oval Office, Conversation No. 464–17)

mechanism with both major and small powers represented in the headquarters but with observer units on the ground along the UAR-Israeli border limited to representatives of small powers (e.g., Dutch, Danes, Canadians). We would support one of the following two alternatives on demilitarization: (a) Israel would accept the presence of UN observers on its territory if Egypt accepts total or almost total demilitarization of the Sinai; (b) if Egypt is willing to accept only a more limited area of demilitarization on its side of the border we would not press Israel to accept demilitarization or a UN force on its side.

—*Gaza.* Israel should have a voice in determining the final disposition of Gaza which at a minimum would bar its return to UAR control and the introduction of any Arab military or para-military forces. It would be supervised by a UN force made up of small powers. We would favor Jordanian acquisition of Gaza but would not exclude an interim UN administration.

—*Freedom of Navigation.* We would support the absolute right of Israel in parity with other nations to freedom of navigation through the Suez Canal and the Straits of Tiran.

—*Refugees.* A solution allowing for return of refugees to Israel only in such numbers and at such rates as are satisfactory to it. We would support an understanding that Israel would be expected to accept no more than 100,000.

—*West Bank.* Anomalies in the border should be corrected and considerations of local security and of administrative and economic convenience should be taken into account in making "insubstantial alterations." Such alterations should be based on the 1949 armistice lines and could not encompass retention of Israeli positions on the Jordan River. The entire West Bank should be demilitarized. The parties should be given reasonable opportunity to work out security arrangements for verifying demilitarization and controlling fedayeen activities on the West Bank, perhaps with joint Jordanian-Israeli arrangements under some kind of UN umbrella. If that did not work out, we would support a UN force consisting of small power representatives with the same guarantees against termination as in the case of the UAR border and Sharm al-Shaikh.

—*Jerusalem.* The city should be united with free access and movement within the city. There must be administrative arrangements which will leave Israel in a position to assure that these principles are not violated while giving Jordan a meaningful role in the administration and economy of the Arab part of the city.

—*Golan Heights.* We would continue to hold that there is no basis for taking up the question of a Syrian-Israeli settlement in the absence of Syrian acceptance of Resolution 242. If the Syrians did join the negotiations, we would support the principle that in negotiations Israel has a right to seek some alteration of the Syrian-Israeli boundary to assure Israel a permanent position on the Golan Heights.

—*Negotiating procedures.* We would support immediate escalation of negotiations to the foreign minister level.

2. If Israel were prepared to concur in these positions, *the US would enter bilateral arrangements with Israel as follows:*

—Long-term arrangements to satisfy Israeli arms requirements under generous financial terms within the context of any arms limitation agreements to which Israel and its neighbors might subscribe. Specifically: delivery beginning this July of the F–4 and A–4 aircraft Israel has requested; $500 million in military sales credits in FY 1972; $500 million in credit and grant in FY 1973.

—Further unilateral US declarations in support of Israel's security by both the Executive and the Congressional branches.

—Formalization of bilateral defense consultations against the contingency that the peace settlement appears on the verge of breaking down. Specifically: (a) a commitment formalized by exchange of letters between the President and Prime Minister to consult on possible joint or parallel action to be taken in the event Israeli security is jeopardized; (b) a formal consultation arrangement between our military representatives for the fullest possible exchange of intelligence information on a continuing basis.

—Major US financial contribution to resettlement of refugees.

—A major US financial contribution to the conversion of the Israeli economy to peace time lines and to regional development schemes

—A US commitment to undertake diplomatic exchanges with the USSR to seek an understanding that a final Arab-Israeli settlement would be paralleled by a US-Soviet agreement not to base operational combat forces on the territory of Israel or any neighboring Arab country. This would require that Soviet air and ground operational units and personnel be withdrawn from the UAR. This would not, however, be a precondition to a settlement along the above lines.

217. Memorandum of Conversation[1]

Washington, March 19, 1971, 12:50 p.m.

PARTICIPANTS

Abba Eban, Foreign Minister of Israel
Yitzhak Rabin, Ambassador of Israel
David Rivlin, Secretary to the Foreign Minister
Shlomo Argov, Minister of Israeli Embassy
Henry A. Kissinger, Assistant to the President
Joseph J. Sisco, Assistant Secretary of State
Harold H. Saunders, NSC Staff

After an exchange of pleasantries, Foreign Minister Eban said that the Prime Minister had asked him to convey her respects both to Dr. Kissinger and to the President. He had just concluded a talk with Secretary Rogers,[2] and he was sure that Dr. Kissinger would be receiving a full report on that, so he could be brief. His remarks are concentrated on where we go from here. There are two problems: progress in the Jarring mission and the possibility of discussing a partial solution in connection with the re-opening of the Suez Canal.

In connection with the Jarring mission, the Foreign Minister had talked with Ambassador Jarring in New York.[3] He had made clear that the Israeli position stands as stated in Israel's February 26 memorandum to the Ambassador.[4] Israel felt that it was necessary to state its position that way. Even with that statement of Israel's position, however, there are a number of things in Israel's view that Ambassador Jarring could do. For instance, he could draft paragraphs on those issues on which there is near harmony between the Egyptian and Israeli positions. Or, he could attempt to work from the present statements of

---

[1] Source: National Archives, Nixon Presidential Materials, NSC Files, Box 656, Country Files, Middle East, Middle East Nodis/Cedar/Plus, Vol. I. Secret; Nodis; Cedar Plus. Drafted by Saunders on March 22. The meeting took place in Kissinger's office. All brackets are in the original.

[2] Eban met with Rogers at 11 a.m. that morning for an hour and 45 minutes. According to telegram 47428 to Tel Aviv, March 20, the Secretary said that the United States and Israel "differed on questions of emphasis and timing but not on basic positions" and that "no agreement was acceptable" to the United States that did not provide for "security for Israel in all of its aspects, including Sharm el-Sheikh, Golan Heights, and West Bank." Rogers added that the Nixon administration recognized that it "could not force Israel to accept something unacceptable from security standpoint." It would not "press Israel," he said. (Ibid., Kissinger Office Files, Box 129, Country Files, Middle East, Middle East—Nodis/Cedar/Plus)

[3] Eban met separately with Jarring and U Thant on March 18 to discuss Israel's position on withdrawal. (*New York Times,* March 19, 1971, p. 1)

[4] See Document 211.

Egyptian and Israeli positions on borders. Israel is prepared to detail its position. Ambassador Jarring could use such a device to begin a specific discussion on the border and withdrawal issue.

The key to Israel's position is that it cannot say that it will undertake withdrawal of all of its troops to pre-war borders. There is one specific sticking point—Sharm al-Shaikh, from which Israel cannot withdraw.

Dr. Kissinger asked whether, in the light of the Foreign Minister's last comment, it is reasonable to conclude that Israel means it wants Israeli forces at Sharm al-Shaikh but would be willing to return to pre-war borders on all other fronts.

The Foreign Minister replied that he could not go beyond his statement about Sharm al-Shaikh. There are other issues, such as Israel's role in demilitarized zones, that remain to be specified. But Israel's position on Sharm al-Shaikh is already enough to preclude his saying that Israel could accept return to pre-war borders.

Dr. Kissinger asked whether Israel could say that it is prepared to go back to pre-war boundaries everywhere except at Sharm al-Shaikh.

The Foreign Minister said that he would not be correct if he said that. The Israeli position is not yet that concrete.

Dr. Kissinger asked the Foreign Minister's opinion on two propositions: (1) that Israel should tell the US what its position is and (2) that Israel should tell Ambassador Jarring something so that there would exist an Israeli position on borders which he could use to keep the negotiations alive.

The Foreign Minister said he had the impression that Ambassador Jarring is not interested in hearing anything from Israel but acceptance of his memorandum seeking Israeli agreement to withdraw to the international UAR-Israeli border. Jarring has certain suggestions that Israel had put before him. One is that he try to have a concrete discussion on the issue of withdrawal and boundaries.

Dr. Kissinger said he had never understood whether Eban was saying that Israel would not commit itself on withdrawal prior to negotiations or whether Israel was saying that it would not ever commit itself to withdrawal.

The Foreign Minister said that at the moment the first statement is true—that Israel will not commit itself prior to negotiation. However, later on if discussions begin, Sharm al-Shaikh will become a sticking point. Also there will be other problems that will need to be negotiated. But Sharm al-Shaikh is a "national sticking point." Dr. Kissinger asked whether this was more of a sticking point than other possible issues. The Foreign Minister said that Prime Minister Meir in her recent interview[5] had tried to indicate that there might be others, but Sharm al-Shaikh is "on top of the list." Many national interests converge at that geographic point. For the moment however the principal Israeli concern is that Israel be given freedom to negotiate.

Dr. Kissinger asked why it would not be possible for Israel to tell Jarring that it is prepared to discuss anything except Sharm al-Shaikh. Eban replied that Israel had not said it refuses to discuss any issue. Mr. Sisco said that the difficulty is that we need a concrete proposition from Israel for discussion. Ambassador Rabin said that Israel has stated a concrete proposition—that there be no withdrawal to pre-1967 lines. Moreover, Israel cannot say that Sharm al-Shaikh alone solves all of Israel's border problems.

The Foreign Minister said that the long and short of it is that Israel, at this point, cannot give a more concrete definition of its position than it has already stated.

Dr. Kissinger asked whether an Israeli proposal on re-opening the Suez Canal fell in that category. The Foreign Minister replied that Israel has received the working paper passed to Ambassador Rabin by Mr. Sisco.[6] Israel has decided not to reply with a critical analysis of that paper but to develop a paper of its own. In response to Dr. Kissinger's question, the Foreign Minister said the Israeli paper would be ready in another week or ten days.[7] The Israeli bureaucracy was working on the subject. [At this point there was a brief and partially humorous exchange on the nature of bureaucracies.] The Foreign Minister concluded his comment on the forthcoming proposal in connection with partial withdrawal from the canal by saying that Israel recognized it had to keep discussions going. It had taken the Egyptians three years to decide that they must make a "peace agreement with Israel." It may take Egypt more time to adjust to the notion of Israel in borders different from those of 1967.[8]

---

[5] Reference is to a March 12 interview that Meir gave in her office in which she outlined her views on the borders that should be established between Israel and its neighbors to prevent another war between them. Specifically, she said that Israel would not relinquish control of Sharm al-Sheikh, the Golan Heights, and East Jerusalem; that the West Bank border would have to be negotiated; and that Arab troops could not be free to cross the Jordan River. (*New York Times*, March 13, 1971, p. 1)

[6] In telegram 38126 to Tel Aviv, March 7, the Department reported the March 6 conversation between Sisco and Rabin during which the Assistant Secretary "informally outlined some preliminary ideas" on reopening the Suez Canal in conjunction with a partial Israeli withdrawal from the Sinai Peninsula. (National Archives, Nixon Presidential Materials, NSC Files, Box 658, Country Files, Middle East, Middle East Nodis/Cedar/Plus, Vol. IV)

[7] See footnote 2, Document 224.

[8] On March 17, Sadat informed Bergus that Egypt, Syria, and Libya would form a federal state called the United Arab Republic, with each country having its own President and administration, but with "top-level coordination" occurring "in some way" among

Dr. Kissinger asked what about the proposition that unless the Egyptians can show some progress, they are likely to relapse into a renewal of hostilities?

The Foreign Minister said he did not see any evidence that President Sadat was preparing to move in that direction. The US had done a good job on the military balance, and there are ways Ambassador Jarring can move forward. He hoped that concrete discussion on the issue of borders could move on. He had made suggestions to Ambassador Jarring which had been passed on to the Egyptians, but there had been no reply yet. If the UAR asked Israel to give greater precision to its position on borders, that would be a legitimate question to which Israel would have to respond.

Dr. Kissinger said he saw two problems:

—at what point Israel becomes more concrete with the UAR;
—at what point Israel becomes more concrete with the US about its position.

The Foreign Minister said that he was obliged to point out that Israeli thinking, when concrete, will not coincide with the US positions of 1969. Israel hoped that the US would be prepared to look at the Israeli positions with understanding. However, Israel would develop them out of its own convictions and recognizing "the full implications of solitude."

Dr. Kissinger said he was sure that Secretary Rogers had told the Foreign Minister that there is no disposition in Washington to force a confrontation with Israel. It would be presumptuous for the US to give Israel its answer on how to balance territory and security. It is difficult to resolve the questions of what is the best mix between physical safety and the moral, bilateral, international and legal guarantees that may also provide some measure of security. We need to discuss this mixture with Israel.

The Foreign Minister replied that Israel is clear about one fact—that the moral, legal and other such arrangements cannot be a substitute for territory. What disturbs Israelis now is the apparent view that geography does not matter. In the Israeli view it is not the only issue, but it is "one of the things that matter" and Sharm al-Shaikh "matters very much."

Mr. Sisco said that he wanted to make clear that whatever the US has said on specific guarantees, it is important to understand the frame-

---

the three. The upshot was that the former United Arab Republic would once again officially be referred to as Egypt. (Telegram 588 from Cairo, March 17; National Archives, Nixon Presidential Materials, NSC Files, Box 1162, Saunders Files, Middle East Negotiations Files, Middle East—Jarring Talks, April 1–20, 1971)

work within which the US has been talking. The press in recent days has spoken as if guarantees would be a substitute for a peace agreement or a substitute for Israel's own means for self-defense. That is incorrect. The US has always spoken about guarantees against the background of an assumption that Israel's own deterrent strength is of central importance to any settlement. Nothing the US has ever said has indicated that the US considers guarantees something that could be provided in lieu of Israel's own strength.

The Foreign Minister replied that strength consists of two elements: (1) there are the elements of military strength itself and (2) there is the question of where that strength is deployed. Dr. Kissinger added that there is also the question of where the enemy deploys its strength, and that raised the question of demilitarized zones.

Ambassador Rabin said that there are three elements which Israel considers important:

—There is the peace agreement itself.
—Since a peace agreement can be broken, Israel wants the capacity to defend itself in local conflict by itself. Israel does not expect anybody to come to its defense in a local war. In this connection, on the one side, Israel needs the US supply channel to remain open. On the other, Israel needs defensible borders.
—Israel needs enough of a guarantee to protect it against the direct involvement of Soviet forces.

Israel's position is an exact exemplification of what is outlined in the Nixon doctrine.[9] In summary, Israel wants peace negotiated in the normal way, an Israeli ability to defend itself and recognition of the fact that Israel is not the only country that cannot defend itself against the Soviet Union.

The Foreign Minister endorsed the Ambassador's comment on the importance of US deterrents against the USSR.

Dr. Kissinger summarized his understanding of Eban's position as follows:

—Israel is going to make a specific proposal on re-opening the Suez Canal soon.
—Israel believes it has opened the door to discussion of the border issue in the Jarring talks.
—Israel does not exclude the possibility of discussing its position with the US.

The Foreign Minister said that Secretary Rogers has requested that Israel discuss its position with the US, and this request will be taken seriously. In fact, however, the Prime Minister has already opened dis-

---

[9] See *Foreign Relations, 1969–1976,* volume I, Foundations of Foreign Policy, 1969–1972, Documents 29 and 30.

cussion of this issue with the President and the Secretary of State in September.[10]

Mr. Sisco said that he did want to inject one point in connection with a statement the Foreign Minister had made earlier. The US judgment remains that the UAR will not make another step in the Jarring talks until Israel makes one. The Egyptians feel that they have laid their cards on the table. We do not expect a UAR response to the Israeli suggestion that detailed negotiations now begin on the basis of positions as stated to date.

Foreign Minister Eban replied that there is another option for Ambassador Jarring. He could put questions to Israel to "elicit our position."

Dr. Kissinger said that the US would find it helpful if Israel would put forward a position that had a reasonable chance of starting discussion. Mr. Sisco added that the US has never told Israel it must say "yes" to Ambassador Jarring's memorandum.

Dr. Kissinger said that he wished to reiterate that the US is not steering this issue toward a confrontation with Israel. The Foreign Minister replied that a confrontation is certainly not in Israel's interest. He added that in accord with the desire not to move into a confrontation, it was desirable that not only that bilateral steps be avoided but that an international climate of confrontation not be created. This has a great deal to do with how the US posture is reflected to others.[11]

Harold H. Saunders[12]

---

[10] See Document 162.

[11] Upon reviewing "detailed accounts" of Eban's talks with Rogers and Bush, Bergus wrote to the Department that the "most disturbing element" of the Foreign Minister's presentation was that Israel's "tenacity'" had "paid off," that "time is on Israel's side." He continued that "such 'tenacity' was to a large extent purchased by US at a considerable cost," adding that "thanks to Israel's 'tenacity,' Soviets have made a quantum jump insofar as their presence and influence in this area is concerned." Bergus later remarked: "But what troubles us most about Eban's thesis is that it does not take into account the highly delicate situation which presently exists in Egypt. Sadat has placed a childlike trust in the United States. Perhaps he was mistaken in doing so. It is our considered view that his future, and the future of that diminishing little band of Egyptians who think like he does is in increasing jeopardy." The United States would suffer the consequences, he concluded. (Telegram 629 from Cairo, March 22; National Archives, Nixon Presidential Materials, NSC Files, Kissinger Office Files, Box 129, Country Files, Middle East, Middle East—Nodis/Cedar/Plus)

[12] Saunders initialed "H.S." above his typed signature.

218. Memorandum of Conversation[1]

Washington, March 25, 1971.

PARTICIPANTS

Ashraf Ghorbal, Head of UAR Interests Section
Henry A. Kissinger, Assistant to the President
Harold H. Saunders, NSC Staff

Dr. Ghorbal explained that he is going to Paris for a meeting with Foreign Minister Riad and other Egyptian chiefs of mission to discuss and assess the present situation. He "wanted to go wiser and had come to seek wisdom."

He said that he needed help in explaining the U.S. position. He cited his visit to the UAR last August. In a conversation with President Nasser and others, Nasser had made some nasty comments about the U.S. and then had turned to Dr. Ghorbal and said, "Forgive me." Dr. Ghorbal said that he expected to be bombarded with questions and similar comments in Paris and wanted the clearest possible view of where the U.S. thinks the situation is going.

Dr. Kissinger said he was familiar with Dr. Ghorbal's talk with Secretary Rogers[2] and he did not have much to add. One thing he did wish to make clear was that there are not two U.S. foreign policies. There is one policy "which we do jointly." He said that no one had to think that there are two strands of policy, with Secretary Rogers following one and Dr. Kissinger following another. Dr. Kissinger said that he did not involve himself deeply in day-to-day tactics, and much that has been done in the Middle East has been tactical.

Dr. Kissinger said that a second point he wished to make is that it is important to be realistic. The U.S. would like an Arab-Israeli settlement. We believe that would be in everybody's interest. The President's foreign policy message to Congress—which after all had been

---

[1] Source: National Archives, Nixon Presidential Materials, NSC Files, Box 656, Country Files, Middle East, Middle East Nodis/Cedar/Plus, Vol. I. Secret; Nodis; Cedar Plus. The conversation took place in Kissinger's office. All brackets are in the original. This memorandum is attached to a March 26 memorandum that Saunders sent to Kissinger both for his approval and to notify him that, at his request, he sent a copy "Eyes Only" to Sisco. Kissinger initialed his approval on it and wrote: "1) What's the sense of approving it if it has already gone to Sisco; 2) Send copy to Rogers eyes only. Never again send unedited copy out."

[2] Ghorbal met with Rogers on March 24 for a half hour. (Telegram 49891 to Cairo, March 25; ibid., Box 1162, Saunders Files, Middle East Negotiations Files, Middle East—Jarring Talks, March 25–31, 1971)

drafted in the White House—reflects that purpose.[3] On the other hand, we sometimes think that the UAR over-estimates the ability of the U.S. to force a settlement in the Middle East. For that reason, we find unhelpful the short deadlines that have been imposed recently.

Dr. Kissinger hastened to add that we recognize the UAR's problem: the UAR does not wish the passage of time to turn the occupation of territory which has historically belonged to it into Israeli territory. The UAR has, however, already opened a debate in Israel and between Israel and the US on the nature of a final settlement. It should allow time for those debates to work themselves out.

Dr. Kissinger said that looking back, one of the sad things in his view was that, on the occasion of Dr. Fawzi's first visit here,[4] the opportunity to improve U.S.–UAR relationships was not seized then. We approach the UAR on the basis of wanting good relations with the Arab Nations. In the present situation, we need to "reconcile our problems with Egyptian necessity."

As an interim measure Dr. Kissinger continued that we hope that something might be done in connection with President Sadat's proposal for partial withdrawal from the Suez Canal.[5] We recognize full well that this would have to be an "interim" arrangement.

Dr. Ghorbal expressed appreciation for Dr. Kissinger's seeing him. When Dr. Ghorbal recognized that Dr. Kissinger has other momentous problems on his desk, Dr. Kissinger replied that this is one of the biggest of them.

Dr. Ghorbal said that he wanted to stress that never has so much been invested by the UAR as in the past few weeks in getting a settlement—in energy and in political risk. The UAR believes that Israel and the U.S.—particularly the U.S.—must do the same. He hoped that the U.S. would not lose this opportunity.

Dr. Kissinger said that Dr. Ghorbal could be assured that we are doing all we can. Dr Ghorbal replied that he hoped the U.S. would grasp the situation with energy commensurate with the opportunity.

Dr. Kissinger asked what concretely Dr. Ghorbal had in mind our doing. Dr. Ghorbal replied that he is gratified to know that there are not two U.S. foreign policies. He certainly understand the tactics of "not firing all your guns at once." But he felt that it is now time for the President to stand up and reiterate what U.S. policy is. Dr. Kissinger asked what more the President could do than he had said in his foreign policy message. Dr. Ghorbal replied that there are many who heard only the

---

[3] See footnote 6, Document 211.
[4] See footnote 2, Document 18.
[5] See Document 203.

President's short radio address and will not read the longer foreign policy message itself.[6] Therefore, there is need for clearer and fuller exposition to the American people of what U.S. policy is.

Dr. Ghorbal said that the last time President Nixon had spoken,[7] the Egyptians had been very disappointed. He spoke in the old balance of power terms. That means to Israel and to the UAR that Israel can go on relying on a continuous flow of arms and economic help regardless of what policy it adopts.

Dr. Kissinger replied that the President had said many things. On the one hand, Israel has to consider what security it may achieve by military means and by territories. On the other, if Israel returns to its pre-war frontiers, it will need security perhaps even more.

Dr. Ghorbal noted that Israel still has $300 million in the President's budget. In other words, there is no U.S. indication that Israel's political stand would affect U.S. support. [There followed a humorous exchange over whether the UAR would shift to U.S. equipment if we offered it.]

Dr. Ghorbal said that a new UAR proposal on debt rescheduling had been put to the U.S. He felt this to be a further sign of Egyptian good will. Also, although there were a few things in the President's state of the world message that the UAR did not like, the UAR had reacted positively emphasizing those things which it had regarded as constructive.

Dr. Kissinger said that he wanted to make clear his feeling—and the President feels the same way, he said—that the UAR's approach in recent weeks has been responsible. We may differ on details of such issues as demilitarization. But the U.S. cannot develop every last formula. The Egyptian attitude has been constructive.

Dr. Ghorbal said that it was now important to translate general policies into action. Dr. Kissinger replied that he had a purely personal suggestion to make. It derived from his thought that sometimes in seeking comprehensive agreements, we create deadlocks for ourselves. He felt that it was sometimes possible to take a series of limited, partial, interim steps thus providing steady progress toward an objective but

---

[6] On the morning that he transmitted his message to Congress, President Nixon delivered a radio address summarizing the report. In the section on the Middle East, he stated: "The policy of the United States will continue to be to promote peace talks—not to try to impose a peace from the outside, but to support the peace efforts of the parties in the region themselves." (*Public Papers: Nixon, 1971*, p. 216)

[7] Reference is presumably to the March 4 press conference at which Nixon responded to a question on the Middle East by saying: "We, of course, will be there to see that the balance of power is maintained in the Mideast—which we will continue to do—because if that balance changes that could bring on war." (Ibid., p. 393)

not creating the deadlocks that result from trying to swallow the whole problem all at once.

He said that the U.S. would continue to try to influence Israel to take positions that could lead to a negotiation. He wondered whether there were cases where the UAR could use its ingenuity in making such proposals. It had already done so to some extent in proposing partial withdrawal and opening the Canal.

Dr. Ghorbal asked whether there were any other ideas. Dr. Kissinger mused for a moment on whether there was anything in the Gulf of Aqaba and then turned to the question of why the Israelis put such store in Sharm al-Shaikh. "Are there not other ways to keep the Straits open?" he asked. Dr. Ghorbal agreed that the Israelis could defend the opening to the Gulf of Aqaba in other ways just as there were ways other than occupying Sharm al-Shaikh that the Gulf could be closed.

Dr. Ghorbal cautioned against seeking "gimmicks" such as Israeli leasing of Sharm al-Shaikh. He felt that a lot of time could be wasted in such talk and that it would end up being an "exercise in futility." Dr. Kissinger asked, "Because you won't have it?" Dr. Ghorbal replied, "Yes." He felt that if the Israelis insisted on staying at Sharm al-Shaikh that would affect the whole atmosphere of negotiations. "How could the UAR trust Israel if it insists on staying at Sharm al-Shaikh?" The only way to solve this problem is to have non-Israeli and non-Egyptian forces there to enforce demilitarization. Half way measures do not solve the problem; they are just issues for talk.

Dr. Kissinger asked whether, supposing the Israelis went back to the international border with the UAR, the UAR would then insist on total Israeli withdrawal on all other fronts. Dr. Ghorbal said that they would not be "more royalist than King Hussein." However, he felt that the U.S. should not try to achieve an agreement which left Israeli forces in Syria. That would just provide the seed for future wars.

Dr. Kissinger said he wanted to summarize by saying that we are happy here that relations between us have taken a turn for the better. He hopes that patience can be shown for some more time. He felt that it was desirable for the moment to concentrate on the subject at hand—a UAR-Israeli settlement.

Dr. Ghorbal said that of course the Egyptians did not wish the Syrians to have a veto over a settlement. If there was to be progress on the proposal for the Suez Canal, it should contribute to a positive atmosphere for a settlement. If Israel put at the end of its proposal the statement that it does not plan to withdraw further, that then would kill the whole idea. There would be no pressures left on Israel. "The mechanics of progress should not be established with a veto at the end." They must undertake that this would be the first step toward a peace settlement.

Dr. Kissinger replied that the U.S. position has always been that both sides should enter the negotiations without pre-conditions. Dr. Ghorbal replied that Ambassador Jarring's proposals to Israel and the UAR had incorporated the U.S. position. He felt the U.S. should press those positions. If the UAR were to receive a positive answer from Israel to Jarring's questions, that would be the testimony the UAR needs of U.S. intentions.

The conversation closed with the usual pleasantries and with Dr. Kissinger's making a general comment that he hoped he would see Dr. Ghorbal sometime after his return.

Harold H. Saunders[8]

---

[8] Printed from a copy that bears this typed signature.

---

219. Telegram From the Department of State to the Interests Section in the United Arab Republic[1]

Washington, April 1, 1971, 0020Z.

54323. Please deliver following message from President Nixon to President Sadat:

Quote: Dear Mr. President:

Thank you for your messages of March 5[2] and 17.[3] I deeply appreciate this thoughtful, personal and candid presentation of your views.

---

[1] Source: National Archives, Nixon Presidential Materials, NSC Files, Box 656, Country Files, Middle East, Middle East Nodis/Cedar/Plus, Vol. I. Secret; Priority; Nodis; Cedar. Drafted by Sterner and Sisco; cleared by Jon Howe, Sterner, and Atherton; and approved by Rogers. A stamped notation on the telegram reads: "Sent to San Clemente."

[2] See footnote 4, Document 215.

[3] Sadat asked Bergus to meet with him on March 17 primarily to convey to Nixon his reaction to the news conference that Rogers held the previous day. A transcript of Rogers's news conference is in the Department of State *Bulletin*, April 5, 1971, pp. 478–486. He wanted the President to know that: 1) he could not agree to the total demilitarization of the Sinai; and 2) Egypt did not intend to annex Gaza but that there should be a vote by its inhabitants to determine its future. He added that he nonetheless "greatly appreciated all Rogers had said regarding borders." Sadat also wanted to make two other points to Nixon, "in an absolutely personal message," first complaining that his March 5 comments to the President "had not been closely held" and then informing him that his soldiers were getting restless as he awaited Israeli action regarding his partial withdrawal proposal. (Telegram 588 from Cairo, March 17; National Archives, Nixon Presidential

I am keenly aware of the problems that you face and the steps you have taken recently to help facilitate the negotiations currently being pursued under Ambassador Jarring's auspices. The steps you have taken with such political skill have strengthened your nation's international position and moved your people closer to peace.

For its part the United States wants one thing: a just and lasting peace agreement that meets the legitimate concerns of both sides and that both sides can accept with honor, dignity, and confidence in their future security. I am under no illusions, Mr. President, that the clouds of suspicion that exist between the Arabs and the Israelis will be easily dispelled. Both sides view the issues as fundamental. But I am struck with the fact that some modest progress has been made during this past year on which, hopefully, more progress can be built in the days ahead.

There is an opportunity today which has not existed since the June war. The political climate and the situation generally in the Middle East have been evolving. I wish there were a better prescription than time, but some time must be allowed for the changes which are occurring to be fully understood by leaders and peoples who live in the area.

Moreover, we both know there is a political process involved, both in Egypt and in Israel. Patience and determination will be required to overcome the difficulties in a manner that best preserves public support for the painful decisions which could eventually make a peace agreement possible. From your own skillful management of your nation's foreign affairs, I believe you understand this point. For our part, I hope I made it clear in my February 25th message to Congress[4] that we intend to remain fully involved and to help both sides move toward a peace agreement which could mean so much for all peoples in the area and for my own country.

I welcome your reaffirmation of the proposal for a partial Israeli withdrawal and the reopening of the Suez Canal. We have told the Israelis that in our view your statement of February 5 on this matter and that made by Prime Minister Golda Meir on February 9[5] are worth careful study. I hope that further explorations can proceed in the days ahead.

Materials, NSC Files, Box 1162, Saunders Files, Middle East Negotiations Files, Jarring Talks—Middle East, March 17–24, 1971)

[4] See footnote 6, Document 211.

[5] That day, Meir officially responded to Sadat's partial withdrawal proposal in a policy speech before the Israeli Knesset, saying that Israel was ready to discuss re-opening the Suez Canal in conjunction with a mutual demilitarization of the Sinai. She reiterated the point, however, that Israel would not withdraw its troops from the Suez Canal zone until it reached a peace agreement with the United Arab Republic. (*New York Times*, February 10, 1971, p. 1) For the text of her February 9 statement, see *Israel's Foreign Policy: Historical Documents*, volumes 1–2, 1947–1974, Chapter XII, The War of Attrition and the Cease Fire, Document 29.

I appreciate very much your confidence in alerting me to the developments which you foresee and mentioned in your message of March 17. We will also give careful consideration to the specific views you express on the disposition of Gaza and the question of demilitarization.

Once again, Mr. President, I would like to thank you for bringing to my personal attention your concerns at this stage of our peace settlement efforts. I place high value on the direct communication we have established in these messages and want to assure you that I reciprocate the sincerity which they so clearly convey.

With my best personal wishes, sincerely, Richard Nixon Unquote.[6]

Rogers

---

[6] Bergus met with Sadat on April 1 for 1½ hours, beginning their discussion by reading Nixon's message to him. In response, Sadat asked Bergus to convey his thanks to the President, remarking that he was "pleased by its warmth." Later, he said that he realized that the U.S. Government "needed time to bring the Israelis around" but added that "there would be no progress along lines his initiative without real pressure on Israelis from US." Sadat believed that he also "needed time to change mental attitudes in Egypt and in Arab world." He declared that he wanted to "make it clear" to Nixon that, in the meantime, "if Israel raided Egyptian heartland, he would raid the interior of Israel." At the end of the conversation, Sadat commented that the "most dangerous idea being floated by Israelis was Eban's statement that 'tenacity' had paid off with Egyptians and that Egyptians would soon be ready to cede territory." Egypt, Sadat concluded, "would not kneel." (Telegram 712 from Cairo, April 1; National Archives, Nixon Presidential Materials, NSC Files, Box 656, Country Files, Middle East, Middle East Nodis/Cedar/Plus, Vol. I)

---

220. Telegram From the Department of State to the Embassy in Jordan[1]

Washington, April 6, 1971, 2058Z.

57631. Subj: Letter from President to King Hussein. Please deliver following letter from President Nixon to King Hussein.

---

[1] Source: National Archives, Nixon Presidential Materials, NSC Files, Box 757, Presidential Correspondence 1969–1974, Jordan King Hussein Corres. Confidential; Priority. Drafted by Seelye and Lloyd W. Sutherland (PA); cleared by Pickering, Hartman, and MacDonald (AID); cleared in substance by Jeanne Davis; and approved by Sisco.

Begin

Your Majesty:

Thank you very much for your letter of March 27[2] which Ambassador Brown forwarded to me. I followed with interest the talks my representatives had with Prince Hassan during his visit to Washington, and I was pleased to hear that his visit was a pleasant and rewarding one for all concerned.

The problems which you outlined in your letter are of great personal concern to me. I recall our mutual efforts over past years to promote the independence of Jordan's economy and the strength of its political structure.

I also recall the impressive growth Jordan was experiencing before the June 1967 war and the great promise it held for the future. With the situation now somewhat different, I can well appreciate that you have your hands full endeavoring to meet your most immediate financial problems.

I certainly want to be helpful, within the limits of resources available. Therefore, in the light of your country's acute financial situation, I have decided to arrange for dols 15 million in supporting assistance funds to be made available to Jordan in early July; and I have proposed that an additional sum of dols 15 million in supporting assistance be made available to Jordan at a later date during this calendar year on the assumption it will be needed. This action is, of course, subject to the usual Congressional appropriation process.[3]

Both our countries will continue to face difficult choices among competing demands for limited resources. Accordingly, I am sure we will both wish to continue our useful dialogue on how these can best be

---

[2] In the letter, Hussein first thanked Nixon for his March 3 message to him and then proceeded to raise the issue of Jordan's economic and financial difficulties, which he described as "the most pressing of all the problems we are facing now." He also addressed the discussions in Washington between U.S. officials and a Jordanian delegation led by Crown Prince Hassan during the first week of March. This included the promise made by Sisco that the United States would "do its best" to cover the Government of Jordan's budget deficit, calculated to be $30 million "above and beyond Saudi and Kuwaiti subsidies" to Jordan. In the end, Hussein asked for Nixon's "personal attention in expediting Congressional consultations and Departmental negotiations, in order to arrive at a firm commitment regarding United States assistance in the present crisis." (Ibid., Box 616, Country Files, Middle East, Jordan, Vol. VII)

[3] In telegram 57630 to Amman, April 6, the Department instructed the Embassy to make several additional points on behalf of the United States regarding its aid package to Jordan, including: "We do not rpt not presume to judge what GOJ's priorities should be at this time, but we do believe that Jordan's case for future assistance will be enhanced to the extent it demonstrates financial responsibility." The instruction continued: "We thus see it as incumbent on GOJ to take very painful measures to cut back, reducing JAF spending to the JD 32.3 million level now budgeted and ensuring that disbursements under the Quote development Unquote budget are made strictly in accordance with priorities assigned by GOJ." (Ibid.)

used. In due time, I will propose that our experts consult with yours to be sure that the steps being taken to address your government's financial problems are the most effective possible.

With warm personal regards,

Sincerely,

Richard Nixon

End quote

Rogers

221. Minutes of a Senior Review Group Meeting[1]

Washington, April 14, 1971, 3:05–4 p.m.

SUBJECT

Middle East Guarantees

PARTICIPATION

Chairman—Henry A. Kissinger

State
U. Alexis Johnson
Joseph Sisco
Alfred Atherton
Tom Thornton

Defense
David Packard
James S. Noyes
G. Warren Nutter

CIA
Richard Helms
David Blee

JCS
Gen. Richard Knowles
Adm. William St. George

NSC Staff
Col. Richard Kennedy
Harold Saunders
Jeanne W. Davis

SUMMARY OF CONCLUSIONS

It was agreed that a Working Group will be created, chaired by Joe Sisco, to spell out our position on guarantees: some sense of priorities among possibilities, how the machinery might function, etc. The

[1] Source: National Archives, Nixon Presidential Materials, NSC Files, NSC Institutional Files (H-Files), Box H–112, Senior Review Group, SRG Minutes (Originals) 1971. Secret. The meeting was held in the White House Situation Room.

Working Group will draw on the paper being prepared by the JCS on the size and composition of a peacekeeping force.[2]

Mr. Kissinger: I'd like to review the guarantees issue so we know where we are going. I have a number of questions. Joe (Sisco), will you sum up where we stand.

Mr. Sisco: As you know, we circulated some papers in January[3] which were designed to do two things: first, to discuss the specifics of the options within the Four-Power framework without making any choices.

Mr. Kissinger: They were damn good papers. However, in SALT we gave the Russians three choices of equal standing. They picked one, and we said "wrong." I don't want to get into the same position here.

Mr. Sisco: The second purpose was to provide a basis for discussion with the Israelis. Since that time, we have started Four-Power discussions, which have been largely a holding action. We haven't tried to reach any decisions because we didn't want the Four Powers to get ahead of the situation. We have also had preliminary discussions with the Israelis, whose reaction was "no sale" on guarantees in any form. Israel is still stonewalling on putting anything new into the context of the Jarring effort. In the light of this, I think we will get a new approach from the Israelis. Rabin has made the point that it must be understood between the two sides that, if the agreement is broken, Israel could reoccupy the presently occupied areas. We believe that is reasonable, and that it will be an element of any Israeli proposal. I think Mrs. Meir will ask if we will support them if they move back into the areas, and we will have to find a way to respond affirmatively without giving her a blank check. I suggest we see what they come up with on the Suez Canal and not talk guarantees in the Jarring context.

Mr. Kissinger: If they come up with a tough position I assume we will talk about it, or would we consider rejecting it?

Mr. Sisco: I believe any proposal will be barely within the ball park. I suggest we transmit it in its pristine form to the Egyptians. We

---

[2] The Working Group paper was not found. Admiral Moorer sent the JCS ad hoc study group's final report, "Middle East Peacekeeping Forces," to Laird on April 29. In a covering memorandum, Moorer addressed the report's key points, including: 1) a peace agreement must satisfy the terms of the signatories, should not be imposed by outside parties, and must establish borders designated by physical and permanent markers; 2) "the establishment of a UN force capable of deterring or suppressing all possible threats to the peace is not feasible in terms of contemporary international peacekeeping"; and 3) "any UN observer/peacekeeping force deployed to the Middle East preferably should be comprised of neutral nation forces." (Washington National Records Center, OSD Files: FRC 330–76–0197, Box 70)

[3] Sisco's group prepared several papers in January and early February. See Documents 198, 202, and 207.

should try to avoid getting into any negotiation with the Israelis on their proposal before communicating it to the Egyptians.

Mr. Kissinger: That's a good idea. Then we can see what to do with the Egyptian reply.

Mr. Sisco: We might even suggest indirectly some counter-points to the Egyptians.

Mr. Kissinger: I think Joe's secret dream is to draft a cable taking three sides.

Mr. Sisco: I think the second point is more difficult. If we decide to talk about guarantees to the Israelis, is there any practical form of guarantee on the ground we should opt for? I think not at this time. The Israelis say they will not permit any Russians on their side of an international border. The British have suggested a four-power force limited to the Suez Canal area. From that, we might detach an American contingent and position it in Sharm el Shaik under a UN umbrella. This could be feasible if we could sell it to the Israelis. Egypt would be hard put to turn it down. There's really no necessity for anything in the Sinai because there is no fedayeen problem there. If anyone crossed the border, the international peace-keeping machinery would come into play, backed by a strong Israel. I expect we will have to put a good deal more into Israel in this event: approximately one-half billion more in arms and one-half billion more credit. With that, Israel could take care of anything in demilitarized Sinai. This would defeat the Israeli argument that an international peace-keeping force is giving the Soviets a greater presence in the area.

Mr. Kissinger: But Egypt wouldn't accept anything like this. Why all the emphasis on Sharm el Shaik? Is this the only place the Gulf can be closed?

Mr. Atherton: It is very narrow here.

Mr. Sisco: The third point, on which we need a paper, is related to what US bilateral inducement we might offer to the Israelis. I think we should look seriously at the pros and cons of a bilateral treaty with Israel. I have strong reservations about such a treaty, but Ambassador Barbour thinks one thing that might induce Israel to talk about a settlement is a bilateral defense treaty with the U.S.

Mr. Kissinger: Against whom? What would we be promising to protect them against?

Mr. Sisco: We would be committing ourselves to support them militarily and financially in the event of a finding of aggression against Israel.

Mr. Kissinger: Couldn't we do that anyway without a treaty?

Mr. Sisco: Yes, in all kinds of ways. A Presidential letter to Golda, for example, with a joint resolution of the Congress to back it up. There are various gradations of formality. The weakness of a formal treaty is that it tends to polarize the area. However, the attitude of the Arab world today is much different than it was five or ten years ago. It might be possible to achieve this alignment and reduce the political repercussions of bipolarization. I'm not making a case for a treaty but I do think we should look seriously at it.

Mr. Kissinger: It's not to our advantage to raise a specific formula for guarantees. But neither is it to our advantage not to know what would be desirable. For internal purposes, we should have some discussion of the possibilities raised in the paper, establish some priorities among them and get a definition of what we want them to do. Suppose someone asked us what we want in the way of guarantees.

Mr. Sisco: There is simply no acceptance of the principle of international guarantees by Israel. We can choose our preferred form—in fact it would be a good thing to know internally—but we would be better advised to retain all the options. Any one of them, or a combination of them, would be satisfactory if it were agreeable to Israel.

Mr. Kissinger: But whether or not it is agreeable to Israel depends in part on the conviction with which we present it to them. What is the hierarchy among the various possibilities? They say they don't want any of them, but this could be part of their stonewalling tactic.

Mr. Sisco: I think it's more fundamental than that.

Mr. Kissinger: Assuming they get their border, and assuming the rest of Sinai is left as a demilitarized zone, how would it be policed?

Mr. Sisco: By Israel and Egypt. They haven't agreed to anything else. I don't think this is tactical on their part; I think it is fundamental. On the Jordanian side, I think there is a good possibility of a joint Israel-Jordanian arrangement. The King seems to be amenable. It is different on the Egyptian side. If you asked me for a coordinated proposal, I could describe what, in combination, would meet more of Israel's concerns than any other. We can be entirely flexible.

Mr. Kissinger: What they prefer, of course, is to stay where they are. Whatever settlement is reached won't be their preference. We will have to become involved to get them to give up anything. We're already in conversation about guarantees in the Four-Power meetings. How can we influence these talks if we don't know what we want?

Mr. Sisco: We don't want any guarantees chosen by the four powers. We want all guarantees open because the option must be chosen by the parties to the dispute. Israel would reject out of hand any proposal coming from the Four Powers. The most we want from the four powers is a list of the options which would not be too different from those listed in our paper. We may want to go to Israel at some point with something concrete.

Mr. Kissinger: The paper contains a good smorgsabord of ideas, but the implications of the various plans are not fully elaborated. Are we clear that we want U.S. forces to be involved?

Mr. Sisco: No. If Israel wants U.S. forces, we would consider it.

Mr. Kissinger: Consider it positively?

Mr. Sisco: Yes.

Mr. Kissinger: Do we want Soviet forces?

Mr. Sisco: It's not a question of whether we want them. We already have an Egyptian proposal to Jarring that Sinai and Sharm el Shaik should be policed by four-power forces.

Mr. Kissinger: Do we have any idea of how these forces would operate?

Mr. Sisco: In a combination of fixed positions with some mobility in between. We have had a good deal of experience with this in a decade of the UN Emergency Force. They would have the right of self-defense, but this would not be a Korea-type peace-keeping force. They would be more in the observer category, with recourse to the Security Council for reporting violations, and recourse to the parties for discussions. They would have small arms and some helicopters. This part is not the problem.

Mr. Kissinger: What do you think, Dick (Helms)?

Mr. Helms: I think this has been a first-class presentation of the problem but I don't see what it gets us. If we choose any one of these possibilities does it get us where we want to go?

Mr. Johnson: We want Israel to accept one of them.

Mr. Helms: I see little chance of Israel's acceptance of any of them.

Mr. Kissinger: It would help if they were more fully fleshed out.

Mr. Helms: I doubt it. I just don't think they would accept any of them.

Gen. Knowles: The mechanical part of the force is easy. It's a question of its saleability. We are doing a paper on this now.

Mr. Kissinger: The desirability of various types of forces can become a problem if we don't understand what we're getting into. Suppose there is a US force at Sharm el Shaik and the Egyptians decide to put us out. Do we go to war?

Mr. Packard: I think it's a good idea to flesh out these possibilities. I agree with Dick (Helms) that it won't work, but we need to know what the problems are and how far we are prepared to go. It may not be useful at this point, but there could be some movement in a short period of time and we should be ready.

Mr. Kissinger: Is any settlement possible? Be realistic.

Mr. Sisco: I don't know. It will certainly require maximum pressure on Israel.

Mr. Kissinger: If we wait until a settlement is acceptable to Israel, we are wasting our time. I don't believe they will accept the old frontiers. I suggest we put together a working group under Joe (Sisco) to spell out our position on the guarantees a little more.

Mr. Packard: They should also take a look at the paper the JCS is preparing.

Mr. Sisco: Yes, we will look at that.

Mr. Packard: We can get the general range of the types of guarantees that might be possible.

Mr. Sisco: The IG paper has that general range.

Mr. Kissinger: But we need some sense of priorities; how the peace-keeping machinery would function and what we would be getting ourselves in for.

Mr. Helms: Are we going to have American troops?

Mr. Kissinger: Suppose the Egyptians started a war of national liberation? Are we prepared to fight Egypt?

Mr. Helms: The scenario you're outlining is very close to what happened in 1967. There was a peace-keeping force in the area; the Egyptians said "get out" and they were out 24 hours later.

Mr. Sisco: This is a different proposition. The Security Council would have to deny to Egypt the unilateral right to terminate the force.

Mr. Kissinger: Suppose they didn't have the right, but they went individually to the Yugoslavs, the Indians, the Canadians and said they wanted their forces out. Would they have pulled out? I think the Yugoslavs and Indians would have.

Mr. Sisco: I agree this is a grey area—whether a country has the right to terminate. The Yugoslavs and Indians would probably have said they wouldn't stay where they were not wanted. I agree that U Thant acted stupidly in not trying to buy time, but it might have happened anyway. But in any Israel-Egyptian agreement, each country will reserve the right to unilateral action if and when the other side breaks the agreement. Also, any guarantee would have a clause calling for consultation in the framework of the Security Council in the event of agreement. This, of course, means absolutely nothing in this kind of commitment.

Mr. Kissinger: If the situation ever unfreezes, I don't want the President hit with short deadlines and faced with various complicated schemes. What is the JCS doing in its paper?

Gen. Knowles: We are taking a hard look to see what size forces would be needed.

Mr. Kissinger: To do what: fight? monitor? observe?

Gen. Knowles: We believe it would take approximately 11,000 observers for the whole area.

Mr. Kissinger: To observe what?

Gen. Knowles: Any hostile activity.

Mr. Helms: There goes the strategic reserve.

Mr. Kissinger: We will have to step up withdrawals.

Gen. Knowles: It would take 24,000 to do the whole job. We're talking about a UN force, not American forces. We would prefer American forces be kept to the absolute minimum and used chiefly for support.

Mr. Kissinger: Are you speaking only of an observer role?

Gen. Knowles: Observe and report any violations.

Mr. Kissinger: What would such violations be?

Gen. Knowles: Movement of hostile forces, for example.

Mr. Kissinger: And they would just report it.

Gen. Knowles: Yes. Although they should be able to protect themselves and to handle small forces.

Mr. Kissinger: The purpose of such an observer force would be what? Once they report the facts, does the other side take military action?

Gen. Knowles: If a force crossed the line, they would report the fact and the other side would take appropriate action.

Mr. Johnson: What is appropriate action?

Gen. Knowles: Repel them.

Mr. Johnson: There's a sharp line between an observer-only force, able to protect itself, and a force with a policing role.

Mr. Sisco: We will look at the JCS paper. I should point out, though, that there is a fundamental constitutional difference between the US and USSR going back to the Article 19[4] issue. The Russians want any international force to be subject to Security Council veto. They would have the SC decide on financing, composition, appointment of the commander, and policy direction. Our approach in the UN for the last 25 years, has been that the SC authorizes the force, but the force re-

---

[4] Article 19 of the UN Charter reads: "A Member of the United Nations which is in arrears in the payment of its financial contributions to the Organization shall have no vote in the General Assembly if the amount of its arrears equals or exceeds the amount of the contributions due from it for the preceding two full years. The General Assembly may, nevertheless, permit such a Member to vote if it is satisfied that the failure to pay is due to conditions beyond the control of the Member." (*Yearbook of the United Nations, 1947–48*, p. 989)

ports to the Secretary General operating under a SC mandate. The international field commanders have to have flexibility within the mandate of the SC. The question rose again in the Article 43[5] issue, over whether we and the USSR would make forces available to the SC as a permanent force. There has been absolutely no progress to bridge the gap between the US and the USSR on this issue.

Mr. Kissinger: All of this reinforces my conviction that we need a check list of what the forces can do and what problems they would face.

Gen. Knowles: Our paper will be a first cut at that.

Mr. Sisco: The question really is reduced to whether we want an international peace-keeping force with the US directly involved or not involved.

Mr. Kissinger: Yes, and the relative merits of various kinds of peace-keeping forces. If it is going to take a special effort to get it, let's get something which improves the situation. When will the JCS finish their study?

Gen. Knowles: The draft will be finished tomorrow, then it has to go to the Chiefs.

Mr. Kissinger: Let's get it and put it in the IG framework. How soon can you get your paper finished, Joe (Sisco).

Mr. Sisco: Two weeks.

---

[5] Article 43 of the UN Charter reads: "1) All Members of the United Nations, in order to contribute to the maintenance of international peace and security, undertake to make available to the Security Council, on its call and in accordance with a special agreement or agreements, armed forces, assistance, and facilities, including rights of passage, necessary for the purpose of maintaining international peace and security. 2) Such agreement or agreements shall govern the numbers and types of forces, their degree of readiness and general location, and the nature of the facilities and assistance to be provided. 3) The agreement or agreements shall be negotiated as soon as possible on the initiative of the Security Council. They shall be concluded between the Security Council and Members or between the Security Council and groups of Members and shall be subject to ratification by the signatory states in accordance with their respective constitutional processes." (Ibid., p. 991)

222. Conversation Between President Nixon and the President's Assistant for National Security Affairs (Kissinger)[1]

Washington, April 20, 1971, 10:13–10:25 a.m.

Kissinger: [Rogers] asked you about going to the Middle East?

Nixon: That's right. He says he has an invitation.[2] I said, "Well [unclear]—

Kissinger: Well. It's a mistake. But—

Nixon: But why is it a mistake?

Kissinger: Well, because he's going—I think we can handle it, Mr. President.

Nixon: No, my point is, my point is, he's going to Europe. And so he's invited to the Mid-East.

Kissinger: Well, you see—

Nixon: I'm not urging him to go.

Kissinger: No, I know you're not. But, they're just never telling us the truth. We've been getting for two months [1 *second not declassified*] that they've been arranging this trip. We've been asking the State Department whether they were. They never—I've talked to Dobrynin. [4 *seconds not declassified*] They denied it. His going there is going to accelerate the diplomatic process. Sisco is such a liar that they're going to promise everything to everybody. And there is going to be a deadlock.

Nixon: When he said to me though, Henry was sent to this—I just talked to him very briefly before he went to some meeting last night. He said he had invitations to go to three countries: to Israel, to Jordan, to Egypt—to the UAR. And he said, "I don't want to be excited now." And he said, "I want to turn it off. If you want me to turn it off," I said, "Fine. Fine. Turn it off."

---

[1] Source: National Archives, Nixon Presidential Materials, White House Tapes, Oval Office, Conversation No. 483–4. No classification marking. Haldeman was also present during the conversation. The editors transcribed the tape recording printed here specifically for this volume. Brackets indicate unclear portions of the original recording or those that remain classified, except "[Rogers]", added for clarity.

[2] In a telephone conversation with Nixon on April 19, Rogers said: "I've been thinking for some time and have been asked by Israel, Egypt, and Jordan to visit their countries. I would like to, at least, have serious consideration given to it. I—So, what I'm calling about is to see if you have any initial reaction that's—that would be opposed to it." Near the end of the call, Nixon said: "If you think it's a good idea, you go," later adding "I think it's a very good thing to, sort of, put the spotlight of attention out there, and if something can come out of it, it'd be great." Rogers replied: "You know, something may come out of it." Earlier in the conversation, he had pointed out that no Secretary of State had been to Egypt since Dulles went in 1953. (Ibid., White House Telephone, Conversation No. 2–4)

Kissinger: Well, the truth is that he's presenting—

Nixon: [unclear]

Kissinger: I know. But I want to tell you what the truth is—because I can show it to you [2 *seconds not declassified*].

Nixon: No, no. I believe.

Kissinger: He has generated those invitations.

Nixon: Sisco has or he has?

Kissinger: Sisco No, Sisco. Sisco generated all these invitations.

Nixon: What do they think he's going to accomplish over there?

Kissinger: Well, what he thinks he'll accomplish is—

Nixon: A settlement?

Kissinger: —is a Suez settlement, which he won't get.[3]

Nixon: Maybe we can get it before he goes there.

Kissinger: Well, not before he goes. I think the way you can get it is after he gets a deadlock, you can step in.

Nixon: Well, [unclear]. Get the goddamn thing settled. I mean, is there a way?

Kissinger: No. I think, you see—

Nixon: See, I was prepared, based on your conversation—Haig told me to say if there's a [unclear] let him go ahead and present the thing. And once there's deadlock, we break it.

Kissinger: That's right.

Nixon: All right. Once there's gridlock, we break it. I'm willing to do it at any time.

Kissinger: Well they have presented—

Nixon: You've got a way to get the deal, I assume?

Kissinger: Well, no. No, no, you can't get the deal.

Nixon: You mean we got to wait till the Israelis make—the Israelis made an offer?

Kissinger: The Israelis have made an offer.

---

[3] In a conversation with Nixon in the Oval Office on April 22, Rogers said that, during his trip, he would try to "get the parties to move closer together on the Suez proposal." He later added: "We don't want to be in the position of superseding Jarring. I've got to be careful about that. I don't want to be in the position of being a mediator on Suez. On the other hand, we're the only ones who can do it. We're the only ones who talk to both sides. So, what we're—what I'm saying, in effect, is that we're playing the role of constructive diplomacy." After Nixon said, "Um-hmm," Rogers continued: "We're trying to encourage discussions; we aren't going to mediate; we aren't twisting anybody's arms. We're, hopefully, going to create a better feeling of understanding, discussing the parts to see if there are possibilities of accommodation, but not pushing it and not being the mediator. And I think that that role—I'm going to say it—entails some risk." (Ibid., Oval Office, Conversation No. 486–7)

Nixon: [unclear]

Kissinger: You see, the only reason the Israelis made an offer was because I told them they had to; they wouldn't have made it otherwise.

Nixon: Yeah.

Kissinger: Now, that offer is unacceptable—

Nixon: Yeah.

Kissinger: —to the Egyptians. Now—

Nixon: But it's a good offer they told me?

Kissinger: It's a pretty good offer. So there is going to be a deadlock, I think. And then—I mean the record is clear, except for again one of these damn records, which we can't surface yet. That it's entirely—

Nixon: Our initiative?

Kissinger: Our initiative. Because, in fact, State told them they didn't want it because the whole thing [unclear].

Nixon: I know that, Bill told me that he didn't—that he says, "Let's not talk about Suez until later." I said, "The Suez is all we can get."

Kissinger: Suez is what you can get now. And then—

Nixon: My goal is to get—

Kissinger: I think—well I think even, if you ever authorized talks with Dobrynin on a realistic basis that the Israelis will rather finally destroy than accept the Rogers Plan.

Nixon: My point is, why would he want to go to Israel? I don't think he's going to get a good reception there.

Kissinger: No, he'll get a good reception, but he'll get no concession.

Nixon: Why would he get a good reception?

Kissinger: Because—

Haldeman: It's the United States.

Kissinger: It's the United States.

Nixon: And they want to play to him?

Kissinger: But they will, in my judgment—he also wants to go to the Soviet Union and that must be turned down.

Nixon: He didn't mention that. Oh, he can't go to the Soviet Union.

Kissinger: That's right.

Nixon: He cannot go there. No, sir.

Kissinger: That's right.

Nixon: Did he say that? Who did he raise it with?

Kissinger: I think he raised it with Dobrynin.

Nixon: Well, don't worry. Nobody is going to the Soviet Union.

Kissinger: And I wouldn't be surprised if Dobrynin brought an invitation back with him from Gromyko.

Nixon: No. No. I will not allow it.

Kissinger: But that, I think, you should get. If you don't go, no one should go.

Nixon: No, sir. We're not going to go.

Kissinger: But I think on the—but what I think you should insist on before he goes is that we have an NSC meeting in which he explains exactly what he intends to say to everybody. And what he expects to get out of it. He isn't so dangerous because he doesn't know exactly what he's saying. But Sisco, I've concluded, is really a menace in that job. He's so energetic and so ruthless. We couldn't—[4 seconds not declassified] we wouldn't know what's going on.

Nixon: [6 seconds not declassified]

Kissinger: [15 seconds not declassified]

Nixon: How do you know about this Soviet Union thing? Cause, Bob, has he ever mentioned going to the Soviet Union to you?

Haldeman: Not since last summer.

Kissinger: I know it—

Haldeman: He came up with this [unclear]—

Kissinger: Well, he wrote a very curious letter to Gromyko,[4] which he gave to Dobrynin, which was a pretty wide-open hint. He didn't—and secondly Dobrynin has been making hints.

Nixon: He's not going to the Soviet Union, I'm sure. Nobody's going to go.

Kissinger: Dobrynin is coming back tomorrow.

Nixon: No one can go.

Haldeman: He's definitely coming?

Nixon: Yeah.

Kissinger: Yeah. We found out at the FBI session.

Nixon: Nobody not only is going, Bob, if I don't go, nobody else is going. We're going to play it under my consent.

Kissinger: That's right.

Nixon: Tough son-of-a-bitch.

Kissinger: I don't think we can settle the Suez issue before he goes there. But we can sure as hell can settle it. I told the Israelis that when you make a request to them, the horsing around has got to stop. They've got to accept whatever you—

---

[4] See *Foreign Relations*, 1969–1976, volume XXIV, Soviet Union, October 1970–October 1971, Document 157.

Nixon: And we won't request anything they shouldn't accept?

Kissinger: That's right.

Nixon: They know that.

Kissinger: And I think—whenever you're ready to have the deal with the Soviets, if we have a summit, I think we have a good crack at getting the Israelis to be much more flexible with us.

Nixon: I know that. Well, let's come to something else.

223. Editorial Note

On April 20, 1971, Israeli Deputy Prime Minister Yigal Allon held separate meetings in Washington with Assistant to the President for National Security Affairs Henry Kissinger and Secretary of State William Rogers. The main purpose of Allon's visit was to "assess the temperature" with respect to 1) a possible interim agreement providing for the opening of the Suez Canal and the partial withdrawal of Israeli forces from the East Bank of the Canal in Sinai; 2) the achievement of an overall settlement of the Arab-Israeli conflict; and 3) the U.S. attitude with respect to future military and economic assistance to Israel. (Memorandum from Kissinger to Nixon, April 26; National Archives, Nixon Presidential Materials, NSC Files, Box 999, Haig Chronological Files, April 24–28, 1971) Allon held the first meeting with Kissinger at the Israeli Ambassador's residence beginning at 7:45 a.m. According to a record of the conversation prepared by Israeli Minister Shlomo Argov, Allon presented the essence of the Israeli consensus on a possible Canal agreement as follows:

"1. Israeli forces will withdraw at the most 7–12 kms from canal in order to be able to act against possible Egyptian breach.

"2. Israel would receive safeguards for maintenance of its fortifications along the canal.

"3. No Egyptian or Soviet forces to cross the canal."

Allon said that while he had confidence in U.S. interest in preventing a Soviet effort to take over the area, the Israeli Government was less confident about its performance in preventing a "salami tactics" takeover, which was why Israel would want U.S. guarantees.

Kissinger responded by telling Allon that the reasoning and need for guarantees was beside the point. "The question is *with whom* you do it," he said. "You have to understand what you are up against. The situation you confronted in December 1970, and which you confront today is that everybody in the U.S. Government wants to impose a settlement on you at least along the Rogers lines. Get that into your heads. You can get all the formal assurances from Sisco and they would be worthless. Right now the need is to prevent war now that the Arabs think they may have carte blanche for you ... You Israelis don't seem to understand that you have only one single hope—the President. Everybody else wants *at least* the Rogers Plan. If some of them could settle your problem on the Biafra model—they would." Allon then asked Kissinger if Israel was a "liability" in the eyes of the State Department, to which Kissinger responded:

"Yes! Most of the Arabists are colonialists who remember the Arabs in their pre-war image and long for those days again. And the State Department is not the worst of the lot! You have today a totally united Government against you. You have never been in such a position here before. If you should be divided on your end then it will be impossible to save you. *You must talk to the U.S. with one voice.* I know that if the Soviets win big in the M.E. it will be a disaster for the U.S. Others don't understand this. Therefore at this moment the question of 7–12 kilometers is irrelevant. The main thing is to agree on a strategy. First thing to understand is the seriousness of your position. Today at lunch you will be told many things. You are considered the dove who will take care of delivering the [Prime Minister] and ultimately of bringing about an acceptance of something close to the Rogers Plan. They say the same thing about your Ambassador. They say he was embarrassed to present some of his Government's positions and some of the papers he had to submit on its behalf ... The main thing is that you have to avoid being maneuvered into a position in which you are totally in the wrong. The ideal thing is for you to prove that if you are treated with confidence you can be reasonable. The tricky pattern is to reach a crisis point in which the White House has to come in, as was the case during the Jordan crisis. At the end of February it was a matter of barely two hours before a public condemnation of Israel by the U.S. was announced. I got this reversed by convincing the President that we should start an honest dialogue with Israel, so that she may tell us what she really wants. A Suez deal is important because if you just stay along the Suez war is inevitable, and I could not guarantee what we could do."

After a brief exchange on what the reaction in Cairo would be, the discussion continued regarding what Israel's strategy should be in the negotiations with the United States and the Egyptians:

"Allon: Let us assume we agree to a partial arrangement involving end of belligerence, partial withdrawal, no Soviet-UAR crossing of canal etc., and State Department then tells us it is unacceptable, can we then at least explain our position to the President?

"Kissinger: The great illusion in Israel is that you can always come over here to explain everything to the President. This is not so. This is not the way to impress him. He is not interested in your problems in the abstract, but only as to how they may affect next year. What impresses him is the kind of pressure that was brought to bear this February and last March. He *was* also impressed by your performance in Jordan. Two weeks before the Jordan crisis I advised that war was on the way and we had two options:

"1. To use American troops

"2. To use Israeli troops

"I recommended Israeli troops. The President was furious with me and wrote on my memorandum to him: 'No! These are pro-Jewish sympathies.' He would not talk to me. I flew to Chicago to try to explain things to him. Then the crisis came and he asked me to get in touch with Rabin.

"Allon: What do we do now?

"Kissinger: You should aim at having complete deadlock with us for two weeks or a month. Then Rogers will come in and ask for pressure on you. By then you should have your Jews organized properly. Then I can come in and intervene, provided of course that you have a fallback position that we can all agree on.

"Allon: Suppose we accept a fallback position. What guarantees will you give us against the Russians?

"Kissinger: On every big decision he himself has made the President has stood firmly, e.g., Cambodia, Laos, etc. He has not yet engaged himself on the M.E.—for obvious reasons. If you can bring about a situation in which he becomes personally involved then he will have a personal stake in it. In March, 1970 your Ambassador came in and made an eloquent statement on the dangers you were going to face (as a result of decision not to supply planes). In July—after Soviet violations—I came in and reminded him of this and he acted—issued a statement and ordered dispatch of Sidewinders etc. We had to bomb the Pentagon to get them out of there.

"Allon: Isn't the pressure already on? Phantom deliveries have stopped. No answer to Rabin's request. If we get a positive answer it will be very important psychologically. It will give Israel a feeling it is not being subjected to pressure. The President will understand the importance of this.

"Kissinger: You will not get the President to touch it before there is a real deadlock.

"Allon: Can't you get in the picture earlier than that?

"Kissinger: All I can say is that without me you are dead!

"Rabin: Sisco said he may propose a letter from President to P.M. supporting an overall settlement along lines he described to me (international force along canal, Americans in Sharm, billion dollar credits etc.) He expects it to be rejected by us.

"Kissinger: This is the first I have heard of it. I think I can prevent this. My influence is that I have always been right on the Middle East. The President is very good on big strategic issues. He has no particular love for Jews. He does not give a damn for Israel in the abstract. It interests him only within the strategic context of the Middle East. He told me so. He has a good conception of the strategic significance of the Middle East.

"Rogers will now be coming to the area. You will find that Sisco will promise you everything. They will want to come back with a triumph. If Sisco gets into the dominant position again then the implementation of anything he brings back will be his as was the case in July of last year.

"Allon: What about a letter from the President?

"Kissinger: If you get anything through Barbour then it means State Department, and then it does not mean a damn thing. Unless you get it from the President directly, or through me, or unless I advise the Ambassador (about its significance) then it does not mean a thing. If you settle with Sisco on this trip he will control things and you will never know the truth. There is no way of telling what he is telling the Egyptians today.

"After the violations were obvious I still could not for three weeks convince people of them and had to commission people to prepare all kinds of studies to prove my point. (Kissinger gave various examples.) They kept saying the missiles were already there. The President was all that time assailed by the others. Now if *he* had given the assurances to Rabin (instead of Sisco) then he would have felt that in violating the standstill the Soviets had double-crossed him and would have acted accordingly. Sisco will agree to any verbal guarantee and will then work to prevent it. If the President makes a deal with you he will watch it. He is tough.

"Allon: What can he give us?

"Kissinger: You must have the right to move in case anybody crosses. You can get something against Russians.

"Allon: Can he act as Commander in Chief without Congress?

"Kissinger: Yes. You can get the President to act if he is convinced that the Soviets are moving against you for great power reasons. He will act provided you don't alienate him before.

"Allon: Is it illogical for the President to accept notion of non-belligerence together with our acceptance of continuation of Jarring?

"Kissinger: No question in my mind that Sisco wants to play the Jarring mission so as to impose a settlement on you.

"Allon: How about non-belligerence?

"Kissinger: I think you should have a demilitarized zone on the canal and I would ask for it and be totally unyielding on it. Otherwise what would keep the Egyptians from crossing it. You have to get the President involved personally on this. At the moment the State Department is acting semi-autonomously on M.E.

"Allon: May I give you my personal thinking on the territorial issue and get your reactions.

"1. Golan Heights: important to us not only because kibbutzim, but for reasons of strategic defense for entire irrigation system of the Jordan Valley. Some territorial compromise can be arranged there too. Part of the Heights can be given back.

"2. Jordan: the main principle is not to annex areas that are heavily populated, this should be part of the solution of the Palestine problem, or may go back to Jordan in return for peace. The major point is to have the changes where there are no Arabs.

"Kissinger: You want to annex that?

"Allon: Yes. We shall hold on to valley and first range of mountains and leave them a desert.

"Kissinger: If you could get that will you go back to the old line with Egypt?

"Allon: Can you connect these?

"Kissinger: I believe that if a complete breakdown takes place and a complete deadlock is brought about then I can get the President with a proposal like this, but only if you wish it. I shall not do anything and shall not be involved in any settlement not acceptable to you. I have always believed that you could not accept the old Egyptian line because it would set a precedent for all the other sectors. If this gets into complete deadlock then it will be necessary to talk to the President directly.

"Allon: We cannot go back to old mandatory lines with Egypt. We must have an airfield west of Eilat, the only place where we can have a field for long range operations. In addition we must have Sharm, Gaza, and Rafah.

"Kissinger: How about giving Gaza to Jordan in return for Allon Plan?

"Allon: My position is that Greater Gaza can be given to Hussein for the Jordan Valley provided he agrees to peace and to considering Palestine refugee problem settled. We have to have less than one third of Sinai, less than one third of West Bank and Jerusalem united under

Israeli sovereignty, giving Jordanians special rights on their holy places there.

"Kissinger: In my view we have to agree first with the Soviets.

"Allon: But before that with us.

"Kissinger: Exactly. Dobrynin is after me to do just that. I won't do it unless we have an understanding with you first. I will never do it unless I spoke to you first. State Department cannot deliver on this. The way to [get] purchase in Jordan is with concessions in Sinai. I will not get involved unless you agree.

"Allon: Do you think this is a good plan (workable)?

"Kissinger: It has a chance. No problem with Golan. Sinai I have to think more. If you want to move on this talk to me. You will face a major problem soon. You will be confronted with a list of promises (by Sisco). Your policy must be to get them from the *President.* You are in mortal danger.

"Allon: Mortal?

"Kissinger: Yes, mortal. And those who will make easy promises to you are only out to get the Rogers Plan implemented.

"Allon: Our defense must be viable. We want to be less dependent on you. We need your political support and deterrence of Russians. Personally I think a bilateral military pact with U.S. must be achieved.

"Kissinger: You will be crazy to want that! It will explode enormous public debate. The Joint Chiefs will fight it. It will only expose you to enormous pressure. You will not be able to act when you have to. You will lose your freedom. A formal U.S. guarantee is counter-productive. A pact is against your interests. Right now your policy must be to resist Rogers. Be tough on Suez opening and if you are ready to make any concessions make them only to the President and only to him." (Israel State Archive, Ministry of Foreign Affairs, 9352/3)

Secretary of State Rogers and Assistant Secretary of State for Near Eastern and South Asian Affairs Joseph Sisco held a meeting at the State Department with Allon and Israeli Ambassador Yitzhak Rabin later in the day beginning at 1:02 p.m. (Personal Papers of William P. Rogers, Appointment Books) Allon began the meeting by explaining Israel's reasons for opposing the interim Canal settlement and its reluctance to cooperate with the Jarring mission. He said the Israelis were under the impression that the opening of the Suez Canal did not serve U.S. interests and therefore Israel did not wish to upset its strongest ally. He also said that because the 1949 armistice lines were "indefensible borders" Israel could not consider any proposal that envisioned a withdrawal to those frontiers. Rogers, however, did not accept Allon's answer, insisting that the United States wanted more cooperation from

Israel. "We don't like your rejecting everything as when your [Prime Minister] rejects this and then rejects that," he said. "You should have some regard for our interests. We do hope you will see this is a time to work out peace. Because of Soviet involvement this has become a major problem giving us the right to play a major role. We don't wish to be rejected ... The PM's territorial conception as reported in the *London Times* and the Rogers Plan is not great. Assuming demilitarization and security arrangements on Sharm and Gaza can be worked out satisfactorily then there are no great differences between us. You never insisted on annexation before and when you do so now you talk to us as if you don't want a settlement ... By talking annexation you are making it impossible for Sadat to negotiate."

Allon then asked why Israel should submit a proposal that the United States did not support when it would just lead to a confrontation between officials in Washington and Jerusalem. But Rogers insisted that "the confrontation already exists." The issue, he told Allon, is coming to the UN Security Council. "If you insist on territorial changes we will vote against you. We took you at your word when you said all you wanted was peace. We made presentations to Arabs and others on their grounds and said that if peace is accomplished you will not insist on annexation." Rogers then added that the United States did not understand why Israel's response to Jarring's February 8 aide-mémoire was in such "arrogant adamant terms." Israel has "created the impression that you were trying to undermine his (Jarring's) mission. You could have answered positively ... You could have said 'Yes provided we have a presence in Sharm el Sheikh, security for Gaza and demilitarization of Sinai.' The way you put it seemed a retrogression. Every nation says this to the US." Sisco agreed, adding "You are alone in the world. You have no friends. Even the Dutch reject your position. You haven't got anybody. We want to support you but have other interests." (Telegram from Washington to the Israeli Foreign Ministry, April 20; ibid., 5971/6)

224. Telegram From the Department of State to the Embassy in Israel[1]

Washington, April 22, 1971, 0237Z.

68413. Ref: Tel Aviv 2220.[2]

1. Following are our replies to points on which GOI seeks establish agreed position with USG. You are authorized to convey these to GOI, leaving piece of paper to assure textual accuracy. Paragraphs below refer to correspondingly numbered sub-paragraphs of para B of Israeli document:

(1) We believe document contains elements which obviously will require further clarification and adjustment during subsequent negotiations. USG is prepared to pass points contained in paragraph A, sub-paragraphs 1–13, of Israeli document to UARG, to recommend that they be given serious consideration and to tell UARG we are prepared to convey its reponse to GOI. We are certain GOI will appreciate that, if we are to play role of constructive diplomacy as both sides have asked us to do, we cannot be advocate for entirety of the positions of either side. Of positions set forth in Israeli document, some are obviously fundamental, others less so. We will, however, emphasize to UAR that we believe Israeli proposal offers positive basis for further discussions and exploration and will urge they reply in positive spirit.

(2) The USG position remains as it was stated in the communications cited (President Nixon's letters to Prime Minister Meir of July 23

---

[1] Source: National Archives, Nixon Presidential Materials, NSC Files, Box 1152, Saunders Files, Middle East Negotiations Files, Middle East—Jarring Talks, April 21–30, 1971. Secret; Priority; Nodis; Cedar Plus. Drafted by Sisco and Atherton, cleared by Haig, and approved by Rogers. Repeated Priority to Cairo and to USUN.

[2] Telegram 2220 from Tel Aviv, April 19, included the text of Israel's proposal for reopening the Suez Canal, which begins: "With a view to facilitating the attainment of durable peace between Israel and the UAR, Israel is prepared to consider entering into a special agreement with the UAR for the opening of the Suez Canal to international navigation, the observance of a cease-fire without limitation of time and non-resumption of fighting, and the stationing of the IDF at some distance east of the Suez Canal." What followed were 13 principles that the Government of Israel believed the agreement had to contain. (Ibid., Box 657, Country Files, Middle East, Middle East Nodis/Cedar/Plus, Vol. II) Meir handed the proposal to Barbour in a meeting with him on the afternoon of April 19, telling him that the proposal "should be understood as a state of clarification between GOI and USG," and that "there would be a need for negotiations to work out details." (Telegram 2221 from Tel Aviv, April 19; ibid., Box 1162, Saunders Files, Middle East Negotiations Files, Middle East—Jarring Talks, April 1–20, 1971)

and December 3, 1970,³ and clarifications conveyed by Assistant Secretary Sisco to Ambassador Rabin July 27, 1970).⁴

(3) The US position remains as previously stated: Quote no Israeli soldiers should be withdrawn from occupied territories until a binding contractual peace agreement satisfactory to Israel has been achieved. Unquote. We understand fully that Israeli willingness to pull back its forces in accordance with an interim agreement does not create an added obligation to make a further withdrawal in the absence of a peace agreement, and we agree that no added commitment would be involved on the part of Israel. If such agreement achieved, it would of course provide basis for progress in Jarring talks.

(4) It follows from 3 above that we understand clearly that a pullback by Israel in accordance with the interim agreement does not imply Israeli willingness to future withdrawal to the international border or any other line not agreed to in the course of the negotiations. Our view regarding borders remains that Resolution 242 neither endorses or excludes the pre-June 5, 1967 lines, in all or in part, as the lines to which Israel will withdraw in accordance with the final agreement to be reached under Ambassador Jarring's auspices.

(5) We are not altogether clear just what Israel is aiming at in question 5. We would be prepared to make clear to the Soviet Union the seriousness of any violation under the terms of any agreement reached on the Canal question, including any Soviet participation in or support of such violations. Other ways and means to deter such moves by the Soviets would depend on the actual circumstances of the situation at the time.

(6) As we have said, the USG is prepared to play constructive diplomatic role in assisting the UAR and Israel in reaching agreement on the Canal question so long as both parties wish us to do so. As previously indicated, we have no plans to involve Jarring or the Four in the negotiations.

2. After conveying foregoing, you should make following additional points orally.

A. We must take exception to the point made which suggests that USG has advocated opening of Suez Canal and that GOI is responding to US wishes in this regard. As records show, idea of interim agreement

---

³ Documents 136 and 187.
⁴ When Sisco met with Rabin on July 27, 1970, the Israeli Ambassador asked him—on instructions from the Government of Israel—to clarify the U.S. position on fundamental points regarding a future peace agreement between Israel and its neighbors. (Telegram 120681 to Tel Aviv, July 28, 1970; National Archives, Nixon Presidential Materials, NSC Files, Box 1155, Saunders Files, Middle East Negotiations Files, U.S. Peace Initiative for the Middle East Vol. II)

on opening of Canal was proposed by President Sadat and responded to by Prime Minister Meir in public statements in early February.[5] USG advocates peace settlement on basis of Resolution 242. We advocate any interim agreement between Israel and UAR that would be step in that direction and would help diminish risk of renewed hostilities. It is in this context that we have said we would favor agreement between the two sides which would result inter alia in reopening of Suez Canal.

B. USG believes Israeli proposal provides basis for negotiating Canal agreement and is prepared to convey it to UARG. In our private view, it contains some constructive elements and some points which UAR will not be able to accept. We have no intention, however, of pre-judging UAR reaction and we ready to communicate Israeli document unchanged to UAR promptly.[6]

Rogers

---

[5] See Document 203.

[6] On April 23, Barbour wrote that Gazit gave Zurhellen this statement: "Regarding your paper yesterday containing responses to our document of April 19, we shall see the Ambassador sometime next week for a further discussion of the matter. We ask that you not rpt not deliver any document to the UAR. We assume that the document is not rpt not being transmitted to other parties." (Telegram 2334 from Tel Aviv; National Archives, RG 59, Central Files 1970–73, POL 27–14 ARAB–ISR)

---

225. Memorandum for the President's File by the President's Assistant (Haldeman)[1]

Washington, April 22, 1971.

This meeting was held at the Secretary's request to discuss matters concerning his forthcoming trip to Europe and the Middle East[2] and to

---

[1] Source: National Archives, Nixon Presidential Materials, NSC Files, Kissinger Office Files, Box 129, Country Files, Middle East. No classification marking. "Top Secret" is handwritten in the upper right-hand corner. All brackets are in the original except those indicating text omitted by the editors.

[2] The President and Rogers met from 3:32 to 4:35 p.m. (Ibid., White House Central Files, President's Daily Diary) A recording of the conversation is ibid., White House Tapes, Oval Office, Conversation No. 486–7. Rogers left Washington on April 27; traveled to London, Ankara, Beirut, Amman, Riyadh, Cairo, Jerusalem, and Rome; and returned on May 9.

review possible questions that will arise at his press conference tomorrow morning.[3]

[Omitted here is material unrelated to the Middle East.]

On the question of Israel, the Secretary made the point that the present Israeli position is that they will continue to operate as they have been; that is, to keep negotiating, talking, and maneuvering, but take no action or arrive at no decision. The Secretary's view is that Israel should be urged continually to come to a settlement, that their position is stronger now than it's going to be in the future, and therefore it's to their advantage to settle now. The Egyptians have basically agreed to give them all that they've demanded and there's no reason for Israel to continue to refuse to settle.

The Secretary then listed his other stops—Paris to touch base with the French—then on to Turkey for the CENTO meetings. It was agreed that he should try to deal with the dope problem while in Turkey and to make some publicity on this since it would be of considerable domestic, political value to do so.

Then on to Saudi Arabia, Jordan and Lebanon, from there to Egypt, then Israel, then a courtesy stop in Italy on the way back.

There was considerable additional discussion of the Egypt-Israeli question all to the same basic point outlined above. The President told the Secretary to make it clear to Mrs. Meir that we will continue to maintain the balance and that we do this in spite of the fact that we have no political support from the American Jewish community.

The Secretary indicated that he feels Ambassador Rabin has a more realistic view than the Israeli government and that it still may be possible to convince the Israelis that continued resistance to a settlement will not serve their own purposes. It was agreed that the Secretary should not push the Israelis, but should make our position clear to them.

The President put the direct question to the Secretary as to whether he felt there was any basis to the danger expressed by Attorney General Mitchell and others recently that the Israelis' threat to go to war was a real one that should be of major concern to us. The Secretary thought there was no such possibility, that the Israelis have nothing to gain from going to war, they have everything they want now and the Egyptians also have nothing to gain from going to war. The Russians have given them full defensive capability and back-up and assured them that they will help them to defend themselves and they know that the Russians don't want a war. So, it's to both parties' interest to avoid war

---

[3] For the transcript of Rogers's press conference on April 23, see the Department of State *Bulletin,* May 10, 1971, pp. 593–600.

at this time and in the Secretary's view, to the Israelis' interest to move to a settlement at this time, if only we can persuade them to do so.

The Secretary made the point that he will urge progress by Israel but in no way will he dictate anything to them. He will make sure that he stays out of the negotiations and avoids getting into the role of a mediator. He will emphasize even balance in all of his activities in Egypt vs. his activities in Israel—spending two days in each and doing the same kinds of things in each country.

He will keep the settlement idea out as a goal, recognizing that it will take a year probably, before we can achieve it, but he will urge something now on the part of Israel—such as a Suez settlement.

[Omitted here is material unrelated to the Middle East.]

At the conclusion the President asked the Secretary to send him a personal, brief report each day from the important countries so that he would be able to keep on top of the major matters covered by the Secretary during the day. He explains the need for this arose from the very high press interest that there will be in the Secretary's trip[4] and the need to keep Ron Ziegler fully posted and coordinated from this end as well as the President's desire to stay current with developments as the Secretary's trip progressed.

---

[4] In an April 26 conversation with Ziegler, Nixon instructed him on how to handle questions from the media about Rogers's trip: "As the Secretary has indicated, you should expect no dramatic breakthroughs in terms of agreement. But the purpose of this trip is to keep the momentum going—to keep the cease-fire going, to listen to both sides, to talk to both sides. The President strongly [unclear]. Here again—that he's particularly—that this will be the Secretary's first visit to Israel. He's glad that the Secretary will have a chance to visit Israel, as the President has done. You can say that. He's also very glad the Secretary is going to Egypt. This is the first time in history that a Secretary of State has visited a country which denies it diplomatic relations. The President urged this. His goal—his long-range goal—is to reestablish diplomatic relations with Egypt." (National Archives, Nixon Presidential Materials, White House Tapes, Oval Office, Conversation No. 488–6)

226. Telegram From the Embassy in Israel to the Department of State[1]

Tel Aviv, April 30, 1971, 1220Z.

2468. Dept Pass Ankara. For Sisco from Ambassador. Ref: Ankara 3002.[2]

1. I have, of course, been devoting a considerable part of my thinking recently to an assessment of GOI strategy at the present time and have not come up with any hard and fast conclusion. As to their attitude with specific reference to the possible opening of the Canal, I believe their concerns focus on two considerations. (1) They are genuinely concerned that the Egyptians and Soviets will take advantage of any Israeli withdrawal to cross the Canal with military forces and that the Israelis will somehow be prevented from countering such a move. They genuinely feel that their own security will require that they not withdraw beyond a distance which they, the Israelis, can publicly police. They are not rpt not interested in any conceivable multilateral guarantee against such violation. Nor would any prospect (which has not been specifically raised on either side but which is presumably the objective of their probing for our support) of unilateral American presence to deter the Egyptians and Soviets be attractive either if it went no further than some kind of American surveillance, etc. (2) They are concerned lest they withdraw and permit clearance of the Canal but then are faced with some further Egyptian demand such as the exclusion of Israeli shipping before the Canal is actually opened. In this case, they see themselves arrayed against the unanimous displeasure of all the world's shipping nations.

2. Perhaps more fundamental to their thinking, however, is an underlying divergence with US as to the effectiveness of various tactics in dealing with the Egyptians and Soviets. Thus, while they recognize that considerable progress has been made since last summer, particularly the continued cessation of hostilities, and they appreciate an American role in this, they attribute this progress more to Israel's hard line than to the various diplomatic maneuvers which have been going on. They don't exactly admit to this assessment but in their discussion or references to the principal Egyptian concessions which have been made—

---

[1] Source: National Archives, Nixon Presidential Materials, NSC Files, Box 1162, Saunders Files, Middle East Negotiations Files, Middle East—Jarring Talks, April 21–30, 1971. Secret; Immediate; Nodis: Cedar Plus. All brackets are in the original except "[with]", added for clarity.

[2] In telegram 3002 from Ankara to Tel Aviv, April 29, Sisco asked Barbour for his "full assessment" of "GOI strategy at present time." (Ibid., RG 59, Central Files 1970–73, POL 27–14 ARAB–ISR)

(A) Nasser's agreement to the ceasefire and (B) Sadat's expression of willingness to conclude a peace arrangement with Israel—the implication is clearly present that they believe these were squeezed out of the Egyptians by Israel's adamancy.

3. The result is that in both channels the Israelis are reluctant to move rapidly. Also, I think they still hope, and at least have not given up on the prospect that, [with] these tactics they will somehow be able to bring about the direct negotiating procedure by which they originally put so much store. They do not wish to terminate the Jarring exercise but are happy to keep it on a back burner with the thought that if triangular negotiation gets complicated enough, Jarring might persuade himself or be persuaded that his March 10, 1968 proposal, involving unconditional talks under his auspices, should be revived as the only way to break the impasse.

4. I appreciate the foregoing analysis is not rpt not very promising, but I am afraid these conclusions are, to a considerable extent anyway, what we are faced with.

Barbour

227. Editorial Note

On May 6, 1971, Secretary of State William Rogers and Assistant Secretary of State for Near Eastern and South Asian Affairs Joseph Sisco met with Egyptian President Anwar al-Sadat and Foreign Minister Mahmoud Riad at Sadat's home in Cairo. It was the first meeting between a U.S. Secretary of State and an Egyptian President since Secretary of State John Foster Dulles visited President Gamal Abdel Nasser in May 1953, and the highest level of contact between Egyptian and U.S. officials since Egypt broke diplomatic relations with the United States during the 1967 Arab-Israeli war. Rogers sent President Nixon a brief report of his meeting with Sadat in a May 7 telegram from Tel Aviv:

"For President from Secretary.

"1. Quote Tell President Nixon that I welcome you, Mr. Rogers, with open mind and open heart Unquote, President Sadat said. Behind these words, which opened my two and one half hour talk with him, at which only FonMin Riad and Sisco joined, is a decision taken by Sadat with some risk to seek a peace agreement by relying heavily on the US and an intention to try to work out an interim Suez Canal settlement.

He views a Suez settlement as a Quote test of peace Unquote. Sadat also said some things about the Soviet presence which I will report to you personally.

"2. Throughout the visit, at all levels, there was warm cordiality evident. Quote We disagree on a number of things, Unquote said the Foreign Minister, Quote but we are not questioning your motives Unquote. This represents a significant change in the psychological atmosphere here. In ten different ways, as you can imagine, they said what is needed is Quote more squeeze Unquote on the Israelis who in their judgement have misled the U.S.; they contend that Israelis have demonstrated anew in recent weeks their greater interest in territory than peace.

"3. Sadat is intelligent, forceful, sensitive, an emotional nationalist, deeply suspicious of the Israelis, and a thoroughly political man. He is obviously attracted to the idea of being the peacemaker and was at pains to say that I should tell you that if he is given something to work with, he Quote has the authority to make the decisions; he is in control Unquote. In this connection, he gives my trip credit for forcing his hand to fire Ali Sabri well before I arrived. He is supremely confident he can control the other members of the Federation, including Qadafi, the young Libyan leader whom he describes as a true patriot, but inexperienced. He is adamant he cannot Quote give up one inch of territory Unquote.

"4. There were two concrete results: first, Sadat gave us enough to keep the negotiations alive on an interim settlement, and there is a considerable amount of bargaining ahead in the coming weeks and no immediate results should be expected. He and Fawzi are both more favorable to a Suez interim settlement than Foreign Minister Riad. Second, on the bilateral side they were anxious to reflect improvement in relations and to hold out hope rather than despair. This is the reason we announced, with their approval, that we were increasing our respective staffs by one in Washington and Cairo, that we would take another look at debt rescheduling, and continue our consultations.

"5. On the physical side, Cairo shows the wear and tear of years of neglect. People are very friendly with Americans, and the Soviets are most inconspicuous. The war seems far away, people are busy doing their thing, the streets are full of Egyptian-assembled Fiat cabs, and the only reminder of hostility are a few non-descript soldiers carrying a shoulder re [*sic*] walking guard in a relaxed manner around the famous Liberation Bridge in the middle of the city." (Telegram 2660/Secto 127 from Tel Aviv, May 7; National Archives, Nixon Presidential Materials, NSC Files, Box 657, Country Files, Middle East, Middle East Nodis/Cedar/Plus Vol. II)

When Rogers returned to Washington after stops in Israel and Italy, he had two conversations at the White House with President Nixon where he provided further details of his meeting with Sadat. Both conversations were recorded on the White House tapes. The first conversation took place in the Oval Office on May 10 from 3:30 to 4:53 p.m. (Ibid., White House Central Files, President's Daily Diary) The editors transcribed the portions of the conversations printed here specifically for this volume.

Rogers: "[Sadat] started out by saying, 'I know what's uppermost in your mind, and I want to talk about it at once. That's the Soviet Union.' He said, 'I don't like the fact that we have to depend on the Soviet Union as much as we do. I am a nationalist. I want to remain a nationalist. I am an Arab. I have deep feelings. I have all the weaknesses that we Arabs have. I love my country; I love the land; it is ours. I don't want to have to depend on anyone else. And, the only reason I have is because we were humiliated and I had no place to turn—we had no place to turn.' But he said that 'I hope that something can result from the initiatives you've been taking. The position that I took with Jarring is because I would like to become much closer with the West.' He said, 'There's no reason why the Arabs should be closer aligned to the Soviet Union.' He said, 'My people like the West better. We appreciate your values and our association with the West—business opportunities.' He said, 'I like American businessmen.' He said, 'My decision to respond as I did to Jarring, my decision to say that we would live with Israel in peace; that we would sign a peace agreement; that we would not interfere with internal affairs etc., was because I thought that would break the logjam; I thought that's what the West wanted. I thought that's what the United Nations wanted. Now we find that Israel won't respond.' He said, 'I have the feeling that you are the only nation who can do anything about it. Everybody else wants to do it, but doesn't have the ability.' He said, 'I realize too that you can't change overnight.' He said, 'You've sort of built a monument in your relationship with Israel that can't be affected quickly, but can be changed over a period of time. And if you can do that, I'm prepared to change our relationship with you.' He said, 'If we can work out some interim settlements on the Suez, we'll renew diplomatic relations with you. Secondly, I think that others will too.'

"Well, we had a long talk and went into a few details, which he spelled out what he would like. He would like to open the Suez; he would like a withdrawal by Israel of some considerable distance—he didn't mention the distance, but he previously talked to some of us—some of his people had—and he's talking, by considerable distance, a number of kilometers. But I think he's willing to bargain on that. He wants Egyptian troops to cross the Canal . . . it's his land and he wants to move his troops. And I argued with him that there's no particular reason why they had to have any troops. It would be unacceptable to Israel to permit large numbers of troops on an interim basis because it would look as if he was trying to take military advantage of the situation on an interim basis."

Nixon: "How'd he react to that?"

Rogers: "Well, it was negative at first instance."

Nixon: "But he's open to it?"

Rogers: "Happened upon the observer force—the peacekeeping force—whatever. He was quite flexible about that. He said, 'Any kind is satisfactory. I don't care.' I said, 'The United States couldn't even fathom the thought of having Russian presence across the Canal.' And he said, 'We wouldn't want it either.' He said, 'That's not a big part; we wouldn't expect that.'"

Nixon: "I don't think they like them."

Rogers: "He said, 'I'll tell you—you may not believe this but this is the truth: I have to pay for everything. All—I pay for. I can't afford it. It's a drain on me. We should be spending money for other—I pay for it in hard currency.' He said, 'I pay for the salaries and expenses of the Russians who are here—all of them.' He said, 'That's very costly.' He said, 'I don't like that; I need the money for other things.'"

Nixon: "They're so damn poor."

Rogers: "In the city it's really poor; it's a sad looking city."

Nixon: "It could be a very nice city; so goddamn poor."

Rogers: "He said he wanted to have diplomatic relations with us; 'we'd like to have diplomatic relations with you. We can't do it now.' I said, 'Why don't we take some steps to indicate that our relations are improving.' He said, 'Fine.' Interestingly, he said, 'I want you know that I am the President; nobody else;' he said 'I rule this country.' He said, 'There's some doubt about this. As long as I'm President, I can make decisions.' But you come away with the impression that he has made a commitment to peace. At least for the short run. Which is going to be difficult for him to back away from. In other words, he's spent a good deal of political capital on paving his step. And if something doesn't happen, then he's going to be in a political dilemma because he's not strong enough to start trouble with Israel. He couldn't carry out his threat. Although, I must say, he didn't make a threat. He never suggested anything in terms of time. He never said this has to be done or else. He never said anything of that kind. And you have a feeling that he knows his limitations in terms of military strength—he's just not prepared to renew hostilities. On the other hand, he realizes the value of some success. And I gave him the talk about what a great statesman he'd be if Suez was open. Pointing out that he would get the credit throughout the world on it.

"So I think he would like to get a settlement on the Suez. He wants to be sure that it's phrased, and described, and explained in such a way that it doesn't seem as if he's lost, he's made a concession, that he's given up something. He wants to make it clear that he still expects a complete withdrawal. And I think that that can be done. I don't think that will be a difficult problem, really.

"The impression that you get from Sadat, he is genuine, at least for the moment, in wanting to improve his relations with the United States. And he is willing to go much farther than any other Arab leader has ever gone in stating what he'll do with Israel.

"He said, 'If the United States wants to do it itself, that's fine with me.' He said, 'If you wanted to move troops in, that's all right with me. I have no interest in violating the security interests in anything you want to do, in anything the United Nations wants to do, or anyone else wants to do. It's all right with me. All I want is my land back. I don't want anything else; I don't want to bother Israel. I've made my decision. I'll live with them in peace. I'll sign an agreement. I'll do all the things they've always said they've wanted. I just want my land back.'" (Ibid., White House Tapes, Conversation No. 496–13)

Rogers returned to the White House on May 19, where he met with the President in the Oval Office from 9:05 to 10:14 a.m. (Ibid., White House Central Files, President's Daily Diary) Although most of their conversation focused on the pending announcement of the recent ABM agreement and U.S.-Soviet relations, the two began with a discussion of the Middle East, and in particular Rogers's May 6 meeting with Sadat:

Rogers: "What we have done up to this point, is to pursue a policy of trying to get the Arabs to have some trust in us. They finally did. They finally accepted the initiative. The only way that could ever be settled is to have the United States play a part. Everything else was hopeless. The United Nations had no chance. Jarring had no chance [unclear]."

Nixon: "No one would."

Rogers: "Now, we had no reason to suspect that it would work out as well as it has to date, although this is what we were trying to do. Now, Sadat is a very forceful man. He has a lot of strength. He is nationalistic as the devil. He probably is untrustworthy, so I don't want you to think that I'm trusting him."

Nixon: "Sure."

Rogers: "But, he is [unclear]. He has decided to—I'm convinced—to change his position. He is determined to become closer to the West for economic and political reasons. He—he's got a hell of a situation there. He's spending his money on his arms. He knows his people can't operate them; can't fly the damn airplanes. He's surrounded with Russians—he doesn't like that very much. Now, what I wanted to say to you, and he told me this in private, and then he told Joe [Sisco] the same thing. And he didn't say it unequivocally; he said it as categorically as you possibly can. And I haven't briefed—I haven't told anybody at the State Department, or anywhere else—"

Nixon: "That's right."

Rogers: "—because it would be a disaster if we did—"

Nixon: "Got out."

Rogers: "He said, 'I have to have this current agreement. It's important for me to have the new agreement. You're the only one who can help us get it—you, the United States. I don't like the presence of the Russians. I am a nationalist, but I had no way of defending our country. We had no way of defending our country, except to get Russian help. You wouldn't give it to us; nobody else would. It's costing me a lot of money. I'm paying the salaries of the Russians. I'm paying cash for the equipment I get.' And, he said, 'I want to give you this promise: that, if we can work out an interim settlement—and it'll take me six months to open the Canal—I promise you, I give you my personal assurance, that all the Russian ground troops will be out of my country at the end of six months. I will keep the Russian pilots to train my pilots, because that's the only way my pilots can learn to fly. But, insofar as the bulk of the Russians are concerned, the ten or twelve thousand, they will all be out of Egypt in six months if we can make a deal.'"

Nixon: "On, on, on Suez?"

Rogers: "On the interim Suez."

Nixon: "'Interim' means Suez, in other words—?"

Rogers: "Suez [unclear]."

Nixon: "I see."

Rogers: "The final peace agreement is—"

Nixon: "The key to [unclear]—"

Rogers: "—the whole ball of wax. The interim is—we're talking about the Suez Canal. Now—and I said, 'Well, Mr. President, you know, based on that, we may be able to work it out.' I said, 'The complicating factor is the Russian—the presence of the Russian troops. If you can assure us that they'll be out in six months, that makes our problem a lot easier.' I said, 'You tell us that we shouldn't be so pro-Israeli. We have to be supportive of Israel's position, because you got the Russians here, in large numbers.' I said, 'For as much as we would like to be friendly as hell with you, we can't as long as you have this number of Russians here. You might as well realize it.' I said, 'We have to supply Israel with arms as long as you've got a large number of Russian troops in your country. On the other hand, once that is not the case, once they've left—or, most of them have left—it's a different ballgame.' Now, when Joe [Sisco] went back, he [Sadat] told him again, he said, 'I told the Secretary, as well as I'll tell you: I give you my assurance; we'll work it out.'"

Nixon: "Um-hmm."

Rogers: "Now, if that should be done—and we have to take it obviously with, with a grain of salt—but, if he stays in power, and he could do that—he could deliver. It would be the greatest thing for, for you, Mr. President, and for the administration, as possible. I mean, to get the Russians out of Egypt—"

Nixon: "The important—the important thing is to get the deal."

Rogers: "It's to get the deal ... And, and then, as we were leaving, I talked to him about it. He said who would communicate with me: 'Don't do it through channels; get in touch with Heikal,' he said, 'on any personal thing.'"

Nixon: "Yeah."

Rogers: "He is, he is relying considerably upon Heikal's judgment, and Heikal's really friendly with the West ... Obviously, [laughs] Sadat, at one point said to me—he took me over to the side. We talked, just the two of us, for a while. He said, 'When this is over with, I'm going to make you pay for a lot of this.' And I said, 'What are you talking about?' 'It's just been done to some of our towns.' He says they were done along the Suez, done by your planes. And he tells us, 'You're going to have to help me rebuild those.' In other words, it's very significant that—"

Nixon: "Yeah. Yeah."

Rogers: "To be thinking down the road. He wasn't—in other words—"

Nixon: "Yeah, yeah, yeah."

Rogers: "—he was thinking about tomorrow—"

Nixon: "It's a very interesting point, Bill. He wants economic assistance from us—"

Rogers: "Of course, of course."

Nixon "And that's, of course, our big stroke in the Middle East, right—?"

Rogers: "Of course ... I think that it's possible, if he stays in power, that we could make a breakthrough here that will have tremendous importance."

[Omitted here is conversation unrelated to Rogers's meeting with Sadat.]

Rogers: "And I think that the thing that I want to close with on this note is that—"

Nixon: "It's the right time—"

Rogers: "—we are going to have to squeeze—"

Nixon: "The Israelis."

Rogers: "—the Israelis."

Nixon: "Yeah."

Rogers: "Sadat said—he's, he's a pretty clever fellow—he said, 'Mr. Secretary, I want you to know—'"

Nixon: "Um-hmm."

Rogers: "'—that I don't expect you to do too much all of a sudden.' He said, 'I know you can't hit 'em; you can't make 'em do things.' He said, 'Just squeeze them!' [laughter]" (Ibid., White House Tapes, Oval Office, Conversation No. 501–4)

228. Telegram From Secretary of State Rogers to the Department of State[1]

Rome, May 8, 1971, 1542Z.

2935. Secto 147. Subj: Sec Visit ME: Bilateral Conversation With Prime Minister Meir May 6. Following is uncleared memcon, FYI, and subject to change upon review.

Begin summary: Secretary reviewed for Mrs. Meir his impression of visits to Arab capitals. Noted Saudi concern re Jerusalem, strength of Jordanian regime but need for settlement if Hussein is to be able to hold out over long period, and Lebanese sense of insecurity and need for better equipment for army. Sadat gave impression of being totally confident of his position and preoccupied with Egypt, had stressed his decision to go for a peace agreement with Israel despite criticism at home and in other Arab countries, but had been adamant that he must get back all Egyptian territory. Sadat had made clear he viewed Suez agreement not as end in itself but merely better way to reach an overall settlement; Secretary had argued UAR should not press for time limita-

---

[1] Source: National Archives, Nixon Presidential Materials, NSC Files, Box 657, Country Files, Middle East, Middle East Nodis/Cedar/Plus, Vol. II. Secret; Nodis; Cedar. All brackets are in the original except those indicating garbled text and "[Egypt]", added for clarity.

tion on cease-fire in connection with Suez agreement. After making these points, Secretary said he very much hoped GOI would make clear its stand and take a position that would make a peace agreement possible. USG feels time is ripe for progress, and as Israel's main supporter believes it has legitimate right to ask GOI to make an effort. Mrs. Meir said Sadat's aim is not to make peace but to get UAR territory back as first step toward destruction of Israel. Prime Minister returned to this theme repeatedly, with references to Heykal articles and Sadat speeches, claiming UAR wants to dictate terms of peace, not negotiate. Secretary reiterated USG support for negotiations through Jarring and strong hope that way be found soon to get negotiations off dead center. Exchange was friendly throughout but frank and lively. *End summary.*

1. Meeting convened at 5:15 p.m. at Prime Minister's office and lasted two and one-quarter hours. In attendance on Israeli side in addition Prime Minister Meir were Deputy PM Allon, FonMin Eban, DefMin Dayan, Herzog and Dinitz of PM's office, and Gazit, Elizur and Rivlin of FonMin. Accompanying Secretary were Ambassador Barbour, Sisco, Pedersen, McCloskey, Atherton, DCM Zurhellen and PolOff Korn.

2. Mrs. Meir welcomed the Secretary and said she and her colleagues were anxious to listen. Secretary said it might be helpful to talk about his impressions as result of his visit to Arab countries. In Saudi Arabia he had gotten impression of young, intelligent and dynamic officials in the government. King Feisal's main concern, as regards the Arab-Israeli conflict, is Jerusalem, and also Palestinian problem. The King feels that the character of Jerusalem is being changed. Secretary said he had not gone deeply into this matter with King but had told him he would be talking with Mrs. Meir and would ask her views on the subject.[2] In Jordan, Secretary said, King Hussein seems to be firmly in control. He too is obviously concerned over Palestinian problem and refugees. Secretary said he had flown with King Hussein from Dead Sea area along Jordan Valley to area of tank battles with Syrians last September. He had not visited refugee camps but he was impressed by the seriousness and the human tragedy of the problem. Hussein's general attitude regarding peace, Secretary said, reflects recognition that he will have to make some territorial adjustments to achieve it. Hussein does not talk about getting back every inch of territory. King gives impression of feeling a little bit left out, since he has not been involved in recent negotiations, and he welcomed Secretary's visit. He desperately hopes some progress can be achieved. He does not want any Russian

---

[2] For a report on Rogers's meeting with King Faisal, see *Foreign Relations, 1969–1976,* volume XXIV, Middle East Region and Arabian Peninsula, 1969–1972; Jordan, September 1970, Document 149.

presence in Jordan and has rejected several Russian offers. Secretary said USG is helping King Hussein and will continue to do so. Hussein feels that he can hold on for time being but there is concern that he may not be able to survive over a long period unless a settlement is worked out.

3. Secretary said main problem in Lebanon is that government feels insecure. There were some demonstrations though no violence during his stay, and Secretary had been encouraged by response that his stop in the street had aroused. However, government is very shaky and it is much concerned over Israeli intentions toward Lebanon. Secretary said he had told Lebanese leaders that any changes in Lebanese-Israeli borders would be absolutely out of the question and he was certain Israel had no intention of attacking Lebanon. Addressing Mrs. Meir, Secretary said he was sure she would not take issue with anything he had said to Lebanese leaders in this regard. Mrs. Meir said Lebanese leadership would do best to worry about Fatah within their own borders than about Israel. Secretary said problem is Lebanese Government does not have military strength to deal with Fatah problem. Army is small and weak, its equipment poor, and GOL is divided, and does not feel it has the ability to deal with fedayeen problem. Deputy Prime Minister Allon said GOL has shown in past that it can do well in handling fedayeen problem when it wants to. Secretary asked whether USG might be helpful to Lebanon by giving it military equipment. Mrs. Meir said there was a time when people talked about Hussein's not being able to handle the fedayeen but then he took them on and won. Secretary said it was not correct to say it had been our view that Hussein was not capable of confronting the fedayeen. Sisco noted there had been two or three occasions before September coup when King had told us he thought he could and should confront fedayeen. But, Mrs. Meir said, Israel was told time and again that it should understand the situation in Jordan and not expect too much of the King. Secretary said the difference between Jordan and Lebanon was that the King had a good army, but the Lebanese people are divided along religious lines.

4. The Secretary said we had been thinking about question of USG providing arms to Lebanon. What would be Israeli attitude? Mrs. Meir said there is no problem between Israel and Lebanon from territorial viewpoint. In 1948 Israel had occupied 40 Lebanese villages but gave them back right away, and until the 1967 war the Israel-Lebanon border "was an ideal border." But after 1967 border area became a Fatah area. Since then there has been shelling, shooting and mining, and Lebanese themselves say there is no Lebanese Government presence in border area even though territory is Lebanese. Lebanese Government reached agreement with Fatah according to which Fatah could not shell Israel

but was free to cross over into Israel. This may be all right for the Lebanese but it is not all right for Israel, Mrs. Meir said. It is Lebanese territory and Lebanese Government must be responsible for actions carried out from its territory. Mrs. Meir reiterated that Lebanon, however, "is the last people we want a war with." "There were good relations after 1948 and we want good relations in the future." Secretary said he thought USG would consider helping Lebanon by providing military equipment. They are weak and need help. It is one thing to implore them to take action against fedayeen, but quite another thing if they do not have arms to do so. Secretary said we would naturally want to make sure that any equipment provided Lebanese be used only for internal security purposes. Mrs. Meir said if Lebanese do get [arms] from USG there must be assurances they will be used responsibly. Eban added that GOI had sent a statement to GOL through Jarring assuring it that Israel considers the present border to be the permanent one.

5. With regard to Egypt Secretary said impression is Sadat is totally confident regarding his own position. Sadat gives the visitor impression that he is well along toward taking Nasser's place. He is intelligent and resourceful although he does have Arab characteristics of emotionalism. Secretary said he and his party had been much impressed by the way Sadat had talked about Egypt, not about UAR, and with extent of Sadat concern for things Egyptian. Mrs. Meir interjected "We always called it Egypt too". Secretary said Sadat definitely gives one the feeling that he is the leader. Sadat had told Secretary that he was the President and could make decisions. He had already decided he wanted a peace agreement even though a lot of people in Egypt and other Arab countries criticized him for it. Sadat had said that in deciding on a peace agreement with Israel he had taken the word straight form Mr. Eban's remarks. He should have read on further, Mrs. Meir commented. Yes, Eban added on to what I said about secure boundaries. Continuing Secretary said Sadat had said he was prepared to do what Israel and US wanted, to make a peace agreement, and would accept any kind of guarantees that anybody wanted to add. He said he did not need these guarantees, but he would [garble] was that he could not give up any of his territories. Sadat had repeated time and again, Secretary said, that he was ready for agreement with Israel, but could not under any circumstances give up territory.

6. Secretary said Sadat had talked very little about Gaza and not at all about Jerusalem problem. He had said in effect that Gaza could be under Arab control, whether under Jordanian or some other arrangement he did not care. He had talked to Secretary about his problems with his military leaders regarding Suez agreement issue, and had said that even his Foreign Minister had not been in favor of an interim Suez agreement, but he had made the proposal anyway. Secretary said Sadat

had asked about Israeli position regarding a peace settlement, and Secretary had answered that we had no information beyond what Israel gave to Jarring. We told Sadat, Secretary said, that Israel had said that if Egypt would be ready for a peace agreement, Israel would lay its cards on the table. Sadat had said that time was passing and the situation will deteriorate if it is not put to good use; he would have a problem and so would King Hussein, so now was the best time to work out a solution. Sadat had said he knew Soviet presence in Egypt was a matter of concern to USG. He could assure Secretary that he had not wanted Sovs in [Egypt].

7. Secretary said he had thought that perhaps Sadat had been thinking of Suez agreement as a half settlement. As it turned out, however, this impression was incorrect. Sadat made clear that he was thinking about Suez agreement in terms of an overall settlement, with Suez opening being merely a better way to reach an overall agreement. Secretary said he had told Sadat we thought there were four areas of general agreement (Secretary cautioned he had made clear that what he was saying did not commit Israel in any way): (1) Israel is willing to have Suez open (Secretary commented parenthetically that as far as USG is concerned there are some advantages and some disadvantages to having Canal open; on the whole it is a standoff); (2) A withdrawal of some kind would be possible under proper conditions; (3) This would be coupled with a ceasefire of some duration; (4) The agreement would not be an end in itself. Secretary said Sadat had taken note of those points. Sadat had talked about need for his forces to cross Canal. Secretary said he and his colleagues had argued against this. Sadat had added that he did not want Russians to cross the Canal. We did not get into specifics, Secretary said, but we also made the argument that if UARG presses for big Israeli withdrawal it will be defeating its own purposes, since that would make it look like a permanent agreement. Secretary said he and his colleagues had argued that even a small Israeli withdrawal would look like a major success for Sadat, and would be striking demonstration of Israel's acceptance of principle of withdrawal. It would also signify that there could be agreement on larger issues as well. Secretary said he and his colleagues had argued these points at length. He could not tell what effect they had made on Sadat, though Sadat had listened intently. We said we had no proposals and no pieces of paper, Secretary said, and he could think of no more senseless procedure than putting down things on pieces of paper and having people then reject them. Secretary said he had told Sadat that we will be ready to convey two sides ideas and to help, but first let us see if we can reach some points of agreement before we start putting things on paper. Sadat had said he accepted that concept, would remain in touch with us, and would convey his thoughts.

8. Secretary said he would tell Mrs. Meir same thing. If your government wants to convey thoughts, we will pass them on. On a more general level, however, we find ourselves in a difficult position because we have said we believe that if Egypt would say it was prepared to make a peace agreement with Israel and say that they recognized Israeli sovereignty and were ready to live with it in peace, do all they could to prevent their territory being used to attack Israel, then we thought a peace agreement might be possible and believed Israel would be ready to state its terms. Secretary said he was sure Mrs. Meir and her colleagues knew that Israeli Government had lost support recently because of its stand; even a government as friendly toward Israel as Turkey had expressed deep concern over the Israeli stand. Israeli international support is deteriorating and Israel and the USG are in the same boat. Secretary said there was no need to do it right now, but he very much hoped that GOI could make clear its stand and take a position that would make a peace agreement possible. Now is the time, Secretary said, and we will help. What would you like us to do, Secretary asked? If you have doubts and think the other side is not sincere, you are not committed until you sign, but it seems to us that you would want to keep the momentum going. Secretary added that we don't care how this is done.

9. Sisco said he would like to make one point. Why does US feel the time is now ripe? Why do we think there is now a chance that might later be lost? Let's look at the conditions. Sisco said he thought GOI agreed that Jordan is now as secure a partner for peace as it likely to be. This could change in the future but King Hussein is now in control and wants a settlement; during September 1970 crisis Israelis realized that if there were no King Hussein there would be no one to make peace with in Jordan. Jordan is now in a position to make peace and run a reasonable chance of having it stick. As regards UAR, Sisco said, we came away with impression that Sadat is a man who would like to try to do business and feels able to do something at present but is not sure what would happen in the circumstance of a continued impasse. Question therefore is, Sisco said, what does Israel expect and what does it want to see develop in these two countries in the future. If you think things will be better in six, twelve, or eighteen months, we would like to know, Sisco said, because our impression is that the longer things continue stalemated the worse the situation becomes. Please tell us if you think we are wrong in this estimate, Sisco said. What are you prepared to do, Secretary asked? The time is now ripe to make a move.

10. Mrs. Meir said she would have to "say something you may not like." People say Sadat wants to make peace with Israel and ask why it is that Israel does not agree. Mrs. Meir said that she could not forget that last year, while at dinner in New York at Ambassador Tekoah's,

Dr. Bunche had told her that if he were really an honest man, he would return his Nobel Peace Prize. Dr. Bunche said in 1949 he had been convinced that there would be a permanent peace within a year, but it had not come. If Dr. Bunche remembers these things, Mrs. Meir said, how can we forget? We all recall these things, Secretary said, and we all have our own emotional reactions, but we must not allow them to get the best of us. When Sadat says he wants peace, Mrs. Meir resumed, all he wants is to get his land back. But we must ask what happened four years ago when all of a sudden Egypt prepared for war. Did Israel provoke Egypt? Why after 1957 had there been war again in 1967? Israel had been happy with the UN force, but then the Egyptians threw it out. I can only say this, Mrs. Meir added, we have to learn from our own experience. Many people came back from talks with Nasser and told us Nasser says he wants peace. Secretary interjected that Nasser had never said this in the way that Sadat had recently said it. Secretary recalled that Israel had said that if Nasser leaves the scene then it would be possible to make peace. Mrs. Meir said she had a collection of things that Sadat had said after he had quoted Eban about a peace agreement. Sadat had described how he pictures a final settlement, i.e. no more Jewish state. Heykal's articles (he is more than just a newspaperman you know, Mrs. Meir said) list the priorities: (1) get Israel out of the occupied territories, (2) get them back to the 1947 lines, and (3) then turn it into a mixed Moslem-Christian-Jewish state. This is no secret; Sadat said the same thing at the Fatah conference in Cairo.[3] So which Sadat are we to believe?

11. Secretary recalled that when she had spoken to Ambassador Barbour, she had said that as soon as Sadat says he will sign peace Israel would lay out its position. We are prepared to do it now, Mrs. Meir rejoined. Israel has wanted peace for 20 years, and it wanted to negotiate for secure and agreed borders. Egypt's answer was the Khartoum formula.[4] We want negotiations, that is what Israel wants, Mrs. Meir said. Jarring handed Israel and Egypt a paper and asked for our commitment. Sadat had said he was prepared to sign on the condition that Israel would withdraw to the pre-Six Day War lines. We won't accept that, Mrs. Meir said, but we are prepared to go on with negotiations.

12. Mrs. Meir said it was not correct to say that nobody knows what Israel wants in regard to a settlement. She had set Israel's position out in public and to the USG. One, it is not coming down from Golan (now there is a better regime in Syria, Mrs. Meir added, but she still must say this); two, it is no secret that Israel must hold on to Sharm el-

---

[3] Reference is to the meeting of the Palestine National Council, a body of the Palestine Liberation Organization, held in Cairo on February 28.

[4] See footnote 4, Document 18.

Sheikh and have a land connection. It is not that we have not said these things, Mrs. Meir said, but you don't accept them. What about the rest, the Secretary asked? Mrs. Meir replied that she had told Ambassador Barbour that Israel did not want all of Sinai, not even half. How wide the area that Israel will hold should be is a question for negotiations, but nobody can say Israel wants all of Sinai. Mrs. Meir recalled her conversation with the Secretary in Washington at which time the Secretary had asked if Israel wants property, or perhaps only a 99-year lease. Her reply had been that she would take the question to the government, but in any case there must be Israeli control, not an international force.[5] The United States well knows what Israel wants, Mrs. Meir said. She was sorry to say, however, that there is a disagreement between Israel and the United States. The disagreement, however, is not because United States does not know what Israel wants. There is nothing more unjust than the accusation that Israel wants territory, Mrs. Meir said, but it does want more defensible borders, borders that are in themselves a deterrent. When the Syrians sit on Golan, we don't feel secure. Secretary said we agreed. Continuing, Mrs. Meir said when Natanya and Tel Aviv were within range of Jordanian guns, Israel also did not feel secure. "We want borders which, if attacked out of the blue, we can defend."

13. Mrs. Meir said that Israel had been called intransigent because it insisted on direct negotiations and then it had accepted the U.S. initiative but, Mrs. Meir asked, what are these negotiations? What is it when Egypt's Ambassador to UN returns Israeli paper because it is labeled a communication from Israel to UAR. Israel states its position, but then UAR says that if that is the case it doesn't want to negotiate. Mrs. Meir said Israel feels that negotiations should now proceed to point by point examination of issues in question. But there is also the problem, Mrs. Meir said, that when you tell me I must believe Sadat when he says peace, I must also believe him when he says what kind of peace he intends.

14. Secretary said we know Israel says it wants control of Sharm el-Sheikh, but GOI has never told us where it would withdraw to if it did get Sharm el-Sheikh. We don't know. President asked me, Secretary said, and I couldn't answer. Definitely not the 1967 borders, Mrs. Meir said. But USG has announced there must be withdrawal to the 1967 borders, she added. Secretary said this was not correct. What we had said was we thought that if satisfactory arrangements could be reached regarding Sharm el-Sheikh and free passage, demilitarization of Sinai and on Gaza, then we thought agreement could be reached on basis of 1967 borders. But, Secretary reiterated, we do not know where you will

---

[5] See Document 162.

withdraw to. Secretary said we hoped that sometime soon, perhaps not tonight or tomorrow, but sometime soon, we would like to know. We are Israel's principal supporter, we feel we do have a legitimate right to know its position. We very much want negotiations to be continued under Ambassador Jarring and hope that an honest and active effort will be made in this direction. U.S. policy has been very adversely affected by Middle East impasse, Secretary said. Israel tells us what it does not want, but we need to know what it does want. Do you not want us to work together and give you our support, Secretary asked? We are prepared to consider any kind of guarantee that Israel thinks will help. Israel and the U.S. are in the same boat, and we think that this is the time to take risks for peace, though we realize that it is easier to do nothing. If it turns out in the end that no agreement is possible, that there is no chance for peace, then we will give it up.

15. Mrs. Meir said this grieved her very much, and was unjust. There had been many unjust accusations made against Israel. Israel refuses peace on dictated terms. Israel had presented to us its ideas regarding opening of Canal, but Sadat had said there must be full withdrawal. This Israel does not accept. Secretary said USG does not accept it either. But he would like to ask if GOI really favors opening of Suez Canal. When we got Israel's response, we had impression that Israel thought of it as a favor to us. But this is matter between Israel and UAR; GUS is ready to help but is not a party. Sisco noted that we had said we were ready to transmit Israel's views. Mrs. Meir asked if Sadat would agree to an end of shooting in connection with Canal agreement. No, Secretary said, for this would mean, for Sadat, giving up everything. Eban commented that Israel had said in its paper that the line the IDF will hold is not to be considered the final line and the special agreement will not affect other agreements which may be reached in the future. Secretary said he did not believe that, in any case, these were the major hurdles. It should be possible to work out positions and language which will overcome the differences between the two sides. Mrs. Meir said it would be ridiculous for Israel to agree to withdrawal without having gotten Egypt's promise that there will be no more shooting, or to let Egypt send its army across the Canal. Eban asked what was Sadat's precise position regarding the ceasefire. Secretary said Sadat wants a specific time limit. Secretary said he had told Sadat it would be wiser not to do that, not to create for himself artificial deadlines. Main thing is to have an agreement. But Secretary added, if Israel says Sadat must foreswear shooting forever in return for Suez opening, then there can be no agreement, since he couldn't do that.

16. Dayan asked whether Sadat had indicated his position regarding other elements of a settlement, i.e. West Bank, and Golan. Secretary said Sadat had not raised these, he had always talked about

Egypt. Sisco added that what struck us most was that Sadat had been so Egypt-oriented there had been none of the old pan-Arab litany. Sadat is preoccupied with Egypt. Mrs. Meir asked rhetorically what people do when they want to make peace. They sit down and talk, argue, but finally reach agreement. But Sadat says he wants peace only on his own conditions. He says no diplomatic relations with Israel, but Israel can live another 100 years without an Egyptian Ambassador. Problem is Sadat really wants no Israel at all. Mrs. Meir then quoted at length from a speech by Sadat (apparently Sadat speech to Palestine Council late in February) calling for Palestinian rights, terming Palestinians "the owners of the country" and saying that there must be an end to the Zionist movement. Sisco interjected that in other Arab countries there is a great concern that Egypt will abandon the Arab cause. Mrs. Meir said we only know what we hear and read. But if we only went by public statements, Sisco said, there would never be any hope for settling the Arab-Israel conflict. We have to be guided not by public statements but by real negotiating positions, Sisco said.

17. Summing up, Secretary reiterated his strong hope that as a result of his visit some way would be found to get off dead center. We think it is in your own national interest, Secretary said; literally there is no other nation that supports you. We hope that Israel will do something to get negotiations going again. Maybe Jarring should try to get the parties together, Mrs. Meir replied. The Secretary answered we hope Israel will not fall back now on the face-to-face argument. USG still holds to position that there can be direct negotiations later, but to insist on that now would kill any chances for agreement. In closing, Secretary reiterated the hope that GOI would take steps to get negotiations moving again. He noted that he had found atmosphere for USG much improved in Arab countries and Israel itself had always said that the more friends USG has in Arab world, the better things would be for Israel. Resumption of negotiations would be of great benefit to all.

18. Both sides agreed to continue talks at next meeting, scheduled for afternoon May 7.[6]

Rogers

---

[6] See Document 229.

229. Editorial Note

On May 7, 1971, Secretary of State William Rogers met with Israeli Prime Minister Golda Meir in Tel Aviv at 4:45 p.m. Also present from the United States were Ambassador Walworth Barbour, Assistant Secretary of State for Near Eastern and South Asian Affairs Joseph Sisco, Deputy Secretary of State for Near Eastern and South Asian Affairs Alfred L. Atherton, and Assistant Secretary of State for Public Affairs Robert McCloskey. Joining Meir on the Israeli side were Deputy Prime Minister Yigal Allon, Defense Minister Moshe Dayan, Foreign Minister Abba Eban, Finance Minister P. Sapir, Ambassador to the United States Yitzhak Rabin, Dr. Herzog, Simcha Dinitz, and Mordechai Gazit. No U.S. record of the meeting has been found, but according to a May 12 memorandum of conversation between Rabin and Assistant to the President for National Security Affairs Henry Kissinger, the Israelis provided Kissinger with "verbatim" minutes of the meeting, as well as the record of Sisco's May 7 meeting with Dayan. (National Archives, Nixon Presidential Materials, NSC Files, Box 997, Haig Chronological Files, Haig Memcons, Dec 1970–Dec 1971 (3 of 3)) The Israeli minutes are ibid., Kissinger Office Files, Box 129, Country Files, Middle East. The Israelis also prepared an abridged record of Rogers's May 7 meeting with Meir in which they recorded that the "talk concentrated almost exclusively on the interim settlement." Sisco emphasized that Sadat was "serious on interim agreement." He said it was "a step towards that overall settlement," but that the door was "completely open to further explanations on interim settlement." Rogers added that he too believed Sadat wanted an interim settlement. "We lose nothing by trying," said Rogers. "Israel is in good position to take risks now. Israel is much stronger than Egypt." Rogers pointed out that Sadat felt an agreement on a Canal settlement would accomplish a "political coup" and allow Sadat to overcome humiliation. "This would put him [in] a frame of mind that he would not want to start war. He would have so much credit politically that he would resist a war that would ruin him."

The conversation then turned to addressing a symbolic Egyptian military presence on the east bank of the Suez Canal. Rogers acknowledged that if Sadat insisted on moving "a lot of troops" across the Canal that would cast doubts on his intentions. "On the other hand, a symbolic military presence is another matter." Meir replied that "military personnel cannot be considered at all." Rogers said that it did not make all that much difference if it were small number of military personnel under U.S. supervision. "If it is just a symbolic number, that is one thing, if it is more that casts doubts on his intentions." But Meir appeared more concerned about whether, if the Egyptians crossed the Canal, they would bring Soviet forces with them, asking Rogers what the U.S. reaction would be to that scenario. Rogers replied that he had told Sadat the United States would not consider Soviet presence on the east side of the Canal. Rogers did not think "it is possible to give answer about what we might do in the event if things happen, but we would take it as a matter of very grave concern. Soviet Union knows that. I do not see them playing that game," he said. "If they do we will have to face it. But I do not think they have that in mind." Rogers added that the United States would have a "major problem" if it looked as if the Soviets were going to move "in a big way to take countries in the region."

Sisco then asked for an elaboration of the distance that Israel was prepared to withdraw its forces from the Canal, emphasizing that "the broader the zone the better the possibility of getting a satisfactory formulation of the cease-fire from Israel's point of view." Dayan said that if Egyptians did not undertake not to resume shooting, then Israeli forces would have to remain "very very close" to the line. Dayan did not rely on the United Nations keeping fortifications and certainly not being behind the passes, which is more than 35 kilometers. Israel, Dayan said, would accept a 10-kilometer withdrawal from the Suez Canal, but "the matter is related to an understanding not to resume fighting." Dayan said he would not recommend a withdrawal at all if the Egyptians did not undertake non-resumption of fighting and non-crossing of the Canal. Sisco replied that it therefore seemed possible to try for a 10-kilometer withdrawal while the Canal is cleared and once the Canal opened to have Israel "simultaneously" withdraw to the passes. Eban interjected that he would like continued U.S. opposition to any idea of military crossing, symbolic or non-symbolic, to which Sisco replied that the Egyptians would then expect a much larger withdrawal from the Israelis, somewhere in the vicinity of 35 kilometers.

After further discussion about the withdrawal, and not relating an interim Canal agreement to Security Council Resolution 242, Prime Minister Meir stated that "we are prepared to move from the Canal, we do not want any more shooting. We do not want military personnel to cross the Canal. If we have to face the Egyptian army we would rather face them across the Canal." Rogers replied that "this was the first time that there had been a good talk on specifics. If U.S. can rub it up so that it would look as if Sadat had been reasonably successful on the agreement, he might do it." With that in mind, Rogers asked Meir about the possibility of having Sisco go back to Cairo to talk with Sadat to explain Israel's position. Meir agreed but emphasized that the United States "had no authority to speak about withdrawal of one mile. Government will not decide until it sees principles are accepted and there are some arrangements. I do not care how you call it. That we are assured that no more shooting, no crossing of Egyptian military and some mechanism, a small civilian group to see to it that Bar Lev Line is not destroyed. And if we have U.S. assurance and Rogers had said so, that U.S. will support us that this does not commit us to anything else. Sadat must know that you accept our position that this [is] no commitment whatsoever."

Before the meeting adjourned, Rogers asked Meir if she thought the Canal agreement was a good idea. Meir replied: "This we think is a good service of the U.S. government if they can do it." (Main Points of Talk Prime Minister with Rogers, May 7; Israel State Archive, Previously Classified Material, 7038/9)

230. Telegram From the Embassy in Italy to the Department of State[1]

Rome, May 8, 1971, 1147Z.

2919. For the President from the Secretary.

1. I have completed the final phase of my Middle East trip—two days in dynamic, creative, intense, worried, suspicious, querulous Israel. After a first day's round with Golda Meir during which she stuck to familiar themes and maintained an immovable steadfastness, we hit pay dirt in our last session in a long, detailed and point-by-point discussion of the interim settlement in which we were able to get some helpful Israeli flexibility on certain key points.[2] It was an arduous process, but in the end we got enough of what we wanted, and represented sufficient clarification and elaboration that I am sending Joe Sisco to report to Sadat[3] and to explore further some of the remaining key points. I am satisfied that this trip has accomplished its principal purposes: to show American interest and leadership in the constant search for peace in the area; to maintain and conceivably even enhance the pace of the peacemaking process particularly with regard to an interim Canal agreement; and to add to the more hopeful atmosphere slowly developing in the Middle East.

---

[1] Source: National Archives, Nixon Presidential Materials, NSC Files, Box 657, Country Files, Middle East, Middle East Nodis/Cedar/Plus Vol. II. Secret; Immediate; Nodis; Cedar.
[2] See Documents 228 and 229.
[3] Sisco met with Sadat on May 9; see Document 231.

2. More concretely, the principal results of the trip seem to be these: our relations with Faisal have had a fresh input; friendly Jordanian-American relations have been reinforced; Lebanon was given a badly needed reminder to adopt a more positive posture with its people before its weakness produces its own demise;[4] we added a measure of confidence in our relations with Egypt; and we reaffirmed our continuing interest in Israel's security, while leaving them with no doubt that our direct interests in the area can be affected adversely unless they adopt a more flexible position on an overall and interim peace settlement. We have finally begun to take the play away from the Russians, and both sides—Arabs and Israelis—see the US as the key—and this is as it should be. So long as we maintain our strength to bulwark this kind of active US diplomacy, we ought to be able in time to move from neutralizing Soviet influence to reversing that trend and at least keep pace with them in the Persian Gulf and the Indian Ocean.

3. Back to Israel. It is clear that this is a divided government, and decisions will come only with painful slowness. Mrs. Meir has great strength, but also great weaknesses. Doubts were expressed that she is the leader who in the end will make any fundamental settlement. She is showing understandable strain, irritation, signs of weariness, and age, but more important, she suffers psychologically from the Quote trauma of 1957 Unquote when as Foreign Minister she announced Israeli withdrawal. She strongly prefers arguing the past, has difficulty talking specifics, and has to be pushed forward rather than lead her platoon of Ministers Allon played a mixed role; Eban was quite silent. Only Dayan came out straightforwardly. His approach to the interim settlement is similar to ours; he believes that it must be conceived as a step towards the overall settlement and based on a permanent ceasefire. He believes that once having left the Canal, Israel should assume it will not return. In a previous detailed meeting with Sisco,[5] he helped break the

---

[4] Haig attached Rogers's reports on his visits to Jordan and Lebanon to a memorandum to the President on May 5. (National Archives, Nixon Presidential Materials, NSC Files, Box 1162, Saunders Files, Middle East Negotiations Files, Middle East—Jarring Talks, May 1–9, 1971) He did not include telegram 1052 from Cairo, May 5, in which Rogers detailed his 2½-hour meeting with King Hussein at al-Hummar Palace on May 3. (Ibid.)

[5] Sisco met with Dayan on May 7 in Tel Aviv. The minutes of their conversation are in the National Archives, Nixon Presidential Materials, NSC Files, Kissinger Office Files, Box 129, Country Files, Middle East, Middle East. Saunders summarized the "main points" that emerged from the Sisco-Dayan meeting in a memorandum to Kissinger on May 17, concluding: "This conversation would seem to reinforce Sisco's prior assumption that peace is not likely to be made with Prime Minister Meir. Even Dayan, however, does not envision a border settlement which Sadat could, under present circumstances, accept in a final settlement." (Ibid., NSC Files, Box 1163, Saunders Files, Middle East—Jarring Talks, May 19–31, 1971)

ice, and this flexibility to a degree got reflected grudgingly at my marathon three hour session with Golda Meir.

4. On substance, the remaining difficult points which will over the coming weeks determine whether we get an interim agreement are these:

A. Length of ceasefire. Dayan injected the positive concept that if unlimited or extended, the area of Israeli withdrawal from the Suez can be greater.

B. Understandable hard-rock Israeli insistence that no UAR military force will move into the evacuated territories. Sadat was equally strong the other way. Israel is likely to accept a UAR civilian presence, and Dayan helped by keeping open possibility of UAR police in symbolic numbers. This point will be tough.

C. Supervision. Meir, aided by Allon, has been suggesting joint Egyptian-Israeli arrangements. This is not feasible. We made a little headway in showing how an augmented UNTSO (UN Truce Supervisory Organization—which could involve a few Americans) with a reinforced mandate deriving from the agreement might be a satisfactory arrangement. There are a number of other points of lesser significance which we believe are negotiable.

5. I have in mind also that if we are able to narrow the gap even further in the next few weeks, the time will soon come when we will wish to tie down the Russians with respect to the agreement as a whole and in particular that Quote no Russian forces will come across the Canal Unquote. I will have some other information for you on this at our Monday meeting.[6]

Martin

[6] Rogers met with Nixon to discuss his trip on May 10 in the Oval Office from 3:30 to 4:53 p.m. For a transcript of the portions of the conversation pertaining to Rogers's May 6 meeting with Sadat, see Document 227.

231. Telegram From the Interests Section in Egypt to the Department of State[1]

Cairo, May 9, 1971, 1746Z.

1108. For Secretary from Sisco. I will report separately on the previous one-hour talk with Foreign Minister Riad and two-hour talks with President Sadat and Prime Minister Fawzi.[2] This is a report on my subsequent two-hour meeting with Sadat alone.

1. It is apparent that you made a hit with Sadat.[3] He is full of praise for you. He was very grateful that you sent me here so promptly after your talks in Israel and that I gave him such a full report. For once we have received what the Israelis will do, he said, not what they will not do.

2. I gave him some of the byplay that we found and what we considered to be Dayan's positive role.[4] He said that he wants you to know that he "prays to God in hopes that Dayan will become Prime Minister some day." I can deal with him, a strong man like him, said Sadat. Throughout the five-hour talk they paid more attention to what Dayan's views are more than anybody else's.

3. As you might expect, he laid great stress in several different ways on two cardinal points: why he must have Egyptian troops across the Canal; and why he needs a commitment to the international border in the context of an overall political settlement. I handled these two hot potatoes with great care. I gave him no encouragement, however, saying candidly these were the two points which the other side laid the greatest stress on. Nevertheless, I said, we would objectively explore all possibilities as to elements of interim settlement, but I could not expect commitment to international border.

4. He offered an alternative proposal "on his own" for US alone which he said he wants the two of us to think about. His alternative is: a limited number of UAR troops crossing the Canal, with a specified limited amount and type of arms, with a wide 50 kilometer buffer zone be-

---

[1] Source: National Archives, Nixon Presidential Materials, NSC Files, Box 1162, Saunders Files, Middle East Negotiations Files, Middle East—Jarring Talks, May 1–9, 1971. Secret; Immediate; Nodis; Cedar Plus.

[2] Telegram 1107 from Cairo, May 9, contains Sisco's reports of his previous talks. (Ibid.)

[3] Rogers sent Sadat a note immediately after leaving Egypt in which he wrote: "I want to tell you how deeply I was impressed with what I heard and saw in your country, and in particular the enlightened leadership you are providing." (Telegram 2675 from Tel Aviv, May 7: ibid., Box 657. Country Files, Middle East, Middle East Nodis/Cedar/Plus Vol. II)

[4] See footnote 5, Document 230.

tween the two sides, with limited arms on the Israeli side of the new line. This has obvious difficulties, but I did not, of course, say anything more than that we would look at all possibilities. I felt it was more important psychologically to leave him with the impression that we were trying to be helpful to him directly rather than express strong doubts at this point. In connection with this proposal, I said in any area evacuated the Israelis had laid great stress on Egyptian-Israeli joint supervisory teams. Much to my surprise, he said this was not ruled out, provided the proposal allowed some crossing of Egyptian troops across the Canal and provided joint Egyptian-Israeli teams were under the supervision "of Jarring," which I later had him to clarify to mean as under the umbrella of the UN.

5. I once again told him that if our intelligence indicates that they are receiving more arms from the Soviets, this would become a matter of major importance in American public opinion, and that this would increase the pressure on us to provide additional arms to Israel. He said we should expect nothing new before May and June, but he did not go beyond this. In connection with the ideas on the Russians which you intend to convey to the President personally,[5] I just want to confirm to you that your interpretation of what he said is absolutely correct. He reiterated this to me in plain language.

6. He went into great detail regarding his internal situation which added some additional information to that which you conveyed to me as a result of your private conversation with him. As you said, he is going to the people, he is going to move politically in order to develop broad mass support for himself in Egypt, including new elections to the Arab Socialist Union from top to bottom since he says about 100 out of 150 are against him. He also says that General Fawzi and the military are very negative and did not favor his February proposal to Jarring and are against an interim settlement unless it provides for some movement of Egyptian troops across the Suez Canal. He was more critical of Foreign Minister Riad than any of his colleagues. I regret to report to you that he says Riad does not want to do anything to improve relations with the United States. He said it is not the case of Riad being anti-American, but rather that over the last twenty years, and particularly as a result of Riad's role in connection with the armistice arrangements, Riad feels himself to be vulnerable since he made some genuine attempts to work out matters in the past and he has been disappointed. For this reason Riad continues to be "hawkish" and oppose him on the interim settlement. Sadat confirmed to me what Bergus had already learned from Heykal in the last 24 hours: that Prime Minister Fawzi will be playing a much more active role in the field of foreign affairs.

---

[5] See Document 227.

"You know Fawzi, Joe," Sadat said, "and you know that he likes Americans, he is flexible, and wants to do something. We will need about two weeks to study the important report that you have given us here today and then I intend to send Fawzi to Washington to give you my answer." In the meantime, he pleaded that we try to do something more with the Israelis on the two cardinal points of concern.

7. In his campaign to develop broad support, he will meet tomorrow with the Arab Socialist Union in order to arrange for elections. He then will meet with the armed forces on Tuesday and Wednesday. He said he will announce all of this on Thursday.[6]

8. He reconfirms that once the interim settlement is achieved he will resume diplomatic relations with the United States immediately. He want you to tell President Nixon that he wants his help in those circumstances to rebuild his country. In his words, he wants room to breathe. He repeated his story in detail of the reasons, with which you are fully familiar, as to why he decided to sack Aly Sabry[7] before you arrived. He implied the same thing would happen to Riad or alternatively he might be kicked upstairs. In any event, he is going to rely on Prime Minister Fawzi primarily in foreign affairs.

9. He told me that inadvertently I had in one way been unhelpful to him. He said that several of the things that I had reported to Ghorbal in the past several weeks had come through the Foreign Office filter and reached him in a distorted fashion. He said if there is anything that we want to get to him, and in a straight way, that we should begin to tell Ghorbal less and have Bergus relay it to Heykal for Sadat. I said we would do this. Sadat, at his initiative, even after five hours of talks today, is sending Heykal to see me tonight. I will report anything new that comes from this meeting.

10. I asked him once again to take a unilateral step and free the few Israeli POW's as a signal. He said he would consider it, but was noncommittal.

11. I did not take up Eban's suggestion re their technical people getting together because of the later Israeli overruling of him on this score.

---

[6] May 13.

[7] According to telegram 990 from Cairo, May 3, which reported on Sadat's "delicate domestic situation," Cairo was "awash with stories about bitter arguments" between Sadat and Ali Sabri, the Egyptian Vice President. Bergus further commented: "Taken as a whole, this is a victory for the 'good guys' in Egypt. It will, however increase Sadat's need for some kind of tangible movement towards peaceful settlement. Basic issue in Sadat's quarrel with Sabri was not federation [with Syria and Libya] but Sabri's accusation that Sadat was being diddled by the Americans. At same time, with Sadat's greater dependence on military support, his flexibility regarding interim settlement on Suez Canal will be impaired." (National Archives, Nixon Presidential Materials, NSC Files, Box 637, Country Files. Middle East, UAR, Vol. VI)

12. There has been no criticism here from any quarter or level as to your trip over international waters to see the Gulf and Sharm el Sheik.

Bergus

232. Conversation Among President Nixon, the President's Assistant for Domestic Affairs (Ehrlichman), and the President's Assistant (Haldeman)[1]

Washington, May 10, 1971, 5:25–6:15 p.m.

Nixon: As long as we've got this problem with the Rogers-Kissinger thing, that—and I've said this before—you've got to allow me to see Rogers alone, particularly—and, in particular, when he reports on the Mideast problem. And, because I didn't, I didn't realize that—I thought I was seeing him alone and say that it's my own schedule [unclear]. In case if Henry came bouncing in, well, we'll have to pretend that it's—I mean, don't, don't raise it with him, now.

Haldeman: I won't raise it with Henry.

[unclear exchange]

Nixon: Yeah, but he—but, but with—when I see Rogers, I just know that I could get a hell of a lot more done without Henry being there. And there's no problem not being there—

Haldeman: Yeah.

Nixon: It's no use to having the two sitting there. You know, they both irritate each other. And, so—and, particularly, the Mideast, Bob [unclear] 'cause Henry's wrong on the Mideast. I mean, he just happens to be wrong. He wants to sit tight and do nothing 'cause of the elections in '72, now. [laughs] Well, we ain't going to do it.

[Omitted here is discussion unrelated to the Middle East.]

Nixon: But I don't want, in case Henry raises the Rogers-Mideast thing, for you to give him any comfort on that. I just don't want you to do it, because the—

---

[1] Source: National Archives, Nixon Presidential Materials, White House Tapes, Oval Office, Conversation No. 496–16. No classification marking. The editors transcribed the portions of the tape recording printed here specifically for this volume. Brackets indicate unclear portions of the recording or those omitted by the editors, except "[laughs]", "[Joseph]", "[million dollar]", and "[Admiral]", added for clarity.

Haldeman: Well, I was planning, pretty much, to sweetheart Henry tonight—

Nixon: Yeah.

Haldeman: —and say that our own—

Nixon: Yeah—

Haldeman: —general stuff that—

Nixon: Well, the, the main thing is that on, on that, is that we, we simply cannot—I mean, Rogers is now working on the Mideast thing. Somebody has to work on it. We cannot just continue to go down the line with the Jews on that, and have no other friends in the world. Now, that's just the cold turkey about it. And, the—so, it's a curious thing, at the present, present time, in the whole world. The United States, at the present time, is the only country that is supporting Israel. There ain't nobody else, now. None. None. Their vote in the UN would be the United States only.

Haldeman: Hmm.

Nixon: Now, goddammit, we just can't continue that way. The Israelis are sitting there, right now, on this offer to open the Suez; just sitting tight, not doing a damn thing. We've got to pressure 'em, and we're going to. They—Bill said today they've denied it—they said that, well, that their real thing is that they all think we're coming up to an election again, and they can sit tight. And I said, "Never." I said, "They pulled that in '70," and I said, "Just forget it." And, now, I want Henry to hear it. Now, Henry's arguments will be that, well, he's worried about the fact that the, the Jewish editorial writers and columnists in this country will be—will be—if we're nice to Israel, will be nicer to us on Vietnam. Who? Maybe one: Joe Alsop. Who? The goddamn Jews are all against us. [Joseph Kraft—[2]

Haldeman: Well, what in the world difference does it make what the columnists do to us, or Democrats—

Nixon That's right.

Haldeman: —on Vietnam anyway. They just—

Nixon: It's working out.

Haldeman: Vietnam is, is—

Ehrlichman: Yeah.

Nixon: We're finished in Vietnam. It's gonna go. But, let me say that on Israel—

Haldeman: [unclear] and there it is—

Nixon: —on Israel, my feelings there just happen to be different. That's, then, very different from Henry's. It's the one thing he's blind

---

[2] Syndicated newspaper columnists Joseph Alsop and Joseph Kraft

on. Now, he doesn't—the Russian thing is brought in, and that's to ensure the Russian thing is in there. But, it's a much different game than that. He just—the United States just cannot continue to sit in there supporting Israel alone against 100 million Arabs, against the British, against the French. Forget the French, but the British, for example—the Italians. There isn't a goddamn government in Europe that supports us on this, on the Israeli thing. You know that? Not one! Now, why in the hell is that? And so, there, there must—we must be doing something wrong. And they're all doing it, because they think that Muskie's gone over to Israel, and Humphrey will be going to Israel, and Teddy Kennedy'll be going to Israel,[3] and everybody else, and I have to go along. Screw 'em. You know, Connally[4] says, "Sometimes, you've got to have an enemy." Well, maybe it'll be the Jews. And this is cold turkey, now. That's what—don't let it be raised. If it's raised, just say, "Well, I don't know anything about it." Don't let him—there's plenty of things wrong with Rogers. We know that. We know that he plays his own game. But, on the other hand, on this particular issue, if—he is squeezing the Israelis because I want him to. You know? Do you understand, John? You see, that's—he's doing it because I want it done.

Ehrlichman: Right.

Nixon: I'm just not—I, I will not—I don't buy Henry's idea of, of just taking the Jewish line. I just don't buy it, and we've, we've, we've gone too far, I mean, on everything. They're out knocking, because they want $500 million more of economic assistance—the Jews do. And they want, they want about another hundred [million dollar] advance. [unclear] They expect us to give 'em that and not do a goddamn thing about opening Suez or anything else. They're not going to get it.

Ehrlichman: Hmm.

Nixon: Now this is it. This is it. And so, another thing, another reason you've got to keep Henry out of it, is that when he gets involved in Israel, he is totally irrational about anything else. We've just got to keep him—keep his mind on, on Vietnam, Soviet-American relations, and China. And it's really for his own benefit. And so, I just—I know that, in here, we don't usually get into that. But, there's plenty of things that—I don't mind discussing his relation with Rogers in other ways, because Rogers is involved in many other places. And the State Department is not to be trusted, and I don't trust them. But, on this one, we—we've just got to realize that Henry is not the fellow that can call the turn. I mean, if, if he would only realize it, we'd be a hell of a lot better

---

[3] Senators Edmund S. Muskie (D–ME), Hubert H. Humphrey (D–MN), and Edward M. Kennedy (D–MA).

[4] Secretary of the Treasury John Connally.

off. That's, that's the way it is. Do you want to weigh in? Do you have any difference on it?

Haldeman: No. I haven't talked to Henry at all, so it's—

Nixon: Well, I don't know what he'll have to say.

Haldeman: I don't know what his—

Nixon: Rogers, as a matter of fact, got—

[unclear exchange]

Nixon: —got quite a—as we would expect, he got a very good reception over there. They're all after [unclear]. They want our support. [unclear] We got that Sino-Soviet thing [unclear]. Otherwise [unclear].

Haldeman: He raise that at all?

Nixon: No.

Haldeman: 'Cause, he, he knew—

Nixon: No.

Haldeman: —when I talked to him about it, then.

Nixon: No, that—

[unclear exchange]

Nixon: It's—

Haldeman: —fully aware of what he had done.

Nixon: It's just too damn bad that, too damn bad that you have, have a situation there with Rogers. I mean, he is—we need at the State Department a Secretary of State that will, will, frankly, be Secretary of State like Connally is Secretary of the Treasury. In other words, tries to do what we want, and tries to play it [unclear]. Rogers isn't that way. On other hand, I—I, I separate out this issue, because I know Henry's wrong on it. He takes the Javits[5] line, and all the rest. He'll say he doesn't, but if [unclear] what do you think the Israelis ought to do? I mean, he won't say another goddamn thing but what Mrs. Meir says. Nothing! Nothing. They—it's a strange thing. It's a—but, I think if we—if any one of us were Jewish, we'd do exactly the same thing. I never found a Jew that was rational about Israel—never one. [Admiral] Lewis Strauss? Half-way, half-way. But, put yourself in their position. And I understand it, I mean. But just—but, on the other hand, we are just damned fools. That's why Johnson's appointment of Goldberg to the UN was a terrible, terrible blunder. Send Goldberg up to negotiate with the Jews and the Arabs at the UN? I mean, geez, he's—he cannot— no Jew can see the Israeli problem, except—just as no Irish, no Irishman can see the Northern Ireland problem. You don't put him in charge of that, do you?

---

[5] Senator Jacob K. Javits (D–NY).

233. Memorandum From President Nixon to Secretary of State Rogers[1]

Washington, May 26, 1971.

Following up on our discussion a few days ago on the Mideast[2] I would like to pass on to you a few observations on our policy in that area which reflect not only my views as to the current situation but also cover some episodes of the past.

I have always supported the State of Israel, as a Congressman, Senator, as Vice President, during the years I was out of office, and as President. My support, however, has in no way been influenced by the Jewish political lobby in the United States. On the contrary, I have made it clear time and time and again to friends in the Jewish community that under no circumstances would I take a position on aid to Israel which I felt would be in conflict with the national security interests of the United States.

I think as a result of the enormous influence of the Jewish lobby in the United States—not only through its financial contributions to Congressmen and Senators but even more because of its enormous influence through the media—we have often subordinated U.S. security interests to the interests of Israel.

There was one glaring exception for which we have to take responsibility in the Eisenhower Administration. In 1956, just before the election, we took a position against the Israelis, British and French which brought an end to that comic opera war.[3] Clearly apart from what effect this action may have had on the nations in the Mideast it had a devastating effect on the British and French. From that time on, they ceased to be major powers in the world and have simply lost their stomach for playing a major role in world affairs. This was a glaring error and at sometime in the future I will have to admit publicly that the little part

---

[1] Source: National Archives, RG 59, Office Files of William Rogers, Entry 5439, Lot 73D443, Box 25, WPR-President Nixon. Top Secret; Eyes Only. Haldeman referred to this memorandum in his diary when recording a conversation that he had with Kissinger on June 1. He wrote: "What really is bothering him [Kissinger] is he thinks Rogers is engaged in secret negotiations, that the P[resident] knows about it and isn't telling Henry. So he asked me to ask the P what he sent to Rogers last week via military aide, which the P mentioned to Rogers on the phone while both Henry and I were in there, and also the direct question: is Rogers conducting a secret negotiation that K[issinger] doesn't know about. Henry says if he is, then he, Henry, will have to quit, that he can't tolerate something of that sort." (*Haldeman Diaries: Multimedia Edition*, June 1, 1971)

[2] Rogers and Nixon discussed the Middle East during a meeting in the Oval Office on May 19 from 9:05 to 10:14 a.m. For a transcript of the portions of the conversation relating to the Middle East, see Document 227.

[3] Nixon was Vice President at the time of the invasion of the Suez Canal Zone.

that I played in supporting it during the campaign was a mistake, (although, of course, as you know, I had no other choice running as a candidate for Vice President with no policy responsibilities.)

On the other side of the coin, the Aswan Dam decision by Dulles[4] was a mistake. Here again, in a moment of pique, he infuriated Nasser and to a certain extent may have contributed to the tragic events of 1956.

Except for the 1956 incident, however, United States' policy has gone overboard in support of the State of Israel against their neighbors. Some of those decisions perhaps have been justified on humanitarian grounds. After all, the Jews were horribly persecuted during World War II and it was the responsibility of all decent people to go an extra mile to rectify that blot on the conscience of mankind. But speaking in humanitarian terms we have almost totally closed our eyes to the terrible condition of Arab refugees. When I was on a brief African trip in 1957 I stepped into this problem without knowing what a sensitive nerve I would be hitting. I did not visit Israel or Egypt on that occasion, but I reported when I returned that leaders in Morocco and Tunisia, the most pro-Western of the Arab countries, had expressed concern about the plight of the refugees. The whole Jewish community in this country jumped down my throat and probably have never forgiven me for mentioning the issue.

These historical references will put my present policy into perspective. It can be summarized quite bluntly as follows:

1. The interests of the United States must be our only consideration in the policy decisions we make with regard to the Mideast.

2. Under absolutely no circumstances are political considerations in this country to affect any decisions I make. I say this not for what many think is the very obvious reason that I get at most 8 to 10 percent of the Jewish votes, but because the stakes for this Nation's peace in the future are too great for us to make decisions abroad based on the political power of a small but very powerful and influential minority at home.

3. There are times when the national security interests of the United States will be served by siding with Israel. For example, where the Soviet Union is obviously siding with Israel's neighbors it serves our interest to see that Israel is able to not only defend itself but to deter further Soviet encroachments in the area. This is what has influenced me in coming down hard on the side of Israel in maintaining the bal-

---

[4] Reference is to Secretary of State John Foster Dulles's decision, in response to Egypt's approach to the Soviet Union, to tell Egypt's Foreign Minister in July 1956 that the United States would no longer fund the Aswan Dam project, prompting Nasser to nationalize the Canal at the end of the month.

ance of power in the area at a time when Soviet influence in Egypt and other countries surrounding Israel has been particularly strong.

4. On the other hand, where on analysis the question becomes primarily one of the interests of Israel and the interest of Israel's neighbors, Egypt, Jordan et al, then we should have a totally even-handed policy. As a matter of fact, the interest of the United States will be served in this case by tilting the policy, if it is to be tilted at all, on the side of 100 million Arabs rather than on the side of two million Israelis. However, I believe that an even-handed policy is, on balance, the best one for us to pursue as far as our own interests are concerned.

5. It is quite apparent that the Israeli leaders have diddled us along through the 1970 election and now are planning to follow the same tactics through the 1972 elections. The statement in the memorandum from the Quaker group that they were just waiting until after '72 when they got a Democratic Administration is a very good indication of what their deepest feelings are. They will be expected to continue to say that they consider RN to be their best friend, that he is a great supporter of Israel, and we will have many well-intentioned Republican supporters in the Jewish community, like Max Fisher,[5] who will be coming in and telling us that we're going to get 35 to 40 percent of the Jewish vote because of the confidence Israeli leaders in their *private* conversations have indicated in RN. This, of course, is all hogwash. They know that I will put the interest of the United States first and they want somebody in the Presidency who will put the interest of Israel first.

6. Under these circumstances, it is essential that no more aid programs for Israel be approved until they agree to some kind of interim action on Suez or some other issue. I shall be interested in what recommendations you have in this respect. It is vitally important that we all recognize that time is of the essence. In the month of June or July at the latest the Israeli leaders must bite the bullet as to whether they want more U.S. aid at the price of being reasonable on an interim agreement or whether they want to go it alone.

7. You should put this proposition to them very hard in your conversations. They will, of course, immediately assume that they can come to me and get me to override you because of the political considerations that will be coming up in 1972. They are already working very hard on John Mitchell in this respect. This memorandum is your assurance that while on the merits I might reach a different conclusion on a recommendation that comes from State on this problem I will never be influenced one iota by political considerations.

---

[5] An oil and real estate magnate who advised Republican Presidents on the Middle East and Jewish issues.

In sum, I am convinced that unless we get some kind of a settlement now with the Israelis on the Suez or some other issue, we aren't going to get any kind of settlement until after the '72 elections. By that time, even though the Israelis don't think this can happen, the Soviet will have had no other choice but to build up the armed strength of Israel's neighbors to the point that another Mideast war will be inevitable. As far as Sadat is concerned, he obviously does not want to have a Soviet presence in Egypt. On the other hand, if his policy of conciliation fails, he will either have to go along with a new program of accepting Soviet aid or lose his head, either politically or physically.

I do not want you to report to me on the day-to-day negotiations you undertake. Just keep me posted when a major decision has to be made. You can also have in mind that by my being somewhat detached from the negotiating procedure you will have me in a position where when the time is ripe I may be able to be the "persuader" in getting Israel to accept what is a reasonable settlement and one which is in the interest of the United States.

Good luck!

234. Telegram From the Department of State to the Interests Section in Egypt[1]

Washington, May 27, 1971, 0038Z.

92945. For Bergus. Ref: Cairo 1245.[2]

1. Sadat's idea of your personally delivering message from him to President and Secretary[3] poses something of a dilemma. On one hand,

---

[1] Source: National Archives, Nixon Presidential Materials, NSC Files, Box 1163, Saunders Files, Middle East Negotiations Files, Middle East—Jarring Talks, May 19–31, 1971. Secret; Priority; Nodis; Cedar Plus. Drafted by Sisco, Sterner, and Atherton; cleared by Kissinger; and approved by Rogers. Repeated to Tel Aviv.

[2] In telegram 1245 from Cairo, May 22, Bergus reported that in his 45-minute meeting with Heikal "quite a lot" had happened since he had met with him on the previous day, particularly that Sadat and Riad had had "some kind of session" in which Mahmoud Riad had "sworn fealty" to Sadat's "partial settlement policy.'" Bergus also believed that, based on Heikal's remarks, the Soviet Union was "putting heavy pressure on Egyptians to get interim settlement out of exclusive American context." At the end of their conversation, Heikal assured him that Sadat was "still very interested" in the interim settlement. (Ibid.)

[3] Heikal conveyed this idea to Bergus on May 23 at 8 p.m. (Telegram 1246 from Cairo, May 24; ibid.)

we do not want to appear to rebuff Sadat and want to make clear we always look forward to receiving any personal message he wishes to send. Our judgment, on which we would appreciate your comment, is that Sadat is playing for time and of course we should do what we can to help in this regard. He may have concluded that for the time being at least, he is too exposed to carry out promptly his undertaking to send Fawzi with his reply to the specific points conveyed to him by Sisco on behalf of the Israelis.

On other hand, we have asked ourselves what sort of a message is Sadat apt to send. On basis Riad's May 20 approach,[4] our estimate is that he will: (A) Reiterate his continuing interest in an interim Suez Canal agreement; (B) stress the three key points of the UAR position, namely, Egyptian troops across the Canal, a commitment of total Israeli withdrawal to the international border, and a limited ceasefire. Unless there is some flexibility on these points, more in the spirit of how Sadat expressed himself rather than Riad, their reiteration can only tend to lock Sadat in, and it unlikely that any response on our part would be helpful in moving on toward an interim Suez Canal agreement. Having you carry such a message and seeing the President would tend to polarize positions rather than maintain the kind of constructive ambiguity which is important at this stage and which in our judgment continues to offer some hope for reconciliation based on picking up certain tentative exploratory thoughts expressed both in Cairo and in Tel Aviv.

2. Our thinking on how to proceed is that we should neither react directly to Riad démarche of May 20, which would only lead to fruitless and argumentative debates, nor convey it in precise terms to Israelis which would strengthen their inclination to stand pat for now. Rather, we believe time has come for us to develop Quote common denominator Unquote proposal that seeks to bridge gap between Egyptian and Israeli positions on key issues and seek to move Israelis and Egyptians toward middle ground. To begin this process, we will need further early consultations with Israelis and meanwhile need to find ways to keep dialogue going with Egyptians which will not lock them further into positions on which there must clearly be some give if there is to be an interim Canal agreement. If our estimate is correct that Sadat is seeking to delay sending Fawzi to Washington at this time, we should

---

[4] Bergus met with Foreign Minister Riad for an hour on May 20. In his abbreviated report on their conversation, he wrote that the position paper the Foreign Minister tried to hand him—and his subsequent remarks—"practically slam the door on further discussion of interim agreement on the Suez Canal." Riad said that the Egyptian Government insisted on three conditions to which Israel had to agree to continue a dialog on the issue: "A) firm linkage between interim settlement and final settlement; B) Israeli withdrawal east of the passes; C) six months' ceasefire during which Jarring will draw up timetable." (Telegram 1230 from Cairo, May 20; ibid.) A detailed account of their meeting is in telegram 1231 from Cairo, May 20. (Ibid.)

also find way to help him in this regard, which could take pressure off his idea of sending you back with message.

3. In light foregoing, you should convey following to Haikal:

A. We can understand that, in view developments since Sisco-Sadat meeting May 9,[5] Sadat may feel time not propitious to send Fawzi here, and President Sadat need feel no concern that we will misinterpret delay.

B. President and Secretary look forward to receiving messages from Sadat at any time in interest of furthering objectives we both seek. They would prefer you not absent yourself from Cairo at this delicate time in efforts work out interim Canal agreement, when your presence on the spot is of great value to us. Furthermore, such trip by you would inevitably be publicized and could lead to unhelpful speculation. We think it better for now to keep discussions in quiet diplomatic channels and therefore want to defer for now decision on your return.

C. Sadat can be assured, however, that any message he may send will get immediate attention of Secretary and President, and that you can use special channels to assure it is fully protected.

D. It would be helpful to have further, concrete Egyptian comments on possible ways of taking into account in any interim settlement following three ideas which Sisco conveyed May 9 and which Riad's comments May 20 did not address. In raising these questions, it important that you prepare ground carefully so that UAR responses not take on rigidity of FonMin Riad's presentation. We want door to remain open on these points and would prefer no concrete response from UAR rather than repetition of FonMin Riad's unhelpful and dogmatic approach

(1) Need to make clear that Canal will not only be cleared but also opened and operated for international navigation, including Israel's once clearance is completed.

(2) Need to express ceasefire in way which avoids explicit deadlines and thus makes possible greater degree of withdrawal.

(3) Need to relate interim agreement to final settlement in way which does not prejudge either side's position on terms of final settlement while at same time assuring that interim arrangements are in fact transitional and temporary leading to full implementation of Security Council Resolution 242.

4. We recognize, of course, that Sadat message may be more substantive than we anticipate in para 1 above and could, for example, deal with such issues as his relations with Soviets or diplomatic relations

---

[5] See Document 231.

with us. We do not want to close door on Sadat's idea of sending message with you, but would want to have some advance idea of its nature before reaching final decision and would also hope in such circumstances its delivery could be handled in way (e.g., in connection your return on leave) which avoided dramatic publicity and risk of awakening undue expectations or speculation that could disrupt rather than help current negotiating process we are seeking to carry forward on interim Canal agreement.

Rogers

235. Editorial Note

On May 27, 1971, after 3 days of secret negotiations, Egypt and the Soviet Union signed a 15-year Treaty of Friendship and Cooperation. Under the terms of the treaty, the two sides agreed to hold regular consultations or in the event of an imminent threat to peace to "immediately contact one another in the interests of removing the threat that has developed or restoring the peace." (*Current Digest of the Soviet Press*, Volume XXIII, No. 21 (June 22, 1971), pages 2–4) Before Secretary of State Rogers could report to President Nixon, Assistant Secretary of State for Near Eastern and South Asian Affairs Joseph Sisco called Assistant to the President for National Security Affairs Henry Kissinger at 11:10 a.m. on May 28 to provide his preliminary analysis of the treaty:

"S: The first part's obviously legal [omission in transcript] around arrangements which are very political and psychologically true in the area. It assures long-range support—political, economic and military over next 15 years. Undoubtedly Soviet initiated due to the internal events in Egypt and to keep them from making overtures to the U.S. I think it will cause waves in other countries in which they hope the influence without treaty will be increased.

"K: What do you mean?

"S: In countries like Lebanon, Saudi Arabia, etc. they may make overtures to the United States if they do not have a treaty with the Soviet Union.

"K: Loosen their ties.

"S: Yes. These are countries which are on our side of the fence anyway. Now where this leaves Sadat. Gives pledge that they will not be involved in the internal affairs and any ex post facto changes made by Sadat are OK with the Russians. There is a firm commitment to consultation with the Egyptian Government. There is an overall packet on consultation. From Sadat's point of view it eases his pressure on the military. The military is dependent on the Soviets and if he has an agreement with the Soviets that solves the army question. This will leave Sadat with as much or as little influence as he had before."

After assessing the impact on Israel, Sisco commented on the implications of the treaty for Moscow: "We will see not so much change on substance—just manifest procedurally because Russians want to be in if there is any settlement. The Russians are saying to us that nothing will happen unless we get in." The two men then briefly discussed the element of surprise in Soviet diplomacy:

"S: This thing looks like it is a Soviet draft. It has been concocted in a hurry.

"K: It seems to have been happening often lately.

"S: We had no advance warning that this was coming. It could be we have lousy intelligence or—

"K: It couldn't be true!!

"S: Or the Russians drafted it and we knew nothing about it. There is no such treaty in existence in other places. In quick capsule form this is a political move to protect their major commitment in that area and they are putting the rest of the world on notice that they plan to be there for a good long time to come." (National Archives, Nixon Presidential Materials, NSC Files, Henry Kissinger Telephone Conversation Transcripts, Box 10, Chronological File)

Later that day, Nixon telephoned Secretary of State Rogers to get his assessment of the treaty. Rogers explained that the Soviets were trying to "make it appear that they have not lost their position with Egypt. And this is the only way they can think of to do it. They don't want to discontinue any support—they don't want to threaten anything because that would really make Sadat mad as hell. So what they are doing is trying to figure out other ways to make it appear that there has been no change in their relationship." As far as Sadat was concerned, Rogers told Nixon that "he's trying to play both ends against the middle. And this is the way to do it. It didn't say a hell of a lot that they didn't have informal treaties; they've got several treaties now. So this is just window dressing, I'm quite convinced of that." (Ibid., White House Tapes, White House Telephone, Conversation No. 3–166)

Rogers forwarded further analysis that afternoon in a memorandum for the President drafted by Sisco. On May 31, Kissinger summarized for Nixon the main points not only of Rogers's memorandum but also of the treaty itself. Kissinger, however, offered an alternative analysis in his memorandum: "The Egyptian army is dependent on Soviet support. In turn, Sadat is at the moment dependent on his military for his base of power, having purged the party and the bureaucracy. Rather than strengthening Sadat's flexibility with respect to negotiating the Canal settlement, the treaty could give the Soviet Union a veto over the future negotiations. Thus, whatever the outcome of the negotiations—and after all the Soviets are the chief beneficiaries of a Suez settlement—recent events may have enhanced Soviet long-term influence. Certainly the Soviets are committed to engage themselves as never before in case of resumption of hostilities." The President noted this passage and wrote the following instructions in the margin: "K—We must not allow this to be a pretext for escalation of arms to Israel. We should act only in response to incontrovertible evidence of a Soviet military aid which we evaluate as *significantly* changing the balance of power." (Ibid., NSC Files, Box 657, Country Files, Middle East, Nodis/Cedar/Plus, Vol. II (2 of 3))

Egyptian President Sadat, meanwhile, sought to reassure the United States about the Soviet role in his country's affairs. On the morning of May 29, Heikal conveyed this oral message from Sadat: "A. President Sadat still considers himself committed to the spirit and letter of what he said to Secretary Rogers during their recent meeting. B. President Sadat's initiative for an interim arrangement remains valid. C. President Sadat continues to welcome the efforts of the United States in assisting the parties in the effort to reach agreement on an interim arrangement. D. The UAR–USSR treaty places no restrictions whatsoever on the US–UAR dialog." Regarding the treaty between Egypt and the Soviet Union, Heikal said that he hoped the United States would not exaggerate its importance and "should not be hesitant" to ask any specific questions as to the "meaning or implications" of the treaty. (Telegram 1311 from Cairo, May 29; ibid., Box 1163, Saunders Files, Middle East Negotiations Files, Middle East—Jarring Talks, May 19–31, 1971)

When Bergus met with Sadat the next day, the Egyptian President was "most anxious" that the Ambassador "personally deliver" his message to Nixon and Rogers. Sadat declared that he needed "this indication that his lines to the United States remain open" and that there was "some hope" for an interim settlement as he proceeded to "reform the Arab Socialist Union and rebuild his internal position." (Telegram 1318 from Cairo, May 30; ibid.) In a June 3 memorandum, Kissinger briefed Nixon on the main points of Sadat's message. According to Kissinger, Sadat told Bergus that the Soviet-Egyptian treaty was "nothing new; it merely set forth the shape of the existing relationship." Kissinger also reported that Sadat promised that Soviet military personnel would leave Egypt "as soon as the first phase agreement (presumably Canal settlement) was reached." After reading the memorandum, Nixon approved the Department's instructions for Bergus to deliver Sadat's message to Rogers in Lisbon (where he was attending a NATO Ministerial meeting) but to warn the Egyptians beforehand that any publicity "would be interpreted by the American public as a Soviet effort" to pressure the United States. (Ibid., Box 657, Country Files, Middle East, Nodis/Cedar/Plus, Vol. II (2 of 3))

236. Letter From President Nixon to King Hussein of Jordan[1]

Washington, June 2, 1971.

Your Majesty:

I was pleased to hear from Secretary Rogers about the warm welcome he received in Jordan and about the usefulness of his visit there and in other countries in that part of the world.[2] His assessment of the results of his trip is encouraging and we are hopeful that progress will be made in the months ahead. You can be sure that we will have Jordanian concerns very much in mind as we do our part to help achieve that goal.

As to our efforts to help achieve a peaceful settlement, we are proceeding on the basis of the policy announced by the Secretary of State on December 9, 1969[3] and my own report to the Congress on February 25 of this year.[4] I know that you have had a full report of where matters stand with respect to current discussions looking towards an interim Suez Canal agreement.[5] Secretary Rogers has reported to me your view, with which we agree, that any interim settlement not become a substitute for a final comprehensive agreement. He has also reported to me fully your concern over developments in Jerusalem.[6] I understand that you have been getting reports on Secretary Rogers' and Assistant

---

[1] Source: National Archives, Nixon Presidential Materials, NSC Files, Box 797, Presidential Correspondence 1969–1974, Jordan—King Hussein. No classification marking.

[2] See footnote 4, Document 230.

[3] See Document 73.

[4] See footnote 6, Document 211.

[5] Sisco briefed Rifai on May 18 and then briefed Sharaf the following day. (Telegram 87901 to Amman, May 20; National Archives, Nixon Presidential Materials, NSC Files, Box 616, Country Files, Middle East, Jordan, Vol. VII; and telegram 88358 to Amman, May 20; ibid., Box 1163, Saunders Files, Middle East Negotiations Files, Middle East—Jarring Talks, May 10–18, 1971)

[6] Rogers first reported Hussein's concerns about Jerusalem in telegram 3692 from Beirut, May 4, which Haig forwarded to the President on May 5; see footnote 4, Document 230.

Secretary Sisco's conversations with the Israelis on this matter,[7] and I believe it is important that we continue to exchange views in light of on-going efforts to achieve an overall settlement of the dispute.

With regard to your letter of May 1,[8] I understand that the subject of increasing and expediting financial assistance to Jordan was discussed in your conversation with Secretary Rogers and that he explained our difficulties in making available sooner the $15 million in supporting assistance which we propose for disposition in July. As you know, on the assumption that it will be needed, I have proposed that an additional sum of $15 million in supporting assistance be made available to Jordan at a later date this calendar year.

I share your concern with the continued non-resumption of the Kuwaiti subsidy. We are prepared to follow up further efforts that you make to bring about a renewal of this subsidy and we hope that this matter can be resolved at an early date.

Please accept my assurance that my Government will continue to view Jordan's needs most sympathetically. We will continue to do our very best to be as forthcoming as possible in providing necessary assistance.[9]

With best personal regards,
Sincerely,

Richard Nixon

---

[7] In their May 18 meeting with Rabin, Rogers and Sisco made it clear that they "tended to agree" with the Jordanian view of "de facto steps being taken in Jerusalem by Israel which in their judgment prejudiced overall settlement." (Telegram 87261 to Tel Aviv, May 19; National Archives, Nixon Presidential Materials, NSC Files, Box 1163, Saunders Files, Middle East Negotiations Files, Middle East—Jarring Talks, May 10–18, 1971)

[8] In his letter, Hussein thanked Nixon for arranging the $30 million in assistance funds for Jordan. The King worried, however, that, since Kuwait's subsidy to Jordan looked "increasingly unlikely to be resumed," the $30 million promised by the United States would no longer be enough to cover Jordan's budget deficit of that same amount. Thus, Hussein asked that the second half of the $30 million not be made "contingent upon any conditions in the future," but rather that Jordan be given a "firm commitment" on the second installment. (Telegram 2122 from Amman, May 1; ibid., RG 59, Central Files 1970–73, ORG 7 S AID (US) JORDAN)

[9] Brown delivered the President's message to Hussein on June 5 at noon, but their conversation revolved around Israeli settlements in Jerusalem and whether to take the issue to the UN Security Council. (Telegram 2662 from Amman, June 5; ibid., Nixon Presidential Materials, NSC Files, Box 1163, Saunders Files, Middle East Negotiations Files, Middle East—Jarring Talks, June 1–18, 1971)

237. Telegram From the Department of State to the Interests Section in Egypt[1]

Washington, June 3, 1971, 2308Z.

98100. Tosec 77. For Bergus.

1. We appreciate having received your full report of your conversation with Sadat.[2] It closely parallels what Sadat told to the Secretary[3] and subsequently to Sisco[4] both as to Sadat's continuing interest in an interim Suez Canal agreement as well as the substance of such an agreement. It tends to confirm our judgment that both sides continue to remain interested in an Canal agreement and both continue to look to us to pursue further its role of quiet constructive diplomacy.

2. We are still some way from agreement, however, since there are a number of fundamental points which may or may not prove reconcilable. In view current situation as indicated above, and your confirmation that Sadat is likely to play any visit by you to Washington as an appeal to us to put the squeeze on Israel, we feel that we should not fall in with this strategy. A trip by you to Washington to make a direct report to the President is therefore in our judgment premature. At the same time, we also feel it is in our interest not to rebuff Sadat's reaffirmation of his desire to maintain and demonstrate continuance of US–UAR dialogue, to have the US continue to play its quiet diplomatic role in helping achieve an interim Suez Canal agreement over the coming months, all of this regardless of the recently concluded treaty of friendship between the USSR and the UAR.[5]

3. We request therefore that you see Heykal immediately and make the following points:

---

[1] Source: National Archives, Nixon Presidential Materials, NSC Files, Box 1163, Saunders Files, Middle East Negotiations Files, Middle East—Jarring Talks, June 1–18, 1971. Secret; Flash; Nodis; Cedar Plus. Drafted by Sisco; cleared by Rogers (in substance) and Saunders; and approved by Sisco. Repeated Flash to Lisbon for Secretary Rogers, who was there June 3–4 attending a NATO Ministerial meeting.

[2] Bergus met with Sadat on the evening of May 30 and reported that the "main thing" that the Egyptian President wanted to tell him was that "the issue of war or peace in the Middle East was in the hands of the United States." Sadat offered some specific ideas for an interim settlement with Israel, which included Egypt's occupation, administration, and control of the Sinai "up to a line east of the three passes" and a 50-kilometer "no-man's land" between Egyptian and Israeli forces that would be controlled by troops of the United Nations or the Four Powers. He concluded by urging Bergus to convey personally the "letter and spirit" of the meeting to Nixon and Rogers. (Telegram 1321 from Cairo, June 1; ibid.)

[3] See Document 227.

[4] See Document 231.

[5] See Document 235.

A. We continue to feel that the original plan of sending Fawzi to Washington to convey specific UAR reaction to detailed points we carried to Cairo from Israel[6] is the most effective way to continue US–UAR dialogue and offers the best hope and opportunity for further progress. We would be prepared to wait to receive him at some appropriate later time. (Or alternatively, Secretary Rogers would be prepared to receive any UAR emissary in next few days in Lisbon.)

B. If indications are, as we expect, that above not immediately feasible and that Sadat attaches great importance to a demonstration that he is keeping open his lines of communication with us, you are authorized to indicate that you would be prepared to carry any message which President Sadat may wish to convey by going immediately to see Secretary Rogers in Lisbon.[7] You can inform Heykal that Secretary Rogers wishes to assure President Sadat that any message from him will receive prompt and careful consideration by USG.

4. You should inform Heykal that it would be your intention to put out the following low-key announcement in Cairo: Quote I am leaving Cairo for a short period. I will be reporting to Secretary Rogers in Lisbon on current developments in UAR and on recent discussions that I have held with UAR officials. Unquote.

5. In this connection, you should stress to Heykal that we want President Sadat to know we feel strongly that the best way to proceed is to continue to keep discussions in quiet diplomatic channels. We therefore do not plan to publicize the fact that you will be carrying message from President Sadat and hope that UARG will not do so. We want to explain frankly why we think such publicity could complicate our efforts, particularly in the wake of a Soviet-UAR treaty.[8]

---

[6] The plan is discussed in Document 234.

[7] The Department of State requested that the White House sanction this approach, which Nixon approved on a June 3 memorandum from Kissinger. (National Archives, Nixon Presidential Materials, NSC Files, Box 657, Country Files, Middle East, Middle East Nodis/Cedar/Plus, Vol. II)

[8] Bergus met with Sadat and Mahmoud Riad on June 4 at 8:30 p.m. Sadat said: "What I need is to know the position of the USG. Is the US going to back Israeli occupation of Egypt? Will the US give Israel aid under the thesis of the 'balance of power?'" After declaring that he did "not accept the idea of the balance of power," Sadat said that he was "ready for peace" and handed Bergus a paper containing his ideas for achieving it. As the meeting concluded, Sadat reaffirmed the importance of Israel's withdrawal "from all repeat all Arab territories" being a part of any future discussion of a 6-month cease-fire extension. At the very end, Riad asked that Bergus tell Rogers that Egypt was "flexible," that it was "not putting everything in a corner." Bergus also told Sadat that he would meet with the Secretary on June 6 in Paris, where Rogers would be attending a meeting of the Organization for Economic Cooperation and Development. (Telegram 1364 from Cairo, June 4; ibid., Box 1163, Saunders Files, Middle East Negotiations Files, Middle East—Jarring Talks, June 1–18, 1971)

6. We accept President Sadat's assurance conveyed to you through Heykal that the treaty places no restrictions whatsoever on US–UAR dialogue. Sadat will have noted that we have kept our public comment on treaty to a minimum. The fact is, however, that the Soviets have been giving extensive publicity to treaty as a major new move which Qte goes beyond normal relations between two countries Unqte and Qte constitutes strong blow to plans of international imperialism Unqte. (Moscow—Arab language broadcast May 25). Emphasis and interpretation which Soviets are giving to treaty will make more difficult achievement of an interim agreement and will strengthen position of those who doubt Egyptian intentions. In saying this, we are not endorsing these views but simply stating what is a political fact of life.

7. In these circumstances, American public would interpret any publicity emanating from Cairo that Bergus was carrying a special message to President Nixon as an effort by Soviets through the UAR to bring pressure on USG. Such publicity therefore could make it more difficult for us to play a constructive role. Again we are not endorsing such an interpretation, we are merely stating a fact with which both of us must deal if our continuing dialogue is to be a useful means to make further progress on an interim settlement.

8. Bergus should be very careful not to indicate to Heykal or to press what his on-going plans will be after Lisbon. This will be decided by Secretary Rogers after your conversation with him in Lisbon. We would hope that Bergus would also be able to carry with him UAR point-by-point response to Israeli points since you indicate in your Cairo 1320[9] that Foreign Office is putting together paper which sets forth UAR position on an interim arrangement in what they consider to be a more positive manner than previously. You should not, however, wait for this if it is not ready.

9. We would suggest that Bergus plan on leaving Cairo on Friday, June 4, or Saturday, June 5, and be available to see Secretary in Lisbon.

Irwin

---

[9] Dated June 1. (Ibid., RG 59, Central Files 1970–73, POL 27–14 ARAB–ISR)

238. Telegram From the Interests Section in Egypt to the Department of State[1]

Cairo, June 10, 1971, 1300Z.

1422. From Wiley to Sisco. Ref: State 101690.[2]

1. When Mohammed Riad gave me copy of paper left with him by Bergus on May 23 (text sent septel),[3] he said he had some other points to raise with me concerning the paper. FonMin Riad wished to know whether we considered this document to be an official U.S. paper. Mohammed said that he had considered Bergus paper as personal and unofficial until Bergus had asked for reply to his paper through Heykal. In eyes of FonMin, by this action, Bergus converted his personal paper into official USG paper. Heykal then transmitted request to the Presidency and reply was prepared and given to Bergus. FonMin wanted USG to realize that the President's speech on May 20[4] and the

---

[1] Source: National Archives, Nixon Presidential Materials, NSC Files, Box 1163, Saunders Files, Middle East Negotiations Files, Middle East—Jarring Talks, June 1–18, 1971. Secret; Immediate; Nodis; Cedar Plus. All brackets are in the original except "[USG?]", added for clarity.

[2] In telegram 101690 to Cairo, June 9, Sisco wrote to Wiley: "In my conversation with Ghorbal yesterday he continually referred to a Qte Bergus paper. Unqte I have just spoken with Don Bergus since I have no knowledge of any such paper. He tells me that this is probably a paper emanating from the informal exchange between himself and Mohammad Riad at Mohammad's house May 23rd. In this conversation Don reports he made some suggestions about how certain points might be formulated in the UAR position. Don reports he had some typed ideas on yellow paper and left it with Mohammad Riad. He does not have a copy with him and therefore requests you to get a copy of what was left with Mohammad and transmit it immediately." (Ibid., Box 657, Country Files, Middle East, Middle East Nodis/Cedar/Plus, Vol. II)

[3] The paper outlined the elements of an interim agreement for Israeli withdrawal from the Sinai Peninsula. The most important provisions included: 1) specific lines behind which Israel would withdraw its forces (east of the passes); 2) a zone to be occupied and administered by UN-authorized observers; 3) a six-month cease-fire; and 4) a mandate for Egypt to clear, open, and operate the Suez Canal "for ships of all nations except for those nations claiming or actually exercising belligerency against the UAR." The entire paper is in telegram 1419 from Cairo, June 10. (Ibid.)

[4] On May 20, Sadat gave a speech before the Egyptian National Assembly ostensibly to announce that subversive elements within the government had been plotting a coup against him and to discuss what he wanted in the preparation of a new constitution for the country. In the address, he took the opportunity to raise the issue of his Suez Canal proposal, comment on Secretary Rogers's recent visit to the Middle East, and criticize Israel, saying: "If they want peace, we are for peace. As for the statements emanating from Israel, they make no difference whatever. These are the statements which Sisco conveyed. This is because Israel continues to be enticed by victory and Nazism. The Israelis continue to attempt to live past dreams and fantasies. All this does not concern me. What concerns me is that the United States should define its stand because we are now facing historical stands that must be fully defined, it being a matter of war or peace." (FBIS 26, May 20; ibid., Box 1163, Saunders Files, Middle East Negotiations Files, Middle East—Jarring Talks, May 19–31, 1971)

communication handed to Bergus on May 20[5] were the official statements of the UAR position. If paper left by Bergus with Riad on May 23 was not an official U.S. paper, there would have been no need for additional reply from President. If USG still considers Bergus paper as personal and unofficial, UAR would have to reconsider its reply.

2. Wiley asked why President's latest paper could not have been in response to informal discussions between Bergus and UAR officials. Mohammed said that this was hypothetical question since Bergus had, in fact, left written document and asked for reply through Heykal. He did not know what the President would have done under such hypothetical circumstances. It quite possible that President would have seen no reason to add to his May 20 statements in absence of official USG paper.

3. Mohammed also said that FonMin had been disturbed over the publicity emanating from Paris after Bergus had met with Secretary. UAR Foreign Ministry had understood that USG wished to conduct quiet diplomacy and had been surprised to note news accounts stating that Bergus had carried message to Rogers.[6] FonMin was particularly disturbed over characterization of message as less rigid than previous UAR position. Mohammed then said that Sulzberger article appearing in *International Herald-Tribune* June 2[7] was obviously based on inside information and he was certain that the UAR had not given such information to any journalist.

4. Mohammed also said that FonMin had been disturbed to find out that Rogers had discussed details of the paper with French FonMin. As a result, GUAR had given paper to French, British, and Soviet Ambassadors in Cairo. Until they learned that Secretary had discussed subject with French FonMin, GUAR had told no one about its position.

5. *Comment*: Above comments were no doubt based partly on pique felt by FonMin over extent to which Heykal has encroached on his official role. At same time, believe FonMin understands that using [USG?] must follow Sadat's instructions on delicate matter of channels. FonMin no doubt feels he also has some legitimate grievances on publicity and that we should be aware of his feelings. We have also been told by several journalists that the FonMin had issued instructions to the press to play down the Bergus-Secretary meetings. In fact, the meetings have received only limited coverage in the UAR.

---

[5] See footnote 4, Document 234.

[6] The *New York Times* reported that Bergus and Rogers met in Paris on June 8, and that Bergus had conveyed a message from Sadat that "slightly advanced the prospects for an interim agreement." (June 9, 1971, p. 14)

[7] The opinion piece argued that while there was hope that Egypt and Israel might achieve an interim settlement that summer, the agreement probably would not be followed by a formal peace. (*New York Times*, June 2, 1971, p. 41)

6. In my meeting with Mohammed I did not receive impression that UAR has any desire to withdraw its latest paper or that concerns expressed above will jeopardize future efforts to negotiate partial settlement. FonMin apparently engaging in legalistic hairsplitting to preserve his own amour-propre and to defend dignity of office of UAR Presidency.

7. I recommend we tell Mohammed that we have no objection to their considering Bergus paper as official paper if they wish to do so.[8] Important thing is not whether paper was official or unofficial but where we go from here in achieving partial withdrawal and opening of Canal.[9]

Wiley

---

[8] On June 12, Kissinger discussed the issue of the Bergus paper with Nixon in the Oval Office and said: "Well, Mr. President, what they've done on the Suez is just screw it up in such an unbelievable way by—I had it all set so that after the deadlock you'd write a letter to Golda Meir, and she was going to make some additional concessions to you, which we could have taken to the Egyptians as proving you could get things out of the Israelis. What I didn't count on was the vanity of these people at State. They went over to the Egyptians instead of presenting the Israeli plan, and forcing them to react to that. They never presented any plan and started dickering with the Egyptians on their own. Then our Chargé in Cairo submitted a written plan—[Nixon interrupted and asked, "Bergus?" and Kissinger affirmed that it was Bergus] submitted a written, unsigned plan, which the Egyptians have now adopted, which, in effect, instead of an interim settlement, ties the interim settlement to the Israelis withdrawing from all of Sinai, which they have already rejected in February. The Israelis don't know yet that we've submitted this piece of paper. But as soon as that surfaces—which it will, because the Egyptians have already proposed it—we'll be at the same deadlock as we were at the end of February. And then, they're going to come in here and ask you to cut off economic and military aid to Israel." (National Archives, Nixon Presidential Materials, White House Tapes, Oval Office, Conversation No. 518–3)

[9] In a meeting with Rogers on June 29, Rabin formally responded to this incident with "surprise and astonishment that action on crucial issue had been taken by US official without approval his government and consultation with Israel." Rogers responded that the United States was "not sure of Israel's purpose in making issue of case which appears to have little substantive impact." (Telegram 118212 to Tel Aviv, July 1; ibid., NSC Files, Box 1164, Saunders Files, Middle East Negotiations Files, Middle East—Jarring Talks, July 1–16, 1971)

239. Memorandum From Secretary of Defense Laird to President Nixon[1]

Washington, June 21, 1971.

SUBJECT

Middle East Arms Policy

The USG public policy of maintaining a Middle East "military balance" should be altered, in my judgment, because:

(1) The policy does not reflect as well as it should the two dominant military realities of the current and prospective situation. First, repeated studies by various DoD components confirm overwhelming Israeli military superiority in relation to Arab forces. The level of military hardware is not the dominant factor in the Arab-Israeli equation. The Arabs already have more planes than pilots, and more advanced equipment than they can handle. They do not have and are unlikely to get, even with Soviet assistance, the leadership, morale, technical aptitude, and individual motivation necessary to match the Israelis. This reality highlights the second and more critical one: we must draw a distinction between Arab forces on the one hand and Arab plus Soviet forces on the other. It is unrealistic to talk of giving Israel enough equipment to maintain a "balance" against present or prospective Soviet forces that may be focused on the Middle East. This is a separate problem which must not be confused with the Arab-Israeli arms balance issue, but instead involves NATO, the Sixth Fleet, and global US security interests.

(2) The policy removes arms supply initiative in the Middle East from US hands. Instead, the Soviets are enabled to increase their penetration of Egypt at will. The Soviets retain a large degree of control over Egyptian military capability because of Egyptian technical deficiency. Therefore, introduction of new weapons almost automatically increases the Soviet presence in Egypt without, however, increasing their risk of losing control. With the USG committed to a balancing response, increased polarization is assured. The USG, moreover, does not retain any degree of control over Israeli capabilities and, for each new round of weapons, the risk for the USG mounts.

(3) The policy has not achieved USG Middle East objectives. New USG weapons commitments to Israel have provoked greater Soviet

---

[1] Source: National Archives, Nixon Presidential Materials, NSC Files, Box 1164, Saunders Files, Middle East Negotiations Files, Middle East—Jarring Talks, July 1–16, 1971. Secret; Sensitive. The President did not receive this memorandum until July 14, when Kissinger forwarded it to him with a memorandum summarizing its contents. (Ibid.)

penetration of Egypt. These same commitments, which were designed to induce Israeli self-confidence toward productive peace negotiations, have, instead, fostered the over-confidence which translates into today's rigid posture.

(4) The policy contradicts the heart of the USG peace initiative by committing us to underwriting continued occupation of Arab territories rather than encouraging withdrawal.

(5) The policy associates the USG dangerously with Israeli weapons developments over which we have no control. Specifically, Israeli production of highly sophisticated and special-purpose weapons introduces a critical new factor in the Middle East military equation which will reflect on the USG most disadvantageously if and when the full story eventually surfaces.

(6) The policy does not lend itself to distinguishing between offensive and defensive capabilities. The bulk of Soviet weapons introduced in the recent past are defensive in character and do not directly enhance Egyptian capability to threaten Israel's survival. USG policy, however, has frequently responded by providing Israel with more highly sophisticated, offensively oriented fighter-bomber aircraft and other offensive weaponry[2] which pose a direct threat to Egyptian survival.

Clearly, the time has come to change our policy. Israel is launching a major public campaign for the additional USG aircraft commitments they have sought for some time. Our response will be a prime tangible by which the Arab world will gauge the sincerity of our spoken desires for an equitable peace settlement.

I recommend that we substitute for our present "military balance" policy a new policy which assures only an appropriate Israeli capability to defend its legitimate borders against Arab attack.

Stress could increasingly be placed on defense of Israel per se, apart from occupied territories. Larger questions of military balance as related to NATO and USG-Soviet postures would be dealt with as issues separated from the Arab-Israeli conflict. This new policy would:

---

[2] Packard met with Rabin on June 24 in the Pentagon to discuss the continuation of aircraft deliveries to Israel, an extension of the U.S.-Israeli data exchange agreement, and the purchase of surplus weapons from Vietnam. When Rabin asked what Israel could "look forward to in the way of sales," Packard responded that "he understood Israel's problem" but could only say, as he had previously, "if Israel could get the negotiations started" the aircraft decisions would be "easier" to make. As of that meeting, 12 of the 54 F–4s that Israel requested the year before had been sold and delivered, and of the 120 A–4s that Israel had requested, 20 had been or were being delivered and 18 were coming from new production. (Memorandum of conversation, June 24; Washington National Records Center, OSD Files: FRC 330–76–0197, Box 66, Israel)

(1) Define USG interests in the Middle East situation more sharply. Israel's survival would remain important, but would be seen in the context of overall US national interest, rather than as an open-ended commitment.

(2) Enable the USG to decide privately, and justify publicly, if necessary, which weapons to allow or not allow as matters separate from the question of Israel's survival.

(3) Introduce greater flexibility for our diplomatic efforts to move Israel toward a more reasonable negotiating stance. Statements of USG interest in Israel's defense could be varied to include "defense of legitimate Israeli borders" if our diplomacy required.

(4) Permit us to exclude further commitments of inflammatory offensive weapons such as attack aircraft, thereby offering greater scope for improvement of our relations with Egypt and the rest of the Arab world and helping reduce opportunities for Soviet penetration.

(5) Place our judgments on justifiable military grounds that can be supported privately, and even publicly, on a professional basis. This would permit a more flexible response to the politicized campaign already beginning on behalf of Israel's security. Key members of Congress could be briefed on the professional considerations behind our policy, and any need to offset the Soviet strategic gains in the Mediterranean would become the responsibility of the Sixth Fleet and NATO rather than the Israeli armed forces.

The US cannot exert sufficient leverage in the Middle East as long as it is locked rigidly into a false concept of military balance that robs the US of the initiative and does not take into account the very real differences between US and Israeli interests. The proposed policy would gain for us the flexibility to support Israel on a more selective basis, disassociating ourselves from political and military positions which are not in the US national interests.[3]

Melvin R. Laird

---

[3] On June 30, the last day of the fiscal year, Nixon approved Kissinger's recommendation that he endorse the Department of State's proposal that $50 million in surplus military assistance funds be passed on to Israel as an add-on to the $500 million already approved for that fiscal year. According to Kissinger, the Department of State argued: 1) "The additional money would help our own services who have been bearing some of the financial burden for last year's exceptional shipments to Israel"; and 2) "This would allay some of the Israeli nervousness that we are cutting off the assistance tap entirely." Kissinger himself added: "It seems desirable to make use of this money rather than have it revert to the Treasury at the end of the fiscal year. Applying it against the Israeli account would, at the very least, allow increased flexibility in the FY 1972 appropriations even if more than the present $300-million is not actually provided to Israel." (Memorandum from Kissinger to Nixon, June 30; National Archives, Nixon Presidential Materials, NSC Files, Box 609, Country Files, Middle East, Israel, Vol. IX)

240. Memorandum From the President's Assistant for National Security Affairs (Kissinger) to President Nixon[1]

Washington, June 23, 1971.

SUBJECT

State of Play in Middle East

We are approaching a confrontation with Israel as the last presently planned shipments of aircraft are made in June (Phantoms) and August (Skyhawks) and as we try to work out next steps on an interim settlement. The purpose of this memo is to review the main elements in the situation.

To begin with, it is worth looking back for a moment at the *purpose for which the idea of an interim settlement on the Canal was originally developed*. I broached the idea to Mrs. Meir when she was here in October[2] as a possible alternative focus for peacemaking given flat Israeli refusal to negotiate a peace based on withdrawal to essentially pre-war borders. The purpose of such an alternative was thought to be:

—to stabilize the Suez front and reduce the possibility of resumed conflict;

—thereby to buy time for a prolonged process of reaching an overall settlement;

—to permit the two sides to begin developing some confidence that they can work out reasonable agreements together.

What has happened since January is that *the original concept of a Canal settlement*—mutual pullback and thin-out forces along the Canal to stabilize the front—*has been transformed into simply a withdrawal on the way to an overall settlement* along the lines of the "Rogers Plan."

—Mrs. Meir initially resisted the idea of interim movement, but Dayan appeared to see advantage in it as a means of reducing UAR

---

[1] Source: National Archives, Nixon Presidential Materials, NSC Files, Box 657, Country Files, Middle East, Middle East Nodis/Cedar/Plus, Vol. III. Secret; Nodis; Cedar Plus. Sent for information; outside system. A stamped notation on the memorandum indicates the President saw it.

[2] Meir visited New York in October 1970, along with 25 other heads of state, to participate in the two-week celebration of the 25th anniversary of the United Nations. She addressed the General Assembly on October 21 with a detailed speech on Israeli policy regarding negotiations with its Arab neighbors, declaring that Israel would not participate in Jarring talks until the cease-fire with Egypt was extended. (*New York Times*, October 22, 1970, p. 1) On October 24, she attended a black-tie dinner hosted by Nixon in the East Room of the White House for the delegates who attended the UN celebrations in New York. (National Archives, Nixon Presidential Materials, White House Central Files, President's Daily Diary) No record of Meir's meeting with Kissinger has been found.

ability to increase pressure on Israel with a credible threat to renew hostilities. Both the Israelis and Ambassador Dobrynin were postured to see the Canal settlement as an alternative to the Jarring negotiations to buy time.

—The Egyptians picked up some of the comments Dayan made publicly on mutual pullback and put out informal feelers to us in January. The idea was put as a "demand" for partial Israeli withdrawal in Sadat's February 4 speech.[3] But it was not until after Israel's negative reply to Jarring[4] that Sadat turned energetically to the Canal alternative.

—In mid-April the Israelis developed a paper and showed it to me. At my inquiry, they softened it a bit and presented it to the State Department.[5] In Israeli eyes State seemed more interested in talking about the Jarring negotiations than in the Canal proposal. In any case, the Israelis asked for certain clarifications of the U.S. position and these were still being discussed at the time of Secretary Rogers' trip. The Israeli paper was not passed to Cairo because Israel wanted to wait for our support. In the meantime Sadat began developing a UAR position calling for Israeli withdrawal east of the passes.

—During and following the Secretary's trip, both sides were drawn out on their positions until we now have two quite different positions. Each side's position was described by Sisco in such a way as to lead the other to believe it was more flexible than it really was. Also, each side was led to believe it had a substantial measure of U.S. support. For example, Bergus passed typewritten notes to a UAR official which became the basis of the latest UAR position paper,[6] which stands far from what the Israelis could accept. These notes were naturally interpreted by the Egyptians as an official U.S. position on the Canal proposal. At the same time, Israel was told that "the ball was in the UAR court" and the next move was up to the Egyptians.

As a result, *two sharply differing positions* have emerged, each with some appearance to its author of a considerable measure of U.S support:

—*The UAR* would extend its control east of the main passes in the Sinai (40–60 miles east of the Canal); extend the ceasefire six months

---

[3] See Document 203.

[4] See Document 211.

[5] See footnote 2, Document 224. In his memoirs, Kissinger asserts that Rabin showed him the proposed paper in "mid-April before surfacing it at the State Department," and that he persuaded Rabin to modify "some elements" of the Israeli proposal that would have made the negotiation "a total non-starter." (Kissinger, *White House Years*, p. 1282)

[6] See Document 238.

with a possibility of renewal; send UAR military forces across the Canal; and state formally that this is the first stage in a settlement along the lines of the "Rogers Plan."

—*Israel* is thinking of a very small withdrawal (perhaps 10, at most 40 miles) staying west of the key passes; insists on an indefinite cease-fire; refuses to agree to UAR military forces crossing the Canal; and resists any linkage between an interim Canal settlement and an overall peace settlement.

The situation now contains these elements:

—In *Egyptian* eyes, the US seems to be supporting them in negotiating for a line east of the passes. The latest UAR paper incorporating this position is based on informal suggestions made by our man in Cairo.[7] The Egyptians have not been told that the Israelis are not likely to accept their position, although they know it would be hard for Israel to accept.

—In *Israeli* eyes, the Egyptian proposal for an interim settlement almost equates to their idea now of a final settlement. They will not accept it short of a peace settlement. They took a position encouraged to think the US would support it and pave the way for it. They will be furious if they find out that the Egyptian position has been encouraged by some Americans.

—The *Soviets* interpreted the active US diplomacy as an effort to displace them in Cairo.

—On the negotiating front, whereas the Canal proposal had been designed to slow the pace and buy time, the pace of diplomacy since early May has speeded it up and shown US anxiety for movement.

In short, we are in a position where both sides will be upset with us when they find out that we have not supported their concept of an interim settlement. On top of this, the Israelis assume we have begun to put the squeeze on them by letting the aircraft pipeline run dry. We have the choice of continuing shipments under their pressure or continuing to delay to gain their agreement on an interim settlement that will either be as hard for them to accept as an overall settlement or close enough to the Israeli position to leave Sadat feeling cheated. Sadat has been told that no commitment was made to Israel on aircraft during Secretary Rogers' trip.

The strategy which State seems to be moving toward is (a) to create concern in Israel that aircraft shipments will end temporarily and (b) to try to move the UAR toward a position that would permit us to try to split the difference between the UAR and Israeli positions. The strategy

---

[7] See footnote 4, Document 234.

behind the initial Canal settlement proposal on the other hand, was to convince the UAR to accept an interim settlement because it recognized that it could not get complete withdrawal now. Instead, the UAR has been encouraged to think that it can get a substantial step to complete withdrawal now.

It seems likely now that we have lost the chance for an interim settlement—unless its relationship to complete withdrawal can be reduced, and that will now be hard for Sadat to accept. If we continue aircraft shipments, we will seem to Sadat to have reversed ourselves. If we do not, we will be in a period of confrontation with Israel. Israel will then have a choice between (a) waiting us out on the assumption that hostilities will resume in six months or so and we will be forced to their side and (b) making a diplomatic concession that, in their view, would just harden the Egyptian/Soviet position.

---

241. Memorandum From the President's Deputy Assistant for National Security Affairs (Haig) to President Nixon[1]

Washington, July 2, 1971.

SUBJECT

New Suez Canal Initiative

Secretary Rogers has sent you a memo [attached][2] recommending that we undertake a "new effort" to reconcile the serious differences which exist between Egypt and Israel on an interim Suez Canal settlement.

The Secretary proposes a scenario in which we would seek to move first the Israelis and then the Egyptians towards a middle ground position. This would require a number of difficult concessions on each side since, as the Secretary points out, there has been a further hardening of both Egyptian and Israeli positions since his trip to the area. *For the Israelis,* it would at a minimum mean:

---

[1] Source: National Archives, Nixon Presidential Materials, NSC Files, Box 657, Country Files, Middle East, Middle East Nodis/Cedar/Plus, Vol. III. Secret; Nodis; Cedar. Sent for action; outside system. A stamped notation on the memorandum indicates the President saw it. All brackets are in the original.

[2] Dated July 1; attached but not printed.

—Agreeing to a much greater withdrawal from the Canal than they now envisage and giving up control of the key strategic passes, probably to a U.N. force.

—Allowing at least a limited Egyptian force to cross the Canal.

—Accepting a formula that would in effect limit the cease-fire to a year if there was no progress towards a final settlement.

For the Egyptians, it would at a minimum mean:

—Giving up the idea of linking the interim settlement to a final settlement, with an Israeli commitment to total withdrawal.

—Agreeing to allow Israeli ships to pass through the Suez Canal after an interim settlement.

—Giving up their hope for an explicit six-month cease-fire deadline.

—Agreeing to strict limitations on their future military presence in the Sinai.

In terms of mechanics, Assistant Secretary Sisco would go to Israel around July 12 (he has already informed the Israelis he would like to come for about a week for "free-wheeling" discussions) and orally probe the Israeli position. He would then report back to you and Secretary Rogers and a decision would be made on whether he should continue on to Cairo. Meanwhile, we would conduct a holding operation with President Sadat in Cairo and make sure he is still interested.

The Secretary's plan amounts to a fairly bold new initiative. But, by his own admission, he does "not believe a complete bridging of the two sides is now possible." His real hope is that the gap can be "narrowed" some and that, "at a minimum, we buy time," and improve the chances for something important coming out of the discussions he will be having with the Egyptian and Israeli foreign ministers at the General Assembly in the fall.

I think, and feel sure that Dr. Kissinger would agree, that we all need to give Secretary Rogers' proposed "new effort" considerable thought. It raises many questions, most of which boil down to whether or not we would be paying too high a price for too small a chance of achieving anything substantial. The Secretary is right when he says that the heart of the present impasse is Israel's unwillingness to be more forthcoming on the territorial aspect and that there is "no possibility" of Israeli movement in this regard in the near future. Yet this is the very heart of the problem, even of an interim settlement. There is also, of course, the problem of raising expectations without any real chance of being able to produce substantial movement. We already have a serious credibility problem with the Israelis and especially the Egyptians. If it increases much more, our whole diplomatic posture in the Middle East could be seriously undermined without anything to show for it.

Another question that needs to be very carefully explored is where this new effort might lead us if we do go through with it. One likely result is that we will move further from our "honest broker" role to become a more active initiator of ideas and consequently with a much more exposed and vulnerable position. This has important implications that need to be thought out. Finally, I believe we should, above all, consider our future initiatives with respect to the Middle East in the light of the events which will occur during and just after Dr. Kissinger's trip[3] when our longer term prospects with respect to the Soviets and Asia will come into sharper focus.

Recommendation: That you authorize me to inform Secretary Rogers that you wish to hold up temporarily on this new initiative until we can consider it in greater depth at a restricted NSC meeting at San Clemente.[4] There is no apparent need for acting in great haste and it seems only prudent to approach this important decision in an orderly manner.[5]

---

[3] Kissinger left Washington on July 1 for his first, secret trip to Beijing. He returned to the United States on July 13 and spent 2 days in San Clemente reporting to President Nixon.

[4] See Document 243.

[5] Nixon initialed his approval. After a "long session" with Rogers, Helms, and Haig on the Middle East during a July 6 flight to San Clemente, Nixon told Haldeman privately that "Rogers is basically right on some of the points that he makes, particularly that we should appear to be doing something rather than just letting the thing sit." (*Haldeman Diaries: Multimedia Edition*, July 6, 1971)

242. Telegram From the Interests Section in Egypt to the Department of State[1]

Cairo, July 7, 1971, 0950Z.

1644. For Secretary and Sisco from Sterner. Ref: Cairo 1639.[2]

1. Atmosphere of our meeting with Sadat last night was genial and personally warm, but below surface we could detect mood of exasperation and puzzlement as to purpose of our mission. With effort, Sadat converted this into humorous treatment, but tension and increasing suspicion that we are merely leading him on were clearly there.

2. We nevertheless emerged with strong impression of a man who still wants, and is still in a position to do business on an interim agreement. When we paid him compliment on his reply to Jarring initiative, but then went on to say that in terms of what was possible we thought we had to concentrate on interim agreement, he nodded vigorously. At no point during conversation did Sadat even mention SC Resolution 242 or Jarring Mission or otherwise reflect any hardening on linkage of interim agreement to question of borders in final settlement. Absence of any warning signals on this leads us to think he fundamentally views purpose of interim agreement in same manner we do—as device that defers judgments on shape of final settlement but wins time for political processes to work on both sides. I think Sadat could buy something along the lines of formulation we have in mind on linkage of interim agreement to on-going efforts achieve overall peace settlement.

3. Although somewhat impatient with the need to cover all this ground again, when we explained value of his renewed assurances, he carefully and unequivocally affirmed his previous position on each of points we were instructed to raise. On important point about with-

---

[1] Source: National Archives, Nixon Presidential Materials, NSC Files, Box 657, Country Files, Middle East, Middle East Nodis/Cedar/Plus, Vol. III. Secret; Priority; Nodis; Cedar Plus.

[2] Telegram 1639 from Cairo, July 6, reported the substance of Sterner and Bergus's 90-minute conversation with Sadat that evening. They explained that they wanted to meet with him to share the U.S. assessment of the situation in the Middle East after having reviewed the results of exchanges with both Egypt and Israel on an interim settlement. They told him that they believed he took a "courageous and statesmanlike step" with his positive reply to the Jarring initiative in February and that the Israeli reply was "unsatisfactory." That said, they thought that the "best avenue for progress in immediate future was in negotiations on an interim settlement" and that "the next order of business should be to explore, in specific terms, how the differences on an interim settlement could be narrowed." They then informed him that "Washington was actively considering how best to carry out early, intensive discussions" with Israel, but before they did so, Rogers wanted to "touch base" with Sadat to "make sure that premises on which we were proceeding were mutually understood." Sterner had been sent, they said, so that he could "report fully to the Secretary on his return." (Ibid.)

drawal of Soviet operational military personnel he was again very explicit: they would be asked to leave upon conclusion of an interim agreement. He made it clear he would not be doing this as favor to U.S. but because he himself would like to see them depart as soon as probability of renewed fighting appreciably decreased.

4. Sadat sounded like a man who is in control of his country and who had few immediate concerns about his ability to stay there in foreseeable future. At one point, as he was talking about May 13 arrests,[3] he said "Nasser could afford to be compassionate; I can't; I'm going to be cruel and severe."

5. We did not get much help when we raised problem of lines of communication with UARG. He dismissed this with wave of hand saying once areas of agreement are achieved with him orally Foreign Ministry could be brought in at appropriate moment. It sounded as if he were talking about briefing some third country. But he was definite in stating his wish that we continue to use Heykal as channel to him. This obviously leaves us with problem of continuing friction with Foreign Ministry. We don't see much to do about it except continue to do business as President desires while conducting handholding operation with Ministry. Perhaps Cabinet reshuffle expected this month will give us line-up in Ministry that will make this whole arrangement easier.

6. One thing that struck us about Sadat's comments was his barely disguised criticism of Soviets for not giving him adequate arms to face Israel. His beef seemed to be about quality rather than quantity. Implication was that he thought Soviets had better stuff to give but were holding out on him, whereas U.S. was giving Israel its first-line equipment.

7. I believe we impressed Sadat when we said Washington saw first step of next phase of intensive discussions as beginning in Israel, and that we were readying Sisco for this purpose. If we can show him some palpable progress, even if it is modest, I think we can keep him on this course through the summer and maintain his negotiating flexibility. We have, however, just about exhausted handholding potential in any further missions to Cairo or talks with him unless we can show him some real substance.

Bergus

---

[3] Sadat announced on May 15 that more than 100 people, including Minister of War Mohamed Fawzi and Minister of Interior Sharay Jumaa, had been arrested for plotting a coup against the government. (*New York Times*, May 16, 1971, p. 1)

243. Memorandum for the Record[1]

San Clemente, July 16, 1971.

SUBJECT

NSC Meeting on the Middle East and South Asia

PARTICIPANTS

The President
Secretary of State, William Rogers
Deputy Secretary of Defense, David Packard
Admiral Thomas Moorer, Chairman JCS
Richard Helms, Director of Central Intelligence
U. Alexis Johnson, Under Secretary of State
Henry A. Kissinger, Assistant to the President
Brigadier General Alexander M. Haig, Jr., Deputy Assistant to the President
Joseph J. Sisco, Assistant Secretary of State
Harold H. Saunders, NSC Staff

The President opened the meeting by pointing out that there are enormous risks in the situation in South Asia for our China policy. There are risks for the Indians and Pakistanis, too. He suggested that the discussion begin with the Middle East and then turn to a briefer discussion of South Asia. That is one problem that must be watched very closely. The Indians are stirring it up. If they mess around on this one, they will not find much sympathy here.

The President then asked Mr. Helms to brief on the situation in the Middle East. [The substance of Mr. Helms' briefing is attached.][2]

At the conclusion of Mr. Helms' briefing, Secretary Rogers said that State had just gone through another extensive review of the military balance in the Middle East with the Defense Department and concluded that the balance still remains slightly in favor of the Israelis. Mr. Sisco expanded on this point by noting that the Israelis define the military balance as one which gives them a margin of advantage. There is no question that it is impossible to recreate the conditions of 1967 in which the Israelis were able to win an overwhelming victory. Now, although the qualitative advantage remains on Israel's side, what the Russians have done to improve Egyptian defenses is impressive. In as-

---

[1] Source: National Archives, Nixon Presidential Materials, NSC Files, NSC Institutional Files (H-Files), Box H–110, NSC Meeting Minutes, NSC Minutes Originals 1971 thru 6–20–74. Top Secret; Nodis. The meeting was held in the Conference Room at San Clemente. According to the President's Daily Diary, the meeting was held from 10:57 a.m. to 12:06 p.m. (Ibid., White House Central Files) All brackets are in the original except those indicating text omitted by the editors.

[2] Attached but not printed.

sessing what equipment Israel needs, it is the old question: How much is enough to deter?

Mr. Helms referred to the statement by Senator Jackson that the military balance had shifted.[3] He pointed out that Senator Jackson had based his statement on the ratio between numbers of aircraft. That is not the important thing. The important thing is the number of pilots. Whereas the Israelis have three pilots for every plane, the Egyptians have one pilot for every three planes.

Mr. Packard said that, in addition to the aircraft balance, it must be remembered that the US has given Israel the best electronics counter-measures equipment it has. While the Egyptians have received new equipment from the Soviets, the Israelis are significantly better than they were a year ago.

The President summarized by concluding that the margin is closer.

Mr. Packard said that the big change had taken place when the Soviets moved missiles into the UAR. The situation would never get back to the way it was before that development.

The President asked Admiral Moorer what he thought. The Admiral replied that if Israel has to operate inside the UAR missile envelope, its losses would naturally be greater than prior to the existence of that envelope. Still, the Israelis enjoy qualitative superiority over the UAR air force. The Admiral noted that Israel is now producing its own Jericho surface-to-surface missile. The Admiral noted that the new planes the Soviets were providing to the Egyptians were suitable primarily for air-to-air combat and the UAR ratio in aircraft is superior, but the Israeli pilots are better. The Admiral concluded by saying that photographs indicate that the UAR is making mock-ups to practice canal crossings.

The President asked, "Where does that leave us?"

Secretary Rogers said that, as a result of Mike Sterner's conversations with President Sadat,[4] we believe President Sadat wants the US to continue playing a role in the negotiation of an interim canal settlement. In addition, President Sadat sent word through the Saudi intelligence chief that he still wants a Canal settlement. The Secretary proposed that Mr. Sisco go to Israel to attempt to narrow the gap between the Egyptian and Israeli positions on an interim settlement.[5] He said

---

[3] In his July 14 statement arguing for an increase in the U.S. supply of jets to Israel, Senator Jackson accused the Nixon administration of allowing the military balance in the region to deteriorate by "degrading" the Israeli defense capability, claiming that Egypt alone possessed half of the 600 total military aircraft in the Middle East. (*New York Times*, July 15, 1971. p. 15)

[4] See Document 242.

[5] Sisco went to Israel from July 28 to August 6. See Document 245.

that Israel would "favor" a visit by Mr. Sisco. He hoped that such a trip would permit a narrowing of the gap between now and September when the UN General Assembly will be the meeting point for a number of Foreign Ministers from the area. Then, hopefully, there could be an agreement by the first of the year.

The Secretary continued that Mr. Sisco would not be authorized to make commitments on aircraft, but he would be authorized to discuss the Israeli view of their requirements. He would report back to the President and then we would see where we go next with the UAR.

The Secretary continued that President Sadat said that there is some flexibility in his position. He also had said, with regard to the Soviets in the UAR, that he is prepared to have the Soviets withdraw from the SAM sites, but he will continue to need Soviet pilots to train his own pilots. As far as whether we should resume discussions with the Russians is concerned, President Sadat has said that he has no objection to our talking to the Russians "at the proper time." The Secretary concluded with the recommendation that Mr. Sisco go to Israel, try to narrow the gap and make no commitments on aircraft.

The President reiterated the Secretary's proposition that Mr. Sisco take the trip to Israel, return and report to the President and then see whether to go on to deal further with the UAR. He said that we did not want to get into a position where we would trigger a confrontation for which we do not have an answer.

The President went on, saying, "I have a thought." This is July 16. The Congress will be out of play for the best part of August. He interjected that we are not going to have a policy governed by a domestic opinion, but we do have "more running room" when Congress is out of session, particularly on the aircraft question. Then he asked Mr. Sisco how long he thought the discussion in Israel would take.

Mr. Sisco replied that he thought about a week, but he could spend 10 days. He agreed that this is not the time for a confrontation with the Israelis. That time will come, perhaps in September when we know more precisely what kind of agreement might be possible and what kind of concessions we might seek from Israel. Some of the issues involved are:

—Are the Israelis willing to buy a symbolic Egyptian military presence in a narrow strip east of the Suez Canal?

—Is a zone of Israeli withdrawal possible where the key passes to the Sinai are neither in Egyptian nor in Israeli hands?

—Is it possible to achieve a relatively open-ended ceasefire?

—What can be done with regard to passage of Israeli ships through the Suez Canal?

Mr. Sisco continued that we have to be sympathetic—and to show sympathy—in meeting Israel's concern about arms. Still, it is difficult to respond to the Israeli requests without destroying the one diplomatic thread still in play. However, we should adopt a sympathetic posture on arms and on an interim settlement. Both sides have put forward some interesting propositions.

The President recapitulated by confirming that Mr. Sisco's thought was that Mrs. Meir would talk about arms and Mr. Sisco would talk about a settlement.

The President then said that we had to put this into the context of the "announcement last night" [that the President would visit Peking]. We do not want to have a fight develop with the Israelis now. That would overshadow the China announcement. So it is very important to schedule the trip to Israel so that Mr. Sisco would still be talking when Congress gets out of town.

The President said he knew how "this lobby" [Zionist] works. There is George Meany;[6] there is the group in New York; there is Senator Jackson; and Senator Muskie has to get back on this issue since he is "hurting for money." Israel plays a shrewd, ruthless political game. They will egg on the Presidential hopefuls as well as their usual friends (like Congressman Celler). The President said he saw this blowing up into strong Israeli pressure. The argument would be that we are allowing the Russians to fish in troubled waters.

Turning to the USSR, the President said that if one puts oneself in the Soviet position, one would be concerned about US initiative toward China. The Soviets will be looking for places to irritate the US. They may send some nuclear submarines back to Cienfuegos.

The President said that, with regard to Mr. Sisco's trip, he would like "a very low-profile." Rather than go out to Israel the first of the very next week, the President suggested that Mr. Sisco go out the following week and then stay there until Congress gets out of town.

The President then said, "Don't promise a damned thing. This is not going to be a free ride this time. From now on it is quid pro quo."

The President reiterated that the visit should be low profile, that Mr. Sisco should be conciliatory on the question of Israel's arms needs, but on the other hand, firm about the need for some diplomatic progress. Then Mr. Sisco would come back and report in Washington. Then we would see whether he would go on to the UAR later in August. At that time we could decide whether it was useful to do anything with the Russians. We have been careful not to bring in the Soviets again, although the Russians would like to play a role. We don't know

---

[6] George Meany, President of the AFL–CIO.

what kind of role they would like to play—whether they would like to mess the situation up or what.

Mr. Sisco said that, looked at from the Mid-East viewpoint, the advantage of the trip would be to keep negotiations alive until mid-September when the UN General Assembly meets. We know what a reasonable settlement on the Canal would look like. At that time—mid-September—in the context of the Secretary's bilateral talks with Foreign Ministers at the UN, the US could make a major effort to force a final interim settlement. But this would have to be done carefully since Israel has said that it does not want the US and the Russians making that settlement.

Secretary Rogers said that this trip would be an effort to "keep the ball in play." President Sadat wants the US to show it is still active.

The President asked when we have to make the decision on arms for Israel. Mr. Sisco replied that he would be testifying before the Symington sub-committee[7] the following week and that he would simply say that he had been authorized to discuss this issue in Israel. Mr. Packard said that he felt the decision should be put off another month or two. The President said that August would be a good month for holding off.

Mr. Sisco said that we could do this consistent with our diplomatic efforts. Domestic pressure might build up, since the Israelis seem to have a case on the merits—that is, the changing military balance.

Dr. Kissinger said that the military balance shifts against Israel when the Israelis can no longer win a war quickly. The Arabs do not have to defeat them; they just have to engage Israel in a prolonged war of attrition.

Dr. Kissinger continued that we have all agreed that at some point we would have to squeeze Israel. The issue is whether we squeeze in making a commitment to provide aircraft or at the time of delivery. If we squeeze in making the commitment, Israel will look at everything in terms of on-going pressure.

Secretary Rogers said, "We can wait a couple of months."

The President said that for the UAR the fact that Mr. Sisco was going to Israel should be enough. He suggested that Mr. Sisco leave around July 26. Secretary Rogers said that the trip can be announced before President Sadat's July 23 speech.[8] The President said Mr. Sisco

---

[7] Stuart Symington (D–MO), Chairman of the Senate Foreign Relations Committee Subcommittee on Near Eastern and South Asian Affairs.

[8] The Department of State announced Sisco's trip on July 19. Sadat delivered the speech on July 23 at the opening of the National Congress of the Arab Socialist Union. Bergus commented that the "most dramatic aspect" of the Egyptian President's remarks was their "lack of drama." He wrote: "Sadat unveiled no new policies, set no new dead-

could tell the Symington sub-committee on Monday and that would get the word around. He acknowledged that there has to be an "appearance of motion."

[Omitted here is discussion of South Asia printed in *Foreign Relations, 1969–1976, volume XI, South Asia Crisis, 1971,* Document 103.]

Harold H. Saunders[9]

---

lines, raised no new issues (and buried no old ones), essentially declared intention of maintaining Egypt on course it has pursued since early months of this year." (Telegram 1853 from Cairo, July 24; National Archives, Nixon Presidential Materials, NSC Files, Box 1164, Saunders Files, Middle East Negotiations Files, Middle East—Jarring Talks, July 16–August 1, 1971)

[9] Printed from a copy that bears Saunders's typed signature.

---

244. Telegram From the Department of State to the Embassy in Israel[1]

Washington, July 21, 1971, 0105Z.

131519. 1. At Rabin's request, Sisco had a long session with him at lunch preparatory to Sisco's trip to Israel next week. Principal purpose of the lunch was for Sisco to seek any advice that Rabin wished to convey as to how best to handle the trip in our mutual interests.

2. Sisco made the following principal points:

A. We reviewed the current situation in the Middle East with the President and the Secretary at San Clemente[2] and Sisco has full authority to discuss both the elements of an interim settlement and the question of outstanding Israeli requests for arms.

B. Both the President and the Secretary will be interested to receive full report from Sisco as to what the current attitude of Israel is on the principal elements of an interim settlement and their current assessment of the present balance in the area.

C. Sisco is prepared to discuss the question of arms fully and to consider carrying back with him recommendations for top level consid-

---

[1] Source: National Archives, Nixon Presidential Materials, NSC Files, Box 1164, Saunders Files, Middle East Negotiations Files, Middle East—Jarring Talks, July 16–August 1, 1971. Secret; Nodis; Cedar Plus. Drafted and approved by Sisco. Repeated to Cairo.

[2] See Document 243.

eration in the United States Government. His approach will be sympathetic taking into account all factors, including President's commitment to maintain the balance. Arms question must also be considered in context of fundamental importance which the United States attaches to avoiding any action which will destroy its role in trying to achieve an interim settlement. We believe interim settlement required if deterioration to hostilities in 1972 is to be avoided.

D. Sisco would like to have exchange of views on recent developments in the area, including the Soviet role and impact politically and militarily of the Soviet-UAR treaty.[3]

E. Sisco has had the benefit of a full detailed Department of Defense intelligence briefing on the question of Soviet arms supply to Egypt and Syria. He would benefit from a similar detailed intelligence briefing from Israel as a preliminary basis for our detailed talks on Israeli arms requests.

F. On the political side, while he assumes that the Prime Minister will wish to meet with him at the outset for a general overall review, Sisco hopes that arrangements can be made for an in-depth exchange with relevant Minister or Ministers or officials—quietly and deliberately—in which ideas on interim settlement can be explored without either side feeling that it is irrevocably committed. Sisco indicated that he intended to fill in the Prime Minister in greater detail and specificity on the current exchanges with Sadat.

G. Sisco will not be carrying a detailed blueprint with him, but he will want to explore various substantive ideas as to how the principal remaining difficulties can be met and would be prepared, if it is appropriate, to try his hand together with Israeli officials to put together certain formulations. This would be without prejudice as to when and how any formulations would be presented to the other side. In this connection, it would be well if the in-depth discussion would attempt to make a common judgment as to what the final elements of an interim settlement would look like; and secondly, how the situation might be played tactically to arrive at that point.

H. Finally, Sisco hopes that the minimal amount will be said to the press of a substantive character by either of us. What he would like have come out of the discussions publicly is that we have had a detailed in-depth talk, that he would report fully to his government, and on this basis the United States will decide what further steps it is to take on an interim settlement and with respect to the Israeli arms request. Sisco expressed hope that ways would be found to prevent leaks; purpose is private, quiet diplomacy. Sisco intends to keep press contacts to an ab-

---

[3] See Document 235.

solute minimum. Would hope that the whole visit can be played in the lowest possible key. Finally, he would hope that social engagements would be kept to an absolute minimum since he would prefer this to be as much a working visit as possible.

3. Rabin said he is doing everything possible to dampen down undue expectations on arms stimulated by recent statement of Foreign Minister.[4] In response to Sisco's thought that he not make any statement upon his arrival in Israel so as to keep matters in lowest possible key, Rabin demurred. He said this would be interpreted as US pouting over fact that Israeli press in the last couple of weeks have expressed some doubts regarding desirability of Sisco trip at this time. Rabin suggested that Sisco make brief statement indicating he pleased to be in Israel, indicating his intention to have in-depth discussions in a friendly and understanding spirit on all aspects of Israeli-American relations and interim Suez Canal agreement. Rabin thought this was the right atmospheric note to strike. Rabin also said that it ought to be possible to explore a number of the specific points of an interim settlement as Sisco indicated he wished, but he cautioned Sisco not to put his queries in the form of a definitive US position. Rabin said his advice would be for Sisco to explain the Israeli position on a given point, the Egyptian position on the same point, and then express any judgment that Sisco might have as to what would be required to meet the differences in the two respective positions. Sisco indicated that he had this kind of an approach very much in mind. When Sisco indicated that he recently had the benefit of a full, detailed Department of Defense intelligence briefing on the military balance, Rabin indicated GOI intention to give a comparable briefing to Sisco based on their own intelligence sources.

4. *FYI:* Sisco told Rabin he expects talks to be deliberate and detailed and expects to remain at least a week in Israel and probably longer. Number of meetings a day should be very limited (perhaps no more than one) and ample time allowed between meetings for reflection by both sides on ideas expressed. *End FYI.*

5. Rabin felt it important for Ambassador Barbour to make all of foregoing points to appropriate Israeli official since he will only report it in briefer form orally on his return.

Rogers

---

[4] Speaking before the Knesset on July 19, Eban appealed to the United States for more Phantom aircraft, saying: "This need is most important and urgent in the light of facts which have been revealed by authoritative American sources that the Soviet Union has been supplying aerial weapons to Egypt and Syria at a very accelerated tempo." (*New York Times,* July 20, 1971, p. 32)

245. Telegram From the Embassy in Israel to the Department of State[1]

Tel Aviv, August 3, 1971, 0630Z.

4626. For Secretary from Sisco.

1. My second session with Prime Minister Meir,[2] which lasted two and one-half hours, and at which she was joined by Allon, Dayan, Eban, Rabin, et al, also went reasonably well in that they said neither yes nor no to any of the ideas I put forward to reconcile presently existing differences on key elements of interim settlement. Israelis listened without interruption to my detailed presentation and at the end posed a number of questions for clarification, with caveat that they might have further questions later, and that failure to express any reservations re specific ideas I floated did not imply consent but merely they wished to reflect.

2. Atmosphere once again was entirely businesslike, unemotional and friendly. My impression is that we have given them serious food for thought, that they recognize it as such, and that they will proceed with great caution to avoid giving impression of knee jerk negative reaction. Many of our ideas I put forward will in my judgement appeal to some within the Israeli establishment and contribute to their internal debate on this issue. They are now going into a deep skull session and Prime Minister has asked me to meet with her again late Wednesday afternoon.[3] She personally wants to actively head up their negotiating team.

---

[1] Source: National Archives, Nixon Presidential Materials, NSC Files, Box 1164, Saunders Files, Middle East Negotiations Files, Middle East—Jarring Talks, August 1–16, 1971. Secret; Priority; Nodis; Cedar Plus.

[2] In the first session, which lasted three hours on the morning of July 30, Sisco told Meir that the United States "attaches importance to achieving interim settlement along Suez Canal by end of year," and that it wanted to avoid a breakdown of the cease-fire as a result of the impasse over the issue. He also outlined Sadat's attitudes on key elements of an interim settlement—although Meir questioned the Egyptian President's "readiness or ability to assume more flexible position" regarding it—and stressed that successfully working toward such an agreement would "strengthen the forces for peace inside Egypt." She agreed to "explore ideas" with Sisco on a "noncommittal basis" to see whether Israeli differences with Egypt could be reconciled. Finally, the Assistant Secretary tried to reassure Meir on the question of aircraft deliveries, stating that the United States did not link aircraft deliveries with progress on the interim settlement. (Telegram 4587 from Tel Aviv, July 31; ibid., RG 59, Central Files 1970–73, POL 27–14 ARAB–ISR)

[3] At their third meeting on August 4, Meir pressed Sisco on further aircraft deliveries from the United States, given the Soviet-Egyptian Treaty of Friendship and the "strengthening" Soviet presence in Egypt. She complained that the United States was not providing "adequate information" on what Egyptian officials were telling their U.S. counterparts and asked that the United States "refrain from putting forward proposals of its own." She explained that ideas that Sisco had aired in Cairo, namely, certain cease-fire

3. As an aid to their discussion, I am forwarding to her an "oral discussion minute" which tries to express in precise language the "ideas" I presented at our meeting. You are fully familiar with how I intend to express these. It is in my judgment encouraging that she is ready to look at and weigh these ideas in precise form, without commitment on either side. It was clear from what she said at the meeting that she would find this useful since we were discussing a considerable number of ideas which will require both subtle and precise formulations. There are also first glimmers—and only glimmers—of preparation of the public through the press for some flexibility on their part, but not so much that they cannot pull back at any moment. She has cancelled tomorrow's Cabinet meeting so that she can discuss the ideas in the first instance with the inner group which was at our meeting.

4. She is very clear that no proposal is being made on our side and it is an "oral discussion minute" that she is receiving. She understands that all that I have been saying is strictly on an ad referendum basis. She understands also that at this stage what we are trying to do is to have a look at the kind of ideas that might have some chance of meeting Israeli and Sadat's principal needs. I made clear that it does not mean that even if we come to a mutual judgment regarding the ideas I expressed that we would necessarily put all of them forward to the Egyptians in the next stage and give away all the concessions that she would feel she had made in order to make this possible. I get the impression that she is trying to find a way to meet us at least part way within the presently approved Knesset position rather than provoke a new crisis in the Cabinet. She of course reiterated in the meeting that their April paper[4] is "our bible." Allon interjected with a smile, "Yes but it is likely to become an Old Testament." I took this to mean that some of the ideas expressed would carry the GOI beyond where they are at the present time. I am under no illusions about how difficult it will be for them to move from their present common denominator position. However, I shall continue my effort to get the Prime Minister to agree to explore and come to an understanding with us on the positions we feel we could reasonably put to Sadat, under the ground rule that the outcome

---

limitations and the notion that Egypt could keep forces east of the Suez Canal, were "contrary to fundamentals of Israeli position." The extent of withdrawal suggested by the United States for the second stage of a two-stage withdrawal process was "fantastic," Meir contended, adding that Israel could not change its position and "current talks could not be reported as reflecting Israeli agreement." Sisco responded that the United States was not hiding anything in its talks with Egyptian officials and that his ideas regarding the interim agreement reflected what Sadat had told him and others. (Telegram 4725 from Tel Aviv, August 6; ibid., Nixon Presidential Materials, NSC Files, Box 1164, Saunders Files, Middle East Negotiations Files, Middle East—Jarring Talks, August 1–16, 1971)

[4] See footnote 2, Document 224.

of the negotiating process, if an interim agreement is arrived at, would be ad referendum to the constitutional processes in Israel. I have also been doing a little work on Allon because I suspect—though I am not sure—that he is a little jealous of the leading role played by Dayan on an interim settlement.

5. My presentation was made in three parts: (A) Discussion of the kind of bilateral consultations, intelligence exchange and military and economic assistance arrangements as well as international positions we might consider if an interim settlement achieved and to reassure Israel against the contingency of violations, (reported more fully in subsequent telegram); (B) Description of the concepts underlying our approach to an interim agreement with emphasis on avoiding military disadvantage to Israel and on the need to make an interim agreement as irrevocable a process towards an overall settlement as possible; (C) A point by point elaboration of the UAR-Israel positions and our own tentative ideas re elements of an interim settlement. It was clear from questions put to me by the Ministers present—and Mrs. Meir made this quite explicit—that stickiest issue for Israel is likely to boil down to the question of a UAR military presence of any kind east of the Canal. Prime Minister Meir said "For us there are two cardinal points: no fighting, no Egyptian troops across the Canal." I have the feeling that our formulation on the ceasefire could do the trick since they openly acknowledged the problems that Sadat has not to appear to be buying a new indefinite armistice arrangement. Surprisingly, they did not seem unduly shocked by the idea that, in final stage of interim agreement, they might be expected to pull back to the vicinity or east of the key Sinai passes. They did not make major point of their right to use the Canal during the interim agreement and seemed taken with the idea of Israeli and UAR representatives participating in an augmented UNTSO supervisory arrangement. Finally I have the impression they are somewhat intrigued with our concept of a two stage withdrawal, whereby second and major stage would depend on Sadat's performance in the first stage in normalizing conditions in the Canal area and getting Canal back into operation.

6. All of these impressions must necessarily remain tentative until we hear their considered reaction at the next session. I expect hard bargaining, including on the question of aircraft commitments which the Israelis raised again today.

7. Before the above meeting took place, I asked for a meeting with the Prime Minister alone to discuss the question of press leaks. I found her most sympathetic and understanding and terribly distressed, as we were, over a *Maariv* article that could not have been written without some backgrounding on the part of Israelis present at our first meeting. I am trying to put as complete a clamp on the contact with the press as

is possible. We are saying absolutely nothing here beyond the agreed communiqués issued at the end of each meeting. After we concluded our detailed meeting today she called in her Ministers and laid down the law about leaks.

8. I have surfaced with her the idea of our trying to arrange secret talks between the UAR and Israel after an interim settlement is achieved. I did this in order to show her that there would be a new situation created after an interim settlement is achieved with fresh opportunities to try to get Jarring unstuck from the present mud he is in and to find other ways as well to get on with discussions on an overall settlement. I will also at the appropriate time raise the possibility with her of secret talks in New York or elsewhere in September as a way to get things moving more rapidly on an interim settlement. I do not want to do this until I have had their reaction to our ideas and have been able to assess it.

9. Here are the ideas in brief which were discussed: I will send you text of "oral discussion minute" in later telegram.[5]

(A) Relation of interim to an overall settlement. I expressed understanding of the Israeli view that Israeli withdrawal on an interim agreement cannot be tied, as Sadat wishes, to total Israeli withdrawal to the June 5 line as part of the overall settlement. I explained that as a minimum what Sadat needs is a link between an interim agreement and ongoing diplomatic efforts under Jarring's auspices towards an overall agreement in accordance with SC Resolution of November 1967. I stressed that an interim agreement would create a completely new situation, that Jarring would have to take this into account, and he would have to see whether some new tack was possible. I also said to Prime Minister Meir that if an interim agreement was achieved, we would be prepared to give thought to trying to get some secret talks going between the UAR and Israel. I gave this as an illustration of possibilities created by a favorable atmosphere resulting from an interim agreement. Her eyes lit up.

(B) Ceasefire. I indicated we understood and appreciated why a six month ceasefire, even on a renewable basis, would be considered a short time fuse for them. I also put to rest the idea of a permanent ceasefire, pointing out no government would take on such a self denying ordinance jeopardizing its sovereignty. After all, the Kellogg-Briand Pact of 1928 certainly proved that legal eschewment of war is not the route. I

---

[5] The "Oral Discussion Minute" covered the ideas on the interim agreement that Sisco and Meir discussed on August 2 and was transmitted in telegram 4655 from Tel Aviv, August 3. (National Archives, Nixon Presidential Materials, NSC Files, Box 1164, Saunders Files, Middle East Negotiations Files, Middle East—Jarring Talks, August 1–16, 1971)

suggested the possibility that the ceasefire might be expressed in an "open ended" or "indefinite" not "permanent" way along side two other but separate provisions in any agreement: . . .

(A) An 18 month "mutual review" clause of the entire agreement, including the stage of negotiations under Jarring's auspices;
(B) A clause reserving the right of each to exercise their right of self defense if a violation of the agreement occurred. The formula would get around the problem which worried them that the UAR could at any given point, after Israeli withdrawal, point to lack of progress in negotiations under Jarring and use this as a pretext to break the agreement.

(C) Use of the Canal. While both Egypt and Israel have agreed that the UAR should clear, open and operate the Canal, Israel wants to be able to use the Canal as part of the interim agreement whereas Sadat would not have them use it until an overall settlement is achieved. I came up with several ways to meet this difference which they are chewing on: (A) UAR acknowledge in principle Israel's right to use the Canal, but Israel agree voluntarily not to exercise the right until a final peace agreement is achieved; (B) UAR simply make an explicit commitment in principle that Israel can use the Canal once an overall settlement is reached; and (C) Israel's merchant vessels and peace time cargoes transiting the Canal as part of an interim arrangement, but its war vessels unable to do so until a final peace agreement.

(D) Zone of withdrawal; nature of supervisory mechanism; Egyptian presence east of the Canal. These three critical issues are so closely linked they were handled together. The idea they are giving serious thought to, after I surfaced it with them bit by bit, boiled down to this two stage proposal: Stage I, Israel would withdraw 10 kilometers from the Canal, in the meantime (6 months) the Canal would be cleared and readied for operation; UNTSO would assure that the Bar Lev Line was maintained during this initial period only and only Egyptian civilians would be permitted east of the Canal. Stage II—after this six month test on the ground, Israel would withdraw to a line "in the vicinity" of the 3 key passes (30–50 kilometers from the Canal); an augmented UNTSO operation with UAR and Israeli liaison representatives included, would be responsible for establishment of posts on the key passes which would leave them in the hands of neither the UAR nor Israel; Egypt would be permitted to occupy the vacated zone up to 10 kilometers with no more than 750 men with rifles.

10. I know that this has been somewhat of a lengthy report but I was sure that you would want all of the relevant details.

11. I spend tomorrow with the Israeli military getting a detailed briefing on the military balance.

Barbour

246. Telegram From the Interests Section in Egypt to the Department of State[1]

Cairo, August 16, 1971, 1220Z.

2048. For Secretary and Sisco from Bergus.

1. State 149349[2] reached me at about 0900 this morning. I immediately got in touch with Heykal, who was in Alexandria. He said he would advance his plans and return to Cairo at once. Later in the morning, he asked me to meet him at the Hilton at 1330 local. (Heykal family, like Bergus family, staying in Hilton temporarily while major repairs being done on their respective houses.)

2. When I met with Heykal he said what I was about to tell Egyptians would affect their attitude far into the future. Egypt must reevaluate its stand prior to the Damascus meeting.[3] Soviets were putting very heavy pressure on Egyptians, saying that U.S. was tempted to make Egypt a pawn in the game among U.S., USSR and People's China. Soviets were still saying they had no objection to Egyptians continuing efforts for interim settlement through USG, but were warning Egyptians U.S. not acting in good faith but simply playing for time. UAR Ambassador to Moscow would shortly arrive in Cairo bearing just that message.

3. Heykal then said Sadat having lengthy meeting with students today and had only 36 hours before leaving for Damascus. He asked I give him highlights of message so he could lay them before Sadat in effort arrange meeting between me and Sadat. I said I was authorized do this but Secretary hoped very strongly I could present these points to Sadat personally.

4. I then began giving highlights of talking points. Heykal took verbatim notes until about half way through my presentation, when he

---

[1] Source: National Archives, Nixon Presidential Materials, NSC Files, Box 1164, Saunders Files, Middle East Negotiations Files, Middle East—Jarring Talks, August 1–16, 1971. Secret; Immediate; Nodis; Cedar Plus.

[2] In telegram 149349 to Cairo, August 13, the Department instructed Bergus to seek an appointment with Sadat, or, if preferable, with Heikal, to report orally on Sisco's talks in Israel the previous week. Rogers wrote: "We obviously want to be frank with Sadat so that he does not feel, as Heikal indicated, that we are trying to tranquilize him. On the other hand, he must understand that Sisco trip was part of on-going process to explore all possibilities of flexibility on remaining key issues, that we did not seek new commitments at this stage, and that this was another phase in process of continuing discussions on this subject with Israelis in weeks ahead. We assume that Sadat continues to prefer interim settlement to other options open to him, and that in particular he wants to find a way to avoid the military option if at all possible." (Ibid.)

[3] Presidents Sadat, Asad, and Qadhafi met in Damascus August 18–20. (*New York Times*, August 21, 1971, p. 3.)

dropped his pen and said it demeaned him to listen to such points. This was kind of stuff I should be passing to Mohammed Riad. I firmly enjoined him to hear me out.

5. Upon conclusion of my presentation we had lengthy, always friendly, never emotional, but very gutsy personal exchange. Heykal took line that it would have been better if Sisco had admitted he had failed. What I had had to say would not convince a child let alone Kaddafi, Assad or ASU Central Committee. I interposed that latter were only people Egypt should really be worrying about.

6. Heykal said that if USG intended proceed along these lines he personally wanted out of the interim settlement business and would so request Sadat. I stressed U.S. intent to continue discussing our ideas with Israelis and expression of our willingness unveil these ideas to Sadat, if he wished, and carry on exploratory discussions with Egyptians without requesting commitment or immediate reaction. As friend of Egypt, I had racked my brain and could not see for the life of me where Egypt had anything to lose by entering into such discussions. We went on at it hot and heavy along these lines for about 20 minutes.

7. Finally, Heykal promised me that he would pass highlights of my presentation to Sadat as soon as possible and urge that Sadat hear what I had to say from my own lips. Heykal promised me that he would volunteer no judgments or recommendations to Sadat so as to permit the President to make his own decisions on these matters so vital to the future of Egypt.

8. Meeting with Sadat may take place this evening.[4]

Bergus

---

[4] Bergus did not meet with Sadat that evening, but rather with Heikal again at 1 p.m. the next day. According to Bergus's message to the Department, Heikal said that he had conveyed Bergus's oral presentation from the day before to Sadat "without comment," causing the Egyptian President to be "very disappointed." Sadat told Heikal that he hoped that the United States would "send him something more reassuring" over the next two days, but that he would understand if it was not in a position to do so. If U.S. officials did not have another message for him, then he wanted Bergus to make the same presentation to Mohammed Riad at the Foreign Office on August 21 that he had made to Heikal, to which Bergus commented: "Sadat well knows that putting question of interim settlement back into hands of Mahmoud Riad's FonOff means writing off this particular exercise." Sadat further remarked that he wanted to be informed about the suggestions that Sisco made to Israeli officials earlier that month, but Bergus wrote that he hesitated to do so without the prospect of being able to "deliver Israel on any one of them." (Telegram 2057 from Cairo, August 17; National Archives, Nixon Presidential Materials, Box 1164, Saunders Files, Middle East Negotiations Files, Middle East—Jarring Talks, August 1–16, 1971)

247. Editorial Note

On September 15, 1971, delegations representing Jordan and the Palestine Liberation Organization arrived in Jidda, Saudi Arabia, to negotiate an agreement that would allow the fedayeen to live peacefully—and to some degree autonomously—in Jordan. The two sides did not begin face-to-face talks until September 20, after Saudi and Egyptian mediators, including Saudi King Faisal, had narrowed the gulf that existed between them on a variety of issues. (*New York Times*, September 21, 1971, page 2) A major sticking point for the Jordanian delegation was the recommendation that Jordan accept a small group of military supervisors on its soil to arbitrate between the government and the fedayeen. (Telegram 3337 from Jidda, September 20; National Archives, Nixon Presidential Materials, NSC Files, Box 629, Country Files, Middle East, Saudi Arabia) With matters still unsettled, Jordanian representatives left the talks on September 24 for consultations in Amman and never returned. The Palestinian delegation left for Beirut two days later, where King Faisal, on a state visit to Lebanon, met with Yasser Arafat as part of a continuing joint Saudi-Egyptian effort to reconcile differences between Jordan and the PLO. (*New York Times*, September 30, 1971, page 15) According to U.S. intelligence sources, the Fatah wing of the PLO had sent a group to Jidda with the "principal aim of sabotaging" the discussions there, hoping to lay blame on Jordan for their failure, and thus prompting Egypt and Saudi Arabia to take punitive action against Jordan, information which the Embassy in Jidda had given to the Jordanian delegation. (Telegram 3282 from Jidda, September 15; National Archives, Nixon Presidential Materials, NSC Files, Box 629, Country Files, Middle East, Saudi Arabia)

248. Editorial Note

On September 18, 1971, President Richard Nixon, President's Assistant for National Security Affairs Henry Kissinger, and Attorney General John Mitchell discussed "some shooting going on along the Suez Canal" in the Oval Office. According to Kissinger, Israel shot down an Egyptian reconnaissance plane "by accident" earlier in the week, not long after which Egypt shot down an Israeli plane "thirty miles inside Israeli territory," leading Israel to strike SAM sites in Egypt on the morning of September 18. Nixon remarked that he was "inclined to stay out" of the matter because he did not think it would "do any good" to get involved. He added, "And I don't want to do anything that's impotent. So they're fighting around a little. Let them fight a little. They aren't going to have a war about this, Henry. The Israelis aren't going to go to war—I mean a war isn't going to come unless the Egyptians start roaring in there." Kissinger agreed, explaining that Israeli Ambassador Yitzhak Rabin had called him earlier that morning to tell him that "unless there's a retaliation, they won't do any more." When Mitchell asked if "the Palestinian raids on the Lebanese border" were "any part of this," Kissinger responded, "Not that we can tell. That's mostly caused by the fact that the fedayeen are getting pushed out of Jordan," to which he added, "The Jordan thing has worked out very well."

Next, they discussed the meetings that Secretary of State William Rogers intended to have with Israeli, Egyptian, and Soviet officials in New York in September at the session of the UN General Assembly. Nixon said, "On the Mideast, it appears that the main thing is to be sure to keep Bill in line." Kissinger worried that Rogers would "pull some spectacular that he isn't telling anybody," explaining that "the danger we have in the Middle East is if we raise expectations." Later, Mitchell said, "On this Middle East thing, Mr. President, I hope that Bill doesn't foolishly come down on our Israeli friends up there," to which Nixon later responded, "I see no reason to push it." Kissinger told them that he instructed Ambassador George Bush "to keep me informed about what's going on at the U.N." When Nixon remarked, "There's no reason to push the Israelis out the window," Mitchell said that Israeli Defense Minister Moshe Dayan sent a message through an intermediary that Israel "would be perfectly happy" with "a secret commitment on future deliveries of their Phantoms." Nixon agreed that "the best thing, probably, is to have a secret deal. Frankly, I would rather have it that way, than for them to raise hell with us in the Senate." Nixon later added, "Well, I don't want—well, the main thing is, John, I don't want Rabin to know. We—this has to be totally secretive. Because I don't want him running to Rogers and the State Department and then saying we blew the deal." (National Archives, Nixon Presidential Materials, White House Tapes, Cabinet Room, Conversation No. 576–6) The editor prepared this transcript of the tape recording specifically for this volume.

249. Memorandum From the President's Assistant for National Security Affairs (Kissinger) to President Nixon[1]

Washington, September 23, 1971.

SUBJECT

Letter from Mrs. Meir

The attached letter from Mrs. Meir[2] reiterates interest in a limited interim settlement and restates "grave concern" over the stoppage of Phantom deliveries. On the interim settlement:

—For Israel, the main purposes of an interim agreement are "the strengthening of the cease-fire, the disengagement of forces and the creation of a better atmosphere for further negotiations, looking towards a final peace settlement."

—She repeats Israel's positions: unlimited ceasefire; no Egyptian or Soviet military forces across the Canal because it would "negate the concept of disengagement;" no prejudice to final positions in a peace agreement; Israeli ships through the Canal.

On aircraft, she notes the Soviet-Egyptian treaty,[3] the flow of Soviet arms and President Sadat's urging that the US press Israel. She concludes citing the danger that a hiatus in US shipments will weaken Israel's "deterrent posture" in Soviet and Egyptian eyes.

This letter highlights the issue that will face Secretary Rogers in his efforts at the UN to revive discussion of the interim settlement. Aircraft shipments to Israel have been allowed to lapse on the theory that this might cause the Israelis to modify their position. Informally, the word comes back that there will be no modification until Mrs. Meir and Gen. Dayan are satisfied that aircraft shipments are secured. Even then, of course, modifications would be in keeping with Israel's view of an interim settlement—that its purpose is to freeze the present situation until the UAR is ready to accept boundary changes.

State Department this week is discussing two general options:

—One would be to allow the hiatus in shipments to go on a while longer. The problem with this is that a time will probably come when the US will be forced by circumstances to resume shipments. The situa-

---

[1] Source: National Archives, Nixon Presidential Materials, NSC Files, Box 756, Presidential Correspondence 1969–1974, Israel Prime Minister Golda Meir. Secret; Nodis; Cedar Plus. Sent for information. A stamped notation on the memorandum indicates the President saw it.

[2] Dated September 17; attached but not printed.

[3] See Document 235.

tion at that time could be more difficult if we appeared to be backing down in the face of Israeli pressure, military action or diplomatic intransigence.

—The other would be to make a new aircraft commitment now with most deliveries a year or more in the future at the end of present production lines. The details would be adjustable to encourage Israeli responsiveness. The problem with this is that it somewhat reduces the pressure on Israel to modify its position.

Secretary Rogers has not yet reached his own decision. Whichever the tactic, the objective would be to induce just enough change in the Israeli position to revive discussion with Egypt.

The problem with the interim settlement is that too much has been attempted. The initial idea was simply a mutual thinning out on both sides. From that it mushroomed to Sadat insisting on moving his forces to the key Sinai passes. To achieve that, the US would have to press Israel almost as hard as to get an overall settlement.

The main hope now, it would seem to me, would be to reduce Egyptian expectations to a point where changes that might realistically be expected in Israel's position could produce an understanding. Because official positions are tied to greater expectations, it may be that the only way of achieving this—if it were possible at all—would be through less official exchanges to see what might be possible.

250. Editorial Note

On September 25, 1971, the United Nations Security Council adopted Resolution 298 regarding the status of Jerusalem by a vote of 14–0–1, with Syria abstaining. It reaffirmed the Security Council's two previous resolutions on Jerusalem, 252 and 267, adopted in 1968 and 1969 respectively, and deplored Israel's failure to respect those resolutions by taking legislative and administrative actions that changed the status of the city. It also called on Israel to both stop and undo such actions, including the expropriation of land and property and the transfer of people. Finally, it requested that the Secretary General, in consultation with the President of the Security Council, report on the progress of the resolution's implementation within at least 60 days. (*Yearbook of the United Nations, 1971,* page 187) Jordan had requested that the Security Council meet to discuss Jerusalem two weeks earlier, prompting Israeli Ambassador Yitzhak Rabin to tell Assistant Secretary of State Joseph Sisco that Israel believed that the United States was "behind this

Jordanian move" and that it would be "the cause for bad blood in U.S.-Israeli relations." (Memorandum from Saunders to Kissinger, September 13; National Archives, Nixon Presidential Materials, NSC Files, Box 647, Country Files, Middle East, Middle East (General), Vol. 8)

In fact, the United States had worked since June 1971 to discourage Jordan from taking the Jerusalem question to the Security Council, fearing that any Security Council meeting on the issue could not be confined to Jerusalem, "however strenuous" its "efforts to that end." (Telegram 114987 to Amman, June 25; ibid., Box 1163, Saunders Files, Middle East Negotiations Files, Middle East—Jarring Talks, June 18–30, 1971) Having accepted that it could not deter Jordan on the matter, U.S. officials decided to work with Jordanian officials throughout July and August to craft the text of a resolution that would be moderate enough for the United States to support once it came up for a vote because, as Secretary of State William Rogers wrote to President Nixon: "The Israeli policy on Jerusalem has continued with such disregard of Jordanian sensibilities that our failure to give modest support to Hussein would have seriously jeopardized our relations with him." (Memorandum from Rogers to Nixon, September 16; ibid., Box 1165, Saunders Files, Middle East Negotiations Files, Middle East—Jarring Talks, September 1–October 1, 1971) Key instructions and commentary to the Mission to the United Nations regarding a draft resolution are in telegrams 120507 to USUN, July 3, and 154569 to USUN and Amman, August 23. (Ibid., Box 1164, Saunders Files, Middle East Negotiations Files, Middle East—Jarring Talks, July 1–16, 1971, and ibid., Box 1165, Saunders Files, Middle East Negotiations Files, Middle East—Jarring Talks, August 16–September 1, 1971, respectively)

251. Conversation Between President Nixon and Soviet Foreign Minister Gromyko[1]

Washington, September 29, 1971.

[Omitted here is discussion unrelated to the Middle East.]

Gromyko: One thing on the Middle East, I would like, if you had not mentioned it, I would mention it. I wish to tell you privately, strictly privately—

Nixon: Yeah?

Gromyko: —two key points. Frankly, some time ago, the United States Government, and you personally—and I think a sufficient decision was made—expressed concern how about delivery of armaments—

Nixon: To Egypt? Right?

Gromyko: Right.

Nixon: Fine.

Gromyko: We think it would be possible to reach understanding, if some kind of framework is reached, which would provide [for] withdrawal of Israeli troops from all occupied territories. We would agree on the limitation, or if you wish, even on stoppage—full stoppage of delivery [of armaments]—

Nixon: Hmm.

Gromyko: —in connection—even in connection with understanding on the first stage—

---

[1] Source: National Archives, Nixon Presidential Materials, White House Tapes, Oval Office, Conversation No. 580–20. No classification marking. The editors transcribed the tape recording printed here specifically for this volume. Brackets indicate unclear portions of the original recording or those omitted by the editors except "[for]", "[of armaments]", "[agreement]", "[United Nations]", "[is]", "[withdrawal]", and "[be]", added for clarity. The conversation was conducted in English without interpreters. According to the President's Daily Diary, this "one-on-one" meeting took place from 4:40 to 5 p.m. (Ibid., White House Central Files) No written U.S. record of the conversation has been found. Although neither was present, Kissinger and Dobrynin both described the meeting in their respective memoirs. See *White House Years*, pp. 838 and 1287, and *In Confidence*, p. 234. Prior to the meeting, Kissinger sent Nixon a memorandum explaining that Dobrynin had informed him on September 20 that Gromyko had a "personal message from Brezhnev" that he would like to deliver in private. "The Soviet leaders are proposing that this issue be handled in the same framework as Berlin was, having concluded that present efforts could not lead anywhere. They recognized that we are stymied in our initiative. They in turn, with their basic commitments to the Arabs, are under pressure to deliver something for them sooner or later if they are to preserve their influence." (Memorandum from Kissinger to Nixon, September 28; *Foreign Relations*, 1969–1976, volume XIII, Soviet Union, October 1970–October 1971, Document 335) For a record of Nixon and Gromyko's conversation prior to the private "one-on-one" meeting, which was attended by Rogers, Kissinger, and Dobrynin, see ibid., Document 337.

Nixon: What to do here—

Gromyko: On the—

Nixon: Exactly. In terms of the—

Gromyko: —even in connection with the interim [agreement]—

Nixon: —interim. Right.

Gromyko: You agree.

Nixon: Right.

Gromyko: Even in connection, provided that this is the—connected with the final, with the withdrawal—

Nixon: Yeah.

Gromyko: —of—from all territories, within a certain period of time. More than this. I would like to tell you, also frankly, confidentially, both this point and then the third one I discussed with Mr. Brezhnev. So this is not the second point here. The second point is this: some time ago, you expressed interest—oh, I don't know—in Egypt, about our presence there, our military—

Nixon: Yeah, yeah, yeah, yeah.

Gromyko: —presence in Egypt.

Nixon: Yeah.

Gromyko: I do not know whether you know precisely our position, or not, on our presence, but, in a sense, we are present there. In a sense—

Nixon: Hm-hmm.

Gromyko: North of Cairo, certain personnel, and certain forces—

Nixon: I see.

Gromyko: —and such presence, the presence is agreed. We are ready, in connection with understanding, full understanding, on the Middle East—

Nixon: Hm-hmm

Gromyko: —we are ready to agree not to have our military units there.

Nixon: Hm-hmm.

Gromyko: Not to have soldiers based there—

Nixon: Not the civilian, I understand.

Gromyko: Not precisely. Not to have military units, you know, there—

Nixon: Not there.

Gromyko: We probably—we would leave a limited number, a limited number of advisers for purely advisory—

Nixon: Advisory purposes.

Gromyko: You know—
Nixon: Technical advisers.
Gromyko: —like you have in Iran.
Nixon: Like we have in Cambodia and the rest.
Gromyko: Yes, that is right.
Nixon: That's right.
Gromyko: I said it's for—
Nixon: I understand.
Gromyko: —for purely advisory purposes.
Nixon: But not for—I see.
Gromyko: Hmm.
Nixon: Right. I understand.
Gromyko: Absolutely right. I know that you—
Nixon: But these are matters that I deal with.
Gromyko: Okay.
Nixon: Yes.
Gromyko: I know. You understand very clearly.
Nixon: Yeah.
Gromyko: I would say limited, and maybe very limited.
Nixon: I understand.
Gromyko: Maybe very.
Nixon: Well, those are matters that could threaten—be discussed, if—but that has to be very private.
Gromyko: And it would be very private, very private—
Nixon: Right. Right. Right. The Mideast is so tense—so touchy, politically, in this country—
Gromyko: All these—
Nixon: —it has to be private here.
Gromyko: All these—
Nixon: Right.
Gromyko: —ideas, we did not put into motion—
Nixon: Sure. Right. Right—
Gromyko: —with anybody. Never. This is—
Nixon: Hm-hmm.
Gromyko: —new, and this is principle.
Nixon: Hm-hmm.
Gromyko: And the third point, whether you attach importance or not, but Israel always stresses anything you don't want to stress. It

would be—we would be ready, even if this accord is written on this basis, even in connection with the interim agreement, in the third stage.

Nixon: Hm-hmm.

Gromyko: And we will be ready to deal—to sign, if you wish, together with you, or with U.S. and other powers, or with all other powers who are on the [United Nations] Seurity Council. This initiative [is] possible in a document, if with additional—

Nixon: Hm-hmm. Hm-hmm.

Gromyko: —agreement and understanding on security for Israel—

Nixon: Sure.

Gromyko: —in connection with the interim. With the interim—

Nixon: I see.

Gromyko: —provided that interim is—

Nixon: All right.

Gromyko: —connected. [unclear] and our own suggestion was that, well, when vis-à-vis the border or finalization of the agreement, only some kind of decision—

Nixon: True.

Gromyko: —should be taken on guarantees. But we are ready to discuss this idea in connection—we can sign any agreement with guarantees in connection with the interim, provided that the interim is linked with Israeli [withdrawal]. The limitation of even—limitation, even stoppage [unclear]—

Nixon: Your arms?

Gromyko: Second—

Nixon: Present?

Gromyko: —not presence of any Soviet units. Not—

Nixon: Sure.

Gromyko: —[unclear] heavy units, intermediate military—

Nixon: Right.

Gromyko: —you could say.

Nixon: Sure.

Gromyko: Some of the limited—I say this would [be] limited number of advisers for purely, purely, purely advisory purposes.

Nixon: I understand.

[unclear exchange]

Gromyko: If you—

Nixon: Let us do a little—as I say, we'll do a private talking on this. And then, on this message that Kissinger brings you tomorrow on Vietnam, I think you'll find very interesting. It could be very—

Gromyko: Good.

Nixon: It could be very important.

Gromyko: Very good.

Nixon: If we could get that out of the way, you could see—and I don't, we don't want to ask you to do anything that's not in your interest—but if we get that out of the way, it opens other doors. You see?

Gromyko: Good. I have to say—what I told you about this Middle East, this is—

Nixon: Comes from—

Gromyko: —result of the conversation personally with Brezhnev. And he wants me to say to you—

Nixon: Yeah.

Gromyko: So we are taking a position.

Nixon: I understand.[2]

[Omitted here is a brief, largely unclear exchange as Nixon and Gromyko evidently left the room.]

---

[2] Following the meeting, Gromyko prepared a memorandum of his "one-on-one" conversation with Nixon for circulation to members and candidate members of the Politburo. Regarding the Middle East, Gromyko wrote the following: "I said that above all, clarity was needed with respect to the withdrawal of Israeli troops. If the U.S. has serious intentions and is genuinely willing to promote a settlement 'on the basis of complete withdrawal of Israeli troops from all occupied Arab territories,' we would be willing to give favorable consideration to the following issues: (1) limiting or even stopping outside arms shipments to the countries of the region once the situation has been fully resolved; (2) withdrawing our actual 'military units' from the region, but 'leaving military advisers in the relevant countries' who would have purely advisory functions, like the military advisers the U.S. has in certain countries, such as Iran; (3) the issue of political security guarantees could even be resolved in connection with the first-stage agreement, the so-called interim agreement, if it is linked to the *complete withdrawal* of Israeli troops from Arab territories within a *specified period of time*. I again explained to Nixon that we are willing to reach agreement on the aforementioned basis only if any agreement, including an interim agreement, is linked to the ultimate total withdrawal of Israeli troops, i.e. to thereby predetermine the final settlement. Without the complete withdrawal of Israeli troops no settlement is possible." (See *Soviet-American Relations, 1969–1972*, Document 204, footnote 3)

---

252. Editorial Note

On the evening of September 30, 1971, President's Assistant for National Security Affairs Henry Kissinger met with Soviet Foreign Minister Andrei Gromyko at the Soviet Embassy for two hours. First, Kissinger wanted to ensure that President Richard Nixon had correctly understood what the Foreign Minister had told him the previous afternoon regarding the cessation in arms deliveries, the withdrawal of Soviet troops, and Soviet participation in guarantee arrangements (see Document 251). After Gromyko had assured him that he had indeed made those points, the two of them discussed the complications of trying to establish a link between an interim and a final settlement. Kissinger said that there was "no possibility of implementing a final agreement" before the Presidential election, since "no American President could engage in the pressures that might be necessary" to achieve it. But Kissinger suggested that they might be able to "get the interim settlement out of the way" by the time of the Moscow Summit in May, where he thought Nixon and Brezhnev might privately agree on the nature of an "ultimate settlement." After Gromyko declared that their discussion had been "very positive" Kissinger informed him that he was prepared to begin talks with Dobrynin in three weeks. (*Foreign Relations, 1969–1976*, volume XIII, Soviet Union, October 1970–October 1971, Document 344)

253. Telegram From the Department of State to the Interests Section in Egypt[1]

Washington, September 30, 1971, 0140Z.

179672. 1. As you will gather from septel[2] reporting conversation over lunch today between Secretary and Foreign Minister Riad, discussion was frank, spirited, and at times even heated. We think, however, overall effect will be beneficial. We believe it helped clear air of some misunderstandings that have grown up between ourselves and Egyptians in recent weeks. At bottom of Riad's concern is misgiving that we are thinking of interim arrangement which in fact accords with what he believes to be Israeli concept—i.e., agreement which has life of its own and provides prolonged opportunity for new status quo without further movement toward final peace settlement. Riad insisted that "in-

---

[1] Source: National Archives, Nixon Presidential Materials, NSC Files, Box 1165, Saunders Files, Middle East Negotiations Files, Middle East—Jarring Talks, September 1–October 1, 1971. Secret; Priority; Nodis; Cedar Plus. Drafted by Sterner on September 29, cleared by Atherton, and approved by Sisco. Repeated to Amman, Beirut, London, Moscow, Paris, Tel Aviv, and USUN.

[2] Telegram 179673 to Cairo, September 29. (Ibid., Box 657, Country Files, Middle East, Middle East Nodis/Cedar/Plus, Vol. III)

terim agreement" just another name for "armistice agreement." Secretary partially lifted veil on some of elements of our specific ideas which should help to dispel these concerns. Point that seemed to make most impression on Egyptians was that, while we do not think short cease-fire extensions are realistic, we have very much in mind that interim agreement should have some built-in time frame for ongoing negotiations looking toward final settlement. Thus analogy with armistice agreements is not rpt not correct.

2. Secretary deliberately took offensive with Riad in attempt to undermine his negativism about interim agreement and get across reasons why we think this is in interests of all—including Egypt. Nevertheless fact emerged plainly that Riad remains almost implacably suspicious of and opposed to interim idea. We think ground covered in today's meeting could be very helpful for Sadat if reliable report of Secretary's comments gets to him. We are concerned that Riad's negativism may cause him to distort and perhaps omit much of what Secretary said. We think it would be good idea, therefore, for you to make an appointment with Heikal as soon as possible to relay following points which we attempted to get across today and which we consider very important. You may supplement these as you see fit with points taken from telegram reporting Secretary's remarks.

3. Secretary was at pains today to try to get across to Riad that our concept of interim agreement was not end in itself but practical starting process toward final peace settlement. Egypt knows how we stand on shape of final peace settlement. But Secretary made point that unfortunately at this time, in our judgment, it is impossible to get agreement between the parties on terms of final peace settlement. This is why we have viewed President Sadat's proposal for an interim agreement as an imaginative and constructive step. It offers the opportunity to make practical progress in a manner that is to the advantage of both sides without requiring at this time that all the answers to a final peace settlement be agreed upon.

4. Secretary and Foreign Minister spent some time today in discussion of semantics as to what was meant by term "interim agreement." Secretary said we would continue to use this term because it was what most other nations used and also because it seemed accurate. To us word "interim" conveys exactly what we think we and Egyptians have in mind: Arrangement of temporary nature leading to further stages of progress toward a final peace settlement. Important thing in our view is not so much term by which this proposition is known but rather certain basic principles about it. These are: (1) that this is not a final agreement but rather one looking toward final settlement; (2) under interim agreement neither side can expect to achieve certain fundamental commitments that it expects in final settlement.

5. Practical choice confronting Egypt and Israel at this juncture of history is either to make practical step-by-step progress toward peace settlement, or to continue clamoring for total solution according to their desires which in our judgment will consign area to another decade and more of bitter, wasteful impasse and perhaps bloody hostility. We hope Secretary's frank exposure today of realities as we see them will help to get this message across to Egyptians.[3]

6. As next step Secretary will see Eban in N.Y. Monday[4] to continue our intensive efforts to move matters forward on interim agreement. Secretary also plans to see Riad again while two men are in New York,[5] but no precise date set. Sisco will also undoubtedly find opportunity to continue discussion with Mohammed Riad in New York.

Rogers

---

[3] Bergus conveyed the Department's message to Heikal on September 30, meeting with him for 90 minutes. Heikal said that he would pass the information along to Sadat that evening but that he would not comment at the time because "so many fundamental questions were involved." Bergus replied that he understood and that he himself did not want to go beyond his instructions "in such a vital matter as this." (Telegram 2379 from Cairo, September 30; ibid.)

[4] Rogers and Eban met in New York at 5:30 p.m. on October 4. Held in a "calm and relaxed atmosphere," the meeting was "devoted largely to reviewing present state of play on interim Canal agreement." Rogers informed Eban that his recent talks with Riad and Gromyko "broke little new ground," but that the Soviet Foreign Minister expressed "great concern about risk of renewed fighting" in the Middle East. He added that the United States believed that Sadat was still interested in an interim settlement and supported U.S. efforts toward that end. He also said that the United States considered the next two to three months "vital" for achieving such an outcome and that he hoped that both Egypt and Israel would "show greater flexibility" in the process of doing so. Eban responded by expressing Israel's "readiness" to work for an interim agreement on the "understanding that such agreement not attempt to obtain for Arab side what Arabs cannot achieve in negotiations on overall settlement." Eban also expressed "concern" that Egypt had no interest in seeking an interim agreement, but, rather, was trying to "change US position in favor Arabs." He also stressed that the "negotiating ball is in Egyptian court" and that the "next move is clearly up to Sadat." (Telegram 3179 from USUN, October 6; ibid., Box 1165, Saunders Files, Middle East Negotiations Files, Middle East—Jarring Talks, October 1–11, 1971)

[5] The two had met on September 29 when Rogers had pointed out to Foreign Minister Riad that unless a partial step leading to a final agreement were taken, the status quo would continue. (Telegram 179673 to Cairo, September 29; ibid., RG 59, Central Files 1970–73, POL 27–14 ARAB–ISR) They met again on October 8; see footnote 4, Document 255.

254. Telegram From the Department of State to the Interests Section in Egypt[1]

Washington, October 2, 1971, 2104Z.

181659. Tosec 31.

1. *FYI:* Mohammed Riad told Newlin in N.Y. that Foreign Minister Riad in speech to GA which scheduled for Wednesday plans to attack interim agreement.[2] We have been considering how we might get to Sadat in effort to head off Foreign Minister's taking line that could constitute serious obstacle to current negotiating efforts. Problem is somewhat delicate, because we want to avoid appearing end run Riad in way which might backfire on what we seek accomplish. Best approach in our view would be for you to seek appointment with President for Monday evening, purpose of which would be to convey, as courtesy to President, text of Middle East portion of Secretary's address to GA Monday morning,[3] together with some comments thereon. USUN will cable text of Middle East portion of Secretary's speech as soon as it is in final form, either later Sunday or early Monday N.Y. time.[4] If appointment with President not possible, we suggest you carry out exercise with Heikal, asking him to pass text and our comments to President. *End FYI.*

2. You should tell Sadat that Secretary's remarks on Middle East occupy prominent place in his speech and constitute important U.S. policy statement. As President will note, Secretary reaffirms that final peace settlement remains goal of our policy, and that our position on shape of final settlement and central role of Jarring mission remains unchanged. His remarks on this occasion underscore our belief, also conveyed by Secretary to Foreign Minister at their lunch, that at this time interim agreement for opening Canal and some Israeli withdrawal is only practical and realistic way to make progress toward final peace settlement. We believe this accords with President Sadat's own view as

---

[1] Source: National Archives, Nixon Presidential Materials, NSC Files, Box 658, Country Files, Middle East, Middle East Nodis/Cedar/Plus, Vol. IV. Secret; Immediate; Nodis; Cedar Plus. Drafted by Sterner and approved by Atherton. Repeated Priority to USUN for Secretary Rogers and to Tel Aviv.

[2] In his October 6 General Assembly speech, Riad announced that Egypt would reject any interim settlement that allowed Israeli forces to continue to occupy Egyptian territory. (*New York Times*, October 7, 1971, p. 1)

[3] See footnote 3, Document 255.

[4] Done in telegram 3116 from USUN to Cairo, October 3. (National Archives, Nixon Presidential Materials, NSC Files, Box 1165, Saunders Files, Middle East Negotiations Files, Middle East—Jarring Talks, October 1–11. 1971)

conveyed to Secretary last May.[5] Our efforts in intervening months have been predicated on this understanding of President's views.

3. Secretary told Foreign Minister on Sept 29,[6] and we want to reinforce this point with President, that we do not think it is possible to achieve as part of interim settlement certain fundamental commitments which each side expects as part of final peace settlement. This means that Egypt cannot expect to get Israeli commitment for total withdrawal from Sinai in interim agreement; it also means that Israel will not be able to achieve its objective of Egyptian commitment to final termination of belligerency in form of permanent ceasefire. At same time, we want to make it equally clear that we do not see interim agreement as end of road. We envisage agreement, as Secretary told Foreign Minister, that has built-in time frame and commitment from parties for on-going negotiations toward final peace settlement. We do not think interim agreement could provide basis for long range stability that US seeks in area and which can only be provided by final peace settlement based on full implementation of SC Res 242. We envisage that following conclusion of interim agreement there would be resumption of negotiations under Jarring on final settlement.

4. We stress this connection between interim agreement and final settlement because it is key point and we sense there may be misunderstanding between our two governments about it. This may be partly problem of semantics and if so we would like to clear it up as soon as possible. We note, for example, statements by Egyptian officials to effect that Egypt rejects "partial settlement." This term does not describe what US is seeking. We do not advocate "partial settlement." To contrary, we envisage interim agreement as practical first step toward final peace settlement and we favor it precisely because it offers prospect of improving conditions for negotiations toward final settlement. Word "interim" to US connotes idea of something temporary, of situation existing between one phase and next phase.

5. President will note that Secretary places heavy emphasis on interim agreement as our best hope for progress. He hopes that his speech will help create momentum toward narrowing gap on this first decisive step toward peace—a step which we want to achieve this year. We hope that Egyptian position, which we assume will be fully treated in Foreign Minister's speech on Wednesday, will also contribute to this end which we both seek and will treat interim agreement in such fashion as to add to this momentum and not close any doors. It is important for both sides to focus on what they can do for peace rather than, as has been case so often in past, what they cannot do. This posi-

---

[5] See Document 227.
[6] See Document 253.

tive quality of President Sadat's proposal last February[7] was precisely what made it such constructive and hopeful development against long background of negative attitudes that have characterized Arab-Israel dispute.

FYI: We leave to you whether and if so how to get across thought that, according to some stories circulating in N.Y., FonMin will attack interim agreement idea.[8]

6. *FYI:* We also want to bring to your attention fact that Egyptians in N.Y. are engaged in campaign to discredit Eban's speech[9] and in doing so misrepresenting what he said, e.g. claiming that speech shows Israel has backed off SC Res 242. On contrary we find speech helpful on certain key points. Referring to interim agreement Eban says Quote The agreement would stand on its own feet, but it would not affect or annul the undertakings which the parties gave in August 1970 to hold discussions under Ambassador Jarring's auspices in conformity with his mandate under the Security Council Resolution 242. Unquote. Discussing benefits of interim agreement Eban says, Quote A new impetus would be given to the Jarring mission which is now in abeyance; and the undertakings which I have given refute the idea that the Canal agreement would be the last word. On the contrary, its conclusion and observance would create a favourable channel for further agreements. Unquote. Again, he says, Quote neither Egypt nor Israel would attain its final objective in this interim framework. But Egypt's right to present its claims in the overall peace negotiations would remain intact, as would Israel's freedom to present its own proposals and reservations. Unquote. These passages indicate Israel does not see interim agreement as end in itself but fully expects resumption Jarring negotiations and reaffirms its commitment to Res 242 under our June, 1970 initiative and Jarring's August 7, 1970 report to SYG.[10] Since we suspect Sadat will be receiving negative interpretations of Eban speech from N.Y., we are providing foregoing for what use you may be able to make of it in your discussions. *End FYI.*

Irwin

---

[7] See Document 203.

[8] Bergus met with Heikal at 1 p.m. on October 4 and presented a copy of the Middle East portion of Rogers's General Assembly speech. Heikal assured Bergus that he would "get to Sadat as urgently as he could" to pass along the presentation. (Telegram 2408 from Cairo; National Archives, Nixon Presidential Materials, NSC Files, Box 1165, Saunders Files, Middle East Negotiations Files, Middle East—Jarring Talks, October 1–11, 1971) Bergus met with Sadat on October 7; see footnote 5, Document 255.

[9] In his September 30 speech before the UN General Assembly, Eban called for Foreign Minister Riad to meet with him under the auspices of the United States to discuss an interim settlement or under the auspices of Jarring to discuss a permanent settlement. (*New York Times,* October 1, 1971, p. 1)

[10] See footnote 5, Document 139.

Proximity Talks and the Backchannel: Separate Department of State and White House Negotiating Tracks

255. Telegram From Secretary of State Rogers to the Department of State[1]

New York, October 7, 1971, 2157Z.

3258/Secto 86. Dept pass Immediate Action USINT Cairo and Priority info AmEmbassy Tel Aviv. For Bergus from Secretary.

1. We note from reporting that Sadat will probably be leaving Cairo by October 10 so that we hope that we can have an answer from him to our proposal to bring the parties closer together in an intensified negotiation with the United States present.[2] We note too that Acting Foreign Minister Ghalib is stressing the desire that the United States get down to discussing substance. We have to handle this with great care in order to avoid getting ourselves committed substantively to the position of one side or the other at this juncture as we proceed with our good offices role. You will have noted that Eban has indicated to us that if there were any give by Egypt on one of the six points cited in the Secretary's speech,[3] Israel would be prepared to consider such Egyptian views.

2. We therefore believe that in connection with your approach on our procedural proposal, and as a follow-up to it, you need to explore with him thoroughly one critical point in particular: Relation of the interim agreement to an overall settlement. In doing so, please do not leave anything in writing. Secretary intends to explore this point with

---

[1] Source: National Archives, Nixon Presidential Materials, NSC Files, Box 658, Country Files, Middle East, Middle East Nodis/Cedar/Plus, Vol. IV. Secret; Priority; Nodis; Cedar Plus.

[2] See Document 254. Bergus made a "preliminary presentation" to Ismail on the morning of October 8. Ismail then conveyed the presentation to Sadat, who did not offer his reaction that day. (Telegram 2453 from Cairo, October 8; ibid., RG 59, Central Files 1970–73, POL 27–14 ARAB–ISR)

[3] In his October 4 address to the General Assembly, Rogers called on Israel and Egypt to accept an interim Suez Canal agreement based on six points: 1) the agreement would be only a step toward complete and full implementation of Resolution 242; 2) maintenance of the cease-fire; 3) determination of a "zone of withdrawal" to establish the "principle" of withdrawal in a permanent agreement; 4) establishment of supervisory arrangements to monitor the agreement; 5) the presence of Egyptian "personnel" east of the Canal; and 6) free passage of the Suez Canal for all nations. (Department of State Bulletin, October 25, 1971, pp. 442–444) Excerpts of the address were printed in the New York Times, October 5, 1971.

Riad in his meeting on Friday,[4] but we have no hope that he is either inclined or has any mandate to make a concession in this regard. We therefore want to get across to Sadat that if he is willing to consider sympathetically the kind of formulation have in mind on the relationship between an interim agreement and an overall settlement, that we would be prepared—hopefully in a negotiation in which the parties are in closer proximity, to come quickly to grips in a specific way on the other outstanding issues as described by the Secretary in his General Assembly statement.

3. In hitting this point, you have to make clear that Egyptian insistence—and we must admit to ourselves they have been absolutely unbending on this point from the start—on getting a commitment on total Israeli withdrawal to the international border as part of the interim agreement, as the Secretary said in his speech, was unrealistic.

4. Your presentation should be along the following lines:

A. We want to call Sadat's attention in particular to two basic principles which Secretary in his speech said would constitute foundation of fair approach to interim Canal agreement: (1) that a Suez Canal agreement is merely a step toward complete and full implementation of Resolution 242 within a reasonable period of time and not an end in itself; and (2) that neither side can realistically expect to achieve, as part of an interim agreement, complete agreement on the terms and conditions of an overall settlement. Those final terms and conditions will have to be worked out by negotiations under Ambassador Jarring's auspices.

B. Since these principles are fundamental to our thinking as we pursue our present diplomatic role with Egypt and Israel, we need to know if they are also acceptable basis from Sadat's viewpoint.

C. We recognize that Sadat would have difficulty answering foregoing question without knowing our thinking about its logical counterpart—namely, nature of commitment by parties to on-going efforts under Jarring's auspices to achieve final settlement and timeframe within which such efforts would take place.

D. We therefore want to share with Sadat our specific thoughts on how these two points might be handled in an interim agreement:

(1) We would envisage both sides explicitly acknowledging that the steps they were taking under the agreement were of an interim na-

---

[4] At their 75-minute meeting in New York on October 8, Rogers emphasized the importance of Egypt's participation in proximity talks in an "effort make faster progress on interim agreement." He also stressed that the United States understood Egypt's concern about the interim agreement becoming the "new status quo," declaring, "we will throw our weight behind ongoing negotiations toward final peace settlement." (Telegram 3358 from USUN, October 9; National Archives, Nixon Presidential Materials, NSC Files, Box 658, Country Files, Middle East, Middle East Nodis/Cedar/Plus, Vol. IV)

ture with a view to facilitating attainment of a just and lasting peace based on full and complete implementation of S.C. Resolution 242 in all its parts. To that end, they would make a commitment to pursue negotiations effectively and expeditiously under Ambassador Jarring's auspices.

(2) We would also envisage both sides explicitly undertaking to refrain from firing or other hostile acts and at the same time continuing their efforts under Jarring's auspices to achieve the peace settlement described above.

(3) Finally, we would envisage both sides explicitly agreeing to review interim agreement in its entirety after specified period if final settlement not achieved during that period. In other words, both sides would reserve their positions with respect to what happens at expiry of a specific period of time in light of progress achieved by them in working out final settlement. Length of timeframe would have to be negotiated, but in our view six months much too short, given complex issues to be resolved and need for reasonable period to give this first step Quote test of peace Unquote time to work.

(4) As Jarring negotiations resume in accordance parties' undertakings in interim agreement, we would obviously try to be as helpful as possible to move matters toward a final agreement.

(5) We urge President Sadat to examine carefully the specific ideas we have outlined above, which we have formulated carefully and precisely to meet what we understand to be one of his principal concerns—namely to make certain that an interim agreement would not lead to an indefinite occupation of Sinai. An indication from Sadat that these ideas formed an acceptable basis for dealing with issues of relationship between interim agreement and final settlement and of ceasefire would give dramatic impetus to our efforts to help parties realize first tangible, concrete step toward peace by end of year.[5]

Rogers

---

[5] Bergus met with Sadat and Ismail for 90 minutes that evening to outline the Department of State's proposal for Egypt and Israel to participate in what would become known as "proximity talks." Sadat reiterated his frustration with "the arrogance of Israel" as well as his fear that the interim settlement initiative was "being diverted towards a partial settlement and a new armistice between U.S. and Israel" by which Israel would occupy Egyptian territory "for an indefinite time." Bergus and Sadat agreed that the interim settlement should never be referred to as the "Suez Canal agreement," as it connoted an avoidance of a final settlement and peace, and Bergus added that he was sure that Rogers would "give clear directive to make certain that all official USG references henceforth and forever more would be to an 'interim agreement.'" (Telegram 2447 from Cairo, October 7; ibid.)

256. Telegram From Secretary of State Rogers to the Department of State[1]

New York, October 7, 1971, 2317Z.

3269/Secto 87. Dept pass AmEmbassy Tel Aviv and USINT Cairo.

1. In a somber mood, Rabin, at his request, met with Sisco in an early morning breakfast meeting. It was obvious that Rabin was under instructions to reflect a very deep and disquieting concern of GOI over Secretary's speech.[2]

2. Rabin said that Egypt had now achieved two very important goals: (A) they had succeeded in getting the U.S. to stop supplying aircraft to Israel; and (B) while it is true that there was nothing in our speech that could be called a proposal, nevertheless, Israel believed there was an erosion in the position of the U.S. on an interim agreement.

3. Rabin said that Israel sees Secretary's speech as a significant departure, a first move by the U.S. to begin to adopt substantive positions on the six points referred to in the Secretary's speech; substantive positions which more closely approximated the Egyptian view; positions which would give Israel great difficulty. Rabin singled out three things in the speech: (A) A re-affirmation by the U.S. of our position on the overall settlement as laid down in the Secretary's December 9, 1969 statement;[3] (B) the question of the ceasefire; and (C) the question of Egyptian forces crossing east of the Suez Canal. Rabin, in a posture more in sorrow than of anger, said he could not emphasize enough the concern that our statement has caused back home. He maintained that the UAR will see in the U.S. speech a turning point, a further move toward them substantively, and would encourage the Egyptians to sit absolutely tight. He stressed that Egypt had not made any concessions from the position that was adopted by them last May.[4] He said that we could not point to any position by the Egyptians on any of the six headings cited by the Secretary where the Egyptian position today is different than that expressed to us in May.

4. Specifically on the question of the ceasefire, while due note was taken that we had said that six months was too short, they interpreted

---

[1] Source: National Archives, Nixon Presidential Materials, NSC Files, Box 658, Country Files, Middle East, Middle East Nodis/Cedar/Plus, Vol. IV. Secret; Nodis; Cedar Plus.

[2] See footnote 3, Document 255.

[3] See Document 73.

[4] See Document 227.

our statement to rule out a ceasefire with an indefinite duration. Insofar as Egyptian forces east of the Canal, he admitted that we had stated that both sides hold opposing views, but was disturbed at the reference that we thought this issue could be compromised.[5]

5. Sisco said insofar as U.S. attitude overall settlement is concerned, it remains what it has been for the last two years. As to an interim agreement, there had been no erosion of our position; we made no proposals in the Secretary's speech and carefully avoided surfacing any of the ideas which were discussed with the GOI in July of this year.[6] Moreover, Sisco pointed out that in adopting the strong public view that Egypt could not expect to get an Israeli commitment of total withdrawal in the context of interim agreement, we were expressing a view which Israel holds. Just as we ruled out that kind of a commitment on the Egyptian side, so we believe it is equally realistic to expect a permanent ceasefire that has the effect of lifting the state of belligerency. Between these views there ought to be found some common ground between the two sides. On the question of Egyptian forces across the Canal, Sisco stated that this is probably the most sensitive point and the most important from the Israeli point of view. But here too while Sisco could understand the concern of Israel in that we indicated our belief that some acceptable compromise could be found, we had been very careful to avoid mentioning any specific proposals in this regard.

6. Sisco readily acknowledged that the Riad speech[7] was intended to apply pressure on the U.S. and to apply additional pressure on Israel. Sisco also acknowledged that as a minimum, the Egyptian strategy is to get the U.S. committed substantively as close as possible to their view, if not for the purpose of achieving an interim agreement of the kind Egypt has in mind, but at least to divorce or divide the United States substantively from Israel on the interim agreement in the same way which we are divided on the overall settlement, but Egypt did not get this in our speech. Sisco expressed regret that Israel did not find it possible in July to have given him even minimal flexibility on one or two of the points which he raised with them. Sisco said this was a mistake by the Israelis. Sisco noted that Eban had said in the last conversa-

---

[5] Specifically, Rogers said: "The question of an Egyptian military presence east of the Canal is one on which the parties hold opposite views. But here too the possibilities of some compromise are not negative."

[6] Reference is to Sisco's meetings in Israel from July 28 to August 6. See Document 245.

[7] Riad addressed the General Assembly on October 6. See footnote 2, Document 254.

tion[8] that Israel would be prepared to consider any new flexibility from Cairo on any one of the six points. We would be meeting with Riad on Friday,[9] and obviously would probe this matter further, and in particular the whole question of the relationship between an interim agreement and an overall settlement.

7. Rabin then turned the discussion to Sadat's Moscow trip[10] and there was an exchange as to whether Sadat would seek and get additional commitments of arms. Rabin indicated strongly he did not feel this was the main point. He stressed that what is more important to Sadat is the Russian commitment to intervene militarily in the defense of Egypt in the event the war of attrition is renewed. Rabin pointed out that unless Israel could in such circumstances strike in depth, costs of the war of attrition to them would be greater. He stressed that the Soviets are committed to this kind of defense to Egypt. He assumed that Sadat would get further arms commitments from the Russians but underscored that this was not as important as the Russian commitment to help the Egyptians defend themselves against in-depth operations. Sisco said our information indicates Soviets counseling restraint.

8. Sisco then raised the question of the Israeli vote on the Chirep question[11] and Rabin was very non-committal, suggesting a discussion with Eban on this matter. Sisco got the distinct impression that Rabin and Eban were at odds on this matter. Rabin has weighed in against an Israeli position which would have the effect of contributing to the expulsion of the Chinese Nationalists. He did not deny reports we had been receiving from other sources that Eban favors abstaining on the Important Question resolution.

9. Sisco said we would view such a vote very seriously since if the principle of expulsion by a majority vote were established, Israel could

---

[8] See footnote 4, Document 253.

[9] See footnote 4, Document 255.

[10] Sadat was in Moscow October 11–13 for talks with Soviet leaders. Kissinger informed the President in an October 16 memorandum that, judging from the public statements and speeches made in Moscow, "Sadat gained assurance of continued military assistance. How specific this is in terms of new equipment remains to be seen." Moving to the Arab-Israeli situation, Kissinger stated that "it is not clear what occurred in Moscow. The speeches and communiqué seem to reflect Soviet-Egyptian differences. Sadat's tough language about the use of force to pressure Israel was not endorsed in the communiqué, and the Soviets generally avoided talking about the dangers of war." The memorandum concluded that "the Soviets will evidently provide some further aid but have continued to hold to the position that a military solution is not feasible at this time." (National Archives, Nixon Presidential Materials, NSC Files, Box 637, Country Files, Middle East, UAR, Vol. VII) For additional analysis of Sadat's trip to Moscow, see *Foreign Relations, 1969–1976*, volume XIV, Soviet Union, October 1971–May 1972, Document 5.

[11] Reference is to the anticipated vote in the UN General Assembly on Chinese representation in the United Nations, specifically the issue of expelling the Republic of China and admitting the People's Republic of China.

not be very far down as a candidate for possible expulsion in circumstances where many in the UN favor application of sanctions. Rabin was unusually mum on this and he clearly gave the impression of a man under wraps. Sisco asked Rabin to convey his view to the FonMin and asked that he be informed that Sisco would be available to discuss this at his convenience.

Rogers

257. Transcript of a Telephone Conversation Between the President's Assistant for National Security Affairs (Kissinger) and the Assistant Secretary of State for Near Eastern and South Asian Affairs (Sisco)[1]

October 9, 1971, 12:50 p.m.

K: Joe, I wanted to tell you something so that you will be the first to be told by me. I have been reading with mounting concern the cables coming from New York which we didn't have even the slightest courtesy of being informed of.[2]

S: We are doing what the Israelis have wanted for three years, bringing it to direct negotiations.

K: But if this fails, you will come to us and ask us to beat the Israelis over the head.

S: What do you mean "if it fails?"

K: You say you are not going to be the mailman any longer, which I don't understand.

---

[1] Source: National Archives, Nixon Presidential Materials, NSC Files, Henry Kissinger Telephone Conversation Transcripts, Box 11, Chronological File. No classification marking. Kissinger was in Washington; Sisco was in New York.

[2] See Documents 255 and 256. Kissinger had telephoned Mitchell at 12:45 p.m. that day and said: "Do you know what that maniac [Rogers] did now? The Egyptians are sending a secret emissary to New York and Sisco is to get the Israelis to do the same and Sisco will send messages back and forth like in 1948. Then they are going to come and ask us to squeeze the Israelis. The Russians will think we are screwing them. The Egyptians will think we are screwing them. There we are with this maniac with not one word to us." Kissinger then added: "I tell you this will kill the Administration. Everyone knows that State is not checking with us. The insolence, incompetence, and frivolity of this exercise is beyond belief. Leave aside the Russians, would you ask for a secret emissary to come and put your prestige on the line as an intermediary when there is nothing to believe that anything is going to happen?" (National Archives, Nixon Presidential Materials, NSC Files, Henry Kissinger Telephone Conversation Transcripts, Box 11, Chronological File)

S: It's more semantics than anything else.

K: Well, the next time a cable goes out in violation of Presidential directives that they must be cleared, I will take the originator into his office and one of us will come out without his job. I will insist that the originator be fired or I will resign. I like you; I think you are the most creative Assistant Secretary we've got. And I don't want you to be a victim.

S: I'm afraid I will be. But I want you to know, I am no longer the principal prime mover on this Henry.

K: Who drafts the cables?

S: Oh, of course, I have to draft them . . . I know how you feel about this, but I can't help you. Honestly, I can't, I have tried for weeks to create a dialogue between you, the President, Secretary Rogers and myself. I have tried to create a White House discussion and I can't do it. It is something you and the Secretary have got to resolve.

K: We are not going to do it. He has got his directives. I am going to create a showdown.[3]

S: I can't advise you on that Henry. Frankly, I am no longer calling the shots.

K: If you try to run around between these two parties without knowing where the President will back you, you'll kill yourself.

S: I know. There has been one basic rule in the problem: if you don't have the backing of the President you don't have anyone. He in-

---

[3] Kissinger telephoned Haldeman at 2:55 p.m. that day and said: "I am telling you, you are going to get into a first class crisis with me. I am not going to let this happen." When Haldeman asked him what the next step should be, Kissinger responded: "I am going to go into the President and tell him we have to play it this way or go without me, when they go wild on the Middle East again." (Ibid.) Later in the evening, Haldeman recorded the following in his diary about the day's events: "Henry called at home this morning and has really blown up regarding Rogers. He feels that we have now thrown away our bargaining position on the Middle East; that up to now we've taken the role as intermediaries; that now Rogers has told Sadat that we will not function simply as mailmen; that we will throw our weight into the process and that we will squeeze the Israelis; in other words, he's told Sadat we'll hold our view regardless of Israeli complaints and that we will not give the Israelis planes or any other new weapons. This cable was sent to Sadat with no word to us. Two days ago, with no word to us again, Rogers proposed secret talks in New York between Egypt and the Israelis under Sisco—without telling us and without asking the Israelis first. Henry's really furious. He feels that our plan depended on the Russians delivering the Egyptians and we delivering the Israelis. If Rogers had tried to clear this with Henry, he would have said we're not ready yet for this move—the same as he did with Sisco's plan to go to Israel in July." Haldeman added that what really seemed to be bothering Kissinger was how he could explain to Brezhnev, right after the Gromyko proposal (see Document 251), that we go out and pull this in New York. "He thinks Rogers' route will inevitably leave the Russians sitting solid in the Mideast, where we can get what we want as the result of a deal with the Russians and without the Israeli's total opposition. We could get it, in other words, without an Israeli confrontation. But now we're on record as having promised Egypt everything, so there's no reason for the Russians to get out." (Ibid., Haldeman Diaries, Cassette Diary)

sists that he has his backing. I don't want to get between you and Rogers on this. Is there any way ... I have done everything I can to create a dialogue between you.

K: If you can, on an informal basis, let him know what's being cooked up ...

S: Ahead of time?

K: Yes. I think what will happen is the President will start squeezing Rogers out of this like he has on everything else.

S: At some point we will have to call the President in, and if he doesn't agree ...

K: He doesn't know what you are doing. How can he agree if he doesn't know?

S: Are they in touch?

K: No.

S: What can I do?

K: Well, first I want you to know what I am going to do, and I don't bluff. I would hate to have you end up as the fall guy.

S: I am going to. I am going to be the fall guy.

K: I will do my best to see that you don't.

S: I am going to.

K: And second, if we can get some advance information ...

S: I don't imagine the Secretary feels this is any new departure. He feels—and I am not arguing, I just want you to know—he is trying to produce the kind of negotiation that the Israelis have wanted. He feels he has carte blanche to do this as he sees fit. He tells me he has an understanding with the President to do this.

K: Well, that could be ...

S: He feels he has a clear line from the President. I wrote a paper four weeks ago to try to create a dialogue. It never got beyond his desk. Not that I am lily white. I have never been comfortable in this job unless the President, the Secretary and you have all known what's being done. I have lost sleep over this.

K: I think we are producing a war the way we are going.

S: No, I don't think it is the wrong direction but ...

K: No, but without coordination everyone ends up furious.

S: Is there any way that you can produce a Presidential dialogue?

K: Not before I go to China.[4]

---

[4] Kissinger was in the People's Republic of China October 20–26. Reports of his meetings with Chinese leaders are in *Foreign Relations, 1969–1976*, volume XVII, China, 1969–1972, Documents 163, 164, and 165.

S: When are you going?

K: About 10 days.

S: Then let's see afterward.

K: Can you slow things down until then?

S: I don't know. The Secretary sees Eban on Thursday.[5] Sadat is going to Moscow around _____.[6]

K: You could let me have the reporting cable of the conversation between the Secretary and Riad.[7]

S: That was sent to you last night.

K: I never saw it.

S: It was sent last night; it goes automatically to you.

K: No it doesn't.

S: We can't send a cable that way without it going to the Situation Room.

K: You did a pretty good job of it on the UN speech.

S: Oh well, that's another ... I know that problem. I'm glad you called; I have been very uneasy.

K: You have every reason to be. It is going to lead to a showdown.

S: And let's say that we never talked today. I don't want to report this.

K: Oh Joe, you know, I never talk to anybody.

S: Okay.

---

[5] Rogers and Sisco met with Eban on October 14 to discuss the interim agreement. The Secretary briefed Eban on his second conversation with Riad in New York on October 8, telling him that the Egyptian Foreign Minister was "less negative" and that he "asked questions and was thoughtful." Much of the discussion, which became heated at times, was dominated by a dispute over the terms of a cease-fire. Eban said that Israel wanted one without a time limit because a "revision date" could be "changed by unilateral decision and not through agreed change." Rogers, on the other hand, believed that "it is unrealistic to talk of a permanent cease fire in an interim agreement." He later added: "I resent the idea that we don't support a permanent cease fire. We hope the interim agreement will lead to a permanent cease fire." They also discussed the Secretary's speech before the UN General Assembly on October 4, particularly Israel's negative reaction to it, which Rogers characterized as a "personal attack." (National Archives, Nixon Presidential Materials, NSC Files, Kissinger Office Files, Box 134, Country Files, Middle East)

[6] See footnote 10, Document 256. The blank underscore is an omission in the original.

[7] See footnote 4, Document 255.

258. Telegram From the Department of State to the Interests Section in Egypt[1]

Washington, October 14, 1971, 2216Z.

188739. Bergus from Secretary. Ref: Cairo 2483.[2]

1. We want to check further Sadat's interest in our proposal for more proximate and expeditious negotiating procedure and at same time obtain early indication whether Sadat's Moscow visit[3] has altered in any way receptive attitude apparent in your conversations with him and Ismail. We also want to get it across to him that we cannot get further into specifics of our ideas at this stage, since this is what the negotiations are all about, and for us to do this would undermine those negotiations. We want to persuade Sadat to signify his willingness to go ahead with procedures we have in mind without further insistence, at this time, for specifics on our ideas on other issues involved in interim agreement. We think there is reasonable chance Sadat can agree to this.

2. You should therefore seek appointment with Sadat as soon after his return from Moscow as possible. We assume Egyptians will expect same procedure to be followed whereby you sketch out your approach beforehand to Ismail. In doing so you should underline importance USG is attaching to this phase of our efforts and desirability of your meeting personally with President to make sure we have full flavor of his views. You should convey following points to Sadat.

3. We appreciate President's latest response conveyed to us through Ismail.[4] We welcome his statement that he can accept as point of departure for discussion ideas we outlined concerning manner in

---

[1] Source: National Archives, Nixon Presidential Materials, NSC Files, Box 658, Country Files, Middle East, Middle East Nodis/Cedar/Plus, Vol. IV. Secret; Priority; Nodis; Cedar Plus. Drafted by Sterner; cleared by Sisco, Davies, and Atherton; and approved by Rogers. Repeated to Tel Aviv and USUN.

[2] In telegram 2483 from Cairo, October 9, Bergus reported his meeting with Ismail that afternoon, during which Ismail conveyed this message from Sadat to Rogers: "In reply to the message you conveyed to me on October 8, 1971, respecting the nature of the commitment between parties towards efforts under Dr. Jarring's auspices to reach a final settlement and the time needed to make this effort. While the ideas by the State Department do not clear the doubts and concerns of the President concerning an indefinite occupation of Sinai or a final agreement about the Arab territories, he considers that they represent a point of departure for an exchange of views and discussions which he hopes will be fruitful. Therefore, he expects in a short time and in a specific way to receive the elaboration (clarification) of the other points contained in the Secretary's speech of October 4, 1971, so that a decision may be taken to nominate an Egyptian representative with a mardate." (Ibid.) For the message that Bergus presented on October 8, see Document 254 and footnote 1, Document 255.

[3] See footnote 10, Document 256.

[4] See footnote 5, Document 255.

which relationship of interim agreement to final peace settlement, and question of ceasefire, could be handled. We also welcome his indication that he views favorably idea of proceeding in near future to more proximate and expeditious negotiating procedure.

4. We note that President, in latest message conveyed to us through Ismail, said that he is awaiting our specific ideas on other aspects of interim agreement before making final decision to name Egyptian negotiator with mandate to intensified talks. In our recent exchanges in Cairo (including message contained State 186256[5] conveyed by you through Ismail Oct 9 subsequent to receiving Sadat's message in Cairo's 2483), in Secretary's speech to UNGA, and also in Secretary's two meetings with Foreign Minister Riad,[6] we have endeavored to convey to Egyptians more specifically our concept of interim agreement. We have also given President Sadat our specific ideas on central issue (para 3 above) involved in interim agreement. From all of this we think it must now be clear to Egyptians where we stand on point of most concern to them—that interim agreement is first step toward final peace settlement and must not become new armistice. We cannot go further at this time in terms of delineating our specific ideas without jeopardizing negotiating process which in our view is only way of making process toward agreement. Purpose of negotiating process we have in mind is in fact to assist two sides in coming to grips with those specifics President Sadat has in mind.

5. We also want to emphasize that as negotiations proceed, US as middleman will obviously be intimately and continuously involved in negotiations. As Secretary Rogers told Foreign Minister Riad at their second meeting, US does not intend to play mere mailman role. We will also try to act as catalyst by putting forward constructive ideas and conveying frankly to each side our assessment of what is within bounds of acceptability to other side. From our exchanges in spring and summer we have good idea of concerns and needs of both sides and therefore of parameters of possible agreement.

6. We hope, therefore, that President Sadat can agree to appointing representative with broad mandate in substance and procedure to facilitate intensified negotiating process we envisage for reaching interim agreement. If he is ready in principle to do this, we would anticipate coming back to him in near future with suggestions for a specific place and date for negotiations in close proximity.

7. We have in mind active and intensive negotiations. If fact that these are under way leaks to press, which will probably happen sooner

---

[5] Not found.

[6] See footnote 4, Document 255 and footnote 5, Document 257.

or later, we would say, as indicated in our last message to President Sadat, that this is merely intensification of present procedures.[7]

Irwin

---

[7] Bergus met with Ismail at 6:30 p.m. on October 15 and told him that he had an important message to convey to Sadat. He then presented the points contained in paragraphs 3–7 of this telegram. Speaking personally, Ismail told Bergus that he was "not happy with process whereby Egypt continually said 'yes, yes' and subsequently found itself in the air." He added that he feared that if Egypt blindly followed the procedure that Rogers had outlined, it would "soon find itself beset by further preconditions." Furthermore, he maintained that Egypt could not reply to Rogers's message until Sadat and his advisers learned the results of U.S. discussions with Israel, at least on the twin issues of linking the interim agreement to an overall settlement and the cease-fire. (Telegram 2538 from Cairo, October 15; National Archives, Nixon Presidential Materials, NSC Files, Box 658, Country Files, Middle East, Middle East Nodis/Cedar/Plus, Vol. IV)

---

259. Letter From Secretary of State Rogers to Secretary of Defense Laird[1]

Washington, October 15, 1971.

Dear Mel:

Your memorandum to me of October 6[2] on Israeli use of American equipment in its September 18 action against Egyptian missile sites[3] makes a number of points which, I agree with you, should be discussed with the Israelis: the technical misuse of the Shrike, and the apparent disregard of two of the conditions under which we had provided the anti-missile package of last year. In our judgment, we should not make too much of the violation of the condition on secrecy, since it was laid down in the context of the delicate ceasefire situation at that time, which has changed considerably since then, and since Israel's possession of the Shrike has in fact been an open secret for some time. Use of the Shrike in the absence of a resumption of hostilities by the other side was clearly, in a literal sense, a violation of one of the conditions of sale.

---

[1] Source: Washington National Records Center, OSD Files: FRC 330–76–0197, Box 66, Israel. Secret; Nodis. A stamped notation on the letter reads: "Sec Def has seen. 15 Oct 1971."

[2] Not found.

[3] See Document 248.

On the other hand, there is no doubt that use of the Shrike was in response to an escalatory hostile act by Egypt (the firing of a SAM across the ceasefire line against an unarmed reconnaissance plane), that it was the second Egyptian violation in a short period (the first being a low level Sukhoi overflight of the ceasefire line), and that it was a relatively restrained reaction in the circumstances. Despite these qualifying considerations, it will serve a useful purpose, I believe, to let the Israelis know that we still take seriously the conditions to which they have agreed. Our own view is that you should bear down particularly hard on Israel's technical misuse of the Shrike in a way and in a mission for which it is not intended. I find your arguments on this point most persuasive.

I am troubled, however, by your intention to hold in abeyance all further action on sale or delivery of equipment covered by these special conditions.[4] As you know, we have moved into a difficult and intensive phase of our efforts to bring about an interim Suez Canal agreement between Israel and Egypt. It becomes doubly important at this time that in matters of high sensitivity to Israel our every action be carefully weighed with a view to the broader effects on the negotiating situation. The Israelis are anxious about the direction of our efforts in the interim agreement negotiations. I believe it is essential that we not give them any signals they might misconstrue. To interrupt our arms relationship, even in such a limited way as you propose would, I fear, compound our difficulties and could have an adverse impact on the diplomatic role we are playing.

I would, therefore, like to request that any proposals to interrupt Israeli arms deliveries be thoroughly discussed and coordinated between us in advance and that, in the present situation, no action be taken to suspend or delay the sale or delivery of any items,

---

[4] On October 8, James H. Noyes, Deputy Assistant Secretary of Defense for Near Eastern, African, and South Asian Affairs, sent a memorandum to the Director of the Defense Security Assistance Agency that reads: "The Secretary of Defense has directed that the sale or delivery of special munitions type weapons to Israel temporarily be held in abeyance effective today. There is no intention at this time to cancel any of these sales. Based on information previously provided by your agency, the attached listing shows the category of items which should not be delivered or offered Israel during this temporary suspension. You are requested to take immediate action to withhold delivery or signing of letters of offer on this equipment. You are further requested to implement this decision on a close hold basis and in such a manner that no speculation will be generated. Further guidance will be provided on this subject within 30 days." (Washington National Records Center, OSD Files: FRC 330–74–0115, Box 5, Israel)

including those subject to the special conditions discussed in your memorandum to me.[5]

With best personal regards,
Sincerely,

William P. Rogers

---

[5] Laird replied to Rogers's letter on October 22. He began by noting that he appreciated the Secretary's concern. He then continued: "We certainly do not intend for this temporary 'hold' to be misinterpreted by Israel, and by keeping the matter in defense-to-defense channels I believe this objective has been accomplished. At the same time, it is precisely because we do not wish to give wrong signals that we have taken this action. We realize that the Israeli military were emotionally distraught by the shooting down of this unarmed aircraft, and could have made a hasty decision which, in comparison with previous Israeli responses, may well be regarded as 'restrained.' Unfortunately, this is the very kind of reaction which is most dangerous and which could lead most directly to escalation and great power confrontation. In short, we want there to be no misunderstanding on the part of the Israel Defense Forces as to the seriousness with which we view the conditions attached to this equipment." (Ibid.)

---

260. **Letter From Secretary of Defense Laird to Secretary of State Rogers**[1]

Washington, October 18, 1971.

Dear Bill:

There is increasing concern here over our continued inability to get distribution—even on a carefully controlled "CEDAR" basis—of key cable traffic on the Arab-Israel situation. I recognize the sensitivity of the present state-of-play, but the *New York Times* and *Washington Post* continue to print reports which, if true, indicate that a good deal of discussion on military-security topics is taking place.

Obviously, any settlement proposal must address security questions, and is thus of concern to DOD. Further, as our experience with the 1970 "stand-still" demonstrates, the military-security aspects of even limited settlement proposals require careful review by military-security experts to ensure they are workable.

In short, while recognizing State's primacy in these critical negotiations, I am sure you will agree that DOD has a real role to play as well.

---

[1] Source: Washington National Records Center, ISA Files: FRC 330–74–0083, Box 23, Middle East. Secret.

This requires that we receive—on at least a "CEDAR" basis—all traffic on this subject. Practically speaking, it is not enough that we be able to see some particular message upon request, nor is it feasible that we receive eleventh hour briefings or selected cables just before NSC meetings.

I would hope that you can arrange for this distribution, at least to my personal office, to Dave Packard, and to Warren Nutter. I also urge you to ensure that your staff take advantage of our capabilities to check out the practicability of any military-security arrangements being considered.[2]

Sincerely,

Mel

---

[2] On October 20, Rogers replied: "I can assure you that you have been receiving and will continue to receive the sensitive cables in the 'CEDAR' series. We will also make available to you any cables which are of direct interest to the Department of Defense, such as those dealing with specific arms transactions. On our side, we will want to continue to seek the counsel of the Department of Defense on the military-security aspects of settlement proposals. On some aspects of our efforts to achieve a settlement, I have decided not to have documents circulated. I have, however, asked Joe Sisco to make certain that you, Dave Packard, and Warren Nutter are kept informed both so that you can fulfill your NSC responsibilities and in order for us to benefit from your counsel. Please let me know with whom in your personal office Joe Sisco should stay in touch." (Ibid., OSD Files: FRC 330–76–0197, Box 70, Middle East) Laird replied to Rogers on November 10, explaining that Warren Nutter was his principal foreign affairs adviser and that Sisco should keep in touch with him on matters contained in the most sensitive documents. (Ibid.)

261. Telegram From the Embassy in Israel to the Department of State[1]

Tel Aviv, October 21, 1971, 1245Z.

6374. Ref State 191731 and State 192032.[2]

1. Gist of presentation contained in paras 3, 4, 5, 6, 7 of State 191731 given Rafael Oct. 20 and communicated by him to Eban on latter's arrival at airport.

2. Chargé saw Eban (who was accompanied by Gazit) morning Oct. 21 and made full detailed presentation which was taken down practically verbatim by Gazit. Eban acknowledged he had had word from Rafael and had also received report from Rabin of Oct. 20 conversation with Sisco, but said he was not rpt not yet in position to make formal reply. He had, however, several questions.

3. Eban asked just what "not negative" meant regarding Sadat's reaction. Chargé replied Sadat reaction had been such as to lead USG to believe it useful to get indication of whether GOI would agree to procedure if final agreement from Sadat obtained. We were not now making formal proposal to GOI, and had not yet done so to Egypt either. Upon affirmative indication from GOI, we would explore further in Cairo and believe there is chance we can sell Sadat on idea. If this proves to be so, we will then so inform GOI with formal proposal to them as well.

4. Eban noted negotiations between countries frequently begin on "documentary basis" and asked whether this would be so in this case. Chargé repeated we are not asking either Israel or Egyptians to modify their present positions in advance or to make any other pre-

---

[1] Source: National Archives, Nixon Presidential Materials, NSC Files, Box 658, Country Files, Middle East, Middle East Nodis/Cedar/Plus, Vol. IV. Secret; Immediate; Nodis; Cedar Plus.

[2] In telegram 191731 to Tel Aviv, October 19, the Department instructed the Embassy to convey a message to Eban from Rogers that the time had come "to get into real negotiations on interim agreement" and there was a limited amount of time before Egypt would decide to "precipitate a UNGA debate" as Sadat's negotiating flexibility began to narrow. Rogers also wanted Eban to know that the Department had broached the idea of proximity talks with Sadat, that his initial reaction was "not negative," and that the Department could "sell" him on the idea. The Secretary stressed: "We are not asking either Israel or Egypt to modify their present positions of April 19 and June 4 in advance on interim agreement, but only that they have open mind and will be prepared seek ways to accommodate present wide differences." Finally, he said that the negotiations stood the best chance of "getting somewhere" if they were "kept out of public limelight." (Ibid. Box 1165, Saunders Files, Middle East Negotiation Files, Middle East—Jarring Talks, October 12–November 1, 1971) In telegram 192032 to Tel Aviv, October 20, the Department authorized the Embassy to make the presentation to Rafael at 6 p.m. on the understanding that it would make the presentation directly to Eban the following day and noted that Sisco would "be making same pitch with Rabin" at noon on October 20. (Ibid., Box 658, Country Files, Middle East, Middle East Nodis/Cedar/Plus, Vol. IV)

commitments other than to enter into negotiations in real give and take spirit and with open mind, prepared to seek ways to accommodate present wide differences. Eban asked whether proposal being made to Egypt in same terms or whether Egypt would expect negotiations to start on basis of Secretary's six points as outlined in GA speech.[3] Chargé replied conversations with Egyptians had extended over longer time than this present short conversation with Eban but that essential elements were same in regard both countries. USG was proposing no rpt no documentary or other basis on which to begin negotiations; question of how each party would look upon this matter the parties had to explore with each other.

5. Eban said that Secretary had stated after their meeting[4] that USG would intensify its efforts concerning Canal arrangement and he, Eban, was already frequently being asked what next steps USG would be undertaking. He understood desire to have no announcement of negotiations in New York but it would be very hard, in his opinion, to keep matter completely quiet since everybody would be looking to see results of Secretary's statement. Nevertheless, this was subsidiary to primary question of whether to begin negotiations.

6. Eban asked whether Chargé knew whom Egyptians might designate as their representative. (Prior to meeting, Gazit (protect) had gone over Rabin's report with Chargé, indicating that Ghaleb and Ismail had been mentioned as possibilities.) Chargé said that since no formal proposal had been made to Egypt and no formal agreement obtained, it followed that there had been no actual designation of a representative. Nevertheless, he had heard that Ghaleb might be considered and also understood that Ismail was intimately involved in discussions. Gazit indicated it already known that Ghaleb was coming to New York for remainder of GA.

7. In closing, Eban said that he would be in touch as soon as possible with more definite GOI reply.

Zurhellen

---

[3] See footnote 3, Document 255.
[4] See footnote 4, Document 253.

262. Editorial Note

On November 4, 1971, Assistant to the President for National Security Affairs Henry Kissinger met in the Map Room of the White House with Soviet Ambassador Anatoly Dobrynin from 1:10 to 3 p.m. to discuss a Middle East peace agreement. (Library of Congress, Manuscript Division, Kissinger Papers, Box 438, Miscellany, 1968–76) It was the third conversation between Kissinger and Dobrynin focused on the Middle East since Foreign Minister Andrei Gromyko had presented to President Nixon a proposal for an Arab-Israeli peace settlement (see Document 251). At their first meeting on October 9, Kissinger informed Dobrynin that recent statements by Secretary of State Rogers at the United Nations and calls for "secret talks" between Egyptians and Israelis under the aegis of Assistant Secretary of State for Near Eastern and South Asian Affairs Joseph Sisco should not be considered as a U S. reply to Gromyko's proposal. Dobrynin said he was very grateful because it would almost certainly have been misunderstood in Moscow and would have had very "unfortunate consequences." (Memorandum of conversation, October 9; *Foreign Relations, 1969–1976*, volume XIII, Soviet Union, October 1970–October 1971, Document 351) On October 15, Dobrynin emphasized the need to focus on Gromyko's proposal, insisting that it was "the most generous offer the Soviet Union would ever make. They were offering withdrawing their forces, limiting arms shipments into the Middle East, and guaranteeing the settlement. What more could Israel possibly want?" Except for the frontier, which the Soviets believed had to be the international frontier, Dobrynin said that the Soviet Union would be "extremely flexible" in the settlement. (Memorandum of conversation, October 15; ibid., volume XIV, Soviet Union, October 1971–May 1972, Document 4)

At the November 4 meeting, Kissinger outlined to Dobrynin two possible procedures for how to proceed: "One was for the United States to tell the Israelis and for the Soviets to tell the Egyptians that we were proceeding along this track." The other was to bring the Israelis in on an interim settlement but to keep vague its relationship to an overall settlement until 1973. Kissinger observed that the first procedure was the "more honorable course"; the second might be the "more effective course." Dobrynin said he would check in Moscow as to their preference and then turned the discussion to Gromyko's proposal:

"The Ambassador then said that the Soviet Union had made major concessions. They were prepared to withdraw their forces, to have an embargo on arms into the Middle East, and to join a Soviet-American force for guarantees. In other words, they would be very flexible about anything that was within the Soviet discretion. Matters that required Egyptian approval were more complex. He therefore hoped that Dr.

Kissinger would be able to concentrate in their discussions on those three items.

"Dr. Kissinger told Dobrynin that the guarantees issue was really quite simple and that it would probably be settled fairly easily. If their talks were to have any chance of success, Dr. Kissinger would have to be able to demonstrate to the Israelis that they were getting something as a result of these talks that they were not getting as a result of the Rogers/Sisco approach. Ambassador Dobrynin responded by noting that the Israelis were getting the withdrawal of Soviet forces and a Soviet arms embargo.

"Dr. Kissinger then said it would also help if the terms of the interim settlement were better than those now being negotiated. Ambassador Dobrynin asked what Dr. Kissinger meant. For example, did he mean that the line should be at the western end of the pass and not on the eastern end, that is on the Suez Canal side of the passes not on the Israeli side of the passes.

"Ambassador Dobrynin also asked whether under those conditions it was conceivable that some Egyptian troops could cross the canal. Dr. Kissinger replied that it was conceivable but that he had no really clear idea, and that issue would have to wait.

"Ambassador Dobrynin then asked for Dr. Kissinger's concept of the final settlement. Dr. Kissinger replied that he did not really believe in shooting blanks and therefore would be very careful. It seemed to him that the demilitarized zones were an essential element. Ambassador Dobrynin commented that it was very tough to get a demilitarized zone that did not include some territory on the other side of the Israeli frontier. Dr. Kissinger stated that in such a case all of Israel would be demilitarized if the zones were equal. He then proposed jokingly that the zones start equi distance [sic] from the capitals. Dobrynin reiterated that it would be very hard not to have a demilitarized zone on the Israeli side. Dr. Kissinger remarked that if Ambassador Dobrynin could, however, get agreement on it this would be a tremendous step forward.

"Dr. Kissinger finally said that it seemed to him that the matters which could represent enormous progress would be: if the Egyptian settlement could be separated from the others, if the demilitarized zones could be kept entirely on the Egyptian side, if the interim settlement could be on terms more favorable to Israel than the present one, and a determination of concessions Sadat ought to be prepared to make if he knew an overall settlement was coming. Dobrynin noted that he would consult Moscow but would like Dr. Kissinger to make a specific proposal at the next meeting." (Ibid., Document 10)

Dobrynin prepared his own record of the November 4 conversation in which he added that President Nixon and Kissinger were reluctant to present a U.S.-Soviet proposal to Israeli Prime Minister Golda Meir until after the U.S. elections the following year. "More precisely," Dobrynin wrote, "they will not inform her during this period about the agreement with us on the second stage (final settlement and complete withdrawal of Israeli forces) but only about the first stage—an interim settlement in connection with the opening of the Suez Canal." The reasoning in the White House in this regard, Dobrynin explained, was that "the Israelis definitely have no interest in returning to their old borders and giving back territory. Therefore, if the White House were to inform Golda Meir of the agreement between the USSR and the U.S. that might possibly be reached, then she, having no interest in the main thing— withdrawal from the presently occupied territories—would almost certainly make this agreement public and, taking advantage of the U.S. election campaign, would try to torpedo it." At the end of his report, Dobrynin offered his assessment, based on his recent meetings with Kissinger, as to where matters stood:

"From the three conversations I have had with Kissinger on a Middle East settlement since A.A. Gromyko's departure from Washington, it is my general impression that the White House—evidently taking into account that the summit meeting is still half a year away—is not really prepared at this time for urgent, detailed discussion of an agreement on all the specific issues of a Middle East settlement. They appear to be exploring and weighing various options, and also trying to take into account possible near-term developments in the region.

"They are apparently not averse to waiting a little to see whether the Egyptians might in the meantime make some concessions. It is obvious they also do not want to stir up the Israelis prematurely. And apparently the fact that they are busy preparing for the first summit meeting—with the Chinese—is also playing a part.

"On the whole—and this needs to be emphasized—the White House is seriously interested in continuing the dialogue with us with a view to reaching a possible agreement. In all probability, however, the White House will begin actively preparing issues for consideration at the Moscow meeting about two or three months before the meeting.

"In this connection, we think it advisable to proceed as follows in discussing a Middle East settlement with the White House in the future: a) Continue in meetings with Kissinger to probe and clarify the U.S. position, even if only its general outlines, thus forcing the White House to approach the various aspects with increasing specificity and nudging them in the direction we need. b) At the same time, start to work on preparing our document on the Middle East, having in mind primarily the summit meeting (for example, in the form of basic principles, provisions, and so forth), a document that would lay out our specific approach to the main issues of an interim and final settlement.

"At some point such a document could be given to Kissinger for transmittal to the President, and further work here on a Middle East settlement, through the confidential channel, could be conducted using this specific document as a starting point. After this preliminary discussion, it could then be adopted as the basis for consideration of the Middle East problem at the summit meeting.

"Our 'Basic Provisions' for a Middle East settlement of June 17, 1969 [see Document 34], could serve as the point of departure for such a document of ours, but after they have been revised to take into account those provisions that have been essentially agreed with the Americans in the course of our almost year-long exchange of views with the State Department. Moreover, it would be desirable, for tactical purposes, not to present this document as a repetition of the "Provisions" that we have already set forth, but rather as a new document reflecting the current state of affairs (taking into account the various contacts and exchanges of views that have occurred, including with the White House).

"In terms of format this document could be presented to Kissinger as a possible draft decision at the summit meeting, on the understanding that the process of reaching preliminary agreement on it would be initiated in advance through the confidential channel. In our first draft we might want to avoid mentioning the issues concerning our military presence that were discussed here by the Minister and the U.S. President. For the time being we might limit ourselves to an oral reaffirmation of this, stating that we will fulfill our part of the agreement if the White House accepts the prologue for an overall Middle East settlement as set out in the document.

"The suggestion that we prepare such a document and present it to Kissinger after a certain period of time is premised on the need to induce the White House to discuss the concrete issues related to a settlement, as well as on the assumption that the White House itself, seeking to protect the confidentiality of our exchanges of views from the State Department and other government agencies, is unlikely to prepare its own detailed document on a Middle East settlement for discussion with us anytime soon (which could require bringing in additional people on their side, something they are clearly avoiding for the moment). Our initiative in this matter is thus all the more appropriate.

"As for the questions Kissinger raised today, he will undoubtedly expect some response from Moscow so that he can brief the President on the progress of the negotiations.

"As noted above, during the conversation we answered two of the questions that were of greatest interest to him—on demilitarized zones and on the need to implement a Middle East settlement as a 'package.'

"Bearing in mind the main objective of further clarifying their position and pushing them towards the solution that we need, it seems to us that at our next meeting with Kissinger we might refrain from re-opening a major discussion of these issues. After briefly reaffirming our position, we could propose continuing the discussion of other issues, including guarantees, within the framework of the understanding that was discussed during A.A. Gromyko's visit to Washington.

"There is one further matter. Not being aware of Egypt's exact position, we have thus far made no comment here on the ideas voiced by Kissinger regarding an interim (Suez) solution as it pertains to the withdrawal of Israeli troops and the crossing of Egyptian forces to the eastern bank of the canal. If our side can (and should) provide our own ideas in response, we would request appropriate guidance." (*Soviet-American Relations, 1969–1972*, Document 220)

Despite telling Dobrynin that he would not bring the proposal to the Israelis, the following day, November 5, Kissinger held a secret meeting with Israeli Ambassador Yitzhak Rabin to inform him of the proposal Gromyko had presented to Nixon on September 29 and to gauge the Israeli reaction. No U.S. record of their meeting has been found. Rabin, however, later described the meeting in his memoirs:

"Kissinger invited me to the White House under 'cloak-and-dagger' conditions. He asked me to come alone, said that he too would be alone, and had me admitted through a side entrance in the West Wing, so that by the time we were face to face my curiosity (not to mention my tension) was at a peak.

"'What I am about to say is on behalf of the president, and you must promise that you will report it to no one other than Prime Minister Meir,' he began in a conspiratorial manner, 'and even to her privately and personally.' An alarm bell went off in my mind because when Kissinger asked me to go to Israel and deliver a message to the prime minister personally, there was usually reason to believe that a crisis was in the offing.

"What he now told me was of a secret proposal from Leonid Brezhnev relayed to President Nixon by Soviet Ambassador Dobrynin. Brezhnev was suggesting a deal between the two powers for an overall solution in the Middle East. The settlement was to be effected in two stages: first a limited agreement for reopening the canal; then, after the 1972 American presidential elections (Brezhnev was not insensitive to Nixon's domestic vulnerabilities in an election year), an overall agreement based on the Jarring document. Brezhnev also offered that if the two powers could reach an agreement on the character of an overall solution, he would be willing to make concessions on everything having to do with the partial agreement. Moreover, once the overall agreement was reached, the Soviet Union would be prepared to eliminate its operational military presence in Egypt, leaving no more than a small number of advisers, and join the United States both in an embargo on weapons shipments to the region and in measures to safeguard the agreement in whatever form the United States found necessary ...

"'I do not intend to negotiate with the Soviet Union, not even at the top level, without close coordination with Israel. I don't think that the United States should negotiate on a matter of fateful importance to Israel without taking into our confidence at all stages of the negotiations. This is why I want an answer from Prime Minister Meir: Does Israel agree to the United States' entering into such negotiations—on the assumption that the future borders will not basically be different from the June 4, 1967 lines and that the boundary between Egypt and Israel must be the international border? ... I understand your difficulties, and if Israel replies to the Soviet proposal in the negative, I won't blame her. I would seek ways of preventing American-Soviet negotiations on Brezhnev's proposals.'" (Rabin, *The Rabin Memoirs,* pages 203-205)

Although Rabin agreed to present the Soviet proposal directly to Prime Minister Meir in Israel, he had his doubts about the proposal. "[Kissinger] depicted the initiative as coming from Brezhnev," he later wrote, "and I in no way doubted his sincerity on this point. But I could not shake free of the vision of Kissinger and Dobrynin closeted away cooking up deals, with Kissinger subsequently announcing the results to us as a fait accompli—much as Sisco had during his earlier talks with the Soviet ambassador." (Ibid., page 205)

---

263. **Telegram From the Department of State to the Interests Section in Egypt**[1]

Washington, November 6, 1971, 1647Z.

203152. For Bergus from Secretary. Subject: Briefing Sadat on Status of Interim Agreement Efforts.

---

[1] Source: National Archives, Nixon Presidential Materials, NSC Files, Box 1165, Saunders Files, Middle East Negotiation Files, Middle East—Jarring Talks, November 1–15, 1971. Secret; Immediate; Nodis; Cedar Plus. Drafted by Sterner, Atherton, and Sisco and approved by Rogers. Repeated Priority to Tel Aviv.

1. *FYI:* Mrs. Meir's reply,[2] conveyed November 1 to Ambassador Barbour, in effect leaves our proposal for negotiations in proximity in abeyance while seeking clarification on questions of (A) when Israel can expect decision on Phantoms and (B) whether Quote six points Unquote in Secretary's UNGA speech[3] will be basis for negotiations. Other Israeli officials have been more explicit in making clear that positive decision on Phantoms, and assurances that six points will not be basis for negotiations, are necessary before Israel will agree to New York talks. We will be considering what our next steps should be in face of this reply, but for moment we must assume that our proposal for intensified negotiations is stalled. We note that Sadat has now set in motion series of meetings to dramatize that decision-making is at hand, and that he is also scheduled to make speech to People's Assembly November 11.[4] We agree with you (Cairo 2637)[5] as to advantages of giving Sadat some kind of progress report before his speech so that at least we don't come in for criticism that he hasn't heard from us recently. We see little further advantage in not telling Sadat with considerable degree of candor what political facts of life are on our interim agreement efforts. We want to be sufficiently frank to leave him with feeling that we are not trying to hide anything from him; at same time we want to make it clear we have not given up on interim agreement, even though this may take longer than we expected. Additional reason for seeing Sadat is to seek to clarify where Egypt stands on idea of negotiations in proximity. Last word we had from Sadat was that he was attracted to this idea and thought New York was best locale. We have therefore been operating on assumption that, if Israelis agreed, prospects were reasonably good that Egyptians would also go along with our proposal and send negotiator to New York. Heykal's November 5 Friday sermon

---

[2] As part of her reply, Meir asked, as instructed by her Cabinet: "Does US agree with Israeli concept that negotiations for partial settlement are basically different from negotiations for overall settlement, in that some Israeli withdrawal from Canal is presupposed in former, which is Israeli concession made in advance involving risks and requiring Israel to insist on certain conditions, whereas in latter set of negotiations, there can be no conditions, only positions?" (Telegram 6602 from Tel Aviv, November 1; ibid., Box 658, Country Files, Middle East, Middle East Nodis/Cedar/Plus, Vol. IV)

[3] See footnote 3, Document 255.

[4] In the speech, Sadat suggested that Egypt and Israel could reach an interim agreement if Israel would withdraw from the Sinai Peninsula, as Jarring had asked Israel if it would have been willing to consider doing during his exchanges with both parties in February. Furthermore, Sadat criticized the United States for what he described as its detachment of his plan for re-opening the Suez Canal from the larger goal of achieving an overall settlement. (*New York Times,* November 12, 1971, p. 9)

[5] Dated October 26. (National Archives, Nixon Presidential Materials, NSC Files, Box 658, Country Files, Middle East, Middle East Nodis/Cedar/Plus, Vol. IV)

(Cairo 2724 and 2729),[6] in which he says it is impossible for Egypt to accept this proposal, throws that assumption into considerable doubt. Before reaching decision on what further approach to make to Israelis, we need best possible current reading of Sadat's attitude toward our proposal. *End FYI.*

2. You should try to get appointment to see Sadat personally for this approach. If necessary we can convey what we have to say to Ismail, but this is one occasion when we think it important for President to have full flavor of our comments, and for us to receive first-hand his reaction and further thoughts. If there appears to be any problem about meeting with President, therefore, you should say that on this occasion Secretary Rogers hopes you can see President personally.

3. Begin talking points. We have now received Israeli reply to our proposal for new phase of intensified negotiations in New York. We are still studying response and what our next steps might be in the light of it, but in meantime we want to give President progress report.

4. As recent Israeli public and press statements have made clear, Israeli Government has not yet agreed to our proposal for Quote negotiations at close proximity Unquote in New York. Israelis say their hesitation is based on two concerns: (A) Absence of US decision with respect to Israel's request for future aircraft deliveries. On this point, Sadat should be told candidly decision on arms in Egyptian-Soviet communiqué[7] has made our task more difficult. (B) Israel is concerned over six points on interim agreement set forth in Secretary Rogers' UNGA speech, which Israelis interpret as giving Egypt advantage in negotiations. Like Egyptians, Israelis too are pressing us to clarify further our position on six points. In addition, each side wants other to make next move. It was against this background that we put forth idea of proximate and intensive negotiating procedures, which we still believe would provide opportunity for better give-and-take between views of two sides and for some simultaneous progress on issues where differences in position must be resolved if interim agreement is to be achieved. We are not asking either Egypt or Israel to abandon their present positions prior to entering such talks. Purpose of talks is to explore whether middle ground on key issues can be arrived at. While

---

[6] In telegram 2724 from Cairo, November 5, Bergus recommended that the Department study a piece by Heikal in that day's *Al-Ahram*, which he noted came "perilously close to slamming the door on negotiations in proximity." He added: "Sadat may be having substantive doubts about value of negotiations in proximity, but more importantly, I believe he deeply resents fact that we have had nothing to tell him since mid-October, while our subsequent discussions with Israelis have been source of continuing series of reports in Israeli, Arab, and world press." (Ibid.) Telegram 2729 from Cairo, November 5, reported the contents of Heikal's weekly column in detail. (Ibid., RG 59, Central Files 1970–73, POL 27–14 ARAB–ISR)

[7] See footnote 10, Document 256.

USG has no blueprint of its own on these issues, Secretary has indicated parameters in GA speech within which we think agreement must be sought. In process of seeking such agreement, we would expect to play more than passive mailman role and would do our best to promote agreement between parties on terms which they find advantageous. In brief, we would envisage playing role of active catalyst.

5. We are carefully studying Prime Minister's response and expect to press this matter further with Israelis in hopes process of negotiations in close proximity can get started at early date in New York, latter site having been suggested by Sadat.

6. As result of President Sadat's reaction to Quote negotiations in proximity Unquote idea during his meeting with Bergus on October 7,[8] we have been proceeding on assumption that he is interested in this idea and that, if Israelis agree to send representative to New York for this purpose, President Sadat will be favorably disposed toward doing the same. But Heykal article November 5 gives a different impression. We will soon be responding to Israel's request for clarifications but first, in light of Heykal article, we need to know: Is Egypt still interested in an interim agreement and in entering negotiations in proximity? We must be certain that Egypt is still interested in further efforts on our part with Israel are to be taken seriously by them. End talking points.[9]

Rogers

---

[8] See footnote 5, Document 255.

[9] Bergus presented the talking points to Ismail at 1:15 p.m. on November 8. Ismail explained that he and Sadat would need time to reflect on the presentation and that the Egyptian President would probably meet with Bergus on November 10. Nonetheless, Ismail had a preliminary response to Bergus's remarks, asking if the U.S. Government planned to adhere to the six points that Rogers raised in his October 4 speech to the UN General Assembly. He also said that he had hoped that the United States "would be coming up with something which could be a basis for discussion if Egyptians and Israelis started talking in proximity." Otherwise, proximity discussions "would be useless," he said. He also addressed the U.S. Government's imminent decision on aircraft for Israel, commenting that "linking aircraft deliveries to negotiations in proximity was a most 'illogical' step and a most 'illogical' request from Israel," as Israel had previously argued that an interim agreement would undermine Israel's security. (Telegram 2757 from Cairo, November 8; National Archives, Nixon Presidential Materials, NSC Files, Box 658, Country Files, Middle East, Middle East Nodis/Cedar/Plus, Vol. IV)

264. Letter From Secretary of Defense Laird to Secretary of State Rogers[1]

Washington, November 10, 1971.

Dear Bill:

Thank you for your letter of 4 November.[2] I share your concern regarding the possible effects of even a limited cutoff of special arms shipments to Israel, but I believe a fundamental issue is involved. What is at stake is our whole contractual relationship with Israel.

The IDF repeatedly has requested sale of sophisticated equipment (e.g., NIKE, LANCE) with the argument, to ease U.S. concern, that special conditions could be attached to its use. However, we are now being asked, in effect, to agree to an unwritten but overriding proviso that "the IDF will always be free to use any equipment supplied as it chooses if it considers the circumstances so warrant." Unless the Israeli military are willing to acknowledge the absolute necessity of honoring their commitments, regardless of circumstances, then there can be none of the mutual respect which must exist if Israel is to trust even marginally U.S. assurances as a substitute for its present borders.

I am attaching copies of our exchange of letters with the Israeli Defense Attaché.[3] As is evident, there is no acknowledgment of a violation. In these circumstances, the assurances provided have a distinctly hollow ring.

It is difficult to continue to approve sales of sophisticated equipment unless we are assured that the conditions of sale will be honored. As I see it, we have only two alternatives: we can complete deliveries of items already agreed to, ignoring the Israeli violations, but approve no more; or, alternatively, we can reach a clear understanding of the mutuality of our commitments, and can continue to consider requests for

---

[1] Source: Washington National Records Center, OSD Files: FRC 330–76–0197, Box 66, Israel. Secret; Sensitive.

[2] On November 4, Rogers wrote to Laird: "Your letter to me of October 22 states that the Department of Defense has placed a hold on the delivery of certain items to Israel. You say that by keeping communication with Israel on the matter in defense-to-defense channels you do not believe the steps we are taking will be misinterpreted by the Israelis. It is our judgment, however, especially in the current state of our relations with Israel, that any interruption of normal procedures or flow of matériel is likely to be attributed by the Israelis to political reasons. Again, with the exception of the special case of aircraft on which a decision is still pending, I must request that there be no interruption in our arms deliveries to Israel at this time." He concluded: "I am confident we can reach a mutually satisfactory arrangement in which your concerns and ours are satisfied." (Ibid.) For Laird's October 22 letter, see footnote 5, Document 259.

[3] Attached but not printed are letters dated October 9 and November 3.

material covered by these or other special conditions. The latter course seems plainly the better one, from all points of view.

Meanwhile, we have asked the Israeli Attaché for a fuller written response. We have not indicated that we are withholding deliveries, and we are not asking for an abject apology. What we do insist on is an acknowledgment that there was at least a limited violation, and assurance that similar violations will not occur in the future. If the IDF feels the conditions themselves are unreasonable, then its proper course of action is not to ignore them, but to request their renegotiation.

I genuinely regret that this problem should have cropped up at this particular time, but, since it did, we should not ignore it. As I indicated in my letter to you earlier this fall on the subject of aircraft sales to Israel,[4] given our long-term military relationship with that country, it becomes most important that our relationship be frank, open, and workable. This requires, first and foremost, the honoring of mutual commitments.

I am hopeful that once the IDF clearly understands this fact, we will receive the assurances we require, and our entire relationship will benefit.

If you have different thoughts or recommendations, I would be more than happy to hear from you.[5]

Sincerely,

Melvin R. Laird[6]

---

[4] Reference is to the October 22 letter.

[5] On November 11, Rogers replied: "As I indicated to you in my letter of October 15, I, too have some reservations about the Israeli action of September 17. I agree completely, moreover, with your feeling that Israel's undertakings to us must be honored. There are, however, mitigating factors, and there is room for honest differences of judgment about the justification for Israel's use of Shrikes in this instance, to which I think you have not given full weight." Later in the letter, Rogers "strongly" suggested that the Department of Defense write to Israeli General Zeira that the Israeli Government had "agreed to abide by the conditions" of the missile sale and that, while the Department of Defense did not believe that it abided by the agreement with its actions on September 17, the Department expected "strict adherence in the future." Rogers then wrote: "By handling it and closing the chapter in this way, I have no doubt that you will have made your point cogently, and we will emerge from this with minimal political damage." (Washington National Records Center, OSD Files: FRC 330–76–0197, Box 66, Israel) Rogers's October 15 letter is Document 259.

[6] Printed from a copy with Laird's stamped signature and an indication he signed the original.

265. Memorandum From the President's Assistant for National Security Affairs (Kissinger) to President Nixon[1]

Washington, November 15, 1971.

SUBJECT

State of Play in Mid-East Diplomacy

A new effort has been made by the State Department to get talks started with the Egyptians and Israelis to break the deadlock on an interim settlement. The purpose of this memo is to assure that you are up to date.

The New Initiative

State sounded out both Sadat and Eban on sending a negotiator to the same location—presumably New York—for intensified talks on an interim settlement.[2]

State's plan would be to have Assistant Secretary Sisco work between the two to try to close the gap between their positions.

The Israelis in reply requested a US response to their aircraft requests; asked whether the points in Secretary Rogers' UN speech still stood since Israel regards those points as limiting Israel's scope for negotiation; and asked for assurance that we see negotiations on an interim settlement as basically different from those on an overall settlement.[3] Ambassador Barbour concluded that this was an Israeli effort to fend off the US initiative.

The State of the Negotiations

The prospects for success are not great if State continues its past practice of trying to minimize differences between the two sides and "splitting the difference" on principles that are fundamental to each.

You will recall that the original proposals for an interim settlement envisioned a quite limited mutual pullback or thinning out along the Suez Canal:

—Dayan saw this as a means of (a) reducing the opportunity for Egyptian military action and (b) perhaps providing enough diplomatic

---

[1] Source: National Archives, Nixon Presidential Materials, NSC Files, Box 658, Country Files, Middle East, Middle East Nodis/Cedar/Plus, Vol. IV. Secret; Nodis; Cedar. Sent for information. A stamped notation on the memorandum indicates the President saw it.

[2] See footnote 5, Document 255 and the text of Document 261.

[3] See footnote 2, Document 263.

movement without jeopardy to Israeli security to permit Sadat to continue the ceasefire.

—Sadat seemed to recognize that reaching an overall settlement could take a long time and apparently felt that some Israeli withdrawal could help buy him the necessary time.

Instead of stopping to recognize that US interests lay in the most modest—and therefore most achievable—arrangement possible, State began talking to both sides in terms of a withdrawal that came to seem almost a half-step to an overall settlement.

—Whereas the essence of an interim arrangement is to avoid issues of a final settlement which cannot be resolved now, State has led Egypt to see an interim settlement as a step toward Israeli withdrawal to the pre-war border. While maintaining in Israel that an interim agreement would not commit Israel to a final border, State has in Cairo and publicly reasserted US support for Israeli withdrawal to the pre-war border. This position has been used to encourage Egypt to accept an interim step.

—Whereas the US interest lies in an indefinite extension of the ceasefire, State has acquiesced in the Egyptian idea of in effect setting a limit on its extension. While first proposing in Israel an indefinite ceasefire, State in a general way has contributed to an atmosphere of arbitrary deadline by speaking repeatedly of 1971 as the "year of decision."[4]

—Whereas the success of an interim agreement lies in keeping the zone of Israeli withdrawal narrow enough to preserve Israeli military access to the canal, State adopted the Egyptian position of Israeli withdrawal to—and eventually beyond—the Sinai passes rather than trying to reduce Egyptian aspirations. Knowing that Israel would not give up the passes, State specifically authorized telling Sadat that withdrawal east of the passes would not be precluded.

—Whereas Israel insists that there be no Egyptian troops across the canal, Secretary Rogers on October 4 publicly stated that there could be "compromise" on this issue, meaning that some Egyptian troops could cross. While State initially presented its view of an interim settlement in terms of no Egyptian troops across the canal. Mr. Sisco in Jerusalem in July began talking of "750 with light arms."

—Whereas Israel in February urged the US to refrain from discussing substance with Egypt, a US representative eventually drafted notes that became the basis for an Egyptian position paper in June, and

---

[4] In a speech on June 22 to Egyptian naval officers, Sadat said that 1971 was a "year of decision" for the conflict with Israel.

Secretary Rogers publicly discussed the possibility for compromise on specific issues before the UN General Assembly in October.

The contrast between these positions is shown sharply in the attached table.[5]

It is also worth recalling how this situation evolved:

—After exchanges with Jarring resumed at the beginning of January, State showed little interest in an interim arrangement despite several Egyptian feelers. At that time, Sadat was still talking even about pulling his own troops back from his side of the canal. If we had moved then, modest agreement might have been achieved.

—After the Jarring talks collapsed with Israel's negative reply on February 26,[6] State became interested in an interim settlement. Then, however, in the drama of Secretary Rogers' trip the proposal became less modest and became a substantial step toward an overall settlement.[7] In addition, the dialogue on the subject has led the Israelis to conclude that US weight would be more on the Egyptian side.

Thus the Israelis were confronted with a decision on sending a negotiator to intensified talks where (1) they could expect from experience that the US would begin to advance substantive positions when a deadlock occurred and (2) they could expect that the US positions would be closer to Arab positions than to theirs. Since a deadlock would be almost certain to develop quickly, an Israeli decision to join the talks would be an Israeli decision to submit themselves to combined US and Egyptian pressures. Confronted with this prospect, it seemed unlikely even before the Israeli reply that they could accept without getting something substantial.

State has, by withholding aircraft, created a situation where it may have to agree to provide additional aircraft simply to persuade the Israelis to come to talks which are bound to deadlock soon. Given the way State has developed the issues since April, it would take a major

---

[5] Dated November 9; attached but not printed. The table, "US Positions on an Interim Settlement as Stated to Israel and the UAR," has two columns—under the headings "What We Told Israel" and "What We Told Egypt"—in which the U.S. positions, the officials who expressed them, to whom the officials expressed them, and when they did so, are detailed. An introduction to the table reads: "The following illustrate three points: (1) The Israelis have reason from the record to expect that the US will not remain simply a go-between in negotiations. We started by simply passing positions back and forth. We have since put forward substantive proposals. (2) As the US has become more active, it has become apparent that the US weight will be more on the Egyptian than on the Israeli side of the scale within the limited context of negotiations on an interim arrangement. (3) One position has been taken with Israel and another with Egypt. A negotiation would bring this out."

[6] See Document 211.

[7] Rogers was in Egypt and Israel May 6–7. See Documents 227, 228, 229, and 230.

confrontation to achieve agreement and yet we will already have used much of our leverage just to get talks started.

In addition, pursuing an overall settlement via State's strategy keeps the Soviets out of the process. State seems to feel that Sadat will push the Soviets out. The Soviets cannot want this, and they can always undercut any agreement that would lead in that direction. Unless the Soviets are involved, a settlement seems unlikely. It would seem easier for us to gain their agreement to withdraw than for the Egyptians to push them out.

In short, what started as a modest and possibly achievable objective to buy some time has become an exercise almost as costly to the US as an overall settlement. If the Israelis resist the pressure without reacting, the Soviet position in Egypt will remain as it is. If the Israelis resist but at some point become desperate enough to exploit an incident to mount an attack, the Soviets will find it difficult not to react.

The Issue on Strategy

The real issue here is whether State's strategy for trying to produce an Arab-Israeli accommodation has any chance of success.

—The 1967 UN resolution premised that all the major issues in a final settlement could be worked out as part of one big package. It assumed that agreement could be achieved in the near term.

—The Israelis do not believe Arab attitudes can change enough in a short period to assure Israel of their peaceful intent. Also, they know the Arabs will not accept border changes now and prefer to try to wear them down. So the Israelis will oppose any settlement terms the Arabs are likely to accept in the near term.

—The Arabs have said they will not be worn down on the border issue but they are prepared to make peace with Israel now within pre-1967 borders. They see allowing time to pass as playing along with Israeli strategy. Sadat, however, seems to recognize that some time is needed.

—The strategy behind an interim settlement, therefore, should be (a) to recognize the longer time frame Israel talks about as more realistic but also (b) to recognize the Arab need to get on with the process, even if it be prolonged.

State's strategy has been confusing to both sides. State has pursued an interim settlement as phase one of a quick package settlement. Thus, what ever Sadat conceived as a tactic for surviving through a longer peace-making process has been portrayed by State as a larger step toward a package settlement in a nearer future. Because of State's past position, the Israelis see in the new US diplomatic effort no US sensitivity to what the Israelis thought was the main purpose of an interim settlement—buying time for a more gradual peace-making settlement, they thought this was the US purpose too.

An alternative to State's strategy would be to acknowledge first to ourselves that we are working in a longer time frame and that we need to re-involve the USSR. If we could then persuade the Soviets that this is the only realistic course for both of us and reach some understanding on the ultimate objective, then we might have a chance of allaying Israeli fears that, as soon as an interim agreement was signed, we would hustle them on to a broader settlement on terms that today could only be Egyptian.

As it now stands, the Israelis see us following an Arab/Soviet strategy, and yet we have none of the possible advantages of Soviet involvement. Until we can persuade them that we are at least partially willing to accommodate their strategy, we can only be in confrontation with them. I see no possibility of avoiding that confrontation—or of getting anything significant from it—as long as the State Department's strategy is followed.

266. Memorandum From the President's Assistant for National Security Affairs (Kissinger) to President Nixon[1]

Washington, November 27, 1971.

SUBJECT

Military Balance in Middle East

In view of the recent public statements and reports concerning the military balance in the Middle East and the role of the Soviets, I thought you might be interested in the conclusions reached in recent intelligence studies on this subject.

Following the Egyptian-Soviet communiqué from Moscow,[2] Secretary Rogers in New York said we would "reconsider" the military balance. Then last week in an interview with *US News* November 11 he said, "Up to now, the military balance has not shifted" and noted that the Soviets had operated "with some restraint" in shipments over the

---

[1] Source: National Archives, Nixon Presidential Materials, NSC Files, Box 647, Country Files, Middle East, Middle East (General), Vol. VIII. Secret; Nodis. Sent for information. A stamped notation on the memorandum indicates the President saw it.

[2] See Document 235.

past four or five months. A few days after that the State Department noted the arrival of TU–16 missile-carrying bombers in Egypt.

I thought you would be interested in the conclusions of the State Department study which, in consultation with CIA and DIA, reviewed and assessed the current balance of Arab and Israeli military forces.[3] The two main conclusions of this study were:

—Israel's military superiority has been reduced because of Egypt's much improved air defense system that would make impossible a preemptive air strike such as that in 1967 and make very costly resumption of deep penetration attacks such as those in early 1970. But even larger numbers of additional aircraft would not enable Israel to attack deep into Egypt without suffering "unacceptable" losses.

—Israel does retain the ability to defeat Arab attacks without sustaining "unacceptable" losses, the ability to break up an Egyptian invasion force at the Suez Canal and a "definite edge" in attack capability. Israel is "qualitatively" superior on the ground and at sea and its air force is capable of inflicting "far more damage" on its Arab neighbors than they can inflict on Israel.

Some of the more important facts that went into the above conclusions were:

—The Israelis have fewer aircraft but they are superior in terms of performance and the Israelis have more and better combat pilots. Thus, for instance, Israel's jet fighters have an average range-load superiority of about 4:1 over the comparable Egyptian aircraft. While Israel has about three qualified pilots per supersonic jet aircraft and more than one pilot for each jet aircraft in their total jet inventory, it is estimated that it will be as much as two to five years before Egypt has one available or qualified pilot per jet aircraft.

—Even in the question of absolute numbers, the Israelis received 119 new jet aircraft from the US in 1970 and 1971 while Egypt received 125. While Egypt retains overall numerical superiority, the increase in numbers of aircraft over the past two years has been almost even, and the Israelis have the capacity to put the entire increase to military use while the Egyptians do not.

—Aircraft overhaul and maintenance capabilities of the Egyptian Air Force are such that only 50–65 percent of its aircraft are operationally ready at any time. The Israelis keep about 85 to 90 percent of their aircraft operational and measure their combat turn-around time in minutes compared to hours for the Egyptians.

---

[3] The study, entitled "Arab-Israeli Military Capabilities," was produced by the Bureau of Intelligence and Research on November 1. (National Archives, Nixon Presidential Materials, NSC Files, Box 647, Country Files, Middle East, Middle East (General), Vol. VIII)

—The Arabs have always outnumbered, out-tanked, and outgunned Israel but they have never been able to defeat it in battle. The poor record stems from qualitative differences in organization, matériel, manpower and leadership which from "all indications" continue to give Israel a "decisive advantage" today and for a "considerable time" into the future.

—There has been a "dramatic" improvement in the Egyptian air defense system since early 1970. Determined to deny the Israelis the freedom to fly with impunity in Egyptian air space, the Soviets have deployed extensive air defense equipment including as many as 10,000 Soviet personnel to man air defense units and five of their own fighter squadrons.

—Israel's air defense system has also improved since 1967 by the installation of new equipment and procurement of additional HAWK launchers and, most important, by retention of the occupied territories which provide strategic depth, added warning time and permit deployment of interceptor aircraft nearer to Egyptian bases.

—The Arab navies pose no significant threat to Israel whose own navy is capable of interdicting Arab naval forces, conducting limited anti-submarine warfare and supporting amphibious operations.

This boils down to three main points:

1. The shift in the balance that has taken place as a result of the Soviet-installed defense capability mainly affects Israel's pre-emptive strike capability. Israel's own defensive capability remains adequate and not in jeopardy. This loss of ability to make a decisive pre-emptive strike is important to Israel because it deprives Israel of the ability to impose a short war. It enhances the Arab ability to prolong a war of attrition, but the Sinai buffer, Israel's defenses and Egyptian offensive inadequacy make it difficult for Egypt to direct such a war at Israel proper. Hence the effect of a war of attrition might be limited.

2. The other important element in the picture is the continuing buildup in the USSR's own position in Egypt. Despite a decline in Soviet shipments this spring—perhaps simply because the massive missile buildup was completed—the Soviets have this year introduced the SA–6 mobile missile system, the Flagon-A supersonic interceptor, the Foxbat reconnaissance aircraft and now the missile-carrying TU–16s. All these improve Soviet capability against the US and even, in an extreme situation, against Israel. While Soviet shipments have declined comparatatively in numbers or tonnage, there seems to be a steady qualitative improvement in the Soviet position rather than any significant "restraint."

3. When all the studies of the military balance are complete, the decision now to provide another complement of Phantoms is political—in both the Egypt-Israel and the US-Soviet contexts. Everyone here admits

that Israel will need more planes over a 1–3 year span to continue normal modernization and upgrading of its air force. The main question is when those planes will be provided and in what political context.[4]

---

[4] On November 23 the Senate voted 81–14 to provide Israel with $500 million in military credits for Israel, half of which was earmarked for the purchase of Phantom jets. (*New York Times*, November 24, 1971, p. 1)

---

267. Memorandum From Secretary of Defense Laird to President Nixon[1]

Washington, November 30, 1971.

SUBJECT

Mrs. Meir's Visit[2] and U.S. National Security Interests

Mrs. Meir's visit will test the credibility of the U.S. commitment to UN Resolution 242 and the Administration's goal for a more even-handed Middle East policy. I urge continued restraint on provision of more F–4 and A–4 fighter-bomber aircraft at this time.

A recently completed assessment by the Joint Chiefs of Staff supports conclusions previously reached in Defense,[3] State,[4] and CIA regarding substantial Israeli military superiority. Israel has utilized the ceasefire period advantageously to an extent not possible for Egypt. The Israelis concur that the Egyptians have no foreseable capability to attack in force across the Canal. "Deterrence" is hardly an issue because an Egyptian attack would constitute an irrational act and the presence or absence of a few additional Israeli aircraft would not be a predominant component in the equation.

In the longer run, Israel will require replacement aircraft, and we should not close the door to all future sales, or to assisting Israel to pro-

---

[1] Source: Washington National Records Center, OSD Files: FRC 330–74–0115, Box 5, Israel. Secret; Sensitive. Drafted by Noyes on November 29.

[2] Meir visited the United States November 30–December 11, meeting with Nixon on December 2; see Document 268.

[3] Moorer attached the appendix to a DIA study entitled "DIA Intelligence Appraisal: The Arab-Israeli Military Balance" to a memorandum to Laird that day. (Washington National Records Center, OSD Files: FRC 330–74–0115, Box 5, Israel)

[4] See footnote 3, Document 266.

duce its own "super Mirage" aircraft—which could be in production by the end of 1974.

However, Israel's immediate aircraft supply requirement is for political, rather than military, advantage. Affirmative U.S. action would symbolically underwrite her preferred option of standing pat, and would serve as a practical repudiation of our own publicly announced position.

In terms of Israeli as well as U.S. and NATO security interests, a new commitment of aircraft would be counterproductive. The Soviets have little to lose in a military sense from such a commitment, but its disclosure would enable them to share with the Israelis the political benefits of increased polarization in the Middle East. Apart from the damage to U.S. credibility, a military price would be paid by NATO, the U.S., and even the Israelis in the long run through the resulting security implications of an increased Soviet presence in Egypt. In meeting the need for a counterpart military supply response, the Soviets would virtually be compelled to increase the numbers of their own personnel in Egypt since Egypt, per se, cannot even absorb the Soviet aircraft already available.

If we are to pursue our own broader national security interests, the U.S. must retain some degree of initiative in the military supply sphere. Likewise, we must be prepared to rely on our own military and political assessments. Otherwise, the Israelis and the Soviets are left with the initiative of wrecking any negotiations to avoid uncomfortable choices or prevent a degree of depolarization that challenges either the Soviet Middle East political posture or Israel's image as an indispensable U.S. cold war instrument.

In the event of an emergency requirement we could make aircraft and other supplies immediately available from our own stocks either from Europe or the U.S. The monitoring of the situation in the Eastern Mediterranean has an exceptionally high priority and we are studying very carefully our military posture in that area, both as it relates to the southern flank of NATO and our own unilateral interests in the Middle East. Therefore, I am confident should a military requirement become paramount we can respond in a timely manner.

As expressed to you before, I believe that our military supply relationship with Israel, in either the private or public context, is by itself inadequate as the principal operative manifestation of U.S. policy toward Israel. The coming UNGA debate[5] will provide another critical test. In the same sense that our present military supply policy suggests a departure from the old path of least resistance, our diplomatic stance

---

[5] See Document 270.

needs to emphasize that our commitment to Israel's basic security is as unswerving as is our unwillingness to live with her present hard line posture. I appreciate the problems that will be generated by the resulting Israeli discomfort, but this price appears justified beside our larger goals of peace and by the prospects for productive dialogue during your Moscow visit.[6]

Melvin R. Laird[7]

[6] Nixon went to Moscow in May 1972 for a summit with Soviet General Secretary Brezhnev.

[7] Printed from a copy that bears Laird's stamped signature with an indication that he signed the original.

268. Editorial Note

On December 2, 1971, in Washington, Israeli Prime Minister Golda Meir met with senior American officials to discuss the delivery of Phantom jets to Israel—shipments of which had not occurred since July—beginning with Secretary of State William Rogers at noon. She warned the Secretary that even though Sadat "might be afraid to go to war" and that the Soviet leadership "might not want war," Israel "had to be ready" nonetheless since Sadat could become a "slave to his own words" and get himself into the kind of trouble that might draw the Soviet Union further into the region. Rogers agreed, and, thus, he argued that the United States and Israel "had to leave way out for Sadat," foremost by "achieving progress toward peace" by "getting negotiations going" after the UN General Assembly convened. He continued by saying that "fundamental U.S. support of Israel had not changed and will not change," but that the timing of such support "was of course important" because the United States "did not want anything to make beginning of negotiating process difficult." Regarding future negotiations, Meir reviewed the differences between the U.S. and Israeli positions and remarked that the U.S. stand on "the territorial aspects of peace" was "harmful" to Israel. She also said that the United States seemed to be "punishing" Israel by withholding Phantoms. After addressing these issues, Rogers ended their session with a discussion of common U.S.-Israeli objectives. (Telegram 219343 to Tel Aviv, December 4; National Archives, Nixon Presidential Materials, NSC Files, Box 658, Country Files, Middle East, Middle East Nodis/Cedar/Plus, Vol. IV) His talking points had been coordinated with President

Richard Nixon and President's Assistant for National Security Affairs Henry Kissinger at a meeting on the previous day, of which there is a tape recording. (Ibid., White House Tapes, Oval Office, Conversation No. 627–4)

After her conversation with Rogers, Meir met with the President in the Oval Office from 3:05 to 4:52 p.m., with Kissinger and Israeli Ambassador Yitzhak Rabin present. Nixon assured her of his commitment to sending Phantoms to Israel and said that Assistant Secretary of State for Near Eastern and South Asian Affairs Joseph Sisco would finalize the details of their delivery in meetings with Rabin scheduled for the end of the month. The President also emphasized that his promise of future Phantom shipments did not depend on a political settlement in the Middle East, foremost because of his dedication to maintaining a military balance in the region. While Meir was pleased that the two issues were not "linked," she and Rabin both expressed their concern over precisely when the aircraft deliveries would re-start. Nixon and Kissinger avoided addressing the issue directly and said only that Sisco and Rabin would negotiate a schedule. The President added: "Let me say this. I do not want the delivery or non-delivery of the planes to be a block to the frank discussions which we should have on the political side. Now, I think that's what we've really come down to."

The subject then turned to the Soviet Union, with Nixon confiding in Meir the offer that Soviet Foreign Minister Andrei Gromyko had privately made to him that the Soviet Union would stop sending arms to Egypt—in addition to removing its forces from the country—in exchange for Israeli withdrawal from Egyptian territory (see Document 251). The President explained that Gromyko "didn't say this in front of the others" and that "this has not gone to the bureaucracy," and, thus, she should not discuss the subject with her Cabinet. As a result of the Soviet offer, Nixon advised Meir: "You have the real negotiations—that's the other end of the spectrum [from proximity talks] and that may be involving the Russians, because let's face it, your Egyptian friends can't do a damn thing unless the Russians back them. You know that, and I know that. Now having said that, we then move to the 'appearance' of negotiations [under the Department of State's auspices]. That's why I use the term appearance. If you were to give us in this an interim period—don't—just the appearance of talking to us—it's the appearance—I can assure you there won't be any pressure. No pressure. Because we will know that this is not—it doesn't mean—I think that if you give the appearance that too will cool. This whole business of the Soviets." Kissinger added: "I think what we have to avoid is a Soviet misunderstanding." In his concluding remarks, Nixon reassured her: "We're not talking about the two of us getting together and pressuring you." (National Archives, Nixon Presidential Materials,

White House Tapes, Oval Office, Conversation No. 628–16; the editors transcribed the portions of the tape recording printed here specifically for this volume) There is a tape recording of a meeting between Nixon and Kissinger earlier that day, during which they set the parameters for this discussion. (Ibid., Conversation No. 628–2)

269. Conversation Between President Nixon and the President's Assistant for National Security Affairs (Kissinger)[1]

Washington, December 9, 1971, 4:55–5:15 p.m.

Kissinger: This Sisco's going to go crazy in these other negotiations coming up with schemes. We've got to slow him down.

Nixon: Well, how do we? Should we let him into the deal? Never.

Kissinger: He's too dangerous. He's too unreliable. Let me think about that, how I can slow him down. We may just have to tell Rogers you don't want that much activity. I can get the Egyptians to slow down a little bit through Dobrynin.

Nixon: [unclear]

Kissinger: He's one of the trickiest ones we've got.

Nixon: [unclear]

Kissinger: Well, I thought, Mr. President—I was really—I was in awe, because you really—that was—there were so many traps into which you could have fallen—

Nixon: Yeah.

Kissinger: —and every one of which would—could have raised enormous political problems for you if—you have no idea with what suspicion, and determination to have a showdown, they [the Israelis] came to this country. And they are, actually, now, from our domestic point of view, in a rather good position to put the heat on us, at least.

Nixon: Yeah, sure they are.

Kissinger: And I think they were floating on air, and we didn't really give them anything other than what we—

---

[1] Source: National Archives, Nixon Presidential Materials, White House Tapes, Oval Office, Conversation No. 628–18. No classification marking. The editors transcribed the portion of the tape recording printed here specifically for this volume. Brackets indicate unclear portions in the original recording or those omitted by the editors except "[laughter]", added for clarity.

Nixon: Well, actually, Henry, what we could get from the Russians, for them, is a hell of a lot.

Kissinger: Yeah. They won't think—

Nixon: If it's in their long-term interests.

Kissinger: They won't think it's enough. And I have no illusions that I can negotiate an agreement they'll like.

Nixon: Yeah, I know, but we're—

Kissinger: And if we've got to squeeze them, '73 is a hell of a lot better than '72—

Nixon: That's right, that's right, that's right. And the Russians understand that.

Kissinger: Oh, yes. I've got that worked out with the Russians.

Nixon: But, then we can do it. Then, in the meantime, you see, the Russians have got to keep the damned Egyptians from screwing around.

Kissinger: What I've got to do is to get the Russians to make some modifications in the Rogers proposal, so that we can tell the Israelis we've met our part of the bargain. And that might be possible. It won't be as much as the Israelis think they can get, but—

Nixon: What do you mean? The Russians? They would make it privately to us?

Kissinger: Yeah.

[unclear]

Nixon: Yeah.

Kissinger: Well, there would be improvements. So, I think no one here should object to our getting a better deal than the—

Nixon: You really thought that she was going to be tougher? [unclear]—

Kissinger: Oh, yes. Oh, yeah. That's why I went to see her yesterday; to condition her a little bit. But, I wasn't making much headway. I mean, she was much harder with me than she was with you. But, I didn't handle her so skillfully. And, of course, I couldn't [unclear]—

Nixon: You couldn't commit so much, I know.

Kissinger: I couldn't commit it—

Nixon: But I think I disarmed her from the beginning by saying, "Now, look here: one track."

Kissinger: Yeah.

Nixon: "Let's do that and forget it." Now, let's talk about the other [unclear] thing.

Kissinger: Well, when I said—what was so effective was when I said there is this relationship between [unclear] this I do for the balance. [laughter] Let's just get that out of the way. I mean—

Nixon: Yeah.

Kissinger: —you were sort of—

Nixon: Yeah.

Kissinger: —overruling what I had said.

Nixon: Yeah. Yeah. Yeah.

Kissinger: It was a terribly effective way, because it showed that you had gone beyond the government.

Nixon: Um-hmm. Yeah. Which, still, is true.

Kissinger: Which is true.

Nixon: But, we know, we know that this is the reason why, frankly, the—the—the—Bill's and Sisco's scheme will not frighten them. They know that apart from the American political situation, that American security requires that we not allow the Russians to change the balance of power in the Mideast. That's always been the heart of the problem.

Kissinger: That's right.

Nixon: See, that's what I know. So, they know damn well, that isn't credible. But, if a Democrat were sitting here, they know it would not be credible, because the Democrats are going to depend on the Jewish vote.

Kissinger: Right.

Nixon: I, as one who doesn't depend on the Jewish vote, they know it's not credible, because they know that I won't let the balance of power be changed. And I think being quite honest with them about that helps a great deal.

Kissinger: That's right.

Nixon: Isn't that an incentive—?

Kissinger: If we can bring this off now, we have, one, solved the security problem. Two, we will have to use these negotiations, which drive the Jewish community crazy, and yet, at the same time, have some real negotiations go on—

Nixon: Hmm?

Kissinger: —which, by early '73, will lead to a result.

Nixon: But you must keep that in the separate channel. I don't want any of that—

Kissinger: Oh, no.

Nixon: What is significant—I want you to tell Dobrynin, "Quit talking to Rogers about that goddamn thing." Has he been talking to Rogers—

Kissinger: No.

Nixon: —about the Mideast?

Kissinger: Well, yes, he talked about—

Nixon: I, I just have to be rough on that. I said, "Now, if it's raised, you just ask what it's all about." But, I said [unclear]

Kissinger: No, we've got to discipline Dobrynin on that.

Nixon: Yeah, Dobrynin. Dobrynin has just got know that for this thing to work, we've got to have that, that two-channel situation.

Kissinger: Yeah.

Nixon: Because, you know, Dobrynin likes to talk to everybody and report back to his government. Now, now—because, you see, if Bill gets involved in this part—

Kissinger: No, no, if—

Nixon: —he'll get involved on the Hill.

Kissinger: No, Bill will do what he did with the others. You see, first of all, Mr. President, my strategy will be to waste as much time as possible, because—so that if there is an interim settlement, you'll make it at the summit.

Nixon: Sure. I should do both.

Kissinger: And, imagine that out of the summit, there comes SALT, an interim arrangement in the Middle East, trade, and, maybe, one or two other things. And on this basis, I can now talk cold turkey to Dobrynin. I'll tell him, "If Vietnam blows up in this interval, the Middle East negotiation is dead."

Nixon: Sure. Your feeling is that they want a Middle East settlement, for: one, they don't want a confrontation with us; two, they want—they don't want the burden of the Egyptians; three, they don't want trouble with us, particularly while they have to deal with the Chinese—

Kissinger: Fourth—

Nixon: And they think that China—they don't want the Chinese messing in the Mideast, is that it?

Kissinger: They think that if [unclear]

Nixon: That's just because [unclear]

Kissinger: That's right. If there is no settlement, say, within two years, the Chinese will take over their position in the Middle East.

Nixon: You think so?

Kissinger: Yeah.

Nixon: I see. Because, they—

Kissinger: They'll radicalize the whole area.

Nixon: They'll radicalize it. So, that's why they want [unclear]

Kissinger: And that—what's even worse, the Russians—the Chinese may drive them into confrontation with which they have [unclear] for issues the Chinese face. The Chinese, on the other hand, are terrified that there'll be a Middle East deal, because on the way to the airport, that Marshal who was taking Lin Biao's place said to me, "We know the Russians want to make a deal with you in the Middle East, so that they can throw everything against us." So, this is the predicament of the China—of the Russians. And we may just pick it off. Now, it will require some painful things early in '73, but I—

Nixon: [unclear] Lin Biao's—

[unclear exchange]

Kissinger: Mr. President—

Nixon: [unclear] but they've got to in their own interest. In the end, they're going to lose. See? [unclear] I'd pit the whole world against them.

Kissinger: Mr. President, I have always said, at the right moment, we've got to put it to Israel.

Nixon: Yeah. Yeah.

Kissinger: As it happens, now could be the right moment.

Nixon: [unclear] at the same time.

Kissinger: At this moment it would lead to a war.

Nixon: Hell, yes.

Kissinger: Next year, or well into '73.

[Omitted here is discussion unrelated to the Middle East.]

---

270. Telegram From the Department of State to the White House[1]

Washington, December 13, 1971, 1713Z.

223761. Tosec 21. Please pass Peter Johnson in the Azores for Secretary Rogers.[2] For Secretary from Sisco.

---

[1] Source: National Archives, Nixon Presidential Materials, NSC Files, Box 1166. Saunders Files. Middle East Negotiations Files, Middle East—Jarring Talks, December 1–14, 1971. Secret; Exdis. Drafted by Sisco, cleared in IO/UNP, and approved by Sisco. Repeated to USUN.

[2] Rogers accompanied the President to the Azores December 13–14 for meetings with French President Pompidou.

1. We expect a vote on the Middle East resolution within the next two or three hours and I want to tell you, as a follow up to our conversation on Sunday,[3] where matters presently stand and my recommendation.

2. The resolution is essentially the same as the one you reviewed on Sunday (septel).[4]

3. As you know, Egyptians are pressing us to vote affirmatively, whereas Israelis have made a major pitch to have us vote negatively.[5] While resolution in septel was originally sponsored by 18 countries, including twelve Africans, we understand four of the Africans have withdrawn their sponsorship. Since then, Egypt has picked up a few other non-Africans and the sponsorship is around 23. They will probably be able to get at least 65 votes for this resolution. The Africans have suggested some changes to the Egyptians to bring their resolution more in line with its own report.[6] Whether Senegal or other Africans are submitting amendments or not is problematical. The important thing is that some difference has occurred within the African group and this

---

[3] December 12. No record of the meeting has been found.

[4] Reported in telegram 223760 to the White House, December 13. (National Archives, RG 59, Central Files 1970–73, POL 27–14 ARAB–ISR) The UN General Assembly adopted Resolution 2799, which had been proposed by 21 members, on the evening of December 13 by a recorded vote of 79 to 7, with 36 abstentions. The United Kingdom, Egypt, France, Jordan, Lebanon, and the Soviet Union voted for the resolution; Israeli voted against it; the United States and Syria abstained. The resolution reaffirmed the inadmissibility of acquisition of territory by force, set forth the principles for a just and lasting peace in the Middle East, and called for the reactivation of Jarring's Mission. The text of the resolution is printed in *Yearbook of the United Nations, 1971*, pp. 176–177, and Bush's report on its adoption was sent in telegram 4996 from USUN, December 14. (Ibid., Nixon Presidential Materials, NSC Files, Box 1166, Saunders Files, Middle East Negotiations Files, Middle East—Jarring Talks, December 1–14, 1971)

[5] Regarding the General Assembly debate, Eban told Bush on December 7 that Israel and the United States would have to "make best of situation" and prevent "certain things from happening" rather than trying to "achieve any specific steps." Eban was adamant that: 1) there be no changes to Security Council Resolution 242; 2) that Israel was under no "obligation" to "accept Egyptian interpretation" of Jarring's February aide-mémoire; and 3) that there be no "support for sanctions." (Telegram 4826 from USUN, December 7; ibid., Box 658, Country Files, Middle East, Middle East Nodis/Cedar/Plus, Vol. IV) The Department instructed Bush to tell Eban that it agreed on the issue of Resolution 242 and sanctions, but that "it is clear that any resolution which omitted all reference to Jarring memorandum would be non-starter for Egyptians and would obtain virtually no support in assembly." (Telegram 221645 to USUN, December 9; ibid., Box 1166, Saunders Files, Middle East Negotiations Files, Middle East—Jarring Talks, December 1–14, 1971) Eban responded to Bush's presentation on December 9 by saying that he "appreciated that parliamentary reasons may dictate need for something" but feared that a "call might be made for Israel to respond to Jarring." (Telegram 4900 from USUN; ibid., RG 59, Central Files 1970–73, POL 27–14 ARAB–ISR) The debate was held in plenary sessions December 3–14. See *Yearbook of the United Nations, 1971*, pp. 170–175.

[6] A Committee of Ten African Heads of State conducted an inquiry on behalf of the OAU and submitted proposals to the Secretary General aimed at breaking the impasse in the Middle East. See ibid., pp. 169–170.

will probably be reflected by some abstentions among them though how many is very difficult to say.

4. Yesterday, Bush put to Riad the changes which you reviewed on Sunday. Without going into technical details, you recall this was an attempt to move the references to the February 8 Jarring memo,[7] the characterization of the Egyptian and Israeli replies,[8] and the call on Israel to reply positively on the preambular paragraphs. As we expected, Riad turned them down.

5. Candidly, I do not believe there is any satisfactory vote for us. Whichever way we go, we will be criticized by one side or the other. Our basic posture has been, as you know, that diplomatic alternatives will be required in the post-GA period. The resolution is likely to carry regardless of how the US votes.

6. I recommend an abstention coupled with the explanation of vote along the following lines:

A. The US agrees with much of the resolution sponsored by the 23 countries

B. However we abstain in the belief that the resolution distorts the balance of Res 242 and will not get Jarring's mission restarted but rather would help to reenforce the impasse.

C. In our efforts we have tried to influence the substance of the resolution in the direction of the OAU report. We regret that the resolution does not approximate more closely that report.

D. We suggested changes in the resolution which would have maintained the balance of Res 242 and, by referring to Jarring's initiative in the preamble, would have reflected the reality that his initiative had not succeeded and would have left open a wider range of options for resumption of his efforts in the future. Regrettably our suggestions were not acceptable.

E. I hope that all of us can draw one lesson from the Assembly proceedings on this matter. The US continues to believe that the way to practical progress towards a peaceful settlement and an interim agreement is by means of quiet diplomacy. We do not believe that the Assembly at this point or the SC subsequently can make a practical contribution to this end at this time. We hope that at the conclusion of these proceedings the parties concerned will come to the common judgment that diplomacy must find a way.

7. There remains one further contingency which we might have to consider. The British on behalf of WEO's may suggest to Riad this

---

[7] See footnote 2, Document 205.

[8] For the Egyptian reply, see footnote 4, Document 206; for the Israeli reply, see Documents 211 and 213.

morning that sixth operative paragraph be amended to read: Qte Calls upon Israel to make a response to the Special Representative's aide-mémoire of February 8, 1971, that would enable the search for a peaceful settlement under the auspices of the Special Representative to continue. Unqte This is essentially the formulation contained in the SYG's report and follows Jarring's suggestion as a means of finessing the impasse and giving the Israelis a means to get off the hook. With this change, the resolution would undoubtedly receive a greater majority of affirmative votes but it nevertheless leaves res basically faulty in other respects noted above, and we would intend to abstain in this contingency even though a smaller group will be with us.

8. We voted against a similar GA res last year[9] which was even less strong than this one. Moreover, vote comes at time PM Meir is reporting at home that things have been patched up between us, and affirmative vote would tend undermine publicly and psychologically constructive results of President's talk with PM Meir. On other hand, I recognize that Sadat will be deeply disappointed and Arabs will play our vote as a backoff from our support of the Jarring initiative.

Irwin

---

[9] See footnote 8, Document 177.

---

271. Memorandum of Conversation[1]

Washington, December 29, 1971.

PARTICIPANTS

    Ambassador Yitzhak Rabin
    Minister Avner Idan

    Assistant Secretary Joseph Sisco
    Mr. H. Stackhouse

Sisco said the President had directed that discussions begin with Ambassador Rabin as a follow-up, through the Ambassador, of the conversation the President and the Prime Minister had had December

---

[1] Source: National Archives, RG 59, Central Files 1970–73, DEF 12–5 ISR. Secret; Nodis; Cedar Plus. Drafted by Stackhouse (NEA/IAI). The meeting was held at 9 a.m. in Rabin's residence.

2,[2] the purpose being to work out an agreement as it relates to Phantoms and Skyhawks.[3]

First, Sisco wanted to tell the Ambassador what production schedules were under normal circumstances. If we were to proceed on the basis of new production, that is, new Phantom production with which Israel could tie in (we were talking here about 42 Phantoms), this would mean that Israel could receive aircraft from new production beginning in April, 1973. Regarding Skyhawks, on the basis of our production line, delivery could begin from new production in July, 1973. as an add-on to the 18 Skyhawks now scheduled for delivery November 1972–June 1973. If we were to proceed on the basis of new production schedules, there were contingencies that could affect delivery, that is, that would dictate earlier delivery to Israel:

A. If we conclude that Soviet deliveries to the Arabs threaten to turn the military balance against Israel;

B. If the Arabs resume the war of attrition or otherwise initiate active hostilities;

C. If there were an interim agreement or some kind of agreement involving Israeli withdrawal, it was obvious this would involve additional military risk for Israel.

Sisco was aware, he continued, that the Prime Minister had talked to the President in terms of a delivery schedule beginning in 1972. Rabin interjected that that was what the Prime Minister had told him. Sisco said that if the Ambassador were going to be in town for a few more days he could have gotten additional information as to what the possibilities were regarding earlier deliveries. Sisco said he would be in touch with the Pentagon while Rabin was away and would see what was possible. Anything in the way of deliveries before the dates he had described—that is deliveries other than those based on new production—would have to be done by diversion from our own inventory. By the time Rabin returned, he hoped to be able to give him some indication as to what might be possible, but he had not had the opportunity to explore this fully with the Pentagon.

Sisco then recalled that the Prime Minister and the President had also discussed political aspects of the situation, the Jarring mission, and the interim agreement. Regarding reactivation of the Jarring mission, Sisco would summarize our position as follows: We see advantage in

---

[2] See Document 268.

[3] A copy of Kissinger's December 28 memorandum to Rogers directing him to begin talks with Rabin is attached to Document 272. On February 2, 1972, after the fifth and final meeting between Sisco and Rabin, Rogers sent Nixon a memorandum to update him on the outcome of the talks. For Kissinger's summary and analysis, see Document 277.

some Jarring activity if for no other reason than that it reinforces the continuance of the ceasefire. It gives Cairo an opportunity to point to ongoing diplomatic activity; such activity tends to blur deadlines which have been of concern to the United States and Israel. So we see reactivation of the Jarring mission as desirable. If there were some new response to Jarring from Israel which would take into account, for example, the OAU approach,[4] this would be helpful not only in reinforcing the ceasefire's continuance but in creating a more satisfactory climate generally. Sisco expressed the hope that Israel would look at this.

Regarding the interim agreement, Sisco went on, our position remains that we remain available to the parties if they desire it. On November 1 the Prime Minister had asked Ambassador Barbour for clarifications.[5]

The first clarification requested was with respect to aircraft. In this regard, Sisco had said what he could say at this time.

The second clarification was regarding the six points the Secretary had outlined in his address at the UNGA.[6] On this, our position was described clearly in the Secretary's interview in the November 22 issue of *U.S. News and World Report*, in which the Secretary said:

"I outlined in my (United Nations) General Assembly speech a few weeks ago the six areas where there are differences. I want to make clear we have made no proposals of our own and we have not adopted any substantive position on any of these six parameters that I outlined. We have no blueprint of our own that we have put forward.

"Both sides have put forward some positive ideas; both sides adhere to certain points strongly, and both sides will have to make adjustments in their positions if an interim agreement is to be achieved.

"There are a number of difficulties, but I would single out one in particular: the nature of any Egyptian presence east of the Canal. On this key point, I also want to make clear that both sides hold strong views, one insisting that military forces cross and the other taking an opposite view. While I expressed in my general debate speech the hope that this and other points might prove reconcilable, I want to make clear that we have taken no substantive position. The fact that I hope the reconciliation is possible should not be understood to mean that we have made a judgment or expressed a substantive view on how it should be resolved. That is a matter for the parties."

This was our response on this point.

---

[4] See footnote 5, Document 270.
[5] See footnote 2, Document 263.
[6] See footnote 3, Document 255.

Sisco said the third clarification related to:

(a) whether the U.S. agrees that negotiations for an interim settlement are basically different from negotiations for an overall settlement; and

(b) what role the U.S. would play in these negotiations.

As to (a), we do not believe there should be any preconditions for entering into negotiations in close proximity. As far as we were concerned the principle of no imposed settlement applies to an interim agreement as it does to an overall settlement. As a minimum, the objective of close proximity talks should be to reinforce the ceasefire; therefore, the pace of these talks should be geared to avoid false deadlines resulting in new crises.

As to (b), the U.S. will seek to identify common ground between the positions of the two sides and use our good offices with both parties to help them develop such common ground. Israel can be assured that we will consult fully step-by-step with it in the spirit of the special relationship that exists between our two countries.

Now in light of these clarifications that we have provided, we seek confirmation that Israel is now prepared to enter into the negotiations at close proximity suggested earlier by the United States Government.

Sisco then said that we requested that Israel review the "Minute of Oral Discussion" of August 2, 1971[7] (this was the paper, he noted, he had left with the Prime Minister) and, in particular, point one of that paper dealing with the relationship of the interim agreement with the final settlement. At this point Sisco said he wanted to say a word about the Egyptian position. We have had no new indication of a change in the Egyptian position regarding an interim agreement. The last formal conveyance by the Egyptians to us, Sisco continued, linked the beginning of proximity talks with a further reply on the part of Israel to the February 8 memorandum of Jarring. When the U.S. first approached Egypt in October regarding talks in close proximity the Egyptian reaction was positive. We did not press for a formal, categorical, 100 percent acceptance of the proximity talk proposal because we wanted to be sure Israel would go along. We had suggested to Israel a specific time and place for such talks. But in view of Israel's reservations, we did not carry the matter further with Egypt. We wanted Israel to know precisely what our understanding was of the Egyptian position on close proximity talks. The last privately conveyed Egyptian position shortly before the opening of the Middle East GA debate (in mid-December) was one of linkage between proximity talks and a further Israeli reply to the Jarring February 8 memorandum.

---

[7] See footnote 5, Document 245.

Finally, if Israel was ready to proceed to proximity talks, Sisco said, we would appreciate any thoughts it might have as to time and place.

Sisco said we had chosen to convey all of this to the GOI and to have Rabin carry this back personally in order to diminish the risk of any leaks. It was essential that there be no government leaks and speculation as it related to these talks and in particular as it related to military assistance.

There was a technical point Sisco wanted to mention. In the President's discussion with the Prime Minister she had referred to F4Fs. Rabin said that this was a two-seat trainer not equipped for fighting but which the Israelis wanted to equip for fighting. Rabin said she had said Israel wanted during 1972 40 A4Es and 10 F4Fs. In 1973, in addition to the 18 A4Ns already scheduled, Israel wanted another 32. As for Phantoms, Rabin continued, Israel wanted three per month, with deliveries beginning early in 1972 and continuing in 1973. Mrs. Meir had talked about beginning deliveries in January. Rabin said that on the political side of Sisco's presentation he preferred not to say anything at the present, but he obviously would report fully to Jerusalem. On the military side, Rabin made clear in several ways Israel's very strong view that deliveries should begin in 1972 and that he could not agree to a later delivery schedule. In short, Rabin again reiterated he would take what Sisco had said back to Israel and Sisco in the meantime would explore matters with the Pentagon. This is a start of talks, Sisco said.

Regarding handling of press queries on this meeting, Sisco and Rabin agreed that nothing would be volunteered to the press. If there was any query from the press to Rabin he would confirm that a meeting had taken place and that there had been a regular, routine exchange of views. If asked whether there had been any discussion of clarifications, Rabin said he would "stay out of it."

In closing comments Sisco asked that General Zeira not raise these matters with the Pentagon in the interim. This was being held very closely within the USG. Rabin reassured Sisco on this point.

Attachment

F-4E DELIVERY SCHEDULE

1972		1973	
Feb	2	Feb	2
Apr	2	Apr	2
Jun	2	May	4
Aug	2	Jun	4
Oct	2	Jul	4
Dec	2	Aug	2
	12	Sep	4
		Oct	2
		Nov	2
		Dec	4
			30

TOTAL = 42

NOTE: Majority of aircraft incorporate leading edge slats

272. **Memorandum From the Assistant Secretary of Defense for International Security Affairs (Nutter) to Secretary of Defense Laird**[1]

Washington, December 30, 1971.

SUBJECT

President's Decision on Aircraft for Israel

By memorandum of 28 December Dr. Kissinger has directed Secretary Rogers to initiate immediate discussions with Ambassador Rabin to conclude an agreement by the U.S. to deliver A–4s and F–4s on a regular monthly schedule beginning February 1972.[2] In a footnote the memorandum indicates that the President received "without contradiction" Mrs. Meir's request for delivery of three F–4s per month from

---

[1] Source Washington National Records Center, OSD Files: FRC 330–76–0197, Box 66, Israel. Secret; Sensitive. A stamped notation on the memorandum reads: "Sec Def has seen, 2 Jan 1972."

[2] Kissinger's memorandum is attached but not printed.

February 1972 through December 1973—a total of 69 aircraft; and delivery of an additional 82 A–4s during the same period. We note, however, that the memorandum itself does not specify numbers of aircraft or a precise delivery schedule.

Dr. Kissinger's directive raises several serious problems:

a. It was addressed to Secretary Rogers and not to yourself—yet it in effect gives away DoD assets.

b. As was the case in the August 1970 and December 1970 A–4 sales decisions, it is physically impossible for the Navy to begin delivery of A–4s by February 1972 in the configuration Israel insists on. Modification takes at least three to six months.

c. The only possible source for either A–4s or F–4s between now and November 1972 (for A–4s) and March of 1973 (for F–4s), when aircraft previously ordered for Israel become available, is to divert them from U.S. operational units. As has been repeatedly emphasized by the Air Force and Navy, and officially endorsed by the JCS, any diversion from short supply U.S. inventories would have a serious adverse impact on U.S. capabilities.

d. Mrs. Meir's request is an inflated one, which exceeds Israel's previous requests (by 24 F–4s) and clearly exceeds Israel's short term requirements. As you will recall the Chiefs have already forwarded to you a carefully worked-out force modernization sales program for Israel, recommending sale of 63 F–4s and 60 A–4s through CY 1975, with all sales coming from new production. Attached is a summary chart showing Israel's original and new requests, plus copies of the JCS proposal, and a proposal forwarded by Mr. Packard to Mr. Sisco show-ing how Israel's original requests could be met from new production.[3]

The Air Force, Navy and Chairman's office are deeply concerned by the implications of Dr. Kissinger's directive, as am I. The adverse consequences for U.S. force readiness and for our own national security objectives in the Middle East are obvious. Accordingly, I recommend that this subject be discussed with the principals concerned after Monday morning's staff meeting.[4] The Secretary of the Navy, Secretary of the Air Force, Chief of Naval Operations, Chief of Staff, Air Force and the Chairman will all be prepared to address the subject at that time. In the meantime, Air Force and Navy are preparing an assessment of the impact of the proposed program, together with various alternatives open to us. These will be available by Monday morning.

---

[3] Attached but not printed.

[4] The minutes of the meeting, which occurred at 9:30 a.m. on January 3, 1972, are in the Washington National Records Center, OSD Files, DB–TS–99–006.

Finally, I recommend you call Secretary Rogers[5] and ask that he delay meeting with Ambassador Rabin until you have had a chance to review Dr. Kissinger's memorandum and prepare recommendations.

G. Warren Nutter

[5] According to a January 3 letter to Rogers from Laird, the two spoke on December 31, and after the conversation, the Secretary of Defense had his staff study the possibility of delivering aircraft to Israel beginning February 1972, as Meir had requested. Laird wrote: "It is our conclusion that we can, to a large measure, meet the delivery schedules requested by Mrs. Meir. However, based on our experience with the Israeli requests over the past months I believe some modifications to her stated schedule would be acceptable, and still be responsive to the President's directive." He attached Meir's delivery schedule and the Department of Defense's alternatives for Rogers to examine and argued that the alternative schedules would alleviate the "delivery and production problems" that the United States would encounter if it rigidly adhered to what Meir wanted. (Ibid., ISA Files: FRC 330–75–0155, Box 3, Israel) At a joint Department of State–Department of Defense meeting on January 4, Sisco approved "in principle" proposing the alternative schedules to Rabin, pending Rogers's approval. (Ibid.)

273. Letter From President Nixon to King Hussein of Jordan[1]

Washington, January 12, 1972.

Your Majesty:

I am always pleased to hear from such a close and valued friend and have read your letter[2] with great concern.

Your letter emphasizes Jordan's urgent need for financial support, while at the same time acknowledging our current legislative difficulties.[3] As a result of these difficulties, we have had to delay action with regard to further financial assistance to several of our friends including Jordan. While our means for responding to world-wide needs

[1] Source: National Archives, Nixon Presidential Materials, NSC Files, Box 797, Presidential Correspondence 1969–1974, Jordan—King Hussein. No classification marking. The letter was transmitted to the Embassy in Amman in telegram 6707, January 13. (Ibid., Box 617, Country Files, Middle East, Jordan, Vol. VIII)

[2] Hussein's letter was transmitted in telegram 5561 from Amman, December 10, 1971. (Ibid., RG 59, Central Files 1970–73, POL 15–1 JORDAN)

[3] Before adjourning for the year on December 17, 1971, Congress passed a stopgap resolution to extend until February 22, 1972, the nation's foreign aid program, the size of which had become the subject of controversy and debate. At the time of this exchange of letters between Nixon and Hussein, Congress was expected to approve an appropriations bill that included $1.2 billion less than the administration had requested. (*New York Times*, December 18, 1971, p 1)

continue to be extremely limited, I am pleased to inform you that we can provide you immediately with an additional $15 million. Regarding the level of possible assistance during 1972,[4] you can be sure that the United States is aware of the urgency of this matter and that we will communicate with your officials about it shortly.

I continue to follow developments in Jordan closely and as you know attach great importance to our close and friendly relationship.

With warmest personal regards,
Sincerely,

Richard Nixon

[4] Saunders informed Kissinger in a January 24 memorandum that, because of public reports that Jordan had transferred F–104 aircraft to Pakistan during the most recent war with India, it had become "immediately ineligible" for further aid under the Foreign Assistance Act. For Jordan to receive the aid that the Nixon administration had intended, the President would have to sign a waiver that allowed Jordan's use of the act's funds as justified by its importance to the security of the United States. (National Archives, Nixon Presidential Materials, NSC Files, Box 617, Country Files, Middle East, Jordan, Vol. VIII)

274. Telegram From the Mission to the United Nations to the Department of State[1]

New York, January 12, 1972, 0004Z.

102. Subj: Bush-Jarring Meeting January 11. Ref: State 3029.[2]

1. Bush called on Jarring AM Jan 11 to ascertain latter's current thinking. Jarring was suffering from one of his gloomy phases.

[1] Source: National Archives, Nixon Presidential Materials, NSC Files, Box 1166, Saunders Files, Middle East Negotiations Files, Middle East—Jarring Talks, January 1–15, 1972. Confidential; Exdis. Repeated to Amman, Beirut, Tel Aviv, Paris, London, Moscow, Jerusalem, and Cairo.

[2] Telegram 3029 to Amman and Moscow, January 5, conveyed the Department's disappointment that Jordan's Foreign Minister was willing to delay the UN Security Council's meeting on Jerusalem for only a week: "We understand Jordanian concern at continuing to be 'left alone' in context Arab-Israeli negotiations and its need at this point to demonstrate its involvement in political settlement efforts. At the same time, we do not want to get into position of appearing to be taking the lead in stimulating Jarring efforts with Jordanians and Israelis, since this could complicate our own efforts, particularly with Israelis, on interim agreement." (Ibid., RG 59, Central Files 1970–73, POL 27–14 ARAB–ISR)

2. Jarring first denied AFP[3] reports from Moscow that he had been holding round of talks there prior to his departure. He had routinely received new Egyptian Ambassador and had seen Kuznetsov but this did not reflect any initiative on his part.

3. Jarring then expressed unhappiness over Israeli campaign to blame him for Feb 8, 1971, memorandum.[4] Ideas in that memo were fully consistent with US positions yet Israel had been at pains to give impression that US no longer supports him. Jarring also indicated he disturbed over US abstention on GA Res 2799(XXVI).[5] Bush assured him that there no question but that US continues to support his mission.[6] We abstained because we were concerned not to worsen the existing impasse.

4. Jarring also indicated that he concerned because Four Powers no longer meeting.[7] This contributed to impression his mission no longer actively supported by Four. Bush said main problem with Four Power meeting was to know what could constructively be done.

5. There had not yet been opportunity for Jarring to talk to new SYG[8] who, he noted, had stated on TV that he had some ideas on ME which he wished to discuss with his Special Rep. Jarring said he would call in Tekoah and el Zayyat in near future but unless Israel was willing to make some kind of statement that would break the impasse, he was pessimistic. In response to question, Jarring said this did not necessarily have to be a positive reply to his Feb 1971 memo. The FonMin of Senegal during GA had shown the way. It could be a statement that Israel does not desire to annex Arab territory but that it desires secure and recognized boundaries. On other hand, if Israel merely repeats that it will withdraw to secure and recognized boundaries to be determined

---

[3] Agence France-Presse.

[4] See Document 211.

[5] See footnote 4, Document 270.

[6] Two weeks later, Sisco briefed Jarring in detail on the "state-of-play" of U.S. efforts to achieve an interim settlement between Egypt and Israel. (Telegram 15308 to USUN, January 27; National Archives, Nixon Presidential Materials, NSC Files, Box 658, Country Files, Middle East, Middle East Nodis/Cedar/Plus, Vol. V)

[7] The Four Powers met twice in both June and July and once in both August and September in 1971. The meetings were marked almost entirely by Soviet accusations—and U.S. denials—that Israeli intransigence, with the support of the United States, was undermining efforts to achieve a settlement between Egypt and Israel. (Telegram 1495 from USUN, June 4; telegram 1700 from USUN, June 25; telegram 1893 from USUN, July 14; telegram 2023 from USUN, July 27; and telegram 2334 from USUN, August 20; all ibid., Boxes 1163–1164, Saunders Files, Middle East Negotiations Files, Middle East—Jarring Talks) The Four Powers had last met on September 9, 1971, a description of which is in telegram 2604 from USUN, September 10. (Ibid., Box 1165, Saunders Files, Middle East Negotiations Files, Middle East—Jarring Talks, September 1–October 1, 1972)

[8] Kurt Waldheim was appointed Secretary General for a term that began on January 1, 1972.

in course of negotiations this would make it impossible for Egyptians to resume discussions.

6. Jarring mentioned that Jordanian Amb had also seen him in Moscow and had made clear that GOJ wants an aide-mémoire similar to the one handed Egypt last Feb. He had taken non-committal attitude and had said he must be careful not to raise entire Palestine question. (He said nothing about needing green light from USG.) Jarring said he would also call in Toukan but latter would have to convince him that such a step would be useful.

7. Bush indicated that this decision was entirely one for Jarring and the parties to make. At same time, we shared his misgivings about another aide-mémoire.

8. In discussion of Toukan's imminent return to Amman, Bush said Toukan told us he would be replaced by Sharaf. Jarring (protect) said this would be ideal from his standpoint but that he was told in Moscow Toukan would be replaced by Munim Rifai.

9. Jarring said he planned to be available to parties in NY for indefinite future. He would have to return to Moscow Feb 8 for a couple of days during visit of his FonMin but otherwise he would be at UNHQ.

Bush

275. Telegram From the Department of State to the Interests Section in Egypt[1]

Washington, January 22, 1972, 0117Z.

12682. Subj: Mid East.

1. On Jan 20 Egyptian Interests Section Chief Dr. Ghorbal accompanied by Counselor Sharara[2] called on Assy Secy Sisco. Ghorbal noted he had just returned from Cairo where he had seen all appropriate officials up to and including President Sadat and noted that what he had to say was on instruction. Sisco offered to bring him up to date since their last conversation and noted that Jarring had announced Jan 20 his in-

---

[1] Source: National Archives, Nixon Presidential Materials, NSC Files, Box 658, Country Files, Middle East, Middle East Nodis/Cedar/Plus, Vol. V. Secret; Nodis; Cedar Plus. Drafted by Seton Shanley (NEA/EGY), cleared in NEA/EGY, and approved by Sisco. Repeated to Tel Aviv, Amman, Beirut, London, Paris, Moscow, and USUN. All brackets are in the original except "[May]", added for clarity.

[2] Yousef Sharara.

tention to go to Africa for consultations and will then see if talks under his auspices can be restarted. Sisco said we continue to support Jarring Mission and would welcome any progress Jarring can make. With reference to the US role in any talks on an interim agreement Sisco said we were unable to tell from Sadat's Jan 13 speech[3] if the door to an interim agreement was closed but have drawn no conclusions from the speech. He noted, however, that we might soon be raising prospect of interim talks with Egypt.

2. Sisco recalled that when US had proposed interim talks in October 1971 Egyptian response was positive whereas Israelis were neither positive nor negative. While considerable time has since elapsed we have intensively consulted with Israelis in the course of the last two weeks and hope soon to have their assent to entering talks in proximity. At that point the US will notify Egypt of this diplomatic opportunity and Egypt will face a decision. Sisco said we shared Egypt's disappointment in lack of progress to date.

3. Sisco noted US did not conceive of these talks in lieu of the Jarring talks but only as complementary to them and as a first step toward full implementation of SC Res 242. We continue to feel that an interim agreement is feasible, that the Israeli and Egyptian positions on an interim agreement are reconcilable and that our role has been and will continue to be a constructive one. We recognized Egypt's disappointment and fact there had been some loss of confidence in US; Egypt would have to decide itself whether we can play useful role. Situation is admittedly currently more complicated than it was in Oct. But Arab-Israel negotiations are a "history of lost opportunities."

4. Sisco called Ghorbal's attention to recent public statements in Israel suggesting more forthcoming attitude toward interim talks. He emphasized DefMin Dayan's call for need to "compromise" and noted PM Meir's more flexible recent statements. Sisco said Israel continues to be interested in an interim agreement. He said while the Arab world assumption has been that an election year circumscribes US diplomatic efforts this in fact not the case. President Nixon had declared this an era of negotiations and the achievement of a peace settlement, even limited partial one, in the Middle East would be popular domestically. Thus no incorrect analyses of US position should be made.

---

[3] In the speech, Sadat criticized the United States for, according to reports, its decision to sell Phantoms to Israel as well as for enabling Israeli territorial ambitions in the Middle East. Furthermore, he warned the Nixon administration that its support for Israel jeopardized U.S. oil interests in the Arab world. (*New York Times*, January 14, 1972, p. 1) Marshall Wiley reported from Cairo, however: "Sadat speech on Jan 13 leaves door open for further USG effort to arrange proximity talks. Sadat emphasized his willingness to seek negotiated settlement and did not rule out possibility of future US role in spite of his attacks on US policy and on Secretary." (National Archives, Nixon Presidential Materials, NSC Files, Box 658, Country Files, Middle East, Middle East Nodis/Cedar/Plus, Vol. V)

5. Ghorbal thanked Sisco for completing the picture. He asked Sisco if he could be told anything specific on the details of recent US discussions with Israel on an interim agreement. Sisco said that the details are not yet buttoned down and that he would defer any discussion of them until such time as he could be more precise. He said that both Egypt and Israel have been anxious to know where US stands but that if the US role is to be constructive the US cannot take a stand on the issues before the parties enter into negotiations. Sisco assured Ghorbal that US will be active when the time comes. Sisco emphasized neither side can attain its desired preconditions before negotiations begin and said he wished Cairo to reflect on this fact. We found it difficult to see an alternative to talks on an interim agreement at this time.

6. Ghorbal said that he was distressed to hear Sisco use phrase "no prior conditions" in context negotiations as this was an Israeli thesis. Egypt felt it had to know what end of the road was, and as far as Cairo was concerned this was overall peace settlement in accordance with SC Res 242. Ghorbal said it was important for Sisco to understand present mood in Cairo. Cairo feels 1971 was a wasted year. The US itself had made 1971 a year of decision and Secretary Rogers' trip to Cairo last June [*May*] was an earnest of US endeavor to achieve peace in the Middle East. But warmth engendered by the Secretary's trip has not totally evaporated. Egypt had said yes to everything US asked of it. What more does Washington want, Egyptians are asking? Sadat had shown great patience and only latterly had explained his and Egypt's grievances against the US in public fora. However Cairo feels that the opportunities lost in 1971 were lost mostly through fault of US.

7. Ghorbal said that US praise for various Egyptian positions taken in course of last year made only more bitter the fact that US was renewing supply of Phantoms and Skyhawks to Israel and now had signed arms licensing agreement with Israel. He said that a significant portion of Egyptian society regarded these as "bellicose actions" against Egypt and emphasized this feeling was held from rank and file to policy levels. He called the Nov Arms Technology Agreement[4] reminiscent of US court decision two years ago permitting US citizens to fight in foreign armies without losing their US citizenship[5] and said this

---

[4] The memorandum of understanding by which the United States agreed to provide technical and manufacturing assistance to Israel's arms industry. It established "streamlined procedures" for American consideration of Israeli arms requests without specifying which weapons the program would include. Its signing in November was not announced at the time. (*New York Times*, January 14, 1972, p. 1)

[5] Reference is probably to the Supreme Court decision, reached on May 29, 1967, that prevented Congress from passing laws that stripped U.S. citizens of their nationality without their consent. The decision was based on the specific case of a U.S. national who had voted in an Israeli election and had had his citizenship revoked in 1960, but it dealt broadly with Congress's efforts to regulate the participation of U.S. nationals in the for-

allowed US citizen Jews to fight side-by-side with the Israelis against Egypt. Why, Ghorbal asked, does US allow Israel to drag the US into new commitments of far-reaching consequence? Not only is the US building Israel's own arsenal, he said, but the recent agreement will allow Israel to export these arms and encourage situations such as those which earlier occurred in the Sudan and in Biafra.

8. Ghorbal said the USG had told Egypt that it had only limited leverage with Israel but now Egypt wonders why US has surrendered even this limited leverage. He noted US interests in the Middle East were immense and cautioned that US policy decisions on the Mideast should be based upon full appreciation of the situation as it exists which was why he was going to such length on this occasion.

9. Continuing Ghorbal said Cairo feels she has been fed nothing but generalities and semantics in the last year and while she has received the praise of the US, Israel got arms and assistance. Cairo no longer is prepared to believe that problem is one of finding right formulae for peace settlement but rather fundamental change not only in Israeli policy, but even more in US policy. While US words mollify Egypt, US in practice is giving Israel guns and butter. Record in last four years shows that when supplied with more armaments Israel does not become readier to negotiate. Thus US argument that it is giving weapons to Israel in order to induce Israel to enter negotiations does not impress Cairo.

10. Ghorbal adverted to announcement in Jan 20 press that Israel intended to establish an Israeli city in the Gaza Strip and said this was but one further example of lack of Israeli intent to withdraw. When President Nixon came to power Cairo's assessment had been that the US wanted better relations with Egypt. At that time he noted Egyptian spokesmen were instructed to emphasize that the Phantoms then being delivered to Israel had been contracted for during the Johnson administration. This is no longer the case. US aid level to Israel in 1971 was $600 million—a new high—and that $80 million was the comparable figure for the Johnson administration.

11. Ghorbal emphasized that picture he had drawn was by instruction brought to Asst Secy Sisco's attention and said that what must now be sought is peace in the Middle East based on security for all. When the US approached Egypt, Egypt would bear this in mind. However the US should bear in mind that in any approach to Egypt on an interim agreement generalities will not suffice nor will ambiguous phrase-

---

eign affairs of other countries. In the case of Israel, the issue once again emerged in October 1969 when the U.S. Embassy in Israel confirmed, in response to questions, that the service of U.S citizens in the Israeli armed forces would not lead to the loss of their nationality. (*New York Times,* October 21, 1969, p. 15)

ology. Either of these will make Cairo think the time is once again being frittered away in preservation of a ceasefire which in Cairo's view is of limited utility. Cairo's feeling is that the ceasefire is all the United States cares about.

12. Sisco replied that US feels ceasefire is in the interests of both Israel and Egypt and that were the ceasefire presently in existence our sole desideratum we would not now be as active diplomatically as we are. He told Dr. Ghorbal that he appreciated and understood his exposition of Cairo's views and emphasized US remains available and willing to play a constructive role should both parties so desire. He said that US would not press Egypt to enter into interim negotiations but when and if time came simply inform Egypt straightforwardly, and frankly that the opportunity existed. Cairo would have to make up its own mind.

Rogers

276. Telegram From the Department of State to the Interests Section in Egypt[1]

Washington, February 12, 1972, 1947Z.

25304. For Greene from Secretary.

1. Message below from Secretary to Sadat informs him of Israeli willingness to enter proximity talks and asks Sadat whether Egypt is itself prepared to enter such talks. We have been considering timing and manner of this presentation, and have reviewed question again in light Cairo 445.[2] On question timing, one possibility would be to wait until Ghaleb-Ismail report is completed and we can see what Sadat says to ASU.[3] We have already seen several indications, however, that Egyp-

---

[1] Source: National Archives, Nixon Presidential Materials, NSC Files, Box 1166, Saunders Files, Middle East Negotiations Files, Middle East—Jarring Talks, February 1–16, 1972. Secret; Immediate; Nodis; Cedar Double Plus. Drafted by Atherton and Sterner, cleared by Sisco, and approved by Rogers and Kissinger. Repeated to Tel Aviv.

[2] In telegram 445 from Cairo, February 11, Greene recommended that he delay his presentation to Ghaleb until February 14 or 15, when he could do so alone—as opposed to doing so with the Spanish Ambassador present, given the local diplomatic protocols associated with Greene's having just assumed his post. (Ibid., Box 658, Country Files, Middle East, Middle East Nodis/Cedar/Plus, Vol. V)

[3] Sadat addressed the Arab Socialist Union on February 16, vowing to resign as President if Egyptians lost confidence in him during the country's "long political and military struggle" to retake territory lost during the 1967 war with Israel. He also remarked

tians are expecting message from US, and we believe it important that Sadat be aware of and in position to weigh option we are offering before he goes public. We also think this is one occasion when there may be positive advantage in not rpt not conveying message to Sadat personally, but rather do so through either Ghaleb or Ismail. Our reasoning here is that we would rather avoid precipitate Presidential reaction in this case and let him give us considered response through one of his subordinates (we would of course make it clear we were available if Sadat wished to talk about message).

2. We agree with Wiley that it may be desirable to begin to do our business with FonMin Ghaleb. On other hand, we have, at Sadat's specific request, been conveying our messages to President through Ismail and we would not want sudden switch of procedure on our part to be misinterpreted by Egyptians. Since you are to pay courtesy call on Ghaleb Monday, one way to handle this would be for you to inform Ghaleb that you have oral message from Secretary to President Sadat and would appreciate being informed whether Sadat preferred that message be conveyed through Ghaleb or Ismail. You would, of course, need to ask for private moment with him in view of fact Spanish Ambassador accompanying you, and we do not want to reveal fact of this approach to anyone at this time.

3. Seems to us foregoing procedure offers opportunity to put matter to Ghaleb at earliest moment without attracting undue attention, but we realize presence of Spanish Ambassador could present complications and leave it to you to decide how best to let Ghaleb know you have message for Sadat and get his advice as to channel through which to convey it. Secretary also wishes you at time you see Ghaleb to convey his appreciation to FonMin Ghaleb for his recent message (Cairo 421)[4] that Quote all endeavors Unquote toward establishing a just and lasting peace in the Middle East will be appreciated and welcomed by Egypt.

4. You should convey verbatim following oral message from Secretary to President Sadat (do not leave anything on paper with Egyptians).

5. *Begin message.* As a result of our discussion with the Israelis during past weeks,[5] we now have Israel's agreement to enter talks in close proximity in a renewed effort to reach agreement on an interim arrangement for partial withdrawal of Israeli forces in Sinai and re-

---

that the United States's further commitment to Israel in the form of Phantom and Skyhawk fighter jets had prevented him from taking early military action to recover that territory. (*New York Times*, February 17, 1972, p. 4)

[4] Not found.

[5] For a summary, see Document 277.

opening of the Suez Canal. I am persuaded the Israelis are now ready to negotiate actively and without preconditions to see whether an interim agreement is possible.

6. When we first broached the idea of talks in proximity with you last October,[6] you said you found the proposal appealing. I know, Mr. President, how disappointed you are that the past year has not yielded greater results in terms of the progress we all hoped for toward a peace settlement. I share this sense of disappointment personally, but we are now offered a fresh opportunity, and past disappointments should not keep us from testing it. The experience of the past year leaves me convinced that the positions of the two sides on an interim agreement leave room for reconciliation and that an agreement is not out of the question.

7. Mr. President, the purpose of this oral message is not repeat not to press you on this matter. We have no interest other than to help facilitate an agreement between Egypt and Israel that meets the concerns of both sides. I realize the situation is more complicated today than last October, but I believe that a diplomatic option nevertheless is available. We are prepared to seek to get talks underway, with Mr. Sisco as go-between, at a time and place agreeable to you. If you would care to we would be pleased to have your views on the matter and particularly any thoughts you might have on the time, place and level of negotiations which we are prepared to discuss with Israel. I am personally satisfied that it is desirable to pursue this effort, but I would understand if you feel you want to take some time to reflect on these questions or to delay any response until a later time.

8. I am aware, Mr. President, of your concern that any interim agreement must not be considered an end in itself but rather the first step toward a final peace settlement in accordance with Security Council Resolution 242. This has also been our conception from the very beginning. You have also indicated in your statements recently that Egypt looks to Ambassador Jarring as the principal focal point for further peace settlement efforts. If Ambassador Jarring can find some way to move ahead constructively with the parties on an overall peace agreement, the US would welcome it. Such talks, as well as any the US may conduct relating to an interim agreement, could be mutually reinforcing.

9. If you believe it would be helpful, nothing need be said for time being that this question of proximity talks has been broached to your government, so that you may have ample opportunity to consider the matter without feeling under any particular time deadline. We can un-

---

[6] See footnote 5, Document 255.

derstand if you should want to discuss further the question of proximity talks with us out of the public spotlight before reaching a decision and would be glad to consider any other channel or means you might suggest.

10. Finally, Mr. President, I do not want the occasion to pass without expressing to you my warm personal regards. I look back with pleasure and appreciation upon the cordiality with which I was received by you personally and your advisors last May. I know the situation now is more difficult. Nevertheless, it is my hope that we can resume our discussions on that foundation of good will and respect and in the same spirit that prevailed at that time. *End message.*[7]

11. We recognize that Ghaleb or Ismail may well respond to foregoing by raising recent reports of US decisions on aircraft supply and defense production arrangements for Israel and may ask how Egypt can be expected any longer to deal through USG when it is Quote arming its enemy Unquote. If reply raises question of US military supply to Israel, we should in most dignified and low-key manner possible decline to enter into discussion of this question. If circumstances are such that you feel it necessary to respond, you should limit yourself to following comments:

A. Question of US military supply to Israel is aspect of US-Israeli bilateral relations, just as Soviet supply to Egypt is aspect of Soviet-Egyptian bilateral relations, and experience has shown that there is no useful purpose served by USG and Egypt getting into discussion or argument about this question with each other.

B. Middle East arms supply relationships are facts of life with dimensions which go beyond Arab-Israel problem. We are sure President Sadat is aware that heavy Soviet involvement in the area complicates matters for us.

C. In our view, efforts to improve US-Egyptian relations and to explore possibilities for interim agreement and overall peaceful settlement are worth pursuing on their own merits.

12. In view number of reports that Egyptians feel our talks with GOI have restricted US role as go-between, you should make it clear to Ghaleb or Ismail that we will be in a position to play a constructive role if Egypt decides to enter into proximity talks. Delay in obtaining Israeli agreement to talks during our intensive discussions with them was in fact largely result of our insistence on retaining such flexibility. We would intend obviously to consult with both sides but are not repeat not barred from putting forth suggestions on ways of reconciling dif-

---

[7] Greene conveyed the Secretary's message on February 23; see footnote 3, Document 278.

ferences if this should prove desirable.[8] At same time, hope you can get across that principal purpose of exercise should be to get a real negotiation (indirect) going between Egypt and Israel, not Egypt and US Government.

Irwin

---

[8] Saunders wrote a comment on this sentence: "*Yes but*—(1) Israelis have it in writing from us that we will discuss *any* 'suggestion' with them first. (2) Israelis have made it abundantly clear and in writing that if they do not *first* agree with anything we want to say to Egyptians it will be a non-starter. In short, while we are not telling the Egyptians a lie nor are we telling them the whole truth. Sisco may think he can outrun the implications *but* my bet is they will catch up with him sooner rather than later."

---

277. Memorandum From the President's Assistant for National Security Affairs (Kissinger) to President Nixon[1]

Washington, February 17, 1972.

SUBJECT

Negotiations with Israel—Aircraft, Talks in Proximity

Secretary Rogers has sent you the attached concluding report on Assistant Secretary Sisco's talks with Ambassador Rabin[2] on the provision of aircraft (delivery schedules at Tab A) and on the talks in proximity (Sisco-Rabin summary at Tab B).[3] Mrs. Meir, with Cabinet approval, has agreed to enter such talks. The following are the essential points of the Secretary's memorandum and attachments.

Aircraft

The Secretary reports that agreement has been reached with Israel on delivery schedules for 42 Phantom and 82 Skyhawk aircraft and that

---

[1] Source: National Archives, Nixon Presidential Materials, NSC Files, Box 658, Country Files, Middle East, Middle East Nodis/Cedar/Plus, Vol. V. Secret; Nodis; Cedar Plus. Sent for information; outside system. A stamped notation on the memorandum indicates the President saw it. All brackets are in the original.

[2] Dated February 2; attached but not printed. Rogers's January 14, 24, and 27 reports to the President are ibid., RG 59, Central Files 1970–73, DEF 12–5 ISR. The memorandum of conversation of the first Sisco-Rabin meeting is Document 271. The memoranda of conversation of their January 10 and 11 meetings are in the National Archives, RG 59, Central Files 1970–73, DEF 12–5 ISR and POL 27–14 ARAB–ISR, respectively.

[3] Tabs A and B are attached but not printed.

an Israeli team is currently discussing the details with Defense preparatory to concluding final contracts.

The final delivery schedule for the Phantoms (Tab A) has been brought into phase with Mrs. Meir's desires of two per month starting this month. [20 are scheduled for 1972 and 22 for 1973.]

Agreement has also been reached on the provision of 82 A–4 Skyhawks. The Secretary notes, however, there may be some mutually agreed upon adjustments of their delivery schedule in the course of the present technical discussions. The Israelis are interested in the option of taking fewer of the older A–4E model this year in order to receive more of the new A–4N model from the production line in early 1974.

Talks in Proximity

On November 1 Mrs. Meir requested certain clarifications pending Israeli agreement to enter talks in "proximity" on an interim canal settlement.[4] In the course of Sisco-Rabin discussions, the Secretary says that our clarifications have been provided in a manner which provides us with sufficient scope to play a "constructive role" in the event the talks get started. The Secretary informs you of his intention to "avoid false deadlines, proceed at a deliberate pace, avoid confrontations with the Israelis on various issues, avoid putting forth American blueprints to resolve the problem." The following summarizes the Israeli requests and the US "clarifications":

—*Aircraft:* As noted above, requests met in full as to types, numbers and delivery schedules.

—*Six Points of Secretary Rogers' UNGA Speech:*[5] These represent areas of difference between the parties. The US has "made no proposals of our own and we have not adopted any substantive position" on any of the six points. We have "no blueprint." Both sides "will have to make adjustments" in their positions to achieve an interim settlement. A particularly difficult problem is "the nature of any Egyptian presence on the East of the Canal." While the US hopes this might prove reconcilable, the US has taken "no substantive position," nor should our hope for agreement on this point be interpreted that we have made a judgment or expressed a substantive view on how it should be resolved.

—*Position of the US on (a) whether it agrees that negotiations for an interim settlement are basically different from those for an overall settlement, and (b) what role it would play in these negotiations:*

(a) The US believes there should be no preconditions laid down for talks in proximity. The principle of no imposed settlement applies both

---

[4] See Document 263.
[5] See footnote 3, Document 255.

to an interim and overall settlement. While we have expressed hope that Israel could find it possible to reply to Jarring's memorandum of February 1971[6] in a way permitting him to relaunch his mission, we agree Israel should not be expected to change its position—as Sadat insists—in order to begin talks in proximity. We will support this view with the Egyptian Government.

(b) The US will use its "good offices" to help the parties develop areas of common ground. In performing this role with Egypt, we will "consult fully with Israel on a step-by-step basis with respect to any ideas we may explore with the Egyptians and will make clear to the latter they are not proposals, are not binding on Israel and are strictly ad referendum." The US "will not forward to Egypt, nor will it support any suggestions or proposals" without making every effort to seek and to achieve full prior understanding" with Israel. Furthermore, the US will not forward to Egypt any proposal on behalf of Israel without prior agreement. (The Israelis have gone on to unilaterally say that prior Israeli agreement on US "suggestion" to Egypt "is essential both in principle and in order to avoid possible complications" for which Israel not be "responsible.")

The US "takes note" that Israel's position objecting to language which would create linkage between the interim agreement and the Egyptian demand for total withdrawal remains unchanged. The US will not make any suggestion to Egypt with regard to "the relation between the interim agreement and the overall agreement" without prior agreement with Israel.

The Secretary envisages approaching the Egyptians after Sadat's trip to Moscow and promises to clear the instructions here.[7]

---

[6] See footnote 2, Document 205.

[7] For the Secretary's message to Sadat, see Document 276. See also footnote 3, Document 278. Sadat visited Moscow February 2–4.

278. Telegram From the Department of State to the Interests Section in Egypt[1]

Washington, February 18, 1972, 0012Z.

28420. 1. There are a number of indications that Egyptians, in reacting to Secretary's message to Sadat,[2] may take position that interim agreement talks should be conducted under Jarring's auspices rather than through USG go-between. On basis of our discussions with Israelis, we are convinced that this would be an absolute non-starter so far as they are concerned. For tactical purposes, however, if Egyptians make this suggestion to you, you should limit yourself to commenting as follows:

A. It is your strong impression that Israel's decisions to explore idea of interim agreement and to enter proximity talks for this purpose were based on understanding that this effort would be conducted through USG representative. FonMin Eban made statement along these lines recently. USG has been operating on assumption that this is also Egyptian approach; change in that approach would create new situation and, in your judgment, could add new complications not likely to be overcome in foreseeable future.

B. You should add that this is your off-cuff visceral reaction and that you have no instructions on this point. You will report Egyptian view to Washington.[3]

Irwin

---

[1] Source: National Archives, Nixon Presidential Materials, NSC Files, Box 658, Country Files. Middle East, Middle East Nodis/Cedar/Plus, Vol. V. Secret; Nodis; Cedar Double Plus. Drafted by Atherton and approved by Sisco. Repeated to Tel Aviv.

[2] See Document 276.

[3] Greene reported Ghaleb's reaction to the Secretary's oral message to Sadat in telegram 552 from Cairo, February 23. Sadat had instructed the Egyptian Foreign Minister to receive Rogers's message on his behalf and told him to emphasize the importance to the Egyptian Government of keeping secret the content of the message and the fact that it had even been delivered. Ghaleb said that his own first impression was that "it was a good and careful message, both in style and psychology." (National Archives, Nixon Presidential Materials, NSC Files, Box 658, Country Files, Middle East, Middle East Nodis/Cedar/Plus, Vol. V) In his analysis of the meeting sent in a separate telegram, Greene's "major comment" was that if there was "any leak at all" regarding Rogers's message, Sadat might well have taken "occasion to walk away" from the current round of discussions. He added: "Ghaleb was equally obviously sensitive about anything reaching the Israelis." (Telegram 554 from Cairo, February 23; ibid.)

279. Telegram From the Mission to the United Nations to the Department of State[1]

New York, February 28, 1972, 0755Z.

710. Lebanon/Israel in SC. PM Feb 27, Amb Bush made following statement in SC:

Quote

The USG views with deep concern the recurrence of incidents along the Lebanese border and the continuing incursions within Lebanon by Israeli defense forces.

Yesterday, we had understood that the military action had ended. We are distressed and very concerned to find that there have been new incidents along the frontier and even more extensive measures by Israel.

We must, Mr. President, express deep regret and concern that Israel has prolonged and intensified its attacks on the territory of Lebanon. We cannot condone such actions. As we have repeatedly made clear, the US fully supports the territorial integrity and political independence of Lebanon. We therefore believe the SC should call upon the Govt of Israel to withdraw its forces immediately from Lebanese territory.[2]

The US deeply regrets the loss of life that has occurred on both sides. We also sympathize fully with Israel's distress at the loss of life at the hands of guerrilla infiltrators which apparently precipitated this latest round. The continuation of such acts of terrorism is not in the interest of any of the people of the area because it can only delay the achievement of a just and lasting peace that all of us here support—in the Security Council and in the United Nations.

At the same time, we know that the Govt of Lebanon has made strenuous efforts over past months to maintain quiet along the border. We recognize the difficulty of sealing the border completely, but unless more effective measures can be taken to do so, a situation is perpetuated in which Israel is exposed to terrorist attacks and feels compelled in self-defense to retaliate.

---

[1] Source: National Archives, Nixon Presidential Materials, NSC Files, Box 1167, Saunders Files, Middle East Negotiations Files, Middle East—Jarring Talks, February 16–March 1, 1972. Unclassified; Immediate. Repeated to Amman and Immediate to Beirut and Tel Aviv.

[2] Israeli shelling and air and ground attacks on Palestinian commando positions in southern Lebanon began on February 25 after guerrillas fired on Israeli positions in the Mt. Hermon area. The Israeli forces withdrew on February 28.

However, the US believes the way to solve the problem lies not in hortatory declarations nor in further recourse to armed force. It lies, rather, through direct liaison and cooperation between the parties to provide the most reliable assurance possible regarding the security of each. It is the parties who must redouble their efforts to avoid a repetition of the cycle of attacks and counter-attacks.

The US, therefore, urges that both Israel and Lebanon have more frequent recourse to the international facilities that exist for the exchange of information and consultation on border matters. Above all, we ask for an end to cross-border attacks and terrorism, without which the cycle of action and reaction cannot be broken.

These events serve to underline the urgency of moving ahead on negotiations for a peaceful settlement for until peace is achieved, failure to satisfy the fundamental and legitimate concerns of all the peoples of the area will perpetuate tensions.

As to the resolution before us, in our statement we have expressed our concern over the loss of life on both sides. Others here have addressed themselves to the events which led to the situation as it stands today. As I look at the resolution, it is brief and to the point, but it would better reflect the genuine concern that we feel for the loss of life—the loss of innocent civilian life—if the resolution were amended to include the words "on both sides" after the word "lives." The preambular sentence would then read: "Deploring all actions which have resulted in the loss of innocent lives on both sides." It can be stated that as written the sentence implies that we deplore actions on both sides, but it would be clearer indeed if the Council would accept this one amendment. This amendment is in keeping with the views expressed here by several countries. I strongly hope the Council will accept our amendment. As the co-sponsors stated, the present text is not entirely satisfactory to all members of the Council. For our part, we strongly believe that the thought implicit in the preamb para should be made explicit. I am most sympathetic with the plea by our colleague from Italy but the addition of these three words seems to us to express more fairly the humanitarian concern we all feel. My govt feels so strongly on this point that I feel I must submit this amendment to the text before us. End quote.

2. Following the defeat of the preambular paragraph (8(US)–4–3),[3] Amb Bush made following statement:

Quote: We find it incomprehensible that people around this table could have failed to support the inclusion of the statement which read "deploring all actions which have resulted in the loss of innocent lives."

---

[3] The preambular paragraph was defeated in a separate vote.

How this Council could object to such fair, humane language leaves us completely baffled. Yes, we voted for the resolution without the preambular paragraph for as we said in our statement, "The SC should call upon the Govt of Israel to withdraw its forces immediately from Lebanese territory." That we have done, but it is our strongly held view that the Council even at this stage knows enough and should have cared enough to deplore among other things the actions which resulted in the loss of innocent lives. Let me be clear, our vote on the final passage of this resolution was in no way a condonation of events that led up to Israel's actions. End quote.[4]

Bush

---

[4] Security Council Resolution 313, unanimously adopted early in the morning of February 28, reads: "The Security Council demands that Israel immediately desist and refrain from any ground and air military action against Lebanon and forthwith withdraw all its military forces from Lebanese territory." For a summary of the Security Council debate, see *Yearbook of the United Nations, 1972*, pp. 158–160. The text of Resolution 313 is ibid., p. 172.

280. Editorial Note

On March 15, 1972, King Hussein of Jordan announced to a gathering of 40 to 50 members of the foreign press and "scores of Jordanian personalities" that Jordan would adopt a new federation plan once it achieved peace with Israel and the West Bank was returned to Jordanian sovereignty. Under the plan, Jordan—which would be renamed the United Arab Kingdom—would consist of two provinces: a Palestinian one on the West Bank of the Jordan River and a Jordanian one on the East Bank. Amman would serve as both the federal capital and the capital of the Jordanian province, and Jerusalem would serve as the capital of the Palestinian province. (Telegram 1112 from Amman, March 15; National Archives, Nixon Presidential Materials, NSC Files, Box 1167, Saunders Files, Middle East Negotiations Files, Middle East—Jarring Talks, March 1–31, 1972) According to the Department of State, public reaction to the plan in the Arab world was "largely hostile," with skeptics viewing it as "a plot concocted by the US, Israel, and King Hussein to undermine Palestinian interests and achieve a Jordanian-Israeli peace on unacceptable terms." (Memorandum from Eliot to Kissinger, March 22; ibid., Box 617, Country Files, Middle East, Jordan, Vol. VIII)

Hussein had sent a letter to Nixon two days earlier to inform him of the announcement as well as of the details of the proposal. He wrote: "We believe the time has come, Mr. President, for us to enter into a new state which will be a further contribution to the cause of peace in our area, bearing in mind that an essential part of any settlement in our area is recognition of the identity of the Palestinian people who have existed for hundreds of years before 1948 and continue to exist." He later added, "It is hoped that the new plan will also enable the Palestinians, through their responsible representative elements, to redress the wrongs done to them." (Telegram 1069 from Amman, March 13; ibid., Box 1167, Saunders Files, Middle East Negotiations Files, Middle East—Jarring Talks, March 1–31, 1972) The King sent similar messages to British, French, and Soviet leaders, Arab Ambassadors, and Arab leaders not represented in Amman. (Telegram 1072 from Amman, March 13; ibid.)

The letter to Nixon merely established officially what the King had already conveyed privately to the United States through secret channels one month earlier, as discussed in a February 17 CIA intelligence memorandum. (Central Intelligence Agency, OCI Files, Job 79B1737A) On April 6, Egypt broke diplomatic relations with Jordan because, as Sadat explained, Egypt would "not allow anyone to liquidate the rights of the Palestinian people." (*New York Times*, April 7, 1972, page 1)

281. Memorandum of Conversation[1]

Washington, March 17, 1972, 1 pm

PARTICIPANTS

The President (at beginning)
Soviet Ambassador Anatoliy F. Dobrynin
Dr. Henry A. Kissinger

---

[1] Source: National Archives, Nixon Presidential Materials, NSC Files, Box 493, President's Trip Files, Dobrynin/Kissinger, 1972, Vol. 10. Top Secret; Sensitive; Exclusively Eyes Only. A stamped notation on the memorandum indicates the President saw it. All brackets are in the original except those indicating text omitted by the editors and "[Dobrynin]", added for clarity. The meeting took place in the White House Map Room. The President left the meeting before the discussion of the Middle East. For the full text of the memorandum of conversation, see *Foreign Relations*, 1969–1976, volume XIV, Soviet Union, October 1971–May 1972, Document 62.

[Omitted here is discussion unrelated to the Middle East.]

The Middle East

He [Dobrynin] then asked, "What about the major items? Let's talk about the Middle East. You told me you would have some proposition to make." I said that the first question that I wanted to raise was: could they give me some expression of how they propose to inform the Egyptians if some agreement were reached between the President and Brezhnev?[2] It seemed to me extremely dangerous to inform the Egyptians at all since they were bound to be penetrated by the Israelis. For us it was a matter of the gravest importance. Dobrynin grew somewhat restless. He said delivering the Egyptians was their problem and they could not be accountable on that. I said that was not the issue; the issue was whether the process of notification would create substantive difficulties that would affect our situation and the possibility of carrying through with any understanding that might be reached. For example, I said, the interim agreement we were discussing was worse than what Bergus had offered them in the bilateral discussions.[3] If they were going to be asked by the Soviets to accept a worse interim agreement, there had to be some argument that would make this plausible. Dobrynin again said that I seem to be producing one red herring after another to avoid facing concrete issues. I said this was not the case, and I insisted that they produce some expression from Moscow of how they would deal with the implementation of any agreement.

Turning to the substance of the settlement, Dobrynin asked whether I had formulated any ideas. I told him that it seemed to me that the irreducible Israeli position was for the airfield just east of Eilat, control over Sharm el Sheikh, and a land connection with Sharm el Sheikh. This perhaps could be wrapped up in some riparian arrangement of the states along the Gulf of Aqaba, which perhaps might pro-

---

[2] Kissinger and Dobrynin were considering items for discussion at the upcoming Nixon-Brezhnev summit and the possible agreements that might be reached. On January 17, Brezhnev wrote Nixon a letter regarding U.S.-Soviet relations in which he addressed the Middle East: "The situation in the Middle East, Mr. President, causes serious concern. The tension there is not diminishing. Rather, to the contrary. Many elements in Israel's behaviour cause apprehension. But it should be clear that attempts to carry out its known designs toward the Arab territories would lead to far-reaching consequences. In conversation with you in Washington our Minister for Foreign Affairs set forth in detail considerations concerning the questions of Middle East settlement. We are prepared, as before, to work in real earnest to find concrete solutions on the basis of the principles set forth in that conversation, and to bring what has been started to successful conclusion. And here it is desirable to act without delay." (Ibid., Document 39) For Gromyko's proposals, see Documents 251 and 252.

[3] See Documents 255, 258, and 263.

vide a fig leaf for Israeli presence in Sharm el Sheikh. (Attached at Tab B[4] is a memorandum explaining this.)

Dobrynin asked my view of demilitarization. I said in my view demilitarization would have to take place at least to the western edge of the passes. Dobrynin said that in effect I was giving him the Israeli position. I said that if he talked to the Israeli Ambassador, he would not get that idea; this would be next to impossible to sell to the Israelis. What I was trying to do was to get a position which the Israelis might accept with some considerable pressure but short of actions that would lead them to conclude that they were better off going to war. Dobrynin said that in effect we were returning to the old position in which all the sacrifices had to be made by Egypt. I said that the pity was that Dobrynin could never seem to understand that these were negotiating arguments that we had already heard in New York and Washington. If he was talking to me, he should face the substance of the problem, and the substance was that we were prepared to use our good offices with the Israelis but only within a framework that we thought would not drive them to acts of total desperation.

Dobrynin asked why the demilitarized zone had to be entirely on the Egyptian side. I said it was because equivalent demilitarized zones would drive the Israelis back to Jerusalem. Dobrynin asked whether we would consider proportional demilitarized zones. I said it seemed to me extremely improbable, but if he wanted to make a proposal this was of course open to him.

Dobrynin indicated that he did not think we were making much progress. He said the difficulty was that we did not take the Soviet proposals sufficiently seriously. The Soviet Union had offered to withdraw all its forces from Egypt, except a number roughly equivalent to what we had in Iran, not to establish bases elsewhere, and to accept limitations on its arms shipments.[5] This responded exactly to what we had said publicly in July 1969 we wanted. Now we were haggling about a few miles of territory.

I responded that Dobrynin always had the great ability to present his position in the form of enormous concessions, without ever looking at what we were doing on our side. For example, the Soviet proposal was a way for the Soviets of extricating themselves from a difficult situation. Their client could not win a war with the Israelis. Therefore, a continuation of the situation would lead to one of two situations: either a conviction on the part of the Arabs that their alliance with the Soviet Union was not adequate to produce a settlement, or a war by the Egyp-

---

[4] Attached but not printed.
[5] See Document 251.

tians which would face the Soviet Union with a decision of military support and a risk out of proportion to anything that could be achieved.

Dobrynin answered that this was partially true, but there was a third possibility that the Soviet Union had to consider. The Soviet Union was now at a watershed; its next move would be a considerable increase of its military presence in Egypt and other Arab states. He could assure me they were deluged with offers, for example, to provide air protection to other Arab countries. The Soviet Union had requests for a massive influx of arms which then could be given with the argument that the Soviet Union would stay there until the local people were in a position to defeat the Israelis militarily. [Note: This seems confirmed by Israeli intelligence.] Also the Soviet Union was well aware of the fact that its proposal really opened up the field for us to compete with them much more effectively in the Arab world than is now the case. In short, it was a major policy act by the Soviet Union, and if we did not pick it up, the consequences might be quite serious. However, he would transmit my suggestions to Moscow and he would give me their reaction.

[Omitted here is discussion unrelated to the Middle East.]

282. Editorial Note

On March 21, 1972, Prime Minister Golda Meir and King Hussein held a secret meeting to discuss their respective requirements for a peace agreement between Israel and Jordan. The meeting was originally scheduled for March 16, but Meir cancelled it to protest the Jordanian federation plan that the King had announced on March 15. After Hussein opened the discussion by explaining his reasons for restructuring Jordan, she replied that she was "shocked" when she had heard about his proposal, especially because "Israel was not even mentioned" and because, by her interpretation, it "would lead to the eventual liquidation" of her country. She later characterized both the territorial aspects of the plan and its position on Jerusalem as "unacceptable," describing the section on Jerusalem as "a tale of horror" and adding that the subject was "not up for discussion."

They both listed the principles on which they were unwilling to compromise. Meir said: 1) "Under no conditions will we return to the boundaries of 1967"; 2) "Secretary Rogers's proposals are totally unacceptable"; 3) "Minor border rectifications are out of the question"; and 4) "Jerusalem must be a unified city, although Jordan can control the

Arab holy places." Hussein responded that he did not agree with the Prime Minister's proposals and listed his own requirements: 1) "A return to the situation as it existed prior to 1967"; 2) "A complete separation and secession of the West Bank"; and 3) "The establishment of the UAK, which I have proposed." He said that the last point was "the only logical solution for our people" and also remarked, "I cannot tell my people to give up Jerusalem."

The discussion then turned to the issue of basic cooperation over the near term. Meir asked Hussein if he was prepared to: 1) "Keep Jordan out of any eastern front command"; 2) "Not allow Syrian or Iraqi troops in Jordan"; 3) "Keep the fedayeen out of Jordan"; and 4) "Continue cooperation with us on contingency planning as before." She added, "This is the best we can do." Hussein replied, "Can't we work jointly to arrive at peace?" to which Meir said, "We can't accept your paper." The conversation concluded with Hussein asking Meir when Israel would provide Jordan with a plan of its own for a settlement between their two countries. The Prime Minister did not offer a time but instead answered: "We will produce a plan outlining the principles and designs which we consider the basis for a settlement. But one final word, Your Majesty, when you are in Washington the question of the Jarring negotiations is bound to come up. Negotiations through Jarring will not lead to anything. The only way we are going to reach a peaceful settlement is through direct negotiations." (Attachment A to a memorandum from Helms to Nixon, March 24; National Archives, Nixon Presidential Materials, White House Special Files, President's Office Files, Box 16, President's Handwriting)

283. Telegram From the Department of State to the Embassy in Israel[1]

Washington, March 23, 1972, 2027Z.

50083. For Ambassador from Sisco.

1. We are increasingly concerned about current Israeli tactics in their dealings with Jarring and Waldheim.[2] We have no desire to precipitate USG–GOI dispute over this matter or to seek to quarterback Israeli moves, but believe it important our concerns and thoughts on this subject get through to them. It occurs to us that best thing would be for you to engage GOI on personal basis in dialogue on this problem, without its having appearance of formal démarche. You know best how to get this across.

2. Following are points we would hope you could get across:

A. As Israel knows, we have stayed out of their current negotiations with Jarring and SYG, and we will continue to stay out. In spirit of close consultations between us, however, we want to share our views for their consideration.

B. We gather Israelis feel that, if clarification process in Jarring talks can be stalled, this will eventually convince Egyptians they have no alternative to entering proximity talks on interim Canal agreement. This may be true, but we think argument can also be made for contrary view—namely, that some substantive activity in Jarring context would make it easier for Sadat to ultimately enter proximity talks on parallel track.

C. Whichever analysis is correct, we see real risk that tactic of temporizing in Jarring talks will lead sooner or later to steps by SYG and Jarring which would cast Israel in most indefensible light, make our own position vulnerable and risk precipitating return of whole Middle East question to Security Council.

---

[1] Source: National Archives, Nixon Presidential Materials, NSC Files, Box 609, Country Files, Middle East, Israel, Vol. 10. Secret; Nodis. Drafted by Atherton and approved by Sisco and Rogers.

[2] Rabin's report to Sisco on Jarring's visit to Israel is in telegram 33722 to Tel Aviv, February 28. (Ibid., Box 658, Country Files, Middle East, Middle East Nodis/Cedar/Plus, Vol. V) According to Bush's account of his March 14 meeting with the Secretary-General, the latter said that Israel had been "engaging in dilatory tactics," which he "could not tolerate." Waldheim was referring specifically to Tekoah's week-long delay in returning to New York from Israel, his lack of communication with Jarring when he did return, and his ultimatum to Jarring that he must "disassociate himself" from his February 8, 1971, memorandum and General Assembly Resolution 2799 when, upon Jarring's request, he finally got in touch with the Special Representative. (Telegram 927 from USUN, March 15; ibid., Box 1167, Saunders Files, Middle East Negotiations Files, Middle East—Jarring Talks, March 1–31, 1972)

D. Israeli position, as we understand it, is that it has not wanted to be confronted in Jarring talks with Jarring's February 8 memorandum and December UNGA Resolution.[3] We can appreciate this view and understand it. In our judgment, Jarring is now offering Israelis precisely this and is in effect saying that he is prepared to resume his mission without pre-conditions. This will have achieved a major step for Israeli point of view: In effect the memo and GA Resolution are being disregarded as condition to get talks started while both sides hold to their own positions substantively as to the settlement.

E. For Israel to press situation still further and ask Jarring in effect to disavow his memorandum and UNGA resolution vis-à-vis Egyptians puts him in humiliating and impossible situation. Furthermore, were he to do so, this would certainly create new obstacles on Egyptian side. Since Jarring is not asking Israel to change its position with respect to his memorandum and UNGA resolution, it would be unreasonable to expect him to ask Egyptians to change their position in this respect.

F. We have no illusions that clarification process Jarring proposes re elements of Resclution 242 will lead to new significant breakthroughs, or that it will not eventually come up against opposing Israeli and Egyptian views on question of prior withdrawal commitment. We believe Jarring knows this, the Egyptians know this, as we and the Israelis know this. It is very much in U.S.-Israeli mutual interests, however, to keep Jarring process going, which will require some semblance of movement in Jarring talks. As long as some diplomatic activity is going on, the ceasefire will be reinforced, the doors to interim Suez Canal talks remain open, and the outside pressures for outside involvement—four or five power talks, Security Council, etc.—will be diminished. In our view, diplomatic activity can only come about if Israelis will drop their present attempt to obtain preconditions from Jarring and agree to engage in clarification process which Jarring is offering them and Egyptians, without seeking to pin Jarring down on relationship of Jarring talks to his February memorandum and UNGA resclution. If Jarring is willing to finesse these documents by getting both sides to resume talks on basis which does not include specific reference to them, we think this protects Israeli position fully.[4]

---

[3] See, respectively, footnote 2, Document 205 and footnote 4, Document 270.

[4] On March 24, before he received this telegram, Barbour met with Eban, who reported to him that contacts with Jarring appeared "to be going on in desultory manner" and remarked that Israel still believed that a partial Suez agreement constituted a "better approach" than the Jarring Mission. Barbour replied that the United States also believed that, at the time, an interim settlement had a better chance of succeeding than Jarring's efforts but emphasized that U.S. officials did not "consider the two incompatible." He added that it would be "disastrous for either Israel or the US to undermine Jarring." Eban agreed that it would not be "good for Israel" to be "charged with responsibility for a breakdown in the Jarring talks." (Telegram 1995 from Tel Aviv, March 24; ibid., RG 59, Central Files 1970–73, POL 27–14 ARAB–ISR) Telegram 1998 from Tel Aviv, March 25, reported that telegram 50083 to Tel Aviv, March 23, arrived after his conversation with Eban. (Ibid.)

3. We are taking every precaution to assure that knowledge of this approach to Israelis does not repeat not get back to other governments or UN officials.

Rogers

284. Editorial Note

On March 26, 1972, King Hussein of Jordan traveled to Washington, his first stop on a six-week trip abroad. (*New York Times*, March 27, 1972, page 10) He met with President Richard Nixon on the morning of March 28 for almost 1½ hours, during which he read from a 45-minute prepared statement that, in part, reintroduced his federation plan for Palestinian autonomy (see Document 280). The King spent the rest of the meeting describing Jordan's financial and military needs, which he hoped the United States would satisfy. (Transcript of telephone conversation between Kissinger and Rogers, March 28, 12:32 p.m.; National Archives, Nixon Presidential Materials, NSC Files, Henry Kissinger Telephone Conversation Transcripts, Box 15, Chronological File) While Nixon would not officially endorse Hussein's plan, he said that the United States would welcome any initiative that would meet the "legitimate aspirations of the Palestinian people." White House Press Secretary Ronald Ziegler later said that, "so far as the Jordanian plan would 'help the Palestinians develop a voice in shaping their own future it would seem to be one step in creating the conditions necessary for peace.'" (*New York Times*, March 29, 1972, page 2)

On March 29, the King and his advisers met for a half hour with Secretary of Defense Melvin Laird and other Department of Defense officials, who told him that the President had instructed them to "be as forthcoming as possible on behalf of Jordan's needs." After discussing his federation plan, which he raised in the context of his efforts to confront multiple threats to regional stability, he mentioned Jordan's "specific military problems." (Washington National Records Center, ISA Files: FRC 330–75–0155, Box 3, Jordan) In a March 31 follow-up letter to the meeting, Deputy Assistant Secretary of Defense for Near Eastern, African, and South Asian Affairs James Noyes informed Jordanian Ambassador Zuhayr Mahmud al-Mufti that the United States would sell Jordan the jet aircraft and other military equipment that it requested if Congress earmarked the credits necessary for Jordan to buy them. Noyes attached a table to the letter, which listed the equipment to be sold and their line-item costs for the fiscal years 1972–1974. (Ibid.: FRC 330–75–0125, Box 14, Jordan)

285. Telegram From the Department of State to the Interests Section in Egypt[1]

Washington, April 1, 1972, 0113Z.

56147. 1. You should ask to see Ghaleb as soon as possible drawing to extent you deem appropriate on following points, without repeat without indicating you are doing so on instruction from Washington.

2. You are concerned that reported remarks by President Sadat in speech at military base in Delta, to effect that he plans to inform special session of People's Assembly about recent contacts with USG, may mean he plans reveal fact if not substance of message from Secretary to Sadat.[2] These special sessions are usually accompanied by full briefings to press afterwards. Even without briefing to press, disclosure of information to audience of several hundred maximizes opportunity for leaks. You wish to recall to Ghaleb that it was Foreign Minister himself who urged us to hold fact and nature of Secretary's message very closely. USG has taken considerable pains to do so and has not revealed its existence even to closest friends. Disclosure of message in Cairo will do nothing to advance prospect of negotiations on any front and on contrary will only weaken confidence in Washington and other capitals that when they have something to convey of private or confidential nature Egyptian Government can be relied upon to respect such communications. It would be shortsighted to assume that there will not be occasions in future when both of our governments will want to have this

---

[1] Source: National Archives, Nixon Presidential Materials, NSC Files, Box 658, Country Files, Middle East, Middle East Nodis/Cedar/Plus, Vol. V. Secret; Nodis; Cedar Double Plus. Drafted by Sterner, cleared by Davies and Atherton, and approved by Rogers.

[2] In Sadat's March 31 speech at an air base in the Nile Delta, he not only said that war with Israel was "inevitable" but also promised to expose exchanges with the United States. (*New York Times*, April 1, 1972, p. 2) For the Secretary's message, see Document 276.

kind of confidence in one another, which is essential for any kind of diplomatic dialogue.[3]

Rogers

---

[3] Greene met with Ghaleb on the morning of April 3. Ghaleb said that when Sadat responded to Rogers's February message to him, Greene would be the "first to know," and that the response could possibly come "in the next few days." Greene explained that the timing was not as important to the United States as the fact that the exchanges remain confidential, as the Government of Egypt had previously mandated. Ghaleb agreed on the importance of confidentiality and said that Sadat's response would concern this question. (Telegram 962 from Cairo, April 3; National Archives, Nixon Presidential Materials, NSC Files, Box 658, Country Files, Middle East, Middle East Nodis/Cedar/Plus, Vol. V)

---

286. Memorandum From the President's Assistant for National Security Affairs (Kissinger) to President Nixon[1]

Washington, April 8, 1972.

SUBJECT

Sadat-Brezhnev Meeting in February, 1972

[2½ lines not declassified] The highlights are as follows:[2]

The overall impression given [less than 1 line not declassified] is a sense of the tension that continues to underline Sadat's relations with the Soviets. From the Egyptian leader's standpoint, the theme of the entire discussion was one of concern that his relations with the Soviets are not what they ought to be. He warned that the internal situation in Egypt will "explode" unless he is able to offer his people more convincing evidence that the USSR is fully committed to the Egyptian-Arab cause.

Sadat expounded on his concept that the United States has created "two belts" of pressure on Egypt, one in the south including Iran, Ethiopia, Chad and the Congo and one in the north which includes Malta, Jordan, Italy, Greece and Israel. Although that concept appeared to be mainly for the sake of argument with the Russians, it does fit with

---

[1] Source: National Archives, Nixon Presidential Materials, White House Special Files, Staff Secretary's Files, Box 37. Secret; Sensitive. Sent for information. All brackets are in the original except those indicating text that remains classified.

[2] Sadat met with Brezhnev on February 3 during his February 2–4 visit to Moscow.

Sadat's other arguments that Egypt is now confronting the U.S. rather than merely Israel. But all this, along with some remarks about his problems with Maoism among Egyptian students, was also aimed at what Sadat believes are Soviet phobias. His effort, however, does not appear to have made much impression on the Soviet leaders.

Sadat's strategy proposals for 1972 are not very exciting. He said he intends to escalate "political action" prior to your visit to Moscow;[3] to prepare to defend against any Israeli attack and to launch a military attack across the Suez Canal—perhaps against the Sinai passes. He noted, however, that he does not have the military means to take such a military action and that he needs a force of fighter-bombers and some ultra-modern tanks (he did not mention the time needed to train with this equipment).

The Egyptian leader further requested an industrial-military complex, financed by the Libyans in order to assure domestically produced ammunition. Given the incongruities between Sadat's requests and what he claimed to be his strategy and timing, it is hard to escape the conclusion that his "military requirements" have a primarily political motivation. They seem to be more to quiet Sadat's critics at home than to prepare for serious military action against the Israelis at an early date.

[less than 1 line not declassified] the Soviet response was essentially playing for time—perhaps to see how our present negotiations were going. [less than 1 line not declassified] Brezhnev underlined the fact that Soviet policy has not changed and that the Soviet leadership sees no need for it to change. The Soviets, in effect, rejected Sadat's grand design. The providing of forty U.S. aircraft to Israel did not change the nature of Soviet-Egyptian "friendship," according to Brezhnev. Moreover, Moscow's policy continues to be one of "solving the crisis peacefully." In this connection, Brezhnev told Sadat that the Arab-Israeli problem is on the Soviets' agenda for your summit meeting in May but he promised nothing except that "in any case we will continue with new initiatives for a political solution in consultation with you."

Brezhnev avoided falling into the trap of enabling Sadat to claim that the Soviets vetoed military action against Israel. He stated that the Soviets had always striven to help the Egyptian army become an offensive army but he reminded Sadat that a decision to make any kind of a military move is a serious one and it is necessary to "weigh many considerations."

There were some sharp exchanges between Brezhnev and Sadat about Egyptian military requirements and Soviet willingness to meet

---

[3] Nixon was in Moscow May 22–28 for the summit with Brezhnev.

them. Brezhnev stated that in Moscow's view, the Arabs need unity as much or more than hardware—even Saudi Arabia and Jordan should be approached by Sadat, and Sadat should work out—with Soviet help—military arrangements with the Syrians for the use of Syrian airfields by the Egyptians. In the end, however, Brezhnev promised hardware:

—100 new-type MIG fighters (70 before June 1972 and 30 in the second half of the year),
—20 TU–22 supersonic bombers,
—200 T–62 tanks, and

more sophisticated communications equipment and arrangements for licensing some military production in Egypt.

Even here, however, the note was one of caution: deliveries are to be paced with training, wasteful industrial projects are to be avoided, etc. At the close of the meeting, Brezhnev once again reminded Sadat that the Soviets were not happy about developments in connection with Libya, the Sudan and the relations between Soviet experts and the Egyptian military.

In sum, [*less than 1 line not declassified*] indicate that the Soviet-Egyptian relationship is considerably more reserved than it was before Nasser's death. Sadat is trying to manipulate the relationship primarily to strengthen his domestic political situation. He does not seem genuinely interested at this time in war with Israel. The Soviets, for their part, are still holding Sadat at arms' length. They are playing for time until they see how our private negotiations develop. The Soviets are clearly keeping their options open. The Soviets are willing to provide new arms to the Egyptians but they are concerned about the Egyptian request for an industrial base which would enable them to produce their own weapons. Such a development obviously would make Egypt less dependent upon the USSR for weapon supply.

287. Memorandum From the President's Assistant for National Security Affairs (Kissinger) to President Nixon[1]

Washington, May 17, 1972.

SUBJECT

A Preliminary Look at the Mid-East in the Moscow Talks

Secretary Rogers has sent you the attached preliminary thoughts on the issues in discussing the Middle East at the Moscow summit.[2] This analysis will be reflected in your briefing book[3] as well.

The essence of the State Department analysis is that the Soviets will make clear their view that there must be progress in the Mid-East or they will be unable to keep the lid on much longer. State feels that the Soviets will be seeking some sort of understanding that the great powers will work together to impose a solution. State's recommendation is that we should insist that the focus of negotiations must remain with the Middle Eastern parties to the dispute and not with the major powers. State says: "Our counter to any Soviet pressure to renew bilateral or Four Power talks should be to keep the focus on the need for Egypt to face up to the necessity of negotiating a settlement with Israel instead of looking to others to do the job for it."

State acknowledges that a standoff such as this approach will produce will leave a very unpredictable situation in the post-summit period since no one can guarantee that Sadat will continue to avoid military action—no matter how foolish—in the absence of hope for diplomatic movement. The State memo offers no suggestions for softening the impact of a standoff.

The premise of the State memo is correct—that we are limited in any effort to reach specific agreements because (a) the Israelis are opposed in principle to the idea of a great-power solution and (b) the Israelis are unlikely to find palatable any specific terms on key issues that the Russians could accept. The problem remains how to avoid the worst effects of a complete stalemate.

---

[1] Source: National Archives, Nixon Presidential Materials, NSC Files, Box 1167, Saunders Files, Middle East Negotiations Files, Middle East—Jarring Talks, May 1–31, 1972. Secret; Nodis; Cedar. Sent for information. A stamped notation on the memorandum indicates the President saw it. All brackets are in the original.

[2] Dated May 1; attached but not printed. For excerpts from the memorandum, see *Foreign Relations, 1969–1976,* volume XIV, Soviet Union, October 1971–May 1972, Document 178.

[3] The briefing book for the Moscow Summit is in the National Archives, Nixon Presidential Materials, NSC Files, Box 476, President's Trip Files.

It is true that we are unlikely to want to make any concessions in the Middle East in the aftermath of Soviet actions in South Asia last year[4] and until there is evidence of a responsible attitude toward Southeast Asia. However, there are some subjects that we could seek understanding on that would serve our interests.

I would rule out getting too deeply into specifics unless an unusual opportunity was offered, and I would want to avoid the atmosphere of total inflexibility since that could lead the Soviets to step up their military program in Egypt. I would suggest exploring points like the following designed to lead toward some understanding on a general framework for future handling of the Middle East problem:

—Our ability to move Israel even in a limited way will depend on our finding a way to avoid the appearance of a US–USSR solution and to create the appearance of Arab-Israeli negotiation. We are not looking for a concession in saying this; we are looking for a solution to a practical problem. We would like to discuss with the Soviets ways in which an Egyptian-Israeli exchange could be set up outside the glare of publicity in which all possible solutions could be aired. The mere fact of the exchange would have significance in Israel, and only if we can break away from present rigid positions does there seem any chance of finding a way to move negotiations forward.

—The US and USSR should each accept the idea that the settlement process will take some time. We should each acknowledge our understanding that the process may even reach over several years. Such an understanding is not an evasion of responsibility but an effort to assure that the two of us at least are not measuring each other's performance against an unrealistic standard.

—One way to buy time over the next few months might be to return to the idea of an interim agreement for opening the Suez Canal. If this were coupled with private Egyptian-Israeli talks, it could provide the outward appearance of movement that Sadat needs. [State recommends that we low-key this subject because the Soviets will oppose our going ahead as the exclusive go-between while the Israelis will oppose Soviet involvement. This problem might be partly met if we were to talk with the USSR as well as to Egypt and Israel.]

—There might be some agreement on discussing the ultimate limitation of US and Soviet forces on Middle Eastern soil.

We would not want to create an impression for the Egyptians that we had renounced the UN resolution of November 1967, the Jarring talks or the Rogers Plan. At the same time, we ought to try to find ways

---

[4] Reference is to Soviet support of India during its war with Pakistan in December 1971.

with the Soviets of exploring new approaches that can break free of the old positions which are at impasse.

288. Memorandum From Director of Central Intelligence Helms to the President's Assistant for National Security Affairs (Kissinger)[1]

Washington, May 18, 1972.

SUBJECT

Further Developments on Egyptian Suggestion for Secret Talks on the Middle East Crisis

1. The following developments have occurred since [2 lines not declassified] 5 April 1972 that secret contact between the Presidencies of our two governments would be a prerequisite to renewing serious discussion on a Middle East settlement, as outlined in my memorandum dated 7 April 1972.[2]

2. On 29 April 1972, [2½ lines not declassified]. This message acknowledged that there was interest in exploring the possibility of a secret, high-level meeting between senior representatives of the two governments; suggested that an emissary of President Sadat would be welcome in the United States, if a meeting were deemed mutually desirable; and indicated that the timing of such a meeting could clearly not be before the President returned from his trip in June. [less than 1 line not declassified] advised that he had given the foregoing message to President Sadat shortly after the latter returned from Moscow in late April.[3]

3. On 16 May 1972, [1 line not declassified] that President Sadat is still considering the matter of new, secret contacts and would respond to our message in June, recognizing that little can happen before then in any case because of President Nixon's trip. In discussing [less than 1 line not declassified] the decision of the Egyptian Government to reduce the size of the U.S. Interest Section in Cairo, [less than 1 line not declassified]

---

[1] Source: National Archives, Nixon Presidential Materials, NSC Files, Kissinger Office Files, Box 131, Country Files, Middle East. Secret; Sensitive. All brackets are in the original except those indicating text that remains classified.
[2] Not found.
[3] Sadat visited Moscow April 27–29.

stressed that this is not related to the pending proposal for secret contacts. [6½ lines not declassified]

4. The Department of State has not been informed of this exchange.[4]

Richard Helms[5]

---

[4] At the beginning of the year, Rogers met with Haldeman and Mitchell to discuss his "lack of trust" in Kissinger because Kissinger had previously "lied to him" and had "admitted it." Haldeman wrote in his diary: "We agreed we had to set up a method so that Rogers would keep us posted on all the meetings he has with the Soviets or the Israelis, etc. Rogers agreed that he would, if K[issinger] would notify Rogers about all of his meetings, unless the P[resident] tells him not to notify. The basic principle to apply is whatever one of the three knows on foreign policy, all three should, between K, Rogers, and the P. (*Haldeman Diaries, Multimedia Edition*, January 11, 1972) On January 16, Rogers had another conversation with Haldeman in which he agreed that "State people have to be kept out of some things" but that he, the Secretary of State, should not. Rogers added that the "main thing" was that Kissinger did not keep him "advised on all that he's doing." (Ibid., January 16, 1972)

[5] Helms signed "Dick" above his typed signature.

---

289. Memorandum From the President's Assistant for National Security Affairs (Kissinger) to President Nixon[1]

Washington, May 22, 1972.

SUBJECT

Sadat Letter to Brezhnev

Director Helms has sent you a memorandum (Tab A)[2] informing you that he has just acquired a copy of a letter written by Sadat to Brezhnev on *12 April* 1972. A translation of the full letter is at Tab B.[3] Director Helms believes that the document is authentic. [2 lines not declassified]

The highlights of Director Helms' appreciation of the letter are as follows. The letter is another reflection of Sadat's frustration with a situation in which the openings for movement seem virtually nil. It is also

---

[1] Source: Library of Congress, Manuscript Division, Kissinger Papers, Box CL–179, Middle East, Chronological File. Secret; Sensitive. Sent for information. A handwritten notation on the memorandum reads: "The President has seen, 6–2–72." All brackets are in the original except those indicating text that remains classified.

[2] Dated May 2; attached but not printed.

[3] Attached but not printed.

an expression of his concern that the Soviet leaders at the summit talks may tacitly or otherwise agree to leave the Arab-Israeli situation as it now stands.

Although Sadat did not refer directly to the possibility of an agreement to limit the quality or quantity of arms supplies to Egypt and Israel, he clearly is concerned that such an agreement might be discussed at the summit. The thrust of his argument is that the balance of power between the Arabs and Israel can only be shifted if Egypt is provided with the means to develop an offensive capability in the air. Failing this, he claims, the Israelis and the United States will be able to freeze the present situation indefinitely. He cites a variety of evidence to support his belief that this is, in fact, Israeli and U.S. policy now.

Sadat pointed to King Hussein's proposal for an eventual Palestine entity[4] as an especially dangerous example of the way in which the U.S. and Israel are working. He also included an implied complaint about the willingness of the Soviets to allow Jews of military age and technical qualifications to emigrate to Israel. Sadat's language indicates that he remains deeply worried that world attention will turn away from the Middle East, leaving him with what he calls "a border dispute" which would lack international support and which would lead to direct negotiations and "defeat."

Here too, Sadat is subtly reminding the Soviets that in talking to the United States, they should not be led into any arrangement that provides for direct negotiations. For his part, he tried to reassure Brezhnev, that he will stick to his "firm decision" to reject negotiations with Israel, if the Soviets will stand firm against U.S. blandishments or pressures. In other words, he will not undercut Moscow by again using the U.S. as an intermediary. He also asserted, however, that if the Soviets continue to fail to change the terms of power between Egypt and Israel, Soviet objectives and even the existence of the "progressive" Arab regimes may be threatened.

On the whole, Sadat's is not a strong letter. It does not offer anything new. It is defensive in tone and very much the plea of a worried client to his patron rather than an argument presented by one partner to another in whom he has real confidence. The Soviet leaders may agree up to a point with Sadat's reasoning but they will hardly welcome his implicit suggestions that their present policy is a failure.

It is still doubtful that under present circumstances, the Soviets will run the risks involved in providing Egypt with the kind of effective, offensive air power Sadat wants. There are indications, however, in the Soviet-Egyptian communiqué following Sadat's Moscow visit

---

[4] See Document 280.

last week that the Soviets are now willing to give at least some rhetorical support to the line Sadat took in this letter. The communiqué omitted the usual stress on the defensive character of Soviet military support for Egypt and supported the view that, in the absence of a settlement, the Arabs have "every reason to use other means" than negotiations to regain territory lost to Israel. Despite that language, there is nothing in Sadat's letter or the communiqué to point to any new diplomatic initiative by the Soviets or the Egyptians.

290. Telegram From the Interests Section in Egypt to the Department of State[1]

Cairo, May 22, 1972, 1215Z.

1506. Ref: Cairo 1009.[2]

1. In reftel USInt reported statement allegedly made by Sadat to his old political crony, Mohammed Dakroury, that Egypt would launch offensive across Suez Canal between April 15 and May 15 of this year. Our source now reports that on May 19 he asked Dakroury about Sadat's statement pointing out that May 15 had passed.

2. Dakroury replied that Sadat had indeed intended to attack but had been dissuaded by the Soviets who had told Sadat he would have to wait at least two years before he could attack and win. Dakroury said that Sadat will not accept a two year delay and will attack much sooner than that.

Greene

---

[1] Source: National Archives, Nixon Presidential Materials, NSC Files, Box 638, Country Files, Middle East, Egypt, Vol. VIII. Secret; Nodis.

[2] Dated April 5. (Ibid., RG 59, Central Files 1970–73, POL 27–14 ARAB–ISR)

291. U.S. Paper[1]

Moscow, undated.

BASIC PROVISIONS FOR A FINAL SETTLEMENT IN THE MIDDLE EAST

Agreements on a final settlement, termination of the state of belligerency and the establishment of peace between Egypt and Israel, Jordan and Israel, Syria and Israel will be governed by the following principles:

a. All signers of the agreements will accept obligations to end the state of belligerency and to establish peace among them.

b. The agreements will contain arrangements for the withdrawal of Israeli troops from Arab territories occupied in 1967.

c. Arrangements for securing the borders will include the establishment of demilitarized zones and security zones and the participation of military units of the signatories in a UN force.

d. The agreements and the security arrangements will assure freedom of navigation for ships of all nations, including Israel, through the Suez Canal and the Straits of Tiran.

e. Completion of these arrangements will at some stage involve negotiations among the potential signers of the agreement.

1. *The withdrawal of the Israeli troops and boundaries*

Israel shall withdraw her troops from Arab territories occupied in 1967 within an agreed period after the signature of the agreements. Withdrawal will take place in agreed stages. Flexibility will be permitted for negotiated changes in borders where those changes enhance agreed security arrangements.

---

[1] Source: National Archives, Nixon Presidential Materials, NSC Files, Kissinger Office Files, Box 73, Country Files, Europe, USSR. No classification marking. "Handed to Brezhnev by President May 26" is handwritten at the top of the first page. After Nixon handed the paper to Brezhnev, Kissinger noted that it was a counterproposal to a proposal that Brezhnev gave to him in Moscow on April 22. For memoranda of conversation of the April 22 and May 26 meetings, see *Foreign Relations, 1969–1976*, volume XIV, Soviet Union, October 1971–May 1972, Documents 141 and 284. The paper is based on a draft written by Saunders, which was in turn based on Saunders's critique of the Soviet proposal. (Memorandum from Saunders to Kissinger, May 19; National Archives, Nixon Presidential Materials, NSC Files, Box 482, President's Trip Files, Middle East Negotiations, Dr. Kissinger, May 19, 1972, Part I) Other meetings at which the Middle East was discussed during the summit include those between Kissinger and Gromyko during the afternoon and evening of May 28, both of which are printed in *Foreign Relations, 1969–1976*, volume XIV, Soviet Union, October 1971–May 1972, Documents 292, 293, and 295.

The withdrawal of Israeli troops from occupied territories will be carried out under the supervision of UN military observers.

2. *Termination of the state of belligerency and the establishment of peace*

The sides in the conflict will agree to terminate the state of belligerency between them and assume the following concrete obligations with respect to the establishment of peace:

to respect and to recognize the sovereignty, territorial integrity, inviolability and political independence of one another, their mutual right to live in peace without being subjected to threats or use of force or to intervention in their domestic affairs by other nations;

to undertake all in their power so that no military or other hostile acts or the use or threat of force against the other side should originate in or be committed from their territories;

to agree on the freedom of movement by people and commerce across international boundaries;

to settle differences peacefully.

3. *The Suez Canal*

In the agreement on the final settlement between Egypt and Israel, Egypt will assume obligation, in exercising its sovereignty over the Suez Canal, to ensure freedom of navigation through the Canal for vessels of all states without discrimination, including Israel. That freedom would not be denied under any circumstances except the outbreak of war between Egypt and Israel.

Israeli ships will begin to exercise their right to passage through the Suez Canal upon the opening of the Canal.

In order to resume at an early date the use of the Suez Canal for international shipping and as a practical step which could either be an integral part of general settlement or an agreed step in advance of a final agreement, Egypt and Israel will agree on the implementation of certain measures which will envisage:

a) an obligation by Israel to withdraw her forces from the Suez Canal within a month (tentatively) after reaching agreement on these measures to the distance of ... kilometers from the Suez Canal;[2]

b) restoration of Egyptian administration and control in the territory to be vacated by Israel and movement across the Suez Canal of Egyptian personnel agreed to be necessary for the exercise of civil authority and security in the area of the Canal consistent with whatever demilitarization arrangements may be agreed;

c) an obligation by Egypt to take measures for the speediest clearing and reopening of the Suez Canal.

---

[2] Omission in the original.

4. *The Gulf of Aqaba and the Straits of Tiran*

The Egyptian-Israeli agreement shall envisage an obligation by Egypt to observe the principle of freedom of navigation through the Straits of Tiran and in the Gulf of Aqaba for vessels of all countries, including Israel. It will also provide for stationing of UN military personnel, including Israeli units, at Sharm El Sheikh and at such other places as may be agreed. The need for the UN post will be reviewed at agreed intervals; it will be removed only by agreement of the signatories to the agreement and of the UN Security Council.

5. *Gaza*

The Gaza strip shall be placed under a transitional administration endorsed by the UN Security Council with the participation of Gazan, Jordanian, Israeli and UN personnel pending a final agreement on the disposition of Gaza. The transitional period would continue until the refugees in Gaza had been resettled and the residual population had decided its own future. A referendum shall take place in Gaza under the United Nations observation five years after refugee resettlement from Gaza is complete so that its population could decide the destiny of this territory. In the period after the withdrawal of Israeli troops until Gaza's final status has been defined security would be provided by a United Nations military unit manned by personnel of the UN and by participants in the transitional administration stationed in Gaza.

6. *Jerusalem*

Jerusalem shall remain a unified city. Jordan shall have a role there, including the administration of the Islamic shrines. The walled city and adjacent shrines shall be demilitarized and freedom of access to the Holy places of all religions shall be ensured by Jordan and Israel. Arrangements shall be negotiated between Jordan and Israel.

7. *Demilitarized and Security Zones*

The agreements shall establish two types of zones. There will be demilitarized zones in which the nature and level of forces and equipment will be limited by agreement. There will also be security zones in which each side will have special rights to station troops, patrol, and maintain facilities. The number, location and size of such zones will be subject to agreement between the sides. The regime of such zones will only contain limitations of a purely military nature.

A UN force with personnel assigned by the UN and by the parties to the agreement will be stationed in the demilitarized zones and in the security zones.

8. *Troops and military observers of the United Nations*

On the decision of the Security Council and by consent of the signatories to the agreement small contingents of forces and military observers of the United Nations will be formed for agreed periods and subject to removal only by agreement of the signatories and approval of the Security Council.

These forces and groups of military observers will be formed from among the military personnel of member states of the United Nations to be determined by the Security Council, including units of the signatories of the agreement and taking into account the opinion of the states in whose territories these contingents or observers will be stationed. The extension of the stationing of these contingents and observers after the expiry of the initial period (5 years tentatively) will be decided by the signatories of the agreement and by the Security Council.

9. *International assurances*

The security of Israel and the neighboring Arab states and, in particular, the boundaries between them established in the agreements on the settlement, shall be assured by the Security Council and the great powers.

Such assurances will legally enter into force after signing of the peace agreements. Corresponding obligations on this score shall be taken by the signatories.

10. *The Palestine problem and ensuring the just rights of the refugees*

In the interests of establishing a just and lasting peace in the Middle East the signatories agree to make efforts for the settlement of the Palestine refugee problem.

In the agreements on the settlement the signatories will express their consent that Palestine refugees will exercise on an individual basis by means of a poll the choice between repatriation to Israel and resettling with compensation on the Western Bank of the Jordan river, in the Gaza strip, other Arab countries or elsewhere.

Israel shall assume an obligation on annual quotas of refugees whom she will admit as well as on the amount of compensation for the property of the Palestine refugees left in her territory.

The implementation of all other parts of the agreements on the final settlement shall not be delayed until practical measures for solving the refugee problem are completed.

11. *Cease-fire*

For the purpose of providing more favorable conditions for the speediest settlement in the Middle East the sides in the conflict shall agree at the beginning of negotiations to continue observing the cease-fire through the negotiations until those negotiations result in an agreement which will replace the cease-fire with a permanent peace.

12. *On the entry into force of the agreements on the final settlement*

The agreements on the final settlement would become effective through their approval by signature of the parties and by the Security

Council. The signatories will act in accordance with the obligations contained in the agreements from the moment of their signature.

13. *A Negotiating Process*

Any reasonable channel of negotiation, secret or public, may be used, and several complementary channels may be used simultaneously. Whatever the channel, it is important that the principal elements and details in the agreements be agreed in exchanges among the signatories. The US and USSR will support these exchanges.

292. Editorial Note

On May 29, 1972, the United States and the Soviet Union concluded the talks in Moscow by issuing a joint communiqué on areas of agreement and disagreement on a range of topics that was meant to establish a new era of stable relations between the two countries. The section on the Middle East reads: "The two Sides set out their positions on this question. They reaffirm their support for a peaceful settlement in the Middle East in accordance with Security Council Resolution 242. Noting the significance of constructive cooperation of the parties concerned with the Special Representative of the UN Secretary General, Ambassador Jarring, the US and the USSR confirm their desire to contribute to his mission's success and also declare their readiness to play their part in bringing about a peaceful settlement in the Middle East. In the view of the US and the USSR, the achievement of such a settlement would open prospects for the normalization of the Middle East situation and would permit, in particular, consideration of further steps to bring about a military relaxation in that area." The full text of the communiqué is printed in *Public Papers. Nixon, 1972*, pages 635–642.

293. Telegram From the Department of State to the Embassy in Israel[1]

Washington, June 1, 1972, 2235Z.

97086. Tosec 257. London for Assistant Secretary Sisco. Subject: Possible Israel Action Against Lebanon.

1. In wake Lod Airport attack[2] and indications possible Israeli reprisal against Lebanon we confront familiar dilemma: whether or not to seek to deter retaliation which could have salutary inhibiting effect on fedayeen and GOL in short run but, given Lebanese circumstances, could also have more far-reaching destabilizing effect in Lebanon with strains on U.S.-Lebanese relations and (as in case of 1968 raid) with ultimate strengthening of fedayeen position in Lebanon. On one hand fact is Israel makes its own decisions and on previous occasions our direct appeals for them to stay their hand have rarely if ever seemed to have effect. Our own feeling is that such appeals for restraint have more often than not aroused Israeli resentment that we were trying to close off a legitimate option and were more sympathetic to Arab than to Israeli concerns. The higher the emotional temperature the more likely this counterproductive emotional reaction will be evoked. On other hand failure by us to indicate we believe further violence could have broader destabilizing political effects in area may well be construed by Israelis as U.S. acquiescence to any action they may choose to take. It clearly not in our interest that this be their understanding.

2. With foregoing considerations in mind we are inclined to think that most effective tack would be low key but unmistakable signal as regards our concerns about Israeli retaliation against Lebanon. Circumstances may favor such an approach now. We slightly encouraged that Knesset debate has been postponed and hope this indicates GOI wants to give time for emotions to cool.

3. We therefore think, unless you have serious reservations, that you should speak to GOI along following lines at high level at earliest opportunity. As we informed GOI we have gone in strongly to Leba-

---

[1] Source: National Archives, Nixon Presidential Materials, NSC Files, Box 609, Country Files, Middle East, Israel, Vol. X. Secret; Immediate; Exdis. Drafted by Stackhouse and Atherton, cleared by Seelye and Davies, and approved by Irwin. Repeated Priority to Beirut, USUN, and London for the Secretary.

[2] On May 31, three Japanese guerrillas fired on a crowd of roughly 250 to 300 people in the Tel Aviv airport, killing 25 and wounding 72. The Popular Front for the Liberation of Palestine claimed sole responsibility for the attack, timing it to coincide with the anniversary of the Arab-Israeli war of 1967 as well as retaliating for the IDF killing of two Arab guerrillas who had hijacked an airplane to Tel Aviv earlier in the month. (*New York Times*, May 31, 1972, pp. 1 and 27)

nese Government. We note that in letter to Security Council Lebanese Government has expressed disapproval such acts of violence and said it was not implicated in any way in the matter. We have since been informed by Lebanese that GOL is planning to move to restrict activities of PFLP. We were not given details as to precisely what GOL would do, but they have said they will keep us advised. In our conversations with Lebanese, while making clear to them we cannot speak for GOI, we have expressed our judgment that their own actions vis-à-vis PFLP will be factor GOI will weigh in considering how to respond to Lod Airport killings.[3] In our view, initial Lebanese response has been so far so good. While doubt obviously remains how effectively GOL will move against PFLP, we believe that they can best do so in atmosphere free of further violence and will be watching closely for evidence of how GOL plans to proceed.[4]

Irwin

---

[3] On June 2, the Embassy in Tel Aviv replied: "Embassy does have serious reservations concerning procedure outlined para 3 reftel. As Department notes, we have already informed GOI, and Eban acknowledged to Ambassador, that we have weighed in strongly with GOL. We have also told GOI initial GOL response was 'positive.' Among other points Department proposes to make to Israelis now, however, there are several which we feel will only excite argument and convince Israelis that we do not take sufficiently grave view of role which GOL permits terrorist organizations in Lebanon." (Telegram 3501 from Tel Aviv, June 2; National Archives, Nixon Presidential Materials, NSC Files, Box 609, Country Files, Middle East, Israel, Vol. X)

[4] Sisco met with Rabin on June 23 to inform him that U.S. officials had "told Lebanon it should not expect support in Security Council from us if it proceeds with its decision in principle to take recent incidents there." The Assistant Secretary added that they had "declined the Lebanese request that we press Israel for release prisoners taken June 21 but we had said we would inquire what Israeli intentions were re these prisoners." Sisco then asked Rabin for more information regarding Israel's patrolling policy on the Lebanese border. The Israeli Ambassador said, "Israeli policy would continue as long as Lebanese territory used as fedayeen base against Israel," defending Israeli patrolling actions as "necessary to forestall fedayeen attacks." As for the prisoners, Rabin said that Israel "wanted package deal covering all Arab and Israeli POWs and was in touch with ICRC." (Telegram 114024 to Tel Aviv, June 24; ibid., Box 1168, Saunders Files, Middle East Negotiations Files, Middle East—Jarring Talks, June 1–30, 1972)

294. Memorandum From Harold Saunders of the National Security Council Staff to the President's Assistant for National Security Affairs (Kissinger)[1]

Washington, June 19, 1972.

SUBJECT

Current State Department Line on the Middle East

Reports of recent conversations that Sisco has held with diplomats here in Washington move me to raise a basic question about the posture we should take toward the Arab-Israeli impasse over the next few months. This question is sharpened by Egyptian rejection this week of Secretary Rogers' February proposal for proximity talks on an interim agreement.[2]

The question is: Do we want to continue prodding the Egyptians gently to respond positively to our proposal for proximity talks on an interim agreement, or do we want to lie low until after the election? It seems obvious to me that the answer is to lie low, and State may be more inclined to do that following the Egyptian reply. But that was not the line Sisco was following before their reply.

The basic line that Sisco is taking comes through in the two attached reports of recent conversations with Ambassador Ortona and with Ashraf Ghorbal.[3] The composite line that emerges from these conversations goes like this:

—We see no immediate hope for Ambassador Jarring's mission to achieve a new breakthrough but continue to hope that an interim agreement might be achieved. We have never had a reply from Egypt and are still awaiting one. [This, of course, was overtaken by the Egyptian reply last weekend.]

---

[1] Source: National Archives, Nixon Presidential Materials, NSC Files, Box 647, Country Files, Middle East, Middle East (General) Vol. IX. Secret. Sent for information. At the top of the page, Kissinger wrote: "Let's get him stopped, HK." Another note by Haig reads: "Eliot informed." All brackets are in the original.

[2] For Rogers's proposal, see Document 276. Egypt's rejection of his proposal was conveyed to Greene by Ismail on June 17. Ismail told Greene that Egypt considered the United States "responsible for the failure of the talks in 1971" and considered Rogers's proposal of February 1972, "unacceptable." (Telegram 1787 from Cairo, June 18; National Archives, Nixon Presidential Materials, NSC Files, Box 658, Country Files, Middle East, Middle East Nodis/Cedar/Plus, Vol. V)

[3] Attached but not printed are telegrams 105507 to Amman, June 14, and 106539 to Cairo, June 15. These telegrams reported Sisco's meeting with the Italian Ambassador and his meeting with Ghorbal.

—In Moscow we stuck with the Rogers Plan, namely that we thought that both the US and the USSR should encourage negotiations and the best way to do this was to press for an interim agreement

—The "next step" after the summit would be for the US to talk with the Egyptians.

—Sadat has three options: renewed hostilities, accepting "our proposals" or continued drift. [This ignores that there could be other ideas for conducting negotiations.]

—If the USG and the Egyptian Government could conduct an objective exchange on the respective positions of Egypt and Israel on an interim agreement, it might come as a surprise to Cairo to see that the gap between them is not as great as has been supposed. [The Egyptian reply over the weekend said the gap would remain wide as long as we rejected a specific link between an interim settlement and total Israeli withdrawal.]

—Sisco would like an opportunity some day to review these exchanges with Foreign Minister Ghaleb, whom he had not met.

The obvious problem consists of the following elements:

—The Egyptians feel strong bitterness over what they consider Sisco's having deceived them last year by misleading them about the breadth of the gap between the Egyptian and Israeli positions.

—The Egyptian and Israeli positions remain far apart, not close as Sisco maintains.

—Ghorbal, at least, reports the Soviet impression following the US–USSR summit that the Administration is placing its emphasis more on the issue of an overall settlement than on the interim settlement. When Sisco talks up the interim settlement, he creates confusion about the real Administration positions and raises questions in Egyptian minds about what the real US position is.

—Each time Sisco has one of these conversations and disseminates it by cable, his line becomes the line picked up around the area. Thus the impression is created that the gap is narrow and that the US continues to press actively for negotiations on an interim settlement.

The operational point is whether someone should suggest either to Secretary Rogers or to Sisco that they should lie low between now and November. This would not necessarily mean that we would have to take a completely negative line. We could say that we have put a variety of proposals on the table and that no one is precluded in the present situation from pursuing one of these. To maintain the reverse—that we are actively seeking to begin negotiations at this time—simply turns the Egyptians off and puts us in the position of appearing to pursue something that the Egyptians have written off, at least in present context.

295. Editorial Note

Violence across the border between Israel and Lebanon prompted both countries to lodge complaints with the UN Security Council, which met on June 23, 1972, to discuss the issue. (*Yearbook of the United Nations, 1972*, page 161) In a statement before the Security Council the following day, U.S. Representative to the United Nations George H.W. Bush said, "To be sure, terrorism in the Middle East breeds its own deplorable reactions," referring to the May 31 terrorist incident at the Lod Airport in Israel and the Israeli reprisals in Lebanon that occurred earlier in the week. He concluded: "As I stated last February in this Council, the United States fully supports the territorial integrity and political independence of Lebanon. My government hopes and expects that the incidents of the type that have occurred along the Israeli-Lebanon border will not recur; that all forces, regular and irregular, will remain on their own side of the frontier; and that quiet will be maintained. We are aware that the Government of Lebanon has made efforts to control terrorist elements on its territory—elements whose activities are as inimical to the interest of many Arab governments as they are to Israel. We are pleased to note the absence of cross-border incidents for nearly four months. We hope that all authorities in the area, including particularly the Government of Israel, will facilitate and not impede these efforts by Lebanon to control terrorism." (Telegram 2330 from USUN, June 25; National Archives, Nixon Presidential Materials, NSC Files, Box 1168, Saunders Files, Middle East Negotiations Files, Middle East—Jarring Talks, June 1–30, 1972)

On June 26, the Security Council adopted Resolution 316—which France, Belgium, and the United Kingdom had introduced—by a vote of 13–0–2, with the United States and Panama abstaining. The resolution condemned the recent Israeli attacks against Lebanon; asked that Israel refrain from resorting to further military actions against Lebanon; deplored the "tragic loss of life resulting from all acts of violence and retaliation" in the region; expressed the "strong desire that appropriate steps will lead" to the release "in the shortest possible time of all Syrian and Lebanese" personnel "abducted" by Israel on June 21; and declared that if these steps did "not result in the release of abducted personnel or if Israel fails to comply with the present resolution," the Security Council would consider further action. (*Yearbook of the United Nations, 1972*, page 173) After the vote, Bush made a statement before the Security Council criticizing the resolution for not being either fair or balanced, for not showing equal concern for casualties on both sides of the Israeli-Lebanese border, and for not giving equal weight to Arab terrorist attacks and strikes by Israel. He said: "Mr. President, that resolution did not fulfill what we strongly believed are the needs of the situation and my delegation therefore was obliged to abstain." (Telegram 2345 from USUN, June 27; National Archives, Nixon Presidential Materials, NSC Files, Box 1168, Saunders Files, Middle East Negotiations Files, Middle East—Jarring Talks, June 1–30, 1972) The United States introduced its own draft resolution, but the Security Council did not put it to a vote.

296. Memorandum of Conversation[1]

Washington, June 27, 1972, 12:15–12:45 p.m.

PARTICIPANTS

Ashraf Ghorbal, Head of UAR Interest Section
Henry A. Kissinger, Assistant to the President
Harold H. Saunders, NSC Staff

Dr. Ghorbal opened the conversation by congratulating Dr. Kissinger on the "tremendous job" that he has been doing in recent months. Ghorbal smiling said he was especially proud of a "fellow Harvard alumnus."

Dr. Kissinger thanked Dr. Ghorbal and said that he hoped it would be possible to make "progress in other areas" as well.

Dr. Ghorbal replied, "I am counting on it."

Dr. Kissinger replied that realistically until after the US election no significant moves are likely on our side. This did not preclude moves initiated by others. But in spite of that, we recognize the need for a peaceful solution of the Middle East problem. It will certainly be a major item on the agenda of the new administration. How that solution will be arrived at, "I don't know." However, we do have to find a way.

Dr. Kissinger continued that his philosophy is to promise less but to deliver on everything we promise. He felt that the trouble with the US-Egyptian dialogue has been that it did not lead to any concrete results. We expected too much.

Dr. Ghorbal said he was glad to hear this. He always likes to look to the horizons. Dr. Kissinger's concern about the dialogue, he felt, was valid. There has been unhappiness over it in Cairo.

---

[1] Source: National Archives, Nixon Presidential Materials, NSC Files, Kissinger Office Files, Box 131, Country Files, Middle East. Secret; Sensitive. Sent for information; outside system. All brackets are in the original except those indicating text that remains classified. The conversation took place in Kissinger's office.

Dr. Kissinger said that, very honestly, he had been afraid this would happen.

Dr. Ghorbal said that he would not report this conversation formally and that if there were anything Dr. Kissinger wanted to say it could be reported orally when Ghorbal returned to Cairo. Dr. Kissinger's conversation with the Foreign Minister Mahmoud Riad in New York[2] had never been reported.

Dr. Kissinger said that the reason negotiations conducted from the White House have been effective is that we have never promised anything we could not deliver. We have never really had a good dialogue with Egypt about what is "do-able" and in what time frame.

Dr. Ghorbal said that he felt that Cairo needs now more than a general promise that the US will try again "after elections." Cairo's patience has been "eaten up." In fact, Dr. Ghorbal felt that Cairo had shown more patience since May than he had expected. He said he would like to take to President Sadat and to Hafez Ismail some indication of what they can hope for.

Dr. Kissinger said he would like to start a dialogue with someone on the Egyptian side "who can keep a secret." He said he frankly had not believed that the road we were on would work. On the one hand, Egypt has asked for too much too soon. On the other hand, the US has "fudged up the differences" between Israel's position and Egypt's to make it seem as if they were smaller than they actually were. He said this had all worked to Israel's advantage—not that anyone here tried to make it turn out that way, but it has been the objective consequence of what we have done that the status quo has been continued, and that is what Israel has hoped for.

Dr. Kissinger reiterated that in principle we are prepared to establish a high-level contact. Out of that we would hope to crystallize some position. This would, however, have to be kept secret—even from our own people.

Dr. Ghorbal [1½ *lines not declassified*].

Dr. Kissinger, [2 *lines not declassified*].

Dr. Ghorbal asked what kind of meetings Dr. Kissinger envisioned. Would it just be Dr. Kissinger and one other to start and where might they be?

Dr. Kissinger said that the negotiations would be conducted "under my supervision." He might be in Europe sometime for Vietnam talks, although he usually makes those trips in secrecy. He might be in

---

[2] Kissinger met with Riad on October 7, 1971, at David Rockefeller's residence in New York City. A memorandum of conversation is ibid., Box 134, Country Files, Middle East.

Europe for a few days in September for the Olympics. Or talks could take place in New York.

Dr. Ghorbal said he would like to come to the substance of the issue. He recognized that Dr. Kissinger could not promise anything at this point. "But what can you give me at this stage?" We had the Rogers proposal two years ago. Where are we in this regard? Where are we on such issues as demilitarized zones, Sharm al Sheikh, Gaza? He asked how Dr. Kissinger could help him to make his case in Cairo.

Dr. Kissinger said that he did not want now to make a concrete proposal The US stands very "generally behind" the Rogers Plan. The problem is, in his view, that we have to start Israel moving. From some points of view making maximum demands plays into Israel's hands because Israel finds it easier to turn those aside.

Dr. Kissinger continued that he could see how the Israeli logic might work: The Israelis could argue that Egypt alone cannot defeat Israel and that the US and USSR will not fight over the Middle East. Therefore, they could justify going on with the status quo rejecting all demands that they could find any reason to reject. If, on the other hand, tensions get too bad, the Israelis can play on the anti-Communist line to get US support.

Dr. Kissinger said that he knew Dr. Ghorbal was familiar with Israel's views on Sharm al Sheikh. "Just thinking out loud," Dr. Kissinger said he felt that it might be possible to work out some formula for a period of time which could meet Israel's security concerns. He said he personally could not be persuaded that Sharm al Sheikh is as essential to maintaining access to the Gulf of Aqaba as the Israelis feel. The strategic question is one problem, but the symbolic problem is another. If we talked informally, we could deal with problems of that kind and seek answers.

Dr. Kissinger said that we do not support the "Israeli possession of the Sinai." What we need is a formula to move Israel back. The US is willing to press Israel back but not to dissociate itself to the extent that it would encourage an attack on Israel.

Dr. Kissinger continued that we have "gone through the Bergus exercise"[3] and "drawn lines on a map until we are sick of it." Two years ago he said he favored an interim settlement if it could be done quickly and with modest terms. He felt that if too much were tried, the withdrawal would be too much for Israel and too little for the Arabs. But if a very small withdrawal had been agreed then Israel would have begun moving and yet the Arabs would have been able to demonstrate that the small Israeli withdrawal was obviously not a final settlement.

---

[3] See Document 238.

Dr. Ghorbal said that it is, frankly, difficult to sell this point of view in Cairo.

Dr. Kissinger said that the important thing is that Israel should give the Sinai back. The US is accused of "balance of power politics" and that is a lot of nonsense. We realize that Egypt is a big country and an important country in the Middle East. We have no conceivable interest in being in a permanent state of estrangement from Egypt. If we can normalize relations with Peking, why can we not do so with Cairo? We have gone against the China lobby in the United States and we will go against "other lobbies" provided we can establish a framework where we both know what we are doing.

Dr. Ghorbal said he would convey this to Hafez Ismail. He jokingly said that he referred to him as Hafez Kissinger.

Dr. Kissinger said with a smile that he had often been referred to as "the American Ismail."

Dr. Ghorbal said that he wanted to explain the apprehension that exists in Cairo that Israel will try to make permanent whatever line is drawn on a map short of a complete withdrawal.

Dr. Kissinger said that he felt that the mistake that had been made was to get into the issue of drawing partial withdrawal lines on a map. What has to be done is for us to sit down and to talk about where we want to come out in the end. Otherwise, we will never get off dead center. The Israelis are "fanatics," and "you are strong minded too." This is a tough problem, and any solution is extremely difficult.

Dr. Ghorbal said that Cairo is apprehensive about the "last mile." That is the most difficult.

Dr. Kissinger agreed. He said the reason he is reluctant to present a final proposal is that he felt we needed to talk about some sort of interim arrangements perhaps. Just speaking hypothetically, he wondered whether we could agree on a final line that would define sovereignty but find some way to provide for Israeli military control for some interim period—"civil bases" or some other such arrangement. The US would be willing to bring some pressure on Israel—but it would have to be pressure that is short of causing a war.

Dr. Kissinger continued that we cannot have an interest in having Egyptian leaders for the next fifty years blaming the US for a settlement that Egypt could not live with. He said he would rather live with the present situation than to have to live with that kind of solution.

Dr. Kissinger went on saying that we have not had an exchange at "our level"—meaning at the level of the two presidencies. Maybe there is nothing at all that can be done. But on our side, we see Egypt as a permanent and important factor in the Middle East. We recognize that there have been many faults on our side. Dr. Ghorbal could convey this in Cairo.

Dr. Ghorbal replied that Cairo does not understand the notion that there have not been high-level exchanges. After all, Secretary Rogers was in Cairo and saw President Sadat.[4]

Dr. Kissinger said that Dr. Ghorbal could tell Cairo—he has been in Washington long enough to observe this—that the question is not a question of whether the level is high or low but that one has to observe where the agreements that have been worked out in this Administration have been negotiated. The things that have been worked out in this Administration have not been negotiated in that channel.

Dr. Kissinger concluded that we would have to wait until after the election for any significant developments, but a meeting could take place before. He again cautioned Dr. Ghorbal that it would be of the utmost importance to maintain the secrecy of any such exchanges.

They parted with an exchange of best wishes.

Harold H. Saunders[5]

---

[4] See Document 227.
[5] Saunders initialed "H.S." above his typed signature.

---

297. Memorandum From the President's Assistant for National Security Affairs (Kissinger) to President Nixon[1]

Washington, June 30, 1972.

SUBJECT

Israeli-Jordanian Settlement

We have received covertly from the political advisor to King Hussein, Zaid al Rifai, a paper which outlines the King's view of the shape of a final peace settlement between Jordan and Israel. Rifai indicates that the paper represents the maximum concessions they believe are

---

[1] Source: Library of Congress, Manuscript Division, Kissinger Papers, Box TS–31, Jordan, Chronological File. Top Secret; Sensitive. Sent for action. A stamped notation on the memo indicates the President saw it.

possible. Our comments are solicited on ways they might improve their position "within the realm of the possible." (Tab A)[2]

The Jordanians believe that if there is to be a movement toward a solution with the assistance of the United States at the highest level, they are willing to go "a little beyond the Rogers proposals."

Although the Jordanians are not willing to make territorial concessions, they are prepared to sign a peace treaty with the Israelis embodying necessary guarantees, including a determination of ways to change the June 4, 1967 demarcation line into a permanent boundary. They will accept rectifications of the line, on a reciprocal basis, in order to make it a permanent boundary. Their position with regard to Guarantees, Jerusalem, Gaza and Refugees has the following basic elements:

—*Guarantees.* The guarantees would include total demilitarization of the West Bank, no outside Arab Armed Forces stationed on Jordanian soil, a peace treaty, eventual establishment of normal relations, participation in joint development projects, and agreements on a procedure for Israelis to reside inside Jordanian territory near Jewish religious shrines.

—*Jerusalem.* Jerusalem would be an open city under dual sovereignty of Israel and Jordan, with complete freedom of movement within the city. The Israelis could occupy the Jewish quarter of the old city in return for one of the Arab quarters in the Israeli sector.

—*Gaza.* Gaza would become part of the Palestine region of the United Arab Kingdom (name for a new Jordan with two autonomous divisions—Palestine and Jordan), with a corridor linking Gaza to the Palestinian region. This would put the majority of the Palestinians in the area under one umbrella.

—*Refugees.* Refugees who fled the West Bank in 1967 could return after any peace treaty. Other refugees would be given the right of repatriation or be compensated. The Jordanians believe that no more than ten percent would choose to live in Israel; the remainder, after proper financial compensation, would be settled in Jordan. With necessary funds the Jordanians are prepared to commence a resettlement of refugees in the East Bank immediately.

The Jordanian position may provide a possibility for movement toward a settlement. I have sent a noncommital reply to Rifai, but it might be worthwhile to explore this in greater detail with a meeting this summer.

---

[2] Not printed.

Recommendation

That you approve my arranging a meeting with Rifai to further examine this initiative.[3] (Meeting will be between Kissinger and Rifai.)

---

[3] Nixon checked the option indicating his approval for a meeting between Kissinger and Rifai. On July 27, Haig forwarded a July 15 letter to Kissinger from Rifai on the most recent secret meeting between Jordan and Israel, which occurred on June 29. Haig wrote: "He [Rifai] is exceedingly gloomy about Israeli inflexibility. He is convinced that: 1) Israel will retain most of the territories, even at the price of perpetual war; 2) Only the U.S. can exert sufficient weight to change Israel's position; 3) Israel not only accepts the inevitability of a new war but is preparing for one, as early as the end of this year; 4) Jordan will not participate in a new war as long as there is any hope of settlement." (National Archives, Nixon Presidential Materials, NSC Files, Box 137, Kissinger Office Files, Country Files, Middle East)

---

298. Telegram From the Department of State to the Interests Section in Egypt[1]

Washington, July 19, 1972, 2253Z.

130867. Subject: Your Meeting with Ghaleb. Ref: Cairo 2040.[2]

1. It is very firm policy view here that USG should not repeat not inject itself in any way into current developments in Egyptian-Soviet relations. In your meeting with Ghaleb you should carefully avoid indicating, even in indirect way you propose reftel, any curiosity about

---

[1] Source: National Archives, Nixon Presidential Materials, NSC Files, Box 658, Country Files, Middle East, Middle East Nodis/Cedar/Plus, Vol. V. Secret; Immediate; Nodis; Cedar Double Plus. Drafted by G. Norman Anderson (NEA/EGY), cleared by Rogers (in substance) and Davies, and approved by Atherton.

[2] In telegram 2040 from Cairo, July 19, Greene informed the Department that Sadat's announcement one day earlier of the expulsion of all Soviet military advisers and experts from Egypt had "substantially" changed the context in which his previously scheduled meeting with Ghaleb would occur. Greene wrote: "All these things considered, my (luckily) postponed meeting with Ghaleb takes on a new perspective and could be markedly significant in determining what happens in next few weeks." He then asked for authorization to, among other things: 1) obtain clarification on the details of the Soviet military withdrawal from Egypt; 2) state that the U.S. Government received Sadat's message to Nixon "with particular interest"; and 3) mention that the U.S. Government had received Saudi Prince Sultan's account of his talk with Sadat. (Ibid.) On July 18, Sadat announced in a speech before the Central Committee of the Arab Socialist Union that he had ordered all Soviet "military advisers and experts" out of Egypt and that all Soviet bases and equipment would be placed under Egyptian control. He did not make clear, however, if the Soviet combat personnel manning the missile emplacements or the Soviet pilots would also be withdrawn. (*New York Times*, July 19, 1972, p. 1)

these developments.³ It follows, therefore, that you should not proceed along lines suggested para 3 reftel. Re para 3(D), You should make no reference at this time to our having received report of Prince Sultan's discussions with President Sadat. While we of course have telegraphic account in Jidda's 2385⁴ of highlights of these discussions, Saudi Ambassador has not yet presented Sultan's report formally and has requested appointment with Secretary in next few days to do so. Furthermore, Jidda's 2385 indicates Sadat has impression from Sultan that USG contemplates early new initiative on Middle East, and we do not want in any way to feed this idea.

2. In making presentation authorized in State 125234,⁵ you should limit yourself to talking points in paras 6–9, eliminating paras 10, 11 and, as you have recommended, para 12. You should also make clear to Ghaleb that points you are making on proximity talks per State 125234 as modified above are based on instructions received week ago, to avoid any risk that they will somehow be interpreted as reaction to current developments in Soviet-Egyptian relations.

3. Re para 3(C) reftel, you should limit yourself at this point to expressing thanks for President Sadat's reply of July 17⁶ and to informing Ghaleb it has been passed to President Nixon.

---

³ In a telephone conversation with Dobrynin on the morning of July 20, Kissinger said: "We don't really know what the hell is going on in Egypt, and we want you to know that, as far as we're concerned, our discussions remain unimpaired. We're not going to play little games there. We have given the strictest orders to our diplomats to stay the hell out of that discussion and not to make any approaches or anything else." (Transcript of a telephone conversation between Kissinger and Dobrynin, July 20, 9:45 a.m.; National Archives, Nixon Presidential Materials, NSC Files, Henry Kissinger Telephone Conversation Transcripts, Box 15, Chronological File)

⁴ Not found.

⁵ In telegram 125234 to Cairo, July 12, the Department instructed Greene to inform Ismail that: 1) U.S. officials conveyed Egypt's negative reply to Rogers's February proposal to Israel, including an account of comments that Ismail made when he presented Egypt's reply (see Document 278); 2) the United States did not think "this is best course for Egypt, but it is Egypt's decision to make"; and 3) Israel had not yet given U.S. officials a reaction to Egypt's reply. (National Archives, Nixon Presidential Materials, NSC Files, Box 658, Country Files, Middle East, Middle East Nodis/Cedar/Plus, Vol. V) Greene's meeting with Ghaleb occurred on the morning of July 20, during which the Egyptian Foreign Minister asked five questions designed to determine how the United States planned to approach the Arab-Israeli dispute in the coming months. The questions concerned: 1) proximity talks for an interim agreement; 2) further U.S.-Soviet discussions; 3) whether Four-Power discussions would be reactivated; 4) how the Jarring Mission would be supported; and 5) what alternatives to what had already been discussed would be considered. They also discussed Sadat's decision to terminate the Soviet military advisory presence in Egypt and the resulting state of Egyptian-Soviet relations. (Telegram 2054 from Cairo, July 20; ibid., Box 638, Country Files, Middle East, Arab Republic of Egypt (UAR), Vol. VIII)

⁶ Sadat's July 17 message to Nixon, contained in telegram 2029 from Cairo, July 18, addressed the President's June 26 oral message to him concerning the Moscow Summit and expressed his appreciation for Nixon's "initiative" to keep him informed about the summit's results. Sadat also commented broadly on the importance of the United States

4. *FYI:* We agree with your assessment that we are in new situation, which will require our keeping antennae finely tuned. Before we begin to draw firm conclusions, we will also be waiting to see what sort of Soviet presence in fact remains in Egypt following implementation of Sadat's decision. Another major factor will be how Egypt decides to treat USG under new circumstances. President Sadat's speech July 24[7] may provide clue in this regard. *End FYI.*

5. Exempt from general declassification schedule of Executive Order 11652.

Rogers

---

and the Soviet Union reaching out to each other to "strengthen cooperation between them" and "for the sake of world peace and the peoples of the world as a whole." (Ibid., Box 763, Presidential Correspondence 1969–1974, UAR President Anwar Sadat, Vol. 3) The Interests Section conveyed Nixon's June 26 oral message to Sadat regarding the Moscow Summit on June 27. (Telegram 1857 from Cairo, June 28; ibid., Box 638, Country Files, Middle East, Egypt, Vol. VIII)

[7] That day, Sadat delivered a 4-hour speech before the Central Committee of the Arab Socialist Union, during which he asserted Egypt's independence from both the Soviet Union and the United States. He declared that he would not steer Egypt toward the United States, which he claimed some had suggested he do, nor would he allow a total rift between Egypt and the Soviet Union to develop. (*New York Times*, July 25, 1972, p 1) In March, the Central Intelligence Agency's Directorate of Intelligence produced a 10-page memorandum entitled "Soviet-Egyptian Relations: An Uneasy Alliance," which concluded: "Egypt is anxious to reduce its dependence upon the Soviet Union, but cannot effectively do so until the Arab-Israeli impasse is resolved. In the meantime, the tenet that 'the enemy of my enemy is my friend' will prevail, and the state of relations between Egypt and the Soviet Union will continue on the uneasy base achieved after the debacle of 1967." (Central Intelligence Agency, OCI Files, Job 79T00832A)

299. Memorandum From Director of Central Intelligence Helms to the President's Assistant for National Security Affairs (Kissinger)[1]

Washington, July 24, 1972.

SUBJECT

Request [1 line not declassified] for Initial Top-Level United States Government Reaction to Egyptian Termination of the Soviet Military Advisory Program

1. The following development has occurred since [2 lines not declassified] 13 July 1972 the thoughts of Egyptian President Anwar Sadat regarding the possibility of secret talks between Egypt and the United States, as outlined in my memorandum dated 18 July 1972.[2]

2. During a 19 July 1972 meeting [2 lines not declassified] asserted that President Sadat's decision to terminate the Soviet military advisory program has created a new opportunity for the USG. [name not declassified] expressed the view that it is of great importance to both his government and to the United States Government that the latter seize this opportunity and make the most of it. [name not declassified] urged that the United States Government move—and with minimal delay—to develop a concrete plan for future action for submission to President Sadat on how to progress towards a peaceful settlement of the Middle East problem. As an opening step [3½ lines not declassified] if I could secure and forward via Agency channels as soon as possible an initial top-level United States Government reaction to the Egyptians' termination of the Soviet military advisory program. [name not declassified] said that he would like the United States Government's reaction as soon as possible and expressed the hope that we would be able to reply by 1 August 1972.

3. [less than 1 line not declassified] asked, as his purely personal question, whether the recent Egyptian decision to terminate the Soviet military advisory program might have any effect on President Sadat's apparently negative position, as set forth in my memorandum dated 18 July 1972, on the possibility of an early, secret, high-level contact between our two governments. [name not declassified] gave as his opinion that high-level contact should be made only in the event that the United States Government is prepared to offer new ideas and some concrete plan.

---

[1] Source: National Archives, Nixon Presidential Materials, NSC Files, Kissinger Office Files, Box 131, Country Files, Middle East. Secret; Sensitive. All brackets are in the original except those indicating text that remains classified.

[2] Not found.

4. [3½ lines not declassified] indicating that the Egyptians remain very much interested in the interim solution for the reopening of the Suez Canal, a partial Israeli withdrawal from the Canal, and an international presence at Sharm As-Shaykh.

5. I would appreciate your advising me what kind of response you prefer that [less than 1 line not declassified] convey to [name not declassified] in this connection.[3]

6. The Department of State has not been informed of this exchange.

Richard Helms[4]

---

[3] See footnote 4, Document 305.
[4] Helms signed "Dick" above his typed signature.

---

300. Conversation Between President Nixon and the President's Assistant for National Security Affairs (Kissinger)[1]

Washington, July 25, 1972, 9:55–10:35 a.m.

Nixon: What's your analysis of the Sadat thing?[2] I read the—
Kissinger: I wanted to talk to you about it. Of course, I—
Nixon: I don't what the hell it was.
Kissinger: It's not concrete. Well first, I'll give you my analysis and then I have a concrete operational proposal I want to give you.
Nixon: Yeah. Yeah.
Kissinger: First of all, I think the guy is highly unstable.
Nixon: Right.
Kissinger: You cannot talk of a coherent long-range strategy.
Nixon: Right. Right.
Kissinger: There could be three basic motivations. One is, it's a blackmail move against the Russians, that he's kicking out some of them—

---

[1] Source: National Archives, Nixon Presidential Materials, White House Tapes, Oval Office, Conversation No. 752–6 (2). No classification marking. The editors transcribed the portion of the tape recording printed here specifically for this volume. Brackets indicate portions of the original recording that remain classified, were omitted by the editors, or were unclear.
[2] See footnote 2, Document 298.

Nixon: Right.

Kissinger: Keeping another batch of them there in order to blackmail them into giving him a long-range offensive weapons and needed supplies. Incidentally, one of the better negotiations we've conducted is the one between this building and the Russians for the last eight months, maneuvering them into a restraint position on the Middle East.

Nixon: Yeah.

Kissinger: Because that is what's adding the fire. The one that started with your talk with Gromyko.[3]

Nixon: Yeah.

Kissinger: Because that's what Sadat is screaming about. He made a speech yesterday saying the Russians were too cautious.[4]

Nixon: I saw that, yeah, blackmail the Russians.

Kissinger: The second possibility is that he wants to make a move towards us.

Nixon: Yeah.

Kissinger: Being dissatisfied with the Russians. And if you remember when we talked about it two years ago when you went on television with I think it was Howard K. Smith—[5]

Nixon: Oh, yeah.

Kissinger: From Los Angeles. We were saying that if the Egyptians get dissatisfied enough with the inability of the Russians to produce something they will be forced to move to us. And that that is the time to brutalize the Israelis. We never said that publicly. The third possibility—and the most worrisome one—is that he is getting rid of the Russians—so that he can jump the Israelis and force the Russians into supporting him.

Nixon: That's what worries me.

Kissinger: That's the one that worries me most. Now—

Nixon: [unclear] need to do something, and then—

Kissinger: The Israelis probably figure we have elections. They might well come to terms with clobbering the bejeezus out of the Egyptians. Now operationally—

Nixon: What's arguing with him about all that?

---

[3] See Document 252.

[4] For Sadat's July 24 speech, see: Henry Tanner, "Egyptian Asserts Moscow Caution Caused Ousters," *New York Times*, July 25, p. 1, and "Excerpts From President Sadat's Speech in Cairo Criticizing Policies of the U.S.," ibid., p. 10.

[5] See footnote 3, Document 134.

Kissinger: He stops all three of them really. He's trying to get offensive weapons. He has [*3 seconds not declassified*] approached Dick Helms[6] and asked us to make a specific proposal. And thirdly he's started harassing Israeli airplanes with SAM batteries from his side. Now, what I would like to do, and I wanted to talk to you about it today—in fact, I was talking to Helms this morning about these messages.

Nixon: Right.

Kissinger: First, I'm going to call in Rabin and tell him we've kept them afloat, we've been the best friend they've ever had, we've saved them from being brutalized.

Nixon: Right.

Kissinger: But they sunk the Egyptians during this campaign.

Nixon: That's right.

Kissinger: [unclear]

Nixon: That's right.

Kissinger: And they must have no illusions.

Nixon: Let me say, I would say that, even though it might jeopardize the elections, I'm not going to fool around.

Kissinger: Exactly.

Nixon: He's got to know that.

Kissinger: And I will tell Mr. Rabin this week. Two, I think we should return the following answer to the Egyptians. We should say, "Look, you've had three years of proposals. You want to deal with the White House, we don't operate that way. The way we like to operate is to have an understanding in principle first of what they are trying to accomplish, to lay out a game plan, and then we can then come up with some proposal. Therefore if you want to talk to us send somebody over late September/early October." Say honestly we can do nothing before the elections. Because we can't, Mr. President. If we made a big proposal on the Middle East, the Jewish community will go up in—

Nixon: Oh, the hell with them. I'm not going to touch the Middle East.

Kissinger: In fact, if we made the proposal now the Russians would consider it an anti-Russian move too.

Nixon: That's correct.

Kissinger: So what I think we should do is to have the—is to propose to the Egyptians that they send my counterpart over here at the

---

[6] See Document 299.

end of September/early October, and then work out a game plan with them—maybe at Camp David or someplace quiet.

Nixon: Good. Good.

Kissinger: That keeps them happy [and] keeps the Russians quiet.

Nixon: Yeah. All right, you'll talk to Rabin and have them send that over. And the other thing is you naturally have got to talk to Dobrynin cold turkey on this too, for him. I don't know what the hell Dobrynin—

Kissinger: Well, I have given Dobrynin an assurance that we would not take advantage of the situation. That we would not move unilaterally.[7]

Nixon: What's he think of it? Or does he—

Kissinger: Well, he hasn't told me. Well, we got sort of a stupid letter from Brezhnev in which Brezhnev points out that they thought up this idea of their own withdrawal[8]—

Nixon: Yeah.

Kissinger: —of having confidence in you. It's a dumb statement and now you owe them something.

Nixon: Yeah. Yeah.

Kissinger: Now that's sort of a stupid thing for them to say because it's so transparent. But what I think we should do is to answer that letter to Brezhnev in a very warm way.

Nixon: Good. Good. Do that.

[Omitted here is conversation unrelated to the Middle East.]

---

[7] During a meeting with Dobrynin the afternoon of July 20, Kissinger told the Soviet Ambassador: "We were not aware of these events beforehand. We had not yet fully understood their significance. Nor did we know the extent of Soviet withdrawal. In any event, I wanted Dobrynin to know that the President had issued the strictest orders that there would be no U.S. initiatives toward Cairo and that we would not try to gain unilateral advantages." The memorandum of conversation is printed in *Foreign Relations, 1969–1976*, volume XV, Soviet Union, June 1972–August 1974, Document 16.

[8] Dobrynin gave Kissinger the letter at their July 20 meeting. Brezhnev wrote: "As a result of the exchange of views between the Egyptian leadership and ourselves it was decided to withdraw part of our military personnel from Egypt. In determining our position in this question we proceeded, on the one hand, from the fact that the contingent now being withdrawn by us, has in the main, fulfilled its functions. On the other hand, I will tell you frankly, we acted with account of the exchange of views which took place between us while discussing the entire range of problems of the Middle East settlement. It seems to me that this will help dispel doubts which may have been there as to how we intend to solve the question of our military personnel in Egypt in case of settlement of the Middle East problem. We believe that you will find the opportunity to use this step for bringing your appropriate influence on the leaders of Israel." (National Archives, Nixon Presidential Materials, NSC Files, Kissinger Office Files, Box 130, Country Files, Middle East, Middle East—Sensitive (RN), 1971–1974)

301. Letter From President Nixon to Soviet General Secretary Brezhnev[1]

Washington, July 27, 1972.

Dear Mr. General Secretary:

I am most grateful for your letter of July 20 sending me your thoughts on the recent events in Egypt.[2] These events impose on us the special obligation to conduct our relations in conformity with the principles of the Moscow declaration and the relationship that has developed between us.

As Dr. Kissinger has already informed Ambassador Dobrynin on my behalf,[3] the United States had no advance knowledge of the recent events in Egypt. The fundamental principle which has guided and will guide American policy in this situation is that an effort by either of us, in the Middle East or elsewhere, to gain unilateral advantage at the expense of the other is incompatible with our broader mutual objectives and mutual responsibility. Experience shows that pursuit of such marginal advantages is futile as well as dangerous. The fundamental improvement in the US-Soviet relationship, to which my Administration is unalterably committed, can be maintained only on the basis of equality and respect for the legitimate security and political interests of both.

Mischievous speculation looking for disruption of our relationship is to be anticipated in such a situation as this. But you and I did not sign the Basic Principles of US-Soviet Relations[4] in order to repudiate them and all that they represent in the first real test of their application.

On the Middle East question specifically, Dr. Kissinger has also assured your Ambassador, at my behest, that nothing that has occurred affects the general principles discussed between your Foreign Minister and Dr. Kissinger to promote a just overall settlement cooperatively. The US will take no unilateral actions in the Middle East. Elaboration of these basic understandings will be carried forward on the schedule agreed upon by the US side. There has not been and will not be any breach on our side of the strictest confidentiality of the US-Soviet exchanges.

---

[1] Source: National Archives, Nixon Presidential Materials, NSC Files, Kissinger Office Files, Box 130, Country Files, Middle East. No classification marking. Written in an unknown hand in the upper right-hand corner of the page is the note: "Handed by K to D[obrynin] 5:45 pm, 7/27/72."

[2] See footnote 8, Document 300.

[3] See footnote 7, Document 300.

[4] Nixon and Brezhnev signed the Basic Principles on May 29 at the Moscow Summit; for the text, see *Public Papers: Nixon, 1972*, pp. 633–635.

In my view, the recent events only dramatize the dangerous volatility of the Middle East, which underscores the urgent US and Soviet interest in helping to resolve the perennial crisis. This is clearly in the interest of peace and in the interest of furthering and safeguarding the great progress we have achieved in US-Soviet relations.[5]

Sincerely,

Richard Nixon

[5] Brezhnev's response was handed to Kissinger on August 11 by Dobrynin; see *Foreign Relations, 1969–1976*, volume XV, Soviet Union, June 1972–August 1974, Document 25.

302. Telegram From the Department of State to the Interests Section in Egypt[1]

Washington, July 31, 1972, 1801Z.

137986. For Greene from Secretary. Subject: Response to Ghalib's Five Questions. Ref: Cairo 2054.[2]

1. You should seek appointment with FonMin Ghalib for purpose of responding to his "five questions" (reftel).

2. *FYI:* We wish to avoid giving Egyptians impression we are inclined to rush in with new diplomatic initiative. Given continued divergence of views between parties directly concerned, we see no evidence that mechanisms such as Four Powers, US-Soviet talks, or four or five power statements would work any better now than before, and we do not favor any such moves. While we are not optimistic re Jarring reactivation, we are continuing to take line that we would welcome any progress he could achieve we believe "proximity talks" on interim Canal agreement continue to offer most practical approach. In this latter connection, Israel wants us to continue to stress importance of in-

[1] Source: National Archives, Nixon Presidential Materials, NSC Files, Box 658, Country Files, Middle East, Middle East Nodis/Cedar/Plus, Vol. V. Secret; Priority; Nodis; Cedar Double Plus. Drafted by Anderson; cleared by Kissinger, Sisco, and Atherton; and approved by Rogers.

[2] See footnote 5, Document 298.

terim Canal talks under US aegis paralleling emphasis given to this in PM Meir's speeches.[3] *End FYI.*

3. Begin talking points:

(A) We appreciate FonMin Ghalib's frank comments conveyed at your last meeting on July 20 on his view that the situation has acquired new momentum. We also understand GOE's particular interest in knowing the attitude of USG regarding the coming period. We have studied FonMin's questions, and wish to deal with them in a spirit of sincerity and desire for a productive exchange of opinion.

(B) We especially wish to stress one fundamental aspect of US policy on the question of peace in the Middle East. We do not believe that a solution of the conflict can be devised by external parties. The experience we have acquired over the past several years has only reinforced this view, along with our further belief that progress toward a settlement can only be made through a genuine negotiating process, in which the parties directly involved in this dispute take an active diplomatic role in coping with their differences. We are not suggesting that talks at outset start face to face, but as Secretary has recently noted in public statements, ME is only area where meaningful negotiations not in train. *FYI* (you should draw as appropriate on what Secretary has said in this regard, pointing to talks on such problems as Vietnam, Indo-Pak, Berlin, etc).

(C) We do not claim that the concept of "proximity talks" without preconditions on an interim Suez Canal agreement is the only way to begin negotiations towards a final settlement but of proposals now on table we feel this most feasible. We are not pressing the GOE on "proximity talks" but hope that in the fullness of time such a concept will be recognized as a way to begin moving along the difficult road to peace. We remain available, as we have repeatedly stated, to play a role in this process if Egypt desires us to do so. As Egypt knows, Israel accepted the proposal of proximity talks without preconditions last February.[4] In this connection, we know one of Egypt's principal concerns has been that any interim agreement not become final settlement. We hope PM Meir's stress in her speech that such an interim agreement would be temporary has been noted in Cairo.

(D) We want to dispel the notion that resolution of the Middle East conflict is of greater importance to the United States than it is to the parties directly involved. We do not agree that our position on need for negotiations favors one side against the other. We see Egypt's bar-

---

[3] For the text of Meir's July 26 speech to the Knesset, see *Israel's Foreign Policy: Historical Documents*, volumes 1–2: 1947–1974, Chapter XII, The War of Attrition and the Cease Fire, Document 38.

[4] See Document 276.

gaining position as one of equality. Egypt can offer Israel what it most wants: Long-term security and acceptance as a Middle Eastern state. We do not view entering negotiations as a "concession" on the part of Egypt. We would not claim that negotiations would be painless. Both sides would have to expect to make difficult decisions. We are speaking frankly because we do not wish to be thought to be attempting to mislead any of the parties.

(E) We note Jarring plans shortly to resume his activity. As we have previously informed GOE, if Jarring can bridge the fundamental chasm that exists between the parties, we would welcome such a success. We see no need for UN resolutions or four or five power declarations at this point in support of Jarring Mission. As Egypt knows, impasse presently exists—with Egypt insisting that mandate for Jarring include his February 1971 memo and GA resolution of December 1971[5] whereas Israel insists that Jarring's mandate rests solely on SC Resolution 242. We doubt this chasm can be bridged at this time, and for this reason feel step-by-step approach envisaged on an interim Suez Canal agreement is most pragmatic way to proceed.

(F) Our previous experience with US-Soviet talks and discussions within the Four Power framework does not lead us to believe that these forums can contribute to starting up negotiations between the parties under present circumstances. We wish again to emphasize that, in our view, negotiations between the parties are the key to a settlement.

(G) Secretary Rogers will be in NY for UNGA and looks forward to meeting FonMin Ghalib at that time and discussing Middle East situation with him.[6]

Irwin

---

[5] See, respectively, footnote 2, Document 205 and footnote 4, Document 270.

[6] Greene met with Ghaleb on August 3, presenting the Department's response to his five questions, as instructed. Ghaleb asked him if his presentation meant that the United States was "moving away from SC Resolution 242," to which Greene responded that "it did not mean that at all." Finally, the Egyptian Foreign Minister commented that a major impediment to an agreement between Egypt and Israel was their "widely different" conceptions of peace. (Telegram 2170 from Cairo, August 4; National Archives, Nixon Presidential Materials, NSC Files, Box 658, Country Files, Middle East, Middle East Nodis/Cedar/Plus, Vol. V)

303. Conversation Between President Nixon and the President's Assistant for National Security Affairs (Kissinger)[1]

Washington, August 2, 1972.

[Omitted here is conversation unrelated to the Middle East.]

Kissinger: Actually, you know, in the Middle East, our negotiations—we can claim 90 percent of the credit. If we had done what State did, the Russians would still be in Egypt. The way they conducted these negotiations created so much frustration in Egypt. I mean, we've now got to move after the election. Incidentally, Sadat sent you a message.[2] I sent him a message, as I told you last week, that I'd be prepared to meet a representative of his [in] early October to—he wanted a private contact with us.[3] I said early October is the earliest. He sent you a message saying he wants you to know he wants you to be re-elected.

Nixon: Hmm.

Kissinger: [laughs] I said [unclear] almost unanimous that he understands why you say early October.

Nixon: Well, our main game there is the Russians, as I told you.

Kissinger: Well, the way I would visualize it is if we could get a deal with the Egyptians, then we can make the same deal with the Russians, and then everybody will be happy.

Nixon: Well, what about the Israelis? [unclear]—

Kissinger: You'll have to brutalize the Israelis.

Nixon: That has to be done in any event.

Kissinger: Mr. President—

Nixon: It's in their own best interests.

Kissinger: —if we're ever going to screw the Israelis—it's not even screwing them—if we're ever going to brutalize them—

Nixon: We're doing what's best for them.

Kissinger: I think the first half of next year is the time to do it. Get it done. Then, by the '76, there'll be a new card.

---

[1] Source: National Archives, Nixon Presidential Materials, White House Tapes, Oval Office, Conversation No. 759–5. No classification marking. According to the President's Daily Diary, Nixon and Kissinger met from 10:34 to 11:47 a.m. (Ibid., White House Central Files) The editors transcribed the portion of the tape recording printed here specifically for this volume. Brackets indicate unclear portions of the original recording or those omitted by the editors except "[in]" and "[laughs]", added for clarity.

[2] See Document 299.

[3] See footnote 4, Document 305.

Nixon: The main thing is to do it for the reason that our interests vis-à-vis the Soviet Union must override everything else in the world today.

Kissinger: My objection to Rogers wasn't that we were brutalizing the Israelis; it's that we were cementing the Russians into the Middle East—

Nixon: That's right.

Kissinger: —and that they were likely to produce a war. If you can pull off—if the Egyptians think that after moving to you that things got fluid—

Nixon: Yeah?

Kissinger: —while when they went to the Russians it didn't work, you have restored the American position among the Arabs. You've— the Israelis trust you enough to know that they get—and we can get them a better deal, I believe, than what Rogers offered them. Not as good as they want, but better than what they were offered two years ago.

Nixon: That's right.

Kissinger: So, while the Israelis won't be happy—

Nixon: That's right—

Kissinger: And this is why we shouldn't make too many moves before November, but after that we should—

[unclear exchange]

[Omitted here is conversation unrelated to the Middle East.]

304. **Telegram From the Department of State to the Interests Section in Egypt**[1]

Washington, August 8, 1972, 1454Z.

143197. Ref: Cairo 2170.[2]

1. Re para 8 reftel, you are correct in assuming that you should not rpt not keep GOE informed of our conversations with Israeli officials

---

[1] Source: National Archives, Nixon Presidential Materials, NSC Files, Box 658, Country Files, Middle East, Middle East Nodis/Cedar/Plus, Vol. V. Secret; Nodis; Cedar Double Plus. Drafted by Sterner and approved by Sisco.

[2] See footnote 6, Document 302.

unless explicitly instructed to do so. Obviously relationship between USG and Israel on one hand, and between USG and Egypt on other, are different requiring different levels of confidence in dealing with these two governments. As to our briefing of Israelis about our exchanges with Egyptians, we carry this out in manner to carefully protect sources or other areas of confidence. We are also aware of desirability of being frank with Egyptians when we can and have sought in the past to keep them informed. We will continue to follow this practice.

2. Exempt from general declassification schedule of Executive Order 11652.

Rogers

305. Memorandum From the President's Assistant for National Security Affairs (Kissinger) to President Nixon[1]

Washington, August 14, 1972.

SUBJECT

Our Strategy Towards Egypt

On my earlier memorandum on the Egyptian expulsion of the Soviets (Tab A)[2] you noted the reports that the Egyptians do not want to wait until the November elections for the US to seize this "new opportunity."

As you know, in late July the Egyptians approached us and sought to open a confidential channel to the White House via Director Helms [*less than 1 line not declassified*].[3] They wanted "new proposals" from us. We agreed to open the channel and agreed in principle to confidential

---

[1] Source: National Archives, Nixon Presidential Materials, NSC Files, Kissinger Office Files, Box 131, Country Files, Middle East. Top Secret; Sensitive; Exclusively Eyes Only. Sent for information. A stamped notation on the memorandum indicates the President saw it. All brackets are in the original except those indicating text that remains classified.

[2] Attached but not printed.

[3] See Document 299.

exchanges.[4] We were willing to begin initial exchanges with someone designated by Sadat at any location, as early as late September.

However, we made clear that we would not accept preconditions. Our approach in these talks would be as follows: In all the previously successful negotiations conducted at the Presidential level, we did not go into detailed substantive negotiation until we had already achieved a preliminary understanding on the direction and general principles that the outcome would follow. In this case we insisted to the Egyptians that we talk initially about what was realistically achievable. This was the essence of the matter and the only justification for the direct involvement of the President.

The Egyptians have welcomed the establishment of the channel but have not yet responded to the above groundrules we proposed.[5]

We have received many reports that Sadat does not want to wait until November. But we have offered him preliminary talks by late September, and we cannot conduct these talks under any groundrules other than the above. The alternative of military action will be suicidal for him. The Israelis plan to behave scrupulously and give him no pretext for such action.

---

[4] On July 29, a U.S. official met [*text not declassified*] in Cairo to present talking points provided by Kissinger's office, in which Kissinger agreed to open a secret channel and also suggested that a secret, high-level meeting occur in late September or early October. (Memorandum from Helms to Kissinger, August 1; National Archives, Nixon Presidential Materials, NSC Files, Kissinger Office Files, Box 131, Country Files, Middle East) On July 30, [*text not declassified*] confirmed that the message from Kissinger had been passed to Sadat. (Memorandum from Helms to Kissinger, August 2; ibid.)

[5] Helms reported to Kissinger on August 3 that [*text not declassified*] had volunteered two suggestions that would "contribute toward creating an optimum climate for U.S.-Egypt relations and, more specifically, have a salutary effect on Sadat" while he weighed his response to the proposal for high-level talks. First, he suggested that the U.S. Government "refrain from making public statements during this period which might have an upsetting effect on Sadat," such as recent calls by Rogers and Sisco for direct negotiations; "overly warm endorsements of Israel;" or "announcements of new aid for Israel." Second, he suggested that Nixon or Kissinger send a personal message to Sadat. (Memorandum from Helms to Kissinger; ibid.) In response to the first recommendation, Kissinger's office passed a message [*text not declassified*] that said that, because only Nixon, Kissinger, and Haig knew about the recent exchanges, he "must understand if some actions from other branches of the government are not finely tuned to this effort." (Memorandum from Haig to Helms, August 8; ibid.)

306. Memorandum From Samuel Hoskinson of the National Security Council Staff to the President's Assistant for National Security Affairs (Kissinger)[1]

Washington, August 29, 1972.

SUBJECT

Middle East Settlement Effort

State has sent over for clearance a cable (Tab A)[2] intended to smoke out current Israeli views on an interim settlement and the extent to which they might serve as a basis for restarting the Israeli-Egyptian dialogue. Put in Sisco's terms, we should now go back to Dayan to (1) make it clear we consider his recent remarks "significant," (2) ascertain whether and to what extent he is speaking for the government and, (3) let him know that we remain available to play a diplomatic role with Egypt if the Israelis so desire.

By way of background, you will recall that last week the Chargé, Zurhellen, invited Dayan over for an informal talk (Tab B)[3] during which Dayan made the following major points:

—If Sadat gave up his demand for an Israeli commitment to full withdrawal as part of an interim settlement, Dayan would recommend to Mrs. Meir that Israel drop all previous positions and start again from scratch with the Egyptians.

—While Israel could not retract its position that the final line of withdrawal could not be the pre-war boundary, he would favor putting that issue aside and simply say nothing about an interim settlement. Dayan said there would be a majority in the cabinet for this approach.

—In addition to specifying in an agreement that the "interim solution" was not a final one, there could be "intrinsic conditions" in the agreement militating against the situation becoming frozen. For instance, he could agree to Egyptian forces crossing the Canal into the

---

[1] Source: National Archives, Nixon Presidential Materials, NSC Files, Box 658, Country Files, Middle East, Middle East Nodis/Cedar/Plus, Vol. V. Secret; Nodis; Cedar Double Plus. Sent for action. In a covering memorandum to Kissinger on September 1, Haig wrote: "State is again off and running. Hoskinson's memorandum is exactly right and the cable at Tab A which has been cleared by Secretary Rogers should not be sent." Haig concluded: "We obviously have another Sisco ploy underway which we must get on top of immediately."

[2] The draft telegram is attached but not printed.

[3] Telegram 5429 from Tel Aviv, August 21, is attached but not printed.

Egyptian-held area of Sinai to the extent required for security, but he would not want, in an interim agreement, freedom for full Egyptian army attack elements to cross the Canal. In return, he would be agreeable to Israel being placed under similar conditions in its zone of occupation, thus making it clear Israel was not to be accorded full sovereign rights on its side of the line.

Sisco believes that Dayan's remarks reflect an Israeli desire to try to build on new developments in the area and to provide Sadat with a politically viable alternative to the military option which Sadat might otherwise be tempted to exercise to put the Middle East back on the U.S. and Soviet front burner. He thinks that the Israelis are also concerned about the possibility that they may soon face a new Waldheim and Egyptian initiative at the UN[4] and would much prefer progress on an interim settlement.

If he gets any hint of encouragement at all from the Israelis, Sisco's next step would undoubtedly be to pass on Dayan's views to the Egyptians. The purpose would be to test the possibility—unlikely as it may seem—that Sadat would be willing to drop his demand for an Israeli commitment to full withdrawal at the outset, if he learned from us that there was a prospect for the Israelis revising their positions on other aspects of an interim settlement and would give reassurance that an interim arrangement would not become final.

At best, any scenario like this would be a fairly long shot. For one thing, there is no real evidence that the Israelis are all that interested in an interim settlement at the moment and Dayan—as has frequently been the case in the past—may simply be floating a few of his own ideas. Even if the Israelis were serious, it seems unlikely that Sadat is prepared to go this far, especially with nothing more concrete from the Israelis than a promise to start from scratch on all issues but the one most important to him. Finally, there is a legacy of distrust of U.S. efforts like this on both sides of the Canal.

---

[4] Bush met with Waldheim on September 7. Responding to the Ambassador's presentation of the Department's views about his possible future initiatives, Waldheim said that "any initiative at present time would be useless, in fact, extremely bad." He remarked that the next year might offer new opportunities but said that he realized that the United Nations could not "simply keep repeating 'Jarring, Jarring, Jarring,'" particularly because of Israel's "lack of confidence" in the Special Representative's "objectivity." Israel had also indicated to him, he said, that it did not want the "big powers involved in any [Middle East] peace conference." Finally, he commented that the proximity talks favored by the United States "would make him very happy," adding that Egypt "made it clear to him" that it was "hoping for more understanding from [the United States] and others following expulsion of Soviets." (Telegram 3121 from USUN, September 7; National Archives, Nixon Presidential Materials, NSC Files, Box 1169, Saunders Files, Middle East Negotiations Files, Middle East—Jarring Talks, September 1–30, 1972)

In short, I feel that any action like this now would be premature, both in terms of our domestic political situation and the situation in the Middle East. If the Israelis really want to pass something along to Sadat they already know we would be willing and would have no need to probe us indirectly. Sadat, for his part, may be looking for us to make a move now that he has expelled the Soviets, but a false step now could well be more damaging than doing nothing and taking a more meaningful step later.

Recommendation: That you call Sisco and inform him that an effort such as this seems premature to you.[5]

---

[5] Attached to a September 5 memorandum from Eliot to Haig is a revised version of the telegram reflecting Kissinger's concerns regarding the original draft. (Ibid., Box 558, Country Files, Middle East, Middle East Nodis/Cedar/Plus, Vol. V) No documentation on whether the telegram was sent has been found.

---

307. Memorandum for the President's Files by the President's Deputy Assistant for National Security Affairs (Haig)[1]

Washington, September 6, 1972, 10 a.m.

SUBJECT

President's Meeting with Secretary of State Rogers, Dr. Kissinger and M/Gen. Haig

PARTICIPANTS

President Nixon
Secretary of State William Rogers
Henry A. Kissinger
M/Gen. Alexander M. Haig, Jr.

---

[1] Source: National Archives, Nixon Presidential Materials, White House Special Files, President's Office Files, Box 77. Secret. The meeting took place in the Oval Office. There are tape recordings of this meeting and an earlier meeting. (Ibid., White House Tapes, Oval Office, Conversation Nos. 771–2 and 771–5) Transcripts are printed in *Foreign Relations, 1969–1976*, volume E–1, Documents on Global Issues, 1969–1972, Documents 93 and 95.

The meeting was held for the purpose of discussing the situation in Munich which resulted in the death of 11 Israeli athletes together with Arab terrorists.[2]

The President stated that he had spoken to Ambassador Rabin the previous evening and found him to be completely rational. The President continued that the US must pursue a delicate line which demonstrated justified sympathy for Israel but which did not serve to encourage Israeli retaliation which could only further escalate tensions and dangers in the Middle East. The President noted that he had called Mrs. Meir from San Clemente the day before and assured her that the United States was working diligently on the terrorist problem.[3] It now remains to outline a number of measures, practical and public, with which to deal with the problem.

Secretary Rogers noted that it was tragic that the German Government had handled the public notification of the situation so poorly with initial reports that the athletes were safe followed by a complete reversal of this news. The Department of State had formed a task force that had been working all the previous day and throughout the night on the situation. There was some indication that the Israeli Government might ask the United States Government to cancel its further participation in the Olympics. This developed earlier that morning and General Haig, Dr. Kissinger and Secretary Rogers coordinated on a position which precluded our becoming involved in this knotty issue. Nevertheless, it could come up again in the hours ahead. The Secretary noted that one of the measures which we might consider would be to direct the US flags in Washington be placed at half mast and declare a day of mourning.

The President stated that the United States should not agree to drop out of the Olympics and that Israel should remain consistent with the position it announced earlier to see the games through.

---

[2] Armed with automatic rifles, members of the Black September Organization (named after Jordan's suppression of the fedayeen uprising two years earlier) invaded the Olympic Village at the Munich games and broke into the quarters of the Israeli team early in the morning on September 5. Two of the Israeli athletes were killed immediately, and nine others were taken hostage. German authorities spent hours negotiating with the guerrillas, who demanded the release of 200 Arab commandos imprisoned in Israel, before eventually providing them with helicopters to take them and their Israeli captives to an airport at Furstenfeldbruck, where a Boeing 707 airplane bound for Cairo was awaiting their arrival. The 23-hour affair ended at 1 a.m. on September 6. In an attempt to rescue the hostages, hidden German sharpshooters exchanged fire with two of the guerrillas as they moved between the helicopter and the plane. All nine of the remaining Israeli athletes as well as four of their captors died.

[3] The President, in San Clemente, spoke on the telephone with Meir on September 5 from 10:33 to 10:37 a.m., after which he returned to Washington. He spoke to Rabin, who was in Vancouver, British Columbia, from 11:15 to 11:27 p.m. (National Archives, Nixon Presidential Materials, White House Central Files, President's Daily Diary)

Secretary Rogers stated that all had agreed on this stand the day before since it would be a terrible slap at the Germans to precipitously withdraw. It appeared that the Germans were in deep difficulty already for their handling of the situation at the NATO airbase. Secretary Rogers stated that most nations were in deep sympathy with Israel but were they to withdraw from the games that sympathy could be reversed. An additional problem was the fact that even if the United States were to accept Israel's logic it could not control either its athletes or the head of the Olympic Committee.

The President directed that Israel be informed that we wished to continue.

Dr. Kissinger commented that it was important that the United States not permit Israel to "put the heat" on us to withdraw. The President noted that withdrawal would be the *New York Times*/McGovern approach.

Secretary Rogers again asked about the propriety of lowering our flags and a day of mourning. The President stated that we had not done similar things when deaths occurred in Ireland or during the earthquake in Peru and we must be careful not to demonstrate a double standard. Secretary Rogers suggested that we could call for a period of silence during the funeral of the Israeli athletes. He added that the Israelis apparently do not want high-level delegations in order to avoid politicization and perhaps we should send some of our athletes such as the US swimmer who is of Jewish descent.[4] In any event, we should abide carefully by Israel's own wishes.

Secretary Rogers stated that the Department of State is not favorably inclined towards the suggestion that we convene the Security Council on the terrorist issue. The President stated that this kind of action would butt us up against China and the Soviet Union but if the US were to go to the Security Council condemning countries which harbor guerrillas, this would in effect support Israel while at the same time not encouraging it to take escalatory retaliatory action.

Secretary Rogers stated that a cable had been prepared to the Prime Minister outlining our disgust and sympathy.[5] He noted that he would make a strong statement at the International Hijacking Confer-

---

[4] Reference is to Mark Spitz, who won a record seven gold medals at the Munich games.

[5] Nixon's September 6 message to Meir is printed in *Public Papers: Nixon, 1972*, p. 858.

ence being conducted at the Department of State that day.[6] The President agreed that the message should go and that the Secretary should make the statement. He inquired what kind of a resolution we would seek should we decide to go to the United Nations.[7]

Dr. Kissinger stated that no resolution would be likely to pass. The question is how to posture ourselves. The resolution should talk about rules of conduct of those who sponsor radicals who operate across international borders. It is probable that the Peoples' Republic of China would veto. On the other hand, this would be a statesmanlike US position. It would likely engender extensive debate and would tend to defuse Israeli emotions during the critical hours ahead. Then when the General Assembly meets the debate could continue. All this tends to control Israeli retaliatory action.

The President stated that we should now turn to the public relations aspects of the problem and following that bring Mr. Ziegler to the meeting.

Secretary Rogers again expressed opposition to the United Nations initiative. Dr. Kissinger stated that the government lawyers could develop a formulation which included something on border crossing, something on countries who harbor organizations which operate beyond their borders and in this way the US would go to the Security Council in a statesmanlike posture and solicit the views of other nations. Secretary Rogers stated that it would be impossible to get any kind of action. Dr. Kissinger stated that this was true but it would serve as a deterrent to Israeli action. Secretary Rogers stated that the Israelis would not be impressed by Security Council action and that for the moment it is important that we keep in close contact with them.

---

[6] At the September 4–15 meeting of the subcommittee of the International Civil Aviation Organization (ICAO) that concerned hijacking, Rogers made a statement on September 6 in which he said: "I know that you share with me the deep sense of outrage and grief at the senseless and tragic events which have so marred the Olympic games. These murders by extremist terrorists are more than crimes against the citizens of one country. The very spirit which the Olympic games represent, the spirit of brotherhood and of friendly competition among people all over the world, has been seriously challenged by this demented action. In this time of sorrow all men of good will must ask, What can we do to help insure that such crimes do not continue?" (Department of State *Bulletin*, October 2, 1972, p. 360)

[7] That evening, Kissinger told Rabin on the telephone that the United States would "absolutely and very strongly" take the initiative on a UN resolution. (Transcript of a telephone conversation between Kissinger and Rabin, September 6, 11:07 a.m.; National Archives, Nixon Presidential Materials, NSC Files, Henry Kissinger Telephone Conversation Transcripts, Box 15, Chronological File) On September 10, Bush addressed the UN Security Council and closed by describing a resolution which he said "could be helpful in addressing" the thrust of the remarks that had been made during that session. (Telegram 3177 from USUN, September 10; ibid., Box 1169, Saunders Files, Middle East Negotiations Files, Middle East—Jarring Talks, September 1–30, 1972) The United States presented, and the Security Council considered, draft resolution S/10785, which did not pass. (*Yearbook of the United Nations, 1972*, p. 173)

The President noted that we had been doing precisely this. He also noted that the public statements made thus far by Israel were also statesmanlike. Dr. Kissinger stated that all of this is true. Nevertheless if we do nothing it is probable that we will see strong Israeli action. Secretary Rogers urged that the President think about this before proceeding with the UN initiative.

The President stated that in his discussions last night with Ambassador Rabin he underlined the fact that despite the disadvantages of the tragedy it would bring the terrorist activity to the attention of the world. Secretary Rogers stated that another advantage of the tragedy was that it will again underline the need for an overall settlement. He noted that Dayan had made some overtures[8] and that Egypt would probably launch some initiatives in conjunction with the General Assembly meeting this fall. This is the basic problem and only a settlement will solve it. If Dayan was actually speaking for Israel then it is important that we get the process started for another round of negotiations.

The President stated that the situation in Munich will not soften up the Israeli attitudes but will strengthen their hawks. Secretary Rogers agreed but said that this only underlined the need for seeking a solution to the Middle East situation and certainly there will be efforts in the fall to get negotiations started.

The President stated that Secretary Rogers should make a strong statement at the hijacking conference. Secretary Rogers stated that with respect to the UN initiative we should leave it open until he has an opportunity to check the Israeli view.

The President instructed the Secretary to see what kind of a game plan we could come up with for the United Nations. Secretary Rogers stated that his people were tired and he hoped that Dr. Kissinger's people would also work on this. Dr. Kissinger stated that if the decision is made to proceed in the UN it must be done quickly.

The President stated that we might also have some legislation for the Congress to get the Conventions for Hijacking, etc. moved. Also we should give some thought to what the Congress could do on terrorism.

---

[8] In an August 11 interview on the Israeli Government television network, Dayan said that the withdrawal of Soviet military forces and advisers from Egypt would allow Israel to redeploy troops along the Suez Canal cease-fire line. He added that Israel would also be able to reduce the call-up of reservists for active duty and remarked that there might be hope for an interim agreement between Israel and Egypt. (*New York Times*, August 12, 1972, p. 1) In his commencement address to graduates of the Armed Forces Command and Staff School on August 17, Dayan pushed Egypt to accept an interim accord with Israel along a line that divided the Sinai Peninsula. (Ibid., August 18, 1972, p. 6) See also Document 306.

The President told Secretary Rogers to consider the UN initiative seriously, since it might just serve to buy time. It serves as a visible reaction to the Israeli outcries. Secretary Rogers said that he would discuss it with Rabin although he does not think the Israelis will support it because of their anti-UN feelings. Secretary Rogers continued to the effect that feelings in Israel are very high against the Germans for three reasons: (1) because they afforded poor protection to the Israeli athletes, (2) because of the reporting of the incident, and (3) because of the trigger-happy performance of the German police.

The President commented that it was ironic that the German Government found itself in the position of protecting Israeli athletes. He stated that in summary the following actions should be undertaken:

1. The cable sent to Mrs. Meir.
2. Secretary Rogers would make a strong statement at the Hijacking Conference.
3. We would look into the feasibility of a UN initiative.
4. We would do whatever remained to be done with our own Congress with respect to pending legislation and the possibility of new legislation.
5. Secretary Rogers should ask Ambassador Rabin about the UN initiative, tell him that we have no illusions but that it would serve to spotlight the issue.[9]

Secretary Rogers asked that Dr. Kissinger keep him informed if he should have any contact with the Israelis. The President told General Haig to do this should Ambassador Rabin contact the White House.

Secretary Rogers then noted as an aside that the President should give a brief speech at the IMF Conference since it was a good platform for an expression of the President's monetary policies. The President stated that Treasury Secretary Shultz was opposed on the convertibility issue but that Mr. Burns favored it. Secretary Rogers agreed that this was a problem.

Secretary Rogers recapitulated noting that he would call Ambassador Rabin, that we should continue to consider lowering our flags and that he would give the speech at the Hijacking Conference.

The President stated that he did not think the flag at half mast was a good idea. Dr. Kissinger agreed. Secretary Rogers said that we would just do this in public buildings. The President stated maybe just the White House. Dr. Kissinger again stated that he disagreed. Secretary Rogers stated that an alternative would be a moment of silence during

---

[9] Rogers and Rabin met on September 6. A report on their meeting is in telegram 164170 to Tel Aviv, September 8, printed in *Foreign Relations,* 1969–1976, volume E–1, Documents on Global Issues, 1969–1972, Document 98. In his September 6 Evening Report to the President, Rogers summarized the actions he and the Department of State were taking; see ibid., Document 97.

the funeral. The President stated that it might be worth considering. Dr. Kissinger stated that it was less troublesome than lowering the flags. The President asked why not do something on a personal basis. He could go to church at the time of the funeral. This looked more spontaneous and more of an individual reaction rather than a government reaction.

Press Secretary Ziegler was then called into the Oval Office and was given the following press guidance. He should discuss the fact of the meeting, the message to the Prime Minister, and the fact that we are considering measures to include consultations with other governments on an urgent basis to see what can be done to prevent terrorist activity. The point should be made that the President, Secretary Rogers and Dr. Kissinger consulted throughout the night and that close consultation was maintained with Israel and Bonn. It should be noted that the President talked to Ambassador Rabin and that Secretary Rogers will see the Ambassador later today. The point should be made that precautionary measures have been ordered by the President to ensure the security of Israeli and other foreign personnel and facilities in the rising tensions.

308. **Telegram From the President's Deputy Assistant for National Security Affairs (Haig) to President Nixon at Camp David, Maryland**[1]

Washington, September 9, 1972, 1950Z.

WH27332. Memorandum for: The President. From: Al Haig. Subject: Rising Tensions in the Mid-East.

Pursuant to your instructions, I conveyed to Israeli Minister Idan (in the absence of Ambassador Rabin who was en route to Israel) our strong concern for the retaliatory action taken by the Government of Israel yesterday against refugee terrorist camps.[2] I added that this action was inconsistent with the assurances given by Ambassador Rabin to Dr. Kissinger yesterday that Israel would do nothing to upset the

---

[1] Source: National Archives, Nixon Presidential Materials, NSC Files, Box 609, Country Files, Middle East, Israel, Vol. X. Secret; Sensitive. Stamped notations on the first page indicate that the telegram was received at Camp David at 4:35 p.m. and that the President saw it.

[2] On September 8, Israeli fighter jets struck 10 Palestinian guerrilla bases deep in both Lebanese and Syrian territory in retaliation for the killing of the Israeli athletes in Munich on September 6. (*New York Times*, September 9, 1972, p. 1)

"trend of tranquility" in the Mid-East. Idan replied that Israel intended to abide by the assurances given but that this did not mean that Israel would stand by idly and not take some action against known terrorist bases. He implied that the targets were precise and well identified beforehand. He estimated that there may have been as many as 90 to 100 casualties inflicted.

Idan pointed out that today's air action over the Golan Heights resulted from efforts by the Syrian Air Force to bomb Israeli territory. During these air battles, which involved as many as 90 aircraft, three Syrian SU–7s were shot down and a fourth was damaged but landed safely. Idan stated that today's actions were purely defensive in nature and that he did not foresee any change in the assessment given by Rabin yesterday. I again reiterated to him that you were concerned and hoped that Israel would not jeopardize the good will built here as a result of the improving situation in the Mid-East, and the sympathy for Israel which had been engendered by the tragic events in Munich. It was made clear to Idan that a continuation of clearly unprovoked military aggressiveness on the part of Israel would not be understood nor condoned by the White House.[3]

---

[3] Nixon wrote "good" next to these last two sentences. In a September 11 memorandum, Butterfield informed Haig that the President read this telegram and "was especially pleased to note that you made it clear to Minister Idan that a continuation of unprovoked military aggression on the part of Israel would not be understood, or condoned, at this end of the line." (National Archives, Nixon Presidential Materials, NSC Files, Box 609, Country Files, Middle East, Israel, Vol. X) On September 16, Kissinger told Idan: "But if you do not stop these actions—I must tell you, you are running an enormous risk in your relations with the President. You launched an action the day before I go to Moscow and you launch an action the day after I come back at a time when we are taking an all-out diplomatic position in your defense and are preventing—going into actions. We cannot take this. Now there is no President who has done more for you, and I can tell you, I have just come from the President and he asked me to call you." (Transcript of telephone conversation, 1:28 p.m.; ibid., Henry Kissinger Telephone Conversation Transcripts, Box 15, Chronological File)

309. Memorandum of Conversation[1]

Washington, September 19, 1972, 3 p.m.

PARTICIPANTS

Richard Helms, Director of Central Intelligence
[name and title not declassified]
Henry A. Kissinger
Thomas K. Latimer

Mr. Kissinger: I appreciate your role in passing these messages to the Egyptians.[2] My first question is technical—can the Egyptians keep these contacts secret or are they penetrated by the Soviets? Is it to their advantage to let the Soviets know of our contacts?

[name not declassified]: They can keep it secret.

Mr. Kissinger: But will they?

[name not declassified]: I think they will despite their past record. It is in their interest to do so.

Mr. Kissinger: You have not passed them pieces of paper? This has all been done orally has it not?

[name not declassified]: Yes, all orally. They take notes as do I when they pass us a message. It is not to Sadat's interest to have these secret contacts known because he fears raising false hopes among his people.

Mr. Kissinger: He might use it as blackmail with the Soviets but so far, he doesn't have anything to tell them. No substance has been exchanged.

---

[1] Source: National Archives, Nixon Presidential Materials, NSC Files, Kissinger Office Files, Box 131, Middle East. Top Secret; Sensitive; Exclusively Eyes Only. All brackets are in the original except those indicating text that remains classified. The conversation took place in Kissinger's office.

[2] Reference is to the exchange of messages between Kissinger and [text not declassified]; see footnotes 4 and 5, Document 305. On September 7, Kissinger received a message from Sadat [text not declassified] in which the Egyptian President discussed "considerations and views" that he wanted taken into account as the United States and Egypt began a new initiative to reach a settlement with Israel. (National Archives, Nixon Presidential Materials, NSC Files, Kissinger Office Files, Box 131, Middle East) Kissinger received another message [text not declassified] on September 13 in which the Egyptian intelligence chief commented that the United States had abetted Israel in its "dangerous escalation" of violence in the Middle East since the guerrilla attack at the Olympic games in Munich. (Ibid.) In response, a message was passed [text not declassified] on September 19 that advocated breaking the "cycle of violence" in the region, to which [text not declassified] remarked that the U.S. Government had "lost much good will in the Arab world" over the previous few days for the September 10 veto of UN Security Council draft resolution S/10784 condemning Israeli air strikes in Lebanon and for "refusing to restrain Israel from killing innocent people in Lebanon." (Memorandum from Helms to Kissinger, September 19; ibid.)

[*name not declassified*]: Most Egyptians think Sadat checked with us before throwing the Soviets out. They do not think he would have been so stupid as to have taken that action without checking with us first.

Mr. Kissinger: I think he was stupid.

[*name not declassified*]: Sadat took that move as part of what he saw as the national interest. He thought that the Soviets could not help Egypt achieve one of the key elements in its national policy, the regaining of the Sinai.

Mr. Kissinger: Why did he not make us an offer to exchange the ouster of the Soviets in exchange for pressure on Israel on our part?

[*name not declassified*]: There you are running into the personality of Sadat. His pride was involved and a lot of what he felt was ...

Mr. Kissinger: Alright. Do you know Ismail?

[*name not declassified*]: [*less than 1 line not declassified*] He has an unusually well organized mind for an Egyptian.

Mr. Kissinger: Do you mean Sadat's mind is not well organized?

[*name not declassified*]: Sadat is more impetuous. [*1½ lines not declassified*]

Mr. Kissinger: What will he expect from me?

[*name not declassified*]: He will ask what the US wants in the Middle East and from Egypt specifically. They think we must want something more than they have delivered on but they think they have expelled the Russians and abided by what the Secretary of State called for. They want to know what they can do to get on the same equal footing with the US as Israel is.

Mr. Kissinger: They can emigrate five million Egyptians. What I want to get away from is both sides espousing impossible positions and then palavering endlessly about technical steps which can never be implemented.

[*name not declassified*]: That is just what the Egyptians want too.

Mr. Kissinger: What can Egypt accept? Israel will not go back to the 1967 borders. Can Egypt accept this as an acceptable position, that they must discuss an agreement which will only represent a slight modification of the present situation?

[*name not declassified*]: One thing you will encounter is Egyptian insistence that we take a specific position on elements of a settlement.

Mr. Kissinger: I will not get into a discussion of a theoretical settlement. Are they capable of a concrete discussion?

[*name not declassified*]: They say that the US has to take a specific stand. They want to know how far the US is prepared to go in pressing Israel.

Mr. Kissinger: That is none of their business. All we need do is tell them we will try our best to get a settlement once they agree to specific, concrete proposals.

[name not declassified]: They felt that last year we did not go far enough in pressing Israel.

Mr. Kissinger: But there never was a specific goal. I never could find out what specific points were under consideration. Nothing concrete was on the table. Now, they want to know: 1) what are we willing to do; 2) are we willing to make concrete suggestions . . .

[name not declassified]: And will we exert maximum pressure. They are convinced that Zionist plans call for gradual expansion and that only the US has enough muscle to get the Arabs a settlement.

Director Helms: Would it be useful for [less than 1 line not declassified] to put down what round one will look like?

Mr. Kissinger: I'd like to get some feel for Ismail, his cast of mind, what does he want, how will he go about getting it. Will he be alone?

[name not declassified]: He might be alone, Ghorbal might be along but Ismail will do the talking.

Mr. Kissinger: How will we get him here? Shouldn't he come openly?

[name not declassified]: He is an anonymous type, not so well known as some Egyptians. He could be less conspicuous than some.

Mr. Kissinger: Dick, should he come openly?

Director Helms: Whatever you want. We can get him here.

Mr. Kissinger: My concern is to protect myself from all these various elements.

Director Helms: If he is to come openly, say in connection with the UN General Assembly.

Mr. Kissinger: Then you can get us a place in New York. He could talk officially with Sisco for that matter. Do they understand how our system works? Do they understand that they should ignore things that come through some channels? Will they now propose a date?

[name not declassified]: They understand that this channel is the genuine one.

Director Helms: We should think through the merits of a public versus a private trip.

Mr. Kissinger: I have to think of what happens if it blows. I'd like to be one stage removed. If he has a plausible reason for being here, I can always say he was here anyway so I saw him.

Director Helms: Let us have a day to think about it.

[name not declassified]: They were thinking of a secret trip but that is not firm.

Mr. Kissinger: I'm not an expert in arranging secret trips, you are the experts.

Director Helms: Judging from the past two years you are now.

Mr. Kissinger: In general I lean toward a theatrical arrangement which provides a plausible reason for his trip.

Director Helms: We probably should get him here publicly.

Mr. Kissinger: That's what I think.

[*name not declassified*]: He is somewhat stiff in his bearing and rather haughty but he is thoroughly loyal to Sadat.

Mr. Kissinger: Well he and I should get along very well. My desire to get next to this is near zero. If it succeeds, it will buy us trouble. However, we cannot go on with highly publicized proposals which go nowhere. We must have workable, concrete proposals.

[*name not declassified*]: Sadat's position is close to that.

Mr. Kissinger: I want to find out what they can really live with. Then, we will see if it can be done. Can you do a paper which 1) will restate what you have said here regarding what they want, 2) give me a little background on Ismail, 3) how to set up the meeting—we can use October to agree on something and then be in a position to move.[3]

[*name not declassified*]: [*less than 1 line not declassified*] understands the problem of moving before November.

Mr. Kissinger: We cannot stop sending Phantoms to Israel or everyone will ask what is up.

[*name not declassified*]: These exchanges have already borne fruit in terms of US-Egypt relations. This was a breath of fresh air to Sadat to learn that the United States at the highest level was interested.

Mr. Kissinger: To be saddled with Le Duc Tho and Ismail in one month is more than one deserves. Will you [*name not declassified*] be around and will you introduce us?

Director Helms: He will be here.

---

[3] See Document 310.

310. Memorandum From Director of Central Intelligence Helms to the President's Assistant for National Security Affairs (Kissinger)[1]

Washington, September 22, 1972.

SUBJECT

Nature of the Exploratory Talks

1. Considerations pertinent to the principal aspects of the proposed talks with the Egyptian government are set forth below, in accordance with your request of 18 September 1972.[2]

2. President Sadat's decision to enter into secret preliminary talks with the United States Government to explore the prospects for peace in the Middle East was determined by certain facts of life in the prevailing situation in Egypt and the Middle East, which considerations will also shape Sadat's approach to these talks. In parlous financial straits and faced with a deterioration of its over-all economic condition that cannot be arrested without peace, Egypt as a whole, at all levels, recognizes its need for peace. Egypt's leadership recognizes and accepts what it was unwilling to accept prior to 1967, that the price it must pay for its 1967 defeat by Israel is Egyptian agreement to allow Israel to exist as a state and in conditions of genuine peace. *The unresolved question for negotiation concerns only that of Israel's existence within what borders.* Sadat unquestionably had the great majority of his people with him when he pursued with the United States in 1971 the possibilities for a peaceful settlement; his political troubles at home began only when those efforts collapsed leaving Sadat and the country in a no war-no peace quandary which it found intolerable to live with indefinitely.

3. The available evidence indicates that the Egyptian leadership recognizes that the regaining of Sinai, which is Egypt's cardinal national objective, is impossible to achieve by military means because of preponderant Israeli military strength. In terminating recently the Soviet military advisory program, Egyptian leadership was well aware that it was weakening itself militarily for an extended period if not permanently. The Egyptian decision in this regard can only be interpreted as reflecting Sadat's conclusion that a military solution was unrealistic even with their former military relationship with the Soviets and that Egypt's main objective therefore can only be achieved through some

---

[1] Source: National Archives, Nixon Presidential Materials, NSC Files, Kissinger Office Files, Box 131, Country Files, Middle East. Secret; Sensitive. All brackets are in the original except those indicating text that remains classified.

[2] The request was actually issued on September 19. See Document 309.

form of peaceful negotiating process. Sadat's whole conduct since his assumption of power supports the conclusion that this has been his belief all along and that for him the chief importance of Egyptian military strength consisted only in developing as much credibility of military threat as was possible for tactical bargaining purposes related to a negotiating process.

4. Among the various considerations that contributed to Sadat's decision to alter their military relationship with the Soviets, another was his awareness that the Soviet presence in Egypt had long been a factor disturbing to the United States and complicating the quest for peace. Indications [*less than 1 line not declassified*] suggest that Sadat probably hoped that one of the effects of his decision concerning the Soviets would be to unlock to some degree the existing deadlock and improve the possibility for a renewal of American interest in seeking a peaceful settlement of the Middle East problem. Sadat very likely interprets in this light the timing of the United States Government's 29 July initiative on preliminary talks.[3] Sadat's termination of the Soviet military program, which evoked a universally favorable reaction in Egypt, eased the internal pressures which had been building around Sadat and bought him time, perhaps as much as a year. But malaise and the same pressures will grow again if the no war-no peace impasse is not eventually resolved.

5. *While there is real urgency therefore about Sadat's need for peace, there are also real limits on how far he can go and how much he can concede to get peace.* In public opinion in Egypt at all levels, the emotionalism attaching to the belief that no land lost in 1967 should be permanently yielded to Israel in a peace settlement and to the belief that no direct negotiations should be conducted with Israel so long as it is in occupation of Egyptian soil, is also a fact of life which Sadat cannot cavalierly ignore without political peril.

6. Against this background, Sadat's approach to the proposed exploratory talks is likely to reflect the following:

a. The Egyptian leadership is so deeply persuaded of the United States Government's total alignment with Israel that it will be entering the proposed talks without optimism, skeptically, doubtful that any major breakthrough will result—but hopeful, nevertheless, because of its great need for peace, and with the feeling that it cannot afford to pass up any opening or conceivable opportunity for movement towards an honorable peace.

b. *It is improbable that Sadat will be undertaking preliminary talks with the illusion that any grandiose, overall plan for a full settlement of the Middle*

---

[3] See footnote 4, Document 305.

East problem will emerge from the talks. [1½ *lines not declassified*] indicated that they are thinking in terms of a partial Israeli withdrawal with concomitant reopening of the Suez Canal as a first step in a gradual piecemeal approach to some eventual final settlement. The Egyptians will be probing to establish what the United States believes to be realistically obtainable from the Israelis in a partial settlement, i.e., the depth of partial withdrawal, Egyptian military presence on the east bank of the Canal, and the nature of the linkage between partial and final settlement.

c. *The Egyptians do not believe however that they can afford to acquiesce in partial steps towards final peace, which do not lead to further movement towards that ultimate end.* Therefore, the Egyptians predictably will press the United States in these talks for the general lines of the sort of eventual final settlement which the United States envisions. They will endeavor to flush out United States positions on the separate elements of a final peace, such as the final border, the status of Sharm ash Shaykh and of Gaza, the nature of international guarantees for the peace, the extent of demilitarization of Sinai, the presence of Egyptian military personnel there. One of their two principal objectives in these talks will be to seek mutual clarifications of the present positions of both governments on the elements of a peaceful settlement. The Egyptians will not wish to talk in generalities in these talks, but will insist on getting down to brass tacks and talking in specific, clear and concrete terms.

d. *Sadat's second principal objective will be to try to pin down the United States as to precisely how far it is prepared to go in bringing pressure to bear on Israel to accept steps towards peace mutually agreed upon privately between the United States and Egypt.* The Egyptians, from Sadat down, have an unshakable conviction which is certain to be articulated in these talks that Israel's dependence on the United States is so great that the United States can turn Israel off and on like a spigot. They are equally convinced that Israel will yield nothing unless constrained to in one way or another and that only the United States can bring that constraint to bear. This consideration will be uppermost in Sadat's mind in entering these talks. If private preliminary talks can result in a meeting of minds by the American and Egyptian governments on mutually acceptable steps towards peace, Sadat will insist upon firm assurances that the United States Government will commit itself to a maximum effort to induce Israeli acceptance before Sadat will agree to enter into any overt negotiating process. Sadat's current preoccupation with this consideration is a direct result of his experience with the United States in 1971 when, he believes, the United States walked away when the going got hot with Israel, leaving Sadat to hold the bag and a shaky political position endangered by the dashing of aroused expectations in his constituency.

e. Senior Egyptian officials [*less than 1 line not declassified*] invariably reflect mystification about United States policy objectives in the Middle East. While professing an ability to grasp the depth of the United States Government's commitment to Israel, they also assert an inability to comprehend why the United States should assume a commitment to Israel to a degree which jeopardizes other interests of the United States in the larger Middle East picture, notably its economic interests in the Arab world. The topmost officials of the Egyptian government surmise therefore that there must be something more, as yet unarticulated to them, which the United States wants and expects of them as a prerequisite to peace and improved bilateral relations with the United States. In one form or another this question will be posed by the Egyptian side in the course of the talks.

7. The holding of these exploratory talks entails two conceivable risks to United States interests. The first of these arises from the possibility that the very holding of the talks might generate unwarranted Egyptian expectations which, if disappointed, could leave the United States' bilateral relations with Egypt in more disarray than before. It is unquestionably true that the exchanges to date between the two governments concerning preliminary talks have evoked a measure of hopefulness in the Egyptian leadership which has had something of a soothing effect on our troubled relations with Egypt. However, several considerations appear to limit this risk to an acceptable degree. The United States' relations with Egypt cannot become much worse than they have been in the past half year or so. More importantly, as indicated above, it is doubtful that the Egyptians will embark on these discussions with any undue optimism. Finally, it is not unrealistic to believe that the risk may be containable to some degree by the atmospherics of the talks. At least part of Sadat's bitterness towards the United States in the past year has derived from his conviction that the United States was neglecting and ignoring him with a couldn't-careless attitude towards Egyptian needs, aspirations and sensitivities. Part of their evident pleasure recently concerning our 29 July initiative was caused by their reading it as a sign of United States interest and concern with the problem. Even if the talks should yield no tangible results at this time, the Egyptian reaction would not necessarily be disastrous from our viewpoint, could in fact prove to be positive, so long as they at least come away with an impression of genuine United States concern with the Middle East problems at the highest level and of a sincere United States desire to continue the effort to locate some reasonable and fair basis for an eventual solution.

8. The second of these risks relates to the possibility that Sadat, if dissatisfied with the outcome of the talks, might later opt to violate his promise to maintain secrecy by either public pronouncements by Sadat

as he has done in the past or by his revealing the talks to the Soviets. To date the Egyptians give every indication of having taken pains to limit awareness of this development as tightly as we have. Our estimate is that the Egyptians will continue to honor their pledge of secrecy. Sadat's past conduct is not in itself necessarily a valid indicator on this score. He has never before given an explicit pledge of secrecy beforehand in his dealings with us; he prides himself on keeping his word and Egyptians who know him well and whom we respect contend that Sadat's personal record in this respect is excellent and that, for example, if he had been president in August 1970 instead of Nasir, the Egyptian violation of the ceasefire-standstill agreement would never have occurred. However that may be, Sadat believes that it was the United States which did not honor its promises to him in 1971 thus releasing him from whatever tacit undertaking there may have been concerning secrecy. A more tangible and compelling reason concerns Sadat's previously noted conviction that only the United States can solve his problems. This creates doubt for us that Sadat will ever totally abandon all hope of a possible change of heart and policy by the United States; his betrayal of the current pledge of secrecy could occur only if he reached such a point of complete despair with the United States. Revelation to the Soviets by Sadat is less likely, in our estimate, than revelation by public pronouncement or leak to the press. The strains and coolness that have marked the course of Egyptian-Soviet relations in the past six months argue for the unlikelihood of Sadat's revealing the talks to the Soviets, particularly when such a move would not appear to serve or advance any significant Egyptian national interest.[4]

Richard Helms[5]

---

[4] In a September 23 memorandum to Helms, Kissinger asked him to pass a message to Egyptian officials informing them that he believed the time had come to "commence definite planning for the conduct of talks between the designated representatives of the two governments." Kissinger continued: "The U.S. side does not favorably view overt or covert travel by Dr. Kissinger to Europe or some other location outside of the United States, because such travel would ultimately involve the arrangements with other governments and possible compromise. On the other hand, the U.S. side is impressed with the advantages of the Egyptian Government's representative traveling overtly to New York with the ostensible purpose of attending the United Nations General Assembly sessions as President Sadat's personal representative." (National Archives, Nixon Presidential Materials, NSC Files, Kissinger Office Files, Box 131, Middle East)

[5] Helms signed "Dick" above his typed signature.

311. Memorandum of Conversation[1]

Washington, October 2, 1972, 1:20–3:45 p.m.

PARTICIPANTS

    Andrei Gromyko, Foreign Minister of the USSR
    Anatoliy F. Dobrynin, Soviet Ambassador
    Victor M. Sukhodrev, Interpreter
    Henry A. Kissinger, Assistant to the President for National Security Affairs
    Peter W. Rodman, NSC Staff

SUBJECTS

    Europe; Nuclear Understanding; Jackson Amendment; Middle East

[The conversation began over cocktails in a room adjoining the dining room.]

[Omitted here is discussion unrelated to the Middle East.]

Middle East

FM Gromyko: Alright. Now the Middle East. I would like to listen to you. I remember what you said to the General-Secretary and the Prime Minister.

Dr. Kissinger: As I told Anatoliy, we think we know how we might get a settlement with Jordan, but we don't think it is a good idea to have a separate settlement with Jordan. So we think a settlement with Egypt is the heart of the problem. We have not spoken with anyone. We are not aware of any secret Israeli plan, whatever you may read, or any secret Israeli/Egyptian talks.

Our view is that it is important to make an initial major step with respect to Egypt. I was never wild about the idea of an interim settlement but I believe the biggest problem is to get Israel to make an initial step back. The longer it stays the way it is, the harder it will be. Therefore, we should try to get the situation into a state of flux. Without a final determination, we should approach the problem from a standpoint of security, of security zones, without raising the issue of sovereignty. For example, the notion that Egyptian sovereignty extends up to the 1967 borders but for a certain period the Sinai will be divided into zones—one zone where both sides can station their forces, other zones

---

[1] Source: National Archives, Nixon Presidential Materials, NSC Files, Box 495, President's Trip Files, Dobrynin/Kissinger, Vol. 13. Top Secret; Sensitive; Exclusively Eyes Only. The conversation took place at the Soviet Embassy. All brackets are in the original except those indicating text omitted by the editors. For the full text of the memorandum of conversation, see *Foreign Relations,* 1969–1976, volume XIV, Soviet Union, June 1972–August 1974, Document 55.

where there can be some patrolling but no stationed forces, and maybe a buffer zone between them. Thus, for example, Sinai could be divided into five regions. In that event Egyptian civil administration would extend immediately to the borders.

I doubt Israel would accept this. In fact I am sure Israel would not accept this without massive pressure. If it is conceivable we could perhaps apply something like it to the Golan Heights. The major problem is to get some movement, or else the situation will be frozen so no movement can ever get started. Once movement starts, other pressures can continue to work.

FM Gromyko: I have two questions. First, does the United States accept the principle of withdrawal from all occupied territory? Second, does the United States accept the principle of a package deal? An all-embracing settlement?

Dr. Kissinger: When you say all-embracing, you mean Syria, because we can get the others.

FM Gromyko: I mean vertical as well as horizontal. I mean that the Suez Canal cannot be separated from withdrawal and the Palestinian question and Gaza and ...

Dr. Kissinger: We would like to separate out the question of the Canal, but I see that the others are related to each other. But in my view the only justified solution is one all sides can accept. We would like to make progress towards a settlement. If it can be achieved only by a global approach, we will consider a global approach. Our view up to now, which has not changed, is that we should see if we can get a settlement on the Suez Canal first.

FM Gromyko: But Egypt will not accept this.

Dr. Kissinger: So we will look at the other approach. My own view, as I have told Anatoliy, is that a global approach will lead to no settlement. This is what Israel would prefer, because it means no settlement will occur. They would love to discuss this.

FM Gromyko: What nonetheless do you think practically can be done? Before November, or after November.

Dr. Kissinger: After November we should take the principles we agreed on in Moscow[2] and apply them concretely to each area, to Egypt, to Jordan and to Syria. And then discuss how one tries to implement the right solution—whether to pass a UN resolution or apply direct pressure. If pressure is ever to be applied to Israel, it is better to do it earlier in the Administration.

---

[2] See Document 292.

FM Gromyko: We have talked with some Arabs in New York, and they have indicated again, they have reiterated, that they can't accept a partial settlement without it being part of a global settlement and without withdrawal of Israeli forces. Then am I right that you are not prepared now to discuss this in a concrete way?

Dr. Kissinger: To discuss what?

FM Gromyko: The whole problem.

Dr. Kissinger: The only thing I mentioned was security zones. I have said I could not come up with a very concrete plan by now. What we should discuss is what do you mean by a concrete proposal.

FM Gromyko: Speaking concretely, what do you think about withdrawal? Are you in favor of complete withdrawal or not? Second, on the question of a partial or all-embracing settlement, it is a fact that without an all-embracing settlement a partial one won't give results, because the Arabs reject it. As for Sharm el-Sheikh you know our position: Egyptian sovereignty plus a temporary stationing of UN personnel. With respect to the Gaza, the people there must determine their own destiny.

Dr. Kissinger: All this is in the paper you gave us.[3]

FM Gromyko: There must be some solution to the problem of the Palestinian refugees. On Suez, Egypt is prepared to allow peaceful passage of Israeli shipping. With respect to Israel's independence and sovereignty and existence, we agree to this, and the Arabs too, although without enthusiasm! With respect to guarantees, we are prepared to join with you in the most rigorous way possible, that is in the United Nations Security Council. Well, if we agreed on this, then we together could bring the necessary influence to bear on the parties concerned.

In short, what is your advice to me? What should I report to the General-Secretary on your views?

Dr. Kissinger: On the problem of guarantees, the history of UN guarantees does not create confidence that they operate when they are needed. This is the President's view: We will work for a common position we can agree to, on the basis of the principles we reached in Moscow. But at some time, it is essential to recognize realities. The Arabs may recognize Israel's right to exist, but the same was true of India and Pakistan before the war.[4] The peculiarity of the Middle East is that war arises among countries who are already at war; everywhere else war arises among countries who are already at peace! What we need is some concern for security. We are prepared to bring pressure on Israel

---

[3] See footnote 1, Document 291.
[4] Reference is to the Indo-Pakistani war of December 1971.

short of military pressure. We will not allow outside military pressure. Economic or moral pressures we are willing to do.

FM Gromyko: You did not reply. What should I tell the General-Secretary?

Dr. Kissinger: On some of the proposals you have suggested, we disagree. On others we agree; on others we should discuss.

FM Gromyko: When?

Dr. Kissinger: Early November, after the election. Say the 15th or the 14th or the 13th.

Amb. Dobrynin: You will need one week after the election for celebration!

[At 3:45 the meeting ended. Dr. Kissinger had to return to the White House and would come back to the Embassy at 4:15 to pick up the Foreign Minister and the Ambassador and accompany them to Camp David.]

312. Memorandum From the Executive Secretary of the Department of State (Eliot) to the President's Assistant for National Security Affairs (Kissinger)[1]

Washington, October 3, 1972.

SUBJECT

    Middle East and Lebanon

I am attaching a long memorandum of conversation between the Lebanese Foreign Minister Khalil Abouhamad and Joe Sisco on September 27th.[2] This conversation was held when the Foreign Minister asked Mr. Sisco to come to the Lebanese Consulate General in New York to have a "discreet" meeting with him. It is perhaps one of the most significant conversations we have held with the Lebanese in recent years for the following reasons.

First, for the first time, the Lebanese have said to us that they are considering the contingency of a military confrontation with the fedayeen in Lebanon and they wish to know what the United States would

---

[1] Source: National Archives, Nixon Presidential Materials, NSC Files, Box 658, Country Files, Middle East, Middle East Nodis/Cedar/Plus, Vol. V. Secret; Nodis; Cedar.
[2] Attached but not printed.

do prior and during such developments with particular reference to the possible contingency that during such a period of confrontation, Syria is apt to send more fedayeen into Lebanon across the borders.

Secondly, the Lebanese Foreign Minister has revealed what it considers to be stepped up pressure by the Soviet Union in the aftermath of Sadat's decision to expel the Soviets. Specifically, the Foreign Minister told Sisco that the Soviet Ambassador had offered Soviet friendship in the following specific terms: (a) the Soviet fleet could be made available to enter Beirut "in the case of an Israeli attack on Lebanese territory"; (b) the USSR would be willing to consider entering into a military agreement with Lebanon; and (c) the Soviet Union was willing to reach an arms agreement with Lebanon at very favorable prices. The Foreign Minister said that Lebanon has refrained from responding to these Soviet approaches for the time being at least. This initiative with the Lebanese coincides with what we believe are parallel Soviet efforts in recent weeks to strengthen its position in Iraq and Syria. This seems to be a Soviet move to compensate for its losses in Egypt.

Thirdly, the Lebanese Foreign Minister made a major pitch for the U.S. at some point to make contact with various Palestinian leaders in Lebanon in order to assure that they do not lose hope and confidence in the U.S. role in the area. The Lebanese Foreign Minister intends to convey to us the names of the specific Palestinians whom they believe are key in the situation in Lebanon.[3]

As you can see from the memorandum of conversation, Mr. Sisco was non-committal, indicating that the questions posed were so fundamental that they would require careful study by the U.S. Government.

Theodore L. Eliot, Jr.

---

[3] Abouhamad's follow-up conversation occurred at Ambassador Buffum's residence in Beirut on October 20. The discussion, which lasted over two hours, focused primarily on the possibility of a confrontation between the Lebanese Government and the local fedayeen. According to Buffum, "Abouhamad said he wished to make clear that it is not GOL policy to push for a confrontation with fedayeen. Such confrontation, he stressed, would have most serious consequences for Lebanon because of country's internal structure, its geographical contiguity with Syria, and its ties with Arab world." (Telegram 11400 from Beirut, October 20; National Archives, Nixon Presidential Materials, NSC Files, Box 658, Country Files, Middle East, Middle East Nodis/Cedar/Plus, Vol. V)

313. Memorandum From the President's Assistant for National Security Affairs (Kissinger) to President Nixon[1]

Washington, October 7, 1972.

SUBJECT

Secretary Laird's Views on the Middle East

Secretary Laird has sent you a memo outlining his current views on the Middle East situation and U.S. policy toward the area (attached).[2]

Secretary Laird is concerned that President Sadat could still slip back into a highly dependent relationship with the Soviets and that a "discreetly stepped up dialogue" might help Sadat over the next three or four critical months.

More specifically, he suggests the following actions with Egypt:

—Open a higher level channel of communication to Sadat than is provided by our Interests Section in Cairo.

—Ask Sadat how we can be helpful, short of all the usual impossible steps he believes we can take vis-à-vis Israel. Specifically, Secretary Laird suggests asking Sadat if we might help identify and "sell" to the Israelis a mutually acceptable substitute for "proximity talks" under our auspices aimed at an interim settlement. Alternatively, Secretary Laird suggests our acting in full secrecy as an "intermediary" with the Egyptian and Israeli negotiators remaining in their own capitals.

—Stress to Sadat how helpful his reduced dependence on the Soviets will be at any point when diplomatic relations are resumed.

With the Israelis, Secretary Laird would:

—"Encourage" the Israelis to make more encouraging public gestures toward the Arabs.

—"Encourage" the Israelis to exercise particular care to avoid allowing new information about their weapons plans or capabilities to surface and urge restraint in action, such as overflights of the Suez Canal, which might complicate things for Sadat.

—"Intercede strongly" to persuade Israel to at least explore Sadat's position should he agree to some form of secret talks.

---

[1] Source: National Archives, Nixon Presidential Materials, NSC Files, Box 647. Country Files, Middle East, Middle East (General) Vol. 9. Secret; Sensitive. Sent for information. Drafted on September 12 by Hoskinson. A stamped notation on the memorandum indicates the President saw it.

[2] Laird's August 26 memorandum is attached but not printed.

With little real prospect of advance along the tracks we have traveled in the Middle East in the past, some of Secretary Laird's suggestions offer some food for further thought.[3] Much more attention, of course, needs to be given to the substance of any renewed effort we might make in the future to promote an Arab-Israeli settlement. Moreover, it is not even clear whether we should continue to concentrate on the Egyptian-Israel aspects or should focus more on the Israel-Jordan problem as King Hussein shows signs of genuine interest in a separate peace.

---

[3] Laird sent another memorandum to Nixon on October 9 under the subject heading, "Dangers in the Middle East," which begins: "I am concerned that Israeli military actions could, before November 7, precipitate a Middle East crisis and do serious long-term damage to peace prospects and to our own position in the area." Kissinger forwarded the memorandum to Nixon on November 1, writing: "After Israel's mid-September raids on Lebanon and Syria we warned them strongly against repeating. Since then, our embassy in Tel Aviv has been reporting that the Israelis may be debating the nature of their current response to the terrorist problem with the hawks arguing along lines described by Secretary Laird. In the past ten days, a qualitative change has taken place in the Israeli position, and they have said they would henceforth attack the fedayeen preemptively and not wait for provocation. There was one round of attacks since that statement. The Israelis are aware that we will not associate ourselves with this Israeli strategy." (National Archives, Nixon Presidential Materials, NSC Files, Box 647, Country Files, Middle East, Middle East (General) Vol. 9)

---

314. Telegram From the Interests Section in Egypt to the Department of State[1]

Cairo, October 16, 1972, 0940Z.

2772. Subject: What Chance Middle East Peace? Ref: USUN 3818 (Secto 73), USUN 3723 (Secto 63), USUN 3651.[2]

---

[1] Source: National Archives, Nixon Presidential Materials, NSC Files, Box 1169, Saunders Files, Middle East Negotiations Files, Middle East—Jarring Talks, October 1–31, 1972. Secret. Repeated to Amman, Jidda, London, Moscow, Paris, Tel Aviv, Tripoli, and USUN.

[2] In telegram 3818/Secto 73 from USUN, October 11, Rogers reported his and Sisco's October 6 meeting with Saudi Foreign Minister Umar Saqqaf, who, after the Secretary's presentation on why the United States continued to support the idea of proximity talks, said he had planned to speak with Egyptian officials on the subject. (Ibid., RG 59, Central Files 1970–73, POL 27–14 ARAB–ISR) In telegram 3723/Secto 63 from USUN, October 6, Rogers reported his and Sisco's October 5 conversation with Mohammed Riad and Mohamed Zayyat, who had recently been appointed Foreign Minister, which considered how Egypt and Israel could make progress toward an interim Suez Canal agreement. (Ibid., Nixon Presidential Materials, NSC Files, Box 1169, Saunders Files, Middle

Summary: Our interim reassessment of the GOE position and policy on Middle East peace finds no prospect of a change in what they continue to regard as the central issues, territory and negotiations, absent evidence of change in US or Israeli positions thereon. The GOE regards such change as something the USG, not the GOE, must produce—or induce.

1. Prompted by reports of New York conversations about Middle East in reftels, among others, we have reassessed what we know and can infer about GOE position on Middle East peace. The fundamental elements of that position continue to be that "peace" or even "progress towards peace" are for Sadat and co. secondary in importance to the territorial issue and the "direct negotiation" issue. Compelling as the logic of the case for unfreezing matters is to us Anglo-Saxons, the logic for the Egyptians and other Arabs closest to their councils is that the present state of affairs is better, or at least no worse, than "submission" to Israel and the United States or either or both of them on what they see as the central issues.

2. The resultant impasse was succintly described by Jarring to Bush (USUN 3651). It strikes us as interesting that Jarring seems to have adopted the Egyptian view of the importance and nature of a "new US initiative" to breaking his efforts loose. "New US initiative" in this part of the Arab world we see as a euphemism for US pressure on Israel; it also has the advantage of passing the buck for doing something from the Govt. of Egypt to the Govt. of the US. Moreover, alas, the more we talk about the need for movement involving either of the central issues, and about opening the Suez Canal, the more Sadat and co. tend to conclude that the US cares more about changing the present state of affairs than they do; ergo, the more they tend to sit tight and await a "US initiative" to change the Israeli position, at least on the territorial issue. As Sadat continues to reiterate, he will not agree to give up one inch of Arab territory—all he has been and is willing to negotiate are the modalities and timetable of Israeli withdrawal to the 1967 border. The "direct negotiation" issue, is in his view a reinforcement for the territorial issue—indeed, they are mutually reinforcing.

3. We have not so far been able to think of any form of inducement or compulsion on GOE open to the United States that would yield Egyptian flexibility in the absence of Israeli agreement to full withdrawal, whether or not overtly induced by a "new US initiative." In e-

---

East Negotiations Files, Middle East—Jarring Talks, October 1–31, 1972) In telegram 3651 from USUN, October 4, the Mission reported that Jarring had told Bush that all the negotiating tracks in the Arab-Israeli dispute were "blocked" and that, unless the United States could "assume initiative" after the November Presidential election, he feared that the Middle East "would become increasingly unstable." (Ibid.)

ther event, the scenario would also have somehow to dispose of or at least neutralize the Egyptian view that "unlimited" US support of Israel—especially military—underlies Israeli intransigence on the central issues. A show of Israeli agreement that was not accompanied by some reassurance about the military dimension might not be enough to budge Sadat. Conversely, of course, a show of US compulsion of Israel would further entrench the Israelis, as the Egyptian leadership well knows even though they do not readily acknowledge it.

4. Our efforts to think of inducement or compulsion open to other governments in better communication with Sadat than the US is are not much more promising. Indeed, the renewed Egyptian effort to restore their political, psychological, and especially economic relationship with the Soviet Union, while cultivating Western Europeans too, looks to us to be calculated to help them hang on in the present impasse without losing or giving away anything of value to them.

5. The importance of these relationships is reinforced by the importance to Sadat of his relationship with Qaddafi. The latter's munificence in return for stonewalling Israel is a major determinant of Sadat's policy and posture, at least as strong as any purely Egyptian factor. The Saudi influence in the opposite direction is there, but the money does not talk as loudly. And while, as Saqqaf said (Secto 73–USUN 3818), Sadat no doubt wants a political solution, the solution he wants, by all the evidence, rhetorical and circumstantial, is one involving a degree of Israeli flexibility that, to put it mildly, is not visible from here.

6. In assessing all this, we have tried to allow for the customary posturing and polemics of the UNGA context, intensified this year by the US election campaign. There are, of course, other issues that are important to Sadat and his friends, and that efforts to move matters would have to take into account; the Palestinian refugees is prominent among these. But one does not, we believe, get to these further issues until the central issues are disposed of—as long as Sadat is in charge. Even with the current context stripped away (or lived through), however, we do not perceive an alteration in the Egyptian constellation of forces that would alone get even an interim solution going. And even if, as Hafez Ismail once enjoined me to remember, "the Arabs are very unpredictable," they can be just as unpredictable in living up to an agreement they do not want or like, as they might prove to be in purporting to make one.

Greene

315. Telegram From the Department of State to the Embassy in Israel[1]

Washington, October 20, 1972, 2115Z.

192092. Subject: Israeli Strategy re Fedayeen. Ref: Tel Aviv 6807.[2]

1. Appreciate your full report of meeting with Eban. Believe after our talks with Israelis there and here they understand well our reservations re their fedayeen strategy as expressed in air attacks October 15.[3] We have no desire therefore to prolong this exchange unnecessarily. Eban made several points to you in course his comments, however, that do not accord with our view of past history and present facts. Lest our silence be misconstrued, you should, in manner you deem most appropriate, register with GOI following points:

2. We are sure that Israel is doing all it can to avoid civilian casualties in its actions against fedayeen targets in Lebanon. But fact is on every such occasion in recent months, including according to our best information Oct 15 raids, there have been civilian casualties. We have greatest respect for Israeli intelligence but it like intelligence of any country can be wrong. It was unaware for example that tents used by fedayeen were on Sept 8 occupied by children many of whom were casualties. (Beirut 9696).[4] We gather it was unaware in Oct 15 action that fedayeen at Mazyef were absent on leave at time of raid.

---

[1] Source: National Archives, Nixon Presidential Materials, NSC Files, Box 610, Country Files, Middle East, Israel, Vol. XI. Secret; Exdis. Drafted by Stackhouse and Atherton, cleared in draft in INR/RNA/NE and AF/N, and approved by Sisco. Repeated to Amman, Beirut, Cairo, Tripoli, and USUN.

[2] In telegram 6807 from Tel Aviv, October 17, the Embassy reported Barbour's meeting with Eban, during which the Israeli Foreign Minister explained his government's thinking behind its recent air raid strategy against fedayeen installations in Lebanon and Syria. Eban said that "Israel will not be limited in its response and will act if it gets information about preparations at a fedayeen base. Israel does not accept logic that Israelis should let fedayeen train because they had not attacked across Israeli border for one month. Just as governments everywhere should act promptly against nests of hijackers and other terrorists abroad, so Israel should not wait if it can act to prevent future casualties on its own side and especially if Israeli action can be taken without causing civilian casualties." (Ibid.)

[3] On October 16, Sisco met with Rabin to discuss Israel's air raids of the previous day. The Assistant Secretary said that, while the United States "understood the objective to be that such raids were intended to 'encourage' GOL to take more effective steps in controlling the guerillas," he wanted to share U.S. "misgivings" about the October 15 strikes. He said that the United States considered the actions "ill-advised" and that "we urge Israel to try and enlarge its exchanges with the Lebanese authorities through appropriate channels," adding that, "in the absence of prior incidents or border crossings," such raids were "more likely to undermine the ability of the GOL to take effective action." Finally, Sisco wanted to emphasize that the United States did not raise this issue on behalf of Lebanon but at its own initiative to share its concern with Israel. (Telegram 188750 to Tel Aviv, October 16; ibid.)

[4] Not found.

3. Eban's remarks suggest that principal reason for Hussein's crackdown on fedayeen was Israeli pressure on fedayeen in Jordan. While undoubtedly Israeli policies had part in Hussein's finally grasping nettle, proximate and probably decisive factor in our view was direct threat fedayeen posed to very existence of Hashemite regime. Lebanese situation is very different—we believe crucially different—from that of Jordan, in number of respects, and it is risky to draw parallels.

4. Eban claims the Lebanese have backtracked on efforts to get fedayeen out of villages. As Israelis know from our exchanges on this subject, our info is that fedayeen have been ejected from and still being kept out of villages.

5. If Lebanon is still bound by Cairo Agreement[5] then it is an agreement reinterpreted from the original. What seems more important to us is not rpt not what overall framework of Lebanese-fedayeen agreement is called, but what actual Lebanese army restrictions are being carried out against fedayeen on the ground. By Israel's own account the Lebanon border has been free of fedayeen incursions for over a month. This is tangible evidence that Cairo Agreement, as originally understood, is not rpt not being fulfilled.

6. Eban asserts that Lebanon is only real base that terrorists now have, and that it is only place where terrorists are free to train and prepare actions. We are in basic disagreement with centrality which GOI accords to Lebanon in problem of terrorism. We believe it overlooks support of all kinds terrorists are receiving from other Arab countries, support without which fedayeen movement would be severely crippled. Eban told Secretary Sept 22 that without Arab governments' support terrorist organizations could not be effective. He spoke of evidence of massive links of terrorist organizations to Cairo, Beirut, Damascus and certain North African states. We agree with this evaluation, which puts Lebanon in proper perspective, and believe it is still valid.

7. Eban states that if fedayeen currently not shooting at Israelis this is not important because they are training to shoot. With due regard for Israel's perception of its own security we cannot agree that quiet along Israel's ceasefire lines is unimportant. It is a positive contribution to area stability and to atmosphere for diplomatic efforts for peace. Of almost equal importance it reflects a prudent and perhaps a constructive attitude on part of Israel's neighbors, in present instance particularly on part of Lebanon.

8. In sum, we agree with Israel that ideal situation would be complete elimination of fedayeen presence and activities on their territories

---

[5] See footnote 6, Document 60.

by all Arab governments. And we think some of Israel's earlier reactions to fedayeen incursions have had salutary effect on GOL determination to prevent such incursions. Where we diverge from GOI analysis is over latter's view that military strikes at fedayeen in Lebanon, even in absence of fedayeen attacks across border, can seriously inhibit terrorist actions in third countries or be carried out in ways that neither cause innocent civilian casualties nor have adverse political repercussions in Lebanon which in long run are counter to broader U.S. and we believe, Israeli interests.

9. On related subject, we note recent comments attributed to "Tel Aviv military sources" by CBS correspondent Wasserthile Oct 16 that Israel does not preclude striking against countries further removed which give support to fedayeen, including Libya. We deplore Libyan attitude re fedayeen activities as much as does GOI. We feel, however, that we must make clear to GOI our very real concern that any military action it might take against Libya—however justified Israel might consider it in light Libyan policies—could trigger emotional mob reactions that would place large American community in Libya in serious physical jeopardy.[6]

Irwin

---

[6] Barbour presented the Department's views to Elizur on the morning of October 23. (Telegram 6918 from Tel Aviv, October 24; ibid.)

---

316. Telegram From the Embassy in Israel to the Department of State[1]

Tel Aviv, November 9, 1972, 1025Z.

7357. Subject: US-Israel: Dayan Visit to Washington.[2]

Summary: Dayan is the one Israeli leader who continues to focus on possibility of interim Suez Canal settlement and by all indications to want it. We believe he should be encouraged. However, Dayan like rest

---

[1] Source: National Archives, Nixon Presidential Materials, NSC Files, Box 658. Country Files, Middle East, Middle East Nodis/Cedar/Plus, Vol. V. Secret; Nodis; Cedar Repeated to Cairo.

[2] Dayan visited New York and Washington November 12–14. The memorandum of conversation of Dayan's meeting with Department of Defense officials is Document 319.

of GOI is probably convinced that Sadat in due course will take his own initiative to bring about such settlement and that nothing should be done meanwhile which might sidetrack him. Dayan also must be concerned about current unrealistic mood of expectation in Cairo that US, with elections over, will help solve Egypt's problem with Israel. GOI for this reason may charge Dayan with making strong pitch in Washington for USG to do and say nothing about Arab-Israeli problem in coming weeks. As for substantive questions involved in interim settlement, it would not be surprising if Dayan's authority to talk with Americans about such matters at this juncture is severely limited; PriMin Meir would not want to risk mistaken impression in Washington that GOI is ready to send signals to Sadat. Dept might consider using occasion of Dayan's visit rekindle his desire to start moving now toward Canal settlement—and to strengthen his hand within GOI as leading proponent of such move—by renewing assurances of US willingness to be helpful in spheres of advance intelligence coordination monitoring and subsequent for any Canal settlement, possible limited observer role in such settlement, and fending off undesirable outside Middle East initiatives in meantime. *End summary.*

1. Dayan is the one Israeli leader who from the fall of 1970 to the present day has wanted strongly to see a partial Suez Canal settlement and who appears to remain convinced that one is achievable. Presumably his strong interest in disengagement with Egypt arises from Dayan's responsibility for military situation at Canal, his appreciation of normalization of life in Israel made possible by past two years of ceasefire at Canal, and his dread of unpredictable situation to which renewed shooting could lead. Dayan therefore is the right Israeli leader for US to encourage on subject of interim Canal settlement.

2. There is no reason to think, however, that Dayan does not share conviction of rest of Israeli leadership that Sadat is being led inexorably by flow of events toward taking an Egyptian initiative aimed at Israelis themselves (and not US). While recognizing that disarray in Cairo's relations with USSR and Egypt's internal unrest have weakened Sadat at the moment, making initiative toward Israel harder for him to undertake, we suspect Israelis like Dayan look upon Sadat's current troubles with his own military and his Soviet allies as sealing once and for all, in Sadat's mind, notion that Egypt can afford to delude itself that it has any military option against Israel for foreseeable future.

3. Israelis clearly have sensed mood of unrealistic anticipation in Cairo, which Minister Greene has so succinctly reported (Cairo 2933),[3] that USG after elections may take major new initiative in Middle East

---

[3] Dated November 1. (National Archives, RG 59, Central Files 1970–73, POL 27–14 ARAB–ISR)

entailing pressure on Israel to bring about settlement acceptable to Egypt. Israelis undoubtedly view such mood not only as regrettable sidetrack for gradual evolution of Egyptian policy in realistic direction, but also as serious potential danger because of instability to which Cairo's inevitable disappointment with US can lead. We therefore believe that if Israeli leadership charges Dayan with conveying any message in Washington on November 14, it will be to emphasize need, as GOI sees it, for US in coming weeks to do and say absolutely nothing concerning Arab-Israeli problem.

4. As we are reporting separately, Israel's pre-election campaign is now getting underway, and Dayan is involved. How involved he is personally is hard to judge, since his numerous supporters have been applying all their talents to do battle for him and may have to some extent helped to create the emanations we are getting to effect that a sparring among leading personalities is underway within Labor Party. Suffice it to say here, in any case, that Washington should not be surprised if Dayan's lips are tightly buttoned Nov 14 with respect to substantive issues involved in any interim Canal settlement. Fact that Dayan at first regretted and later accepted Secretary's invitation to come to Washington during his visit to US could conceivably mean that Dayan's colleagues in Cabinet have hammered out with him set of guidelines for his talks with US officials. Given Dayan's propensity to speak his mind on terms of an accommodation with Egypt and GOI's concern not to encourage US to say anything on this subject because of Cairo's current mood of expectation, one of guidelines might well be injunction to stay off subject of Suez Canal.

5. If Dayan while in Washington cannot be drawn out on substantive aspects of Canal settlement, and if as we expect he takes view that US and Israel should do absolutely nothing at this time to prime the Egyptian pump, US talks with Dayan Nov 14 can still be turned to good advantage, in our view, if they serve the purpose of reviving and strengthening Dayan's interest in seeing Canal settlement come to pass. Dept might therefore consider renewing to Dayan assurances of US readiness to: A) Enter into detailed discussion with Israel at any time of intelligence aspects of interim settlement, to give Israel added assurance that it can safely carry out partial withdrawal; B) provide Israel with meaningful, ongoing assistance in monitoring good performance on obligations undertaken by Egypt in any Canal agreement, if desired, C) serve in limited supervisory or observer capacity on ground as part of Canal settlement arrangements, if desired; and D) assist Israel meanwhile in fending off any unhelpful outside initiatives on Middle East arising in UN or other contexts.

Barbour

317. Memorandum From Harold Saunders of the National Security Council Staff to the President's Assistant for National Security Affairs (Kissinger)[1]

Washington, November 13, 1972.

SUBJECT

A Proposal for a New Step Toward Arab-Israeli Peace Negotiations—How to Use This Book

A *table of contents* immediately follows this memo.[2]

The purpose of this book is to give you a take-off point for thinking about where we might go from here in looking afresh at the Arab-Israeli problem. I have done this (a) by putting together *one possible approach to Israel followed by approaches to the Egyptians and Jordanians* and (b) by giving you a series of variations which could suggest modifications to the basic approach. I am not pushing any one approach, but I thought it would be most helpful to put something together as a starting point for discussion.

Many refinements would be necessary if this were to become a basis for any kind of action. But it seemed desirable to start looking at general approaches now.

There is more material included in this book than you will need initially. *I suggest that you glance over the first memo under the next tab marked "Strategy—Considerations and Approach." Then read fairly carefully Sub-tab 1 marked "Israel," which is a full set of talking points for an initial approach to the Israelis. This will give you a sense of the essence of the approach put forward for discussion. The heart of the proposal is at the red tabs in those two papers.* Following the Israeli talking paper are similar papers for use with the Egyptians, Jordanians and Soviets, but they are all elaborations of the approach initially outlined to the Israelis.

If you want to pursue the subject in more detail, you can later move on to the other tabs which outline the main broad options for settlements between Egypt-Israel and Jordan-Israel.

---

[1] Source: National Archives, Nixon Presidential Materials, NSC Files, Box 1190, Saunders Files, Middle East Negotiations Files, Arab-Israeli Negotiations A Review of the Present Situation and Options for the Future Mr. Saunders. Secret. All brackets are in the original. This memorandum is attached to a November 14 covering memorandum from Saunders to Kissinger under the subject heading, "The Middle East, 1973–1976," which begins: "I have prepared this book over the past couple of months with the thought that new attention would have to be given to the Middle East—one way or another—after the President's re-election. It is consistent with your desire for memos on where we might go over the next four years." The book is attached but not printed.

[2] Attached but not printed.

While the approach below will sound as if it is directed primarily at an Egypt-Israel settlement, it is one of the premises of the papers in this book that *we should simultaneously develop strategies toward both the Jordanian and Egyptian fronts,* even though those strategies may be quite different.

In a nutshell, *the proposed approach on Egypt-Israel negotiations would differ from the Rogers Plan in three important respects.*

1. It would begin by trying to establish with Israel a genuinely reciprocal alliance relationship, in substance though not in name. This would require a *change in style* from the past four years. Instead of hitting the Israelis with a big initiative on a more or less take-it-or-leave-it basis, we would move through a period of consultation with them before putting a new initiative in final form for presentation to the Egyptians or Jordanians.

2. Then, it would move to try to reach an understanding in *private talks* with both sides *on the general objectives* of a negotiation *before either negotiating details or going public.* Any interim step will founder, as in 1971, on these issues eventually anyway.

3. Since it is unlikely that the central issue of borders can be resolved before negotiation, this approach would seek a statement of objective that could help meet Sadat's need while actually accepting the fact that he cannot reach final terms without negotiating. We would try to *shift the issue from "withdrawal" to "restoration of Egyptian sovereignty"* so as to allow flexibility for phasing withdrawal and even the stationing of Israeli troops on Egyptian soil. Thus, we would not commit ourselves in advance of a negotiation to total Israeli withdrawal from the Sinai.

The following are the main elements of what I have put forward as a suggested approach on the Egypt-Israel front:

—Any new initiative would start with *an approach to Israel:*

—*We would propose dealing with Israel as an ally in substance, if not in name.* The purpose would be to increase confidence and response since we would make clear that any such relationship would have to be reciprocal.

—We would *buy the Israeli strategy of stretching the settlement process over as long a time period as possible* with the pullback of troops staged through agreed phases, but at the same time we would state that *our interests require that some process of negotiation begin soon.* We would say that we are prepared to press for mixed direct and indirect negotiations as early as possible so that the role of outsiders would be minimized.

—We would say that, *before launching a new initiative, we want to consult with the Israelis* in detail on the nature of that initiative. [This is significantly different in style from what State is initially considering.]

—During those consultations, we would seek Israeli authorization for us to convey a *message to President Sadat* outlining the agreed approach. We believe it is essential to tell him that Israel will negotiate without preconditions and will not at the outset of negotiation preclude any particular outcome, *including restoration of Egyptian sovereignty in the Sinai*. We would tell the Israelis frankly that this would be our preference but that we will not try to force it on Israel. In using the word "sovereignty," we would deliberately try to shift the issue from "withdrawal" to the question of sovereignty because this would allow flexibility for maintaining Israeli troops on Egyptian soil over agreed periods while perhaps beginning to meet Egyptian requirements for getting most of their land back. Its purpose would be to provide *enough discussion of a final settlement to try to meet Sadat's need and then to permit detailed negotiations on a first step*, presumably opening the Canal and pulling Israeli troops away from it.

—We would say that, while the (probably secret) talks on general objectives would have to precede any negotiation of a partial settlement on the Canal, we would be prepared to see them continue simultaneously with more open talks on a Canal settlement.

—To *Egypt* we would privately convey the position outlined above. We would promise that this new initiative would be tightly controlled from the White House and would outline our philosophy of not promising to deliver more than is possible to achieve. We would offer several secret talks on overall objectives and on procedures for getting talks started if the Egyptians wish. With Israeli concurrence, we would tell the Egyptians that we see the objective of negotiation as the restoration of Egyptian sovereignty in the Sinai, but that we are not prepared or able to force this objective on Israel. If the approach is to work, Sadat will have to decide that the time has come to negotiate, but he will have to have some confidence that we are serious about pushing beyond an interim settlement on the Canal.

—Unlike previous initiatives, we would propose *paying simultaneous attention to moving negotiations on both the Jordanian and the Egyptian fronts*. Over the past three years we have concentrated almost exclusively on the Egyptian front. We should now at least do what we can to facilitate parallel negotiations between Israel and Jordan. King Hussein will be here in February to see the President and to ask what support he can count on, and we will have to be prepared for that. The *main choice to be discussed with Hussein at that time is between:*

—a settlement that might be called "interim," would give Hussein much less than he wants on the West Bank, but would let him start building his United Arab Kingdom with its autonomous Palestinian province there *and*

—a strategy whereby Israel, in agreement with Jordan or not, would prepare the West Bank for autonomy and ultimate choice of allegiance over time.

—We would *inform the Soviets* of our general approach to the problem, indicate willingness to go on discussing the approach outlined last May, *but suggest that we leave details to Egypt and Israel and concentrate our own talks on issues which are appropriate for the superpowers to address.* These might include the nature of major power or Security Council guarantees, the nature of US and USSR support for UN observer missions in the Sinai, and perhaps the nature of our ultimate military relationship to the Middle Eastern nations.

—We would *leave the Syrian front aside for the moment.* Our primary interest is to keep Syria from preventing progress on other fronts and to avoid deep Soviet involvement. This may require that we offer the prospect of an eventual Syrian involvement in a settlement provided the Syrians themselves are interested. However, if the Jordanians wanted to try drawing the Syrians into an interim settlement, then we might find ourselves sounding out the Israelis on a token pullback or partial demilitarization on the Golan Heights.

If you wished to develop this idea, two sets of approaches would have to be made which are not included in this book:

—We would want to develop support for Sadat and Hussein in those other parts of the Arab world where we have access.

—We would want to develop support in key European countries.

One final point is that *timing will be critical.* We will lose Israeli confidence if we move too quickly because they do not want us to do anything that will lighten the pressure on Sadat to negotiate with them. On the other hand, pressure on Sadat will mount to heat up the Suez front, perhaps before the next US–USSR summit, in order to force the superpowers to act.

318. Telegram From the Interests Section in Egypt to the Department of State[1]

Cairo, November 14, 1972, 1110Z.

3060. (Note: Since content of this message does not strictly speaking fall into any of the special distribution captions of which I am aware, I have not used one of them. I request, however, that distribution be as closely limited as if I had.)

1. *Summary:* During routine call on Undersecretary Ismail Fahmy at Ministry Foreign Affairs November 13, subject of next moves re peace in Middle East came up. In response to my statement that US view remains as previously expressed (State 205883),[2] Fahmy made standard, resistant rejoinder but then allowed himself "personal" observation that "it is up to us (Egypt)" to devise something new to inject into situation. Although he would not specify what this might be, I do not rpt not on reflection think we can prudently assume he was talking about politico-diplomatic initiative, nor that he was speaking as "personally" as he professed. Even though he would not signal what Egypt's hole card is, he wanted me to believe there is one. *End summary.*

2. As conversation developed, each of us acknowledged that following US elections, and in part stimulated by reports of Secretary Rogers' statement on "Meet the Press" November 5[3] and Egyptian re-

---

[1] Source: National Archives, Nixon Presidential Materials, NSC Files, Box 638, Country Files, Middle East, Egypt, Vol. VIII. Secret; Nodis. A typed notation at the top of the first page reads: "Our Interests Section in Cairo reports that during a routine call on Undersecretary Fahmy at the Ministry of Foreign Affairs yesterday, Fahmy indicated that Egypt has a hole card and wants the U.S. to think it is potent, in the hope that this will bring us to produce a change in Israeli policy. Fahmy observed that it is up to us (Egypt) to devise something new to inject into the situation."

[2] Telegram 205883 to USUN, November 10, reads in part: "A. As we have consistently made clear, we do not think Middle East debate at this time can serve any practical purpose. If anything, it is more likely to delay time when parties face up to fact that there is no realistic alternative to getting down to some kind of meaningful negotiating process. B. We take it as forgone conclusion that no resolution, however carefully formulated to avoid exacerbating sensitivities of either side, will emerge of the kind that could help in any way to get such negotiating process started. In these circumstances we believe the best possible outcome, after all concerned have had their say during debate, would be to adjourn debate without any resolution. This would leave matters where they now stand and avoid further complicating the atmosphere for getting negotiations started." (Ibid., Box 1169, Saunders Files, Middle East Negotiations Files, Middle East—Jarring Talks, November 1–30, 1972) The UN General Assembly discussed the Middle East in plenary meetings November 29–December 8. See Document 320.

[3] When asked about the Middle East, Rogers said: "There isn't as much attention focused on peace as there is on war, but we have had a cease-fire in the Middle East now for about 27 months. We are going to do what we can diplomatically to see if we can get negotiations started between Egypt and Israel, and very soon now we will be very active in discussions of that kind to see if we can get negotiations started. We think that the Secu-

sponse thereto (Cairo 2988),[4] publicists and diplomats in Cairo have been busily trying to get out of each of us what is new. I said that I have responded to such queries by restating importance USG attaches to inauguration of process which engages parties to Arab-Israeli conflict in discussion of settlement—as before. Fahmy allowed as how he too has been replying that he has heard nothing new, but he went on to say that both Cairo diplomats and reports from Khalil in Washington have it that the diplomatic pundits there believe something new is actually in the making. He supposed, what with President's announced intention to re-organize this administration, it would be at least January before new policy approaches surface. I simply repeated what has been communicated to me and said I did not think it would be useful for me to join in speculation about anything else.

3. Fahmy responded with acknowledgment of latter point, disparaging comment about possible "trial balloons," and standard statement of inability to understand why USG has moved from '69 to its present position. After a pause, however, he said he did not expect change in US stance, so in his personal view "it is up to us." Egypt's next move, he continued, is going to "require a lot of work" on their part; he would not be drawn on what that would involve. I said at one point that just as I was not going to try to anticipate what if anything new USG might say, I would not keep asking GOE what they have that is new; I assumed that if they have anything new to say, they will let me know.

4. Fahmy said that this might not be necessary. He said I would be able to perceive the "new" situation when it develops, and "they will feel it in Washington, Moscow and Jerusalem too." Fahmy continued that "we will have to pull ourselves together here" and get a lot of work done, and he wound up, as he had started, saying he knows that the next move is Egypt's.

5. In response to my reiteration of the "negotiating process" point, Fahmy rather briskly said that this is not the heart of the matter. Egypt's leadership, in the eyes not only of other Arab states but also of

---

rity Council Resolution 242 has to be implemented fully, but we think that a good beginning is to attempt to work out an agreement between Egypt and Israel that would open the Suez Canal, have a partial withdrawal, and have a commitment to full implementation of Security Council Resolution 242." (Department of State *Bulletin*, November 27, 1972, p. 622)

[4] Telegram 2988 from Cairo, November 7, transmitted the Egyptian Minister of Information's statement: "Egypt has previously declared on several occasions her rejection of the holding of direct negotiations with Israel. She has also declared her rejection of partial solutions to the Middle East problem. The last of these occasions was the opening session of the present People's Assembly session, when President Anwar El Sadat stated that America has obstructed every attempt to achieve peace based on justice and wants to face us with acceptance of a fait accompli. The President also stated in his speech that we would not cede one inch of Arab land and that there would be no negotiations with Israel." (National Archives, RG 59, Central Files 1970–73, POL 27–14 ARAB–ISR)

the people of Egypt, could not at the present stage be seen to be seeking a deal. (*Comment:* This part of the conversation was the most elliptical, but I thought it prudent, all things considered, not to try to nail Fahmy down; his role in the policy-making on this issue is not clear anyway.)

6. Fahmy's remarks about forthcoming UNGA debate I am reporting separately.[5] In the foregoing context, he seemed to be saying that this was something GOE figures it has to get through tactically, with as large a friendly vote on a resolution as possible. He said he assumed the US would abstain rather than wind up in small, negative minority.

7. *Comment:* Fahmy is too accomplished a pro to embark solo on what has all the earmarks of the first round of a poker hand. (He said at one point he would not be making a record of this part of our talk; maybe not. I would be surprised if he believed I would not.) He was, I think, saying Egypt has a hole card, and wants US to believe it is potent, in the hopes this will bring US to produce a change in Israeli policy. The thought (also reflected in government inspired press) that US policy cannot be expected to change can plausibly (if illogically) be read as part of an effort to make us take seriously the threat of Egyptian action, thus (hopefully) impelling the change they seek.

Greene

---

[5] Telegram 3065 from Cairo, November 14. (Ibid.)

319. Memorandum of Conversation[1]

Washington, November 14, 1972, 12:15 p.m.

SUBJECT

Discussions with MOD Dayan

PARTICIPANTS

Israeli Side
Minister of Defense Dayan
Ambassador Rabin
Mr. Dror, Israeli Mission
Major General Gur, Israeli Attaché
LtCol Bar-on, Aide to MOD

United States Side
Deputy Secretary of Defense
Admiral Moorer, Chairman, JCS *
Assistant Secretary of Defense Nutter
Assistant Secretary of Defense Henkin *
Vice Admiral Peet, Director/DSAA *
Deputy Assistant Secretary of Defense Noyes
Major General Brett, OASD/ISA
Mr. Kubal, OASD/ISA **
Col Jones, Military Assistant **

* Lunch only
** Pre-lunch discussion only

Following introductory comments and a discussion of some of the MOD's experience with the British (Rabin: "The British are very good losers"), conversation turned to Egypt and Israeli-Egyptian relations. Dayan acknowledged Israel was relatively much stronger than Egypt, and felt Egypt realized it would lose if it started a war. He believed the present impasse was a result of Sadat's lack of real leadership, his unwillingness to face reality and turn to negotiations. Instead, since he couldn't do what he wanted, he did nothing. Secretary Rush referred to President Nixon's difficult decision to bomb North Vietnam and mine the harbors, despite the risks of undercutting his trip to Moscow, détente with the Soviets, and loss of the election. (Dayan: "I'm not sorry about the result of the election"). This strong action of the President, to almost everyone's surprise, received very strong popular backing in

---

[1] Source: Washington National Records Center, OSD Files: FRC 330–77–0094, Box 62, Israel. Secret; Sensitive. Drafted on November 16 by Brett and approved by Nutter. The conversation took place in Rush's office and the Secretary's Dining Room. Dayan also met with Rogers and Helms that day. (*New York Times*, November 15. 1972, p. 1) The meeting with Rogers is summarized in the President's Wednesday Briefing, November 21. (National Archives, Nixon Presidential Materials, NSC Files, Box 1283, Saunders Files, Subject Files, Israel) No record of the meeting with Helms has been found.

this country, the trip to Moscow was not cancelled, and the President has been overwhelmingly re-elected. Perhaps, Sadat might receive surprising support also if he had the courage to negotiate.

Dayan agreed, but felt Sadat was unwilling to take any such risks. He felt Sadat was weak and getting weaker. The Russians are not out completely and indeed are coming back a bit, but probably not with combat personnel and pilots. They probably will, over time, introduce new weapons but he felt the Soviets had been deeply offended by the expulsion and would insist on Egypt meeting Soviet terms. Thus the Soviets might insist on a voice in selection of MOD, Chief of Staff, etc. He was not sure that the Egyptian military had been involved in Sadat's expulsion decision, even though they did not like the Russians. Rather Sadat had gotten himself in a hole with his promises of a year of decision, and blamed the Russians for his failures. Mr. Rush noted that the Soviets were vitally interested in a détente for a number of reasons, so there was hope they would be a moderating influence in the Middle East. Dayan agreed the Soviets were not interested in a confrontation with the U.S. or backing a loser in the Arabs, but would still seek to keep their position in Egypt. To do this they knew they had to give something, to meet some Egyptian demands at least for arms if not for personnel. He thought the Russians would support better aircraft, perhaps more SAM 6s, etc.

The discussions in the Dining Room commenced with Dayan discussing the current relationship between Jordan and Israel.[2] Mr. Noyes asked Dayan whether an interim settlement could be formulated for Jordan that might be pursued simultaneously to the well known interim canal settlement proposal. Dayan responded that he did not believe it would be possible for Hussein to be satisfied and to be able to retain his position in the Arab world as well as his position in his own government.

To do so he would have to get major concessions from Israel, concessions which Israel was not prepared to make. Dayan added that for

---

[2] The next day, November 15, Meir and King Hussein held a secret meeting. As reported in a November 27 memorandum from Helms to Kissinger, Meir presented Hussein with Israel's minimum demands for a settlement with Jordan, which included: 1) Israel's retention of the "unpopulated areas along the 1967 Israeli-Jordanian border in addition to unspecified agricultural settlements along the Jordan River; 2) Jordan's resumption of control of the rest of a demilitarized West Bank, which meant a total absence of Jordanian army forces west of the Jordan River; and 3) Israel's retention of sovereignty over the entire, undivided city of Jerusalem. Meir added that Israel would never relinquish the Golan Heights and would have to retain a strip along the eastern coast of the Sinai Peninsula, including Sharm el-Sheikh. Hussein and Zaid Rifai, who was also present, believed that the Israeli Prime Minister was on the defensive, "spending a great deal of time emphasizing how the U.S. could not pressure Israel in a settlement." (Ibid., Box 610, Country Files, Middle East, Israel)

some time an informal arrangement had been under way with Jordan. This is clearly indicated by the fact that the "bridges are open." He considered that this accommodation was a satisfactory one for the time being to both Israel and Jordan, and that in the near term he could not see any other solution. Mr. Rush pointed out that King Hussein was certainly one of the most moderate leaders in the Arab world. Rabin countered that "Yes, he was moderate to the Western world, but this was not necessarily the case in his relations with Israel." Rabin stressed that Hussein unilaterally entered into the 1967 war even ahead of the Syrians. Dayan and Rabin then reviewed on a moment-by-moment basis the actions that Hussein had taken in the initial stages of the Six Day War. Stress was placed on the fact Hussein struck on the ground before any other Arab army. The conversation then turned to a general discussion of the situation in the Middle East.

About half way through the meal Dayan commented that it was a working luncheon and that to earn his meal he believed it advisable to turn the discussion toward some specific subjects of interest to Israel. He stated that his government was very interested in procuring additional F–4s and A–4s so deliveries would continue at about the current rate, this being at 2–3 a month. He did not indicate the overall numbers but he did state that these aircraft would be needed as attrition aircraft. Mr. Rush responded that the respective staffs could discuss this in greater detail and that the subject would be taken under consideration by the USG.

Dayan then turned to the subject of the production of the Mirage type aircraft (MX79), and the need for Israel to have the approval in principle of the USG for the support of this aircraft. He emphasized this was a subject of great importance to Israel. He stated that it is Israel's desire to produce a simple Mirage type aircraft which would be available to the IAF by 1976, and one that would be better than the Mirage. He expected that this airplane would not be available until some time in 1976 and would be built in small numbers and not for export. At the same time, he said, this airplane in no way is considered a substitute for the requirement for additional A–4s and F–4s. Dayan then emphasized that what his government needed was a decision on the principle of the USG supporting production of this aircraft. Mr. Rush commented that this was a decision of major importance which affected both governments. He pointed out that the manufacture of an aircraft was difficult and expensive, and could have very grave economic consequences. He emphasized this by pointing out the recent problems that Lockheed Aircraft Corporation had encountered and the necessity for the USG to help the company out. He said there have been several companies in the past that have come close to bankruptcy or gone bankrupt in attempting to produce competitive military aircraft. Therefore, it was of considerable concern to the USG that Israel undertake this major step only with full knowledge of the economic problems that could be encountered. Mr. Rush added that he would be very candid and that such an undertaking also presented certain additional problems, not only of an international political nature but also domestic in regard to our own manufacturers and labor force. He explained that we cannot back an aircraft that would be competitive with our own aircraft industries. Dayan responded that he was not prepared to discuss the economics of the situation but that he was certain such information could be made available to the USG. He again emphasized that Israel felt that within the next decade it must produce its own aircraft. Such an Israeli-produced aircraft should be of some advantage to the USG in that it would no longer be necessary for Israel to come to the U.S. for all its aircraft and thus create international political problems. Rabin interjected that his government fully understood Dr. Nutter's letter in that the USG was prepared to support a prototype program but not production. Rabin stated that no one builds just prototypes but the purpose is to build prototypes to support production. With this in mind it was essential that Israel get approval in principle for USG production support of the Israeli Mirage-type aircraft. Dr. Nutter responded that our government handled such undertakings on a step by step basis and that our policy currently was that we "fly before we buy". In the case of Israel the initial decision was to support a retrofit program for the older Mirage aircraft, by furnishing certain requested equipment. The second step which was recently approved was the release of equipment and certain know-how to support a prototype program. Based on a review of the prototype, a logical decision could be made on whether or not to support production.

MOD Dayan then indicated that Ambassador Rabin had a subject that he wished to discuss. The Ambassador stated that there was a critical requirement for Israel to secure certain additional intelligence capability, and that this could be done by the release of two USAF C–130s. The Secretary responded that this subject would be taken under advisement along with the Israeli views.[3]

Dayan then stated that Israel was most interested in securing the Lance or the Hawk to achieve an effective surface-to-surface capability to use against missile sites. He added he would like Major General Gur to address this subject in greater detail. General Gur stated that the Israelis were interested in Lance, "smart bombs," and the Maverick and

---

[3] On November 22, Rush informed Helms that the Secretary of Defense had determined, based on a review by the Middle East Task Group, that the United States would not be able to release the two C–130 planes to Israel. (Washington National Records Center, OSD Files: FRC 330–77–0094, Box 62, Israel)

that these had been put before the METG. General Gur emphasized that the release of these weapons to the Israelis would greatly increase the accuracy of their attacks while resulting in minimizing casualties to both sides. He added that they also desire additional Shrikes. Mr. Rush responded that this would be taken into consideration. Dayan also cited the need for a weapon to counter the Foxbat which the Russians prior to their departure from Egypt had flown at will over the Sinai.

Dayan then turned to Mr. Dror and indicated that he, too, had a subject that he wished to raise. Dror stated that since the problem had arisen in regard to the aircraft production know-how, that all other normal know-how had slowed down. Specifically, he said that requests for production know-how for parts unrelated to the MX79 had not been forthcoming. In fact, it appeared that there was a 360° check on all the production know-how for the J–79 engine parts as well as other F–4 parts. He stated that he had a specific problem with the environmental control units for which they already had much of the production data. They needed these units in order to increase their expertise on assembling and disassembling these units. Major General Brett responded that this was correct, that all this information was being held because in our view it related directly to production know-how for the MX79. However, in the case of the environmental control units, units had been released sufficient to support the prototype program.

After a few additional amenities the luncheon was concluded.

G. Warren Nutter

320. Memorandum From the President's Deputy Assistant for National Security Affairs (Haig) to the President's Assistant for National Security Affairs (Kissinger)[1]

Washington, November 21, 1972.

SUBJECT

Message from the Egyptians

Attached at Tab A is a message from Ismail which was delivered through the secret channel.[2] After handing over the note, Ismail elaborated on several points orally. The following are the significant points in his presentation:

—The Egyptians attach great importance to future exploratory talks but these can be adversely affected by a positive response to further demands by Israel for arms, a blocking position during the coming discussions in the UN, and the continuation of Israeli air strikes against Syria and Lebanon.

—The Egyptians wish to have the first round of discussions conducted in a third country and publicly announced at the conclusion.

—Although the Egyptian Foreign Minister will be in New York, this channel remains the sole channel for the discussion of the Middle East problem between the two Presidents.

In elaborating on the above points, Ismail noted that:

—Anywhere in Europe such as London, Rome or Paris would be acceptable for the first meeting. Future sessions could be held both in the US and Egyptian capitals.

—Since the talks would be announced, it would be necessary to have the third country agree to host the talks before they begin.

—With regard to the forthcoming UN Middle East debate, the Egyptians hope the US will not obstruct the resolution but rather will accept and live with the fact that the resolution will come to pass just as it did last year.[3]

—These procedural modifications in no way lessen the Egyptian's desire for talks with Dr. Kissinger.

---

[1] Source: National Archives, Nixon Presidential Materials, NSC Files, Kissinger Office Files, Box 131, Country Files, Middle East. Secret; Sensitive; Exclusively Eyes Only. Kissinger initialed the memorandum and wrote "OBE" at the top of the first page.

[2] Dated November 20; attached but not printed.

[3] Reference is to Resolution 2799 adopted December 13, 1971. See footnote 4, Document 270.

It is my understanding that in the UN debate which begins next week, we are presently postured to take a neutral and low-key position. You may, however, want to call George Bush to ensure that our delegation is properly postured for the debate.

321. Telegram From the Department of State to the Interests Section in Egypt[1]

Washington, December 4, 1972, 2349Z.

219619. Ref: Cairo 3247. Tel Aviv 7927.[2]

1. *FYI.* Rabin interview, although unfortunate in sense that he chose to make it at all at this time and thereby reveal existence of US-Israeli memorandum on ground rules for our role in proximity talks, nevertheless contains essentially accurate description of some points in this understanding. Careful reading of Rabin comments reveals little more than confirmation of well-known tenets of US policy: That (para four second reftel) there will be no Israeli withdrawal without agreement between the two sides, that the US wants to preserve the ceasefire, that US assistance to Israel is to prevent enforced evacuation from the ceasefire lines; that (para five) solution cannot be imposed from outside, but must be negotiated on basis SC Res 242, that gap between two sides on overall settlement is too great to bridge at this juncture (which is why we favor interim agreement as means of facilitating negotiations on overall settlement); that (para six) principal obstacle pres-

---

[1] Source: National Archives, Nixon Presidential Materials, NSC Files, Box 658, Country Files, Middle East, Middle East Nodis/Cedar/Plus, Vol. V. Secret; Nodis; Cedar Plus. Drafted by Sterner, cleared by Atherton, and approved by Sisco. Repeated to Tel Aviv.

[2] Telegram 3247 from Cairo, December 2, reported the negative reaction of the Egyptian press to an interview that Rabin gave to the Israeli newspaper *Ma'ariv* on November 30, and conveyed Greene's concerns that the Egyptian Government would be "less disposed than ever to pick up the opportunity for talks under US aegis." (Ibid.) Telegram 7927 from Tel Aviv, December 1, transmitted the translation of Rabin's replies in the interview, including this comment: "In contacts which have been held lately between representatives of Israel and the US, both in the US and in Israel, it has been clear that there has been no change in the US position. Our clarification talks with the Americans at the beginning of 1972 were even formalized through a written aide-mémoire between the two governments. This aide-mémoire was used and is used today as the agreed policy between the United States and Israeli Governments on all things connected with progress on a political solution regarding the conflict between Israel and Egypt in the Middle East." (Ibid., RG 59, Central Files 1970–73, POL 27–24 ARAB–ISR) Regarding the U.S.-Israeli understanding on the proximity talks, see Documents 276 and 277.

ently blocking interim agreement talks is question linkage between that agreement and on-going negotiations for final peace settlement (which everybody recognizes); that (para seven) Egypt's demand for Israeli commitment to total withdrawal as part of interim agreement is "unacceptable" (if "unobtainable" is substituted here this is in effect what Secretary said in his 1971 UNGA speech[3] and what we have stressed to Egyptians privately on many occasions subsequently).

2. Problem is created by immediate rush by Egyptian press to distort understanding to fit their worst fears and to cast it in unfavorable light. We see little profit in trying to refute specific distortions that appear publicly; we will, however, be sending you text of line that we propose to use here which you and other posts can also use.[4] *End FYI.*

3. We do not feel you should take initiative to seek appointment for specific purpose of discussing Rabin interview. However, during any future calls you may have with FonMin officials or in any next informal contact, you may draw on following.

4. *Begin talking points.* Understanding which Rabin refers to in his interview resulted from Israel's desire for clarifications about US position concerning interim agreement and role USG would play in proximity talks we had proposed. As we told Ghaleb when delivering Secretary's message to Sadat, delay in obtaining Israeli agreement to proximity talks was largely result of our insistence on retaining freedom of action that would enable US to play such role effectively without being an advocate of either side.[5] We are satisfied that understanding reached with Israel at this time does not impair this flexibility. This point was also reaffirmed in talks with Zayyat in October at UN.[6]

5. We wish particularly to make it clear that certain allegations appearing in the Cairo press are without foundation. On question of linkage between interim agreement and overall settlement, which US regards as a key issue, our views are well known to GOE. We view interim agreement as practical first step that would facilitate negotiations for final peace settlement in accordance with S.C. Res. 242. We do not accept thesis that interim agreement should be end in itself or that there should be no linkage between it and final peace settlement. Secondly, understanding reached with Israelis last winter concerned U.S. role in negotiations on interim agreement talks and did not deal with terms of either interim agreement or final peace settlement. Allegation appearing in one Cairo newspaper that US agreed to support Israel on question location of final borders is without foundation. We went no

---

[3] See footnote 3, Document 255.
[4] Not found.
[5] See Document 276.
[6] See footnote 2, Document 314.

further than reaffirming what we have frankly told Egyptians on number of occasions—namely that Israel cannot be expected to agree to total withdrawal to pre-June 5, 1967 lines in context of interim agreement.

Rogers

---

322. Telegram From the Department of State to the Embassy in Israel[1]

Washington, December 16, 1972, 0145Z.

227505. Subj: Secretary-Allon Meeting December 12.

Summary: Secretary-Allon conversation December 12 concentrated on outlook for negotiations with Jordan and Egypt.[2] Atmosphere was extremely warm, cordial and positive. Throughout talk Secretary stressed conviction time is ripe for beginning negotiating process: this is in Israel's interest and ours, and we should be thinking how to get process started. Allon made clear he felt Israel ready to discuss comprehensive or limited agreements with Jordan, or an interim agreement reached through talks under U.S. aegis with Egypt, or both. It evident however that Allon himself personally attracted—as he has indicated in public statements—to effort begin negotiations with Hussein. He spoke approvingly of Hussein's reaction to Munich incident[3] and said Hussein's plan for West Bank was good "except for its territorial concepts." In spite of this Allon was anxious that U.S. not give Hussein any "illusions" when he comes early next year, or appear over eager to move. To suggestion that Israel might give reassurance re Jerusalem's future that would make settlement more feasible, Allon said maximum

---

[1] Source: National Archives, Nixon Presidential Materials, NSC Files, Box 610, Country Files, Middle East, Israel, Vol. XI. Secret; Exdis. Drafted by Stackhouse and approved in draft by Sisco, and by Atherton. Repeated to Amman, Beirut, Cairo, Jerusalem, London, Paris, Moscow, Jidda, and USUN. All brackets are in the original except those indicating text omitted by the editors.

[2] During a phone call with Haldeman on November 17, Kissinger said that Rogers would "now run wild and try to win one," to which Haldeman commented: "And that's probably true, because Rogers did talk about wanting to get into the Middle East thing before he leaves, at least get negotiations started." Kissinger told him that "it's a disaster for the second term and he's affronted that it was done without discussion from him." The new administration should start "with a clear slate," Kissinger added. (*Haldeman Diaries, Multimedia Edition,* November 17, 1972)

[3] See footnote 2, Document 307.

Israel could give would be extraterritoriality to Hussein as Muslim representative for Holy Places under Israeli sovereignty, and it would not be easy to persuade Israeli public of this. Secretary reassured Allon we would not give Hussein illusions but went on to stress U.S. respect for him, our continuing support of Jordan, including military support, and our hope King and Israel will find ways to move toward peace.[4] Re Egypt, Allon expressed concern Egyptians may undertake out of frustration some kind of limited military action in coming weeks. Secretary and Sisco said everything Egyptians said indicated they well aware military options not practical. Sadat, we believed, would be responsive to effort that would enable him to show his people he was getting something. Allon asked what Israel could do. Were proximity talks for an interim agreement the answer? Allon stressed he was not against interim agreement, he was for it. Secretary replied we believed this was most promising and feasible approach. Way had to be found to get around obstacle created by Israel's reply to Jarring 2/71 memo.[5] We were not proposing anything at this time but trying to convey our frame of mind. While stressing Israel ready for negotiations, Allon introduced no new ideas except to suggest rather tentatively that the U.S. might be instrumental in bringing Mrs. Meir and President Sadat into direct and secret talks. Secretary made clear he did not think this kind of premature summitry was really a practical alternative. At close, Allon expressed gratification current state U.S.-Israel relations and improvement U.S. relations with Arabs (it proves Israeli theory, he said, former does not preclude latter). He said he hoped U.S. deliveries of aircraft would continue. And he urged we continue to express to Soviets our interest in exodus under decent conditions of Soviet Jews. Secretary noted recent record level of Soviet Jewish emigration and assured Allon we would continue be active in what we thought would be most helpful way, i.e. through quiet efforts. *End summary.*

[Omitted here is the remainder of the telegram.]

Rogers

---

[4] Hussein visited the United States February 5–7, 1973, meeting with both President Nixon and Secretary Rogers on February 6. See *Foreign Relations,* 1969–1976, volume XXV, Arab-Israeli Crisis and War, 1973, Documents 14 and 15.

[5] For Jarring's memorandum, see footnote 2, Document 205. For Israel's reply, see Document 211.

323. Telegram From the Embassy in Jordan to the Department of State[1]

Amman, December 17, 1972, 0805Z.

5622. Subject: Jordan-Israeli Peace Negotiations. Ref: Tel Aviv 8090.[2]

Summary: Gap between Hussein and Israeli positions on peace terms so great that prospects look slim.[3] Yet Hussein would try direct negotiations if he saw reasonable prospect and he could go first, given independent, nationalist line to which he is committed. Internally, he is strong enough to have negotiating latitude but attitude of Arab moderates, especially Faisal, would be constraint. Outside, especially US, help essential with both Israel and Arabs. Durability of agreement should not be problem; GOJ stability such that any successor regime to Hussein almost surely will continue same conservative, nationalist policy. Indications of Israeli flexibility are hopeful, but Israelis unrealistic in appraising Hussein incentive to negotiate. Critical issue is Jerusalem, and Hussein has little incentive to accept mutilated West Bank while abandoning claim to Jerusalem, would probably prefer continue indefinitely as champion of Arab cause rather than formalize humiliating deal. If, however, Israelis have real incentive to compromise with Jordan, secret exploratory discussion probably possible, if judged worthwhile even with slim prospect of success. Would require Israeli signals of greater flexibility, particularly on Jerusalem; would have to deal with both Jerusalem and West Bank as inseparable package; and U.S. would have to accept some public onus (and real responsibility) for "imposing" settlement. *End summary.*

1. Gap between Israeli and Jordanian asking price for settlement is so great and incentives on both sides to compromise so modest that prospects for successful negotiations slim. Nevertheless, Tel Aviv reftel raises points that require consideration. Unlike complex Israeli politics, Jordan position depends almost entirely on one man and Hussein plays his cards very close to the chest; we have little basis for stating his views other than public record. This much said, we think Hussein could and would negotiate, but only if he saw reasonable prospect of

---

[1] Source: National Archives, Nixon Presidential Materials, NSC Files, Box 617, Country Files, Middle East, Jordan, Vol. VIII. Secret; Exdis. Repeated to Beirut, Cairo, Jidda, Jerusalem, Kuwait, Tel Aviv, and USUN.

[2] Telegram 8090 from Tel Aviv, December 8, reported the Embassy's analysis of the Israeli public's attitude toward a settlement with Jordan. (Ibid., Box 1169, Saunders Files, Middle East Negotiations Files, Middle East—Jarring Files, December 1–31, 1972)

[3] See footnote 2, Document 319.

settlement satisfactory to him, which he does not now see. As he told Rouleau of *Le Monde* recently,[4] direct negotiation is not problem; problem is what there is to negotiate about. Hussein is realist enough to recognize that overwhelming Israeli preponderance of power ensures Israel can dictate terms of settlement. Hard line coming out of Jerusalem till now, particularly on Jerusalem (assuming no softer line is being signalled privately) offers him no inducement to a negotiation which would, in effect, be capitulation to terms neither his inter-Arab relations nor his own convictions could tolerate.

2. Assuming adequate incentive to do so, Hussein could go first. Since September, 1970, he has increasingly followed line independent of other Arabs, hewing to tough line on Jordan national interests. It has been so successful he is deeply committed and very confident his line is right. He would not let Egyptian or radical Arab criticism steer him from profitable negotiation. In fact, he would probably get personal satisfaction from being leader and key figure and not averse to scoring over Egyptians. While he would be somewhat constrained by reaction of local Palestinians, he has sufficient internal stability and support from army and East Bankers to give him considerable latitude. Bigger constraint would be reaction of Arab moderates and, crucially, of Faisal (recent Hussein-Faisal conversation, Amman 5564,[5] underlines difficulties). Any deal would have to be sufficiently respectable, cosmetically and factually, for him to defend it effectively to these constituencies. Faisal's political and economic support, hints of possible Kuwaiti thaw, Syrian border opening, and general warming of Arab climate are assets he will not jeopardize lightly. If he were to go first, he would need assurance of real help from USG and other friends, not only with Israelis but among moderate Arabs.

3. Jordanians are following with moderate interest Dayan-Allon debate on West Bank future but show little inclination to discuss it seriously. They recognize it is primarily a domestic debate and, in any event, they see little in it that would provide a basis for serious negotiation. At same time, they have never liked interim Canal initiative, feeling that it would leave them with little leverage and diminish chances of satisfactory Jordan-Israel negotiation. Thus if Israelis showed any signs of real flexibility on issues with Jordan, Hussein would have incentive to preempt negotiating initiative from Egyptians. If Israelis themselves visibly more interested in West Bank/Jerusalem than Canal settlement, this too might encourage Hussein to negotiate.

---

[4] Eric Rouleau's interview with Hussein was published in the November 4 edition of *Le Monde*. (*New York Times*, December 4, 1972, p. 1)

[5] Not found.

4. Issue of Hussein's durability and of what comes after him does not seem to us so great a problem. Most regimes in world pose same problems in more serious form. Certainly, Egypt does. Even were Hussein to go, succession issue would be decided within small group at top with army holding decisive hand. Army, the potential rivals within leadership group, the powerful and conservative East Bank clans and tribes, and the local establishment are all sufficiently like-minded and cohesive that successor regime will almost certainly be army-based, East Bank dominated, conservative and nationalist, and will continue Hussein policies and commitments. More important, it will probably have power and stability to do so. We would judge Jordanian regime to have less succession problem, more durability of policy, than almost any Arab regime in area. Indeed, Hussein might raise same issue re hardening of Israeli line over past several years. Since Israel will retain de facto power to modify and harden any settlement agreed to (e.g. through continued military/security control of West Bank) what assurance can he have that Israeli right wing, at a future time, may not force GOI to renege.

5. What is interesting about Israeli situation as portrayed reftel is not specifics of Israeli internal dialogue which, framed within domestic preoccupations, still offers Hussein choice between little and nothing—even the little is on the wrong, i.e. West Bank end of bargain. Interest lies in hints of Israeli flexibility and apparent incentive to negotiate, even though issues are tougher than Egypt-Israeli issue. As reftel points out, however, Israelis lack appreciation of Hussein's limited incentive to negotiate. To East Bankers (and Arabs such as Faisal) Jerusalem, not West Bank, is big issue. West Bank settlement is viewed by many East Bankers as primarily means to get some of Palestinians here off their necks and back across river. For Hussein, return of maximum Palestine population and minimum territory, with mutilated sovereignty and with onus of being Hashemite who sold out Arab claim to Jerusalem is worst of all worlds, a bargain conceivable only in wishful perspective of Israeli domestic politics. At best, West Bankers are, for Hussein, politically a mixed blessing. Even as an economic asset their value is limited and Hussein is not man to put economic ahead of political considerations. As things are going now, with durable and substantial backing from USG and Saudis, with Arab trend apparently vindicating his policy, and with internal situation in good shape, Hussein probably more inclined to go along indefinitely with existing de facto détente and favorable evolution in economic relation to West Bank and Israel. He is better off for present as resolute, if unsuccessful, defender of Arab claims, than stirring up political trouble for himself to no purpose or accepting humiliation of settling on present Israeli terms.

6. Nevertheless it may be that with diminishing Egyptian (and especially Soviet) threat on Canal front Israelis are more interested in set-

tlement on Jordan side, where they perceive vital interests to be served, than on Canal (where limited withdrawal might be easier but serves lesser Israeli interests). There may also be, in Israeli views and pressures reflected reftel, enough flexibility to warrant renewed exploration on Jordanian side. To do so, however, it would be necessary to accept several conditions.

A) Initial probes would have to be secret. Hussein would be very disinclined to stir up public trouble for himself over an initiative with so little prospect of success.

B) There would have to be some Israeli signals of greater flexibility, particularly on Jerusalem. Hussein has already given a number of public signals of his own—flexibility about Jerusalem, about direct negotiations, about interest in a real and substantive peace which would provide example and perhaps bridge toward real Arab-Israeli comity over time. Mrs. Meir has unfailingly taken an uncompromising stand, particularly on Jerusalem.

C) Contrary to past tactical thinking, negotiation would have to engage both Jerusalem and West Bank issues at same time, with Jerusalem as controlling factor. Extent to which Israelis could give Hussein a respectable and defensible (particularly with Faisal) Jerusalem settlement would be decisive. We doubt that any meaningful discussion of West Bank compromise possible without Jerusalem concessions as bait.

D) Given yawning gap between two sides, we would have to decide that exploratory initiative is worthwhile even given high probability of ultimate failure. Thus exploration would have to be publicly invisible, noncommittal and open-ended, accepting that we do not see end of road but betting that, once exploration begins, both sides will find more incentive and more flexibility than so far demonstrated.

E) Hussein will have a hard time accepting even best bargain we might hope Israelis could give. We may well find that he needs appearance (and even reality) of a settlement imposed from outside—and that means primarily by Americans and imposed on both repeat both sides—as defense against Arab critics. Are we prepared to accept that role and take heat; even, if necessary, to impose some real pressure on Hussein and Israelis?

7. Basic question, obviously, is negotiability of Jerusalem and on this we find reftel para 8 thought provoking. Everything we have seen indicates Mrs. Meir dictum that nothing is negotiable on Jerusalem is an absolute and is universally shared even by Israel moderates. But reftel suggests that definition of what is Jerusalem and what is negotiable may be open to discussion. We have no idea what Hussein reaction might be. Clearly, however, there are three distinct areas—historical holy precincts, including walled city; balance of former (modern Arab Jerusalem); and modern western Jerusalem. Dayan himself

argues that Jews should be able to live in Arab (West Bank) areas even after settlement; thus Israeli "facts" in East Jerusalem are by same argument not conclusive. Israeli signal that within limits of unified city and administration, formal sovereignty over modern Arab city or some portion, and special ordinance re Muslim Holy Places and access thereto are discussable would probably provide sufficient incentive at least to initiate dialogue. How far dialogue could be sustained could only be revealed by course of events; yet there may be more room for ingenuous compromise than we have supposed. Cosmetics are important and there are ways for Israelis to help Hussein save face if face is less important to them than real peace.

8. Whether, as reftel suggests, this is a momentarily favorable conjunction or more durable trend, we inclined to agree that outside push would be necessary to move either party toward initiating dialogue; and while prospects for success are slim, climate is for moment probably more favorable than at any time in recent years. With Soviet threat on Egyptian side at least diminished, and Palestinian problem (solvable only in Jordanian context) persistent and perhaps growing, it may be worth at least considering an initiative on Jordan-Israel front as complement or as alternative to renewed Canal initiative, it might even, by rousing Egyptian fear of being left out, ease path to Canal negotiation.

Brown

---

324. Telegram From the Interests Section in Egypt to the Department of State[1]

Cairo, December 22, 1972, 1305Z.

3435. Subject: Egyptian View of Peace Issue.

Summary: Foreign Office Under Secretary Fahmy in conversation he initiated December 22 said he thought UNGA resolution of De-

---

[1] Source: National Archives, Nixon Presidential Materials, NSC Files, Box 633, Country Files, Middle East, Egypt, Vol. VIII. Secret; Exdis.

cember 8[2] would be of more help to USG even than to GOE in period immediately ahead. He said situation has so changed in recent weeks that it is "too late" for USG only to continue to say it is available for peace discussions. In reply to a question, he seemed to be trying to leave inference that in the absence of movement on the political front, the military option might be a serious possibility.

1. Fahmy opened our December 22 conversation (which he had requested to discuss bombing in Hanoi) with discussion of state of play of ME peace questions. He expressed interest in my forthcoming visit to Washington, and confirmed I expect to have consultations as well as do some family and personal business.

2. Fahmy expounded at some length the thesis that recent UNGA resolution had been the product of long and careful consideration by the Egyptian and many other governments at the highest levels and that USG should take this into account. He expressed gratification that US had abstained on the vote, and said he thought the resolution and the whole exercise would be even more useful to USG than to GOE in stimulating movement on the political front. He did not point to any particular paragraph of the resolution nor offer detailed reasoning.

3. He also said that he did not think the USG could any longer continue to say only that it is available to assist in getting discussions under way. I pressed several times for a reason but Fahmy confined himself to repeating the point and deferring an explanation until I return. He persisted even when I said it would be more useful to know now.

4. I recalled that several weeks ago he had said that he recognized the next move is up to Egypt and asked whether he was now saying something else. He said yes, the situation has changed. So I asked whether I could be clear that GOE is still interested in a political settlement and he again temporized; he said the political possibility is up to the USG.

---

[2] The UN General Assembly adopted Resolution 2949 on December 8 by a roll-call vote of 86 to 7, with 31 abstentions (including the United States). The resolution reaffirmed Security Council Resolution 242 and General Assembly Resolution 2799 (see footnote 4, Document 270) and expressed the General Assembly's deep perturbation that neither resolution had been implemented, and, thus, the previously "envisaged just and lasting peace" in the Middle East had not been achieved. The thrust of the resolution criticized Israel for its non-compliance with previous resolutions—resulting in its negative vote—particularly on the issue of the acquisition of territory by force. For a summary of the debate in the General Assembly and the text of the resolution, see *Yearbook of the United Nations, 1972*, pp. 175–181. After the vote, Bush made a statement that begins: "We regret very much that the resolution which has just been voted constitutes precisely the kind of resolution we had so much hoped could be avoided at this Assembly. This resolution cannot render constructive assistance to the processes of diplomacy. It cannot offer encouragement to the parties to reach a peaceful accommodation of their differences." (Department of State *Bulletin,* January 1, 1973, p. 27)

5. Conversation trailed off into pleasantries.

6. Italian Ambassador Plaja has come in to say that he gets from conversations with both Zayyat and Fahmy in last few days that they are much interested in my visit to Washington; they have even asked Plaja what I am going for and he has told them what I have said. Plaja has little to add to the substance of the matter except that on UNGA resolution he has found the Egyptians concentrating their attention on para 8. Plaja himself thinks that para 6 on nonannexation by force will in the long run be more useful. (This puts this point in somewhat different light than that reported Rome 7745,[3] in which the Italians attribute to the Egyptians the importance of the nonannexation paragraph).

7. Department repeat as desired.

Greene

---

[3] Dated December 19. (National Archives, Nixon Presidential Materials, NSC Files, Box 1169, Saunders Files, Middle East Negotiations Files, Middle East—Jarring Talks, December 1–31, 1972)

Index

References are to document numbers

40 Committee, 91
303 Committee, 60, 91

Abouhamad, Khalil, 312
Ad Hoc Special Review Group on the
    Israeli Nuclear Weapons Program,
    20, 31, 35, 37, 59, 63, 79, 86, 94, 117,
    119, 133, 150, 153, 160
Agnew, Spiro:
    Four-Power negotiation proposals, 5
    Jarring mission (1971), 209
    Meeting with King of Jordan, 189
    Military contingency planning, 4
    U.S. Middle East policy, 74, 124
    U.S. military aid to Israel, 102
    U.S. settlement proposals, 26
al-Aqsa mosque fire (1969), 48
Allon, Yigal, 2, 4, 13, 188, 223, 228, 229,
    230, 245, 322, 323
Allon Plan, 4, 13, 32, 36, 182, 192, 223
American Jewish community:
    Ad Hoc Special Review Group
        discussions, 117
    Dayan U.S. visit (1970), 190
    Government-organized protests, 54
    Israeli withdrawal and, 66
    Nixon-Ehrlichman/Haldeman
        discussions, 232
    Nixon-Kissinger discussions, 269
    Nixon memoranda, 233
    Rogers memoranda, 67
    Sisco memoranda, 81
    U.S. military aid to Israel, 101
Arab-Israeli military balance (see also
    U.S. military aid to Israel):
    Kissinger memoranda, 113, 266
    Laird memoranda, 239
    National Security Study Memoranda,
        103, 108
    Nixon press conference (Mar. 4,
        1969), 218
    NSC discussions, 4, 48, 124, 243
    U.S.-Israeli communications, 106
    Yariv meetings, 108, 110
Arab-Israeli War (1967), 14, 19, 21
Arab League, Rabat Summit (1969), 67,
    70, 73, 74

Arafat, Yassir (see also Fatah;
    Palestinians), 168, 174, 183, 185,
    186, 192, 247
Argov, Shlomo:
    Ceasefire efforts, 144
    Interim settlement proposals (1971),
        217, 223
    Israeli nuclear capabilities, 41
    Jarring mission (1971), 217
    Meir U.S. visit, 52
    Soviet military aid to Egypt, 110
    Soviet peace plan (Dec. 30, 1968), 1
    U.S.-Israeli bilateral negotiations, 14,
        78, 84
    U.S. military aid to Israel, 46, 118, 192
    U.S. peace initiative (Jun. 1970), 140,
        142, 143
Asad, Hafez el-, 184
Aswan Dam, 233
Atherton, Alfred L. "Roy":
    Egypt-Israel ceasefire (Aug. 1970),
        143, 146
    Egypt-Israel ceasefire violations, 154,
        177, 178
    Four-Power negotiation proposals,
        13, 71
    Hussein U.S. visit (1970), 189
    Interim settlement proposals (1971),
        234, 253, 254
    International guarantees, 195, 199,
        221
    Israeli incursions in Lebanon (1972),
        293
    Israeli nuclear capabilities, 20, 41
    Jarring mission (1969–1970), 13
    Jarring mission restart proposals
        (1970), 149
    Jarring mission (1971), 195, 196, 199,
        200, 204, 208, 209, 219
    Jordanian-Israeli bilateral
        negotiations, 322
    Lebanese crisis (1969), 64
    Military contingency planning, 134
    Nixon-Meir correspondence, 33
    Proximity talk proposals, 258, 263,
        276, 278, 285, 322
    Rogers Plan, 80

1095

Atherton, Alfred L. "Roy"—*Continued*
  Soviet-Egyptian relations, 298
  Soviet peace plan (Dec. *30, 1968*), 1, 2
  UN General Assembly meeting (Oct. *1970*), 177
  U.S.-Israeli bilateral negotiations, 52
  U.S. Jordan-Israel settlement proposal, 78
  U.S. Middle East policy, 74, 117, 119, 124, 172
  U.S. military aid to Israel, 94, 124, 150, 153, 188, 195, 204
  U.S. military aid to Jordan, 187
  U.S. peace initiative (Jun. *1970*), 129, 133
  U.S. settlement proposals, 26, 48, 84
  U.S.-Soviet negotiations, 15, 22, 61, 111
  U.S. statement of principles, 13
Atlantic Alliance, 269

Bar-On, Lt. Col. Aryeh, 319
Barbour, Walworth:
  Border incidents, 64
  Dayan U.S. visit (*1972*), 316
  Egypt-Israel ceasefire (Aug. *1970*), 143, 146
  Egypt-Israel ceasefire violations, 154
  Interim settlement proposals (*1971*), 224, 226, 245, 283, 316
  Israeli incursions in Lebanon (*1972*), 315
  Israeli nuclear capabilities, 20, 42
  Jarring mission restart proposals (*1970*), 187
  Jarring mission (*1971*), 205, 209, 226
  Jarring mission (*1972*), 283
  TWA hijacking (Aug. *1969*), 46
  U.S.-Israeli bilateral negotiations, 33, 52
  U.S.-Israeli bilateral treaty proposals, 221
  U.S. military aid to Israel, 106, 130, 136, 245
  U.S. military aid to Jordan, 24
  U.S. peace initiative (Jun. *1970*), 136
  U.S. settlement proposals, 84
  U.S.-Soviet negotiations, 29
Beam, Jacob D., 49, 109, 111, 138, 155, 157, 172, 193
Begin, Menachem, 149
Behr, Col. Robert M., 56, 60, 68, 90, 91
Beirut airport attack (*1969*), 64
Bennett, Lt. Gen. Donald, 178, 183

Bérard, Armand, 7, 50, 72, 75
Bergus, Donald C.:
  Egypt-Israel ceasefire (Aug. *1970*), 146
  Egypt-Israel ceasefire violations, 154, 158
  Egyptian political situation, 217, 231
  Interim settlement proposals (*1971*):
    Heikal discussions, 215, 234, 246, 253
    Sadat discussions, 237, 255
    Sterner-Sadat discussions, 242
    Voice of Egypt paper, 238, 240
  Jarring mission (*1971*), 196, 200, 206, 213, 215, 219
  Nixon-Sadat correspondence, 197
  Proximity talk proposals, 255, 258, 263
  Rogers Egypt visit (*1971*), 231
  U.S.-Egyptian bilateral negotiations, 237
  U.S. Middle East policy, 61, 134
  U.S. military aid to Israel, 92
Bitan, Moshe, 36, 42, 52
Black September (*1970*), 160, 161, 168, 190
Black September organization, 307
Blee, David H.:
  Egypt-Israel ceasefire violations, 160, 183
  International guarantees, 195, 199, 221
  Jarring mission (*1971*), 195, 199, 208
  Jordan intervention contingency planning, 126
  Jordan U.S. personnel evacuation, 125
  Military contingency planning, 134
  Palestinians, 183, 192
  U.S. Middle East policy, 172
  U.S. military aid to Israel, 150, 160, 183, 188, 195
  U.S. military aid to Jordan, 168, 183, 192
Border incidents (*see also* Ceasefire efforts; Egypt-Israel ceasefire (Aug. *1970*); Egypt-Israel ceasefire violations; Israeli incursions in Lebanon (*1972*)):
  Ad Hoc Special Review Group discussions, 94, 119
  Beirut airport attack (*1969*), 64
  Kissinger memoranda, 127
  Nixon-Hussein correspondence, 82
  Nixon-Kissinger discussions, 248

References are to document numbers

Border incidents (*see also* Ceasefire
  efforts; Egypt-Israel ceasefire (Aug.
  1970); Egypt-Israel ceasefire
  violations; Israeli incursions in
  Lebanon (*1972*))—*Continued*
 Nixon-Kosygin correspondence, 88,
  93, 94
 Porter-Helou discussions, 98
 U.S.-Israeli communications, 142, 308
 U.S. military aid to Israel and, 93,
  259, 264
 U.S.-Soviet communications, 120
Borders. *See* Israeli withdrawal; Sharm
 el-Sheikh; West Bank.
Brett, Maj. Gen. Devol, 188, 319
Brezhnev, Leonid Ilyich, 42, 65, 88, 99,
 155, 157, 251, 252, 257, 262, 267,
 281, 286, 289, 291, 300, 301
Brown, L. Dean, 168, 185, 189, 201, 220,
 236, 323
Buckley, William F., 102
Buffum, William B., 138, 312
Bunche, Ralph, 50, 61, 138
Bush, George H.W.:
 Four-Power negotiations, 213
 Israeli incursions in Lebanon (*1972*),
  279, 295
 Jarring meetings, 274, 314
 Jarring mission (*1971*), 209, 274
 Jarring mission (*1972*), 283
 Munich massacre (Sep. *1972*), 307
 Proximity talk proposals, 306
 Rogers New York meetings (Sep.
  1971), 248
 UN General Assembly Resolution
  2799, 270
 UN General Assembly Resolution
  2949, 324
Butterfield, Alexander, 308

Cairo Accord (*1970*), 168
Cairo Agreement (*1969*), 60, 64, 315
Cairo communiqué (Feb. 9, *1970*), 92
Caradon, Lord (Hugh Foot), 50, 72, 75
Cargo, William, 56
Ceasefire efforts (*see also* Egypt-Israel
 ceasefire (Aug. *1970*); Egypt-Israel
 ceasefire violations; Interim
 settlement proposals (*1971*)):
 Ad Hoc Special Review Group
  discussions, 94, 117, 119, 133
 Dayan proposal (Dec. *1970*), 188
 Kissinger memoranda, 127
 Kissinger-Rabin discussions, 103

Ceasefire efforts (*see also* Egypt-Israel
  ceasefire (Aug. *1970*); Egypt-Israel
  ceasefire violations; Interim
  settlement proposals (*1971*))—
  Continued
 Kissinger-Rogers discussions, 144
 Kissinger-Sisco discussions, 141
 Nixon aide-mémoire, 102
 NSC staff summaries, 112
 Rogers memoranda, 123
 U.S.-Israeli communications, 103, 142
 U.S. peace initiative (Jun. *1970*) and,
  129, 133
 U.S.-Soviet communications, 120
 Washington Special Actions Group
  discussions, 90
Celler, Emanuel, 94, 102, 243
Central Intelligence Agency (CIA) (*see
 also* Helms, Richard M.), 298
China, People's Republic of (PRC), 242,
 256, 269
Cline, Ray, 155, 177, 178, 183
Conger, Clinton, 48
Conger, Pat, 74
Congress, U.S.:
 U.S. economic aid to Jordan, 274
 U.S. military aid to Israel, 101, 124,
  150, 157, 195, 243
Connally, John, 232
Constantinople Convention, 53
Crocker, Chester, 195
Crowe, Colin, 199
Cushman, Lt. Gen. Robert E., Jr., 126,
 131, 168, 172

Dakroury, Mohammed, 290
Davies, Rodger P.:
 Egypt-Israel ceasefire violations, 160
 Israeli incursions in Lebanon (*1972*),
  293
 Israeli nuclear capabilities, 31, 35
 Lebanese crisis (*1969*), 60, 68
 Military contingency planning, 4, 56,
  90, 126, 131
 Nixon-Meir correspondence, 33
 Proximity talk proposals, 258, 285
 Soviet-Egyptian relations, 298
 Soviet military aid to Egypt, 91
 U.S. military aid to Israel, 160
 U.S. military aid to Jordan, 87
Davis, Jeanne W., 27, 37, 133, 150, 153,
 160, 168, 172, 178, 183, 188, 192,
 195, 199, 204, 220, 221

References are to document numbers

Day, Arthur R., 2
Dayan, Moshe:
  Border incidents, 120, 124, 134, 149
  Ceasefire proposal (Dec. *1970*), 188, 192, 202
  Contingency planning, 4, 13, 36, 48
  Egypt-Israel ceasefire (Aug. *1970*), 146, 162, 183
  Egypt-Israel ceasefire violations, 160, 183
  Interim settlement proposals (*1971*), 228, 229, 230, 240, 245, 307
  Proximity talk proposals, 306
  Rogers visit (*1971*), 230
  Sharm el-Sheikh, 208
  Soviet-Egyptian relations, 307
  U.S. military aid to Israel, 160, 167, 188, 190, 248, 319
  U.S. visit (*1970*), 187, 189, 190
  U.S. visit (*1972*), 316, 319
De Gaulle, Charles, 4, 8, 14, 189
De la Barre de Nanteuil, Luc, 13
De Palma, Samuel, 17, 29, 83, 197
De Seynes, Phillippe, 50
Defense, U.S. Department of (DOD) (*see also* Laird, Melvin R.), 260
Demilitarized zone proposals, 2, 23, 25, 26, 58, 199, 216
Dinitz, Simcha, 52, 106, 162, 228, 229
Dobrynin, Anatoly F.:
  Israeli withdrawal, 1
  Moscow Summit (*1972*), 291
  Rogers Plan, 58, 74, 80, 240
  Soviet-Egyptian relations, 269, 298, 301
  U.S. peace initiative (Jun. *1970*), 120, 122, 137, 210, 298, 300
  U.S.-Soviet negotiations:
    Kissinger-Gromyko talks, 138, 311
    Kissinger talks, 96, 99, 134, 135, 137, 177, 212, 222, 223, 251, 253, 262, 269, 281, 298, 300, 301
    Nixon-Gromyko talks, 173
    Nixon talks, 281
    Rogers talks, 97, 104, 105, 111, 120, 127, 129, 214, 251
    Sisco talks (*1969*), 5, 11, 13, 15, 18, 22, 26, 27, 28, 29, 34, 49, 52, 53, 57, 58, 61
    Sisco talks (*1970*), 95, 96, 107, 127
Doolin, Dennis J., 126
Douglas-Home, Sir Alec, 183
Dubs, Adolph, 107, 120, 137

Dulles, John Foster, 222, 227, 233

Eban, Abba:
  Egypt-Israel ceasefire violations, 154, 157, 169
  Four-Power negotiation proposals, 8, 11, 13, 14, 15, 29, 70
  Interim settlement proposals (*1971*), 217, 245, 253, 254, 256, 257, 283
  Israeli incursions in Lebanon (*1972*), 293, 315
  Israeli withdrawal, 2, 13
  Jarring mission (*1969–1970*), 2, 8, 12, 13
  Jarring mission restart proposals (*1970*), 129, 187
  Jarring mission (*1971*), 195, 205, 217, 254
  Jarring mission (*1972*), 283
  Nixon discussions, 14, 118
  Proximity talk proposals, 261
  Rogers visit (*1971*), 228, 229, 230
  Soviet involvement in Egypt, 118
  UN General Assembly Resolution 2799, 270
  UN General Assembly speech (Sep. 30, *1971*), 254
  U.S.-Israeli bilateral negotiations, 13, 14, 36, 47, 71, 74, 77, 78
  U.S. military aid to Israel, 106, 117, 118, 130, 187, 244
  U.S. peace initiative (Jun. *1970*), 136, 138, 140
  U.S. settlement proposals, 11, 13, 14, 26, 29, 74, 84, 129
  U.S.-Soviet negotiations, 29, 61, 187
Egypt (*see also* Egypt-Israel ceasefire (Aug. *1970*); Egypt-Israel ceasefire violations; Interim settlement proposals (*1971*); Jarring mission (*1969–1970*); Jarring mission (*1971*); Proximity talk proposals; Rogers Plan; Soviet-Egyptian relations; Soviet military aid to Egypt; U.S.-Egyptian bilateral negotiations):
  Cairo Agreement (*1969*), 60
  Jordanian relations with, 280
  Nasser peace appeal speech (May 1, *1970*), 112, 115, 116, 117, 129
  Nixon-Sadat correspondence, 165, 197, 215, 219, 298
  Political situation, 14, 39, 51, 217, 231, 238, 286

References are to document numbers

Egypt (*see also* Egypt-Israel ceasefire (Aug. 1970); Egypt-Israel ceasefire violations; Interim settlement proposals (*1971*); Jarring mission (*1969–1970*); Jarring mission (*1971*); Proximity talk proposals; Rogers Plan; Soviet-Egyptian relations; Soviet military aid to Egypt; U.S.-Egyptian bilateral negotiations)—*Continued*
   Rogers visit (*1971*), 225, 227, 228, 229
   TWA hijacking (Aug. 1969) and, 46
   U.S. peace initiative (Jun. *1970*) response, 136
   U.S. relations with, 19, 225, 227, 228, 229, 231
Egypt-Israel ceasefire (Aug. *1970*) (*see also* Egypt-Israel ceasefire violations):
   Ad Hoc Special Review Group discussions, 160
   Agreement text, 145
   Israeli response, 147
   NSC staff summaries, 170, 175, 181
   Sadat speech (Feb. 4, *1971*), 203, 204
   Sadat speech (Mar. 7, *1971*), 215
   Sadat speeches (Jan. *1971*), 197
   Soviet responses, 155
   UN General Assembly discussions, 177
   U.S. aerial reconnaissance, 146, 155, 159
   U.S.-Egyptian communications, 215
   Washington Special Actions Group/Senior Review Group discussions, 172
Egypt-Israel ceasefire violations:
   Israeli suspension of Jarring mission and, 161
   Johnson, U. Alexis, memoranda, 157
   Kissinger memoranda, 169, 179
   Meir Knesset speech (Nov. 16, 1970), 185
   NSC discussions, 156
   NSC staff summaries, 175, 181
   Rogers press conference statement, 177
   Saunders-Hoskinson memoranda, 159
   Senior Review Group discussions, 177, 178, 183
   UN General Assembly discussions, 177
   U.S.-Egyptian communications, 154, 157, 158, 169

Egypt-Israel ceasefire violations—*Continued*
   U.S.-Israeli communications, 154, 157, 162, 169
   U.S.-Soviet communications, 157, 169, 173
   Washington Special Actions Group/Senior Review Group discussions, 172
Egypt-Israel proximity talk proposals. *See* Proximity talk proposals.
Ehrlichman, John, 232
Eisenhower, Dwight D., 4, 5, 21, 124, 233
Eliot, Theodore L., Jr., 46, 106, 140, 280, 294, 306, 312
Elizur, Michael, 106, 228, 315
Ellsworth, Robert, 1
Eshkol, Levi, 13, 26, 30. 36, 41, 42, 55

Fahmy, Ismail, 318, 324
Faisal ibn Abd al-Aziz al Saud (King of Saudi Arabia), 61, 70, 112, 117, 228, 230, 247, 323
Fatah, 4, 42, 47, 52, 168. 171, 174, 180, 185, 186, 188, 247
Fawzi, Mahmoud, 18, 21, 26, 197, 218 227, 231, 234, 237
Fawzi, Gen. Mohamed, 158, 165, 231, 242
Fisher, Max, 95, 233
Foreign Assistance Act, 274
Foreign Military Sales Act, 166
Four-Power negotiation proposals (*see also* Four-Power negotiations):
   Ad Hoc Special Review Group discussions, 133
   Kissinger memoranda, 11
   National Security Study Memoranda, 6
   Nixon press conference (Mar. 4, *1969*), 77
   NSC discussions, 4, 5, 26, 74
   NSC Interdepartmental Group papers, 8
   NSC staff summaries. 198
   Rogers-Foreign Ministers meeting discussions, 50
   Rogers memoranda, 67, 70, 71
   Sisco memoranda, 39
   UN representative discussions, 23
   U.S.-French communications, 7, 8, 13
   U.S.-Israeli communications, 13, 14, 33

References are to document numbers

1100 Index

Four-Power negotiation proposals (see also Four-Power negotiations)—Continued
  U.S. settlement proposals and, 25
  U.S.-Soviet communications, 1, 15
  U.S. working paper, 17
  Yost memoranda, 23
Four-Power negotiations, 72, 75, 98
  Bush-Jarring discussions, 273
  Egypt-Israel ceasefire (Aug. *1970*) and, 145
  Kissinger memoranda, 76, 89
  Kissinger-Sisco discussions, 73
  Nixon-Kissinger discussions, 210, 212
  NSC discussions, 209
  NSC staff summaries, 202
  Rogers memoranda, 83, 111, 193, 213
  Senior Review Group discussions, 183, 199, 208
  Sisco memoranda, 81
  U.S.-Israeli communications, 77, 78, 84
  U.S. peace initiative (Jun. *1970*) and, 129, 139
France (see also Four-Power negotiation proposals; Four-Power negotiations), 50, 86, 94
Freeman, John, 98
Freeman, Adm. Mason B., 172
Fulbright, J. William, 102, 151, 195

Garment, Leonard, 54, 77, 95
Gaza Strip, 53, 58, 216
Gazit, Mordechai, 154, 224, 228, 229, 261
Ghaleb, Mohammed Murad, 261, 276, 278, 285, 294, 298, 302, 321
Ghorbal, Ashraf, 21, 61, 218, 231, 238, 275, 294, 296, 309
Glick, Brig. Gen. Jacob E., 126
Golan Heights (see also Israeli withdrawal), 74, 117, 162, 198, 202, 204, 207, 208, 210, 212, 214, 216, 217, 223, 308, 311, 317, 319
Goldberg, Arthur J., 81, 232
Goldwater, Barry, 102
Goodell, Charles, 102
Greece, 46, 124, 146, 286
Greene, Joseph N., Jr.:
  Proximity talk proposals, 276, 278, 285, 290, 294, 302
  Soviet-Egyptian relations, 298
  U.S.-Egyptian bilateral negotiations, 316, 318, 321, 324
  U.S. Middle East policy, 314

Greene, Joseph N., Jr.—*Continued*
  War, possible, 290
Gromyko, Andrei A.:
  Egypt-Israel ceasefire violations, 156, 169
  Egypt visit (*1968*), 1, 34
  Interim settlement proposals (*1971*), 251
  Jarring mission, 138, 173
  Rogers-Foreign Ministers meeting, 50
  Rogers talks, 52, 53, 169
  Soviet military aid to Egypt, 251, 268
  U.S.-Soviet negotiations:
    Kissinger talks, 49, 172, 252, 292, 300, 311
    Nixon talks, 28, 173, 221, 251, 262
    Rogers talks, 47, 48, 50, 52, 53, 74, 83, 85, 86, 169, 253
    Sisco Moscow talks (*1969*), 28, 39, 47, 48, 49, 71, 86, 133
Gur, Maj. Gen. Mordechai, 319
Guthrie, D. Keith, 68, 90, 91, 125, 126, 131, 177, 208

Haig, Gen. Alexander M., Jr.:
  American Jewish community government-organized protests, 54
  Arab-Israeli military balance, 97, 243
  Dayan U.S. visit (*1970*), 190
  Egypt-Israel ceasefire violations, 156, 162
  Four-Power negotiation proposals, 5, 70
  Interim settlement proposals (*1971*), 241, 243
  Israeli incursions in Lebanon (*1972*), 308
  Jarring mission restart proposals (*1970*), 187
  Jarring mission (*1971*), 209, 210
  Jordan U.S. personnel evacuation, 125
  Meir U.S. visit (*1970*), 162
  Military contingency planning, 4, 26
  Munich massacre (Sep. *1972*), 307
  Proximity talk proposals, 306
  Rogers Middle East trip (*1971*), 227, 228, 229
  Soviet military aid to Egypt, 99, 162
  U.S.-Egyptian backchannel (*1972*), 305, 320
  U.S. Middle East policy, 124
  U.S. military aid to Israel, 79, 160, 162, 187, 190

References are to document numbers

Haig, Gen. Alexander M., Jr.—*Continued*
  U.S. military aid to Jordan, 113
  U.S. military aid to Lebanon, 100
  U.S. peace initiative (Jun. *1970*), 142
  U.S. settlement proposals, 26, 48
  War of attrition, 51
  White House-Department of State divisions, 216
Haldeman, H.R.:
  Egypt-Israel ceasefire violations, 156
  Interim settlement proposals (*1971*), 227, 228, 229, 241
  Jordanian-Israeli bilateral negotiations, 322
  White House-Department of State divisions, 96, 144, 156, 162, 216, 222, 225, 232, 233, 257, 288
Hart, Parker T., 4
Hartman, Arthur A., 172, 220
Hassan bin Talal, el- (Crown Prince of Jordan). 220
Hassan Muhammed ibn Yusuf, Mawlay al- (King Hassan II of Morocco), 201
Heath, Edward, 168, 182, 188
Heikal, Mohamed, 165, 215, 227, 228, 231, 234, 237, 238, 246, 253, 254, 263
Helms, Richard M.:
  Ad Hoc Senior Review Group discussions, 35, 86, 94, 117, 119, 133, 150, 153, 160
  Arab-Israeli military balance, 243
  Dayan U.S. visit (*1972*), 319
  Egypt-Israel ceasefire violations, 160, 177, 178, 183
  Four-Power negotiation proposals, 5, 48
  Hussein U.S. visit (*1970*), 189
  Interim settlement proposals (*1971*), 241, 243
  International guarantees, 195, 199, 221
  Israeli nuclear capabilities, 10, 20, 31, 37, 38
  Jarring mission (*1971*), 195, 199, 204, 208, 209, 210
  Jordan U.S. personnel evacuation, 125
  Jordanian-Israeli bilateral negotiations, 319
  Military contingency planning, 4, 16, 44, 134
  Moscow Summit (*1972*), 289

Helms, Richard M.—*Continued*
  Palestinians, 174, 180, 183, 185, 186, 192
  Soviet-Egyptian relations, 310
  UN General Assembly meeting (Oct. *1970*), 177
  U.S.-Egyptian backchannel (*1972*), 288, 299, 300, 305, 309, 310
  U.S.-Israeli bilateral negotiations, 216
  U.S. Middle East policy, 3, 6, 26, 39, 74, 117, 119, 124
  U.S. military aid to Israel, 163, 166
    National Security Study Memoranda, 63, 148, 150
    Nixon memoranda, 163
    NSC discussions, 124, 209
    Senior Review Group discussions, 183, 195, 199, 204, 208
  U.S. military aid to Jordan, 24, 192
  U.S. peace initiative (Jun. *1970*), 133
  U.S. settlement proposals, 26, 48
Helou, Charles, 26, 60, 61, 64, 70, 98, 100
Henkin, Daniel Z., 319
Herzog, Chaim, 42, 52, 106, 228, 229
Hillenbrand, Martin J., 56
Holdridge, John H., 44
Hoskinson, Samuel M., 145, 159, 306
Humphrey, Hubert H., 232
Hussein bin Talal (King of Jordan; *see also* Jordan):
  Border incidents, 82
  Federation plan (*1972*), 280, 282, 284, 289
  Jarring mission restart proposals (*1970*), 189
  Jarring mission (*1971*), 197
  Jordanian-Israeli bilateral negotiations, 30, 32, 282, 319, 323
  Nixon correspondence, 82, 220, 236, 272, 273
  Palestinians, 185, 188
  Sisco Jordan visit cancellation, 109
  Soviet military aid, 69
  U.S. economic aid to Jordan, 220, 236, 274
  U.S. military aid to Jordan, 24, 87, 113, 284
  U.S. visit (*1969*), 14, 19
  U.S. visit (*1970*), 189
  U.S. visit (*1972*), 284
Hyland, William G., 56, 99

References are to document numbers

Idan, Avner, 271, 308
Interim settlement proposals (*1971*; see also Proximity talk proposals):
  Barbour memoranda, 226, 316
  Bergus:
    Bergus-Heikal discussions, 215, 234, 246, 253
    Bergus-Ismail discussions, 258
    Bergus paper, 238, 240
    Bergus-Riad discussions, 196, 234
    Bergus-Sadat discussions, 237, 255
  Dayan interview, 307
  Eban UN General Assembly speech (Sep. *30, 1971*), 254
  Israeli response, 219
  Kissinger-Ghorbal discussions, 218
  Kissinger memoranda, 216, 240, 265
  Nixon:
    Nixon-Ehrlichman/Haldeman discussions, 232
    Nixon-Kissinger discussions, 222, 227
    Nixon-Meir correspondence, 249
    Nixon-Rogers discussions, 227
    Nixon-Sadat correspondence, 219
  NSC discussions, 209, 243
  Riad UN General Assembly speech (Oct. *6, 1971*), 254, 256
  Rogers:
    Rogers-Eban discussions, 253, 257
    Rogers *Meet the Press* statement (Nov. *5, 1972*), 318
    Rogers memoranda, 241, 258
    Rogers-Riad discussions, 253, 255
    Rogers-Sadat discussions, 227
    UN General Assembly speech (Oct. *4, 1971*), 249, 254, 256, 277
  Sadat speech (Feb. *4, 1971*), 203, 204
  Sadat speech (Nov. *11, 1971*), 263
  Senior Review Group discussions, 208
  Sisco:
    Sisco-Ghorbal discussions, 275
    Sisco Israel trip, 228, 229, 241, 243, 244, 245, 246
    Sisco-Rabin discussions, 244
    Sisco-Sadat discussions, 231
  Sterner-Sadat discussions, 242
  U.S.-Israeli communications, 211, 217, 223, 224, 228, 229, 230, 244, 245, 249, 256, 261, 263, 268
  U.S.-Soviet communications, 212, 251, 252, 262
International guarantees:
  Four-Power discussions, 193, 198

International guarantees—*Continued*
  Four-Power UN representative discussions, 23
  Nixon speech (Feb. *25, 1971*), 211
  NSC discussions, 5
  NSC Interdepartmental Group papers, 8
  NSC staff summaries, 198
  Senior Review Group discussions, 195, 199, 221
  U.S.-Israeli communications, 14, 217
  U.S.-Jordanian communications, 189
  U.S.-Soviet communications, 18, 311
Iraq, 4, 21, 42, 48, 51, 52, 93, 94, 106, 161, 167, 172, 177, 182, 186, 188, 282, 312
Irwin, John N., II:
  Interim settlement proposals (*1971*), 254
  International guarantees, 195, 199
  Israeli incursions in Lebanon (*1972*), 293, 315
  Jarring mission (*1971*), 195, 199, 208, 209
  Proximity talk proposals, 258, 270, 276, 278, 302
  U.S.-Egyptian bilateral negotiations, 237
  U.S. military aid to Israel, 124, 178, 195
Ismail, Hafez, 255, 258, 261, 263, 276, 294, 296, 298, 309, 314, 320
Israel (*see also* Border incidents; Jordanian-Israeli bilateral negotiations; U.S.-Israeli bilateral negotiations; U.S.-Israeli relations; U.S. military aid to Israel):
  Political situation, 8, 48, 316
  U.S. economic aid, 62, 79, 86, 93, 96, 164
  U.S. peace initiative (June *1970*) response, 130, 136, 139, 141, 142
Israeli incursions in Lebanon (*1972*):
  Laird memoranda, 313
  UN Security Council discussions, 279, 295
  UN Security Council Resolution *316*, 295
  U.S.-Egyptian communications, 309
  U.S.-Israeli communications, 293, 308, 315
Israeli nuclear capabilities:
  Ad Hoc Special Review Group discussions, 35, 37, 86, 94, 117, 119, 113, 150, 153, 160

References are to document numbers

Israeli nuclear capabilities—*Continued*
  Kissinger memoranda, 38, 40, 47, 54, 55
  Laird memoranda, 10, 45
  National Security Study Memoranda, 20, 31
  NSC discussions, 5, 26, 35, 37, 48
  U.S.-Israeli communications, 41, 42, 52, 55
Israeli withdrawal (*see also* Interim settlement proposals (*1971*); Jarring mission (*1971*)):
  Ad Hoc Special Review Group discussions, 117, 119
  Four-Power UN representative discussions, 23
  Jarring-Eban discussions, 2
  Kissinger memoranda, 27, 66, 127
  Meir interview (Mar. 12, *1971*), 217
  Nasser peace appeal speech (May 1, *1970*), 112, 115
  NSC discussions, 209
  NSC Interdepartmental Group papers, 8
  Rogers memoranda, 25
  Rogers Plan on, 34
  Senior Review Group discussions, 208
  UN General Assembly Resolution 2799, 270, 274, 283, 324
  U.S.-Egyptian communications, 2, 218, 237
  U.S.-Israeli communications, 13, 136, 162, 211, 217
  U.S.-Jordanian communications, 189
  U.S.-Soviet communications, 1, 2, 15, 49, 107, 251, 311
Italy, 4, 8, 46, 57, 146, 166, 169, 225, 227, 230, 279, 286

Jackson, Henry M. "Scoop", 157, 209, 243
Jackson Amendment, 157, 162, 166, 195, 311
Jadid, Saleh al-, 184
Jarring, Gunnar V. (*see also* Jarring mission), 1
  Bush meetings, 274, 314
  Cyprus location proposals, 193
  Egypt-Israel ceasefire violations, 157
  Four-Power negotiation proposals, 4
Jarring mission (*1969–1970*):
  Cyprus location proposals, 193

Jarring mission (*1969–1970*)—*Continued*
  Four-Power discussions, 4, 7, 13, 17, 23, 50, 72, 75, 83, 111
  Israeli resumption decision (Dec. *1970*), 193
  Israeli suspension (Sep. *1970*), 161
  Jarring discouragement, 185
  Jarring questions, 12, 15
  Kissinger memoranda, 11, 25, 167, 169
  Meir Knesset speech (Nov. 16, *1970*), 185
  Meir UN speech (Oct. 21, *1970*), 240
  NSC discussions, 4, 43, 124, 133, 150, 156, 172, 177, 183, 188
  NSC Interdepartmental Group papers, 8, 10
  NSC staff papers, 116, 152
  NSC staff summaries, 112, 170, 175, 176, 181, 182
  Restart proposals (*see also* Jarring mission (*1971*)), 3, 75, 88, 120, 122, 129, 133, 137, 138, 139, 145, 149, 187
  Rogers memoranda, 34, 67, 70, 83, 84, 123, 149, 193
  U.S.-Israeli communications, 13, 29, 33, 36, 52, 84, 95, 140, 143, 151, 157, 187, 190
  U.S.-Jordanian communications, 189
  U.S.-Soviet communications, 1, 2, 15, 22, 28, 34, 39, 49, 61, 80, 85, 99, 107, 120, 122, 136, 137, 138, 173
  U.S.-Soviet working paper, 58
  Yost correspondence, 43
Jarring mission (*1971*):
  Barbour memoranda, 205, 226, 245
  Bergus memoranda, 231, 242, 246
  Bush-Jarring discussions, 274
  Eban UN General Assembly speech (Sep. 30, *1971*), 254
  Nixon-Kissinger discussions, 210, 212, 222
  Nixon-Sadat correspondence, 197, 219
  NSC discussions, 209
  NSC staff papers, 202, 207, 214
  Rogers memoranda, 197, 200, 201, 206, 211, 213, 215, 219, 220, 224, 228, 230, 234, 235, 241, 244, 250, 253, 255, 256, 259, 263
  Rogers press conference (Mar. 16, *1971*), 219
  Senior Review Group discussions, 195, 199, 204, 208

References are to document numbers

Jarring mission (1971)—Continued
  Thant report, 198
  UN General Assembly Resolution 2799, 270, 274
  U.S.-Egyptian communications, 196, 200, 206, 213, 215, 218
  U.S.-Israeli communications, 205, 211, 217, 271
  U.S.-Jordanian communications, 201
Jarring mission (1972), 275, 283, 292
Javits, Jacob K., 4, 232
Jerusalem:
  al-Aqsa mosque fire (1969), 48
  Brown memoranda, 323
  NSC Interdepartmental Group papers, 8
  Department of State proposal (1971), 216
  UN Security Council Resolution 298, 250
  U.S.-Israeli communications, 78, 228
  U.S.-Jordanian communications, 19, 236, 274
Jewish community. See American Jewish community.
Johnson, Lyndon B., 2, 8, 41, 42, 48, 55, 79, 81
Johnson, Adm. Nels, 44, 56, 60, 68
Johnson, Peter, 270
Johnson, U. Alexis:
  Arab-Israeli military balance, 243
  Egypt-Israel ceasefire violations, 154, 157, 177, 178, 183
  Four-Power negotiation proposals, 71
  Interim settlement proposals (1971), 243
  International guarantees, 221
  Jarring mission (1971), 204, 209
  Lebanese crisis (1969), 60, 68
  Military contingency planning, 44, 56, 125, 126, 131
  Soviet military aid to Egypt, 91
  UN General Assembly meeting (Oct. 1970), 177
  U.S. Middle East policy, 172, 209
  U.S. military aid to Israel, 150, 160, 183, 188, 204
  U.S. military aid to Jordan, 168, 188
  U.S. peace initiative (Jun. 1970), 133
Johnson mission, 4
Johnston mission, 4
Jordan (see also Border incidents; Jordanian-Israeli bilateral negotiations; U.S.-Jordanian bilateral negotiations):
  Allon Plan, 4, 13, 192

Jordan (see also Border incidents; Jordanian-Israeli bilateral negotiations; U.S.-Jordanian bilateral negotiations)—Continued
  Black September (1970), 160, 161, 162, 163, 168
  Egyptian relations with, 21, 28, 280
  Hassan U.S. visit (1971), 220
  Hussein federation plan (1972), 280, 282, 284, 289
  Hussein U.S. visit (1969), 14, 19
  Hussein U.S. visit (1970), 189
  Hussein U.S. visit (1972), 284
  Jerusalem, 17, 19, 236, 249, 274
  Jidda PLO talks (Sep. 1971), 247
  Kissinger memoranda, 24, 25, 47, 54, 76, 77, 81, 84, 89, 114, 115, 127, 169
  National Security Study Memorandum 33, 16
  National Security Study Memorandum 103, 164
  NSC discussions, 4, 26, 48, 74, 124
  Palestinian settlement proposals, 181, 182, 183, 185, 186, 192
  Political situation, 52, 161, 174, 185, 323
  Sisco memorandum, 39
  Sisco visit cancellation, 109
  Soviet military aid, 113
  U.S. economic aid, 220, 236, 273
  U.S. military aid:
    Ad Hoc Special Review Group discussions, 86, 119, 133
    National Security Decision Memoranda, 192
    NSC staff papers, 93, 112, 170, 176, 181, 182, 191
    Rogers memoranda, 64, 69, 70, 71, 78, 80, 83, 87, 123, 129, 137, 147
    Senior Review Group discussions, 168, 172, 183, 188, 192
    U.S.-Jordanian communications, 19, 30, 32, 82, 87, 189, 220, 236, 284
    Washington Special Actions Group discussions, 125, 126, 131
  U.S. peace initiative (Jun. 1970), 139, 140
  U.S. personnel evacuation, 125, 126
Jordan Crisis. See Black September (1970).
Jordanian-Israeli bilateral negotiations:
  Brown memoranda, 323
  Hussein-Meir communications, 32

Jordanian-Israeli bilateral negotiations—Continued
Hussein-Meir secret meetings (1972), 282, 319
Rogers-Allon discussions, 322
U.S.-Egyptian backchannel (1972), 317
U.S.-Jordanian communications, 30, 32

Karame, Rashid, 26
Karamessines, Thomas:
Lebanese crisis (1969), 60, 68
Military contingency planning, 44, 56, 90, 126, 131
Soviet military aid to Egypt, 91
U.S. military aid to Israel, 160, 188
U.S. military aid to Jordan, 188
Kennedy, David M., 4, 74
Kennedy, Edward M., 232
Kennedy, Col. Richard T.:
Egypt-Israel ceasefire violations, 160, 177, 178, 183
International guarantees, 221
Jarring mission restart proposals (1970), 187
Jarring mission (1971), 204, 208, 209
Military contingency planning, 131
UN General Assembly meeting (Oct. 1970), 177
U.S. Middle East policy, 172
U.S. military aid to Israel, 153, 160, 183, 187, 188, 204
U.S. military aid to Jordan, 168, 188
U.S. peace initiative (Jun. 1970), 133
Kettlehut, Col. Marvin C., 125
Khartoum declaration (Aug. 1967), 18, 50
Kissinger, Henry A. (see also White House-Department of State divisions):
American Jewish community, 54, 269
Arab-Israeli military balance, 113, 266
Laird memoranda, 239
National Security Study Memoranda, 108
NSC discussions, 243
Border incidents, 88, 127, 248
Ceasefire efforts, 104, 127, 141, 142, 144, 188
Egypt-Israel ceasefire (Aug. 1970), 43, 172
Egypt-Israel ceasefire violations, 169, 179

Kissinger, Henry A. (see also White House-Department of State divisions)—Continued
Egypt-Israel ceasefire violations—Continued
Ad Hoc Special Review Group discussions, 160
NSC discussions, 156
Saunders-Hoskinson memoranda, 159
Senior Review Group discussions, 177, 178, 183
Four-Power negotiations, 5, 7, 11, 74, 76, 81, 89, 210, 212
Hussein U.S. visit (1969), 19
Hussein U.S. visit (1970), 189
Interim settlement proposals (1971), 216, 240, 265
Nixon discussions, 222
NSC discussions, 243
U.S.-Egyptian communications, 218
U.S.-Israeli communications, 217, 249
U.S.-Soviet communications, 252
International guarantees, 195, 199, 221
Israeli incursions in Lebanon (1972), 308, 309, 313
Israeli nuclear capabilities, 10, 20, 31, 35, 38, 40, 47, 55
Jarring mission (1971):
Nixon discussions, 210, 212, 222
NSC discussions, 209
NSC staff summaries, 202
Senior Review Group discussions, 195, 199, 204, 208
U.S.-Egyptian communications, 206, 218
U.S.-Israeli communications, 212, 217
Lebanese crisis (1969), 60, 65, 68
Lebanese-Palestinian confrontation plans, 312
Military contingency planning:
National Security Study Memoranda, 16
NSC discussions, 4, 5
Washington Special Actions Group discussions, 44, 60, 90, 125, 126, 131
Moscow Summit (1972), 252, 269, 287, 291
Munich massacre (Sep. 1972), 307

1106 Index

Kissinger, Henry A. (*see also* White House-Department of State divisions)—*Continued*
  Nasser peace appeal speech (May 1, 1970), 115
  Palestinians, 172, 174, 180, 183, 186, 192
  Proximity talk proposals, 265
    Egyptian rejection, 294
    Nixon discussions, 269
    Sisco discussions, 257
    Sisco-Rabin discussions, 277
  Rogers Middle East trip (1971), 222, 229
  Rogers Plan, 127
  Soviet-Egyptian relations, 286, 299, 300
  Soviet military aid to Egypt, 127, 266
    NSC discussions, 124
    Sadat-Brezhnev discussions, 286
    U.S.-Israeli communications, 110, 142
    U.S.-Soviet communications, 135, 252
    Washington Special Actions Group discussions, 91
  UN General Assembly meeting (Oct. 1970), 177
  U.S. economic aid to Israel, 62, 79, 95, 96
  U.S.-Egyptian backchannel (1972), 305
    Classified asset report, 309
    Haig memoranda, 320
    Helms memoranda, 288, 299, 310
    Nixon discussions, 300, 303
    Saunders memoranda, 317
    U.S.-Egyptian communications, 296
  U.S.-Egyptian bilateral negotiations, 21
  U.S.-Israeli bilateral negotiations, 14, 52, 53, 77, 216
  U.S. Middle East policy, 95, 127
    Ad Hoc Special Review Group discussions, 117, 119
    Domestic political considerations, 9
    Laird memoranda, 313
    National Security Study Memoranda, 6, 164
    NSC discussions, 74, 124
    NSC Interdepartmental Group papers, 8
    Sisco memoranda, 114

Kissinger, Henry A. (*see also* White House-Department of State divisions)—*Continued*
  U.S. Middle East policy—*Continued*
    Washington Special Actions Group/Senior Review Group discussions, 172
  U.S. military aid to Israel, 38, 40, 59, 79, 95, 127, 166, 167, 266
    Ad Hoc Special Review Group discussions, 86, 94, 133, 150, 153, 160
    Dayan memoranda, 248
    Laird memoranda, 45
    Meir U.S. visit (1971) discussions, 268
    National Security Decision Memoranda, 128
    National Security Study Memoranda, 63, 148
    Nixon discussions, 96
    Nixon-Meir correspondence, 249
    NSC discussions, 124
    Nutter memoranda, 272
    Proximity talk proposals and, 265
    Rabin discussions, 102, 110, 133, 142
    Senior Review Group discussions, 183, 188, 195, 204
    Sisco discussions, 141
    Sisco-Rabin discussions, 277
  U.S. military aid to Jordan, 24, 113, 168, 188, 192
  U.S. peace initiative (Jun. 1970), 142
  U.S. settlement proposals, 27, 47, 127
    Jordan-Israel settlement proposal, 76, 77
    NSC discussions, 26, 48
    Rogers memoranda, 25
  U.S.-Soviet negotiations, 66, 127
    Dobrynin talks, 135
    Gromyko talks, 53, 252, 300, 311
    Nixon-Dobrynin talks, 281
    Nixon-Gromyko talks, 173
    Yost memoranda, 43
  War of attrition, 49, 51, 104, 110, 113
Knowles, Lt. Gen. Richard T.:
  Egypt-Israel ceasefire violations, 177, 178, 183
  International guarantees, 195, 199, 221
  Jarring mission (1971), 195, 199
  Palestinians, 183

References are to document numbers

Knowles, Lt. Gen. Richard T.—
Continued
UN General Assembly meeting (Oct. 1970), 177
U.S. military aid to Israel, 150, 183, 188, 195
U.S. military aid to Jordan, 188
Kosygin, Alexei, 2, 48, 88, 93, 94, 99, 214
Kraft, Joseph, 232
Krimer, William D., 173
Kubal, Robert, 319
Kutakov, Leonid N., 50
Kuwait, 86, 93, 124, 129, 131, 168, 176, 236, 323

Laird, Melvin R.:
Arab-Israeli military balance, 108, 239
Dayan ceasefire proposal (Dec. 1970), 188
Dayan U.S. visit (1970), 187, 190
Egypt-Israel ceasefire violations, 177
Four-Power negotiation proposals, 5
Hussein U.S. visit (1969), 19
Hussein U.S. visit (1970), 189
Israeli incursions in Lebanon (1972), 313
Israeli nuclear capabilities, 10, 20, 31, 37
Jarring mission (1971), 209, 210
Military contingency planning, 4, 16
Palestinians, 188
Proximity talk proposals, 260
Soviet military aid to Egypt, 239
U.S. economic aid to Israel, 62
U.S.-Israeli bilateral negotiations, 216
U.S. Middle East policy, 3, 6, 74, 313
U.S. military aid to Israel, 10, 45, 86, 94, 121, 239, 267
    Kissinger memoranda, 166
    Kissinger-Rabin discussions, 132
    National Security Decision Memoranda, 128, 166
    National Security Study Memoranda, 63, 148
    Nixon-Dayan discussions, 190
    Nixon memoranda, 163, 195
    Nutter memoranda, 142, 272
    Rogers communications, 259, 264
U.S. military aid to Jordan, 113, 284
U.S. peace initiative (Jun. 1970), 121, 128
U.S. settlement proposals, 26
Latimer, Thomas K., 309
Lebanese crisis (1969), 56

Lebanese crisis (1969)—Continued
Cairo Agreement (1969), 60, 64, 315
Military contingency planning, 60, 68
NSC discussions, 26, 48
Porter memoranda, 100
Rogers memoranda, 98
Soviet statement (1969), 65
U.S. military aid, 60. 68, 98, 100
Washington Special Actions Group discussions, 60, 68
Lebanon (see also Israeli incursions in Lebanon (1972); Lebanese crisis (1969)):
Palestinian confrontation plans (1972), 312
Soviet relations with, 312
U.S. intervention (1958), 124
Leprette, Jacques, 1
Lewis, William, 192
Libya, 4, 21, 57, 60, 86, 94, 112, 119, 124, 127, 131, 168, 176, 217, 227, 231, 286, 315
Lincoln, Gen. George A., 4, 5, 26, 48, 74, 124
Lindsay, John, 102
Lucet, Charles, 13

MacDonald, Donald, 220
Malik, Yakov, 22, 50, 72, 75, 181
Mansfield, Mike, 102
McCloskey, Robert J., 144, 158, 228, 229
McCloy, John J., 74, 94
McConnell, Gen. John P., 5
McPherson, Lt. Gen. John, 117
Meany, George, 243
Meir, Golda, 13
Arab-Israeli military balance, 106, 108, 117
Egypt-Israel ceasefire (Aug. 1970), 143, 145, 147, 149, 151
Egypt-Israel ceasefire violations, 151, 154, 185
Hussein federation plan (1972), 282
Interim settlement proposals (1971), 203, 216, 219, 221, 224, 230, 240, 245, 249, 262, 306
Israeli nuclear capabilities, 42, 55
Israeli withdrawal interview (Mar. 12, 1971), 217
Jarring mission, 175, 185, 187, 188, 195, 240
Jarring mission (1971), 205, 207, 209, 211

References are to document numbers

Meir, Golda—*Continued*
  Jordanian-Israeli bilateral negotiations, 32, 282, 319
  Munich massacre (Sep. *1972*), 307
  Nixon correspondence, 33, 101, 102, 103, 130, 136, 142, 151, 163, 187, 188, 224, 238, 249, 307
  Proximity talk proposals, 263, 277
  Rogers correspondence, 67, 78, 129, 213, 224
  Rogers discussions, 122, 144, 225
  Rogers visit (*1971*), 208, 225, 228, 229, 230
  Sisco Israel trip (*1970*), 109, 114
  Sisco Israel trip (*1971*), 228, 229, 243, 245
  TWA hijacking (Aug. *1969*), 46
  United Kingdom visit, 183
  U.S. military aid to Israel, 51, 52, 59, 79, 86, 94, 95, 96, 99, 104, 106, 109, 117, 166, 190, 271, 272, 277
    U.S. visit (*1969*) discussions, 52, 57
    U.S. visit (*1971*) discussions, 268
  U.S. peace initiative (Jun. *1970*), 120, 129, 136, 140
  U.S. visit (*1969*), 33, 35, 36, 37, 39, 47, 48, 51, 52, 73, 77
  U.S. visit (*1970*), 151, 162, 240
  U.S. visit (*1971*), 267, 268
Mikhailov, V.V., 15, 22
Military contingency planning:
  Ad Hoc Special Review Group discussions, 133
  National Security Study Memoranda, 16
  NSC discussions, 4, 5
  Washington Special Actions Group discussions, 44, 56, 60, 68, 90, 91, 125, 126, 131
Mitchell, John N.:
  Egypt-Israel ceasefire violations, 160
  Rogers New York meetings (Sep. *1971*), 248
  U.S. Middle East policy, 124
  U.S. military aid to Israel, 160, 233
  U.S. settlement proposals, 48
  White House-Department of State divisions, 225, 257, 288
Moorer, Adm. Thomas H.:
  Arab-Israeli military balance, 243, 267
  Dayan U.S. visit (*1972*), 319
  Egypt-Israel ceasefire violations, 160
  Hussein U.S. visit (*1970*), 189

Moorer, Adm. Thomas H.—*Continued*
  Interim settlement proposals (*1971*), 243
  International guarantees, 221
  Jarring mission (*1971*), 204, 209
  Jordan intervention contingency planning, 125, 126
  Jordan U.S. personnel evacuation, 125, 126
  Military contingency planning, 131
  Palestinians, 192
  U.S.-Israeli bilateral negotiations, 216
  U.S. Middle East policy, 124, 172, 208, 209
  U.S. military aid to Israel, 132, 150, 153, 160, 163, 204
  U.S. military aid to Jordan, 192
Mosbacher, Emil, 14, 21, 96, 189
Moscow Summit (*1972*):
  Communiqué, 292, 311
  Kissinger-Gromyko discussions, 252
  Kissinger memoranda, 287, 294
  Laird memoranda, 267
  Nixon-Kissinger discussions, 269
  U.S. settlement proposal, 291
Mufti, Zuhayr Mahmud al-, 284
Munich massacre (Sep. *1972*), 307
Munn, Robert, 86
Muskie, Edmund S., 232, 243

Narasimhan, C.V., 50
Nasser, Gamal Abdel:
  Ad Hoc Special Review Group discussions, 117, 119, 133, 160
  Black September mediation, 168
  Death of, 165, 168, 169, 170, 172, 184, 192, 197, 286
  Dulles meeting (*1953*), 227
  Four-Power discussions, 23, 70
  Jordanian-Israeli bilateral negotiations, 30
  Kissinger memoranda, 19, 25, 47, 51, 66, 76, 88, 89, 114, 127, 169, 286
  NSC discussions, 4, 8, 26, 47, 48, 74, 86, 124
  NSC papers, 93, 112, 116, 170
  Peace appeal speech (May 1, *1970*), 112, 115, 116, 117, 129
  Political situation, 14, 19, 39, 47, 51, 114, 124, 184,
  Senior Review Group discussions, 168, 172, 192
  Soviet military aid to Egypt, 109, 111, 286

References are to document numbers

Nasser, Gamal Abdel—*Continued*
  Soviet peace plan, 1
  Soviet Union visit (*1970*), 104, 133, 142
  U.S. Middle East policy, 4, 8, 25, 26, 29, 36, 57, 60, 66, 67, 83, 116, 117, 118, 129, 149
  U.S. military aid to Israel, 92, 104, 105, 112, 115, 116, 124
  U.S.-Israeli communications, 14, 29, 36, 52, 99, 104, 106, 109, 110, 118, 142, 226, 228
  U.S.-Jordanian communications, 19, 189
  U.S.-Soviet communications, 1, 18, 39, 111, 120
  U.S.-United Arab Republic communications, 21, 109, 112, 115, 158, 196, 197, 218, 242
National Security Council (NSC):
  Arab-Israeli military balance, 4, 48, 124, 243
  Egypt-Israel ceasefire violations, 156
  Four-Power negotiation proposals, 4, 5, 26, 74
  Interim settlement proposals (*1971*), 209, 243
  Jarring mission (*1971*), 209
  Military contingency planning, 4, 5
  NSC papers, 93, 112, 116, 152, 156, 170, 175, 176, 181, 182, 191, 194, 198, 202, 207, 214
  Senior Review Group discussions, 168
  U.S. Middle East policy, 4, 74, 124
  U.S. military aid to Israel, 124, 209, 243
  U.S. settlement proposals, 26, 48, 306, 317
  U.S.-Soviet negotiations, 4, 5, 26, 48, 74
National Security Decision Memoranda (NSDM):
  NSDM 8, "Crisis Anticipation and Management," 16
  NSDM 19, 44
  NSDM 40, "Responsibility for Conduct, Supervision, and Coordination of Covert Action Operations," 91
  NSDM 61, 113
  NSDM 66, "Next Steps in the Middle East," 128

National Security Decision Memoranda (NSDM)—*Continued*
  NSDM 87, "Military and Financial Assistance to Israel," 171
  NSDM 100, "Military Equipment Package for Jordan," 192
National Security Study Memoranda (NSSM):
  NSSM 2, "Middle East Policy," 3
  NSSM 17, "Further Studies on Middle East Policy," 6
  NSSM 33, "Contingency Planning for the Middle East," 16
  NSSM 40, "Israeli Nuclear Weapons Program," 20
  NSSM 81, "U.S. Arms Transfer Policy Toward Israel," 63
  NSSM 82, "U.S. Economic Assistance Policy Toward Israel," 62
  NSSM 93, "The Arab-Israeli Military Balance," 104, 108
  NSSM 98, "Further Review of Israeli Arms Requests," 148
  NSSM 103, "Future Options in the Middle East," 164
  NSSM 105, "Addendum to NSSM 103," 164
Newlin, Michael H., 254
Nixon, Richard M.:
  40 Committee, 91
  American Jewish community, 54, 81, 232, 233, 269
  Arab-Israeli military balance, 108, 218, 239, 243, 266
  Black September (*1970*), 161, 190
  Border incidents, 82, 88, 94, 248
  Brezhnev correspondence, 281, 301
  Dayan ceasefire proposal (Dec. *1970*), 188
  Dayan U.S. visit (*1970*), 190
  Eban U.S. visit (*1970*), 118
  Egypt-Israel ceasefire violations, 156, 162, 169, 179
  Europe trip (Feb.-Mar. *1969*), 5, 8
  Four-Power negotiation proposals, 4, 11, 14, 67, 70, 77
  Four-Power negotiations, 76, 81, 89, 210, 212
  Heath meetings, 269
  Hussein correspondence, 82, 220, 236, 273, 280
  Hussein federation plan (*1972*), 280, 284
  Hussein U.S. visit (*1969*), 19

References are to document numbers

Nixon, Richard M.—*Continued*
  Hussein U.S. visit (*1970*), 189
  Hussein U.S. visit (*1972*), 284
  Interim settlement proposals (*1971*), 209, 216
    Bergus paper, 238, 240
    Ehrlichman/Haldeman discussions, 232
    Gromyko discussions, 251
    Kissinger discussions, 222, 233
    Kissinger memoranda, 240
    Meir correspondence, 249
    NSC discussions, 243
    Sadat correspondence, 219
    U.S.-Egyptian communications, 227
  International guarantees, 211
  Israeli incursions in Lebanon (*1972*), 308, 313
  Israeli nuclear capabilities, 38, 41, 55
  Jarring mission restart proposals (*1970*), 187, 189
  Jarring mission (*1971*), 197, 209, 210, 212, 219, 222
  Kosygin correspondence, 88, 94, 99, 214
  Meir correspondence, 33, 101, 106, 130, 136, 187, 188, 249, 307
  Meir U.S. visit (*1969*), 52
  Meir U.S. visit (*1970*), 162
  Military contingency planning, 4, 5
  Moscow Summit (*1972*), 269, 287, 289, 291, 298
  Munich massacre (Sep. *1972*), 307
  Nasser peace appeal speech (May 1, *1970*), 112, 115
  Oil company executives meeting, 74
  Press conference statement (Mar. 4, *1969*), 14, 77, 218
  Proximity talk proposals, 265, 269, 277
  Rogers Middle East trip (*1971*), 222, 225, 227, 230
  Rogers New York meetings (Sep. *1971*), 248
  Rogers Plan, 58
  Sadat correspondence, 165, 197, 219, 298
  Soviet-Egyptian relations, 233, 286, 300, 301
  Soviet military aid to Egypt, 124, 127, 162, 197, 233, 251, 286
  Soviet military aid to Jordan, 69
  Soviet role, 1, 4, 34, 65, 269
  Syrian political situation, 184

Nixon, Richard M.—*Continued*
  U.S. economic aid to Jordan, 220, 236, 273
  U.S.-Egyptian backchannel (*1972*), 300, 303, 305
  U.S.-Egyptian bilateral negotiations, 237
  U.S.-Israeli bilateral negotiations, 14, 51, 77, 216
  U.S. Middle East policy, 233
    Domestic political considerations, 9
    Kissinger memoranda, 11, 24, 25, 27, 38, 45, 47, 51, 54, 55, 59, 65, 66, 76, 77, 79, 81, 89, 95, 113, 114, 115, 127, 134, 166, 167, 169, 179, 216, 223, 240, 249, 265, 266, 277, 286, 287, 289, 297, 305, 313
    Laird memoranda, 121, 239, 267, 313
    National Security Study Memoranda, 3, 6, 20, 62, 63, 104, 108, 148, 164
    NSC discussions, 48, 74, 124, 209, 243
    Rogers memoranda, 34, 58, 67, 69, 70, 97, 123, 184, 227, 235
    Sisco memoranda, 39, 114
    CBS network interview (Jul. 1, *1970*), 134
  U.S. military aid to Israel, 101, 163, 233
    Ad Hoc Special Review Group discussions, 86, 94
    Aide-mémoire, 102, 103
    Congressional leadership meeting, 94, 140
    Dayan discussions, 190
    Dayan memoranda, 248
    Ehrlichman/Haldeman discussions, 232
    Jordanian response, 92
    Kissinger discussions, 73, 96, 104
    Kissinger memoranda, 59, 79, 95, 127, 166, 167, 168
    Kissinger-Rabin discussions, 103
    Laird memoranda, 121, 239, 267
    Meir correspondence, 101, 106, 187, 188, 249
    Meir U.S. visit discussions, 162, 268
    NSC discussions, 124
    Rabin discussions, 151
    Sisco-Rabin discussions, 271, 277

References are to document numbers

Nixon, Richard M.—*Continued*
  U.S. military aid to Jordan, 24, 113, 192
  U.S. military aid to Lebanon, 100
  U.S. peace initiative (Jun. *1970*), 121, 128, 129, 136, 139
  U.S. settlement proposals, 25, 26, 27, 47, 48, 76, 77
  U.S.-Soviet negotiations, 84
    Dobrynin talks, 281
    Gromyko talks, 173, 251
    Kissinger-Dobrynin talks, 135
    Kissinger memoranda, 127
    NSC discussions, 4, 5, 26, 48, 74
    Rogers-Dobrynin talks, 97
    Rogers memoranda, 34
    Sisco Moscow talks (*1969*), 39
  War of attrition, 51
  White House-Department of State divisions, 134, 144, 216, 223, 227, 232
  Wilson U.S. visit (*1970*), 83
Nixon Doctrine, 217
Noujaim, Gen. Jean, 100
Noyes, James H.:
  Egypt-Israel ceasefire violations, 177, 178, 183
  International guarantees, 195, 199, 221
  Jarring mission (*1971*), 195, 199, 204, 208
  Palestinians, 183, 192
  UN General Assembly meeting (Oct. *1970*), 177
  U.S. Middle East policy, 172
  U.S. military aid to Israel, 183, 188, 195, 204, 259, 319
  U.S. military aid to Jordan, 188, 191, 192, 284
NSC Interdepartmental Group for the Near East and South Asia, 8
  Papers, NSCIG/NEA 69-2A (Revised), "Further Studies on Middle East Policy," 8
NSC Review Group, 3, 6, 20
Nuclear Nonproliferation Treaty (NPT), 4, 31, 35, 37, 38, 41, 42, 52, 55, 86
Nuclear weapons. *See* Israeli nuclear capabilities.
Nutter, G. Warren:
  Dayan U.S. visit (*1972*), 319
  Egypt-Israel ceasefire violations, 177, 183
  International guarantees, 199, 221

Nutter, G. Warren—*Continued*
  Jarring mission (*1971*), 199, 204
  Lebanese crisis (*1969*), 60, 68
  Military contingency planning, 44, 56, 131
  Palestinians, 183, 192
  Proximity talk proposals, 260
  UN General Assembly meeting (Oct. *1970*), 177
  U.S. Middle East policy, 117, 119, 172
  U.S. military aid to Israel, 132, 142, 183, 204, 272
  U.S. military aid to Jordan, 113, 168, 192
  U.S. peace initiative (Jun. *1970*), 133

Oil company executives, 74
Operation Even-Steven, 146, 155, 159
Organization of African Unity (OAU), 270

Packard, David:
  Arab-Israeli military balance, 243
  Egypt-Israel ceasefire violations, 160, 177, 178
  Interim settlement proposals (*1971*), 243
  International guarantees, 195, 199, 221
  Israeli nuclear capabilities, 10, 20, 35, 37, 38, 41
  Jarring mission (*1971*), 195, 199, 204, 208
  Jordan U.S. personnel evacuation, 125
  Palestinians, 192
  UN General Assembly meeting (Oct. *1970*), 177
  U.S. Middle East policy, 48, 117, 119, 124, 172
  U.S. military aid to Israel:
    Ad Hoc Special Review Group discussions, 86, 94, 133, 150, 153, 160
    Israeli discussions, 55, 167
    Kissinger-Sisco discussions, 141
    NSC discussions, 124
    Nutter memoranda, 132
    Senior Review Group discussions, 188, 195, 204, 208
  U.S. military aid to Jordan, 168, 188, 192
  U.S. peace initiative (Jun. *1970*), 133
  U.S. settlement proposals, 48
Pakistan, 48, 73, 243, 273, 287, 311

1112   Index

Palestine Liberation Organization (PLO), 4, 60, 247
Palestinian refugees:
  Four-Power UN representative discussions, 23
  Johnson mission, 4, 314
  Kissinger memoranda, 47, 216, 297
  Nixon memoranda, 233
  NSC discussions, 26, 124, 209
  NSC Interdepartmental Group papers, 8
  NSC staff summaries, 112, 181, 202, 207
  Rogers Plan on, 58
  Sisco memoranda, 114
  U.S.-Israeli communications, 1, 140, 142, 187, 223, 228
  U.S.-Soviet communications, 49, 53, 311
Palestinians (see also Palestine Liberation Organization or PLO; or Popular Front for the Liberation of Palestine or PFLP; Jordan; Lebanese crisis (1969); Palestinian refugees):
  Black September, 160, 161, 168
  Fatah state plans, 186, 188
  Hussein federation plan (1972), 280, 284, 289
  Jidda Jordan talks (Sep. 1971), 247
  Jordanian role, 181, 182, 183, 192, 280, 297
  Lebanese confrontation plans, 312
  NSC staff summaries, 112, 170, 175, 176, 181, 182, 191
  Senior Review Group discussions, 177, 183, 188, 192, 195, 204
  U.S.-Fatah contacts, 174, 180, 185, 186
  U.S.-Israeli communications, 228, 248, 279
  U.S.-Jordanian communications, 185, 189, 192, 247, 280, 284
  Washington Special Actions Group/Senior Review Group discussions, 172
Parmenter, William, 177, 204
Pastinen, Ilkka, 138
Peacekeeping force proposals. See International guarantees.
Pederson, Richard F., 4
Peet, Vice Adm. Raymond E., 319
Plaja, Eugenio, 324
Pompidou, Georges, 67, 96, 102, 270

Popular Front for the Liberation of Palestine (PFLP), 4, 46, 48, 60, 124, 293
Porter, William J., 60, 61, 98, 100
Pranger, Robert J.:
  Egypt-Israel ceasefire violations, 160
  Jordan U.S. personnel evacuation, 125
  Military contingency planning, 90, 131, 133
  Soviet military aid to Egypt, 91
  U.S. Middle East policy, 117, 119
  U.S. military aid to Israel, 150, 160
  U.S. peace initiative (Jun. 1970), 133
Proximity talk proposals:
  Bush-Waldheim discussions, 306
  Defense Department role, 260
  Egyptian rejection, 294
  Kissinger memoranda, 265
  Kissinger-Sisco discussions, 257
  Nixon-Kissinger discussions, 269
  Rabin interview (Nov. 30, 1972), 321
  Sadat speech (Jan. 13, 1972), 275
  Sadat speech (Mar. 31, 1972), 285
  Saunders memoranda, 294
  Soviet role, 265, 269
  U.S.-Egyptian communications, 255, 258, 263, 275, 276, 278, 285, 302
  U.S.-Israeli communications, 257, 261, 263, 277, 306, 322
  U.S.-Saudi discussions, 314

Qadhafi, Muammar, 246, 314

Rabin, Yitzhak, 26, 166
  Border incidents, 248
  Ceasefire efforts, 103, 144
  Dayan U.S. visit (1970), 190
  Dayan U.S. visit (1972), 319
  Eban U.S. visit (1970), 118
  Egypt-Israel ceasefire (Aug. 1970), 147
  Egypt-Israel ceasefire violations, 157, 162
  Interim settlement proposals (1971), 217, 223, 238, 244, 245, 248, 256
  Israeli incursions in Lebanon (1972), 293, 315
  Israeli nuclear capabilities, 31, 35, 36, 37, 38, 41, 47, 55
  Jarring mission restart proposals (1970), 129, 187
  Jarring mission (1971), 206, 209, 211, 212, 213, 214, 216, 217
  Jerusalem, 250

References are to document numbers

Rabin, Yitzhak—*Continued*
  Meir U.S. visit (*1970*), 162
  Munich massacre (Sep. *1972*), 307
  Nixon-Meir correspondence, 33, 101, 130, 187, 224
  Proximity talk proposals, 261, 277, 321
  Sisco Israel trip (*1971*), 229, 244, 245
  Soviet military aid to Egypt, 110, 142, 162, 256
  U.S.-Israeli bilateral negotiations, 14, 36, 52, 78, 99, 151
  U.S.-Israeli communications, 1, 4, 5, 10, 13, 31, 33, 35, 37, 38, 48, 54, 55, 61, 64, 70, 78, 84, 86, 96, 102, 103, 104, 129, 140, 147, 151, 154, 166, 167, 204, 211, 300
  U.S. Jordan-Israel settlement proposal, 78
  U.S. military aid to Israel, 86, 93, 94, 95, 96, 106, 117, 141, 160, 166, 167, 272
    Dayan U.S. visit (*1972*) discussions, 319
    Kissinger discussions, 103, 104, 110, 132, 133, 142, 143, 144, 147, 151, 262
    Meir U.S. visit (*1971*), 268
    Meir U.S. visit discussions, 162
    Nixon-Meir correspondence, 187
    Packard discussions, 167, 239
    Rogers discussions, 106, 129, 130, 209, 225, 229, 272
    Senior Review Group discussions, 119, 140
    Sisco discussions, 129, 157, 224, 244, 245, 256, 261, 271, 277, 283, 293
  U.S. peace initiative (Jun. *1970*), 140, 141, 142, 151
  U.S.-Soviet negotiations, 27, 29
Rafael, Gideon, 36, 46, 261
Raviv, Moshe, 41
Rhea, Col. Frank W., 131
Rhodes formula, 52, 53, 58, 61, 67, 71, 74, 80, 83, 85, 107
Riad, Mahmoud, 1, 165, 195
  Bergus discussions, 237, 238, 246
  Egypt-Israel ceasefire (Aug. *1970*), 215
  Egypt-Israel ceasefire violations, 154, 157, 158, 169
  Interim settlement proposals (*1971*), 234, 253, 254, 256

Riad, Mahmoud—*Continued*
  Israeli withdrawal, 2, 237
  Jarring mission (*1969–1970*), 8, 12, 15, 26, 139, 143
  Jarring mission (*1971*), 196, 200, 206, 213
  Nasser speech (May 1, *1970*), 115
  Nixon-Sadat correspondence, 197
  Proximity talk proposals, 255
  Rogers communications, 52, 74, 136, 137, 172, 177, 178, 188, 253
  Rogers visit (*1971*), 227
  Sisco discussions, 231
  UN General Assembly speech (Oct. 6, *1971*), 254, 256
Riad, Mohammed, 21, 146, 154, 196, 200, 206, 215, 238, 254
Richardson, Elliot L.:
  Four-Power negotiation proposals, 5
  Four-Power negotiations, 70, 78
  Israeli nuclear capabilities, 20, 31, 35, 37, 38, 40, 41, 55
  Military contingency planning, 4
  U.S. Middle East policy, 73, 74, 117, 119, 124
  U.S. military aid to Israel, 86, 94
  U.S. settlement proposals, 26, 48, 78
  U.S.-Soviet negotiations, 61, 111
Rifai, Abdul Munim, 12, 82, 87
Rifai, Zaid, 30, 32, 74, 109, 113, 188
Rogers, William P. (*see also* Rogers Plan *and* White House-Department of State divisions):
  Arab-Israeli military balance, 108, 243, 266
  Border incidents, 64, 82, 88, 259, 264
  Ceasefire efforts, 123, 140, 142, 143, 144
  Dayan ceasefire proposal (Dec. *1970*), 188
  Dayan U.S. visit (*1972*), 319
  Egypt-Israel ceasefire (Aug. *1970*), 146, 147, 155, 215
  Egypt-Israel ceasefire violations, 88, 156, 163, 173, 177
  Foreign Ministers meeting, 50
  Four-Power negotiation proposals, 5, 13, 17, 50, 67, 70, 71, 76, 83
  Four-Power negotiations, 7, 17, 78, 83, 111, 193, 213
  Hussein U.S. visit (*1969*), 19
  Hussein U.S. visit (*1970*), 189
  Interim settlement proposals (*1971*), 209, 215, 241, 258

References are to document numbers

Rogers, William P. (*see also* Rogers Plan *and* White House-Department of State divisions)—*Continued*
  Interim settlement proposals (*1971*)—*Continued*
    Eban discussions, 253, 257
    Meet the Press statement (Nov. 5, *1972*), 318
    Nixon discussions, 227
    NSC discussions, 243
    Sisco Israel trip, 228, 229, 244, 246
    UN General Assembly speech (Oct. 4, *1971*), 249, 254, 256, 277
    U.S.-Egyptian communications, 227, 234, 237, 238, 253, 255
    U.S.-Israeli communications, 224, 230, 238, 256
    U.S.-Soviet communications, 251
  Israeli nuclear capabilities, 10, 24, 37
  Jarring mission (*1969–1970*), 13
  Jarring mission restart proposals (*1970*), 123, 138, 149, 187, 193
  Jarring mission (*1971*), 213
    Nixon-Kissinger discussions, 210
    NSC discussions, 209
    Press conference (Mar. 16, *1971*), 219
    U.S.-Egyptian communications, 196, 200, 206, 215, 218, 219, 242
    U.S.-Israeli communications, 209, 211, 217
    U.S.-Jordanian communications, 197, 201
  Jarring mission (*1972*), 283
  Jerusalem, 236
  Jordanian-Israeli bilateral negotiations, 32, 322
  Kissinger memoranda, 11, 25, 27, 47, 77, 113, 114, 127, 134, 166, 169, 216, 240, 249, 277
  Lebanese crisis (*1969*), 64, 98
  Middle East trip (*1971*), 222, 225, 227, 228, 229, 230, 231
  Military contingency planning, 4
  Munich massacre (Sep. *1972*), 307
  New York meetings (Sep. *1971*), 248
  Nixon-Meir correspondence, 33, 130, 136, 187
  Nixon-Sadat correspondence, 197
  Palestinians, 182, 185
  Proximity talk proposals, 255, 258
    Defense Department role, 260
    Rabin interview (Nov. 30, *1972*), 321

Rogers, William P. (*see also* Rogers Plan *and* White House-Department of State divisions)—*Continued*
  Proximity talk proposals—*Continued*
    U.S.-Egyptian communications, 263, 275, 276, 285
    U.S.-Israeli communications, 261, 263, 322
  Soviet-Egyptian relations, 233, 235, 298
  Soviet military aid to Egypt, 123, 124
  Soviet military aid to Jordan, 69
  Soviet peace plan (Jun. 17, *1969*), 34
  Syrian political situation, 184
  UN General Assembly Resolution 2799, 270
  U.S. economic aid to Israel, 62
  U.S. economic aid to Jordan, 220, 236
  U.S.-Egyptian bilateral negotiations, 18, 74
  U.S.-Israeli bilateral negotiations, 13, 52, 118, 223, 228, 229, 230, 304
  U.S. Jordan-Israel settlement proposal, 82
  U.S. Middle East policy, 7, 9, 57, 74, 111, 123, 124, 175, 233
  U.S. military aid to Israel, 96, 123, 163, 188
    Kissinger memoranda, 166, 169
    Laird communications, 259, 264
    Meir U.S. visit (*1971*) discussions, 268
    National Security Decision Memoranda, 128, 166
    National Security Study Memoranda, 63, 148
    Nixon-Meir correspondence, 130, 136, 187
    Nixon memoranda, 163, 233
    NSC discussions, 86, 124
    Press conference (Mar. 23, *1970*), 94, 95, 99, 105
    Rabin discussions, 96, 106, 142
    Sisco-Ghorbal discussions, 275
    Sisco-Rabin discussions, 244, 271
  U.S. military aid to Jordan, 69, 87, 113, 192
  U.S. peace initiative (Jun. *1970*), 123, 128, 129, 136, 139, 143, 175
    Israeli response, 138, 140, 142, 151
    Soviet response, 137
    U.S.–UN discussions, 138
    U.S. settlement proposals, 25, 27

References are to document numbers

Index   115

Rogers, William P. (*see also* Rogers Plan *and* White House-Department of State divisions)—*Continued*
  U.S. settlement proposals—*Continued*
    Jordan-Israel settlement proposal, 67, 76
    NSC discussions, 26, 48
    Speech (Dec. 9, *1969*), 73, 74, 75, 181, 182
    U.S.-Israeli communications, 77, 78, 84
    U.S.-Soviet communications, 85
  U.S.-Soviet negotiations, 15, 34, 39, 67, 84, 111
    Dobrynin talks, 80, 97, 105, 122
    Gromyko talks, 52, 53, 173
    Nixon-Gromyko talks, 173, 251
    Sisco-Dobrynin talks (Mar.-Apr. *1969*), 18, 22, 29
    Sisco-Dobrynin talks (*1970*), 107, 135
    Sisco Moscow talks (*1969*), 39
    U.S.-Israeli communications, 29
  U.S. statement of principles, 13
Rogers Plan:
  Development of, 25, 28, 58
  Kissinger memoranda, 127
  NSC discussions, 74
  Presentation to Dobrynin, 58, 61
  Rogers memoranda, 71
  Rogers speech (Dec. 9, *1969*), 73, 74, 75
  Sisco memoranda, 39
  Soviet peace plan (Jun. 17, *1969*) and, 34
  Soviet response, 84, 85
  Text a, 58
  U.S.-Israeli communications, 29, 78, 162, 205
  U.S.-Soviet communications, 80
Rostow, Eugene V., 1, 2, 15, 74
Rush, Kenneth, 319
Rusk, Dean, 1, 2, 5, 8, 15, 26, 28, 36, 61, 81, 209

Sabri, Ali, 165, 227, 231
Sadat, Anwar al-:
  Accession of, 165
  Egypt-Israel ceasefire (Aug. *1970*), 197, 203, 204, 215
  Hussein federation plan (*1972*), 280, 289

Sadat, Anwar al-—*Continued*
  Interim settlement proposals (*1971*), 201, 202, 208, 213, 216, 217, 229, 240, 241, 245, 246, 253, 254
    Bergus discussions, 200, 219, 237, 255
    Bergus-Heikal discussions, 234, 246
    Nixon correspondence, 215, 219
    Rogers discussions, 227, 257
    Sisco discussions, 230, 231, 242, 244
    Speech (Feb. 4, *1971*), 203, 204, 218, 224, 240
    Speech (Mar. 7, *1971*), 215
    Speech (May 20, *1971*), 238
    Speech (Nov. 11, *1971*), 263
    Speech (Jan. 13, *1972*), 275
    Speech (Feb. 16, *1972*), 276
    Sterner discussions, 242, 243
  Jarring mission (*1971*), 181, 195, 197, 212, 215, 219, 223, 226, 270
  Moscow Summit (*1972*), 287, 289, 294, 298
  Nixon correspondence, 165, 197, 215, 219, 298
  Political situation, 217, 229, 231, 238, 306, 318
  Proximity talk proposals, 258, 261, 263, 265, 275, 277, 278, 283, 285, 317
  Rogers visit (*1971*), 227, 228, 231
  Soviet-Egyptian relations, 215, 227, 228, 233, 235, 256, 257, 268, 286, 287, 298, 300, 312, 313, 314
  U.S. diplomatic relations renewal, 231, 234, 288, 305
  U.S.-Egyptian backchannel (*1972*), 296, 299, 303, 309, 310
  U.S. military aid to Israel, 245, 275, 276
  War, possible, Dakroury discussions, 289, 290
Saint George, R. Adm. William R., 153, 177, 183, 188, 192, 195, 199, 204, 208, 221
Sapir, Pinchas, 106, 229
Saqqaf, Umar, 61, 314
Saudi Arabia, 17, 42, 43, 47, 52, 57, 61, 67, 74, 86, 93, 117, 124, 127, 129, 131, 168, 177, 182, 186, 189, 220, 225, 228, 235, 243, 247, 286, 298, 314, 323
Saunders, Harold H., 74, 124
  Ad Hoc Special Review Group discussions, 86, 94, 150, 153, 160

References are to document numbers

Saunders, Harold H.—*Continued*
  Arab-Israeli military balance, 243
  Egypt-Israel ceasefire violations, 159, 160, 177, 178, 183
  Four-Power negotiation proposals, 5, 70
  Interim settlement proposals (*1971*), 217, 243
  International guarantees, 195, 198, 199, 221
  Israeli nuclear capabilities, 35
  Jarring mission restart proposals (*1970*), 188
  Jarring mission (*1971*):
    NSC discussions, 209
    NSC staff summaries, 202
    Senior Review Group discussions, 195, 199, 204, 208
    U.S.-Egyptian communications, 218
    U.S.-Israeli communications, 217
  Jordan intervention contingency planning, 126
  Lebanese crisis (*1969*), 60, 68
  Military contingency planning, 4, 57, 90, 125, 131
  Moscow Summit (*1972*), 291
  Palestinians, 176, 183, 192
  Proximity talk proposals, 276, 294
  Rogers Plan, 28
  Soviet military aid to Egypt, 91, 110, 124
  UN General Assembly meeting (Oct. *1970*), 177
  U.S. economic aid to Jordan, 273
  U.S.-Egyptian backchannel (*1972*), 296, 317
  U.S.-Egyptian bilateral negotiations, 21
  U.S.-Israeli bilateral negotiations, 14, 36, 52
  U.S.-Israeli desalting project, 77
  U.S. Middle East policy, 117, 119, 172
  U.S. military aid to Israel:
    Kissinger-Rabin discussions, 110, 132
    NSC discussions, 124
    NSC staff summaries, 152
    Senior Review Group discussions, 183, 188, 195, 204
    Yariv meetings, 108
  U.S. military aid to Jordan, 113, 168, 188, 192
  U.S. peace initiative (Jun. *1970*), 133

Saunders, Harold H.—*Continued*
  U.S. settlement proposals, 26, 48, 291
  U.S.-Soviet negotiations, 15, 22, 53
Schumann, Robert, 39, 50, 74
Secret Egypt-Israel backchannel meeting proposals. *See* U.S.-Egyptian backchannel (*1972*).
Seelye, Talcott, 168, 188, 189, 192
Selden, Armistead I., 178, 183, 195, 208
Semyanov, Victor, 1
Senior Review Group, 168, 172
  Dayan ceasefire proposal (Dec. *1970*), 188
  Egypt-Israel ceasefire violations, 172, 177, 178, 183
  International guarantees, 195, 199, 221
  Jarring mission (*1971*), 195, 199, 208
  Palestinians, 183, 192
  UN General Assembly meeting (Oct. *1970*), 177
  U.S. military aid to Israel, 183, 188, 195, 204
  U.S. military aid to Jordan, 168, 188, 192
Shakespeare, Frank J., Jr., 189, 209
Sharaf, Abdul Hamid, 32, 189, 236, 274
Sharara, Yousef, 275
Sharm el-Sheikh:
  Department of State proposal (*1971*), 216
  Kissinger memoranda, 25, 47, 77, 216
  NSC discussions, 26, 47, 48, 74, 209
  NSC papers, 112, 198, 202, 207, 214
  Rogers Plan on, 17, 58
  Rogers travel, 231
  Saunders memoranda, 53, 57
  Senior Review Group discussions, 208, 221
  UN role proposals, 18, 23, 53, 221, 291, 299
  U.S.-Egyptian communications, 67, 81, 218, 296, 310
  U.S.-Israeli communications, 13, 36, 77, 208, 211, 217, 223, 228, 319

References are to document numbers

Sharm el-Sheikh—*Continued*
  U.S.-Soviet communications, 1, 2, 18, 28, 34, 49, 53, 57, 61, 80, 97, 107, 281, 311
Shriver, Sargent, 13
Sinai control and demilitarization proposals, 2, 14, 18, 23, 25, 26, 27, 28, 47, 53, 57, 67, 74, 107, 110, 118, 124, 127, 146, 153, 157, 178, 188, 198, 199, 200, 207, 208, 211, 213, 214, 215, 216, 217, 219, 221, 223, 228, 237, 238, 240, 241, 243, 245, 249, 254, 255, 258, 263, 265, 266, 276, 286, 296, 306, 307, 309, 310, 311, 317, 319
Sisco, Joseph J.:
  Ad Hoc Special Review Group discussions, 86, 94, 117, 119, 133, 150, 153, 160
  American Jewish community, 81
  Arab-Israeli military balance, NSC discussions, 243
  Border incidents, 82
  Ceasefire efforts, 141, 188
  Egypt-Israel ceasefire (Aug. *1970*), 147
  Egypt-Israel ceasefire violations, 157, 160, 162, 177, 178, 183
  Four-Power negotiation proposals, 4, 7, 13, 17, 39, 71
  Four-Power negotiations, 73, 81
  Hussein U.S. visit (*1970*), 189
  Interim settlement proposals (*1971*):
    Barbour memoranda, 226
    Bergus paper, 238
    Ghorbal discussions, 275
    NSC discussions, 243
    U.S.-Egyptian communications, 227, 231, 234, 253
    U.S.-Israeli communications, 217, 230, 244, 245, 256
  International guarantees, 221
  Israel trip (*1971*), 228, 229, 241, 243, 244, 245
  Israeli incursions in Lebanon (*1972*), 293, 315
  Israeli nuclear capabilities, 55
  Jarring mission restart proposals (*1970*), 149, 187
  Jarring mission (*1971*):
    Barbour memoranda, 226
    Nixon-Kissinger discussions, 210, 212
    NSC discussions, 209

Sisco, Joseph J.—*Continued*
  Jarring mission (*1971*)—*Continued*
    NSC staff summaries, 202, 207
    Rogers memoranda, 209
    Senior Review Group discussions, 195, 208
    U.S.-Egyptian communications, 196, 200, 206, 215, 218, 219
    U.S.-Israeli communications, 208, 211, 217
    U.S.-Jordanian communications, 197
  Jarring mission (*1972*), 275
  Jerusalem, 236, 250
  Jordan U.S. personnel evacuation, 125
  Jordanian-Israeli bilateral negotiations, 32, 322
  Lebanese crisis (*1969*), 64
  Lebanese-Palestinian confrontation plans, 312
  Meir discussions, 109, 245
  Meir U.S. visit (*1970*), 162
  Middle East trip (Apr. *1970*), 109, 114
  Military contingency planning, 4
  Nixon-Meir correspondence, 33
  Nixon-Sadat correspondence, 197
  Proximity talk proposals:
    Kissinger discussions, 257
    Rabin discussions, 277
    Rogers-Allon discussions, 322
    Rogers memoranda, 258
    Saunders memoranda, 294
    U.S.-Egyptian communications, 275, 276, 278
    U.S.-Israeli communications, 257, 263, 306
  Rogers Middle East trip (*1971*), 222, 227, 228, 231
  Rogers Plan, 28, 39, 58, 61, 66, 80
  Soviet military aid to Egypt, 124, 162
  Soviet peace plan (Dec. 30, *1968*), 2
  UN General Assembly meeting (Oct. *1970*), 177
  UN General Assembly Resolution 2799, 270
  U.S. economic aid to Jordan, 220
  U.S.-Egyptian bilateral negotiations, 21
  U.S.-Israeli bilateral negotiations, 14, 52, 216, 304
  U.S. Jordan-Israel settlement proposal, 78
  U.S. Middle East policy, 8, 74, 114, 117, 119, 124, 181

Sisco, Joseph J.—*Continued*
  U.S. military aid to Israel, 46, 95, 243
    Ghorbal discussions, 275
    Kissinger discussions, 141
    Meir discussions, 109, 245
    Meir U.S. visit discussions, 162
    Nixon-Meir correspondence, 187
    NSC discussions, 124
    NSC staff summaries, 152, 194
    Rabin discussions, 244, 271, 277
    Senior Review Group discussions, 183, 188, 195
    Yariv meetings, 108
  U.S. military aid to Jordan, 86, 87, 113, 188, 191, 192
  U.S. peace initiative (Jun. *1970*), 129, 133, 137
  U.S. settlement proposals, 26, 48, 84, 85
  U.S.-Soviet negotiations:
    Dobrynin talks (*1969*), 13, 15, 18, 22, 27, 28, 29, 49, 57, 61
    Dobrynin talks (*1970*), 107, 127
    Moscow talks (*1969*), 39, 48
    NSC discussions, 48
    Rogers-Dobrynin talks, 120
    Rogers memoranda, 111
  U.S. statement of principles, 13
  White House-Department of State divisions, 223, 257
Smith, Walter B., 22, 85
Sonnenfeldt, Helmut, 48, 56, 65, 95, 117, 187
Soviet-Egyptian relations (*see also* Soviet military aid to Egypt):
  Dayan interview, 307
  Joint communiqué (*1970*), 142
  Nasser Soviet Union visit (*1970*), 142
  Nixon-Brezhnev correspondence, 301
  Sadat-Brezhnev meeting (*1972*), 286
  Sadat Soviet Union visit (*1971*), 215, 256
  Soviet adviser expulsion, 298, 299, 300, 307, 310
  Treaty of Friendship and Cooperation (*1971*), 233, 235, 237
  U.S.-Egyptian communications, 228, 302
  U.S.-Soviet communications, 298, 300
Soviet military aid to Egypt (*see also* Egypt-Israel ceasefire violations):
  Kissinger memoranda, 127, 266
  Laird memoranda, 239

Soviet military aid to Egypt (*see also* Egypt-Israel ceasefire violations)—*Continued*
  Nasser peace appeal speech and, 112, 115
  Nixon memoranda, 233
  Nixon-Sadat correspondence, 197
  NSC discussions, 124
  NSC staff summaries, 112
  Rogers memoranda, 123
  Sadat-Brezhnev discussions, 286
  U.S.-Egyptian communications, 109, 197, 231, 242
  U.S.-Israeli communications, 106, 108, 110, 142, 162, 256, 268
  U.S.-Soviet communications, 39, 111, 120, 134, 135, 251, 268
  Washington Special Actions Group discussions, 91
Soviet role (*see also* Four-Power negotiation proposals; Soviet military aid to Egypt; U.S.-Soviet negotiations):
  Border incidents and, 88, 93, 94
  Egypt-Israel ceasefire (Aug. *1970*), 155, 159
  Interim settlement proposals (*1971*), 235, 240
  International guarantees and, 221
  Lebanese crisis (*1969*), 60, 65
  Nixon-Kissinger discussions, 269
  NSC discussions, 4, 26, 48, 124
  NSC staff papers, 198, 214
  Peace plan (Dec. *30, 1968*), 1, 2, 4, 15
  Peace plan (Jun. *17, 1969*), 34
  Proximity talk proposals and, 265, 269
  Response to U.S. settlement proposals, 84, 85
  Rogers-Foreign Ministers meeting, 50
  Senior Review Group discussions, 195
  U.S.-Israeli communications, 1, 14, 190
  U.S. military contingency planning, 4
  U.S. peace initiative (Jun. *1970*) response, 137, 138
Soviet Union (*see also* Soviet-Egyptian relations; Soviet role):
  Ad Hoc Special Review Group:
    Egypt-Israel ceasefire violations, 160
    Military contingency planning, 133

References are to document numbers

Index 1119

Soviet Union (*see also* Soviet-Egyptian relations; Soviet role)—*Continued*
  Ad Hoc Special Review Group—*Continued*
    U.S. military aid to Israel, 86, 94, 117, 119, 133, 150, 153, 160
    Lebanese relations with, 312
    Military aid to Jordan, 69, 92
Spitz, Mark, 307
Stackhouse, Haywood, 140, 149, 183, 206, 271, 293, 315, 322
Stans, Maurice H., 62
Stark, Andrew, 50
State, U.S. Department of. *See* Proximity talk proposals; White House-Department of State divisions; Rogers, William P.; Sisco, Joseph J.
Sterner, Michael E.:
  Egypt-Israel ceasefire violations, 154, 157
  Interim settlement proposals (*1971*), 234, 242, 253, 254
  Jarring mission restart proposals (*1970*), 149
  Jarring mission (*1971*), 200, 206
  Nixon-Meir correspondence, 33
  Nixon-Sadat correspondence, 197, 219
  Proximity talk proposals, 258, 263, 276, 285
  U.S.-Israeli bilateral negotiations, 304, 321
Stewart, Michael, 39, 50, 67
Suez Canal, freedom of navigation (*see also* Interim settlement proposals (*1971*)), 1, 2, 4, 8, 17, 19, 23, 25, 39, 47, 48, 53, 57, 58, 66, 80, 107, 115, 121, 216
Suez crisis (*1956*), 21, 124, 233
Suez partial-withdrawal proposal. *See* Interim settlement proposals (*1971*).
Sukhodrev, Viktor M., 173, 311
Sultan (Crown Prince of Saudi Arabia), 298
Symington, Stuart, 102, 243
Symmes, Harrison:
  Border incidents, 82
  Hussein U.S. visit (*1969*), 19
  Jarring mission (*1969–1970*), 12
  Jordan intervention contingency planning, 125, 126
  Jordan U.S. personnel evacuation, 125

Symmes, Harrison—*Continued*
  Jordanian-Israeli bilateral negotiations, 30, 32
  Sisco Jordan visit cancellation, 109
  Soviet military aid to Jordan, 69
  U.S. military aid to Israel, 92
  U.S. military aid to Jordan, 24, 87
Syria, 1, 4, 15, 21, 36, 39, 42, 46, 47, 48, 51, 52, 60, 66, 67, 73, 80, 93, 104, 124, 127, 161, 168, 177, 182, 183, 184, 186, 188, 190, 202, 204, 208, 210, 213, 216, 217, 218, 228, 244, 250, 270, 280, 286, 288, 291, 295, 308

Tcherniakov, Yuri, 1, 2, 34
Tekoah, Yosef, 84, 140, 157, 228, 274, 283
Territorial settlement proposals. *See* Israeli withdrawal.
Terrorism:
  Black September and, 160, 161
  Lod airport attack (May *1972*), 293, 295
  Munich massacre (Sep. *1972*), 307
  TWA hijacking (Aug. *1969*), 46
  U.S.-Soviet communications, 2
Thant, U:
  Four-Power negotiations, 213
  Jarring mission restart proposals (*1970*), 129, 138, 140, 143, 145, 170, 185
  Jarring mission (*1971*), 198, 199, 201, 203, 213, 217, 221
  Nasser peace appeal, 115
  Rogers-Foreign Ministers meeting, 50
Thornton, Thomas:
  International guarantees, 221
  Jarring mission (*1971*), 195, 199, 204, 208
  U.S. military aid to Israel, 183, 195, 204
  U.S. military aid to Jordan, 192
Tiran Straits, 2, 14, 23, 25, 47, 48, 57, 58, 74, 107, 121, 208, 216, 291
Treasury, U.S. Department of, 166
TWA hijacking (Aug. *1969*), 46
Two-Power discussion proposals. *See* U.S.-Soviet negotiations.

United Nations (*see also* International guarantees):
  Charter, 58, 92, 198, 221
  Rogers-Foreign Ministers meeting, 50

1120 Index

UN General Assembly meeting (1970), 122, 133, 154, 169, 172, 175, 177, 181, 182, 183
UN General Assembly Resolution 2628, 177, 181, 183, 189
UN General Assembly Resolution 2799, 270, 283, 320, 324
UN General Assembly Resolution 2949, 324
UN Security Council (see also specific resolutions):
  Israeli incursions in Lebanon (1972), 279, 295
  Munich massacre (Sep. 1972), 307
UN Security Council Resolution 242:
  Israeli acceptance, 120
  Jarring formula on, 1, 8, 12, 17, 22, 85, 116
  Rogers speech (1969), 73
  Soviet peace plan (Dec. 30, 1968), 1
  U.S.-Israeli communications, 84, 107
  U.S.-Jordanian communications, 92
  U.S.-Soviet working paper on, 58
UN Security Council Resolution 262, 8
UN Security Council Resolution 298, 250
UN Security Council Resolution 313, 279
UN Security Council Resolution 316, 295
Unger, Lt. Gen. F.T., 94, 119
United Arab Republic (UAR). See Egypt.
United Kingdom (see also Four-Power negotiation proposals; Four-Power negotiations), 13, 50, 83, 146, 183, 209
U.S. domestic political considerations (see also American Jewish community), 9, 113, 209, 233, 269, 318
U.S.-Egyptian backchannel (1972):
  Classified asset report, 309
  Haig memoranda, 320
  Helms memoranda, 288, 299, 310
  Kissinger memoranda, 305
  Nixon-Kissinger discussions, 300, 303
  Saunders memoranda, 317
  U.S.-Egyptian communications, 296
U.S.-Egyptian bilateral negotiations (see also U.S.-Egyptian backchannel (1972)):
  Greene-Fahmy discussions, 318, 324
  Irwin memoranda, 237

U.S.-Egyptian bilateral negotiations (see also U.S.-Egyptian backchannel (1972))—Continued
  Laird memoranda, 313
  Nixon-Fawzi talks, 21
  NSC discussions, 74, 124
  NSC staff papers, 112
  Rogers-Fawzi talks, 18
U.S. elections (1972). See U.S. domestic political considerations.
U.S.-Israeli bilateral negotiations:
  Department of State proposal (1971), 216
  Kissinger-Eban talks, 13, 77
  Kissinger memoranda, 51
  Meir U.S. visit (1969), 52
  Nixon-Eban discussions, 14
  NSC discussions, 124
  NSC staff papers, 112
  Richardson-Rabin talks, 78
  Rogers-Eban talks, 13
  Rogers-Meir talks, 52
  Saunders-Rabin talks, 36
  U.S. peace initiative (Jun. 1970), 129
U.S.-Israeli relations:
  Bilateral treaty proposals, 216, 221
  Dayan U.S. visit (1970), 190
  Dayan U.S. visit (1972), 316, 319
  Desalting project, 77
  Meir U.S. visit (1969), 33, 35, 36, 37, 39, 47, 48, 51, 52, 73, 77
  Meir U.S. visit (1970), 151, 162, 240
  Meir U.S. visit (1971), 267, 268
  Nixon-Meir correspondence, 33, 130, 133, 136, 142, 151, 163, 187, 188, 224, 238, 249, 307
  NSC Interdepartmental Group papers, 8
  Rogers visit (1971), 230
U.S.-Jordanian bilateral negotiations, 129
U.S. Middle East policy (see also White House-Department of State divisions):
  Ad Hoc Special Review Group discussions, 117, 119
  Bergus memoranda, 134
  Domestic political considerations, 9, 113, 209
  Greene memoranda, 314
  Kissinger memoranda, 95, 127, 134
  Laird memoranda, 313
  National Security Study Memoranda, 3, 6, 164

References are to document numbers

U.S. Middle East policy (see also White House–Department of State divisions)—Continued
  Nixon memoranda, 233
  NSC discussions, 4, 74, 124
  NSC Interdepartmental Group papers, 8
  NSC staff papers, 112, 116, 170, 181
  Rogers memoranda, 123
  Sisco memoranda, 114
  Statement of principles, 13
  Washington Special Actions Group/Senior Review Group discussions, 172

U.S. military aid to Israel:
  Ad Hoc Special Review Group discussions, 35, 37, 86, 94, 117, 119, 133, 150, 153, 160
  Barbour-Meir discussions, 106, 136
  Border incidents and, 93, 259, 264
  Dayan memoranda, 248
  Dayan U.S. visit (1972) discussions, 319
  Department of State proposal (1971), 216
  Jackson Amendment, 157, 162, 166, 195, 311
  Johnson, U. Alexis memoranda, 157
  Kissinger memoranda, 38, 40, 59, 79, 95, 127, 166, 167, 240, 265, 266
  Kissinger-Rabin discussions, 102, 110, 133, 142
  Kissinger-Sisco discussions, 141
  Laird memoranda, 10, 45, 121, 239, 267
  Meir U.S. visit (1969) discussions, 52, 57
  Meir U.S. visit (1971) discussions, 268
  Nasser peace appeal speech (May 1, 1970), 112, 115, 116
  National Security Decision Memoranda, 128, 171
  National Security Study Memoranda, 20, 63, 148
  Nixon aide-mémoire, 102, 103
  Nixon-congressional leadership meeting, 94, 140
  Nixon-Dayan discussions, 190
  Nixon-Ehrlichman/Haldeman discussions, 232
  Nixon-Kissinger conversations, 73, 96, 104
  Nixon-Meir correspondence, 101, 106, 187, 188, 249

U.S. military aid to Israel—Continued
  Nixon memoranda, 163, 233
  NSC discussions, 124, 209, 243
  NSC staff papers, 93, 112, 116, 152, 194, 207
  Nutter memoranda, 132, 142, 272
  Packard-Rabin discussions, 167
  Rogers-Laird communications, 259, 264
  Rogers memoranda, 123
  Rogers-Rabin discussions, 106, 129, 130, 209, 225, 229, 272
  Sadat Arab Socialist Union speech (Feb. 16, 1972), 276
  Sadat speech (Jan. 13, 1972), 275
  Senior Review Group discussions, 183, 188, 195, 204
  Sisco-Ghorbal discussions, 275
  Sisco Israel trip discussions, 228, 229, 241, 243, 244, 245
  Sisco-Meir discussions, 109, 245
  Sisco-Dayan discussions, 228, 229
  Sisco-Rabin discussions, 244, 271
  TWA hijacking (Aug. 1969) and, 46
  U.S.-Egyptian communications, 218
  U.S. peace initiative (Jun. 1970) and, 123, 128, 129
  Washington Special Actions Group discussions, 90
  Yariv meetings, 108

U.S. peace initiative (Jun. 1970) (see also Egypt-Israel ceasefire (Aug. 1970); Jarring mission restart proposals (1970)):
  Ad Hoc Special Review Group discussions, 133
  Egyptian response, 136
  Israeli response, 130, 136, 139, 141, 142, 162
  Jordanian response, 139
  Laird memoranda, 121
  National Security Decision Memoranda, 128
  NSC staff summaries, 175
  Rogers memoranda, 123, 129, 138, 139
  Soviet response, 137, 138
  U.S.-Israeli communications, 142, 144
  White House-Department of State divisions and, 134, 144

U.S. settlement proposals (see also Rogers Plan):
  Jordan-Israel settlement proposal, 67, 75, 76, 78, 85, 89, 127
  Kissinger memoranda, 27, 47, 76, 127

U.S. settlement proposals (*see also* Rogers Plan)—*Continued*
    Moscow Summit (*1972*), 291
    NSC discussions, 26, 48
    Rogers memoranda, 25, 67
    Rogers speech (Dec. *9, 1969*), 73, 74
    Soviet response, 84, 85
    U.S.-Israeli communications, 84
    Working paper, 17, 21
U.S.-Soviet negotiations (*see also* Rogers Plan):
    Ad Hoc Special Review Group discussions, 133
    Egypt-Israel ceasefire violations, 173
    Kissinger-Dobrynin talks, 135, 300
    Kissinger-Gromyko talks, 252, 311
    Kissinger memoranda, 66, 127
    National Security Study Memoranda, 6
    Nixon-Brezhnev correspondence, 281, 310
    Nixon-Dobrynin talks, 281
    Nixon-Gromyko talks, 173, 251
    NSC discussions, 4, 5, 26, 48, 74
    NSC Interdepartmental Group papers, 8
    Rogers-Dobrynin talks, 97, 105, 122
    Rogers-Foreign Ministers meeting discussions, 50
    Rogers-Gromyko talks, 52, 53, 173
    Rogers memoranda, 34, 67, 84, 111
    Senior Review Group discussions, 195
    Sisco-Dobrynin talks (*1969*), 13, 15, 18, 22, 27, 28, 29, 49, 58, 61
    Sisco-Dobrynin talks (*1970*), 107, 127
    Sisco Moscow talks (*1969*), 39, 48
    U.S.-Israeli communications, 13, 29, 33, 77
    U.S. peace initiative (Jun. *1970*) and, 129, 137
    U.S. settlement proposals and, 25
    Yost memoranda, 43

Vinogradov, Vladimir, 39, 111, 155, 157
Vogt, Lt. Gen. John W., 90, 91, 160, 168
Vorontsov, Yuly M., 111, 120

Waldheim, Kurt, 274, 283, 306
Walsh, John P., 27, 29, 31
War, possible, 290
War of attrition, 49, 51, 104, 110, 113, 119
Ware, Richard A., 90, 91, 126

Warnke, Paul, 31, 35, 37, 41
Washington Special Actions Group (WSAG):
    Lebanese crisis (*1969*), 60, 68
    Military contingency planning, 44, 56, 60, 68, 90, 125, 126, 131
    Soviet military aid to Egypt, 91
    U.S. Middle East policy, 172
    U.S. military aid to Jordan, 168
Watts, William, 74
Weinberger, Caspar W., 166
West Bank (*see also* Israeli withdrawal):
    Allon Plan, 4, 13, 192
    Department of State proposal (*1971*), 216
    NSC Interdepartmental Group papers, 8
    Sisco memoranda, 81
    U.S.-Israeli communications, 36
Westmoreland, Gen. William, 26, 96, 168
Wheeler, Gen. Earle G.:
    Israeli nuclear capabilities, 20, 31, 35, 37, 38
    Military contingency planning, 4
    U.S. Middle East policy, 74, 119
    U.S. military aid to Israel, 86
    U.S. peace initiative (Jun. *1970*), 121
    U.S. settlement proposals, 48
White House-Department of State divisions:
    Haldeman memoranda, 96, 144, 156, 162, 216, 222, 225, 232, 233
    Jordanian-Israeli bilateral negotiations and, 322
    Nixon-Ehrlichman/Haldeman discussions, 232
    Nixon-Kissinger discussions, 233
    Proximity talk proposals and, 257
    Rogers-Haldeman/Mitchell discussions, 288
    U.S.-Egyptian backchannel (*1972*) and, 288
    U.S. peace initiative (Jun. *1970*) and, 134, 144
Wiley, Marshall W., 158, 196, 197, 238, 275, 276
Wilson, Harold, 8, 13, 67, 83, 89

Yariv, Gen. Aharon, 35, 108, 110, 146, 160
Yost, Charles W.:
    Egypt-Israel ceasefire violations, 157

Yost, Charles W.—*Continued*
- Four-Power negotiation proposals, 5, 7, 8, 15, 17
- Four-Power negotiations, 67, 72, 75, 78, 81, 83, 193, 198, 199
- Four-Power UN representative discussions, 23, 24
- Jarring mission (1971), 84, 183, 185, 205
- Military contingency planning, 4
- Palestinians, 182
- Rogers-Foreign Ministers meeting, 50
- U.S. Middle East policy, 73, 74, 124

Yost, Charles W.—*Continued*
- U.S. military aid to Jordan, 24
- U.S. settlement proposals, 26, 48, 76, 140
- U.S.-Soviet negotiations, 43, 49

Yugoslavia, 4, 169

Zayyat, Mohamed Hassan el-, 200, 274, 314, 321, 324
Zeira, Maj. Gen. Eliyahu, 264, 271
Ziegler, Ronald L., 143, 162, 225, 284, 307
Zurhellen, Z.O., Jr., 157, 228, 261, 306

ISBN 978-0-16-092847-5